S. Haykin

COMPUTER ARCHITECTURE
AND PARALLEL PROCESSING

McGraw-Hill Series in Computer Organization and Architecture

Bell and Newell: *Computer Structures: Readings and Examples*
Gear: *Computer Organization and Programming*
Hamacher, Vranesic, and Zaky: *Computer Organization*
Hayes: *Computer Architecture and Organization*
Hayes: *Digital System Design and Microprocessors*
Hwang and Briggs: *Computer Architecture and Parallel Processing*
Kogge: *The Architecture of Pipelined Computers*
Siewiorek, Bell, and Newell: *Computer Structures: Principles and Examples*
Stone: *Introduction to Computer Organization and Data Structures*
Stone and Siewiorek: *Introduction to Computer Organization and Data Structures: PDP-11 Edition*

McGraw-Hill Computer Science Series

COMPUTER ARCHITECTURE AND PARALLEL PROCESSING

Kai Hwang

Purdue University

Fayé A. Briggs

Rice University

McGraw-Hill Book Company

New York   St. Louis   San Francisco   Auckland   Bogotá   Hamburg
Johannesburg   London   Madrid   Mexico   Montreal   New Delhi
Panama   Paris   São Paulo   Singapore   Sydney   Tokyo   Toronto

This book was set in Times Roman.
The editors were Eric M. Munson and Jonathan Palace;
the production supervisor was Leroy A. Young.
The drawings were done by ANCO/Boston.
Halliday Lithograph Corporation was printer and binder.

COMPUTER ARCHITECTURE AND PARALLEL PROCESSING

2 3 4 5 6 7 8 9 0 HALHAL 8 9 8 7 6 5 4

ISBN 0-07-031556-6

Library of Congress Cataloging in Publication Data

Hwang, Kai.
Computer architecture and parallel processing.

(McGraw-Hill series in computer organization and
architecture)
Bibliography: p.
Includes index.
1. Computer architecture. 2. Parallel processing
(Electronic computers) I. Briggs, Faye A. (Faye Alaye)
II. Title. III. Series.
QA76.9.A73H88 1984 001.64 83-23867
ISBN 0-07-031556-6

ABOUT THE AUTHORS

Kai Hwang is a professor of computer engineering at the School of Electrical Engineering, Purdue University. He received the Ph.D. in EECS from the University of California at Berkeley in 1972. His current research and teaching interest lies mainly in vector supercomputers, multiprocessors, VLSI and dataflow computing structures, and image understanding systems. Dr. Hwang has published about 60 scientific papers and books. He is the author of *Computer Arithmetic Principles, Architecture and Design* (Wiley, 1979) and the editor of *Supercomputer Design and Applications* (Computer Society Press, 1984). Dr. Hwang is the coeditor-in-chief of the *Journal of Parallel and Distributed Computing*. He has been involved in advanced studies on supercomputer architectures and large-scale scientific computations for U.S. National Science Foundation, IBM Fishkill Facilities, Fujitsu in Japan, Academia Sinica, and NATO Advanced Study Institute. He has been a distinguished visitor of IEEE Computer Society since 1981.

Fayé A. Briggs is an associate professor of electrical engineering at Rice University. He received the Ph.D. degree in electrical engineering from the University of Illinois, Urbana. Prior to joining the faculty at Rice University, Dr. Briggs was an assistant professor and the systems manager of the Advanced Automation and Research Laboratory at Purdue University. He has also served as a consultant to IBM Watson Research Center and Exxon Production Research Company. Since 1983 he has been a distinguished visitor of the IEEE Computer Society. Dr. Briggs' current research interests include performance evaluation of advanced computer architectures such as pipeline computers, multiprocessors, and VLSI computing structures. He has published over 30 technical papers and book chapters in the areas of multiprocessing computer architectures, memory organizations, and performance modeling techniques.

To my parents,
Hwang Yuan-Chung and Liu Cheng Fong,
my wife, Pu Fong,
and my sons, Tony and Andy.

Kai Hwang

黄鑑

To my grandparents,
Rev. P. B. Harry and Mrs. B. P. Harry.

Fayé A. Briggs

Fayéofori   Alayé   Nimifa-ā

CONTENTS

Chapter 5 Structures and Algorithms for Array Processors 325

Chapter 6 SIMD Computers and Performance Enhancement 393

PREFACE

High-performance computers are increasingly in demand in the areas of structural analysis, weather forecasting, petroleum exploration, fusion energy research, medical diagnosis, aerodynamics simulations, artificial intelligence, expert systems, industrial automation, remote sensing, military defense, genetic engineering, and socioeconomics, among many other scientific and engineering applications. Without superpower computers, many of these challenges to advance human civilization cannot be made within a reasonable time period. Achieving high performance depends not only on using faster and more reliable hardware devices but also on major improvements in computer architecture and processing techniques. This book is devoted to studying advanced computer architectures, theories of parallel computing, optimal resource allocation, fast algorithms, efficient programming languages, and application requirements of cost-effective computer systems to meet the above demands.

Advanced computer architectures are centered around the concept of parallel processing. State-of-the-art parallel computer systems can be characterized into three structural classes: *pipelined computers*, *array processors*, and *multiprocessor systems*. The development and application of these computer systems require a broad knowledge of the underlying hardware and software structures and close interactions between parallel computing algorithms and the optimal allocation of machine resources. This book provides the readers with the necessary knowledge to design a new computer system; to improve an existing one; to develop fast computing algorithms; and to allocate hardware-software resources in solving large-scale computing problems.

The book is designed to be used by seniors and/or graduate students in computer science, electrical engineering, industrial engineering, and in any other fields demanding the use of high-performance mainframe computers, attached vector processors, scientific supercomputers, and multiprocessors to solve specific applications problems. Parallel processing can be applied at the hardware/software system level or at the algorithmic and programming level. It demands concurrent execution of many programs in the computer. Parallel-processing computers provide a cost-effective means to achieve high system performance through concurrent activities.

Computer scientists, system designers, advanced programmers, application engineers, computational experimentalists, and computer professionals should find the material useful in their respective lines of work. Results obtained by many researchers, designers, and users of parallel-processing computers have been included in the text. The material being presented is the outgrowth from several courses in Computer Architecture and Advanced Computing taught by both authors, at Purdue University and Rice University. The book is organized into 10 chapters. Chapter 1 introduces the basic concepts of parallel processing and computer structures and prepares readers with an overview of parallelism in computer systems and various application areas. Chapter 2 presents memory hierarchy and input-output subsystems needed in parallel processing computers.

Chapters 3 and 4 are devoted to the design principles and applications of pipelined supercomputers. Systems to be studied include Star-100, TI-ASC, Cray-1, Cyber-205, Fujitsu VP-200, CDC-NASF, and attached scientific processors AP-120B (FPS-164), IBM 3838, and Datawest MATP. Language and compiler requirements are assessed toward optimized vectorization. Pipelined vector processing methods and performance evaluation of pipeline computers are also provided.

Chapters 5 and 6 present the interconnection structures of processor arrays. Such array processors can handle single instruction stream over multiple data streams. Several parallel algorithms are presented for array processors and associative processors. Case study systems include the Illiac-IV, Burroughs Scientific Processor (BSP), the STARAN, and PEPE, and the massively parallel processor (MPP). Performance enhancement methods are also provided for synchronous array processors.

In Chapters 7, 8, and 9, we study hardware system architectures, operating system controls, parallel algorithms, and performance evaluation of multiprocessor systems. Design experiences of three exploratory research multiprocessors, C.mmp, S-1, and Cm*, will be presented. Commercial multiprocessors to be studied include the IBM 370/168 MP, 3033, and 3081, Univac 1100/80 and 1100/90, Cray X-MP, Tandem/16, and Denelcor's HEP. Research issues toward designing tightly coupled multiprocessors are discussed.

Chapter 10 is devoted to studying new computing concepts and their realization issues. Principles of data-driven computations are introduced. Functional languages and existing data flow computer architectures are reviewed. Finally, we study parallel computing algorithms that are suitable for VLSI hardware implementations. Applications of VLSI architectures for image processing are presented.

The prerequisite for reading this book is an introductory undergraduate course in computer organization and programming. We use Fortran and its extensions in Chapters 3 to 6, because most vector supercomputers are Fortran machines. For multiprocessors in Chapters 7 to 9, we use concurrent Pascal as the illustrative language. Sections marked with asterisk (*) are research-oriented topics. Readers are expected to have some background on discrete mathematics and probability theory in studying these research topics. These difficult sections can be skipped in the first reading without loss of continuity. Homework problems are essential to provide readers with in-depth thinking and hands-on experience in the design, application, and evaluation of parallel computers.

Parallel processing and computer architecture are two wide-open areas for research and development. We hope that this book will inspire further advances in these frontier computer areas. Bibliographic notes are attached at the end of each chapter to help interested readers find additional references for extended studies. The authors are fully responsible for any errors or omissions. We apologize to those computer specialists whose original works are not included in this volume. The computer area is changing so rapidly that no book can cover every new progress being made. However, we do welcome inputs and criticisms from our readers. Readers are invited to send their comments directly to the authors, so that improvement can be made in future printings or revisions of the book.

This book can be used as a text when offering a sequence of two courses on computer architecture and parallel processing. Each course contains 45 lectures, each 50 minutes long. We suggest the following materials be covered in the first course of a two-course sequence. The remaining sections are reserved for the second course.

Material suggested for the first course

Chapter	Sections and subsections
1	1.1, 1.2, 1.3.1–3, 1.3.5, 1.4.1, 1.5
2	2.1.1, 2.1.3, 2.2.1–2, 2.4.1–2, 2.5.1
3	3.1.1–2, 3.2.1–2, 3.3.1–2, 3.4.1
4	4.1, 4.2.1, 4.3.1, 4.4.1–3
5	5.1, 5.2.1–2, 5.3.1, 5.4.1
6	6.1, 6.2.1–2, 6.3.1, 6.4.1
7	7.1, 7.2.1–2, 7.4.1, 7.5.1
8	8.1.1, 8.2.1, 8.3.1, 8.4.1
9	9.1, 9.2.1, 9.5.1–2, 9.6.1
10	10.1.1, 10.2.1, 10.3.1

The first course is suitable for senior and first-year graduate students. The second course is mainly for graduate students. The first course is a prerequisite for the second course. If the book is adopted for only one course offering, the instructor can move some sections from the second course to the first one to give more complete coverage of some selected topics which are of special interest to the instructor and students. This may necessitate trading some sections listed above with the added sections from the second course. A Solutions Manual to this book will be available from McGraw-Hill for instructors only. The manual contains solutions to all problems plus a number of design projects suitable for use as term projects. Instructors are welcome to communicate directly with the authors or with McGraw-Hill representatives for suggestions or sharing their experiences in using this book as either a required text or as a research reference.

The authors are grateful to a number of individuals whose professional encouragement and assistance have made the long writing and production process a very pleasant endeavour. In particular, we wish to thank Harold S. Stone, Jean Loup Baer, C. V. Ramamoorthy, Tse-yun Feng, John P. Hayes, King-Sun Fu, Clarance L. Coates, V. Carl Hamacher, Herschel H. Loomis, Jr., Bart Sinclair, J. Robert Jump, Edward S. Davidson, H. J. Siegel, Tom Mowbray, Wolfgang Händler, Kenichi Miura, Lional M. Ni, Michel Dubois, and Shun-Piao Su for their valuable comments and suggestions. Many of our students helped us in improving the manuscript. In particular, we thank Chi-Yuan Chin, Zhiwei Xu, and William Carlson for their assistance. Finally, we wish to thank the typing, drafting, and secretarial assistance from Andy Hughes, Wanda Booth, Linda Stovall, Vicki Johnson, Pat Loomis, Mickey Krebs, Sharon Katz, Nancy Lein, and D. Ringe. Last but not least we appreciate the McGraw-Hill editing staffs and production professionals for their excellent work in producing the book. Without the timely efforts of the above individuals, this book might be still in preparation.

Kai Hwang
Fayé A. Briggs

CHAPTER ONE

INTRODUCTION TO PARALLEL PROCESSING

Basic concepts of parallel processing on high-performance computers are introduced in this chapter. We will review the architectural evolution, examine various forms of concurrent activities in modern computer systems, and assess advanced applications of parallel processing computers. Parallel computer structures will be characterized as *pipelined computers*, *array processors*, and *multiprocessor systems*. Several new computing concepts, including data flow and VLSI approaches, will be introduced. The material presented in this introductory chapter will provide an overview of the field and pave the way to studying in subsequent chapters the details of theories of parallel computing, machine architectures, system controls, fast algorithms, and programming requirements.

1.1 EVOLUTION OF COMPUTER SYSTEMS

Over the past four decades the computer industry has experienced four generations of development, physically marked by the rapid changing of building blocks from relays and vacuum tubes (1940–1950s) to discrete diodes and transistors (1950–1960s), to small- and medium-scale integrated (SSI/MSI) circuits (1960–1970s), and to large- and very-large-scale integrated (LSI/VLSI) devices (1970s and beyond). Increases in device speed and reliability and reductions in hardware cost and physical size have greatly enhanced computer performance. However, better devices are not the sole factor contributing to high performance. Ever since the stored-program concept of von Neumann, the computer has been recognized as more than just a hardware organization problem. A modern computer system is really a composite of such items as processors, memories, functional units, interconnection networks, compilers, operating systems, peripheral devices, communication channels, and database banks.

To design a powerful and cost-effective computer system and to devise efficient programs to solve a computational problem, one must understand the underlying hardware and software system structures and the computing algorithms to be implemented on the machine with some user-oriented programming languages. These disciplines constitute the technical scope of *computer architecture*. Computer architecture is really a system concept integrating hardware, software, algorithms, and languages to perform large computations. A good computer architect should master all these disciplines. It is the revolutionary advances in integrated circuits and system architecture that have contributed most to the significant improvement of computer performance during the past 40 years. In this section, we review the generations of computer systems and indicate the general trends in the development of high performance computers.

1.1.1 Generations of Computer Systems

The division of computer systems into generations is determined by the device technology, system architecture, processing mode, and languages used. We consider each generation to have a time span of about 10 years. Adjacent generations may overlap in several years as demonstrated in Figure 1.1. The long time span is intended to cover both development and use of the machines in various parts of the world. We are currently in the fourth generation, while the fifth generation is not materialized yet.

The first generation (1938–1953) The introduction of the first electronic analog computer in 1938 and the first electronic digital computer, ENIAC (Electronic Numerical Integrator and Computer), in 1946 marked the beginning of the first generation of computers. Electromechanical relays were used as switching devices

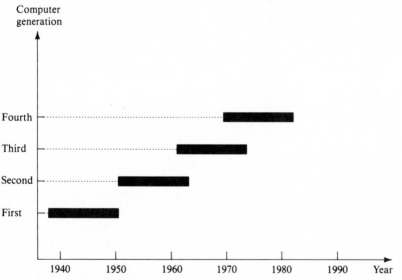

Figure 1.1 The evolution of computer systems.

in the 1940s, and vacuum tubes were used in the 1950s. These devices were interconnected by insulated wires. Hardware components were expensive then, which forced the CPU structure to be *bit-serial*: arithmetic is done on a bit-by-bit fixed-point basis, as in a ripple-carry addition which uses a single full adder and one bit of carry flag.

Only binary-coded machine language was used in early computers. In 1950, the first stored-program computer, EDVAC (Electronic Discrete Variable Automatic Computer), was developed. This marked the beginning of the use of system software to relieve the user's burden in low-level programming. However, it is not difficult to imagine that hardware costs predominated and software-language features were rather primitive in the early computers. By 1952, IBM had announced its 701 electronic calculator. The system used Williams' tube memory, magnetic drums, and magnetic tape.

The second generation (1952–1963) Transistors were invented in 1948. The first *tra*nsistorized *di*gital *c*omputer, TRADIC, was built by Bell Laboratories in 1954. Discrete transistors and diodes were the building blocks: 800 transistors were used in TRADIC. Printed circuits appeared. By this time, coincident current magnetic *core* memory was developed and subsequently appeared in many machines. Assembly languages were used until the development of high-level languages, Fortran (*for*mula *tran*slation) in 1956 and Algol (*algo*rithmic *l*anguage) in 1960.

In 1959, Sperry Rand built the Larc system and IBM started the Stretch projeet. These were the first two computers attributable to architectural improvement. The Larc had an independent I/O processor which operated in parallel with one or two processing units. Stretch featured instruction lookahead and error correction, to be discussed in Section 1.2. The first IBM scientific, transistorized computer, IBM 1620, became available in 1960. Cobol (*com*mon *b*usiness *o*riented *l*anguage) was developed in 1959. Interchangeable disk packs were introduced in 1963. Batch processing was popular, providing sequential execution of user programs, one at a time until done.

The third generation (1962–1975) This generation was marked by the use of small-scale integrated (SSI) and medium-scale integrated (MSI) circuits as the basic building blocks. Multilayered printed circuits were used. Core memory was still used in CDC-6600 and other machines but, by 1968, many fast computers, like CDC-7600, began to replace cores with solid-state memories. High-level languages were greatly enhanced with intelligent compilers during this period.

Multiprogramming was well developed to allow the simultaneous execution of many program segments interleaved with I/O operations. Many high-performance computers, like IBM 360/91, Illiac IV, TI-ASC, Cyber-175, STAR-100, and C.mmp, and several vector processors were developed in the early seventies. Time-sharing operating systems became available in the late 1960s. Virtual memory was developed by using hierarchically structured memory systems.

The fourth generation (1972–present) The present generation computers emphasize the use of large-scale integrated (LSI) circuits for both logic and memory sections. High-density packaging has appeared. High-level languages are being extended to handle both scalar and vector data, like the extended Fortran in many vector processors. Most operating systems are time-sharing, using virtual memories. Vectorizing compilers have appeared in the second generation of vector machines, like the Cray-1 (1976) and the Cyber-205 (1982). High-speed mainframes and supers appear in multiprocessor systems, like the Univac 1100/80 (1976), Fujitsu M 382 (1981), the IBM 370/168 MP, the IBM 3081 (1980), the Burroughs B-7800 (1978), and the Cray X-MP (1983). A high degree of pipelining and multiprocessing is greatly emphasized in commercial supercomputers. A massively parallel processor (MPP) was custom-designed in 1982. This MPP, consisting of 16,384 bit-slice microprocessors, is under the control of one array controller for satellite image processing.

The future Computers to be used in the 1990s may be the next generation. Very-large-scale integrated (VLSI) chips will be used along with high-density modular design. Multiprocessors like the 16 processors in the S-1 project at Lawrence Livermore National Laboratory and in the Denelcor's HEP will be required. Cray-2 is expected to have four processors, to be delivered in 1985. More than 1000 *mega float-point operations per second* (megaflops) are expected in these future supercomputers. We will study major existing systems and discuss possible future machines in subsequent chapters.

1.1.2 Trends Towards Parallel Processing

According to Sidney Fernbach: " *Today's large computers* (*mainframes*) *would have been considered 'supercomputers' 10 to 20 years ago. By the same token, today's supercomputers will be considered 'state-of-the-art' standard equipment 10 to 20 years from now.*" From an application point of view, the mainstream usage of computers is experiencing a trend of four ascending levels of sophistication:

- Data processing
- Information processing
- Knowledge processing
- Intelligence processing

The relationships between data, information, knowledge, and intelligence are demonstrated in Figure 1.2. The data space is the largest, including numeric numbers in various formats, character symbols, and multidimensional measures. Data objects are considered mutually unrelated in the space. Huge amounts of data are being generated daily in all walks of life, especially among the scientific, business, and government sectors. An information item is a collection of data objects that are related by some syntactic structure or relation. Therefore, information items form a subspace of the data space. Knowledge consists of information items plus some semantic meanings. Thus knowledge items form a subspace of the information

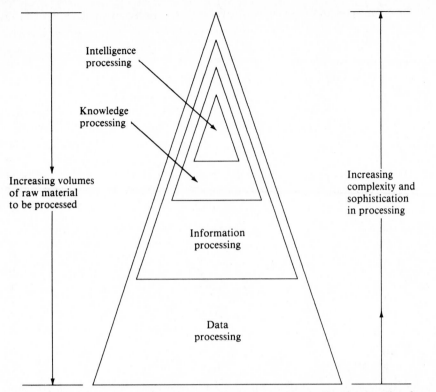

Intelligence
processing

Knowledge
processing

Increasing volumes
of raw material
to be processed

Increasing
complexity and
sophistication
in processing

Information
processing

Data
processing

Figure 1.2 The spaces of data, information, knowledge, and intelligence from the viewpoint of computer processing.

space. Finally, intelligence is derived from a collection of knowledge items. The intelligence space is represented by the innermost and highest triangle in the Venn diagram.

Computer usage started with *data processing*, which is still a major task of today's computers. With more and more data structures developed, many users are shifting to computer roles from pure data processing (mainly number crunching) to *information processing*. Most of today's computing is still confined within these two processing levels. A high degree of parallelism has been found at these levels. As the accumulated knowledge bases expanded rapidly in recent years, there grew a strong demand to use computers for *knowledge processing*. For example, the various expert computer systems listed in Table 1.1 are used for problem solving in specific areas where they can reach a level of performance comparable to that of human experts. It has been projected by some computer scientists that knowledge processing will be the main thrust of computer usage in the 1990s.

Today's computers can be made very knowlegeable but are far from being intelligent. Intelligence is very difficult to create; its processing even more so. Today's computers are very fast and obedient and have many reliable memory cells to be qualified for data-information-knowledge processing. But none of the

Table 1.1 Some existing expert computer systems for knowledge processing

System name	Expertise
AQ11	Diagnosis of plant diseases
Internist, casnet	Medical consulting
Dendral	Hypothesizing molecular structure from mass spectrograms
Dipmeter, advisor	Oil exploration
EL	Analyzing electrical circuits
Macsyma	Mathematical manipulation
Prospector	Mineral exploration
R1	Computer configuration
SPERIL	Earthquake damage estimation

existing computers can be considered a really intelligent thinking system. Computers are still unable to communicate with human beings in natural forms like speech and written languages, pictures and images, documents, and illustrations. Computers are far from being satisfactory in performing theorem proving, logical inference, and creative thinking. We are in an era which is promoting the use of computers not only for conventional data-information processing, but also toward the building of workable machine knowledge-intelligence systems to advance human civilization. Many computer scientists feel that the degree of parallelism exploitable at the two highest processing levels should be higher than that at the data-information processing levels.

From an operating system point of view, computer systems have improved chronologically in four phases:

- Batch processing
- Multiprogramming
- Time sharing
- Multiprocessing

In these four operating modes, the degree of parallelism increases sharply from phase to phase. The general trend is to emphasize parallel processing of information. In what follows, the term *information* is used with an extended meaning to include data, information, knowledge, and intelligence. We formally define *parallel processing* as follows:

Definition Parallel processing is an efficient form of information processing which emphasizes the exploitation of concurrent events in the computing process. Concurrency implies parallelism, simultaneity, and pipelining. Parallel events may occur in multiple resources during the same time interval; simultaneous events may occur at the same time instant; and pipelined events may occur in overlapped time spans. These concurrent events are attainable in a computer system at various processing levels. Parallel processing demands concurrent execution of many programs in the computer. It is in contrast to sequential processing. It is a cost-effective means to improve system performance through concurrent activities in the computer.

The highest level of parallel processing is conducted among multiple jobs or programs through multiprogramming, time sharing, and multiprocessing. This level requires the development of parallel processable algorithms. The implementation of parallel algorithms depends on the efficient allocation of limited hardware-software resources to multiple programs being used to solve a large computation problem. The next highest level of parallel processing is conducted among procedures or tasks (program segments) within the same program. This involves the decomposition of a program into multiple tasks. The third level is to exploit concurrency among multiple instructions. Data dependency analysis is often performed to reveal parallelism among instructions. Vectorization may be desired among scalar operations within DO loops. Finally, we may wish to have faster and concurrent operations within each instruction. To sum up, parallel processing can be challenged in four programmatic levels:

- Job or program level
- Task or procedure level
- Interinstruction level
- Intrainstruction level

The highest job level is often conducted algorithmically. The lowest intra-instruction level is often implemented directly by hardware means. Hardware roles increase from high to low levels. On the other hand, software implementations increase from low to high levels. The trade-off between hardware and software approaches to solve a problem is always a very controversial issue. As hardware cost declines and software cost increases, more and more hardware methods are replacing the conventional software approaches. The trend is also supported by the increasing demand for a faster real-time, resource-sharing, and fault-tolerant computing environment.

The above characteristics suggest that parallel processing is indeed a combined field of studies. It requires a broad knowledge of and experience with all aspects of algorithms, languages, software, hardware, performance evaluation, and computing alternatives. This book concentrates on parallel processing with centralized computing facilities. Distributed processing on physically dispersed and loosely coupled computer networks is beyond the scope of this book, though a high degree of concurrency is often exploitable in distributed systems.

Parallel processing and distributed processing are closely related. In some cases, we use certain distributed techniques to achieve parallelism. As data communications technology advances progressively, the distinction between parallel and distributed processing becomes smaller and smaller. In this extended sense, we may view distributed processing as a form of parallel processing in a special environment.

To achieve parallel processing requires the development of more capable and cost-effective computer systems. This book emphasizes the design and application of parallel processing computers, including various architectural configurations, functional capabilities, operating systems, algorithmic and programming requirements, and performance limitations of parallel-structured computers. The ultimate goal is to achieve high performance at lower cost in performing large-scale scientific-engineering computing tasks in the various application areas to be introduced in Section 1.5.

Most computer manufacturers started with the development of systems with a single central processor, called a *uniprocessor system*. We will reveal various means to promote concurrency in uniprocessor systems in Section 1.2. Uniprocessor systems have their limit in achieving high performance. The computing power in a uniprocessor can be further upgraded by allowing the use of multiple processing elements under one controller. One can also extend the computer structure to include multiple processors with shared memory space and peripherals under the control of one integrated operating system. Such a computer is called a *multiprocessor system*.

As far as parallel processing is concerned, the general architectural trend is being shifted away from conventional uniprocessor systems to multiprocessor systems or to an array of processing elements controlled by one uniprocessor. In all cases, a high degree of pipelining is being incorporated into the various system levels. We will introduce these parallel computer structures in Section 1.3. After learning the parallelism in both uniprocessor and multiprocessor systems, we will then study several architectural classification schemes based on the machine structures and operation modes.

1.2 PARALLELISM IN UNIPROCESSOR SYSTEMS

Most general-purpose uniprocessor systems have the same basic structure. In this section, we will briefly review the architecture of uniprocessor systems. The development of parallelism in uniprocessors will then be introduced categorically. It is assumed that readers have had at least one basic course in the past on conventional computer organization. Therefore, we will provide only concise specifications of the architectural features of two popular commercial computers. Parallel-processing mechanisms and methods to balance subsystem bandwidths will then be described for a typical uniprocessor system. Details of these structures, mechanisms, and methods can be found in references suggested in the bibliographic notes.

1.2.1 Basic Uniprocessor Architecture

A typical uniprocessor computer consists of three major components: the *main memory*, the *central processing unit* (CPU), and the *input-output* (I/O) *subsystem*. The architectures of two commercially available uniprocessor computers are given below to show the possible interconnection of structures among the three subsystems. We will examine major components in the CPU and in the I/O subsystem.

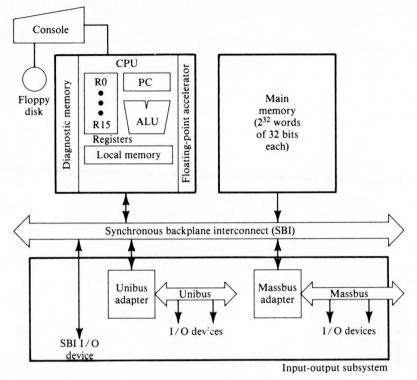

Figure 1.3 The system architecture of the supermini VAX-11/780 uniprocessor system (Courtesy of Digital Equipment Corporation).

Figure 1.3 shows the architectural components of the super minicomputer VAX-11/780, manufactured by Digital Equipment Company. The CPU contains the *master controller* of the VAX system. There are sixteen 32-bit general-purpose registers, one of which serves as the *program counter* (PC). There is also a special *CPU status register* containing information about the current state of the processor and of the program being executed. The CPU contains an *arithmetic and logic unit* (ALU) with an optional *floating-point accelerator*, and some local *cache memory* with an optional *diagnostic memory*. The CPU can be intervened by the operator through the console connected to a floppy disk.

The CPU, the main memory (2^{32} words of 32 bits each), and the I/O subsystems are all connected to a common bus, the *synchronous backplane interconnect* (SBI). Through this bus, all I/O devices can communicate with each other, with the CPU, or with the memory. Peripheral storage or I/O devices can be connected directly to the SBI through the *unibus* and its controller (which can be connected to PDP-11 series minicomputers), or through a *massbus* and its controller.

Another representative commercial system is the mainframe computer IBM System 370/Model 168 uniprocessor, shown in Figure 1.4. The CPU contains the

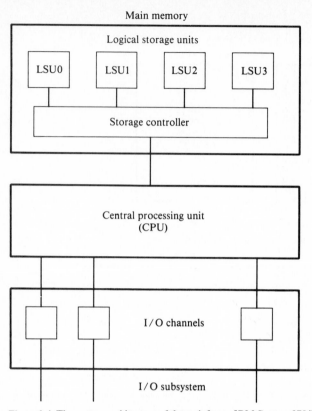

Figure 1.4 The system architecture of the mainframe IBM System 370/Model 168 uniprocessor computer (Courtesy of International Business Machines Corp.).

instruction decoding and execution units as well as a cache. Main memory is divided into four units, referred to as *logical storage units* (LSU), that are four-way interleaved. The *storage controller* provides multiport connections between the CPU and the four LSUs. Peripherals are connected to the system via high-speed I/O *channels* which operate asynchronously with the CPU. In Chapter 9, we will show that this uniprocessor can be modified to assume some multiprocessor configurations.

Hardware and software means to promote parallelism in uniprocessor systems are introduced in the next three subsections. We begin with hardware approaches which emphasize resource multiplicity and time overlapping. It is necessary to balance the processing rates of various subsystems in order to avoid bottlenecks and to increase total *system throughput*, which is the number of instructions (or basic computations) performed per unit time. Finally, we study operating system software approaches to achieve parallel processing with better utilization of the system resources.

1.2.2 Parallel Processing Mechanisms

A number of parallel processing mechanisms have been developed in uniprocessor computers. We identify them in the following six categories:

- Multiplicity of functional units
- Parallelism and pipelining within the CPU
- Overlapped CPU and I/O operations
- Use of a hierarchical memory system
- Balancing of subsystem bandwidths
- Multiprogramming and time sharing

We will describe below the first four techniques and discuss the remaining two approaches in the subsections to follow.

Multiplicity of functional units The early computer had only one arithmetic and logic unit in its CPU. Furthermore, the ALU could only perform one function at a time, a rather slow process for executing a long sequence of arithmetic logic instructions. In practice, many of the functions of the ALU can be distributed to multiple and specialized functional units which can operate in parallel. The CDC-6600 (designed in 1964) has 10 functional units built into its CPU (Figure 1.5). These 10 units are independent of each other and may operate simultaneously. A *scoreboard* is used to keep track of the availability of the functional units and registers being demanded. With 10 functional units and 24 registers available, the instruction issue rate can be significantly increased.

Another good example of a multifunction uniprocessor is the IBM 360/91 (1968), which has two parallel *execution units* (E units): one for fixed-point

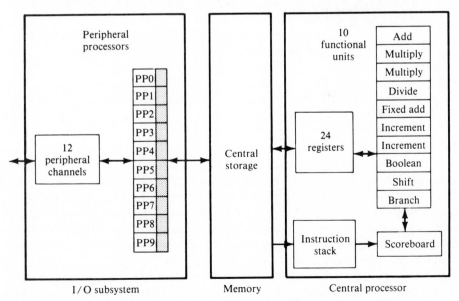

Figure 1.5 The system architecture of the CDC-6600 computer (Courtesy of Control Data Corp.).

arithmetic, and the other for floating-point arithmetic. Within the floating-point E unit are two functional units: one for floating-point add-subtract and the other for floating-point multiply-divide. IBM 360/91 is a highly pipelined, multifunction, scientific uniprocessor. We will study 360/91 in detail in Chapter 3. Almost all modern computers and attached processors are equipped with multiple functional units to perform parallel or simultaneous arithmetic logic operations. This practice of functional specialization and distribution can be extended to array processors and multiprocessors, to be discussed in subsequent chapters.

Parallelism and pipelining within the CPU Parallel adders, using such techniques as carry-lookahead and carry-save, are now built into almost all ALUs. This is in contrast to the bit-serial adders used in the first-generation machines. High-speed multiplier recoding and convergence division are techniques for exploring parallelism and the sharing of hardware resources for the functions of multiply and divide (to be described in Section 3.2.2). The use of multiple functional units is a form of parallelism with the CPU.

Various phases of instruction executions are now pipelined, including instruction fetch, decode, operand fetch, arithmetic logic execution, and store result. To facilitate overlapped instruction executions through the pipe, instruction prefetch and data buffering techniques have been developed. Instruction and arithmetic pipeline designs will be covered in Chapters 3 and 4. Most commercial uniprocessor systems are now pipelined in their CPU with a clock rate between 10 and 500 ns.

Overlapped CPU and I/O operations I/O operations can be performed simultaneously with the CPU computations by using separate I/O controllers, channels, or I/O processors. The direct-memory-access (DMA) channel can be used to provide direct information transfer between the I/O devices and the main memory. The DMA is conducted on a *cycle-stealing* basis, which is apparent to the CPU. Furthermore, I/O multiprocessing, such as the use of the 10 I/O processors in CDC-6600 (Figure 1.5), can speed up data transfer between the CPU (or memory) and the outside world. I/O subsystems for supporting parallel processing will be described in Section 2.5. Back-end database machines can be used to manage large databases stored on disks.

Use of hierarchical memory system Usually, the CPU is about 1000 times faster than memory access. A hierarchical memory system can be used to close up the speed gap. Computer memory hierarchy is conceptually illustrated in Figure 1.6. The innermost level is the register files directly addressable by ALU. Cache memory can be used to serve as a buffer between the CPU and the main memory. Block access of the main memory can be achieved through multiway interleaving across parallel memory modules (see Figure 1.4). Virtual memory space can be established with the use of disks and tape units at the outer levels.

Details of memory subsystems for both uniprocessor and multiprocessor computers are given in Chapter 2. Various interleaved memory organizations are given in Section 3.1.4. Parallel memories for array processors are treated in

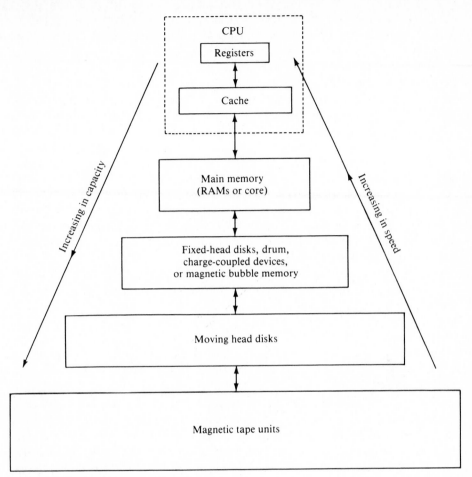

Figure 1.6 The classical memory hierarchy.

Section 6.2.4, along with the description of the Burroughs Scientific Processor (1978). Multiprocessor memory and cache coherence problems will be treated in Section 7.3. All these techniques are intended to broaden the memory bandwidth to match that of the CPU.

1.2.3 Balancing of Subsystem Bandwidth

In general, the CPU is the fastest unit in a computer, with a processor cycle t_p of tens of nanoseconds; the main memory has a cycle time t_m of hundreds of nanoseconds; and the I/O devices are the slowest with an average access time t_d of a few milliseconds. It is thus observed that

$$t_d > t_m > t_p \tag{1.1}$$

For example, the IBM 370/168 has $t_d = 5$ ms (disk), $t_m = 320$ ns, and $t_p = 80$ ns. With these speed gaps between the subsystems, we need to match their processing bandwidths in order to avoid a system bottleneck problem.

The *bandwidth* of a system is defined as the number of operations performed per unit time. In the case of a main memory system, the memory bandwidth is measured by the number of memory words that can be accessed (either fetch or store) per unit time. Let W be the number of words delivered per memory cycle t_m. Then the maximum memory bandwidth B_m is equal to

$$B_m = \frac{W}{t_m} \quad \text{(words/s or bytes/s)} \tag{1.2}$$

For example, the IBM 3033 uniprocessor has a processor cycle $t_p = 57$ ns. Eight double words (8 bytes each) can be requested from an eight-way interleaved memory system (with eight LSEs in Figure 1.7) per each memory cycle $t_m = 456$ ns. Thus, the maximum memory bandwidth of the 3033 is $B_m = 8 \times 8$ bytes/456 ns $= 140$ megabytes/s. Memory access conflicts may cause delayed access of some of the processor requests. In practice, the utilized memory bandwidth B_m^u is usually lower than B_m; that is, $B_m^u \leq B_m$. A rough measure of B_m^u has been suggested as

$$B_m^u \doteq \frac{B_m}{\sqrt{M}} \tag{1.3}$$

where M is the number of interleaved memory modules in the memory system (to be described in Section 3.1.4). For the IBM 3033 uniprocessor, we thus have an approximate $B_m^u = 140/\sqrt{8} = 49.5$ megabytes/s.

For external memory and I/O devices, the concept of bandwidth is more involved because of the sequential-access nature of magnetic disks and tape units. Considering the latencies and rotational delays, the data transfer rate may vary. In general, we refer to the average data transfer rate B_d as the bandwidth of a disk unit. A typical modern disk may have a data rate of 1 megabyte/s. With multiple disk drives, the data rate can increase to 10 megabytes/s, say for 10 drives per channel controller. A modern magnetic tape unit has a data transfer rate around 1.5 megabytes/s. Other peripheral devices, like line printers, readers/punch, and CRT terminals, are much slower due to mechanical motions.

The bandwidth of a processor is measured as the maximum CPU computation rate B_p, as in 160 megaflops for the Cray-1 and 12.5 *million instructions per second* (MIPS) for IBM 370/168. These are all peak values obtained by $1/t_p = 1/12.5$ ns and $1/80$ ns respectively. In practice, the utilized CPU rate is $B_p^u \leq B_p$. The utilized CPU rate B_p^u is based on measuring the number of output results (in words) per second:

$$B_p^u = \frac{R_w}{T_p} \quad \text{(words/s)} \tag{1.4}$$

where R_w is the number of word results and T_p is the total CPU time required to generate the R_w results. For a machine with variable word length, the rate will vary. For example, the CDC Cyber-205 has a peak CPU rate of 200 megaflops for

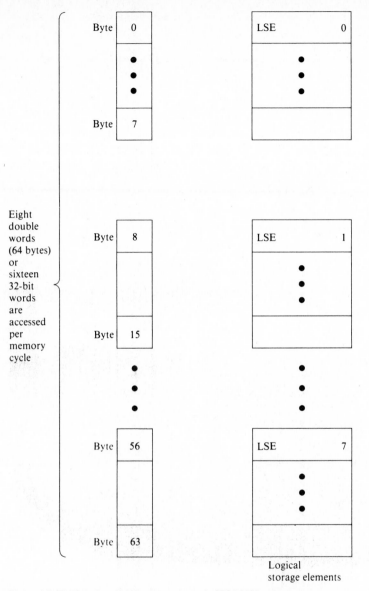

Eight double words (64 bytes) or sixteen 32-bit words are accessed per memory cycle

Logical storage elements

Figure 1.7 The interleaved memory structure in IBM 3033 uniprocessor.

32-bit results and only 100 megaflops for 64-bit results (one vector processor is assumed).

Based on current technology (1983), the following relationships have been observed between the bandwidths of the major subsystems in a high-performance uniprocessor:

$$B_m \geq B_m^u \geq B_p \geq B_p^u > B_d \tag{1.5}$$

This implies that the main memory has the highest bandwidth, since it must be updated by both the CPU and the I/O devices, as illustrated in Figure 1.8. Due to the unbalanced speeds (Eq. 1.1), we need to match the processing power of the three subsystems. Two major approaches are described below.

Bandwidth balancing between CPU and memory The speed gap between the CPU and the main memory can be closed up by using fast cache memory between them. The cache should have an access time $t_c = t_p$. A block of memory words is moved from the main memory into the cache (such as 16 words/block for the IBM 3033) so that immediate instructions/data can be available most of the time from the cache. The cache serves as a data/instruction buffer. Detailed descriptions of cache memories will be given in Sections 2.4 and 7.3

Bandwidth balancing between memory and I/O devices Input-output channels with different speeds can be used between the slow I/O devices and the main memory. These I/O channels perform buffering and multiplexing functions to transfer the data from multiple disks into the main memory by stealing cycles from the CPU. Furthermore, *intelligent disk controllers* or *database machines* can be used to filter out the irrelevant data just off the tracks of the disk. This filtering will alleviate the I/O channel saturation problem. The combined buffering, multiplexing, and filtering operations thus can provide a faster, more effective data transfer rate, matching that of the memory.

In the ideal case, we wish to achieve a totally balanced system, in which the entire memory bandwidth matches the bandwidth sum of the processor and I/O devices; that is,

$$B_p^u + B_d = B_m^u \tag{1.6}$$

where $B_p^u = B_p$ and $B_m^u = B_m$ are both maximized. Achieving this total balance requires tremendous hardware and software supports beyond any of the existing systems.

1.2.4 Multiprogramming and Time Sharing

Even when there is only one CPU in a uniprocessor system, we can still achieve a high degree of resource sharing among many user programs. We will briefly review the concepts of *multiprogramming* and *time sharing* in this subsection. These are software approaches to achieve concurrency in a uniprocessor system. The

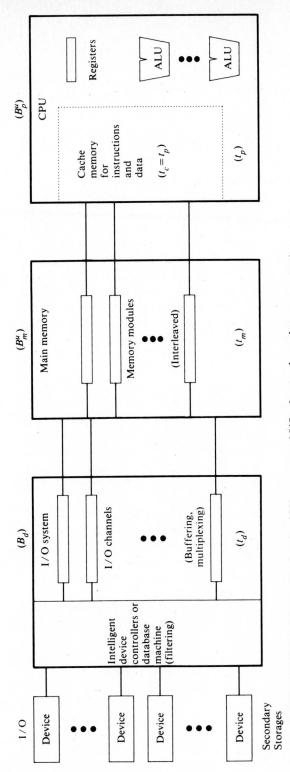

Figure 1.8 Bandwidth balancing mechanisms between CPU, memory, and I/O subsystem in a uniprocessor computer.

17

conventional batch processing is illustrated by the sequential execution in Figure 1.9a. We use the notation *i*, *c*, and *o* to represent the *input*, *compute*, and *output* operations, respectively.

Multiprogramming Within the same time interval, there may be multiple processes active in a computer, competing for memory, I/O, and CPU resources. We are aware of the fact that some computer programs are *CPU-bound* (computation intensive), and some are *I/O-bound* (input-output intensive). We can mix the execution of various types of programs in the computer to balance bandwidths among the various functional units. The program interleaving is intended to promote better resource utilization through overlapping I/O and CPU operations.

As illustrated in Figure 1.9b, whenever a process P_1 is tied up with I/O operations, the system scheduler can switch the CPU to process P_2. This allows the simultaneous execution of several programs in the system. When P_2 is done, the CPU can be switched to P_3. Note the overlapped I/O and CPU operations and the CPU wait time are greatly reduced. This interleaving of CPU and I/O operations among several programs is called *multiprogramming*. The programs can be mixed across the boundary of user tasks and system processes, in either a mono-programming or a multiprogramming environment. The total execution time is reduced with multiprogramming. The processes $P_1, P_2, \ldots$, may belong to the same or different programs.

Time sharing Multiprogramming on a uniprocessor is centered around the sharing of the CPU by many programs. Sometimes a high-priority program may occupy the CPU for too long to allow others to share. This problem can be overcome by using a *time-sharing* operating system. The concept extends from multiprogramming by assigning fixed or variable *time slices* to multiple programs. In other words, equal opportunities are given to all programs competing for the use of the CPU. This concept is illustrated in Figure 1.9c. The execution time saved with time sharing may be greater than with either batch or multiprogram processing modes.

The time-sharing use of the CPU by multiple programs in a uniprocessor computer creates the concept of *virtual processors*. Time sharing is particularly effective when applied to a computer system connected to many interactive terminals. Each user at a terminal can interact with the computer on an instantaneous basis. Each user thinks that he or she is the sole user of the system, because the response is so fast (waiting time between time slices is not recognizable by humans). Time sharing is indispensable to the development of real-time computer systems.

Time sharing was first developed for a uniprocessor system. The concept can be extended to designing interactive time-sharing multiprocessor systems. Of course, the time sharing on multiprocessors is much more complicated. We will discuss the operating system design considerations for multiprocessor systems in Chapters 7, 8, and 9. The performance of either a uniprocessor or a multiprocessor system depends heavily on the capability of the operating system. After all, the major function of an operating system is to optimize the resource allocation and management, which often leads to high performance.

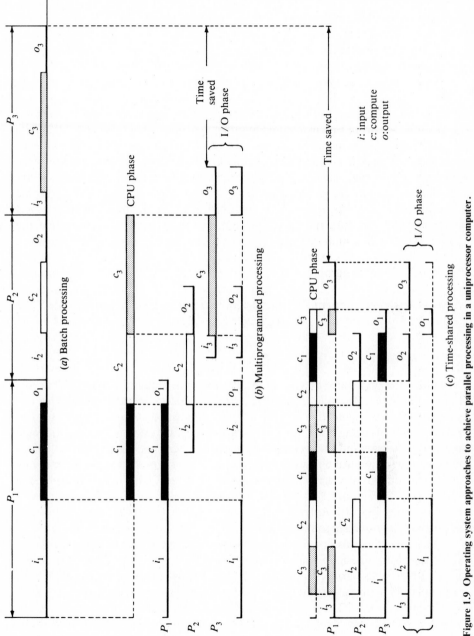

(a) Batch processing

(b) Multiprogrammed processing

(c) Time-shared processing

i: input
c: compute
o: output

Figure 1.9 Operating system approaches to achieve parallel processing in a uniprocessor computer.

1.3 PARALLEL COMPUTER STRUCTURES

Parallel computers are those systems that emphasize parallel processing. The basic architectural features of parallel computers are introduced below. We divide parallel computers into three architectural configurations:

- Pipeline computers
- Array processors
- Multiprocessor systems

A pipeline computer performs overlapped computations to exploit *temporal parallelism*. An array processor uses multiple synchronized arithmetic logic units to achieve *spatial parallelism*. A multiprocessor system achieves *asynchronous parallelism* through a set of interactive processors with shared resources (memories, database, etc.). These three parallel approaches to computer system design are not mutually exclusive. In fact, most existing computers are now pipelined, and some of them assume also an "array" or a "multiprocessor" structure. The fundamental difference between an array processor and a multiprocessor system is that the processing elements in an array processor operate synchronously but processors in a multiprocessor system may operate asynchronously.

New computing concepts to be introduced in this section include the *data flow computers* and some *VLSI algorithmic processors*. All these new approaches demand extensive hardware to achieve parallelism. The rapid progress in the VLSI technology has made these new approaches possible.

1.3.1 Pipeline Computers

Normally, the process of executing an instruction in a digital computer involves four major steps: *instruction fetch* (IF) from the main memory; *instruction decoding* (ID), identifying the operation to be performed; *operand fetch* (OF), if needed in the execution; and then *execution* (EX) of the decoded arithmetic logic operation. In a nonpipelined computer, these four steps must be completed before the next instruction can be issued. In a pipelined computer, successive instructions are executed in an overlapped fashion, as illustrated in Figure 1.10. Four pipeline stages, IF, ID, OF, and EX, are arranged into a linear cascade. The two space-time diagrams show the difference between overlapped instruction execution and sequentially nonoverlapped execution.

An *instruction cycle* consists of multiple pipeline cycles. A pipeline cycle can be set equal to the delay of the slowest stage. The flow of data (input operands, intermediate results, and output results) from stage to stage is triggered by a common clock of the pipeline. In other words, the operation of all stages is synchronized under a common clock control. Interface latches are used between adjacent segments to hold the intermediate results. For the nonpipelined (non-overlapped) computer, it takes four pipeline cycles to complete one instruction. Once a pipeline is filled up, an output result is produced from the pipeline on each

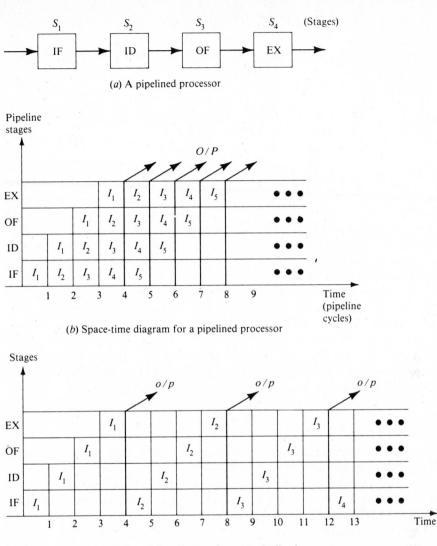

(a) A pipelined processor

(b) Space-time diagram for a pipelined processor

(c) Space-time diagram for a nonpipelined processor

Figure 1.10 Basic concepts of pipelined processor and overlapped instruction execution.

cycle. The instruction cycle has been effectively reduced to one-fourth of the original cycle time by such overlapped execution.

Theoretically, a k-stage linear pipeline processor could be at most k times faster. We will prove this in Chapter 3. However, due to memory conflicts, data dependency, branch and interrupts, this ideal speedup may not be achieved for out-of-sequence computations. What has been described so far is the *instruction pipeline.* For some CPU-bound instructions, the execution phase can be further partitioned into a multiple-stage arithmetic logic pipeline, as for sophisticated floating-point operations. Some main issues in designing a pipeline computer include job sequencing, collision prevention, congestion control, branch handling, reconfiguration, and hazard resolution. We will learn how to cope with each of these problems later.

Due to the overlapped instruction and arithmetic execution, it is obvious that pipeline machines are better tuned to perform the same operations repeatedly through the pipeline. Whenever there is a change of operation, say from *add* to *multiply*, the arithmetic pipeline must be drained and reconfigured, which will cause extra time delays. Therefore, pipeline computers are more attractive for vector processing, where component operations may be repeated many times. Most existing pipeline computers emphasize vector processing. We will study basic vector processing requirements in Chapter 3. Various vectorization methods will be presented in Chapter 4, after learning the structure and capability of commercially available pipeline supercomputers and attached processors.

A typical pipeline computer is conceptually depicted in Figure 1.11. This architecture is very similar to several commercial machines like Cray-1 and VP-200, to be described in Chapter 4. Both scalar arithmetic pipelines and vector arithmetic pipelines are provided. The instruction preprocessing unit is itself pipelined with three stages shown. The OF stage consists of two independent stages, one for fetching scalar operands and the other for vector operand fetch. The scalar registers are fewer in quantity than the vector registers because each vector register implies a whole set of component registers. For example, a vector register in Cray-1 contains 64 component registers, each of which is 64 bits wide. Each vector register in Cray-1 requires 4096 flip-flops. Both scalar and vector data could appear in fixed-point or floating-point format. This means different pipelines can be dedicated to different arithmetic logic functions with different data formats. The scalar arithmetic pipelines differ from the vector arithmetic pipelines in structure and control strategies. Modern vector processors are usually augmented with a powerful scalar processor to handle a mixture of vector and scalar instructions.

Pipelined computers to be studied in Chapter 4 include the early vector processors, Control Data's Star-100 and Texas Instruments' Advanced Scientific Computer (ASC); the attached pipeline processors, AP-120B and FPS-164 by Floating Point Systems, Datawest MATP, and IBM 3838; and recent vector processors, Cray-1, Cyber-205, and Fujitsu VP-200. Vectorization methods to be studied include resource reservation, pipeline chaining, vector segmentation, vectorizing compiler design, and optimization of compilers for vector processing. A performance evaluation model for pipeline processors will also be presented.

1.3.2 Array Computers

An *array processor* is a synchronous parallel computer with multiple arithmetic logic units, called *processing elements* (PE), that can operate in parallel in a lock-step fashion. By replication of ALUs, one can achieve the spatial parallelism. The PEs are synchronized to perform the same function at the same time. An appropriate data-routing mechanism must be established among the PEs. A typical

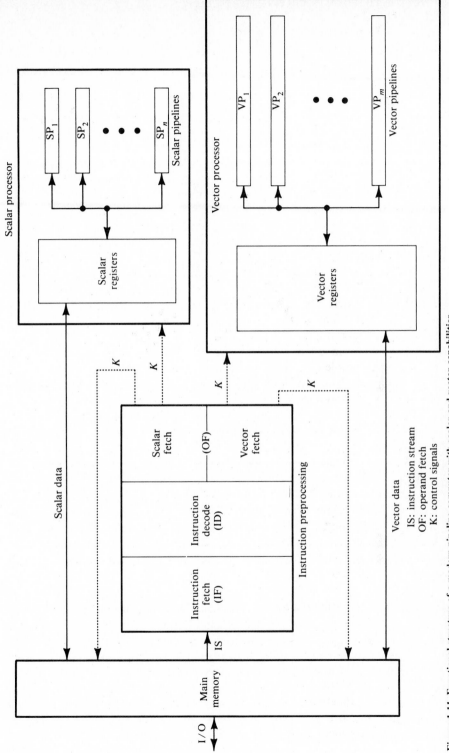

Figure 1.11 Functional structure of a modern pipeline computer with scalar and vector capabilities.

IS: instruction stream
OF: operand fetch
K: control signals

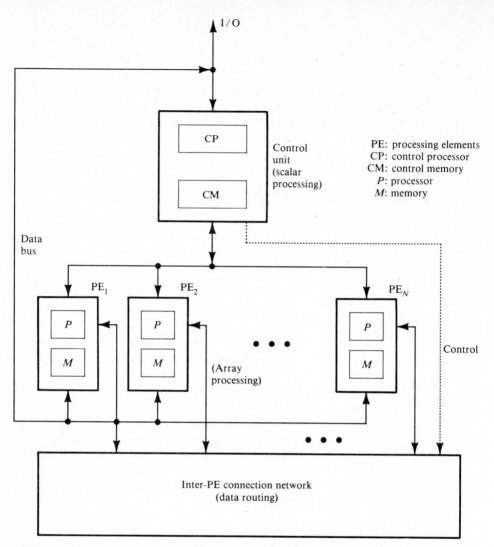

Figure 1.12 Functional structure of an SIMD array processor with concurrent scalar processing in the control unit.

array processor is depicted in Figure 1.12. Scalar and control-type instructions are directly executed in the *control unit* (CU). Each PE consists of an ALU with registers and a local memory. The PEs are interconnected by a data-routing network. The interconnection pattern to be established for specific computation is under program control from the CU. Vector instructions are broadcast to the PEs for distributed execution over different component operands fetched directly from the local memories. Instruction fetch (from local memories or from the control memory) and decode is done by the control unit. The PEs are passive devices without instruction decoding capabilities.

Various interconnection structures for a set of PEs will be studied in Chapter 5. Both recirculating networks and multistage networks will be covered. *Associative memory*, which is content addressable, will also be treated there in the context of parallel processing. Array processors designed with associative memories are called *associative processors*. Parallel algorithms on array processors will be given for matrix multiplication, merge sort, and fast Fourier transform (FFT). A performance evaluation of the array processor will be presented, with emphasis on resource optimization.

Modern array processors will be described in Chapter 6. Different array processors may use different interconnection networks among the PEs. For example, Illiac-IV uses a mesh-structured network and Burroughs Scientific Processor (BSP) uses a crossbar network. In addition to Illiac-IV and BSP, we will study a bit-slice array processor called a *massively parallel processor* (MPP). Array processors are much more difficult to program than pipeline machines. We will study various performance enhancement methods for array processors, including the use of skewed memory allocation, language extensions for vector-array processing, and possible future architectural improvements.

1.3.3 Multiprocessor Systems

Research and development of multiprocessor systems are aimed at improving throughput, reliability, flexibility, and availability. A basic multiprocessor organization is conceptually depicted in Figure 1.13. The system contains two or more processors of approximately comparable capabilities. All processors share access to common sets of memory modules, I/O channels, and peripheral devices. Most importantly, the entire system must be controlled by a single integrated operating system providing interactions between processors and their programs at various levels. Besides the shared memories and I/O devices, each processor has its own local memory and private devices. Interprocessor communications can be done through the shared memories or through an interrupt network.

Multiprocessor hardware system organization is determined primarily by the interconnection structure to be used between the memories and processors (and between memories and I/O channels, if needed). Three different interconnections have been practiced in the past:

- Time-shared common bus
- Crossbar switch network
- Multiport memories

These organizations and their possible extensions for multiprocessor systems will be described in detail in Chapter 7. Techniques for exploiting concurrency in multiprocessors will be studied, including the development of some parallel language features and the possible detection of parallelism in user programs.

Special memory organization for multiprocessors will be treated in Section 7.3. We will cover hierarchical virtual memory, cache structures, parallel memories,

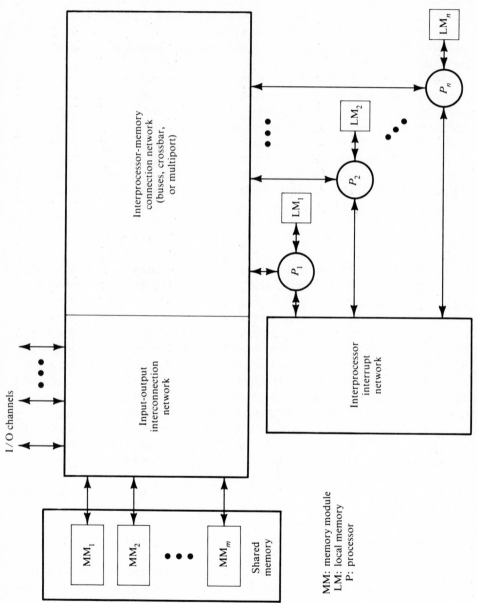

MM: memory module
LM: local memory
P: processor

Figure 1.13 Functional design of an MIMD multiprocessor system.

paging, and various memory management issues. Multiprocessor operating systems will also be studied in Chapter 8. Important topics include protection schemes, system deadlock resolution methods, interprocess communication mechanisms, and various multiple processor scheduling strategies. Parallel algorithms for multiprocessors will also be studied. Both synchronous and asynchronous algorithms will be specified and evaluated.

We will present several exploratory and commercial multiprocessor systems in Chapter 9, including the C.mmp system and Cm* system developed at Carnegie Mellon University, the S-1 multiprocessor system developed at the Lawrence Livermore National Laboratory, the IBM System 370/Model 168 MP system, the IBM 3081, the Univac 1100/80 and 90 MP, the Tandem multiprocessor, Denelcor HEP system, and the Cray X-MP and Cray-2 systems.

What we have discussed so far are *centralized* computing systems, in which all hardware-software resources are housed in the same computing center with negligible communication delays among subsystems. The continuing decline of computer hardware and communication costs has made possible the decentralization of hardware, controls, and databases in a computer system. Claims made for *distributed processing* systems include fast response, high availability, graceful degradation, resource sharing, high adaptability to changes in work load, and better expandability. Distributed computing is being widely practiced in banking institutions, airline companies, government services, nationwide dealership, and chain department stores. Computer networks and distributed processing are beyond the scope of this book.

1.3.4 Performance of Parallel Computers

The speedup that can be achieved by a parallel computer with n identical processors working concurrently on a single problem is at most n times faster than a single processor. In practice, the speedup is much less, since some processors are idle at a given time because of conflicts over memory access or communication paths, inefficient algorithms for exploiting the natural concurrency in the computing problem, or many other reasons to be discussed in subsequent chapters. Figure 1.14 shows the various estimates of the actual speedup, ranging from a lower-bound $\log_2 n$ to an upper-bound $n/\ln n$.

The lower-bound $\log_2 n$ is known as the *Minsky's conjecture*. Most commercial multiprocessor systems have from $n = 2$ to $n = 4$ processors. Exploratory research multiprocessors have challenged $n = 16$ processors in the C.mmp and S-1 systems. Using Minsky's conjecture, only a speedup of 2 to 4 can be expected from existing multiprocessors with 4 to 16 processors. This sounds rather pessimistic. A more optimistic speedup estimate is upper bounded by $n/\ln n$ as derived below.

Consider a computing problem, which can be executed by a uniprocessor in unit time, $T_1 = 1$. Let f_i be the probability of assigning the same problem to i processors working equally with an average load $d_i = 1/i$ per processor. Furthermore, assume equal probability of each operating mode using i processors, that is $f_i = 1/n$, for n operating modes: $i = 1, 2, \ldots, n$. The average time required to solve

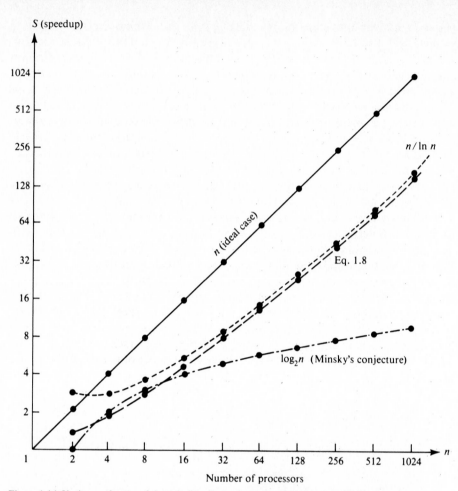

Figure 1.14 Various estimates of the speedup of an *n*-processor system over a single processor.

the problem on an *n*-processor system is given below, where the summation represents *n* operating modes.

$$T_n = \sum_{i=1}^{n} f_i \cdot d_i = \frac{\sum_{i=1}^{n} \frac{1}{i}}{n} \tag{1.7}$$

The average speedup S is obtained as the ratio of $T_1 = 1$ to T_n; that is,

$$S = \frac{T_1}{T_n} = \frac{n}{\sum_{i=1}^{n} \frac{1}{i}} \leq \frac{n}{\ln n} \tag{1.8}$$

For a given multiprocessor system with 2, 4, 8, or 16 processors, the respective average speedups (using Eq. 1.8) are 1.33, 1.92, 3.08, and 6.93. The speedup obtained in Eq. 1.8 can be approximated by $n/\ln n$ for large n. For example, $S = 1000/\ln 1000$ $= 144.72$ for a system with $n = 1000$ processors. We have plotted the upper bound, the lower bound, and the speedup using Eq. 1.8 in Figure 1.14.

The above analysis explains the reason why a typical commercial multi-processor system consists of only two to four processors. Dr. John Worlton of the United States Los Alamos Scientific Laboratory said once: "The designers of supercomputers will do better at exploiting concurrency in the computing problems if they use a small number of fast processors instead of a large number of slower processors." This conclusion coincides with the analytical prediction given in Eq. 1.8.

To measure the real performance of a computer system, one cannot ignore the computation cost and the ease in programming. Comparing multiprocessor systems with other computer structures, we conclude the following: Pipelined uniprocessor systems are still dominating the commercial market in both business and scientific applications. Pipelined computers cost less and their operating systems are well developed to achieve better resource utilization and higher performance. Array processors are mostly custom designed. For specific applications, they might be effective. The performance/cost ratio of such special-purpose machines might be low. Programming on an array processor is much more difficult due to the rigid architecture. Multiprocessor systems are more flexible in general-purpose applications. Pipelined multiprocessor systems represent state-of-the-art design in parallel processing computers. Many of the computer manu-facturers are taking this route in upgrading their existing systems.

1.3.5 Data Flow and New Concepts

New approaches to parallel processing are briefly outlined in this section. Details of these approaches will be treated in Chapter 10.

Data flow computers The conventional von Neumann machines are called *control flow computers* because instructions are executed sequentially as controlled by a program counter. Sequential program execution is inherently slow. To exploit maximal parallelism in a program, *data flow computers* were suggested in recent years. The basic concept is to enable the execution of an instruction whenever its required operands become available. Thus no program counters are needed in data-driven computations. Instruction initiation depends on data availability, independent of the physical location of an instruction in the program. In other words, instructions in a program are not ordered. The execution follows the data dependency constraints. Theoretically, maximal concurrency can be exploited in such a data flow machine, constrained only by the hardware resource availability.

Programs for data-driven computations can be represented by *data flow graphs*. An example data flow graph is given in Figure 1.15 for the calculation of the following expression:

$$z = (x + y) * 2 \tag{1.9}$$

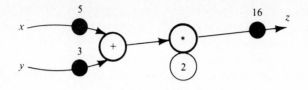

(a) Data flow program graph

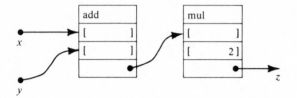

(b) Template implementation

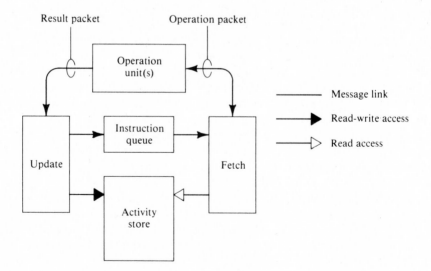

(c) Basic data flow mechanism

Figure 1.15 Data flow graph, language, and architectural concept (Courtesy of Dennis *IEEE Computer*, 1980).

Each instruction in a data flow computer is implemented as a *template*, which consists of the operator, operand receivers, and result destinations. Operands are marked on the incoming arcs and results on the outgoing arcs. The template implementation of the program graph in part *a* is shown in part *b* of Figure 1.15. The firing rule of an instruction requires that all receivers be filled with operand values.

The basic mechanism for the execution of a data flow program is conceptually illustrated in Figure 1.15c. Activity templates are stored in the *activity store*. Each activity template has a unique address which is entered in the *instruction queue* when the instruction is ready for execution. Instruction fetch and data access are handled by the *fetch* and *update* units. The *operation* unit performs the specified operation and generates the result to be delivered to each destination field in the template. This basic structure can be extended to a data flow multiprocessor, to be described in Chapter 10.

VLSI computing structures The rapid advent of very-large-scale integrated (VLSI) technology has created a new architectural horizon in implementing parallel algorithms directly in hardware. The new high-resolution lithographic technique has made possible the fabrication of 10^5 transistors in an NMOS chip. It has been projected that by the late eighties it will be possible to fabricate VLSI chips which contain more than 10^7 individual transistors. One such chip may contain more functions than one of today's large minicomputers. The VLSI development phases and definitions are summarized in Table 1.2.

The use of VLSI technology in designing high-performance multiprocessors and pipelined computing devices is currently under intensive investigation in both industrial and university environments. The multiprocessors are expected to be regularly interconnected. Pipelining makes it possible to overlap I/O with internal computations. Pipelined multiprocessing is a distinct feature of most of the VLSI computing structures that have been proposed in the literature. Most proposed VLSI arithmetic devices are for vector and matrix type computations. Both globally structured arrays and modular computing networks have been suggested for signal and image processing. We will study VLSI computing algorithms and architectures in Chapter 10.

Table 1.2 VLSI domain and definition phases

Domain / Phase	Gate equivalent count ($> 10^3$ G/C)†	Line width ($< 2.5\ \mu M$)	Storage density ($> 30\ KB/CM^2$)	Circuit complexity ($> 16\ KD$)
VLSI-1	10^3–10^4 G/C	2–4 μM	30–100 KB/CM^2	16–64 KD
VLSI-2	10^4–10^5 G/C	1–2 μM	100–300 KB/CM^2	64–256 KD
VLSI-3	10^5–10^6 G/C	0.5–1 μM	300–1000 KB/CM^2	256–1024 KD
VLSI-4	$> 10^6$ G/C	$< 0.5\ \mu M$	> 1000 KB/CM^2	> 1024 KD

† G/C = gates/chip, μM = micron (10^{-6} meter), KB = 1024 bits, and KD = 1024 devices (transistors or diodes).

1.4 ARCHITECTURAL CLASSIFICATION SCHEMES

Three computer architectural classification schemes are presented in this section. *Flynn's classification* (1966) is based on the multiplicity of instruction streams and data streams in a computer system. *Feng's scheme* (1972) is based on serial versus parallel processing. *Händler's classification* (1977) is determined by the degree of parallelism and pipelining in various subsystem levels.

1.4.1 Multiplicity of Instruction-Data Streams

In general, digital computers may be classified into four categories, according to the multiplicity of instruction and data streams. This scheme for classifying computer organizations was introduced by Michael J. Flynn. The essential computing process is the execution of a sequence of instructions on a set of data. The term *stream* is used here to denote a sequence of items (instructions or data) as executed or operated upon by a single processor. *Instructions* or *data* are defined with respect to a referenced machine. An *instruction stream* is a sequence of instructions as executed by the machine; a *data stream* is a sequence of data including input, partial, or temporary results, called for by the instruction stream.

Computer organizations are characterized by the multiplicity of the hardware provided to service the instruction and data streams. Listed below are Flynn's four machine organizations:

- Single instruction stream-single data stream (SISD)
- Single instruction stream-multiple data stream (SIMD)
- Multiple instruction stream-single data stream (MISD)
- Multiple instruction stream-multiple data stream (MIMD)

These organizational classes are illustrated by the block diagrams in Figure 1.16. The categorization depends on the multiplicity of simultaneous events in the system components. Conceptually, only three types of system components are needed in the illustration. Both instructions and data are fetched from the *memory modules*. Instructions are decoded by the *control unit*, which sends the decoded instruction stream to the *processor units* for execution. Data streams flow between the processors and the memory bidirectionally. Multiple memory modules may be used in the shared memory subsystem. Each instruction stream is generated by an independent control unit. Multiple data streams originate from the subsystem of shared memory modules. I/O facilities are not shown in these simplified block diagrams.

SISD computer organization This organization, shown in Figure 1.16a, represents most serial computers available today. Instructions are executed sequentially but may be overlapped in their execution stages (pipelining). Most SISD uniprocessor systems are pipelined. An SISD computer may have more than one functional unit in it. All the functional units are under the supervision of one control unit.

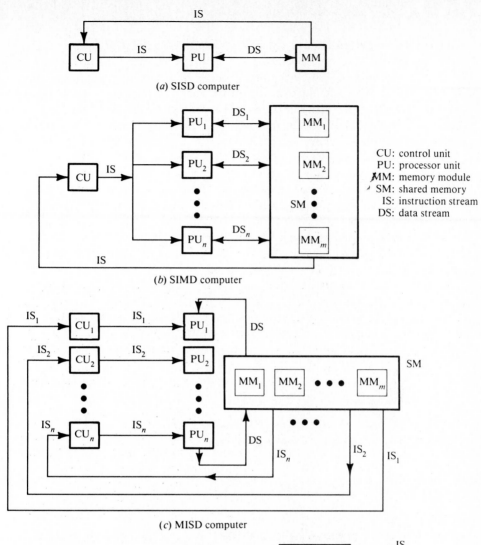

CU: control unit
PU: processor unit
MM: memory module
SM: shared memory
IS: instruction stream
DS: data stream

(a) SISD computer

(b) SIMD computer

(c) MISD computer

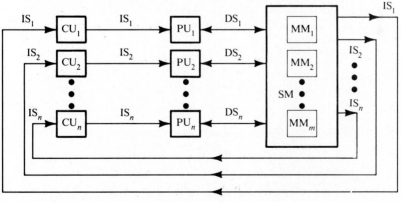

(d) MIMD computer

Figure 1.16 Flynn's classification of various computer organizations.

33

SIMD computer organization This class corresponds to array processors, introduced in Section 1.3.2. As illustrated in Figure 1.16*b*, there are multiple processing elements supervised by the same control unit. All PEs receive the same instruction broadcast from the control unit but operate on different data sets from distinct data streams. The shared memory subsystem may contain multiple modules. We further divide SIMD machines into *word-slice* versus *bit-slice* modes, to be described in Section 1.4.2.

MISD computer organization This organization is conceptually illustrated in Figure 1.16*c*. There are *n* processor units, each receiving distinct instructions operating over the same data stream and its derivatives. The results (output) of one processor become the input (operands) of the next processor in the macropipe. This structure has received much less attention and has been challenged as impractical by some computer architects. No real embodiment of this class exists.

MIMD computer organization Most multiprocessor systems and multiple computer systems can be classified in this category (Figure 1.16*d*). An *intrinsic* MIMD computer implies interactions among the *n* processors because all memory streams are derived from the same data space shared by all processors. If the *n* data streams were derived from disjoint subspaces of the shared memories, then we would have the so-called multiple SISD (MSISD) operation, which is nothing but a set of *n* independent SISD uniprocessor systems. An intrinsic MIMD

Table 1.3 Flynn's computer system classification

Computer class	Computer system models (chapters where the system is quoted or described)
SISD (uses one functional unit)	IBM 701 (1); IBM 1620 (1); IBM 7090 (1); PDP VAX11/780 (1).
SISD (with multiple functional units)	IBM 360/91 (3); IBM 370/168UP (1); CDC 6600 (1); CDC Star-100 (4); TI-ASC (4); FPS AP-120B (4); FPS-164 (4); IBM 3838 (4); Cray-1 (4); CDC Cyber-205 (4); Fujitsu VP-200 (4); CDC-NASF (4); Fujitsu FACOM-230/75 (4).
SIMD (word-slice processing)	Illiac-IV (6); PEPE (1); BSP (6)
SIMD (bit-slice processing)	STARAN (1); MPP (6); DAP (1).
MIMD (loosely coupled)	IBM 370/168 MP (9); Univac 1100/80 (9); Tandem/16 (9); IBM 3081/3084 (9); C.m* (9)
MIMD (tightly coupled)	Burroughs D-825 (9); C.mmp (9); Cray-2 (9). S-1 (9); Cray-X MP (9); Denelcor HEP (9)

computer is *tightly coupled* if the degree of interactions among the processors is high. Otherwise, we consider them *loosely coupled*. Most commercial MIMD computers are loosely coupled.

In Table 1.3, we have listed several system models under each of the three existing computer organizations. Some of these machines will be studied in subsequent chapters. Readers should check the quoted chapters for details or references related to the specific machines.

1.4.2 Serial Versus Parallel Processing

Tse-yun Feng has suggested the use of the *degree* of parallelism to classify various computer architectures. The maximum number of binary digits (bits) that can be processed within a unit time by a computer system is called the *maximum parallelism degree P*. Let P_i be the number of bits that can be processed within the ith processor cycle (or the ith clock period). Consider T processor cycles indexed by $i = 1, 2, \ldots, T$. The average parallelism degree, P_a is defined by

$$P_a = \frac{\sum_{i=1}^{T} P_i}{T} \tag{1.10}$$

In general, $P_i \leq P$. Thus, we define the *utilization rate* μ of a computer system within T cycles by

$$\mu = \frac{P_a}{P} = \frac{\sum_{i=1}^{T} P_i}{T \cdot P} \tag{1.11}$$

If the computing power of the processor is fully utilized (or the parallelism is fully exploited), then we have $P_i = P$ for all i and $\mu = 1$ for 100 percent utilization. The utilization rate depends on the application program being executed.

Figure 1.17 demonstrates the classification of computers by their maximum parallelism degrees. The horizontal axis shows the word length n. The vertical axis corresponds to the bit-slice length m. Both length measures are in terms of the number of bits contained in a word or in a bit slice. A *bit slice* is a string of bits, one from each of the words at the same vertical bit position. For example, the TI-ASC has a word length of 64 and four arithmetic pipelines. Each pipe has eight pipeline stages. Thus there are $8 \times 4 = 32$ bits per each bit slice in the four pipes. TI-ASC is represented as (64, 32). The maximum parallelism degree $P(C)$ of a given computer system C is represented by the product of the word length w and the bit-slice length m; that is,

$$P(C) = n \cdot m \tag{1.12}$$

The pair (n, m) corresponds to a point in the computer space shown by the coordinate system in Figure 1.17. The $P(C)$ is equal to the area of the rectangle defined by the integers n and m.

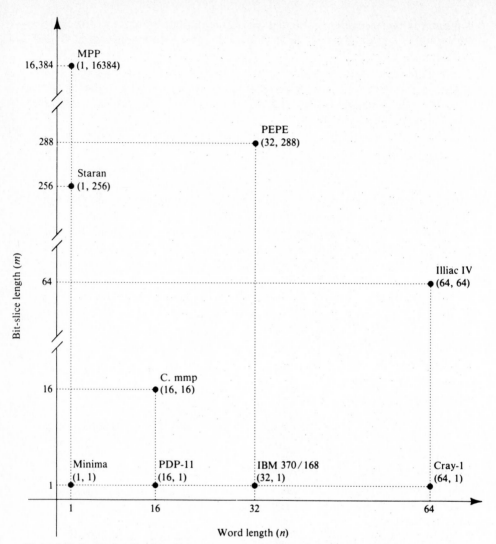

Figure 1.17 Feng's classification of computer systems in terms of parallelism exhibited by word length and bit-slice length.

There are four types of processing methods that can be seen from this diagram:

- Word-serial and bit-serial (WSBS)
- Word-parallel and bit-serial (WPBS)
- Word-serial and bit-parallel (WSBP)
- Word-parallel and bit-parallel (WPBP)

WSBS has been called *bit-serial processing* because one bit ($n = m = 1$) is processed at a time, a rather slow process. This was done only in the first-generation

Table 1.4 Feng's computer systems classification

Mode	Computer model (manufacturer)	Degree of parallelism (n, m)
WSPS $n = 1$ $m = 1$	The "MINIMA" (unknown)	(1, 1)
WPBS $n = 1$ $m > 1$ (bit-slice processing)	STARAN (Goodyear Aerospace) MPP (Goodyear Aerospace) DAP (ICL, England)	(1, 256) (1, 16384) (1, 4096)
WSBP $n > 1$ $m = 1$ (word-slice processing)	IBM 370/168 UP CDC6600 Burrough 7700 VAX 11/780 (DEC)	(64, 1) (60, 1) (48, 1) (16/32, 1)
WPBP $n > 1$ $m > 1$ (fully parallel processing)	Illiac IV (Burroughs) TI-ASC C.mmp (CMU) S-1 (LLNL)	(64, 64) (64, 32) (16, 16) (36, 16)

computers. WPBS ($n = 1, m > 1$) has been called *bis* (*bit-slice*) *processing* because an m-bit slice is processed at a time. WSBP ($n > 1, m = 1$), as found in most existing computers, has been called *word-slice processing* because one word of n bits is processed at a time. Finally, WPBP ($n > 1, m > 1$) is known as *fully parallel processing* (or simply *parallel processing*, if no confusion exists), in which an array of $n \cdot m$ bits is processed at one time, the fastest processing mode of the four. In Table 1.4, we have listed a number of computer systems under each processing mode. The system parameters n, m are also shown for each system. The bit-slice processors, like STARAN, MPP, and DAP, all have long bit slices. Illiac-IV and PEPE are two word-slice array processors. Some of these systems will be described in later chapters.

1.4.3 Parallelism Versus Pipelining

Wolfgang Händler has proposed a classification scheme for identifying the parallelism degree and pipelining degree built into the hardware structures of a computer system. He considers parallel-pipeline processing at three subsystem levels:

- Processor control unit (PCU)
- Arithmetic logic unit (ALU)
- Bit-level circuit (BLC)

The functions of PCU and ALU should be clear to us. Each PCU corresponds to one processor or one CPU. The ALU is equivalent to the processing element (PE) we specified for SIMD array processors. The BLC corresponds to the combinational logic circuitry needed to perform 1-bit operations in the ALU.

A computer system C can be characterized by a triple containing six independent entities, as defined below:

$$T(C) = \langle K \times K', D \times D', W \times W' \rangle \tag{1.13}$$

where $K =$ the number of processors (PCUs) within the computer
$D =$ the number of ALUs (or PEs) under the control of one PCU
$W =$ the word length of an ALU or of a PE
$W' =$ the number of pipeline stages in all ALUs or in a PE
$D' =$ the number of ALUs that can be pipelined (pipeline chaining to be described in Chapter 4)
$K' =$ the number of PCUs that can be pipelined (macropipelining to be described in Chapter 3)

Several real computer examples are used to clarify the above parametric descriptions. The Texas Instrument's Advanced Scientific Computer (TI-ASC) has one controller controlling four arithmetic pipelines, each has 64-bit word lengths and eight stages. Thus, we have

$$T(\text{ASC}) = \langle 1 \times 1, 4 \times 1, 64 \times 8 \rangle = \langle 1, 4, 64 \times 8 \rangle \tag{1.14}$$

Whenever the second entity, K', D', or W', equals 1, we drop it, since pipelining of one stage or of one unit is meaningless.

Another example is the Control Data 6600, which has a CPU with an ALU that has 10 specialized hardware functions, each of a word length of 60 bits. Up to 10 of these functions can be linked into a longer pipeline. Furthermore, the CDC-6600 has 10 peripheral I/O processors which can operate in parallel. Each I/O processor has one ALU with a word length of 12 bits. Thus, we specify 6600 in two parts, using the operator $\times$ to link them:

$$\begin{aligned} T(\text{CDC } 6600) &= T(\text{central processor}) \times T(I/O \text{ processors}) \\ &= \langle 1, 1 \times 10, 60 \rangle \times \langle 10, 1, 12 \rangle \end{aligned} \tag{1.15}$$

Another sample system is the C.mmp multiprocessor system developed at Carnegie-Mellon University. This system can be used in a number of ways, as illustrated in Figure 1.18. The system consists of 16 PDP-11 minicomputers of a word length of 16 bits. Normally, it will operate in MIMD mode, as shown in Figure 1.18a. Theoretically, it can also operate in SIMD mode, provided all the minicomputers are synchronized by one master controller, as illustrated in Figure 1.18b. Finally, the system can be rearranged to operate in MISD mode, as shown in Figure 1.18c. Based on these three operating modes, we specify C.mmp in three parts, using the operator $+$ to separate them.

$$T(\text{C.mmp}) = \langle 16, 1, 16 \rangle + \langle 1 \times 16, 1, 16 \rangle + \langle 1, 16, 16 \rangle \tag{1.16}$$

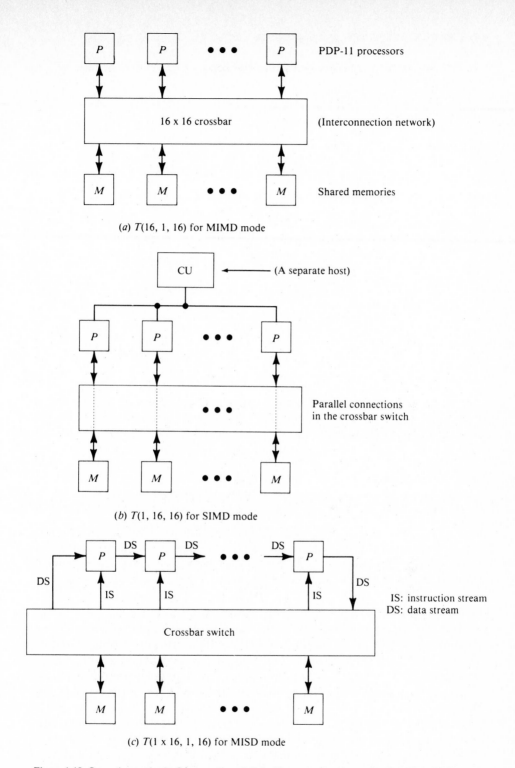

(a) $T(16, 1, 16)$ for MIMD mode

(b) $T(1, 16, 16)$ for SIMD mode

IS: instruction stream
DS: data stream

(c) $T(1 \times 16, 1, 16)$ for MISD mode

Figure 1.18 Operation modes in C.mmp system (all double-arrowed paths are for both IS and DS).

Table 1.5 Händler's computer system classification

Computer model $T(C)$	System specification† $\langle K \times K', D \times D', W \times W' \rangle$
T(TI-ASC)	$\langle 1, 4, 64 \times 8 \rangle$
T(CDC-6600)	$\langle 1, 1 \times 10, 60 \rangle \times \langle 10, 1, 12 \rangle$
	central I/O
	processor processors
T(Illiac IV)	$\langle 1, 64, 64 \rangle$
T(MPP)	$\langle 1, 16384, 1 \rangle$
T(C.mmp)	$\langle 16, 1, 16 \rangle + \langle 1 \times 16, 1, 16 \rangle + \langle 1, 16, 16 \rangle$
T(PEPC)	$\langle 1 \times 3, 288, 32 \rangle$
T(IBM 360/91)	$\langle 1, 3, 64 \times (3 \sim 5) \rangle$
T(Prime)	$\langle 5, 1, 16 \rangle$
T(Cray-1)	$\langle 1, 12 \times 8\ddagger, 64 \times (1 \sim 14) \rangle$
T(AP-120B)	$\langle 1, 2, 38 \times (2 \sim 3) \rangle$

† K', D', and W' are omitted when equal to 1.

‡ For Cray-1, the pipeline chaining degree is a variable with a maximum value equal to 8.

In Table 1.5, we use Händler's classification scheme to specify some computer systems. It should be noted that many computers have variable numbers of stages in different functional units. Under such circumstances, we indicate the range of pipeline stages within parentheses.

1.5 PARALLEL PROCESSING APPLICATIONS

Fast and efficient computers are in high demand in many scientific, engineering, energy resource, medical, military, artificial intelligence, and basic research areas. Large-scale computations are often performed in these application areas. Parallel processing computers are needed to meet these demands. In this section, we introduce some representative applications of high-performance computers. Without using superpower computers, many of these challenges to advance human civilization could hardly be realized. To design a cost-effective super-computer, or to better utilize an existing parallel processing system, one must first identify the computational needs of important applications. With rapidly changing application trends, we introduce only the major computations and leave the readers to identify their own computational needs in solving each specific problem.

Large-scale scientific problem solving involves three interactive disciplines: theories, experiments, and computations, as shown in Figure 1.19. Theoretical scientists develop mathematical models that computer engineers solve numerically; the numerical results may then suggest new theories. Experimental science provides

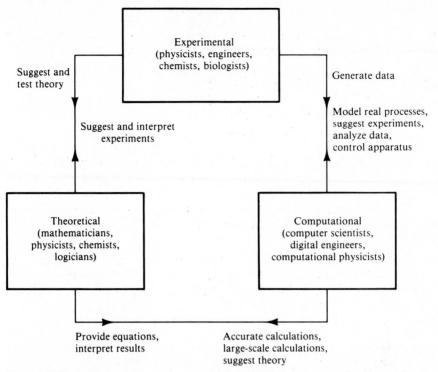

Figure 1.19 Interaction among experiments, theories, and computations to solve large-scale scientific problems (Courtesy of Rodrique et al., *IEEE Computer*, 1980).

data for computational science, and the latter can model processes that are hard to approach in the laboratory. Using computer simulations has several advantages:

1. Computer simulations are far cheaper and faster than physical experiments.
2. Computers can solve a much wider range of problems than specific laboratory equipments can.
3. Computational approaches are only limited by computer speed and memory capacity, while physical experiments have many practical constraints.

Theoretical and experimental scientists are users of large program codes provided by the computational scientist. The codes should yield accurate results with minimal user effort. The computer scientists must apply advanced technologies in numerical modeling, hardware engineering, and software development. In what follows, we will review parallel processing applications in four categories, according to their objectives. Within each category, we will then identify several representative application areas that have been challenged by scientists, engineers, and programmers throughout the world.

1.5.1 Predictive Modeling and Simulations

Multidimensional modeling of the atmosphere, the earth environment, outer space, and the world economy has become a major concern of world scientists. Predictive modeling is done through extensive computer simulation experiments, which often involve large-scale computations to achieve the desired accuracy and turnaround time. Such numerical modeling requires state-of-the-art computing at speeds approaching 1000 million megaflops or beyond.

A. Numerical weather forecasting Weather and climate researchers will never run out of their need for faster computers. Weather modeling is necessary for short-range forecasts and for long-range hazard predictions, such as flood, drought, and environmental pollutions. The weather analyst needs to solve *general circulation model* equations with the computer. The atmospheric state is represented by the surface pressure, the wind field, temperature, and the water vapor mixing ratio. These state variables are governed by the Navier-Stokes fluid dynamics equations in a spherical coordinate system.

The computation is carried out on a three-dimensional grid that partitions the atmosphere vertically into K levels and horizontally into M intervals of longitude and N intervals of latitude (Figure 1.20). A fourth dimension is added as the number P of time steps used in the simulation. Using a grid with 270 miles on a side, a 24-hour forecast would need to perform about 100 billion data operations. This forecast could be done on a 100 megaflops computer in about 100 minutes.

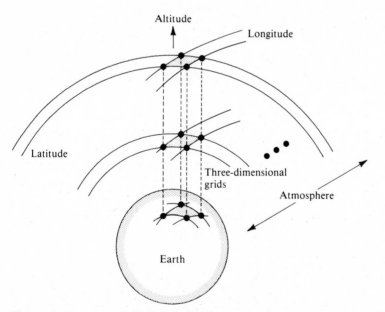

Figure 1.20 The general circulation model for three-dimensional global atmosphere simulation used in numerical weather forecasting and climate studies.

This 270-mile grid gives the forecast between New York and Washington, D.C., but not for Philadelphia, about halfway between.

Increasing the forecast by halving the grid size in all four dimensions would take the computation at least 16 times longer. The 100 megaflops machine, like a Cray-1, would therefore take 24 hours to complete the 24-hour forecast. In other words, to halve the grid size, giving the Philadelphia weather, requires a computer 16 times more powerful (1.6 gigaflops) to finish the forecast in 100 minutes. Reliable long-range forecasts require an even finer grid for a lot more time steps, and thus demand a much more powerful computer than the 1.6 gigaflops machine.

B. Oceanography and astrophysics Since oceans can store and transfer heat and exchange it with the atmosphere, a good understanding of the oceans would help in the following areas:

- Climate predictive analysis
- Fishery management
- Ocean resource exploration
- Coastal dynamics and tides

Oceanographic studies use a grid size on a smaller scale and a time variability on a larger scale than those used for atmospheric studies. To do a complete simulation of the Pacific Ocean with adequate resolution (1° grid) for 50 years would take 1000 hours on a Cyber-205 computer.

The formation of the earth from planetesimals in the solar system can be simulated with a high-speed computer. The dynamic range of astrophysic studies may be from billions of years to milliseconds. Interesting problems include the physics of supernovae and the dynamics of galaxies. Three-dimensional, n-body integrations ran in such a study, involving 10^5 particles moving self-consistently under Newtonian forces. The Illiac-IV array processor was used in this study.

C. Socioeconomics and government use Large computers are in great demand in the areas of econometrics, social engineering, government census, crime control, and the modeling of the world economy for the year 2000. Nobel laureate W. W. Leontief (1980) has proposed an input-output model of the world economy which performs large-scale matrix operations on a CDC scientific computer. This United Nations–supported world economic simulation suggests how a system of international economic relations that features a partial disarmament could narrow the gap between the rich and the poor.

In the United States, the FBI uses large computers for crime control; the IRS uses a large number of fast mainframes for tax collection and auditing. There is no doubt about the use of supercomputers for national census and general public opinion polls. It was estimated that 57 percent of the large-scale computers manufactured in the United States have been used by the U.S. government in the past.

1.5.2 Engineering Design and Automation

Fast supercomputers have been in high demand for solving many engineering design problems, such as the finite-element analysis needed for structural designs and wind tunnel experiments for aerodynamic studies. Industrial development also demands the use of computers to advance automation, artificial intelligence, and remote sensing of earth resources.

A. Finite-element analysis The design of dams, bridges, ships, supersonic jets, high buildings, and space vehicles requires the resolution of a large system of algebraic equations or partial differential equations. Conventional approaches using predeveloped software packages (written in sequential codes) require intolerable turnaround times. Many researchers and engineers have attempted to build more efficient computers to perform finite-element analysis or to seek finite difference solutions. This would imply a fundamental change of engineering design tools and higher productivity in the future.

Computational engineers have developed finite-element code for the dynamic analysis of structures. High-order finite elements are used to describe the spatial behavior. The temporal behavior can be approximated by using a central difference explicit scheme. Vectorization procedures can be used to generate the element stiffness and mass matrices, to decompose the global matrices, and to multiply the global stiffness matrix by a vector. The CDC Star-100 and Cyber-205 have been used to implement these computations for structural analysis.

B. Computational aerodynamics Large-scale computers have made significant contributions in providing new technological capabilities and economies in pressing ahead with aircraft and spacecraft lift and turbulence studies. NASA's Ames Research Center is seeking to supplement its Illiac-IV to do three-dimensional simulations of wind tunnel tests at gigaflop speeds. The fundamental limitations of wind tunnels and of numerical flow simulations are compared in Table 1.6. Every wind tunnel is limited by the "scale effects" attributed to the

Table 1.6 Fundamental limitations of wind tunnel experiment and of numerical flow simulations

Wind tunnel experiment	Numerical flow simulation
Model size	Processor speed
Wind velocity	
Density	Memory capacity
Temperature	
Wall interference	
Aeroelastic distortions	
Atmosphere	
Stream uniformity	

listed factors. In contrast, computer flow simulations have none of these physical constraints, but have their own: computational speed and memory capacity.

Two gigaflops supercomputers, known as the *Numerical Aerodynamic Simulation Facilities* (NASF), have been proposed by the Burroughs Corporation and by the Control Data Corporation. These are specialized "Navier-Stokes" machines, capable of simulating complete aircraft design for both the U.S. government and commercial aircraft companies. We will study the proposed designs, along with their predecessor vector processors, in Chapters 4 and 6.

C. Artificial intelligence and automation Intelligent I/O interfaces are being demanded for future supercomputers that must directly communicate with human beings in images, speech, and natural languages. Listed below are intelligence functions which demand parallel processing:

- Image processing
- Pattern recognition
- Computer vision
- Speech understanding
- Machine inference
- CAD/CAM/CAI/OA
- Intelligent robotics
- Expert computer systems
- Knowledge engineering

Special computer architectures have been developed or proposed for some of the above machine intelligence applications. Recently, Japan launched a national project to develop the fifth-generation computers to be used in the 1990s. The Japanese envision the new generation computers to possess highly intelligent input-output subsystems, capable of most of the above functions. CAD/CAM/CAI stands for *computer-aided design, computer-aided manufacturing, and computer-assisted instruction*, respectively. OA stands for *office automation*.

The projected computing power of the system being developed is 100 mega to 1 giga *logical inferences per second* (LIPS). The time to execute one logical inference equals that of executing 100 to 1000 machine instructions. Therefore, the machine should be able to execute 10,000 to 1 mega *million instructions per second* (MIPS). Such an ultrapower computer is expected to process knowledge-based information and to serve as the multipurpose expert systems demanded by applicationers in the future.

D. Remote sensing applications Computer analysis of remotely sensed (via satellite, for example) earth-resource data has many potential applications in agriculture, forestry, geology, and water resources. Explosive amounts of pictorial information need to be processed in this area. For example, a single frame of LANDSAT imagery contains 30 million bytes; it takes 13 such images to cover the

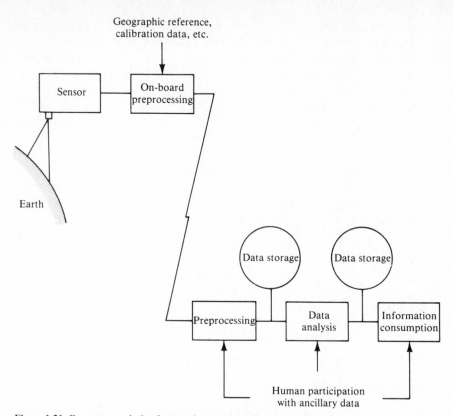

Figure 1.21 Computer analysis of remotely sensed earth resource data (Courtesy of Swain, *McGraw-Hill International*, 1978).

state of Alabama. What is even more demanding is the production of a complete new set of imageries for the entire earth surface every 15 days (Figure 1.21).

NASA has ordered a *massively parallel processor* (MPP) for earth resources satellite image processing. This MPP has a peak computing rate of 6 billion 8-bit integer operations per second. It can almost provide real-time, time-varying scene analysis, for example, where the sensor interacts with the scene. We will study MPP in detail in Chapter 6.

1.5.3 Energy Resources Exploration

Energy affects the progress of the entire economy on a global basis. Computers can play an important role in the discovery of oil and gas and the management of their recovery, in the development of workable plasma fusion energy, and in ensuring nuclear reactor safety. Using computers in the energy area results in less production costs and higher safety measures.

A. Seismic exploration Many oil companies are investing in the use of attached array processors or vector supercomputers for seismic data processing, which accounts for about 10 percent of the oil finding costs. Seismic exploration sets off a sonic wave by explosive or by jamming a heavy hydraulic ram into the ground and vibrating it in a computer-controlled pattern. A few thousand phones scattered about the spot are used to pick up the echos. The echo data are used to draw two-dimensional cross sections that display the geometrical underground strata. Reconstruction techniques are being used to identify the types of strata that may bear oil. Such seismic exploration may save the drilling of many dry holes.

A typical field record for the response of the earth to one sonic input has 3000 different time values, each at about 48 different locations. This produces about 2 to 5 million floating-point numbers per kilometer along a survey line. In 1979 alone, 10^{15} bits of seismic data were processed. One geophysical company in Houston has about 2 million magnetic reels of seismic data in inventory and 300,000 reels awaiting processing. The demand of cost-effective computers for seismic signal processing is increasing sharply.

B. Reservoir modeling Supercomputers are being used to perform three-dimensional modeling of oil fields. The reservoir problem is solved by using the finite difference method on the three-dimensional representation of the field. Geologic core samples are examined to project forward into time the field's expected performance. Presently at least 1000 flops needs to be processed per data point in the three-dimensional model of an oil field. This means a superpower computer must be employed to achieve an accurate performance evaluation in a reasonable time period for a large field.

Due to the importance of the Prudhoe Bay oil field, SOHIO Petroleum Company has constructed a numerical simulator for the whole field on a vector computer (Cyber-203). The field is about 168 meters thick and has been subdivided into 12 layers. With an aerial grid no finer than 160 acres, a model of 16,421 active subsurface blocks can cover 1000 oil wells. The finite difference equations for the reservoir model are solved iteratively on the Cyber-203. A simulated year requires 33 minutes of computer time. The success in this large modeling is attributed to both high speed and the large main memory built into a supercomputer.

C. Plasma fusion power Nuclear fusion researchers are pushing to use a computer 100 times more powerful than any existing one to model the plasma dynamics in the proposed Tokamak fusion power generator. Magnetic fusion research programs are being aided by vector supercomputers at the Lawrence Livermore National Laboratory and at Princeton's Plasma Physics Laboratory. The potential for magnetic fusion to provide an alternate source of energy has become closer as a result of the cooperative effort of the experimental program with the computational simulation program.

Synthetic nuclear fusion requires the heating of plasma to a temperature of 100 million degrees. This is a very costly effort. The high-temperature plasma, consisting of positively charged ions and negatively charged electrons, must be magnetically confined. The United States National Magnetic Fusion Energy Computer Center is currently using two Cray-1's and one CDC-7600 to aid the controlled plasma experiments. Supercomputers have become an indispensable tool in magnetic fusion energy exploration.

D. Nuclear reactor safety Nuclear reactor design and safety control can both be aided by computer simulation studies. These studies attempt to provide for:

- On-line analysis of reactor conditions
- Automatic control for normal and abnormal operations
- Simulation of operator training
- Quick assessment of potential accident mitigation procedures

The importance lies in the above operations being done in real time. For light reactor safety analysis, a TRAC code has been developed to simulate the non-equilibrium, nonhomogeneous flow of high-temperature water and steam. Another code, Simmer II, has been developed to analyze core melting in a fast breeder reactor. Only supercomputers can make these calculations possible in real time.

1.5.4 Medical, Military, and Basic Research

In the medical area, fast computers are needed in computer-assisted tomography, artificial heart design, liver diagnosis, brain damage estimation, and genetic engineering studies. Military defense needs to use supercomputers for weapon design, effects simulation, and other electronic warfare. Almost all basic research areas demand fast computers to advance their studies.

A. Computer-assisted tomography The human body can be modeled by *computer-assisted tomography* (CAT) scanning. The Mayo Clinic in Rochester, Minnesota, is developing a research CAT scanner for three-dimensional, stop-action, cross-action viewing of the human heart. At the Courant Institute of Mathematical Sciences, research scientists are seeking an array processor for time-sequence, three-dimensional modeling of blood flow in the heart, with the goal of pursuing the artificial heart. Similar approaches can be applied to reveal the secrets of other human organs in real time.

Cross-sectional CAT images used to take 6 to 10 minutes to generate on a conventional computer. Using a dedicated array processor, the processing time can be reduced to 5 to 20 s. The image reconstruction of human anatomy in present CAT scanners is two-dimensional. It is generated too slowly (5 s) to freeze the motion of organs such as the heart or the lungs. The Mayo Clinic's super CAT scanner is expected to have 2000 to 3000 megaflops speed. It will produce three-dimensional images of the beating heart, within a few seconds, with 60 to 240 thin adjacent cross sections stacked one upon the other. Because of the short processing and exposure time, three-dimensional and stop-motion pictures of a beating heart will be possible for the first time. Dye injection may be used to trace the blood flow.

B. Genetic engineering Biological systems can be simulated on supercomputers. Genetic engineering is advancing rapidly in recent years. There is a growing need for large-scale computations to study molecular biology for the synthesis of complex organic molecules, such as proteins. Crystallography also can be aided by computer processing.

A highly pipelined machine, called the Cytocomputer, has been developed at the Michigan Environmental Research Institute for biomedical image processing. It can be used to search for genetic mutations. Sophisticated biomedical and computer techniques are being applied to derive an accurate estimate of the mutation rate for the human species. Gel matching between the father, mother, and child is done in the Cytocomputer using some parallel graph-matching techniques.

C. Weapon research and defense So far, military research agencies have used the majority of the existing supercomputers. In fact, the first Cray-1 was installed at the Los Alamos Scientific Laboratories in 1976. By 1981, four upgraded Cray 1's had been acquired by Los Alamos. Listed below are several defense-related military applications of supercomputers.

- Multiwarhead nuclear weapon design (Cray-1)
- Simulation of atomic weapon effects by solving hydrodynamics and radiation problems (Cyber-205)
- Intelligence gathering, such as radar signal processing on the associative processor for the antiballistic missile (ABM) program (PEPE)
- Cartographic data processing for automatic map generation (Staran)
- Sea surveillance for antisubmarine warfare (the S-1 multiprocessor)

D. Basic Research Problems Many of the aforementioned application areas are related to basic scientific research. Below are several additional areas that demand the use of supercomputers:

1. Computational chemists solve problems on quantum mechanics, statistical mechanics, polymer chemistry, and crystal growth.
2. Computational physicists analyze particle tracks generated in spark chambers, study fluid dynamics, examine quantum field theory, and investigate molecular dynamics.
3. Electronic engineers solve large-scale circuit equations using the multilevel Newton algorithm, and lay out VLSI connections on semiconductor chips.

1.6 BIBLIOGRAPHIC NOTES AND PROBLEMS

Parallel processing computers have been treated in parts of the books by Hayes (1978), Kuck (1978), Stone (1980), and Baer (1980). Enslow (1974) and Satyanarayanan (1980) devoted their books to multiprocessor systems. The book by Hockney and Jesshope (1982) covers only pipeline and array processors.

The introductory material on data flow computers is based on Dennis (1980). A recent survey of vector processing computers can be found in Hwang, et al. (1981). Additional material on supercomputer applications can be found in Rodrique, et al. (1980) and Sugarman (1980). Bode and Händler (1980, 1982) have written two computer architecture books in German.

Other surveys on parallel processing and supercomputer systems appeared in Kuhn and Padua (1981), IEEE *Computer Magazine* (Nov. 1981), and *Communications of ACM* (Jan. 1978). The computer architectural classifications are based on Flynn (1966), Feng (1972), and Händler (1977). Interested readers should regularly check the proceedings of the *Annual Symposium on Computer Architecture*, and of the *International Conference on Parallel Processing* for frontier research development. The *Journal of Parallel/Distributed Computing* is a dedicated publication in this area.

Problems

1.1 Distinguish among computer terminologies in each of the following groups:
- (*a*) Data processing, information processing, knowledge processing, and intelligence processing.
- (*b*) Batch processing, multiprogramming, time sharing, and multiprocessing.
- (*c*) Parallel processing at the job level, the task level, the interinstruction level, and the intra-instruction level.
- (*d*) Uniprocessor systems versus multiprocessor systems.
- (*e*) Parallelism versus pipelining.
- (*f*) Serial processing versus parallel processing.
- (*g*) Control flow computers versus data flow computers.

1.2 Existing computer systems are classified in Tables 1.3, 1.4, and 1.5, based on the three architectural specification schemes given in Section 1.4. The listing in each table is not complete. Enter the specification of at least two additional computer systems under each architectural category of each of the three tables. Use the same specification format for the existing entries in making the new entries.

1.3 The speedup of using n processors over the use of one processor in solving a computing problem was analyzed in Section 1.3.4 under various assumptions, such as $f_i = 1/n$ and $d_i = 1/i$ for $i = 1, 2, \ldots, n$.

(*a*) Repeat the performance speedup analysis to derive a new speedup equation (similar to Eq. 1.8), under the following new probability distributions of operating modes.

$$f_i = \frac{i}{\sum\limits_{i=1}^{n} i} \qquad \text{for } i = 1, 2, \ldots, n \qquad (1.17)$$

(*b*) Repeat part (*a*) for another probability distribution:

$$f_i = \frac{n - i - 1}{\sum\limits_{i=1}^{n} i} \qquad \text{for } i = 1, 2, \ldots, n \qquad (1.18)$$

(*c*) The case in (*a*) favors the assignment of the computing task to a larger number of processors, whereas the case in (*b*) favors the assignment to a smaller number of processors. The case presented in Section 1.3.4 treats all possible task divisions equally. Plot the new speedup curves obtained in case (*a*) and in case (*b*) along with plots given in Figure 1.14. Can you find new upper bounds for the new speedup curves? Derive the upper bound, if it exists.

1.4 Name three distinct characteristics that exist in the ith generation computers for $i = 1, 2, 3,$ and 4 but not in the jth generation for $j = 0, 1, 2, \ldots, i - 1$, where the 0th generation corresponds to prior electronic computers.

1.5 Match each of the following computer systems to the phrase that best describes it.

___ Illiac-IV	(1) A cluster of microprocessors
___ TI-ASC	(2) A vector processor made in Japan
___ CDC-7600	(3) A supermini computer with virtual memory
___ IBM 360/91	(4) The first MIMD multiprocessor consisting of 16 PDP II minicomputers
___ AP-120B	(5) The first IBM computer using the thermal conduction modules
___ Cray-1	(6) A multiprocessing vector processor by Cray Research
___ B-5500	(7) A major computer project at IBM in the 1960s
___ PEPE	(8) An array processor with 64 PEs
___ Cyber-205	(9) A multifunction computer with multiprocessing in I/O subsystem
___ C.mmp	(10) The first operational electronic digital computer
___ BSP	(11) An associate processor with 288 PEs
___ MPP	(12) A commercial multiprocessor with a packet switched interconnection network
___ Cray X-MP	(13) The first IBM scientific processor with multiple functional units
___ HEP	(14) An attached array processor for minicomputers
___ VP-200	(15) A first-generation pipelined vector processor
___ ENIAC	(16) An array processor with 16384 PEs
___ Stretch	(17) A CDC vector processor enhanced from the STAR-100
___ C.m*	(18) One of the first stack computers
___ VAX 11/780	(19) An array processor with 16 PEs and shared memories
___ IBM 3081	(20) A vector processor with 12 pipes and large register files

1.6 You were briefed about 15 important applications of parallel processing computers in Section 1.5. Choose the one of these application areas that interests you most for an indepth study. Dig out more information from the library or request the source information from any application site of supercomputers that you know of. Prepare a study report based on your readings and observations in the chosen area of supercomputer applications.

1.7 In the following block of computations, a and b are two external inputs and z is the final output. Two intermediate results are labelled x and y.

$$x \leftarrow a * a; \quad y \leftarrow b * b; \quad z \leftarrow (x + y)/(x - y)$$

(a) Draw a data flow graph for this code block, where $*, +, -,$ and $/$ are arithmetic operators.

(b) Show a template implementation of the data flow graph in (a).

(c) Indicate the events that can be done in parallel in the execution of the above block of codes.

1.8 Describe at least four characteristics of MIMD multiprocessors that distinguish them from multiple computer systems or computer networks.

1.9 Prove that a k-stage linear pipeline can be at most k times faster than that of a nonpipelined serial processor.

1.10 Summarize all forms of parallelism that can be exploited at different processing levels of a computer system, including both uniprocessor and multiprocessor approaches. Discuss hardware, firmware, and software supports needed to achieve each form of parallelism. Indicate example computers that have achieved various forms of parallelism.

CHAPTER
TWO

MEMORY AND INPUT-OUTPUT SUBSYSTEMS

In this chapter, we describe memory organizations and input-output subsystems, material needed to study subsequent chapters. Memories are organized in a hierarchical order of access times. The basic techniques used to create a large virtual address space and the necessary translation mechanisms to the physical space are discussed. Some memory allocation and management schemes are presented for multiprogrammed systems. Various organizations of cache memories are presented. Techniques for estimating the effective bandwidth of such memories are developed. Finally, techniques for exploiting concurrency in input-output subsystems are summarized. Memory and I/O subsystems are needed in uniprocessors, pipeline machines, array processors, and multiprocessors. Special parallel memory structures for each class of machines are treated separately in their respective chapters.

2.1 HIERARCHICAL MEMORY STRUCTURE

Memory systems for parallel processor computers are described in this section. We begin with the hierarchical memory structures and the concept of virtual memory. Virtual memory concepts are discussed for paged systems, segmented systems, and systems with paged segments.

2.1.1 Memory Hierarchy

The design objectives of hierarchical memory in a parallel processing system and a multiprogrammed uniprocessor system are basically the same. The objectives are to attempt to match the processor speed with the rate of information transfer or the *bandwidth* of the memory at the lowest level and at a reasonable cost. However, one major difference exists in the hierarchical memory structures of the two systems. This difference is due to the memory reference characteristics of multi-programmed uniprocessors and parallel processors. In the latter case, the existence of multiple processors necessitates the arrival of concurrent memory requests to memory at the same level of the hierarchy. If two or more of these concurrent requests reference the same section of memory at the same level, a *conflict* is said to occur, which could degrade the performance of the system. Hence, memory for a parallel processing system must be organized to reduce the potential conflicts at each level of the hierarchy. This is usually done by partitioning the memory at a given level into several modules so that some degree of concurrent access can be achieved.

Memories in a hierarchy can be classified on the basis of several attributes. One common attribute is the accessing method, which divides the memories into three basic classes: *random-access memory* (RAM), *sequential-access memory* (SAM), and *direct-access storage devices* (DASDs). In RAM, the access time t_a of a memory word is independent of its location. In SAMs, information is accessed serially or sequentially, as in shift-register memory such as a first-in, first-out (FIFO) buffer, *charged-coupled devices* (CCDs), and *magnetic bubble memories* (MBMs). DASDs are rotational devices made of magnetic materials where any block of information can be accessed directly. The DASDs are accessed via special interfaces called channels, which are discussed in Section 2.5.

Another attribute often used to classify memory is the speed or access time of the memory. In most computer systems, the memory hierarchy is often organized so that the highest level has the fastest memory speed and the lowest level has the slowest speed. On the basis of access time, memory can be further classified into primary memory and secondary memory. Primary memory is made of RAMs and secondary memories are made of DASDs and optional SAMs. In characterizing the access times of memories in the hierarchy we will concentrate on RAMs and DASDs.

The three most common DASDs are drums, fixed-head disks, and moveable-arm disks. For these cases, the time to transfer a block of information is $t_a + t_B$, where t_a is the access time and t_B is the block-transfer time. For drums and fixed-head disks, t_a is the time it takes for the initial word of the desired block to rotate into position. For moveable-arm disks, an additional "seek time" t_s is required to move the arms into track position. Table 2.1 depicts some of the characteristics of the different memories used in a hierarchy.

In general, the memory hierarchy is structured so that memories at level i are "higher" than those at level $i + 1$. If c_i, t_i, and s_i are respectively the cost per byte, average access time, and the total memory size, at level i, the following relationships normally hold between levels i and $i + 1$: $c_i > c_{i+1}$, $t_i < t_{i+1}$, and $s_i < s_{i+1}$, for $i \geq 1$. Figure 2.1 illustrates the typical relative cost-access time relationship of some memory technologies.

Figure 2.2 illustrates an example of a two-processor system with a three-level memory. Memory module $M_{1,j}$ is the *local* or *private* memory of processor j since it is exclusively used by that processor. The local memory is often implemented as a high-speed buffer or *cache* memory using bipolar technology and hence is the

Table 2.1 Characteristics of memory devices in a memory hierarchy

Level i	Memory type	Technology	Typical size s_i	Average access time t_i	Unit of transfer
1	Cache	Bipolar, HMOS, ECL	2K–128K bytes	30–100 ns	1 word
2	Main or primary memory	MOS core	4K–16M bytes	0.25–1 μs 0.5–1 μs	2–32 words
3 (optional)	Bulk memory (LCS, ECS)	Core	64K–16M bytes	5–10 μs	2–32 words
4	Fixed head disk or drums	Magnetic	8M–256M bytes	5–15 ms	1K–4K bytes
5	Moveable arm disk	Magnetic	8M–500M bytes	25–75 ms	4K bytes
6	Tape	Magnetic	50M bytes	1–5 s	1K–16K bytes

fastest memory. The cache is used to capture the segments of information which are most frequently referenced by the processor. Information transfer between the processor and the cache is on a word basis. Cache memories will be discussed in detail in Section 2.3. The next lower level of memory consists of modules $M_{2,0}$ to $M_{2,3}$ and constitutes the main memory. The four modules are usually designed with *metal oxide semiconductor* (MOS) or ferromagnetic (core) technology, and the

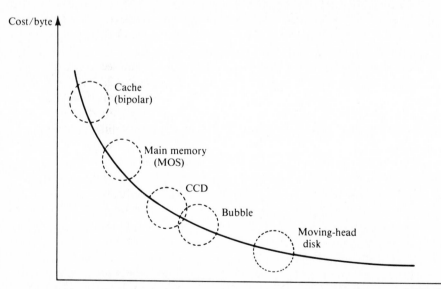

Figure 2.1 Cost and access time relationship.

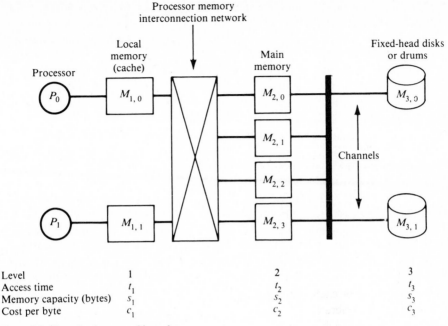

Level	1	2	3
Access time	t_1	t_2	t_3
Memory capacity (bytes)	s_1	s_2	s_3
Cost per byte	c_1	c_2	c_3

Figure 2.2 Three-level memory hierarchy.

unit of information transfer between the main memory and cache is a block of contiguous information (typically 2 to 32 words). The primary memory may be extended either with the so-called *large core storage* (LCS) or with *extended core storage* (ECS), both of which are made of slower core memories. The average access time of the primary memory and its extensions are in the order of 0.5 μs and 5 μs, respectively.

There exists a technological gap between the primary and secondary memory, as evidenced by the access time characteristics shown in Table 2.1. Average access time of secondary memories is 1000 to 10,000 times slower than that of primary memories. Electronic disks, such as CCDs and MBMs, have not proved cost-effective in closing the technological gap and thus have had little impact in the design of memory systems. Hence, as shown in Figure 2.2, the secondary memories most often used are disks and drums.

The processor usually references an item in memory by providing the location or address of that item. A memory hierarchy is usually organized so that the address space in level i is a subset of that in level $i + 1$. This is true only in their relation, however; address A_k in level i is not necessarily address A_k in level $i + 1$, but any information in level i may also exist in level $i + 1$. However, some of the information in level i may be more current than that in level $i + 1$.

This creates a *data consistency* or *coherence* problem between adjacent levels because they have different copies of the same information. Usually level $i + 1$ is eventually updated with the modified information from level i. The data consistency problem may also exist between the local memories or caches when two cooperating processes, which are executing concurrently or on separate processors, interact via one or more shared variables. One process may update the copy of a shared variable in its local memory while the other process continues to access the previous copy of the variable in its local memory. This situation may result in the incorrect execution of the cooperating processes. In general, a memory hierarchy encounters such a coherence problem as soon as one of its levels is split into several independent units which are not equally accessible from faster levels or processors. Solutions to data consistency problems are discussed in Sections 2.3, 2.5, and 7.3.

In modeling the performance of a hierarchical memory, it is often assumed that the memory management policy is characterized by a *success function* or *hit ratio* H, which is the probability of finding the requested information in the memory of a given level. In general, H depends on the granularity of information transfer, the capacity of memory at that level, the management strategy, and other factors. However, for some classes of management policies, it has been found that H is most sensitive to the memory size s. Hence the success function may be written as $H(s)$. The *miss ratio* or probability is then $F(s) = 1 - H(s)$. Since copies of information in level i are assumed to exist in levels greater than i, the probability of a hit at level i and of misses at higher levels 1 to $i - 1$, is:

$$h_i = H(s_i) - H(s_{i-1}) \tag{2.1}$$

where h_i is the access frequency at level i and indicates the relative number of successful accesses to level i. The missing-item fault frequency at level i is then $f_i = 1 - h_i$.

2.1.2 Optimization of Memory Hierarchy

The goal in designing an n-level memory hierarchy is to achieve a performance close to that of the fastest memory $M_{1,j}$ and a cost per bit close to that of the cheapest memory $M_{n,j}$. The performance of the hierarchy may be indicated by the effective hierarchy access time per each memory reference. However, it should be noted that the performance depends on a variety of interrelated factors. These include the program behavior with respect to memory references, the access time and memory size of each level, the granularity of information transfer (block size), and the management policies. One other important factor that also affects the effective access time is the design of the processor-memory interconnection network, which is discussed in Sections 5.2 and 7.2.

The interrelation among some of these factors can be used to derive a criterion for optimizing the performance of the memory hierarchy. One performance measure is the effective memory access time. Another measure may include the utilization of the processor. The effective access time T_i from the processor to the ith level of the memory hierarchy is the sum of the individual average access times t_k of each level from $k = 1$ to i:

$$T_i = \sum_{k=1}^{i} t_k \tag{2.2}$$

In general, t_k includes the wait time due to memory conflicts at level k and the delay in the switching network between levels $k - 1$ and k. The degree of conflicts is usually a function of the number of processors, the number of memory modules, and the interconnection network between the processors and memory modules. In most systems, a request for a word which is not in memory level i causes the block of information which contains the requested word to be transferred from level $i + 1$ to level i. When the block transfer to level 1 has been completed, the requested word is accessed in the local memory.

The effective access time for each memory reference in the n-level memory hierarchy is

$$T = \sum_{i=1}^{n} h_i T_i \qquad (2.3)$$

Substituting h_i and T_i into Eq. 2.3,

$$T = \sum_{i=1}^{n} [H(s_n) - H(s_{i-1})]t_i \qquad (2.4)$$

Assuming that there is a copy of all requested information in the lowest level n, $H(s_n) = 1$. In the derivation of Eq. 2.4, it is convenient to define $H(s_0) = 0$, hence $F(s_0) = 1$. Rewriting Eq. 2.4:

$$T = \sum_{i=1}^{n} [1 - H(s_{i-1})]t_i$$

Since $1 - H(s_{i-1}) = F(s_{i-1})$, we obtain

$$T = \sum_{i=1}^{n} F(s_i - 1)t_i \qquad (2.5)$$

If $c(t_i)$ is the cost per byte of memory at level i which is expressed as a function of its average access time, the total cost of the memory system is

$$C = \sum_{i=1}^{n} c(t_i)s_i \qquad (2.6)$$

A typical memory-hierarchy design problem involves an optimization which minimizes the effective hierarchy access time T, subject to a given memory system cost C_0 and size constraints. That is, minimize $T = \sum_{i=1}^{n} F(s_{i-1})t_i$, subject to the constraints $C = \sum_{i=1}^{n} c(t_i)s_i \leq C_0$, where $s_i > 0$ and $t_i > 0$, for $i = 1, 2, \ldots, n$. In practice, the cost constraints should include the cost of the processor-memory interconnection network.

In the memory types we have discussed so far, the contents of a memory location is accessed by specifying the memory location or address of the item. In another type of memory, *associative memory*, the data stored in the memory can be accessed by specifying the contents or part of the contents. In this sense, associative memory has also been known as *content-addressable memory* and *parallel search memory*. The major advantage of associative memory over the RAM is its capability of performing parallel search and comparison operations, which are needed in many important applications, such as table lookup, information storage and retrieval of rapidly changing databases, radar-signal tracking and processing, image processing, and real-time artificial intelligence computations. The major disadvantage of associative memory is its much increased hardware cost. Currently, associative memories are much more expensive than RAMs, even though both are built with integrated circuitry. However, with the rapid advent of VLSI technology, the price gap between these types of memories may be reduced in the future. Associative memories and associative processors will be treated in Section 5.4.

2.1.3 Addressing Schemes for Main Memory

In a parallel processing environment, main memory is a prime system resource which is normally shared by all the processors or independent units of a pipelined processor. Care must be taken in the organization of the memory system to avoid severe performance degradation because of memory interference caused by two or more processors simultaneously attempting to access the same modules of the memory system. It would be undesirable to have one monolithic unit of memory to be shared among several processors, as this would result in serious memory interference. Hence, the main memory is partitioned into several independent memory modules and the addresses distributed across these modules. This scheme, called *interleaving*, resolves some of the interference by allowing concurrent accesses to more than one module. The interleaving of addresses among M modules is called M-*way* interleaving.

There are two basic methods of distributing the addresses among the memory modules. Assume that there are a total of $N = 2^n$ words in main memory. Then the physical address for a word in memory consists of n bits, $a_{n-1}a_{n-2} \cdots a_1a_0$. One method, *high-order* interleaving, distributes the addresses in $M = 2^m$ modules so that each module i, for $0 \le i \le M - 1$, contains consecutive addresses $i2^{n-m}$ to $(i + 1)2^{n-m} - 1$, inclusive. The high-order m bits are used to select the module while the remaining $n - m$ bits select the address within the module, as depicted in Figure 2.3.

The second method, *low-order* interleaving, distributes the addresses so that consecutive addresses are located within consecutive modules. The low-order m bits of the address select the module, while the remaining $n - m$ bits select the address within the module, as shown in Figure 2.4. Hence, an address A is located in module A mod M.

The two schemes depicted in Figures 2.3 and 2.4 represent extremes in the choice of the address decoding. The first scheme permits easy memory expansion by the addition of one or more memory modules as needed to a maximum of $M - 1$. However, the placement of contiguous memory addresses within a module may cause considerable memory conflicts in the case of pipelined, vector, or array (SIMD) processors. The sequentiality of instructions in programs and the sequentiality of data in vector processors cause consecutive instructions or data to be in the same module. Since memory cycle time is much greater than the pipeline clock

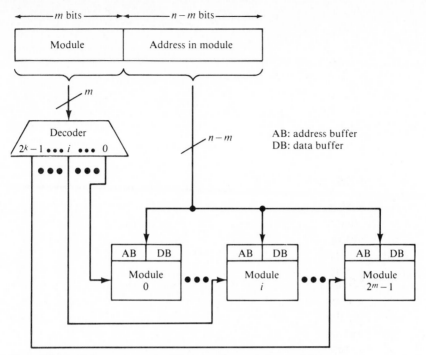

Figure 2.3 Parallel memory system with consecutive words in a module.

time, a previous memory request would not have completed its access before the arrival of the next request, thereby resulting in a delay.

In array processors, if the data elements of a vector reside in the same module, there will be insignificant parallelism in computation because the elements cannot be fetched simultaneously by all processors for the "lock-step" manipulation. The high-order interleaving can be used without conflict problems in multiprocessors if the modules are partitioned according to disjoint or noninteracting processes. In practice, however, processes interact and share instructions and data in multiprocessor systems and will thereby encounter considerable conflicts in a high-order interleaved memory subsystem. For the above reasons, low-order interleaving is frequently used to reduce memory interference.

An advantage of high-order interleaving is that it provides better system reliability, since a failed module affects only a localized area of the address space and therefore provides graceful degradation in performance. The failed module can be logically isolated from the system and the memory manager can be informed so that no process address space is mapped into the failed module. A failure of any single module in the second scheme will almost certainly be catastrophic to the whole system. The second scheme, however, seems preferable if memory interference is the only basis of choice.

A compromise interleaving technique is to partition the module address field into the two sections S_{m-r} and S_r so that section S_r is the least significant

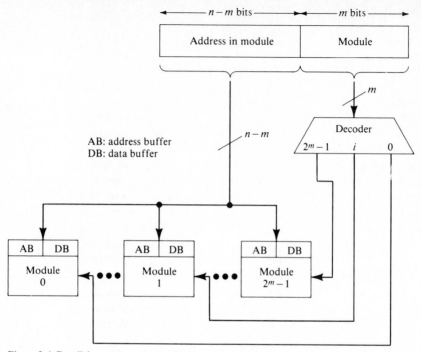

Figure 2.4 Parallel memory system with consecutive words in consecutive modules.

r bits of the memory address and section S_{m-r} is the high-order $m\text{-}r$ bits of the address. Notice that the module address is formed by the concatenation of section S_{m-r} and S_r. In this scheme, the addresses are interleaved among groups of 2^r memory modules. This tends to reduce memory interference to a segment of shared data. The memory system is expandable in blocks of 2^r modules; however, a single module failure disables an entire block of 2^r modules. This scheme is appealing for systems with a large number of memory modules if r is chosen to be very small.

2.2 VIRTUAL MEMORY SYSTEM

In many computer systems, programmers often realize that some of their large programs cannot fit in main memory for execution. Even if there is enough main memory for one program, the main memory may be shared with other users, causing any one program to occupy some fraction of memory which may not be sufficient for the program to execute. The usual solution is to introduce management schemes that intelligently allocate portions of memory to users as necessary for the efficient running of their programs. The use of virtual memory to achieve this goal is described in this section.

2.2.1 The Concept of Virtual Memory

Memory management is distributed over several overlapping phases. It begins with the program structure and design, the naming function performed by the compiler in translating the program modules from programming language into modules of machine code or *unique identifiers*. A linker then combines these modules of unique identifiers and the composite is translated by a loader into main memory locations. The set of unique identifiers defines the *virtual space* or the *name space* and the set of main memory locations allocated to the program defines the *physical memory space*. The last phase of memory management is the dynamic memory management required during the execution of the program.

In earlier computers, when the entire program would not fit into memory space at one time, a technique called *overlay* was used. Phases of the program were brought into memory when needed, overlaying those that were no longer needed.

Memory requirements of some programs are difficult to predict, a factor that influences memory management during executions. Another and perhaps the strongest influence is that high-performance computer systems are often operated in multiprogramming mode. The result of these influences is that the fraction of main memory which is assigned to any one program is unpredictable outside the execution environment. Only at execution time are physical addresses assigned, for only then are the total memory size, the currently unused memory space, and the sizes of the various routines from called libraries known.

Virtual memory gives programmers the illusion that there is a very large memory at their disposal, whereas the actual (physical) memory available may be small. This illusion can be accomplished by allowing the programmer to operate in the name space while the architecture provides a mechanism for translating the program-generated (virtual) addresses (during execution) into the memory-location addresses. In multiple processor systems with virtual memory, this mechanism must be provided for each processor. Assume that the name space V_j generated by the jth program running on a processor consists of a set of n unique identifiers. Hence

$$V_j = \{0, 1, \ldots, n - 1\}$$

Assume that the memory space allocated to the program in execution has m locations. This space can be represented as a sequence of addresses:

$$M = \{0, 1, \ldots, m - 1\}$$

since main memory can be regarded as a linear array of locations, where each location is identified by a unique memory address. Also, since the allocated memory space may vary with program execution, m is a function of time.

At any time t and for each referenced name $x \in V_j$, there is an *address map*

$$f_j(t): V_j \rightarrow M \cup \{\phi\}$$

which identifies a mapping between names and memory addresses at instant t so as to *bind* them. The function $f_j(t)$ is defined by

$$f_j[x, t] = \begin{cases} y & \text{if at time } t \text{ item } x \text{ is in } M \text{ at location } y \\ \phi & \text{if at time } t \text{ item } x \text{ is missing from } M \end{cases}$$

When $f_j[x, t] = \phi$, an *addressing exception* or *missing item* fault is said to occur, which causes a fault handler to bring in the required item from the next lower level of memory. The fault handler also updates the f_j map to reflect the new binding of names to memory addresses. In a general hierarchy, the missing item is retrieved by sending a memory request for the item to successive lower levels until it is found in a level, say k. Three basic policies define the control of the transfer of the missing item from a lower level to the desired level. A *placement* policy selects a location in memory where the fetched item will be placed. Where the memory is full, a *replacement* policy chooses which item or items to remove in order to create space for the fetched item. A *fetch policy* decides when an item is to be fetched from lower level memory. These policies and their impact on memory management will be discussed fully in Section 2.3.

Program locality The sequence of references made by the jth program in execution can be represented by a *reference string* $R_j(T) = r_j(1)r_j(2) \ldots r_j(T)$, where $r_j(t) \in V_j$ is the tth virtual address generated by process j. It is common knowledge that the virtual addresses generated are nonrandom but behave in a somewhat predictable manner. Such characteristics of programs are due to looping, sequential and block-formatted control structures inherent in the grouping of instructions, and data in programs. These properties, referred to as the *locality of reference*, describe the fact that over an interval of virtual time, the virtual addresses generated by a typical program tend to be restricted to small sets of its name space, as shown in Figure 2.5. For example, if one considers the interval Δ in Figure 2.5, the subset of pages referenced in that interval is less than the set of pages addressable.

There are three components of the locality of reference, which coexist in an active process. These are *temporal, spatial*, and *sequentiality* localities. In temporal locality, there is a tendency for a process to reference in the near future the elements of the reference string referenced in the recent past. Program constructs which lead to this concept are loops, temporary variables, or process stacks. In spatial locality there is a tendency for a process to make references to a portion of the virtual address space in the neighborhood of the last reference. The principle of sequentiality states that if the last reference was $r_j(t)$, then there is a likelihood that the next reference is to the immediate successor of element $r_j(t)$. Traversals of a sequential set of instructions and arrays of data enforce spatial and sequentiality localities. It should be noted that each process exhibits an individual characteristic with respect to the three types of localities.

Each type of locality aids or influences the characterization of an efficient memory hierarchy. The principle of spatial locality permits us to determine the size of the block to be transferred between levels. The principle of temporal

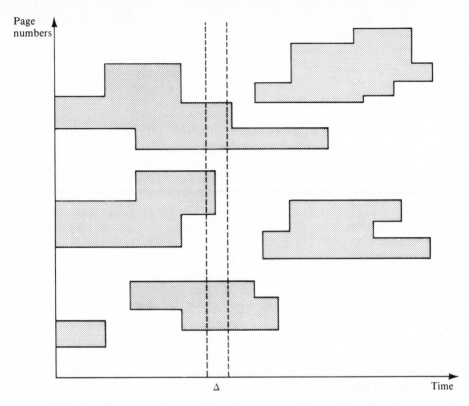

Figure 2.5 An example of a page reference map for a process.

locality aids in identifying the number of blocks to be contained at each level. Sequentiality locality permits the distribution of the unique identifiers to concurrently operating devices at certain levels of the hierarchy for concurrent accesses.

From Figure 2.5, if the reader considers a hypothetical interval time window Δ which moves across the virtual time axis, it can be seen that only a subset of the virtual address space is needed during the time interval of the history of the process. The subset of virtual space referenced during the interval t, $t + \Delta$ is called the *working set* $W(t, \Delta)$. During the execution of a process, the working set quickly accumulates in the highest level of the memory hierarchy to reduce the effective memory access time of a reference. In general, the time window Δ is a critical parameter which may be chosen to optimize the working set of the process over its lifetime.

Program relocation During the execution of a program, the processor generates logical addresses which are mapped into the physical address space in the main memory. The address mapping, considered as the function $f_j: V_j \rightarrow M$, is performed both when the program is initially loaded and during the execution of the program. The former case is called *static relocation*; the latter is called *dynamic relocation*. Static relocation makes it difficult for processes to share information which is modifiable during execution. Furthermore, if a program is displaced from main memory by mapping, it must be reloaded into the same set of memory locations, thereby fixing or binding the physical address space of the program for the duration of the execution. This constraint causes inefficient memory management policies. Multiprogramming systems do not generally use static relocation because of these and other disadvantages. In order to effectively utilize memory resources, dynamic relocation is often used, in which the function f_j is varied during the execution of the programs.

One technique in performing dynamic relocation is to use a set of base or relocation registers in which the content of a relocation register is added to the virtual address at each memory access. In this case, the programs may be initially loaded into memory using static relocation, after which they may be displaced within memory and the contents of the relocation register adjusted to reflect the displacement. Two or more processes may share the programs by using different relocation registers.

Address map implementation The address map f can be implemented in several ways. The simplest implementation, *direct mapping*, is a table with n entries so that the xth entry contains y whenever $f(x) = y$ and is null (ϕ) otherwise. The time to access the element identified by x involves an additional memory access; the time to look up the xth entry in the table. If the table is implemented in main memory, the effective access time of the element may be intolerable. Fast registers may be used at a great expense. Since the virtual space size n may be much greater than the physical space size m in practice, the table would contain $n - m$ null entries. Even if we created a table with only m entries, the execution time variation of m may present some management problems, as we shall see later. Another implementation, *associative mapping*, uses an *associative memory* (AM) that contains those pairs (x, y) for which $f(x) = y$ and the search is by content. Since the search time in an AM increases with an increase in the number of entries, a small high-speed buffer is often used. This buffer, often called the *translation lookaside buffer* (TLB), maintains the mapping between recently used virtual and physical memory addresses.

The implementation discussed above for the address map is still impractical because the virtual memory size n is usually too large, so that even the locality set of the program cannot be stored in a practical AM. In the following three sections, we examine methods that result in considerable reduction in the amount of mapping information that must be stored. Each method groups information into nonoverlapping blocks, so that the entries in the address may refer to blocks instead of individual addresses in the address space. The first method organizes the address space into blocks of fixed size, called a *page*. The second method organizes the name space into blocks of arbitrary size, called a *segment*. In the third method, we combine paging and segmentation.

Virtual memory in perspective The principle of locality of reference has proved virtual memory to be effective for the given access times and costs. That is, users have been willing to accept the overhead and burden of a page management system in order to have the benefits of an apparently large memory. If the cost of a large memory is so inexpensive that the user is willing to buy it in the first place regardless of the inefficiency in its use because the references are local, then virtual memory may be unimportant. The microcomputers used in offices and small businesses probably fit in this category today and will certainly be in this category when 256K and possibly 1M random-access memory chips are in high production.

At this point, it may be more effective to have large real memory for a small computing system than virtual memory in a two-level system, although paging hardware for automatic relocation will still be useful. Whereas virtual memory was present on the majority of interactive, time-shared systems in the 1970s, it may disappear from use on small personal systems. However, virtual memory will continue to be used in many large systems, such as large database systems or computing facilities, where the program-size requirements are extremely large and do not fit into real memory at an economical cost.

2.2.2 Paged Memory System

In this scheme, the virtual space is partitioned into pages, which can be resident in matching size blocks (called *page frames*) in memory. Each virtual address that is generated by a program in execution consists of two fields: a virtual page number i_p, which is the mapped field, and the displacement i_w of the word within the page, which is the unmapped field. The address map consists of a *page table* (PT), from which is read the corresponding base address of the page frame if the page exists in the main memory. The simplest page table may contain one entry for each possible virtual page.

There is one page table for each process, and the page table is created in main memory at the initiation of the process. A page table base register (PTBR) in each processor contains the base address of the page table of the process that is currently running on that processor. The page table entry may be accessed by indexing into the page table array. Figure 2.6 shows how the page table is used by direct mapping to implement the mapping of a virtual address to a physical address. Each *page table entry* (PTE) consists of a *valid bit* (F), a *permissible access code* (RWX), a *memory-disk bit* (M) and a *page-frame address* (PFA).

The valid bit, if set, indicates that the page *exists*, or is *nonnull*. A page which is null (valid bit cleared) would have to be created when referenced. A page is said to be active with respect to a process if it is resident in main memory. The memory bit (M) flag is set in the page table entry of that process and the PFA field of the PTE contains the address of the page in memory. In contrast, a nonnull page is inactive with respect to a process if the memory bit (M) is cleared. Then the PFA field of the PTE contains the disk address of the page.

The page table mapping mechanism is rather inefficient since it requires two memory accesses for each data accessed. This may be improved by using a fast

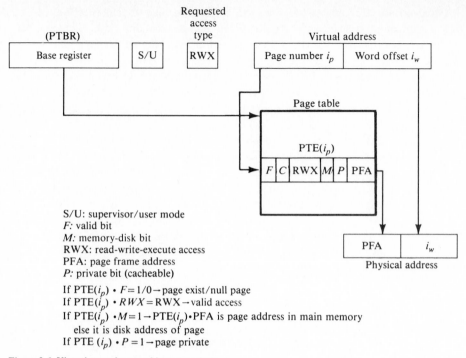

S/U: supervisor/user mode
F: valid bit
M: memory-disk bit
RWX: read-write-execute access
PFA: page frame address
P: private bit (cacheable)

If $PTE(i_p) \cdot F = 1/0 \rightarrow$ page exist/null page
If $PTE(i_p) \cdot RWX = RWX \rightarrow$ valid access
If $PTE(i_p) \cdot M = 1 \rightarrow PTE(i_p) \cdot PFA$ is page address in main memory
    else it is disk address of page
If $PTE(i_p) \cdot P = 1 \rightarrow$ page private

Figure 2.6 Virtual to real page address translation.

random-access memory or register set to store the page table. For example, the Xerox Sigma 7 processor has a 256 register-set of nine bits each and a page size of 512 words. This corresponds to a virtual memory of 2^{17} words (128 K). A better solution is to exploit the locality of reference property of programs and use an associative map which consists of an N-entry translation lookaside buffer (TLB). Hence the TLB may contain the N most recently accessed virtual page numbers and their corresponding page-frame addresses.

In a system with a single virtual address space, all users reside in the same virtual memory. Another method is to partition the virtual space into several independent areas, allocating one to each active process. This can be accomplished by using the high-order bits of the virtual page number as a process identification. These bits with the PTBR can be used to select the page table of a process.

Yet another technique of maintaining multiple virtual address spaces is to fix the virtual space and concatenate a system-generated process identification with the virtual address. This is illustrated in Figure 2.7. For a multiprogrammed processor, a page map entry typically consists of six fields: a virtual page number i_p, a process identification, the RWX, a modified bit (C), and the PFA in shared memory. The process identification of the currently running process is in the current process register (CPR) of the processor.

When a virtual address is generated by a running process, the virtual-to-real address translation involves the associative comparison of the virtual page number

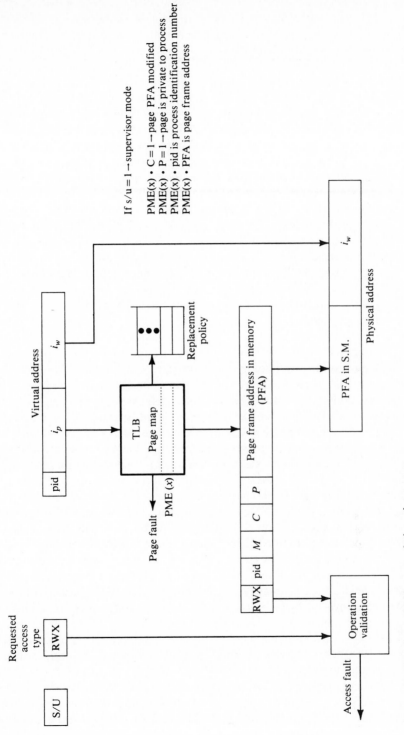

If s/u = 1 → supervisor mode

PME(x) • C = 1 → page PFA modified
PME(x) • P = 1 → page is private to process
PME(x) • pid is process identification number
PME(x) • PFA is page frame address

Figure 2.7 Virtual to real address translation using page map.

i_p with all the *page map entries* (PME) that contain the same process identification as the current running process. If there is a match, the page-frame number is retrieved and the physical address formed by concatenating the displacement with the PFA. If there is no match, a page fault interrupt occurs, which is serviced to locate the page. Moreover, if the page-access key presented by the virtual address does not match the RWX field of the PME with a corresponding virtual page number and PID, an access violation is trapped. When a referenced page is modified, the modified bit C of the corresponding PME is set in the page map. This bit may be used by the replacement and memory update policies.

When a page fault occurs because the virtual page number i_p was not found in the TLB, a *dynamic address translation* is requested, using the page table which is resident in main memory. The virtual page number i_p, used as an index, is added to the page table address in the PTBR and the resulting address is used to access the PTE as described earlier. If the PTE indicates that the page is not in main memory, the running process is *blocked* or suspended. A *context switch* is then made to another ready-to-run process while the page is transferred from drum or disk to memory and the PTE entry updated. The page address on disk or drum may be found in the address field of the PTE. The context or task switch involves the saving of the state of the faulting process and restoring the state of the runnable process in the processor.

The TLB is invalidated or its contents are saved in memory as part of the faulting process. The task switch is made because the page-transfer operation is slow compared to the processor speed. If the page is in memory, the TLB is updated with the virtual page number and the page's page-frame address pair before the process resumes execution. Updating the TLB involves replacing one of its entries if it is full. The entry chosen for replacement is usually the least recently used entry. Additional control bits, such as a set of usage bits, are associated with each page map entry. The usage bits determine which entry is overwritten during the replacement policy. Sometimes a private bit P is associated with each page to indicate that the page is private to a process or shared by a set of processes.

Pure paged memory systems can become very inefficient if the virtual space is large. The size of a page table can become unreasonably large. For example, consider a system with a 32-bit virtual address and a 1024 (1 K)-byte page size. The page address field is thus 22 bits, assuming byte addressability. Hence, we have 2^{22} page table entries! Assuming that we have an 8M-byte main memory, there are $2^{23}/2^{10} = 2^{13}$ page frames. Therefore, in the PTE we have a 13-bit page-frame field, or approximately 4 bytes per PTE. The total space consumed by a page table is thus 2^{24} bytes! In such cases, the page table may have to be paged also.

There are other disadvantages of a pure paged system. There are no mechanisms for a reasonable implementation of sharing. The size of a program space is not always an integral number of pages hence, oftentimes, *internal fragmentation* occurs in memory because the last part of the last page is wasted. In addition, there is another type of storage fragmentation called *table fragmentation*, which occurs because some of the physical memory are occupied by the page tables and so are unavailable for assignment to virtual pages. The VAX 11/780 virtual memory system is described below as an example of a paged memory system.

The virtual address of the VAX 11/780 is 32 bits wide and the page size is $2^9 = 512$ bytes. For each reference, this address is translated, via a page map, to a physical address that is 30 bits wide. The entry format of the page table is shown in Figure 2.8. Bit 31 of the PTE represents the valid bit which, when set, indicates that the referenced page is in main memory. Therefore, bits $\langle 20:0 \rangle$ of the PTE contain the physical page-frame number of the page. If the valid bit is reset, bits $\langle 20:0 \rangle$ of the PTE contain the invalid memory address of the referenced page. Thus a page fault occurs and bits $\langle 25:0 \rangle$ of the PTE are used to determine the location of the page on disk.

The modified bit (bit 26) of the PTE, if set, indicates that the page was modified. Hence, the disk copy of the page must be updated when the page frame is de-allocated. The modified bit is set on the first reference to the page. Bits $\langle 30:27 \rangle$ of the PTE contain the protection mask or access privileges permitted on that page. The protection mask is defined for four process types: kernel, executive, supervisor, and user processes. In a memory reference, the requested access type for the process is compared to the allowable accesses, if any. Access is denied if an unpermitted access was requested.

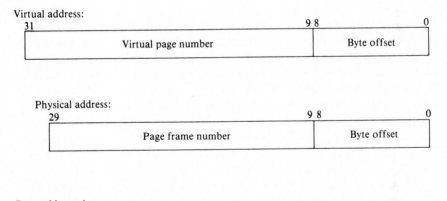

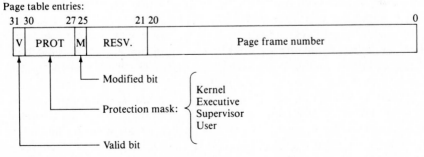

Figure 2.8 Address and page table entry formats of VAX-11/780 virtual memory (Courtesy of Digital Equipment Corp.).

Virtual address space regions:

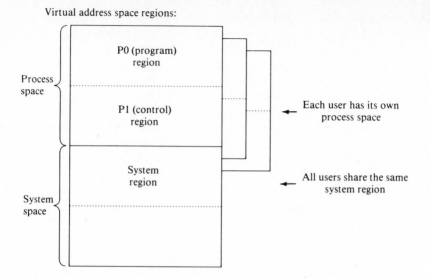

Figure 2.9 Partitions of virtual address space (Courtesy of Digital Equipment Corp.).

For further memory protection, the virtual address is partitioned into two spaces, process and system. Each of the two spaces are further partitioned into two regions. The process space consists of program (P0) and control (P1) regions, as shown in Figure 2.9. These regions permit two directions of growth. The system space consists of a system and unused regions. Bits of the virtual address $\langle 31:30 \rangle$ are used to specify the addressed region. A page table is established for each region. Each user process is assigned its own process space and, therefore, page tables for its private program and control regions. However, all user processes share the same system space.

Since all users share the same system space, there is only one page table for the system space. This page table is called the *system page table* (SPT). The SPT is described by two hardware registers: the system base register (SBR) and the system length register (SLR). The SBR contains the starting physical address of the SPT, which must be contiguous and cannot be paged.

Similarly, two hardware registers are allocated to each of the program and control regions' page tables of the user process. These registers are P0BR and P0LR for the program region's page table, and P1BR and P1LR for the control region's page table, as shown in Figure 2.10. These registers are always loaded with the address and length of the page tables for the process in execution.

The process page tables are stored in the contiguous system space's virtual memory, therefore, the page table's base registers contain system space addresses so that the process-space page tables can be paged. An address reference in the process space requires a two-level address translation. The address translation process is illustrated in Figure 2.11. To speed up the translation process, an associative page map (address translation buffer) is provided. It has 128 entries divided

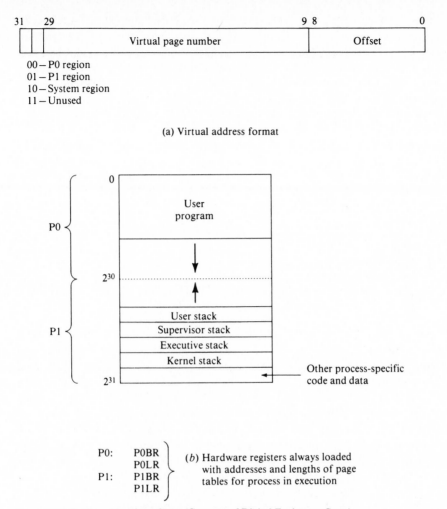

(a) Virtual address format

Figure 2.10 Region addressing scheme (Courtesy of Digital Equipment Corp.).

into two 64-entry groups for process and system spaces. On a context switch, only the process space entries are purged.

2.2.3 Segmented Memory System

Programs which are block-structured and written in languages such as Pascal, C, and Algol yield a high degree of modularity. These modules may include procedures or subroutines which call other procedures. The modules are compiled to produce machine codes in a logical space which may be loaded, linked, and executed. The set of logically related contiguous data elements which are produced is commonly called a *segment*, which is given a segment name. Segments are allowed to grow and shrink almost arbitrarily, unlike pages, which have fixed sizes. Segmentation is a technique for managing virtual space allocation, whereas paging is a concept used to manage the physical space allocation. In a segmented system, a user can define a very large logical space, which can be managed efficiently. An element in a segment is referenced by the segment name–element name pair ($\langle s \rangle$, $[i]$). During program execution, the segment name $\langle s \rangle$ is translated into a segment address by the operating system. The element name maps into a relative address or displacement within the segment during program compilation.

A program consists of a set of linked segments where the links are created as a result of procedure segment calls within the program segment. The method of

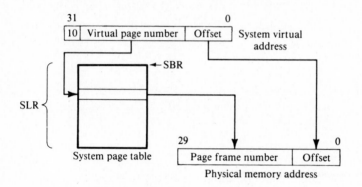

(a) System address translation

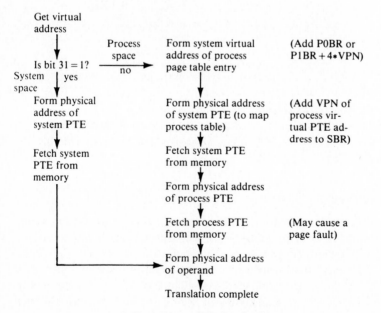

(b) The address translation algorithm

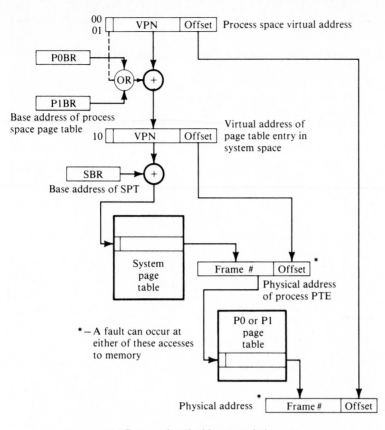

(*c*) Process virtual address translation

Figure 2.11 Address translation mechanisms in VAX-11/780 virtual memory (Courtesy of Digital Equipment Corp.).

linking the segments is an implementation problem. There are other implementation problems in the segmentation concept, including the determination of the number of segments to be allowed in the system and the maximum size of each segment. The method for sharing and protecting the segments and for mapping the virtual address into a physical address is also a design factor.

Segmentation was used in the Burroughs B5500. Each process in the system has a *segment table* (ST), pointed to by a segment table base register (STBR), in the processor when the process is active. The STBR permits the relocation of the ST, a segment itself, which is stored in main memory when the process is active. The ST consists of *segment table entries* (STE), each of which has a node structure shown in Figure 2.12.

The address field contains the absolute base address of the segment in memory if the segment is present, as indicated by the missing segment flag *F*. If the segment is missing from memory, the address field may point to the location of the segment in disk. L and RWX fields contain the length and access rights (read, write, execute)

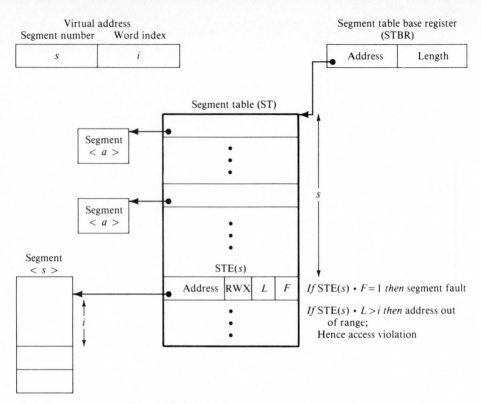

Figure 2.12 Address mapping in a segmented system.

attributes of the segment, respectively. Figure 2.12 illustrates how the physical address is determined from the segmented virtual address, which consists of the segment number s and the index i of the word within the segment. Segments may be shared by several processes, as shown in Figure 2.13 for two processes in separate processors. Notice that the relative positions of a shared segment need not be the same in different segment tables.

When a segment $\langle s \rangle$ is initially referenced in a process, its segment number s is not established. The segment must therefore be *made known* to the process by providing a corresponding segment number as an entry in the ST to be used in subsequent references. Using the segment name (directory pathname) $\langle s \rangle$ as a key, a global table, called the *active segment table* (AST), which is shared by all processes, is searched to determine whether the segment is active in memory. If it is, the absolute base address of the segment and its attributes are returned and an entry is made in the AST to indicate that the process is using this segment. If $\langle s \rangle$ does not exist in AST, a file directory search is initiated to retrieve the segment and its attributes. The returned absolute base address of the segment and its attributes are entered into the AST and a newly created node of the ST. A segment number s, which is the displacement of the node, is assigned by the operating system from the set of unused segment numbers for that process.

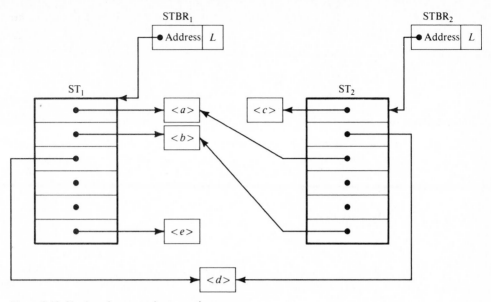

Figure 2.13 Sharing of segments by two active processes.

Associated with each process is a *known segment table* (KST), which contains entries on a set of segments known to the process. Each entry in the table contains a segment name–segment number pair. This is used to obtain the segment number when subsequent references are made to the segment name in the process. The address mapping mechanism shown for the segmented system involves a method of indirection to access each word that is referenced. This inefficiency may be resolved by the use of associative mapping techniques, as discussed in the paged system.

When a segment is copied from disk to memory, it is moved in its entirety. This is also true when the segment is relocated in memory. An appropriate size of contiguous data area must be found and allocated to that segment before the transfer operation is initiated. It is not often that a contiguous block of memory is found to fit the segment. In many cases, there are unused fragments of space, called *holes*, each of which may not always fit the segment to be placed. Various placement algorithms have been proposed. We present four of them.

Let $s_1, s_2, \ldots, s_n$ be the sizes of the n holes available in memory, and let s be the size of the segment to be placed. If the holes are listed in order of increasing size, $s_1 \leq s_2 \leq \cdots \leq s_n$, then the *best fit* algorithm finds the smallest i, such that $s \leq s_i$. Similarly, the *worst fit* algorithm can be defined if the holes are listed in order of decreasing size. This algorithm places the segment in the first hole and links the hole formed by the remaining space into the appropriate position in the list. In a third algorithm, called the *first fit*, the hole table lists holes in order of increasing initial address. The hole with the smallest i, such that $s \leq s_i$, is selected.

The fourth algorithm is the *buddy system*. In this case we assume that the segment size is $s = 2^k$ for some $k \leq n$. This policy maintains n hole lists, one for each size hole, $2^1, 2^2, \ldots, 2^n$. A hole may be removed from the $(i + 1)$th list by splitting it into half, thereby creating a pair of "buddies" of size 2^i, which are entered in the i list. Conversely, a pair of buddies may be removed from the i list, coalesced, and the new hole entered in the $(i + 1)$th list. With this scheme, we can develop an algorithm to find a hole of size 2^k.

The best fit algorithm appears to minimize the wastage in each hole it selects, since it selects the smallest hole that will fit the segment to be placed. However, the worst fit algorithm is based on the philosophy that the allocation of a larger hole will probably leave a hole large enough to be useful in the near future. It also assumes that making an allocation from a small hole will leave an even smaller hole, which will probably be useless without coalescing with other holes. The first fit and the buddy system are the most efficient algorithms.

In most cases, a time-consuming *memory compaction* is used to collect fragments of unused space into one contiguous block for the appropriate segment size. Moreover, since in the process of compaction segments in use are moved, the corresponding segment table entries must be modified. The unoccupied holes of various sizes which tend to appear between successive segments give rise to a phenomenon called *external fragmentation*. This causes memory management inefficiencies. Moreover, a whole segment may be brought into memory when only a small fraction of its address space will be referenced during the lifetime of the process, resulting in *superfluity*. These problems can be alleviated by combining segmentation with paging. It should be noted that table fragmentation also occurs in segmented systems.

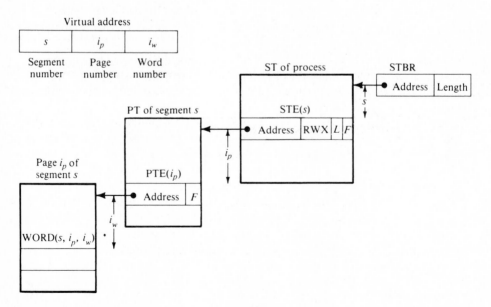

Figure 2.14 Address mapping in a system with paged segments.

2.2.4 Memory with Paged Segments

In this case, paging and segmentation are combined to gain the advantages of both. There are two types of paged segment schemes. One uses *linear segmentation*, in which the paging characteristics dominate, and the other is *segmented name space*, in which the segmentation characteristics dominate. In both cases, each segment is divided into pages and is referenced by the processor via a page table for that segment. An entry in the PT of a segment s contains an address field and a page presence bit, F. If the page is present in main memory, the address field contains the absolute base address of the page. A referenced page which is absent in memory causes a *page-fault* interrupt, which invokes the page-fault handler to retrieve the page from disk to the memory. Figure 2.14 illustrates the mapping of the initial address triple (s, i_p, i_w) to the physical address. The mapping of a virtual address to a physical address requires two levels of indirection, which is inefficient. Again, the mapping operation can be improved dramatically by using the associative mapping technique in each processor as illustrated in Figure 2.15. However, the improvement may be at a considerable cost. The Multics system, IBM 370/168, and the Amdahl 470 V/6 are examples of systems with segmentation and paging.

During the mapping of a virtual address of a known segment to the physical address, an access fault may occur in the TLB because of the absence of the segment or page number in the associative memory. Using the segment number, the information about the page address could be obtained from the page table, which is stored in main memory, and possibly from a local table memory (LTM) for a nonconflicting access. However, storing the page table in LTM may not facilitate the sharing of the segment. It may also create table consistency problems. An entry

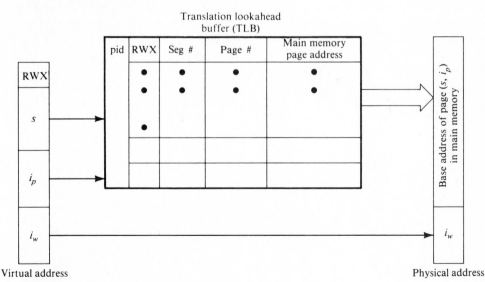

Figure 2.15 Associative map for paged segments.

in the TLB is chosen for replacement with the new segment number, page number, and page address triple.

If the segment number is not known when using segmented name space, a segment fault occurs, which invokes a procedure to make the segment known and causes the processor to perform a context switch to another process. The segment is made known by searching for the segment pathname in the AST. If it exists, the segment is in memory and is being used by an active process. Hence, its PT location in shared memory is known and is obtained from the AST entry. An unused segment number for the faulting process is obtained and an entry is made in the process control block of the process to prepare the process for subsequent execution. However, if the segment is not known to any active process, a directory search is performed to find the location of the segment in the file memory. A free PT and an unused AST entry are obtained. These segment attributes are copied to the PT and a pointer is established in the AST entry to point to the PT. A page of the segment is then copied to the memory and the appropriate entries are made in the ST of the process, as described previously.

In a virtual memory system, a *page-fault* interrupt typically violates the assumption made about interrupts on a processor. While interrupts occur asynchronously, they are constrained to be serviced at the end of an instruction cycle. However, a page fault interrupt which occurs within an instruction cycle must be serviced before the instruction cycle can be completed. This problem occurs, for example, when an instruction encoding crosses a page boundary or when a reference is made to an operand which is outside the page. Hence, at the point of interrupt, the page-fault handler must determine how far the instruction has progressed and what it must do to restart or continue the instruction cycle.

In some systems, many instructions can be restarted simply by backing up the program counter and reexecuting the instruction from the beginning. However, the partial execution of other instructions may have already made irrevocable changes to the registers and memory states. Such instructions must be restarted from the point of interruption. In general, this requires the saving of many "atomic" processor states, such as machine cycles, or the prohibition of any instructions which cannot be "backed out" of.

There are certain problems involved with using an associative map (TLB) in a multiprogrammed processor. The size of a TLB is fixed and hence can contain only a limited number of entries. If a segment number–page number pair $\langle s, i_p \rangle$ does not exist in the TLB at the time of reference, it is accessed from the PT of the segment in memory and is used to replace an entry in the TLB. When a page fault or segment fault occurs because the page or segment is not in memory, the processor suspends the faulting process and switches to a ready-to-run process.

The new process creates its own address space, which is different from the suspended process. Therefore, all the entries in the TLB map become invalid. The mapping mechanism must ensure that no old TLB entry is used in the new address space, as this may result in incorrect access to physical words of the suspended process and thereby create a hole in the protection mechanism. This problem can be solved by the context switch mechanism, which can invalidate all entries of the

TLB by the use of a special instruction, as was done in the original GE-645 Multics system. This technique degrades the performance of the system since the new process goes through initial slow indirect accesses to retrieve the $\langle s, i_p \rangle$ entries from the STs and PTs of the process.

Further problems exist when all TLB entries are invalidated. As the new process slowly fills up the TLB map with the valid entries, it may be interrupted or page faulted again, which will cause the TLB entries to be invalidated once more. Processes may continuously undergo the TLB reload cost and severely degrade the system performance. This problem can be solved by introducing in each TLB entry a process identification field which contains a short encoding of the process identification number. This technique, as implemented in the IBM 370/168, permits the associative map to contain more than one process entry (address space). However, only the entry that matches the currently running process is used. A process may therefore be restarted with part of its mapping entries in the TLB, thereby reducing the reload cost.

Choice of page size In purely segmented memory systems, we found that external fragmentation is a potential cause of memory under-utilization. The external fragmentation can theoretically be avoided by paging. However, paged segments reduce the utilization of memory by using additional storage space for segment and page tables (table fragmentation) and by rounding up the memory requirements for a segment to an integral number of pages (internal fragmentation). If z words is the size of a page and s is the segment size in words, the number of pages allocated to the segment is

$$n(s, z) = \left\lceil \frac{s}{z} \right\rceil$$

Hence, the amount of space

$$I(s, z) = n(s, z)z - s$$

usually called the internal fragmentation is wasted in the last page allocated to the segment because of the rounding off effect, assuming that $z > 1$. The page table for the segment occupies the following number of words:

$$T(s, z) = cn(s, z)$$

where c is a constant.

The fraction w of memory wasted because of paging in a segmented system is

$$w = \frac{n(s, z)z - s + cn(s, z)}{s} \tag{2.7}$$

The expectation of the numerator of w is $(c + z)E[n(s, z)] - E[s]$ and that of the denominator is $E[s]$. If we denote the ratio of the expectations by $\bar{w}$, we have

$$\bar{w} = \frac{(c + z)E[n(s, z)] - E[s]}{E[s]}$$

If we let $\bar{s} = E[s]$, it can be shown that $E[n(s, z)] = \bar{s}/z + \frac{1}{2}$. Hence

$$\bar{w} = \frac{(c + z)(s/z + \frac{1}{2})}{\bar{s}} - 1 \tag{2.8}$$

By setting $d\bar{w}/dz = 0$, we find that the optimum page size z_0 and the minimum fractional wasted space $\bar{w}_0$ are $z_0 = \sqrt{2c\bar{s}}$ and $\bar{w}_0 = \sqrt{2c/\bar{s}} + c/2\bar{s}$. In general, the fractional wasted space decreases when the segments (and pages) increase in size. This is in contrast to the requirements for contiguous segments, which should be small in size to reduce external fragmentation.

The choice of the page size z is a critical parameter which affects the perform-ance of a virtual memory system. Assuming that $\bar{s} = 8192$ bytes and $c = 4$, $z_0 = 256$ bytes. This seems rather small when it is known that typical values of z are 256 to 2048 bytes. In practice, the choice of z depends mostly on the efficiency of the paging device.

2.3 MEMORY ALLOCATION AND MANAGEMENT

In this section, we discuss the various models and classification of memory manage-ment schemes. Basically, two policies, fixed and variable partitioning, are identified to manage the allocation of memory pages to active processes. In the fixed alloca-tion scheme, the partition of memory allocated to an active process is fixed during the lifetime of the process. The variable allocation scheme permits the partition to vary dynamically during the lifetime of the process and according to the memory requirements of the active process. Various paging algorithms are discussed for both the fixed and variable partitioning policies.

2.3.1 Classification of Memory Policies

In general, the page-fault rate f is not a value entirely intrinsic to the process. It is a critical parameter which depends on the memory management policy, which in turn determines: (1) how many pages of main memory are allocated to the process, and (2) what policy is chosen to decide which of the process's pages reside in main memory. A memory policy's *control parameter* can be used to trade paging load against resident set size.

A memory management policy change which improves the page-fault rate without changing the system load or other system parameters is expected to im-prove processor utilization, increase the system throughput, and decrease the response time. To show whether a change in the memory policy improves process-ing efficiency, it is usually sufficient to show that the change does not increase a process-paging rate. We will now discuss the various memory management policies.

Two classes of memory management policies are often used in multiprogram-ming systems, *fixed partitioning* and *variable partitioning*. These have been treated comprehensively by Denning and Graham and the terminologies used here are borrowed from their work. Let us denote by $A = \{P_1, P_2, \ldots, P_d\}$ the set of active processes during the interval in which the level of multiprogramming is fixed $[d = d(t)]$. To each P_i at time t is associated its *resident set* $Z_i(t)$ (which is the set of the page frames of the process present in memory) containing $z_i(t) \geq 1$ pages. In general, the resident sets $Z_i(t)s'$ overlap because of the sharing that takes place among active processes. The management configuration is represented by a *partition vector* $Z(t) = [Z_1(t), \ldots, Z_d(t)]$. Hence, the *size vector* $z(t) = [z(t), \ldots, z_d(t)]$.

The total set of page frames used by the d processes is

$$Z(t) = Z_1(t) \cup Z_2(t) \cup \cdots \cup Z_d(t) = \bigcup_{i=1}^{d} Z_i(t) \qquad (2.9)$$

Let $z_{ij}(t)$ represent the number of pages shared by processes P_i and P_j such that $P_i \neq P_j$ and let $z_{ijk}(t)$ represent the number of pages shared by processes $i, j,$ and $k,$ at $t.$ That is, ignoring the t's, we write

$$z_i = n(Z_i), z_{ij} = n(Z_i \cap Z_j), z_{ijk} = n(Z_i \cap Z_j \cap Z_k).$$

where $n(z)$ is the number of pages in a set z. The sum of all $z(t)$'s with r subscripts represents the total number of pages shared by r processes at time t. We will denote this by $N_r(t)$. Hence, $N_1(t) = \sum z_i(t),$ $N_2(t) = \sum z_{ij}(t),$ $N_3(t) = \sum z_{ijk}(t),$ where $1 \leq i < j < k < \cdots \leq d.$ Note that $N_r(t)$ has $\binom{d}{r}$ terms and the last sum, $N_d(t),$ reduces to a single term that indicates the number of pages shared by all the d processes. If M is the total number of page frames available for allocation in memory, then Feller (1970) found

$$\sum_{r=1}^{d} (-1)^{r+1} N_r(t) \leq M$$

at every time instant t. The pages of main memory which are unused by any active process is called the *resource memory* and is denoted by

$$R(t) = M - \sum_{r=1}^{d} (-1)^{r+1} N_r(t) \qquad (2.10)$$

Analytical modeling of the sharing concept is very difficult. Most results obtained to date assume that there is no sharing and $N_r = 0$ for $r > 1$. This simplifies the problem greatly and the reserve memory becomes $R(t) = M - N_1(t)$. A memory management policy includes a method of estimating programs' locality sets. The estimates obtained are used to specify the content (and size, if adjustable) of each process resident set.

If the resident set size $z_i(t)$ is a fixed constant z_i for all t during which process P_i is active, then the size vector $Z(t)$ is constant during any interval in which the set of active processes is fixed; this is known as the fixed-partition approach. In variable partitioning, the partition vector $Z(t)$ varies with time. The important advantage of fixed partitioning is the apparent low overhead of implementation, since partition changes occur as infrequently as possible; that is, when the set of active processes changes. This advantage can be very easily offset (even if the memory requirements of each process can be predicted prior to processing) when one accounts for the changing locality in a process. Consider the behavior of a fixed partition when each process of the set of active processes $(P_1, \ldots, P_d)$ has a large variance in locality set size as the time varies.

Since the partition is fixed, there is no way to reallocate page frames from Z_i to Z_j at a time when P_i's locality is smaller than z_i and P_j's locality is larger than z_j, even though such a reallocation would not degrade the performance of P_i but would improve the performance of P_j. This effect has been analyzed by comparing fixed versus variable memory-partitioning strategies in terms of the probability that the memory space a process demands exceeds the allocated space. A study suggests that the variable-partitioning strategy is much better than the fixed-partitioning strategy because there is a severe loss of memory utilization for processes that exhibit a wide variance of locality size.

In addition to the fixed- and variable-partitioning strategies, a memory policy can either be *global* or *local*. A local policy involves only the resident set of the faulting process; the global policy considers the history of the resident sets of all active processes in making a decision.

We describe the behavior of programs being executed in terms of certain parameters which define various memory management policies for fixed- and variable-partitioning strategies. Recall that a program in execution generates a sequence of references (known as an *address trace*) to information in its virtual address space. The ith process's behavior is described in terms of its reference string, which is a sequence:

$$R_i(T) = r_i(1)r_i(2) \cdots r_i(T)$$

in which $r_i(k)$ is the number of the page containing the virtual address references of the process P_i at time k, where $k = 1, 2, \ldots, T$ measures the execution time or virtual time. The set of pages that P_i has in main memory just before the kth reference is denoted by $Z_i(k - 1)$, and its size (in pages) by $z_i(k - 1)$. A page fault occurs at virtual time k if $r_i(k)$ is not in $Z_i(k - 1)$.

There are basically two memory-fetching policies used in fetching the pages of a process when a page fault occurs, *demand prefetching* and *demand fetching*. In demand prefetching, a number of pages (including the faulting page) of the process are fetched in anticipation of the process's future page requirements. In general, prefetching can, if properly designed, improve performance by permitting an overlap between the execution and the fetching of the same program. Prefetching techniques will be discussed later. In demand fetching, only the page referenced is fetched on a miss. Demand fetching can result in an increase in superfluity. Under the assumption of demand fetching, $Z_i(k)$ is the same as $Z_i(k - 1)$ plus $r_i(k)$, less any pages $\{y_i\}$ of $Z_i(k - 1)$ replaced by the memory policy. Hence, using set notations,

$$Z_i(k) = Z_i(k - 1) + \{r_i(k)\} - \{y_i\}$$

$$z_i(k) \leq z_i(k - 1) + 1$$

(2.11)

The memory policy, or paging algorithm A, is a mechanism for processing the reference string $R_i(T)$ and for determining the sequence of resident sets $Z_i(1)Z_i(2) \cdots Z_i(T)$ and, hence, the paging rate experienced by process P_i. We should note that although the behavior of a process is formulated with respect to its virtual time, the behavior of the system is formulated with respect to real time.

The concept of program locality usually applies to *phases* of the program execution. Although there is a strong correlation between adjacent phases of the execution of the program, there are *transitions* between phases which do not always satisfy the concept of locality. The transitions between phases are usually characterized by fairly disruptive changes in the set of favored pages, which cannot be predicted from the past behavior. Although intraphase behavior covers the majority of the virtual time, it is the interphase behavior that produces the majority of the misses or faults. This enforces the reason for some type of anticipatory fetch policy.

A number of models for program locality have been developed. Two examples are the *independent reference model* (IRM) and the *least recently used stack model* (LRUSM). The IRM regards the reference string as a sequence of independent random variables with a common stationary reference distribution. Hence the probability that the $r_i(k)$ reference is in page j is written as:

$$Pr[r_i(k) = j] = a_j \qquad \text{for all } t$$

This model predicts a geometric interreference distribution:

$$I_j(k) = (1 - a_j)^{k-1}a_j \qquad \text{for } k = 1, 2 \dots$$

The optimal memory policy for IRM replaces the page with the smallest value of a_j among the pages present in the resident set. The IRM is the simplest way of accounting for the nonlinearities observed in the swapping curves of real programs. Note that an assumption of completely random references would imply linear swapping curves. The IRM is not a good model of overall program behavior.

It has been shown that the LRUSM is a result of the LRU memory policy. This model uses an "LRU stack," which is a vector that orders the pages by decreasing recency of reference. Just after referencing $r(t)$, the first position will contain $r(t)$. A stack distance $g(t)$ is associated with the reference $r(t)$. $g(t)$ is the position of $r(t)$ in the stack just after $r(t - 1)$. The LRU stack has the property that (a) the LRU policy's resident set of capacity s pages always contains the first s elements of the stack, and (b) the missing-page rate is the frequency of occurrences of the event $g(t) > s$. The LRUSM assumes that the distances are independent random variables with a common stationary distribution. Thus the probability of referencing a page in stack at distance j is

$$Pr[g(t) = j] = b_j \qquad \text{for all } t$$

If $b_1 \geq b_2 \geq \cdots \geq b_j \geq \cdots \geq b_s$, then the LRU policy is optimal both in fixed-space and variable-space strategies. The LRUSM is slightly better than the IRM.

The above models do not adequately capture the essence of program behavior, which demands the changing need for memory from one phase to another. A realistic model must account for multiple program phases over locality sets of significantly different sizes and must not rule out strong correlations between distant phases. Some phase-transition models of program behavior have been developed which are more realistic than the last two models. Briefly, the program model consists of a *macromodel* and a *micromodel*. The macromodel is a semi-Markov chain whose "states" are mutually disjoint locality sets and whose "holding times" are phases. The macromodel is used to generate a sequence of locality-set–holding-time pairs (S, T). The micromodel is used to generate a reference substring of length T over the pages of locality set S. For the micromodel, the IRM or LRUSM may be used.

The *page-fault rate function* for process P_i, denoted by $f_i(A, s)$, is the expected number of page faults generated per unit of virtual time when a given reference string R_i is processed by memory policy A, subject to the memory space constraints s. The page-fault rate function is one of the most important parameters in the study of memory management. Most studies performed indicate that this function is relatively independent of R_i. For the fixed-memory allocation, the space constraints are interpreted to mean that the resident set sizes must satisfy $z_i(k) \leq s$ for all virtual times k. For the case of variable-space allocation, the space constraint s is interpreted as the *average resident set size* of process P_i, that is

$$s = \frac{1}{d} \sum_{k=1}^{d} z_i(k) \tag{2.12}$$

for a system with d active processes. In both allocation schemes, the *page-fault rate* for the total page is

$$f = \sum_{i=1}^{d} f_i(A, s) \tag{2.13}$$

which is the figure of merit to be minimized, subject to the allocation constraints

$$\sum_{r=1}^{d} (-1)^{r+1} N_r \leq M$$

where N_r is the number of pages shared by r processes and M is the total number of page frames in the main memory.

Another measure of the page-fault rate is the *lifetime function* $e_i(z_i)$, which gives the mean execution interval (in virtual time) between successive page faults for process P_i when it has z_i of its pages in shared memory. The derivation of this function assumes a given memory policy. A *knee* of a lifetime curve is a point at which $e_i(z_i)/z_i$ is locally maximum. The primary knee is the global maximum of $e_i(z_i)/z_i$. A typical lifetime curve is shown in Figure 2.16.

Several empirical models of the lifetime curve have been proposed. One is the *Belady model*:

$$e_i(z_i) = a \cdot z_i^k \tag{2.14}$$

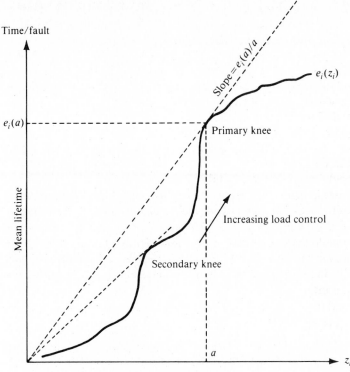

Figure 2.16 A lifetime curve.

where z_i is the mean resident set size, a is a constant, and k is normally between 1.5 and 3. In general, a and k depend on the program characteristics. This model is often a reasonable approximation of the portion of the lifetime curve below the primary knee, but it is otherwise poor.

A second model is the *Chamberlin model*:

$$e_i = \frac{2b_i}{1 + (c_i/z_i)^2} \tag{2.15}$$

This model was derived empirically as a result of many measurements performed on computer systems. It was observed that the lifetime curve $e_i(z_i)$ is concave for small values of z_i and becomes convex as z_i increases, as shown in Figure 2.16. Two parameters characterize the behavior of a process P_i in the concave-convex model: c_i, the number of pages for which $e_i = b_i$, that is, for which the mean execution interval is half of the longest interval for P_i; and b_i, the mean execution interval between page faults when the process P_i is allocated a memory space of c_i page frames. The parameter c_i gives a relative measure of the memory space needed to enable the process to be executed efficiently. It can be seen from Eq. 2.15 that the transition from the concave to the convex region occurs at $z_i = c_i/\sqrt{3}$, and that in $z_i = c_i$ the curvature in the convex region is maximum. Therefore, e_i could be considered a reasonable approximation to the memory demand of P_i.

Although this model has a knee, it is not a very good match for real programs. It is generally quite easy to measure lifetime curves from real data and such measurements are generally more reliable than estimates from models. If the page transfer time is S then the *page-fault rate* for process P_i is

$$f_i = \frac{1}{e_i + S} \tag{2.16}$$

This equation can be used to derive an optimization problem, which can then be solved to obtain optimum memory space allocation in a multiprogramming system.

Another measure that is often used is the *space-time product* of an active process. This product is the integral of a program's resident set size over the time T it is running or waiting for a missing page to be swapped into shared memory. Let $z(t)$ be the size of the resident set at time t, t_i be the time of the ith page fault ($i = 1, \ldots, K$), and D be the mean swapping delay. The *space-time product* is

$$ST = \sum_{t=1}^{T} z(t) + D \sum_{i=1}^{K} z(t_i) \tag{2.17}$$

If s is the mean resident set size, we can approximate ST by noting that the first sum becomes sT. If we approximate the second sum by sK and note that $sK = s(K/T)T = sf(s)T$, where $f(s)$ is the missing page rate, the space-time product is approximated by

$$ST = Ts[1 + Df(s)] \tag{2.18}$$

Although Eq. 2.18 is simple to compute, the approximation is not very reliable. Note that $sf(s) = s/e_i(s)$ is minimum at the primary knee of the lifetime curve. If D is large, choosing s at this knee will approximately minimize the space-time product.

2.3.2 Optimal Load Control

Main memory is considered a prime system resource which is used dynamically by the active processes in a multiprogramming environment. The number of active processes (degree of multiprogramming) in a parallel processor system is usually greater than the number of available processors so that when one of the running processes is suspended the processor may switch to another active process. This capability requires the memory be able to hold the pages of the active processes in order to reduce the context switching time. In general, multiprogramming improves concurrency in the use of all system resources, but the degree of multiprogramming should be varied dynamically to maintain both a low overhead on the system and a high degree of concurrency.

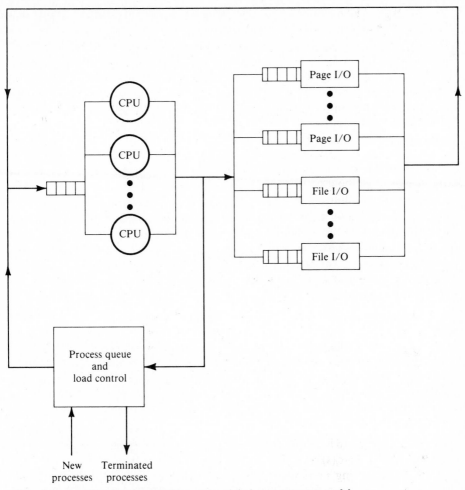

Figure 2.17 A multiprogrammed multiprocessing virtual memory system model.

Usually these are two conflicting requirements. Increasing the degree of multiprogramming may overcommit the memory to holding sets of only a few pages or segments of the active processes. In such a case, a context switch to a process with too small a working set may almost immediately encounter another page fault, which would necessitate another context switch to get another process with a small working set. If these activities occur continuously, the system is said to be *thrashing*, whereupon its performance is degraded considerably as it spends most of its time page-faulting and context-switching. The number of active processes or the *degree of multiprogramming* (DOM) will be denoted by a time-dependent variable $d(t)$.

Figure 2.17 depicts the model of the multiprogrammed multiprocessor system. This network consists of two main portions: the *active network* which contains the processors, memory and the file memory, and the *passive network* which contains a process queue and the policies for admitting new processes to active status. A process is considered active if it is in the active network, where it is eligible to receive processing and have pages in main memory. Each active process is waiting or in service at one of the three classes of resources in the active network. It waits at the file I/O class whenever it requires a segment to be transferred between main memory and the disk memory. An active process waits at the paging device modules whenever it requires a page to be transferred between main memory and a paging device, such as a drum or fixed-head disk. Otherwise it is in the CPU station.

The box labeled "Process queue" contains a set of enabled (passive) processes, a decision policy for activating them, and a load-control mechanism for controlling $d(t)$. Notice that each CPU node is usually considered to have a cache whose action is transparent, i.e., a cache miss does not necessitate a context switch. When a process either issues a file I/O request or creates a page fault, it will release its processor to another ready process and wait for the completion of the I/O transaction. Such a model, as depicted in the Figure 2.17, is called a closed queueing network model with d processes, where d is the steady-state degree of multiprogramming.

In addition to the DOM, another parameter used in the memory management model is the average total time used to service each process which requested paging device i. This time, which is denoted D_i, is the demand per process for the ith device. For each device, D_i is the product of the mean number of requests per process for that device and the mean time to service one request. For the paging device, the demand per process grows with d because higher DOMs imply smaller resident sets and higher rates of paging. For devices such as CPU and I/O, the demand per process does not depend on d. The demand for each CPU is the mean execution time E of a process. The average number of page faults per process is $E/L(d)$, where $L(d)$ denotes the lifetime or mean time between faults for a DOM of d.

The demand for the paging device is $D_i = ES/L(d)$, where S is the mean time to service one page transfer (exclusive of queueing delays). If the function $L(d)$ is not available from a direct measurement of the system, it can be estimated from the lifetime curve of a typical program. One method to estimate $L(d)$ is to set $L(d) = e_i(M/d)$, where $e_i(x)$ is the mean time between page faults for a typical program when the given memory policy produces a mean resident set size of x pages and M is the number of available pages of main memory.

The queueing network model of Figure 2.17 can be used to estimate the system's throughput X_0, which is the number of processes completed per second. The throughput is proportional to the average utilization of the CPUs, U, and is given by $X_0 E$. Figure 2.18 illustrates typical CPU utilization curves as a function of the DOM. The curve rises toward CPU saturation as the degree of multiprogramming d increases, but is eventually depressed by the ratio $L(d)/S$, the utilization of the saturated paging device. As suggested in Figure 2.18a, the DOM d_1, at which $L(d) = S$, is slightly better than the optimum d_0. Note that beyond d_0, the system begins to thrash.

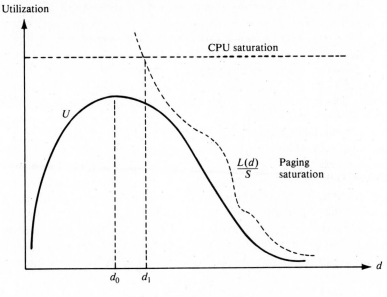

(a) Small main memory

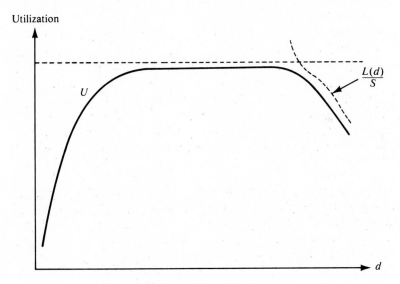

(b) Large main memory

Figure 2.18 Optimum degrees of multiprogramming.

This is known as the $L = S$ *criterion*, which can be used as an adaptive load control. It keeps the averaged lifetime at least as great as the page-transfer time for a page fault. The size of the main memory certainly affects the $L = S$ criterion. A very large main memory offsets the instabilities in memory policies and overheads created when the resident sets attempt to overflow the available memory space. The degree of multiprogramming can increase considerably in a system with a very large main memory without significant overhead because of swapping, as illustrated in Figure 2.18*b*. Once the main memory is large enough to allow the CPU utilization to be near one for some *d*, further increases of memory cannot increase the system throughput or decrease the response time.

An approximation of the optimum DOM, as characterized by the relation $L = aS$ for some constant, is not quite adequate. This approximation fails when the system is I/O bound or when the maximum lifetime L does not exceed the page-swapping time. The optimum DOM is actually achieved by running each process at its minimum space-time product, which is more difficult to achieve than the $L = aS$ criterion. Recall that if the total delay (queueing time plus swap time S) per page fault is large, the space-time product will be minimized approximately at the primary knee of the lifetime curve.

This *knee criterion* can be used as a basis for load control. It is more robust than the $L = S$ criterion. The knee criterion is a memory allocation strategy which achieves the maximum ratio of the lifetime to the memory allotment for process in a multiprogramming set. To limit the drop of CPU utilization, a maximum limit d_{max} is set on the DOM. The function of the load controller is to attempt to set d_{max} near the current optimum. If the number of submitted processes at a

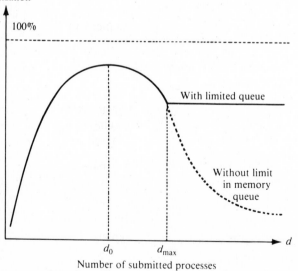

CPU utilization

Figure 2.19 **Effect of the load control on CPU utilization.**

given time does not exceed d_{max}, all are active; otherwise, the excess processes are held inactive in a memory queue. The limit effect of the memory queue is illustrated in Figure 2.19. In practice, the optimum DOM varies with the work load, therefore an adaptive control is required to adjust d_{max}.

The load control is accomplished by a component of a dispatcher, which is part of the operating system. The purpose of the dispatcher is to control the scheduling of processes and allocation of main memory so that the throughput for each work load is maximum. The dispatcher consists of three components: the *scheduler*, the *memory policy* and the *load controller*. The scheduler determines the composition of the active set of processes. It does this by activating processes from the passive process queue into the active set. The memory policy determines a resident set for each active process and, as we have seen, the load controller adjusts the limit d_{max} on the degree of multiprogramming. All memory policies manage a pool of unused space in main memory. The pool contains the pages of resident sets of recently deactivated processes. Under a fixed-space policy, the pool also contains pages which have recently left the resident sets of active processes. By comparing the measured memory demand of a process with the pool's size, the scheduler avoids activating a process if the activation would overload the system.

2.3.3 Memory Management Policies

The following definitions will be used in describing various paging algorithms. Given a reference string $R(t) = r(1)r(2)\cdots r(t)$, the *forward distance* $d_t(x)$ at time t for page x is the distance of the first reference to x after time t. That is,

$$d_t(x) = \begin{cases} k & \text{if } r(t + k) \text{ is the first occurrence of } x \text{ in } R(\infty) - R(t) \\ \infty & \text{if } x \text{ does not appear in } R(\infty) - R(t) \end{cases} \qquad (2.19)$$

Similarly, we define the *backward distance* $b_t(x)$ as the distance to the most recent reference of x in $R(t)$. Hence

$$b_t(x) = \begin{cases} k & \text{if } r(t - k) \text{ is the last occurrence of } x \text{ in } R(t) \\ \infty & \text{if } x \text{ never appeared in } R(t) \end{cases} \qquad (2.20)$$

Let $Q(Z)$ be the page replaced from resident set Z when a page fault occurs. Below we list examples of commonly used demand-paging page-replacement memory policies for fixed-space and local-policy allocation schemes:

1. *Least recently used (LRU)*—At page fault replaces the page in $Z(t)$ with the largest backward distance:

$$Q(Z(t)) = y \qquad \text{if and only if } b_t(y) = \max_{x \varepsilon Z(t)} [b_t(x)] \qquad (2.21)$$

2. *Belady's optimal algorithm (MIN)*—At page fault replaces the page in $Z(t)$ with the largest forward distance:

$$Q(Z(t)) = y \qquad \text{if and only if } d_t(y) = \max_{x \varepsilon Z(t)} [d_t(x)] \qquad (2.22)$$

This algorithm minimizes the number of page faults.

3. *Least frequently used (LFU)*—Replaces the page in $Z(t)$ that has been referenced the least number of times.

4. *First-in, first-out (FIFO)*—Replaces the page in $Z(t)$ that has been in memory for the longest time.

5. *Clock algorithm (CLOCK)*—A disconcerting feature with the FIFO algorithm is that it may end up replacing a frequently referenced page because it has been in memory for the longest time. This problem is alleviated by associating a *usage bit* with each entry in the FIFO queue, which is made circular, and establishing a pointer for the circular queue. The usage bit for an entry in the queue is set upon initial reference. On a page fault, the pointer resumes a cyclic scan through the entries of the circular queue, skipping used page frames and resetting their usage bits. The page frame in the first unused entry is selected for replacement. This algorithm attempts to approximate LRU within the simple implementation of FIFO.

6. *Last-in, first-out (LIFO)*—Replaces the page in $Z(t)$ that has been in memory for the shortest time.

7. *Random (RAND)*—Chooses a page in $Z(t)$ at random for replacement.

Since the LRU policy is one of the most popular algorithms, we will describe its implementation. Associated with this policy is a dynamic list known as the *LRU stack*, which arranges the referenced pages from top to bottom by decreasing order of recency of reference. At a page replacement time, the LRU policy chooses the lowest-ranked page in the stack, therefore, the contents of an s-page resident set must always be the pages occupying the first s stack positions. When a page is referenced, the stack is updated by moving the referenced page to the top and pushing down the intervening pages by one place. The position at which the referenced page was found before being promoted to the top is called the *stack distance*. A page fault occurs in an s-page resident set at a given reference if and only if the stack distance of that reference exceeds s. In the fixed partitioning strategy, each active process has its own LRU stack.

Algorithms such as LRU, LFU, LIFO, FIFO, and RAND, which are called *nonlookahead* algorithms, are realizable. MIN is a lookahead page-replacement algorithm and is not realizable, but provides a benchmark on which we can measure the relative performance of the realizable algorithms. Figure 2.20 illustrates the typical relative page-fault rates for various paging algorithms. The page-fault rate $f(A, s)$ for a given algorithm A and resident size constraint s can be computed from the reference string R.

Let $S_j(A, s, R)$ represent the set of pages in the resident set-size constraint s at time instant j when processing a reference string R. A natural expectation is that if the size constraint s increases, the following *inclusion property* would hold:

$$S_j(A, s, R) \subseteq S_j(A, s + 1, R) \tag{2.23}$$

However, the FIFO algorithm has the disadvantage of exhibiting erratic and undesirable behaviors under certain circumstances and does not always satisfy

$f(A, s)$

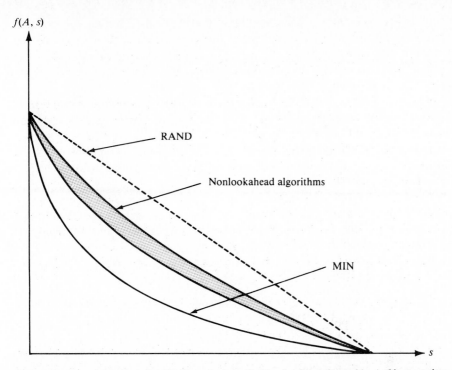

Figure 2.20 Page fault rates of realizable and nonrealizable algorithms for various resident set sizes.

the inclusion property. For example, consider the processing of the reference string $R = 12314$, using the FIFO algorithm, when the address space of the process is the set $M = \{1, 2, 3, 4\}$ for two resident size constraints, $s = 2$ and $s = 3$. Below we show the sequence of S_j states generated as a result of the processing of the string R. In this illustration, an asterisk ($*$) after a reference indicates that no page fault occurred, otherwise, a page fault did occur.

$$
\begin{array}{c|ccccc}
 & S_1 & S_2 & S_3 & S_4 & S_5 \\
R = & 1 & 2 & 3 & 1 & 4 \\
\hline
 & 1 & 1 & 2 & 3 & 1 \\
 & & 2 & 3 & 1 & 4 \\
\hline
 & 1 & 1 & 1 & 1* & 2 \\
 & & 2 & 2 & 2 & 3 \\
 & & & 3 & 3 & 4
\end{array}
\quad
\begin{array}{l}
\left. \right\} \; s = 2 \\[2ex]
\left. \right\} \; s = 3
\end{array}
$$

Notice that $S_5(\text{FIFO}, 2, R) \not\subseteq S_5(\text{FIFO}, 3, R)$ and, hence, does not satisfy the inclusion property. The *normalized page-fault rate* can be obtained from the expression

$$
f(A, s) = \frac{N(A, s, R)}{|R|} \tag{2.24}
$$

where $N(A, s, R)$ is the number of page faults which occurred in the processing of the reference string R using algorithm A and a resident set-size constraint of s. $|R|$ is the cardinality of R or the number of references in R. For the example above, $f(\text{FIFO}, 2) = 1.0$ and $f(\text{FIFO}, 3) = 0.8$. Algorithms which satisfy the inclusion property are called *stack algorithms*.

Although this method of derivation of the page-fault rate for a given reference is adequate, it does not account for the mechanisms by which programs generate reference strings. Moreover, the procedures do not readily extend to the analysis of variable-space policies which use the locality of reference model. We will now consider the paging algorithms for variable-space partitioning strategy using a global policy.

Several important algorithms for implementing variable-space partitioning strategies have been used. One approach to the memory management commonly used extends the idea of a fixed-space replacement policy simply by applying the replacement rule to the entire contents of main memory, without identifying which process is using a given page. Examples of this approach are:

1. *Global LRU* — which arranges all the pages of the active processes into a single global LRU stack. Whenever an active process runs, it will reference its locality set pages and move them to the top of the global LRU stack.
2. *Global FIFO* — which arranges all the pages of the active programs into a single global FIFO list.

A load control is necessary for the successful implementation of the global LRU policy, for if there are too many active processes, pages will be taken from the resident set of the least recently run process (whose pages will tend to occupy the lowest stack positions), whereupon that process, when run, will soon experience a page fault. This type of policy has been found highly susceptible to thrashing and may not perform better than fixed-space partition policies.

There is a variation of the global LRU policy which uses a *usage bit u* and a *changed bit c*, which are associated with every resident page. The bit u is set to 1 by the addressing hardware on any reference to the given page and is cleared to 0 by the memory management routine. The bit c is set to 1 by the addressing hardware on the first write reference to the given page and is cleared when the page is loaded or when the disk copy is updated. At intervals, the memory management process scans all resident set pages and maintains them in four lists according to the possible values of the bits (u, c). At a page fault, the first page of the first non-empty list in the order $(u, c) = [(0, 0), (0, 1), (1, 0), (1, 1)]$ is selected for replacement. This policy, which approximates LRU, is subject to the same problems as LRU when used for multiprogramming.

Another variation of the global LRU and FIFO combines elements of both policies. It is called *global FINUFO* (first-in, not-used, first-out). In this policy, all the pages of the active processes are linked in a circular list with a pointer designating the current position. Each page has a usage bit which is set by the hardware to 1 when the page is referenced. Whenever a page fault occurs, the memory policy advances the current-position pointer around the list clearing set usage bits and stopping at the first page whose usage bit is already cleared to 0: this page is selected for replacement. This paging algorithm was used in the Multics system. The above variable-space allocation policies do not attempt to identify locality sets and protect them from preemption.

Another example of the variable memory partitioning is the *working-set* (WS) algorithm, which takes into account the varying memory requirements during the execution of a process. Denning (1968) introduced the concept of working set to describe program behavior in virtual memory environments. The working set $W(t, \theta)$ is used to denote an estimator of a locality set. $W(t, \theta)$ of a process at time t is defined as the set of distinct pages which are referenced during the execution of the process over the interval $(t - \theta, t)$, where θ is the window size. The working-set size $w(t, \theta)$ is the number of pages (cardinality) of the set $W(t, \theta)$.

This algorithm retains in memory exactly those pages of each process that have been referenced in the preceding θ seconds of process (virtual) time. If an insufficient number of page frames are available, then a process is deactivated in order to provide additional page frames. Notice that the working-set policy is very similar to the LRU policy in that the working-set algorithm specifies the removal of the LRU page when that page has not been used for the preceding θ time units, whereas the LRU algorithm specifies the removal of the sth least recently used page when a page fault occurs in a memory of capacity s.

The success of the working-set algorithm is based on the observed fact that a process executes in a succession of localities; that is, for some period of time the process uses only a subset of its pages and with this set of pages in memory, the program will execute efficiently. This is because, at various times, the number of pages used in the preceding θ seconds (for some appropriate θ) is considered to be a better predictor than simply the set of K (for some K) pages most recently used. Thus for example, a compiler may need only 25 pages to execute efficiently during parsing, but may need 50 during code generation. A working set with the correct choice of the parameter θ would adapt well to this situation, whereas a constant K over both phases of the compiler would either use excess space in the syntax phase or insufficient space in the code-generation phase. The working-set paging algorithm, although efficient, is difficult to implement, however.

Yet another variable-partitioning strategy which can use local or global policy is the *page-fault frequency* (PFF) replacement algorithm. The PFF also attempts to follow variations in localities when allocating memory space to processes. This policy is implemented using hardware usage bits and an interval timer and is invoked only at the time of a page fault. Let t' and t for $t > t'$ denote two successive (virtual) times at which page faults occur in a given process. Also, let $R(t, \theta)$ denote the PFF resident set just after time t, given that the control parameter of PFF has the value θ. Then

$$R(t, \theta) = \begin{cases} W(t, t - t') & \text{if } t - t' > \theta \\ R(t', \theta) + r(t) & \text{otherwise} \end{cases} \qquad (2.25)$$

where $r(t)$ is the page referenced at time t (and found missing from the resident set). The interfault interval $t - t'$ is used as a working-set window and the parameter θ acts as a threshold to guard against underestimating the working set in case of a short interfault interval. Hence, if the interval is too short, the resident set is augmented by adding the fault page $r(t)$. The usage bits, which are reset at each page fault, are used to determine the resident set if the timer reveals that the interfault interval exceeds the threshold. Note that $1/\theta$ can be interpreted as the maximum tolerable frequency of page faults.

Various experimental studies have shown that WS and PFF, when properly "tuned" by good choices of their control parameters, perform nearly the same as each other and considerably better than LRU. The PFF may display anomalies for certain programs since it does not satisfy the inclusion property. Since global memory policies make no distinctions among programs, their load controls have no dynamically adjustable parameters. However, these controls cannot ensure that each active program is allocated a space-time minimizing resident set. Local memory policies such as WS and PFF offer a much finer level of control and are capable of much better performance than global policies. These policies, however, present the problem of selecting a proper value of the control parameter θ for each program.

Finally, we present an ideal variable-space memory policy which could be local or global. This is the *optimal variable replacement* algorithm called VMIN. The VMIN generates the least possible fault rate for each value of mean resident-set size. At each reference $r(t) = i$, VMIN looks ahead: if the next reference to page i occurs in the interval $(t, t + \theta)$, VMIN keeps i in the resident set until that reference; otherwise, VMIN removes i immediately after the current reference. Page i can be reclaimed later when needed by a fault. In this case, θ serves as a window for lookahead, analogous to its use by WS as a window for lookbehind. VMIN anticipates a transition into a new phase by removing each old page from residence after its last reference prior to the transition. This results in a behavior depicted in Figure 2.21. In contrast, WS retains each segment for as long as θ time units after the transition. VMIN and WS generate exactly the same sequence of page faults for a given reference string. The suboptimality of WS results from resident set "overshoot" at interphase transitions, as shown in Figure 2.21. However, since VMIN is a lookahead algorithm, it is not practical.

Prefetching techniques Prefetching is a technique to reduce the paging traffic during locality phase transitions. Recall that there are two aspects of phase transition behavior. The first aspect is the removal of the pages of the old locality set; the second aspect is the fetching of the pages of the new locality set. A prefetch policy must dictate three main issues:

1. When do you initiate a prefetch?
2. Which block or blocks do you prefetch?
3. What replacement status do you give the prefetched block?

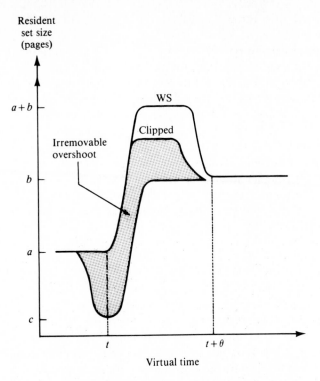

Resident
set size
(pages)

$a+b$

WS

Clipped

Irremovable
overshoot

b

a

c

t

$t+\theta$

Virtual time

Figure 2.21 Behavior of policies near a transition between phases.

One prefetch technique is the well-known *swapping*, commonly used in multi-programmed or time-sharing systems. If we do not use swapping, in such systems a context switch occurring because of the end of a time slice is followed by a slow purge of the process's blocks from memory. Similarly, later reactivation of the process is followed by a slow and tedious recognition of the locality set. This behaves as a transition of localities. A compromise between demand fetching and swapping is to demand fetch during a process's active intervals and use swapping at the end and beginning of the time slice to save and restore, respectively, the working set of the process.

Another type of prefetching technique is based on the frequently observed principles of spatial locality and sequentiality of references in programs. An example of a prefetching algorithm exploiting this property is the so-called one block lookahead (OBL) algorithm. We illustrate this algorithm by considering a stack of s pages, where s is the page allotment to the process. The demanded page is placed at the top of the stack in the usual manner. When a page fault occurs, the page that is the sequential successor of the demanded page in the virtual address space is prefetched, provided it is not resident in main memory. When such a prefetching occurs, an additional replacement is done and the prefetched page is placed at the bottom of the stack. Thus, if another page fault occurs before the prefetched page is referenced, then the prefetched page is replaced. In all other respects, this stack is maintained like an LRU stack.

This algorithm, when applied to database systems and vector operations, performs adequately where a high degree of sequentiality is present. It has been observed that common programs in execution do not possess adequate spatial locality unless the page size is rather small. As we shall see in Section 2.4, systems with caches employ a small block size so the OBL algorithm may be used to advantage in them. Also, since the units of information transfer from memory to the processor are quite small, and the instruction stream tends to exhibit a high degree of sequentiality, sequential prefetching of instructions into an instructor buffer is commonplace. Sequentiality may be induced in the data streams for vector instructions. Prefetching algorithms must be designed carefully so as not to nullify the potential gain in the reduction of page faults or misses by a disproportionate increase in the number of fetches.

2.4 CACHE MEMORIES AND MANAGEMENT

Cache memories are high-speed buffers which are inserted between the processors and main memory to capture those portions of the contents of main memory which are currently in use. They can also be inserted between main memory and mass storage. Since cache memories are typically five to 10 times faster than main memory, they can reduce the effective memory access time if carefully designed and implemented. This section discusses the characteristics of cache memories and the various cache management strategies. Four cache organizations—direct, fully associative, set associative, and sector mappings—are discussed. Cache replacement policies are used to decide what cache block to replace when a new block is to be brought into the cache.

2.4.1 Characteristics of Cache Memories

The success of cache memories can be attributed to its property of locality of references. The effectiveness of the cache in capturing localities is measured by the asymptotic fraction of program references found in the cache, called the *hit ratio h*.

The design of a cache memory for a concurrent computer system usually involves the minimization of a number of parameters, such as the miss ratio $(1 - h)$, the access time, the delay due to a miss, and the penalty for updating main memory. It also involves maintaining data consistency between the cache and main memory and, in the case of a multicache system, maintaining data consistency between the multiple caches. These and other aspects are discussed below. First, we describe the functional operation of a cache.

Operation of a cache The cache memory generally consists of two parts, the *cache directory* (CD) and the *random-access memory* (RAM). The memory portion is partitioned into a number of equal-sized blocks called *block frames*. The directory, which is usually implemented as some form of associative memory, consists of block address tags and some control bits such as a "dirty" bit, a "valid" bit, and protection bits. The address tags contain the block addresses of the blocks that are currently in the cache memory. The control bits are used for cache management and access control. Hence, the cache contains a set of address-data pairs, each of which consists of the main memory block address and a copy of the contents of the main memory block corresponding to that address.

The cache directory can be implemented as either an *implicit* or *explicit* lookup table. In the explicit directory, the referenced data is fetched from the memory portion of the cache only after the corresponding address tag has been searched. The implicit lookup table permits the simultaneous searching of the address tags and the fetching of the corresponding data. However, the presence of the desired block and its location in the cache are only detected at the end of the cache cycle.

The operation of the cache is simple in concept, as illustrated in Figure 2.22, for a fetch operation. The processor generates is a virtual address which is mapped into a physical memory address via a *translation lookaside buffer* (TLB). If there is a TLB hit, the corresponding physical page address is retrieved to form the physical address and the replacement status of the TLB entries is updated. If the TLB does not contain the ⟨virtual, physical⟩ address pair required for translation, the virtual address is passed along to the address translator to determine the physical address. This translation is performed, as discussed in Section 2.2, by using the high-order bits of the virtual address as an entry into the segment and page tables. The address pair is returned to the TLB (possibly replacing an existing TLB entry).

From the cache's viewpoint, the physical address formed consists of two components: the block-frame address and the byte within the block. The block-frame address is used to search the cache directory. If there is a *match* (cache hit), the block (or part of it) containing the target locations is copied from the RAM portion of the cache into a shift register. Concurrently, the replacement status of the cache entries is updated. The shift register is shifted to select the target bytes which are transmitted to the CPU. If a miss occurs during the fetch operation, the block is fetched from main memory by using the physical address. The fetched block is stored in the cache and also passed to the shift register for selection of the target bytes.

Recall that, in a paging system, a *miss* in main memory (page fault) necessitates a context switch to another runnable process because the time to service a page fault is usually much greater than the context switch overhead. In a cache, however, the time to service a miss is comparatively smaller than the context switch time and, because of the small size of the cache, misses are more frequent than page faults. Also, context switching will invariably cause the new process to encounter initial cache misses in an attempt to restore its "locality set" in the cache. For these reasons, the process does not context switch on a cache miss.

Design aspects In general, the design of a cache is subject to different constraints and trade-offs than that of main memory. One of the important parameters in the

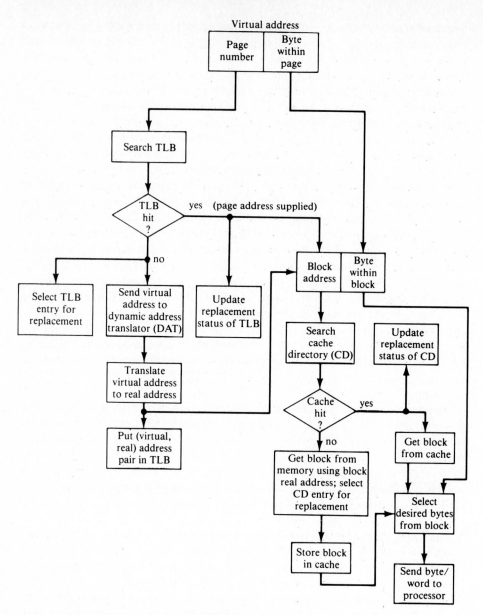

Figure 2.22 Simplified flowchart of cache operation for a fetch.

design of a cache memory is the *placement policy*, which establishes the correspondence between the main memory block and those in the cache. Other organizational parameters are the *fetch policy*, the *replacement policy*, the *main memory update policy*, *homogeneity*, the *addressing scheme*, cache and block sizes, and the *cache bandwidth*. The main memory update policy decides the time the information in memory is to be updated once the processor has requested a modification of the information. The fetch policy denotes how, when, and what information is to be fetched into the cache. The cache could be partitioned into several independent caches to segregate various types of references. An unpartitioned cache is said to be homogeneous. The cache could be multiported so that two or more requests can be made to the cache concurrently. In this case, a priority algorithm must exist to select one of the arbitrating requests. Furthermore, the cache accesses can be pipelined as in many mainframes, so that more than one cache access can be in progress concurrently. For example, four cache requests can each be in a unique phase of completion if the cache cycle is partitioned into four segments as follows: priority selection, TLB access, cache access, and replacement status update.

Cache bandwidth The cache bandwidth is the rate at which information can be transferred from or to the cache. The bandwidth must be sufficient to support the rate of instruction execution and I/O. The bandwidth can be improved by increasing the data-path width, interleaving the cache for concurrency, and decreasing the access time. The cache bus width affects the cost, reliability, and throughput of the system. An increase in bus width increases the access time because of packaging problems and additional gate delays because of line drivers and receivers. It also diminishes the signal-switching noise immunity. However, the wider the bus, the faster the data transfer. The number of fetches to main memory required to load a block of a given size depends on the bus width. Interleaving the cache can keep the bus width low while maintaining the bandwidth.

Effects of multiprogramming Most cache-based concurrent computers are, in fact, multiprogrammed. In most cases, each process gets to use the processor for a time slice or quantum in a round-robin fashion until the process terminates. Because of the alternate use of the processor, a significant fraction of the cache misses is due to the loading of the data and instructions for the new process which is assigned to the processor at the end of an intertask interval. This assumes that there is only one context in the cache in a given time slice and cache is purged at the end of the time slice. However, if the cache contains multiple contexts, a context switch may still increase the "cold-start" miss ratio because some of the new process's context may have been displaced in the cache. Note that the contexts can be distinguished in the cache by augmenting the address space of each context with a unique address space identification or process identification.

The problem of high cold-start miss ratios can be alleviated in a number of ways. A large cache can be used so that several processes' contexts will exist in it simultaneously. The scheduling policy can be modified to give priority to a task most likely to have its context in the cache. The time slice can be increased so that the frequency of task switches is reduced and a task, once assigned to the processor, will get a chance to reach a steady-state ("warm-start") miss ratio before the next context switch. Another solution is to save the process's context in main memory on a context switch and reload it *en masse* the next time it is assigned to the processor.

Data consistency The problem of having several different copies of the same block in a system is referred to as the *cache coherence* or data consistency problem. This problem exists in a uniprocessor with cache when the processor can be active after modifying a word in the cache and before the copy in memory has been updated. The effect of the main memory update policy on data consistency will be discussed in Section 2.4.3. If the processor is the only unit to access memory, then the coherence problem is a mere theoretical observation without practical bearing on the correctness of the program execution. However, practical systems contain I/O units which require access to the memory. The method in which the I/O unit accesses the memory in a system with cache may create consistency problems, as will be seen in Section 2.5. In a multiple processor system with caches, the data consistency problems may also exist between caches. Solutions to such coherence problems will be discussed in detail in Chapter 7.

2.4.2 Cache Memory Organizations

The cache is usually designed to be user-transparent. Therefore, in order to locate an item in the cache, it is necessary to have some function which maps the main memory address into a cache location. For uniformity of reference, both cache and main memory (MM) are divided into equal-sized units, called blocks in the memory and block frames in the cache. The placement policy determines the mapping function from the main memory address to the cache location.

Placement policies There are basically four placement policies: *direct, fully associative, set associative,* and *sector* mappings. In discussing the mapping functions, we will consider a specific running example in which each processor's cache is of size 2K (2048) words with 16 words per block. Thus the cache has 128 block frames. Let the main memory have a capacity of 256K words or 16,384 blocks. The physical address is representable in 18 bits.

Direct mapping This is the simplest of all organizations. In this scheme, block i of the memory maps into the block frame i modulo 128 of the cache. The memory address consists of three fields: the tag, block, and word fields, as depicted in Figure 2.23. Each block frame has its own specific tag associated with it. When a block of memory exists in a block frame in the cache, the tag associated with that frame contains the high-order 7 bits of the MM address of that block. When a physical memory address is generated for a memory reference the 7-bit block address field is used to address the corresponding block frame. The 7-bit tag address field is compared with the tag in the cache block frame. If there is a match, the information in the block frame is accessed by using the 4-bit word address field.

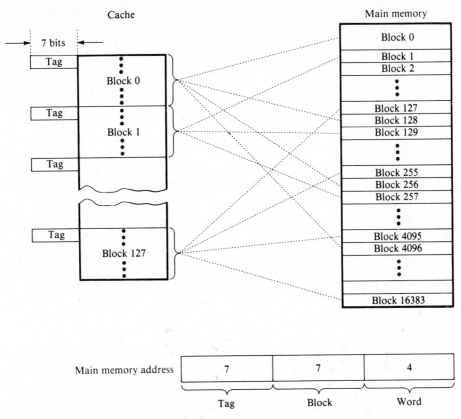

Figure 2.23 Direct mapping cache organization.

This scheme has the advantage of permitting simultaneous access to the desired data and tag. If there is no tag match, the output data is suppressed. No associative comparison is needed and, hence, the cost is reduced. The direct mapping cache also has the advantage of a trivial replacement algorithm by avoiding the overhead of record keeping associated with the replacement rule. Of all the blocks that map into a block frame, only one can actually be in the cache at a time. Hence, if a block caused a miss, we would simply determine the block frame this block maps onto and replace the block in that block frame. This occurs even when the cache is not full.

A disadvantage of direct-mapping cache when associated with a processor is that the cache hit ratio drops sharply if two or more blocks, used alternately, happen to map onto the same block frame in the cache. The possibility of this contention may be small in a uniprocessor system if such blocks are relatively far apart in the processor-generated address space. The possibility of this contention in a multiple-stream shared cache system may be much higher than that in a uniprocessor because many concurrently active streams are sharing the cache. The instruction cache in the IBM System/370 Model 158 uses direct mapping.

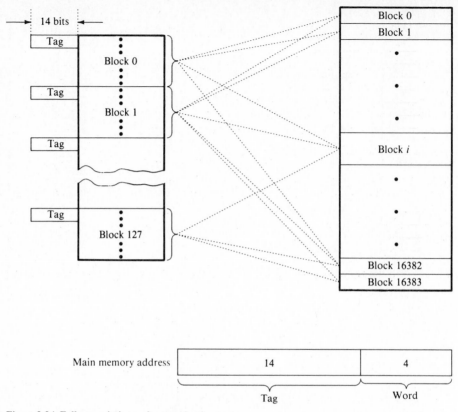

Figure 2.24 Fully associative cache organization.

Fully associative In terms of performance, this is the best and most expensive cache organization. The mapping is such that any block in memory can be in any block frame. When a request for a block is presented to the cache, all the map entries are compared simultaneously (associatively) with the request to determine if the request is present in the cache. In the running example, 14 tag bits are required to identify the memory block when it is present in the cache. Figure 2.24 illustrates the fully associative buffer. The mapping flexibility permits the development of a wide variety of replacement algorithms, some of which may be impractical. Although the fully associative cache eliminates the high block contention, it encounters longer access time because of the the associative search.

Set associative This represents a compromise between direct- and associative-mapping organization. In this scheme, the cache is divided into S sets with $E = M/S$ block frames per set, where M is the total number of block frames in the cache. A block i in memory can be in any block frame belonging to the set i modulo S, as shown in Figure 2.25 for the running example, where $M = 128$ and $S = 64$.

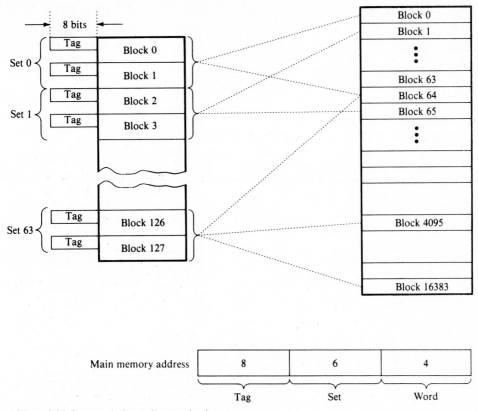

Figure 2.25 Set associative cache organization.

Several possible schemes are used for mapping a physical address into a set number. The simplest and most common is the *bit-selection* algorithm. In this case, the number of sets S is a power of 2 (say 2^k). If there are 2^j words per block, the first j bits, $0, \ldots, j - 1$, select the word within the block, and bits $j, \ldots, j + k - 1$ select the set via a decoder. Hence, for the example, the 6-bit set field of the memory address defines the set of the cache which might contain the desired block, as in the direct-mapping scheme. The 8-bit tag field of the memory address is then associatively compared to the tags in that set. If a match occurs, the block is present. The cost of the associative search in a fully associative cache depends on the number of tags (blocks) to be simultaneously searched and the tag field length. The set-associative cache attempts to cut this cost down and yet provide a performance close to that of the fully associative cache. For this reason, it is the most commonly used placement policy for cache memories.

The main consideration in choosing the values for S and E depends on directory lookup time, cost, miss ratio, and addressing. Note that S and E are inversely related, assuming a constant $M = SE = 2^m$. The set size defines the degree of associative search and thus the cost of the search. The addressing scheme used can indicate whether an overlap in cache lookup and the translation operation (via TLB) is possible in order to reduce the cache access time. Recall that the only address bits of a virtual address that get mapped in a virtual memory system are the ones that specify the page address. In order to illustrate how an overlap may occur, assume that there are 2^j bytes per block and 2^k sets in the cache. Let the page size be 2^p bytes. Assuming bit selection mapping, $p - j$ bits are immediately available to choose the set, since the low-order p bits, which specify the byte within the page, are invariant with respect to the mapping. It is quite advantageous to make $p - j \geq k$ so that the set can be selected immediately, in parallel with the translation process. This overlap is shown in Figure 2.26. However, if $p - j < k$, then the search for the cache block can only be narrowed down to a small number, $2^{(k-p+j)}$, sets.

The effect S and E have on the miss ratio can only be measured by trace-driven simulation on a typical work load. However, Smith (1978) derived a relationship between the miss ratio for fully associative and set associative cache organizations. Assuming an LRU stack-programming model with coefficients drawn from the linear paging model, it was shown that the ratio of the miss ratios between the set associative and the fully associative cache is

$$R(E, S) = \frac{E - 1/S}{E - 1} \qquad \text{for } E \geq 3 \qquad (2.26)$$

Figure 2.27 shows an example on the effect of S and E on the miss ratio. Experimental results have shown for uniprocessors that a set size in the range of 2 to 16 performs almost as well as fully associative mapping at little cost increase over direct mapping. Notice that when $E = m$, it is the fully associative mapping and when $E = 1$, it is the direct-mapping scheme. Table 2.2 shows some examples of systems that use set-associative cache and the choices of S and E.

Sector mapping In this scheme, the memory is partitioned into a number of sectors, each composed of a number of blocks. Similarly, the cache also consists of sector frames, each composed of a set of block frames. The memory requests are for blocks, and if a request is made for a block not in cache, the sector to which this block belongs is brought into the buffer with the following constraints: A sector from memory can be in any sector in the buffer, but the mapping of blocks in a sector is congruent. Also, only the block that caused the fault is brought into the cache, and the remaining block frames in this sector frame are marked invalid. A valid bit is associated with each block frame to indicate the blocks in a sector that have been referenced and hence retrieved from memory. Figure 2.28 illustrates the sector-cache organization for the running example with 16 blocks per sector and, hence, eight sector frames in the cache. This cache also attempts to reduce the cost of the map since it requires relatively few tags, which permits simultaneous comparisons with all tags. The IBM System/360 Model 85 has a sector-cache organization with 16 sectors and 16 blocks per sector.

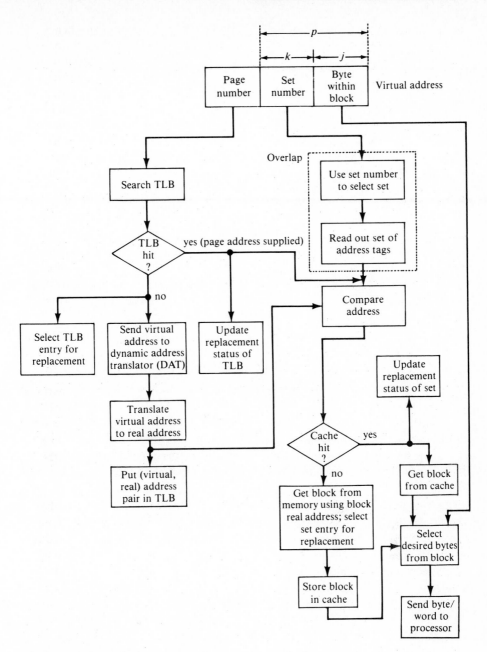

Figure 2.26 Set associative cache operations.

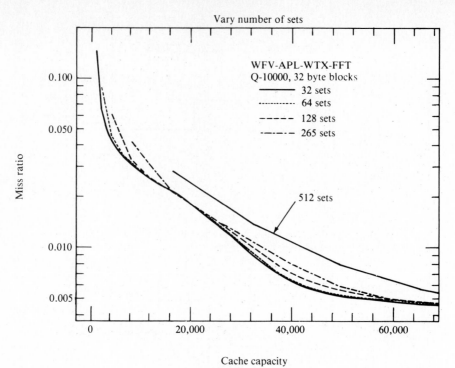

Figure 2.27 Miss ratios as a function of the number of sets and cache capacity (Smith, *ACM Surveys*, 1982).

Block and cache size selection In caches, a block is so small that spatial locality effects are the main consideration in the choice of the block size. The effect of cache size and block size on the hit ratio relates to spatial and temporal localities. For a given cache size, the miss ratio improves as the block size increases, because an increase in the block size captures more of the spatial locality. This improvement is achieved to the detriment of the temporal locality, because the total number of

Table 2.2 Typical values of S and E in example systems

System	(S, E)
Amdahl 470v/6	(2, 256)
Amdahl 470v/7	(8, 128)
Amdahl 470v/8	(4, 512)
IBM 370/168-3	(8, 128)
IBM 3033	(16, 64)
DEC VAX 11/780	(2, 512)
Honeywell 66/60	(4, 128)

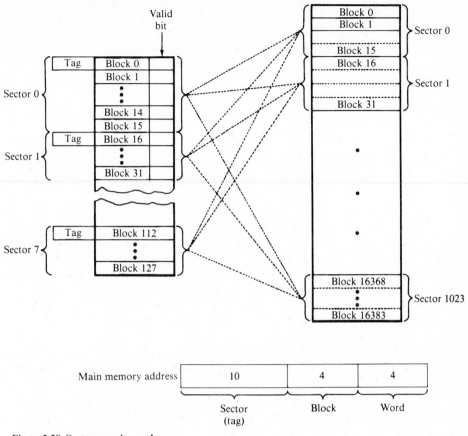

Figure 2.28 Sector mapping cache.

blocks in the cache is diminished proportionally. At some point, the miss ratio curve levels off for a block size such that the effects of a block-size increase on both localities compensate each other. Beyond this block size, most of the spatial locality has been captured and the miss ratio curve inflects, as the cache is not capable of holding the temporal locality of the program.

When the number of blocks in the cache is so small that blocks are swapped constantly between the cache and the memory, the efficiency of the cache goes to zero. The block size corresponding to the minimum miss ratio depends not only on the cache and its organization but also on the program behavior or work load. Because properties of programs vary widely, the choice of block and cache sizes must result from extensive simulations based on traces of programs constituting a representative work load. In Figure 2.29, we show two example miss ratio curves for a given work load in which the time slice Q is varied and represented in a number of memory references. It can be seen that Q also affects the selection of the block and cache sizes.

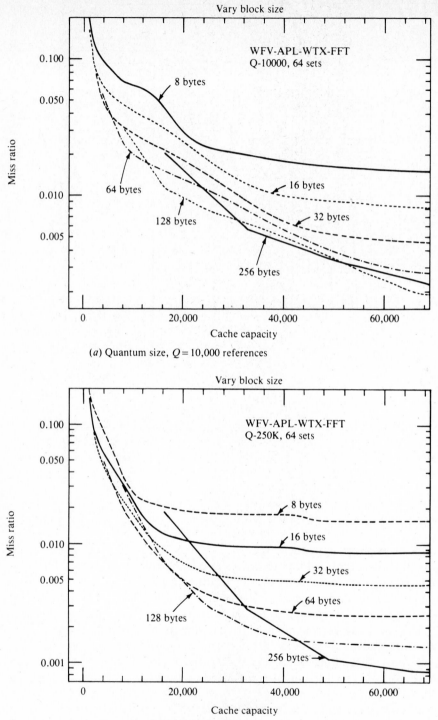

(a) Quantum size, $Q = 10,000$ references

(b) Quantum size, $Q = 250K$ references

Figure 2.29 Miss ratios as a function of block size and cache capacity (Smith, *ACM Surveys*, 1982).

For a given block size, a cache size increase is accompanied by an improvement in the miss ratio as more of the temporal locality is contained in the cache. Finally, the size and behavior of supervisor programs are a major factor in the selection of the cache size, as the supervisor typically uses the processor 25 to 60 percent of the time.

Practical translation lookaside buffers The TLB is typically designed as a small set-associative memory. However, the design is somewhat different from a set-associative cache. Unlike the set-associative cache, the input to the TLB is the virtual page number with no offset. However, if bit-selection algorithms were used, the low-order TLB entries would not be used efficiently. Therefore, the virtual page number is first randomized by hashing and the result applied as input to the TLB. Hashing can be performed rapidly by a set of exclusive-or logic on some bits of the virtual page number. However, the overhead due to hashing can be avoided, as in the VAX 11/750, which has a TLB with 256 sets and a set size of two. In this case, the set is selected with the high-order address bits and five low-order bits of the page number. Other examples of systems with TLB are the IBM 3033 (with 64 sets and two elements each), Amdahl 470V/6 (with 128 sets and two elements each), and the Amdahl 470V/7 and V/8 (with 256 sets and two elements each).

During a context switch, the entries of the TLB become invalid if only one context's *address-space identifications* reside in the TLB. Hence, the TLB is purged or invalidated at context switch. The purge operation, usually initiated by a privileged instruction, may create and extra overhead. For example, in the IBM 3033, it takes 16 machine cycles to purge the TLB.

Virtual versus physical addressing We have seen that the cache is addressed using the physical address. Although in the set-associative caches the translation of the virtual address can be overlapped with the lookup in the cache, the lookup cannot be completed until the physical address is available. The cache access time could be significantly reduced if the translation step could be eliminated. In this case, the cache would have to be addressed directly using the virtual address. The major problem with using virtual addresses to access the cache is that these names are defined within a process. Two processes may know the same physical word under different virtual names. Conversely, the same virtual name may designate different blocks for different processes. If the processor is multiprogrammed, a context switch is accompanied by a cache sweep or purge. Otherwise, the new process may issue a reference with a virtual name which will hit on a block that had the same name for the previously running process. This problem can be avoided by augmenting the virtual address with an address-space identification, which makes it unique.

However, there is still a possibility that several copies of the same physical block may exist in the cache under different names. This is called the *synonym problem* and causes coherence problems within the cache. If a block is shared among several active processes, several of its copies can be present in the cache under different names. The solution is to avoid multiple copies of the same block in the same cache by detecting the synonym when it occurs and enforcing consistency. Synonyms can be detected by mapping the virtual address into a physical address via a TLB and determining if there exist other virtual addresses in the cache that have the same physical address. This can be accomplished by a mapping device that is inverse to the TLB and is called an *inverse translation buffer* (ITB). The ITB is accessed on a physical address and indicates all the virtual addresses associated with that physical address that is in the cache.

To reference memory, the virtual address is applied to the TLB at the same time as the cache. If a miss occurs in the cache, the physical address obtained from the TLB is used to request a fetch of the block from main memory. Simultaneously, the physical address is also used to search the ITB to determine if that block is already in the cache under a different name (virtual address). If it is, the virtual address is renamed and moved to its new location to avoid multiple copies of the same block for consistency reasons. Also, the block-fetch request to memory is discarded. Otherwise, the block fetched from memory is used and the ITB and cache updated accordingly. The addressing of the cache by virtual addresses may decrease the cache access time on a hit at the cost of increased hardware complexity.

Partitioned cache Another issue in the design of a cache is the partitioning of the cache into several independent caches in order to segregate various types of references. Usually, segregation is limited to reference types that are hardware-detectable: for example, instructions versus data, or references in user mode versus references in supervisor mode. It could be extended to compiler-imposed segregation, in which references could be tagged at compile time. This extension, however, violates the principle of cache transparency, which simplifies the compiler. Splitting the cache generally improves the cache bandwidth and access time.

In a pipelined system, the processor is usually physically partitioned into two units, the I unit and the E unit. The I unit performs instruction fetch and decode and forwards the decoded instruction to the E unit, which executes it. In the execution phase, the E unit may fetch and store operands. By splitting the cache into data (D) and instruction (I) caches, the I cache (D cache) can be placed next to the I unit (E unit) to permit simultaneous access and reduce the access time. While one instruction is being fetched from the I cache, another instruction in the E unit can be accessing its operands from the D cache.

It is generally known that a significant fraction of misses is due to task switching for the execution of supervisor tasks. In order to reduce these miss transients, the cache can be split between a user cache and a system cache. Depending on the mode of execution, one cache or the other is referenced. Note, however, that the supervisor cache may still have a high-miss ratio because of its large working set.

The most obvious problem with split-cache organization is the consistency problem, because two copies of an information may now exist in separate caches. For example, in a pipelined processor, instructions being modified by the E unit must be stored in the I cache before they can be fetched. However, the E unit can access the D cache. Even if we assume that programs are not self-modifying, a cache block may contain instructions and data. Presumably, this effect can be minimized by designing compilers to insure that instructions and data are in separate blocks. Another problem with split cache results in possible inefficient use of cache memory. Locality properties of instructions and data are not homogeneous in this case. The miss ratio may increase as a result of splitting the cache. However, this depends on the work load. Examples of systems with split cache are the S-1 and the Amdahl 580.

2.4.3 Fetch and Main Memory Update Policies

As discussed earlier, this policy is used to decide when and what information to fetch into the cache. There are three basic types of fetch policies which are applied to cache: *demand*, *anticipatory*, and *selective* fetches. Demand and anticipatory fetch techniques used for paging systems can be applied to caches. In selective fetch, some information, such as shared writeable data, may be designated as unfetchable; further, there may be no fetch-on-write when a miss occurs, as discussed below.

Prefetching can be successfully used to prefetch the needed blocks ahead of time so that the cache miss ratio can be reduced. The major factor in determining the usefulness of prefetching in a cache is the block size. It has been found that a block size of less than 512 bytes results in useful prefetching. Only the OBL prefetch algorithm is usually considered because of its ease of implementation at cache speeds. Several possibilities exist for deciding when to initiate a prefetch. For example, for all i, prefetch block $i + 1$ if a reference is made to block i for the first time.

This technique, termed *always prefetch*, while good in reducing the miss ratio, creates more traffic to the cache and main memory. In multiprocessor systems, this may be detrimental. A refined technique is to prefetch block $i + 1$ only on a miss to block i. Yet another technique is *tagged prefetch* which, in addition to prefetching on a miss, also prefetches block $i + 1$ if a reference to a previously prefetched block i is made for the first time. Prefetching has been found to be very effective in pipelined systems such as the Amdahl 470 V/8, which uses *prefetch on a miss*.

One technique used to reduce the wait time of the processor during the fetching of a missed block is to forward the requested word directly to the processor first and then complete the fetching of the block in a wraparound fashion. This technique is called *load-through* or *read-through*.

The time when a word in memory is updated after a write depends on the write policy. One possibility, *write-through* (WT), is to update directly the memory copy of the data word. In this case, the copy of a block in the cache is never different from its copy in memory. Two variations of write-through are possible. The first is the *write-through-with-write-allocate* (WTWA) policy, in which a block is loaded into the cache on a write-miss. In WTWA, both read and write references contribute to the hit ratio. The second possibility is the *write-through-with-no-write-allocate* (WTNWA) policy, in which blocks are loaded into the cache on read-misses but not on write-misses. In WT, the effectiveness of the cache is limited by the fact that 5 to 30 percent of all memory references are write operations. When no buffer is provided at the memory, the processor is blocked during the write-through. In general, one can consider that the memory address and data registers form a buffer of size one. If another write-through or a miss occurs when a previous write has not been completed, the processor is blocked.

In order to estimate the effect of the write policies on the average memory access time, let ω_t be the fraction of writes in the system and assume a nonread-through fetch policy. Also, let t_c, t_m, and t_B be the cache cycle time, the memory cycle time ($t_c < t_m$), and the block transfer time, respectively. Assuming a WTWA policy, the *average time* to complete a reference when no buffer is present is

$$t_c + (1 - h)t_B + \omega_t(t_m - t_c) \tag{2.27}$$

Note this assumes that the writes to cache and main memory are performed simultaneously in the case of a hit and the miss ratio is $1 - h$. For WTNWA policy, the *average cycle time* is

$$t_c + (1 - h)(1 - \omega_t)t_B + \omega_t(t_m - t_c) \tag{2.28}$$

Note that the hit ratios in Eqs. 2.27 and 2.28 are not equal because of the difference in block-frame allocation. However, both equations have the same lower bound $t_c + \omega_t(t_m - t_c)$, which occurs when $h = 1$. This lower bound limits write-through policies to low-performance caches.

To improve the effectiveness of WT, increased buffering must be provided at the memory. The processor stores the write request in a FIFO buffer and then proceeds. To take full advantage of the buffering capability, block transfers due to cache misses should have a higher priority in accessing memory than write requests. Additional hardware checks the write buffer to ensure that a block requested by the processor does not contain any word waiting in the FIFO buffer. If the buffer contains such a word, the block is updated accordingly before it reaches the cache. At the limit, if the buffer has infinite size, the processor never waits for the completion of a write request, and thus the cache with WT policy can potentially achieve an *average reference time* of

$$t_c + (1 - h)t_B \tag{2.29}$$

The alternate policy is *write-back* (WB). The WB always allocates a cache block frame on a miss. When a write-hit occurs, only the block in the cache is modified. The memory update takes place when a block is replaced and swapped back to memory. Note that since the block-frame allocations in WB and WTWA are the same, the hit ratios are equal for both policies. The policy in which all replaced blocks are written back to memory is called *simple write-back* (SWB). Of course, the SWB results in many redundant swaps, during which the processor waits. To improve performance, a replaced block is written back only if it has been modified. A "dirty" bit is included in the directory with the tag of each cache frame. The dirty bit is reset when the block is loaded in the cache and is set when any word of the block is modified. This strategy is called *flagged write-back* (FWB), and it increases performance at low cost by reducing the average time the processor waits on a cache miss.

To further improve the performance, the write-backs on misses have to be buffered. In a technique called *flagged register write-back* (FRWB), the modified block selected for replacement is first written in a fast register to avoid interfering with the fetch. The new block is then brought into the freed cache block frame. The block write-back to the memory is activated later and is completed "in the background." In an extension to this policy, the blocks to write back could be buffered, as the modified words are in WT. The fetching of blocks from memory to cache on misses is given higher priority, and special hardware checks for the possible presence of a requested block in the write-back queue. The cost effectiveness of such an extension depends on the relative improvement achieveable beyond FRWB.

As for WT, we can estimate the efficiency of write-back strategies for some special cases. For SWB, the *average reference time* is

$$t_c + 2(1 - h)t_B \tag{2.30}$$

For FWB, it is

$$t_c + (1 - h)(t_B + w_b t_B) = t_c + (1 - h)(1 + w_b)t_B \tag{2.31}$$

where w_b is the probability that a replaced block has been modified.

The comparison between WT and WB is rather complex and depends on the program behavior. However, three major factors influence the effectiveness of WT or WB in a given system: the extent of memory traffic, data consistency, and reliability. WT usually results in more memory traffic, which can be very detrimental to the performance of a system with multiple processors. However, when the WT is used, main memory is always consistent with the cache, since the memory always has the updated copy of the data. Thus the failure of a processor and its cache permits recoverability.

2.4.4 Block Replacement Policies

When a miss occurs in a cache and a new block has to be brought in, a decision must be made as to which of the old blocks is to be overwritten if the cache is full. Various *replacement algorithms* have been proposed to select the block to be displaced. The property of locality of reference in programs gives a clue as to the types of algorithms that may result in a reasonable strategy. We would expect that a good replacement rule would appropriately treat a program's pages, depending on their reference probabilities. Since the cache has a small size it is generally overcommitted; that is, it is generally impossible to keep the working set of even one program in the cache at a time, except for some systems, such as Amdahl 470 V/8 and IBM 3033, with a 32K or more byte cache. Also, because of the constrained mapping mechanisms, only fixed-space replacement algorithms are generally considered. For example, in the set-associative cache, the block to be replaced is within a set and thus the replacement algorithm is invoked for block frames within that set.

Examples of commonly used fixed-space policies are *least recently used* (LRU) which, at a cache miss, replaces the least recently referenced block of the resident set; *first-in, first-out* (FIFO) which, at a miss, replaces the longest resident block; and *random* (RAND) which, at a miss, replaces a randomly chosen block from the set in the cache. It has been found that, on the average, LRU performs better than FIFO or RAND and is therefore preferred.

We will discuss the implementation of the LRU policy, which is used very often as a cache-replacement policy. Associated with an instance in this policy is a dynamic list, called the *LRU stack*, in which is arranged the referenced block-frame numbers from top to bottom by decreasing recency of reference. At a block replacement time, the LRU policy chooses the lowest-ranked block-frame number in the stack. Each time a block frame of the cache is referenced, the stack is updated by moving the referenced block-frame number x to the top and pushing down the intervening blocks by one position, thereby giving x a new lease on its life in the cache. The position at which the referenced block frame x was found in the stack before being promoted to the top is called the *stack distance* of x.

For small set sizes, the LRU policy may be implemented efficiently in hardware so as to operate at cache speeds. Three implementation schemes are discussed. The first scheme employs a set of fast counters, called *age registers*. Each age register is associated with every block in a set. As an example, consider the LRU stack implementation of a four-block set. Associate a 2-bit counter with each block, which can therefore count from 0 to 3. Each time a reference results in a hit and a block frame with count j is referenced, its counter is reset to 0 and all other counters with a value less that j are incremented by 1. The other counters are unmodified. If a reference results in a miss and the set is full, the block with counter value $j = 3$ is overwritten with the new block and its counter is reset to 0. The counters of the other three blocks are incremented by 1. The block with a counter value of 3 can be obtained by an associative search of the counters. If the set is not full when the miss occurs, the counter associated with the new block loaded from main memory is reset to 0 and all others incremented by 1. A little thought will show that the counter values of occupied blocks are always distinct.

A second implementation employs a set of D flip-flops to maintain the status of the blocks which currently reside in the cache. A few logic gates can achieve the updating function. Since there is plenty of time to update the LRU stacks for cache misses, only the updating for hit requests is considered in the example. For a set containing E blocks, that is, for a set of size E, $\log_2 E$ bits will be sufficient to address any given block in the set and a total of $E \log_2 E$ bits are enough to keep all the necessary information for LRU replacement operation. Figure 2.30 shows one example of an LRU stack with set size equal to 4. In this example, the four words of the stack are denoted as X, Y, Z, and W. Register X corresponds to the top of the stack and register W the bottom of the stack. Register X contains the block number $X_1 X_0$, register Y contains the block number $Y_1 Y_0$, and so on.

The number of the block just accessed is available on lines I_1 and I_0, and the number of the least-recently-used block is available as $W_1 W_0$. Three control signals, NX, NY, and NZ, are provided, each of which controls its corresponding

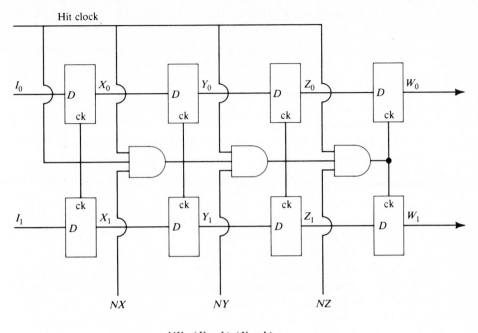

$$NX = (X_1 \oplus I_1)v(X_0 \oplus I_0)$$
$$NY = (Y_1 \oplus I_1)v(Y_0 \oplus I_0)$$
$$NZ = (Z_1 \oplus I_1)v(Z_0 \oplus I_0)$$

Figure 2.30 An implementation of the LRU algorithm.

block in the LRU stack. NX is 1 if the block that has just been accessed is not block number X; otherwise, NX is 0. The values of NY and NZ can be obtained similarly. Whenever a request results in a hit, a hit clock is generated immediately to control the updating process. Each of these three control signals, together with the hit clock, determine if the corresponding block should be shifted to the right in the LRU stack. The number of the block that has just been accessed is loaded into the leftmost pair of D flip-flops every time a hit in this set occurs. The contents of the other pairs are shifted to the right until the previous position of the just-accessed block is reached. The rightmost pair of the D flip-flops always indicates the number of the least recently used block in the set associated with this LRU stack.

A third implementation uses $E(E\text{-}1)$ active bits of status for a set with E elements. These $E(E - 1)$ active bits are derived from an E-by-E binary matrix in which the diagonal elements are passive and always zero. When the block in the jth block frame is referenced, the jth row of the binary matrix is first set to all 1's and then the jth column is set to all 0's. It is easy to show that, using such a scheme, the most recently used block is always the block in the block frame that has the largest number of 1's in its row. Similarly, the least recently used block is in the block frame with the smallest number of 1's in its row.

The three implementation schemes discussed above require a number of status bits that increase with the square of the set size. For a small set size (4 or 6), it is acceptable. However, for machines with a large set size (8 for IBM 370/168-3; and 16 for IBM 3033), it may be too expensive and slow. In such systems, the set of elements is partitioned into nonoverlapping groups. The LRU group is determined and the LRU element within the group is selected for replacement. If this scheme were applied to a set size of 8, in which the groups consist of 2 elements each, the implementation would use 20 active status bits instead of 56.

It has been shown that, in general, the effect of cache replacement algorithms on the performance of the cache is secondary when compared to the effect of the mapping on performance. The fully associative cache is most sensitive to the replacement algorithm (and least sensitive to mapping), while the direct-mapping cache is the most sensitive to mapping (and least sensitive to the replacement algorithm).

2.5 INPUT-OUTPUT SUBSYSTEMS

In this section, we review techniques for handling I/O processing. Several schemes are presented to handle different types of I/O transactions. Interfacing methodologies for slow, moderate, and fast devices are given. Methods for handling single, multiple, and priority interrupt requests are discussed. Techniques used to achieve maximum concurrency of I/O and CPU processing are introduced. Architectures of some intelligent I/O subsystem controllers are presented. Example I/O processors discussed include the IBM channels, the CDC integrated peripheral processing units, and the Intel I/O processor.

2.5.1 Characteristics of I/O Subsystems

The performance of a computer system can be limited by compute-bound jobs or input-output (I/O) bound jobs. The emphasis in the following discussion is on the I/O problem and various techniques which can be used to manage I/O data transfer. An example I/O subsystem for a dual processor system is shown in Figure 2.31. The subsystem consists of I/O interfaces and peripheral devices. Sometimes the distinction between the device and its associated interface is fuzzy. The I/O interface controls the operation of the peripheral device attached to it. The control operations are initiated by commands from the CPU. The set of commands used to accomplish an I/O transaction is called the *device driver* or *software*. The functions of the interface are to buffer and perform data conversion into the required format. It also detects transmission errors and requests regeneration of an I/O transaction in case of error. Moreover, the interface can interrogate, start, and stop the device according to commands issued by the CPU. In some cases, the interface can also interrogate the CPU if an urgent attention is requested by the device. Not all interfaces possess these capabilities and many design options are available depending on the device characteristics. Below, we outline a few devices and their speed characteristics.

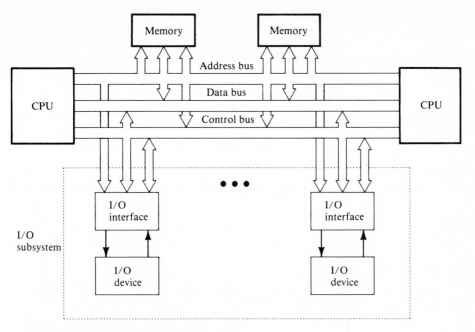

Figure 2.31 I/O subsystem in a dual processor system.

There are many different types of peripheral devices. Most of them are electromechanical devices and hence transfer data at a rate often limited by the speed of the electromechanical components. Table 2.3 shows some typical peripheral devices. Bubble memories, disk drums, and tape devices are mass storage devices which store data cheaply for later retrieval. Typical capacities of mass storage devices are: fixed-head and moving-head disks 512M bytes; floppy disks, 1M bytes; 9-track tape, 46M bytes; and cassette tape, from 64K to 512K bytes. Display terminals are input-output devices which consist of keyboards and cathode ray tubes (CRT). The keyboard acts as input while the CRT is the output display. In some cases where the CRT is replaced by a printer, the terminals are called teletypes.

Since terminals are often used interactively and are relatively slow devices, a reliable technique for transmitting characters between the processor and the terminal is *serial data transmission*. This method is cheaper than parallel transmission of characters because only one signal path is required. Data communication over long distances is usually done serially. For this reason, remote communication can be done over telephone lines by using a *modem* (*mo*dulator-*dem*odulator) interface. The modem is used at each end of the transmission line. There are a variety of character codes used in the transmission of data. However, one of the standard codes often used is the American Standards Committee on Information Interchange (ASCII), which uses seven-bit characters.

Table 2.3 Some I/O devices

I/O device	Function	Data rate
Bubble memories	Mass storage	300K, 4M cps
Charged-coupled devices	Mass storage	500K, 4M cps
Disk	Mass storage	
Fixed head		300K, 2M cps
Moving head		30K, 1M cps
Floppy		25K cps
Display terminal	Input-output	10–300 cps
Line printer	Output	
Impact		100–3000 lpm
Electrostatic		300–40,000 lpm
Ink jet		100–3000 lpm
Tape drive	Mass storage	
Reel to reel		15–300K cps
(7, 9 tracks)		
Cassette		10–400 cps

I/O subsystems may be classified according to the extent to which the CPU is involved in the I/O transaction. An I/O transaction can be the transfer of a single bit, byte, word, or block of bytes of information between the I/O device and the CPU, or between the I/O device and the main memory. The simplest I/O architecture is one in which all processing is performed sequentially. In such systems, the CPU executes programs that initiate, test the status of the device, perform the data transfer, and terminate I/O operations. In this case, the I/O transaction is performed using *program-driven* I/O. Most computers provide this option, as it requires minimal hardware. However, as the action of the program-driven I/O is illustrated in Figure 2.32, the CPU can spend a significant amount of time testing the status of the device. This *busy-wait* feature of the program-driven I/O scheme has the disadvantage that the time required to transfer a unit of information between main memory and an I/O device is typically several orders of magnitude greater than the average instruction cycle. Therefore, even a moderate I/O transfer rate will significantly degrade the useful cycles of the CPU in performing actual computations. Hence, the system performance may be degraded significantly.

A solution to this possible degradation is to permit concurrent CPU and I/O processing. This can be achieved by a modest increase in the hardware complexity of the interface. As the degree of concurrency is increased, the complexity of the hardware will have to be increased to match the data transfer requirements. One scheme uses a "pseudo" program-driven I/O method. In this scheme, the CPU initiates the I/O transaction and resumes its regular computation. When the device is ready with the data, in an input operation, the device controller notifies the CPU of the presence of the data in the controller's buffer. The CPU can then service the device to retrieve the data. A similar description can be made regarding an output operation. The notification signal is referred to as an *interrupt request*. An interrupt capability relieves the CPU from the task of periodically testing the I/O device status.

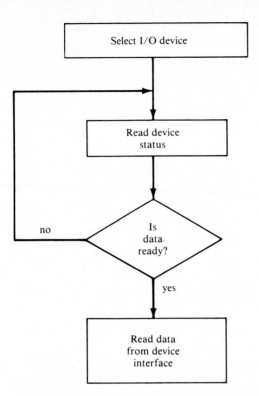

Figure 2.32 Programmed-driven I/O.

Although an interrupt request may arrive asynchronously during an instruction cycle, most processors permit the current instruction cycle in progress to be completed before the interrupt request is serviced. When an interrupt request is issued by a device to the CPU, the CPU may not be willing to accept the interrupt. It indicates its willingness (or unwillingness) to receive interrupts by setting (or resetting) an interrupt-enable flag in the CPU by executing an enable (or disable) interrupt instruction. This flag informs the device of the CPU's interruptibility status. When the CPU receives an interrupt, it acknowledges the interrupt by issuing an interrupt acknowledge signal to the device controller. At the same time, it saves the status of the interrupted process. The CPU then transfers control to a specified location in memory where the service routine of the device resides. The transfer of control is similar to a procedure call. The device is serviced and the status of the interrupted process is restored before its execution resumes. More details on interrupts will be given later.

The ultimate degree of concurrency in I/O processing can be achieved if the device controller is intelligent enough to perform the I/O transaction between the device and the main memory without the intervention of the CPU. This parallelism is very effective when a block of data is to be transferred. This requires the device controller to be capable of generating a sequence of memory addresses. However, the CPU is still responsible for initiating the block transfer. As an example, we illustrate a typical sequence of operations required to transfer a block of data from a device to main memory. The CPU initializes a buffer in main memory which will receive the block of data after the I/O transaction is complete. The address of the buffer and its size are transmitted to the device controller, and the address of the required block of data in the device, is also given to the controller.

The CPU then executes a special "start I/O" command which causes the I/O subsystem to initiate the transfer. While the transfer is in progress, the CPU will be free to perform basic computations, thereby improving overall system performance. When the block transfer is complete, the CPU is notified. Notice that since the CPU and the controller share the main memory, the device will periodically "steal" memory cycles from the CPU to deposit the data in memory. The cycle-stealing is very effective since the devices are often slower than the CPU. When the CPU and the device controller conflict in accessing the bus or a memory module, the device is given priority over the CPU in the access since it is a more time-critical component. This type of I/O data transfer scheme is called *direct*

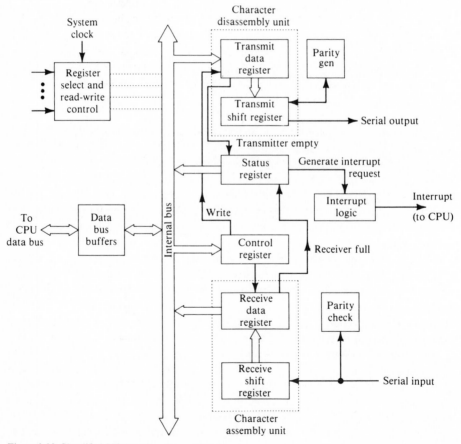

Figure 2.33 Simplified I/O interface for serial data.

memory access (DMA). The I/O controller often used for DMA operations is called an *I/O data channel*.

Notice that the DMA facility does not yield total control of the I/O transaction to the I/O subsystem. The I/O subsystem can assume complete control of the I/O transactions if a special unit, called an *I/O processor* (IOP) is used. The IOP has a direct access to main memory and contains a number of independent data channels. It can execute I/O programs and can perform several independent I/O transactions between main memory and devices or between two devices without the intervention of the CPU.

2.5.2 Interrupt Mechanisms and Special Hardware

An example of an interface used for slow I/O devices is the *universal asynchronous receiver-transmitter* (UART), often used in a microcomputer system. Its architecture is depicted in Figure 2.33. Its function is to buffer and translate between the parallel word format used by the CPU and the asynchronous serial format used by most slow-speed devices. The interface consists of addressable I/O registers or ports. The formats of the status and control registers are shown in Figure 2.34. The control register is a write-only register which is used to program the command specification. The status register contains the current state of the device and the outcome of the I/O transaction. Of importance is the device's busy-ready flag, which indicates whether the device is busy servicing an I/O transaction or is ready to receive the next transaction. This is the flag used when performing I/O transactions in busy-wait mode.

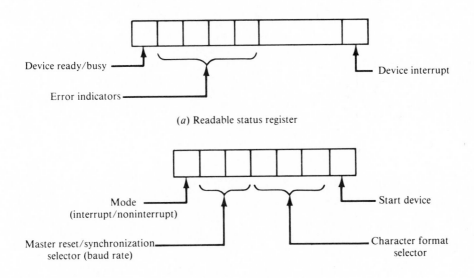

(*a*) Readable status register

(*b*) Writeable control register

Figure 2.34 Format of control and status registers in interface of Figure 2.33.

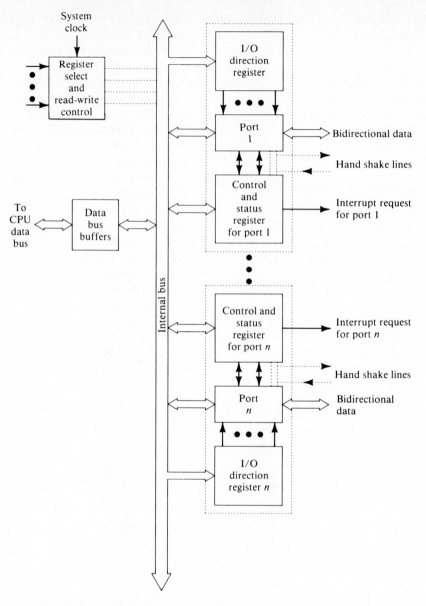

Figure 2.35 Simplified I/O interface for parallel data.

Figure 2.35 shows an example of a simplified parallel interface which contains *n* programmable data ports. Each data port is controlled by two associated control-status and I/O direction registers. By loading the appropriate command into the control-status register, the CPU can define the characteristics of the data port. Some definable characteristics are *I/O direction*, *I/O mode*, and *interrupt mode*. For the I/O direction, each bit, group of bits of the data port can be individually programmed as either input or output. For the I/O mode, each port can be programmed as *direct* I/O, *strobed* I/O, or *bidirectional* I/O. Moreover, each port can be programmed as interrupting or noninterrupting. In direct I/O, the device acts as a passive unit. Strobed and bidirectional I/O modes are used with active devices which must have established I/O communication protocols. A procedure, called *handshaking*, of mutual communication and cooperation between the CPU and a device is established so that the CPU knows when the input data is ready or when the output port is vacant.

In a handshake interface, the circuitry that receives data must first indicate its willingness to do so with a "ready" signal. For the example in Figure 2.36, this willingness is indicated by the INPUT LATCH EMPTY signal. Hence, if the input latch is empty, the sender can strobe in the data into the interface and indicate the presence of the data to the receiver (the CPU in this case) by generating an interrupt request. Note that the interrupt request is generated only if the CPU is willing to be interrupted (by the indication of the interrupt-enable signal from the CPU).

There are basically three classes of interrupts in a computer system: *internal*, *external*, and *software* interrupts. Internal interrupts, often called *traps*, are generated

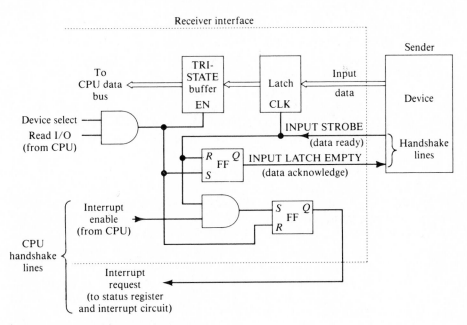

Figure 2.36 Input interface with handshaking.

within the CPU as a result of certain internal processor events. Traps may occur because of arithmetic-exception conditions, such as overflow and underflow (divide by zero) operations. It may also occur as a result of program faults, such as page faults, protection violation or the execution of an illegal instruction. Hardware faults, such as memory-parity errors and power failures, can also generate a trap. On the occurrence of a trap, the processor saves the state of the current process and transfers control to a *trap vector* location in memory, where the trap event is handled. Different trap vectors are often provided for different conditions or set of conditions.

Software interrupts, or system calls, affect the processor state in much the same way as a hardware interrupt. An example of a software interrupt occurs in the execution of the SVC system call instruction provided in IBM System 370. System call instructions are often used as a convenient and efficient method of calling operating system utilities.

External interrupts can be further classified as *maskable interrupts* (MI) and *nonmaskable interrupts* (NMI). Nonmaskable interrupts are considered the highest priority interrupts because they cannot be ignored, even if the CPU interrupt system is not enabled. NMI is particularly useful in monitoring a watchdog timer. It is also used in handling power failures. Maskable interrupts are accomplished through the use of an interrupt-enable flag associated with each device or set of devices. When this flag is set by the CPU, the flag permits the interrupt issued by the corresponding device to be received by the CPU. Otherwise, the device interrupt request is masked and does not reach the CPU until the interrupt-enable flag is set. The interrupt-enable flag is often incorporated in the device interface, as shown in the example of Figure 2.36.

In many applications, more than one device operating in interrupt mode may be connected to the computer. When an interrupt request reaches the CPU, it is known that at least one device caused the interrupt. Notice that since interrupts are asynchronous, there is a possibility that two or more devices will generate interrupts simultaneously. For the moment, assume that only one device caused the interrupt. In the simple I/O bus configuration of Figure 2.31, the I/O devices are identified by their addresses. The address lines can also be used to identify the interrupting device. The interrupting device can be identified by a simple *polling* arrangement, as shown in Figure 2.37.

In this scheme, called the *polled interrupt method*, the interrupt received by the CPU causes it to transfer control to a specified location, where the interrupt service routine is stored. The interrupt service routine consists of an interrupt polling routine which polls the devices in order to establish the identity of the interrupting device. The polling is performed by testing the interrupt bit of the status register of each device controller. When the interrupting device is determined, a call is made to the particular device handling procedure. If more than one device caused the interrupt, these devices are serviced in the order established by the polling direction. Hence all the devices that caused interrupt within the unpolled subcycle are serviced.

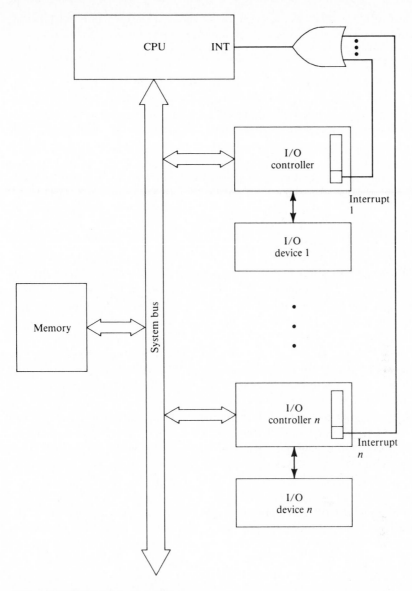

Figure 2.37 Polled interrupt method.

This method is effective for slow- to moderate-speed devices. However, the order of polling may have inherently established some form of fixed priority levels. The various methods used for establishing bus-control priority will be discussed in Section 7.2: that is, rotating daisy chaining, fixed-time slice, dynamic priority, and independently using a built-in hardware that automatically selects the highest priority device from the set of interrupting devices and also supplies the unique starting address or *interrupt vector* of the device. This interrupt vector permits the CPU to transfer control to the device service routine at the corresponding vector location in main memory. A system that possesses this capability is said to have *vectored interrupts*.

A vectored-interrupt system requires a priority scheme to be provided in the hardware. This priority scheme could be fixed, rotating, or dynamic priority. When the CPU accepts an interrupt request, it sends an acknowledgement to the vectored-interrupt controller. The controller, upon receipt of this acknowledgement, sends the unique interrupt vector of the highest priority device of the set of unmasked-interrupting devices. This action is illustrated in Figure 2.38. The interrupt-acknowledge signal can in turn be transmitted to the highest priority device controller, which caused the interrupt in order to reset the interrupt request from that device.

2.5.3 I/O Processors and I/O Channels

The logical solution to the problem of obtaining maximum concurrency in I/O processing is to deploy an intelligent I/O system which isolates the CPU from the I/O peripherals. The CPU is therefore free to proceed at full speed with its primary task of internal program processing and data manipulation. The intelligent I/O subsystem is facilitated by an I/O processor (IOP). Basically, an I/O processor is one which is capable of executing a small set of commands to service the I/O request. Figure 2.39 illustrates the principal architectural components of an intelligent I/O subsystem. As shown in the figure, the I/O processor is attached directly to the system bus and is responsible for selecting and retrieving individual I/O commands from main memory. IOP generally contains a processor specifically designed for I/O processing and a number of I/O channels. The channels provide a communication path from the I/O processor to the device controllers and devices. I/O channels can also exist without the IOP, as shown in the figure.

In its simplest form, and when it exists alone, a channel may be a small processor that performs DMA operations for a small set of devices. If the channel is incorporated within an IOP, it is essentially a passive component with no logical processing capacity of its own. When the channel possesses processing capability, it is often used as an IOP. Notice that a number of devices and their controllers can be connected to an active channel. Hence, the channel must be capable of selecting the highest priority requesting device and also servicing it. The stand-alone channels in the I/O subsystem are used in various mainframes such as the IBM 370. IOPs are used in such systems as the CDC 6600 and the 8- and 16-bit Intel microcomputers.

Channel architecture There are basically two types of channels: *selector* and *multiplexor*, as used in the IBM 370 systems. A selector channel is an IOP designed to handle one I/O transaction at a time. Once the device is selected, the set of I/O operations for a given transaction runs to completion before the next transaction is initiated. The selector channel is thus normally used to control high-speed I/O

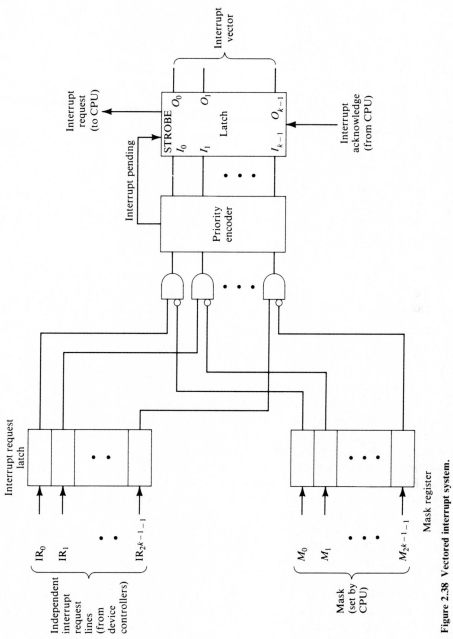

Figure 2.38 Vectored interrupt system.

129

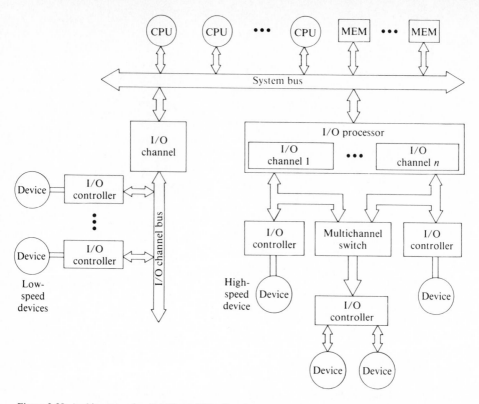

Figure 2.39 Architecture of an intelligent I/O subsystem.

devices such as fixed-head disks and drums. Figure 2.40 shows the architecture of a typical selector channel. The channel consists of word assembly and disassembly registers (WAR and WDR), which store the current word being received from the external device and the current word being transferred to the device, respectively. The channel can be made to receive or transmit data in character, halfword, or fullword mode. Thus, the assembly-disassembly registers can operate accordingly. The devices could be operating too fast (in the case of input) for the channel to handle the data reliably. For example, the next character could arrive before the current one in the WAR has been transmitted to the CPU. If this occurs, an overrun error or buffer full interrupt is generated to the CPU, which can request retransmission. One way to alleviate this problem is to double-buffer the input data. This discussion can also apply to the WDR when operating on a slow output device.

The initialization of the selector channel requires the definition of the location of the first word in memory, the length of the block to be transferred, and the device address. The initialization program is stored in memory and can be executed by the channel in order to initialize its internal registers. The registers used in this case are the device address register (DAR), the block count register (BCR),

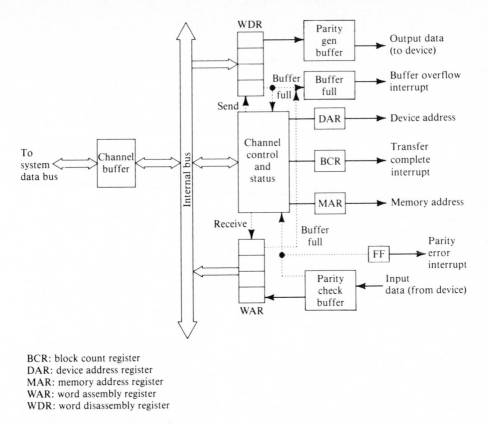

BCR: block count register
DAR: device address register
MAR: memory address register
WAR: word assembly register
WDR: word disassembly register

Figure 2.40 Selector channel architecture.

and the memory address register (MAR). In order to perform an I/O transaction, the CPU transmits a START signal and the device address to the channel on which the selected device is attached. The channel then fetches the *channel address word* (CAW) from a prespecified location in memory. This word, which was stored prior to initiation of the I/O transaction, contains the starting address of the I/O program (called *channel program*) to be executed by the channel.

The channel program consists of *channel command words* (CCW) or control words or instructions. In most sophisticated channels, the channel programs may include commands for positioning the read-write heads of disk drives, rewinding tapes, and selecting or testing the status of a device. In addition, the set of CCWs may contain instructions which permit looping and branching. The concept of the single-channel program can be extended to the CPU preparing an arbitrary number of I/O transactions to be executed by the I/O subsystem as a sequence of I/O transactions. This feature is known as *command chaining*.

If the addressed device is available, the channel executes the channel program to perform the I/O transaction; otherwise, the request may be queued or the CPU notified of the unavailability of the device. If the channel program is executed, the DAR, BCR, and MAR are initialized and the block transfer initiated. Subsequently, the MAR contains the current memory address and the BCR contains the remaining block length. After the transfer of a word between the main memory and the channel, the MAR and BCR are incremented and decremented by one, respectively, to reflect the updated values. When the BCR counts down to zero, a "transfer-complete" interrupt is generated and sent to the CPU. In case of errors (parity or lost character), an error interrupt is also generated. The typical maximum data rate of a selector channel is on the order of 1 to 3 megabytes/s.

A multiplexor channel is an IOP which can control several different I/O transactions concurrently. In this case, the data transfers are time-multiplexed over the I/O interface. This type of channel can be further divided into *block* and *character multiplexors*. The character multiplexors are used to handle low-speed devices, whereas block multiplexors are used for medium- and high-speed devices. The block or character multiplexor consists of a set of *subchannels*, each of which can act as a low-speed selector channel, as shown in Figure 2.41.

Each subchannel contains a buffer, device address register, request flag, and some control and status flags. However, the subchannels share global channel control. Each subchannel is required to have a memory address register (to maintain the current memory address) and a block count register (to maintain the length of block remaining to be transferred). In a character multiplexor channel with a large number of subchannels, as in the IBM 370 system with 256 subchannels, it is cost prohibitive to maintain these pairs of registers in the subchannels. Hence, these registers are maintained in main memory and are accessed by the channel control, as shown in Figure 2.41. The channel controller can select a subchannel for a burst mode or multiplex mode. In the multiplex mode, the scan control cyclically polls the request flag of each subchannel. If the flag is set, the subchannel is selected for a character or block transfer. The subchannel mode control is checked to determine the direction of the transfer operation. When the character or block is transferred, the next subchannel is polled. The block multiplexor interleaves by blocks instead of characters as in a character multiplexor.

For example, suppose that three successive I/O transactions X, Y, and Z are requested. Assume that each transaction is required to transfer a string of n characters. X, Y, and Z are sequences of characters $X_0, X_1, \ldots, X_{n-1}, Y_0, Y_1, \ldots, Y_{n-1}$, and $Z_0, Z_1, \ldots, Z_{n-1}$, respectively. If these transactions are initiated on a selector channel, then the selector channel transmission appears as $X_0 X_1 \ldots X_{n-1} Y_0 Y_1 \ldots Y_{n-1} Z_0 Z_1 \ldots Z_{n-1}$. On a character multiplexor with at least three subchannels, they may appear as $X_0 Y_0 Z_0 X_1 Y_1 Z_1 \ldots X_{n-1} Y_{n-1} Z_{n-1}$. On a block multiplexor programmed for k characters per blocks (assuming that $k < n$), the sequence may appear as $X_0 X_1 \ldots X_{k-1} Y_0 Y_1 \ldots Y_{k-1} Z_0 Z_1 \ldots Z_{k-1}$ $X_k X_{k-1} \ldots X_{2k-1} Y_k Y_{k+1} \ldots Y_{2k-1} Z_k Z_{k+1} \ldots, Z_{2k-1} \ldots$ and so on. The frequent switching and the associated overhead degrade the performance of the character multiplexor. The maximum data rate for the character multiplexor is typically on the order of 100K to 200K bytes p/s. The maximum data rate of the block multiplex or channel approaches that of the selector channel as the block size k approaches the string length n.

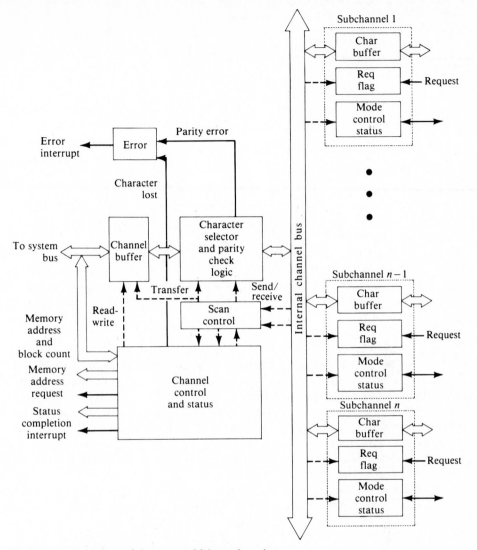

Figure 2.41 Architecture of character-multiplexor channel.

With current technology, an I/O processor can be implemented on a single chip for microcomputer and minicomputer systems. An example of an IOP on a chip is the INTEL 8089 integrated IOP, which is capable of being interfaced to 8-bit and 16-bit systems. This IOP contains two independent I/O channels and a processor on the same chip, as shown in Figure 2.42. It also contains a bus interface, an assembly-disassembly register file and an instruction fetch unit. In order to enable autonomous operation of the I/O channels, each channel maintains its own register set, control and status registers, and a flexible channel controller.

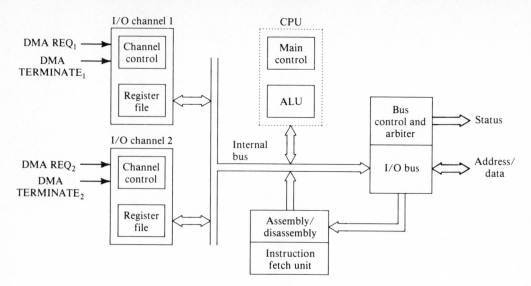

Figure 2.42 The Intel-8089 I/O processor with two separate I/O channels (El-Ayat, *IEEE Computer*, 1979).

Both channels may operate concurrently, executing channel programs or performing high-speed DMA transfers by time multiplexing the access and use of the external bus. The bus control and interface logic are shared by the two channels. The IOP is capable of alternating between the two channels with every internal cycle (4 to 8 clock cycles). This permits very fast service response times to the channel requesting service. A priority algorithm is used by the IOP to select a channel when concurrent requests are made.

Each register set of a channel contains eight user-programmable registers, four of which are 21-bit-wide address registers. The other four registers are 16 bits wide. This is illustrated for a single channel in Figure 2.43. The address registers can be used to address 1 megabyte of system memory or 64K bytes of I/O space. Bit 20 of the address register is used to select the address space as system or local I/O space. The GA and GB registers are used to reference the source and destination locations during any data transfer operation. The GC register can also be used as a general register pointer by the channel program. The task pointer (TP) serves as the channel program counter, which is initialized whenever the channel is started. Using the TP, the instruction unit in the IOP can fetch the next CCW. The TP can also be manipulated by the channel program.

The byte register (BC) contains the number of bytes to be transferred during DMA operation. BC can also be set up to terminate the DMA transfer if this mode is selected. The index register (IX) is used as an index in the indexed addressing mode. The mask-compare register is used to perform masked-byte comparisons during channel program execution and DMA operations. During program execution, the comparisons are used for conditional branching, and in the DMA mode,

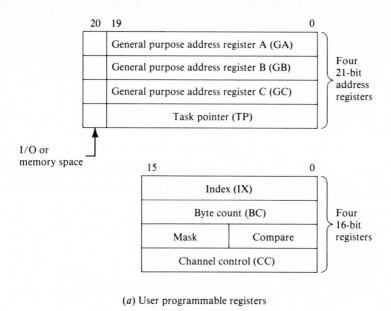

(*a*) User programmable registers

(*b*) Nonuser programmable registers

Figure 2.43 Register set of a channel in Intel IOP (Courtesy of *IEEE Computer*, 1979, El-Ayat).

they may terminate the current DMA transfer. The channel control register (CC) is a special 16-bit register which defines the channel's operation during DMA transfer operations. In addition to the user-programmable registers, there are two non-user programmable 20-bit registers, also shown in Figure 2.43.

The assembly-disassembly register file is used in the DMA transfer mode. For example, when data is transferred during a DMA operation from an 8-bit bus to a 16-bit bus, the IOP assembles 2 bytes in its assembly register file before transferring a word to the destination. A simplified computational model of the INTEL IOP is given in Figure 2.44. After reset, a channel attention (CA) input pulse forces an internal initialization sequence. Then the processor is ready to dispatch an I/O transaction request to either of the two channels to perform the desired I/O task. The I/O channel normally begins its operation in the task block (TB) state with the execution of the I/O program and enters the DMA state under IOP program control. In this state, the channel proceeds with high-speed data

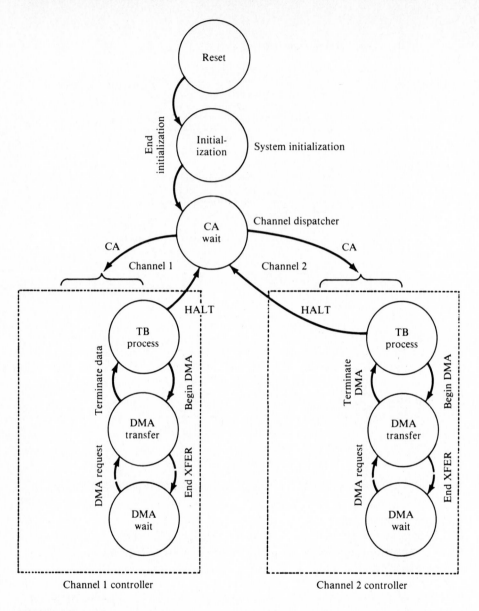

CA: channel attention

Figure 2.44 Simplified computational model of the Intel I/O processor (Courtesy of *IEEE Computer*, 1979, El-Ayat).

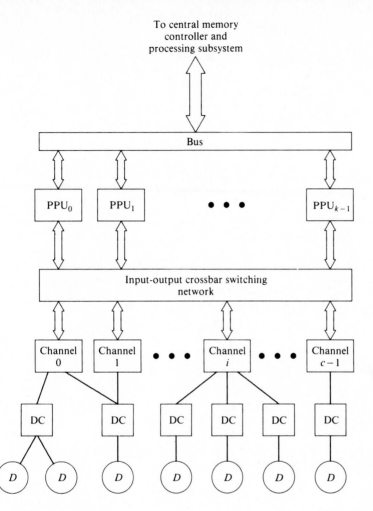

To central memory
controller and
processing subsystem

DC: device controller
D: device

Figure 2.45 Logical representation of peripheral processing subsystem for CDC-6600 and Cyber-170 (Courtesy of Control Data Corp.).

transfers in either burst or request-synchronized mode until the occurrence of a valid termination condition, which returns the channel to the TB state. HALT commands force the channel into the idle state until further dispatching occurs.

Another example of an integrated IOP is in the CDC 6600 I/O subsystem. The integrated IOP is also used as the peripheral processing subsystem (PPS) in the Cyber 170 multiprocessor system. It consists of a set of 10 peripheral processing units (PPU) which share a set of channels to which devices and their controllers are connected. A logical representation of such an I/O subsystem is shown in Figure 2.45.

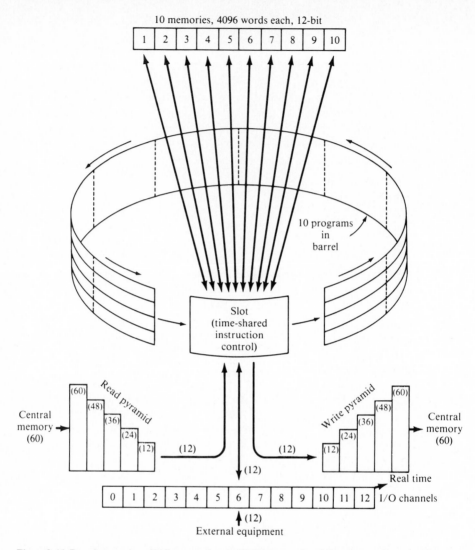

Figure 2.46 Barrel processing of I/O transactions in CDC integrated peripheral processing units (Courtesy of Control Data Corp.).

The CDC 6600 integrated peripheral processor uses a so-called barrel design to share logical units within the IOP. It uses a set of registers to share a common arithmetic logic unit and a data distribution system in a synchronous fashion. The barrel contains 10 peripheral processing units (PPUs) and a PPU is 12-bits wide. A PPU instruction requires a number of steps for its execution. The execution in each step is performed in a distinct "slot" which logically represents a PPU. Hence, the PPU instruction is executed as in a cyclic pipeline process, as shown in Figure 2.46. This execution sequence is possible because each instruction cycle is an integral number (up to 10) of minor cycles. A minor cycle is 100 ns and a major cycle is 1000 ns; hence, the choice of 10 PPUs.

In each minor cycle, all information in the barrel is moved one position (synchronously) after each step is executed in its current slot. The information in each PPU is moved through the shared slot position once every major cycle. Since each PPU operates once per major cycle, the maximum data rate is 12 bits $\div$ 1000 ns = 12×10^6 bits/s. Therefore, the 10 PPUs are time-shared by the slot hardware without significant degradation in performance. However, since the CDC 6600 is a 60-bit computer, five PPU transfers are required to form a 60-bit word. Also, since the I/O processing is synchronized in the CDC system, no handshaking is necessary as in the IBM channels.

I/O configuration in systems with cache   There are two basic methods of connecting an I/O subsystem to the processor-memory complex in a system with a cache. In the first configuration, the I/O channel can be attached to the cache so that the cache is shared by the processor and channel, as shown in Figure 2.47a. The channel competes with the processor for access to the cache. An I/O channel is often slower than the processor. Thus connecting the channel to the cache does not significantly improve the performance of I/O transfers. I/O transfers have little locality and they increase the traffic between the cache and memory. This increase is caused by three main effects: main memory update of memory-bound I/O data; misses caused by channel fetches from memory; and channel programs (and I/O data) occupying cache, reducing the effective cache aggregate miss ratios seen by processor-bound jobs. The configuration of Figure 2.47a may also encounter cache *data-overrun*, in which the data transfer occurs at a rate higher than the cache controller can sustain.

An alternate configuration is to connect the channel to the memory directly, as shown in Figure 2.47b. In this case, the channel competes with the cache controller for access to the memory. However, the I/O channel and processor executions conflict at miss times only, assuming a write-back memory update policy. Also, the cache is not encumbered with the data blocks destined to I/O. It has, however, one major drawback: data consistency or coherence problems. To illustrate, consider a cache which uses write-back main memory update policy. Assume that the processor has modified a copy of a data element X in the cache so that the value of the copy in the cache is NEWX and the memory has not been updated.

Let OLDX be the value of X in memory. Before the memory is updated, the I/O channel requests a fetch from location X in the memory, which delivers OLDX instead of NEWX. A coherence problem has occurred. One solution is to keep a dynamic table in the memory controller which, at any time, indicates the set of blocks in the cache and their status (whether modified or unmodified). Let the modified status be denoted by RW. When the I/O channel makes a reference to a memory block which is also in the cache, the status is checked by the memory controller. If it is RW and the channel requests a read, the data is fetched from the cache. However, if the channel requests a write to the block, the corresponding

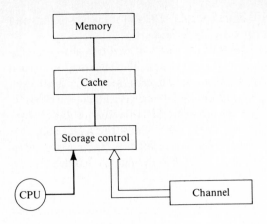

(*a*) The I/O processor accesses the cache

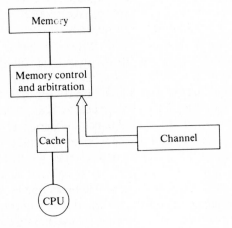

(*b*) The I/O processor accesses the memory

Figure 2.47 Two I/O configurations for a uniprocessor with cache.

cache block frame is invalidated before the memory block is modified by the chan-nel. A similar description can be given for a processor reference.

Note that for a system with buffered write-through update policy, the coherence problem is automatically corrected in the second configuration if the write queue is maintained within the memory controller. However, this configuration may also encounter the data-overrun problem. More cache coherence studies will be given in Chapter 8.

2.6 BIBLIOGRAPHIC NOTES AND PROBLEMS

A model of memory hierarchies in which the memory management strategy is characterized by the hit ratio was given by Chow (1974). Storage systems are covered in detail by Matick (1977, 1980). The Vax 11/780 paging system was discussed in DEC (1979) and Levy and Eckhouse (1980). Cache memories for multiprocessors was studied by Dubois and Briggs (1982a). A discussion of virtual memory and the concept of locality of reference are given in Denning (1970), Denning and Graham (1975) and Baer (1980). A treatment of paged, segmented memory systems and systems with paged segments can be found in Watson (1970). These concepts and their implementations were also described thoroughly in Bensoussan et al. (1972).

Characteristics of cache memories and their organizations have been studied by various authors as in Conti (1969), Mead (1970), Bell et al. (1974). An introduction of the characteristics of cache memories is given in Kaplan and Winder (1974). Recently, Smith (1982) presented a comprehensive survey paper on cache memories. The LRU hardware diagram and its description were given in Yeh (1981). The relationship between the miss ratios for set-associative and fully associative cache was derived in Smith (1978) assuming a linear paging model of program behavior which was studied in Saltzer (1974).

The effect of sharing in the resident set of pages was developed by using the results on union of events in Feller (1970). The demonstration of the flexibility and efficiency of the variable partitioning strategy was given in Coffman and Ryan (1972). Details of some fixed allocation strategies and stack algorithms are given in Coffman and Denning (1973). The two-parameter fit for the lifetime function was proposed in Chamberlin, Fuller, and Lin (1973). The variable-partitioning strategies are presented in Denning and Graham (1975). The working-set model was presented in Denning (1968) and its properties in Denning and Schwartz (1972). The reader is encouraged to read Denning (1980) and Baer (1980) for a complete study of memory management policies.

A general overview of I/O architecture was presented in Buzen (1975). There are good treatments of I/O subsystems and their organizations in Baer (1980), Hayes (1978), and Kuck (1979). Details of I/O subsystems in IBM System/370 and the CDC 6600 integrated peripheral processing subsystem can be found in IBM (1974) and Thorton (1970), respectively. Another overview on I/O channel architectures can be found in Lane (1980). A description of the architecture of Intel IOP is given in El-Ayat (1979). The reader is encouraged to read this reference for typical applications and programming example of the I/O processor.

Problems

2.1 Consider a two-level memory hierarchy (M_1, M_2) for a computer system, as depicted in the following diagram. Let C_1 and C_2 be the costs per bit, S_1 and S_2 be the storage capacities, and t_1 and t_2 be the access times of the memories M_1 and M_2, respectively. The hit ratio H is defined as the probability that a logical address generated by the CPU refers to information stored in M_1. Answer the following questions associated with this virtual memory system.

(a) What is the average cost C per bit of the entire memory hierarchy?

(b) Under what condition will the average cost per bit C approach C_2?

(c) What is the average access time t_a for the CPU to access a word from the memory system?

(d) Let $r = t_2/t_1$ be the speed ratio of the two memories. Let $E = t_1/t_2$ be the access efficiency of the virtual memory system. Express E in terms of r and H. Also plot E against H for $r = 1, 2, 10$, and 100 respectively on a grid-graph paper.

(e) Suppose that $r = 100$, what is the required minimum value of the hit ratio to make $E > 0.90$?

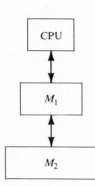

2.2 A page trace is a sequence of page numbers $P = r_1, r_2, r_3, \ldots, r_{k-1}, r_k, r_{k+1}, \ldots$, where r_k is the page number of the kth address in a sequence of addresses

Page trace	a	a	b	b	c	c	a	b
Page faults	*		*		*		*	*
Mp contents	a	a	a	a	c	c	c	b
	–	–	b	b	b	b	a	a

The fault rate F is the number of page faults divided by the number of page addresses (length of the page trace). For this example, $F = \frac{5}{8} = 0.625$. The hit ratio H is $1 - F$. For the remainder of this problem, let $P = abacabdbacd$.

(a) Produce a table similar to the above table for page trace P under a FIFO replacement algorithm with memory size, $|Mp| = 2$ page frames. What is the hit ratio?

(b) Do the same for an LRU replacement algorithm.

(c) Repeat (a) and (b) for $|Mp| = 3$ page frames.

(d) Intuitively, both FIFO and LRU would seem to be "good" algorithms. A *most recently used* (MRU) algorithm intuitively sounds like a bad algorithm. Repeat (a) with an MRU replacement algorithm. Compare this with the results obtained in (a) through (c). What does this say about the particular page trace P and about the generality of results obtained by comparing replacement algorithms based on a single page trace?

2.3 In a uniprocessor with cache, the processor issues its memory access requests to the cache controller (CC). In the case of a miss or a write-through, the CC interacts with the memory controller (MC). Draw the flowcharts describing the operations of a CC for a read and a write operation. Consider the write-back-write-allocate with flagged swap and the write-through-write-allocate strategies. Assume that no read-through is implemented. Indicate how to modify the flowcharts for (a) a write-back-write-allocate with simple WB and with flagged register WB and for (b) write-through without write-allocation.

2.4 Consider the following search algorithm:

```
begin
ifound→N+1;i→0;
while (ifound≠i) do
    begin
        i←i+1;
        if (template=data [i])
            then ifound←i;
    end
end
```

In this program, $data[i]$ is an array of $N(=2^n)$ floating-point numbers; *template* is a floating-point number; N,i, and *ifound* are integers. A floating-point number occupies two memory words, while an integer occupies one memory word only. Assume that the program code as well as the variables N,i, *ifound*, and *template* fit on the same memory page. *Data* [*] is stored in a set of consecutive pages, starting at the beginning of a page. A page is $P = 2^p$ words long. The memory is $M = 2^m$ words long ($M \ll N$). Assume that there is one and only one element equal to *template* in the array *data*. The algorithm is run on a uniprocessor with a paged virtual memory system. The replacement policy is LRU.

(*a*) If Probability[$ifound = i$] $= (1/N)$ ($1 \le i \le N$), determine the mean number of page faults in the cases where the memory does not contain any of the process pages at the beginning of the process, and where the memory is preloaded to capacity with the program page and the first $2^{m-p} - 1$ data pages of the process.

(*b*) Repeat (*a*) if Probability[$ifound = i$] $= G(N)q(1 - q)^{i-1}$ for $1 \le i \le N$, $0 < q < 1$, where $G(N) = 1/[1 - (1 - q)^N]$.

2.5 A computer architect is considering the adoption of write-through-with-write-allocate (WTWA) or write-back (WB) cache management strategy. Assuming no read-through, each block consists of b words, which can be transferred between main memory (MM) and cache in $b + c - 1$ time units, where c is the MM cycle time. The cache is independent of the strategy and is given by h. The probability that a memory reference is a write is w_t and the probability that the block being replaced in the cache was modified (in WB strategy) is w_b. Usually $w_b > w_t$.

(*a*) Using each strategy, give a formula for the expected time to process a reference in terms of the above variables.

(*b*) Assuming $w_t = 0.16$ and $w_b = 0.56$, what is the performance of the WB strategy in comparison to WTWA strategy when (1) $h \to 1$ and (2) $h \to 0$.

(*c*) Give a general expression describing when WTWA is better than WB as a function of h and b. Assume that $w_t = 0.16$, $w_b = 0.56$, and $c = 10$.

(*d*) Does w_t depend on h? Give intuitive reasons.

2.6 A certain uniprocessor computer system has a paged segmentation virtual memory system and also a cache. The virtual address is a triple (s, p, d) where s is the segment number, p is the page within s, and d is the displacement within p. A translation lookaside buffer (TLB) is used to perform the address translation when the virtual address is in the TLB. If there is a miss in the TLB, the translation is performed by accessing the segment table and then a page table, either or both of which may be in the cache or in main memory (MM).

Address translation via the TLB requires one clock cycle. A fetch from the cache requires two clock cycles (one clock cycle to determine if the requested address is in the cache plus one clock cycle to read the data). A read from MM requires eight clock cycles. There is no overlap between TLB translation and cache access. Once the address translation is complete, the read of the desired data may be from either the cache or MM. This means that the fastest possible data access requires three clock cycles:

one for TLB address translation and two to read the data from the cache. There are nine other ways in which a read can proceed, all requiring more than three clock cycles.

(*a*) Assuming a TLB hit ratio of 0.9 and a cache hit ratio of h, enumerate all 10 possible read patterns, the time taken for each, and the probability of occurrence for each pattern. What is the average read time in the system? (Assume that when a word is fetched from memory, a read-through policy is used.)

(*b*) The above discussion assumes that the cache is always given a physical memory address. Suppose that the cache is presented with the virtual address of the data being requested rather than its physical address in memory. In this case, the TLB translation and cache search can be done concurrently. This means that whenever the requested data is in the cache, no address translation is necessary and only two clock cycles are required for the fetch. If the data is not in the cache, either a TLB translation segment table–page table access is needed to generate the physical address of the data. When data is written into the cache, it is tagged with its virtual address. Find the average read time for a system organized in this fashion. Assume that only one clock cycle is required to establish that an item is not in the cache.

(*c*) What are the disadvantages of a cache using virtual addresses?

2.7 In the LRU stack model, assume that the stack distances are independently and identically drawn from a distribution $\{g(j)\}, j = 1, 2, \ldots, n$, for a stack of size n_o. Since each set in the cache constitutes a separate associative memory, it can be managed with LRU replacement. Show that the probability $p(i, S)$ of referencing the ith most recently referenced block in a set, given S sets, is

$$ p(i, S) = \sum_{j=i}^{\infty} g(j) \cdot \left(\frac{1}{S}\right)^{i-1} \cdot \left(\frac{S-1}{S}\right)^{j-i} \cdot \binom{j-1}{i-1} $$

2.8 Consider three interleaved memory organizations for a main memory system containing 8 memory modules, $M_0, M_1, \ldots, M_7$. Each module has a capacity of 2K words. In total, the memory capacity is 16K words. The maximum memory bandwidth is 8 words/cycle. In each of the following organizations, first specify the memory address format (14 bits), then show the address assignment patterns in each memory module, and finally indicate the maximum bandwidth when one of the 8 modules fails to function. Comment on the relative merits of the three interleaved memory organizations.

(*a*) Eight-way interleaved memory organization (one group).

(*b*) Grouped four-way interleaved organization (two groups).

(*c*) Grouped two-way interleaved organization (four groups).

THREE

PRINCIPLES OF PIPELINING AND VECTOR PROCESSING

In this chapter, the structures of pipeline computers and vector processing principles are studied. It begins with the basic properties of pipelining, classifications of pipeline processors, and the required memory supports. Both instruction pipelines and arithmetic pipelines are studied in Section 3.2 with design examples. Pipeline design problems will be studied in Section 3.3, including instruction prefetch, branch control, interrupt handling, data buffering, busing structures, internal forwarding, register tagging, hazard detection and resolution, and reconfiguration control. Vector processing requirements and related optimization problems will be introduced with illustrative examples in Section 3.4. Various pipeline supercomputer systems, attached scientific processors, vectorization techniques, and performance evaluation of pipeline computers will be studied in Chapter 4.

3.1 PIPELINING: AN OVERLAPPED PARALLELISM

Pipelining offers an economical way to realize temporal parallelism in digital computers. The concept of pipeline processing in a computer is similar to assembly lines in an industrial plant. To achieve pipelining, one must subdivide the input task (process) into a sequence of subtasks, each of which can be executed by a specialized hardware stage that operates concurrently with other stages in the pipeline. Successive tasks are streamed into the pipe and get executed in an overlapped fashion at the subtask level. The subdivision of labor in assembly lines has contributed to the success of mass production in modern industry. By the same token, pipeline processing has led to the tremendous improvement of system throughput in the modern digital computer. In this section, a sample design of a floating-point adder is used to illustrate the concept of linear pipelining. Basic properties and speedup of a linear-pipeline processor are characterized. Various types of pipeline processors are then classified according to pipelining levels and functional configurations. Finally, we introduce the reservation table as a design tool of general pipelines with either linear or nonlinear data-flow patterns.

3.1.1 Principles of Linear Pipelining

Assembly lines have been widely used in automated industrial plants in order to increase productivity. Their original form is a flow line (pipeline) of assembly stations where items are assembled continuously from separate parts along a moving conveyor belt. Ideally, all the assembly stations should have equal processing speed. Otherwise, the slowest station becomes the bottleneck of the entire pipe. This bottleneck problem plus the congestion caused by improper buffering may result in many idle stations waiting for new parts. The subdivision of the input tasks into a proper sequence of subtasks becomes a crucial factor in determining the performance of the pipeline.

In a uniform-delay pipeline, all tasks have equal processing time in all station facilities. The stations in an ideal assembly line can operate synchronously with full resource utilization. However, in reality, the successive stations have unequal delays. The optimal partition of the assembly line depends on a number of factors, including the quality (efficiency and capability) of the working units, the desired processing speed, and the cost effectivness of the entire assembly line.

The precedence relation of a set of subtasks $\{T_1, T_2, \ldots, T_k\}$ for a given task T implies that some task T_j cannot start until some earlier task T_i $(i < j)$ finishes. The interdependencies of all subtasks form the *precedence graph*. With a linear precedence relation, task T_j cannot start until all earlier subtasks $\{T_i,$ for all $i \leq j\}$ finish. A *linear pipeline* can process a succession of subtasks with a linear precedence graph.

A basic linear-pipeline processor is depicted in Figure 3.1a. The pipeline consists of a cascade of processing stages. The *stages* are pure combinational circuits performing arithmetic or logic operations over the data stream flowing through the pipe. The stages are separated by high-speed interface *latches*. The latches are fast registers for holding the intermediate results between the stages. Information flows between adjacent stages are under the control of a common clock applied to all the latches simultaneously.

Clock period The logic circuitry in each stage S_i has a time delay denoted by τ_i. Let τ_l be the time delay of each interface latch. The *clock period* of a linear pipeline is defined by

$$\tau = \max\{\tau_i\}_1^k + \tau_l = \tau_m + \tau_l \tag{3.1}$$

The reciprocal of the clock period is called the *frequency* $f = 1/\tau$ of a pipeline processor.

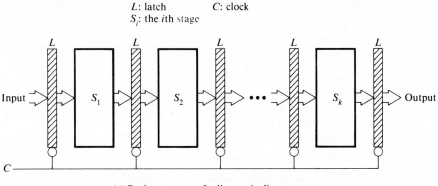

(a) Basic structure of a linear pipeline processor

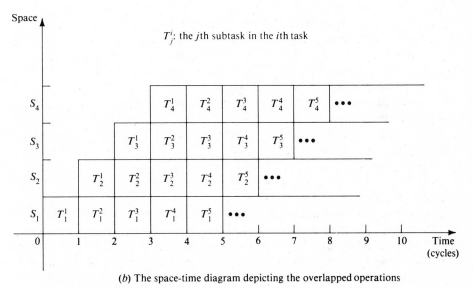

(b) The space-time diagram depicting the overlapped operations

Figure 3.1 Linear pipeline processor for overlapped processing of multiple tasks.

One can draw a *space-time diagram* to illustrate the overlapped operations in a linear pipeline processor. The space-time diagram of a four-stage pipeline processor is demonstrated in Figure 3.1b. Once the pipe is filled up, it will output one result per clock period independent of the number of stages in the pipe. Ideally, a linear pipeline with k stages can process n tasks in $T_k = k + (n - 1)$ clock periods, where k cycles are used to fill up the pipeline or to complete execution of the first task and $n - 1$ cycles are needed to complete the remaining $n - 1$ tasks. The same number of tasks (operand pairs) can be executed in a nonpipeline processor with an equivalent function in $T_1 = n \cdot k$ time delay.

Speedup We define the *speedup* of a k-stage linear-pipeline processor over an equivalent nonpipeline processor as

$$S_k = \frac{T_1}{T_k} = \frac{n \cdot k}{k + (n - 1)} \tag{3.2}$$

It should be noted that the maximum speedup is $S_k \rightarrow k$, for $n \gg k$. In other words, the maximum speedup that a linear pipeline can provide is k, where k is the number of stages in the pipe. This maximum speedup is never fully achievable because of data dependencies between instructions, interrupts, program branches, and other factors to be revealed in later sections. Many pipeline cycles may be wasted on a waiting state caused by out-of-sequence instruction executions.

To understand the operational principles of pipeline computation, we illustrate the design of a pipeline floating-point adder in Figure 3.2. This pipeline is linearly constructed with four functional stages. The inputs to this pipeline are two normalized floating-point numbers:

$$A = a \times 2^p$$
$$B = b \times 2^q \tag{3.3}$$

where a and b are two fractions and p and q are their exponents, respectively. For simplicity, base 2 is assumed. Our purpose is to compute the sum

$$C = A + B = c \times 2^r = d \times 2^s \tag{3.4}$$

where $r = \max(p, q)$ and $0.5 \leq d < 1$. Operations performed in the four pipeline stages are specified below:

1. Compare the two exponents p and q to reveal the larger exponent $r = \max(p, q)$ and to determine their difference $t = |p - q|$.
2. Shift right the fraction associated with the smaller exponent by t bits to equalize the two exponents before fraction addition.
3. Add the preshifted fraction with the other fraction to produce the intermediate sum fraction c, where $0 \leq c < 1$.
4. Count the number of leading zeros, say u, in fraction c and shift left c by u bits to produce the normalized fraction sum $d = c \times 2^u$, with a leading bit 1. Update the large exponent s by subtracting $s = r - u$ to produce the output exponent.

The comparator, selector, shifters, adders, and counter in this pipeline can all be implemented with combinational logic circuits. Detailed logic design of these boxes can be found in the book by Hwang (1979). Suppose the time delays of the four stages are $\tau_1 = 60$ ns, $\tau_2 = 50$ ns, $\tau_3 = 90$ ns, and $\tau_4 = 80$ ns and the interface latch has a delay of $\tau_l = 10$ ns. The cycle time of this pipeline can be chosen to be at least $\tau = 90 + 10 = 100$ ns (Eq. 3.1). This means that the clock frequency of the pipeline can be set to $f = 1/\tau = 1/100 = 10$ MHz. If one uses a non-pipeline floating-point adder, the total time delay will be $\tau_1 + \tau_2 + \tau_3 + \tau_4 =$

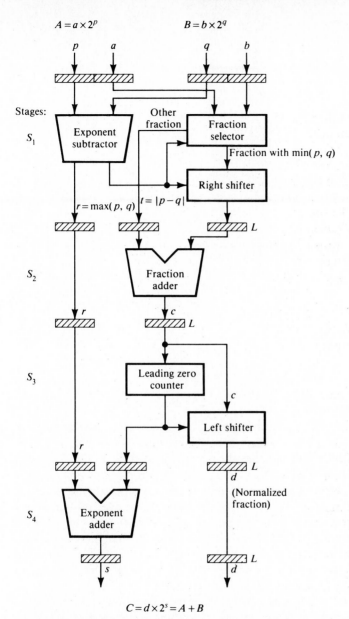

$$C = d \times 2^s = A + B$$

Figure 3.2 A pipelined floating-point adder with four processing stages.

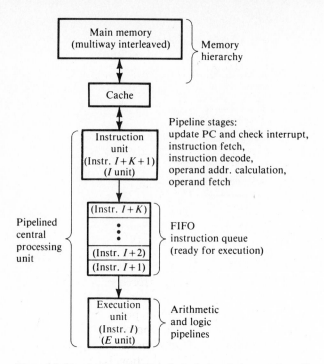

Figure 3.3 The pipelined structure of a typical central processing unit.

300 ns. In this case, the pipeline adder has a speedup of $300/100 = 3$ over the non-pipeline adder design. If uniform delays can be achieved in all four stages, say 75 ns per stage (including the latch delay), then the maximum speedup of $300/75 = 4$ can be achieved.

The central processing unit (CPU) of a modern digital computer can generally be partitioned into three sections: the *instruction unit*, the *instruction queue*, and the *execution unit*. From the operational point of view, all three units are pipelined, as illustrated in Figure 3.3. Programs and data reside in the main memory, which usually consists of interleaved memory modules. The cache is a faster storage of copies of programs and data which are ready for execution. The cache is used to close up the speed gap between main memory and the CPU.

The instruction unit consists of pipeline stages for instruction fetch, instruction decode, operand address calculation, and operand fetches (if needed). The instruction queue is a first-in, first-out (FIFO) storage area for decoded instructions and fetched operands. The execution unit may contain multiple functional pipelines for arithmetic logic functions. While the instruction unit is fetching instruction $I + K + 1$, the instruction queue holds instructions $I + 1, I + 2, \ldots, I + K$, and the execution unit executes instruction I. In this sense, the CPU is a good example of a linear pipeline. We will describe the detailed design of a pipeline CPU for instruction execution and arithmetic computations in Section 3.3.

After defining the clock period and speedup in Eqs. 3.1 and 3.2, we need to introduce two related measures of the performance of a linear pipeline processor. The product (area) of a *time interval* and a *stage space* in the space-time diagram (Figure 3.1*b*) is called a *time-space span*. A given time-space span can be in either a *busy* state or an *idle* state, but not both. We use this concept to measure the performance of a pipeline.

Efficiency The efficiency of a linear pipeline is measured by the percentage of busy time-space spans over the total time-space span, which equals the sum of all busy and idle time-space spans. Let n, k, τ be the number of tasks (instructions), the number of pipeline stages, and the clock period of a linear pipeline, respectively. The *pipeline efficiency* is defined by

$$\eta = \frac{n \cdot k \cdot \tau}{k \cdot [k\tau + (n-1)\tau]} = \frac{n}{k + (n-1)} \tag{3.5}$$

Note that $\eta \to 1$ as $n \to \infty$. This implies that the larger the number of tasks flowing through the pipeline, the better is its efficiency. Moreover, we realize that $\eta = S_k/k$ from Eqs. 3.2 and 3.3. This provides another view of the efficiency of a linear pipeline as the ratio of its actual speedup to the ideal speedup k. In the steady state of a pipeline, we have $n \gg k$, the efficiency η should approach 1. However, this ideal case may not hold all the time because of program branches and interrupts, data dependency, and other reasons to be discussed in Section 3.2.

Throughput The number of results (tasks) that can be completed by a pipeline per unit time is called its throughput. This rate reflects the computing power of a pipeline. In terms of the efficiency η and clock period τ of a linear pipeline, we define the *throughput* as follows:

$$w = \frac{n}{k\tau + (n-1)\tau} = \frac{\eta}{\tau} \tag{3.6}$$

where n equals the total number of tasks being processed during an observation period $k\tau + (n-1)\tau$. In the ideal case, $w = 1/\tau = f$ when $\eta \to 1$. This means that the maximum throughput of a linear pipeline is equal to its frequency, which corresponds to one output result per clock period. We will further evaluate the performance of pipeline processors in Section 4.4.4.

3.1.2 Classification of Pipeline Processors

According to the levels of processing, Händler (1977) has proposed the following classification scheme for pipeline processors, as illustrated in Figure 3.4.

Arithmetic pipelining The arithmetic logic units of a computer can be segmentized for pipeline operations in various data formats (Figure 3.4*a*). Well-known arithmetic pipeline examples are the four-stage pipes used in Star-100, the eight-stage pipes used in the TI-ASC, the up to 14 pipeline stages used in the Cray-1, and the

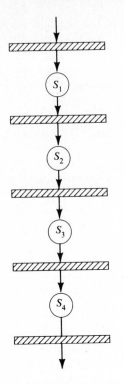

(a) Arithmetic pipelining

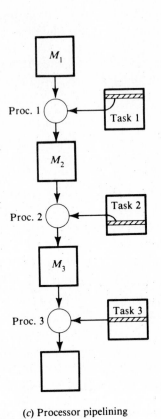

(c) Processor pipelining

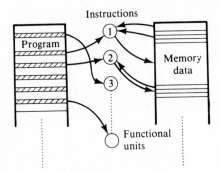

(b) Instruction pipelining

Figure 3.4 Händler classification of pipelined processors.

up to 26 stages per pipe in the Cyber-205. These arithmetic logic pipeline designs will be studied subsequently.

Instruction pipelining The execution of a stream of instructions can be pipelined by overlapping the execution of the current instruction with the fetch, decode, and operand fetch of subsequent instructions (Figure 3.4*b*). This technique is also known as *instruction lookahead*. Almost all high-performance computers are now equipped with instruction-execution pipelines.

Processor pipelining This refers to the pipeline processing of the same data stream by a cascade of processors (Figure 3.4*c*), each of which processes a specific task. The data stream passes the first processor with results stored in a memory block which is also accessible by the second processor. The second processor then passes the refined results to the third, and so on. The pipelining of multiple processors is not yet well accepted as a common practice.

According to pipeline configurations and control strategies, Ramamoorthy and Li (1977) have proposed the following three pipeline classification schemes:

Unifunction vs. multifunction pipelines A pipeline unit with a fixed and dedicated function, such as the floating-point adder in Figure 3.3, is called *unifunctional*. The Cray-1 has 12 unifunctional pipeline units for various scalar, vector, fixed-point, and floating-point operations. A *multifunction* pipe may perform different functions, either at different times or at the same time, by interconnecting different subsets of stages in the pipeline. The TI-ASC has four multifunction pipeline processors, each of which is reconfigurable for a variety of arithmetic logic operations at different times.

Static vs. dynamic pipelines A *static pipeline* may assume only one functional configuration at a time. Static pipelines can be either unifunctional or multifunctional. Pipelining is made possible in static pipes only if instructions of the same type are to be executed continuously. The function performed by a static pipeline should not change frequently. Otherwise, its performance may be very low. A *dynamic pipeline* processor permits several functional configurations to exist simultaneously. In this sense, a dynamic pipeline must be multifunctional. On the other hand, a unifunctional pipe must be static. The dynamic configuration needs much more elaborate control and sequencing mechanisms than those for static pipelines. Most existing computers are equipped with static pipes, either unifunctional or multifunctional.

Scalar vs. vector pipelines Depending on the instruction or data types, pipeline processors can be also classified as scalar pipelines and vector pipelines. A *scalar pipeline* processes a sequence of scalar operands under the control of a DO loop. Instructions in a small DO loop are often prefetched into the instruction buffer. The required scalar operands for repeated scalar instructions are moved into a data cache in order to continuously supply the pipeline with operands. The IBM

System/360 Model 91 is a typical example of a machine equipped with scalar pipelines. However, the Model 91 does not have a cache.

Vector pipelines are specially designed to handle vector instructions over vector operands. Computers having vector instructions are often called *vector processors*. The design of a vector pipeline is expanded from that of a scalar pipeline. The handling of vector operands in vector pipelines is under firmware and hardware controls (rather than under software control as in scalar pipelines). Pipeline vector processors to be studied in Chapter 4 include Texas Instruments' ASC, Control Data's STAR-100 and Cyber-205, Cray Research's Cray-1, Fujitsu's VP-200, AP-120B (FPS-164), IBM's 3838, and Datawest's MATP.

3.1.3 General Pipelines and Reservation Tables

What we have studied so far are linear pipelines without feedback connections. The inputs and outputs of such pipelines are totally independent. In some computations, like linear recurrence, the outputs of the pipeline are fed back as future inputs. In other words, the inputs may depend on previous outputs. Pipelines with feedback may have a nonlinear flow of data. The utilization history of the pipeline determines the present state of the pipeline. The timing of the feedback inputs becomes crucial to the nonlinear data flow. Improper use of the feedforward or feedback inputs may destroy the inherent advantages of pipelining. On the other hand, proper sequencing with nonlinear data flow may enhance the pipeline efficiency. In practice, many of the arithmetic pipeline processors allow nonlinear connections as a mechanism to implement recursion and multiple functions.

In this section, we characterize the interconnection structures and data-flow patterns in *general pipelines* with either feedforward or feedback connections, in addition to the cascaded connections in a linear pipeline. We use a two-dimensional chart known as the *reservation table* which is borrowed from the Gantt charts used in operation research to show how successive pipeline stages are utilized (or reserved) for a specific function evaluation in successive pipeline cycles. This reservation table was originally suggested by Davidson (1971). It is very similar to the space-time diagram introduced by Chen (1971) (Figure 3.1b).

Consider a sample pipeline that has a structure with both feedforward and feedback connections, as shown in Figure 3.5a. Assume that this pipeline is dual-functional, denoted as function A and function B. We will number the pipeline stages S_1, S_2, S_z from the input end to the output end. The one-way connections between adjacent stages form the original linear cascade of the pipeline. A *feedforward connection* connects a stage S_i to a stage S_j such that $j \geq i + 2$ and a *feedback connection* connects a stage S_i to a stage S_j such that $j \leq i$. In this sense, a "pure" linear pipeline is a pipeline without any feedback or feedforward connections. The crossed circles in Figure 3.5a refer to data multiplexers used for selecting among multiple connection paths in evaluating different functions.

The two reservation tables shown in Figure 3.5b and 3.5c correspond to the two functions of the sample pipeline. The rows correspond to pipeline stages and the columns to clock time units. The total number of clock units in the table is

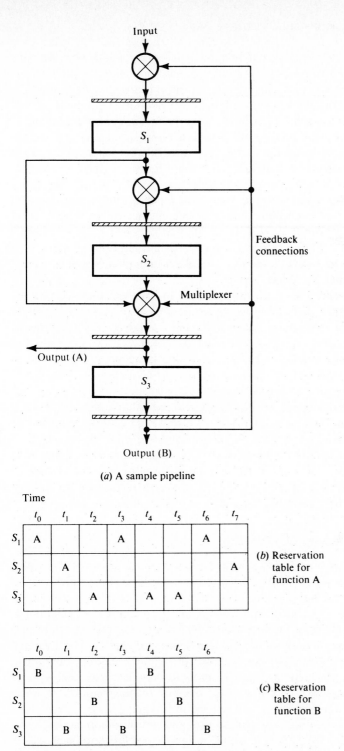

(a) A sample pipeline

Time

	t_0	t_1	t_2	t_3	t_4	t_5	t_6	t_7
S_1	A			A			A	
S_2		A						A
S_3			A		A	A		

(b) Reservation table for function A

	t_0	t_1	t_2	t_3	t_4	t_5	t_6
S_1	B				B		
S_2			B			B	
S_3		B		B			B

(c) Reservation table for function B

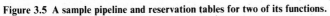

Figure 3.5 A sample pipeline and reservation tables for two of its functions.

155

called the *evaluation time* for the given function. A reservation table represents the flow of data through the pipeline for one complete evaluation of a given function.

A marked entry in the (i, j)th square of the table indicates that stage S_i will be used j time units after the initiation of the function evaluation. For a unifunctional pipeline, one can simply use an " $\times$ " to mark the table entries. For a multifunctional pipeline, different marks are used for different functions, such as the A's and B's in the two reservation tables for the sample pipeline. Different functions may have different evaluation times, such as 8 and 7 shown in Figure 3.5b and 3.5c for functions A and B, respectively.

The data-flow pattern in a static, unifunctional pipeline can be fully described by one reservation table. A multifunctional pipeline may use different reservation tables for different functions to be performed. On the other hand, a given reservation table does not uniquely correspond to one particular hardware pipeline. One· may find that several hardware pipelines with different interconnection structures can use the same reservation table.

Many interesting pipeline-utilization features can be revealed by the reservation table. It is possible to have multiple marks in a row or in a column. Multiple marks in a column correspond to the simultaneous usage of multiple pipeline stages. Multiple marks in a row correspond to the repeated usage (for marks in distant columns) or prolonged usage (for marks in adjacent columns) of a given stage. It is clear that a general pipeline may have multiple paths, parallel usage of multiple stages, and nonlinear flow of data.

In order to visualize the flow of data along selected data paths in a hardware pipeline for a complete function evaluation, we show in Figure 3.6 the snapshots of eight steps needed to evaluate function A in the sample pipeline. These snapshots are traced along the entries in reservation table A. Active stages in each time unit are shaded. The darkened connections are the data paths selected in case of multiple path choices. We will use reservation tables in subsequent sections to study various pipeline design problems.

3.1.4 Interleaved Memory Organizations

Pipeline or vector processors require effective access to linear arrays or sequential instructions, hence the memory must be designed to avoid access conflicts. There is a basic attribute to measure the effectiveness of a memory configuration, called the *memory bandwidth*, which is the average number of words accessed per second. The primary factors affecting the bandwidth are the processor architecture, the memory configuration, and the memory-module characteristics. The memory configuration is characterized by the number of memory modules and their addressing structure and bus width. The module characteristics include the memory-module size, access time, and cycle time. The memory bandwidth must match the demand of the processors as discussed in Chapter 1.

The *demand rate* of a processor architecture and its matching memory configuration is illustrated with an example: Consider a pipeline computer which operates with four independent 32-bit floating-point arithmetic pipelines. Each

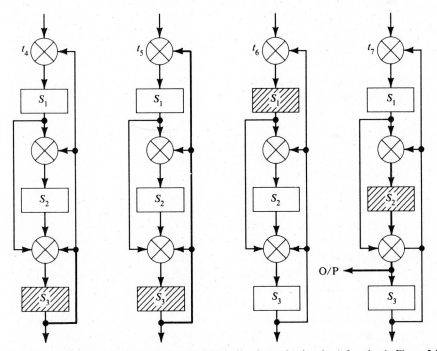

Figure 3.6 Eight snapshots of using the sample pipeline for evaluating the A function in Figure 3.5*b*.

157

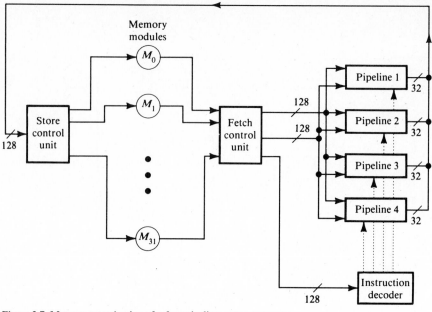

Figure 3.7 Memory organization of a four-pipeline vector processor.

pipeline requires two 32-bit operands every pipeline clock of 40 ns to produce one 32-bit result. Four parallel 32-bit results are produced for every 40 ns. We assume that one 32-bit instruction is fetched for each arithmetic operation. Therefore, the demand rate of the four pipelines is to fetch $3 \times 4 \times 32$ bits every 40 ns and store 4×32 bits of result in the same 40 ns. Hence 512 bits of information need to be accessed every 40 ns. Since each set of operands or instructions consists of four 32-bit elements, the bus width to main memory for each access (fetch or store) can be made $4 \times 32 = 128$ bits (Figure 3.7). Since there are two operand fetches, one operand-store and one instruction fetch for each pipeline and in each 40-ns interval, the main memory should have four 128-bit wide unidirectional buses. If the memory cycle time is 1.28 μs, then 1.28 μs/40 ns or 32 memory modules are required to match the demand rate. Each memory configuration is controlled by a memory controller that defines the *storage scheme* for every memory reference. The storage scheme is the set of rules that determine the module number and the address of the element within each module.

The S access memory organization One of the simplest memory configurations for pipeline vector processors uses low-order interleaving and applies the higher $(n - m)$ bits of the address to all $M = 2^m$ memory modules simultaneously in one access. The single access returns M consecutive words of information from the M memory modules. Using the low-order m address bits, the information from a particular modules can be accessed. This configuration, which is shown in Figure 3.8a, is called *S access* because all modules are accessed simultaneously.

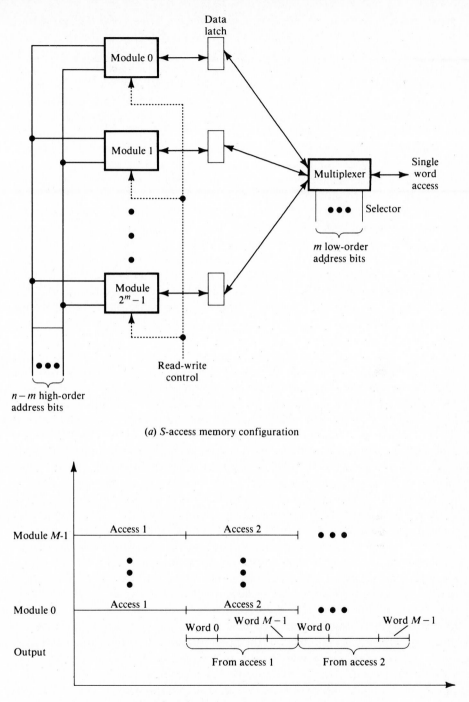

(a) S-access memory configuration

(b) Timing diagram for S-access configuration

Figure 3.8 The S-access interleaved memory configuration.

A data latch is associated with each module. For a fetch operation, the information from each module is gated into its latch, whereupon the multiplexer can be used to direct the desired data to the single-word bus. Figure 3.8b depicts the timing diagram for sample multiple-word read accesses using the S-access configuration. Notice that with a memory-access time T_a and a latch delay of τ, the time to access a single word is $T_a + \tau$. However, the total time it takes to access k consecutive words in sequence, starting in module i, is $T_a + k\tau$ if $i + k \le M$, otherwise it is $2T_a + (i + k - M)\tau$. In both cases, $1 \le k \le M$. For effective access of long vectors, $M\tau \le T_a$; otherwise, there would be a data overrun. S-access configuration is ideal for accessing a vector of data elements or for prefetching sequential instructions for a pipeline processor. It can also be used to access a block of information for a pipeline processor with a cache.

When nonsequentially addressed words are requested, the performance of the memory system deteriorates rapidly. To provide a partial remedy for nonsequential accesses, some concurrency can be introduced into the configuration by providing an address latch for each memory module so that the effective address cycle (hold time) t_a is much smaller than the memory cycle time t_c. Since the address is typically held on the address bus at least as long as data is held on the data bus, the data buses do not pose a limiting constraint on the performance. By providing the address latch, the group of M modules can be multiplexed on an internal memory address bus, called a *bank* or a *line* as to be studied in Chapter 7.

The C access memory organization When a memory operation is initiated in a module, it causes the bank to be active for t_a seconds and the module to be active for t_c seconds. If t_a is much less than t_c, the initiated module uses the bank for a duration much less than one memory cycle per access. Therefore, more than one module can share a bank, increasing the bank utilization and reducing the bank cost. This configuration is called *C access* because modules are accessed concurrently, as illustrated in Figure 3.9a. The low-order m bits are used to select the module and the remaining $n - m$ bits address the desired element within the module. The memory controller is used to buffer a request which both references a busy module and initiates service when the module completes its current cycle. Figure 3.9b shows an example timing diagram where K consecutive words are fetched in $T_a + k \cdot \tau$, assuming that the address cycle $t_a = \tau = T_a/M$.

The effectiveness of this memory configuration is revealed by its ability to access the elements of a vector. Consider a vector of s elements $V[0:s-1]$ in which every other element is accessed; that is, the *skip distance* is 2. Assuming that element $V[i]$ is stored in module i (mod M) for $0 \le i \le s - 1$, the timing diagram in Figure 3.10a for $M = 8$ illustrates the performance. After the initial access, the access time for each sequential element is one per every 2τ seconds, where $\tau = T_a/M$. If the skip distance is increased to 3, the performance is one element per every τ seconds after the initial access. This is shown in Figure 3.10b.

In general, if an address sequence is generated with a skip distance d and there are M modules arranged in C access configuration such that M and d are relatively

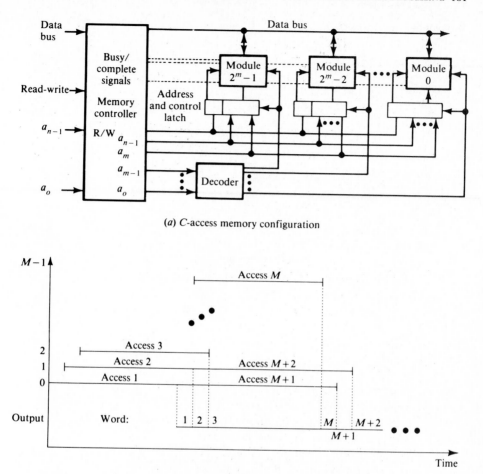

(*a*) C-access memory configuration

(*b*) Timing diagram for accesses to consecutive addresses

Figure 3.9 The C-access interleaved memory configuration.

prime, the elements can be accessed at the maximum rate of T_a/M per word. It is obvious that the S access configuration will perform worse for such address sequences. In the S access scheme, an address sequence which is generated with a skip distance of d has an *average data rate* of dT_a/M when $d \leq M$, and of T_a, when $d > M$.

The storage scheme for a vector can be extended to two and higher dimensional arrays. As an example, consider a two-dimensional array $A[0: R - 1, 0: C - 1]$. The elements can be mapped into a one-dimensional vector $[0: s - 1]$, in two basic ways: *row-major* form or *column-major* form. In row-major form, the index element $A[i, j]$ in the vector V is given by the $iC + j$. Similarly, the index of $A[i, j]$ in column-major form is $jR + i$. The storage scheme for the two-dimensional array can then be derived from the storage schemes for V, as described earlier.

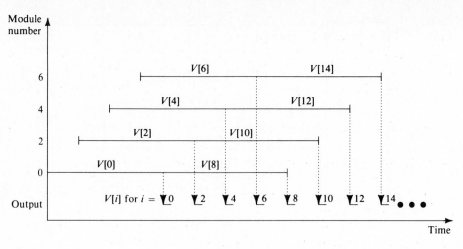

(a) Skip distance, $d = 2$

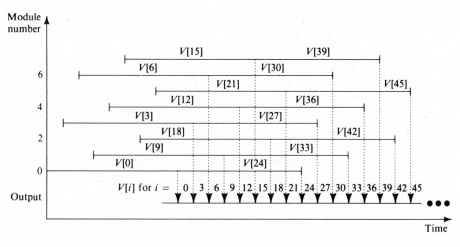

(b) Skip distance, $d = 3$

Figure 3.10 Timing diagrams for accessing the elements of a vector $V[0: s - 1]$ with skip distances $d = 2$ and $d = 3$, respectively.

The C/S access memory organization It is also possible to construct a configuration that consists of a combination of the S access and C access schemes. In such a configuration, which we call *C/S access*, the modules are organized in a two-dimensional array. If the S access is M-way interleaved and the C access is L-way interleaved, up to L different accesses to blocks of M conservative words can be in progress simultaneously. This scheme is effective for multiple pipeline processors.

Memory bandwidth estimation Various analytical models have been developed to evaluate the performance of interleaved memory configurations in a parallel-processing environment. All the models presented here assume some form of memory interleaving and evaluate the access-conflict problem. First, we summarize the memory bandwidth when a single processor is used. A sequence of memory requests from a process can be considered as an ordered set of memory-module numbers from 0 to $m - 1$.

Hellerman presented a model in which a single stream of independent instructions and data-memory requests is scanned in the order of their arrival until the first duplicate memory module is found. These first k-distinct requests are then accessed in parallel. The steady-state bandwidth can be taken to be the average length of an initial string of duplicate-free integers; that is, the distance between the first duplicates. The probability that k is the length of a string of distinct integers is $P(k) = k \cdot (m - 1)!/[m^k \cdot (m - k)!]$ for an m-way interleaved memory system. The *average bandwidth* for the single processor and m memory modules is

$$B(1, m) = \sum_{k=1}^{m} k \cdot P(k) = \sum_{k=1}^{m} \frac{k^2 \cdot (m - 1)!}{m^k \cdot (m - k)!} \tag{3.7}$$

$B(1, m)$ has a good numerical approximation of $m^{0.56}$ when $1 \le m \le 45$. Knuth and Rao showed a closed-form solution of Eq. 3.7, which shows that Hellerman's bandwidth is asymptotic to $\sqrt{m}$.

Burnett and Coffman improved the model by exploiting the principle of sequentiality of instructions. To model this effect, the instruction requests are separated from the data requests. The memory bandwidth can thus be increased considerably because of the locality of programs. This was modeled by introducing two parameters, α and β, where α is the probability of a request addressing the next module in sequence (modulo m) and $\beta = (1 - \alpha)/(m - 1)$. Assume that the memory requests at the start of a memory cycle can be represented as a sequence of m addresses $r_1, r_2, \ldots, r_m$ such that $0 \le r_i \le m - 1$ for $1 \le i \le m$. Assume the following properties for the address sequence:

$$\text{Prob}[r_1 = k] = \frac{1}{m} \qquad \text{for } 0 \le k \le m - 1$$

$$\text{Prob}[r_{i+1} = (r_i + 1) \bmod m] = \alpha \qquad \text{for } 1 \le i \le m$$

$$\text{Prob}[r_{i+1} \ne (r_i + 1) \bmod m] = \beta \qquad \text{for } 1 \le i \le m$$

The first property indicates that the first reference is made randomly to any memory module. The second property indicates the probability that the next reference is made to the next sequential module. The last property indicates the probability that the next reference is made to a nonsequential module.

Since the first request can be made to any module randomly, let us assume it is made to module 0. Assume that the first k requests are made to distinct modules for $1 \le k \le m$. Since the first request is to module 0, an arbitrary number j of the $k - 1$ requests will be of the α type and $(k - j - 1)$ requests will be of the β type. For example, suppose $m = 8$ and a sequence of eight distinct requests

$r_1, r_2, r_3, r_4, r_5, r_6, r_7, r_8$ reference modules 2, 5, 6, 7, 0, 3, 4, 5, respectively. Notice that the first seven requests are to distinct modules. Thus $\text{Prob}[r_1] = 1/m = \frac{1}{8}$; $\text{Prob}[r_2] = \text{Prob}[r_6] = \beta$; $\text{Prob}[r_3] = P[r_4] = P[r_5] = P[r_7] = \alpha$. Hence, the sequence has a probability $(1/m)\alpha^4\beta^2$. A generalization of this concept leads to an *expected bandwidth* of

$$B(1, m) = \sum_{k=1}^{m} \sum_{j=0}^{k-1} \alpha^j \beta^{k-j-1} C_m(j, k) \tag{3.8}$$

where $C_m(j, k)$ is the total number of sequences of length k with j and $(k - j - 1)$ requests of types α and β respectively. A combinational analysis shows that

$$C_m(j, k) = \sum (-1)^n \binom{j + n}{n} \binom{k - 1}{j + n} (m - j - n - 1)_{k-j-1}.$$

where $(m - j - 1)(m - j - 2) \cdots (m - k + 1)$ is denoted $(m - j - 1)_{k-j-1}$.

The bandwidth in Eq. 3.8 increases exponentially to m with α. As the program behavior exhibits more sequentiality, $B(1, m)$ increases exponentially to m. Such a behavior is more representative of instruction streams but does not adequately represent the overall program behavior, which must include the data references. The above model assumes a single processor with instruction lookahead capabilities. It has been called an *overlap processor model*. In general, there may be some *dependency* between any two addresses requested from a process. The bandwidth can further increase if consideration of data dependencies among program segments is included in the analysis.

3.2 INSTRUCTION AND ARITHMETIC PIPELINES

Before studying various pipeline design techniques and examining vector processing requirements, we need to understand how instructions can be overlapped, executed, and how repeated arithmetic computations can be done with pipelining. Instruction pipelining is illustrated with the designs in the IBM 360/91. Arithmetic pipelining will be studied in detail with four design examples for multiple-number addition, floating-point addition, multiplication, and division. Finally, multifunction-pipeline designs and array pipelining for matrix arithmetic will be introduced.

3.2.1 Design of Pipelined Instruction Units

Most of today's mainframes are equipped with pipelined central processors. We will study the instruction pipeline in the IBM System/360 Model 91 as a learning example. The IBM 360/91 incorporates a high degree of pipelining in both instruction preprocessing and instruction execution. It is a 32-bit machine specially designed for scientific computations in either fixed-point or floating-point data formats. Multiple pipeline functional units are built into the system to allow parallel arithmetic computations in either data format.

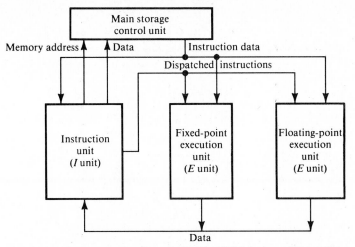

Figure 3.11 The central processing unit (CPU) of IBM System 360/Model 91.

A block diagram of the CPU in the IBM 360/91 is depicted in Figure 3.11. It consists of four major parts: the *main storage control unit*, the *instruction unit*, the *fixed-point execution unit*, and the *floating-point execution unit*. The instruction unit (I unit) is pipelined with a clock period of 60 ns. This CPU is designed to issue instructions at a burst rate of one instruction per clock cycle, and the performance of the two execution units (E units) should support this rate. The storage control unit supervises information exchange between the CPU and the main-memory major functions of the I unit, including instruction fetch, decode, and delivery to the appropriate E unit, operand address calculation and operand fetch. The two E units are responsible for the fixed-point and floating-point arithmetic logic operations needed in the execution phase.

From memory access to instruction decode and execution, the CPU is fully pipelined across the four units shown in Figure 3.11. Concurrency among successive instructions in the Model 91 is illustrated in Figure 3.12. It is desirable to overlay separate instruction functions to the greatest possible degree. The shaded boxes correspond to circuit functions and the thin lines between them refer to delays caused by memory access. Obviously, memory accesses for fetching either instructions or operands take much longer time than the delays of functional circuitry. Following the delay caused by the initial filling of the pipeline, the execution results will begin emerging at the rate of one per 60 ns.

For the processing of a typical floating-point storage-to-register instruction, we show the functional segmentation of the pipeline in Figure 3.13 along with the clock-time divisions. The basic time cycle accommodates the pipelining of most hardware functions. However, the memory and many execution functions require a variable number of pipeline cycles. In general, these storage and execution functions require a large portion of time cycles, as revealed in Figure 3.13. After decoding, two parallel sequences of operation may be initiated: one for operand

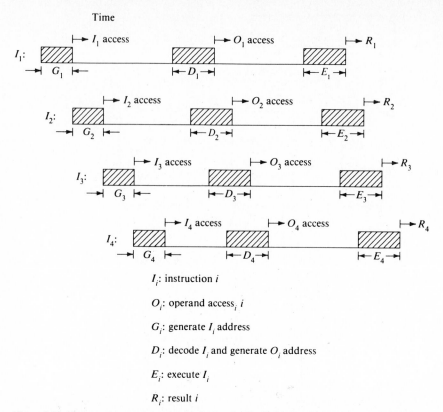

Figure 3.12 Concurrency among successive instruction fetch-decode-execute in the IBM 360/91.

access and the other for the setup of operands to be transmitted to an assigned execution station in the selected arthmetic unit. The effective memory access time must match the speeds of the pipeline stages.

Because of the time disparities between various instruction types, the Model 91 utilizes the organizational techniques of memory interleaving, parallel arithmetic functions, data buffering, and internal forwarding to overcome the speed gap problems. The depth of interleaving is a function of the memory cycle time, the CPU storage request rate, and the desired effective-access time. The Model 91 chooses a depth of 16 for interleaving 400 ns/cycle storage modules to satisfy an effective access time of 60 ns. We will examine pipeline arithmetic and data-buffering techniques in subsequent sections.

Concurrent arithmetic executions are facilitated in the Model 91 by using two separate units for fixed-point execution and floating-point execution. This permits instructions of the two classes to be executed in parallel. As long as no cross-unit data dependencies exist, the execution does not necessarily flow in the sequence in which the instructions are programmed. Within the floating-point E unit are an *add unit* and a *multiply/divide unit* which can operate in parallel. Furthermore, pipelining is practiced within arithmetic units, as will be described in Section

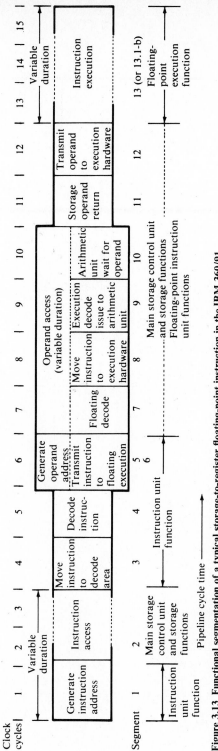

Figure 3.13 Functional segmentation of a typical storage-to-register floating-point instruction in the IBM 360/91.

167

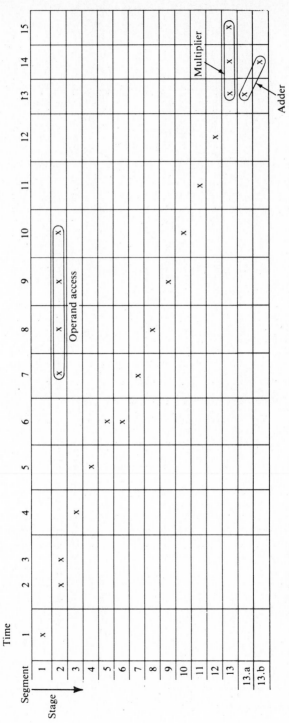

Figure 3.14 The reservation table for a typical Add or a Multiply function evaluated in the instruction pipeline of IBM 360/91.

3.2.2. Figure 3.14 shows a reservation table for the instruction pipeline in Figure 3.13. At stage 13, the path to follow depends on the instruction types, one using the floating-point adder and the other using the floating-point multiplier-divider. The adder requires two cycles and the multiplier requires six cycles.

The I unit in the Model 91 is specially designed (Figure 3.15) to support the above pipeline operations. A buffer is used to prefetch up to eight double words of instructions. A special controller is designed to handle instruction-fetch, branch, and interrupt conditions. There are two target buffers for branch handling. Sequential instruction-fetch branch and interrupt handling are all built-in hardware features. After decoding, the I unit will dispatch the instruction to the fixed-point E unit, the floating-point E unit, or back to the storage control unit. For memory reference instructions, the operand address is generated by an address adder. This adder is also used for branch-address generation, if needed. The performance of a pipeline processor relies heavily on the continuous supply of

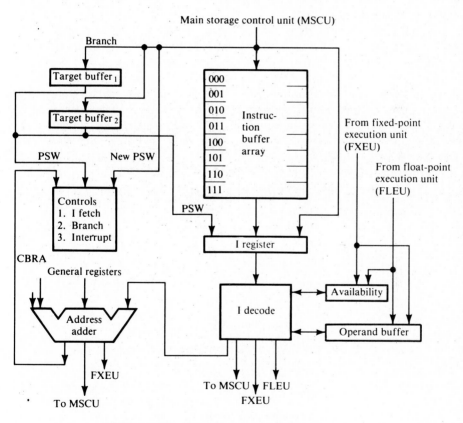

CBRA: conditional branch recovery address

PSW: present state word

Figure 3.15 The instruction unit (I unit) in IBM 360/91 CPU.

instructions and data to the pipeline. When a branch or interrupt occurs, the pipeline will lose many cycles to handle the out-of-sequence operations. Techniques to overcome this difficulty include instruction prefetch, proper buffering, special branch handling, and optimized task scheduling. We will study these techniques in Section 3.3 and check their applications in real-life system designs in Chapter 4.

3.2.2 Arithmetic Pipeline Design Examples

Static and unifunction arithmetic pipelines are introduced in this section with design examples. We will study the pipeline design of Wallace trees for multiple-number addition, which can be applied to designing pipeline multipliers and dividers. Then we will review the arithmetic pipeline designs in the IBM 360/91 for high-speed floating-point addition, multiplication, and division. The method of *convergence division* will be introduced, since it has been widely applied in many commercial computers.

Traditionally, the multiplication of two fixed-point numbers is done by repeated add-shift operations, using an *arithmetic logic unit* (ALU) which has built-in add and shift functions. The number of add-shift operations required is proportional to the operand width. This sequential execution makes the multiplication a very slow process. By examining the multiplication array of two numbers in Figure 3.16, it is clear that the multiplication process is equivalent to the addition of multiple copies of shifted multiplicands, such as the six shown in Figure 3.16.

Multiple-number addition can be realized with a multilevel tree adder. The conventional *carry propagation adder* (CPA) adds two input numbers, say A and B, to produce one output number, called the sum $A + B$. A *carry-save adder* (CSA) receives three input numbers, say A, B, and D, and outputs two numbers,

$$
\begin{array}{ccccccccl}
 & a_5 & a_4 & a_3 & a_2 & a_1 & a_0 & & = A \\
\times) & b_5 & b_4 & b_3 & b_2 & b_1 & b_0 & & = B \\
\hline
 & a_5b_0 & a_4b_0 & a_3b_0 & a_2b_0 & a_1b_0 & a_0b_0 & & = W_1 \\
 & a_5b_1 & a_4b_1 & a_3b_1 & a_2b_1 & a_1b_1 & a_0b_1 & & = W_2 \\
 & a_5b_2 & a_4b_2 & a_3b_2 & a_2b_2 & a_1b_2 & a_0b_2 & & = W_3 \\
 & a_5b_3 & a_4b_3 & a_3b_3 & a_2b_3 & a_1b_3 & a_0b_3 & & = W_4 \\
 & a_5b_4 & a_4b_4 & a_3b_4 & a_2b_4 & a_1b_4 & a_0b_4 & & = W_5 \\
+) & a_5b_5 & a_4b_5 & a_3b_5 & a_2b_5 & a_1b_5 & a_0b_5 & & = W_6 \\
\hline
P_{11}\ P_{10}\ P_9\ P_8 & P_7 & P_6 & P_5 & P_4 & P_3 & P_2 & P_1 & P_0 & = A \times B = P
\end{array}
$$

Figure 3.16 The multiplication array of two 6-bit numbers ($A \times B = P$).

the *sum vector S* and the *carry vector C*. Mathematically, we have $A + B + D = S \oplus C$, where $+$ is arithmetic addition and $\oplus$ is bitwise exclusive-or operation.

$$
\begin{array}{rrccccccc}
 & A & = & 1 & 1 & 1 & 1 & 0 & 1 \\
 & B & = & 0 & 1 & 0 & 1 & 1 & 0 \\
+) & D & = & 1 & 1 & 0 & 1 & 1 & 1 \\
\hline
 & C & = 1 & 1 & 0 & 1 & 1 & 1 & \\
\oplus) & S & = & 0 & 1 & 1 & 1 & 0 & 0 \\
\hline
\end{array}
$$

$$
\begin{array}{l}
A + B + D \\
\text{or} \quad C \oplus S = 1 \quad 1 \quad 1 \quad 0 \quad 0 \quad 1 \quad 0
\end{array}
$$

A carry-propagate adder can be implemented with a cascade of full adders with the carry-out of a lower stage connected to the carry-in of a higher stage. A carry-save adder can be implemented with a set of full adders with all the carry-in terminals serving as the input lines for the third input number D, and all the carry-out terminals serving as the output lines for the carry vector C. In other words, the carry lines of all full adders are not interconnected in a carry-save adder. For the present purpose, we can simply view a CPA as a two-to-one number converter and a CSA as a *three-to-two* number converter.

Now we are ready to show how to use a number of CSAs for multiple-number addition. This, in turn, serves the purpose of pipeline multiplication. This pipeline is designed to multiply two 6-bit numbers, as illustrated in Figure 3.17. There are five pipeline stages. The first stage is for the generation of all $6 \times 6 = 36$ immediate product terms $\{a^i b^j | 0 \leq i \leq 5 \text{ and } 0 \leq j \leq 5\}$, which form the six rows of shifted multiplicands $\{W^i | i = 1, 2, \ldots, 6\}$. The six numbers are then fed into two CSAs in the second stage. In total, four CSAs are interconnected to form a three-level *carry-save adder tree* (from stage two to stage four in the pipeline). This CSA tree merges six numbers into two numbers: the sum vector S and the carry vector C. The final stage is a CPA (carry lookahead may be embedded in it, if the operand length is long) which adds the two numbers S and C to produce the final output, the product $P = A \times B$.

If we restrict the CSA tree to adding only multiple single-bit numbers, we have the well-known bit-slice Wallace trees. In general, a v-level CSA tree can add up to $N(v)$ input numbers, where $N(v)$ is evaluated by the following recursive formula:

$$
N(v) = \left\lfloor \frac{N(v) - 1}{2} \right\rfloor \times 3 + N(v - 1) \bmod 2 \qquad \text{with } N(1) = 3 \qquad (3.9)
$$

For example, one needs a 10-level CSA tree to add 64 to 94 numbers in one pass through the tree. In other words, a pipeline with 10 stages on the CSA tree is needed to multiply two 64-bit fixed-point numbers in one pass. The floor notation $\lfloor x \rfloor$ refers to the largest integer not greater than x.

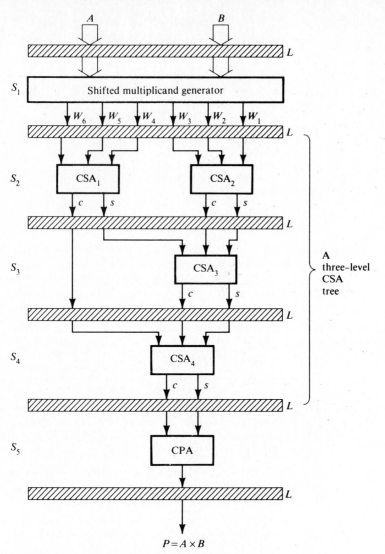

Figure 3.17 A pipelined multiplier built with a CSA tree.

The CSA-tree pipeline can be modified to allow multiple-pass usage by having feedback connections. The concept is illustrated in Figure 3.18. Two input ports of the CSA tree in Figure 3.17 are now connected with the feedback carry vector and sum vector. Suppose that the CPA expanded to require pipeline stages because of increased operand width. We can use this pipeline to merge four additional multiplicands per iteration. If one wishes to multiply two 32-bit numbers, only eight iterations would be needed in this CSA tree with feedback. A complete evaluation of the multiply function in this six-stage pipeline is represented by the reservation table in Figure 3.19. The total evaluation time of this function equals

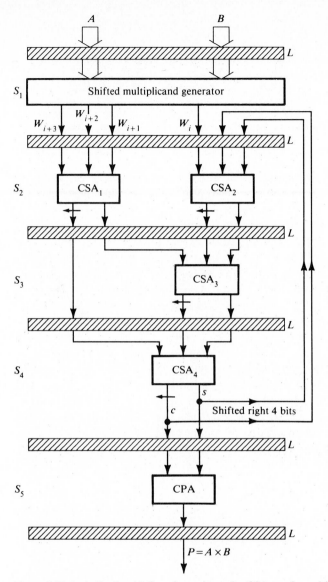

Figure 3.18 A pipelined multiplier using an interative CSA tree for multiple-shift multiplication.

26 clock periods, out of which 24 cycles are needed in the iterative CSA-tree hardware.

This iterative approach saves significantly in hardware compared to the single-pass approach. As a contrast, one-pass 32-input CSA-tree pipeline requires the use of 30 CSAs in eight pipeline stages. The increase in hardware is 26 additional CSAs (each 32-bits wide). The gain in total evaluation time is the saving of

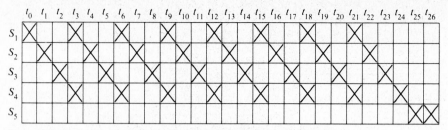

Figure 3.19 The reservation table for the pipelined multiplier in Figure 3.18.

$26 - 11 = 15$ clock periods, where $11 = 1 + 8 + 2$ corresponds to one cycle for the input stage, eight cycles for the one-pass CSA tree, and two cycles for the CPA stages.

We are now ready to present floating-point arithmetic units in the IBM 360/91. A block diagram of the floating-point execution unit in the Model 91 is given in Figure 3.20. *The floating-point instruction unit* (FLIU) communicates with the main storage and the I unit in the CPU (Figure 3.7) in receiving instructions and data retrieval. Successively arrived instructions are queued in the instruction stack. A data buffer (FLB) is used to hold the block of data fetched from the memory. High-speed data registers (FLR) are used to hold operands and intermediate results. A common data bus is used to connect the three components in this E unit. This bus consists of a group of instruction lines and two groups of data lines, one for the FLB and the other for the FLR.

The Add unit can execute all floating-point add and subtract instructions in two machine cycles (120 ns). The M/D unit can execute a floating-point multiply instruction in six machine cycles (360 ns), and a floating-point divide instruction in 18 cycles (1.8 μs). A floating-point operand in the IBM 360/91 can be either short (32 bits) or long (64 bits) with the following two floating point data formats:

Short floating-point data format

Sign	Exponent	Fraction
0	1–7	8–31 (24 bits)

Long floating-point data format

Sign	Exponent	Fraction
0	1–7	8–63 (56 bits)

The Add unit allows three pairs of numbers to be loaded into the three reservation stations. The M/D unit has two reservation stations for two pairs of numbers. The pipeline floating-point adder in the Add unit has physically segmented into two stages. Logically, this pipeline adder can be separated into three algorithmic

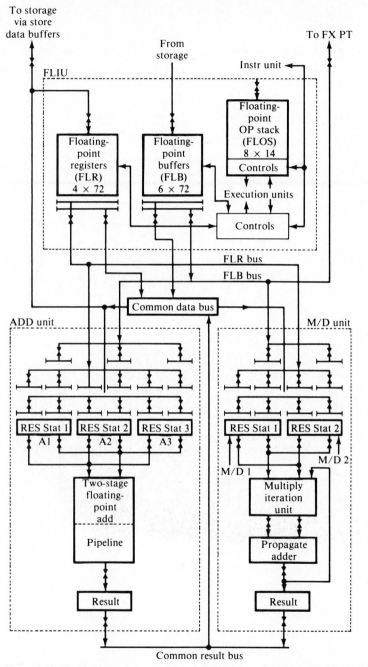

Figure 3.20 The floating-point execution unit in IBM System 360/Model 91. (Courtesy of International Business Machines Corp.)

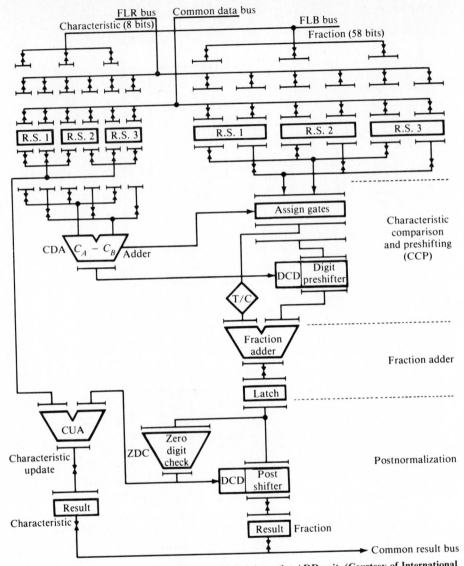

Figure 3.21 Pipelined structure of the IBM 360/91 floating-point ADD unit. (Courtesy of International Business Machines Corp.)

stages, as depicted in Figure 3.21. The functions of these three sections are very similar to what we have discussed in Figure 3.2. Exponent arithmetic and fraction addition and subtraction can be done in parallel. The fraction adder is 56 bits wide and the two exponent adders are each 7 bits wide. Both normalized and unnormalized instructions can be executed, as listed in Table 3.1. The two-cycle speed for double-precision (long-format) floating-point addition matches the instruction-issuing rate of the CPU.

Table 3.1 Typical floating-point instructions in IBM System/360 Model 91

Floating-point instruction	Processing unit	Pipeline cycles needed
Load (S/L)	FLIU	1
Load and test (S/L)	FLIU	1
Store (S/L)	FLIU	1
Load complement (S/L)	Add unit	2
Load positive (S/L)	Add unit	2
Load negative (S/L)	Add unit	2
Add normalized (S/L)	Add unit	2
Add unnormalized (S/L)	Add unit	2
Subtract normalized (S/L)	Add unit	2
Subtract unnormalized (S/L)	Add unit	2
Compare (S/L)	Add unit	2
Halve (S/L)	Add unit	2
Multiply	M/D unit	6
Divide	M/D unit	18

Note: S = short data format; L = long data format; FLIU = floating-point instruction unit; M/D = multiply/divide. Each pipeline cycle is 60 ns.

Floating-point multiply and divide share the same hardware M/D unit in the Model 91. Multiplier recoding techniques are used to speed up the multiplication process. Six multiplicand multiples are generated after the recoding. The complete pipeline structure of the M/D unit is shown in Figure 3.22. The hardware resources can be separated into two parts: the *iterative hardware* for multiple multiplicand addition through a CSA tree, as shown within the dashed-line box, and the *peripheral hardware* for input reservation, prenormalization, multiplier recoding, exponent arithmetic, carry propagation, and output storage. A quadratic convergence division method is applied to generate $Q = N/D$ through dual sequences of the multiplication of N and D by a series of converging factors until the denominator converges to unity. The resulting numerator becomes the desired quotient. Therefore, the aforementioned iterative-multiply hardware can do the job without additional facilities.

The convergence division method has been implemented in many models of the IBM 360/370 and in the CDC 6600/7600 systems. The method is briefly described below. We want to compute the ratio (quotient) $Q = N/D$, where N is the numerator (dividend) and D is the denominator (divisor). Consider normalized binary arithmetic in which $0.5 \leq N < D < 1$ to avoid overflow. Let R_i for $i = 1, 2, \ldots$, be the successive *converging factors*. One can select

$$R_i = 1 + \delta^{2^{i-1}} \qquad \text{for } i = 1, 2, \ldots, k$$

where $\delta = 1 - D$ and $0 < \delta \leq 0.5$.

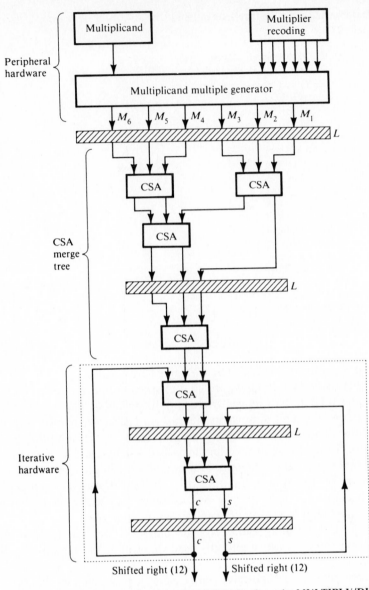

Figure 3.22 Pipelined structure of the IBM 360/91 floating-point MULTIPLY/DIVIDE unit. (Courtesy of International Business Machines Corp.)

To evaluate the quotient Q, we multiply both N and D by R_i, starting from $i = 1$ until a certain stage, say k. Mathematically, we have

$$Q = \frac{N}{D} = \frac{N \times R_1 \times R_2 \times \cdots \times R_k}{D \times R_1 \times R_2 \times \cdots \times R_k}$$

$$= \frac{N \times (1 + \delta) \times (1 + \delta^2) \times \cdots \times (1 + \delta^{2^{k-1}})}{(1 - \delta) \times (1 + \delta) \times (1 + \delta^2) \times \cdots \times (1 + \delta^{2^{k-1}})} \quad (3.10)$$

where $D = 1 - \delta$ is being substituted. Denote $D \times R_1 \times R_2 \times \cdots \times R_i = D_i$ and $N \times R_1 \times R_2 \times \cdots \times R_i = N_i$ for $i = 1, 2, \ldots, k$. We have

$$D_i = (1 - \delta)(1 + \delta)(1 + \delta^2) \cdots (1 + \delta^{2^{i-1}})$$

$$= (1 - \delta^2)(1 + \delta^2)(1 + \delta^4) \cdots (1 + \delta^{2^{i-1}})$$

$$= 1 - \delta^{2^i}$$

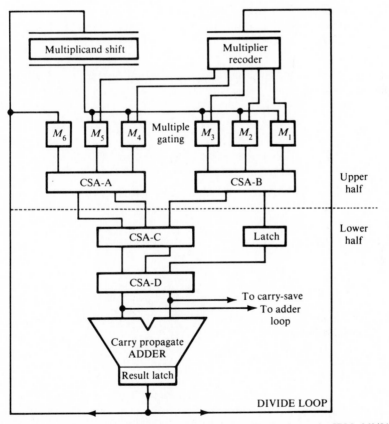

Figure 3.23 Convergence divide loop using the iterative hardware in IBM 360/91 floating-point MULTIPLY/DIVIDE unit. (Courtesy of International Business Machines Corp.)

It is clear that $0.5 \le D < D_1 < D_2 < \cdots < D_k \to 1$, because of the fact $0.5 > \delta > \delta^2 > \delta^4 > \cdots > \delta^{2k} > 0$. When the number of iterations k is sufficiently large, $\delta^{2k} \to 0$ and thus $D_k \to 1$. We end up with

$$N_k = N \times (1 + \delta) \times (1 + \delta^2) \times \cdots \times (1 + \delta^{2^{k-1}}) \tag{3.11}$$

which equals the desired quotient $Q = N/D = N_k$. The smaller the fraction δ, the faster will be the convergence process.

The multiply hardware in the M/D unit can be used iteratively to carry out the above convergence division of two 56-bit fractions in the Model 91. Figure 3.23 shows the *divide loop* when utilizing the iterative hardware in Figure 3.18 for convergence division. A time chart is given in Figure 3.24 to show the two over-lapped sequences of multiplications (Eq. 3.9) carried out simultaneously by the upper half and the lower half of the divide loop. Five iterations are needed ($k = 5$) to converge the numerator into the desired quotient, the factor $\delta^{2^5} = \delta^{32}$ becoming small enough to be considered as zero within the limit of machine precision. In the M/D unit, 12 bits are being shifter per iteration by the *multiplier recoding* logic. The theory of multiplier recoding using redundant number representation can be found in Hwang's book on Computer Arithmetic (1979).

Concurrency in arithmetic operations has been exploited in the IBM 360/91 in four areas:

1. Concurrent operations of the Add unit and the M/D unit within the floating-point E unit

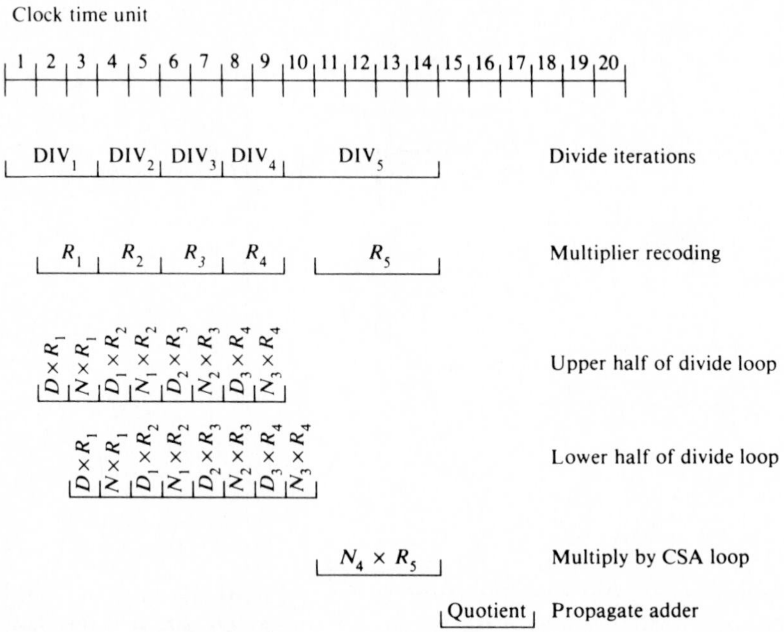

Figure 3.24 Timing chart showing the overlapped execution in the divide loop shown in Figure 3.23.

2. Pipelined executions in the Add unit and the M/D unit
3. Concurrent execution within the iterative multiply hardware
4. Concurrent operations of the fixed-point E unit and floating-point E unit

The hardware examines multiple instructions and optimizes the program execution by allowing simultaneous execution of multiple independent instructions.

3.2.3 Multifunction and Array Pipelines

In this section, we study static and multifunction-arithmetic pipelines and introduce the concept of *array pipelining*, with an example in matrix arithmetic. By definition, a multifunction pipeline can perform different functions at different times upon program control or firmware control. We present a four-function pipeline proposed by Kamal, et al (1974). This pipeline can perform *multiply*, *divide*, *squaring*, and *sqrt* (*square root*) operations. Two types of building cells are used in this four-function pipeline construction. The two cell types are specified in Figure 3.25 by boolean equations. The A cell is a controlled 1-bit adder-subtractor with bypass signal lines. The K cells are for function selection and boundary carry control.

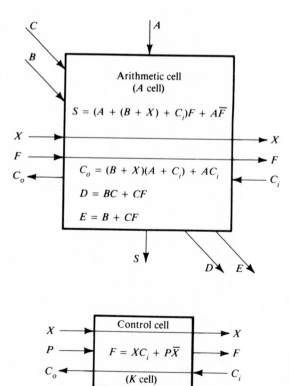

Figure 3.25 Building blocks used in the construction of the four-function arithmetic pipeline in Figure 3.26.

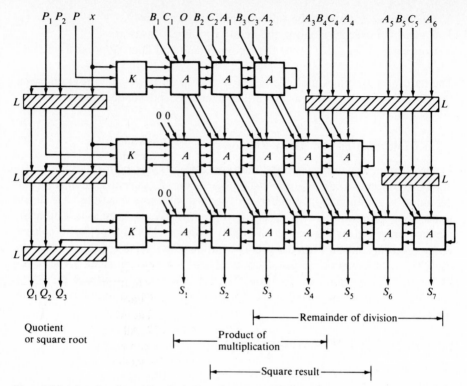

Figure 3.26 A four-function arithmetic pipeline. (Courtesy of *IEEE Trans. Computers*, Kamal et al. 1974.)

The schematic design of the four-function pipeline with A cells, K cells, and interface latches is shown in Figure 3.26. Arithmetic computations being implemented are specified below in terms of input and output relationships. A, B, and P lines are for operand inputs. All pairs of B and C lines can be tied together (with the same input value) except for the *sqrt* operation. K and X are function control signals. S and Q lines are for outputs. In the following arithmetic I/O equations, all unspecified input lines assume a zero input value (unless otherwise noted). The control signal $X = 1$ is for *divide* and *sqrt* operations.

Multiply operation

$$(A_1 A_2 A_3 A_4) + (B_1 B_2 B_3) \times (P_1 P_2) = (S_1 S_2 S_3 S_4) \qquad (3.12)$$

Divide operation

$$(A_1 A_2 A_3 A_4) - (B_1 B_2 B_3) = (Q_1 Q_2 Q_3) \text{ plus } (S_3 S_4 S_5) \qquad (3.13)$$

$$\qquad\qquad\qquad\qquad \text{Quotient} \qquad \text{remainder}$$

Squaring operation

$$(P_1 P_2)^2 = (S_2 S_3 S_4 S_5) \qquad (3.14)$$

Square rooting operation

$$\sqrt{(A_1 A_2 \cdots A_6)} = (Q_1 Q_2 Q_3) \text{ plus } (S_3 S_4 \cdots S_7) \qquad (3.15)$$

$$\underbrace{\qquad\qquad}_{\text{Root}} \qquad \underbrace{\qquad\qquad}_{\text{Remainder}}$$

provided $B_2 C_2 = 01$ and $B_i C_i = 10$ for $i > 3$.

Each stage of the pipeline is essentially a ripple-carry adder-subtractor. Results for multiply, squaring, and for the remainders of *divide* and *sqrt* are generated at the bottom stage of the pipeline. Quotient bits and root bits are generated at the left end of each pipeline stage in a sequential manner.

We have only shown three pipeline stages in Figure 3.26. One can add additional stages at the bottom of the pipeline. The number of A cells used in the kth stage equals $2k + 1$. Of course, more pipeline stages imply higher precision in input-output number representations. This four-function pipeline must operate in a static manner, one function at a time. In this sense, it is not a dynamic pipeline. So far, dynamic pipelines have never been implemented in commercial computers.

Texas Instruments' Advanced Scientific Computer (ASC) was the first vector processor that was installed with multifunction pipelines in its arithmetic processors. We will review the system architecture of ASC in Chapter 4. Only the pipeline arithmetic units of ASC are studied in this section. The ASC arithmetic pipeline consists of eight stages, as illustrated in Figure 3.27. All the interconnection routes among the eight stages are shown. This pipeline can perform either fixed-point or floating-point arithmetic functions and many logical-shifting operations over scalar and vector operands of lengths 16, 32, or 64 bits. The basic pipeline clock period is 60 ns. One to four such pipelines can be installed in the ASC system. The maximum speed is about 0.5 to 1.5 megaflops for scalar processing and 3 to 10 megaflops for vector processing. The results of previous executions can be routed back as future inputs, such as those needed in vector dot product operations.

Different arithmetic logic instructions are allowed to use different connecting paths through the pipeline. Figure 3.28 shows four interconnection patterns of the ASC pipeline for the evaluation of the functions: *fixed-point add*, *floating-point add*, *fixed-point multiply*, and *floating-point vector dot product*. The receiver and output stages are used by all instructions. Simple instructions like *load, store, and,* and *or* only use these two stages. The multiply stage performs 32×32 multiplication. The multiply stage produces two 64-bit results, called *pseudo sum* and *pseudo carry*, which are sent to the accumulate stage or the 64-bit add stage to produce the desired product. The accumulator can also feed its output back to itself when double-precision multiply or divide operations are demanded. This feedback is also used to implement fixed-point vector dot product instruction.

The exponent subtract stage determines the exponent difference and sends this shift count to the align stage to align fractions for *floating-point add* or *subtract* instructions. All right-shift operations are also implemented in this align stage. The normalize stage does the floating-point normalization, all left-shift operations, and conversions between fixed-point and floating-point operands. With many functions, the ASC pipeline is still a static one, performing only one

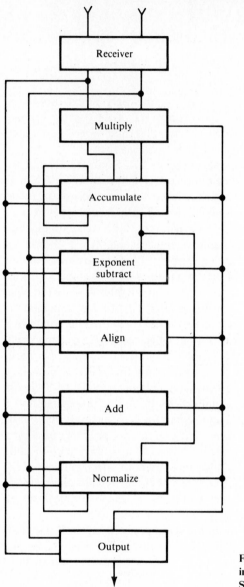

Figure 3.27 All possible interstage connections in the TI-ASC arithmetic pipeline. (Courtesy of Stephenson 1973.)

function at a time. Reconfiguration is needed when the pipeline switches its function from one to another. Multifunction pipelines offer better resource utilization and higher application flexibility. However, their control is much more complicated than their unifunction counterparts. Most of today's pipeline computers choose to use unifunction pipes because of cost effectiveness.

Array pipelines are two-dimensional pipelines with multiple data-flow streams for high-level arithmetic computations, such as matrix multiplication, inversion,

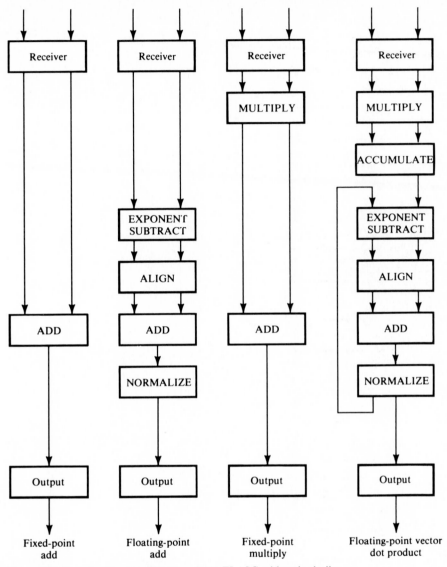

Figure 3.28 Four functional configurations in the TI-ASC arithmetic pipeline.

and L-U decomposition. The pipeline is usually constructed with a cellular array of arithmetic units. The cellular array is usually regularly structured and suitable for VLSI implementation. Presented below is only an introductory sample design of an array pipeline. This array is pipelined in three data-flow directions for the repeated multiplication of pairs of compatible matrices. The basic building blocks in the array are the *M cells*. Each *M* cell performs an additive inner-product operation as illustrated in Figure 3.29.

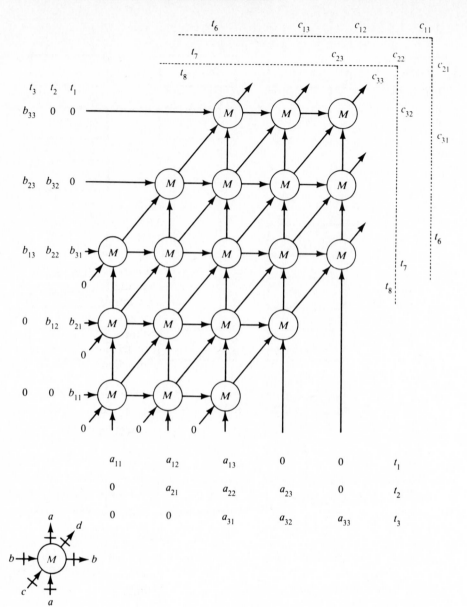

$$d = a * b + c$$

Figure 3.29 A cellular array for pipelined multiplication of two dense matrices.

Each M cell has the three input operands a, b, and c and the three outputs $a' = a$, $b' = b$, and $d = a \times b + c$. Fast latches (registers) are used at all input-output terminals and all interconnecting paths in the array pipeline. All latches are synchronously controlled by the same clock. Adjacency between cells is defined in three orientations: horizontal, vertical, and diagonal (45°) directions. The array shown in Figure 3.29 performs the multiplication of two 3×3 dense matrices $A \cdot B = C$.

$$A \cdot B = \begin{bmatrix} a_{11} & a_{12} & a_{13} \\ a_{21} & a_{22} & a_{23} \\ a_{31} & a_{32} & a_{33} \end{bmatrix} \cdot \begin{bmatrix} b_{11} & b_{12} & b_{13} \\ b_{21} & b_{22} & b_{23} \\ b_{31} & b_{32} & b_{33} \end{bmatrix} = \begin{bmatrix} c_{11} & c_{12} & c_{13} \\ c_{21} & c_{22} & c_{23} \\ c_{31} & c_{32} & c_{33} \end{bmatrix} = C \quad (3.16)$$

The input matrices are fed into the array in the horizontal and vertical directions. Three clock periods are needed for inputing the matrix entries: one row at a time for the A matrix and one column at a time for the B matrix. Dummy zero inputs are marked at unused input lines. "Don't care" conditions at the output lines are left blank. In general, to multiply two $(n \times n)$ matrices requires $3n^2 - 4n + 2$ M cells. It takes $3n - 1$ clock periods to complete the multiply process. When the matrix size becomes too large, the global array approach will pose a serious problem for monolithic chip implementation because of density and I/O packaging constraints. For a practical design of array pipelines, a block-partitioning approach will be introduced in Chapter 10 for VLSI matrix arithmetic. VLSI array-pipeline structures will be treated there with the potential real-time applications.

3.3 PRINCIPLES OF DESIGNING PIPELINE PROCESSORS

Key design problems of pipeline processors are studied in this section. We begin with a review of various instruction-prefetch and branch-control strategies for designing pipelined instruction units. Data-buffering and busing structures are presented for smoothing pipelined operations to avoid congestion. We will study internal data-forwarding and register-tagging techniques by examining instruction-dependence relations. The detection and resolution of logic hazards in pipelines will be described. Principles of job sequencing in a pipeline will be studied with reservation tables to avoid collisions in utilizing pipeline resources. Finally, we will consider the problems of designing dynamic pipelines and the necessary system supports for pipeline reconfigurations.

3.3.1 Instruction Prefetch and Branch Handling

From the viewpoint of overlapped instruction execution sequencing for pipelined processing, the instruction mixes in typical computer programs can be classified into four types, as shown in Table 3.2. The arithmetic load operations constitute 60 percent of a typical computer program. These are mainly data manipulation

Table 3.2 Typical instruction mix and pipeline cycle allocation

Segment function	Instruction type and mix rate	Arithmetic/load type, 60%	Store type, 15%	Branch type, 5%	Conditional branch type	
					Yes, 12%	No, 8%
Instruction fetch		6	6	6	6	6
Decode		2	2	2	2	2
Condition test					1	1
Operand address calculation		2	2	2	2	2
Operand fetch(es)		6–12				
Arithmetic logic execution		4–8				
Store result			6			
Update PC and flags		1	1	1	1	1
Total pipeline cycles		21–31	17	11	12	12

operations which require one or two operand fetches. The execution of different arithmetic operations requires a different number of pipeline cycles. The store-type operation does not require a fetch operand, but memory access is needed to store the data. The branch-type operation corresponds to an unconditional jump. There are two possible paths for a conditional branch operation. The *yes* path requires the calculation of the new address being branched to, whereas the *no* path proceeds to the next sequential instruction in the program. The arithmetic-load and store instructions do not alter the sequential execution order of the program. The branch instructions (25 percent in typical programs) may alter the program counter (PC) in order to jump to a program location other than the next instruction. Different types of instructions require different cycle allocations. The branch types of instructions will cause some damaging effects on the pipeline performance.

Some functions, like interrupt and branch, produce damaging effects on the performance of pipeline computers. When instruction I is being executed, the occurrence of an interrupt postpones the execution of instruction $I + 1$ until the interrupting request has been serviced. Generally, there are two types of interrupts. *Precise interrupts* are caused by illegal operation codes found in instructions, which can be detected during the decoding stage. The other type, *imprecise interrupts*, is caused by defaults from storage, address, and execution functions.

Since decoding is usually the first stage of an instruction pipeline, an interrupt on instruction I prohibits instruction $I + 1$ from entering the pipeline. However, those instructions preceding instruction I that have not yet emerged from the pipeline continue to run until the pipeline is drained. Then the interrupt routine is serviced. An imprecise interrupt occurs usually when the instruction is halfway through the pipeline and subsequent instructions are already admitted into the pipeline. When an interrupt of this kind occurs, no new instructions are allowed to enter the pipeline, but all the incompleted instructions inside the pipeline, whether they precede or follow the interrupted instruction, will be completed before the processing unit is switched to service the interrupt.

In the Star-100 system, the pipelines are dedicated to vector-oriented arithmetic operations. In order to handle interrupts during the execution of a vector instruction, special interrupt buffer areas are needed to hold addresses, delimiters, field lengths, etc., that are needed to restart the vector instructions after an interrupt. This demands a capable recovery mechanism for handling unpredictable and imprecise interrupts.

For the Cray-1 computer, the interrupt system is built around an *exchange package*. To change tasks, it is necessary to save the current processor state and to load a new processor state. The Cray-1 does this semiautomatically when an interrupt occurs or when a program encounters an *exit* instruction. Under such circumstances, the Cray-1 saves the eight scalar registers, the eight address registers, the program counter, and the monitor flags. These are packed into 16 words and swapped with a block whose address is specified by a hardware exchange address register. However, the exchange package does not contain all the hardware state information, so software *interrupt handlers* must save the rest of the states. "The rest" includes 512 words of vector registers, 128 words of intermediate registers, a vector mask, and a real-time clock.

The effect of branching on pipeline performance is described below by a linear instruction pipeline consisting of five segments: *instruction fetch, decode, operand fetch, execute,* and *store results*. Possible memory conflicts between overlapped fetches are ignored and a sufficiently large cache memory (instruction-data buffers) is used in the following analysis.

As illustrated in Figure 3.30, the instruction pipeline executes a stream of instructions continuously in an overlapped fashion if branch-type instructions do not appear. Under such circumstances, once the pipeline is filled up with sequential instructions (nonbranch type), the pipeline completes the execution of one instruction per a fixed latency (usually one or two clock periods).

On the other hand, a branch instruction entering the pipeline may be halfway down the pipe (such as a "successful" conditional branch instruction) before a branch decision is made. This will cause the program counter to be loaded with the new address to which the program should be directed, making all prefetched instructions (either in the cache memory or already in the pipeline) useless. The next instruction cannot be initiated until the completion of the current branch-instruction cycle. This causes extra time delays in order to drain the pipeline, as depicted in Figure 3.26c. The overlapped action is suspended and the pipeline must be drained at the end of the branch cycle. The continuous flow of instructions into the pipeline is thus temporarily interrupted because of the presence of a branch instruction.

In general, the higher the percentage of branch-type instructions in a program, the slower a program will run on a pipeline processor. This certainly does not merit the concept of pipelining. An analytical estimation of the effect of branching on an n-segment instruction pipeline is given below. The instruction cycle is assumed to

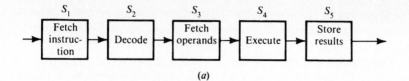

(a)

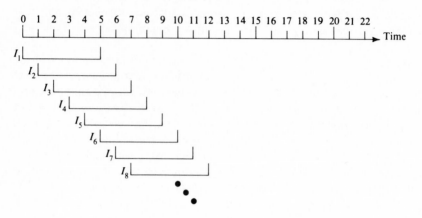

(b) Overlapped execution of instructions without branching

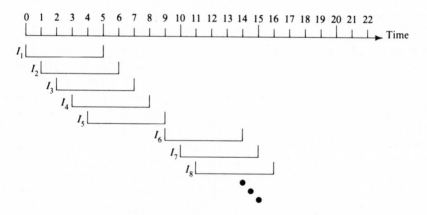

(c) Instruction I_5 is a branch instruction

Figure 3.30 The effect of branching on the performance of an instruction pipeline.

include n pipeline cycles. For example, one instruction cycle is equal to five pipe-line clock periods in Figure 3.30. Clearly, if a branch instruction does not occur, the performance would be one instruction per each pipeline cycle. Let p be the probability of a conditional branch instruction in a typical program (20 percent by Table 3.2) and q be the probability that a branch is successful ($\frac{12}{20} = 60$ per-cent by Table 3.2). Suppose that there are m instructions waiting to be executed through the pipeline. The number of instructions that cause successful branches equals $m \cdot p \cdot q$. Since $(n - 1)/n$ extra time delay is needed for each successful branch instruction, the total instruction cycles required to process these m instructions equal $(1/n)(n + m - 1) + (m \cdot p \cdot q)(n - 1)/n$. As m becomes very large, the performance of the instruction pipeline is measured by the average number of instructions executed per instruction cycle:

$$\lim_{m \to \infty} \frac{m}{(n + m - 1)/n + m \cdot p \cdot q \cdot (n - 1)/n} = \frac{n}{1 + pq(n - 1)} \tag{3.17}$$

When $p = 0$ (no branch instructions encountered), the above measure reduces to n instructions per n pipeline clocks, which is ideal. In reality, the above ratio is always less than n. For example, with $n = 5$, $p = 20$ percent, and $q = 60$ percent, we have the performance of 3.24 instructions per instruction cycle (or 5 pipeline cycles), which is less than the ideal execution rate of 5 instructions per 5 pipeline cycles. In other words, an average of 35.2 percent cycles may be wasted because of branching. In order to cope with the damaging effects of branch instructions, various mechanisms have been developed in pipeline computers.

We have studied instruction prefetch in Section 3.2.1, where the I unit in the IBM 360/91 was described (Figure 3.15). Formally, a prefetching strategy can be stated as follows: Instruction words ahead of the one currently being decoded are fetched from the memory before the instruction-decoding unit requests them. The prefetch of instructions is modeled in Figure 3.31. The memory is assumed to be interleaved and can accept requests at one per cycle. All requests require T cycles to return from memory.

There are two prefetch buffers of sizes s and t instruction words. The s-size buffer holds instructions fetched during the sequential part of a run. When a *branch* is successful, the entire buffer is invalidated. The other buffer holds instructions fetched from the target of a conditional branch. When a conditional branch is resolved and determined to be unsuccessful, the contents of this buffer are invalidated. The decoder requests instruction words at a maximum rate of one per r cycles. If the instruction requested by the decoder is available in the sequential buffer for sequential instructions, or is in the target buffer if a conditional branch has just been resolved and is successful, it enters the decoder with zero delay. Otherwise, the decoder is idle until the instruction returns from memory.

Except for *jump* instructions, all decoded instructions enter the execution pipeline, where E units are required to complete execution. If the decoded instruction is an unconditional branch, the instruction word at the target of the *jump* is requested immediately by the decoder and decoding ceases until the target instruction returns from the memory. The pipeline will see the full memory latency time T, since there was no opportunity for target prefetching.

If the decoded instruction is a *conditional branch*, sequential prefetching is suspended during the E cycles it is being executed. The instruction simultaneously enters the execution pipeline, but no more instructions are decoded until the branch is resolved at the end of E units. Instructions are prefetched from the target memory

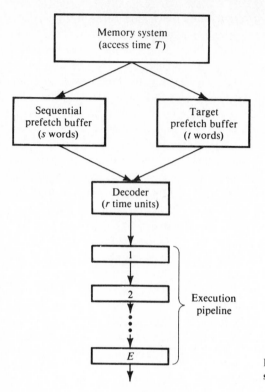

Figure 3.31 An instruction pipeline with both sequential and target prefetch buffers.

address of the conditional branch instruction. Requests for t target instructions are issued at the rate of one per cycle. Once the branch is resolved, target prefetching becomes unnecessary.

If the branch is successful, the target instruction stream becomes the sequential stream, and instructions are requested every r time units from this stream. Execution of this new stream begins when the target of the branch returns from memory, or whenever E units have elapsed, whichever is later. If the branch is unsuccessful, instruction requests are initiated every r units of time following the branch resolution and continue until the next branch or jump is decoded.

Instruction prefetching reduces the damaging effects of branching. In the IBM 360/91, a loop mode and back-eight test are designed with the help of a branch-target buffer. The idea is to keep a short loop of eight instruction double words or less completely in the branch-target buffer so that no additional memory accesses are needed until the loop mode is removed by the final branching out. This replacement of the condition mode by the local loop mode is established once a successful branch results and the back-eight test is satisfied. The load lookahead mechanism in the ASC system follows a similar approach. Another approach is to prefetch into the instruction buffer one (by guess) or even both instruction sequences forked at a conditional branch instruction. After the test result becomes available, one of the two prefetched instruction sequences will be executed and the other discarded. This branch-target prefetch approach may increase the utilization of the pipeline CPU and thus increase the total system throughput.

3.3.2 Data Buffering and Busing Structures

The processing speeds of pipeline segments are usually unequal. Consider the example pipeline in Figure 3.32a, with three segments having delays T_1, T_2, and T_3, respectively. If $T_1 = T_3 = T$ and $T_2 = 3T$, obviously segment S_2 is the bottleneck. The throughput of the pipeline is inversely proportional to the bottleneck. Therefore, it is desirable to remove the bottleneck which causes the unnecessary congestion. One obvious method is to subdivide the bottleneck. Figure 3.32b shows two different subdivisions of segment S_2. The throughput is increased

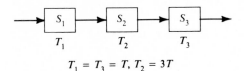

$$T_1 = T_3 = T, T_2 = 3T$$

(a) Segment 2 is the bottleneck

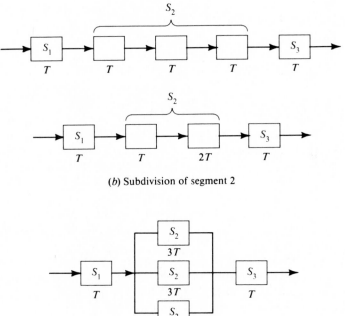

(b) Subdivision of segment 2

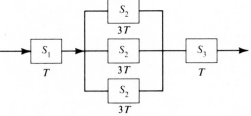

(c) Replication of segment 2

Figure 3.32 Subdivision or replication to alleviate the bottleneck in a pipeline.

in either case. However, if the bottleneck is not subdivisible, using duplicates of the bottleneck in parallel is another way to smooth congestions, as depicted in Figure 3.32c. The control and synchronization of tasks in parallel segments are much more complex than those for cascaded segments.

Data and instruction buffers Another method to smooth the traffic flow in a pipeline is to use buffers to close up the speed gap between the memory accesses for either instructions or operands and the arithmetic logic executions in the functional pipes. The instruction or operand buffers provide a continuous supply of instructions or operands to the appropriate pipeline units. Buffering can avoid unnecessary idling of the processing stages caused by memory-access conflicts or by unexpected branching or interrupts. Sometimes the entire loop's instructions can be stored in the buffer to avoid repeated fetch of the same instruction loop, if the buffer size is sufficiently large. The amount of buffering is usually very large in pipeline computers.

The use of instruction buffers and various data buffers in the IBM System/ 360 Model 91 is shown in Figure 3.33. Three buffer types are used for various instruction and data types. Instructions are first fetched to the instruction-fetch buffers (64 bits each) before sending them to the instruction unit (Figure 3.15). After decoding, fixed-point and floating-point instructions and data are sent to their dedicated buffers, as labeled in Figure 3.33. The store-address and data buffers are used for continuously storing results back to the main memory. We have already explained the function of target buffers for instruction prefetches. The storage-conflict buffers are used only when memory-access conflicts are taking place.

In the STAR-100 system, a 64-word (of 128 bits each) buffer is used to temporarily hold the input data stream until operands are properly aligned. In addition, there is an instruction buffer which provides for the storage of thirty-two 64-bit instructions. Eight 64-bit words in the instruction buffer will be filled up by one memory fetch. The buffer supplies a continuous stream of instructions to be executed, despite memory-access conflicts.

In the TI-ASC system, two eight-word buffers are utilized to balance the stream of instructions from the memory to the execution unit. A *memory buffer unit* has three double buffers, X, Y, and Z. Two buffers (X and Y) are used to hold the input operands and the third (Z buffer) is used for the output results. These buffers greatly alleviate the problem of mismatched bandwidths between the memory and the arithmetic pipelines.

In the Floating-Point Systems AP-120B, there are two blocks of registers serving as operand buffers for the pipeline multiplier and adder. In the Cray-1 system, eight 64-bit scalar registers and sixty-four 64-bit data buffers are used for scalar operands. Eight 64-word vector registers are used as operand buffers for vector operations. There are also four instruction buffers in the Cray-1, each consisting of sixty-four 16-bit registers. With four instruction buffers, substantial program segments can be prefetched to allow on-line arithmetic logic operations through the functional pipes.

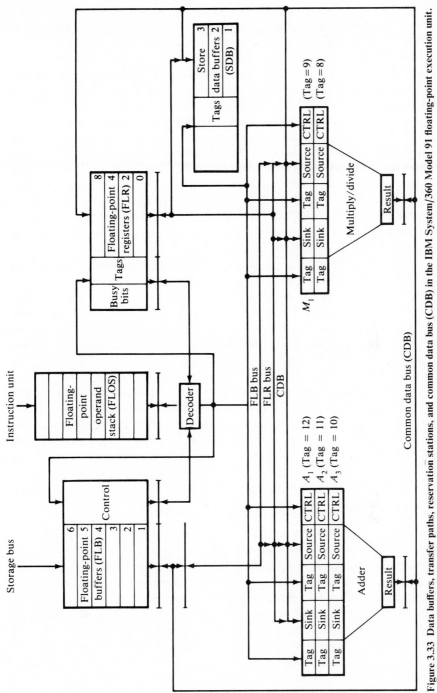

Figure 3.33 Data buffers, transfer paths, reservation stations, and common data bus (CDB) in the IBM System/360 Model 91 floating-point execution unit. (Courtesy of International Business Machines Corp.)

195

Busing structures Ideally, the subfunction being executed by one stage should be independent of the other subfunctions being executed by the remaining stages; otherwise, some processes in the pipeline must be halted until the dependency is removed. For example, when one instruction waiting to be executed is first to be modified by a future instruction, the execution of this instruction must be suspended until the dependency is released. Another example is the conflicting use of some registers or memory locations by different segments of a pipeline. These problems cause additional time delays. An efficient internal busing structure is desired to route results to the requesting stations with minimum time delays.

In the TI-ASC system, once instruction dependency is recognized, only independent instructions are distributed over the arithmetic units. Update capability is incorporated into the processor by transferring the contents of the Z buffer to the X buffer or the Y buffer. With such a busing structure, time delays due to dependency are significantly reduced. In the STAR-100 system, direct routes are established from the output transmit segment to the input receive segment. Thus, no registers are required to store the intermediate results, which causes a significant saving of data-forwarding delays.

In the AP-120B or FPS-164 attached processors, the busing structures are even more sophisticated. Seven data buses provide multiple data paths. The output of the floating-point adder in the AP-120B can be directly routed back to the input of the floating-point adder, to the input of the floating-point multiplier, to the data pad, or to the data memory. Similar busing is provided for the output of the floating-point multiplier. This eliminates the time delay to store and to retrieve the intermediate results to or from the registers.

In the Cray-1 system, multiple data paths are also used to interconnect various functional units and the register and memory files. Although efficient busing structures can reduce the damaging effects of instruction interdependencies, a great burden is still exerted on the compiler to produce codes exposing parallelism. If independent and dependent instructions are intermixed appropriately, more concurrent processing can take place in a multiple-pipe computer.

3.3.3 Internal Forwarding and Register Tagging

Two techniques are introduced in this section for enhancing the performance of computers with multiple execution pipelines. *Internal forwarding* refers to a "short-circuit" technique for replacing unnecessary memory accesses by register-to-register transfers in a sequence of fetch-arithmetic-store operations. *Register tagging* refers to the use of tagged registers, buffers, and reservation stations for exploiting concurrent activities among multiple arithmetic units. We will explain how these techniques have been applied in the IBM System/360 Model 91, which has multiple execution units with common data buffers and data paths. The application of these techniques is not limited to floating-point arithmetic or the System/360 architecture. It may be used in almost any computer that has multiple functional pipelines and accumulators.

It is well understood that memory access is much slower than register-to-register operations. The computer performance can be greatly enhanced if one can eliminate unnecessary memory accesses and combine some transitive or multiple fetch-store operations with faster register operations. This concept of internal data forwarding can be explored in three directions, as illustrated in Figure 3.34. We use the symbols M_i and R_j to represent the ith word in the memory and the jth register in the CPU. We use arrows $\leftarrow$ to specify data-moving operations such as fetch, store, and register-to-register transfer. The contents of M_i and R_j are represented by (M_i) and (R_j), respectively.

Store-fetch forwarding The following sequence of the two operations store-then-fetch can be replaced by two parallel operations, one store and one register transfer, as shown in Figure 3.34a:

$$\left.\begin{array}{ll} M_i \leftarrow (R_1) & \text{(store)} \\ R_2 \leftarrow (M_i) & \text{(fetch)} \end{array}\right\} \text{Two memory accesses}$$

being replaced by

$$\left.\begin{array}{ll} M_i \leftarrow (R_1) & \text{(store)} \\ R_2 \leftarrow (R_1) & \text{(register transfer)} \end{array}\right\} \text{Only one memory access}$$

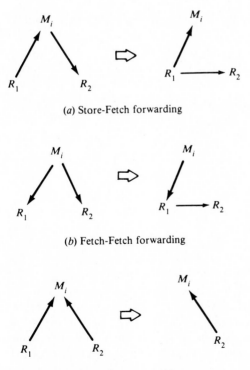

(a) Store-Fetch forwarding

(b) Fetch-Fetch forwarding

(c) Store-Store overwriting

Figure 3.34 Internal forwarding examples (thick arrows for slow memory accesses and thin arrows for fast register transfers).

Fetch-fetch forwarding The following two fetch operations can be replaced by one fetch and one register transfer, as shown in Figure 3.34b. Again one memory access has been eliminated:

$$\left. \begin{array}{ll} R_1 \leftarrow (M_i) & \text{(fetch)} \\ R_2 \leftarrow (M_i) & \text{(fetch)} \end{array} \right\} \text{Two memory accesses}$$

being replaced by

$$\left. \begin{array}{ll} R_1 \leftarrow (M_i) & \text{(fetch)} \\ R_2 \leftarrow (R_1) & \text{(register transfer)} \end{array} \right\} \text{One memory access}$$

Store-store overwriting The following two memory updates (stores) of the same word (Figure 3.34c) can be combined into one, since the second store overwrites the first:

$$\left. \begin{array}{ll} M_i \leftarrow (R_1) & \text{(store)} \\ M_i \leftarrow (R_2) & \text{(store)} \end{array} \right\} \text{Two memory accesses}$$

being replaced by

$$M_i \leftarrow (R_2) \quad \text{(store)} \quad \text{One memory access}$$

The following example shows how to apply internal forwarding to simplify a sequence of arithmetic and memory-access operations. Figure 3.35 depicts these simplification steps, in which adjacent steps are combined to minimize memory references. Nodes in the graph correspond to the memory cells, registers, an adder, or a multiplier.

Example 3.1 The inner loop of a certain program is completed to perform the following operations in a sequence:

1. $R_0 \leftarrow (M_1)$ (fetch)
2. $R_0 \leftarrow (R_0) + (M_2)$ (add)
3. $R_0 \leftarrow (R_0) * (M_3)$ (multiply)
4. $M_4 \leftarrow R_0$ (store)

After the internal forwarding, we end up handling a compound function (macroinstruction) $M_4 \leftarrow [(M_1) + (M_2)] * (M_3)$, as represented by the simplified data-flow graph in Figure 3.35d.

Both internal forwarding and resource tagging have been practiced in the IBM Model 91 floating-point execution unit. The data registers, transfer paths, floating-point adder and multiply-divide units, reservation stations, and the *common data bus* (CDB) in the Model 91 were shown in Figure 3.33. The three reservation stations for the adder are denoted as A_1, A_2, A_3. The two reservation stations in the multiply-divide unit are M_1 and M_2. Each station has the source and sink registers and their tag and control fields. The stations can hold operands for the next execution while the functional unit is busy executing current instruction.

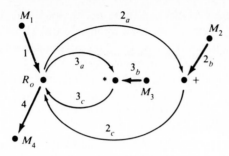

(a) Original data flow sequence

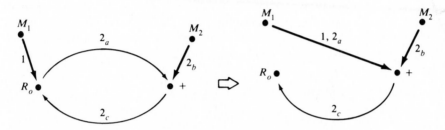

(b) Step 1 and step 2 forwarded

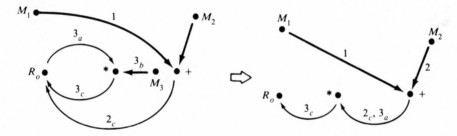

(c) Step 2 and step 3 forwarded

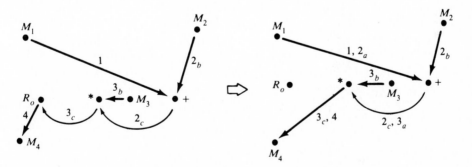

(d) Step 3 and step 4 forwarded

Figure 3.35 Internal data forwarding in Example 3.1 (memory accesses: thick arrows; register transfers: thin arrows).

Three *store data buffers* (SDB) and four *floating-point registers* (FLR) are all tagged. The busy bits in the FLRs marking their status (1 for busy and 0 for idle) can be used to determine the dependence of instructions in subsequent executions.

The CDB is used to transfer operands to the FLRs, the reservation stations, and the SDB. There are 11 units that can supply information to the CDB, including six floating-point buffers (FLB), three adder stations, and two multiply-divide stations. The tag fields of these units are binary-coded as FLBs $1 \sim 6$, add stations $10 \sim 12$, and multiply-divide stations $8 \sim 9$. A tag is generated by the CDB priority controls to identify the unit whose result will next appear on the CDB.

This common data busing and register-tagging scheme permits simultaneous execution of independent instructions while preserving the essential precedences inherent in the instruction stream. The CDB can function with any number of execution units and any number of accumulators. It provides a hardware algorithm for the automatic efficient exploitation of multiple arithmetic units. The following example shows how internal forwarding can be achieved with the tagging scheme on the CDB.

Example 3.2 Consider the consecutive execution of two floating-point instructions in the Model 91 (Figure 3.33), where F refers to an FLR which is being used as an accumulator and B_i stands for the ith FLB. Their contents are represented by (F) and (B_i), respectively:

$$\text{ADD} \quad \text{F, B}_1 \quad \text{F} \leftarrow (\text{F}) + (\text{B}_1)$$
$$\text{MPY} \quad \text{F, B}_2 \quad \text{F} \leftarrow (\text{F}) * (\text{B}_2)$$

In the processing of the *add* instruction, set the busy bit of F to 1, send the contents (F) and (B_1) to the adder station A_1, set the tag field of F to 1010 (the tag value of station A_1), and then carry out the addition.

In the meantime, the decode of the *mpy* (multiply) instruction reveals the fact that F is busy. This implies that the *mpy* depends on the result of the *add*. However, the execution should not be halted. Instead, the tag of F should be sent to the multiply station M_1 to set the tag of M_1 to be also 1010. Then the tag of F should be changed to 1000 (the tag value of station M_1) and the content (B_2) sent to M_1. When the *add* instruction is completed, the CDB finds that the addition result should be sent directly to M_1 (instead of F). The multiply-divide unit begins its execution when both operands become available. After the *mpy* operation is done, the CDB finds F via the tag 1000 of M_1, and thus sends the multiply result to F. In this process, the intermediate result (after addition) will not be sent to F before sending it to M_1. This is exactly a consequence of internal forwarding, using the tag as a vehicle to identify source and destination in successive computations.

3.3.4 Hazard Detection and Resolution

Pipeline hazards are caused by resource-usage conflicts among various instructions in the pipeline. Such hazards are triggered by interinstruction dependencies. In this section, we characterize various hazard conditions. Hazard-detection methods and approaches to resolve hazards are then introduced. Hazards discussed in this section are known as *data-dependent hazards*. Methods to cope with such hazards are needed in any type of lookahead processors for either synchronous-pipeline or asynchronous-multiprocessing systems. Another type of hazard is due to a job scheduling problem and will be described in Section 3.3.5.

When successive instructions overlap their fetch, decode and execution through a pipeline processor, interinstruction dependencies may arise to prevent the sequential data flow in the pipeline. For example, an instruction may depend on the results of a previous instruction. Until the completion of the previous instruction, the present instruction cannot be initiated into the pipeline. In other instances, two stages of a pipeline may need to update the same memory location. Hazards of this sort, if not properly detected and resolved, could result in an *interlock* situation in the pipeline or produce unreliable results by overwriting.

There are three classes of data-dependent hazards, according to various data update patterns: *write after read* (WAR) hazards, *read after write* (RAW) hazards, and *write after write* (WAW) hazards. Note that *read-after-read* does not pose a problem, because nothing is changed.

We use *resource objects* to refer to working registers, memory locations, and special flags. The contents of these resource objects are called *data objects*. Each instruction can be considered a mapping from a set of data objects to a set of data objects. The *domain* $D(I)$ of an instruction I is the set of resource objects whose data objects may affect the execution of instruction I. The *range* $R(I)$ of an instruction I is the set of resource objects whose data objects may be modified by the execution of instruction I. Obviously, the operands to be used in an instruction execution are retrieved (read) from its domain, and the results will be stored (written) in its range. In what follows, we consider the execution of the two instructions I and J in a program. Instruction J appears after instruction I in the program. There may be none or other instructions between instructions I and J. The latency between the two instructions is a very subtle matter. Instruction J may enter the execution pipe before or after the completion of the execution of instruction I. The improper timing and data dependencies may create some hazardous situations, as shown in Figure 3.36.

A RAW hazard between the two instructions I and J may occur when J attempts to read some data object that has been modified by I. A WAR hazard may occur when J attempts to modify some data object that is read by I. A WAW hazard may occur if both I and J attempt to modify the same data object. Formally, the necessary conditions for these hazards are stated as follows (Figure 3.32):

$$R(I) \cap D(J) \neq \phi \qquad \text{for RAW}$$

$$R(I) \cap R(J) \neq \phi \qquad \text{for WAW} \qquad (3.18)$$

$$D(I) \cap R(J) \neq \phi \qquad \text{for WAR}$$

Possible hazards for the four types of instructions (Table 3.1) are listed in Table 3.3. Recognizing the existence of possible hazards, computer designers wish to detect the hazard and then to resolve it effectively. Hazard detection can be done

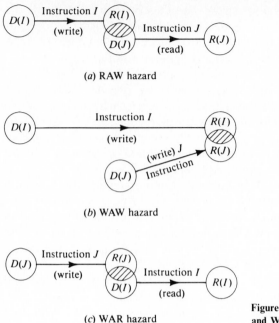

(a) RAW hazard

(b) WAW hazard

(c) WAR hazard

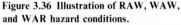

Figure 3.36 Illustration of RAW, WAW, and WAR hazard conditions.

in the instruction-fetch stage of a pipeline processor by comparing the domain and range of the incoming instruction with those of the instructions being processed in the pipe. Should any of the conditions in Eq. 3.18 be detected, a warning signal can be generated to prevent the hazard from taking place. Another approach is to allow the incoming instruction through the pipe and distribute the detection to all the potential pipeline stages. This distributed approach offers better flexibility at the expense of increased hardware control. Note that the necessary conditions in Eq. 3.18 may not be sufficient conditions.

Table 3.3 Possible hazards for various instruction types

	Instruction I (first)			
Instruction J (second)	Arithmetic and load type	Store type	Branch type	Conditional branch type
Arithmetic and load type	RAW WAW WAR	RAW WAR	WAR	WAR
Store type	RAW WAR	WAW		
Branch type	RAW		WAW	WAW
Conditional branch type	RAW		WAW	WAW

Once a hazard is detected, the system should resolve the interlock situation. Consider the instruction sequence $\{\ldots I, I + 1, \ldots, J, J + 1, \ldots\}$ in which a hazard has been detected between the current instruction J and a previous instruction I. A straightforward approach is to stop the pipe and to suspend the execution of instructions $J, J + 1, J + 2, \ldots$, until the instruction I has passed the point of resource conflict. A more sophisticated approach is to suspend only instruction J and continue the flow of instructions $J + 1, J + 2, \ldots$, down the pipe. Of course, the potential hazards due to the suspension of J should be continuously checked as instructions $J + 1, J + 2, \ldots$ move ahead of J. Multilevel hazard detection may be encountered, requiring much more complex control mechanisms to resolve a stack of hazards.

In order to avoid RAW hazards, IBM engineers developed a *short-circuiting* approach which gives a copy of the data object to be written directly to the instruction waiting to read the data. This concept was generalized into a technique, known as *data forwarding*, which forwards multiple copies of the data to as many waiting instructions as may wish to read it. A data-forwarding chain can be established in some cases. The internal-forwarding and register-tagging techniques presented in the previous section should be helpful in resolving logic hazards in pipelines.

3.3.5 Job Sequencing and Collision Prevention

Once a task is initiated in a static pipeline, its flow pattern is fixed. An *initiation* refers to the start of a single function evaluation. When two or more initiations attempt to use the same stage at the same time, a *collision* results. Thus the job-sequencing problem is to properly schedule queued tasks awaiting initiation in order to avoid collisions and to achieve high throughput. The reservation table introduced in Section 3.1.3 identifies the space-time flow pattern of one complete data through the pipeline for one function evaluation. In a static pipeline, all initiations are characterized by the same reservation table. On the other hand, successive initations for a dynamic pipeline may be characterized by a set of reservation tables, one per each function being evaluated.

Figure 3.37 shows the reservation table for a unifunction pipeline. The multiple $\times$'s in a row pose the possibility of collisions. The number of time units between two initiations is called the *latency*, which may be any positive integer. For a static pipeline, the latency is usually one, two, or greater. However, zero latency is allowed in dynamic pipelines between different functions. The sequence of latencies between successive initiations is called *latency sequence*. A latency sequence that repeats itself is called a *latency cycle*. The procedure to choose a latency sequence is called a *control strategy*. A control strategy that always minimizes the latency between the current initiation and the very last initiation is called a *greedy strategy*. A greedy strategy is made independent of future initiations.

A collision occurs when two tasks are initiated with a latency (initiation interval) equal to the column distance between two $\times$'s on some row of the reservation table. The set of column distances $F = \{l_1, l_2, \ldots, l_r\}$ between all possible

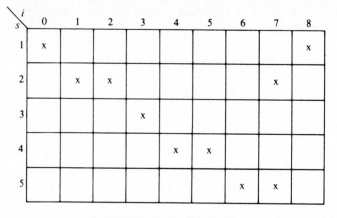

Forbidden list: $F = \{1,5,6,8\}$
Collision vector: $C = (10110001)$

(a) Reservation table and related terms

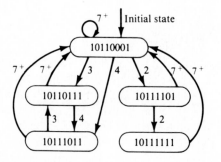

The notation 7^+ means any integer (latency) equal to 7 or greater than 7.

(b) State diagram with MAL = (3 + 4)/2 = 3.5

Figure 3.37 Reservation table and state diagram for a unifunction pipeline.

pairs of ×'s on each row of the reservation table is called the *forbidden set of latencies*. The forbidden set contains all possible latencies that cause collisions between two initiations. The *collision vector* is a binary vector, shown below:

$$C = (C_n \cdots C_2 C_1) \qquad \text{where } C_i = 1 \text{ if } i \in F \text{ and } C_i = 0 \text{ if otherwise} \quad (3.18)$$

For the example in Figure 3.37, the forbidden list $F = \{1, 5, 6, 8\}$, and the collision vector $C = (10110001)$, where $n = 8$ is the largest forbidden latency obtained from the reservation table. This means $C_n = 1$ is always true. The collision vector shows both permitted and forbidden latencies from the same reservation table. One can use an n-bit shift register to hold the collision vector for implementing a control strategy for successive task initiations in the pipeline. Upon initiation of the first task, the collision vector is parallel-loaded into the shift register as the initial state. The shift register is then shifted right one bit at a time, entering 0s from the left end. A collision-free initiation is allowed at time instant $t + k$ if, and only if, a bit "0" is being shifted out of the register after k shifts from time t. A *state diagram* is used to characterize the successive initiations of tasks in the pipeline in order to find the shortest latency sequence to optimize the control strategy. A *state* on the diagram is represented by the contents of the shift register after the proper number of shifts is made, which is equal to the latency between the current and next task initiations.

As shown in Figure 3.37b, the initial state corresponds to the collision vector (10110001). There are four outgoing branches from the initial state, labeled by latencies 2, 3, 4, and 7, corresponding to, respectively, zero-bit positions C_2, C_3, C_4, and C_7 in the vector (10110001). By shifting right the vector (10110001) two positions, we obtain the vector (00101100). This vector is then bitwise *ored* with the collision vector (10110001) to produce a new collision vector (10111101) as the new state pointed to by the arc labeled 2. Similarly, one obtains the new state vectors (10110111) and (10111011) after shifting the latencies 3 and 4, respectively. The arc 7 branches back to the initial state. This shifting process should continue until no more new states can be generated. The shift register will be set to the initial state, if the latency (shift) is greater than or equal to n.

The successive collision vectors are used to prevent future task collisions with previously initiated tasks, while the collision vector C is used to prevent possible collisions with the current task. If a collision vector has a "1" in the ith bit (from the right) at time t, then the task sequence should avoid the initiation of a task at time $t + i$. The bitwise *oring* operations will avoid collisions in any workable latency sequence that can be traced on the state diagram. Closed loops or cycles in the state diagram indicate the steady-state sustainable latency sequences of task initiations without collisions. The *average latency* of a cycle is the sum of its latencies (period) divided by the number of states in the cycle. Any cycle can be entered from the initial state.

The cycle consisting of states (10110111) and (10111011) in Figure 3.37b has two latencies, three and four. This cycle has a period equal to $7 = 3 + 4$. The average latency of this cycle is $\frac{7}{2} = 3.5$. Another cycle, which consists of the states (10110001), (10111101), and (10111111), has the three latencies 2, 2, and 7, with a period of 11. Its average latency cycle equals $\frac{11}{3} = 3.66$. The throughput of a pipeline is inversely proportional to the reciprocal of the average latency. A latency sequence is called *permissible* if no collisions exist in the successive initiations governed by the given latency sequence. The maximum throughput is achieved by an optimal scheduling strategy that achieves the *minimum average latency* (MAL) without collisions. Thus, the job-sequencing problem is equivalent to finding a permissible latency cycle with the MAL in the state diagram. The maximum number of $\times$'s in any single row of the reservation table is a lower bound of the MAL. In other words, the MAL is always greater than or equal to the maximum number of check marks in any row of the reservation table.

Table 3.4 Simple cycles in Figure 3.37b

Simple cycle	Average latency
(7)	7
(3, 7)	5
(3, 4)†	3.5
(4, 3, 7)	4.6
(4, 7)	5.5
(2, 7)	4.5
(2, 2, 7)†	3.6
(3, 4, 7)	4.6

† Greedy cycles.

Simple cycles are those latency cycles in which each state appears only once per each iteration of the cycle. Listed in Table 3.4 are simple cycles and their average latencies for the state diagram shown in Figure 3.37b. A simple cycle is a *greedy cycle* if each latency contained in the cycle is the minimal latency (outgoing arc) from a state in the cycle. For Figure 3.37b, the cycles (3, 4) and (2, 2, 7) are both greedy, with average latencies of 3.5 and 3.6, respectively. A good task-initiation sequence should include the greedy cycle.

The procedure to determine the greedy cycles on the state diagram is rather straightforward. From each node of the state diagram, one simply chooses the arc with the smallest latency label until a closed simple cycle can be formed. The average latency of any greedy cycle is no greater than the number of latencies in the forbidden set, which equals the number of 1s in the initial collision vector. The average latency of any greedy cycle is always lower-bounded by the MAL. In the above example, the greedy cycle (3, 4) has an average latency equal to the MAL = 3.5, which is smaller than 4, the number of 1s in the initial collision vector.

The job-sequencing method for static unifunction pipelines can be generalized for designing multifunction pipelines. A pipeline processor which can perform p distinct functions can be described by p reservation tables overlaid together. In order to perform multiple functions, the pipeline must be reconfigurable. One example of a static multifunction pipeline is the arithmetic pipelines in TI-ASC, which has eight stages with about 20 possible functional configurations. Each task to be initiated can be associated with a function tag identifying the reservation table to be used. Collisions may occur between two or more tasks with the same function tag or from distinct function tags.

The stage-usage pattern for each function can be displayed with a different tag in the overlaid reservation table. For a p-function pipeline, an overlaid reservation table is formed by overlaying p unifunctional reservation tables. An overlaid reservation table for a two-function pipeline is shown in Figure 3.38a, where A and B stand for two distinct functions. Each task-requesting initiation must be associated with a function tag. A *forbidden set of latencies* for a multifunction pipeline is the collection of collision-causing latencies. A task with function tag

t s	0	1	2	3	4
1	A	B		A	B
2		A		B	
3	B		AB		A

(*a*) Reservation table of a two-function pipeline

Cross collision vectors:

$$
\begin{array}{ll}
& C_4\ C_3\ C_2\ C_1 \\
V_{AA} = & (0\ \ 1\ \ 1\ \ 0) \\
V_{BA} = & (1\ \ 0\ \ 1\ \ 0)
\end{array}
\qquad
\begin{array}{ll}
& C_4\ C_3\ C_2\ C_1 \\
V_{AA} = & (1\ \ 0\ \ 1\ \ 1) \\
V_{BA} = & (0\ \ 1\ \ 1\ \ 0)
\end{array}
$$

Collision matrices:

$$
M_A = \begin{pmatrix} 0110 & \text{(AA)} \\ 1010 & \text{(BA)} \end{pmatrix}
\qquad
M_B = \begin{pmatrix} 1011 & \text{(AB)} \\ 0110 & \text{(BB)} \end{pmatrix}
$$

(*b*) Cross collision vectors and collision matrices

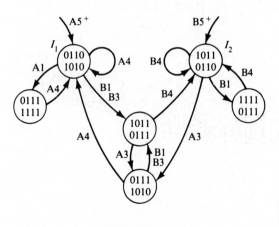

(*c*) State diagram

Figure 3.38 Reservation table, cross collision vectors, collision matrices, and state diagram for a multifunction pipeline.

A may collide with a previously initiated task with function tag B if the latency between these two initiations is a member of the forbidden list.

A *cross-collision vector* V_{AB} marks the forbidden latencies between the function pair A and B. The binary vector V_{AB} may be calculated by overlaying the reservation tables for A and B. A component $C_k = 1$ if some row of the overlaid reservation table contains an A in column t (for some t) and a B in column $t + k$; the component C_k equals 0, if otherwise. Thus, Figure 3.38 has four cross-collision vectors: $V_{AA} =$ (0 1 1 0), $V_{AB} = $ (1 0 1 1), $V_{BA} = $ (1 0 1 0), and $V_{BB} = $ (0 1 1 0). In general, there are p^2 cross-collision vectors for a p-function pipeline. The p^2 cross-collision vectors can be rewritten into p *collision matrices*, as shown in Figure 3.34b. The collision matrix M_R indicates forbidden latencies for all functions initiated after the initiation of a task with the function tag R. The ith row in matrix M_R is the cross-collision vector V_{IR}, where $i = 1, 2, \ldots, p$.

A p-function pipeline can be controlled by a bank of p shift registers. Shift register Q controls the initiation of function Q. The control bits for function initiations are the righmost bit of each shift register. Initiation of a task with function tag Q is allowed at the next time instant if the rightmost bit of the corresponding shift register Q is 0. The shift registers shift right one position per each cycle, with 0s entering from the left. Immediately after the initiation of a task with function tag Q, the collision matrix M_Q is *or*ed with the matrix formed by the bank of shift registers. The state of the shift register Q is bitwise *or*ed with the cross-collision vector V_{IQ} for all $1 \le Q \le p$.

A state diagram is constructed in Figure 3.38c for the two-function pipeline. Arcs are labeled with the latency and the function tag of the initiation. The initial state can be one of the p collision matrices. Cycles in the state diagram correspond to collision-free patterns of task initiations. Any cycle can be entered from at least one of the initial states. For example, the cycle (A3, B1) in Figure 3.38c can be reached by an arc labelled A3 from initial state I_2 or by an arc B1 from initial state I_1. The method of finding the greedy cycles and the MAL on the state diagram of a multifunction pipeline can be extended from that for a unifunction pipeline.

3.3.6 Dynamic Pipelines and Reconfigurability

A dynamic pipeline may initiate tasks from different reservation tables simultaneously to allow multiple numbers of initiations of different functions in the same pipeline. Two methods for improving the throughput of dynamic pipeline processors have been proposed by Davidson and Patel (1978). The reservation of a pipeline can be modified with the insertion of *noncompute delays* or with the use of internal buffers at each stage. The utilization of the stages and, hence, the throughput of the pipe can be greatly enhanced with a modified reservation table yielding a more desirable latency pattern.

It is assumed that any computation step can be delayed by inserting a non-compute stage. We consider first a unifunction pipeline. A *constant latency cycle* is a cycle with only one latency. A latency between two tasks is said to be *allowable* if these two tasks do not collide in the pipeline. Consequently, a cycle is allowable in a pipeline if all the latencies in the cycle are allowable. Our main concern so far has been to find an allowable cycle which results in the MAL. However, an allowable cycle with the MAL does not necessarily imply 100 percent utilization of the pipeline where utilization is measured as the percentage of time the busiest stage remains busy. When a latency cycle results in a 100 percent utilization of at least one of the pipeline stages, the periodic latency sequence is called a *perfect cycle*. Of course, pipelines with perfect cycles can be better utilized than those with nonperfect initiation cycles. It is trivial to note that constant cycles are all perfect.

Consider a latency cycle C. The set G_C of all possible time intervals between initiations derived from cycle C is called an *initiation interval set*. For example, $G_C = \{4, 8, 12, \ldots\}$ for $C = (4)$, and $G_C = \{2, 3, 5, 7, 9, 10, 12, 14, 15, 17, 19, 21, 22, 24, 26, \ldots\}$ for $C = (2, 3, 2, 5)$. Note that the interval is not restricted to two adjacent initiations. Let $G_C(\bmod\ p)$ be the set formed by taking mod p equivalents of all elements of set G_C. For the cycle $(2, 3, 2, 5)$ with period $p = 12$, the set $G_C(\bmod\ 12) = \{0, 2, 3, 5, 7, 9, 10\}$. The complement set $\bar{G}_C$ equals $Z - G_C$ where Z is the set of positive integers. Clearly, we have $\bar{G}_C(\bmod\ p) = Z(\bmod\ p) - G_C(\bmod\ p)$, where Z_p is the set of positive integers of modulo p. A latency cycle C with a period p and an initiation interval set G_C is allowable in a pipeline with a forbidden latency set F if, and only if,

$$F(\bmod\ p) \cap G_C(\bmod\ p) = \phi \qquad (3.19)$$

This means that there will be no collision if none of the initiation intervals equals a forbidden latency. Thus, a constant cycle (l) with a period $p = l$ is allowed for a pipeline processor if, and only if, l does not divide any forbidden latency in the set F. Another way of looking at the problem is to choose a reservation table whose forbidden latency set F is a subset of the set $\bar{G}_C(\bmod\ p)$. Then the latency cycle C will be an allowable sequence for the pipeline. For example, the latency cycle $C = (2, 3, 2, 5)$, $G_C(\bmod\ 12) = \{0, 2, 3, 5, 7, 9, 10\}$ and $\bar{G}_C(\bmod\ 12) = \{1, 4, 6, 8, 11\}$, so C can be applied to a pipeline with a forbidden latency set F equal to any subset of $\{1, 4, 6, 8, 11\}$. This condition is very effective to check the applicability (allowability) of an initiation sequence (or a cycle) to a given pipeline, or one can modify the reservation table of a pipeline to yield a forbidden list which is confined within the set $\bar{G}_C(\bmod\ p)$, if the cycle C is fixed.

Adding noncompute stages to a pipeline can make it allowable for a given cycle. The effect of delaying some computation steps can be seen from the reservation table by writing a d before the step being delayed. Each d indicates one unit of delay, called an *elemental delay*. It is assumed that all steps in a column must complete before any steps in the next column are executed. In Figure 3.39a, the effect of delaying the step in row 0 and column 2 by two time units and the step in row 2 and column 2 by one time unit is shown in Figure 3.39b. The elemental delays d_1, d_2, and d_3 require the use of the additional delays d_4, d_5, and d_6 to make all the outputs simultaneously available in column 2 of the original reservation table.

For a given constant latency cycle (l), a pipeline can be made allowable by delaying some of the steps if, and only if, there are no more than l marks in each

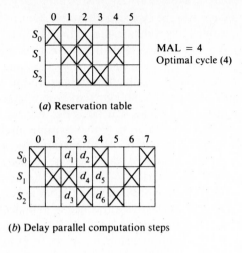

(a) Reservation table

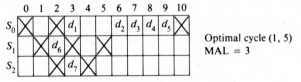

(b) Delay parallel computation steps

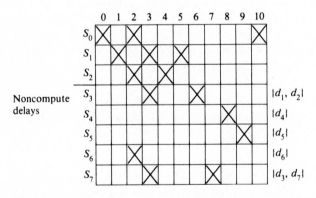

(c) Inserting delays to make the pipeline allowable for the optimal cycle (1, 5)

(d) Assignment of elemental delays to noncompute segments

Figure 3.39 Pipeline with inserted noncomputer delays.

row of the table. Thus by adding elemental delays, a unifunction pipeline can always be fully utilized through the use of a cycle that has a constant latency equal to the maximum number of marks in any row of the reservation table. The maximum achievable throughput of that pipeline is thereby attained. On the other hand, for an arbitrary cycle, a pipeline can be made allowable by delaying some steps. The reservation table of Figure 3.39a can be made allowable with respect to the optimal cycle (1, 5) by adding some elemental delays. The resulting table is shown in Figure 3.39c. Once a modified table is obtained, it is necessary to assign the elemental delays to noncompute stages. Noncompute stages may be shared by various elemental delays. Figure 3.39d shows the modified reservation table after the introduction of the noncompute stages S_3, S_4, S_5, S_6, and S_7.

The task arrivals in a pipeline processor may be periodic for a program with inner loops. If we assume that each task can only occupy one stage at a time, no parallel computations can be done within a single task. Such an assumption stems from the practical difficulties encountered in implementing a priority scheme involving parallel computations of a task. Once some buffers are provided internally, the task-scheduling problem can be greatly simplified. Whenever two or more tasks are trying to use the same stage, only one of the tasks is allowed to use the stage, while the rest wait in the buffers according to some priority schemes.

There are two different implementations of internal buffers in a pipeline: The first uses one buffer for each stage (Figure 3.40a), and the second uses one buffer per computation step (Figure 3.40b). For one buffer per stage, two priority schemes, *FIFO-global* and *LIFO-global*, can be used. In the FIFO-global scheme, a task has priority over all tasks initiated later. In the LIFO-global scheme, a task has priority over all tasks initiated earlier. For one buffer per computation step, multiple buffers may be used in each segment with the following priorities: MPF: most processed first; LPF: least processed first; LWRF: least work remaining first; and MWRF: most work remaining first.

Reconfigurable pipelines with different function types are more desirable. Such an approach requires extensive resource-sharing among different functions. To achieve this, a more complicated structure of pipeline segments and their inter-connection controls is needed. Bypass techniques can be used to avoid unwanted

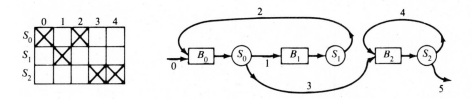

(a) Insert one buffer for each segment of a unifunction pipeline

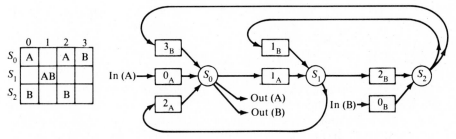

(b) Insert one buffer for each computation step of a two-function pipeline

Figure 3.40 Inserting buffers to improve the pipeline utilization rate.

stages. This may cause a collision when one instruction, as a result of bypassing, attempts to use the operands fetched for preceding instructions. To alleviate this problem, one solution has each instruction activate a number of consecutive stages down the pipeline which satisfy its need.

A dynamic pipeline would allow several configurations to be simultaneously present. For example, a dynamic-pipeline arithmetic unit could perform addition and multiplication at the same time. Tremendous control overhead and increased interconnection complexity would be expected. None of the existing pipeline processors has achieved this dynamic capability. Most commercial pipelines are static. In TI-ASC, the desired control allows different instructions to assume different data paths through the arithmetic pipeline at different times. All path-control information is stored in a *read-only memory* (ROM), which can be accessed at the initiation of an instruction.

The configuration for floating-point addition in TI-ASC (Figure 3.28b) requires four ROM words for its path-interconnection information. This forces the instruction execution logic to access the ROM for control signals. The ROM words for a *floating-point add* may be located at 100, 101, 102, and 103, while the words for a *floating-point subtract* could be located at 200, 101, 102, and 103. The common ROM words (101, 102, 103) used by both operations represent similar suboperations contained in these two instructions. The starting ROM address is supplied by the instruction-execution logic directly after the decode of the instruction.

The pipeline configuration for a floating-point vector *dot product* in TI-ASC was depicted in Figure 3.28c. If the dot product operated upon 1000 operands, the pipeline would be in this configuration for 1000 clock periods. Scalar instructions in ASC use different control sequences. When several scalar instructions in a sequence are of a common type, the instructions streaming through the arithmetic pipeline can be treated as vectors. This requires a careful selection of ROM output signals to allow the maximum overlapping of instructions. The ability to overlap instructions of the same type is achieved by studying the utilization of each pipeline segment. Overlaying identical patterns gives the minimum number of clock periods per result. The two static arithmetic pipeline processors in STAR-100 are reconfigurable with variable structures. Variable structure and resource sharing are of central importance to designing multifunction pipelines. Systematic procedures are yet to be developed for designing dynamically reconfigurable pipelines.

3.4 VECTOR PROCESSING REQUIREMENTS

In this section, we explain the basic concepts of vector processing and the necessary implementation requirements. We distinguish vector processing from scalar processing, present the characteristics of vector instructions, and define the performance measures of vector processors. We present a parallel vector scheduling model for multipipeline supercomputers. Three vector processing methods will be introduced for pipeline computers. After examining the architectures of various pipeline computers, we will study in Chapter 4 various vectorization methods and compiler-optimization problems.

3.4.1 Characteristics of Vector Processing

A vector operand contains an ordered set of n elements, where n is called the *length* of the vector. Each element in a vector is a scalar quantity, which may be a floating-point number, an integer, a logical value, or a character (byte). Vector instructions can be classified into four primitive types:

$$f_1 : V \to V$$
$$f_2 : V \to S$$
$$f_3 : V \times V \to V$$
$$f_4 : V \times S \to V$$

(3.20)

where V and S denote a vector operand and a scalar operand, respectively. The mappings f_1 and f_2 are unary operations and f_3 and f_4 are binary operations. As shown in Table 3.5, the VSQR (*vector square root*) is an f_1 operation, VSUM (*vector summation*) is an f_2 operation, SVP (*scalar-vector product*) is an f_4 operation, and VADD (*vector add*) is an f_3 operation. The *dot product* of two vectors $V_1 \cdot V_2 = \sum_{i=1}^{n} V_{1i} \cdot V_{2i}$ is generated by applying f_3 (vector multiply) and then f_2 (vector sum) operations in sequence. Listed in Table 3.5 are some representative vector operations that can be found in a modern vector processor. Pipelined implementation of the four basic vector operations is illustrated in Figure 3.41. Note that a feedback connection is needed in the f_2 operation.

Table 3.5 Some representative vector instructions

Type	Mnemonic	Description ($I = 1$ through N)	
f_1	VSQR	Vector square root:	$B(I) \leftarrow \sqrt{A(I)}$
	VSIN	Vector sine:	$B(I) \leftarrow \sin(A(I))$
	VCOM	Vector complement:	$A(I) \leftarrow \overline{A(I)}$
f_2	VSUM	Vector summation:	$S = \sum_{I=1}^{N} A(I)$
	VMAX	Vector maximum:	$S = \max_{I=1,N} A(I)$
f_3	VADD	Vector add:	$C(I) = A(I) + B(I)$
	VMPY	Vector multiply:	$C(I) = A(I) * B(I)$
	VAND	Vector and:	$C(I) = A(I)$ and $B(I)$
	VLAR	Vector larger:	$C(I) = \max(A(I), B(I))$
	VTGE	Vector test $>$:	$C(I) = 0$ if $A(I) < B(I)$
			$C(I) = 1$ if $A(I) > B(I)$
f_4	SADD	Vector-scalar add:	$B(I) = S + A(I)$
	SDIV	Vector-scalar divide:	$B(I) = A(I)/S$

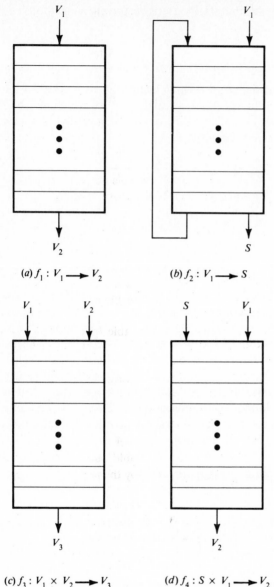

$(a) f_1 : V_1 \longrightarrow V_2$

$(b) f_2 : V_1 \longrightarrow S$

$(c) f_3 : V_1 \times V_2 \longrightarrow V_3$

$(d) f_4 : S \times V_1 \longrightarrow V_2$

Figure 3.41 Four vector instruction types for pipelined processor.

Some special instructions may be used to facilitate the manipulation of vector data. A *boolean vector* can be generated as a result of comparing two vectors, and can be used as a *masking vector* for enabling or disabling component operations in a vector instruction. A *compress* instruction will shorten a vector under the control of a masking vector. A *merge* instruction combines two vectors under the control of a masking vector. Compress and merge are special f_1 and f_3 operations because the resulting operand may have a length different from that of the input operands. Several examples are shown below to characterize these special vector operations.

Example 3.3 Let $X = (2, 5, 8, 7)$ and $Y = (9, 3, 6, 4)$. After the *compare* instruction $B = X > Y$ is executed, the boolean vector $B = (0, 1, 1, 1)$ is generated.

Let $X = (1, 2, 3, 4, 5, 6, 7, 8)$ and $B = (1, 0, 1, 0, 1, 0, 1, 0)$. After the execution of the *compress* instruction $Y = X(B)$, the compressed vector $Y = (1, 3, 5, 7)$ is generated.

Let $X = (1, 2, 4, 8)$, $Y = (3, 5, 6, 7)$, and $B = (1, 1, 0, 1, 0, 0, 0, 1)$. After the *merge* instruction $Z = X, Y, (B)$, the result is $Z = (1, 2, 3, 4, 5, 6, 7, 8)$. The first 1 in B indicates that $Z(1)$ is selected from the first element of X. Similarly, the first 0 in B indicates that $Z(3)$ is selected from the first element of Y.

In general, machine operations suitable for pipelining should have the following properties:

a. Identical processes (or functions) are repeatedly invoked many times, each of which can be subdivided into subprocesses (or subfunctions).
b. Successive operands are fed through the pipeline segments and require as few buffers and local controls as possible.
c. Operations executed by distinct pipelines should be able to share expensive resources, such as memories and buses, in the system.

These characteristics explain why most vector processors have pipeline structures. Vector instructions need to perform the same operation on different data sets repeatedly. This is not true for scalar processing over a single pair of operands. One obvious advantage of vector processing over scalar processing is the elimination of the overhead caused by the loop-control mechanism. Because of the startup delay in a pipeline, a vector processor should perform better with longer vectors. Vector instructions are usually specified by the following fields:

1. The *operation code* must be specified in order to select the functional unit or to reconfigure a multifunctional unit to perform the specified operation. Usually, microcode control is used to set up the required resources.
2. For a memory-reference instruction, the *base addresses* are needed for both source operands and result vectors. If the operands and results are located in the vector register file, the designated *vector registers* must be specified.
3. The *address increment* between the elements must be specified. Some computers, like the Star-100, restrict the elements to be consecutively stored in the main memory, i.e., the increment is always 1. Some other computers, like TI-ASC, can have a variable increment, which offers higher flexibility in application.
4. The *address offset* relative to the base address should be specified. Using the base address and the offset, the effective memory address can be calculated. The offset, either positive or negative, offers the use of skewed vectors to achieve parallel accesses.

5. The *vector length* is needed to determine the termination of a vector instruction. A masking vector may be used to mask off some of the elements without changing the contents of the original vectors.

We can classify pipeline vector computers into two architectural configurations according to where the operands are retrieved in a vector processor. One class is the *memory-to-memory* architecture, in which source operands, intermediate and final results are retrieved directly from the main memory. For memory-to-memory vector instructions, the information of the base address, the offset, the increment, and the vector length must be specified in order to enable streams of data transfers between the main memory and the pipelines. Vector instructions in the TI-ASC, the CDC STAR-100, and the Cyber-205 have a memory-to-memory format. The other class has a *register-to-register* architecture, in which operands and results are retrieved indirectly from the main memory through the use of a large number of vector or scalar registers. Vector instructions in the Cray-1 and the Fujitsu VP-200 use a register-to-register format. The example below demonstrates the difference between these two vector-instruction formats.

To examine the efficiency of vector processing over scalar processing, we compare the following two programs, one written for vector processing and the other written for scalar processing.

Example 3.4 In a conventional scalar processor, the Fortran DO loop

```
        DO 100 I=1, N
        A(I)=B(I)+C(I)
100     B(I)=2*A(I+1)
```

is implemented by the following sequence of scalar operations:

```
        INITIALIZE I=1
10      READ B(I)
        READ C(I)
        ADD B(I)+C(I)
        STORE A(I)←B(I)+C(I)
        READ A(I+1)
        MULTIPLY 2*A(I+1)
        STORE B(I)←2*A(I+1)
        INCREMENT I←I+1
        IF I≤N GO TO 10
        STOP
```

In a vector processor, the above DO loop operations can be vectorized into three vector instructions in a sequence:

```
A(1:N)=B(1:N)+C(1:N)
TEMP(1:N)=A(2:N+1)
B(1,N)=2*TEMP(1:N)
```

where $A(1:N)$ refers to the N-element vector $A(1)$, $A(2)$, ..., $A(N)$. The introduction of the TEMP$(1:N)$ vector is necessary to enable the vectorization.

The execution of the scalar loop repeats the loop-control overhead in each iteration. In vector processing using pipelines, the overhead is reduced by using hardware or firmware controls. A vector-length register can be used to control the vector operations. The overhead of pipeline processing is mainly the *setup time*, which is needed to route the operands among functional units. For example, in the ASC and Star-100 systems, each vector instruction needs to get some vector-parameter registers or control vectors before the instruction can be initiated. Thus, many additional memory fetches are needed to load the control registers. Another overhead is the *flushing time* between the decoding of a vector instruction and the exit of the first result from the pipeline. The flushing time exists for both vector and scalar processing; however, a vector pipe has to check the termination condition and the control vectors. Therefore, a vector pipe may have a longer flush time than its sequential counterpart.

The vector length affects the processing efficiency because of the additional overhead caused by subdividing a long vector. In order to enhance the vector-processing capability, an optimized object code must be produced to maximize the utilization of pipeline resources. The following approaches have been suggested:

Enrich the vector instruction set With a richer instruction set, the processing capability will be enhanced. One can avoid excessive memory accesses and poor resource utilization with an improved instruction set. The compress instruction in Example 3.3 was a good example of saving memory.

Combine scalar instructions Using a pipeline for processing scalar quantities, one should group scalar instructions of the same type together as a batch instead of interleaving them. The overhead due to the pipeline reconfiguration can be greatly reduced by grouping scalar instructions.

Choose suitable algorithms Often a fast algorithm that is implemented in a serial processor may not be at all effective in a pipelined processor. For example, the merge-sort algorithm is more suitable for pipelining because the machine can merge two ordered vectors in one pass.

Use a vectorizing compiler An intelligent compiler must be developed to detect the concurrency among vector instructions which can be realized with pipelining or with the chaining of pipelines. A vectorizing compiler would regenerate parallelism lost in the use of sequential languages. It is desirable to use high-level programming languages with rich parallel constructs on vector processors. The following four stages have been recognized in the development of parallelism in advanced programming. The parameter in parentheses indicates the degree of parallelism explorable at each stage:

- Parallel *a*lgorithm (A)
- High-level *l*anguage (L)
- Efficient *o*bject code (O)
- Target *m*achine code (M)

The degree of parallelism refers to the number of independent operations that can be performed simultaneously. We wish to find a suitable algorithm with a high parallelism (A) to solve large-scale matrix problems. We also need to develop *parallel languages* to express parallelism (L). Unfortunately, no parallel language standards have yet been universally accepted. At present, most users still write their source code in sequential languages.

In sequential languages like Fortran, Pascal, and Algol, we still have $L = 1$. The natural parallelism in a machine is determined by the hardware. For example, the Cray-1 has $O = M = 64$ or 32. In the ideal situation with well-developed parallel user languages, we should expect $A \geq L \geq O \geq M$, as illustrated in Figure 3.42*a*. At present, any parallelism in an algorithm is lost when it is expressed in a sequential high-level language. In order to promote parallel processing in machine hardware, an intelligent compiler is needed to regenerate the parallelism through vectorization, as illustrated by Figure 3.42*b*. The process to replace a block of sequential code by vector instructions is called *vectorization*. The system software which does this regeneration of parallelism is called a *vectorizing compiler*. In Chapter 4, we will study attempts at developing parallel constructs in high-level languages and then discuss desired features in vectorizing compilers.

3.4.2 Multiple Vector Task Dispatching

A parallel task-scheduling model is presented for multi-pipeline vector processors. This model can be applied to explore maximum concurrency in vector supercomputers. The functional block diagram of a modern multiple-pipeline vector computer is shown in Figure 3.43. This structure is generalized from the existing modern vector processors. The main memory is often interleaved to minimize the access time of vector operands. Instructions and data may appear in either vector or scalar formats. The *instruction processing unit* (IPU) fetches and decodes scalar and vector instructions. All scalar instructions are dispatched to the *scalar processor* for execution. The scalar processor itself contains multiple scalar pipelines.

A *task system* contains a set of vector instructions (tasks) with a precedence relation determined only by data dependencies. A long vector task can be partitioned into many subvectors, to be processed by several pipelines concurrently. An increase in system overhead may be incurred with vector segmentations. It has been proved by Hwang and Su (1983) that the multi-pipeline scheduling problem is *NP*-complete, even for restricted task classes. Heuristic-scheduling algorithms are thus desirable for parallel vector processing.

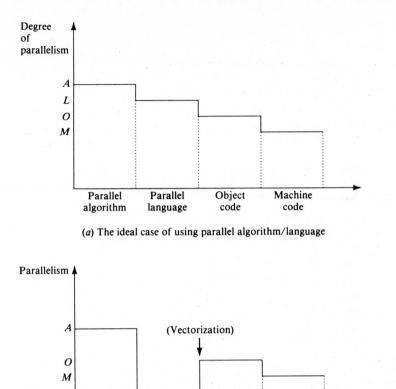

(a) The ideal case of using parallel algorithm/language

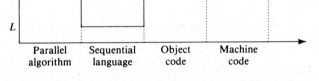
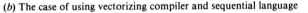

(b) The case of using vectorizing compiler and sequential language

Figure 3.42 Parallelism regeneration in using a vectorizing compiler for programs written in sequential language.

After a vector instruction is recognized by the IPU, the *vector instruction controller* takes over in supervising its execution. The functions of this controller include decoding vector instructions, calculating effective vector-operand address-es, setting up the vector access controller and the *vector processor*, and monitoring the execution of vector instructions. We consider here a very capable vector in-struction controller which can partition a vector task and schedule different instructions to different functional pipelines. In most commercial vector processors, identical pipelines must execute the same vector instruction at the same time. The vector machine model being presented has a structure generalized from the commercial machines. The *vector access controller* is responsible for fetching vector operands by a series of main memory accesses. The *vector registers* are used to close up the speed gap between the main memory and the vector processor. In

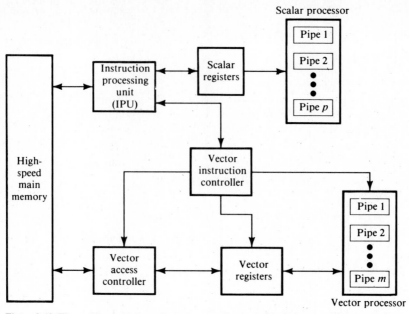

Figure 3.43 The architecture of a typical vector processor with multiple functional pipes.

the following discussions, we assume m homogeneous vector pipelines in the vector processor, each of which is unifunctional or static-multifunctional.

We shall concentrate on scheduling vector tasks exclusively. The vector instruction controller in Figure 3.43 is capable of scheduling several vector instructions simultaneously. The time required to complete the execution of a single vector task is measured by $t_o + \tau$, where t_o is the *pipeline overhead time* due to startup and flushing delays, $\tau = t_l \cdot L$ is the *production delay*, t_l is the *average latency* between two successive operand pairs, and L is the *vector length* (the number of component operands in a vector). The startup time is measured from the initiation of the vector instruction to the entrance of the first operand pair into the pipeline. Parameters t_o and t_l vary with different vector instructions. The overhead time t_o may vary from tens to several hundreds of pipeline cycles. The average latency t_l is usually one or two pipeline cycles. It is reasonable to assume that $t_o \gg t_l$.

Given a task system, we wish to schedule the vector tasks among m identical pipelines such that the total execution time is minimized. To simplify the modeling, we assume equal overhead time t_o for all vector tasks. A *vector task system* can be characterized by a triple:

$$V = (T, <, \tau) \tag{3.21}$$

where

1. $T = \{T_1, T_2, \ldots, T_n\}$ is a set of n vector tasks.

2. $<$ is a partial ordering relation, specifying the precedence relationship among the tasks in set T.
3. $\tau: T \rightarrow R^+$ is a time function defining the production delay $\tau(T_i)$ for each T_i in T. We shall denote the value $\tau(T_i)$ simply as τ_i for all $i = 1, 2, \ldots, n$.

Let $P = \{P_1, P_2, \ldots, P_m\}$ be the set of vector pipelines and R^2 be the set of possible time intervals. The utilization of a pipeline P_i within interval $[x, y]$ is denoted by $P_i(x, y)$. The set of all possible pipeline-utilization patterns is called the *resource space*, which is equal to the cartesian product $P \times R^2 = \{P_i(x, y) | P_i \in P$ and $(x, y) \in R^2\}$. A parallel schedule f for a vector task system $V = (T, <, \tau)$ is a total function defined by

$$f : T \rightarrow 2^{P \times R^2} \tag{3.22}$$

where $2^{P \times R^2}$ is the power set of the resource space $P \times R^2$. Typically, we have the following mapping for each $T_i \in T$. The index $i_j \in \{1, 2, \ldots, n\}$ could be repeated

$$f(T_i) = \{P_{i1}(x_1, y_2), P_{i2}(x_2, y_2), \ldots, P_{ip}(x_p, y_p)\} \tag{3.23}$$

This mapping actually subdivides the task T_i into p subtasks $T_{i1}, T_{i2}, \ldots, T_{ip}$. Subtask T_{ij} will be executed by pipeline P_{ij} for each $j = 1, 2, \ldots, p$. We call $\{T_{ij} | j = 1, 2, \ldots, p\}$ a *partition* of the task T_i. The following conditions must be met in order to facilitate multiple pipeline operations:

1. For all intervals $[x_j, y_j], j = 1, 2, \ldots, p$, $y_j - x_j > t_o$ and the total production delay $\tau_i = \sum_{j=1}^{p} (y_j - x_j - t_o)$.
2. If $P_{ij} = P_{il}$, then $[x_j, y_j] \cap [x_l, y_l] = \phi$. This implies that each pipeline is static, performing only one subtask at a time.

The *finish time* for vector task T_i is $F(T_i) = \max\{y_1, y_2, \ldots, y_p\}$. The finish time ω of a parallel schedule for an n-task system is defined by

$$\omega \equiv \max\{F(T_1), F(T_2), \ldots, F(T_n)\} \tag{3.24}$$

The purpose is to find a "good" parallel schedule such that ω can be minimized. This deterministic scheduling concept is clarified by the following example:

Example 3.5 Given a vector task system V, as specified in Figure 3.44a, $T = \{T_1, T_2, T_3, T_4\}$, $t_0 = 1$, $\tau_1 = 10$, $\tau_2 = 2$, $\tau_3 = 6$, and $\tau_4 = 2$. These delays are marked beside each node of the task graph. We want to schedule four tasks on two ($m = 2$) pipelines. A parallel schedule f is shown in Figure 3.44b, where the shaded area denotes the idle periods of the pipelines. The vector task T_1 is partitioned into the two subtasks T_{11} and T_{12}, with $\tau_{11} = 7$ and $\tau_{12} = 3$. Similarly, the vector task T_3 is partitioned into the two subtasks

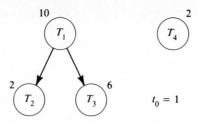

(a) The precedence graph of a vector task system

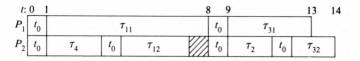

(b) A parallel schedule for the task system in (a)

Figure 3.44 Parallel scheduling of the task system of vector instructions in Example 3.5.

T_{31} and T_{32}, with $\tau_{31} = 4$ and $\tau_{32} = 2$. The parallel schedule f is specified by the following mappings with a finish time $\omega = F(T_3) = 14$:

$$f(T_1) = \{P_1(0, 8), P_2(3, 7)\} \quad \text{with } S(T_1) = 0 \text{ and } F(T_1) = 8$$

$$f(T_2) = \{P_2(8, 11)\} \quad \text{with } S(T_2) = 8 \text{ and } F(T_2) = 11$$

$$f(T_3) = \{P_1(8, 13), P_2(11, 14)\} \quad \text{with } S(T_3) = 8 \text{ and } F(T_3) = 14$$

$$f(T_4) = \{P_2(0, 3)\} \quad \text{with } S(T_4) = 0 \text{ and } F(T_4) = 3$$

The multiple-pipeline scheduling problem can be formally stated as a feasibility problem: *Given a vector task system V, a vector computer with m identical pipelines, and a deadline D, does there exist a parallel schedule f for V with finish time ω such that $\omega \leq D$?* This scheduling problem has been proven to be computationally intractable. In practice, the production delays of different vector tasks are different. These unequal production delays lead to the intractability of the multi-pipeline scheduling problem. Therefore, we have to seek heuristic algorithms in real-life system designs. The heuristics must be simple to implement, with low system overhead, and with nearly optimal performance.

Consider a vector processor with m pipelines with a fixed overhead time t_o for all instructions. The input to the scheduler is an independent task system V with n vector tasks which are totally unrelated. The task scheduler is a built-in part of the vector instruction controller. The output is the parallel schedule f for V. Let t_j be the time span of using pipeline P_j for the execution of various tasks in a given task system V. This time span includes the overhead time t_o every time the pipeline is reconfigured to assume a new task (or a new subtask), the production times τ_i (or τ_{ij}), and some idle times between successive tasks.

We denote the number of subtasks in a partition of task T_i as p_i. This task partitioning process requires $p_i - 1$ subdivisions of the original task. The total number of subdivisions of all tasks in a parallel schedule is expressed by:

$$k = \sum_{i=1}^{n} (p_i - 1) = \sum_{i=1}^{n} p_i - n \qquad (3.25)$$

The average time span $t_a(k)$ for partitioning n tasks into $n + k$ subtasks over m pipelines is defined by

$$t_a(k) = \frac{\sum_{i=1}^{n} (\tau_i + t_o) + k t_o}{m} \qquad (3.26)$$

If there is no subdivision of the original tasks in a schedule, the average time span $t_a(k)$ is reduced as follows, when $k = 0$.

$$t_a(0) = \sum_{i=1}^{n} \frac{\tau_i + t_o}{m} \qquad (3.27)$$

This quantity $t_a(0)$ is an absolute lower bound of the finish time ω, defined in Eq. 3.24. This means that an optimal schedule is generated when $\omega = t_a(0)$. Scheduling n independent tasks among the m pipelines is done by making the time span t_j (for $j = 1, 2, \ldots, m$) as close to $t_a(k)$ as possible. As demonstrated in Figure 3.45, a *bin-packing* approach is used to generate a parallel schedule for independent tasks. First, we assign some tasks to pipeline P_1 until time $t_1 \geq t_a(0) - t_o/2$. Then we switch to pipeline P_2 for assigning the remaining tasks until $t_2 \geq t_a(k) - t_o/2$, where $k = 0$ or 1 depending on how many subdivisions of tasks have been

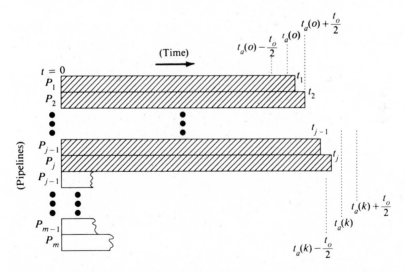

Note: shaded areas correspond to pipelines that have been assigned with vector tasks.

Figure 3.45 Multipipeline scheduling for independent vector tasks with a bin-packing approach.

performed. This generating process will repeat in a sequential manner for the remaining pipelines.

In general, we will switch to the next pipeline, P_{j+1}, when the following boundary condition is met:

$$t_j \leq t_a(k) - \frac{t_o}{2} \tag{3.28}$$

Furthermore, we will subdivide the current task and update $t_a(k)$ if the following condition is met, before switching to pipeline P_{j+1}:

$$t_j \geq t_a(k) + \frac{t_o}{2} \tag{3.29}$$

We consider below, as an example, the schedule of a tree structured task system based on the partitioned bin-packing procedure. This procedure generates a partition, $\{E_1, E_2, \ldots, E_l\}$, of all n tasks in the tree system. The first block E_1 consists of all tasks on leave nodes. The second block E_2 consists of those tasks on the "new" leave nodes after removing tasks in E_1 from the tree. This process continues until reaching the root, which forms the last block E_l where l equals the tree height. We shall process tasks in E_i before E_j, if $i < j$. In this sense, each E_i can be considered as a set of independent tasks, which can be dispatched concurrently as described above.

Example 3.6 We are given a tree task system $V = (T, \theta, \tau)$, where $T = \{T_1, \ldots, T_9\}$ follows the tree relationship shown in Figure 3.46a. Suppose $t_o = 1, \tau_1 = 2, \tau_2 = 4, \tau_3 = 6, \tau_4 = 8, \tau_5 = 8, \tau_6 = 2, \tau_7 = 6, \tau_8 = 4,$ and $\tau_9 = 4$, as marked in the tree graph. To schedule this tree task system on $m = 4$ identical pipelines, we first obtain the partition $E_1 = \{T_1, T_2, T_3, T_4\}, E_2 = \{T_5, T_6, T_8\}, E_3 = \{T_7\}, E_4 = \{T_9\}$ as circled by dashed lines in the figure. A parallel schedule f_B is generated, as depicted in Figure 3.46b. Shaded areas indicate the idle periods of pipelines. Tasks $T_2, T_3, T_4, T_5, T_7,$ and T_9 have been subdivided into subtasks:

$$f_B(T_1) = \{P_1(0, 3)\}$$

$$f_B(T_2) = \{P_1(3, 6.5), P_2(0, 2.5)\}$$

$$f_B(T_3) = \{P_2(2.5, 6.75), P_3(0, 3.75)\}$$

$$f_B(T_4) = \{P_3(3.75, 7), P_4(0, 6.75)\}$$

$$f_B(T_5) = \{P_1(7, 11.75), P_2(7, 12), P_3(7, 8.25)\}$$

$$f_B(T_6) = \{P_3(8.25, 11.25)\}$$

$$f_B(T_8) = \{P_4(7, 12)\}$$

$$f_B(T_7) = \{P_i(12, 14.5): 1 \leq i \leq 4\}$$

$$f_B(T_9) = \{P_i(14.5, 16.5): 1 \leq i \leq 4\}$$

The finish time $\omega = 16.5$ has the same order of magnitude as $\omega_o = 13.25$, the finish time of an optimal schedule.

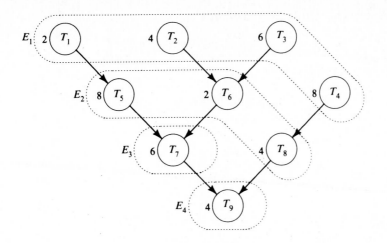

(a) A tree system of vector instructions and its partition

	0			7			12	14.5		16.5
P_1	t_0	T_1	t_0 T_{21}		t_0	T_{51}		t_0 T_{71}	t_0	T_{91}
P_2	t_0	T_{22}	t_0	T_{31}	t_0	T_{53} T_{52}		t_0 T_{72}	t_0	T_{92}
P_3	t_0	T_{32}	t_0	T_{41}	t_0	t_0 T_6		t_0 T_{73}	t_0	T_{93}
P_4	t_0	T_{42}			t_0	T_8		t_0 T_{74}	t_0	T_{94}

(b) A parallel schedule

Figure 3.46 A tree task system of vector instructions and a parallel schedule for it.

Concurrent processing allows a vector to be partitioned into several subvectors for simultaneous execution by parallel pipelines. The fact that the parallel pipeline-scheduling problem is *NP*-complete precludes us from insisting on finding an optimal pipeline-scheduling algorithm. Since the average time span of all tasks is usually much longer than the overhead time, nearly optimal performance is guaranteed in the above heuristic-scheduling algorithms. With proper refinement of the precedence relations on the task graphs, one can extend this method to schedule vector task systems with arbitrary precedence relations. The partitioning of a vector by time units is equivalent to partitioning by vector lengths. The above pipeline-scheduling methodology can be applied to the design and evaluation of pipeline supercomputers for parallel vector processing.

3.4.3 Pipelined Vector Processing Methods

Vector computations are often involved in processing large arrays of data. By ordering successive computations in the array, we can classify vector (array) processing methods into three types:

1. *Horizontal processing*, in which vector computations are performed horizontally from left to right in row fashion
2. *Vertical processing*, in which vector computations are carried out vertically from top to bottom in column fashion
3. *Vector looping*, in which segmented vector loop computations are performed from left to right and top to bottom in a combined horizontal and vertical method

We use a simple vector-summation computation to illustrate these vector processing methods.

Let $\{a_i$ for $1 \le i \le n\}$ be n scalar constants, $\mathbf{x}_j = (x_{1j}, x_{2j}, \ldots, x_{mj})^T$ for $j = 1, 2, \ldots, n$ be n column vectors, and $\mathbf{y} = (y_1, y_2, \ldots, y_m)^T$ be a column vector of m components. We need to compute the following linear combination of n vectors:

$$\mathbf{y} = a_i \cdot \mathbf{x}_1 + a_2 \cdot \mathbf{x}_2 + \cdots + a_n \cdot \mathbf{x}_n \tag{3.30}$$

One needs to perform $m \cdot n$ multiplications and $m \cdot (n-1)$ additions in the above vector computations. Expanding all component computations will help visualize different computation orderings to be used. For simplicity, we specify all multiplications by the shorthand notation: $z_i = a_j \cdot x_{ji}$ for $i = 1, 2, \ldots, m$ and $j = 1, 2, \ldots, n$. We can expand Eq. 3.30 into the following array of additions:

$$
\begin{aligned}
y_1 &= z_{11} + z_{12} + \cdots + z_{1n} \\
y_2 &= z_{21} + z_{22} + \cdots + z_{2n} \\
&\cdots\cdots\cdots\cdots\cdots\cdots\cdots\cdots\cdots\cdots \\
y_m &= z_{m1} + z_{m2} + \cdots + z_{mn}
\end{aligned}
\tag{3.31}
$$

Let us now consider the implementation of the above array computations in a pipeline processor. This processor has a static two-function arithmetic pipeline with five stages. Suppose that the pipeline can perform either addition or multiplication of two numbers, but not both simultaneously. One should first implement the mn multiplications through the pipeline, then follow with the implementation of the $m(n-1)$ additions specified in Eq. 3.31. This separation of multiply and add functions will result in a minimum reconfiguration cost by eliminating unnecessary pipeline setup delays and, thus, increasing the overall pipeline throughput.

In a nonpipeline scalar processor, each addition or multiplication requires $5t$, where t is the clock period or one stage delay. The total execution time (without pipelining) is thus equal to

$$T_1 = [mn + m(n-1)] \cdot 5t = (10mn - 5m)t \tag{3.32}$$

We will compare the total execution times of various pipeline processing methods with T_1 in order to reveal their relative speedups.

The way that addition pairs (operands) are scheduled distinguishes the three processing methods. In what follows, we assume that all multiplications have already been carried out by the pipeline in T_m pipeline cycles:

$$T_m = 5t \text{ (setup time) } + 5t \text{ (time for the first product to come out of the pipe)}$$
$$+ (mn - 1)t(\text{time for producing all the remaining products})$$
$$= mnt + 9t \tag{3.33}$$

It is assumed that the main memory is large enough to hold all intermediate results. There is a feedback path from the output of the pipeline to one of the two inputs if needed for cumulative additions. Let T_a be the total number of clock periods needed for the pipelined addition in each of the following methods. It is assumed $m \gg 5$ and $n \gg 5$.

Horizontal vector processing In this method, all components of the vector **y** are calculated in a sequential order, y_i for $i = 1, 2, \ldots, m$. Each summation $y_i = \sum_{j=1}^{n} z_{ij}$ involving $(n - 1)$ additions must be completed before switching to the evaluation of the next summation $y_{i+1} = \sum_{j=1}^{n} z_{i+1,j}$. To evaluate each y_i requires $(n + 14)t$ clock periods. The total *add time* for m outputs equals

$$T_a(\text{horizontal}) = (mn + 14m)t \tag{3.34}$$

This method is frequently used in a scalar pipeline processor. The above sequence of computations corresponds to the following Fortran program, provided that all initial values of y_i for $i = 1, 2, \ldots, n$, are set to zero.

```
DO 100 i=1,m,1
   DO 100 j=1,n,1
   y_j=y_j+a_i*x_ij
100 CONTINUE
```

The speedup of this horizontal pipelining on a vector processor over serial processing in a uniprocessor is derived below:

$$S_{\text{horizontal}} = \frac{T_1}{T_m + T_a(\text{horizontal})} = \frac{(10mn - 5m)t}{(2mn + 14m + 9)t} = \frac{10mn - 5m}{2mn + 14m + 9} \tag{3.35}$$

Vertical vector processing The sequence of additions in this method is specified below with respect to the m-by-n array shown in Eq. 3.31:

Step 1. Compute the partial sums $(z_{i1} + z_{i2}) = y_{12}^i$ for $i = 1, 2, \ldots, m$ sequentially through the pipeline.

Step 2. Compute the partial sums $(y_{12}^i + z_{i3})$ for $i = 1, 2, \ldots, m$ by loading y_{12}^i into one input port in stage 1 and loading z_{i3} into the second input port.

Step 3 to Step $n - 1$. Repeat Step 2 for $n - 3$ times by feeding successive columns $(z_{1j}, z_{2j}, \ldots, z_{mj})^T$ for $j = 4, 5, \ldots, n$, into the second input port. The values of y_i for $i = 1, 2, \ldots, m$ emerge from the pipeline at the end of Step $n - 1$.

The total add time of this vertical approach equals

$$T_a(\text{vertical}) = (mn - m + 10)t \qquad (3.36)$$

Therefore, the speedup of vertical vector processing over uniprocessing equals

$$S_{\text{vertical}} = \frac{T_1}{T_m + T_a(\text{vertical})} = \frac{10mm - 5m}{2mn - m + 19} \qquad (3.37)$$

This method has been applied to vector processing in the STAR-100.

Vector looping method This method combines the horizontal and vertical approaches into a "block" approach. The steps are specified below.

Step 1. Apply the vertical processing method to generate the first block of five outputs, $y_1, y_2, \ldots, y_5$, in column fashion.

Step 2 to Step k. Repeat Step 1 for generating the remaining five-output blocks as listed below:

$$\text{Step 2:} \quad y_6, \quad y_7, \quad \ldots, y_{10}$$

$$\text{Step 3:} \quad y_{11}, \quad y_{12}, \quad \ldots, y_{15}$$

$$\cdots\cdots\cdots\cdots\cdots\cdots\cdots\cdots\cdots$$

$$\text{Step } k: y_{5k-4}, y_{5k-3}, \ldots, y_{5k}$$

Step $k + 1$. Repeat Step 1 for generating the last block of r outputs, y_{5k+1}, $y_{5k+2}, \ldots$, and y_{5k+r}, where $m = 5k + r$ and $0 < r < 5$.

The total add time of this vector-looping method is given below, where $k = (m - r)/5$.

$$T_a(\text{vector looping}) = 5t + (5n - 1)t + (k - 1)[5(n - 1)t] + 5t$$

$$= mnt - mt - nrt + rt + 14t \qquad (3.38)$$

The speedup of the vector-loop method over a uniprocessing method equals:

$$S_{\text{vector looping}} = \frac{T_1}{T_m + T_a(\text{loop})} = \frac{10mn - 5m}{2mn - m - rn + r + 23} \qquad (3.39)$$

This method has been applied in the Cray-1 for segmented vector processing.

The horizontal method is suitable for use in scalar processors but unfit for parallel processing in a vector processor. Both vertical and vector-looping methods are attractive for vector processors. In vertical processing, the number of vector components m is unrestricted. However, many intermediate results (partial sums in the example) have to be stored in the memory. This poses the problem of increased demand for memory bandwidth. Vertical processing is more suitable for memory-to-memory pipeline operations, like those in the Star-100 and the Cyber-205. The vector-looping method is also not restricted by vector length. Since the intermediate results appear as small blocks of data, one can use a cache memory or fast-register arrays to hold the intermediate results. Thus vector looping is more suitable for register-to-register pipeline operations, such as in the Cray-1 and the Fujitsu VP-200. It is interesting to note that all the speedups approach 5, the number of stages in the sample pipeline, when n and m are very large in the performance analysis.

The speed of a scalar processor is usually measured by the number of instructions executed per unit time, such as the use of a *million instructions per second* (MIPS) as a measure. For a vector processor, it is universally accepted to measure the number of arithmetic operations performed per unit time, such as the use of *mega floating-point operations per second* (megaflops). Note that the conversion between mips and megaflops depends on the machine type. There is no fixed relationship between the two measures. In general, to perform a floating-point operation in a scalar processor may require two to five instructions. If we consider the average as three, then one megaflops may imply three mips. This conversion constant is machine dependent. Other authors compare the speeds of different computers by choosing a reference machine. Readers should be aware of the difference between the *peak speed* and the *average speed* when benchmark programs or test computations are executed on each machine. The peak speed corresponds to the maximum theoretical CPU rate, whereas the average speed is determined by the processing times of a large number of mixed jobs including both CPU and I/O operations.

3.5 BIBLIOGRAPHIC NOTES AND PROBLEMS

An earlier survey of pipeline computer architecture was given by Ramamoorthy and Li (1977). A recent assessment of pipeline processors and vectorization methods can be found in Hwang et al. (1981). The concept of overlapped parallelism was studied in Chen (1971a, b; 1975). Pipeline processors were described in Hayes (1978), Kuck (1978), and Stone (1980). The classification of pipeline computers is based on the work of Händler (1977). Good examples of instruction and arithmetic pipelines can be found in Anderson et al. (1967), Hintz and Tate (1972), Majithia (1976), Hwang (1979), and Waser and Flynn (1982). Interleaved memory systems for pipelining and parallel computers have been studied in Hellerman (1967), Burnett and Coffman (1970), Knuth and Rao (1975), Chang et al., (1977), Briggs and Davidson (1977), and Briggs and Dubois, (1983). A comprehensive treatment of pipeline computer systems can be found in Kogge (1981).

Pipeline models and task scheduling problems have been studied in Davidson (1971), Reddi (1972), Thomas and Davidson (1974), Ramamoorthy and Kim (1974), Li (1975), and Lang et al. (1979). Instruction prefetch techniques were treated by Rau (1977) and Grohoski and Patel (1982). Different aspects of busing, branching, and interrupt-handling of pipeline operations were also treated in Ramamoorthy and Li (1977). The dynamic pipelines with improved throughput using noncompute delays and internal buffers were proposed by Patel (1976, 1978a, b). Lookahead techniques such as hazard resolution and data forwarding have been treated by Keller (1975) and Tomasulo (1967). The modeling of a vector processor with multiple pipelines is based on the work of Hwang and Su (1983). Static pipes are commercially designed because of less control and hardware costs. However, systems requiring reliable and flexible designs may have to use dynamic pipes in order to enhance fault-tolerance capability and to increase the resource utilization.

Problems

3.1 Describe the following terminologies associated with pipeline computers and vector processing:

(a) Static pipeline	(k) Minimum average latency
(b) Dynamic pipeline	(l) Precise vs. imprecise interrupts
(c) Unifunctional pipeline	(m) Perfect cycle
(d) Multifunctional pipeline	(n) Greedy cycle
(e) Instruction pipeline	(o) Data-dependent hazards
(f) Arithmetic pipeline	(p) Short circuiting
(g) Pipeline efficiency	(q) Internal forwarding
(h) Pipeline throughput	(r) Vectorizer
(i) Forbidden latencies	(s) Branch target buffering
(j) Collision vector	(t) Register tagging

3.2 Compare the advantages and disadvantages of the three interleaved memory organizations: the S-access, the C-access, and the C/S-access described in Section 3.1.4 for pipelined vector accessing. In the comparison, you should be concerned with the issues on effective memory bandwidth, storage schemes used, access conflict resolution, and cost-effectiveness tradeoffs.

3.3 Consider a four-segment normalized floating-point adder with a 10-ns delay per each segment, which equals the pipeline clock period.

(a) Name the appropriate functions to be performed by the four segments.

(b) Find the minimum number of periods required to add 100 floating-point numbers $A_1 + A_2 + \cdots + A_{100}$ using this pipeline adder, assuming that the output Z of segment S_4 can be routed back to any of the two inputs X or Y of the pipeline with delays equal to any multiples of the period.

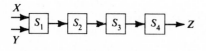

3.4 A certain dynamic pipeline with the four segments S_1, S_2, S_3, and S_4 is characterized by the following reservation table:

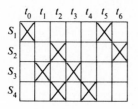

(a) Determine latencies in the forbidden list F and the collision vector C.

(b) Determine the minimum constant latency L by checking the forbidden list.

(c) Draw the state diagram for this pipeline. Determine the *minimal average latency* (MAL) and the *maximum throughput* of this pipeline.

3.5 For the following reservation table of a pipeline processor, give the forbidden list of avoided latencies F, the lower bound on latency, the collision vector, the state diagram, the MAL and all greedy cycles.

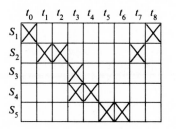

3.6 The following overlayed reservation table corresponds to a two-function pipeline:

	t_0	t_1	t_2	t_3	t_4
S_1	A	B		A	B
S_2		A		B	A
S_3	B	AB			

(a) List all four cross forbidden lists of latencies and corresponding combined cross-collision matrices.

(b) Draw the state diagram for the two-functional pipeline.

3.7 Assume that instructions are executed in a k-segment pipeline. The delay of each segment is one time unit. If an instruction depends on one or more of its predecessors, then all these predecessors must complete execution before the current instruction can begin execution. If such a predecessor is N instructions preceding the current instruction, a delay is added as $k - N$ time units for $N \leq k$ and no delay for $N > k$. Let p_n be the probability of encountering a data dependency from the nth predecessor. Assume an integer $L > k$. Suppose that p_n has the distribution $P_n = 1/L$ for $n = 1, 2, \ldots, L$ and p_n equal zero otherwise.

(a) Find the expected value of the total time T to execute a block of M instructions.

(b) Determine the performance P of the instruction pipeline, where

$$P = \lim_{M \to \infty} \frac{M}{T}$$

3.8 (a) Suppose that only two 4-segment pipelined adders and a number of noncompute delay elements are available. The delay of each segment is one time unit and the noncompute delay element can have either a one- or two-time unit delay. Using available resources, construct a pipeline with only one input, a's, to compute $b(i) = a(i) + a(i - 1) + a(i - 2) + a(i - 3)$. Show the schematic block diagram of your design.

(b) Given one additional four-segment pipelined adder, use this adder together with the pipeline obtained from (a) to design a pipeline for computing the recurrence function $x(i) = a(i) + x(i - 1)$. The pipeline constructed should have a feedback. Show your schematic block diagram. *Hint:* $x(i) = a(i) + x(i - 1) = a(i) + [a(i - 1) + x(i - 2)] = a(i) + a(i - 1) + [a(i - 2) + x(i - 3)] = a(i) + a(i - 1) + a(i - 2) + [a(i - 3) + x(i - 4)] = b(i) + x(i - 4)$.

3.9 Consider the following pipelined processor with four stages. All successor stages after each stage must be used in successive clock periods.

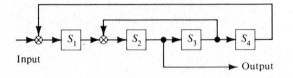

Answer the following questions associated with using this pipeline with an *evaluation time* of six pipeline clock periods.

(a) Write out the reservation table for this pipeline with six columns and four rows.

(b) List the set of forbidden latencies between task initiations.

(c) Show the initial collision vector.

(d) Draw the state diagram which shows all the possible latency cycles.

(e) List all the simple cycles from the state diagram.

(f) List all the greedy cycles from the state diagram.

(g) What is the value of the minimal average latency (MAL)?

(h) Indicate the minimum constant latency cycle for this pipeline.

(i) What is the maximal throughput of this pipeline?

3.10 (a) How does the IBM 360/91 avoid problems due to data dependencies involving the contents of floating-point registers within the floating-point execution unit? In your answer, especially address each type of hazard, indicating how each is controlled.

(b) The floating-point execution unit in the 360/91 handles data dependencies involving floating-point register contents. What data dependencies can arise in the execution of floating-point instructions (including loads to and stores from the floating-point registers) that involve the contents of some memory word? How can these dependencies be managed? Efficiency is a prime consideration. Use a block diagram to illustrate the organization of the major hardware units that your solution requires. Explain the operation of each of these units.

3.11 Answer the following equations related to the task initiation cycle (2, 3, 7) for a given pipelined processor.

(a) What are the period p and the average latency l_a of this initiation cycle?

(b) Specify the initiation interval set $G \pmod{p}$.

(c) What is the necessary and sufficient condition that a given task initiation cycle is allowed by a pipeline with a forbidden latency set F? Repeat the same question for a constant initiation cycle with period p.

3.12 Suppose that scalar operations take 10 times longer to execute per result than vector operations. Given a program which is originally written in scalar code:

(a) What are the percentages of the code needed to be vectorized in order to achieve the speedup factors of 2, 4, and 6 respectively?

(b) Suppose the program contains 15% of code that cannot be vectorized such as sequential I/O operations. Now repeat question (a) for the remaining code to achieve the three speedup factors.

FOUR

PIPELINE COMPUTERS AND VECTORIZATION METHODS

This chapter describes the system architectures and vector processing techniques developed with existing pipeline computers. The first section gives a historical retrospective of pipeline computers in two architectural categories: *vector supercomputers* and *attached array processors*. We will examine three attached processors: the AP-120B (FPS-164), the IBM 3838, and the MATP. Vector supercomputers to be studied include the early systems Star-100 and TI-ASC, and the recent systems Cray-1, Cyber-205, and VP-200, and their possible extensions. Finally, we will study vectorizing compiling techniques, optimization methods, and performance evaluation issues in designing or using pipeline computers.

4.1 THE SPACE OF PIPELINE COMPUTERS

Pipeline computers refer to those digital machines that provide overlapped data processing in the central processor, in the I/O processor, and in the memory hierarchy. Pipelining is practiced not only in program execution but also in program loading and data fetching operations. Univac-1 was the first machine that overlapped program execution with some I/O activities. With the development of interleaved memory, memory words in successive memory modules could be fetched in a pipelined fashion. These pipeline memory fetches prompted the overlapped instruction fetches and instruction executions as pioneered in the IBM 7094 series in the Stretch project and in the Univac-Larc system.

The performance of a pipeline processor may be significantly degraded by the data dependency holdup problem. The evolution of the CDC 6000/7000 series has contributed to the development of hardware/software mechanisms to overcome this difficulty. In addition to further partitioning the instruction execution process, the CDC 6000 series uses a "status checkboard" to indicate the availabilities of various resources in the computer required to execute various stages of subsequent instructions. Resource conflicts are recorded in the checkboard. Instructions being interrupted are temporarily queued for deferred executions. A single instruction may be deferred several times because of sequence of resource conflicts. Multiple arithmetic units are employed in the CDC 6600/7600 to alleviate the resource-conflict problem in the overlapped executions of multiple instructions in the system.

The development of the IBM System/360 Model 91 scientific processor has greatly enhanced the design methodology of pipeline computers. A hierarchy of pipelines is employed in the Model 91 for instruction fetch, preprocessing, and execution, as described in Chapter 3. Mechanisms are provided to prefetch instructions at both alternative program paths after a conditional branch instruction. Continued instruction execution can be sustained with prefetching to increase the system throughput. High-speed instruction and data buffers are used to make the above approach possible. Fast internal data forwarding techniques were also implemented in the IBM System/360 Model 91 and its successor IBM System/370 models to overcome the difficulty caused by hazards or out-of-sequence executions. Many of these pipeline design techniques have appeared in later machines like the Amdahl 470 V/6 and the IBM 3081.

4.1.1 Vector Supercomputers

A *supercomputer* is characterized by its high computational speed, fast and large main and secondary memory, and the extensive use of parallel structured software. Most of today's supercomputers are designed to perform large-scale vector or matrix computations in the areas of structural engineering, petroleum exploration, VLSI circuit design, aerodynamics, hydrodynamics, meteorology, nuclear research, tomography, and artificial intelligence. The demand for high speed and large internal memory is obvious in these scientific applications. Large amounts of data are often processed by a supercomputer. Usually the data elements are arranged in array, vector, or matrix forms. The large data arrays are collected from, for example, seismic echo signals after the set off of a sonic shock wave into the ground. In 1979 alone, 10^{15} bits of seismic data were processed in the United States. Similar examples can be found in radar and sonar signal processing for detection of space and underwater targets, in remote sensing for earth resource exploration, in computational wind tunnel experiments, in three-dimensional stop-action computer-assisted tomography, in numerical weather forecasting, and in many real-time applications. In terms of speed, current supercomputers should be able to operate at a speed of 100 megaflops or higher.

The first generation of vector supercomputers is marked by the development of the Star-100, TI-ASC, and the Illiac-IV in the 1960s. By 1978, there were seven installations of ASC, four installations of Star-100, and only one Illiac-IV system installed at user sites. We will first study the Star-100 and ASC systems. Both the Star-100 and the ASC systems are equipped with multiple functional pipeline processors to achieve parallel vector processing. The Star-100 has a memory-to-memory architecture with two pipeline processors. The ASC can handle up to three-dimensional vector computations in pipeline mode. The peak speed of both systems is around 40 megaflops. We will study Illiac-IV in Chapter 6.

Vector processors entered the second generation with the development of the Cray-1, the Cyber-200 series, and the Fujitsu VP-200. The Cray-1, evolved from the CDC 6600/7600 series, is considered one of the fastest supercomputers that has ever been built. The maximum CPU rate of the Cray-1 is 160 megaflops if all the resources are fully utilized. The Cyber-200 series is extended from the Star-100. The Cyber 205 has both vector and scalar pipelines, with the potential to perform 800 megaflops. As of September 1982, there were over 60 Cray-1 and Cyber-205 machines installed all over the world. Recently, Fujitsu in Japan announced a vector processor, VP-200, which can perform up to 500 megaflops.

For the future, it is highly necessary to have a vector processor which can perform 1000 megaflops or more. Cray Research is currently extending the Cray-1 to a multiprocessor configuration, called Cray X-MP. This Cray X-MP, consisting of dual processors, is expected to be five times more powerful than the Cray-1, with an expected peak speed of 400 megaflops. Eventually, Cray Research plans to further upgrade Cray X-MP to a four-processor model, called Cray-2, which will be 12 times more powerful than Cray-1 in vector processing mode. CDC has proposed to upgrade the Cyber-205 eventually to a vector processor that can provide 3000 megaflops for numerical aerodynamic simulations. Each uni-processor in the multiprocessor system S-1, under construction at the Lawrence Livermore National Laboratory, is also highly pipelined, with an expected CPU rate twice as fast as the Cray-1. Cray X-MP, Cray-2, and S-1 will be introduced in Chapter 9, along with other multiprocessor systems.

4.1.2 Scientific Attached Processors

Most scientific processors are designed as back-end machines attached to a host computer. Most of these *attached processors* are pipeline structured. The most used system is the AP-120B and FPS-164 array processors manufactured by Floating-Point Systems. We will study three attached processors, including the AP-120B (FPS-164), the IBM 3838, and the Datawest array transform processor.

These attached processors are mostly designed to enhance the floating-point and vector-processing capabilities of the host machine. They can be attached to minicomputers and mainframes. For example, an AP-120B can be attached to a VAX 11/780, increasing the computing power of the VAX to 12 megaflops. Attached processors cost much less than the mainframes or supercomputers. However, most attached array processors must be microcoded for specific vector applications. The application software costs are much higher than the bare hardware costs, especially when microcode packages must be developed by users for special-purpose computations.

In a host back-end computer organization, the host is a program manager which handles all I/O, code compiling, and operating system functions, while the back-end attached processor concentrates on arithmetic computations with data supplied by the host machine. High-speed interface is often needed between the host and the back-end machine. In this sense, the supercomputers Cray-1 and Cyber-205 are also back-end machines driven by a host machine.

The projected speed performances of the aforementioned pipeline super-computers and attached processors are compared in Figure 4.1. We use the measure *million operations per second* (mops) to refer to either megaflops or a million integer operations per second. All speeds indicated within the parentheses refer to the theoretical peak performance, if the machine is used sensibly. In the late sixties, only pipeline scalar processors were available with a maximum speed of 5 mops, as represented by the IBM 360/91 and 370/195 series, and by the CDC 6600/7600 series. The first-generation vector processors Star-100 and TI-ASC have a speed ranging from 30 to 50 mops. The second-generation vector processors Cray-1, Cyber-205, and VP-200 have a speed between 100 and 800 mops.

The attached processors AP-120B and FPS-164 have a peak speed of 12 megaflops. The FACOM 230/75 can perform 22 megaflops. MATP is a four-pipeline multiprocessor which can operate up to 120 megaflops. The IBM 3838 has a peak speed of 30 megaflops. The Fujitsu VP-200 is extended from its predecessor FACOM 230/75. The first Cray X-MP became available in 1983.

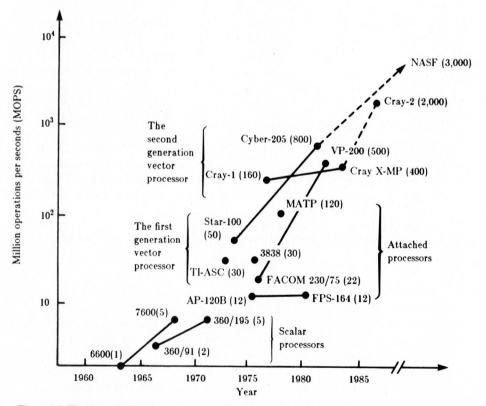

Figure 4.1 The theoretical peak performance of pipelined supercomputers and attached scientific processors.

The future supercomputers Cyber 2xx, Cray 2, and S-1 are expected to perform over 3000 megaflops for applications in the 1990s.

Of course, the peak speeds in Figure 4.1 may not always be attainable. For average programs written by nonspecialists, the speed is much lower than those peak values indicated. For mixed programs, it has been estimated that the average rate of the Cray-1 is 24 megaflops, of the Star-100 is 16 megaflops, and of the AP-120B is only 6 megaflops. These measured operating speeds are low because the software is not properly tuned to explore the hardware. These issues will be studied in Section 4.5 along with language, compiling, vectorization, and optimization facilities for vector processors.

4.2 EARLY VECTOR PROCESSORS

Dedicated computers for vector processing started with the introduction of two supercomputer systems known as the CDC-Star and the TI-ASC, both of which have multiple pipeline processors for stand-alone operations. Based on the employed technology and architectural features, the two generations of vector processors differ in many aspects. In this section, architectural structures, pipelined arithmetic designs and vector processing in the Star and ASC are described. In the next section, we will study more recent vector processors.

4.2.1 Architectures of Star-100 and TI-ASC

The Star-100 is a vector-oriented processor with two nonhomogeneous arithmetic pipelines. Control Data Corporation started the design of Star in 1965 and delivered it to user sites in 1973. It is structured around a four million byte (eight million optional) high-bandwidth core memory for stand-alone operations. Special features designed in the Star-100 include stream processing, virtual addressing, hardware microinstructions, semiconductor memory-register file, and pipelined floating-point arithmetic. The core memory in the Star has a cycle time of 1.28 μs. It has 32 interleaved memory banks, each containing 2048 words of 512 bits each. The memory cycle is divided into 32 minor cycles, with a rate of 40 ns each. This implies that the memory supplies 512 bits of data per minor cycle.

The pipelined arithmetic units are especially designed for sequential and parallel operations on single bits, 8-bit bytes, and 32- or 64-bit floating-point operands and vectors. Virtual addressing employs a high-speed mapping technique to convert a logical address to an absolute memory address. In the ideal case, the system has the capability of producing 100 million 32-bit floating-point results per second. The system architecture of the Star-100 is shown in Figure 4.2. The memory banks are organized into eight groups of four banks each. During the streaming operations, all four buses will be active, with each bus transferring data at a rate of 128 bits per minor cycle. Two of the buses are used for transferring

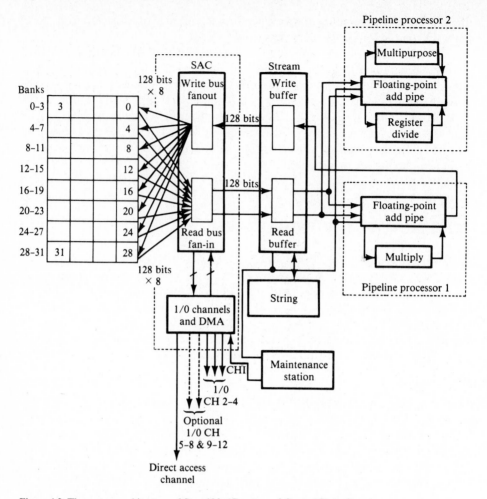

Figure 4.2 The system architecture of Star-100. (Courtesy of Control Data Corp.)

operand streams to the pipeline processors. The third bus is used for storing the result stream, and the fourth bus is shared between input-output storage requests and the references of control vectors.

The *Storage Access Control* unit controls the transmission of all data to and from the memory. It is responsible for memory sharing among the various buses shared by the stream and I/O units. Its principal function is to perform virtual memory address comparison and translation. The *Stream unit* provides basic control for the system. All memory references and many control signals originate from this unit. It has the facilities for instruction buffering and decoding. The *Read Buffer* and *Write Buffer* are used to synchronize the four active buses to maintain a smooth data transfer. The memory requests are buffered eight banks apart to avoid access conflicts. As a result, the maximum pipeline rate can be sustained regardless of distribution of addresses on the four active buses.

Other functional units in the Stream unit include the register file and the microcode memory. The register file supplies necessary addressing for all source operands and results. It also has the capability of performing simple logical and arithmetic operations. The semiconductor microcode memory is used as part of the stream control. The control signals and enable conditions produced by the microcode are used together with the hardwired control to process instructions and interrupts. The *String unit* processes strings of decimal or binary digits and performs bit-logical and character-string operations. It contains several adders to execute binary coded decimal (BCD) and binary arithmetic.

In the Star-100 are two independent arithmetic pipelines (Figure 4.3). The pipeline processor 1 consists of a 64-bit *floating-point* (henceforth FLP) *add unit* and a 32-bit FLP *multiply unit*. The add pipeline on the right contains four segment groups in cascade. The *exponent compare* segment compares exponents and saves the larger. The difference between the exponents is then saved as a shift count by which the fraction with the smaller exponent is right-shifted in the *coefficient alignment* segment. In the add segment, the shifted and unshifted fractions are added. The sum and the larger exponent are then gated to the *normalized* segments. The *transmit* segment selects the desired upper or lower half of the sum, checks for any fraction overflow, and transmits the results to the designated data bus. There is a path from the output of the transmit segment to the input of the *receive* segment. This feedback feature is especially useful for continuous addition of multiple floating-point numbers. However, when nonstreaming-type operations are performed, the execution time can be decreased by 50 percent if the output of an operation is needed as an input operand for subsequent operations.

With little additional hardware, it is possible to split the 64-bit add pipeline into two independent 32-bit ones. Consequently, half-width (32-bit) arithmetic can be available. The 32-bit *multiply pipeline* is implemented with multiplier-recoding logic, multiplicand-gating network, and several levels of carry-save adders. A resultant product of the multiplication is formed by adding the final partial sum and the saved carry vector. The required post-normalization after FLP multiply is done using the normalize segments of the add pipeline on the right.

Processor number 2, depicted in Figure 4.3b, contains a pipelined *add unit*, a nonpipelined *divide unit*, a pipelined *multipurpose unit*, and some pipelined *merge units*. The add pipeline in processor number 2 is similar to that in processor number 1. The multipurpose pipeline has 24 segments and is capable of performing multiply, divide, square root, and a number of other arithmetic logic operations. The *register divide unit* is a nonpipelined divider which can also perform BCD arithmetic.

Two 32-bit multiply pipelines can be combined to form a 64-bit multiply pipeline. This combined unit can simultaneously execute two 32-bit multiplications or execute one 64-bit multiplication. In order to perform a 64-bit multiplication, the multiplicand A and multiplier B are each split into two parts, $A = A_0 + A_1 \cdot 2^w$,

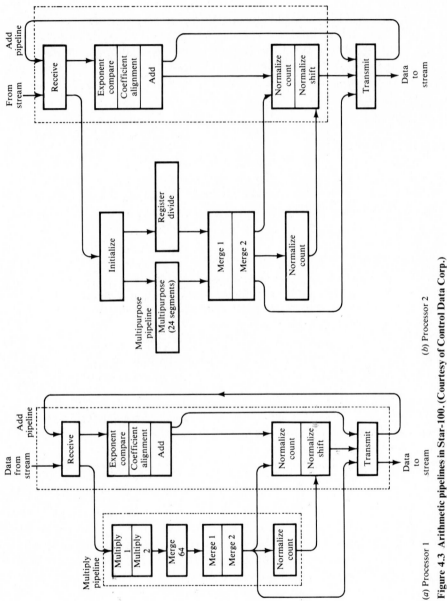

(a) Processor 1

(b) Processor 2

Figure 4.3 Arithmetic pipelines in Star-100. (Courtesy of Control Data Corp.)

and $B = B_0 + B_1 \cdot 2^w$, where $w = 32$ bits, the width of the basic multiply pipeline. Then the following four multiplications are performed:

$$A \times B = A_0 \times B_0 + (A_0 \times B_1 + A_1 \times B_0) \cdot 2^w + (A_1 \times B_1) \cdot 2^{2w} \quad (4.1)$$

$A_0 \times B_0$ and $A_0 \times B_1$ are executed during the first cycle of multiplication, and $A_1 \times B_0$ and $A_1 \times B_1$ during the second cycle. Afterward, all partial sums and partial carries are merged in a 64-bit merge section, which is essentially a set of carry-save adder trees (pipelines). The partial sum and partial product from the 64-bit merge section are then added together by two adders to yield the final 64-bit product.

The Star-100 has 130 scalar instructions and 65 vector instructions, as categorically listed in Table 4.1. Vectors in the Star-100 are formed as *strings* of binary numbers or characters, or as *arrays* of 32- or 64-bit FLP numbers. The *sparse vector* instructions can process compressed sparse vectors. When the pipeline enters streaming operations, it is possible to maintain a 40-ns output rate. The input-to-output time for the FLP add pipeline is 160 ns, because there are essentially four pipeline segments. The time delay of the FLP multiply pipeline equals 320 ns. The maximum throughput for different arithmetic operations is summarized in Table 4.2. These are peak CPU speeds. In practice, the measured average speed of the Star-100 is only 0.5 to 1.5 megaflops for scalar operations and 5 to 10 megaflops for vector operations, lower than its designed capabilities. It is quite obvious that double-precision FLP operations require more time to complete, twice the add/subtract time and four times the multiply or divide time compared to their single-precision counterparts.

Texas Instruments *Advanced Scientific Computer* (ASC) was delivered in 1972. The central processor of ASC is incorporated with a high degree of pipelining in both instruction and arithmetic levels. The basic components of the ASC system

Table 4.1 Instruction types in Star-100

Scalar instructions	Vector instructions
Load and Store	Arithmetic
Arithmetic	Compare
Index	Search
Increment and Test	Move
Bit operations	Normalize
Normalize	Data type conversion
Data type conversion	Sparse vector
Branch	Vector macros
String	Dot product
Logical	Polynomial evaluation
Monitor call	Average difference
	Average
	Adjacent mean

Table 4.2 Maximum numbers of arithmetic operations executable in the CDC Star-100 system for short and long word lengths (in mops)

Floating-point operations	32-bit (short)	64-bit (long)
Add-subtract	100	50
Multiply	100	25
Divide	50	12.5
Square root	50	12.5

are shown in Figure 4.4. The central processor is used for its high speed to process a large array of data. The peripheral processing unit is used by the operating system. Disk channels and tape channels support a large number of storage units. Data concentrators are included for support of remote batch and interactive terminals. The memory banks and an optional memory extension are managed by the memory control unit. The main memory has eight interleaved modules, each with a cycle time of 160 ns and a word length of 32 bits. Eight memory words can be transferred in one memory access. The memory control unit is an interface between eight independent processor ports and nine memory buses. Each processor port has full accessibility to all memories.

The central processor can execute both scalar and vector instructions. Figure 4.5 illustrates the functional pipelines in the central processor. The processor includes the instruction processing unit (IPU), the memory buffer unit

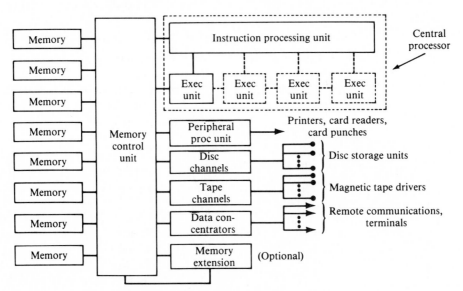

Figure 4.4 Basic Texas Instruments ASC systems configuration.

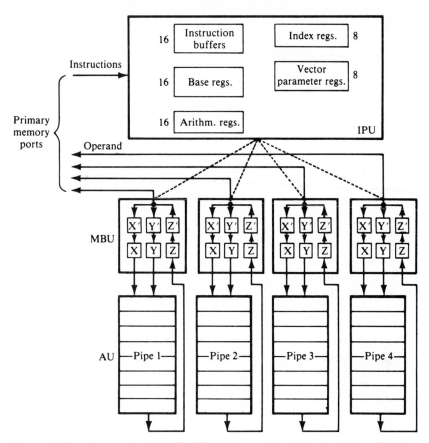

Figure 4.5 Central processor of the TI-ASC with four arithmetic logic pipelines. (Courtesy of Texas Instruments, Inc.)

(MBU), and the arithmetic unit (AU). Up to four arithmetic pipelines (MBU-AU pairs) can be built into the central processor. The ASC instruction types are listed in Table 4.3. The maximum ASC speed per arithmetic pipeline is given in Table 4.4. On the average, only 0.5 to 1.5 megaflops and 3 to 10 megaflops per pipeline can be expected for scalar and vector operations, respectively.

The primary function of the IPU is to supply the rest of the central processor with a continuous stream of instructions. Internally, the IPU is a multisegment pipeline which has 48 program-addressable registers for fetching and decoding instructions and generating the operand address. Instructions are first fetched in *octets* (8 words) from memory into the instruction buffers of 16 registers. Then the IPU performs assignment of instructions to the MBU-AU pairs to achieve optimal use of the arithmetic pipelines. The MBU is an interface between main memory and the arithmetic pipelines. Its primary function is to support the arithmetic units with continuous streams of operands. The MBU has three double buffers, with each buffer having eight registers. X and Y buffers are used for inputs, and a Z buffer is used for output. The fetch and store of data are made in 8-word

Table 4.3 TI-ASC instruction types

Scalar instructions	Vector instructions
Load and Store	Arithmetic
Arithmetic	Logical
Logical	Shift
Shift	Compare
Compare	Merge and Order
Branch	Move
Increment and Test	Search
Stack	Normalize
Normalize	Data conversion
Data type conversion	Peak picking
Monitor call	Select
	Replace

Table 4.4 Maximum floating-point speed of TI-ASC (in mops)

Arithmetic operations	32-bit operands	64-bit operands
Add	16.6	9.5
Multiply	16.6	9.5
Divide	1.1	0.67

Table 4.5 Comparison of major architectural features between Star-100 and TI-ASC

Characteristic	STAR-100	ASC
Data word size	1/8/32/64/128 bits	16/32/64 bits
Instruction size	32/64 bits	32 bits
Memory size	1 M 64-bit words	8 M 64-bit words
Clock rate	40 ns	60 nsec
Functional pipeline unit	2 nonhomogeneous pipelines (1) Add pipe + Multiply pipe in parallel (2) Add pipe + Divide pipe + Multipurpose pipe	1 to 4 homogeneous pipelines: eight exclusive segments in each pipe with bypasses to execute a number of arithmetic functions in FLP or FXP formats
Average speed per pipeline	0.5–1.5 Mflops/s (scalar) 5–10 Mflops/s (vector)	0.5–1.5 Mflops/s (scalar) 3–10 Mflops/s (vector)

increments. The AU has a pipeline structure to enable efficient arithmetic computations. This unit is reconfigurable with variable interconnecting paths among eight segments, as described in Section 3.2.3. Many similarities exist between the Star-100 and the ASC systems. Table 4.5 summarizes the major architectural features of these two early vector processors.

4.2.2 Vector Processing in Streaming Mode

Continuous streaming of data from the high-bandwidth interleaved memories to multiple pipelines makes Star very efficient for the processing of long vectors. The key issue here is to structure the computations into vector mode, such as those frequently done in matrix multiplication, polynomial evaluation, and the solution of large-scale linear systems of equations. The system software of Star provides aids to enable the user to take full advantage of hardware capabilities. The Fortran compiler in Star has been extended to detect loops and vectorize them into simplified vector codes. The lines of Fortran code which can be vectorized must be well isolated and easy to recognize. Of course, the programmer can escape from Fortran code by directly using the mnemonic assembly language to achieve maximal hardware performance.

The vector instruction format of the Star-100 is shown in Figure 4.6. Each instruction has 64 bits divided into eight fields. Fields F and G specify function

F (8X, 9X)	G (subfunc- tion)	X (offset for A)	A (field length 8: base address)	Y (offset for B)	B (field length 8: base address)	Z (CV base address)	C (field length 8: base address)	$C+1$ (offset for C, Z)

Field	Contents of the field in the cited register
X	The offset of source operand 1
Y	The offset of source operand 2
A	The base address and field length of source operand 1
B	The base address and field length of source operand 2
Z	The base address of the control vector
C	The base address and field length of the result vector
$C+1$	The offset of the control or result vector

Figure 4.6 The instruction format of Star-100.

and subfunction codes. The rest of the fields designate the working registers to be used. The field $C + 1$ automatically specifies the register holding the offset for control of the result vectors. The effective starting address is calculated as the sum of the base address and the offset. The effective field length is calculated as the offset subtracted from the field length. Thus, the ending address is the sum of the effective starting address and the effective field length. With offset capability, the ith element in the source operand can operate with the $(i + d)$th element of another source operand, where d is the difference between the two offsets. The following example shows the streaming operations for vector addition in the Star-100:

Example 4.1 Consider the execution of a *Vector Add* instruction in the Star-100:

$$\text{VADD A,B,C} \qquad (\text{A}+\text{B}\rightarrow\text{C}) \qquad\qquad (4.2)$$

where A = field length of A vector = 12 halfwords (32 bits each)
   B = field length of B vector = 4 halfwords, base address = 20000_{16}
   X = offset for A vector = 4 halfwords
   Y = offset for B vector = -4 halfwords
   Z = base address of control vector = 40004_{16}
   C = base address of result vector = 30000_{16}, field length = 12 half-words
   C + 1 = control vector and result vector offset = 4 halfwords

The starting address and effective field length of the A vector are calculated in Figure 4.7. Note that bit addressing is used and a "1" in the control vector permits storing the corresponding element in the resulting vector. For example, the memory location 40005 is stored with a "1," so C_5 is transformed into $A_5 + B_{-3}$. The skewing effect is apparent in this example. After the instruction has been decoded at the stream unit, the appropriate microcode sequence is initiated by the *microcode unit* (MIC) in the stream unit.

When the CPU initiates an instruction requiring microcode control, it sends the F (function) code and a microcode pulse to the MIC. The MIC then takes over control of the startup and termination of the instruction. In case of interrupts, it has to branch to save all the operands and parameters necessary to resume execution afterward. The MIC is the heart of the vector processing control, consisting of the following sequence of control steps:

1. The reading of addresses from the register file (in the stream unit) for the vector parameters according to designations specified in the instruction
2. The calculation of the effective addresses and field lengths for monitoring the starting of vector operations
3. The setting up of the usage of read-write buses as specified by the G (sub-function) field for the operands and results

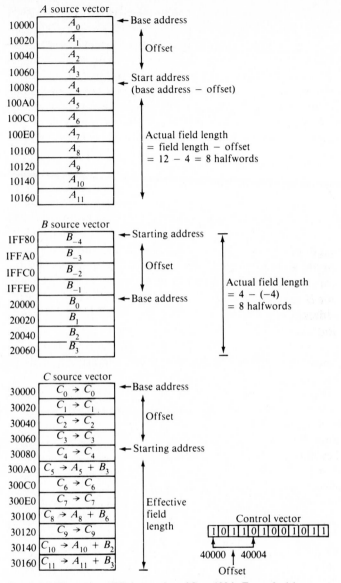

Figure 4.7 The vector ADD instruction of Star-100 in Example 4.1.

4. The transfer of addresses and other information whenever needed to appropriate interrupt-count registers

Once effective addresses are computed, the operand elements are fetched and paired for the operations involved. The static configuration of the execution pipe will remain active until vector instruction is terminated. A termination is marked by either of the following events: (a) a vector is exhausted when the effective field length becomes 0; (b) some other data fields or strings have been exhausted.

To support vector and scalar processing in Star, its operating system provides time sharing, utilizing the concepts of virtual memory. Prepaging is allowed by a feature known as *advise* to alleviate the I/O-bound problem. The Star operating system handles the functions of input, compilation, assembly, loading, execution, and output of all programs submitted, as well as the allocation of main memory. In addition to Star Fortran, an interactive interpreter called Star APL is also implemented in the system, which upgrades system capability to handle a large area of scientific computations.

Instructions in TI-ASC have 32 bits, as shown in Figure 4.8, where F is the opcode, R, T, and M specify the arithmetic, index, and base registers, and N is the symbolic address. ASC differs from Star in the way vector instructions are implemented. Instead of using certain registers to retrieve the operand addresses and control information, the ASC uses a *vector parameters file* (VPF), which consists of eight 32-bit registers in the IPU, as shown in Figure 4.5. The function of each VPR register is fixed, as shown in Figure 4.8. The register V_0 holds the opcode, the vector-operand type, and the length; V_1, V_2, and V_3 indicate the base address and the displacement of each operand vector; V_4 and V_5 hold the increment of the vector index and the interaction number of inner loops; and V_6 and V_7 hold similar information for outer loops.

The above control information is loaded into these V registers from the main memory before the execution of each vector instruction. Microcode will be

8	4	4	4	12
F	R	T	M	N

(a) Instruction format

V_0	OPR	ALCT	SV	L
V_1	$-$	XA		SAA
V_2	HS	XB		SAB
V_3	VI	XC		SAC
V_4	DA$_1$			DB$_1$
V_5	DC$_1$			N_1
V_6	DA$_0$			DB$_0$
V_7	DA$_0$			N_0

(b) Vector parameter file (VPF)

Figure 4.8 The TI-ASC instruction format and vector parameter file.

generated by the timing-sequence circuitry in the MBU to control the entire pipeline processing in the AU. This sequence includes the fetch of operands, the sending of pairs of operands to the pipeline, the execution phase, and the return of successive results. The increment in ASC is variable, while only an increment of 1 is possible in Star. This offers more flexibility in addressing operands. Three-dimensional indexing is also possible in ASC to process the inner loop and outer loop more efficiently. However, ASC does not use control vector, sparse, and macro-vector instructions, as found in Star. Both the Star and ASC are structured to execute memory-to-memory instructions in streaming mode.

4.3 SCIENTIFIC ATTACHED PROCESSORS

Attached processors are becoming popular because their costs are low and yet they provide significant improvement on the host machines. The AP-120B and FPS-164 are back-end attached arithmetic processors specially designed to process large vectors or arrays (matrices) of data. Operationally, these processors must work with a host computer, which can be either a minicomputer (such as the VAX-11 series) or a mainframe computer (IBM 308X series). While the host computer handles the overall system control and supervises I/O and peripheral devices, the attached processor is responsible for heavy floating-point arithmetic computations. Such a functional distribution can result in a 200 times speedup over a minicomputer, and a 20 times speedup over a mainframe computer. Other scientific attached processors include the IBM 3838 and the low-cost Datawest processor. We describe in this section the architectural features of these attached processors and assess their potential applications in the scientific and engineering areas.

4.3.1 The Architecture of AP-120B

The combination of an AP-120B and a host computer is shown in Figure 4.9. All the peripheral devices like printers, display terminals, disk and tape units are attached to the host computer. In fact, the AP-120B is itself a peripheral attachment to the host. Since the host and back-end may have different data formats and even unequal word lengths, an *interface unit* is needed to convert the data "on the fly" and to help implement the *direct-memory access* (DMA) and *programmed input-output* (PIO) data transfers. These are two sets of registers in the interface unit. One set is devoted to control functions via programmed I/O; the other to block data transfers via the DMA. The programmed I/O section of the interface unit provides the array processor with a simulated front panel of the host. It contains a *switches register* used by the host to enter control or parameter data and addresses into the array processor, a *light register* to display contents of registers in the array processor, and a *functional register* for typical front panel commands such as *start*, *stop*, or *reset*.

The DMA register set includes a *host memory address* register, an *AP memory address* register, a *word count* register, a *control* register, and a *format* register. The

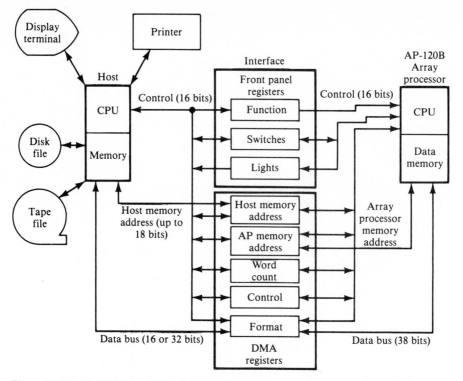

Figure 4.9 The AP-120B host and interface organization.

control register governs the direction of data transfer and the mode of transfer. The format register performs conversion between the FLP format of the host and that of the AP-120B. Interface logic permits data transfer to occur under control of either the host or the AP-120B. The floating-point format in the AP-120B is 38 bits long, with a 28-bit 2's complement mantissa and a 10-bit exponent biased by 512. Using such a format, the precision and dynamic range are improved over the conventional 32-bit floating-point format. If the host has different floating-point data formats, the format conversion is done "on the fly" through the interface. Consequently, the AP-120B can concentrate on useful computational tasks.

A detailed functional diagram of the AP-120B processor is shown in Figure 4.10. The processor is divided into six sections, the *I/O section, memory section, control memory, control unit, data bus,* and two *arithmetic units.* The memory section consists of the *data memory* (MD), *table memory* (TM), and two *data pads* (DPX and DPY). The control memory or *program memory* (PM) has 64-bit words with a 50-ns cycle time. The program memory consists of up to 4K words in 256-word increments. Instructions residing in the PM are fetched, decoded, and executed in the control unit. The data memory is interleaved with a cycle time of either 167 or 333 ns. The choice of a particular speed depends on the trade-off between cost

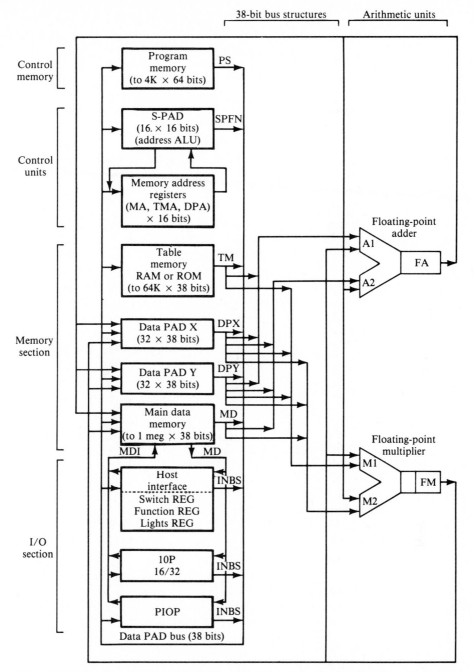

Figure 4.10 The block diagram of an AP120B processor. (Courtesy of Floating-Point Systems, Inc.)

and performance. The data memory is the main data storage unit with 38-bit words. It is directly addressable by the 1 million words in 2K-word (167 ns) or 8K-word (333 ns) increments. The TM has up to 64K 38-bit ROM or RAM words of 167-ns cycle time. The table memory is used for the storage of frequently used constants (e.g., FFT constants). It is associated with a special data path which does not interfere with the data path associated with the data memory. The data pads X and Y are two blocks of 38-bit accumulators. There are 16 accumulators in each block. These accumulators are directly addressable by the AP processor. Any accumulator can be accessed in a single machine cycle of 167 ns. Simultaneous *read* and *write* are possible in each data pad within the same cycle.

The S pad in the control unit contains two parts: an *S-pad memory* and an *integer ALU*. The S-pad memory contains 16 directly addressable integer registers. These registers feed the address ALU to produce effective operand addresses. The address ALU performs 16-bit integer arithmetic. The outputs of the address ALU can be routed to any one of the following address registers: MA for the data memory, TMA for the table memory, and DPA for the data pads. Other functions of the address ALU include *clear, increment, decrement, logical and,* and *logical or*.

Two pipeline arithmetic units are the *FLP adder* (FA) and the *FLP multiplier* (FM). The FA consists of two input registers, A1 and A2, and a two-segment pipeline, as shown in Figure 4.11. The sum output is a 38-bit normalized floating-point number. The FM has M1 and M2 input registers and a three-segment pipeline which performs floating-point multiply operations. Once the pipeline is

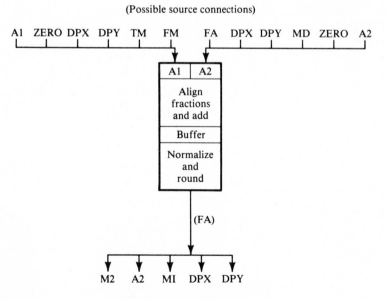

(Possible source connections)

(Possible destination connections)

Figure 4.11 The floating-point adder in AP-120B.

full, a new result (sum or product) is produced for every machine cycle of 167 ns. Consequently, the maximum throughput rate for the AP-120B is 12 mega floating-point computations per second.

The AP-120B derives its high computing power from multiplicities in all sections of its processor organization. It uses two pipeline arithmetic units (FA and FM), one integer ALU, multiple memories (PM, MD, TM) which can be independently addressed, a large number of registers and accumulators (A1, A2, M1, M2, MA, TMA, DPA, DPXs, and DPYs), and seven data paths, as shown in the bus structures section of Figure 4.10.

The two floating-point arithmetic units FA and FM can operate simultaneously and the 16-bit integer ALU can operate independently of the FA and FM. The use of two independent blocks of accumulators (DPX and DPY) provides the desired flexibility in handling operands and intermediate and final results. For instance, each block can hold a vector operand with 16 components so that a 16-element dot product can be performed within the FA and the FM in pipeline mode. In other cases, one block provides data for the FA or FM, while the other block transfers data to and from data memory or table memory.

The pipeline structures of the FA and FM are described below. The first stage of the FA compares exponents, shifts the fraction of the smaller number, and adds the fractions. In the second stage, the resulting fraction is normalized and rounded. Because of different processing speeds in the two stages, a buffer is inserted to hold the intermediate result. The output of the FLP adder, denoted by FA, can be routed to five different destinations. Possible source connections to the input registers A1 and A2 are shown at the top of Figure 4.11. The FM has three stages. In the first stage, the 56-bit product of the two 28-bit fractions is partially completed. The second stage completes the product of the fractions. The third stage adds the exponents, rounds, and normalizes the fraction of the product. All possible source and destination connections to the FLP multiplier are identified in Figure 4.12.

Seven buses are used in the AP-120B simultaneously to enable parallel processing. Both the FA and the FM have multibus input ports. In other words, multiple operands and results can be moved between different functional units at the same machine cycle. Thereby, the total data path bandwidth will match the execution speed of the pipeline adder and multiplier.

Several levels of parallelism in the AP-120B have been described. Another aspect worthy of mentioning is the control of parallel functional units. This is provided by the long instruction word of the AP-120B. An AP-120B instruction has 64 bits, which are subdivided into 10 command fields (Figure 4.13). Each command field controls a specific unit; therefore, a single AP-120B instruction can initiate as many as ten operations per machine cycle, as listed in Figure. 4.13. Multiple memory accesses, register transfers, integer arithmetic, and floating-point computations can occur at the same time.

In summary, multiple memories, multiple functional units, parallel data paths, and the multiple command fields in the instruction have made the AP-120B a fast attached processor for scientific computations.

(Possible source connections)
DPX DPY TM FM
FA DPX DPY MD
M1
M2
Start product of fractions
Buffer 2
Complete product of fractions
Buffer 3
Add exponents Normalize and Round
(FM)
M1 A1 MI DPX DPY
(Possible destination connections)

Figure 4.12 The floating-point multiplier in AP-120B.

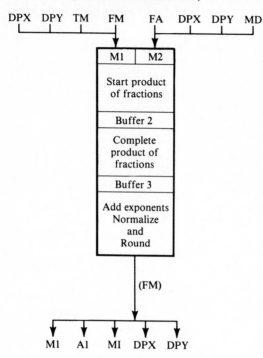

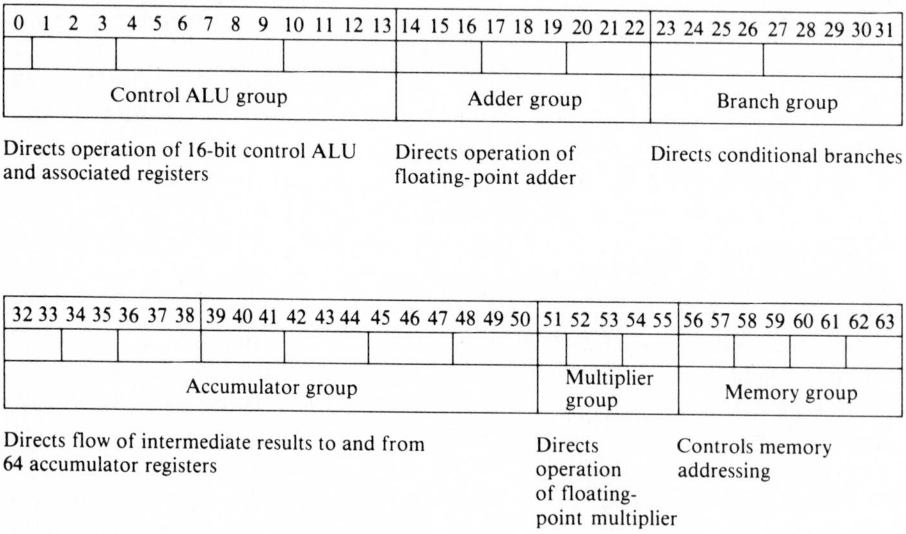

0 1 2 3 4 5 6 7 8 9 10 11 12 13
14 15 16 17 18 19 20 21 22
23 24 25 26 27 28 29 30 31
Control ALU group
Adder group
Branch group
Directs operation of 16-bit control ALU and associated registers
Directs operation of floating-point adder
Directs conditional branches
32 33 34 35 36 37 38
39 40 41 42 43 44 45 46 47 48 49 50
51 52 53 54 55
56 57 58 59 60 61 62 63
Accumulator group
Multiplier group
Memory group
Directs flow of intermediate results to and from 64 accumulator registers
Directs operation of floating-point multiplier
Controls memory addressing

Figure 4.13 The instruction format in AP-120B.

4.3.2 Back-End Vector Computations

The AP-120B, unlike vector supercomputers, does not have vector instructions. Instead, long instructions containing many concurrent microoperations are used to specify the parallel activities. More than 200 application software packages have been developed for complicated vector computations. These routines are called a *mathematical library*, which is devoted to mainly vector and matrix manipulations. These vector-processing routines are Fortran callable from the host computer. All calls are handled by the *array processor executive* (APEX) software, which decodes the subroutine calls from Fortran programs residing in the host and automatically passes control parameters and routines to the AP-120B for execution. After completing the computation of a routine, the AP-120B returns the results to the host computer for further use. The user can add new or special routines to the mathematics library in Fortran or in AP assembly language code. Some program development software have been provided for such purposes. In addition, there is the *signal processing library*, dedicated to digital signal-processing applications. Important Fortran callable routines in these libraries are summarized in Table 4.6, with the time measured in microseconds and the program sizes in numbers of AP-120B microinstruction words.

In the AP-120B, different functions can be performed by the floating-point adder at different times. Listed below are some typical functions:

1. A1 + A2
2. A1 − A2
3. A2 − A1
4. A1 EQV A2
5. A1 AND A2
6. A1 OR A2
7. Convert A2 from signed magnitude to 2's complement format
8. Convert A2 from 2's complement to signed magnitude format
9. Scale A2
10. Absolute value of A2
11. Fix A2

Table 4.6 Floating-point arithmetic timing for some functions in AP-120B

Operation	Travel time	Pipeline interval
Add-subtract	333 ns	167 ns
Multiply	500 ns	167 ns
Multiply-add	833 ns	167 ns
Complex add-subtract	500 ns	333 ns
Complex multiply	1.333 ns	667 ns
Complex multiply-add	1.667 ns	667 ns

Table 4.7 Important FORTRAN callable routines for AP-120B

Operation	Name	Timing (μs per point)	Size (AP-120B prog. words)
Real vector operations			
Vector add	VADD	1.2	8
Vector subtract	VSUB	1.2	8
Vector multiply	VMUL	1.2	11
Vector divide	VDIV	1.8	44
Vector exponential	VEXP	5.1	42
Vector sine	VSIN	5.1	46
Vector cosine	VCOS	5.6	46
Sum of vector squares	SVR	0.4	11
Dot product of two vectors	DOTPR	0.8	9
Sum of vector elements	SVE	0.4	7
Complex vector operations			
Complex vector multiply	CVMUL	2.0	26
Complex vector reciprocal	CVRCIP	5.0	51
Matrix operations			
Matrix transpose	MTRANS	0.8	17
Matrix multiply	MMUL	*	58
Matrix multiply (dimension $\leq$ 32)	MMUL32	*	27
Matrix inverse	MATINV	*	130
Matrix vector multiply (3 $\times$ 3)	MVML3	2.5/vector	30
Matrix vector multiply (4 $\times$ 4)	MVML4	4.6/vector	39
Fast fourier transform operations			
Complex FFT	CFFT	*	187
Real FFT	RFFT	*	235
Signal processing operations			
Convolution (or correlation)	CONV	*	102
Wiener-Levinson algorithm	WIENER	*	68
Bandpass filter	BNDPS	*	287
Power spectrum	PWRSPC	*	268

* Timing unknown.

Similarly, the FM can perform many different functions. The timing for some floating-point arithmetic operations in the AP-120B is summarized in Table 4.7, where the *travel time* is the total time required to transfer data from source to destination, and the *pipeline interval* is the time between successively available results. The pipeline interval indicates the maximum throughput rate for vector-oriented computations.

A detailed example of vector processing in the AP-120B is given below. First some notations are established. A semicolon " ; " separates parallel operations within an instruction word. A comma "," is used to separate operands. A double slash bar "//" denotes a comment. An arrow "←" refers to the replacement operator for data transfers. Some operations required in presenting the example are specified below:

```
FADD   A1,A2        //A1+A2 (floating-point add)
DPX(m)←FA           //Save FA in location m of data pad DPX.
FMUF   M1,M2        //M1×M2 (floating-point multiply)
DPY(m)←FM           //Save FM in location m of data pad DPY.
```

where the inputs A1, A2, M1, and M3 to the adder and multiplier come from the input sources specified in Figures 4.11 and 4.12, respectively.

Example 4.2 The following sequence is used to compute the dot product of two vectors, $\sum_{i=0}^{4} X_i Y_i$, where X_i and Y_i are obtained from DPX and DPY, respectively. The resulting sum of the products is to be stored in DPX:

(1) FMUL DPX(0), DPY(0)   //Multiply $X_0 Y_0$.

(2) FMUL DPX(1), DPY(1)   //Multiply $X_1 Y_1$.

(3) FMUL DPX(2), DPY(2)   //Multiply $X_2 Y_2$.

(4) FMUL DPX(3), DPY(3); //Multiply $X_3 Y_3$, $X_0 Y_0$ is now done. Save it in adder.

FADD FM, ZERO

(5) FMUL DPX(4), DPY(4); //Multiply $X_4 Y_4$, $X_1 Y_1$ is now done. Save it in adder.

FADD FM, ZERO

(6) FMUL; FADD FM, FA   //$X_2 Y_2$ is coming out of the multiplier and $X_0 Y_0$ from the adder. Add them together.

(7) FMUL; FADD FM, FA   //$X_3 Y_3$ is coming out of the multiplier and $X_1 Y_1$ from the adder. Add them together.

(8) FADD FM, FA   //$X_4 Y_4$ is coming out of the multiplier and $(X_0 Y_0 + X_2 Y_2)$ from the adder. Add them together.

(9) FADD; DPX(4)←FA   //$(X_1 Y_1 + X_3 Y_3)$ is coming out of the adder. Save it in DPX(4).

(10) FADD DPX(4), FA   //$(X_0 Y_0 + X_2 Y_2 + X_4 Y_4)$ is coming out of the adder. Add it to $(X_1 Y_1 + X_3 Y_3)$.

(11) FADD   //Push result out of adder pipeline.

(12) DPX(4)←FA   //The result $\sum_{i=0}^{4} X_i Y_i$ is stored in DPX(4).

In the above sequence of computations, cycles 1 to 3 are used to fill the FM pipeline; cycles 4 to 5 to fill the FA pipeline; cycles 6 to 8 to drain the FM pipeline; cycles 9 to 11 to drain the FA pipeline, and the final result is stored in data pad X.

The dummy add "FADD" without arguments in cycle 11 is used only to push the last computation out of the pipeline. Remember that there are three stages and two buffer registers in the FM pipeline, hence two dummy multiplies are needed to push the last two computations out of the pipeline. For long vectors, the speed to execute dot product in the AP-120B is much faster than in a serial processor.

The AP-120B has been applied extensively in the field of digital-signal processing. The execution sequence of *fast Fourier transform* (FFT) in the AP-120B is shown below as an example. The FFT program resides in the program memory of the AP-120B. The array of data to be transformed is stored in the main memory of the host computer. The FFT computation sequence consists of the following steps:

1. The host computer issues an I/O instruction to initiate the FFT program in the AP-120B.
2. The AP-120B requests host DMA cycles to transfer the array of data from host memory to data memory in the AP-120B. The floating-point format is converted during the flow of data through the interface unit.
3. The FFT computations are performed over a 38-bit floating-point data array.
4. The AP-120B requests the host DMA cycles to return the results of the FFT frequency-domain coefficients array.

Example 4.3 The above operations are called by a host machine with the following four Fortran statements:

```
CALL APCLR              //Clear AP-120B.
CALL APPUT (······)     //Transfer data to AP-120B.
CALL CFFT (······)      //Perform FFT.
CALL APGET (······)     //Transfer results to host.
```

where "······" denotes the parameters used in the routines.

For the convolution of two arrays, say A and B, all required operations can also be done by the AP-120B. Once the transfer of data arrays is initiated, there is no need to wait until completion of the entire array transfer. Such convolution requires a sequence of forward FFT and inverse FFT operations, as listed below:

1. Transfer arrays A and B to AP-120B.
2. Perform FFT on A array.
3. Perform FFT on B array.
4. Multiply the results of steps 2 and 3.
5. Perform inverse FFT of the result obtained from step 4.
6. Return the final result to the host computer.

4.3.3 FPS-164, IBM 3838 and Datawest MATP

The FPS-164 is evolved from the proven architecture of its predecessor products, the AP-120B, the AP-190L, and the FPS-100 by Floating-Point Systems, Inc. It is attached to either the input-output channel or the DMA channel of a host computer by means of a hardware and software interface similar to that for the AP-120B. The host machine can be a DEC VAX 11/780, an IBM 4341, or an IBM 3081, ranging from superminis to large mainframes. The FPS-164 improves its performance over the AP-120B by extended precision (64-bit floating-point numbers instead of 38 bits, as in the AP-120B) and a much enlarged memory of 16 million 64-bit words. The FPS-164 can be programmed with either a Fortran-77 subset, FPS-164 symbolic assembly language, or the extensive library of preprogrammed mathematics, matrix, and applications routines.

A functional block diagram of the FPS-164 is given in Figure 4.14. There are eight independent pipeline functional units (the FLP multiplier, the FLP adder, the data pads X and Y, table memory, main memory, integer ALU, and the data pad bus) interconnected by seven dedicated data paths. The peak speed is still 12 megaflops. The 64-bit data word provides 15 decimal-digit accuracy. The 64-bit address space covers 16 million words. Multi-user protection is provided by using memory base and limit registers and privileged instructions. The vectored priority interrupts allow real-time applications. The dynamic range and accuracy of the FPS-164 improves significantly over the AP-120B. Furthermore, the processor has instructions which assist software implementation of double-word floating-point arithmetic. Diagnostic and reliability features are also built into the FPS-164 to enhance dependability of the system in case of hardware or software failures.

The IBM 3838 is a multiple-pipeline scientific processor. It is evolved from the earlier IBM 2938 array processor. Both processors are specially designed to attach to IBM mainframes, like the System/370, for enhancing the vector-processing capability of the host machines. These attached pipeline processors reflect recent progress in scientific processing at IBM beyond the level of the 360/91 and the 370/195. Vector instructions that can be executed in the 3838 include the componentwise *vector add, vector multiply,* the *inner product,* the *sum of vector components, convolving multiply, vector move, vector format conversion, fast Fourier transforms, table interpolations, vector trigonometric* and *transcendental* functions, *polynomial* evaluation, and *matrix* operations. Like the AP-120B and the FPS-164, both the IBM 2938 and the 3838 are microprogrammed pipeline processors which can be supplied with custom-ordered instruction sets for specific vector applications.

The hardware architecture of the IBM 3838 array processor is shown in Figure 4.15. The processor can attach to a System/370 via a block-multiplexer I/O channel with a data transfer rate of 1.5 M bytes per second. With an optional two-type interface, the maximum data-transfer rate can be doubled to 3 M bytes/s. The 3838 appears to the host processor I/O channel as a shared control unit. Up to seven users can be simultaneously active in the 3838. The tasks defined by each user are pipelined at various subsystems in the 3838. The control processor can assist the user with a set of scalar instructions and the necessary registers in preparing vector instructions. The *bulk memory* is used to hold a large volume of vector operands. The *I/O unit* supervises the transfer of data or programs between

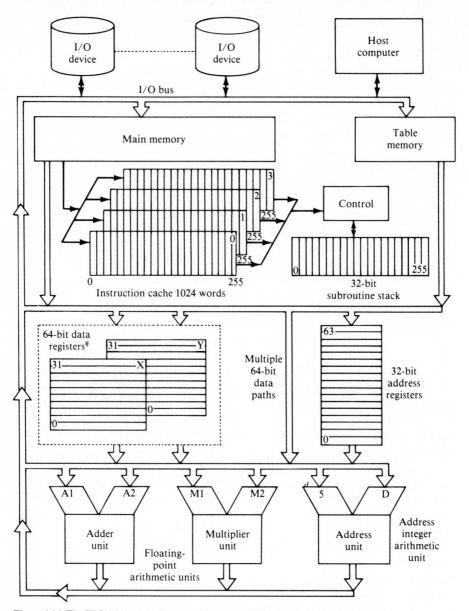

Figure 4.14 The FPS-164 system diagram. (Courtesy of Floating-Point Systems, Inc.)

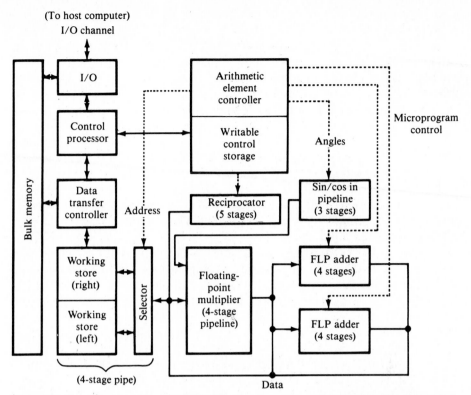

Figure 4.15 The arithmetic processor in IBM/3838. (Courtesy of International Business Machines Corp.)

the host and the bulk memory. Data-word size of the 3838 is 32 bits, matching that of the System/370 machines.

The transfer of the working sets of the vector segments between the bulk memory and the *working stores* is supervised by the *data transfer controller* (DTC). Each working store can hold 8192 bytes. Vector-addressing parameters are supplied to the DTC by the control processor. This DTC is microprogrammed to generate the effective memory addresses for both the bulk and working memories before data can be properly transferred. Furthermore, the DTC can perform data-format conversion during the data flow. The *arithmetic controller* is also a microprogrammed unit. The microprogram sequences performed by the arithmetic pipelines are initialized by this controller. The use of the working stores by the arithmetic pipelines and by the DTC is synchronized. The basic pipeline cycle time is 100 ns in the 3838.

There are five pipeline arithmetic units in the 3838. The pipeline units as diagrammed in Figure 4.15 include two floating-point adders of four stages each; a four-stage floating-point multiplier; a three-stage sine/cosine pipeline; and a five-stage reciprocal estimator. Even the working stores appear as a four-stage pipeline. The delay of each stage is 100 ns. The interconnection paths between these functional pipes are under the microprogrammed control of the *arithmetic element controller.* The access of the writable control storage is also pipelined with two stage delays.

The programs and data to be processed by the 3838 are prepared by the host computer. Both vector and scalar instructions can be contained in these 3838 programs. The host sends the programs and data to the 3838 through the I/O channel. Data will be stored in the bulk store. The instructions will be executed by the control processor. After the decoding of each instruction, the control processor provides linked lists of microprogram sequences for supervising the pipelined execution of the instructions. While the arithmetic pipelines are updating vector data from one working store, the DTC can load the other working store. Therefore, data loading and instruction execution can be done simultaneously at the two banks of the working stores. This facilitates the multiprogrammed use of the 3838. Concurrent pipelinings allow multiple users to share the hardware resources in achieving high system throughput. The maximum speed of the 3838 has been estimated to be 30 megaflops.

Datawest, Inc. at Scottsdale, Arizona, has built a very sophisticated attached processor called MATP for large scientific computations. The MATP consists of up to four pipeline processors. These processors, forming a hybrid MIMD-SIMD system, are microprogrammable and share a common data memory. Each processor can be controlled by separate writable control stores. The primary means of host communication is through a set of program channels that connect to host I/O channels.

A schematic functional block diagram of the Datawest MATP is shown in Figure 4.16. This processor is designed to work with a Univac 1184 computer. Using a Univac and an MATP at a cost of $4 million, Datawest claims that it can attain a peak rate of 120 megaflops. This compares favorably with the 160-megaflop Cray-1 with a $10 million cost. The Fujitsu FACOM 230/75 is another attached array processor with a peak performance of 22 megaflops when attached to a FACOM 200M mainframe.

A comparison of three competing attached processors manufactured in the United States is given in Table 4.8. All three processors, FPS' AP-120B, IBM's 3838, and Datawest's MATP, are pipelined and microprogrammable. The speeds shown are theoretical peak speeds in megaflops. The speed of the MATP corresponds to a maximum configuration of four processors. It is interesting to note the multiprocessor structure in the MATP. This concept of pipelining in a multiprocessing mode is also seen in other supercomputers like the Cray X-MP and HEP to be introduced in Chapter 9.

Attached array processors are effective in seismic-signal processing. If one enlarges the instruction repertoire of array processors, they can be turned into general-purpose scientific processors. The attempt by Datawest is a good example. Most scientific computers remain outside the mainstream of developing large computers for business use. The peak speed shows only a theoretical limit. It is the degree to which parallelism is exploited in the application programs that determines the effectiveness of a scientific processor. In general, attached processors have specialized architectures that appeal better to programs containing many

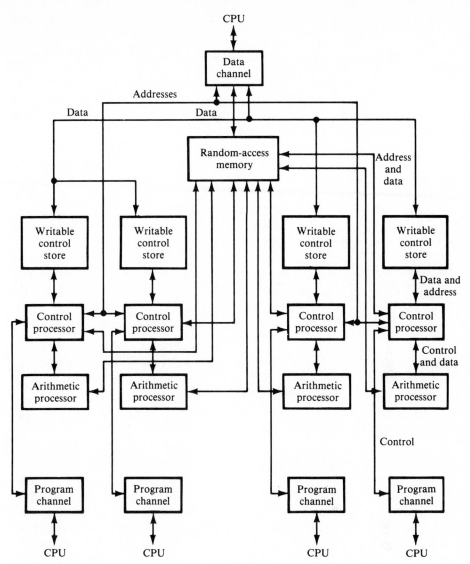

Figure 4.16 The architecture of the MATP: an MIMD/SIMD processor with shared data memory space. (Courtesy Datawest, Inc.)

Table 4.8 Comparison of attached processor capabilities

Features	AP-120B	IBM 3838	MATP
Data word size	38 bits	32bits	32 bits
Processor	Pipelined	Pipelined	Pipelined
Number of controllers	1	1	1 to 4
Number of processors	1	1	1 to 4
Memory size	32K to 1M bytes	2 16K-byte sections	65K bytes
Clock rate	167 ns	100 ns	100 ns
Microprogrammed	Yes	Yes	Yes
Writable control store	Yes	Manufacturer only	Yes
Architecture	Pipeline	Pipeline	Pipeline MIMD/SIMD
Maximum speed (in megaflops)	12	30	120
Add	6	20	2 × 40
Multiply	6	10	40

vector or matrix instructions with regularly structured parallelism. Programs with arbitrary scalar operations may not be suitable for execution in attached scientific processors that are available in the computer market.

4.4 RECENT VECTOR PROCESSORS

The three most recently developed vector processors are described in this section, namely Cray Research's Cray-1, Control Data's Cyber-205, and Fujitsu's VP-200. All three are commercial supercomputers with multiple pipelines for concurrent scalar and vector processing. Possible extensions to these vector supercomputers will be elaborated at the end. We focus on the architectural structures, special hardware functions, software supports, and parallel processing techniques that have been developed with these second generation vector processors.

4.4.1 The Architecture of Cray-1

The Cray-1 has been available as the first modern vector processor since 1976. The architecture of Cray-1 consists of a number of working registers, large instruction buffers and data buffers, and 12 functional pipeline units. With the "chaining" of pipeline units, interim results are used immediately once they become available. The clock rate in the Cray-1 is 12.5 ns. The Cray-1 is not a "stand-alone" computer. A front-end host computer is required to serve as the system manager. A Data General Eclipse computer or a Cray Research "A" processor has been used as the front end, which is connected to the Cray-1 CPU via I/O channels. Figure 4.17 shows the front-end system interface and the Cray-1 memory and functional sections. The CPU contains a *computation section, a memory section*, and an *I/O section*. Twenty-four I/O channels are connected to the front-end computer, the I/O stations, peripheral equipment, the mass-storage subsystem, and a *maintenance control unit* (MCN). The front-end system will collect data, present it to the Cray-1 for processing, and receive output from the Cray-1 for distribution to slower devices. Table 4.9 summarizes the key characteristics of the three sections in the CPU of the Cray-1.

The memory section in the Cray-1 computer is organized in 8 or 16 banks with 72 modules per bank. Bipolar RAMs are used in the main memory with, at most, one million words of 72 bits each. Each memory module contributes 1 bit of a 72-bit word, out of which 8 bits are parity checks for *single error correction and double error detection* (SECDED). The actual data word has only 64 bits. Sixteen-way interleaving is constructed for fast memory access with small bank conflicts. The bipolar memory has a cycle time of 50 ns (four clock periods). The transfer of information from this large bipolar memory to the computation section can be done in one, two, or four words per clock period. With a memory cycle of 50 ns, the memory bandwidth is 320 million words/s, or 80 million words per clock period.

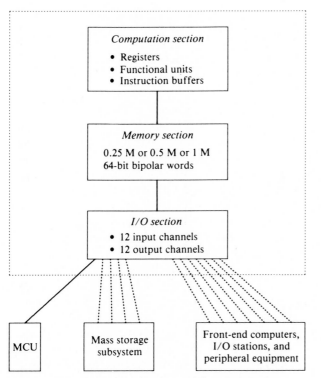

Figure 4.17 Front-end system interface and Cray-1 connections.

Table 4.9 Characteristic of the Cray-1 computer system

Computation section
  64-bit word length
  12.5-ns clock period
  2's complement arithmetic
  Scalar and vector processing modes
  Twelve fully segmented functional units
  Eight 24-bit address (A) registers
  Sixty-four 24-bit intermediate address (B) registers
  Eight 64-bit scalar (S) registers
  Sixty-four 64-bit intermediate scalar (T) registers
  Eight 64-element vector (V) registers, 64-bits per element
  Four instruction buffers of 64 16-bit parcels each
  Integer and floating-point arithmetic
  128 instruction codes

Memory section
  Up to 1,048,576 words of bipolar memory
    (64 data bits and eight error correction bits)
  8 or 16 banks of 65,536 words each
  Four-clock-period bank cycle time
  One word per clock period transfer rate to B, T, and V registers
  One word per two clock periods transfer rate to A and S registers
  Four words per clock period transfer rate to instruction buffers
  Single error correction and double error detection (SECDED)

Input-output section
  Twelve input channels and twelve output channels
  Channel groups contain either six input or six output channels
  Channel groups served equally by memory (scanned every four clock periods)
  Channel priority resolved within channel groups
  Sixteen data bits, three control bits per channel, and four parity bits
  Lost data detection

Such high-speed data-transfer rates are necessary to match the high processing bandwidth of the functional pipelines.

The I/O section contains 12 input and 12 output channels. Each channel has a maximum transfer rate of 80 M bytes/s. The channels are grouped into six input or six output channel groups and are served equally by all memory banks. At most, one 64-bit word can be transferred per channel during each clock period. Four input channels or four output channels operate simultaneously to achieve the maximum transfer of instructions to the computation section. The MCU in Figure 4.17 handles system initiation and monitors system performance. The mass storage subsystem provides large secondary storage in addition to the one million bipolar main memory words.

A functional block diagram of the computation section is shown in Figure 4.18. It contains 64×4 instruction buffers and over 800 registers for various purposes. The 12 functional units are all pipelines with one to seven clock delays except for the reciprocal unit, which has a delay of 14 clock periods. Arithmetic operations include 24-bit integer and 64-bit floating-point computations. Large

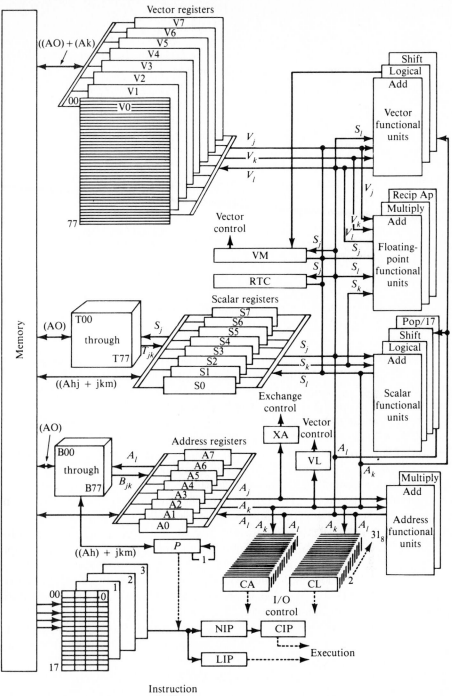

Figure 4.18 Arithmetic logic pipelines, registers, buffers, memory, and data paths in the Cray-1. (Courtesy of Cray Research, Inc.)

numbers of high-speed registers contribute to the vector and scalar processing capability of the Cray-1. Without these many registers, the functional units cannot operate with a clock rate of 12 ns. According to usage, there are five types of registers: three primary types and two intermediate types. The three primary types of registers are *address* (A), *scalar* (S), and *vector* (V) *registers*. The functional units can directly access primary registers. To support the scalar and address registers, an intermediate level of registers exists which is not accessible directly by the functional units. These registers act as buffers between the bipolar memory and the primary registers. The intermediate registers that support address registers are called *address-save registers* (B), and those supporting scalar registers are called *scalar-save registers* (T). Block transfers are made possible between B and T registers and the bipolar memory banks.

There are eight address registers with 24 bits each used for memory addressing, indexing, shift counting, loop control, and I/O channel addressing. Data can be moved directly between bipolar memory and A registers or can be placed in B registers first and then moved into A registers. There are sixty-four 24-bit B registers. The B registers hold data to be referenced repeatedly over a sufficiently long period. It is not desirable to retain such data in the A registers or in the bipolar memory. Examples of such uses are loop counts, variable array base addresses, and dimension control.

There are eight 64-bit S registers serving as the storage of source and destination operands for the execution of scalar arithmetic and logical instructions. S registers may furnish one operand in vector instructions. Data can be moved directly between memory and S registers or can be placed in T registers as an intermediate step before transfer to S registers. There are sixty-four 64-bit T registers. T registers access the bipolar memory by block read or block write instructions. Block transfers occur at a maximum rate of one word per clock period.

There are eight V registers; each has 64 component registers. A group of data is stored in component registers of a V register to form a vector operand. Vector instructions demand the iterative processing of components in the subregisters. A vector operation begins with fetching operands from the first component of a V register and ends with delivering the vector result to a V register. Successive component operands are supplied for each clock period and the result is delivered to successive elements of the result V register. The vector operation continues until the number of operations performed equals a count specified by the *vector length* (VL) register. Vectors having a length greater than 64 are handled under program control in groups of 64 plus a remainder. The contents of a V register are transferred to or from memory in a block mode by specifying the address of the first word in memory, the increment for the memory address, and the vector length.

All instructions, either 16 or 32 bits long (Figure 4.19a), are first loaded from memory into one of four instruction buffers, each having sixty-four 16-bit registers. Substantial program segments can be prefetched with the large instruction buffers. Forward and backward branching within the buffers is possible. When the current instruction does not reside in a buffer, one instruction buffer is replaced with a new block of instructions from memory. Four memory words are

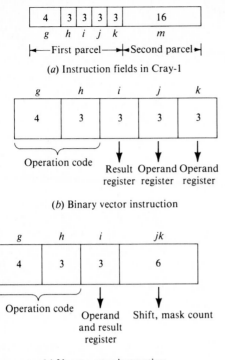

(a) Instruction fields in Cray-1

(b) Binary vector instruction

(c) Unary vector instruction

Figure 4.19 Instruction format of the Cray-1.

fetched per clock period to the least recently used instruction buffer. To allow fast issuing of instructions, the memory word containing the current instruction is the first to be fetched. The Cray-1 has 120 instructions with 10 vector types and 13 scalar types, the majority of which are three-address instructions (Figure 4.19b). Figure 4.19c shows the format of a unary vector instruction.

The P register is a 22-bit program counter indicating the next parcel of program code to enter the *next instruction parcel* (NIP) register in a linear program sequence. The P register is entered with a new value on a branch instruction or on an exchange sequence. The *current instruction parcel* (CIP) register is a 16-bit register holding the instruction waiting to be issued. The NIP register is a 16-bit register which holds a parcel of program code prior to entering the CIP register. If an instruction has 32 bits, the CIP register holds the upper half of the instruction. The *lower instruction parcel* (LIP) register, which is also 16 bits long, holds the lower half. Other registers, such as the *vector mask* (VM) registers, the *base address* (BA), the *limit address* (LA) registers, the *exchange address* (XA) register, the *flag* (F) register, and the *mode* (M) register, are used for masking, addressing, and program control purposes.

The twelve functional units in the Cray-1 are organized into four groups: *address, scalar, vector,* and *floating-point pipelines,* as summarized in Table 4.10. Each functional pipe has several stages. The register usage and the number of pipeline stages for each functional unit are specified in the table. The number of

Table 4.10 Cray-1 functional pipeline units

Functional pipelines	Register usage	Pipeline delays (clock periods)
Address functional units		
Address add unit	A	2
Address multiply unit	A	6
Scalar functional units		
Scalar add unit	S	3
Scalar shift unit	S	2 or 3 if double-word shift
Scalar logical unit	S	1
Population/leading zero count unit	S	3
Vector functional units		
Vector add unit	V or S	3
Vector shift unit	V or S	4
Vector logical unit	V or S	2
Floating-point functional units		
Floating-point add unit	S and V	6
Floating-point multiply unit	S and V	7
Reciprocal approximation unit	S and V	14

required clock periods equals the number of stages in each functional pipe. Each functional pipe can operate independently of the operation of others. A number of functional pipes can operate concurrently as long as there are no register conflicts. A functional pipe receives operands from the source registers and delivers the result to a destination register. These pipelines operate essentially in three-address mode with limited source and destination addressing.

The *address pipes* perform 24-bit 2's complement integer arithmetic on operands obtained from A registers and deliver the results back to A registers. There are two address pipes: the *address add* pipe and the *address multiply* pipe. The *scalar pipes* are for *scalar add, scalar shift, scalar logic,* and *population-leading zero count,* performing operations over 64-bit operands from S registers, and in most cases delivering the 64-bit result to an S register. The exception is the population-leading zero count, which delivers a 7-bit integer result to an A register. The scalar shift pipe can shift either the 64-bit contents of an S register or the 128-bit contents of two S registers concatenated together to form a double precision word. The population count pipe counts the number of "1" bits in the operand, while the leading zero count counts the number of "0" preceding a 1 bit in the operand. The scalar logical pipe performs the mask and boolean operations.

The *vector pipes* include the *vector add, vector logic,* and *vector shift.* These units obtain operands from one or two V registers and an S register. Results from a vector pipe are delivered to a V register. When a floating-point pipe is used for a vector operation, it can function similar to a vector pipe. The three *floating-point pipes* are for FLP *add,* FLP *multiply,* and *reciprocal approximation* over floating-point operands. The reciprocal approximation pipe finds the approximated reciprocal of a 64-bit operand in floating-point format. Note that no divide pipe exists in the Cray-1. The Cray-1 performs floating-point division by multiplying the reciprocal of the divisor with the dividend. Add pipes of various types have each two, three, or six stages. All logical pipes have only one or two stages. Multiply pipes require six or seven clocks for completion. The reciprocal approximation pipe has the longest delay of 14 clock periods. The two shifters have two, three, or four clock delays.

The scalar add pipe and vector add pipe perform 64-bit integer arithmetic in 2's complement mode. Multiplication of two fractional operands is accomplished by the floating-point multiply pipe. The floating-point multiply pipe recognizes as a special case the condition of both operands having zero exponents and returns the upper 48-bits of the product of the fractions as the fraction of the result, leaving the exponent field zero. Division of integers would require that they first be converted to FLP format and then divided by the floating-point reciprocal approximation pipe. The floating-point data format contains a 48-bit binary coefficient and a 15-bit exponent field. Sign magnitude mantissa is assumed. Double-precision computations having 95-bit fractions are performed with the aid of software routines, since the Cray-1 has no special hardware supporting multiple precision operations. Logical functions are bitwise *and*, exclusive *or*, and inclusive *or* operations.

In the Cray-1, the startup time for vector operations is nominal; thereby, even for short vectors the performance is quite good. Because of the short startup time of the vector pipes, there is little loss of speed in processing short vectors. For typical operations, vector lengths of three elements or less run faster in scalar mode, while those of four elements or more run faster in vector mode. The vector mode is definitely faster than scalar mode for long vectors. Of course, a vector operation can also be processed as an iterative scalar operation, as it is done on any scalar processor.

4.4.2 Pipeline Chaining and Vector Loops

The Cray-1 is designed to allow many arithmetic operations performed on operands that are resident in registers before returning them to memory. Resources like registers and functional pipes must be properly reserved to enable multiple vector processing. In register-to-register architecture, all vector operands are preloaded into fast vector registers before feeding them into the pipelines. Intermediate and final results (outputs from pipeline) are also loaded into vector registers before storing them in the main memory. We consider below the resource reservation problem associated with a register-to-register vector processor like the Cray-1. As illustrated in Figure 4.20, vector instructions can be classified into four types. The *type 1* instruction obtains operands from one or two vector registers and returns results to another vector register. The *type 2* vector instruction consumes a scalar operand from an S_j register and a vector operand from a V_k register and returns the vector results to another vector register, V_i. The *type 3* and *type 4* instructions transfer data from memory to a vector register and vice versa, respectively. A data

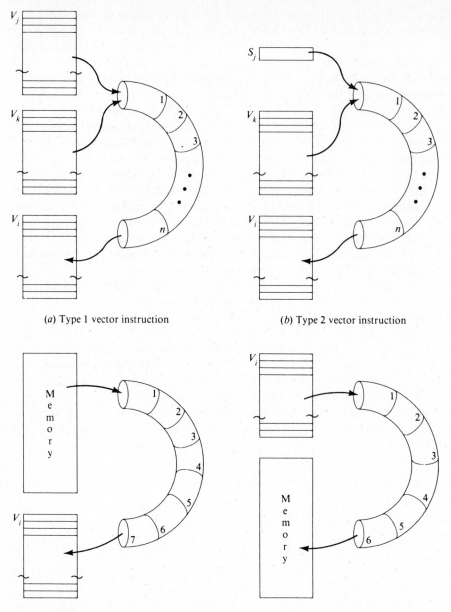

(a) Type 1 vector instruction

(b) Type 2 vector instruction

(c) Type 3 vector instruction

(d) Type 4 vector instruction

Figure 4.20 Four types of vector instruction in the Cray-1.

path between memory and working registers can be considered a *data transmit pipeline* with a fixed-time delay.

When a vector instruction is issued, the required functional pipes and operand registers are reserved for a number of clock periods determined by the vector length. Subsequent vector instructions using the same set of functional units or operand registers cannot be issued until the reservations are released. Two or more vector instructions may use different functional pipelines and different vector registers at the same time, if they are independent. Such concurrent instructions can be issued in consecutive clock periods. Figure 4.21*a* shows two independent instructions, one using the add pipe and the other using the multiply pipe. Figure 4.21*b* depicts the demand on the add pipe by two independent vector additions. When the first *add* instruction is issued, the add pipe is reserved. Therefore, the issue of the second *add* instruction is delayed until the add pipe is freed. Figure 4.21*c* shows two different vector instructions sharing the same operand register V_1. The first *add* instruction reserves the operand register V_1, causing the issue of the *multiply* instruction to be delayed until the operand register V_1 is freed. Figure 4.21*d* illustrates the reservations of both the add pipe and the operand register V_1. Like the reservation required for operand registers, the result register needs also to be reserved for the number of clock periods determined by the vector length and the pipeline delays. This reservation ensures the proper transmittal of the final result to the result register.

A result register may become the operand register of a succeeding instruction. In the Cray-1, the technique is called *chaining* of two pipelines. Pipeline chaining

$$V_0 \leftarrow V_1 + V_2$$
$$V_3 \leftarrow V_4 * V_5$$

(*a*) Independent instructions

$$V_3 \leftarrow V_1 + V_2$$
$$V_6 \leftarrow V_4 + V_5$$

(*b*) Functional unit reservation

$$V_3 \leftarrow V_1 + V_2$$
$$V_6 \leftarrow V_1 + V_5$$

(*c*) Operand register reservation

$$V_0 \leftarrow V_1 + V_2$$
$$V_3 \leftarrow V_1 + V_5$$

(*d*) Functional unit and operand register reservations

Figure 4.21 The reservation of functional units and operand registers.

is expanded from the concept of internal forwarding, discussed in Section 3.3.3. Basically, chaining is a linking process that occurs when results obtained from one pipeline unit are directly fed into the operand registers of another functional pipe. In other words, intermediate results do not have to be restored into memory and can be used even before the vector operation is completed. Chaining permits successive operations to be issued as soon as the first result becomes available as an operand. Of course, the desired functional pipes and operand registers must be properly reserved; otherwise, chaining operations have to be suspended until the demanded resources become available. The following example is used to illustrate pipeline chaining in the Cray-1. Because only eight vector registers are available, the number of pipeline functions that can be linked together is bounded by eight. Usually only two to five functions can be linked in a cascade.

Example 4.4 The following sequence of four vector instructions are chained together to be executed as a compound function:

$$V_0 \leftarrow \text{Memory} \qquad \text{(Memory fetch)}$$

$$V_2 \leftarrow V_0 + V_1 \qquad \text{(Vector add)}$$

$$V_3 \leftarrow V_2 < A_3 \qquad \text{(Left shift)}$$

$$V_5 \leftarrow V_3 \wedge V_4 \qquad \text{(Logical product)}$$

A pictorial illustration is given in Figure 4.22 to show the chaining of the *memory fetch* pipe, the *vector add* pipe, the *vector shift* pipe, and the *vector logical* pipe into a longer pipeline processor. The contents of the register A_3 determine the shift count. A timing diagram of the chaining operations is shown in Figure 4.23. The memory fetch instruction is issued at time t_0. Each horizontal line shows the production of one component of the result in register V_5. The time spans in four pipelines are indicated by solid heavy line sections (marked by b, e, h, and k). The dashed lines represent the transit times (marked by a, c, d, f, g, i, j, and l) between memory fetch and functional pipelines or between transfers among vector registers. One operand is fetched from memory to the pipeline cascade per clock period. The first result emerges at clock period t_{23} and a new component result enters the V_5 register for each clock period thereafter.

In a vector operation, the results are normally not restored to the same vector register used by the source operands. Under certain circumstances, it may be desirable to route results directly back to one of the operand registers. Such recursive operations on functional pipelines require special precautions to avoid the data-jamming problem. To see how recursive computation can be realized in a pipeline, component operations must be properly monitored. Associated with each vector register is a *component counter*. When a vector instruction is issued, all component counters are set to zero. Normally, sending an operand from a source register to a functional pipeline causes the associated component counter

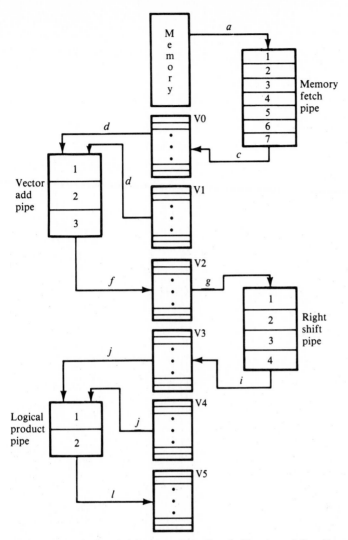

Figure 4.22 A pipeline chaining example in Cray-1. (Courtesy of Cray Research, Inc., Johnson 1977.)

to be incremented by one. Similarly, a component result arriving at a vector register from a functional pipe causes the associated component counter to be incremented by one. When a vector register serves as both operand and result register, its component counter will not be updated until the first result returns from the functional pipe. While the counter is held at zero, the same operand component is repeatedly sent to the functional pipe.

The recursive use of functional pipelines can be applicable to many vector operations, either arithmetic or logical. The initial value in a component register depends on the operation to be performed. Since each vector register in the Cray-1

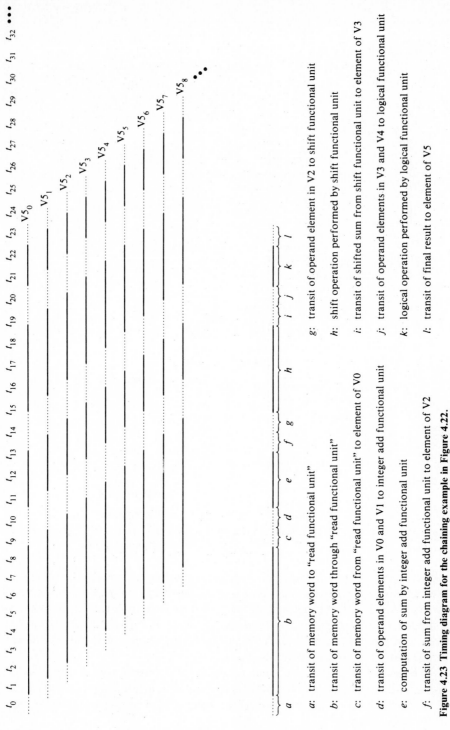

t_0 t_1 t_2 t_3 t_4 t_5 t_6 t_7 t_8 t_9 t_{10} t_{11} t_{12} t_{13} t_{14} t_{15} t_{16} t_{17} t_{18} t_{19} t_{20} t_{21} t_{22} t_{23} t_{24} t_{25} t_{26} t_{27} t_{28} t_{29} t_{30} t_{31} t_{32}

$V5_0$ $V5_1$ $V5_2$ $V5_3$ $V5_4$ $V5_5$ $V5_6$ $V5_7$ $V5_8$

a b c d e f g h i j k l

a: transit of memory word to "read functional unit"

b: transit of memory word through "read functional unit"

c: transit of memory word from "read functional unit" to element of V0

d: transit of operand elements in V0 and V1 to integer add functional unit

e: computation of sum by integer add functional unit

f: transit of sum from integer add functional unit to element of V2

g: transit of operand element in V2 to shift functional unit

h: shift operation performed by shift functional unit

i: transit of shifted sum from shift functional unit to element of V3

j: transit of operand elements in V3 and V4 to logical functional unit

k: logical operation performed by logical functional unit

l: transit of final result to element of V5

Figure 4.23 Timing diagram for the chaining example in Figure 4.22.

can accommodate at most 64 elements, long vectors are processed in segments. The program construct for processing long vectors is called a *vector loop*. The segmentation of long vectors into loops is done by the system hardware and software control. The programmer never sees this segmentation into vector loops. Each pass through the loop processes a 64-element (or smaller) section of the long vectors. Generally, the loop count is computed from the vector length before entering the loop. Inside the loop, each of the twelve functional pipes can be fully utilized to process the current section. The following is an implemented example demonstrating vector looping in the Cray-1.

Example 4.5 Let A and B be vectors of length N. Consider the following loop operations:

$$\text{DO } 10 \text{ I}=1,N$$
$$10 \ A(I)=5.0*B(I)+C$$

When N is 64 or less, a sequence of seven instructions generates the A array:

$S_1 \leftarrow 5.0$	Set constant in scalar register
$S_2 \leftarrow C$	Load constant C in scalar register
$\text{VL} \leftarrow N$	Set vector length into VL register
$V_0 \leftarrow B$	Read B vector into vector register
$V_1 \leftarrow S_1 * V_0$	Multiply each component of the B array by a constant
$V_2 \leftarrow S_2 + V_1$	Add C to $5 * B(I)$
$A \leftarrow V_2$	Store the result vector in A array

The fourth and sixth instructions use different functional pipelines with shared intermediate registers. They can be chained together. The outputs of the chain are finally stored in the A array. When N exceeds 64, vector loops are required. Before entering the loop, N is divided by 64 to determine the loop count. If there is a remainder, the remainder elements of the A array are generated in the first loop. The loop consists of the fourth to the seventh instructions for each 64-element segment of the A and B arrays.

Recursion can be implemented by vector operations in the Cray-1 with the help of the component counters. Let C_1 be the component counter associated with a vector register V1. To introduce recursions, one vector register, say V0, must serve as both an operand register and a result register. Under such circumstances, C_0 will be held to zero until the first component result is returned from the functional pipe to V0. In other words, C_0 updates according to its function as a result register. During this period, the same component operand from $C0_0$, the first component register in V0, is repeatedly sent to the functional pipe until C_0 increments after the first result. The use of the same component from V0 can repeat for

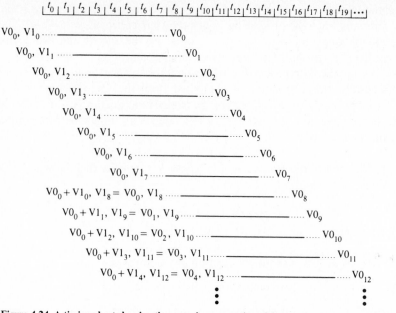

Figure 4.24 A timing chart showing the recursive summation of the vector components in Example 4.6.

subsequent components in V0 until the entire vector operation is done. The following example will clarify this recursion concept.

Example 4.6 Consider the use of the floating-point add pipe for the recursive vector summation $V0 \leftarrow V0 + V1$, where the vector register V1 holds an array of floating-point numbers to be added recursively. The timing chart of the recursion is shown in Figure 4.24. Initially, both counters C_0 and C_1 are set to be zero. The initial value in the first component register $V0_0$ of V0 is also set to zero. The FLP add pipe requires six clock periods to pass through. Register transfer to or from the FLP add pipe takes another clock period. Therefore, the total cycle is $1 + 6 + 1 = 8$ clock periods, as shown in Figure 4.24. The vector-length register is assumed to have a value of 64 for a single vector loop.

The counter C_0 is kept at zero until time t_8. During this cycle, $V0_0$ (which is set to 0) is sent to the pipeline. However, the counter C_1 keeps incrementing after each clock period. Therefore, $V1_0, V1_1, \ldots, V1_{63}$ are sent to the pipeline in subsequent 64 clock periods after t_0. After t_8, C_0 gets incremented by one after each clock period. This means the successive output sums are added recursively with one additional component from V1 in every eight clock periods. When the computations are completed, the component registers of V0 should be loaded as shown in Table 4.11. The 64 components are divided into eight groups of eight component sums each. The last summation group from $V0_{56}$ to $V0_{63}$ holds the eight summations of the eight components of V1, each.

Table 4.11 Successive contents of vector register V0 in Example 4.6

$$(V0_0) = (V0_0) + (V1_0) = 0 + (V1_0)$$
$$(V0_1) = (V0_0) + (V1_1) = 0 + (V1_1)$$
$$(V0_2) = (V0_0) + (V1_2) = 0 + (V1_2)$$
$$(V0_3) = (V0_0) + (V1_3) = 0 + (V1_3)$$
$$(V0_4) = (V0_0) + (V1_4) = 0 + (V1_4)$$
$$(V0_5) = (V0_0) + (V1_5) = 0 + (V1_5)$$
$$(V0_6) = (V0_0) + (V1_6) = 0 + (V1_6)$$
$$(V0_7) = (V0_0) + (V1_7) = 0 + (V1_7)$$

The first group

$$(V0_8) = (V0_0) + (V1_8) = (V1_0) + (V1_8)$$
$$(V0_9) = (V0_1) + (V1_9) = (V1_1) + (V1_9)$$
$$(V0_{10}) = (V0_2) + (V1_{10}) = (V1_2) + (V1_{10})$$
$$(V0_{11}) = (V0_3) + (V1_{11}) = (V1_3) + (V1_{11})$$
$$(V0_{12}) = (V0_4) + (V1_{12}) = (V1_4) + (V1_{12})$$
$$\vdots$$
$$(V0_{15}) = (V0_7) + (V1_{15}) = (V1_7) + (V1_{15})$$

The second group

$$(V0_{16}) = (V0_8) + (V1_{16}) = (V1_0) + (V1_8) + (V1_{16})$$
$$\vdots$$
$$(V0_{55}) = (V0_{47}) + (V1_{55}) = (V1_7) + (V1_{15}) + (V1_{23}) + (V1_{31}) + (V1_{30})$$
$$+ (V1_{47}) + (V1_{55})$$

↑ Group 3
· through
↓ group 7

$$(V0_{56}) = (V0_{48}) + (V1_{56}) = (V1_0) + (V1_8) + (V1_{16}) + (V1_{24}) + (V1_{32})$$
$$+ (V1_{40}) + (V1_{48}) + (V1_{56})$$
$$(V0_{57}) = (V0_{49}) + (V1_{57}) = (V1_1) + (V1_9) + (V1_{17}) + (V1_{25}) + (V1_{33})$$
$$+ (V1_{41}) + (V1_{49}) + (V1_{57})$$
$$(V0_{58}) = (V0_{50}) + (V1_{53}) = (V1_2) + (V1_{10}) + (V1_{18}) + (V1_{26}) + (V1_{34})$$
$$+ (V1_{42}) + (V1_{50}) + (V1_{58})$$
$$(V0_{59}) = (V0_{51}) + (V1_{59}) = (V1_3) + (V1_{11}) + (V1_{19}) + (V1_{27})$$
$$+ (V1_{35}) + (V1_{43}) + (V1_{51}) + (V1_{59})$$
$$(V0_{60}) = (V0_{52}) + (V1_{60}) = (V1_4) + (V1_{12}) + (V1_{20}) + (V1_{28})$$
$$+ (V1_{36}) + (V1_{44}) + (V1_{52}) + (V1_{60})$$
$$(V0_{61}) = (V0_{53}) + (V1_{61}) = (V1_5) + (V1_{13}) + (V1_{21}) + (V1_{29})$$
$$+ (V1_{37}) + (V1_{45}) + (V1_{53}) + (V1_{61})$$
$$(V0_{62}) = (V0_{54}) + (V1_6) + (V1_{14}) + (V1_{22}) + (V1_{30})$$
$$+ (V1_{36}) + (V1_{46}) + (V1_{54}) + (V1_{62})$$
$$(V0_{63}) = (V0_{55}) + (V1_{63}) = (V1_7) + (V1_{15}) + (V1_{23}) + (V1_{31})$$
$$+ (V1_{39}) + (V1_{47}) + (V1_{55}) + (V1_{63})$$

The eighth group
(result)

The above recursive vector summation is very useful in scientific computations. For an example, the dot product of vectors $A \cdot B = \sum a_i \cdot b_i$ can be implemented in the Cray-1 by chaining the following two operations: a *vector multiply* $V1 \leftarrow V3 * V4$ followed by a *floating-point add* $V0 \leftarrow V0 + V1$. If the vector length is 64, the dot product can be reduced to 8 sums (from 64) after the *chained multiply and add* operations. The next iteration is to find the sum of the eight subsums to product the final result. For *recursive vector multiplication*, similar operations can be implemented with a floating-point multiple pipe, except the initial value of $V0_0$ should be 1 instead of 0. This operation should be useful in polynomial evaluations.

The performance of the Cray-1 may vary from 3 to 160 megaflops, depending on the applications and programming skills. Scalar performance of 12 megaflops was observed for matrix multiplication. Vector performance of 22 megaflops was observed in vector dot product operations. Supervector performance of 153 megaflops was observed in assembly-code matrix multiplication. These speeds are special peak values. The Cray-1 will more likely have an average vector-supervector performance in the range of 20 to 80 megaflops, depending of course on the work load distribution.

In order to achieve even better supercomputer performance, Cray Research has extended the Cray-1 to the Cray X-MP, a dual-processor system with loosely coupled multiprogramming and single-program multiprocessing. The Cray X-MP has eight times the Cray-1 memory bandwidth and a reduced clock period of 9.5 ns. It has guaranteed chaining. Furthermore, the software for the Cray X-MP is compatible with that of the Cray-1. The first customer shipments of the Cray X-MP took place in 1983, with full production in 1984.

The Cray X-MP offers impressive speedup over the Cray-1. For mixed jobs, it has been estimated that the Cray X-MP has a 2.5 to 5 times throughput gain over the Cray-1. For scalar processing, it is 1.25 to 2.5 times faster than the Cray-1. Again, it is excellent for both short and long vector processing, as is the Cray-1. When the Cray X-MP gets upgraded to the Cray-2 after the mid-80s, the performance is expected to increase six times in scalar and 12 times in vector operations over the Cray-1. The Cray-2 will have four processors with a basic pipeline clock rate of 4 ns, 32 M words of main memory, and 20 times improved I/O. We will study various Cray Research's multiprocessors in detail in Chapter 9.

4.4.3 The Architecture of Cyber-205

The Cyber-205 represents more than 20 years of evolution in scientific computing by the Control Data Corporation from the early CDC-1604, through the CDC 6600/7600 series, to the Star-100 and Cyber-203. The Cyber-203 improves over the Star-100 by the use of semiconductor memory, concurrent scalar processing, and a memory-interface design that permits instructions to be issued every 20 ns. The improvements of the Cyber-205 over the 203 stem from the use of entire LSI circuitry with large bipolar memory, additional vector instructions, and support by the NOS-based operating system. The Cyber 205 became available in 1981.

The system architecture of Cyber-205 (Figure 4.25) differs from that of the Star-100 (Figure 4.2) in the addition of a powerful scalar processor and two more vector pipelines (for a total of four vector pipes). The basic pipeline clock period of the Cyber-205 pipelines is 20 ns and the memory cycle is 80 ns, half of that of the Star. Only 26 distinct LSI-chip types are used, which significantly increases system reliability and maintainability. Instead of using slow core memory, the Cyber-205 uses bipolar main memory of up to four million 64-bit words with an 80-ns cycle time. Memory-access patterns include 512-bit superwords (eight 64-bit words) for vector operands and fullwords (64 bits) and halfwords (32 bits) for scalar operands. The main memory bandwidth is 400 MW/s, significantly

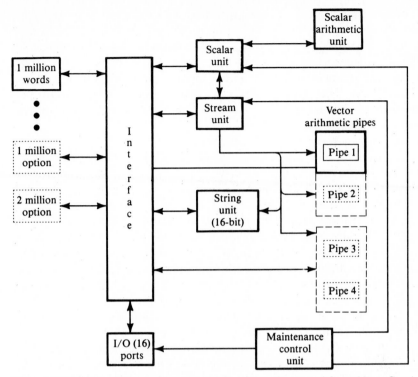

Figure 4.25 The Cyber-205 computer system configuration. (Courtesy of Control Data Corp.)

higher than that in the Cray-1. The high memory bandwidth is needed to support the memory-to-memory pipeline operations.

Instruction-execution control resides in the *scalar unit,* which receives and decodes all instructions from memory, directly executes scalar instructions, and dispatches vector and string instructions to the four *vector pipes* and the *string unit* for execution. It also provides orderly buffering and execution of the data and instructions. With independent vector and scalar instruction controls to a single-instruction stream, the scalar unit can execute scalar instructions in parallel with the execution of most vector instructions.

The *scalar arithmetic unit* contains five independent functional pipes for *add/subtract, multiply, log, shift,* and *divide/sqrt* operations over 32- or 64-bit scalars. The peak speed of the scalar processor is 50 megaflops. The *vector processor* has the option of having one, two, or four floating-point arithmetic pipes. The *stream unit* manages the data streams between central memory and the vector pipelines. A vector arithmetic pipe can perform *add/subtract, multiply, divide, sqrt, logical,* and *shift* over 32- or 64-bit vector operands. Each vector pipeline is directly connected to the main memory without using vector registers (Figure 4.25a). The *string unit* processes the control vectors during streaming operations. It provides the capability for BCD and binary arithmetic-address arithmetic and boolean operations.

The vector startup time in the Cyber-205 is much longer than that of the Cray-1. A vector may comprise up to 65,635 consecutive memory words. Control vectors are used to address data that is stored in nonconsecutive locations. Each pipeline receives two input streams and generates one output stream of floating-point numbers. Each stream is 128 bits wide, supporting a 100-megaflops computation rate of 32-bit results or 50 megaflops for 64-bit results per each vector processor. With four vector pipes, the Cyber-205 can produce 200 megaflops for 64-bit results and 400 megaflops for 32-bit results in *vector add/subtract* or in *vector multiply* operations. The Cyber-205 can also be used to perform *linked vector multiply* and *vector add/subtract* operations with a maximum rate of 800 or 400 megaflops for 64- or 32-bit results, respectively, on a four-processor configuration. The vector divide and *square root* operations are much slower than the *add/subtract* or *multiply* operations.

Each vector arithmetic unit consists of five functional pipes, as shown in Figure 4.26a. The detailed pipeline stages in the floating-point *add unit* and the *multiply unit* are shown in Figure 4.26b and c. Both pipeline units have feedback connections for accumulative add or multiply operations. These two units are improved over the designs in the Star-100 (Figure 4.3). The pipeline delays in both vector-scalar units are summarized in Table 4.12. With a 20-ns clock rate, the number of required clock periods is also shown in each case. The *load/store* is also pipelined. Pipelining produces one result per each clock period of 20 ns. The result from any of the above units can be routed directly to the input of other units without stopping in some intermediate registers. This process is called *short-stopping*, as facilitated by the feedback connections in Figure 4.25. The theoretical peak performance of the Cyber-205 is summarized in Table 4.13 for 32- and 64-bit results.

The bipolar memory is four-way interleaved, giving an effective cycle time of 20 ns per word. The central memory is a virtual memory system with advanced memory management features such as *key* and *lock* for memory protection and separation, hardware mapping from virtual to physical address, and user program-data sharing capability. The page sizes vary from small (1K, 2K, 8K words) to large (65K words). The Cyber-205 has 16 I/O channels, each 16 bits wide. The I/O system consists of multiple minicomputers for handling up to 10 disk stations.

Table 4.12 Pipeline delays in the Cyber-205

Functional pipe	Time delays (ns)	Clock periods
Load-store	300	15
Add-subtract	100	5
Multiply	100	5
Logical	60	3
Divide-square root	1080 (64 bits)	54
Conversion	600 (32 bits)	30

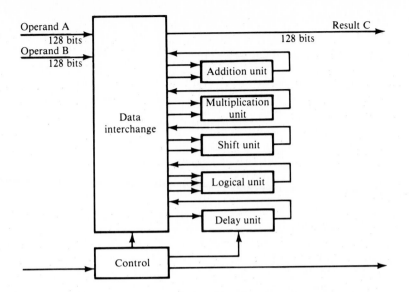

(*a*) One vector arithmetic processor

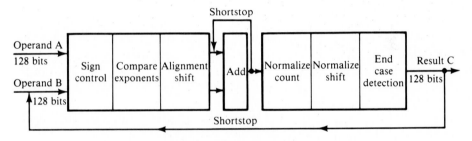

(*b*) The floating-point addition pipeline

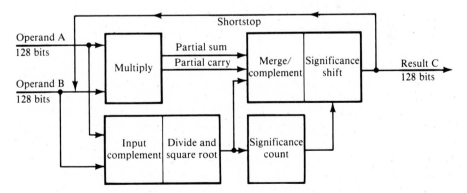

(*c*) The floating-point multiply pipeline

Figure 4.26 Pipelined structure of one vector processor in the Cyber-205. (Courtesy of Control Data Corp.)

Table 4.13 Peak performance of Cyber-205

Vector instructions	Operand length	Peak performance (megaflops)		
		One pipe	Two pipes	Four pipes
Vector add-subtract	32 bits	100	200	400
	64 bits	50	100	200
Vector multiply	32 bits	100	200	400
	64 bits	50	100	200
Vector linked multiply and add or subtract	32 bits	200	400	800
	64 bits	100	200	800
Vector divide-square root	32 bits	15.3	30.6	61.2
	64 bits	8	16	32
Vector divide-square root (high-speed option)	32 bits	—	61.2	122.4
	64 bits	—	32	64

Each station can accommodate eight disk drives. Fifty megabaud serial line interfaces and network access devices can be used to connect the Cyber-205 with the Cyber net.

Software support for the Cyber-205 consists primarily of the Cyber-200-OS, the Cyber-200 Fortran, the Cyber-200 Assembler META, and Cyber-200 utility programs. The Cyber-205 Fortran compiler provides code optimization, loop collapsing into vector instructions whenever possible, effective utilization of the large register file, and accessibility to 256 Cyber-205 instructions, divided into 16 vector types and 10 scalar types.

The most obvious architectural improvement of the second generation vector processors over the first generation is the inclusion of a scalar processor for non-vector operations. By far, the Cray-1 and Cyber-205 are the fastest processors manufactured in the United States, with cycle times of 12.5 and 20 ns, respectively. Both systems use bipolar ECL circuits. Only four chip types are used in the Cray-1 versus 26 chip types in the Cyber-205. Multiple unifunction pipelines are used in the Cray-1, while the Cyber-205 is equipped with multifunction static pipelines. In both systems, fast bipolar main memory is used.

To compare the vector-processing capabilities of the Cray-1 and Cyber-205, we consider the parallel execution of the following program.

Example 4.7

$$\text{DO } 10 \text{ I}=1, 1024$$
$$10 \text{ Y(I)}=\text{A(1)}*\text{B(1)}$$

On the Cray-1, the above DO loop would be computed at a CPU rate of

$$\frac{1000}{12.5 \text{ ns/answer}} = 80 \text{ megaflops}$$

For the Cyber-205, the corresponding CPU rate would be

$$\frac{1000}{20 \text{ ns/answer}} = 50 \text{ megaflops/pipe}$$

If two vector pipelines are used in the Cyber-205, then 100 megaflops could be achieved. The entire operation must be grouped in 16 successive segments of 64 operations each, since 64 is the loop vector length in both systems.

The Cyber-205 has richer vector instructions than the Cray-1, whereas the latter has better scalar instructions. With two pipeline processors, the Cyber has a 10-ns effective burst rate. The Cray-1 can be attached to IBM, CDC, or Univac front-end host computers. The Cyber-205 can be driven by the Cyber-170 series or the IBM 303X. A major difference between the two supercomputers is the all-LSI chip technology in the Cyber-205 as opposed to the SSI logic parts in the Cray-1, except for the LSI 4K RAM chips in the Cray-1. The two systems differ also in the arithmetic pipes, masked vector operations, and in the I/O linkage operation to the front-end host.

4.4.4 Vector Processing in Cyber-205 and CDC-NASF

In this section, we describe several special features in the Cyber-205. These features are necessary to facilitate memory-to-memory vector pipelining. We shall first review memory-mapping schemes in the Cyber-205. Then we illustrate the use of bit vectors for controlled vector processing. The effect of startup delays on the Cyber-205 will be evaluated. We describe the improvement of the I/O configurations in the Cyber-205 as compared with the earlier Star-100 system. Finally, we study the enhanced model proposed by Control Data for future supercomputing.

The Cyber-205 provides high-speed memory-to-memory vector operations. Consider a Fortran declaration DIMENSION A(4, 4), B(4, 4, 4). In a normal Fortran memory-allocation system, the entire array **A** could be considered a vector of length 16 and **B** could be a vector of length 64 if all the data were to be processed as a unit with all elements independent of one another. If every other plane of the **B** array were to be processed, one could view the data as being in four vectors, each of length 16 elements (Figure 4.27a). The requirement for contiguous storage of data in memory arises from the engineering solution to achieve high bandwidth (Figure 4.27b), but the conceptual notion of dealing with problem solutions in vector form is being exploited by mathematicians in the development of new algorithms.

The concept of memory-to-memory vector pipelining in the Cyber-205 is illustrated in Figure 4.28. Since the data arriving at the arithmetic pipeline are usually contiguous, every segment in a pipeline will be performing useful work except at the very beginning and end of a vector operation. From an engineering point of view, this makes very efficient use of the circuitry employed, at a cost of some time to "get the operation rolling" (first result returned to memory or registers) due to the length (in number of clock cycles) of the pipeline.

Experience has shown that few supercomputers totally operate on a single massive problem in a dedicated manner. The normal installation finds the waking hours being consumed by algorithm development, program debugging, and interactive execution of research programs and even large production programs. The evening and midnight hours are usually more structured, with one or more major programs monopolizing the machine's resources and with, perhaps, a modest amount of interactive debugging being pursued in a background mode.

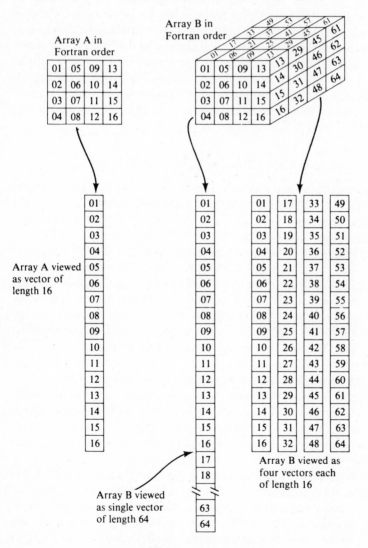

(*a*) Fortran arrays as vectors

Figure 4.27 Memory mapping examples in the Cyber-205.

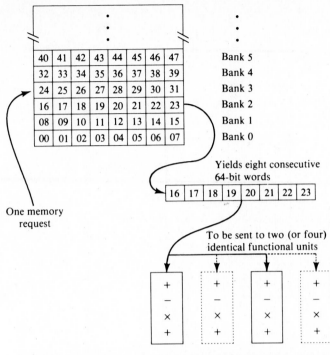

(b) Cyber-20 memory allocation

Figure 4.27 (continued) (Courtesy of *IEEE Trans. Computers*, Lincoln 1982.)

Virtual memory plays a major supporting role in a supercomputer. Listed below are the important memory functions in the Cyber-205:

1. *Assist in memory management*: The operating system can commit and de-commit arbitrary blocks of real memory without having to ensure the physical contiguity of a user's workspace. This reduces overhead for actions such as the accumulation of unused space, which could be quite costly in large memory systems (on the order of eight million words).
2. *Provide identically appearing execution of all jobs*: This means that a program's *dimension* statements and input parameters can remain unchanged whether or not a 4-hour run is being contemplated or a simple debugging run of a particular phase is intended.
3. *Eliminate working space constraints from algorithm development*: Mathematicians and programmers can begin developing an algorithm as if they had available an infinite workspace in which to put data and temporary results. Once the algorithm is developed, the programmer must introduce the means to handle paging of the information in order to optimize the performance of the system and to eliminate the thrashing that can occur in virtual memory machines moving data to and from real central memory.

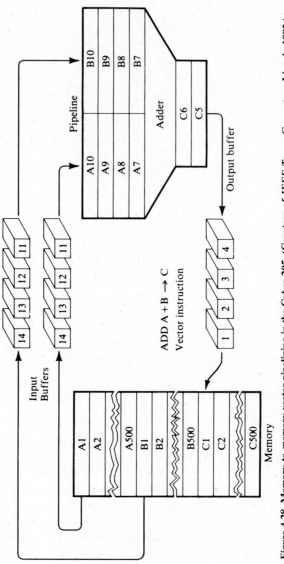

ADD A + B → C
Vector instruction

Figure 4.28 Memory-to-memory vector pipelining in the Cyber-205. (Courtesy of *IEEE Trans. Computers,* Lincoln 1982.)

A most significant contribution of the Cyber-205 was the notion that strings of binary bits (called *bit vectors*) could be used to carry information about vectors and could be applied to those vectors to perform some key functions. Since the bit strings became the key to the vector-restructuring concept, a means had to be provided to manipulate bit vectors as well as numeric vectors; thus was added the *string functional unit* to the hardware ensemble in both the Star-100 and the Cyber-205. The functions of *compress, mask, merge, scatter,* and *gather* were incorporated. In addition, many of the reduction operations like *sum, product,* and *inner product* were implemented directly in the hardware.

Two special vector instructions using the control bit vectors are illustrated in Figure 4.29. In part *a*, the two source vectors A and B are merged under the control of the bit vector C to give the result vector R. The merging is conducted so as to select from A on "1" in C, and from B on "0" in C. In part *b* the source vector A

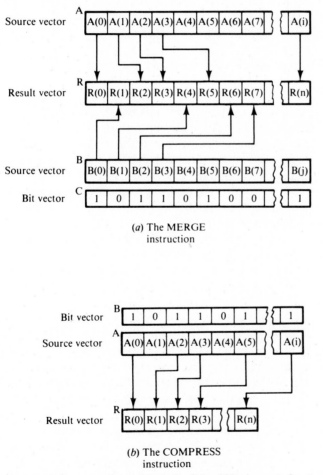

(*a*) The MERGE instruction

(*b*) The COMPRESS instruction

Figure 4.29 Two vector instructions in the Cyber-205 using control vectors.

is being compressed to give the result vector **R** under the bit vector **B**. The compression is done on "0" in **B**. These instructions are extremely useful in manipulating sparse matrices.

Startup time of vector operations includes the instruction translation time and the delay imposed by fetching and aligning the input streams and by aligning and moving output streams to memory. Figure 4.30 illustrates the impact of startup time on the effective performance of the Cyber-205 architecture. A major improvement in the overall performance of this type of memory-to-memory vector architecture requires careful attention to startup time. In addition to the raw improvement in clock speed, the designers were directed to other methods for reducing the delay in vector initiation.

The actions of address setup and management of vector arithmetic control lines require substantial speedup. In addition, providing separate and independent functional units in each of the scalar and vector processors permits execution of those functions in parallel. Hence, the apparent startup time becomes smaller than what the hardware provides. This feature, in the best cases, results in parallel execution of both scalar and vector floating-point operations with a consequent increase in overall performance.

Identified below are three major changes in the architecture of the Star-100 to yield the Cyber-205:

1. In the Star-100, the operation of the scalar unit was coupled with the vector unit such that only one type of operation could be performed at a time. The Cyber-205 has the ability to run both vector unit and scalar unit in parallel.
2. To fit a variety of operating environments, the Cyber-200 family was provided with a range of small page sizes beginning with 4096 bytes and ending with 65,536 bytes. The large page size of the Star-100 was retained since it appeared to be optimum for large production programs.
3. The input-output system employed in the Star-100 was of the "star network" type, with node-to-node communication between the CPU and attached peripherals. The change to a network form of I/O which is called the *loosely coupled network* (LCN), was a major switch for hardware and software alike on the Cyber-205.

Figure 4.31 illustrates the star network connection of the Star-100 and attached peripherals and contrasts this with the Cyber-205. Note that the connectivity of the Cyber-205 is potentially much greater than that of its predecessor. In addition, data transfers between elements of the Cyber-205 system can bypass the front-end elements; in the Star-100, data rates between permanent file storage and the CPU are limited by the capacity of the front-end processor, which typically is on the order of 1 to 4 Mbits/s.

Transmission of data is accomplished on a high-speed, bit-serial trunk to which 2 to 16 system elements can be coupled. The method of establishing a link is based on addresses in the serial message which can be recognized by the hardware trunk coupler, called the *network access device* (NAD). The most significant

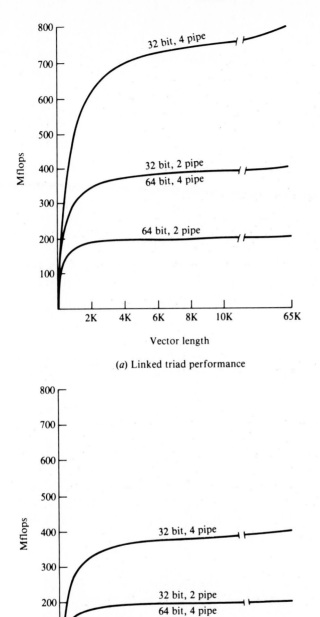

(a) Linked triad performance

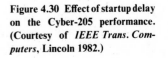

(b) Multiply-add performance

Figure 4.30 Effect of startup delay on the Cyber-205 performance. (Courtesy of *IEEE Trans. Computers*, Lincoln 1982.)

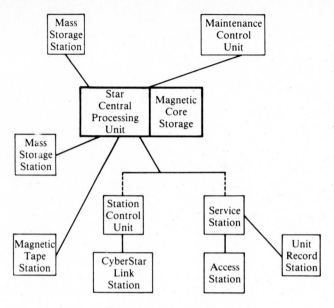

(*a*) The "star-network" for Star-100

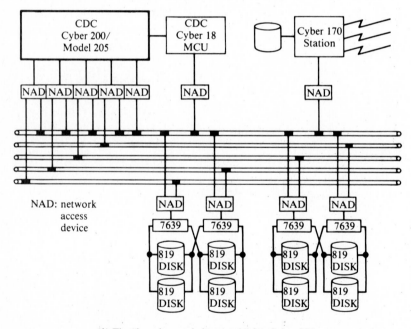

(*b*) The "loosely coupled network" for Cyber-205.

Figure 4.31 Input-output subsystem configurations in the Star-100 and the Cyber-205. (Courtesy of *IEEE Trans. Computers*, Lincoln 1982.)

aspect of this decision has been the philosophical departure from dedicated peripherals to shared peripherals, which are accessed on a "party line" basis. Once this change has been incorporated in the system software, the actual transmission media and hardware form of NAD is invisible to the user.

In 1979, Control Data Corporation proposed to the NASA Ames Research Center a supercomputer design, called the *Numerical Aerodynamic Simulation Facility* (NASF), to be used in the 1990s for aerospace vehicle or superjet designs. The purpose is to provide predictive three-dimensional modeling of the wind tunnel experiments characterized by viscous Navier-Stokes fluid equations. This computational approach to solve fluid dynamic problems is only constrained by processor speed and memory space. It costs much less than building a huge wind tunnel, which is limited by so many physical factors. The speed requirement of the NASF was set to be at least 1000 megaflops. Feasibility has been established and U.S. government funding is being awaited before proceeding with the design and construction of such a supercomputer.

The CDC/NASF design extends the structure of the Cyber-205, as shown in Figure 4.32*a*. There are five vector pipelines in NASF, with one serving as a spare unit. Functional components in one vector pipeline are shown in Figure 4.32*b*. A separate scalar processor is used. The clock rate of this proposed design is 8 ns. The memory hierarchy has three levels: an 8 M word of ECL cache, a 32 M word MOS intermediate memory, and a CCD sequential memory of 128 M words. Within each vector pipeline, adders, multipliers and complementers are all duplicated in pairs to facilitate parallel real or complex number calculations and error checkings. The spare vector pipe can be switched in automatically whenever a failure is detected. This allows on-line repairing of the failing unit.

With an 8-ns clock rate, the CDC/NASF can operate with a rate of 500 megaflops for 64-bit results and 1000 megaflops for 32-bit results. Since each result may be produced with one to three floating-point operations, depending on whether real or complex operands are involved, the theoretical peak performance of the NASF should be tripled, as 1500 megaflops for 64-bit results and 3000 megaflops for 32-bit results. Besides CDC, Burroughs has also submitted a proposal to build the NASF as an SIMD array processor.

4.4.5 Fujitsu VP-200 and Special Features

Fujitsu announced the FACOM vector processors VP-100 and VP-200 in July 1982. High performance in this machine is achieved by LSI technology, improved architecture, a sophisticated compiler, and a number of advanced features in both the hardware and software areas. It can be used as a loosely coupled back-end system. The block diagram of the VP-200 is shown in Figure 4.33. The system has a scalar processor and a vector processor which can operate concurrently. Like in the Cray-1, large and fast registers, buffers, and multiple pipes are used to enable register-to-register operations. The main memory has up to 256 M bytes connected to the vector registers via two load-store pipelines. Each of the two load-store pipes

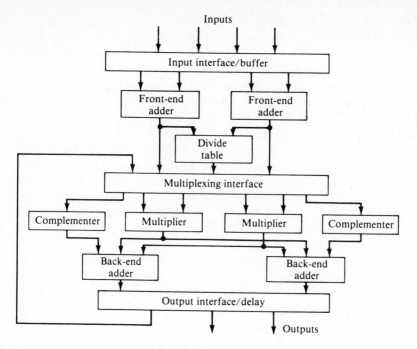

(*a*) Functional design of one vector pipeline

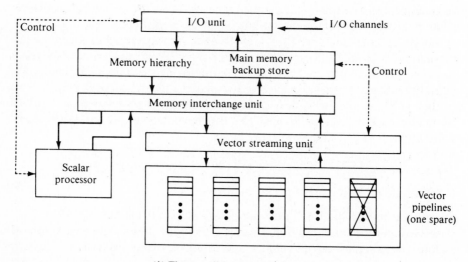

(*b*) The overall system architecture

Figure 4.32 The proposed CDC NASF supercomputer. (Courtesy of Control Data Corp.)

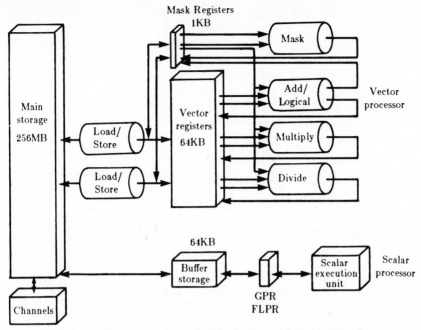

Figure 4.33 The FACOM vector process VP-200. (Courtesy of Fujitsu Limited, Japan.)

has a data bandwidth of 267 M words in either direction. This rate matches the maximum throughput of the arithmetic pipes. There are four execution pipelines in the vector processor. Data format for vector instructions can be bit strings, 32-bit fixed-point, and 32- or 64-bit floating-point operands. There are 83 vector instructions and 195 scalar instructions in the VP-200. Most of the scalar instructions are IBM 370 compatible and the scalar unit interfaces with the main memory via larger buffer storage.

In the VP-200, the vector registers can be dynamically reconfigured by concatenation to assume variable lengths up to 1024 words. Vector instructions include *vector compare, masking, compress, expand, macros,* and *controls,* in addition to arithmetic logic operations. Concurrent operations include two load-store, mask, two out of three arithmetic pipes, and scalar operations. The throughput of the *add-logical* pipe and the *multiply* pipe is 267 megaflops each, whereas that of the *divide* pipe is 38 megaflops. Hence 533 megaflops is the maximum throughput when the add-logical and the multiply pipes run concurrently. The VP-200 has advanced optimization facilities to generate efficient object code through vectorization of sequential constructs, pipeline parallelization, vector-register allocation, and generation optimization.

The strength of the VP-200 lies in its impressive throughput and easy programming environment. The Fortran 77 compiler is developed with advanced automatic optimization feature and convenient tuning tools and application library. The system can be a simple add-on to a front-end processor with MVS/OS as a loosely coupled multiprocessor. It can utilize many of the existing software assets. With more reliable circuit and packaging technology, the system can self-recover from hardware errors. The Fortran 77/VP components in the VP-200 include language processors for both scalar and vector objects, tuning tools, debugging tools, and subroutine packages for special scientific computations, such as for solving linear systems, eigenvalues, differential equations, fast Fourier transform, etc.

Although high-speed components, high degree of parallelism and/or pipelining, and large-sized main memory are the basic requirements to stretch the computational capabilities of a supercomputer, the VP-200 designers consider the following features as also important for such a machine to be versatile enough for a wide range of applications:

1. Efficient processing of DO loops which contain IF statements
2. Powerful vector editing capabilities
3. Efficient utilization of the vector registers
4. Highly concurrent vector-vector and scalar-vector operations

Technology, architecture, compiling algorithms, and the implementation of special hardware and software features in the VP-200 are described below. Readers may find some of these features similar to those in the Cray-1 and Cyber-205, and some features are uniquely developed in the Fujitsu machine.

Technologies utilized Fujitsu's latest technologies are utilized in the FACOM vector processor. Logic LSIs contain 400 gates per chip, with some special functional chips such as the register files containing 1300 gates. Signal propagation delay per gate of these LSIs are 350 picoseconds (ps). Memory LSIs containing 4K bits per module with an access time of 5.5 ns are used where extremely high speed is necessary. Up to 121 LSIs can be mounted on a 14-layered printed circuit board called MCC (multichip carrier). Forced air cooling is employed throughout the system. These are well-proven technologies with Fujitsu's FACOM M-380 mainframes. It is with these technologies that a 7.5-ns clock is realized for the vector unit and a 15-ns clock is realized for the scalar unit. As for the main memory, 64K-bit MOS static RAM LSIs are used with chip access time of 55 ns. The main memory is 256-way interleaved. Vectors can be accessed in contiguous, constant-strided, and indirect addressed fashion.

Vectorizing compiler—Fortran 77/VP A vectorizing compiler, Fortran 77/VP, has been developed for the FACOM vector processor. Fortran 77 has been chosen as the language for this machine so that the large software assets can become readily available. In order to obtain high vectorization ratio for a wide range of application programs, the Fortran 77/VP compiler vectorizes not only the simple DO loops but nested DO loops and the macro operations such as the inner product efficiently. It also detects and separates the recurrences.

Ease of use is another objective of the compiler. Debugging aids, a performance analyzer, an interactive vectorizer, and a vectorized version of the scientific subroutine library are some of the software included in Fortran 77/VP. With the interactive feature, for example, a programmer can provide the compiler with useful information for higher vectorization.

Conditional vector operations The analysis of the application programs indicates that the conditional statements are frequently encountered within DO loops. The FACOM vector processor provides three different methods to efficiently execute conditional branch operations for vectors: masked arithmetic operations, compress-expand functions, and vector indirect addressing.

In order to control conditional vector operations and vector editing functions, bit strings (called mask vectors) are also provided. A total of 256 mask registers, 32 bits each, the store mask vectors, and the *mask pipe* perform logical operations associated with the mask vectors.

Example 4.8 This example describes the *masked* operations in VP-200:

1	1	0	1	0	0	1	1	Mask vector
A_1	A_2	A_3	A_4	A_5	A_6	A_7	A_8	Vector A
B_1	B_2	B_3	B_4	B_5	B_6	B_7	B_8	Vector B
+	+		+			+	+	Add operation
A_1	A_2	C_3	A_4	C_5	C_6	A_7	A_8	Result on vector C
+	+		+			+	+	
B_1	B_2		B_4			B_7	B_8	

In the case of the masked arithmetic operations, the add-logical pipe generates mask vectors to indicate the true-false values of conditional statements, and the arithmetic pipeline units take such mask vectors via mask registers as the control inputs. The arithmetic pipeline units store the results back to vector registers only for the elements having 1s in the corresponding locations of the mask vector: Old values are retained otherwise. For a given vector length, the execution time of a masked arithmetic operation is constant regardless of the ratio of true values to the vector length (called "true ratio").

Since the true ratio of conditional statements widely varies from one case to another, the compiler must select the best method for individual cases. More precisely, there are two key parameters in selecting the best one to use: the *true ratio* and the *relative frequency of load-store instruction executions* over the total instruction executions within the DO loop. If the true ratio is medium to high, the masked arithmetic operation is selected; otherwise, the compress-expand method is selected when the frequency of load-store operations is low, and the indirect addressing is selected when such frequency is high. The Fortran 77/VP compiler analyzes the DO loop, compares the estimated execution times for all three methods, and selects the best one. A programmer can also interactively provide the compiler with the information on the true ratio.

Vector editing functions The FACOM vector processor provides two types of editing functions: compress-expand operations and vector indirect addressing.

These functions can be used not only for the conditional vector operations but for sparse matrix computations and other data editing applications. Vectors on vector registers can be edited by compress and expand functions by using load-store pipes as data alignment circuits; no access to the main memory is involved in these cases. Compressing a vector A means that the elements of A marked with 1s in the corresponding locations of the mask vector are copied into another vector B, where these elements are stored in contiguous locations with their order preserved. Expanding a vector means the opposite operation, as the example below shows:

Example 4.9 This example describes the *compress* operation in VP-200.

1	1	0	1	0	0	1	1	Masked vector
A_1	A_2	A_3	A_4	A_5	A_6	A_7	A_8	Vector A
A_1	A_2	A_4	A_7	A_8				Compress A

In the vector indirect addressing, a vector J on vector registers holds the indices for the elements of another vector A stored in the main memory, which is to be loaded into vector C defined on vector registers. Namely, $C(I) = A(J(I))$. This is a very versatile and powerful operation, since the order of the elements can be scrambled in any manner. The data transfer rate for vector indirect addressing, however, is lower than that for the contiguous vectors, due to possible bank and/or bus conflicts.

Example 4.10 This example describes the *vector indirect addressing* in VP-200.

1	1	0	1	0	0	1	1	Mask vector
1	2	4	7	8				List vector generation
A_1	A_2	A_4	A_7	A_8				Indirect vector load A

Vector compress-expand operations are performed in two steps: mask vector generation and actual operations. Frequently used mask patterns may be stored in mask registers. The compiler also checks whether the domains occupied by the source vector and the destination vector overlap. The indirect addressing, on the other hand, takes three steps: mask vector generation, index list vector generation from the mask vector, and loading the vector from the main memory. Frequently used list vectors may also be stored in the main memory.

Vector registers optimization One of the most unusual features of the FACOM vector processor is the dynamically configurable vector registers. The concept of vector register is very important for efficient vector processing, since it drastically reduces the frequency of accesses to the main memory. The results of our study indicate that the requirements for the length and the number of vectors vary from one program to another. To make the best utilization of the total size of 64K bytes, the vector registers can be concatenated to take the following configurations: 32 (length) × 256 (vector counts), 64 × 128, 128 × 64, ..., 1024 × 8. The length of vector registers is specified by a special hardware register, and it can be altered by an instruction in the program.

The compiler must know the frequently used hardware vector length for each program, or even within one program the vector length may have to be adjusted. When the vector length is too short, load-store instructions will be issued more frequently, whereas if it is unnecessarily long, the number of available vectors will be small and vector registers will be wasted. As a general strategy, the compiler puts a higher priority on the number of vectors in determining the register configuration. A programmer can also interactively provide the compiler with the information on the vector length.

High-level concurrency The FACOM vector processor allows concurrent operations at different levels. In the vector unit, five functional pipelines can operate concurrently: two out of three arithmetic pipeline units, two load-store pipes, and mask pipe. Within each arithmetic pipeline unit, vector operands associated with consecutive instructions can flow continuously without flushing the pipe.

The vector unit and the scalar unit can also operate concurrently, as illustrated in Figure 4.34. Without such a feature, the scalar operations between the vector operations could cause considerable performance degradation. Serialization instructions are provided to preserve the data dependency relations among instructions.

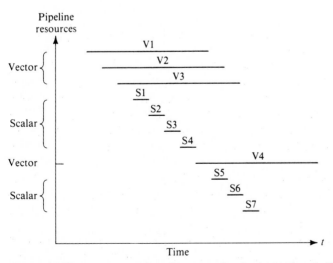

Figure 4.34 Concurrent processing of vector and scalar instructions in VP-200. (Courtesy of Fujitsu Limited, Japan.)

The compiler performs the extensive data-flow analysis of the Fortran source programs and schedules the instruction stream, so that the vector arithmetic pipeline units are kept as busy as possible. This process includes the reordering of instruction sequence, balanced assignments of two load-store pipes, and insertion of serialization instructions, wherever necessary.

A comparison of the modern pipeline vector supercomputers that we have studied is given in Table 4.14. This table summarizes the instruction repertoire, basic system specifications, functional pipes, vector registers, main memory, peak CPU speed, vectorizing facilities, front-end host computers, and possible future extensions for the Cray-1, the Cyber-205, and the VP-200. The option of one vector processor in the Cyber-205 is assumed in the comparison. With the introduction of the Cray X-MP and the options of having two or four vector processors in a Cyber-205, one can conclude that the three vector supercomputers have essentially the same computing power. It is interesting to watch for their future upgraded models.

Table 4.14 Comparison of three pipeline vector supercomputers

Architecture and capability	Cray Research's Cray-1	Control Data's Cyber-205 (1 vector processor)	Fujitsu's VP-200
Organization	Register-to-register	Memory-to-memory	Register-to-register
Instruction repertoire	128 instructions, 10 vector types 13 scalar types	256 instructions, 16 types 10 scalar types	83 vector and 195 scalar instructions
Functional pipelines, pipeline cycle	12 pipelines: 3 vector, 4 scalar, 2 floating point, and 2 integer, clock period: 12.5 ns	11 pipelines: 6 vector and 5 scalar functions, clock period: 20 ns	6 pipelines: add-logical, multiply, divide, mask, and two load-store, clock period 7.5 ns
Vector registers, main memory	8 × 64 × 8 = 4K bytes, 32 Mbytes	Vector register unused, 32 Mbyte main memory	32 × 256 × 8 = 64K bytes, 256 Mbytes
Peak CPU speed	160 mflops	200 mflops	500 mflops
Vectorizing facilities	Cray Fortran compiler (CFT) with automatic vectorization by user intervention	Vector arithmetic with automatic vectorization	Fortran 77/VP compiler with interactive vectorizer
Front-end host computers	IBM/MVS, CDC/NOS, Univac	Cyber-170 series IBM 303x	FACOM M series IBM/MVS
Possible future extended models	Cray X-MP with 420 megaflops, Cray-2 with 2000 megaflops	CDC Cyber 2XX with over 10 gegaflops	(unknown)

In the next 10 years (1984 to 1994), a new generation of supercomputer will emerge, driven by customer demands and other competitive pressures. Memory capacities will be 2 to 4 times greater than now possible, and processing speeds will be improved from 2.5 to 20 times current rates. These goals will be achieved by employing another generation of device technology, with emphasis on larger scales of integration.

The major element of this next generation will be continued evolution of architectures involving parallelism and the incorporation of many artificial intelligence functions and more intelligent I/O interfaces. Vector processors, multiprocessors, and similar parallel structures will be required to keep pace with the demand for computational power. The exploitation of these architectures through new algorithms, operating systems, and compiler technology is the key to achieving the goals of the next generation consumers.

4.5 VECTORIZATION AND OPTIMIZATION METHODS

In this section, we study four issues towards performance enhancement of vector processors. We begin with an introduction of parallel language features for vector processing. Parallel constructs in extending high-level languages are described by examples, instead of abstract declarations. The design phases of a vectorizing compiler for generating vector codes from sequentially written source codes are characterized with various vectorizing facilities. Then we study various optimization methods to generate efficient object code. Finally, analytical tools for evaluating the performance of a pipeline computer are presented.

4.5.1 Parallel Languages for Vector Processing

In recent years, substantial efforts are being exerted on developing high-level languages with parallel constructs to facilitate vector processing. As discussed in Section 3.5.1, the use of sequential languages will lose the parallelism specified in a good algorithm. Thus vectorization (Figure 3.28) is highly needed to restore the concurrency in parallel algorithms so that they can be efficiently implemented on a vector processor. Most commercial vector processors have built-in hardware to support extended high-level languages, like the extended Fortran in the Cray-1, and the Fortran 77 extension in the FACOM VP-200.

Two vector processing languages have been proposed recently: one is the *Actus* by Perrott (1979) and the other is the *Vectran* by Paul and Wilson (1975). Unfortunately, neither of these parallel languages has been successfully tested on a real machine. Parallel languages are far from being standardized. The desired features include *flexibility* in declaring and selecting array objects in columns, rows, blocks, diagonals, and in various subarray expressions; *effectiveness* in manipulating sparse and dense matrices; *array conformity* to allow transportability; and mechanisms to break *vectorization barriers.*

Of course, the usefulness of a new language depends on its application areas. We briefly characterize below, by Fortran extension examples, some of the attractive features in a typical parallel language. A vector may be identified implicitly by the appearance of an array name followed by specific subscripts. The extended notation may be specified through an implied DO notation as follows:

$$e_1 : e_2 : e_3$$
$$e_1 : e_2$$
$$*$$
$$e_1 : * : e_3$$

(4.3)

where e_1, e_2, and e_3 are expressions of indexing parameters as they appear in a DO statement: e_1 indicates the first element or the *initial index* value, e_2 indicates the *terminal index* value, and e_3 is the *index increment* or skip distance. If e_3 is omitted, the increment is one; this includes all of the elements from e_1 to e_2. The single symbol "*" indicates that all of the elements are in a particular dimension. If the elements are to be used in reverse order, the notation "-*" may be used.

Example 4.11 *Given*: DIMENSION X(8), Y(10, 4)
Then: X(2:8:2) represents the elements X(2), X(4), X(6), X(8);
Y(3:5, 3) represents the elements Y(3,3), Y(4,3), Y(5,3);
Y(*,3) represents the third column of the matrix Y;
Y(5,2:*) represents the elements Y(5,2), Y(5,3), Y(5,4).

A vector statement allows different portions of an array to be identified explicitly by separate names. No extra storage is allocated for an identified vector. Each identified vector is simply a virtual name for a collection of elements in the original vector.

Example 4.12 *Given*: REAL X(10,10)
Then: VECTOR X ROW 2(1:10) is a vector consisting of the second row of X;
VECTOR X DIAG(1:10) represents the diagonal elements of X;
VECTOR X COL 5(1:10:3) is a vector consisting of X(1,5), X(4,5), X(7,5)

In a binary vector operation, the two operands must have equal length with only a few exceptions. Each vector operation may be associated with a logical array that serves as a control vector. A WHERE statement may allow the programmer to indicate the assignment statements to be executed under the control of a logical array. The following PACK and UNPACK operations demonstrate the use of control vectors.

Example 4.13 *Given*: DIMENSION A(6), B(6), C(B); DATA A/−3, −2,1,3, −2,5/
Then: PACK WHERE (A .GT. 0) B=C causes elements of C in positions corresponding to "trues" in A.GT.0 to be assigned to B elements such that B(1) = C(3), B(2) = C(4), B(3) = C(6);

UNPACK WHERE (A.GT.0) A = B inserts the elements of B into A in positions indicated by A.GT.0. Thus, A(3) = B(1), A(4) = B(2), A(6) = B(3).

An intrinsic function needs to compute with each element of a vector operand. For example A(1:10) = SIN(B(1:10)) is a vector intrinsic function. Several special vector instructions are shown in the following example:

Example 4.14 *Given*: DIMENSION A(50), B(50), C(50)
Then: C(2:9) = VADD(A(2:9),B(1,8)) performs the *vector addition*;
  S = SIZE(A(1:50:4)) equals the *length* of the sparse vector A(1:50:4)
  S = DOTPD(A,B) forms the *dot product* of vectors A and B;
  S = MAXVAL(A) finds the *largest value* of vector A.

A *Fortran vectorizer* has the capability of detecting parallelism in serially coded Fortran programs. It recognizes Fortran constructs that can be executed in parallel. Basic operations performed by the vectorizer program are precedence analysis and code generation. In performing the analysis, the vectorizer analyzes Fortran instruction sequences for possible translation into a vector syntax. This phase is extremely machine dependent since it must consider special characteristics of the hardware. An ideal vectorizer performs sophisticated analysis of data dependencies and determines the possibility of vectorization. General guidelines in designing a vectorizer include:

1. Determining the flow pattern between subprograms
2. Checking the precedence relationship among the subprograms
3. Checking the locality of variables
4. Determining the loop variables
5. Checking the independence of variables
6. Replacing the inner loop with vector instructions

Described below are six examples for converting conventional Fortran statements into vectorized codes, presumably by a vectorizing compiler.

Example 4.15 A simple DO loop containing independent instructions and no branch statements can be converted to a single vector instruction. The following DO-loop statements:

$$DO\ 20\ 1 = 8,120,2$$
$$20\ A(1) = B(1+3) + C(1+1)$$

are being converted into a single vector statement:

$$A(8:120:2) = B(11:123:2) + C(9:121:2) \qquad (4.4)$$

Example 4.16 A recurrence computation can be converted into vector form, subject only to precedence constraint. The recursion

$$A(0)=X$$
$$DO\ 20\ I=1,N$$
$$20\ A(I)=A(I-1)*B(I)+C(I+1)$$

is being converted to be:

$$A(0)=X$$
$$A(1:N)=A(0:N:1)*B(1:N)+C(2:N+1) \tag{4.5}$$

Example 4.17 An IF statement in a loop can be eliminated by setting a corresponding control vector together with a WHERE statement, such as converting

$$DO\ 20\ I=1,N$$
$$20\ IF(L(I).NE.0)\ A(I)=A(I)-1$$

to

$$WHERE\ (L(I).NE.0)\ A(1:N)=A(1:N)-1 \tag{4.6}$$

Example 4.18 Exchanging the execution sequence sometimes will enable parallel computations, such as converting

$$DO\ 20\ I=1,N$$
$$A(I)=B(I-1)$$
$$20\ B(I)=2*B(I)$$

to the following code:

$$B(1:N)=2*B(1:N)$$
$$A(1:N)=B(0:N-1) \tag{4.7}$$

Example 4.19 Temporary storage can be used to enable parallel computations, such as converting the statements

$$DO\ 20\ I=1,N$$
$$A(I)=B(I)+C(I)$$
$$20\ B(I)=2*A(I+1)$$

to vector code

$$TEMP\ (1:N)=A(2:N+1)$$
$$A(1:N)=B(1:N)+C(1:N) \tag{4.8}$$
$$B(1:N)=2*TEMP(1:N)$$

Example 4.20 Prolonging the vector length is always desirable for pipeline processing. The two levels of array computations

DO 20 I=1,80
DO 20 J=1,10
20 A(I,J)=B(I,J)+C(I,J)

can be rearranged to promote better pipelining:

DO 20 J=1,10
DO 20 I=1,80
20 A(I,J)=B(I,J)+C(I,J)

Other techniques such as register allocation, vector hazard, and instructions rearrangement are also machine dependent. For example, we want to allocate the vector registers in the Cray-1 to result in minimal execution time. Rearranging the execution sequence to execute the same vector operations repeatedly can reduce the pipeline reconfiguration overhead in a multifunctional pipe. A vectorizer informs the programmer of the possibility of parallel operations. It provides also a learning tool, in that the programmer can examine the output of the vectorizer and tune the computations for better pipelining. Automatic vectorization and code optimization will increase the programming productivity on vector processors.

4.5.2 Design of a Vectorizing Compiler

A vectorizing compiler analyzes whether statements in DO loops can be executed in parallel and generates object codes with vector instructions. The higher the vectorization ratio, the higher will be the performance. To achieve this, the compiler vectorizes complicated data accesses and restructures program sequences, subject to machine hardware constraints. Barriers to vectorization exist in conditional and branch statements, sequential dependencies, nonlinear and indirect indexing, and subroutine calls within loops. In this subsection, we outline the design considerations of a vectorizing compiler and illustrate some vectorization techniques.

Let us first review the phases of a conventional Fortran compiler. The first is a lexical-scan and *syntax-parsing* phase which converts the source program to some intermediate code, quadruples, for example. Quadruples usually have fields for specifying the operations, up to two source operands, a result operand, and auxiliary information; the auxiliary field will be used by the next two phases of *code optimization* and *code generation*. The purpose is to specify which operands are found in registers, which registers are occupied, whether the instruction should be deleted, and so on. For an example, the lexical parser converts a Fortran statement $A = A + B * C$ to the following quadruples:

T1←B∗C
A←A+T1

where T1 is a compiler generated temporary identifier.

In the second phase for optimization, the compiler accepts quadruples as inputs and produces modified quadruples as outputs. The optimizer might find that the subexpression B * C is redundant, one whose value had been previously computed and called as identifier T2. The multiplication can thus be eliminated:

$$T1 \leftarrow T2$$
$$A \leftarrow A + T1$$

The optimizer may also discover that T1 will never be used again, so all of its use can be directly replaced by the original T2 and its definition be eliminated, resulting in the single statement $A \leftarrow A + T2$. A register allocator attempts to assign heavily used quantities to CPU registers. If it is discovered that A is frequently used, A will probably be assigned to a register, say R3, and will be recorded as auxiliary information:

$$A(R3) \leftarrow A(R3) + T2$$

In the third phase, the code generator translates the final intermediate code into a machine-language program based on the auxiliary information. A code fragment is selected to represent the quadruple in machine code. The code fragment, along with all other fragments and some initializing code, would be written in linkage-editor format. In the above example, machine addresses have been assigned to identifiers A and T2. Thus we can write the quadruple in a machine code:

$$\text{ADD R3, M(T2)}$$

where M(T2) refers to the memory location of the identifier T2.

In a vectorizing Fortran compiler, the scanner and parser need not be modified. With the scalar code already in place, we want to convert a series of scalar operations into vector code. Let us consider some optimization techniques which can extend the intermediate code. Since the optimization techniques are machine dependent, we will consider a Cray-like structure in which all the vector operations are register-to-register.

A vectorizing compiler will analyze the structure of Fortran programs being compiled. We have seen many examples in previous sections on converting DO loops and other scalar operations in the source program to vector instructions in the object code. In general, the higher the *vectorizing ratio*, the better will be the performance. This is due to the fact that vector speed is much higher than scalar speed in a vector processor. As illustrated in Figure 4.35, we assume the speed ratio of vector to scalar operations to be 50. The shaded areas correspond to reduced execution time for vector instructions; one vector process is reduced from 50 scalar processes as shown. Two levels of vectorization are shown in the figure.

Simple scalar operations like inner product, random-access integer operations, and simple DO arithmetic can be vectorized easily at the first level for a vectorizing ratio of 50 percent. The remaining complicated operations like scatter, conditional statements, gather and others can only be vectorized by a very intelligent

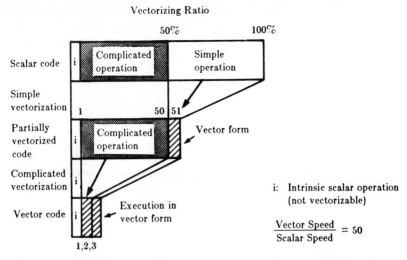

Figure 4.35 Vectorization ratio and saving in execution time. (Courtesy of Fujitsu Limited, Japan.)

compiler which can efficiently access complicated data structures and tune branch-disturbed program structures. The compiler requires sophisticated optimization techniques and improved hardware architecture. Major optimizing functions are listed below according to the levels of sophistication in generating efficient scalar and vector code modules.

1. General optimization
   (a) Common expression elimination
   (b) Invariant expression movement
   (c) Strength reduction
   (d) Register optimization
   (e) Constant folding
2. Extended optimization
   (a) Intrinsic function integration such as SQRT, SINE, etc.
   (b) User Fortran subprogram integration
   (c) Reductions of iteration numbers in nested DO loops
   (d) Reorder of execution sequence to reduce pipeline overhead
   (e) Temporal storage management
   (f) Code avoidance
3. Vector extended optimization
   (a) Full vectorization
   (b) Pipeline chaining
   (c) Pipeline antichaining
   (d) Vector register optimization
   (e) Parallelization

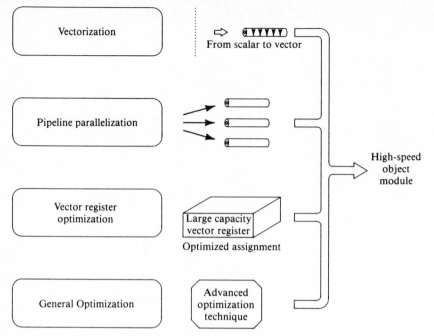

Figure 4.36 Vectorizing compiler design techniques in the Fujitsu FACOM VP-200. (Courtesy of Fujitsu Limited, Japan.)

The *general optimization* and *extended optimization* contribute to the generation of efficient scalar code. The *vector extended optimization* is added to produce fast vector instructions. The three levels of optimization features are demonstrated in Figure 4.36. The *vectorization* converts scalar to vector. The *parallelization* utilizes multiple pipes simultaneously. The vector *register optimization* allocates large-capacity registers properly. The *general optimization* can be achieved with many of the existing compiler assets. The above optimizing features have been implemented in vectorizer packages in most commercial supercomputers.

4.5.3 Optimization of Vector Functions

Described below are nine common practices in optimizing the vector functions. Some of these techniques apply not only to pipeline computers but also to array processors. Tuning tools for an interactive vectorizer are then introduced. Again, we use some examples to illustrate various optimization functions and tuning facilities.

(A) Redundant expression elimination After the scan and parse phase, some redundant operations in the intermediate code could be eliminated. The number of memory accesses and the execution time can be reduced by often eliminating redundant expressions.

Example 4.21 Consider the following extended Fortran code:

```
DIMENSION A(100), B(50), C(50)
C(1:50)=A(1:99:2)*B(1:50)+A(1:99:2)*C(1:50)
```

A possible set of intermediate code is generated on the left below. With elimination of redundant statements, the simplified code is generated on the right below, if the compiler detected the fact that the B array and C array are identical.

$$
\begin{array}{lll}
V1 \leftarrow A(1:99:2) & & \\
V2 \leftarrow B(1:50) & & \\
V3 \leftarrow V1*V2 & V1 \leftarrow A(1:99:2) & \\
V4 \leftarrow A(1:99:2) & V2 \leftarrow B(1:50) & (4.9) \\
V5 \leftarrow C(1:50) \quad \rightarrow & V1 \leftarrow V1*V2 & \\
V6 \leftarrow V4*V5 & V1 \leftarrow 2*V1 & \\
V7 \leftarrow V3+V6 & C(1:50) \leftarrow V1 & \\
C(1:50) \leftarrow V7 & &
\end{array}
$$

(B) Constant folding at compile time In its full generality, constant folding means shifting computations from run time to compile time. Although the opportunities to perform operations on constant arrays is not often, such opportunities will crop up occasionally, particularly as initialized tables. For example, a DO loop for generating the array $A(I) = I$ for $I = 1, 2, \ldots, 100$ can be avoided in the execution phase because the array $A(I)$ can be generated by a constant vector $(1, 2, 3, \ldots, 100)$ initialized in the compile time.

(C) Invariant expression movement The innermost loops are often just scalar encodings of vector operations. In such a case, the innermost loop can be replaced by some vector operations if there is no data dependence relation or no loop variance. If some of the statements are loop-variant, the loop-invariant expressions may be moved out of the loop. This is called *code motion*. Consider the following two-level DO loop:

```
DO 20 I=1,N
   ...
DO 20 J=1,M
   ...
B(I,J)=B(I,J)+A(J)*C(J)
20 CONTINUE
```

Assuming no other computations affecting the variables A, B, C, I and J, the above program can be vectorized as follows:

$$
\begin{aligned}
&\text{DO 20 I=1,N}\\
&\quad\cdots\\
&\text{B(I,*)=B(I,*)+A(*)*C(*)}\\
&\text{DO 20 J=1,M}\\
&\quad\cdots\\
&\text{20 CONTINUE}
\end{aligned}
$$

The vector multiplication can be moved out of the outer loop using a temporary vector T(*):

$$
\begin{aligned}
&\text{T(*)=A(*)*C(*)}\\
&\text{DO 20 I=1,N}\\
&\quad\cdots\\
&\text{B(I,*)=B(I,*)+T(*)}\\
&\text{DO 20 J=1,M}\\
&\quad\cdots\\
&\text{20 CONTINUE}
\end{aligned}
$$

(D) Pipeline chaining and parallelization In a vector processor with multiple functional pipes, the performance can be upgraded by chaining several pipelines. The result from one pipeline may be directed as input to another pipeline. The time delays due to storing intermediate results are thus eliminated. The intermediate results need not be stored back into the memory with the chaining. An intelligent compiler should have the capability of detecting sequences of operations that can be chained together. We have seen some chaining operations of multiple pipelines in Section 3.4.1. Figure 4.37 shows the parallel use of two load-store pipes which are chained with the *multiply pipe* and then the *add pipe* in the VP-200.

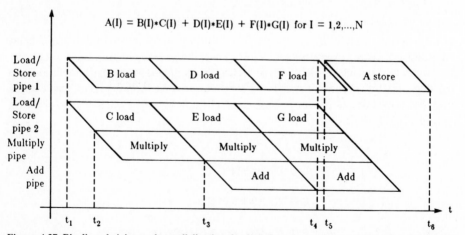

Figure 4.37 Pipeline chaining and parallelization for linked vector operations. (Courtesy of Fujitsu Limited, Japan.)

Example 4.22 Based on the hardware architecture of the VP-200 in Figure 4.33, we can implement the following vector operations, as demonstrated in Figure 4.37.

$$A(I) = B(I) * C(I) + D(I) * C(I) + F(I) * G(I) \quad \text{for } I = 1, 2, \dots, N \quad (4.10)$$

Three pairs of *vector load* operations, (B, C), (D, E), and (F, G), are done in two load-store pipelines. Three *vector multiply* operations, B * C, D * E, and F * G, are carried out in the multiply pipeline from time t_2. The two *vector add* operations are executed in the add pipeline from time t_3. The first result becomes available at t_4. With a minor pipeline reconfiguration delay, the *store* operation begins at t_5. The entire operation requires $t_6 - t_1 = 4N + \Delta_1$ where $\Delta_1 = t_2 - t_1$ is the delay of one pipeline. It was assumed that all pipes have equal delays.

(E) Vector register allocation On a machine like the Cray-1 allowing the chaining of vector operations, the importance of register allocation cannot be overstated. To achieve the maximum computing power, the execution units must be fed a continuous stream of operands. Retaining vectors in registers between operations is one way to achieve this. However, the strategy of vector register allocation emphasizes local allocation rather than global allocation, because of the limited number of available vector registers in a system.

Example 4.23 The vector expression $A - B * C$ can be executed in the Cray-1 by using the three vector registers V1, V2, and V3 as follows:

$$V1 \leftarrow A$$
$$V2 \leftarrow B$$
$$V3 \leftarrow C$$
$$V2 \leftarrow V2 * V3$$
$$V1 \leftarrow V1 - V2$$

If we do the multiply before loading the vector A into a register, only two vector registers are required:

$$V1 \leftarrow B$$
$$V2 \leftarrow C$$
$$V1 \leftarrow V1 * V2$$
$$V2 \leftarrow A$$
$$V2 \leftarrow V2 - V1$$

This sequence of five instructions requires 31 clock periods on the Cray-1, as opposed to 26 clock periods for the sequence using three vector registers.

In general, an optimizing compiler will simulate the instruction timing and keep assigning intermediate results to new registers until a previously assigned register becomes free. In the absence of a careful timing simulation, the best strategy that a compiler can adopt is the "round-robin" allocation of registers. Another solution to the register allocation problem is to generate code for a group of arithmetic expressions using large numbers of virtual registers, then to schedule the resulting code to minimize issue delays and map the virtual registers into a finite number of real registers. This process has the danger of requiring more than the number of available registers, in which case some spilling must be done. Besides, moving instructions around to minimize issue delays may destroy the use of common subexpressions. As done in FACOM VP-200, register concatenation offers another approach to processing vectors of variable lengths.

(F) Reorder the execution sequence In a multifunction pipeline, reconfiguring the pipe for different functions requires the overhead of flushing the pipe, establishing new data paths, etc. Instructions of the same type may be grouped together for pipeline execution. The instructions on the left of the following code block can be regrouped to yield the sequence on the right:

$$
\begin{array}{ccc}
\begin{aligned}
A1 &\leftarrow A2+A3 \\
A4 &\leftarrow A5*A6 \\
B1 &\leftarrow A7+A8 \\
B2 &\leftarrow B3*B4 \\
B5 &\leftarrow C1+C2
\end{aligned}
& \rightarrow &
\begin{aligned}
A1 &\leftarrow A2+A3 \\
B1 &\leftarrow A7+A8 \\
B5 &\leftarrow C1+C2 \\
A4 &\leftarrow A5*A6 \\
B2 &\leftarrow B3*B4
\end{aligned}
\end{array}
\tag{4.11}
$$

The sequence on the left requires three pipeline reconfigurations, while the right one requires only one. An intelligent compiler should be able to reorder the execution sequence to minimize the number of required pipeline reconfigurations.

(G) Temporary storage management In the optimization phase of a vectorizing compiler, the generation of too many intermediate vector quantities can quickly lead to a serious problem. For example, the execution of the vector instruction $A(1:4000) = A(1:4000)*B(1:4000) + C(1:4000)$ in the Cray-1 may need 63 vector registers (with 64 components each) to temporarily hold all intermediate product terms. The Cray-1 does not have this many vector registers to store all the intermediate results. Therefore, the intermediate results must be temporarily stored in the memory. For this reason, the compiler must allocate and deallocate temporary storage dynamically since vector registers may be thought of as temporaries and spillage out of them needs memory. Temporary storage management is closely related to the policy of register allocation. A vector loop can be used to solve the storage allocation problems. Since each vector register can handle 64 elements, we partition the 4000-component vectors into 64-element groups as follows:

```
    DO 20 K=1,4000,64
    L=MIN(K+63,4000)
    A(K:L)=A(K:L)*B(K:L)+C(K:L)
20 CONTINUE
```

In any case, run-time storage management is an expensive feature to be included in a Fortran-based language. There are two techniques to reduce the design cost. First, if the compiler allocates a specific area to fixed-length and variable-length temporaries, the allocation of the fixed-length area can be done at compile time, eliminating some run-time overhead and permitting access of the temporaries by some generated codes. Second, the number of fixed-length temporaries can be increased by "strip mining" with a width equal to the length of vector registers in the target machine.

(H) Code avoidance A somewhat radical approach to the optimization of vector operations is based on the technique of copy optimization. The idea is to avoid excessive copying arrays unless forced to do so by the semantics of the language. Consider the following code sequence:

$$A(1:50)=B(1:99:2)$$
$$\cdots$$
$$\cdots$$
$$C(1:50)=2.0*A(1:50)$$

A copy is avoided (or at least delayed), if the compiler adjusts the storage-mapping function for array A to reference the storage for array B. Thus, instead of producing the following code:

$$V1 \leftarrow B(1:99:2)$$
$$A(1:50) \leftarrow V1$$
$$\cdots$$
$$\cdots$$
$$V1 \leftarrow A(1:50)$$
$$V1 \leftarrow 2.0*V1$$
$$C(1:50) \leftarrow V1;$$

it would generate the following simplified code:

$$V1 \leftarrow B(1:99:2)$$
$$V1 \leftarrow 2.0*V1$$
$$C(1:50) \leftarrow V1$$

(I) Tuning for interactive vectorization Tuning tools are necessary to provide some user interactions in advanced vectorization. Both the Cray-1 and the VP-200 have some tuning facilities. The tuning facility in the VP-200 is illustrated in Figure 4.38. From the displayed tuning information and vectorizing effects, the user can modify the source program with the help of an *interactive vectorizer* package. The modified source program will be optimized towards full vectorization by the vectorizing compiler. A number of compiler directive lines are useful to check whether recurrence appeared in the source code, the true ratio in IF statements, the vector length distribution, and others. The vectorizing compiler generates the

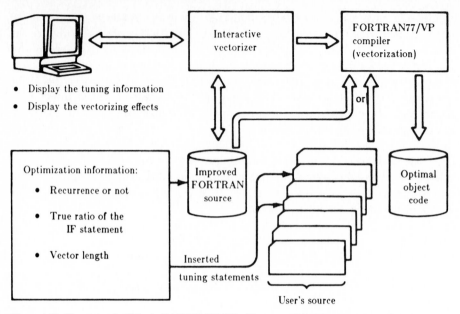

Figure 4.38 The tuning facilities in FACOM VP-200. (Courtesy of Fujitsu Limited, Japan.)

optimal object code with vector instructions after the tuning process is completed. An example is given below to illustrate the tuning concept realized in the VP-200.

Example 4.24 Consider the following DO loop containing an IF statement:

```
DO 20 I=1,N
   IF(A(I).GE.10) GO TO 20
   T=C1*A(I)+C2*B(I)
   A(I)=SIN(T)
20 CONTINUE
```

If one realizes the true ratio is 90 percent, the compiler chooses vector indirect addressing which results in several times better performance than the case without information for tuning. The compiler chooses masked arithmetic, if the optimization information is not available.

4.5.4 Performance Evaluation of Pipeline Computers

In this section, we evaluate the performance of pipelined vector processors. The system performance is measured in terms of *processor utilization* and the *speedup* over a serial computer. The efficiency of a computer depends heavily on the inherent parallelism in the programs it executes. Fully exploring the embedded parallelism is the responsibility of both system designers and programmers. The performance of a pipeline computer depends on the pipeline rate, the work load distributions, the vectorization ratio, and the utilization rate of system resources.

The system performance of a vector processor is measured by the *maximum throughput* (*W*), that is, the maximum number of results that can be generated per unit time, such as the *megaflops* we have used. The processing of a vector job in a pipeline occupies the equipment (segments) over a certain length of time. The enclosed area in a space-time diagram depicts the pipeline hardware utilization as a function of time. The segments of a pipeline may operate on distinct data operands simultaneously. Pipelining increases the bandwidth by a factor of k, since it may carry k independent operand sets in the k segments concurrently. A pipeline computer requires more hardware and complex control circuitry than a corresponding serial computer. The following notations are used in the performance analysis:

- k: the number of stages in a functional pipe
- T: the total pipeline delay in one instruction execution
- n: the number of instructions contained in a task (program)
- N_i: the length of vector operands used in the ith instruction $(1 \leq i \leq n)$
- W: the throughput of a pipeline computer
- T_i: the time required to finish the ith instruction in a pipeline computer $(1 \leq i \leq n)$
- T_p: the total time required to finish a task consisting of n instructions
- S_k: the speedup of a pipeline computer (with k stages) over a corresponding serial computer
- η: the efficiency of a pipeline computer

The parameter T is assumed to be independent of the type of instructions. $N(i) = 1$ means a scalar instruction; $N(i) > 1$ refers to a vector instruction. The average delay in a stage is $\tau = T/k$. We can write

$$T_i = (k - 1) \cdot \tau + N_i \cdot \tau = (N_i + k - 1) \cdot \frac{T}{k} \qquad (4.12)$$

where $(k - 1)\tau$ is the time required to fill up the pipe. As N_i becomes long, T_i approaches $N_i \cdot \tau$ because k is usually a small integer. The system throughput W then approaches k/T, accordingly. The above derivation is for a single vector instruction with vector length N_i.

Consider a sequence of n vector instructions. The degree of parallelism in each vector instruction is represented by its vector length N_i, for $i = 1, 2, \ldots, n$. Suppose that the execution of different types of vector instructions takes the same amount of time if they have the same vector length. The total execution times required in a pipeline processor is equal to

$$T_p = \sum_{i=1}^{n} T_i = \frac{T}{k} \cdot \left[(k - 1) \cdot n + \sum_{i=1}^{n} N_i \right] \qquad (4.13)$$

The same code if executed on an equivalent-function serial computer needs a time delay $T_s = T \cdot \sum_{i=1}^{n} N_i$. The following speedup is obtained over a serial computer that does the same job:

$$S_k = \frac{T_s}{T_p} = \frac{T \cdot \sum_{i=1}^{n} N_i}{T \cdot \left[(k-1)n + \sum_{i=1}^{n} N_i \right] / k} = \frac{k \cdot \sum_{i=1}^{n} N_i}{(k-1)n + \sum_{i=1}^{n} N_i} \quad (4.14)$$

The *efficiency* of the pipeline computer is defined as the total space-time product required by the job divided by a total available space-time product:

$$S_k = \frac{T_s}{T_p} = \frac{S_k}{k} \quad (4.15)$$

The pipeline efficient can be interpreted as the ratio of the actual speedup to the maximum possible speedup k. A numerical example is used to demonstrate the analytical measures. Consider a vector job with a vector length distribution $N_i = 7, 3, 10, 1, 4, 6, 2, 5, 2, 4$ for $n = 10$ vector instructions. Figure 4.39 plots S_k and η against different values of k with respect to the above distribution. When k increases beyond the average vector length of N_i (i.e., 4.4 in this example), the increase in speedup becomes rather flat while the processor utilization continues to decline.

In general, pipeline processors are in favor of long vectors. The longer the vector fed into a pipeline, the less the effect of the overhead will be exhibited. Figure 4.40 shows the relation between the vector length and the system performance on a pipeline computer with $k = 8$ stages. The speedup increases monotonically until reaching the maximum value of $k = 8$, where the length approaches infinity. The dashed line in Figure 4.41 displays the effect due to partitioning the vector operand into 16-element segments. The maximum speedup drops to $8 * 16/(16 + 7) = 5.5$ with vector looping. This occurs when the vector length is a multiple of 16, the number of component registers in the vector register.

The pipeline efficiency depends also on the vector length distribution. Too many scalar operations of different types will definitely downgrade the system performance. To overcome this drawback, an intelligent vectorizer can help improve the situation. The Cray-1 has a scalar processor which is more than two times faster than the CDC 7600. When the vector length is short, execution by a scalar processor should be faster than execution in a vector pipeline.

The throughput rate reflects the processing capability of a pipeline processor. A higher throughput rate may be obtained at the expense of higher hardware cost. Therefore, the cost effectiveness of a pipeline design should not be ignored. Cost effectiveness can be measured by *megaflops per million dollars*. Table 4.15 presents the performance and cost ratio of several pipeline computers. The efficiency of a pipeline computer may depend on both hardware cost and the

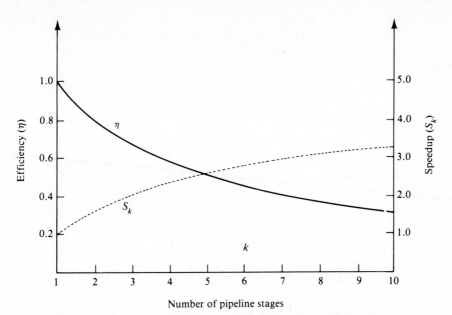

Figure 4.39 The speedup (S_k) and efficiency (η) of a pipelined processor with k stages.

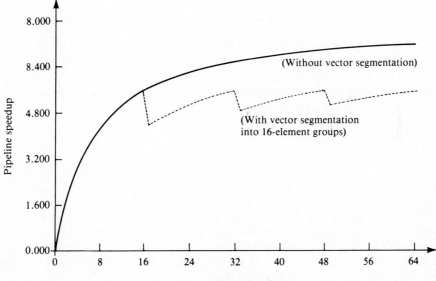

Figure 4.40 Pipeline speedup with and without vector looping. (Courtesy of *Advances in Computers*, Vol. 20, Hwang et al, 1981.)

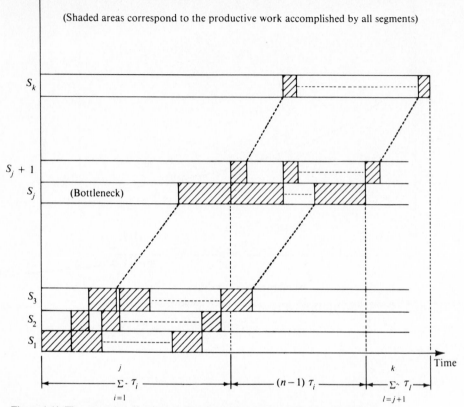

Figure 4.41 The space-time diagram of a linear pipeline with nonuniform stage delays.

delay of each pipeline stage. Let C_i be the cost and τ_i be the delay of the ith stage S_i in a pipeline having k stages. Let n be the total number of jobs streamed into the pipeline during the period of measurement (assuming continuous input of jobs). Let τ be the pipeline clock period equal to the delay of the bottleneck stage ($\tau = \tau_j$ in Figure 4.41). The efficiency η in Eq. 4.15 can be refined to be:

$$\eta = \frac{n \cdot \sum\limits_{i=1}^{k} C_i \cdot \tau_i}{\sum\limits_{i=1}^{k} C_i \cdot \left[\sum\limits_{i=1}^{k} \tau_i + (n-1) \cdot \tau \right]} \tag{4.16}$$

As illustrated in Figure 4.41, the numerator in Eq. 4.16 corresponds to the total weighted space-time span of n productive jobs. The denominator designates the total weighted space-time span of all k stages, including both productive and idle periods of all hardware facilities. In the ideal case with uniform delay ($\tau_i = \tau$ for all i), this efficiency can be reduced to the form in Eq. 3.5:

$$\eta = \frac{n}{k + (n-1)} \tag{4.17}$$

Table 4.15 Performance and cost of several pipeline computers

Pipeline computer	CPU cost (millions of of dollars)	Average performance (megaflops)	Performance and cost ratio (megaflops per millions of dollars)	Relative performance cost ratio
CDC6600	$1.5	0.63	0.42	1
Star-100	$8.0	16.6	2.10	5
AP-120B	$0.1	7.9	79.0	188
Cray-1	$4.5	20.0	4.44	11

Note that $\eta = S_k/k$, where S_k is the speedup defined in Eq. 4.14. When the pipeline approaches the steady state with sufficiently long vector input, the *limiting efficiency* becomes

$$\lim_{n \to \infty} \eta = \frac{\sum_{i=1}^{k} C_i \cdot \tau_i}{\tau \cdot \sum_{i=1}^{k} C_i} \tag{4.18}$$

In the ideal case of uniform delay, $(\tau_i = \tau$ for all $i)$, the above limit will be 1 and the *maximal speedup* will be achieved $(S_k \to k)$.

The cost effectiveness is indicated by the potential throughput performance relative to the total processor cost. The optimal pipeline design will maximize such a performance-cost ratio. Let T_s be the total time required to process a job in a nonpipeline serial processor. Consider the execution of the same job in an equivalent pipeline processor with k stages. The pipeline clock period is set to be $\tau = T_s/k + \theta$, where θ is the latch delay. Thus, in $n \cdot \tau = T_s + n \cdot \theta$ time units, n results can be produced. This implies the following system throughput:

$$W = \frac{n}{n \cdot (T_s/k + \theta)} = \frac{1}{T_s/k + \theta} \tag{4.19}$$

Let $C = \sum_{i=1}^{k} C_i$ be the total cost of all pipeline stages and d be the average latch cost. The cost of the entire pipeline is equal to $C + (k \cdot d)$. A *performance-cost ratio* (PCR) for the pipeline processor is defined as

$$\text{PCR} = \frac{W}{C + k \cdot d} = \frac{1}{(T_s/k + \theta) \cdot (C + k \cdot d)} \tag{4.20}$$

The optimal design of a static linear pipeline processor requires k_0 stages such that the PCR is maximized. Differentiating the PCR with respect to k, we obtain the first-order derivative

$$\frac{\partial (\text{PCR})}{\partial k} = \frac{T_s \cdot C/k^2 - \theta \cdot d}{(T_s/k + \theta)^2 \cdot (C + kd)^2} \tag{4.21}$$

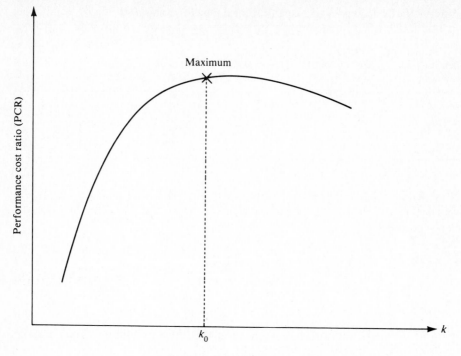

Number of pipeline stages

Figure 4.42 The performance/cost ratio (PCR) as a function of the number of stages in a pipeline.

When $\partial(\text{PCR})/\partial k = 0$, we have $k = k_0$ from $T_s \cdot C/k_0^2 - \theta \cdot d = 0$. Therefore, the optimal design should have k_0 pipeline stages, where

$$k_0 = \sqrt{\frac{T_s \cdot C}{\theta \cdot d}} \tag{4.22}$$

This is indeed the maximum, because one can prove that $\partial^2(\text{PCR})/\partial k^2 < 0$ when evaluated at $k = k_0$.

This optimal stage number is always greater than one for a reasonably complex pipeline. In the above discussion, we have emphasized local optimization of the pipeline processor. In practical design, one has to consider the global performance of the entire computer system, which may include parameters on memory access and program behavior. The PCR given in Eq. 4.20 is plotted in Figure 4.42 as a function of the number k of pipeline stages. The peak of the curve corresponds to the optimal number, k_0, of pipeline stages.

4.6 BIBLIOGRAPHIC NOTES AND PROBLEMS

Comparative studies of the early vector processors Star-100 and TI-ASC were given by Higbie (1973) and Theis (1974). The Cray-1 and Cyber-205 have been characterized in Kozdrawicki and Theis (1980). Hockney and Jesshope (1981) have treated pipeline vector processors and array processors. Others can be found in Thurber (1976, 1979a, b), Kuck (1977), Chen (1980), and Kogge (1981). Literature devoted to the CDC Star-100 and TI-ASC can be found in CDC manuals, Hintz and Tate (1972), Purcell (1974), Stone (1978), Ginsberg (1977), Watson (1972a, b), Watson and Carr (1974), and Texas Instruments manuals.

The Cray-1 computers were studied in Johnson (1978), Peterson (1979), Russell (1978). Cray Research manuals, Dorr (1978), and Baskett and Keller (1976). The Cyber-205 is described in Kascic (1979). The material presented in Section 4.4.4 is based on the work by Lincoln (1982). Manual information on the Cyber-205 can be found in CDC manuals. Material on the VP-200 is based on the report by Miura and Uchida (1983). The AP-120B has been described and assessed in Wittmayer (1978), and Floating Point Systems manuals. Other attached processors were reported in Datawest (1979), IBM (1977), and Thurber (1979b).

Vectorization methods for pipeline computers can be found in CDC and Cray Research manuals, Paul and Wilson (1978), Kennedy (1979), Loveman (1977), and Hwang et al. (1981). Vectorizing compilers are also studied in Arnold (1982), Brode (1981), and Kuck et al. (1983). Parallel programming languages and the optimization of vector operations are still wide open areas for further research and development. Performance of pipeline processors has been evaluated in Chen (1975), Bovet and Varneschi (1976), Baskett and Keller (1977), Larson and Davidson (1973), Ramamoorthy and Li (1975), Hwang and Su (1983), and Stokes (1977).

Problems

4.1 Design a pipeline multiplier using carry-save adders and a carry-lookahead adder to multiply a stream of input numbers $X_1, X_2, X_3, \ldots$, by a fixed number Y. You may assume that all X_i and Y are n-bit positive integers. The output should be a stream of n-bit products $X_1 \cdot Y, X_2 \cdot Y, X_3 \cdot Y, \ldots$. Determine the pipeline clock rate in terms of the delays α, β, and γ, where

α = delay of one stage of a 3-input and 2-output carry-save adder

β = delay of the carry-lookahead adder

γ = delay of the interface latch between stages

4.2 Consider a static multifunctional pipeline processor with k stages, each stage having a delay of $1/k$ time units. The pipeline must be drained between different functions, such as addition and multiplication. Memory-access time, control-unit time, etc., can be ignored. There are sufficient numbers of temporary registers to use.

    (*a*) Determine the number of unit-time steps T_1 required to compute the product of two $n \times n$ matrices on a nonpipeline scalar processor. Assume one unit time per each addition or each multiplication operation in the scalar processor.

    (*b*) Determine the number of time steps T_k required to compute the matrix product, using the multifunction pipeline processor with a total pipeline delay of one time unit.

    (*c*) Determine the speedup ratios T_1/T_k, when $n = 1$, $n = k$, and $n = m \cdot k$ for some large m.

4.3 Compare the second-generation vector processors Cray-1, Cyber-205, and VP-200 in the following aspects:

    (*a*) Instruction sets: vector versus scalar instructions

    (*b*) Functional pipeline structures and usage

(c) Register files and main memory organization

(d) Vectorization and optimization methods

(e) Strengths and weaknesses in using the machine

4.4 Pipeline chaining has demonstrated its advantages in many vector processors. From the viewpoints of resource reservation (registers and functional pipes) and the precedence graphs of arithmetic expressions, find necessary and sufficient conditions that allow the chaining of functional pipes. For different task systems, different chaining conditions may be found for different types of data dependence graphs. Assume some fixed delays of the pipes, registers and memory and some fixed vector-length distribution.

4.5 Conduct a thorough survey of various vectorizing compilers in existing vector supercomputers and compare their special features and relative strengths for a number of representative kernel computations such as those for solving partial differential equations, oil reservoir modeling, electric power flow analysis, linear programming, etc.

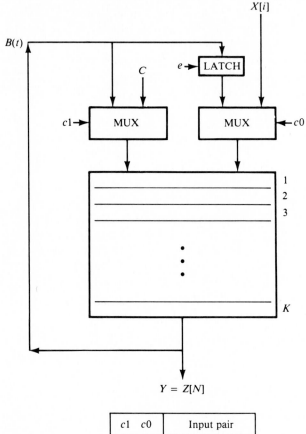

$c1$	$c0$	Input pair
0	0	$C, X[i]$
0	1	$C, B(t-j)$
1	0	$B(t), X[i]$
1	1	$B(t), B(t-j)$

Figure 4.43 The hardware organization of a vector reduction pipeline.

4.6 Conduct a thorough comparison of back-end computer systems, including both *vector super-computers* and the *attached scientific processors*, in the following aspects:

    (*a*) Peak scalar performance
    (*b*) Peak vector performance
    (*c*) Pipeline clock rate
    (*d*) Memory bandwidth
    (*e*) Cost of central processing unit
    (*f*) Performance/cost ratio
    (*g*) Main memory capacity
    (*h*) Register files/buffers
    (*i*) Functional pipelines

4.7 Let $A(1:2N)$, $B(1:2N)$, $C(1:2N)$ and $D(1:2N)$ be each a $2N$-element vector stored in the main memory of a vector processor. Each vector register in the processor has N components. There are two *load-store* pipes, one *multiply* pipe, and one *add* pipe that are available to be used. Draw a space-time diagram (similar to that in Figure 4.37 for Example 4.22) to show the *pipeline chaining* and *parallelization* operations to be performed in the execution of the following linked vector instructions with minimum time delay:

$$A(I) = B(I) * C(I) + D(I)$$
$$\text{for } I = 1, 2, \ldots, N, N+1, \ldots, 2N$$

Assume that all pipeline units, regardless of their functions, have equal delays as assumed in Figure 4.37. Sufficient numbers of vector registers are assumed available, and they can be cascaded together to hold longer vectors, such as $2N$, $3N$, $\ldots$, etc.

4.8 A *vector arithmetic reduction unit* is shown in Figure 4.43. This multifunction pipeline can accept vector inputs and produce a single scalar output at the end of computation. The feedback connection is needed for accumulated arithmetic operations. Develop four fast algorithms for scheduling the successive computations (*multiply*'s and *add-subtract*'s), needed in the following vector reduction arithmetic operations:

    (*a*) The summation of the n components in a vector
    (*b*) The dot product of two n-element vectors
    (*c*) The multiplication of two $n \times n$ matrices
    (*d*) The searching of the maximum among n components of a vector

Hint: Algorithm (*a*) may be used in algorithm (*b*). Both (*a*) and (*b*) may be used in algorithm (*c*). In part (*d*), comparison is done by subtraction through the pipeline unit.

4.9 Let D be a stream of data (tasks or operand sets). Suppose that we wish to perform two functions f_1 and f_2 on every task in D. That is, for each operand set x in D, we want to compute $f_2(f_1(x))$. The computations are to be performed on a machine with multiple pipeline functional units, one of which computes the function f_1 and another which computes f_2. The reservation tables for f_1 and f_2 are given below.

f_1:	1	2	3	4	5	6	7	8
S1	x							x
S2		x	x					
S3				x				
S4		x			x			x
S5						x		

f_2:	1	2	3	4	5	6	7	8	9	10
S1	x									x
S2		x								x
S3			x				x			
S4				x			x			
S5					x			x		
S6						x			x	

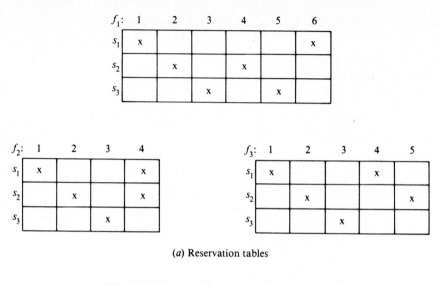

f_1:

	1	2	3	4	5	6
S_1	x					x
S_2		x		x		
S_3			x		x	

f_2:

	1	2	3	4
S_1	x			x
S_2		x		x
S_3			x	

f_3:

	1	2	3	4	5
S_1	x			x	
S_2		x			x
S_3			x		

(a) Reservation tables

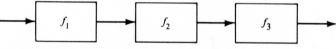

(b) Pipeline chaining

Figure 4.44 The chaining of three pipelines in Problem 4.10.

(a) What are the maximum throughputs for the f_1 and g_2 pipelines, assuming that they work completely independently on one another? That is, assume that the two pipelines work on completely independent data streams D_1 and D_2.

(b) In chaining, the output of one pipeline is applied directly to the input of another pipeline. One can think of this as configuring the pipelines such that the output latch or buffer of the first pipeline becomes the input latch or buffer of the second. What is the maximum throughput for tasks in D if the f_1 and f_2 pipeline functional units are chained together?

(c) What can you conclude about the general effectiveness of chaining pipelines that have feedback? Consider the effect on memory contention and the demand on memory bandwidth as part of your answer.

4.10 Consider three functional pipelines f_1, f_2, and f_3 characterized by the reservation tables in Figure 4.44a.

(a) What are the *minimal average latencies* in using the f_1, f_2, and f_3 pipelines independently?

(b) What is the *maximum throughput* if three pipelines are chained into a linear cascade as shown in Figure 4.44b?

4.11 Show the timing diagrams for implementing the two sequences of vector instructions (described in Example 4.23) on the Cray-1 machine. Verify the total clock periods required in each of the two computing sequences.

CHAPTER FIVE

STRUCTURES AND ALGORITHMS FOR ARRAY PROCESSORS

This chapter deals with the interconnection structures and parallel algorithms for SIMD array processors and associative processors. The various organizations and control mechanisms of array processors are presented first. Interconnection networks used in array processors will be characterized by their routing functions and implementation methods. We then study the structure of associative memory and parallel search in associative array processors. SIMD algorithms are presented for matrix manipulation, parallel sorting, fast Fourier transform, and associative search and retrieval operations.

5.1 SIMD ARRAY PROCESSORS

A synchronous array of parallel processors is called an *array processor*, which consists of multiple processing elements (PEs) under the supervision of one control unit (CU). An array processor can handle *single instruction and multiple data* (SIMD) streams. In this sense, array processors are also known as *SIMD computers*. SIMD machines are especially designed to perform vector computations over matrices or arrays of data. In this book, the terms array processors, parallel processors, and SIMD computers are used interchangeably.

SIMD computers appear in two basic architectural organizations: *array processors*, using random-access memory; and *associative processors*, using content-addressable (or associative) memory. The first three sections of this chapter deal primarily with array processors. We will study associative processors in Section 5.4 as a special type of array processor whose PEs correspond to the words of an associative memory.

5.1.1 SIMD Computer Organizations

In general, an array processor may assume one of two slightly different configurations, as illustrated in Figure 5.1. Configuration I was introduced in Chapter 1. It has been implemented in the well-publicized Illiac-IV computer. This configuration is structured with N synchronized PEs, all of which are under the control of one CU. Each PE_i is essentially an arithmetic logic unit (ALU) with attached

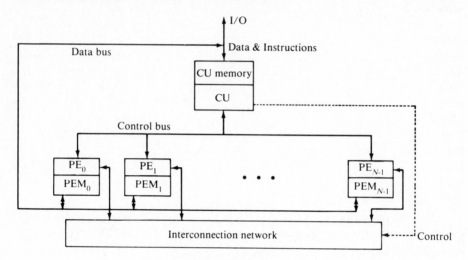

(a) Configuration I (Illiac IV)

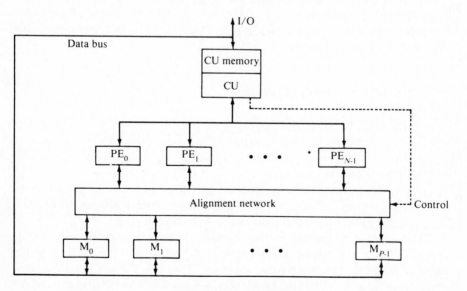

(b) Configuration II (BSP)

Figure 5.1   Architectural configurations of SIMD array processors.

working registers and local memory PEM$_i$ for the storage of distributed data. The CU also has its own main memory for the storage of programs. The system and user programs are executed under the control of the CU. The user programs are loaded into the CU memory from an external source. The function of the CU is to decode all the instructions and determine where the decoded instructions should be executed. Scalar or control-type instructions are directly executed inside the CU. Vector instructions are broadcast to the PEs for distributed execution to achieve spatial parallelism through duplicate arithmetic units (PEs).

All the PEs perform the same function synchronously in a lock-step fashion under the command of the CU. Vector operands are distributed to the PEMs before parallel execution in the array of PEs. The distributed data can be loaded into the PEMs from an external source via the system data bus, or via the CU in a broadcast mode using the control bus. Masking schemes are used to control the status of each PE during the execution of a vector instruction. Each PE may be either *active* or *disabled* during an instruction cycle. A masking vector is used to control the status of all PEs. In other words, not all the PEs need to participate in the execution of a vector instruction. Only enabled PEs perform computation. Data exchanges among the PEs are done via an inter-PE communication network, which performs all necessary data-routing and manipulation functions. This interconnection network is under the control of the control unit.

An array processor is normally interfaced to a host computer through the control unit. The host computer is a general-purpose machine which serves as the "operating manager" of the entire system, consisting of the host and the processor array. The functions of the host computer include resource management and peripheral and I/O supervisions. The control unit of the processor array directly supervises the execution of programs, whereas the host machine performs the executive and I/O functions with the outside world. In this sense, an array processor can also be considered a back-end, attached computer, similar in function to those pipeline attached processors studied in Chapter 4.

Another possible way of constructing an array processor is illustrated in Figure 5.1b. This configuration II differs from the configuration I in two aspects. First, the local memories attached to the PEs are now replaced by parallel memory modules shared by all the PEs through an alignment network. Second, the inter-PE permutation network is replaced by the inter-PE memory-alignment network, which is again controlled by the CU. A good example of a configuration II SIMD machine is the Burroughs Scientific Processor (BSP). There are N PEs and P memory modules in configuration II. The two numbers are not necessarily equal. In fact, they have been chosen to be relatively prime. The alignment network is a path-switching network between the PEs and the parallel memories. Such an alignment network is desired to allow conflict-free accesses of the shared memories by as many PEs as possible.

Array processors became well publicized with the hardware-software development of the Illiac-IV system. Since then, many SIMD machines have been constructed to satisfy various parallel-processing applications. The Burroughs *Parallel Element Processing Ensemble* (PEPE) and the Goodyear Aerospace

Staran are two associative array processors. Extended from the Illiac-IV design are the *Burroughs Scientific Processor* (BSP) and the Goodyear Aerospace *Massively Parallel Processor* (MPP).

Formally, an SIMD computer C is characterized by the following set of parameters:

$$C = \langle N, F, I, M \rangle \qquad (5.1)$$

where N = the number of PEs in the system. For example, the Illiac-IV has $N = 64$, the BSP has $N = 16$, and the MPP has $N = 16{,}384$.

F = a set of data-routing functions provided by the interconnection network (in Figure 5.1a) or by the alignment network (in Figure 5.1b).

I = the set of machine instructions for scalar-vector, data-routing, and network-manipulation operations.

M = the set of masking schemes, where each mask partitions the set of PEs into the two disjoint subsets of enabled PEs and disabled PEs.

This model provides a common basis for evaluating different SIMD machines. We will characterize various data-routing functions in the next section when we study interconnection networks for SIMD machines. The instruction sets of important array processors will be discussed with those example SIMD computers in Chapter 6.

In addition to regular SIMD machines, several algorithmic array processors have been developed as back-end attachments to host machines. Among them are the IBM 3838 and the Datawest MATP. These attached array processors are highly pipelined for array processing. They are not SIMD machines as discussed above. The reason that these pipeline attached processors are commercially known as "array" processors lies in the fact that they are used for processing arrays of data. Details of the Illiac-IV, BSP, MPP and multiple-SIMD computers using a shared pool will be treated in Chapter 6.

5.1.2 Masking and Data-Routing Mechanisms

In this chapter, we consider only configuration I of an SIMD computer. Each PE_i is a processor (Figure 5.2) with its own memory PEM_i; a set of working registers and flags, namely A_i, B_i, C_i, and S_i; an arithmetic logic unit; a local index register I_i; an address register D_i; and a data-routing register R_i. The R_i of each PE_i is connected to the R_j of other PEs via the interconnection network. When data transfer among PEs occurs, it is the contents of the R_i registers that are being transferred. We shall denote the N PEs as PE_i for $i = 0, 1, 2, \ldots, N - 1$, where the index i is the address of PE_i. To facilitate future illustrations, we assume $N = 2^m$ or $m = \log_2 N$ binary digits are needed to encode the address of a PE. The address register D_i is used to hold the m-bit address of the PE_i. This PE structure is essentially based on the design in Illiac-IV.

Some array processors may use two routing registers, one for input and the other for output. We will simply consider the use of one R_i per PE_i in which the

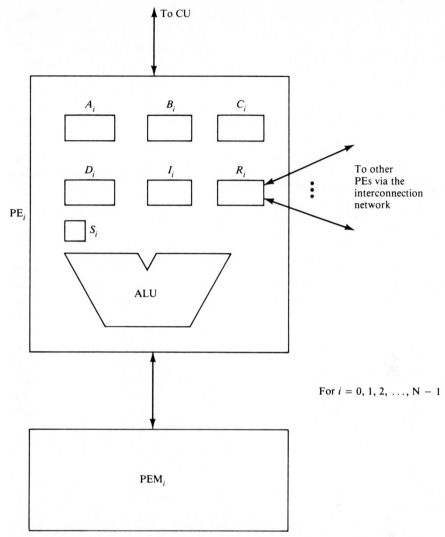

Figure 5.2 Components in a Processing Element (PE$_i$).

inputs and outputs of R_i are totally isolated by using master-slave flip-flops. Each PE$_i$ is either in the active or in the inactive mode during each instruction cycle. If a PE$_i$ is active, it executes the instruction broadcast to it by the CU. If a PE$_i$ is inactive, it will not execute the instructions broadcast to it. The masking schemes are used to specify the status flag S_i of PE$_i$. The convention $S_i = 1$ is chosen for an active PE$_i$ and $S_i = 0$ for an inactive PE$_i$. In the CU, there is a global index register I and a masking register M. The M register has N bits. The ith bit of M will be denoted as M_i. The collection of S_i flags for $i = 0, 1, 2, \ldots, N - 1$ forms a status register S for all the PEs. Note that the bit patterns in registers M and S are exchangeable upon the control of the CU when masking is to be set.

From the hardware viewpoint, the physical length of a vector is determined by the number of PEs. The CU performs the segmentation of a long vector into vector loops, the setting of a global base address, and the offset increment. Distributing vector elements to different PEMs is crucial to the efficient utilization of an array of PEs. Ideally, N elements of a vector are retrieved from different PEMs simultaneously. In the worst case, all the vector elements are all in a single PEM. They must be fetched sequentially one after another. A one-dimensional linear vector of n elements can be stored in all PEMs if $n \leq N$. Long vectors $(n > N)$ can be stored by distributing the n elements cyclically among the N PEMs. Difficulty may arise in using high-dimensional arrays. For example, in matrix computations, rows and columns may both be needed in intermediate calculations. The matrix should be stored in a way to allow the parallel fetch of either a row, a column, or a diagonal in one memory cycle. Skewed storage methods will be discussed in Section 6.4 to overcome the access-conflict problem.

In an array processor, vector operands can be specified by the registers to be used or by the memory addresses to be referenced. For memory-reference instructions, each PE_i accesses the local PEM_i, offset by its own index register I_i. The I_i register modifies the global memory address broadcast from the CU. Thus, different locations in different PEMs can be accessed simultaneously with the same global address specified by the CU. The following example shows how indexing can be used to address the local memories in parallel at different local addresses.

Example 5.1 Consider an array of $n \times n$ data elements:

$$A = \{A(i, j), 0 \leq i, j \leq n - 1\} \tag{5.2}$$

Elements in the jth column of A are stored in n consecutive locations of PEM_j, say from location 100 to location $100 + n - 1$ (assume $n \leq N$). If the programmer wishes to access the principal diagonal elements $A(j, j)$ for $j = 0$, $1, \ldots, n - 1$ of the array A, then the CU must generate and broadcast an effective memory address 100 (after offset by the global index register I in the CU, if there is a base address of A involved). The local index registers must be set to be $I_j = j$ for $j = 0, 1, \ldots, n - 1$ in order to convert the global address 100 to local addresses $100 + I_j = 100 + j$ for each PEM_j. Within each PE, there should be a separate memory address register for holding these local addresses. However, if one wishes to address a row of the array A, say the ith row $A(i, j)$ for $j = 0, 1, 2, \ldots, n - 1$, all the I_j registers will be reset to be for all $j = 0, 1, 2, \ldots, n - 1$ in order to ensure the parallel access of the entire row.

Example 5.2 To illustrate the necessity of data routing in an array processor, we show the execution details of the following vector instruction in an array of N PEs. The sum $S(k)$ of the first k components in a vector A is desired for each k from 0 to $n - 1$. Let $A = (A_0, A_1, \ldots, A_{n-1})$. We need to compute the following n summations:

$$S(k) = \sum_{i=0}^{k} A_i \quad \text{for } k = 0, 1, \ldots, n - 1 \tag{5.3}$$

These n vector summations can be computed recursively by going through the following $n - 1$ iterations defined by:

$$S(0) = A_0$$

$$S(k) = S(k - 1) + A_k \qquad \text{for } k = 1, 2, \ldots, n - 1 \qquad (5.4)$$

The above recursive summations for the case of $n = 8$ are implemented in an array processor with $N = 8$ PEs in $\lceil \log_2 n \rceil = 3$ steps, as shown in Figure 5.3. Both data routing and PE masking are used in the implementation. Initially, each A_i, residing in PEM_i, is moved to the R_i register in PE_i for $i = 0, 1, \ldots, n - 1$ ($n = N = 8$ is assumed here). In the first step, A_i is routed from R_i to R_{i+1} and added to A_{i+1} with the resulting sum $A_i + A_{i+1}$ in R_{i+1}, for $i = 0, 1, \ldots, 6$. The arrows in Figure 5.3 show the routing operations and the shorthand notation $i - j$ is used to refer to the intermediate sum $A_i + A_{i+1} + \cdots + A_j$. In step 2, the intermediate sums in R_i are routed to

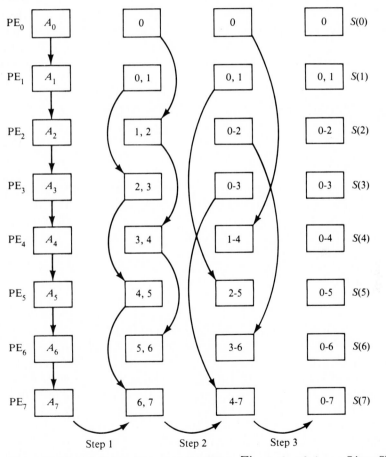

Figure 5.3 The calculation of the summation $S(k) = \sum_{i=0}^{k} A_i$, $k = 0, 1, \ldots, 7$ in an SIMD machine.

R_{i+2} for $i = 0$ to 5. In the final step, the intermediate sums in R_i are routed to R_{i+4} for $i = 0$ to 3. Consequently, PE_k has the final value of $S(k)$ for $k = 0, 1, 2, \ldots, 7$, as shown by the last column in Figure 5.3.

As far as the data-routing operations are concerned, PE_7 is not involved (receiving but not transmitting) in step 1. PE_7 and PE_6 are not involved in step 2. Also PE_7, PE_6, PE_5, and PE_4 are not involved in step 3. These unwanted PEs are masked off during the corresponding steps. During the *addition* operations, PE_0 is disabled in step 1; PE_0 and PE_1 are made inactive in step 2; and PE_0, PE_1, PE_2, and PE_3 are masked off in step 3. The PEs that are masked off in each step depend on the operation (data-routing or arithmetic-addition) to be performed. Therefore, the masking patterns keep changing in the different operation cycles, as demonstrated by the example. Note that the masking and routing operations will be much more complicated when the vector length $n > N$.

Array processors are special-purpose computers for limited scientific applications. We will describe the detailed structures of the CU and PEs with several SIMD computer designs in Chapter 6. The array of PEs are passive arithmetic units waiting to be called for parallel-computation duties. The permutation network among PEs is under program control from the CU. The above general structures of SIMD computers may be modified in the specific SIMD machines to be presented in Chapter 6. However, the principles of PE masking, global versus local indexing, and data permutation are not much changed in the different machines.

5.1.3 Inter-PE Communications

Network design decisions for inter-PE communications are discussed below. These are fundamental decisions in determining the appropriate architecture of an interconnection network for an SIMD machine. The decisions are made between *operation modes, control strategies, switching methodologies*, and *network topologies*.

Operation mode Two types of communication can be identified: *synchronous* and *asynchronous*. Synchronous communication is needed for establishing communication paths synchronously for either a data manipulating function or for a data instruction broadcast. Asynchronous communication is needed for multiprocessing in which connection requests are issued dynamically. A system may also be designed to facilitate both synchronous and asynchronous processing. Therefore, the typical operation modes of interconnection networks can be classified into three categories: synchronous, asynchronous, and combined. All existing SIMD machines choose the synchronous operation mode, in which lock-step operations among all PEs are enforced.

Control strategy A typical interconnection network consists of a number of switching elements and interconnecting links. Interconnection functions are realized by properly setting control of the switching elements. The control-setting function can be managed by a centralized controller or by the individual switching element. The latter strategy is called *distributed control* and the first strategy corresponds to *centralized control*. Most existing SIMD interconnection networks choose the centralized control on all switch elements by the control unit.

Switching methodology The two major switching methodologies are *circuit switching* and *packet switching*. In circuit switching, a physical path is actually established between a source and a destination. In packet switching, data is put in a packet and routed through the interconnection network without establishing a physical connection path. In general, circuit switching is much more suitable for bulk data transmission, and packet switching is more efficient for many short data messages. Another option, integrated switching, includes the capabilities of both circuit switching and packet switching. Therefore, three switching methodologies can be identified: circuit switching, packet switching, and integrated switching. Most SIMD interconnection networks are handwired to assume circuit switching operations. Packet switched networks have been suggested mainly for MIMD machines.

Network topology A network can be depicted by a graph in which nodes represent switching points and edges represent communication links. The topologies tend to be regular and can be grouped into two categories: *static* and *dynamic*. In a static topology, links between two processors are passive and dedicated buses cannot be reconfigured for direct connections to other processors. On the other hand, links in the dynamic category can be reconfigured by setting the network's active switching elements.

The space of the interconnection networks can be represented by the cartesian product of the above four sets of design features: {operation mode} × {control strategy} × {switching methodology} × {network topology}. Not every combination of the design features is interesting. The choice of a particular interconnection network depends on the application demands, technology supports, and cost-effectiveness.

5.2 SIMD INTERCONNECTION NETWORKS

Various interconnection networks have been suggested for SIMD computers. In this section, we distinguish between single-stage, recirculating networks and multi-stage SIMD networks. Important network classes to be presented include the Illiac network, the flip network, the n cube, the Omega network, the data manipulator, the barrel shifter, and the shuffle-exchange network. We shall concentrate on inter-PE communications as modeled by configuration I in Figure 5.1. The interprocessor-memory communication networks will be studied in Chapter 7 for MIMD operations.

5.2.1 Static Versus Dynamic Networks

The topological structure of an SIMD array processor is mainly characterized by the data-routing network used in interconnecting the processing elements. Formally, such an inter-PE communication network can be specified by a set of data-routing functions. If we identify the addresses of all the PEs in an SIMD machine by the set $S = \{0, 1, 2, \ldots, N - 1\}$, each routing function f is a *bijection* (a one-to-one and onto mapping) from S to S. When a routing function f is executed via the interconnection network, the PE_i copies the contents of its R_i register into the $R_{f(i)}$ register of $PE_{f(i)}$. This data-routing operation occurs in all active PEs simultaneously. An inactive PE may receive data from another PE if a routing function is executed, but it cannot transmit data. To pass data between PEs that are not directly connected in the network, the data must be passed through intermediate PEs by executing a sequence of routing functions through the interconnection network.

The SIMD interconnection networks are classified into the following two categories based on network topologies: *static networks* and *dynamic networks*.

Static networks Topologies in the static networks can be classified according to the dimensions required for layout. For illustration, one-dimensional, two-dimensional, three-dimensional, and hypercube are shown in Figure 5.4. Examples of one-dimensional topologies include the *linear array* used for some pipeline architectures (Figure 5.4a). Two-dimensional topologies include the *ring, star, tree, mesh,* and *systolic array*. Examples of these structures are shown in Figures 5.4b through 5.4f.

Three-dimensional topologies include the *completely connected chordal ring, 3 cube,* and *3-cube-connected-cycle* networks depicted in Figures 5.4g through 5.4j. A *D*-dimensional, *W*-wide hypercube contains *W* nodes in each dimension, and there is a connection to a node in each dimension. The mesh and the 3 cube are actually two- and three-dimensional hypercubes, respectively. The cube-connected-cycle is a deviation of the hypercube. For example, the 3-cube-connected-cycle shown in Figure 5.4j is obtained from the 3 cube.

Dynamic networks We consider two classes of dynamic networks: *single-stage* versus *multistage*, as described below separately:

Single-stage networks A single-stage network is a switching network with *N input selectors* (IS) and *N output selectors* (OS), as demonstrated in Figure 5.5. Each IS is essentially a 1-to-*D* demultiplexer and each OS is an *M*-to-1 multiplexer where $1 \leq D \leq N$ and $1 \leq M \leq N$. Note that the crossbar-switching network is a single-stage network with $D = M = N$. To establish a desired connecting path, different path control signals will be applied to all IS and OS selectors.

The single-stage network is also called a *recirculating* network. Data items may have to recirculate through the single stage several times before reaching their final destinations. The number of recirculations needed depends on the

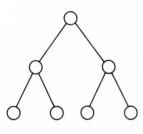
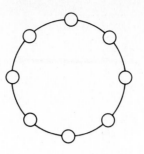
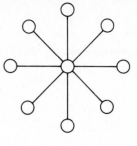

(*a*) Linear array   (*b*) Ring   (*c*) Star

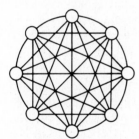
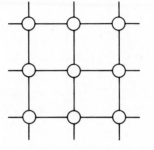
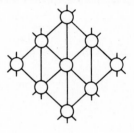

(*d*) Tree   (*e*) Near-neighbor mesh   (*f*) Systolic array

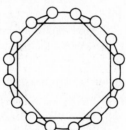
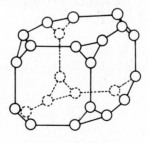

(*g*) Completely connected   (*h*) Chordal ring   (*i*) 3 cube

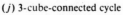

(*j*) 3-cube-connected cycle

Figure 5.4 Static interconnection network topologies. (Courtesy of Feng, *IEEE Computer*, December 1981.)

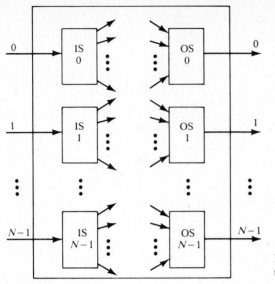

Figure 5.5 Conceptual view of a single-stage interconnection network.

connectivity in the single-stage network. In general, the higher is the hardware connectivity, the less is the number of recirculations. The crossbar network is an extreme case in which only one circulation is needed to establish any connection path. However, the fully connected crossbar networks have a cost $O(N^2)$, which may be prohibitive for large N. Most recirculating networks have cost $O(N \log N)$ or lower, which is definitely more cost-effective for large N.

Multistage networks Many stages of interconnected switches form a *multistage SIMD network*. Multistage networks are described by three characterizing features: the *switch box*, the *network topology*, and the *control structure*. Many switch boxes are used in a multistage network. Each box is essentially an interchange device with two inputs and two outputs, as depicted in Figure 5.6. Illustrated are four states of a switch box: *straight, exchange, upper broadcast*, and *lower broadcast*. A two-function switch box can assume either the straight or the exchange states. A four-function switch box can be in any one of the four legitimate states.

A multistage network is capable of connecting an arbitrary input terminal to an arbitrary output terminal. Multistage networks can be one-sided or two-sided. The *one-sided networks*, sometimes called full switches, have input-output ports on the same side. The *two-sided multistage networks*, which usually have an input side and an output side, can be divided into three classes: blocking, rearrangeable, and nonblocking.

In *blocking networks*, simultaneous connections of more than one terminal pair may result in conflicts in the use of network communication links. Examples of a blocking network are the *data manipulator, Omega, flip, n cube*, and *baseline*.

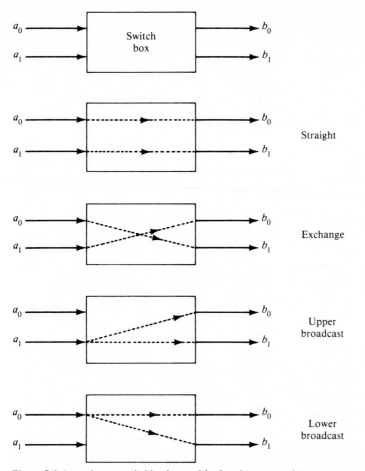

Figure 5.6 A two-by-two switching box and its four interconnection states.

Some of these networks will be introduced in subsequent sections. Figure 5.7a shows the interconnection pattern in the baseline network.

A network is called a *rearrangeable network* if it can perform all possible connections between inputs and outputs by rearranging its existing connections so that a connection path for a new input-output pair can always be established. A well-defined network, the Benes network, shown in Figure 5.7b, belongs to this class. The Benes rearrangeable network topology has been extensively studied for use in synchronous data permutation and in asynchronous interprocessor communication.

A network which can handle all possible connections without blocking is called a *nonblocking network*. Two cases have been considered in the literature. In the first case, the *Clos network*, shown in Figure 5.7c, a one-to-one connection is made between an input and an output. The other case considers one-to-many connections. Here, a generalized connection network topology is generated to

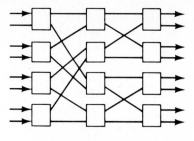

(*a*) 8 × 8 baseline network

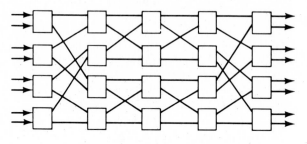

(*b*) 8 × 8 Benes network

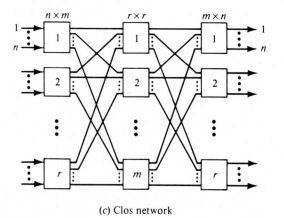

(*c*) Clos network

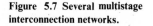

Figure 5.7 Several multistage interconnection networks.

pass any of multiple mappings of inputs onto outputs. The *crossbar switch network* can connect every input port to a free output port without blocking.

Generally, a multistage network consists of n stages where $N = 2^n$ is the number of input and output lines. Therefore, each stage may use $N/2$ switch boxes. The interconnection patterns from stage to stage determine the network topology. Each stage is connected to the next stage by at least N paths. The network delay is proportional to the number n of stages in a network. The cost of a size N multistage network is proportional to $N \log_2 N$. The control structure of a network determines how the states of the switch boxes will be set. Two types of control structures are used in a network construction. The *individual stage control* uses the same control signal to set all switch boxes in the same stage. In other words, all boxes at the same stage must be set to assume that same state. Therefore, it requires n sets of control signals to set up the states of all n stages of switch boxes.

Another control philosophy is to apply *individual box control*. A separate control signal is used to set the state of each switch box. This offers higher flexibility in setting up the connecting paths, but requires $n^2/2$ control signals, which will significantly increase the complexity of the control circuitry. A compromise design is to use *partial stage control*, in which $i + 1$ control signals are used at stage i for $0 \leq i \leq n - 1$. Various network topologies and control structures of both recirculating and multistage inter-PE communication networks are described in subsequent sections.

5.2.2 Mesh-Connected Illiac Network

A single-stage recirculating network has been implemented in the Illiac-IV array processor with $N = 64$ PEs. Each PE_i is allowed to send data to any one of PE_{i+1}, PE_{i-1}, PE_{i+r}, and PE_{i-r} where $r = \sqrt{N}$ (for the case of the Illiac-IV, $r = \sqrt{64} = 8$) in one circulation step through the network. Formally, the Illiac network is characterized by the following four routing functions:

$$R_{+1}(i) = (i + 1) \bmod N$$
$$R_{-1}(i) = (i - 1) \bmod N$$
$$R_{+r}(i) = (i + r) \bmod N \tag{5.5}$$
$$R_{-r}(i) = (i - r) \bmod N$$

where $0 \leq i \leq N - 1$. In practice, N is commonly a perfect square, such as $N = 64$ and $r = 8$ in the Illiac-IV network.

A reduced Illiac network is illustrated in Figure 5.8a for $N = 16$ and $r = 4$. The real Illiac network has a similar structure except larger in size. All the index arithmetic in Eq. 5.5 is modulo N. Comparing with the formal model shown in Figure 5.5, we observe that the outputs of IS_i are connected to the inputs of OS_j for $j = i + 1$, $i - 1$, $i + r$, and $i - r$. On the other hand, OS_j gets its inputs from IS_i for $i = j - 1, j + 1, j - r$, and $j + r$, respectively.

Each PE_i in Figure 5.8 is directly connected to its four nearest neighbors in the mesh network. In terms of permutation cycles, we can express the above routing functions as follows: Horizontally, all the PEs of all rows form a linear circular list as governed by the following two permutations, each with a single cycle of order N. The permutation cycles $(a\ b\ c)\ (d\ e)$ stand for the permutation $a \to b$, $b \to c$, $c \to a$ and $d \to e$, $e \to d$ in a circular fashion within each pair of parentheses:

$$R_{+1} = (0\ 1\ 2\ \cdots\ N{-}1)$$
$$R_{-1} = (N{-}1\ \cdots\ 2\ 1\ 0) \tag{5.6}$$

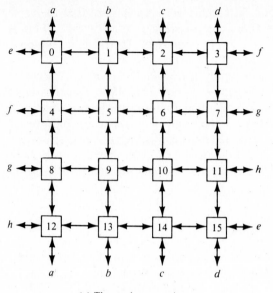

(*a*) The mesh connections

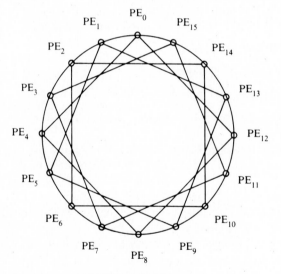

(*b*) The mesh redrawn

Figure 5.8 An Illiac network with $N = 16$ PEs.

Vertically, the distance r shifting operations are characterized by the following two permutations, each with r cycles of order r each:

$$R_{+r} = \prod_{i=0}^{r-s} (i \ \ i+r \ \ i+2r \ \cdots \ i+N-r)$$

$$R_{-r} = \prod_{i=0}^{r-1} (i+N-r \ \cdots \ i+2r \ \ i+r \ \ i)$$

(5.7)

For the example network of $N = 16$ and $r = \sqrt{16} = 4$, the shift by a distance of four is specified by the following two permutations, each with four cycles of order four each:

$$R_{+4} = (0 \ 4 \ 8 \ 12)(1 \ 5 \ 9 \ 13)(2 \ 6 \ 10 \ 14)(3 \ 7 \ 11 \ 15)$$

$$R_{-4} = (12 \ 8 \ 4 \ 0)(13 \ 9 \ 5 \ 1)(14 \ 10 \ 6 \ 2)(15 \ 11 \ 7 \ 3)$$

It should be noted that when either the R_{+1} or R_{-1} routing function is executed, data is routed as described in Eq. 5.6 only if all PEs in the cycle are active. When the routing function R_{+r} or R_{-r} is executed, data are permuted as described in Eq. 5.7 only if PE_{i+kr} where $0 \le k \le r - 1$ are active for each i. The shifting operation in a cycle will be suspended if any PE required in the cycle is disabled. For an example, the cycle (1 5 9 13) in the above permutation R_4 will not be executed if one or more among PE_1, PE_5, PE_9, and PE_{13} is disabled by masking.

The Illiac network is only a partially connected network. Figure 5.8b shows the connectivity of the example Illiac network with $N = 16$. This graph shows that four PEs can be reached from any PE in one step, seven PEs in two steps, and eleven PEs in three steps. In general, it takes I steps (recirculations) to route data from PE_i to any other PE_j in an Illiac network of size N where I is upper-bounded by

$$I \le \sqrt{N} - 1$$

(5.8)

Without a loss of generality, we illustrate the cases when PE_0 is a source node in Figure 5.8. PE_1, PE_4, PE_{12}, or PE_{15} is reachable in one step from PE_0. In two steps, the network can route data from PE_0 to PE_2, PE_3, PE_5, PE_8, PE_{11}, PE_{13}, or PE_{14}. In the worst case of three routing steps, the following eight routing sequences take place in the network:

$$0 \xrightarrow{R_{+1}} 1 \xrightarrow{R_{+1}} 2 \xrightarrow{R_{+4}} 6 \qquad 0 \xrightarrow{R_{+4}} 4 \xrightarrow{R_{+4}} 8 \xrightarrow{R_{-1}} 7$$

$$0 \xrightarrow{R_{-4}} 12 \xrightarrow{R_{-1}} 11 \xrightarrow{R_{-4}} 7 \qquad 0 \xrightarrow{R_{-4}} 12 \xrightarrow{R_{-4}} 8 \xrightarrow{R_{-1}} 7$$

$$0 \xrightarrow{R_{-4}} 12 \xrightarrow{R_{-4}} 8 \xrightarrow{R_{+1}} 9 \qquad 0 \xrightarrow{R_{-1}} 15 \xrightarrow{R_{-4}} 11 \xrightarrow{R_{-1}} 10$$

$$0 \xrightarrow{R_{+1}} 1 \xrightarrow{R_{-4}} 13 \xrightarrow{R_{-4}} 9 \qquad 0 \xrightarrow{R_{-1}} 15 \xrightarrow{R_{-1}} 14 \xrightarrow{R_{-1}} 10$$

In the Illiac-IV computer, at most seven ($\sqrt{64} - 1$) steps are needed to route data from any one PE to another PE. Of course, if we increase the connectivity in Figure 5.8, the upper bound given in Eq. 5.8 can be lowered. We shall demonstrate this by other network types in subsequent sections. When the network is strongly connected (i.e., with 15 outgoing links per node in Figure 5.8), the upper bound on recirculation steps can be reduced to one at the expense of significantly increased hardware in the crossbar network.

5.2.3 Cube Interconnection Networks

The cube network can be implemented as either a recirculating network or as a multistage network for SIMD machines. A three-dimensional cube is illustrated in Figure 5.9a. Vertical lines connect vertices (PEs) whose addresses differ in the most significant bit position. Vertices at both ends of the diagonal lines differ in

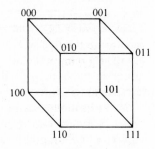

(a) A 3 cube of 8 nodes

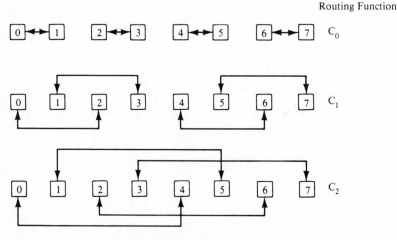

(b) The recirculating cube network

Figure 5.9 The cube interconnection network.

the middle bit position. Horizontal lines differ in the least significant bit position. This unit-cube concept can be extended to an n-dimensional unit space, called an n *cube*, with n bits per vertex. A cube network for an SIMD machine with N PEs corresponds to an n cube where $n = \log_2 N$. We shall use the binary sequence $A = (a_{n-1} \cdots a_2 \, a_1 a_0)_2$ to represent the vertex (PE) address for $0 \le A \le N - 1$. The complement of bit a_i will be denoted as $\bar{a}_i$ for any $0 \le i \le n - 1$.

Formally, an n-dimensional cube network of N PEs is specified by the following n routing functions:

$$C_i(a_{n-1} \cdots a_1 a_0) = a_{n-1} \cdots a_{i+1} \bar{a}_i a_{i-1} \cdots a_0 \qquad \text{for } i = 0, 1, 2, \ldots, n-1 \quad (5.9)$$

In the n cube, each PE located at a corner is directly connected to n neighbors. The neighboring PEs differ in exactly one bit position. Pease's binary n cube, the flip network used in STARAN, and the programmable switching network proposed for the Phoenix project are examples of cube networks.

In a recirculating cube network, each IS_A for $0 \le A \le N - 1$ is connected to n OSs whose addresses are $a_{n-1} \cdots a_{i+1} \bar{a}_i a_{i-1} \cdots a_0$ for $0 \le i \le n - 1$. On the other hand, each OS_T with $T = t_{n-1} \cdots t_1 t_0$ gets its inputs from ISs whose addresses are $t_{n-1} \cdots t_{i+1} \bar{t}_i t_{-1} \cdots t_0$ for $0 \le i \le n - 1$. To execute the C_i routing function, IS_j selects the $C_i(j)$ output line and the OS_j selects the $C_i(j)$ input line for all j such that $0 \le j \le N - 1$.

The implementation of a single-stage cube network is illustrated in Figure 5.9b for $N = 8$. The interconnections of the PEs corresponding to the three routing functions C_0, C_1, and C_2 are shown separately. If one assembles all three connecting patterns together, the 3 cube shown in Figure 5.9a should be the result.

The same set of cube-routing functions, C_0, C_1, and C_2, can also be implemented by a three-stage cube network, as modeled in Figure 5.10 for $N = 8$.

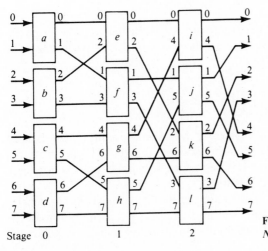

Figure 5.10 A Multistage cube network for $N = 8$.

Two-function (*straight* and *exchange*) switch boxes are used in constructing multistage cube networks. The stages are numbered as 0 at the input end and increased to $n - 1$ at the output end. Stage i implements the C_i routing function (Eq. 5.9) for $i = 0, 1, 2, \ldots, n - 1$. This means that switch boxes at stage i connect an input line to the output line that differs from it only at the ith bit position. Based on this interconnection requirement, individual box control is assumed in a multistage cube network.

The STARAN flip network and Pease's binary n-cube networks are both implemented with multiple stages. These two cube networks have the same topology, as shown in Figure 5.10. They differ from each other only in their control structures. The flip network has two control mechanisms, the flip control and the shift control. Under the individual-stage flip control, an n-bit vector $F = f_{n-1} \cdots f_1 f_0$ determines how stages will be set. Stage i switch boxes are set to exchange if $f_i = 1$, and set to straight if $f_i = 0$. For example, if $F = 001$ (for $N = 8$), the network connects input line $a_2 a_1 a_0$ to output line $a_1 a_2 \bar{a}_0$. This partial-stage shift control allows barrel shifts of data from input A to output $(A + 2^m) \pmod{2^p}$ where $0 \le m \le p \le n$, using $i + 1$ control lines at stage i for $0 \le i \le n - 1$. The individual box control of the Pease's n-cube network is much more flexible than the partial-stage control in the flip network. In other words, the n-cube network can perform not only all the connections that STARAN can, but also some connections it cannot.

The cube-routing function C_i for each i in Eq. 5.9 corresponds to performing the following permutation on N PEs:

$$P_i = \prod_{j=0}^{N-1} (j \quad C_i(j)) \tag{5.10}$$

where the ith bit of j equals zero and PE_j and $\text{PE}_{C_i(j)}$ are both active. For an example, the routing function C_2 executed on a 3-cube network corresponds to the following permutation over eight PEs:

$$P_2 = (0 \quad 4)(1 \quad 5)(2 \quad 6)(3 \quad 7)$$

If all the switch boxes in stage i are set to exchange, the network performs the P_i permutation at stage i. In general, the following multistage permutation is conducted in an n-stage cube network:

$$P = \prod_{i=0}^{n-1} \left(\prod_{j=0}^{N-1} (j \quad C_i(j)) \right) \tag{5.11}$$

where the ith bit j equals 0 and the stage i switch boxes whose inputs are labeled as j and $C_i(j)$ are set to exchange. For the example design in Figure 5.10, the permutation $(0\ 1)(0\ 2)(0\ 4) = (0\ 1\ 2\ 4)$ is performed only if the top row boxes are set to exchange and the rest are set to straight.

Masking may change the data-routing patterns in a cube network. The general practice is to disable all PEs belonging to the same cycle of a permutation. In the above example, if both PE_2 and PE_6 become inactive by masking, the cycles $(2\ 6)$

are removed and the cube-routing function C_2 performs only the partial permutation (0 4) (1 5) (3 7). However, if only PE_2 is disabled in the above example, the above partial permutation will still be performed, but data in both PE_2 and PE_6 will be transferred to PE_2, causing a two-to-one conflicting transfer. PE_6 will not receive any data, so the mapping will not be onto either. Masking should be carefully applied to cube networks because of the *send-active* and *receive-inactive* nature of data transfers among the PEs.

5.2.4 Barrel Shifter and Data Manipulator

Barrel shifters are also known as *plus-minus-2^i* (PM2I) networks. This type of network is based on the following routing functions:

$$B_{+i}(j) = (j + 2^i) \,(\text{mod } N)$$
$$B_{-i}(j) = (j - 2^i) \,(\text{mod } N) \tag{5.12}$$

where $0 \le j \le N - 1$, $0 \le i \le n - 1$, and $n = \log_2 N$. Comparing Eq. 5.12 with Eq. 5.5, the following equivalence is revealed when $r = \sqrt{N} = 2^{n/2}$:

$$B_{+0} = R_{+1}$$
$$B_{-0} = R_{-1}$$
$$B_{+n/2} = K_{+r} \tag{5.13}$$
$$B_{-n/2} = R_{-r}$$

This implies that the Illiac routing functions are a subset of the barrel-shifting functions. In addition to adjacent (± 1) and fixed-distance ($\pm r$) shiftings, the barrel-shifting functions allow either forward or backward shifting of distances which are the integer power of two, i.e., $\pm 1, \pm 2, \pm 4, \pm 8, \ldots, \pm 2^{n/2}, \ldots, \pm 2^{n-1}$. Instead of having just four nearest neighbors as in the Illiac mesh networks, each PE in a barrel shifter is directly connected to $2(n - 1)$ PEs. Therefore, the connectivity in a barrel shifter is increased from the Illiac network by having $(2n - 5) \cdot 2^{n-1}$ more direct links. As demonstrated in Figures 5.8b and 5.11 for $N = 16$ ($n = 4$, $r = 4$), the Illiac network has 32 direct links and the same size barrel shifter has 56 links. The two networks are identical only when the size is reduced to be no greater than $n = 2$ or $N = 5$.

The barrel shifter can be implemented as either a recirculating single-stage network or as a multistage network. Figure 5.12 shows the interconnection patterns in a recirculating barrel shifter for $N = 8$. The barrel shifting functions $B_{\pm 0}$, $B_{\pm 1}$, and $B_{\pm 2}$ are executed by the interconnection patterns shown. For a single-stage barrel shifter of size $N = 2^n$, the minimum number of recirculations B is upper bounded by

$$B \le \frac{\log_2 N}{2} \tag{5.14}$$

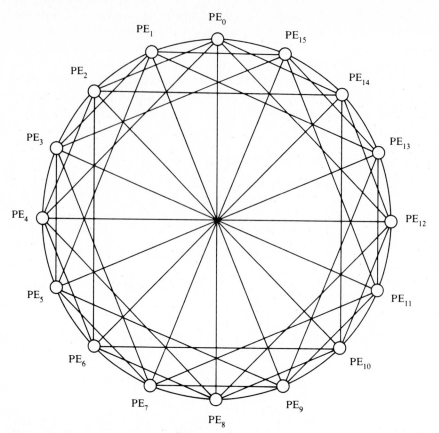

Figure 5.11 Connectivity of a barrel shifter for $N = 16$.

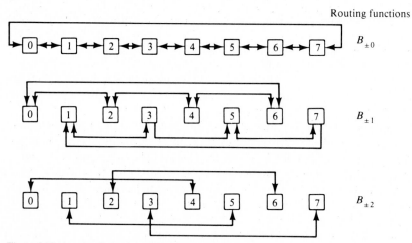

Figure 5.12 A recirculating barrel shifter for $N = 8$.

For the example barrel shifter with $N = 16$, it takes at most two steps to route data from a PE to any other PE. If we assume PE_0 as the source node, PE_0 can reach PE_1, PE_2, PE_4, PE_8, PE_{12}, PE_{14}, or PE_{15} in one step. In two steps, PE_0 can reach PE_3, PE_5, PE_6, PE_7, PE_9, PE_{10}, PE_{11}, or PE_{13}. Thus, one step is saved by using the same size Illiac network. If one replaces the 64-node Illiac-IV network by a 64-node barrel shifter, at most three routing steps are needed (instead of seven steps). The speedup of a barrel shifter over the Illiac network of the same size can be expressed by

$$S_N = \frac{\sqrt{N} - 1}{(\log_2 N)/2} = \frac{2^k - 1}{k} \tag{5.15}$$

where $N = 2^{2k}$. Therefore, the larger the network, the higher the speedup ratio. For very large networks with $N = 2^{2k}$, the speedup approaches $2^k/k$, as demonstrated in Table 5.1.

A barrel shifter has been implemented with multiple stages in the form of a *data manipulator*. As shown in Figure 5.13, the data manipulator consists of n stages of N cells. Each cell is essentially a controlled shifter. This network is designed for implementing data-manipulating functions such as *permuting*, *replicating*, *spacing*, *masking*, and *complementing*. To implement a data-manipulating function, proper control lines of the six groups ($u_1^{2^i}$, $u_2^{2^i}$, $h_1^{2^i}$, $h_2^{2^i}$, $d_1^{2^i}$, $d_2^{2^i}$) in each column must be properly set through the use of the control register and the associated decoder.

The schematic logic circuit of a typical cell in a data manipulator is shown in Figure 5.14. For $0 \le k \le N - 1$ and $0 \le i \le n - 1$, the kth cell at stage i (column 2^i) has three inputs, three sets of outputs, and three control signals. Individual stage control is used with three sets of control signals per stage. The control lines u^i, h^i, and d^i are connected to the AND gates in each cell of stage i. The u^i line controls the backforward barrel shifting (-2^i) and the d^i line controls forward barrel shifting ($+2^i$). The horizontal line corresponds to no shifting under the control of the h^i signal. Note that stage i performs the distance 2^i shiftings. By passing data through the n stages from left to right, the shifting distance decreases from 2^{n-1} to 2^{n-2} and eventually to 2^1 and 2^0 at the output end. Note that all the

Table 5.1 A comparison of bounds on the minimum routing steps in Illiac network and in barrel shifter of various sizes

k	Network size $N = 2^{2k}$	Illiac network (Eq. 5.5)	Barrel shifter (Eq. 5.14)	Speed up (Eq. 5.15)
2	16	3	2	1.50
3	64	7	3	2.33
4	256	15	4	3.75
5	1024	31	5	6.20

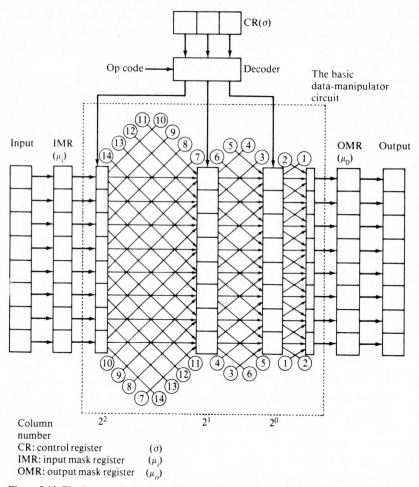

Input   IMR (μ_i)

OMR (μ_0) Output

The basic data-manipulator circuit

Op code ⟶ Decoder

CR(σ)

Column number $\quad 2^2 \qquad\qquad 2^1 \qquad\qquad 2^0$

CR: control register $\qquad\qquad (\sigma)$
IMR: input mask register $\qquad (\mu_i)$
OMR: output mask register $\quad (\mu_o)$

Figure 5.13 The data manipulator for $N = 14$. (Courtesy of IEEE Trans. Computers, Feng 1974.)

shifting operations at all stages are module N. This is reflected by the wraparound connections in the data manipulator.

In terms of permutations, the B_{+i} routing function can be expressed by the following product of 2^i cycles by size 2^{n-i} each:

$$\prod_{k=0}^{2^i-1} (k \quad k+2^i \quad k+2\cdot 2^i \quad k+3\cdot 2^i \quad \cdots \quad k+N-2^i) \qquad (5.16)$$

For the example network of $N = 8$, the B_{+1} function is represented by the following permutation $(0\ 2\ 4\ 6)(1\ 3\ 5\ 7)$. Similarly, for B_{-1} we have the following permutation in cycle notation:

$$\prod_{k=0}^{2^i-1} (k+N-2^i \quad \cdots \quad k+3\cdot 2^i \quad k+2\cdot 2^i \quad k+2^i \quad k) \qquad (5.17)$$

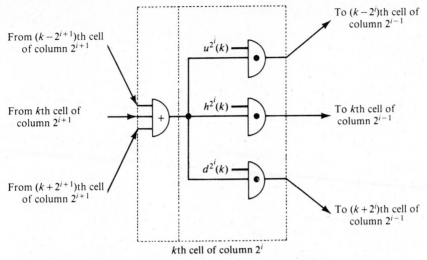

To $(k-2^i)$th cell of
column 2^{i-1}

From $(k-2^{i+1})$th cell
of column 2^{i+1}

$u^{2^i}(k)$

From kth cell of
column 2^{i+1}

$h^{2^i}(k)$

$+$

To kth cell of
column 2^{i-1}

From $(k+2^{i+1})$th cell
of column 2^{i+1}

$d^{2^i}(k)$

To $(k+2^i)$th cell of
column 2^{i-1}

kth cell of column 2^i

Figure 5.14 The logic design of an intermediate cell in the data manipulator.

Listed in Table 5.2 are data-manipulation functions that are implementable with the data manipulator. The network can perform various types of permutations such as *shift, flip, shuffle, merge,* and *sort*. It can be also used to *replicate* and *space* the data. The network does not provide the capability of masking or complementing. However, we include them in the table for the sake of completeness. Primitive operations among the aforementioned data-manipulation functions are listed below:

1. Total shift up, end around
2. Total shift up, end off
3. Spaced substrings shift up, end around
4. Contiguous substring shift up, end off
5. Spaced substrings shift up, end off
6. Substring flip
7. Multiplicate spaced substring up
8. Spread substrings with 2^s spacing up

Additional data-manipulating functions can be generated by using different sequences of primitive operations. One can augment the data manipulator by introducing individual cell control instead of individual stage control. This relaxation in control will increase the functional flexibility at the expense of significantly increased control cost. A prototype data manipulator has been implemented and attached as an interface device to the STARAN computer at the Rome Air Force Development Center in New York. Because of the uniform structure and low wire density buildup, the data manipulator is a good candidate for VLSI implementation.

Table 5.2 Data-manipulating function (Feng)

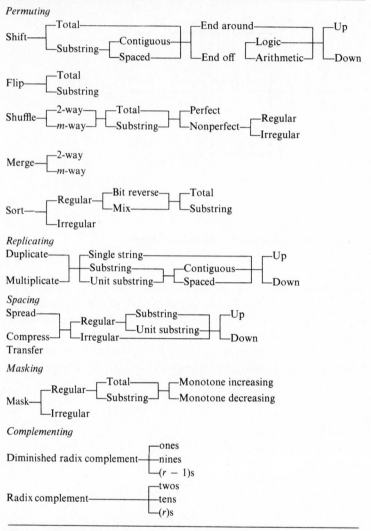

Permuting

Shift — Total / Substring — Contiguous / Spaced — End around / End off — Logic / Arithmetic — Up / Down

Flip — Total / Substring

Shuffle — 2-way / m-way — Total / Substring — Perfect / Nonperfect — Regular / Irregular

Merge — 2-way / m-way

Sort — Regular / Irregular — Bit reverse / Mix — Total / Substring

Replicating

Duplicate / Multiplicate — Single string / Substring / Unit substring — Contiguous / Spaced — Up / Down

Spacing

Spread / Compress — Regular / Irregular — Substring / Unit substring — Up / Down

Transfer

Masking

Mask — Regular / Irregular — Total / Substring — Monotone increasing / Monotone decreasing

Complementing

Diminished radix complement — ones / nines / $(r-1)$s

Radix complement — twos / tens / (r)s

(Courtesy of *IEEE Trans. Computers*, March 1974.)

5.2.5 Shuffle-Exchange and Omega Networks

The class of shuffle-exchange networks is based on two routing functions *shuffle (S)* and *exchange (E)*. Let $A = a_{n-1} \cdots a_1 a_0$ be a PE address:

$$S(a_{n-1} \cdots a_1 a_0) = a_{n-2} \cdots a_1 a_0 a_{n-1} \qquad (5.18)$$

where $0 \le A \le N - 1$ and $n = \log_2 N$. The cyclic shifting of the bits in A to the left for one bit position is performed by the S function. This action corresponds to perfectly shuffling a deck of N cards, as demonstrated in Figure 5.15. The *perfect*

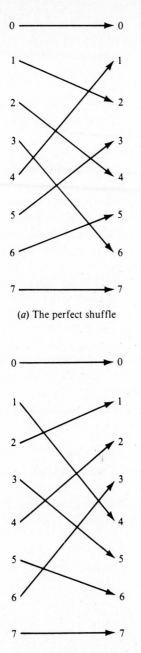

(a) The perfect shuffle

(b) The inverse perfect shuffle

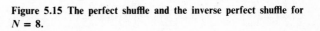

Figure 5.15 The perfect shuffle and the inverse perfect shuffle for $N = 8$.

shuffle cuts the deck into two halves from the center and intermixes them evenly. The *inverse perfect shuffle* does the opposite to restore the original ordering. The exchange-routing function E is defined by:

$$E(a_{n-1} \cdots a_1 a_0) = a_{n-1} \cdots a_1 \bar{a}_0 \qquad (5.19)$$

The complementing of the least significant digit means the exchange of data between two PEs with adjacent addresses. Note that $E(A) = C_0(A)$, where C_0 was the cube routing function defined in Eq. 5.9.

These shuffle-exchange functions can be implemented as either a recirculating network or a multistage network. For $N = 8$, a single-stage recirculating shuffle-exchange network is shown in Figure 5.16. The solid line indicates *exchange* and the dashed line indicates *shuffle*. The use of a recirculating shuffle-exchange network for parallel processing was proposed by Stone. There are a number of parallel algorithms that can be effectively implemented with the use of the shuffle and exchange functions. The examples include the fast Fourier transform (FFT), polynomial evaluation, sorting, and matrix transposition, etc.

The shuffle-exchange functions have been implemented with the multistage Omega network by Lawrie. The Omega network for $N = 8$ is illustrated in Figure 5.17. An $N \times N$ Omega network consists of n identical stages. Between two adjacent stages is a perfect-shuffle interconnection. Each stage has $N/2$ switch boxes under independent box control. Each box has four functions (straight, exchange, upper broadcast, lower broadcast), as illustrated in Figure 5.6. The switch boxes in the Omega network can be repositioned as shown in Figure 5.17*b* without violating the perfect-shuffle interconnections between stages.

The *n*-cube network shown in Figure 5.10 has the same interconnection topology as the repositioned Omega (Figure 5.17*b*). The two networks differ in two aspects:

1. The cube network uses two-function switch boxes, whereas the Omega network uses four-function switch boxes.
2. The data-flow directions in the two networks are opposite to each other. In other words, the roles of input-output lines are exchanged in the two networks.

Based on the above differences, the *n*-cube and Omega networks have different capabilities even with isomorphic topologies. Suppose we wish to establish the

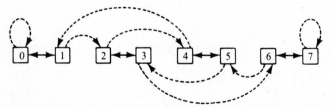

Figure 5.16 Shuffle-exchange recirculating network for $N = 8$. (Solid lines are *exchanges* and dashed lines are *shuffle*.)

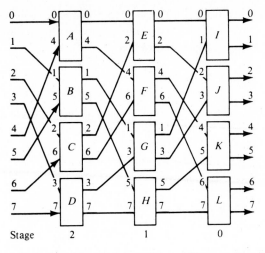

(a) The shuffle-exchange network for $n = 8$ (Omega network)

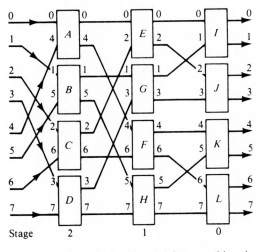

(b) the Omega network with switch box repositioned

Figure 5.17 The multistage Omega network proposed by Lawrie (1975).

I/O connections zero to five and one to seven. The Omega network (Figure 5.17a) can perform this task, whereas the n-cube (Figure 5.10) network cannot. On the other hand, the n-cube network can connect five to zero and seven to one, but the Omega network cannot. In general, the Omega network can perform one to many connections, while the n-cube network cannot. However, if one considers only bijections (one-to-one connections), the n-cube and Omega networks are functionally equivalent by some relabeling techniques.

If one applies the shuffle function S i times, written as S^i, the binary sequence in Eq. 5.18 will be shifted cyclically to the left i bit positions. The shuffle function S (Eq. 5.18) corresponds to the following permutation cycles:

$$\prod_{j=0}^{N-1} (j \ S(j) \ S^2(j) \ \cdots) \tag{5.20}$$

where, for each cycle, j has not appeared in a previous cycle. The largest cycle in the above permutation has order n. For $N = 8$, the shuffle function corresponds to the permutation (0) (1 2 4) (3 5 6) (7).

The exchange function E (Eq. 5.19) can be expressed as a product of $N/2$ cycles of order two, provided that the index j is even:

$$\prod_{j=0}^{N-2} (j \ j+1) \tag{5.21}$$

For $N = 8$, the exchange function results in the following permutation function: (0 1) (2 3) (4 5) (6 7).

Comparing various multistage SIMD networks, we conclude that increasing flexibilities in interconnection capabilities are found in the following order: the flip network, the binary n cube, Omega, and data manipulator. The increased flexibility is obtained with increased cost. The flip network is the only network among the four that has been commercially constructed for a large network size of $N = 256$. The cost-effectiveness of a network for a particular application is the fundamental question to be answered before entering the design and construction phases. One can always use a single-stage recirculating network to simulate the multistage counterpart. Table 5.3 shows the lower and upper bounds for all such simulations. Entries in row i and column j are the lower and upper bounds on the number of recirculations needed for the single-stage network i to simulate the multistage network j, where $n = \log_2 N$. These simulation bounds can be used to analyze network suitability and capability for a particular class of applications.

Table 5.3 Lower and upper bounds on the number of transfers for the network in row i to simulate the network in column j, where $n = \log_2 N$

	Bound	Illiac	Barrel	Shuffle-exchange	Cube
Illiac	Lower	—	$\sqrt{N/2}$	$1 + \sqrt{N/2}$	$1 + \sqrt{N/2}$
	Upper	—	$\sqrt{N/2}$	$3\sqrt{N} - 4$	$1 + \sqrt{N/2}$
Barrel	Lower	1	—	n	2
	Upper	1	—	$2n - 2$	2
Shuffle-exchange	Lower	$2n - 1$	$2n - 1$	—	$n + 1$
	Upper	$2n$	$2n$	—	$n + 1$
Cube	Lower	n	n	n	—
	Upper	n	n	n	—

5.3 PARALLEL ALGORITHMS FOR ARRAY PROCESSORS

The original motivation for developing SIMD array processors was to perform parallel computations on vector or matrix types of data. Parallel processing algorithms have been developed by many computer scientists for SIMD computers. Important SIMD algorithms can be used to perform matrix multiplication, fast Fourier transform (FFT), matrix transposition, summation of vector elements, matrix inversion, parallel sorting, linear recurrence, boolean matrix operations, and to solve partial differential equations. We study below several representative SIMD algorithms for matrix multiplication, parallel sorting, and parallel FFT. We shall analyze the speedups of these parallel algorithms over the sequential algorithms on SISD computers. The implementation of these parallel algorithms on SIMD machines is described by *concurrent* ALGOL. The physical memory allocations and program implementation depend on the specific architecture of a given SIMD machine.

5.3.1 SIMD Matrix Multiplication

Many numerical problems suitable for parallel processing can be formulated as matrix computations. Matrix manipulation is frequently needed in solving linear systems of equations. Important matrix operations include matrix multiplication, L-U decomposition, and matrix inversion. We present below two parallel algorithms for matrix multiplication. The differences between SISD and SIMD matrix algorithms are pointed out in their program structures and speed performances. In general, the inner loop of a multilevel SISD program can be replaced by one or more SIMD vector instructions.

Let $A = [a_{ik}]$ and $B = [b_{kj}]$ be $n \times n$ matrices. The multiplication of A and B generates a product matrix $C = A \times B = [c_{ij}]$ of dimension $n \times n$. The elements of the product matrix C is related to the elements of A and B by:

$$c_{ij} = \sum_{k=1}^{n} a_{ik} \times b_{kj} \qquad \text{for } 1 \leq i \leq n \text{ and } 1 \leq j \leq n \qquad (5.22)$$

There are n^3 cumulative multiplications to be performed in Eq. 5.22. A cumulative multiplication refers to the linked multiply-add operation $c \leftarrow c + a \times b$. The addition is merged into the multiplication because the multiply is equivalent to multioperand addition. Therefore, we can consider the unit time as the time required to perform one cumulative multiplication, since add and multiply are performed simultaneously.

In a conventional SISD uniprocessor system, the n^3 cumulative multiplications are carried out by a serially coded program with three levels of DO loops corresponding to three indices to be used. The time complexity of this sequential program is proportional to n^3, as specified in the following SISD algorithm for matrix multiplication.

Example 5.3: An $O(n^3)$ algorithm for SISD matrix multiplication

> For $i = 1$ to n **Do**
>
> > For $j = 1$ to n **Do**
> >
> > $c_{ij} = 0$ (initialization)
> >
> > For $k = 1$ to n **Do**
> >
> > $c_{ij} = c_{ij} + a_{ik} \cdot b_{kj}$ (scalar additive multiply)
> >
> > **End** of k loop
> >
> > **End** of j loop
>
> **End** of i loop

$$(5.23)$$

Now, we want to implement the matrix multiplication on an SIMD computer with n PEs. The algorithm construct depends heavily on the memory allocations of the A, B, and C matrices in the PEMs. Suppose we store each row vector of the matrix across the PEMs, as illustrated in Figure 5.18. Column vectors are then stored within the same PEM. This memory allocation scheme allows parallel access of all the elements in each row vector of the matrices. Based in this data distribution, we obtain the following parallel algorithm. The two **parallel do** operations correspond to *vector load* for initialization and *vector multiply* for the inner loop of additive multiplications. The time complexity has been reduced to $O(n^2)$. Therefore, the SIMD algorithm is n times faster than the SISD algorithm for matrix multiplication.

Example 5.4: An $O(n^2)$ algorithm for SIMD matrix multiplication

> For $j = 1$ to n **Do**
>
> **Par for** $k = 1$ to n **Do**
>
> $c_{ik} = 0$ (*vector load*)
>
> For $j = 1$ to n **Do**
>
> **Par for** $k = 1$ to n **Do**
>
> $c_{ik} = c_{ik} + a_{ij} \cdot b_{jk}$ (*vector multiply*)
>
> **End** of j loop
>
> **End** of i loop

$$(5.24)$$

It should be noted that the *vector load* operation is performed to initialize the row vectors of matrix C one row at a time. In the *vector multiply* operation, the same multiplier a_{ij} is broadcast from the CU to all PEs to multiply all n elements $\{b_{ik}$ for $k = 1, 2, \ldots, n\}$ of the ith row vector of B. In total, n^2 *vector multiply*

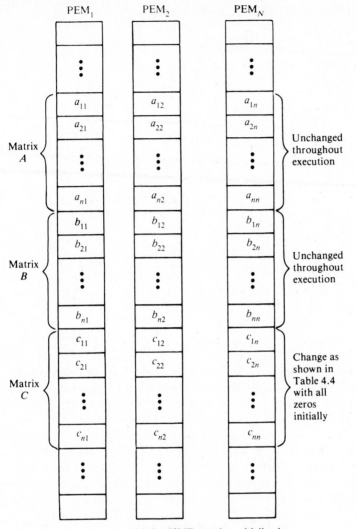

Figure 5.18 Memory allocation for SIMD matrix multiplication.

operations are needed in the double loops. The successive memory contents in the execution of the above SIMD matrix multiplication program are illustrated in Table 5.4. Each *vector multiply* instruction implies n parallel scalar multiplications in each of the n^2 iterations. This algorithm in Example 5.4 is implementable on an array of n PEs.

If we increase the number of PEs used in an array processor to n^2, an $O(n \log_2 n)$ algorithm can be devised to multiply the two $n \times n$ matrices A and B. Let $n = 2^m$ and recall the binary cube network described in Section 5.2.3. Consider an array processor whose $n^2 = 2^{2m}$ PEs are located at the 2^{2m} vertices of a $2m$-cube network. A $2m$-cube network can be considered as two $(2m - 1)$-cube networks linked

Table 5.4 Successive contents of the C array in memory

Outer loop i	Inner loop j	Parallel SIMD operations on $k = 1, 2, \ldots, n$			
		$c_{i1} \leftarrow c_{i1} + a_{ij} \times b_{j1}$	$c_{i2} \leftarrow c_{i2} + a_{ij} \times b_{j2}$	$\cdots$	$c_{in} \leftarrow c_{in} + a_{ij} \times b_{jn}$
1	1	$c_{11} \leftarrow c_{11} + a_{11} \times b_{11}$	$c_{12} \leftarrow c_{12} + a_{11} \times b_{12}$		$c_{1n} \leftarrow c_{1n} + a_{11} \times b_{1n}$
	2	$c_{11} \leftarrow c_{11} + a_{12} \times b_{21}$	$c_{12} \leftarrow c_{12} + a_{12} \times b_{22}$	$\cdots$	$c_{1n} \leftarrow c_{2n} + a_{12} \times b_{2n}$
	$\vdots$	$\vdots$	$\vdots$		$\vdots$
	n	$c_{11} \leftarrow c_{11} + a_{1n} \times b_{n1}$	$c_{12} \leftarrow c_{12} + a_{1n} \times b_{n2}$		$c_{1n} \leftarrow c_{1n} + a_{1n} \times b_{nn}$
2	1	$c_{21} \leftarrow c_{21} + a_{21} \times b_{11}$	$c_{22} \leftarrow c_{22} + a_{21} \times b_{12}$		$c_{2n} \leftarrow c_{2n} + a_{21} \times b_{1n}$
	2	$c_{21} \leftarrow c_{21} + a_{22} \times b_{21}$	$c_{22} \leftarrow c_{22} + a_{22} \times b_{22}$	$\cdots$	$c_{2n} \leftarrow c_{2n} + a_{22} \times b_{2n}$
	$\vdots$	$\vdots$	$\vdots$		$\vdots$
	n	$c_{21} \leftarrow c_{21} + a_{2n} \times b_{n1}$	$c_{22} \leftarrow c_{22} + a_{2n} \times b_{n2}$		$c_{2n} \leftarrow c_{2n} + a_{2n} \times b_{2n}$
$\vdots$	$\vdots$	$\vdots$	$\vdots$	$\vdots$	$\vdots$
n	1	$c_{n1} \leftarrow c_{n1} + a_{n1} \times b_{11}$	$c_{n2} \leftarrow c_{n2} + a_{n1} \times b_{12}$		$c_{nn} \leftarrow c_{nn} + a_{n1} \times b_{1n}$
	2	$c_{n1} \leftarrow c_{n1} + a_{n2} \times b_{21}$	$c_{n2} \leftarrow c_{n2} + a_{n2} \times b_{22}$		$c_{nn} \leftarrow c_{nn} + a_{n2} \times b_{2n}$
	$\vdots$	$\vdots$	$\vdots$	$\cdots$	$\vdots$
	n	$c_{nn} \leftarrow c_{nn} + a_{nn} \times b_{n1}$	$c_{n2} \leftarrow c_{n2} + a_{nn} \times b_{n2}$		$c_{nn} \leftarrow c_{nn} + a_{nn} \times b_{nn}$
Local memory		PEM$_1$	PEM$_2$	$\cdots$	PEM$_n$

together by $2m$ extra edges. In Figure 5.19, a 4-cube network is constructed from two 3-cube networks by using $8 = 2^3$ extra edges between corresponding vertices at the corner positions. For clarity, we simplify the 4-cube drawing by showing only one of the eight fourth dimension connections. The remaining connections are implied.

Let $(p_{2m-1} p_{2m-2} \cdots p_m p_{m-1} \cdots p_1 p_0)_2)$ be the PE address in the $2m$ cube. We can achieve the $O(n \log_2 n)$ compute time only if initially the matrix elements are favorably distributed in the PE vertices. The n rows of matrix A are distributed over n distinct PEs whose addresses satisfy the condition

$$p_{2m-1} p_{2m-1} \cdots p_m = p_{m-1} p_{m-2} \cdots p_0 \qquad (5.25)$$

as demonstrated in Figure 5.20a for the initial distribution of four rows of the matrix A in a 4×4 matrix multiplication ($n = 4$, $m = 2$). The four rows of A are then broadcast over the fourth dimension and front to back edges, as marked by row numbers in Figure 5.20b.

The n columns of matrix B (or the n rows of matrix B^t) are evenly distributed over the PEs of the $2m$ cubes, as illustrated in Figure 5.20c. The four rows of B^t are then broadcast over the front and back faces, as shown in Figure 5.20d. Figure 5.21 shows the combined results of A and B^t broadcasts with the inner product ready to be computed. The n-way broadcast depicted in Figure 5.20b and 5.20d takes $\log n$ steps, as illustrated in Figure 5.21 in $m = \log_2 n = \log_2 4 = 2$ steps. The matrix multiplication on a $2m$-cube network is formally specified below.

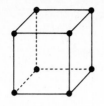

(*a*) A 3 cube

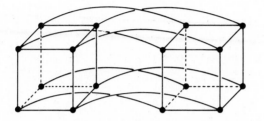

(*b*) A 4 cube formed from two 3 cubes

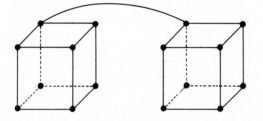

(*c*) The 4 cube showing only one of eight fourth-dimension connections.

Figure 5.19 The construction of $(m + 1)$-cube from two m-cubes. (Courtesy of Thomas, 1981.)

Example 5.5: An $O(n \log_2 n)$ algorithm for matrix multiplication

1. Transpose B to form B^t over the m cubes $x_{2m-1} \cdots x_m 0 \cdots 0$ in $n \log_2 n$ steps (Figure 5.20c).
2. N-way broadcast each row of B^t to all PEs in the m cube

$$p_{2m-1} \cdots p_m x_{m-1} \cdots x_0$$

in $n \log_2 n$ steps (Figure 5.20d).
3. N-way broadcast each row of A residing in PE $p_{2m-1} \cdots p_m p_{m-1} \cdots p_0$ to all PEs in the m cube $x_{2m-1} \cdots x_m p_{n-1} \cdots p_0$ in $n \log_2 n$ steps (Figure 5.20b). All the n rows can be broadcast in parallel.
4. Each PE now contains a row of A and a column of B and can form the inner product in $O(n)$ steps (Figure 5.21). The n elements of each result row can be brought together within the same PEs which initially held a row of A in $O(n)$ steps.

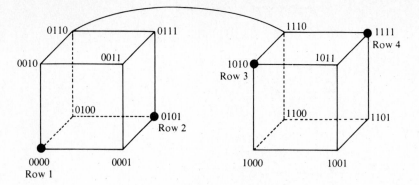

(a) Initial distribution of rows of A

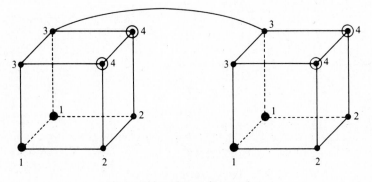

(b) 4-way broadcast of rows of A

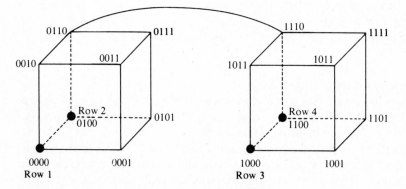

(c) Initial distribution of rows of B^t

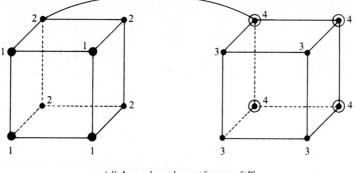

(*d*) 4-way broadcase of rows of B'

Figure 5.20 Allocation of the elements of two 4 × 4 matrices in a 4-cube of 16 PEs.

The above algorithm takes a total of $3n \log_2 n + O(n)$ time steps to complete, which equals $O(n \log_2 n)$. This demonstrates a gain in speed over the $O(n^2)$ algorithm in Example 5.4 at the expense of using n^2 PEs over the use of only n PEs in the slow algorithm. In Chapter 10, we shall further show a VLSI hardware approach to complete the n-by-n matrix multiplication in $O(n)$ time using $O(n^2/m^2)$ VLSI processor arrays, each consisting of an array of $O(m^2)$ PEs for pipelined inner-product computations.

5.3.2 Parallel Sorting on Array Processors

An SIMD algorithm is to be presented for sorting n^2 elements on a mesh-connected (Illiac-IV-like) processor array in $O(n)$ routing and comparison steps. This shows a speedup of $O(\log_2 n)$ over the best sorting algorithm, which takes $O(n \log_2 n)$ steps on a uniprocessor system. We assume an array processor with $N = n^2$ identical PEs interconnected by a mesh network (Figure 5.22) similar to Illiac-IV except that the PEs at the perimeter have two or three rather than four neighbors. In other words, there are no *wraparound* connections in this simplified mesh network.

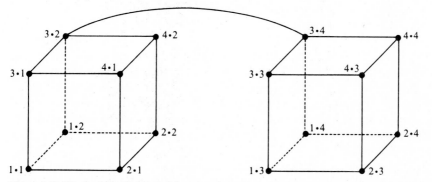

Figure 5.21 The final distributions of the rows of matrix A and the columns of matrix B ready for inner product in the 16 PEs of a 4-cube array processor.

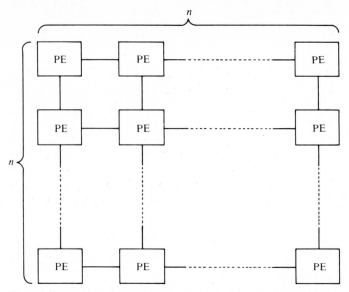

Figure 5.22 A mesh connection of PEs without boundary wraparound connections for SIMD sorting.

Eliminating the wraparound connections simplifies the array-sorting algorithm. The time complexity of the array-sorting algorithm would be affected by, at most, a factor of two if the wraparound connections were included.

Two time measures are needed to estimate the time complexity of the parallel-sorting algorithm. Let t_R be the *routing time* required to move one item from a PE to one of its neighbors, and t_C be the *comparison time* required for one comparison step. Concurrent data routing is allowed. Up to N comparisons may be performed simultaneously. This means that a comparison-interchange step between two items in adjacent PEs can be done in $2t_R + t_C$ time units (route left, compare, and route right). A mixture of horizontal and vertical comparison interchanges requires at least $4t_R + t_C$ time units.

The sorting problem depends on the indexing schemes on the PEs. The PEs may be indexed by a bijection from $\{1, 2, \ldots, n\} \times \{1, 2, \ldots, n\}$ to $\{0, 1, \ldots, N - 1\}$, where $N = n^2$. The sorting problem can be formulated as the moving of the jth smallest element in the PE array for all $j = 0, 1, 2, \ldots, N - 1$. Illustrated in Figure 5.23 are three indexing patterns formed after sorting the given array in part *a* with respect to three different ways for indexing the PEs. The pattern in part *b* corresponds to a *row-majored indexing*, part *c* corresponds to a *shuffled row-major* indexing, and is based on a *snake-like row-major indexing*. The choice of a particular indexing scheme depends upon how the sorted elements will be used. We are interested in designing sorting algorithms which minimize the total routing and comparison steps.

The longest routing path on the mesh in a sorting process is the transposition of two elements initially loaded at opposite corner PEs, as illustrated in Figure 5.24. This transposition needs at least $4(n - 1)$ routing steps. This means that no

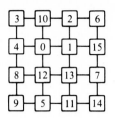

(a) Initial loading pattern
before sorting

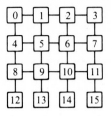

(b) Sorted pattern with
row-major indexing

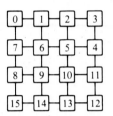

(c) Sorted pattern with
shuffled row major
indexing

(d) Sorted pattern with snakelike
row-major indexing

Figure 5.23 Sorting patterns with respect to three ways of indexing the PEs.

algorithm can sort n^2 elements in a time of less than $O(n)$. In other words, an $O(n)$ sorting algorithm is considered optimal on a mesh of n^2 PEs. Before we show one such optimal sorting algorithm on the mesh-connected PEs, let us review Batcher's *odd-even merge sort* of two sorted sequences on a set of linearly connected PEs shown in Figure 5.25. The *shuffle* and *unshuffle* operations can each be implemented with a sequence of interchange operations (marked by the double-arrows in Figure 5.26). Both the perfect shuffle and its inverse (unshuffle) can be done in $k - 1$ interchanges or $2(k - 1)$ routing steps on a linear array of $2k$ PEs.

Batcher's odd-even merge sort on a linear array has been generalized by Thompson and Kung to a square array of PEs. Let $M(j, k)$ be a sorting algorithm for merging two sorted j-by-$k/2$ subarrays to form a sorted j-by-k array, where j and k are powers of 2 and $k > 1$. The snakelike row-major ordering is assumed in all the arrays. In the degenerate case of $M(1, 2)$, a single comparison-interchange step is sufficient to sort two unit subarrays. Given two sorted columns of length $j \geq 2$, the $M(j, 2)$ algorithm consists of the following steps:

Example 5.6: The $M(j, 2)$ sorting algorithm

J1: Move all odds to the left column and all evens to the right in $2t_k$ time.
J2: Use the *odd-even transposition sort* to sort each column in $2jt_k + jt_c$ time.
J3: Interchange on each row in $2t_k$ time.
J4: Perform one comparison-interchange in $2t_k + t_c$ time.

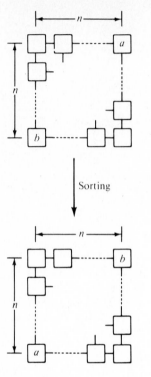

Sorting

Figure 5.24 The transposition of two elements at opposite corner PEs.

Sorted   Sorted

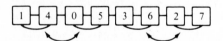

L1. Unshuffle: Odd-indexed elements of left, evens to right.

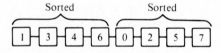

L2. Merge the subsequence of length 2.

L3. Shuffle

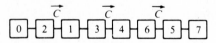

L4. Comparison-interchange (the C's indicate comparison-interchanges).

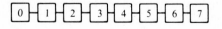

Figure 5.25 Batcher's odd-even merge of two sorted sequences on a linear array of PEs.

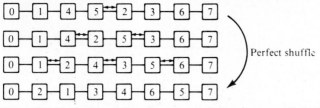

Figure 5.26 The implementation of a perfect shuffle by a sequence of interchange operations.

The above $M(j, 2)$ algorithm is illustrated in Figure 5.27 for an $M(4, 2)$ sorting. When $j > 2$ and $k > 2$, the $M(j, k)$ sorting algorithm for a meshed-connected array processor is recursively specified as follows:

Example 5.7: The $M(j, k)$ sorting algorithm

M1: If $j > 2$, perform a single interchange step on even rows so that columns contain either all evens or all odds. If $j = 2$, the columns are already segregated, so nothing else needs to be done (time: $2t_k$).

M2: Unshuffle each row [time: $(k - 2) \cdot t_k$].

M3: Merge by calling algorithm $M(j, k/2)$ on each half of the array [time: $T(j, k/2)$].

M4: Shuffle each row [time: $(k - 2) \cdot t_k$].

M5: Interchange on even rows (time: $2t_k$).

M6: Comparison-interchange adjacent elements (every *even* with the next *odd*) (time: $4t_k + t_c$).

For $j > 2$ and $k > 2$, the $M(j, k)$ sorting algorithm is illustrated in Figure 5.28 for the case of $M(4, 4)$. Steps M1 and M2 unshuffle the elements. Step M3 recursively merges the *odd subsequences* and the *even subsequences*. Steps 4 and 5 shuffle the *odd* and *even* together. M6 performs the final comparison interchange. Two sorted 4-by-2 subarrays are being merged to form a 4-by-4 sorted array in snakelike row-major ordering. Let $T(j, k)$ be the time required to perform all the steps in the $M(j, k)$ sorting algorithm. In the degenerated case of $k = 2$, we have

$$T(j, 2) = (2j + 6)t_R + (j + 1)t_C \qquad (5.26)$$

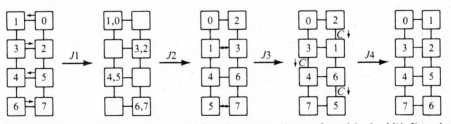

Figure 5.27 Data routing, comparison, and interchange operations performed in the $M(4, 2)$ sorting algorithm. (Courtesy of *IEEE Trans. Computers*, Thompson and Kung 1977.)

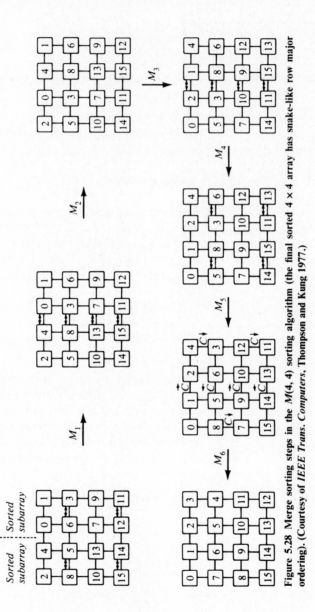

Figure 5.28 Merge sorting steps in the $M(4, 4)$ sorting algorithm (the final sorted 4×4 array has snake-like row major ordering). (Courtesy of *IEEE Trans. Computers*, Thompson and Kung 1977.)

For $k > 2$, the time function is recursively computed by:

$$T(j, k) = (2k + 4)t_R + t_C + T(j, k/2) \tag{5.27}$$

By repeated substitution, we have the following time bound:

$$T(j, k) \leq (2j + 4k + 4\log_2 k)t_k + (j + \log_2 k)t_c \tag{5.28}$$

For an $n \times n$ array of PEs, the $M(n, n)$ sort algorithm can be done in $T(n, n)$ time, which is proportional to $O(n)$:

$$T(n, n) = (6n + 4\log_2 n)t_R + (n + \log_2 n)t_c = O(n) \tag{5.29}$$

Combining an *upwards* merge with the *sideways* merge (just described), one can further tighten the above bound to within a factor of $6n$ under the assumption that $t_C \leq t_R$. This parallel sorting algorithm has a speedup of $\log_2 n$ over the best $O(n \log_2 n)$ algorithm for serial sorting.

5.3.3 SIMD Fast Fourier Transform

SIMD algorithms for performing one-dimensional and two-dimensional *fast Fourier transform* (FFT) are presented in this section. Let $s(k), k = 0, 1, \ldots, M - 1$ be M samples of a time function. The discrete Fourier transform of $s(k)$ is defined to be the discrete function $x(j), j = 0, 1, \ldots, M - 1$ where

$$x(j) = \sum_{k=0}^{M-1} s(k) \cdot W^{jk} \qquad j = 0, 1, \ldots, M - 1 \tag{5.30}$$

and $W = e^{2\pi i/M}$ and $i = \sqrt{-1}$.

Consider the use of an SIMD machine with $N = M/2$ PEs to perform an M-point FFT of the discrete signal sequence $\{s(m), 0 \leq m \leq M - 1\}$. The algorithm is a parallel implementation of the *decimation-in-frequency* (DIF) technique illustrated in Figure 5.29 for the case of $M = 16$ sampling points. The DIF algorithm divides the input sequence $\{s(m)\}$ into two half subsequences $\{f(m)\}$ and $\{g(m)\}$ such that $f(m) = s(m)$ and

$$g(m) = s\left(m + \frac{M}{2}\right) \qquad \text{for } m = 0, 1, \ldots, \frac{M}{2} - 1$$

The FFT of the M-point sequence can be computed in terms of the two $M/2$-point FFTs of the two sequences $\{f(m) + g(m)\}$ and $\{[f(m) - g(m)] \cdot W^m\}$, where $0 \leq m < M/2$. For M being a power of 2, repeated applications of this dividing process require $O(M \log_2 M)$ array operations.

For the parallel FFT algorithm, PE_i initially contains $s(k)$ and $s(k + M/2)$, where $0 \leq k < N$. As in the serial method, $\log_2 M$ stages of computations are needed. At each stage, $M/2$ *butterfly* operations, shown in Figure 5.30, are executed. The items being paired in a butterfly at stage k where $0 \leq k < \log_2 M$ are those whose indices differ in the $(\log_2 M - k - 1)$th bit position of the binary representation. Because of this difference in a given bit position, the cube interconnection

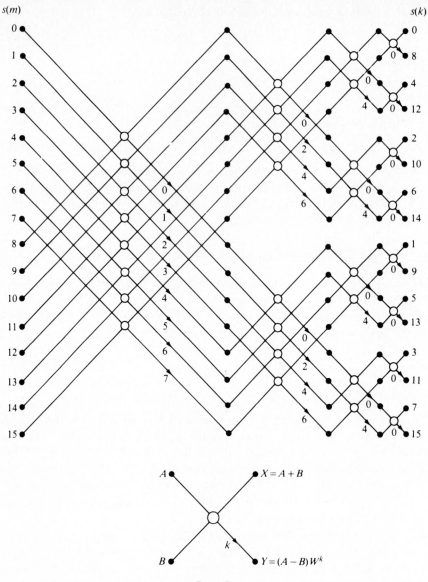

Butterfly

Figure 5.29 Operations in a 16-point FFT based on the decimation-in-frequency algorithm.

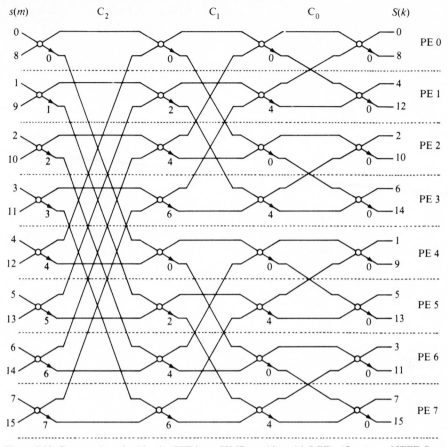

Figure 5.30 Computation of a 16-point FFT in an SIMD machine with 8 PEs. (Courtesy of IEEE *Proc. 5th Int'l Conf. on PRIP*, Mueller, et al. 1980.)

network provides a natural means for specifying the interprocessor data transfers required for the FFT algorithm. This network consists of n routing functions C_i for $0 \le i < \log_2 N$ as in Eq. 5.9. Figure 5.30 illustrates data transfers and computations performed in the one-dimensional FFT algorithm for an SIMD machine with $N = M/2$ PEs.

The above algorithm performs the M-point FFT calculations using $\log_2(M/2)$ parallel data transfers. This is a lower bound on the number of data transfers required to perform an M-point FFT when the M points are initially distributed over $M/2$ PEs. The number of parallel butterfly operations performed is $\log_2 M$, where each butterfly involves two complex additions and one complex multiplication in each PE. The number of butterfly steps is reduced from $(M/2)\log_2 M$ in a serial FFT algorithm to $\log_2 M$ for a parallel FFT algorithm, using $M/2$ PEs.

Because $M/2$ PEs may not be available for the computation of an M-point FFT, it is of interest to consider FFT algorithms which use fewer PEs. A simple solution for using fewer PEs is to replicate the steps in the $M/2$ PE algorithm. For example, if $N = M/4$, two computations that were performed in parallel in different PEs in the $M/2$ PE algorithm are now performed sequentially in the same PE, as shown for $N = 16$ in Figure 5.31. The number of butterfly steps performed is $2\log_2 M$. $2(\log_2 M - 2) = 2[\log_2(M/4)]$ parallel data transfers are required. This approach can be generalized to perform an M-point FFT in $M/2^k$ PEs for $2 \le k \le \log_2 M$. For $N = M/2^k$ PEs, each PE will initially contain 2^k elements. The number of parallel butterfly steps performed will be $2^{k-1}\log_2 M$. The data transfers will be performed the C_i functions for $\log_2 M - k - 1 \ge i \ge 0$; each C_i function will be replicated 2^{k-1} times. The total number of parallel data transfers will therefore be $2^{k-1}(\log_2 M - k)$.

We consider next the two-dimensional FFT algorithm for processing an M-by-M signal array. A standard approach to computing the two-dimensional FFT of a signal array S is to perform the one-dimensional FFT on the rows of S, giving an intermediate matrix G, then performing the one-dimensional FFT on the columns of G. The resulting matrix F is the two-dimensional FFT of S. An SIMD algorithm which uses $N = M^2/2$ PEs is presented below.

The implementation of a two-dimensional FFT makes use of the previous work done for one-dimensional FFTs. The PEs are logically partitioned into M rows of $M/2$ PEs. Each row of PEs is given a row of the input matrix S, with two matrix elements in each PE. The two-dimensional FFT is implemented by simultaneously having each row of PEs compute the FFT of its row of the input matrix to obtain G. The PEs are then logically reconfigured to form M columns of $M/2$ processors, with each column of PEs having a column of G. Then each column of PEs computes the FFT of its column of G to obtain F, the FFT of the input matrix. This approach can be considered a row-column method in that it transforms the rows of the matrix S to produce G, then transforms the columns of the intermediate matrix G to produce F.

Initially, the PEs are logically configured as M rows of $M/2$ PEs, logically numbered (i, j), where $0 \le i < M$ and $0 \le j < M/2$. The physical address of PE (i, j) is $i(M/2) + j$. The physical address can be represented in binary as

$$p_{2\mu-2} p_{2\mu-3} \cdots p_{\mu-1} p_{\mu-2} \cdots p_1 p_0$$

where $\mu = \log_2 M$. Bits $p_{\mu-2} \cdots p_0$ are the binary representation of j, and bits $p_{2\mu-2} \cdots p_{\mu-1}$ are the binary representation of i. The input matrix S is distributed such that PE (i, j) has $S(i, j)$ and $S(i, j + M/2)$. Thus, each row of PEs can perform the one-dimensional FFT on its row of S with $N = M/2$. In this case, the cube functions required for data transfers will exchange data based on the lower order $\mu - 1$ bits of the physical address; i.e., the functions will act on j independently of i. Thus, the one-dimensional FFT can be performed on each row independently and simultaneously. The result G is distributed to each column of PEs which holds two columns of G, with each PE holding one element from each of the two columns of G.

The PEs are now logically reconfigured to form M columns of $M/2$ PEs, with each column of PEs having one column of G. Two matrix elements are in each PE.

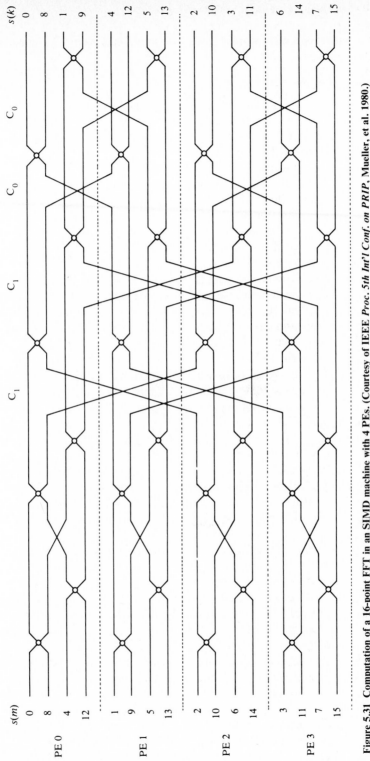

Figure 5.31 Computation of a 16-point FFT in an SIMD machine with 4 PEs. (Courtesy of IEEE *Proc. 5th Int'l Conf. on PRIP*, Mueller, et al. 1980.)

Table 5.5 SIMD machine reconfiguration for two-dimensional FFT computations [notation (i, j) denotes the PE_{ij}]

Configuration: M-by-$M/2$ array

$(0, 0)$	$(0, 1)$	$\cdots$	$(0, M/2 - 1)$
$(1, 0)$	$(1, 1)$	$\cdots$	$(1, M/2 - 1)$
$\vdots$			$\vdots$
$(M - 1, 0)$	$(M - 1, 1)$	$\cdots$	$(M - 1, M/2 - 1)$

Configuration: $M/2$-by-M array

$(0, 0)$	$(M/2, 0)$	$(0, 1)$	$(M/2, 1)$	$\cdots$	$(0, M/2 - 1)$	$(M/2, M/2 - 1)$
$(1, 0)$	$(M/2 + 1, 0)$	$(1, 1)$	$(M/2 + 1, 1)$	$\cdots$		
$\vdots$						$\vdots$
$(M/2 - 2, 0)$	$(M - 1, 0)$	$(M/2 - 1, 1)$	$(M - 1, 1)$	$\cdots$	$(M/2 - 1, M/2 - 1)$	$(M-1, M/2-1)$

To do this, PE (i, j) is renumbered (k, l) where $k = i \bmod (M/2)$ and $l = 2j + [i/(M/2)]$. Effectively, this renumbering takes each column of the original configuration, divides it in half, and aligns the halves to form two columns, as shown in Table 5.5. In terms of the binary representation of the physical address, the binary representation of k is $p_{2\mu-3} \cdots p_{\mu-1}$, and the binary representation of l is $p_{\mu-2} \cdots p_0 p_{2\mu-2}$.

After the renumbering, G is distributed to each pair of PE columns PE$(k, 2\lambda)$ and PE$(k, 2\lambda + 1)$, where $0 \le k$, $\lambda < M/2$. Within such a pair of PE columns, PE$(k, 2\lambda)$ has two points from the kth row of G, and PE$(k, 2\lambda + 1)$ has two corresponding points from the $(k + M/2)$th row of G, for $0 \le k < M/2$. Within each of the two columns of G, these are precisely the points which must be paired at the start of the one-dimensional M-point, $M/2$ PE algorithm. Using the $C_{2\mu-2}$ function, PE$(k, 2\lambda)$ and PE$(k, 2\lambda + 1)$, where $0 \le k$, $\lambda < M/2$, can exchange data so that each column of PEs gets a different column of G with each PE holding the two elements of G needed to start the one-dimensional FFT. In terms of physical PE addresses, $p_{2\mu-2}$ corresponds to the high order position and the routing function $C_{2\mu-2}$ equals C_{n-1}. In terms of logical numbering, $p_{2\mu-2}$ is the low order bit in the binary representation of the logical column index, so the $C_{2\mu-2}$ routing function effects the exchange of elements between the corresponding rows in columns 2λ and $2\lambda + 1$, for $0 \le \lambda < M/2$.

Each column of PEs now performs the one-dimensional FFT on its column of G. However, to perform the FFT on a column, it is necessary to perform data transfers based on the row index, which is given by k and represented by $p_{2\mu-3} \cdots p_{\mu-1}$ of the physical PE address. Therefore, whenever C_i is executed in the original algorithm, $C_{i+\mu-1}$ is executed in this algorithm. In this way, the cube routing functions allow communication within a column instead of within a row.

The complexity of this SIMD algorithm has been derived from the one-dimensional FFT case. The number of multiplication steps required is $2\log_2 M$; the number of addition steps required is $2(2\log_2 M)$; and the number of data transfer steps required is $2\log_2(M/2) + 1 = 2\log_2 M - 1$. The complexity of a serial FFT algorithm is $M^2 \log_2 M$ multiplications and $2M^2 \log_2 M$ additions. To sum up, the speedup of a parallel two-dimensional FFT algorithm is $M^2/2$ over a serial FFT algorithm. Without surprise, this speedup equals the number of PEs in the SIMD array processor.

5.3.4 Connection Issues for SIMD Processing

SIMD array processors allow explicit expression of parallelism in user programs. The compiler detects the parallelism and generates object code suitable for execution in the multiple processing elements and the control unit. Program segments which cannot be converted into parallel executable forms are executed in the control unit; program segments which can be converted into parallel executable forms are sent to the PEs and executed synchronously on data fetched from parallel memory modules under the control of the control unit. To enable synchronous manipulation in the PEs, the data is permuted and arranged in vector form. Thus, to run a program more efficiently on an array processor, one must develop a technique for vectorizing the program codes. The interconnection network plays a major role in vectorization. Several connection issues in using SIMD interconnection networks are addressed below.

Permutation and connectivity In array processing, data is often stored in parallel memory modules in skewed forms that allow a vector of data to be fetched without conflict. However, the fetched data must be realigned in a prescribed order before it can be sent to individual PEs for processing. This alignment is implemented by the routing functions of the interconnection network, which also realigns the data generated by individual PEs into skewed form for storage in the memory modules.

A rearrangeable network and the nonblocking network can realize every permutation function, but using these networks for alignment requires considerable effort to calculate control settings. A recursive routing mechanism has been suggested for a few families of permutations needed for parallel processing; however, the problem remains for the realization of general permutations. Many attempts have been made on the permutation capabilities of single-stage networks and blocking multistage networks. These networks cannot realize arbitrary permutations in a single pass. Recent results show that the baseline network can realize arbitrary permutations in just two passes while other blocking multistage networks, such as the Omega network, need at least three passes. Wu and Feng (1981) have proved that the shuffle-exchange network can realize arbitrary permutations in $3(\log_2 N) - 1$ passes where N is the network size.

Partitioning and reconfigurability A configuration concept has been proposed to better use the interconnection network. Under this concept, a network is just a configuration in the same topologically equivalent class. To configure a permutation function as an interconnection network, we can assign input-output link names in a way that realizes the permutation function in one conflict-free pass. Assigning logical names that realize various permutation functions without conflicts is called a reconfiguration problem. Through the reconfiguration process, the baseline network can realize every permutation in one pass without conflicts.

This means that concurrent processing throughout could be enhanced by the proper assignment of tasks to processing elements and data to memory modules.

When dividing an SIMD interconnection network into independent subnetworks of different sizes, each subnetwork must have all the interconnection capabilities of a complete network of the same type and size. Hence, with a partitionable network, a system can support multiple SIMD machines. By dynamically reconfiguring the system into independent SIMD machines and properly assigning tasks to each partition, we can use resources more efficiently. Siegel (1980) has proved that single-stage networks such as the shuffle-exchange and Illiac networks cannot be partitioned into independent subnetworks, but blocking multistage networks such as a data manipulator can be partitioned.

Reliability and bandwidth The reliable operation of interconnection networks is important to overall system performance. The reliability issue can be thought of as two problems: *fault diagnosis* and *fault tolerance*. The fault-diagnosis problem has been studied for a class of multistage interconnection networks constructed of switching elements with two valid states. The problem is approached by generating suitable fault-detection and fault-location test sets for every fault in the assumed fault model. The test sets are then trimmed to a minimal or nearly minimal set. The second reliability problem concerns mainly the degree of fault tolerance. It is important to design a network that combines full connection capability with graceful degradation in spite of the existence of faults.

A high network bandwidth is often desired at reasonably low network cost. The *network bandwidth* is defined as the number of PE requests honored per unit of time. Several analytical methods have been used to estimate network bandwidth. We shall treat some of them in Section 7.2.4. Most analytical models suggested by researchers are too simplified and closed-form solutions are not attainable. Numerical experiments can simulate actual PE-connection requests by tracing the program to be executed. Continued research efforts are needed in this area to accurately estimate the bandwidth of various interconnection networks.

The cost of a network is primarily determined by the switching complexity. To achieve a cost-effective network design, one must find the optimal trade-off between performance (bandwidth) and cost (complexity). The main difficulty lies in the fact that bandwidth analysis depends on unpredictable program behavior and cost varies rapidly with progress in technology. Cost effectiveness must also insure flexibility in application programming and reliability in achieving fault tolerance. These are wide open areas of further research on interconnection networks for both SIMD and MIMD computers.

5.4 ASSOCIATIVE ARRAY PROCESSING

Two SIMD computers, the Goodyear Aerospace STARAN and the Parallel Element Processing Ensemble (PEPE), have been built around an *associative memory* (AM) instead of using the conventional *random-access memory* (RAM). The fundamental distinction between AM and RAM is that AM is content-addressable, allowing parallel access of multiple memory words, whereas the RAM must be sequentially accessed by specifying the word addresses. The inherent parallelism in associative memory has a great impact on the architecture of *associative processors*, a special class of SIMD array processors which update with the associative memories.

In this section, we describe the functional organization of an associative array processor and various parallel processing functions that can be performed on an associative processor. We classify associative processors based on associative-memory organizations. Finally, we identify the major searching applications of associative memories and associative processors. Associative processors have been built only as special-purpose computers for dedicated applications in the past.

5.4.1 Associative Memory Organizations

Data stored in an associative memory are addressed by their contents. In this sense, associative memories have been known as *content-addressable memory*, *parallel search memory*, and *multiaccess memory*. The major advantage of associative memory over RAM is its capability of performing parallel search and parallel comparison operations. These are frequently needed in many important applications, such as the storage and retrieval of rapidly changing databases, radar-signal tracking, image processing, computer vision, and artificial intelligence. The major shortcoming of associative memory is its much increased hardware cost. Presently, the cost of associative memory is much higher than that of RAMs.

The structure of a basic AM is modeled in Figure 5.32. The associative memory array consists of n words with m bits per word. Each bit cell in the $n \times m$ array consists of a flip-flop associated with some comparison logic gates for pattern match and read-write control. This logic-in-memory structure allows parallel read or parallel write in the memory array. A *bit slice* is a vertical column of bit cells of all the words at the same position. We denote the jth bit cell of the ith word as B_{ij} for $1 \leq i \leq n$ and $1 \leq j \leq m$. The ith word is denoted as:

$$W_i = (B_{i1}B_{i2} \cdots B_{im}) \qquad \text{for } i = 1, 2, \ldots, n$$

and the jth bit slice is denoted as:

$$B_j = (B_{1j}B_{2j} \cdots B_{nj}) \qquad \text{for } j = 1, 2, \ldots, m$$

Each bit cell B_{ij} can be written in, read out, or compared with an external interrogating signal. The parallel search operations involve both comparison and masking and are executed according to the organization of the associative memory. There are a number of registers and counters in the associative memory. The *comparand* register $C = (C_1, C_2, \ldots, C_m)$ is used to hold the key operand being searched for or being compared with. The *masking* register $M = (M_1, M_2, \ldots, M_m)$ is used to enable or disable the bit slices to be involved in the parallel comparison operations across all the words in the associative memory.

The *indicator* register $I = (I_1, I_2, \ldots, I_n)$ and one or more *temporary* registers $T = (T_1, T_2, \ldots, T_n)$ are used to hold the current and previous match patterns,

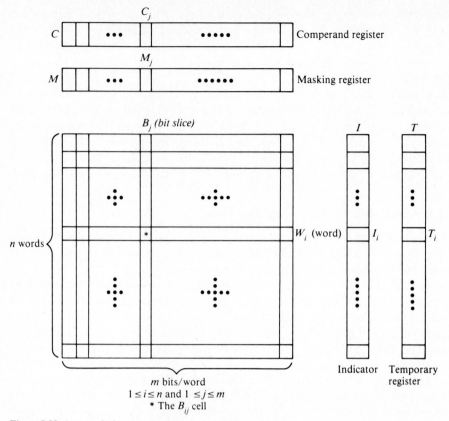

Figure 5.32 An associative memory array and working registers.

respectively. Each of these registers can be set, reset, or loaded from an external source with any desired binary patterns. The counters are used to keep track of the i and j index values. There are also some match detection circuits and priority logic, which are peripheral to the memory array and are used to perform some vector boolean operations among the bit slices and indicator patterns.

The search key in the C register is first masked by the bit pattern in the M register. This masking operation selects the effective fields of bit slices to be involved. Parallel comparisons of the masked key word with all words in the associative memory are performed by sending the proper interrogating signals to all the bit slices involved. All the involved bit slices are compared in parallel or in a sequential order, depending on the associative memory organization. It is possible that multiple words in the associative memory will match the search pattern. Therefore, the associative memory may be required to tag all the matched words. The indicator and temporary registers are mainly used for this purpose. The interrogation mechanism, read and write drives, and matching logic within a typical bit cell are depicted in Figure 5.33. The interrogating signals are associated with each bit slice, and the read-write drives are associated with each word. There are

Interrogation information	Mask*	Information stored	
		0	1
0	0	0	0
1	0	0	0
0	1	0	1
1	1	1	0

*Mask = 0 means that no comparison is performed at that bit position for all words.

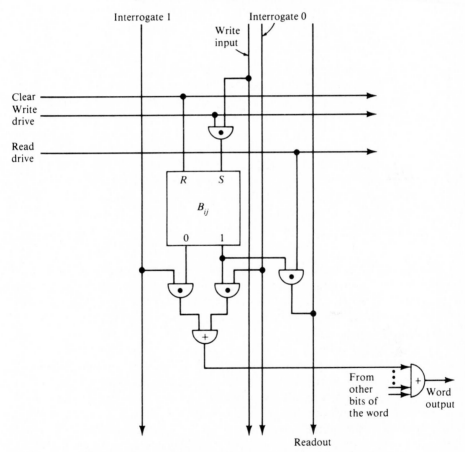

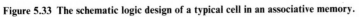

Figure 5.33 The schematic logic design of a typical cell in an associative memory.

two types of comparison readouts: the bit-cell readout and the word readout. The two types of readout are needed in two different associative memory organizations.

In practice, most associative memories have the capability of *word parallel* operations; that is, all words in the associative memory array are involved in the parallel search operations. This differs drastically from the *word serial* operations encountered in RAMs. Based on how bit slices are involved in the operation, we consider below two different associative memory organizations:

The bit parallel organization In a bit parallel organization, the comparison process is performed in a parallel-by-word and parallel-by-bit fashion. All bit slices which are not masked off by the masking pattern are involved in the comparison process. In this organization, word-match tags for all words are used (Figure 5.34*a*). Each cross point in the array is a bit cell. Essentially, the entire array of cells is involved in a search operation.

Bit serial organization The memory organization in Figure 5.34*b* operates with one bit slice at a time across all the words. The particular bit slice is selected by an extra logic and control unit. The bit-cell readouts will be used in subsequent bit-slice operations. The associative processor STARAN has the bit serial memory organization and the PEPE has been installed with the bit parallel organization.

The associative memories are used mainly for search and retrieval of non-numeric information. The bit serial organization requires less hardware but is slower in speed. The bit parallel organization requires additional word-match detection logic but is faster in speed. We present below an example to illustrate the search operation in a bit parallel associative memory. Bit serial associative memory will be presented in Section 5.4.3 with various associative search and retrieval algorithms.

Example 5.8 Consider a student-file search in a bit parallel associative memory, as illustrated in Figure 5.35. The query needs to search all students whose age is not younger than 21 but is younger than 31. This requires performing the *not-less-than* search and the *less-than* search on the age field of the file. Two matching patterns are used in the two subsequent searches. The masking pattern selects the age field. The lower-bound 21 is loaded into the C register as the first key word. Parallel comparisons are performed on all student records (words) in the file. Initially, the indicator register is cleared to be zero.

After the first search, those students who are not younger than 21 are marked with a *1* in the indicator register, one bit per each student word. This matching vector is then transferred to one of the T registers. Then the upper-bound 31 is loaded into C as the second matching key. After the second search, a new matching vector is sent to the I register. A bitwise ANDing operation is then performed between the I and T registers with the resulting vector residing in the I register as the final output of the search process. The whole search process requires only two accesses of the associative memory. An output circuit (shown in Figure 5.34) is used to control the reading out of the result.

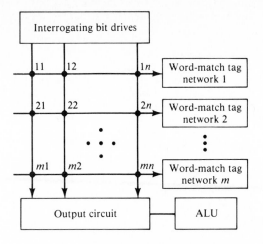

(*a*) Bit-parallel organization

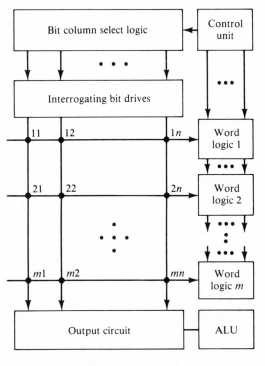

(*b*) Bit-serial organization

Figure 5.34 Associative memory organizations.

Query: Search for those students whose ages are in the range (21, 31)

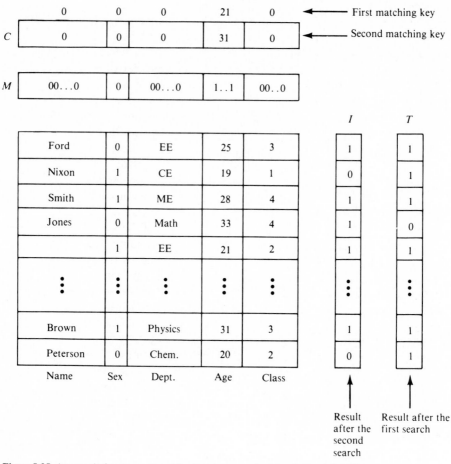

Figure 5.35 An associative memory used for the storage and retrieval of a student file.

5.4.2 Associative Processors (PEPE and STARAN)

An associative processor is an SIMD machine with the following special capabilities: (1) Stored data items are content-addressable, and (2) arithmetic and logic operations are performed over many sets of arguments in a single instruction. Because of these content-addressable and parallel processing capabilities, associative processors form a special subclass of SIMD computers. Associative processors are effective in many special application areas. We classify associative processors into two major classes, the *fully parallel* versus the *bit serial organizations*, depending on the associative memory used. Two associative processors are functionally described below along with their potential applications.

The PEPE architecture There are two types of fully parallel associative processors: *word-organized* and *distributed logic*. In a word-organized associative processor, the comparison logic is associated with each bit cell of every word and the logical decision is available at the output of every word. In a distributed-logic associative processor, the comparison logic is associated with each character cell of a fixed number of bits or with a group of character cells. The most well-known example of a distributed-logic associative processor is the PEPE. Because of the requirement of additional logic-per-cell, a fully parallel associative processor may be cost prohibitive. A distributed-logic associative processor is less complex and thus less expensive. The PEPE is based on a distributed-logic configuration developed at Bell Laboratories for radar signal-processing applications.

A schematic block diagram of PEPE is given in Figure 5.36. PEPE is composed of the following functional subsystems: an output data control, an element memory control, an arithmetic control unit, a correlation control unit, an associative output control unit, a control system, and a number of processing elements. Each processing element (PE) consists of an arithmetic unit, a correlation unit, an associative output unit, and a 1024×32-bit element memory. There are 288 PEs organized into eight element bays. Selected portions of the work load are loaded from a host computer CDC-7600 to the PEs. The loading selection process is determined by the inherent parallelism of the task and by the ability of PEPE's unique architecture to manipulate the task more efficiently than the host computer. Each processing element is delegated the responsibility of an object under observation by the radar system, and each processing element maintains a data file for specific objects within its memory and uses its associative arithmetic capability to continually update its respective file.

PEPE represents a typical special-purpose computer. It was designed to perform real-time radar tracking in the antiballistic missile (ABM) environment. No commercial model was made available. It is an attached array processor to the general-purpose machine CDC 7600, as demonstrated in Figure 5.36.

The bit-serial STARAN organization The full parallel structure requires expensive logic in each memory cell and complicated communications among the cells. The bit serial associative processor is much less expensive than the fully parallel structure because only one bit slice is involved in the parallel comparison at a time. Bit serial associative memory (Figure 5.34b) is used. This bit serial associative processing has been realized in the computer STARAN (Figure 5.37). STARAN consists of up to 32 associative array modules. Each associative array module contains a 256-word 256-bit *multidimensional access* (MDA) memory, 256 processing elements, a flip network, and a selector, as shown in Figure 5.38a. Each processing element operates serially bit by bit on the data in all MDA memory words. The operational concept of a STARAN associative array module is illustrated in Figure 5.38b.

Using the flip network, the data stored in the MDA memory can be accessed through the I/O channels in bit slices, word slices, or a combination of the two. The flip network is used for data shifting or manipulation to enable parallel

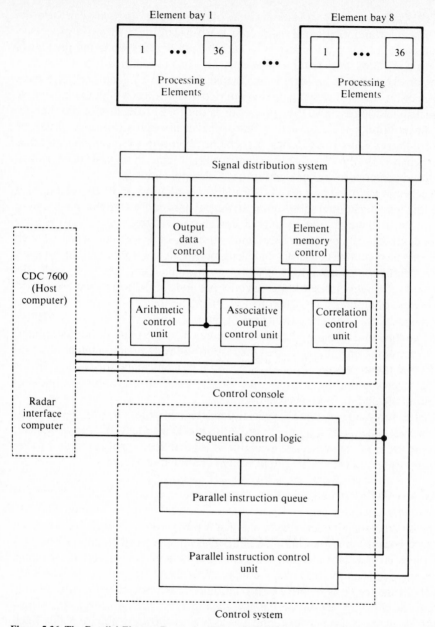

Figure 5.36 The Parallel Element Processing Ensemble (PEPE). (Courtesy of *Proc. of National Electronics Conference*, Berg et al. 1972.)

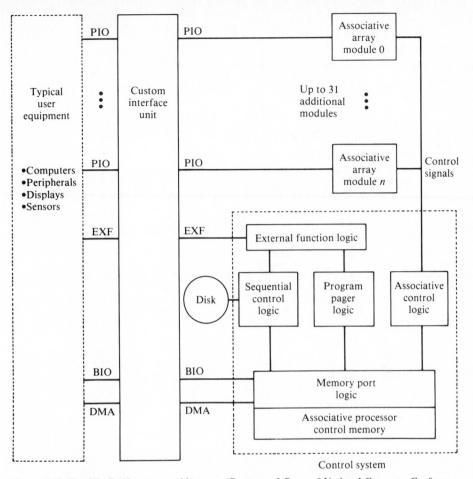

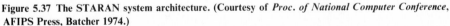

Figure 5.37 The STARAN system architecture. (Courtesy of *Proc. of National Computer Conference*, AFIPS Press, Batcher 1974.)

search, arithmetic or logical operations among words of the MDA memory. The MDA was implemented by Goodyear Aerospace using random-access memory chips with additional XOR logic circuits. The first STARAN was installed for digital image processing in 1975. Since then, Goodyear Aerospace has announced some enhanced STARAN models. The size of the MDA memory has increased to 9216×256 per module in the enhanced model with improved I/O and processing speed.

To locate a particular data item, STARAN initiates a search by calling for a match specified by the associative control logic. In one instruction execution, the data in all the selected memories of all the modules is processed simultaneously by the simple processing element at each word. The interface unit shown in Figure 5.37 involves interface with sensors, conventional computers, signal processors, interactive displays, and mass-storage devices. A variety of I/O options are

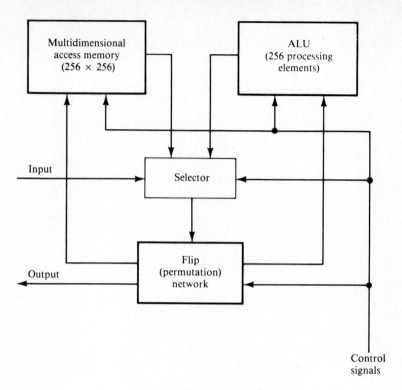

(a) STARAN associative array module

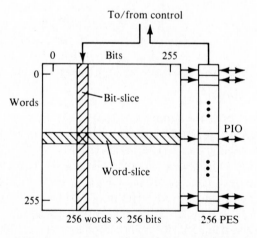

(b) Bit-slice versus word-slice operations in the STARAN

Figure 5.38 Associative memory and parallel operations in the STARAN.

implemented in the custom-interface unit, including the direct-memory access, buffered I/O channels, external function channels and parallel I/O.

Each associative array module can have up to 256 inputs and 256 outputs into the custom-interface unit. They can be used to increase the speed of inter-array data communication to allow STARAN to communicate with a high-bandwidth I/O device and to allow any device to communicate directly with the associative array modules. In many applications, such as matrix computation, air-traffic control, sensor-signal processing and data-management systems, a hybrid system composed of an associative processor and a conventional sequential processor can increase the throughput rate, simplify the software complexity, and reduce the hardware cost.

STARAN has high-speed input-output capabilities and the ability to interface easily with conventional computers. In such a hybrid system, each associative array module performs the tasks best suited to its capabilities. STARAN handles the parallel processing tasks and the conventional computer handles the tasks that must be processed in a single sequential data stream.

PEPE and STARAN are two large-scale associative processors that have been implemented for practical applications. The high cost-performance ratio of associative processors has limited them to be used mainly in military applications. Associative memories and processors have also been suggested for the design of text retrieval computers and back-end database machines. Several exploratory database machines are based on the use of associative memory, as reported in the book by Hsiao (1982).

5.4.3 Associative Search Algorithms

Associative memories are mainly used for the fast search and ordered retrieval of large files of records. Many researchers have suggested using associative memories for implementing relational database machines. Each relation of records can be arranged in a tabular form, as illustrated in Example 5.8. The tabulation of records (relations) can be programmed into the cells of an associative memory. Various associative search operations have been classified into the following categories by T. Y. Feng (1976).

Extreme searches

The *Maxima*: The largest among a set of records is searched.
The *Minima*: The smallest among a set of records is searched.
The *Median*: Search for the median according to a certain ordering.

Equivalence searches

Equal-to: Exact match is searched under a certain equality relation.
Not-equal-to: Search for those elements unequal to the given key.
Similar-to: Search for a match within the masked field.

Proximate-to: Search for those records that satisfy a certain proximity (neighbor-hood) condition.

Threshold searches

Smaller-than: Search for those records that are strictly smaller than the given key.
Greater-than: Search for those records that are strictly greater than the given key.
Not-smaller-than: Search for those records that are equal to or greater than the given key.
Not-greater-than: Search for those records that are equal to or smaller than the given key.

Adjacency searches

Nearest below: Search for the nearest record which is smaller than the key.

Between-limits searches

$[X, Y]$: Search for those records within the closed range $\{z \mid X \leq z \leq Y\}$.
(X, Y): Search for those records within the open range $\{z \mid X < z < Y\}$.
$[X, Y)$: Search for those records within the range $\{z \mid X \leq z < Y\}$.
$(X, Y]$: Search for those records within the range $\{z \mid X < z \leq Y\}$.

Ordered retrievals

Ascending sort: List all the records in ascending order.
Descending sort: List all the records in descending order.

Listed above are primitive search operations. Of course, one can always combine a sequence of primitive search operations by some boolean operators to form various query conjunctions. For examples, one may wish to answer the queries *equal-to-A* but *not-equal-to-B*; the *second largest from below*; *outside the range* $[X, Y]$; etc. Boolean operators AND, OR, and NOT can be used to form any query conjunction of predicates. A predicate consists of one of the above relational operators plus an attribute such as the pairs $\{\leq, A\}$ or $\{\neq, A\}$. The above search operators are frequently used in text retrieval operations.

Two examples are given below to show how to perform associative search operations. We consider the use of a bit serial associative memory (Figure 5.34) in which all the memory words can be accessed (read) in parallel, but where bit slices of all words or within a specified field of all words must be processed sequentially one slice after another from let to right in the AM array. The following notations are used to designate any specific *field* of a word:

- s: The starting bit address of a field, where $1 \leq s \leq n$.
- f: The field length in bits.

- k: The index within the field, where $1 \leq k \leq f$.
- i: The index for different bit slices, where $1 \leq i \leq n$.
- j: The index for successive words, where $1 \leq j \leq m$.

Furthermore, we use $\mathbf{1} = (1, 1, \ldots, 1)$ and $\mathbf{0} = (0, 0, \ldots, 0)$ to denote the binary vectors of all 1s or of all 0s, respectively. The indicator register I is formed with S-R flip-flops I_i for $i = 1, 2, \ldots, n$. The reset and set signals of flip-flop I_i are denoted as R_i and S_i, respectively. In the specification of the following algorithms, we use $I_i(k)$ to refer to the contents of flip-flop I_i at the kth step. The same convention applies to $T_i(k)$, $R_i(k)$, and $S_i(k)$. The initial contents of the working registers are indicated by $I(0)$ and $T(0)$.

Example 5.9: The MINIMA search This algorithm searches for the smallest number among a set of n positive numbers stored in a bit serial AM array. Each number has f bits stored in a field of a word from the bit position s to the bit position $s + f - 1$:

1. Initialize

$$C \leftarrow I; I(0) \leftarrow \mathbf{1}; T(0) \leftarrow \mathbf{0}; k = 1, j = s + k - 1, M \leftarrow (0 \ldots \underbrace{11 \ldots 10}_{f \text{ bits of 1s}} \ldots 0).$$

2. Load $T_i(k) = I_i(k - 1) \cap (C_j \oplus B_{ij})$ for all $i = 1, 2, \ldots, n$.

3. Detect $Q(k) = \bigcup_{i=1}^{n} T_i(k)$.

4. Reset T by applying $r_i(k) = \overline{T_i(k)} \cap Q(k)$ for all $i = 1, 2, \ldots, n$.
5. Increment $k \leftarrow k + 1$. Then proceed to step 2 if $k \leq f - 1$, or read out the work W_i indicated by $I_i(f) = 1$ if $k = f$.

Example 5.10: The NOT-SMALLER-THAN search This algorithm searches for those numbers that are greater than or equal to a given number N. Assume the same field format as in Example 5.9.

1. Initialize

$$C \leftarrow N; I(0) \leftarrow \mathbf{1}; T(0) \leftarrow \mathbf{1}, k = 1, j = s + k - 1, M \leftarrow 0 \ldots \underbrace{011 \ldots 10}_{f \text{ bits of 1s}} \ldots 0.$$

2. If $C_j = 0$, then load $T_i(k)$ with $T_i(k - 1) \cap (C_j \oplus B_{ij})$; else modify I by applying $R_i(k) = T_i(k) \cap (C_j \oplus B_{ij})$ for all $i = 1, 2, \ldots, n$.
3. Increment $k \leftarrow k + 1$. Then test if $k = f$. If no, proceed to step 2. If yes, read out those qualified numbers indicated by $I_i(f) = 1$.

In steps 2 and 4 of Example 5.9 and in step 2 of Example 5.10, all n words are involved in the specified operations. The bit-slice operations are governed by the increment of index k in the loop. When a bit parallel associative memory is used, the above algorithms have to be modified. The bit parallel associative memories were only used in nonnumeric text retrieval operations. The bit serial associative memories were mostly used to perform associative numeric computations.

5.5 BIBLIOGRAPHIC NOTES AND PROBLEMS

General discussions of array processors can be found in the texts by Thurber (1976), Kuck (1978), and Stone (1980). Interconnection networks for SIMD networks have been surveyed in Feng (1981) in a comparative manner. The SIMD computer model was proposed by Siegel (1979). A comprehensive treatment of interconnection networks can be found in the book by Siegel (1984). Multi-stage cube-type networks and their capabilities are discussed in Batcher (1976), Pease (1977), and Wu and Feng (1980). The barrel shifter and data manipulator are based on the work of Feng (1974) and Bauer (1974). The shuffle-exchange networks are discussed in Stone (1971) and Lang and Stone (1976). The Omega network was introduced by Lawrie (1975). Wu and Feng (1981) have studied the universality of shuffle-exchange networks. Network partitioning has been studied by Siegel (1980). Network reliability and fault tolerance were studied in Wu and Feng (1979) and in Shen and Hayes (1980).

A comparative study of large-scale array processors was given in Paul (1978), Thurber (1979), and Hwang et al. (1981). Associative search algorithms are based on the unpublished notes by Feng (1977). Stone (1980) has described the $O(n^2)$ algorithm for matrix multiplication. The parallel sorting method for mesh-connected array processors is developed by Thompson and Kung (1977). The FFT algorithms on SIMD computer are based on the work of Mueller, et al. (1980). The $O(n \log_2 n)$ algorithm for matrix multiplication on a cube network is based on the work of Thomas (1981).

Associative memories and associative processors have been surveyed in Yau and Fung (1977). There are also two published books, Thurber (1976) and Foster (1976), which are devoted to associative processors. More detailed information of PEPE can be found in Vick and Merwin (1973). The STARAN system architecture and applications are discussed in Batcher (1974) and Rohrbacher and Potter (1977). Additional SIMD computer algorithms can be found in Stone (1980), Kuck (1977), Thurber and Masson (1979), and Hockney and Jesshope (1981).

Problems

5.1 Explain the following terminologies associated with SIMD computers:

(a) Lock-step operations
(b) Masking of processing elements
(c) Routing functions for Illiac network
(d) Recirculating networks
(e) Cube-routing functions
(f) Barrel-shifting functions
(g) Shuffle-exchange functions
(h) Associative memory
(i) Bit serial associative processor
(j) Adjacency search

5.2 You are asked to design a data routing network for an SIMD array processor with 256 PEs. Barrel cyclic shifters are used so that a route from one PE to another requires only one unit of time per integer-power-of-two shift in either direction.

(*a*) Draw the interconnection barrel shifting network, showing all directly wired connections among the 266 PEs. In the drawing, at least one node (PE) must show all its connections to other PEs.

(*b*) Calculate the minimum number of routing steps from any PE_i to any other PE_{i+k} for the arbitrary distance $1 \le k \le 255$. Indicate also the upper bound on the minimum routing steps required.

5.3 Consider 64 PEs (PE_0 to PE_{63}) in the Illiac-IV. Determine the minimum number of data-routing steps needed to perform the following inter-PE data transfers: PE_i to $PE_{(i+k) \bmod 64}$ where $0 \le i \le 63$ and $0 \le k \le 63$.

5.4 Consider the use of a four-PE array processor to multiply two 3×3 matrices. The interconnection structure of the four PEs is shown in Figure 5.39. Wraparound connections appear in all rows and columns of the array. You need to map the matrix elements initially one to each of the processors. All the 3 multiplications needed for each output element c_{ij} must be performed in the same PE in order to accumulate the sum of products. Of course, you are allowed to shift the matrix elements around if needed.

(*a*) Show the initial mapping of the A and B matrix elements to the processors before the first multiplication is carried out. (You may have to wrap around the matrix.)

(*b*) What are the initial multiplications to be carried out in each processor (there may be more than one multiplication in each processor) without any data shifting?

(*c*) Parallel shifts are carried out in the horizontal and vertical directions. Show the mapping of the A and B matrix elements to the processors before the second group of multiplications can be carried out.

(*d*) What are the multiplications to be carried out in each processor without any further shifting? (Don't bother with summing with the previous terms. Summation operations in dot product operations are embedded in the multiply hardware automatically.)

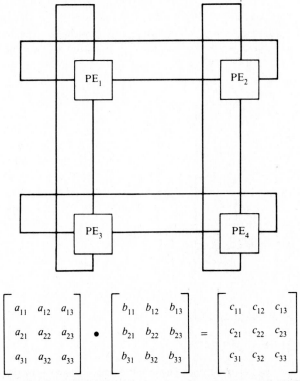

$$
\begin{bmatrix} a_{11} & a_{12} & a_{13} \\ a_{21} & a_{22} & a_{23} \\ a_{31} & a_{32} & a_{33} \end{bmatrix} \bullet \begin{bmatrix} b_{11} & b_{12} & b_{13} \\ b_{21} & b_{22} & b_{23} \\ b_{31} & b_{32} & b_{33} \end{bmatrix} = \begin{bmatrix} c_{11} & c_{12} & c_{13} \\ c_{21} & c_{22} & c_{23} \\ c_{31} & c_{32} & c_{33} \end{bmatrix}
$$

Figure 5.39 The multiplication of two 3×3 matrices on a mesh of 4 PEs in Problem 5.4.

(*e*) Suppose the two matrices have already been allocated as in part (*a*). Assume each processor can perform one multiplication per unit time or one shift in a single direction per unit time for each number. (If you shift two numbers, it takes two units of time.) Determine the time units needed to complete parts (*b*), (*c*), and (*d*), respectively. Minimizing the total time delay is the design goal.

5.5 Let A be a $2^m \times 2^m$ matrix stored in row-major order in the main memory. Prove the transposed matrix A^T can be obtained by performing m perfect shuffles on A.

5.6 Given an $n \times n$ matrix $A = (a_{ij})$, we want to find the n column sums:

$$S_j = \sum_{i=0}^{n-1} a_{ij} \qquad \text{for } j = 1, 2, \ldots, n-1$$

using an SIMD machine with n PEs. The matrix is stored in a skewed format, as shown in Figure 5.40. The jth column sum S_j is stored in location β in PEM_j at the end of the computation. Use the machine organization as shown in Figures 5.1*a* and 5.2. Write an SIMD algorithm and indicate the successive memory contents in the execution of the algorithm.

5.7 Consider the use of the associative memory array in Figure 5.32 for implementing a Not-Equal-To search. Assume bit-slice parallel-word operations similar to those described in Examples 5.9 and 5.10. Write out the detailed steps. Initial conditions in registers and the intermediate and final indicator pattern must be interpreted.

5.8 (*a*) Benes binary network is a type of multistage network which is *rearrangeable* and *nonblocking* because it can perform all possible connections between inputs and outputs by rearranging its existing connections so that a new path for a new input-output pair can always be established. Develop a routing algorithm to realize the following permutation in an 8×8 Benes network:

$$p = \begin{pmatrix} 0 & 1 & 2 & 3 & 4 & 5 & 6 & 7 \\ 3 & 7 & 4 & 0 & 2 & 6 & 1 & 5 \end{pmatrix}$$

Control setting of the input and output switching elements is shown in Figure 5.41 from the first iteration of the algorithm. The algorithm to be developed is *recursive* in nature. It can be applied recursively to the two middle subnetworks, labelled a and b in the figure.

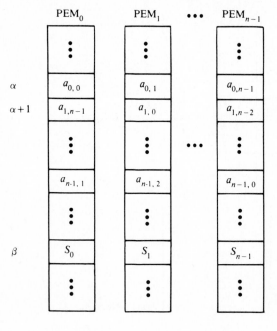

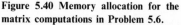

Figure 5.40 Memory allocation for the matrix computations in Problem 5.6.

Subnetwork a

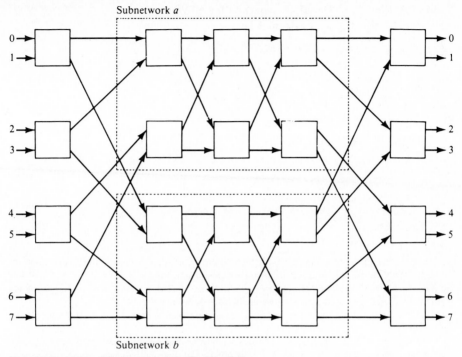

Subnetwork b

Figure 5.41 An 8 × 8 Benes network for Problem 5.8.

(*b*) Classify those multistage SIMD interconnection networks you have studied according to the three distinct features *blocking*, *rearrangeable*, and *nonblocking*.

5.9 Consider an N-input Omega network where each switch cell is individually controlled and $N = 2^n$.

(*a*) How many different permutation functions (one-to-one and onto mapping) can be defined over N inputs?

(*b*) How many different permutation functions can be performed by the Omega network in one pass? If $N = 8$, what is the percentage of permutation functions that can be performed in one pass?

(*c*) Given any source-destination $(S - D)$ pair, the routing path can be uniquely controlled by the destination address. Instead of using the destination address (D) as the routing tag, we define $T = S \oplus D$ as the routing tag. Show that T alone can be used to determine the routing path. What is the advantage of using T as the routing tag?

(*d*) The Omega network is capable of performing broadcasting (one source and multiple destinations). If the number of destination PEs is a power of two, can you give a simple routing algorithm to achieve this capability?

5.10 How many steps are required to broadcast an information item from one PE to all other PEs in each of the following single-stage interconnection networks? ($N = 2^n$ PEs).

(*a*) A shuffle-exchange network. Each step could be either a shuffle or an exchange but not mixed.

(*b*) A cube network. The C_i routing is performed for each step $i, 0 \leq i \leq n - 1$.

5.11 Prove or disprove that the Omega network can perform any shift permutation in one pass. The *shift permutation* is defined as follows: given $N = 2^n$ inputs, a shift permutation is either a circular left shift or a circular right shift of k positions, where $0 \leq k < N$.

5.12 A polynomial, $p(x) = \sum_{i=0}^{N-2} a_i x^i$ can be evaluated in $2 \log_2 N$ steps in an SIMD computer with N PEs, where N is a power of 2. Assume that each PE can perform either an *add* or a *multiply* under masking control. A shuffle interconnection exists among the N PEs. Each PE has a data register and

Table 5.6 The shuffle-multiply sequence for SIMD polynomial evaluation in Problem 5.12.

Data	Mask	Data	Mask	Data	Mask	Data
a_0	0	a_0	0	a_0	0	a_0
a_1	1	$a_1 x$	0	$a_1 x$	0	$a_1 x$
a_2	0	a_2	1	$a_2 x^2$	0	$a_2 x^2$
a_3	1	$a_3 x$	1	$a_3 x^3$	0	$a_3 x^3$
a_4	0	a_4	0	a_4	1	$a_4 x^4$
a_5	1	$a_5 x$	0	$a_5 x$	1	$a_5 x^5$
a_6	0	a_6	1	$a_6 x^2$	1	$a_6 x^6$
x	1	x^2	1	x^4	1	x^8

First iteration	Second iteration	Third iteration
Multiply by x	Multiply by x^2	Multiply by x^4

a mask flag. The machine is equipped with both *broadcasting* and *masking* capabilities (instructions). To evaluate the polynomial requires first to generate all the product terms; $a_i x^i$ for $i = 0, 1, \ldots, N - 1$, by a sequence of $\log_2 N$ shuffle-multiply operations as listed in Table 5.6, and then to generate the sum of all product terms by a sequence of $\log_2 N$ shuffle-add operations.

(a) Show the major components and interconnection structure of the desired SIMD machine for the size of $N = 8$.

(b) Figure out the exact sequence of SIMD machine instructions needed to carry out the shuffle-multiply sequence in Table 5.6. The *shuffle* instruction is used to generate the successive mask vectors. The PE operates by broadcasting the successive multipliers, x, x^2, and x^4, retrieved from the eighth data register.

(c) Before entering the shuffle-add sequence, the eighth data register should be reset to zero. Repeat question (b) for the summing sequence. At the end, the final sum can be retrieved from any one of the eight PE registers.

(d) Explain the advantages of using the shuffle interconnection network for the implementation of the polynomial evaluation algorithm, as compared with the use of the Illiac mesh network for the same purpose.

CHAPTER SIX

SIMD COMPUTERS AND PERFORMANCE ENHANCEMENT

This chapter is devoted to array-structured SIMD computer systems. Three milestone array processors, Illiac-IV, BSP, and MPP, will be studied in detail. These systems represent two decades of development of array processors. The three systems differ not only in their hardware-software structural features but also in their programming and application requirements. The Illiac-IV uses local memories attached to the processing elements. The BSP has parallel memory modules shared by all arithmetic elements. The Illiac-IV uses the mesh network and the BSP uses the crossbar network. The MPP is a bit-slice array processor built with VLSI technology.

After studying these SIMD computers, we discuss general methods to enhance the performance of SIMD array processors. These include parallel memory allocation, language extensions for array processing, and improvement of the system throughput. Finally, multiple-SIMD computer organizations are presented for parallel vector processing in multiarray processors with shared resources.

6.1 THE SPACE OF SIMD COMPUTERS

In this section, we review major SIMD computers that have been constructed, designed, or proposed up to early 1983. We use the term *array processor* exclusively for SIMD computers using conventional (nonassociative) random-access memory and the term *associative processor* for SIMD computers using associative memory.

We divide the space of SIMD computers into five subspaces, based on word-slice and bit-slice processing and the number of control units used:

- Word-slice array processors
- Bit-slice array processors
- Word-slice associative processors
- Bit-slice associative processors
- Multiple-SIMD computers

Known SIMD computers in each class will be briefly surveyed below, among which only the Illiac-IV, the BSP, and the MPP will be described in detail. SIMD computer architectures and example systems are summarized in Table 6.1. Section numbers are identified within the parentheses for SIMD computers covered in this book. For those systems that are not covered, major reference books and articles are identified by the author's name and the year of publication.

6.1.1 Array and Associative Processors

In 1958, Unger conceived a computer structure for spatial problems. The Unger spatial computer is conceptually shown in Figure 6.1. A two-dimensional array of PEs is controlled by a common master. Unger's machine was proposed for pattern-recognition applications. The concept of lock-step SIMD operation was further consolidated in the Solomon computer proposed by Slotnick, et al., in 1962. The Solomon computer, though never built, motivated the development of the Illiac series and many later SIMD machines. In 1965, Senzig and Smith designed a *vector arithmetic multiprocessor* (VAMP) which consists of a linear array of PEs with shared memory modules and a shared arithmetic pipeline, as illustrated in Figure 6.2. Each PE is a virtual processor, having only a few working registers in it. This pipeline-array processor was designed to save hardware in vector processing.

The Illiac-IV evolved from several predecessors in the Illiac series. It was the first major array supercomputer developed in the late 1960s. We shall study the Illiac-IV system and its successor system, the BSP, in Section 6.2. Both systems are no longer operational. However, we wish to learn the design methodologies and the application experiences accumulated with the development of these two systems. In 1979, two proposals were made to extend the Illiac IV-BSP architecture to meet the future demand of gigaflop machines. The Phoenix project suggested a multiple-SIMD computer consisting of 16 Illiac-IV arrays with a total of 1024 PEs. Burroughs proposed an array architecture which upgrades the BSP to 512 PEs sharing 521 memory modules. This Burroughs computer proposal was for the Numerical Aerodynamic Simulation Facilities demanded by the NASA Ames Research Center in the United States.

Several bit-slice array processors have been developed in Europe and the United States. The latest CLIP-4 is a bit-slice array processor built with a cellular mesh of 96×96 PEs with eight neighbors per PE. The CLIP series is designed for bit-slice image-processing applications. The Distributed Array Processor (DAP)

Table 6.1 SIMD computer systems

Computer	Architecture[1]	Developer and references
Unger	wos array	Proposed by Unger (1958)
Solomon	wos array	Proposed by Slotnick (1962)
VAMP	wos array	Proposed by Senzig and Smith (1965)
ILLIAC	wos array[2]	Illiac-IV operational 1972 (Section 6.2)
BSP	wos array	Developed by Burroughs and suspended in 1979 (Section 6.2)
CLIP	bis array	Developed at University College, London, See Duff (1976)
DAP	bis array	Developed by ICL, England, section 3.3 in Hockney and Jesshope (1981)
MPP	bis array	Developed by Goodyear Aerospace (Section 6.3)
PEPE	wos ass	Developed by Burroughs Corp. and System Dev. Corp. (Section 5.4.2)
STARAN	bis ass	Developed by Goodyear Aerospace Corp. (Section 5.4.2)
OMEN	bis ass	Developed by Sanders Associates, chapter 7 in Thurber (1976)
RELACS	bis ass	Proposed for database machine in Berra and Oliver (1979)
MAP	wos MSIMD	Proposed by Nutt (1977) (Section 6.4.4)
PM[4]	wos MSIMD	Proposed by Briggs and Hwang et al. (1979) (Section 6.4.4)
Phoenix	wos MSIMD	Proposed by Feierbach and Stevenson (1979)
NASF	wos array	Proposed in Stevens (1979)

[1] wos (word slice), bis (bit slice), ass (associative), array (array processor).
[2] Original Illiac design had MSIMD with 4 CUs and 256 PEs.

was developed by International Computer Limited in England. The DAP can be constructed in groups of 16 PEs in various sizes, such as 32×32, 64×64, 128×128 and 256×256. The MPP is a 128×128 bit-slice array processor, to be described in Section 6.3. The MPP represents state-of-the-art construction of large-scale SIMD computers in the early 1980s. It will be used to process satellite images for NASA applications.

Four associative processors are listed in Table 6.1. The PEPE is the only word-slice associative processor that we know of. The rest are bit-slice array processors. In Thurber (1976), details of the PEPE, the STARAN, and the OMEN

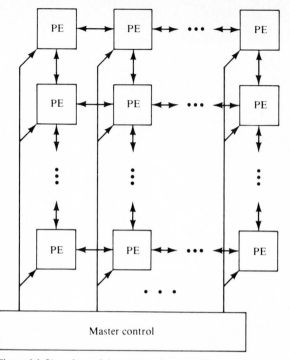

Figure 6.1 Unger's spatial computer concept. (Courtesy of *Proc. of IRE*, **October 1958.)**

are given. At present, most associative processors are designed to perform fast information retrieval and database operations. The RELACS is an associative database machine proposed by researchers at Syracuse University in 1979. It is based on using staged memory between the disks and the host processor. Associative memories are used to implement relational database operations. We have already studied the PEPE and the STARAN architecture in Section 5.4.2. The STARAN is the only commercial associative processor that has several installations in operation at present.

6.1.2 SIMD Computer Perspectives

It is quite clear that SIMD computers are special-purpose systems. For a specific problem environment, they may perform impressively. However, array processors have some programming and vectorization problems which are difficult to solve. The reality is that array processors are not popular among commercial computer manufacturers. The performances of several array processors are compared in Figure 6.3. Only the peak performance is indicated under ideal programming and resource allocation conditions. As the size of the PE-array increases, the performance should increase linearly. Of course, the peak speed is also a function of the word length especially foɪ bit-slice operations. For vector processing, the performance depends also on thᴗ vector length.

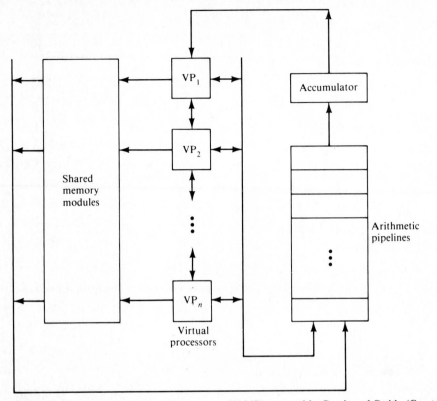

Figure 6.2 The vector arithmetic multiprocessor (VAMP) proposed by Senzig and Smith. (Courtesy of AFIPS *Proc. FJCC*, **1965.)**

Multiple-SIMD (MSIMD) computers form a special subclass of MIMD computers. Multiple instruction streams exist in a multiple-array processor. Each instruction stream handles multiple data sets, as does an SIMD array. The Illiac-IV was originally proposed as an MSIMD machine. There are also other MSIMD computers, such as the Pheonix project and the PM^4 proposed in the literature. We shall briefly introduce these systems in Section 6.4.4. The MSIMD computers can offer higher application flexibility than can a single SIMD machine. So far, none of the proposed MSIMD machines has been built.

Listed below are some application areas that have been challenged or suggested for array processors and, in particular, for the Illiac-IV, the BSP, the MPP, and the STARAN systems:

- Matrix algebra (multiplication, decomposition, and inversion)
- Matrix eigenvalue calculations
- Linear and integer programming
- General circulation weather modeling
- Beam forming and convolution

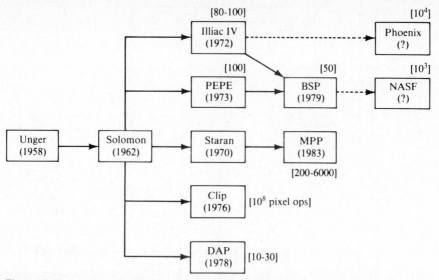

Figure 6.3 The family tree of SIMD array processors (numbers in brackets are estimated peak performance in mflops).

- Filtering and Fourier analysis
- Image processing and pattern recognition
- Wind-tuned experiments
- Automated map generation
- Real-time scene analysis

Some of these applications will be studied with the architectural descriptions in subsequent sections. The above listing is by no means exhaustive. Most of these applications need to process spatially distributed data.

6.2 THE ILLIAC-IV AND THE BSP SYSTEMS

Presented below are the system architecture, hardware and software features, and application requirements of the Illiac-IV and the BSP computer systems. The Illiac-IV system was developed at the University of Illinois in the 1960s. The system was fabricated by the Burroughs Corporation in 1972. The original objective was to develop a highly parallel computer with a large number of arithmetic units to perform vector or matrix computations at the rate of 10^9 operations per second. In order to achieve this rate, the system was to employ 256 PEs under the supervision of four CUs. Due to cost escalation and schedule delays, the system was ultimately limited to one quadrant with 64 PEs under the control of one CU. The speed of the 64-PE quadrant is approximately 200 million operations per second. The Illiac-IV computer has been applied in numerical weather forecasting and in nuclear engineering research, among many other scientific applications.

6.2.1 The Illiac-IV System Architecture

The 64 PEs in the Illiac computer are interconnected as a two-dimensional mesh network, shown in Figure 6.4. The PEs are numbered from 0 to 63. The data flow through the Illiac-IV array includes the CU bus for sending instructions or data in blocks of eight words from the PEMs to the CU. Data is represented in either 64- or 32 bit floating-point, 64-bit logical, 48- or 24-bit fixed point, or 8-bit character mode. By utilizing these data formats, the PEs can hold vectors of operands with 64, 128, or 512 components. The instructions to be executed are distributed throughout the PEMs. The operating system supervises the execution of instructions fetched from the PEMs.

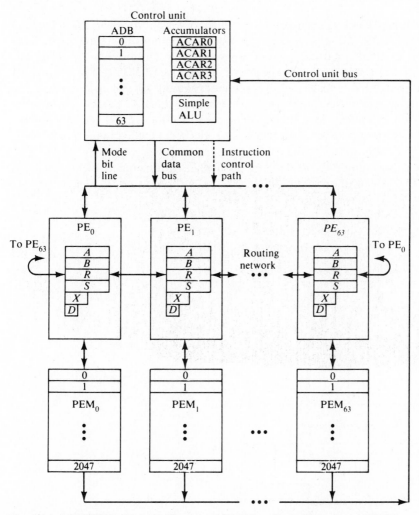

Figure 6.4 A 64-PE Illiac IV array. (Courtesy of _IEEE Proc_. Bouknight et al., April 1972.)

The common data bus is used to broadcast information from the CU to the entire array of 64 PEs. For example, a constant multiplier need not be stored 64 times in each PEM; instead, the constant can be stored in a CU register and then broadcast to each enabled PE. Special routing instructions are used to send information from one PE register to another PE register via the routing network. Standard load or store instructions are used to transfer information from PE registers to PEM. At most, seven routing steps are needed to transfer information among the PEs via the mesh network. The software figures out the shortest routing path in each data-routing operation. The *mode-bit line* consists of one line coming from the *A* register of each PE in the array. These lines can transmit the mode bits of the *D* register in the array to the accumulator register in the CU. There are CU instructions which can test the mask vector and branch on a zero or nonzero condition.

The Illiac-IV communicates with the outside world through an I/O subsystem (Figure 6.5), a disk file system, and a B6500 host computer which supervises a large laser memory (10^{12} bits) and the ARPA network link. The disk has 128 heads, one per track, with a 40-ms rotation speed and an effective transfer rate of 10^9 bits per second. The B6500 manages all programmer requests for system resources. The operating system, including compilers, assemblers, and I/O service routines, are residing in the B6500. As a total system, the Illiac-IV array is really a special-purpose back-end machine of the B6500. The ARPA net linkage makes the Illiac-IV available to all members of the ARPA network.

The control unit (CU) of the Illiac-IV array performs the following functions needed for the execution of programs:

1. Controls and decodes the instruction streams.
2. Transmits control signals to PEs for vector execution.
3. Broadcasts memory addresses that are common to all PEs.

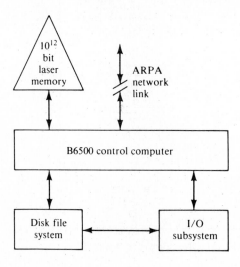

Figure 6.5 The Illiac IV I/O System.

4. Manipulates data words common to the calculations in all PEs.
5. Receives and processes trap or interrupt signals.

A block diagram of the CU is shown in Figure 6.6. The CU by itself is a scalar processor, in addition to its capability of concurrently controlling the PE-array operations. The *instruction buffer* (PLA) and *local data buffer* (LDB) are 64-word fast-access buffers. The PLA is associatively addressed to hold current and pending instructions. The LDB is a data cache with 64 bits per word. There are four *accumulator registers* (ACAR). The CU *arithmetic unit* performs 64-bit scalar

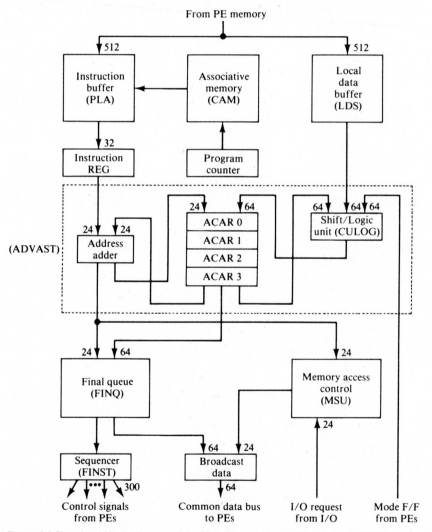

Figure 6.6 Functional block diagram of the Illiac IV control unit. (Courtesy of *IEEE Proc*. Bouknight et al., April 1972.)

addition, subtraction, shift and logic operations. More complex and vector arithmetic logic operations are relegated to the PEs. Address arithmetic is performed by the 24-bit address adder. The *final queue* is used to stack the addresses and data waiting to be transmitted to the PEs.

All instructions are 32 bits wide and classified as either CU instructions or PE instructions. CU instructions are for program control (indexing, jumps, etc.) and scalar operations. PE instructions are decoded by the *adva*nced instruction *st*ation (ADVAST) and then transmitted via control signals to all PEs. In fact, the ADVAST decodes all instructions and executes the CU instructions. The ADVAST constructs the necessary address and data operands after decoding a PE instruction. The PLA instruction buffer can hold 128 instructions, sufficient to hold the inner loop of many programs.

A block diagram of the processing element is shown in Figure 6.7. The PE computes with the distributed data and reforms local indexing for skewed memory fetch. Major components in a PE include:

1. Four 64-bit registers: A is an accumulator, B is the operand register, R is the data-routing register, and S is a general-storage register.
2. An adder/multiplier, a logic unit, and a barrel switch for arithmetic, boolean, and shifting functions, respectively.
3. A 16-bit index register and an adder for memory address modification and control.
4. An 8-bit mode register to hold the results of tests and the PE masking information.

Each PE has a 64 bit wide routing path to four neighbors. To minimize the physical routing distance, the PEs are grouped as shown in Figure 6.7. This drawing has been logically described in Figure 6.8 for a smaller network size. Routing by a distance of plus or minus eight occurs interior to each group of eight PEs. The CU data and instruction fetches require blocks of eight words, which are accessed in parallel. The individual PEM is a thin-film memory with a cycle time of 240 ns and an access time of 120 ns. Each has a capacity of 2048 words. Each PEM is independently accessible by its attached PE, the CU, or other I/O connections. The computing speed and memory of the Illiac-IV arrays require a substantial secondary storage for program and data files. A backup memory is used for programs with data sets exceeding the fast-memory capacity.

6.2.2 Applications of the Illiac-IV

The Illiac-IV was primarily designed for matrix manipulation and for solving partial differential equations. Many ARPA net users attempt to use the Illiac-IV for their own applications. The main difficulties in programming the Illiac-IV are the exploitation of identical arithmetic computations in user programs and the proper distribution of data sets in the PEMs to allow parallel accesses. In this section, we examine several programming problems of the Illiac-IV.

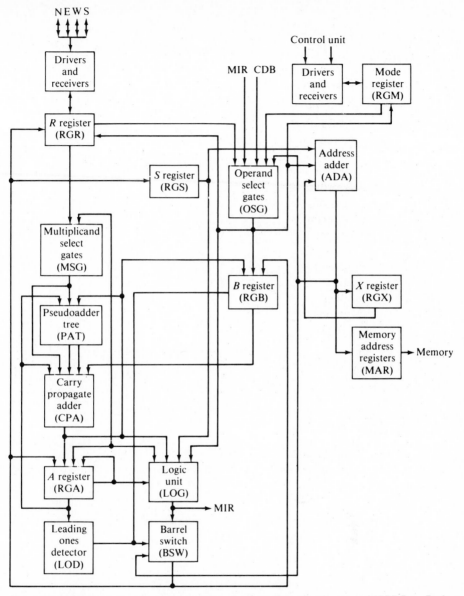

Figure 6.7 The internal structure of the processing element in Illiac IV. (Courtesy of *IEEE Proc*. Bouknight et al., April 1972.)

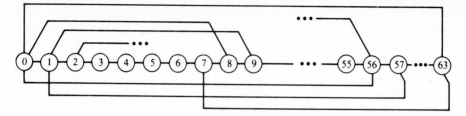

(*a*) Electrical connectivity

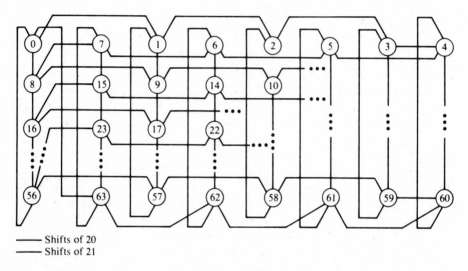

────── Shifts of 20
────── Shifts of 21

(*b*) The physical layout

Figure 6.8 The Illiac IV routing network. (Courtesy of *IEEE Trans. Computers*, Barnes et al., August 1968.)

In a conventional serial computer, the addition of two arrays (vectors) is realized by the following Fortran statements:

$$\text{DO } 100 \text{ I}=1,\text{N}$$
$$100 \text{ A(I)} = \text{B(I)} + \text{C(I)} \tag{6.1}$$

These two Fortran statements will be compiled into a sequence of machine instructions which include the initialization of the loop, the looping-control instructions, the component-addition instruction, and the storage of the result. The initialization instructions are outside the loop. All the remaining machine instructions must be executed N times in the loop.

The Illiac-IV can perform the additions in the loop simultaneously by involving all 64 PEs in synchronous lock-step fashion. The data must be allocated in the

PEMs to support parallelism in the PEs. We consider below the programming of the computations in Eq. 6.1 on the Illiac-IV.

Example 6.1
Case 1: $N = 64$ **(The array matches the problem size)** Only three Illiac-IV machine instructions are needed to implement the Eq. 6.1 loop. The 64 components of the A, B, and C arrays are allocated in memory locations α, $\alpha + 1$, and $\alpha + 2$ of the PEMs, respectively, as shown in Figure 6.9. The machine instructions are:

LDA $\alpha + 2$ (*Load* the accumulators of all PEs with the C array).
ADRN $\alpha + 1$ (*Add* to the accumulators the contents of the B array)
STA α (*Store* the result in the accumulators to the PEMs)

Note that all the 64 *loads* in LDA, the 64 *adds* in ADRN, and the 64 *stores* in STA are performed in parallel in only three machine instructions. This means a speedup 64 times faster than a conventional serial computer.

Case 2: $N < 64$ **(The problem size is smaller than the array size)** In this case, only a subset of the 64 PEs will be involved in the parallel operations. The same memory allocation and machine instructions as in case 1 are needed, except some of the memory space and PEs will be masked off. The smaller the value

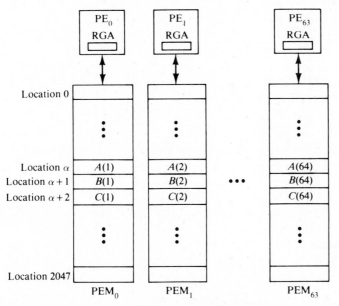

Figure 6.9 Data allocation in PEMs to execute the program:

DO 10 I = 1, 64
10 A(I) = R(I) = C(I)

N compared to 64, the severer the idleness of the disabled PEs and PEMs in the array.

Case 3: $N > 64$ **(The problem size is greater than the array size)** The memory allocation problem becomes much more complicated in this case. The case of $N = 66$ is illustrated in Figure 6.10. The first 64 elements of the A, B, and C arrays are stored from locations α, $\alpha + 2$, and $\alpha + 4$, respectively, in all PEMs. The two residue elements A(65), A(66); B(65), B(66); and C(65), C(66) are stored in locations $\alpha + 1$, $\alpha + 3$, and $\alpha + 5$, respectively, in PEM_0 and PEM_1. The unused memory locations are indicated by question marks. Six machine-language instructions are needed to perform the 66 load, add, and store operations:

1. *Load* the accumulator from location $\alpha + 4$.
2. *Add* to the accumulator the contents of location $\alpha + 2$.
3. *Store* the result to location α.
4. *Load* the accumulator from location $\alpha + 5$.
5. *Add* to the accumulator the contents of location $\alpha + 3$.
6. *Store* the result to location $\alpha + 1$.

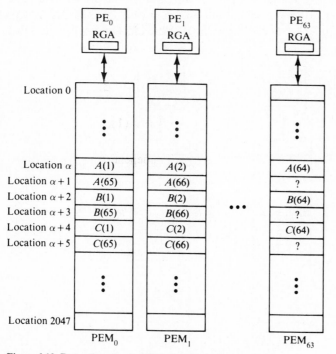

Figure 6.10 Data allocation in PEMs to execute the program.

```
DO 10 I = 1, 66

10 A(I) = R(I) + C(I)
```

The two residue data items in the A, B, and C arrays require three additional Illiac instructions. In fact, the above six instructions can be used to perform any vector addition of dimensions $65 \leq N \leq 128$ in Illiac-IV. The particular storage scheme shown in Figure 6.10 wastes almost three rows of storage ($62 \times 3 = 186$ words).

Next, we consider the implementation of a linear recurrence in the Illiac-IV:

$$
\begin{aligned}
& \text{DO 100 I=2,64} \\
& \text{100 A(I)=B(I)+A(I-1)}
\end{aligned}
\qquad (6.2)
$$

This recursive loop demands the following set of Fortran statements to be executed sequentially:

$$
\begin{aligned}
& \text{A(2)=B(2)+A(1)} \\
& \text{A(3)=B(3)+A(2)} \\
& \qquad \vdots \\
& \text{A(63)=B(63)+A(62)} \\
& \text{A(64)=B(64)+A(63)}
\end{aligned}
$$

We can rewrite the above sequential statements as follows:

$$
\begin{aligned}
& \text{A(2)=B(2)+A(1)} \\
& \text{A(3)=B(3)+B(2)+A(1)} \\
& \text{A(4)=B(4)+B(3)+B(2)+A(2)} \\
& \qquad \vdots \\
& \text{A(N)=B(N)+B(N-1)+}\cdots\text{+B(2)+A(1)}
\end{aligned}
$$

The above 63 computations can be computed independently and simultaneously in the Illiac-IV. We write

$$
A(k) = A(1) + \sum_{I=2}^{k} B(I) \qquad \text{for } 2 \leq k \leq 63 \qquad (6.3)
$$

A Fortran code is given below to perform the above expanded computations:

$$
\begin{aligned}
& \text{S=A(1)} \\
& \text{DO 100 K=2,64} \\
& \text{S=S+B(K)} \\
& \text{100 A(K)=S}
\end{aligned}
$$

The implementation of this decoupled Fortran program on the Illiac-IV requires the following machine instructions, based on the memory allocation shown in Figure 6.11.

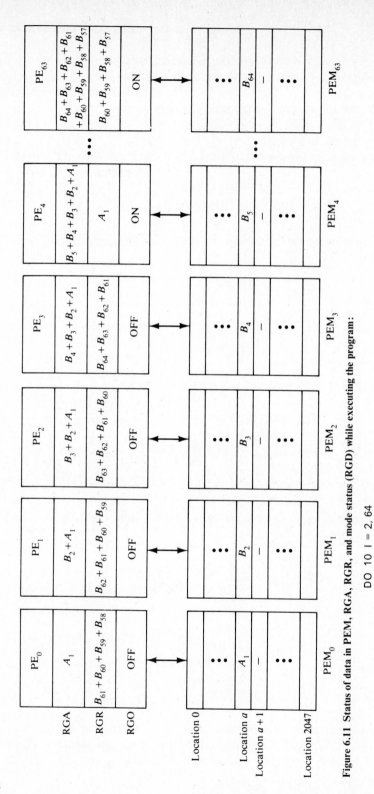

Figure 6.11 Status of data in PEM, RGA, RGR, and mode status (RGD) while executing the program:

DO 10 I = 2, 64

10 A(I) = B(I) + A(I − 1)

1. Enable all PEs.
2. All PEs load accumulators from memory location α.
3. Set index $i \leftarrow 0$.
4. All PEs load registers from their accumulators.
5. All PEs route their register contents to the right for a distance of 2^i.
6. Set index $j \leftarrow 2^i - 1$.
7. Disable PEs from 0 through j.
8. All enabled PEs add to accumulators the contents of routing registers.
9. Reset $i \leftarrow i + 1$.
10. If $i < 6$, go to step 4.
11. Enable all PEs.
12. All PEs store results in accumulators to memory location $\alpha + 1$.

Figure 6.11 shows the status of data in the PEM, the accumulator, the routing register, and the mode-status registers from those enabled and disabled instructions after step 8 is executed, when $i = 2$. Parallelism has been revealed after decoupling in this example.

Most of the Illiac-IV system software is executed by the host processor B6500. This system manager performs the standard B6500 operations, handles user-seeking Illiac-IV services, and implements the necessary features to support the operation of the PE array, the disk-file system, and the I/O subsystem. The Illiac-IV array can be visualized as the highest priority time-sharing user of the B6500 among many users connected via the ARPA net. Results produced by the B6500 or by the Illiac-IV programs may be printed locally or transmitted over the ARPA net to remote output devices local to the user. The Illiac-IV array has a small resident operating system executed by its CU which will allow the fast processing of traps and other special loading operations.

The Illiac-IV operating system runs between a *diagnostic mode* and a *normal mode*. The main task of the diagnostic mode is the testing and diagnosis of possible faults in the I/O subsystem and in the Illiac-IV array itself. The Illiac-IV operating system consists of a set of asynchronous processes which run under the control of the B6500 master-control program. The following events may take place when a user submits an Illiac-IV job to the B6500:

1. The B6500 translates Algol or Fortran programs into binary input files to be used by the Illiac-IV array processor.
2. The Illiac-IV programs written in Ask, Glypnir, or Illiac-IV Fortran will operate on the files prepared by the B6500 programs and prepare binary output files.
3. The B6500 transforms the binary files from the Illiac-IV to the required external form for use or storage.
4. An Illiac control-language program controls the operating system for the job which it defines.

The B6500 programs and the Illiac-IV programs communicate via the disk files (for data) and via the 48-bit path for CU interrupt signals. The protocol for these signals over the 48-bit path is administered by two modules. The first is a small executive program residing in the Illiac-IV itself (called OS4) which processes all interrupts for the array, handles all communications between the user programs and the rest of the operating system, and provides a few standard functions for use in the array. The OS4 communicates with a module (known as the *job partner*) in the B6500, which acts as a clearing house for all communication between the OS4 and thus the user program running on the Illiac-IV. The job partner thus initiates all data transfers between the B6500 and the Illiac-IV disk. This arrangement emphasizes the B6500 as an I/O processor for the Illiac-IV or, conversely, the Illiac-IV as a peripheral processor for the B6500.

The Illiac-IV is very difficult to program properly if one does not banish nearly all serial machine preconceptions and habits. It is worth pointing out the differences between the Illiac-IV high-level languages and the existing languages:

1. The natural method of addressing PEMs is by rows of 64 words, since the words of PEMs may be addressed in parallel. However, a column of words in one PEM may not be addressed at once.
2. The vector elements are operated upon based on the mode pattern. The Illiac-IV language should allow efficient manipulation of the mode patterns.
3. The Illiac language should allow reasonable expression of routing and indexing independently in each PE.

The design experiences of the Illiac-IV are very useful in developing later SIMD array processors. The performance of the Illiac-IV is about two to four times faster than the CDC-7600. The Illiac-IV has limited scalar capability; it uses a recirculating mesh network with fixed size. Some of these difficulties have been overcome in later array processors like the BSP and the MPP. We shall discuss some performance enhancement methods, including the skewed-memory allocations and some language extensions, in Section 6.4.

6.2.3 The BSP System Architecture

The BSP was a commercial attempt made by the Burroughs Corporation beyond the Illiac-IV in order to meet the increasing demand of large-scale scientific and engineering computers. It improves in many aspects on the Illiac-IV design. We describe below the parallel architecture of the BSP and its conflict-free memory organization. Even though the BSP has been suspended by Burroughs, it is a well-designed array supercomputer that we can still learn much from. The BSP extends the array processing capability of the Illiac-IV to a vectorizing Fortran machine. With a maximum speed of 50 megaflops, the BSP was designed to perform large-scale computations in the fields of numerical weather prediction, nuclear energy, seismic signal processing, structure analysis and econometric modeling.

The BSP is not a stand-alone computer. It is a back-end processor attached to a host machine, a *system manager*, such as the B7800 depicted in Figure 6.12. The motivation for attaching the BSP to a system manager is to free the BSP from

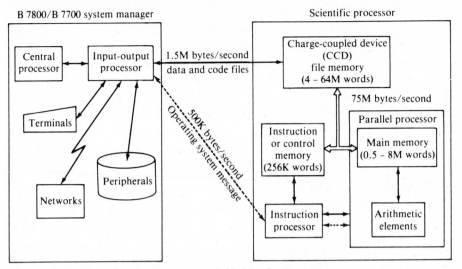

Figure 6.12 The Burroughs scientific processor attached to a host processor.

routine management and I/O functions in order to concentrate on arithmetic computations. The system manager provides time-sharing services, data and program-file editing, data communication to remote job-entry stations, terminals and networks, vectorizing compiling and linking of the BSP programs, long-term data storage, and database-management functions. Major components in the BSP include the control processor, the parallel processors, a file memory, parallel-memory models, and the alignment network shown in Figure 6.13.

The *control processor* provides the supervisory interface to the system manager in addition to controlling the parallel processor. The *scalar processor* processes all operating system and user-program instructions, which are stored in the *control memory*. It executes some serial or scalar portions of user programs with a clock rate of 12 MHz and is able to perform up to 1.5 megaflops. All vector instructions and certain grouped scalar instructions are passed to the *parallel processor controller*, which validates and transforms them into microsequences controlling the operation of the 16 *arithmetic elements* (AEs). The bipolar control memory has 256K words with a 160-ns cycle time. Each word has 48 bits plus 8 parity-check bits to provide the SECDED capability. The *control and maintenance unit* is an interface between the system manager and the rest of the control processors for initiation, communication of supervisory command and maintenance purposes.

The parallel processors perform vector computations with a clock period of 160 ns. All 16 AEs must execute the same instruction (broadcast from the parallel processor controller) over different data sets. Most arithmetic operations can be completed in two clock periods (320 ns). The BSP is capable of executing up to 50 megaflops. Data for the vector operations are stored in 17 parallel *memory modules*, each of which contains up to 512 K words with a cycle time of 160 ns. The data transfer between the memory modules and the AEs is 100 M words per

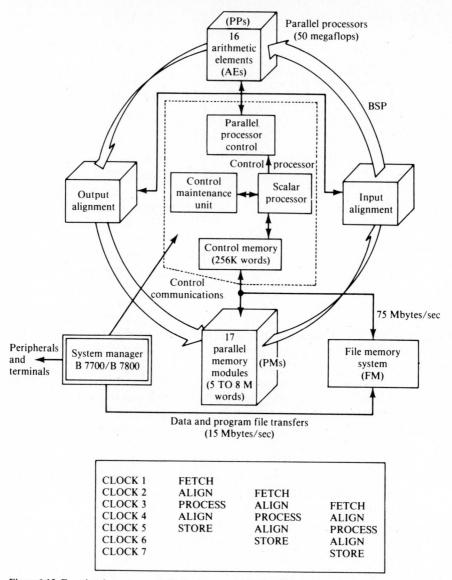

Figure 6.13 Functional structure and pipelined processing in the BSP. (Couresy of *IEEE Trans. Computers*, Lawrie and Vora, 1982.)

second. The organization of the 17 memory modules provides a conflict-free memory that allows access to vectors of arbitrary length and with a skip distance which is not a multiple of 17.

Memory-to-memory floating-point operations are pipelined in BSP. The pipeline organization of the BSP consists of five functional stages. First, 16 operands are fetched from the memory modules, routed via the *input alignment network* into the AEs for processing, and routed via the *output alignment network* into the modules for storage. These steps are overlapped, as illustrated in Figure 6.13. Note that the input alignment and the output alignment are physically in one alignment network. The division shown here presents only a functional partition of the pipeline stages. In addition to the spatial parallelism exhibited by the 16 AEs and the pipeline operations of the fetch, align, and store stages, the vector operations in the AEs can overlap with the scalar processing in the scalar processor. This results in a powerful and flexible system suitable for processing both long and short vectors and isolated scalars as well.

Both alignment networks contain full crossbar switches as well as hardware for broadcasting data to several destinations and for resolving conflicts if several sources seek the same destination. This permits general-purpose interconnectivity between the arithmetic array and the memory-storage modules. It is the combined function of the memory-storage scheme and the alignment networks that supports the conflict-free capabilities of the parallel memory. The output alignment network is also used for interarithmetic element switching to support special functions such as the data compress and expand operations and the fast Fourier transform algorithm.

The *file memory* is a semiconductor secondary storage. It is loaded with the BSP task files from the system manager. These tasks are then queued for execution by the control processor. The file memory is the only peripheral device under the direct control of the BSP; all other peripheral devices are controlled by the system manager. Scratch files and output files produced during the execution of a BSP program are also stored in the file memory before being passed to the system manager for output to the user. The file memory is designed to have a high data-transfer rate, which greatly alleviates the I/O-bound problem.

In summary, concurrent computations in the BSP are made possible by four types of parallelism:

1. The parallel arithmetic performed by the 16 arithmetic elements
2. Memory fetches and stores, and the transmission of data between memory and arithmetic elements
3. Indexing, vector length, and loop-control computations in the parallel processor controller
4. The generation of linear vector operating descriptions by the scalar processor

The 16 AEs operate synchronously under the control of a single micro-sequence in SIMD mode. Each AE has only the most primitive operators hard-wired. The control word is 100 bits wide. Besides being a floating-point machine, the AE has substantial nonnumeric capability as well.

Floating-point add, subtract, and *multiply* each take two memory clocks. The use of two clocks balances the memory bandwidth with the AE bandwidth for triadic operations. A *triadic operation* is defined as having three operands and one result. The *floating-point divide* (requiring 1200 ns) is implemented by generating the reciprocol in a Newton-Raphson iteration. ROMs exist in each AE to give the first approximations for the divide and the square root iterations. The floating-point format is 48 bits long. It has 36 bits of a significant fraction and 10 bits of a binary exponent. This gives 11 decimal digits of precision. The AE has double-length accumulators and double-length registers in key places. This permits the direct implementation of double-precision operators in the hardware. The AE also permits software implementations of triple-precision arithmetic operations. It has been estimated that 20 to 40 megaflops could be achieved for a broad range of Fortran computations in the BSP.

6.2.4 The Prime Memory System

The BSP parallel memory consists of 17 memory modules, each with a 160-ns cycle time. Since we access 16 words per cycle, this provides a maximum effective 10-ns memory-cycle time. This is well balanced with the arithmetic elements which perform floating-point addition and multiplication at the rate of 320 ns/16 operations = 20 ns per operation, since each operation requires two arguments and temporary registers are provided in the arithmetic elements.

Only array accessing (including I/O) uses parallel memory, since programs and scalars are held in the control memory. Thus, perfect balance between parallel memory and floating-point arithmetic may be achieved for trial vector forms since three arguments and one result (four memory accesses) are required for two arithmetic operations. For longer vector forms, since temporaries reside in registers, only one operand is required per operation, so there is substantial parallel-memory bandwidth remaining for input and output of information.

The main innovation in the parallel memory of the BSP is its 17 modules. In past supercomputers it has been common to use a number of parallel-memory modules, but such memory systems are vulnerable to serious bandwidth degradation due to conflicts. For example, if 16 memories were used and a 16×16 array were stored with rows across the units and one column in each memory unit, then column access would be sequential.

The BSP offers a linear vector approach to parallelism. Memory addressing methods of achieving such parallelism are described in this section. The basic quantity susceptible to parallelism in the BSP is the *linear vector*. A linear vector is a vector whose elements are mapped into the main memory in a linear fashion. The linear-vector components are separated by a constant distance d. For example, in a Fortran columnwise mapping, columns have $d = 1$, rows have $d = n$, and forward diagonals have $d = n + 1$. The manipulation of linear vectors in a BSP utilizes both spatial and temporal parallelism.

A unique feature of the BSP is its conflict-free memory system which delivers a useful operand to each AE per each memory cycle. The distance between elements of a vector need not be unity. Therefore, DO loops may contain nonunity increments, or the program may access rows, columns, or diagonals of matrices without penalty. Supercomputer designers have elected either to use memories with severe access restrictions or have used expensive fast-memory parts to attain a degree of conflict-free access through memory-bandwidth overkill.

The hardware techniques used to ensure conflict-free access in the BSP include a prime number of memory ports, full crossbar switches between the memory ports and the AEs, and a special memory address generation which computes the proper addresses for a particular address pattern. This address pattern is the one used by orthodox serial computers. That is, each higher memory address refers to the "next" word in memory. With this pattern, the parallel memory is completely compatible with all the constructs of present programming languages. In particular, Fortran EQUIVALENCE, COMMON, and array-parameter passing can be implemented in the same way as on a conventional computer.

Consider a BSP-like machine with N AEs and M memory modules, where M is a prime number. The *modular number* μ specifies which memory unit a data element associated with a linear address a is stored. This module number can be computed by

$$\mu = a(\mathrm{mod}\ M) \tag{6.4}$$

The *address offset i* within the assigned memory module is calculated by

$$i = \left\lfloor \frac{a}{N} \right\rfloor \tag{6.5}$$

Figure 6.14 shows a 4-by-5 matrix mapped columnwise into the memory of a serial machine. For simplicity of illustration, assume $N = 6$ and $M = 7$ in the hypothetical machine. (The BSP has $N = 16$ and $M = 17$.) The module and offset calculations are shown in the illustration. The module number will remain constant for a cycle equal to the number of AEs, then it will increment by one value. The offset corresponds to repeated cycles of the same module with no value repeating in one cycle and the length of the cycle equal to the number of memory banks.

Example 6.2 As long as the number of AEs is less than or equal to the number of memory banks, the sequence of offset values will cause a different memory bank to be connected to each AE. Thus, each AE may receive or send a unique data object. The particular storage pattern produced in this six AE, seven memory bank system for the 4-by-5 example array is shown in Figure 6.14. The module and offset calculations for the second row of the array is explained below. The starting address is 1 and the skip distance is $d = 4$. We obtain the following module numbers and address offsets:

$$\mu = 1(\mathrm{mod}\ 7),\ 5(\mathrm{mod}\ 7),\ 9(\mathrm{mod}\ 7),\ 13(\mathrm{mod}\ 7),\ 17(\mathrm{mod}\ 7)$$
$$= 1, \qquad 5, \qquad 2, \qquad 6, \qquad 3 \tag{6.6}$$

The offsets within each memory module are obtained accordingly as

$$i = \lfloor \tfrac{1}{6} \rfloor,\ \lfloor \tfrac{5}{6} \rfloor,\ \lfloor \tfrac{9}{6} \rfloor,\ \lfloor \tfrac{13}{6} \rfloor,\ \lfloor \tfrac{17}{6} \rfloor$$
$$= 0,\ 0,\ 1,\ 2,\ 2 \tag{6.7}$$

The decision of using $M = 17$ memory modules for the $N = 16$ AEs will provide conflict-free array access to most common array partitions and yet have

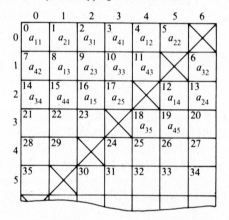

For example, if $M=7$, $N=6$, the 4×5 array is mapped

Array elements	a_{11}	a_{21}	a_{31}	a_{41}	a_{12}	a_{22}	a_{32}	a_{42}	a_{13}	a_{23}	a_{33}	a_{43}	a_{14}	a_{24}	a_{34}	a_{44}	a_{15}	a_{25}	a_{35}	a_{45}
Linear address: $a=$	0	1	2	3	4	5	6	7	8	9	10	11	12	13	14	15	16	17	18	19
memory module number $\mu=$	0	1	2	3	4	5	6	0	1	2	3	4	5	6	0	1	2	3	4	5
offset within module $i=$	0	0	0	0	0	0	1	1	1	1	1	1	2	2	2	2	2	2	3	3

Figure 6.14 The BSP memory mapping for a linearized vector of matrix elements. (Courtesy of Burroughs Corp. 1978.)

little redundant memory bandwidth, since only one memory module is unused per cycle. It is clear that conflict-free access to one-dimensional arrays is possible for any arithmetic sequence index pattern except every 17th element. For two-dimensional arrays with a skewing distance of four, conflict-free access is possible for rows, columns, diagonals, back-diagonals, and other common partitions, including arithmetic-sequence indexing of these partitions. The method can be extended to higher numbers of dimensions in a straightforward manner.

The unused memory cells are the result of having one less AE than there are memory banks. However, the example case is not a useful occurrence. For the real BSP with 16 AEs and 17 memory banks, division by 16 is much simpler and faster than division by 17. One then pays the penalty of supplying some extra memory to reach a given usable size. The above equations yield an AE-centrist vantage point. As long as the same set of equations is always applied to the data from the first time it comes in as I/O onward, then the storage pattern is completely invisible to the user. This applies to program dumps as well because the hardware always obeys the same rules.

Conflict does occur if the addresses are separated by an integer multiple of the number of memory banks. In this case, all the values one wants are in the same memory bank. For the BSP, this means that skip distances of 17, 34, 51, etc., should be avoided. In practice, 51 is a likely problem skip. This is because it is the skip of a forward diagonal of a matrix with column length 50. If conflict occurs in the BSP, the arithmetic is performed correctly, but at $\frac{1}{16}$ the normal speed. The system logs the occurrence of conflicts and their impact on the total running time. This information is given to the programmer for corrective action if the impact was significant.

6.2.5 The BSP Fortran Vectorizer

The BSP has a total of 64 vector instructions, which can be grouped in four types:

- Array expression statements
- Recurrence and reduction statements
- Expand, compress, random store, and fetch
- Parallel data transmissions between control memory and file memory

Array expression statements include indexing and evaluating righthand side array expressions ranking from monad to pentad (five righthand side operands), plus the assignment of the resulting values to parallel memory. The array operations are performed in an element-by-element fashion and allow scalars and array variables of one or two dimensions to be mixed on the righthand side. For example:

$$
\begin{aligned}
&\text{DO 5 I=1,30} \\
&\quad\text{DO 5 J=7,25} \\
&5\qquad\text{X(I,J)=(A(I,J+1)*0.5+B(I+1,J))} \\
&\qquad\qquad\text{*X(I,J+1)+C(J)}
\end{aligned}
\tag{6.8}
$$

would be compiled as a single vector form. This vector form can be regarded as a six-address instruction that contains the four array arithmetic-operation specifications and the assignment operation.

Recurrence vector instructions correspond to assignment statements with data-dependence loops. For example:

$$\text{DO 3 I=1,25}$$
$$3 \qquad Y(I)=F(I)*Y(I-1)+G(I) \tag{6.9}$$

has a righthand side that uses a result computed on the previous iteration. This recurrence produces an array of results while others lead to a scalar result. For example, a polynomial evaluation by Horner's rule leads to the following reduction:

$$P=C(0)$$
$$\text{DO 5 I=1,25}$$
$$5 \qquad P=C(I)+Y*P. \tag{6.10}$$

The third type of vector instructions involves various sparse-array operations. For example, in the case of a Fortran variable with subscripted subscripts, e.g., A(B(I)), no guarantee can be made concerning conflict-free access to the array A. In this case, the indexing hardware generates a sequence of addresses that allows access to one operand per clock. These are then processed in parallel in the arithmetic elements. Such accesses are called *random store* and *random fetch* vector forms.

Sparse arrays may be stored in memory in a compressed form and then expanded to their natural array positions using the input-alignment network. After processing, the results may be compressed for storage by the output-alignment network. These are called *compressed vector operand* and *compressed vector result* vector forms and use control-bit vectors that are packed in such a way that one 48-bit word is used for accesses to three 16-element vector slices.

The fourth class of vector instructions is used for I/O. Scalar and array assignments are made to control memory and parallel memory, depending on whether they are to be processed in the scalar processor unit or the parallel processor, respectively. However, it is occasionally necessary to transmit data back and forth between these memories. Transmissions to file memory are standard I/O types of operations. In Table 6.2, representative vector instructions in the BSP are listed. These four types of vector instructions comprise the entire array functions performed by the BSP.

In ordinary Fortran programs, it is possible to detect many array operations that can easily be mapped into BSP vector instructions. This is accomplished in the BSP compiler by a program called the Fortran vectorizer. We will not attempt a complete description of the vectorizer here, but we will sketch its organization, emphasizing a few key steps.

First, consider the generation of a program graph based on data dependencies. Each assignment statement is represented by a graph node. Directed arcs are drawn between nodes to indicate that one node is to be executed before another. The BSP does a detailed subscript analysis and builds a high-quality graph with few redundant arcs, thereby leading to more array operations and fewer recurrences.

Example 6.3 Consider the following program which explains the problem of scoping and data dependence:

$$
\begin{array}{ll}
& \text{DO 5 I=1,25} \\
& \quad \text{A(I)=3*B(I)} \\
1 & \\
& \qquad \text{DO 3 J=1,35} \\
3 & \\
& \qquad\quad \text{X(I,J)=A(I)*X(I,J-1)+C(J)} \\
5 & \quad \text{B(I)=2*B(I+1)}
\end{array}
\tag{6.11}
$$

A dependence graph for this problem is shown in Figure 6.15a, where nodes are numbered according to the statement label numbers of the program. Node 1 has an arc to node 3 because of the $A(I)$ dependence, and node 3 has a self-loop because $X(I, J - 1)$ is used one J iteration after it is generated. The crossed arc from node 1 to node 5 is an antidependence arc indicating that statement 1 must be executed before statement 5 to ensure that $B(I)$ on the righthand side of statement 1 is an initial value and not one computed by statement 5. Arcs from above denote initial values being supplied to each of the three statements: array B to statements 1 and 5, and array C to statement 3. The square brackets denote the scope of loop control for each of the DO statements.

Given a data-dependence graph, loop control can be distributed down to individual assignment statements or collections of statements with internal loops of data dependence. In our example, there is one loop (containing just one statement) and two individual assignment statements. After the distribution of loop control, the graph of Figure 6.15a may be redrawn, as shown in Figure 6.15b, which can easily be mapped into BSP vector instructions. Statements 1 and 5 go directly into array-expression vector forms since they are both dyads.

Besides vectorizing loops which do not contain branches or cyclic dependencies, the BSP vectorizer (executed by the system manager) can issue vector instructions even for BRANCH and IF statements as long as the branch paths are known to be under the control of bit vectors. The vectorizer also detects cyclic dependencies and converts them to vector recurrence statements. The following example shows the vectorization of a program containing an IF statement in a loop:

$$
\begin{array}{ll}
& \text{DO 1 I=1,92,} \\
& \quad \text{DO J=1,46} \\
1 & \qquad \text{IF(A(I,J).LT.0)B(I,J)=A(I,J)*3.5.}
\end{array}
\tag{6.12}
$$

This loop can be mapped into a single array-expression-statement vector form with bit-vector control that performs the parallel tests and makes the appropriate assignments to $B(I, J)$. By using loop distribution, many of the IFs found in ordinary Fortran programs can be transformed into vector operations that

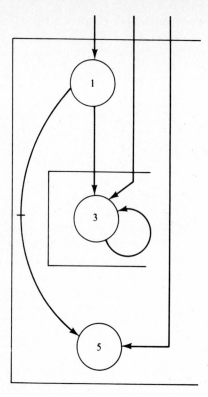

(a) A data dependence graph

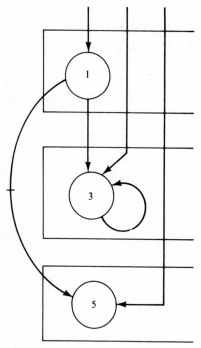

(b) Graph with distributed loop control

Figure 6.15 Dependence graph description of the Loop program in Eq. 6.11.

420

Table 6.2 Vector forms in the BSP

MONAD	It accepts one vector set operand, does one monadic operation on it, and produces one vector set result.	$Z \leftarrow op\ A$
DYAD	It accepts two vector set operands, does one operation on them, and produces one vector set result.	$Z \leftarrow A\ op\ B$
VSDYAD	It is similar to the DYAD except operand B is a scalar.	$Z \leftarrow A\ op\ B$
EXTENDED DYAD	It accepts two vector set operands, does one operation, and produces two vector set results.	$(Z1, Z2) \leftarrow A\ op\ B$
DOUBLE PRECISION DYAD	It accepts four vector set operands (i.e., two double-precision operands), performs one operation, and produces two vector set results.	$(Z1, Z2) \leftarrow (A1, A2)\ op\ (B1, B2)$
DUAL-DYAD	It accepts four vector set operands, does two operations, and produces two vector set results.	$Z \leftarrow A\ op_1\ B \quad Y \leftarrow C\ op_2 D$
TRIAD	It accepts three vector set operands, does two operations, and produces one vector set result.	$Z \leftarrow (A\ op_1\ B)\ op_2\ C$
TETRADI	It accepts four set operands, does three operations, and produces one vector set result.	$Z \leftarrow ((A\ op_1\ B)\ op_2\ C)\ op_3\ D$
TETRAD2	It is similar to the TETRADI except for the order of operations.	$Z \leftarrow (A\ op_1\ B)\ op_2\ (C\ op_3\ D)$
PENTADI	It accepts five vector set operands, does four operations, and produces one vector set result.	$Z \leftarrow (((A\ op_1\ B)\ op_2\ C)\ op_3\ D)\ op_4\ E$
PENTAD2	It is similar to the PENTADI except for the order of operations.	$Z \leftarrow ((A\ op_1\ B)\ op_2\ (C\ op_3\ D))\ op_4\ E$
PENTAD3	It is similar to the PENTADI except for the order of operations.	$Z \leftarrow ((A\ op_1\ B)\ op_2\ C)\ op_3\ (D\ op_4\ E)$
AMTM	It is similar to the MONAD and is used to transmit from parallel memory to control memory.	$Z \leftarrow op\ A$
TMAM	It accepts 6 vector set operands from control memory to transmit to parallel memory.	$Z \leftarrow A1(0, 0),\ A2(0, 0),$ $A3(0, 0),\ A4(0, 0),$ $A5(0, 0),\ A6(0, 0)$
COMPRESS	It accepts a vector set operand, compresses it under a bit vector operand control, and produces a vector set result.	$X \leftarrow A, BVO$
EXPAND	It accepts a vector operand, expands it under a bit vector control, and produces a vector set result.	$X \leftarrow V, BVO$

Table 6.2 (*Cont.*)

MERGE	It is the same as the EXPAND except that the vector set result elements corresponding to a zero bit in BV are not changed in the parallel memory.	$X \leftarrow V, BVO$
RANDOM FETCH	It performs the operation $Z(j, k) \leftarrow U(I(j, k))$, where U is a vector and I is an index vector set.	
RANDOM STORE	It performs the operation $X(I(j, k)) \leftarrow A(j, k)$, where X is a vector and I is an index vector set.	
REDUCTION	It accepts one vector set operand and produces one vector result given by $X(i) \leftarrow A(i, 0) \text{ op } A(i, 1) \text{ op } A(i, 2) \text{ op } A(i, 3) \dots A(i, L)$, where op must be a commutative and associative operator.	
DOUBLE PRECISION REDUCTION	It accepts two vector set operands (one double-precision vector set) and produces two vector results (one d.p. vector) given by $(X_1(i), X_2(i)) \leftarrow (A_1(i, 0), A_2(i, 0)) \text{ op } (A_1(i, 1), A_2(i, 1)) \text{ op} \dots (A_1(i, L), A_2(i, L))$, where op must be a commutative and associative operator.	
GENERALIZED DOT PRODUCT	It accepts two vector set operands and produces one vector result given by $X(i) \leftarrow \{A(i, 0) \text{ op}_2 B(i, 0)\} \text{ op}_1 \{A(i, 1) \text{ op}_2 B(i, 1)\}$ $\text{op}_1 \dots \{A(i, L) \text{ op}_2 B(i, L)\}$, where op_1 must be a commutative and associative operator.	
RECURRENCE-1L	It accepts two vector set operands and produces one vector result given by $X(i) \leftarrow (\{\dots\{(B(i, 0) \text{ op}_1 A(i, 1)) \text{ op}_2 B(i, 1)\} \text{ op}_1 \dots\} \text{ op}_1 A(1, L)) \text{ op}_2 B(i, L)$ where op_2 can be ADD or IOR and op_1 can be MULT or AND.	
PARTIAL REDUCTION	It accepts one vector set operand and produces one vector set result given by $Z(i, j) \leftarrow Z(i, j - 1) \text{ op } A(i, j)$, where op must be a commutative and associative operator.	
RECURRENCE-1A	It accepts two vector set operands and produces one vector set result given by $Z(i, j) \leftarrow \{Z(i, j - 1) \text{ op}_1 A(i, j)\} \text{ op}_2 B(i, j)$, where op_1 can be MULT or AND and op_2 can be ADD or IOR.	

allow substantial speedups on the BSP. Of course, there is also a residual set of IFs that must be compiled as serial code. Fortran language extensions have also been made in the BSP to facilitate vector processing.

6.3 THE MASSIVELY PARALLEL PROCESSOR

A large-scale SIMD array processor has been developed for processing satellite imagery at the NASA Goddard Space Flight Center. The computer has been named *massively parallel processor* (MPP) because of the $128 \times 128 = 16,384$ microprocessors that can be used in parallel. The MPP can perform bit-slice arithmetic computations over variable-length operands. The MPP has a microprogrammable control unit which can be used to define a quite flexible instruction set for vector, scalar, and I/O operations. The MPP system is constructed entirely with solid-state circuits, using microprocessor chips and bipolar RAMs.

6.3.1 The MPP System Architecture

In 1979, NASA Goddard awarded a contract to Goodyear Aerospace to construct a massively parallel processor for image-processing applications. The major hardware components in MPP are shown in Figure 6.16. The *array unit* operates

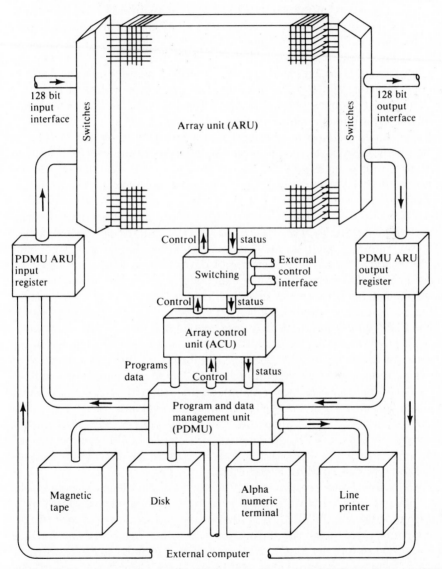

Figure 6.16 The system architecture of the MPP system. (Courtesy of *IEEE Trans. Computers*, Batcher, 1980.)

with SIMD mode on a two-dimensional array of 128 × 128 PEs. Each PE is associated with a 1024-bit random-access memory. Parity is included to detect memory faults. Each PE is a bit-slice microprocessor connected to its nearest neighbors. The programmer can connect opposite array edges or leave them open so that the array topology can change from a plane to a horizontal cylinder, a vertical cylinder, or a torus. This feature reduces routing time significantly in a number of imaging applications.

For improved maintainability, the array has four redundant columns of PEs. The physical structure of the PE array is 132 columns by 128 rows. Hardware faults are masked out with circuitry to bypass a faulty column and leave a logical array structure of 128 × 128. Arithmetic in each PE is performed in bit serial fashion using a serial-by-bit adder and a shift register to recirculate operands through the adder. This increases the speed of multiplication, division, and floating-point operations significantly. The PE array has a cycle time of 100 ns. The *array control unit* (ACU) is microprogrammable. It supervises the PE array processing, performs scalar arithmetic, and shifts data across the PE array.

The *program and data management unit* is a back-end minicomputer. It manages data flow in the array, loads programs into the controller, executes system-test and diagnostic routines, and provides program-development facilities. A Digital Equipment PDP-11/34 minicomputer is used with interfaces to the array and the MPP external computer interface. Peripherals include a magnetic tape drive (9-track, 800/1600 BPI), two 67-megabyte disks, a line printer, and an alphanumeric terminal with CRT display. The I/O interface can reformat the data so that images are transferred in and out of the array in specific formats. These registers are built with the *multidimensional access* memories developed earlier in the STARAN computer. The MDA memory provides data buffering as well as performing some data manipulations between the PE array, the database-management machine, and the external host computer.

The MPP system has more than one operational mode. In the *stand-alone* mode, all program development, execution, test, and debug is done within the MPP system and controlled by operator commands on the user terminal. The array can transfer data in and out through the disks and tape units or through the 128-bit MPP interfaces. In the *on-line* mode, the external computer can enter array data, constants, programs and job requests. It will also receive the output data and status information about the system and the program. Data can be transferred between the MPP and the external computer at 6M bytes per second. In the *high-speed data* mode, data is transferred through the 128-bit external interfaces at a rate of 320M bytes per second.

The PEs are bit-slice processors for processing arbitrary-length operands. The array clock rate is 10 MHz. With 16,384 PEs operating in parallel, the array has a very high processing speed (Table 6.3). Despite the bit-slice nature of each PE, the floating-point speeds compare favorably with other fast number-crunching machines. Figure 6.17 shows the array unit, which includes the PE array, the associated memory, the control logic, and I/O registers. The PE array performs all logic, routing, and arithmetic operations. The *Sum-OR* module provides a zero test of any bit plane. Control signals from the array controller are routed to all

Table 6.3 Speed of typical operations in MPP

	Peak speed (mops*)
Addition of arrays	
8-bit integers (9-bit sum)	6553
12-bit integers (13-bit sum)	4428
32-bit floating-point numbers	430
Multiplication of arrays (element-by-element)	
8-bit integers (16-bit product)	1861
12-bit integers (24-bit product)	910
32-bit floating-point numbers	216
Multiplication of array by scalar	
8-bit integers (16-bit product)	2340
12-bit integers (24-bit product)	1260
32-bit floating-point numbers	373

* Million operations per second (mops)

PEs by the *fan-out* module. The *corner-point* module selects the 16 corner elements from the array and routes them to the controller. The I/O registers transfer array data to and from the 128-bit I/O interfaces, the database machine, and the host computer. Special hardware features of the array unit are summarized below:

1. Random-access memory of 1024 bits per PE
2. Parity on all array-processor memory
3. Extra four columns of PEs to allow on-line repairing
4. Program-controlled edge interconnections
5. Hardware array resolver to isolate array errors
6. A buffer memory with corner-turning capability

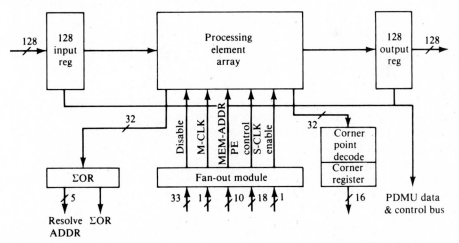

Figure 6.17 The PE array and supporting devices of the array unit. (Courtesy of Goodyear Aerospace Corp.)

Each PE in the array communicates with its nearest neighbor up, down, right, and left—the same routing topology used in the Illiac-IV. The ability to access data in different directions can be used to reorient the arrays between the bit-plane format of the array and the pixel format of the image. The edges of the array can be left open to have a row of zeros enter from the left edge and move to the right or to have the opposite edges wrap around. Since cases have been found where open edges were preferred and other cases have been found where connected edges were preferred, it was decided to make edge-connectivity a programmable function.

A topology register in the array control unit defines the connections between opposite edges of the PE array. The top and bottom edges can either be connected or left open. The connectivity between the left and right edges has four states: *open* (no connection), *cylindrical* (connect the left PE of each row to the right PE of the same row), *open spiral* (for $1 \leq n \leq 127$, the left PE of row n is connected to the right PE of row $n - 1$), and *closed spiral* (like the open spiral, but also connects the left PE of row 0 to the right PE of row 127). The spiral modes connect the 16,384 PEs together in a single linear-circuit list.

The PEs in the array are implemented with VLSI chips. Eight PEs are arranged in a 2×4 subarray on a single chip. The PE array is divided into 33 groups, with each group containing 128 rows and 4 columns of PEs. Each group has an independent group-disable control line from the array controller. When a group is disabled, all its outputs are disabled and the groups on either side of it are joined together with 128 bypass gates in the routing network.

6.3.2 Processing Array, Memory, and Control

Each PE has six 1-bit flags (A, B, C, G, P, and S), a shift register with a programmable length, a random-access memory, a data bus (D), a full adder, and some combination logic (Figure 6.18). The P register is used for logic and routing operations. A logic operation combines the state of the P register and the state of the data bus (D) to form the new state of the P register. All 16 boolean functions of the two variables P and D are implementable. A routing operation shifts the state of the P register into the P register of a neighboring PE (up, down, right, or left). The G register can hold a mask bit that controls the activity of the PE. The data-bus states of all 16,384 enabled PEs are combined in a tree or inclusive-OR elements. The output of this tree is fed to the ACU and used in certain operations such as finding the maximum or minimum value of an array in the array unit.

The full adder, shift register, and registers A, B, and C are used for bit serial arithmetic operations. To add two operands, the bits of one operand are sequentially fed into the A register, least-significant-bit first; corresponding bits of the other operand are fed into the P register. The full adder adds the bits in A and P to the carry bits in the C register to form the sum and carry bits. Each carry bit is stored in C to be added in the next cycle, and each sum bit is stored in the B register. The sum formed in B can be stored in the random-access memory and/or in the shift register. Two's complement subtaction is performed.

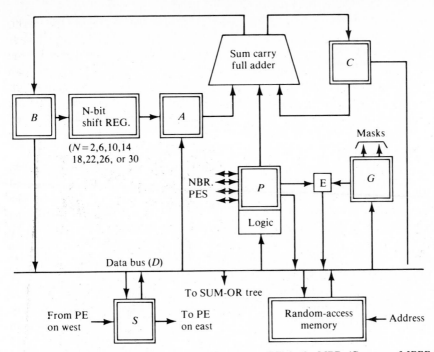

Figure 6.18 Functional structure of a processing element (PE) in the MPP. (Courtesy of *IEEE Trans. Computers*, Batcher, September 1980.)

Multiplication in the MPP is a series of addition steps where the partial product is recirculated through the shift registers A and B. Appropriate multiples of the multiplicand are formed in P and added to the partial product as it recirculates. Division in the MPP is performed with a nonrestoring division algorithm. The partial dividend is recirculated through the shift register and registers A and B while the divisor or its complement is formed in P and added to it. The steps in floating-point addition include comparing exponents, placing the fraction of the operand with the least exponent in the shift register, shifting to align the fraction with the other fraction, storing the sum of the fractions in the shift register and normalizing it. Floating-point multiplication includes the multiplication of the fractions, the normalization of the product, and the addition of the exponents.

The S register is used to input and output array data. While the PEs are processing data in the random-access memories, successive columns of input data can be shifted from the left into the array via the S registers. Although S registers in the entire plane are loaded with data, the data plane can be dumped into the random-access memories by interrupting the array processing in only one cycle time. Planes of data can move from the memory elements to the S registers and then be shifted from left to right column by column. Up to 160 megabytes/s can be transferred through the array I/O ports. Processing is interrupted for only 100 ns for each bit plane of 16,384 bits to be transferred.

The random-access memory stores up to 1024 bits per PE. Standard RAM chips are available to expand the memory planes. Parity checking is used to detect memory faults. A parity bit is added to the eight data bits of each 2×4 subarray of PEs. Parity bits are generated and stored for each memory-write cycle and checked when the memories are read. A parity error sets an error flip-flop associated with each 2×4 subarray. A tree of logic elements gives the array controller an inclusive-OR of all error flip-flops. By operating the group-disable control lines, the controller can locate the group containing the error and disable it.

Standard 4×1024 RAM chips are used for the PE memories. As shown in Figure 6.19, 2×4 subarrays of PEs are packaged on a custom VLSI CMOS-SOS chip. The VLSI chip also contains the parity tree and the bypass gates for the subarray. Each printed circuit board contains 192 PEs in an 8×24 array. Sixteen boards make up an array slice of 128×24 PEs. Five array slices (80 boards) make up the bulk of the entire PE array. The remaining 12 PE columns are packaged on 16 I/O-processor boards, which also contain the topology switches, the I/O switches, and the I/O interface registers. The 96 boards of the array are packaged in one cabinet with forced-air cooling.

Like the control unit of other array processors, the array controller of the MPP performs scalar arithmetic and controls the operation of the PEs. It has three sections that can operate in parallel, as depicted in Figure 6.20. The *PE*

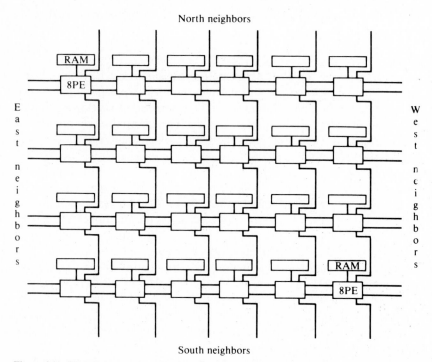

Figure 6.19 The interconnection of VLSI PE and RAM chips in the MPP array. (Courtesy of Goodyear Aerospace Corp. 1980.)

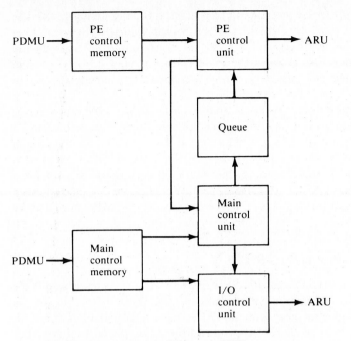

Figure 6.20 The control unit of the PE array in MPP.

control performs all array arithmetic in the application program. The *I/O control* manages the flow of data in and out of the array. The *main control* performs all scalar arithmetic of the application program. This arrangement allows array arithmetic, scalar arithmetic, and input-output to take place concurrently.

The PE control generates all array control signals except those associated with the I/O. It contains a 64-bit common register to hold scalars and eight 16-bit index registers to hold the addresses of bit planes in the PE memory elements to count loop executions and to hold the index of a bit in the common register. The PE control reads 64-bit-wide microinstructions from the PE control memory. Most instructions are read and executed in 100 ns. One instruction can perform several PE operations, manipulate any number of index registers, and branch conditionally. This reduces the overhead significantly so that PE processing power is not wasted.

The PE control memory contains a number of system routines and user-written routines to operate on arrays of data in the array. The routines include both array-to-array and scalar-to-array arithmetic operations. A queue between the PE control and the main control queues up to seven calls to the PE control routines. Each call contains up to eight initial index-register values and up to 64 bits of scalar information. Some routines extract scalar information from the array (such as a maximum value) and return it to the main control.

The I/O control shifts the S registers in the array, manages the flow of information in and out of the array ports, and interrupts PE control momentarily to transfer data between the S registers and buffer areas in the PE memory elements. Once initiated by the main control, the I/O control can chain through a number of I/O commands. The main control is a fast scalar processor which reads and executes the application program in the main control memory. It performs all scalar arithmetic itself and places all array arithmetic operations on the PE control call queue.

The MPP being delivered to NASA uses a DEC VAX-11/780 computer as the host. The interface to the host has two links: a high-speed data link and a control link. The *high-speed data link* connects the I/O interface registers of the MPP to a DR-780 high-speed user interface of the VAX-11/780. Data can be transferred at the rate of 6 megabytes/s. The *control link* is the standard DECNET link between a PDP-11 and a VAX-11/780. The DECNET hardware and software allow the VAX users to transfer their program requests to the MPP from remote stations.

6.3.3 Image Processing on the MPP

In this section, some proposed image processing applications are described for the MPP. The intent is to familiarize our readers with the MPP instruction set, the data access in the staging memory, and parallel processing potentials of the MPP system. The speed power of the MPP promises the development of new image processing techniques, such as for real-time time-varying scene analysis. We shall restrict ourselves to the computation aspects of image processing rather than the statistical or syntactic theories behind image processing and pattern recognition.

The MPP organization described in previous sections can be functionally simplified to consist of only three major components, as shown in Figure 6.21. The PE array and the staging memory are connected by a high-speed I/O bus

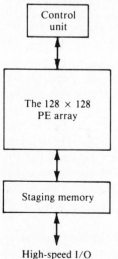

High-speed I/O   **Figure 6.21 The staging memory concept in the MPP.**

capable of transferring 320M bytes/s. The staging memory acts as a data buffer between the parallel and the outside world. The staging memory can accept data from conventional and special-purpose peripherals at rates up to 320M bytes/s. Its internal controller allows it to pack and reformat data so that the parallel array can more efficiently process them.

The staging memory can randomly address any individual datum but, for any given address, it fetches a block of 16K data elements and sends it to the array, where each microprocessor memory receives one datum. The exact configuration of the block of data fetched by the staging memory is under program control. For example, if k is the specific address, data are fetched from the following addresses:

$$k, \qquad k + n, \qquad k + 2n, \qquad \ldots k + 127n,$$

$$k + m, \quad k + n + m, \quad k + 2n + m, \quad \ldots k + 127n + m,$$

$$\vdots \qquad \vdots \qquad \vdots \qquad \vdots$$

$$k + 127m, \; k + n + 127m, \; k + 2n + 127m, \ldots k + 127n + 127m$$

The parameters n and m as well as the address k can be specified by the programmer. Figure 6.22 illustrates the accessing of a block of 128×128 pixels, starting at (x, y), from a 512×512 image stored in the staging memory.

Instruction set of the MPP The instruction set for the MPP can be divided into three subsets: sequential, parallel, and interface. The sequential instructions are similar to those of any other sequential computer. They consist of *load, store, add, subtract, compare, branch, logical operations*, etc. Executed by the sequential controller alone, these instructions are used primarily to direct program flow and to calculate individual parameters and constants that will be broadcast to the parallel array.

The parallel instructions, also similar to conventional sequential instruction sets, consist of *load, store, add, subtract, compare*, and *logical operations*, but not *branch*. The parallel instructions are stored in the sequential controller's memory

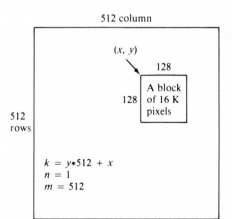

Figure 6.22 Parallel access to the staging memory. (Courtesy of *IEEE* Computer, Potter, January 1983.)

intermingled with the other instructions. When the sequential controller detects a parallel instruction, it passes it via the interface registers to the parallel array, where it is executed by all 16K processors simultaneously. This fundamental form of parallelism provides the incredible computing power of the MPP.

The MPP, like most SIMD processors, has a set of interface instructions that allows the movement of data between the sequential and parallel portions. Constants and parameters can be broadcast to each of the parallel processors by the sequential controller with a special version of the parallel instructions. But the inverse operation—moving parallel results to the sequential portion—can be more complex. The key is the ability to select a unique processor of the 16K to be active.

Each of the PEs is assigned a unique identification number. The STEP instruction selects the lowest-numbered PE to be active and thus enables it to communicate with the sequential controller. The STEP instruction can be combined with a previously executed comparison or other logical operation so that only those PEs satisfying the logical conditions are involved in the operation.

The STEP instruction can also be combined with other instructions to sequence through specified subsets of PEs. This allows the data from each PE to be processed in turn by the sequential controller and by the PE array that is under program control. Described below are several planned image processing applications of the MPP. Performance results on the MPP were not available at the time this book was produced.

Feature extraction The first step in many image-pattern recognition problems is to extract features such as edges, regions, and texture measurements on which to base classifications. Two-dimensional or areal functions such as two-dimensional convolution and correlation are frequently used to extract this information. For these situations, the 16K processors are interconnected into a grid in which each processor can communicate with its four neighbors, as illustrated in Figure 6.23. Using these interconnections, feature extraction functions can be efficiently executed.

Pattern classification The statistical classification of pixels based on multispectral data is quite straightforward in an SIMD computer like the MPP. Data for 16K pixels are input to the parallel array so that all the multispectral data associated with one pixel are stored in the memory of one processor, as illustrated in Figure 6.24. One iteration of the classification algorithm then uses the 16K classification results to be calculated.

Syntactic pattern analysis In addition to feature extraction, the parallel array can be used very effectively to guide linguistic techniques. In general, these techniques consist of a large number of production or reduction rules that must be selectively applied. If one rule is stored in each PE, then 16K rules can be updated and searched in parallel without being ordered.

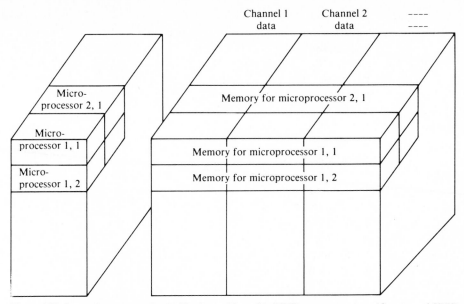

Figure 6.23 Image data storage in the bit-plane addressable MPP memory system. (Courtesy of *IEEE Computer*, Potter, January 1983.)

In the MPP and other SIMD processors, a different rule can be assigned to each PE. Consequently, when a feature is found, all of the rules can be considered in parallel to determine those that apply; the STEP instruction can then be used to sequence through the rules that require processing. Since the addition and deletion of rules in the array memory is a simple operation requiring no sorting, data packing, or garbage collection, this approach will be extremely useful in situations where the grammar is undergoing modification.

Real-time scene analysis The existence of new special-purpose image processing hardware like the MPP allows the development of new techniques for scene analysis. Since imagery can be processed in real time by these machines, the rich information content of time-varying imagery can be trapped for scene analysis. Real-time interaction with the three-dimensional world scene itself means that scene analysis need no longer involve the difficult task of producing detailed exact models of the real world from a single frame of imagery.

Capable of over 6 billion operations per second, the MPP is useful for pattern-recognition tasks such as image processing where large numbers of values must be calculated. The parallel-search aspect of SIMD computers promises to be extremely useful in more complex algorithm areas, too, such as linguistic scene analysis, where large grammars are used. The speed of the MPP not only makes real-time scene analysis possible, but also offers the prospect of real-time time-varying scene analysis with an interactive moving sensor.

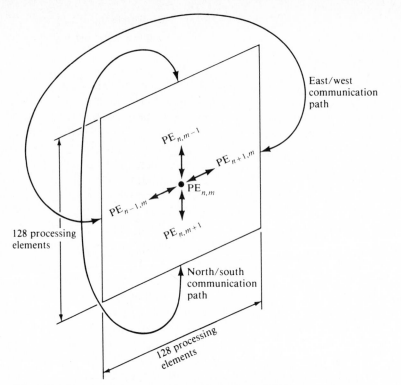

Figure 6.24 The PE-grid and end-around connection in the MPP.

6.4 PERFORMANCE ENHANCEMENT METHODS

The effectiveness of an SIMD array processor depends on the computation types, the interconnection network, the data storage schemes, the vectorization of programs, the language features, and the compiling techniques. Several performance enhancement methods are introduced below for array processors. The performance of SIMD array processors is then evaluated from the viewpoint of system throughput versus work-load distributions. Finally, we study multiple-SIMD computer organizations and related design issues.

6.4.1 Parallel Memory Allocation

An array processor is effective only for those computations that can be vectorized. The program must try to take advantage of the spatial parallelism exhibited by multiple PEs. A high-speed interconnection network is needed to route data among the PEs quickly. Furthermore, vector operands to be used by the PE must be properly stored in the data memories to allow for parallel fetch of certain specific array patterns. Array processors have been considered special-purpose computers in the sense that only matrix computations of fixed sizes can fully explore the hardware parallelism. In order to increase application flexibility and enhance performance, efficient memory allocation schemes have been sought by many researchers and users of SIMD machines.

Consider a parallel memory system of M memory modules. Each of the M memories contains K words and has its own index register. The desirability of fetching matrix elements in rows, columns, or diagonals is clear from most matrix operations. While many computations on arrays may be formulated as row and column operations, operations on squares and blocks (submatrices) are often performed. Matrix multiplication by partitioning is an obvious example. Square (or nonsquare) submatrices become very important when an array is much larger or smaller than the number of available memory modules. One would like to have a parallel memory with as fine a resolution as possible. For example, an M module memory system can be used to access $M \times M$ arrays one row at a time or one $\sqrt{M} \times \sqrt{M}$ block at a time. In the latter case, the subarray $\sqrt{M} \times \sqrt{M}$ should be fetched in one memory cycle. Large arrays of dimension $p\sqrt{M} \times q\sqrt{M}$ can also be handled in parallel steps if p and q are integers. If p and q are not integers, then some fetches yield less than M useful array elements.

Consider the storage of a two-dimensional array of, at most, $M \cdot K$ elements. The dimensions of the original array are $P \times Q$, such that $P > M$ and $Q > K$. The standard arrangement of matrix elements is called a *matrix space*, as illustrated in Figure 6.25. We are interested in fetching M words in parallel, one word from each memory. We call any vector of M words (not necessarily one from each memory) an M vector. Among all possible M vectors, we want to determine those that can be accessed in a single memory cycle. The total number of possible M vectors equals $[MK/M]$. Any particular mapping of the MK elements into the M memory modules will allow the access of any one of K^M different M vectors in a single memory cycle. Thus, the ratio of all possible M vectors to those one can access with a particular allocation scheme is approximated below using Stirling's formula:

$$\begin{bmatrix} MK \\ M \end{bmatrix} \cdot K^M \cong \sqrt{\frac{1}{2\pi M}} \cdot e^M \tag{6.13}$$

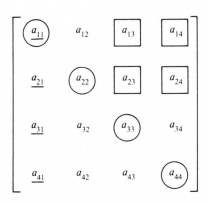

Figure 6.25 Matrix space: column 1 is underlined, a square block is in squares, and the main diagonal is circled.

This ratio means that there is no guarantee we will find one or a limited number of allocation schemes that will allow us to access an arbitrary M vector in a single memory cycle.

Define d as the distance (mod M) measured in columns between adjacent elements of a subarray in the $P \times Q$ space. For example, the elements of a row or of a diagonal have $d = 1$, the elements of a column have $d = 0$, and the even-subscripted elements of a row or diagonal have $d = 2$. If $Q \leq M$, stored arrays can be mapped into memory modules by placing the adjacent elements of rows in the same relative locations of adjacent memory modules (i.e., rows across the memory). If $Q > M$, the above mapping can be performed on partitions of Q.

Furthermore, we define s, the *skewing degree* of a storage scheme, as the distance measured in columns that each row has been shifted with respect to the row above it. All shifting must be done mod M. One value of s is used for an entire array. Figure 6.26 illustrates the storage of an array with skewing degrees $s = 0$ and $s = 1$.

The elements of an M vector fetched in one memory cycle will have the same order they had in matrix space if, and only if, $1 = d + (j - 1)s(\text{mod } M)$ for all $i \leq j$, where i and j are the subsequent rows in $P \times Q$ space from which elements are fetched. Let $j - i = r$. Note that $d + r \times s(\text{mod } M)$ is the displacement between successive elements to be fetched. If this is not one, the elements are not in successive memory modules. For each stored M vector, we define an ordered set as

$$S = \{k_i | 1 \leq k_i \leq M, 1 \leq i \leq M\} \tag{6.14}$$

The ith element of the M vector is stored in memory module k_i. Let $s^j = d + r \times s(\text{mod } M)$ be the displacement between successive M-vector elements. If an M vector is relatively prime to s', then we can access the M vector in one memory cycle. It follows that if some stored M vector is not relatively prime to g, then M/g elements may be accessed at once and g fetches are required to complete the access of that vector.

If we restrict ourselves to $M = 2^L$ for some integer L, we can access rows and diagonals with $s = 0$ or rows and columns with $s = 1$. However, if $s = 1$ and $d = 1$ for diagonals and $d + s = 2$, we cannot access diagonals (Figure 6.25) in parallel. In fact, for any s, s or $s + 1$ must be even. This proves the impossibility of fetching rows, columns, and diagonals using one storage scheme when M is an even integer.

With the following nonuniform skewing scheme, it is possible to access rows, columns, and some square blocks. Suppose we choose $t = \sqrt{M} + \delta_i(\text{mod } M)$, where $\delta_i = 1$ if row index $i = k\sqrt{M} + 1$ for $k \geq 1$, and $\delta_i = 0$ otherwise. Within a strip of width $\sqrt{M}$, we can clearly access a $\sqrt{M} \times \sqrt{M}$ block in one cycle. Across these strip boundaries, conflicts arise in fetching square blocks. However, due to the additional skewing by one at strip boundaries, it is possible to access columns because t is relatively prime to M, as shown in Figure 6.26. Sometimes an access to rows or columns of a square block may be desired. Then blocks may be regarded as one memory access and the above method can be applied. This

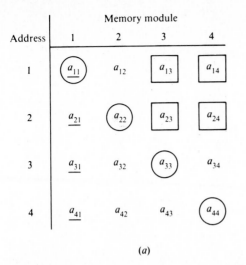

(a)

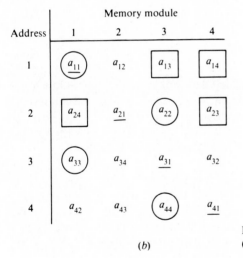

(b)

Figure 6.26 A stored array with skewing degree
(a) $S = 0$ and (b) $S = 1$.

strategy may be useful in parallel memories in which each memory module produces several processor words as one superword.

In some programs, not every element of a row or column is to be accessed at each step. Instead, some index set is used to produce a partition. Let us restrict such index sets to arithmetic sequences with c being the difference between successive elements of the arithmetic sequence. Then to fetch indexed rows, for example, we have $r = 0$ and $d = c$. By the accessibility condition, c must be relatively prime to M. The only safe value for M in this case is a prime number. Consider several values of $M = 2^{2L} + 1$, such as $M = 17$ and $M = 257$, which are both prime, and $M = 65$, which is not. Thus 17, 67 (the next prime greater than 65), or 257 may be considered as good candidates for the selection of M. The number 127 is

Table 6.4 A skewed memory allocation for the prime memory

Module Address	M_0	M_1	M_2	M_3	M_4
0	00	10	20	30	x
1	50	60	70	x	40
2	21	31	x	01	11
3	71	x	41	51	61
4	x	02	12	22	32
5	42	52	62	72	x
6	13	23	33	x	03
7	63	73	x	43	53
8	34	x	04	14	24
9	x	44	54	64	74
10	05	15	25	35	x
11	55	65	75	x	45
12	26	36	x	06	16
13	76	x	46	56	66
14	x	07	17	27	37
15	47	57	67	77	x

also interesting, being an odd power of two minus one and not much larger than a perfect square.

A *storage scheme* is a set of rules which determines the module number and address within that module where a given array element is stored. We will restrict our attention to two-dimensional arrays. However, generalization of these storage schemes is simple for higher-dimensioned arrays. Described below is the storage scheme successfully developed by Lawrie and Vora (1982) for the BSP.

Example 6.4 Table 6.4 shows an 8 × 8 array stored in five memory modules using column major storage. Any five consecutive elements of a row, column, diagonal, etc., lie in separate modules and thus can be accessed in parallel without conflict. For example, the second through sixth elements of the first row are stored in module numbers 3, 1, 4, 2, 0, and at addresses 2, 4, 6, 8, 10, respectively.

Let M be the number of memory modules and P be the number of processors, where we assume $P < M$ and M is prime. The two storage equations $f(i, j)$ and $g(i, j)$ determine the module number and address, respectively, of element (i, j) of the array. In our case we have the following equations:

$$f(i, j) = [j \times I + i + \text{base}] \bmod M \tag{6.15}$$

$$g(i, j) = \frac{[j \times I + i + \text{base}]}{P} \tag{6.16}$$

where we assume the array is dimensioned (I, J), *base* is the base address of the array, and the number of processors P is the greatest power of two less than M.

Notice that these equations require a mod M operation where M is a prime number. They also require an integer divide by P operation. However, P is a power of two, which makes this divide easily implementable. This simplification is made possible by the "holes" shown in the table.

The number of holes in each row of the memory is equal to $M - P$ in general. For example, if $M = 37$ and $P = 32$, then $\frac{5}{37}$ of the memory is wasted. These holes could be filled with other data, e.g., scalar data, but a cleaner solution is available at the expense of an increase in the complexity of the indexing equations.

A *P vector* is defined as a set of elements of the array formed by the linear subscript equations:

$$V(a, b, c, e) = \{A(i, j): i = ax + b, j = cx + e, 0 \leq x < P \leq M\} \quad (6.17)$$

where the array is dimensioned $A(I, J)$. Thus, if $a = b = 0$ and $c = e = 1$, then the P vector ($P = 5$) is the second through sixth elements of the first row of A: $A(0, 1), A(0, 2), \ldots, A(0, 5)$. If $a = c = 2$ and $b = e = 0$, then the P vector ($P = 4$) is every other element of the main diagonal of $A(0, 0), A(2, 2), \ldots, A(6, 6)$. Note that the elements of the P vector are ordered with index x.

The index equation is defined below for the P vector V. We define $\alpha(x)$ to be the address in module $\mu(x)$ of the xth element of the P vector. Thus, combining Eqs. 6.15 through 6.17, we obtain

$$\mu(x) = f(ax + b, cx + e)$$
$$= [(cx + e) * I + (ax + b) + base] \bmod M$$
$$= [rx + B] \bmod M \quad (6.18)$$

where $r = a + cI$ and $B = b + eI + base$. We define r to be the *order* of the P vector and B to be the *base* address. Next, we define

$$\alpha(x) = g(ax + b, cx + e)$$
$$= \frac{[(cx + e) * I + (ax + b) + base]}{P}$$
$$= \frac{[rx + B]}{P} \quad (6.19)$$

It is easy to show that if r is relatively prime to the number of memory modules, then access to the P vector can be made without memory conflict.

Since it is most convenient to generate the address $\alpha(x)$ in memory $\mu(x)$, we solve for x in terms of μ and get

$$x(\mu) = [(\mu - B)r'] \bmod M \quad (6.20)$$

where $r \times r' = 1 \bmod M$. Substituting this into Eq. 6.19, we get

$$\alpha(\mu) = \frac{\{(a + Ic)[(\mu - B)r' \bmod M] + b + eI + base\}}{P}$$
$$= \frac{\{r[(\mu - B)r' \bmod M] + B\}}{P} \quad (6.21)$$

Example 6.5 Consider the P vector $V(0, 0, 1, 1)$, i.e., the second through sixth elements of the first row of $A(8 \times 8)$. We have $B = 8$ and $d = 8$; thus

$$\mu(x) = [(x) \times 8 + 8] \bmod 5$$

$$\alpha(x) = \frac{[(x) \times 8 + 8]}{4}$$

Since $r' = 2$ (i.e., $2 \times 8 = 1 \bmod 5$), $B = 8$, and $M = 5$, the following addresses are obtained as shown in Table 6.4:

$$\alpha(\mu) = \frac{\{8[2(\mu - 8) \bmod 5] + 8\}}{4}$$

$$\mu(x) = (3, 1, 4, 2, 0)$$

$$\alpha(x) = (2, 4, 6, 8, 10)$$

$$\alpha(\mu) = (10, 4, 8, 2, 6)$$

The proper addresses in memories $M_0, M_1, \ldots, M_4$ are 10, 4, 8, 2, 6, respectively.

We use the $\mu(x)$ equation in the xth processor to determine the module number of the memory containing the xth element of the desired N vector. At the same time, addressing hardware in memory μ uses the $\alpha(\mu)$ equation to determine the necessary address of the desired element. We use $\alpha(\mu)$ instead of $\alpha(x)$ because this eliminates the need to route the addresses from the processors through the switch.

The design of the access conflict-free memory is based on the use of a prime number of memories. Crucial to this design is the simplification of the offset equations. Most of the mod M operations and offset calculations can be done with ROMs or with some indexing hardware. The design of this memory system fits nicely in the context of the BSP. The indexing hardware carries out the necessary addressing and alignment calculations automatically once the initial vector-set descriptors have been set up. The problem of indexing overhead and memory-access conflicts may seriously deteriorate the system performance if not properly controlled.

6.4.2 Array Processing Languages

Three high-level languages have been proposed for Illiac-IV: *Tranqual, Glypnir,* and *Illiac-IV Fortran.* The Tranqual is the first Algol-like language proposed for Illiac-IV. It was designed to allow programmers to manipulate arrays of data in a parallel fashion, independent of the machine organization. However, the development of Tranqual was halted by the demand for an extended Fortran for Illiac-IV. Glypnir is also an Algol-like block-structured language, but it is specially designed to be compatible with B6500 Algol in the sense that it was written to better exploit the parallelism in the Illiac-IV architecture.

All arithmetic operations are carried out under the control of a mask pattern. The mask provides 64 true-false values of a boolean vector to be associated with each of the PEs. When a bit of the mask pattern is true, the corresponding PE is enabled and may thus deliver the results of an operation. Consider the Glypnir expression

$$A := B * C \tag{6.22}$$

When A, B, and C are vector-valued PE variables (vectors), each may have up to 64 components. The above multiplication means that each component of B is multiplied by the corresponding element of C and the resulting product vector is stored in A. However, when C is a CU variable (a scalar), the multiplication will be repeated 64 times in an invisible PE variable.

Special facilities exist to allow the rotation and shifting of rows to the right and left in a way similar to the more familiar operations conventionally carried out on words, thus allowing the Route instruction to be utilized. **For** and **if** statements are also provided, but often give unconventional results. For instance, given the PE variables A, B, and C, the statement

$$\textbf{If } A > B \textbf{ then } C := A \textbf{ else } C := B \tag{6.23}$$

will deliver the maximum elements of A and B to C and may result in both the **then** and **else** statements to be executed.

Blocks of assembler language can be explicitly embedded in a Glypnir program for the optimization of any section of code. It has also facilities to refer to selected hardware registers for lower-level code optimization. However, the language demands that the programmer undertakes the detailed supervision of storage allocation and be constrained to only Illiac-IV rows (64 components) or vectors of rows. To remove these restrictions, the Illiac-IV Fortran allows the user to program with vectors of any length in either "straight" or "skewed" storage allocations. Skewed allocation allows equal accessibility of rows or columns in an array.

In Illiac-IV Fortran, the binary data type can be used to specify bit-control vectors for masking purpose. The DO statement has been extended to allow parallel execution of arithmetic expressions, and extra constructs have been added to the language to allow the shifting and rotation of vectors and array rows. The only significant change are the EQUIVALENCE and COMMON statements, where the two-dimensional STORE of Illiac-IV imposes reactions on the usual serial definition.

A parallel-processing programming language *Actus* has been introduced by R. H. Perrott (1979) for array processors. Most parallel computers use extensions of existing languages, such as the extended Fortran for the Star-100, the CFT for Cray-1, and Glypnir language for the Illiac-IV. The language SL-1 is one of the few languages that has tried to bring some of the benefits of structured programming to the Star-100 system. More recently, *Vectran* has been developed by the IBM research group to facilitate the application of vector-array processing algorithms. Actus offers a theoretical extension of the language Pascal. Actus attempts to redress the technology imbalance between hardware and software development for synchronous parallel machines. It is aimed at exploiting parallelism and incorporating some software engineering approaches. The main features in Actus are briefly introduced. The algorithmic and data constructs in Actus are of sufficient generality to make efficient use of parallel resources.

The array is declared in Actus by indicating the maximum extent of parallelism. The syntax can support any number of dimensions. For example, a scalar array is represented by:

$$var \ \textbf{scalara}: \ array[1. .m, 1. .n] \text{ of integer};$$ (6.24)

i.e., **scalara** contains $m \times n$ (predefined) integer numbers. The low indices are restricted to one for convenience. The maximum extent of parallelism is introduced by replacing only one pair of sequential dots "$. .$" by a parallel pair "$:$"

$$var \ \textbf{para}: \ array[1:m, 1. .n] \text{ of real};$$ (6.25)

indicates an array **para** of $m \times n$ real numbers for which the maximum extent of parallelism is m. The array **para** can be manipulated m elements at a time since it has been declared as a parallel variable with that extent of parallelism. The array is thus the main data structure to indicate variables which can be manipulated in parallel. Thus $\alpha[1:4, 2]$ is equivalent to referencing in parallel, $\alpha[1, 2]$, $\alpha[2, 2]$, $\alpha[3, 2]$, $\alpha[4, 2]$, and $\alpha[2:3, 1]$ is equivalent to referencing in parallel $\alpha[2, 1] \ \alpha[3, 1]$.

Identifiers can be used to represent a sequence of integer numbers. They are used to assign values to parallel variables with an extent of parallelism equal to the number of values. The form of a parallel constant is

$$const \ identifier = \textbf{start}: (\text{increment}) \text{ finish};$$ (6.26)

where the values of **start**, increment, and finish must be integers and the sequence is "**start, start** + increment, **start** + $2 \times$ increment,..., finish." If the increment is unity, it may be omitted, e.g., "const $n = 50$; **seq** $= 1:n$; **oddseq** $= 1:(2)31$." Parallel constants can be used to assign values to parallel variables; for example, "**seq**" with an extent of parallelism 50 and "**oddseq**" with an extent 16.

The extent of parallelism can be changed by the use of an index set which identifies the data elements that are to be altered. The members of an index set are (ordered) integer values, each of which identifies a particular element of a data type that can be accessed in parallel. An index set is defined with the data declarations

$$index \ index = i: j;$$ (6.27)

where i and j are constant integer values such that $i \leq j$. The elements i to j inclusive will be accessed whenever the index-identifier index is used as a parallel-array index.

The advantages of using index sets are that (*i*) statements become more readable since they use the identifier name, and the (*ii*) extent of parallelism involved can be evaluated before the statement is encountered. Index-set identifiers cannot be redefined, but they can be operated upon by union ($+$), intersection (*), and difference ($-$) in order to facilitate parallel computations. The complement ($-$) gives the other members of the declared extent of parallelism.

In order to enable the movement of data between elements of the same or different parallel variables, two primitive data-alignment operators are included in the Actus language. These are

1. The *shift operator*, which causes movement of the data within the range of the declared extent of parallelism
2. The *rotate operator*, which causes the data to be shifted circularly with respect to the extent of parallelism

A single extent of parallelism can be associated with each simple or structured statement of the language which involves one, or more than one, parallel variable; this must be less than or equal to the declared extent of parallelism for the parallel variables involved. Hence, during program execution, the smallest unit for which the extent of parallelism can be defined is the single assignment statement. This does not exclude the use of scalar and parallel variables in the same statement, but facilitates testing and data alignment of the parallel variables.

In order to avoid repeatedly indicating the extent of parallelism for a series of assignment statements in which the extent will not change, the **within** construct has been introduced. This, in turn, will avoid a calculation of the extent of parallelism for each of the statements individually. It takes the form:

$$\textbf{within } \textit{specifier} \textbf{ do } \textit{statement} \tag{6.28}$$

where "*specifier*" is either an index-set identifier or an explicit extent of parallelism. The specifier defines the extent of parallelism for the "*statement*." This construct avoids a calculation of the extent of parallelism until another extent-setting construct is encountered or the construct is exited. If another extent-setting construct is encountered, the current extent of parallelism is stacked and the new extent evaluated and applied. This is the rule which governs the nesting of all extent-setting constructs. The **within** construct also serves another purpose when it is embedded in a loop: the *specifier* can consist of variables which are changed each time through the loop, thus, for example, enabling the examination of various subgrids within a larger grid.

To allow for those situations where selection or repetition is concerned, the structured programming concepts of **if**, **case**, **while**, and **for** were expanded to enable the test or loop variables to contain parallel as well as scalar variables. Selective statements are used to spread the extent of parallelism between two or more execution paths, as determined by a test expression in the **if** or **case** constructs.

If a test expression involves parallel variables, the test is evaluated for each indicated element of the variables. For an example:

$$\textbf{if } a[0:49] > b[0:49] \textbf{ then } a[\#]^* := a[\#]- \tag{6.29}$$

In this example, 50 elements of a are tested to see which are greater than the corresponding elements of b; those elements that are greater are decremented by 1.

There are two types of repetitive statements, depending upon whether the number of times the statement is to be executed is known before the statement is encountered or whether the number is dependent on conditions generated by the statement.

The parallel quantifiers **any** and **all** can be used with parallel test variables, in which case the extent of parallelism must be explicitly defined in the statements of the construct (as with a test which involves scalar variables only). For an example:

$$\textbf{while any } (a[1:50] < b[1:50]) \textbf{ do } a[1:50] := a[1:50] + 1 \qquad (6.30)$$

all the elements of a are incremented by one until none of the elements of a are less than their corresponding element in b.

Functions and *procedures* can be declared using the data declarations and statements previously defined; the maximum extent of parallelism of all variables must be known at compile time. The Pascal scope rules for procedures and functions apply; hence, local variables cannot have their extent of parallelism altered by a *function* or *procedure* call.

The formal parameter list for both functions and procedures was expanded to allow for parameters which are parallel variables. The actual parameters can then be either of the same extent of parallelism or a section of the same extent of a larger parallel variable. Only procedures and functions involving scalar variables may be parameters. In the case of a function, either a scalar or parallel variable can be returned as a result of its execution; the extent of parallelism can be different from that of the parameter(s). Procedures can be used to return one or more results which can be either scalar or parallel variables or a mixture of both.

The features of Actus have been described using a syntax similar to that of Pascal; this was due to a plan to use an existing Pascal compiler for its implementation at the Institute of Advanced Computation, NASA/Ames Research Center in California. The Pascal P compiler was used in the creation of the Actus compiler. This P compiler is being modified and enhanced with the new features to form an Actus P compiler which also generates code for a hypothetical stack computer. Since this code is machine independent, the Actus P compiler can be used as a basis for the implementation of Actus on other parallel machines. Preliminary results of the implementation indicate that the features of Actus can be mapped onto the instruction set of the Illiac-IV.

Another consideration in implementing the Actus language is to automate the management of the memory. It is important to determine either from the user or by the compiler the size of the working set; the *working set* is the minimum amount of the database required to be resident in the fast store so that processing can continue without excessive interruptions. On the basis of such information, the fast store can be divided into buffers and processing can be overlapped with backing store transfers. Thus, the compiler rather than the user is responsible for the organization of data transfers.

In summary, two research objectives were achieved by the Actus language and by its compiler. The first objective was achieved by introducing the concept of the extent of parallelism, whose maximum size is defined in the data declarations and subsequently manipulated (in parallel) either in part or in total by the statements and constructs of the language. Using this concept, it was found to be possible to adapt a unified approach for both types of computers. The second objective was achieved by modifying existing data and program-structuring constructs of Pascal to accommodate the special demands of a parallel environment.

6.4.3 Performance Analysis of Array Processors

A space-time approach is used below to evaluate the performance of SIMD array processors. The execution of a vector job in an array processor occupies the equipment space of PEs over a period of the time space. An analysis of an SIMD machine with m PEs is presented below. Ideally, data operands in an array processor should be uniformly distributed among the PEMs. This effectively creates m separate data streams. Theoretically, the maximum speedup cannot exceed m when compared with a functionally equivalent SISD computer. We use the following notations to formulate expressions in measuring the *speedup*, the *throughput*, and the *utilization* of an array processor:

m: The number of PEs in an array processor
t_a: The time required by a PE to complete the execution of a broadcast instruction from the CU
n: The number of instructions to be executed in a specific job
N_i: The length of a vector operand in the ith instruction ($1 \leq i \leq n$)
W_a: The throughput of an array processor
t_i: The time required to finish the ith instruction in an array processor
T_a: The total time required to finish the execution of a job in an array processor
S_m: The speedup of an array processor (with m PEs) over a serial computer
ϕ: The efficiency of an array processor

Note that this list of performance parameters is very similar to those for pipeline computers studied in Section 4.5.4. The m PEs correspond to the k pipeline segments. In fact, the vector job parameters n and N_i are the same in analyzing both types of vector processors. The instruction execution time t_a of a PE is assumed to be a constant equal to the average time for typical instructions. Figure 6.27 shows the space-time diagram for the execution of the ith vector instruction on an array processor with $m = 3$ PEs, where $N_i = 10$ operands are contained in the ith vector instruction. The PE arrays are used four times to complete the execution of the 10 operations. During the fourth iteration, two PEs are disabled.

In an array processor, the time required to finish the ith instruction is computed by

$$t_i = \left\lceil \frac{N_i}{m} \right\rceil \cdot t_a \tag{6.31}$$

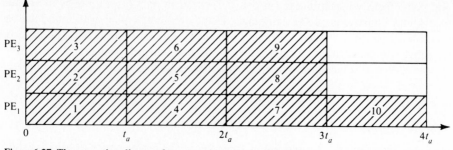

Figure 6.27 The space-time diagram for an array processor with 3 PEs.

for a vector job consisting of n vector instructions having various numbers N_i of operands for $i = 1, 2, \ldots, n$. The total time required to complete the execution of the vector job in an array processor is

$$T_a = \sum_{i=1}^{n} t_i = t_a \cdot \sum_{i=1}^{n} \left[\frac{N_i}{m} \right] \qquad (6.32)$$

The same job if executed on a serial SISD computer requires

$$T_s = t_a \cdot \sum_{i=1}^{n} N_i \qquad (6.33)$$

where t_a was assumed to be independent of instruction types (in an average sense). The improvement in speed is represented by the following speedup ratio:

$$S_m = \frac{T_s}{T_a} = \frac{\displaystyle\sum_{i=1}^{n} N_i}{\displaystyle\sum_{i=1}^{n} [N_i/m]} \qquad (6.34)$$

The *efficiency* ϕ of an array processor is displayed by the utilization rate of the available resources (PEs). The PE utilization rate shows the percentage of PEs being actively involved in the execution of the vector job. The space-time product offers a measure of this utilization of resources. Formally, we have

$$\phi = \frac{t_a \cdot \displaystyle\sum_{i=1}^{n} N_i}{m \cdot t_a} = \frac{S_m}{m} \qquad (6.35)$$

This shows that the efficiency ϕ corresponds to the ratio of the actual speedup S_m to the maximum speedup m. In the ideal case $\phi \to 1$, when $S_m \to m$.

Example 6.6 To illustrate the above performance measures, we choose the same vector distribution as in Figure 4.39. The mean vector length of the job distribution is 4.4. On the average, 4.4 PEs are needed to execute a vector instruction among a set of 10 instructions. Similar to that plotted in Figure 4.39, we calculate the efficiency (using Eq. 6.35) and the speedup (Eq. 6.34) of an array processor having m PEs ($1 \leq m \leq 10$). The numerical results are plotted in Figure 6.28. The speedup increases monotonically with respect to the number of available PEs, whereas the efficiency declines with the increase of PEs.

For an array processor, not only the vector length but also the residue of the vector length will affect the system performance. For example, to execute a vector instruction of length 65 on the Illiac-IV computer with 64 PEs requires one additional instruction cycle to execute the residue of one component operation. The system performance will be degraded due to small residues. Degradation results mainly from many idle PEs. Figure 6.29 shows the speedup (utilization) against vector length on an array processor with eight PEs. Here we consider only the execution of a single vector instruction ($n = 1$). The maximum speedup is achieved when N_1 is a multiple of $m = 8$.

For small residues, the speedup drops rapidly. When N_1 approaches infinity, the ill effect of residue becomes less severe. The PE utilization will approach one when the vector length goes to infinity, as shown by the envelope of the saw-tooth curve. Parallel algorithms, good memory-allocation schemes, and optimizing compilers are needed in array processors. Whether a large array processor will perform as ideally projected depends heavily on the skill of the users. The failure of promoting the Illiac-IV and the BSP into the commercial market was mainly due to user reluctance in accepting SIMD computers for general-purpose applications.

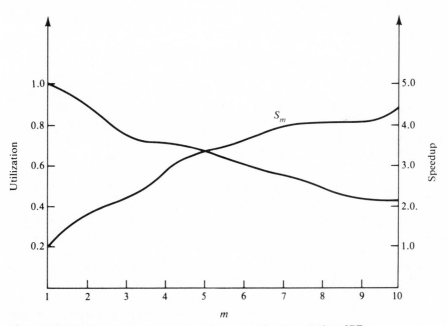

Figure 6.28 Efficiency and speedup of an array processor with various number of PEs.

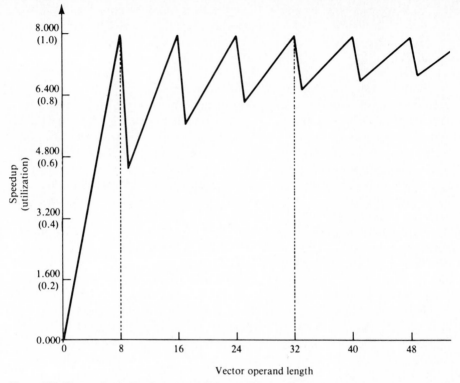

Figure 6.29 The speedup (utilization) of an 8-PE array versus vector length.

6.4.4 Multiple-SIMD Computer Organization

A shared-resource array processor consists of two or more CUs sharing a pool of dynamically allocatable PEs. Such a parallel computer is depicted in Figure 6.30. The system operates with *multiple single-instruction multiple-data* (MSIMD) streams. Each CU must be allocated with a subset of PEs for the execution of a single vector job (an SIMD process). The only way vector jobs can interact with each other is through their independent use of the same PE resources.

Examples of MSIMD array processors include the original Illiac-IV design with four CUs sharing 256 PEs (Figure 6.31), the Multi-Associative Processor (MAP) with eight CUs sharing 1024 PEs, and the PM⁴ system proposed at Purdue University (Figure 6.32). The PM⁴ was proposed as a reconfigurable computer system which can operate in either MSIMD mode, multiple SISD mode, or in MIMD mode. A typical configuration of the PM⁴ consists of 16 CUs with, say, 1024 PMUs. The system was intended to be used for computer imaging applications. The PM⁴ has been upgraded to a generalized research multiprocessor system, called PUMPS, at Purdue University. In the Phoenix computer project, the coupling of sixteen 64-PE arrays is being considered to extend the Illiac-IV design for MSIMD array processing.

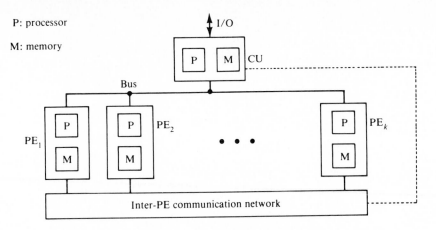

(a) The conventional SIMD array processor

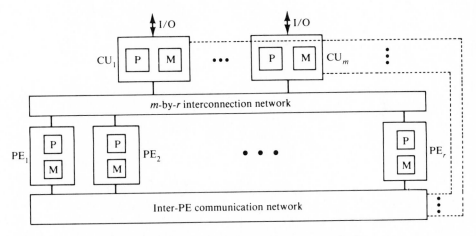

(b) The multiple SIMD (MSIMD) computer organization

Figure 6.30 SIMD versus MSIMD computer organization. (Courtesy of *IEEE Trans. Computers*, Hwang and Ni, September 1980.)

There are three possible multiarray Illiac configurations, as shown in Figure 6.31. This provides some flexibility in matching array size to problem (matrix) size. The end connection of the PEs in each array can be reconnected to the ends of other arrays to form dual two-quadrant arrays with 128 PEs each, or to form a single four-quadrant array of 256 PEs. For multiarray configurations, all CUs receive the same instruction string and any data centrally accessed. The CUs execute the instructions independently. Inter-CU synchronization takes place only on those instructions in which data on control information must cross the array boundaries. The multiplicity of array configurations introduces additional complexities in program control and memory addressing.

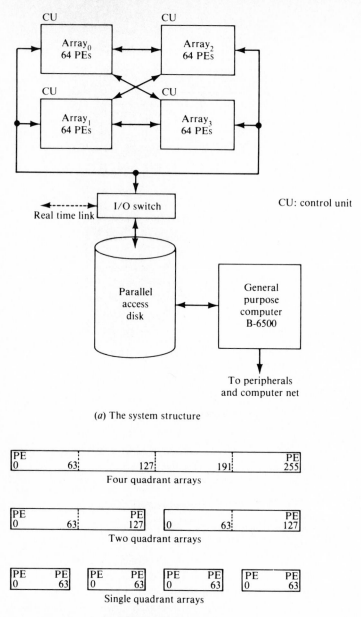

(a) The system structure

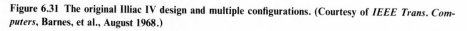

Four quadrant arrays

Two quadrant arrays

Single quadrant arrays

(b) Multiconfigurations

Figure 6.31 The original Illiac IV design and multiple configurations. (Courtesy of *IEEE Trans. Computers*, Barnes, et al., August 1968.)

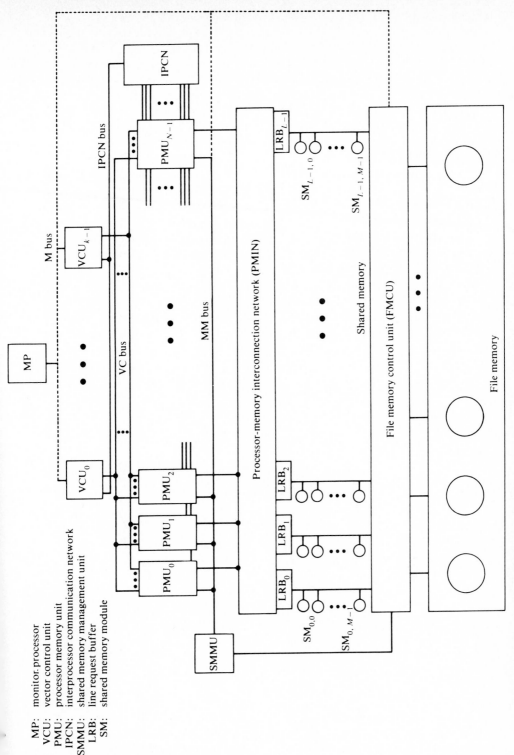

MP: monitor processor
VCU: vector control unit
PMU: processor memory unit
IPCN: interprocessor communication network
SMMU: shared memory management unit
LRB: line request buffer
SM: shared memory module

Figure 6.32 The PM⁴ multiple-SIMD/MIMD computer organization. (Courtesy of AFIPS NCC Proc., June 1979.)

The scheduling of PE resources in an MSIMD computer can be modeled by the queueing network in Figure 6.33. There are m identical CUs in the system, each of which handles an instruction stream. An available CU enters the busy state only if there is a vector job and the PEs demanded by that job are available from the PE pool, otherwise it remains in the wait state. There are n identical PEs shared by all the CUs. Each subarray of PEs can be allocated to one CU through a partitionable interconnection network. All instructions are stored in the CU memory and decoded by the CUs. Only the vector-type instructions are broadcast to the allocated subarray of PEs for execution. Control-type or scalar instructions are directly executed through the CUs. All the PEs can independently accept one assignment at a time. The local memory of each PE is used to store only the distributed data sets to be used for SIMD processes.

The subset of PEs allocated to a CU may vary in size for different jobs. In the case of the original Illiac-IV design, the three multi-array configurations (i) {64, 64, 64, 64} (4 active CUs), (ii) 128, 128 (2 active CUs), and (iii) 256 (1 active CU) corresponds to four, two, and one instruction streams, respectively. Note that some of the CUs may be left idle due to the limited number of available PEs in the resource pool. In the Phoenix extension, the increased reconfiguration capability offers better application flexibility than the Illiac-IV. The PE array partitioning in the Illiac-IV is called *block* reconfigurable. Each block of PE corresponds to one quadrant of the array. In a generalized MSIMD computer, all the PEs should be

λ: arrival rate of input processes

μ: service rate of each control unit

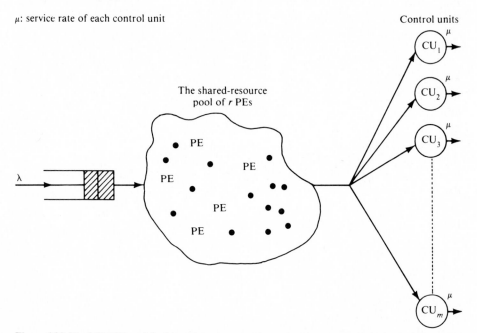

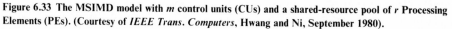

Figure 6.33 The MSIMD model with m control units (CUs) and a shared-resource pool of r Processing Elements (PEs). (Courtesy of *IEEE Trans. Computers*, Hwang and Ni, September 1980).

dynamically partitionable into subarrays of various sizes. The PM^4 was proposed to operate in this fashion.

Several research issues of MSIMD computers are identified below. The goal is to design MSIMD computers for multiple array processing in an interactive manner. These design issues must be properly addressed in order to achieve high performance at reasonable system cost. The operating system of an MSIMD computer is much more complicated than that of a single SIMD machine.

Performance optimization The performance of an MSIMD computer is measured by the utilization rates of the CUs and PEs and by the average job response time. The computer is modeled in Figure 6.30 as a multiserver queueing system. Based on reasonable assumptions of the job arrival distribution, the CU service rate, and the queueing discipline used, one can predicate the expected performance.

The optimal choice of the size of the PE resource pool is a fundamental issue for a given number of CUs in the system. The selection depends on the input workload distribution, the cost of the PEs and their interconnection networks, and the queueing discipline used in allocating the shared PEs to the CUs. The resource allocation can be optimized by promoting the CU-PEs utilization rates at reduced system cost. The results obtained from theoretical queueing analysis need to be verified with machine simulation experiments before meaningful system sizes can be decided for specific application problem environments.

Partitioning the routing network The allocation of PE blocks to multiple CUs demands the use of some partitionable inter-PE routing networks. With a large number of PEs, the network size may become too large to be cost effective. With partitioning, smaller networks may be interconnected to route the data at much lower hardware cost. Of course, the partitionability from large permutation networks to multiple but disjoint subnetworks depends on the network type, the increased delay and blocking rate after partitioning, and the emulation capabilities. among reconfigured network topologies. Without a partitionable interconnection network, the MSIMD computer cannot operate flexibly and efficiently.

Algorithms and system control Multiple SIMD operations need to decompose a large computation problem by algorithmic partitioning. Of course, the algorithm decomposition must be constrained by the hardware resource configuration and availability. Furthermore, none of the proposed array-processing languages can handle multiple data arrays. Designing an effective operating system to coordinate the multiple CU operations is a very challenging effort. The experience in developing an MSIMD operating system will help develop an intrinsic MIMD operating system, especialy for scientific applications.

Due to inexperience in the aforementioned problem areas, MSIMD machines are still in the proposal stage among computer architects. Extensive research and development efforts are necessary towards the production of multiple array processing systems. MSIMD computers are more suitable for regularly structured scientific computations.

6.5 BIBLIOGRAPHICAL NOTES AND PROBLEMS

The original SIMD concept can be traced to Unger (1958) and Slotnick, et al. (1962). The structure of the original 256-PE Illiac-IV computer was first reported in Barnes, et al. (1968). The Illiac-IV software and applications programming was reported by Kuck (1968). A more recent report of the Illiac-IV system was given in Bouknight, et al. (1972). The Actus language extensions for array processors are based on the work of Perrott (1979). Assessments of the first-generation vector processors, including the Illiac-IV, were given by Stokes (1977) and Theis (1974). The language Glypnir was described in Lawrie, et al. (1975). The Fortran-like language CFD was reported by Stevens (1975). Programming experiences on the Illiac-IV are summarized in Stevenson (1980). Possible extension of the Illiac-IV to the Phoenix array processor was discussed in Feierbach and Stevenson (1978).

The Burroughs Corporation has published a series of technical notes on the BSP architecture (1978a, b, c). The BSP was comprehensively reported in Kuck and Stokes (1982). Arithmetic design of the BSP was reported in Gajski and Rubinfield (1978). The prime memory system is based on the work of Lawrie and Vora (1982). The MPP has been reported in Batcher (1980). Detailed design features of the MPP are described in a final report by Goodyear Aerospace Corporation (1979). The image processing applications of the MPP are reported by Potter (1983). The skewed allocation of parallel memories is based on the work of Budnik and Kuck (1971). A good summary of BSP features is given in Kozdrowicki and Theis (1980), where comparisons of the BSP to Cyber-205 and Cray-1 are provided. The throughput analysis of array processors is based on the comparative study by Hwang, et al. (1981). Multiple SIMD computer organizations are modeled in Hwang and Ni (1979, 1980). The partitioning of permutation network for MSIMD machine has been studied in Siegel (1980).

Problems

6.1 Explain the following system features associated with the Illiac-IV, the BSP, and the MPP array processors.

    (a) Multi-array configurations of the Illiac-IV

    (b) The prime memory for the BSP

    (c) The bit-slice operations in the MPP

    (d) Concurrent scalar-array operations in the BSP

    (e) Concurrent I/O and arithmetic logic operations in the MPP array

    (f) The staging memory configurations in the MPP

    (g) Host computers for the Illiac-IV, the BSP, and the MPP

    (h) The I/O facilities in the Illiac-IV, the BSP, and the MPP

6.2 Prove that the Illiac recirculating network cannot be partitioned into independent subnetworks, each of which would have the properties of a complete Illiac network. (Hint: Use the rotating functions defined in Section 5.2.2.)

6.3 Devise an SIMD algorithm for finding the inverse of an 8×8 triangular matrix $A = (a_{ij})$ on the Illiac-IV computer with 64 PEs. Show the memory allocation and CU instructions needed to implement the algorithm. Minimizing the number of instruction steps and the required data memory words is the primary design goal. The given matrix A is assumed to be nonsingular. The successive contents of the involved PE registers and of the PEMs should be demonstrated along with the instruction steps. Masking can be used to enable and disable the PEs.

6.4 Using the vector instruction forms specified in Table 6.2, devise a BSP program for solving a linear triangular system of algebraic equations with n unknowns. You can assume $n \gg p = 16$, the number of arithmetic elements in the BSP. A "block" back substitution method is suggested to solve the triangular system. Memory allocation for the characteristic matrix must be specified among the $m \times 17$ memory modules.

6.5 Given an $n \times m$ image, the gray level for each pixel (picture element) is between 0 and $b - 1$. Let $A[i, j]$ denote the gray level at the pixel (i, j). An algorithm to construct a histogram in an SISD computer is shown below:

$$
\begin{aligned}
&\textbf{For } i = 0 \textbf{ to } b - 1 \textbf{ do}\\
&\quad \text{Histog}(i) \leftarrow 0;\\
&\textbf{For } i = 1 \textbf{ to n do}\\
&\quad \textbf{For } j = 1 \textbf{ to m do}\\
&\qquad \text{Histog}(A[i, j]) \leftarrow \text{Histog}(A[i, j]) + 1;
\end{aligned}
$$

Suppose we want to use an SIMD machine with p PEs to construct the histogram. Assume $n, m \gg p$, n, m, and $p(p = 2y)$ are powers of 2, and $n/p = k$ is an integer. Each PEM stores k rows of image data, e.g., PEM_0 stores rows one to k, etc. The storage formats are shown in Figure 6.34, where

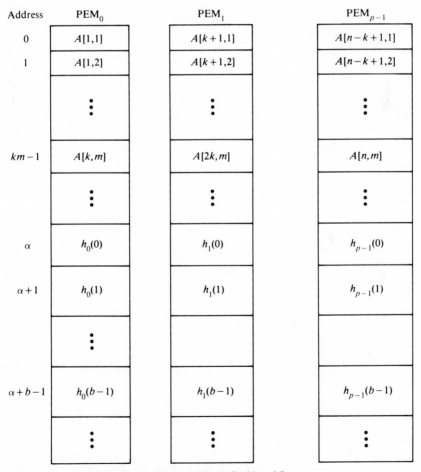

Figure 6.34 Data storage for the histogramming in Problem 6.5.

Table 6.5 Sample vector-scalar instruction set for Problem 6.5

Instruction	Description		Instruction	Description
VLOAD r (3 cycles)	Indexed addressing $(r) \leftarrow ((D_i) + (I_j))$ $r \; \varepsilon \; \{A_i, B_i, C_i, R_{ij}\}$		VADDI r, # (3 cycles)	Immediate adding $(r) \leftarrow (r) + \#$ $r \; \varepsilon \; U_i$
VMOV r_1, r_2 (1 cycle)	Register transfer $(r_1) \leftarrow (r_2)$ $r_1, r_2 \; \varepsilon \; U_i$ where $U_i = \{A_i, B_i, C_i, R_i, I_i, R_{ij}\}$		LCYCLE r (s cycles)	Left cyclic shift $(R_{i-s}) \leftarrow (R_i)$ where $s = 2^d$, $d = (r)$ $r \; \varepsilon \; \{A_i, B_i, C_i\}$
VMVI r, # (2 cycle)	Immediate operand $(r) \leftarrow \#$ $r \; \varepsilon \; U_i$		MVI INX, # (1 cycle)	Immediate operand $(INX) \leftarrow \#$ INX ε Z, where $Z = \{INX_1, INX_2, \ldots, INX_5\}$
VSTORE r (3 cycles)	Indexed addressing $((D_i) + (I_j)) \leftarrow (r)$ $r \; \varepsilon \; \{A_i, B_i, C_i, R_{ij}\}$		ICR INX, 1 (1 cycle)	Increment index register $(INX) \leftarrow (INX) + 1$ INX ε Z
VADD r_1, r_2 (2 cycles)	Register adding $(r_1) \leftarrow (r_1) + (r_2)$ $r_1 r_2 \; \varepsilon \; U_i$		JLT INX_i, INX_j, LOOP (2 cycles)	Conditional branch if $(INX_i) < (INX_j)$ then go to LOOP INX_i, $INX_j \; \varepsilon$ Z

the memory locations from $\alpha + b - 1$ in each PEM are used to store a local histogram. The method to construct the histogram consists of forming a local histogram in each PE and then combining local histograms to get a global histogram.

The organization of each PE_i is shown in Figure 5.2. Each PE_i can communicate with its neighboring PE_{i+1} and PE_{i-1} in one routing step. You are allowed to use the vector instructions and scalar instructions listed in Table 6.5. The number below each instruction indicates the instruction cycle time. Also, we assume that there are five global index registers in the control unit.

(a) Using these instructions, write a program to construct a histogram in the SIMD machine. The resulting data should be stored in the memory locations $\alpha, \alpha + 1, \ldots, \alpha + b - 1$ in PEM_0.

(b) Compute the total number of cycles required in your program. What is the speedup of your program over a conventional one in an SISD computer, which consists of the CU and one PE? Assume the scalar counterpart of each vector instruction consumes the same time as each vector instruction. Note that there is no communication cost in an SISD computer.

6.6 Consider the evaluation of the following inner-product expression in an SISD machine with one PE or in an SIMD machine with m PEs connected by a linear circular ring:

$$S = \sum_{i=1}^{n} A_i \cdot B_i \qquad (6.36)$$

It is assumed that each ADD operation requires two time units and each MULTIPLY operation requires four time units. Data shifting along the bidirectional ring between any adjacent PEs requires one time unit.

(a) What is the evaluation time of S on the SISD computer?

(b) What is the evaluation time of S on the SIMD computer?

(c) What is the speedup of using the SIMD machine over the SISD machine for the evaluation of S?

6.7 Consider K couples of vectors. The ith couple consists of a row vector R_i and a column vector C_i, each of dimension $N = 2^n$. To compute the pairwise inner product for the ith couple, we perform the following:

$$IP[i] = \sum_{j=1}^{N} R_i[j] * C_i[j] \qquad (6.37)$$

Below is the algorithm to perform $IP[i]$ for all $i = 1, 2, \ldots, K$.

```
For i ← 1 to K do
begin
IP[i]←0;
    For j←1 to N do
    IP[i]←IP[i]+R_i[j]*C_i[j];
end
```

(a) Neglecting the initialization step, index updating and testing, find the total compute time on a uniprocessor as a function of K and N. Assume that multiplication and addition take the same unit time to complete.

(b) To speedup this computation, an SIMD machine can be used by exploiting the parallelism in the computation. Two different implications are suggested below. Find the compute time in each case.

(i) Use $P = N$ processing elements (PEs) to compute $IP[i]$ successively for each couple of vectors R_i, C_i.

(ii) A couple of vectors are allocated to each PE, which computes one inner product. The number of PEs is $P = K$ in this case.

6.8 Consider an SIMD machine with 256 PEs using a perfect shuffle interconnection network. If the shuffle interconnection function is executed 10 times, where will the data item originally in PE_{123} be located?

6.9 We have learned that an SIMD machine with $P = 2^{2n}$ PEs can access without conflict the rows, columns, diagonal, and reverse diagonal of a matrix from $M = 2^{2n} + 1$ parallel memory modules, if the skewing distance $S = 2^n$. Prove that it is also possible to access any 2^n-by-2^n square block in one memory cycle under the same condition.

6.10 Table 6.4 shows the skewed memory allocation for an 8×8 matrix in an array processor with $M = 5$ memory modules and $P = 4$ processors.

   (a) List all patterns that can be accessed in one memory cycle.

   (b) Give a P vector $V(1, 1, 1, 1)$. Calculate the word addresses in the memory modules involved.

CHAPTER SEVEN

MULTIPROCESSOR ARCHITECTURE AND PROGRAMMING

This chapter covers multiprocessor system architectures and multiprocessing requirements. Hardware-software factors which limit the performance are presented. The interconnection topologies between the processors and the main memory are discussed. Models are shown to evaluate the performance of these interconnection structures. We present some memory configurations and a classification of operating systems for multiprocessors. Language and programming issues in using multiprocessor systems are discussed at the end.

7.1 FUNCTIONAL STRUCTURES

In this section, we introduce the functional structures of multiprocessor systems. Example systems discussed below include the Cm*, Cyber-170, Honeywell 60/66, and the PDP-10 multiprocessor configurations. More example systems will be given in Chapter 9. Functional characteristics of processor architecture for multiprocessors are presented.

Multiprocessors can be grossly characterized by two attributes: first, a multiprocessor is a single computer that includes multiple processors and second, processors may communicate and cooperate at different levels in solving a given problem. The communication may occur by sending messages from one processor to the other or by sharing a common memory.

There are some similarities between multiprocessors and multicomputer systems since both are motivated by the same basic goal—the support of concurrent operations in the system. However, there exists an important distinction between multiple computer systems and multiprocessors, based on the extent of resource sharing and cooperation in the solution of a problem. A *multiple computer system* consists of several autonomous computers which may or may not communicate with each other. An example of a multiple computer system is the IBM Attached Support Processor System. A *multiprocessor system* is controlled by one operating system which provides interaction between processors and their programs at the process, data set, and data element levels. An example is the Denelcor's HEP system.

Two different sets of architectural models for a multiprocessor are described below. One is a *tightly coupled* multiprocessor and the other is a *loosely coupled* multiprocessor. Tightly coupled multiprocessors communicate through a shared main memory. Hence the rate at which data can communicate from one processor to the other is on the order of the bandwidth of the memory. A small local memory or high-speed buffer (cache) may exist in each processor. A complete connectivity exists between the processors and memory. This connectivity can be accomplished either by inserting an interconnection network between the processors and the memory or by a multiported memory. One of the limiting factors to the expansion of a tightly coupled system is the performance degradation due to memory contentions which occur when two or more processors attempt to access the same memory unit concurrently. In Chapter 2, we have seen some configurations of interleaved main memory suitable for multiprocessors. The degree of conflicts can be reduced by increasing the degree of interleaving. However, this must be coupled with careful data assignments to the memory modules. Another limiting factor is the processor-memory interconnection network itself. This will be discussed in more detail later.

7.1.1. Loosely Coupled Multiprocessors

Loosely coupled multiprocessor systems do not generally encounter the degree of memory conflicts experienced by tightly coupled systems. In such systems, each processor has a set of input-output devices and a large local memory where it accesses most of the instructions and data. We refer to the processor, its local memory and I/O interfaces as a *computer module*. Processes which execute on different computer modules communicate by exchanging messages through a message-transfer system (MTS). The degree of coupling in such a system is very loose. Hence, it is often referred to as a distributed system. The determinant factor of the degree of coupling is the communication topology of the associated message-transfer system. Loosely coupled systems (LCS) are usually efficient when the interactions between tasks are minimal. Tightly coupled systems (TCS) can tolerate a higher degree of interactions between tasks without significant deterioration in performance.

Figure 7.1a shows an example of a computer module of a nonhierarchical loosely coupled multiprocessor system. It consists of a processor, a local memory, local input-output devices and an interface to other computer modules. The interface may contain a channel and arbiter switch (CAS). Figure 7.1b illustrates the connection between the computer modules and a message-transfer system. If requests from two or more different computer modules

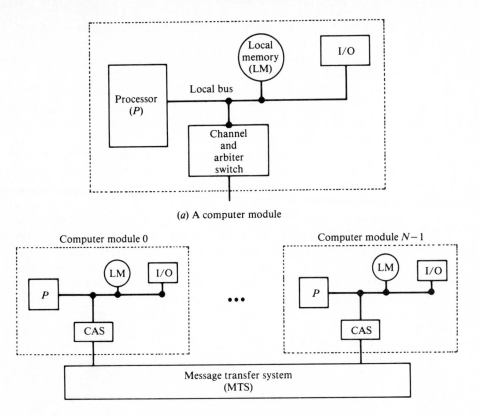

(a) A computer module

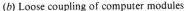

(b) Loose coupling of computer modules

Figure 7.1 Nonhierarchical loosely coupled multiprocessor system.

collide in accessing a physical segment of the MTS, the arbiter is responsible for choosing one of the simultaneous requests according to a given service discipline. It is also responsible for delaying other requests until the servicing of the selected request is completed. The channel within the CAS may have a high-speed communication memory which is used for buffering block transfers of messages. The communication memory is accessible by all processors. With the advent of VLSI technology, the computer module can be fabricated on a single integrated circuit and be used as the building block of a multiprocessor system.

The message-transfer system for a nonhierarchical LCS could be a simple time shared bus, as in the PDP-11, or a shared memory system. The latter case can be implemented with a set of memory modules and a processor-memory interconnection network or a multiported main memory. In a multiported memory system, the arbitration and selection logic of the switch are distributed into the memory modules. The MTS is one of the most important factors that determine the performance of the multiprocessor system. For LCS configurations that use a single time shared bus, the performance is limited by the message arrival rate on the bus, the message length, and the bus capacity (in bits per second).

Contentions for the bus increase as the number of computer modules increases. For the LCS with a share memory MTS, the limiting factor is the memory conflict problem imposed by the processor-memory interconnection network.

The communication memory may also be centralized and connected to a time shared bus, or be part of the shared memory system. Conceptually, a distributed or centralized communication memory can be considered as consisting of logical ports which can be accessed by the processors. Processes (tasks) can communicate with other processes allocated to the same processor, or with tasks allocated to other processors. Associated with each task is an input port stored in the local memory of the processor to which the task is allocated. Every message issued by the task is directed to the input port of the destination task. Communication between tasks allocated to the same processor takes place through the local memory only. Communication between tasks allocated to different processors is through a communication port residing in the communication memory. One communication port is associated with each processor as its input port.

The logical structure of the communication between tasks is shown in Figure 7.2. A process allocated to processor P_1 puts a message into the input port of another task in P_1, as illustrated by the arrow marked with **a**. The **b** arrows show a two-step action in transferring messages between processors. Arrow $\mathbf{b}_1$ sends a message to the input port of processor P_2. Arrow $\mathbf{b}_2$ shows the moving of a message to the input port of the destination process.

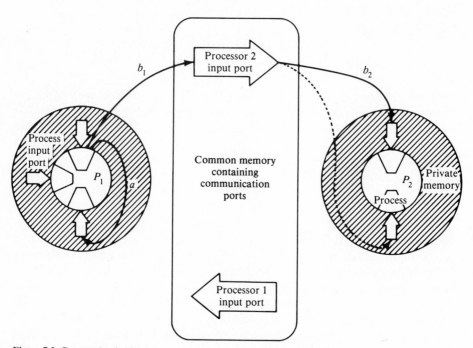

Figure 7.2 Communication between processes in a multiprocessor environment.

The Cm* Architecture For a hierarchical LCS, we consider the example of a computer system project at Carnegie Mellon University called the Cm*. Each computer module of the Cm* includes a local switch called the *Slocal*, as shown in Figure 7.3a. The switch is somewhat similar to the CAS in Figure 7.1a. The Slocal intercepts and routes the processor's requests to the memory and I/O devices outside the computer module via a map bus, shown in Figure 7.3b. It also accepts references from other computer modules to its local memory and I/O devices. The address translation is shown in Figure 7.4. It uses the four high-order bits of the processor's address along with the current address space, as indicated by the X-bit of the LSI-11 processor status word (PSW), to access a mapping table

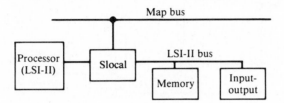

(*a*) A computer module

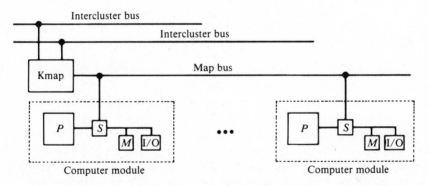

(*b*) A cluster of computer modules

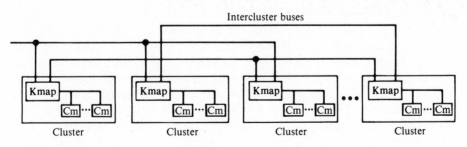

(*c*) A network of clusters

Figure 7.3 **Hierarchically structured multiprocessor system.**

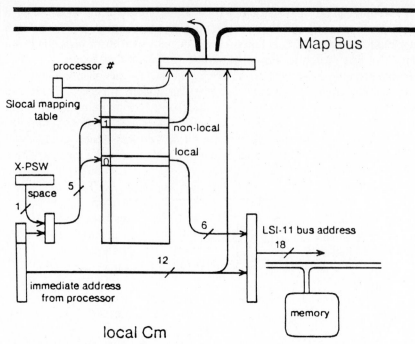

Figure 7.4 Address mapping in the Slocal of the Cm*. (Courtesy of Cm* project at Carnegie-Mellon University, 1980.)

which determines whether the reference is local or nonlocal. A virtual address of the nonlocal reference is formed by concatenating the nonlocal address field given by the mapping table and the source processor's identification. This virtual address is subsequently fetched by the Kmap via the map bus in response to a service request for nonlocal access. A number of computer modules may be connected to a map bus so that they share the use of a single Kmap. The *Kmap* is a processor that is responsible for mapping addresses and routing data between Slocals.

The computer modules are connected in hierarchical clusters by two-level buses, as shown in Figures 7.3*b* and 7.3*c*. A *cluster*, which is regarded as the lowest level, is made up of computer modules, a Kmap and the map bus. Clustering can enhance the cooperative ability of the processors in a cluster to operate on shared data with low communication overhead. It also provides hardware facilities to execute a group of tightly coupled cooperating processes. Any nonlocal reference to memory is handled by the Kmap in the cluster of the target memory module. The map bus may create a bottleneck since only one transaction can take place at a time. The performance of the system is facilitated by interconnecting the clusters of computer modules in a hierarchy. Clusters communicate via *inter-cluster buses* which are connected between Kmaps, as shown in Figure 7.3*c*. In general, a cluster need not have a direct intercluster bus connection to every other cluster in the configuration. Hence the complexity of the interconnection network can be simplified.

The Kmap is a microprogrammed, 150-ns cycle, three-processor complex with a common data memory. The Kmap provides the address mapping, communication, and synchronization functions within the system. Moreover, key operating system primitives can be moved into the Kmap, thereby relieving the computer modules from major supervisor functions. The data memory is used to cache address translation tables and mechanisms for synchronization and other resource management functions.

The three processors in the Kmap are the *Kbus*, the *Linc*, and the *Pmap*, as shown in Figure 7.5. The Kbus is the bus controller which arbitrates requests to the map bus. The Linc manages communication between the Kmap and other Kmap. The Pmap is the mapping processor which responds to requests from the Kbus and Linc. It also performs most of the request processing. The Pmap communicates with the computer modules in its cluster via the map bus which is a packet-switched bus. Three sets of queues provide interfaces between the Kbus, Linc, and the Pmap. Since the Kmap is much faster than the memory in the computer modules, it is multiprogrammed to handle up to eight concurrent requests. Each of the eight partitions is called a *context* and exists in the Pmap. Typically, each context processes one transaction. If one context needs to wait for a message packet to return with the reply to some request, the Pmap switches to another context that is ready to run so that some other transaction can proceed concurrently.

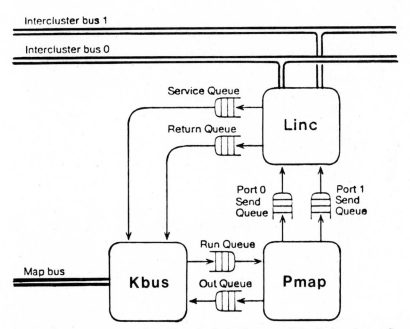

Figure 7.5 The components of the Kmap in Cm*. (Courtesy of the Cm* project at Carnegie-Mellon University, 1980.)

A service request is signaled to the Kbus whenever the processor of a computer module makes a nonlocal memory reference. Such a computer module (Cm) is called the *master* Cm. In response to the service requests, the Kbus allocates a Pmap context and fetches the virtual address of the memory reference via the map bus. Furthermore, the Kbus activates the new context by placing an entry, which contains the virtual address, in the Pmap run queue. The Pmap context performs the vritual to physical address translation via a microsubroutine. Using the physical address, it can initiate a physical memory access in any of the computer modules in its cluster.

The initiation is performed when the context invokes the appropriate Kbus operation by loading a request (with the physical address) into the Kbus *out queue*, shown in Figure 7.5. After loading the request into the out queue, the Pmap makes a context switch to another runnable context. The Kmap services the out requests by sending the physical address of the memory request via the map bus to the destination Cm. When the destination Cm completes the memory access, it signals a return request to the Kmap, which fetches the result of the memory access via the map bus and reactivates the request context. These steps, which are taken in an intracluster memory access, are depicted in Figure 7.6.

The intercluster bus is also a packet-switched bus which is jointly controlled by the Linc processors in each of the Kmaps directly connected to the bus. The Linc maintains queues of incoming and outgoing messages and interacts with the Kbus to activate and reactivate Pmap contexts. Each Linc interfaces to two independent intercluster buses, as shown in Figure 7.5. An intercluster message is sent from an immediate source Kmap to an immediate destination Kmap (in one

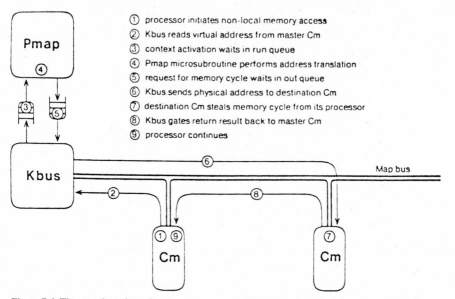

① processor initiates non-local memory access
② Kbus reads virtual address from master Cm
③ context activation waits in run queue
④ Pmap microsubroutine performs address translation
⑤ request for memory cycle waits in out queue
⑥ Kbus sends physical address to destination Cm
⑦ destination Cm steals memory cycle from its processor
⑧ Kbus gates return result back to master Cm
⑨ processor continues

Figure 7.6 The steps in an intracluster memory access. (Courtesy of the Cm* project at Carnegie-Mellon University, 1980.)

hop). These intercluster messages were designed to be used as a mechanism for remote procedure calls between Kmaps. The identity of the destination is encoded in the message so that the Linc can determine which message is sent to its cluster. If the final destination is several hops away from the initial source, the message is handled by intermediate Kmaps until it reaches the final destination.

Intercluster messages are of two types: *forward* messages, which invoke a new context at the destination Kmap, and *return* messages, which return to a waiting context also at the destination Kmap. A return message contains the context number of the context which is to be reactivated in the Pmap. When a Pmap context desires to invoke some operation in another Kmap, it prepares a forward intercluster message, instructs the Linc to transmit it on a specified intercluster bus and then swaps context. The forward message includes the source Kmap number and the originating Pmap context number so that the remote Kmap will be able to send back a return message.

When the remote Linc receives a forward message, it causes the Kmap to activate a new Pmap context to decode the message and respond to the request. It is assumed that the message contains some operation code which the Pmap context can identify and execute. After performing the operation, the context prepares a return intercluster message, and instructs the Linc to transmit it on a specified intercluster bus. The Pmap also informs the Kbus that the context is now free and switches context. As an example of such a cross-cluster operation, we consider the mapping of a nonlocal memory reference to a location in the physical memory of another cluster. Some computer module initiates the nonlocal memory reference which activates a context in its cluster's Kmap. This context becomes the master context and the Kmap becomes the master Kmap. The destination Kmap is the slave Kmap and the new context activated at the slave Kmap is the slave context. Figure 7.7 depicts the steps involved in performing a multicluster operation.

Collectively, the Kmaps and the Slocals form the distributed memory switch. They mediate each nonlocal reference, thus sustaining the appearance of a single large, uniformly addressed memory. However, memory reference times may have large variations. Approximate interreference times for local, intracluster, and intercluster references are 3, 9, and 26 μs, respectively. The distributed memory switch makes the Cm* structure potentially more reliable than tightly coupled systems because the system can still be operational in a degraded mode when an intercluster bus fails. The LSI-11 processor used in the Cm is a relatively slow processor (approximately a 0.1 MIPS) in comparison to the Kmap. It is not quite obvious how the design of the Kmap would be affected if a faster processor is used in the Cm. The Kmap technology and design affect the service rate it provides. In large systems, it can be a limiting factor. The Cm* architecture seems well suited for parallel algorithms with high locality in an intracluster bus. If locality is poor and the processes requests frequently cross intercluster buses, the performance of the algorithm may become poor.

The two-level hierarchy can be extended to an *n*-level hierarchy. An example could consist of a binary tree structure with *n* levels. In such a structure, the tree has a root node and each node which represents a cluster has six branches, with

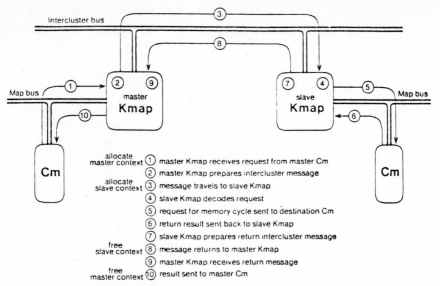

Figure 7.7 The steps in a cross-cluster memory access. (Courtesy of the Cm* project at Carnegie-Mellon University, 1980.)

the exception of the leaf nodes. The total number of nodes is $(b^n - 1)/(b - 1)$, and the number of links is $(b^n - b)/(b - 1)$. In a binary tree, each cluster is connected strictly to its two children and to a single parent. Communication between leaf nodes faces a bottleneck toward the top of the tree. Hence, such tree structures perform well on a large range of problems. Binary tree structures have been shown to be theoretically promising for sorting, matrix multiplication, and for solving some NP-hard problems. The basic scheme involves divide-and-conquer techniques.

7.1.2 Tightly Coupled Multiprocessors

Because of the large variability of interreference times, the throughput of the hierarchical loosely coupled multiprocessor may be too low for some applications that require fast response times. If high-speed or real-time processing is desired, tightly coupled systems (TCS) may be used. Two typical models of a TCS are discussed. The first model is shown in Figure 7.8a. It consists of p processors, l memory modules, and d input-output channels. These units are connected through a set of three interconnection networks, namely, the processor-memory interconnection network (PMIN), the I/O-processor interconnection network (IOPIN), and the interrupt-signal interconnection network (ISIN). The PMIN is a switch which can connect every processor to every memory module. Typically, this switch is a p by l crossbar which has pl sets of cross points. A set of cross points for a particular processor-memory pair includes $(n + k)$ cross points, where n is the width of the address within a module and k is the width of the data path. Hence the crossbar switch for a p by l multiprocessor system has a complexity $O(pl(n + k))$. For large p and l, the crossbar may dominate the cost of the multiprocessor system. If the crossbar switch is distributed across the memory modules, a multiported memory results. The complexity of the multiported memory is similar to that of the crossbar. Alternately, the PMIN could be a multistage network, some examples of which were discussed in Chapter 5.

A memory module can satisfy only one processor's request in a given memory cycle. Hence, if two or more processors attempt to access the same memory module, a conflict occurs which is resolved or arbitrated by the PMIN. If necessary the PMIN may be designed to permit broadcasting of data from one processor to two or more memory modules. To avoid excessive conflicts, the number of memory modules l is usually as large as p. Another method used to reduce the degree of conflicts is to associate a reserved storage area with each processor. This is the unmapped local memory (ULM) in Figure 7.8a. It is used to store Kernel code and operating system tables often used by the processes running on that processor. For example, if each processor is multiprogrammed, each time a task switch is desired the state of the process to be blocked may be saved in the ULM. The ULM helps in reducing the traffic in the PMIN and hence the degree of conflicts,

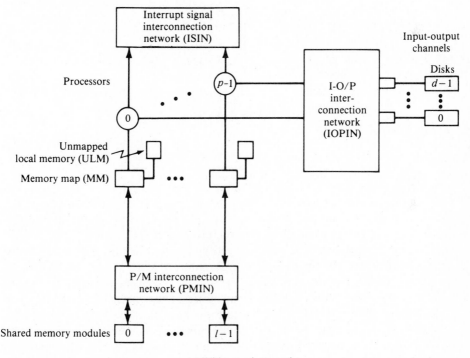

(a) Without private cache

Figure 7.8 Tightly coupled multiprocessor configurations.

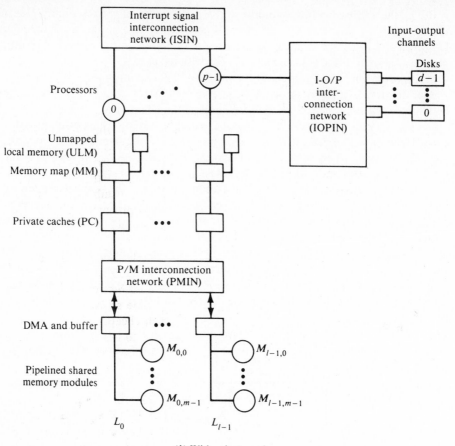

(b) With private cache

Figure 7.8 (*continued*)

provided process migration is not permitted. An example of a multiprocessor system with similar processor memory configuration to that shown in Figure 7.8a is the C.mmp multiprocessor designed at Carnegie Mellon University with 16 processors. Details of this system are given in Chapter 9.

In the multiprocessor organization of Figure 7.8a, each processor may make memory references which are accessed in main memory. These memory references contribute to the memory conflicts at the memory modules. Since each memory reference goes through the PMIN, it encounters delay in the processor memory switch and, hence, the instruction cycle time increases. The increase in the instruction cycle time reduces the system throughput. This delay can be reduced by associating a cache with each processor to capture most of the references made by a processor. Another consequence of the cache is that the traffic through the crossbar switch can be reduced, which subsequently reduces the contention at the cross points. A multiprocessor organization which uses a private cache with each processor is shown in Figure 7.8*b*. This multiprocessor organization encounters the cache coherence problem. More than one inconsistent copy of data may exist in the system. Various solutions to the cache coherence problem are given in Section 7.3. Examples of multiprocessors with private caches are the IBM 3084 and the S-1.

In Figure 7.8, there is a module attached to each processor that directs the memory references to either the ULM or the private cache of that processor. This module is called the *memory map* and is similar in operation to the Slocal discussed earlier. The general scheme for implementing memory maps was discussed in Chapter 2. The ISIN permits each processor to direct an interrupt to any other processor. Synchronization between processors is facilitated by the use of such an interprocessor network. The ISIN can also be used by a failing processor to broadcast a hardware-initiated alarm to the functioning processors. The IOPIN permits a processor to communicate with an I/O channel which is connected to peripheral devices.

The complexity of the ISIN may vary from a simple time shared bus to a complex crossbar switch. For example, in the Univac 1100/80 and Honeywell 60/66 multiprocessor systems, a connection is established between every pair of processors for the ISIN. The C.mmp system uses a time shared bus for inter-processor communication. A time shared bus is much cheaper than a crossbar switch but encounters more contentions and delays due to bus-arbitration logic. However, the interrupt request rate to the bus is usually low enough to make the shared bus an attractive solution to interprocessor communication.

The set of processors used in a multiprocessor system may be homogeneous or heterogeneous. It is homogeneous if the processors are functionally identical. For example, the multiprocessor system of the IBM 3081K has two identical processors. Even if the processors are homogeneous, they may be asymmetric. That is, two functionally identical components may differ along other dimensions, such as I/O accessibility, performance or reliability. Examples with symmetric multiprocessor configurations are the Honeywell 60/66 and the Univac 1100/80. Examples of the asymmetric multiprocessors are the attached processor systems such as the IBM 3084 AP and the C.mmp.

In most cases, the asymmetry or symmetry of the multiprocessor system is usually transparent to the user processes. It is only of interest to the operating system, especially with respect to load balancing and other scheduling considerations. In general, a homogeneous system is easier to program and eliminates the connector problem, which arises in getting two dissimilar processors to effectively communicate. The symmetric system usually can better facilitate error recovery, in case of failure.

Input-output asymmetricity The asymmetricity of the processors can also be extended to the input-output devices with respect to the connectivity of these devices to the processors. An I/O interconnection network that has complete connectivity is symmetric. Because symmetric systems are usually expensive, some multiprocessors have a high degree of asymmetry in the I/O subsystem. Figure 7.9 is an example of an asymmetric I/O subsystem. In such systems, devices attached to one processor cannot be directly accessed by another processor. This is the example I/O subsystem used in the C.mmp. A fully symmetric subsystem is more flexible and provides more accessibility.

In a fully symmetric structure, the failure of a central processor does not preclude the accessibility of a given device by any other processor. In the asymmetric case, the failure of a CPU causes all devices attached to that processor to become inaccessible. Furthermore, a request for data transfer to an I/O device which is attached to a given processor causes undesirable task switching overhead if the request is made by another processor. The inaccessibility problem encountered by a set of devices attached to a faulty processor can be slightly overcome by having redundant connections, as exemplified in Figure 7.10. In this example,

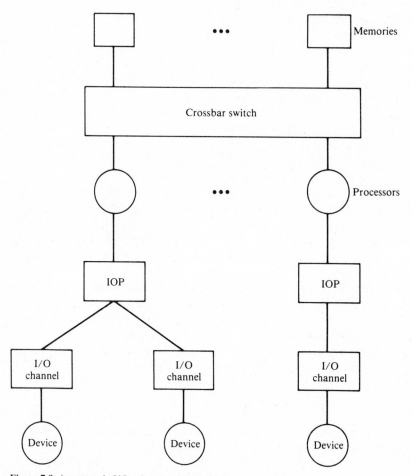

Figure 7.9 Asymmetric I/O subsystem in a multiprocessor system.

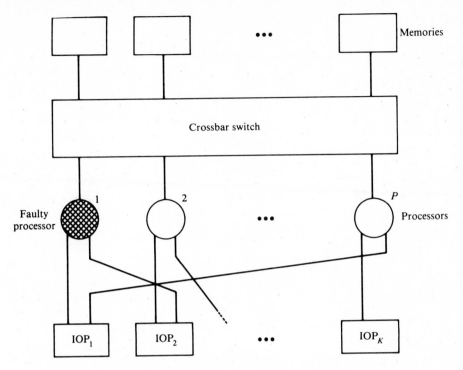

IOP$_1$ still accessible in the event of processor 1 failure

Figure 7.10 Increased availability in an asymmetric I/O subsystem through redundant connections.

IOP$_1$ is still accessible through processor P when processor 1 fails. The availability is provided at the cost of additional arbitration logic required for the multiple paths. Also, the extra logic must be sufficiently reliable that the degradation it introduces is more than compensated by the extra reliability of redundant paths. However, if the reliability of the extra logic is poor, then the reliability and availability of the system in Figure 7.10 will be poorer than that of the original system. The disadvantage of the fully symmetric case is the cost of the crossbar switch. This cost can be reduced without significant sacrifice in availability by using a multistage network such as the delta network discussed in the previous section, or a multiported system. Three examples of a tightly coupled multiprocessor system are the Cyber-170, the Honeywell 60/66, and the PDP-10. These examples are briefed below and details can be found in Satyanarayanan (1980).

The Cyber-170 architecture Figure 7.11 shows an example configuration of a Cyber-170 multiprocessor system. This configuration consists of two subsystems—the central processing subsystem and the peripheral processing subsystem. These subsystems have access to a common central memory (CM) through a central memory controller, which is essentially a high-speed crossbar switch. In addition to the central memory, there is an optional secondary memory called the extended

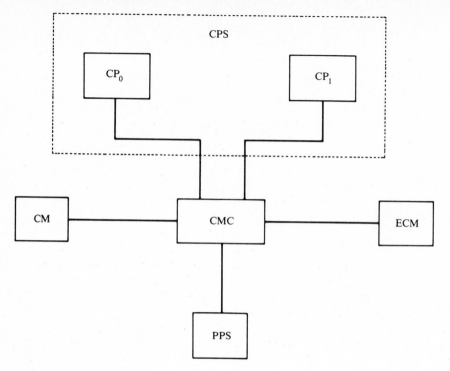

CM: central memory

CMC: central memory controller

CP_i: ith central processor

CPS: central processing subsystem

ECM: extended core memory

PPS: peripheral processing subsystem

Figure 7.11 A Cyber-170 multiprocessor configuration with two processors. (Courtesy of Control Data Corp.)

core memory (ECM), which is a low-speed random-access read-write memory. The ECM and the CM form a two-level memory hierarchy. In this configuration, the CMC becomes the switching center, which performs the combined functions of the ISIN, IOPIN, and PMIN described in Figure 7.8.

Honeywell 60/66 architecture A configuration of a Honeywell 60/66 multiprocessor system is shown in Figure 7.12. In this system, every central processor and every I/O multiplexer is connected to every controller (SC). This provides adequate redundancy in paths for high availability. In the event of a failure on the SC, all IOMs are still accessible by each processor. The system controller acts as a memory controller for its associated pair of memory modules. It also acts as an

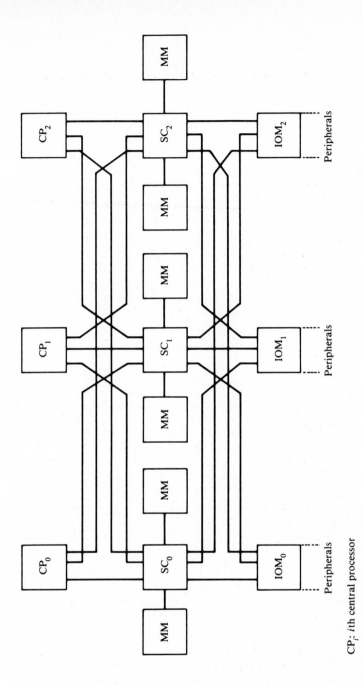

CP_i: ith central processor

IOM: I/O multiplexer

MM: memory

SC_i: ith system controller

Figure 7.12 A Honeywell 60/66 multiprocessor system. (Courtesy of Honeywell Corp.)

intelligent switch to route interrupts and other communications among the various system components. When more than one element attempts to access the same memory module, the corresponding system controller resolves the conflict. This triple redundancy organization is particularly designed to enhance availability and fault tolerance.

The PDP-10 multiprocessor Figure 7.13 shows two configurations of the PDP-10 multiprocessor with multiported memory modules. Each CPU has a cache of 2K words where each word is 36 bits. Figure 7.13a illustrates the asymmetric master-slave configuration. The two processors are identical, but the asymmetry is a result of the connection of the peripherals to the master only. Hence, the slave cannot initiate peripheral operations nor respond to an interrupt directly. The symmetrical configuration of the PDP-10 multiprocessor is shown in Figure 7.13b. Both processors are connected to a set of shared fast and slow peripherals. However, each data channel is attached to one processor, which is the only processor that can use it. Note that slow peripherals are connected to both processors via a switch. There is no cache invalidate interface between them. It is assumed that a software solution is used to enforce cache consistency.

The three tightly coupled multiprocessors discussed above are just a few of the commercial systems available. There is a trend to achieve improved performance

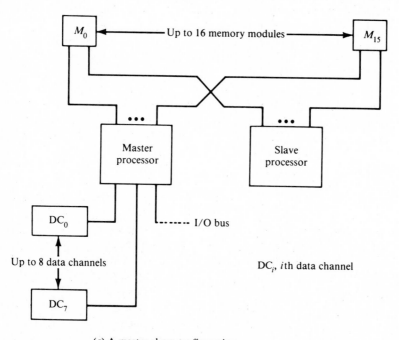

(a) A master-slave configuration

Figure 7.13 Two architectural configurations of the PDP-10 multiprocessor system. (Courtesy of Digital Equipment Corp.)

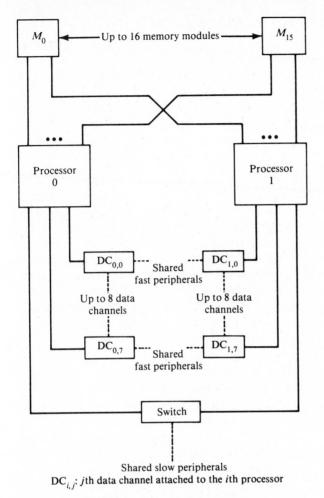

DC$_{i,j}$: jth data channel attached to the ith processor

(*b*) A symmetric configuration

Figure 7.13 (*continued*)

of new generation mainframes and supercomputers by tightly coupling a number of identical processors. Other commercial systems discussed in Chapter 9 are UNIVAC 1100/94, IBM 3081, HEP, and Cray X-MP. The relative merits of tight coupling depend on cost effectiveness, which is technology dependent.

One of the advantages of a multiprocessing system is its potential for effective error recoverable capability. Recoverability, however, is not synonymous with reliability. The number of interconnections and the multiplicity of processing units and other system modules may, in fact, cause a higher probability of failure on a multiprocessor than on a uniprocessor. However, the inherent redundancy in a multiprocessor system probably increases its ability to be fault tolerant.

7.1.3 Processor Characteristics for Multiprocessing

Most multiprocessors have been built using processors not originally designed for multiprocessor architecture. Two examples of these are the C.mmp system, which uses DEC's PDP-11 processors, and the Cm* multiprocessor, which uses LSI-11 microprocessors. One reason for using off-the-shelf components is to shorten development time. However, these off-the-shelf components can create undesirable features in the system. A number of desirable architectural features are described below for a processor to be effective in a multiprocessing environment.

Process recoverability The architecture of a processer used in a multiprocessor system should reflect the fact that the process and the processor are two different entities. If the processor fails, it should routinely be possible for another processor to retrieve the interrupted process state so that execution of the process can continue. Without this feature, the potential for reliability is substantially reduced. Most processors contain the process state of the current-running process in internal registers which are not accessible from outside the processor and are not written to memory in the event of a fault. With current technology, it should be possible to separate the general-purpose registers from the processor itself without much loss of speed. It is desirable to have a register file shared by all processors in the event of a gracefully degraded operation mode.

Efficient context switching Another reason for having a shared general-purpose register is that a large register file can be used in a multi-programmed processor. For effective utilization, it is necessary for the processor to support more than one addressing domain and, hence, to provide a domain-change or context-switching operation. Such switching operations require extensive queueing and stack operations. The context switch operation saves the state of the current process and switches to a selected ready-to-run process by restoring the state of the new process. The state of a running process is indicated by the contents of the processor registers. An example of a processor with multiple domains is the IBM 370/168. Two domains, the supervisor and user modes of operation, are available. A user process can communicate with the operating system by using a mechanism provided through a supervisor call (SVC) instruction.

A special instruction can be created to accomplish the context switch efficiently. An example of such an instruction is the *central exchange jump* (CEJ) provided in the Cyber-170 processor, which has a single set of registers. The execution of the CEJ results in the saving of the context or state of the current process and the register set replaced by the state of another process taken from an area in the central memory. This area is called the exchange package. Such save are restore operations for all processor registers can, if not properly designed, significantly contribute to the overhead in establishing concurrency in the system.

By providing an ample number of register sets, a task switch can be accomplished efficiently by changing the contents of the *current process register* in the processor to point to the register set containing the state of the selected process, as shown in Figure 7.14. The current process register points to the register set currently in use. For example, each processor in the S-1 multiprocessor system has 16 sets of registers. Stack instructions which rapidly save and restore the processor status word tend to minimize switching overheads. The implementation of reentrant procedure calls is related to the stack manipulative structure of the processor.

Large virtual and physical address spaces A processor intended to be used in the construction of a general-purpose medium to large-scale multiprocessor must support a large physical address space. Even when an algorithm is decomposed so that it can be implemented using very small amounts of code, processes sometimes need to access large amounts of data objects. The 16-bit address space of the processor used in the C.mmp hampered effective programming of the system.

In addition to the need for a large physical address space, a large virtual address space is also desirable. If possible, the virtual address space should be segmented to promote modular sharing and the checking of address bounds for memory protection and software reliability. For example, the processor used in the S-1 multiprocessor system has 2 gigabytes of virtual memory and 4 gigawords of physical memory, where each word is 36 bits wide.

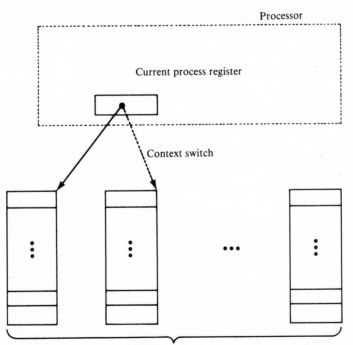

Figure 7.14 Context switching in a processor with multiple register sets.

Effective synchronization primitives The processor design must provide some implementation of indivisible actions which serve as the basis for *synchronization primitives*. These synchronization primitives require efficient mechanisms for establishing mutual exclusion. Mutual exclusion is required when two or more processes are in execution concurrently and must cooperate to exchange data during the computation. Mechanisms for establishing mutual exclusion involve some form of read-modify-write memory cycle and queueing. One such mechanism is the *semaphore*. Each semaphore has a queue associated with it and the entries in the queue refer to processes which were suspended because of the semaphore value of the variable. A semaphore operation requires an indivisible operation, which can be accomplished by using the read-modify-write memory cycle to test and update a semaphore. The queue manipulations should also be done indivisibly. Some instructions which are used to accomplish mutual exclusion are the *test-and-set* and *compare-and-swap*. These primitives will be discussed in Chapter 8.

Interprocessor communication mechanism The set of processors used in a multi-processor must have an efficient means of interprocessor communication. This mechanism should be implemented in hardware. A hardware mechanism is very useful for drawing the attention of the target processor. The need for such a mechanism is even more apparent when, in an asymmetric multiprocessor system, there are frequent requests for services exchanged between different processors. The hardware interprocessor mechanism can also facilitate synchronization between processors. This mechanism could, for example, be used in the event of a processor failure to initiate a hardware signal to all functioning processors, which would then become aware of the faulty processor and start an error recovery or diagnostic procedure.

Since the processors in a tightly coupled system share memory, it is possible to have software interprocessor communication without an explicit hardware mechanism. This method is inefficient as each processor will have to periodically poll its "mailbox" to see if there is a message for it. Such polling will result in intolerable response times for a large number of processors. Examples of systems with hardware interprocessor-communication mechanisms are the IBM 370/168 MP, Cray X-MP, and the C.mmp, which will be discussed in Chapter 9. It is possible that two or more processors may simultaneously attempt to access a common path in the interprocessor mechanism. Each processor must be capable of participating in the arbitration of the requests to use the path. Since arbitration implies that on simultaneous requests one or more processors must wait, the processor must have a wait state or some mechanism to suspend the processor in a queue.

Instruction set The instruction set of the processor should have adequate facilities for implementing high-level languages that permit effective concurrency at the procedure level and for efficiently manipulating data structures. Instructions should be provided for procedure linkage, looping constructs, parameter manipulation, multidimensional index computation, and range checking of addresses. Furthermore, the instruction set should also include instructions for creating and terminating parallel execution paths within a program. Thus, a full set of addressing modes are desirable. Hardware counters and real-time clocks should be provided to generate a unique name of process identification and time-out signals required for process management. These timers can also be used in a multiprocessing system to detect many errors by associating a "watchdog" timer with important system resources, as done in the C.mmp. A multiprocessor system provides a natural environment where each component can monitor each other relatively easily. There are different implementations of the error-detection technique, but the basic idea is that the timer will in some way raise an error-condition indicator if it is not reset within a specified time limit. Various techniques used to interrupt a processor will be discussed later.

7.2 INTERCONNECTION NETWORKS

The principal characteristic of a multiprocessor system is the ability of each processor to share a set of main memory modules and, possibly, I/O devices. This sharing capability is provided through a set of two interconnection networks. One is between the processors and memory modules and the other, between the processors and the I/O subsystem. There are several different physical forms available for the interconnection network (IN). Four basic organizations of the IN are discussed in this section. The classification scheme presented here is due to Enslow (1977). Techniques are presented to evaluate the effective bandwidth of some interconnection networks.

7.2.1 Time Shared or Common Buses

The simplest interconnection system for multiple processors is a common communication path connecting all of the functional units. An example of a multiprocessor system using the common communication path is shown in Figure 7.15. The common path is often called a time shared or common bus. This organization is the least complex and the easiest to reconfigure. Such an interconnection network is often a totally passive unit having no active components such as

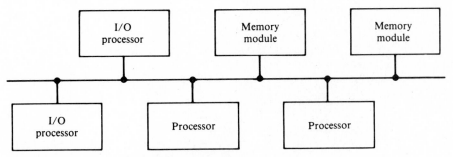

Figure 7.15 A single-bus multiprocessor organization.

switches. Transfer operations are controlled completely by the bus interfaces of the sending and receiving units. Since the bus is a shared resource, a mechanism must be provided to resolve contention.

The conflict-resolution methods include static or fixed priorities, first-in, first-out (FIFO) queues and daisy chaining. A centralized bus controller or arbiter, though simplifying the conflict resolution, may have negative effects on system reliability and flexibility. A unit (processor or I/O) that wishes to initiate a transfer must first determine the availability status of the bus, then address the destination unit to determine its availability and capability to receive the transfer. A command is also issued to inform the destination unit what operation it is to perform with the data being transferred, after which the data transfer is finally initiated. A receiving unit recognizes its address placed on the bus and responds to the control signals from the sender. These concepts, although basic, typify the operations on the bus.

An example of a time shared bus is the PDP-11 Unibus, which has 56 signal lines to provide the control, address lines, and data paths necessary to transfer 16-bit words. The function of each of the signals is shown in Table 7.1. The five bus-request signals are used for requesting bus control by a "master" at four different priority levels. They are also used for *attention signals* by a "slave." The master-slave assignment is dynamic. When a requester is granted control of the bus, it becomes a temporary master until it relinquishes control. The master can then select certain devices as slaves to control the transfer of data. Each of the request signals has a corresponding bus-grant signal. The functions of these signals are described in more details later.

Although the single-bus organization is quite reliable and relatively inexpensive, it does introduce a single critical component in the system that can cause complete system failure as a result of a malfunction in any of the bus interface circuits. Moreover, system expansion, by adding more processors or memory,

Table 7.1 PDP-11 unibus signals

Signal	Number of lines	Function
Address	18	Identifies destination of information (memory location or device address)
Data	16+ 2 parity	Information value
Control	2+ 1 master sync 1 slave sync	Data transfer control
	1	Initialization
Bus request	5	Priority interrupt request
Bus grant	5 (unidirectional)	Bus assignment (made by CPU)
Bus busy	1	Bus status
Interrupt	1	Interrupt request
Selection acknowledge	1	Acknowledgment signal
Power fail	2	Power failure detection

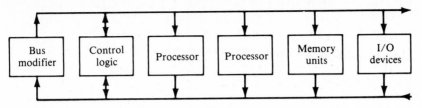

Figure 7.16 **Multiprocessor with unidirectional buses.**

increases the bus contention, which degrades system throughput and increases arbitration logic. The total overall transfer rate within the system is limited by the bandwidth and speed of this single path. For this reason, private memories and private I/Os are highly advantageous. Interconnection techniques that overcome these weaknesses add to the complexity of the system.

An extension of the single path organization to two unidirectional paths, as shown in Figure 7.16, alleviates some the problems mentioned above without an appreciable increase in system complexity or decrease in reliability. However, a single transfer operation in such a system usually requires the use of both buses, hence not much is actually gained.

The next step in alleviating the limitations of the time shared bus is to provide multiple bidirectional buses, as shown in Figure 7.17, to permit multiple simultaneous bus transfers; however, this increases the system complexity significantly. In this case, the interconnection subsystem becomes an active device. A number of computer systems, such as the Tandem-16 and Pluribus, employ variations of the time shared system of buses discussed above. In general, the above organizations are usually appropriate for small systems.

In view of the increasing numbers and speeds of devices attached to a central bus as a result of changing technology and applications, the bus can become heavily loaded. Therefore, the bus impairs the performance of the devices and, thus, of the overall system. There are several factors that affect the characteristics and performance of a bus. These include the number of active devices on the bus, the bus-arbitration algorithm, centralization (or distribution) of control, data width, synchronization of data transmission, and error detection. We will examine several

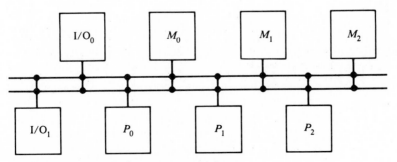

Figure 7.17 **Multi-bus multiprocessor organization.**

bus-arbitration algorithms which control access to the bus by the competing devices.

Current technology (processing speed) requires relatively simple algorithms for bus arbitration. These algorithms are usually implemented in the hardware and allow the arbitration for a bus cycle to be overlapped with the previous transfer.

(A) The static priority algorithm Many digital buses used today assign unique static priorities to the requesting devices. When multiple devices concurrently request the use of the bus, the device with the highest priority is granted access to it. This approach is usually implemented using a scheme called *daisy chaining*, in which all services are effectively assigned static priorities according to their locations along a bus grant control line. The device closest to a central bus controller is assigned the highest priority (Figure 7.18). Requests are made on a common request line, BRQ. The central bus control unit propagates a bus grant signal (BGT) if the acknowledge signal (SACK) indicates that the bus is idle.

The first device which has issued a bus request that receives the BGT signal stops the latter's propagation. This sets the bus-busy flag in the controller and the device assumes bus control. On completion, it resets the bus-busy flag in the controller and a new BGT signal is generated if other requests are outstanding. The DEC PDP-11 Unibus uses this approach. The Motorola MC68000 processor incorporates such a bus control unit.

Another DEC bus called the synchronous backplane interconnect (SBI) and used in the VAX 11/780 computer implements static priorities using a distributed scheme called *parallel priority resolution*, in which the time required to determine which requesting device has the highest priority is fixed (unlike daisy chaining). Using static priorities clearly gives preferences and, thus, lower wait times to devices with higher priorities.

(B) The fixed time slice algorithm Another common bus-arbitration algorithm divides the available bus bandwidth into fixed-length time slices that are then sequentially offered to each device in a round-robin fashion. Should the selected

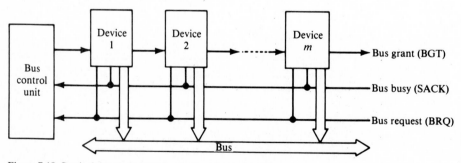

Figure 7.18 Static daisy chain implementation of a system bus.

device elect not to use its time slice, the time slice remains unused by any device. This technique, called *fixed time slicing* (FTS) or *time division multiplexing* (TMD), is used by Digital's Parallel Communications Link, which also allows a flexible assignment of available time slices to the devices. This scheme is usually used with synchronous buses in which all devices are synchronized to a common clock.

The service given to each device in the FTS scheme for access to the bus is independent of that device's position or identity on the bus; schemes with this characteristic are said to be symmetric. In particular, all m devices are given one out of every m time slices at fixed intervals in this scheme. Symmetric bus-arbitration algorithms optimally load-balance all bus requests because no preference is given to any device. It further delivers a bounded maximum wait time to the devices. However, it suffers a high average wait time (and, thus, a lower bus utilization).

When the bus is not heavily loaded, FTS incurs a substantially higher standard deviation from all wait times than does the static priority scheme, although the variability of service is lower and remains constant regardless of the bus load. Both algorithms offer good performance under light bus loading; these characteristics and their relative simplicity explain their widespread popularity.

(C) Dynamic priority algorithms The following dynamic priority algorithms allow the load-balancing characteristics of symmetric algorithms such as fixed time slicing to be achieved without incurring the penalty of high wait times. The devices are assigned unique priorities and compete to access the bus, but the priorities are dynamically changed to give every device an opportunity to access the bus. If the algorithm used to permute the priorities favors no individual device (is symmetric), then the system load balances the bus requests. Further, using priorities overcomes the inefficiency inherent in the fixed time slice scheme of allocating full time slices to the devices before requests are placed. Two algorithms for dynamically permuting priorities are the *least recently used* (LRU) and the *rotating daisy chain* (RDC).

The LRU algorithm gives the highest priority to the requesting device that has not used the bus for the longest interval. This is accomplished by reassigning priorities after each bus cycle. The second dynamic priority algorithm generalizes the daisy chain implementation of static priorities. Recall that in the daisy chain scheme all devices are given static and unique priorities according to their priorities on a bus-grant line emanating from a central controller.

In the RDC scheme, no central controller exists, and the bus-grant line is connected from the last device back to the first in a closed loop (Figure 7.19). Whichever device is granted access to the bus serves as bus controller for the following arbitration (an arbitrary device is selected to have initial access to the bus). Each device's priority for a given arbitration is determined by that device's distance along the bus-grant line from the device currently serving as bus controller; the latter device has the lowest priority. Hence, the priorities change dynamically with each bus cycle.

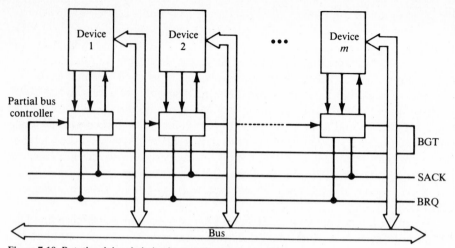

Figure 7.19 Rotating daisy chain implementation of a system bus.

(D) The first-come first-served algorithm In the *first-come, first-served* (FCFS) scheme, requests are simply honored in the order received. This scheme is symmetric because it favors no particular processor or device on the bus; thus, it load balances the bus requests. It has been shown that, under the condition of fixed service times by the central resource (fixed bus-transfer times in this case), FCFS yields the smallest possible average wait time and standard deviation of all wait times. In essence, FCFS is the optimal bus-arbitration algorithm with respect to these performance measures.

Unfortunately, FCFS is difficult to implement for at least two reasons. Any implementation of FCFS must provide a mechanism to record the arrival order of all pending bus requests, unlike the previous algorithms. More important, it is always possible for two bus requests to arrive within a sufficiently small interval so their relative ordering cannot be correctly distinguished. Hence, any implementation can only approximate the behavior of FCFS. Despite the above difficulties in realizing an implementation, it is important to measure the performance of FCFS as an indicator of the best possible performance that a bus-arbitration algorithm can achieve with respect to the above criteria.

Two other techniques used in bus-control algorithms are *polling* and *independent requesting*. In a bus-controller that uses polling, the bus grant signal (BGT) of the static daisy chain implementation is replaced by a set of $\lceil \log_2 m \rceil$ polling lines, as shown in Figure 7.20. The set of poll lines is connected to each of the devices. On a bus request, the controller sequences through the device addresses by using the poll lines. When a device D_i which requested access recognizes its address, it raises the SACK line (to indicate bus busy).

The bus-control unit acknowledges by terminating the polling process and D_i gains access to the bus. The access is maintained until the device lowers the SACK line. Note that the priority of a device is determined by its position in the polling sequence. In the independent requesting technique, a separate bus request (BRQ_i)

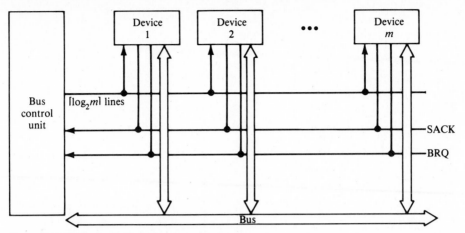

Figure 7.20 Polling implementation of a system bus.

and bus grant (BGT$_i$) line are connected to each device i sharing the bus, as shown in Figure 7.21. This requesting technique can permit the implementation of LRU, FCFS, and a variety of other allocation algorithms.

7.2.2 Crossbar Switch and Multiport Memories

If the number of buses in a time-shared bus system is increased, a point is reached at which there is a separate path available for each memory unit, as shown in Figure 7.22. The interconnection network is then called a *nonblocking* crossbar.

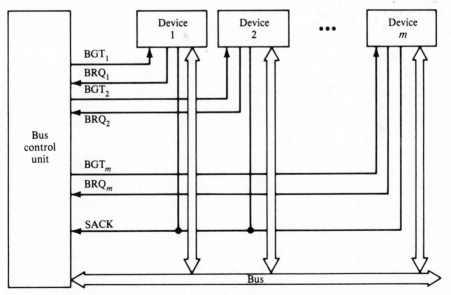

Figure 7.21 Independent request implementation of a system bus.

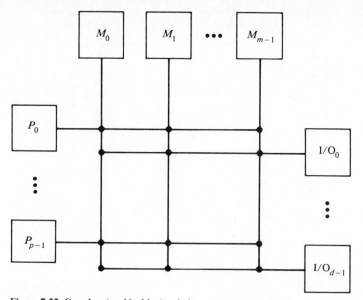

Figure 7.22 Crossbar (nonblocking) switch system organization for multiprocessors. (Courtesy of *ACM Computing Surveys*, Enslow 1977.)

The crossbar switch possesses complete connectivity with respect to the memory modules because there is a separate bus associated with each memory module. Therefore, the maximum number of transfers that can take place simultaneously is limited by the number of memory modules and the bandwidth-speed product of the buses rather than by the number of paths available.

The important characteristics of a system utilizing a crossbar interconnection matrix are the extreme simplicity of the switch-to-functional unit interfaces and the ability to support simultaneous transfers for all memory units. To provide these features requires major hardware capabilities in the switch. Not only must each cross point be capable of switching parallel transmissions, but it must also be capable of resolving multiple requests for access to the same memory module occurring during a single memory cycle. These conflicting requests are usually handled on a predetermined priority basis. The result of the inclusion of such a capability is that the hardware required to implement the switch can become quite large and complex. Although very large scale integration (VLSI) can reduce the size of the switch, it will have little effect on its complexity.

In a crossbar switch or multiported device, conflicts occur when two or more concurrent requests are made to the same destination device. In the following discussion, we assume that there are 16 destination devices (memory modules) and 16 requestors (processors). The implementation to be described can also be used for a processor to device connection. Figure 7.23 shows an example functional design of a crossbar switch element or multiported memory for one module. The switch consists of arbitration and multiplexer modules. Each processor generates a memory module request signal (REQ) to the arbitration unit, which selects the

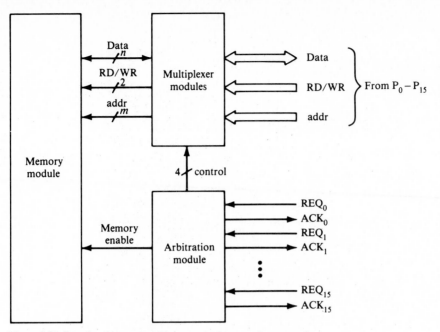

Figure 7.23 Functional structure of a crosspoint in a crossbar network.

processor with the highest priority. The selection is accomplished with a priority encoder. The arbitration module returns an acknowledge signal (ACK) to the selected processor. After the processor receives the ACK, it initiates its memory operation.

The multiplexer module multiplexes data, addresses of words within the module, and control signals from the processor to the memory module using a 16-to-1 multiplexer. The multiplexer is controlled by the encoded number of the selected processor. This code was generated by the priority encoder within the arbitration module.

Such a scheme was used to implement the processor-memory switch for the C.mmp, which has 16 processors and 16 memory modules. The switch consists of 16 sets of cross points from one processor port to the 16 memory ports, and another 16 sets of cross points from one memory port to the 16 processor ports. Theoretically, expansion of the system is limited only by the size of the switch matrix, which can often be modularly expanded within initial design or other engineering limitations. One effect of VLSI on the crossbar interconnection system is the feasibility of designing crossbar matrices for a larger capacity than initially required and equipping them only for the present requirements. Expansion would then be facilitated, since all that is required is the addition of the missing cross points.

In order to provide the flexibility required in access to the input-output devices, a natural extension of the crossbar switch concept is to use a similar switch on the device side of the I/O processor or channel, as shown in Figure 7.24. The

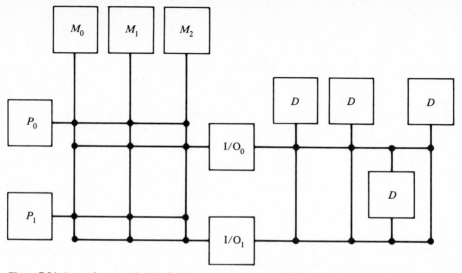

Figure 7.24 A crossbar organization for inter-processor-memory-I/O connections.

hardware required for the implementation is quite different and not nearly so complex because controllers and devices are normally designed to recognize their own unique addresses. The effect is the same as if there were a primary bus associated with each I/O channel and crossbuses for each controller or device.

The crossbar switch has the potential for the highest bandwidth and system efficiency. However, because of its complexity and cost, it may not be cost-effective for a large multiprocessor system. The reliability of the switch is problematic; however, it can be improved by segmentation and redundancy within the switch. In general, it is normally quite easy to partition the system to logically isolate malfunctioning units. There are a number of examples of systems utilizing the crossbar interconnection systems. Some of these are the C.mmp and the S-1 multiprocessor systems, which are to be discussed in Chapter 9.

If the control, switching, and priority arbitration logic that is distributed throughout the crossbar switch matrix is distributed at the interfaces to the memory modules, a multiport memory system is the result, as the example shows in Figure 7.25. This system organization is well suited to both uni- and multiprocessor system organizations and is used in both. The method often utilized to resolve memory-access conflicts is to assign permanently designated priorities at each memory port. The system can then be configured as necessary at each installation to provide the appropriate priority access to various memory modules for each functional unit, as shown in Figure 7.26. Except for the priority associated with each, all of the ports are usually electrically and operationally identical. In fact, the ports are often merely a row of identical cable connectors, and electrically it makes no difference whether an I/O or central processor is attached.

The flexibility possible in configuring the system also makes it possible to designate portions of memory as private to certain processors, I/O units, or com-

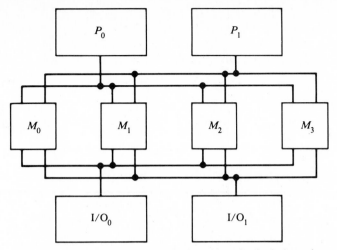

Figure 7.25 Multiport memory organization without fixed priority assignment. (Courtesy of *ACM Computing Surveys*, Enslow 1977.)

binations thereof, as shown in Figure 7.27. In this figure, memory modules M_0 and M_3 are private to processors P_0 and P_1, respectively. This type of system organization can have definite advantages in increasing protection against unauthorized access and may also permit the storage of recovery routines in memory areas that are not susceptible to modification by other processors; however, there are also serious disadvantages in system recovery if the other processors are not able to access control and status information in a memory block associated with a faulty processor.

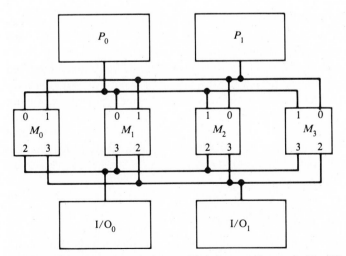

Figure 7.26 Multiport-memory system with assignment of port priorities. (Courtesy of *ACM Computing Surveys*, Enslow 1977.)

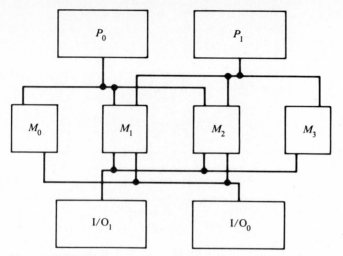

Figure 7.27 Multiport memory organization with private memories. (Courtesy of *ACM Computing Surveys*, Enslow 1977.)

The multiport memory system organization also can support nonblocking access to the memory if a *full-connected* topology is utilized. Since each word access is a separate operation, it also permits the exploitation of interleaved memory addresses for access by a single processor. However, for multiple processors, interleaving may actually degrade memory performance by increasing the number of memory-access conflicts that occur as all processors cycle through all memory following a sequence of consecutive addresses. Interleaving also results in the effective loss of more than one module of memory when there is a failure. There are a number of examples of multiport memory systems such as the Univac 1100/90 and IBM System 370/168 to be discussed in Chapter 9.

It is very difficult to justify the use of a crossbar switch or multiport memories for large multiprocessing systems. The absence of a switch with reasonable cost and performance is one of the reasons that has prevented the growth of large multimicroprocessor systems. The high cost of the switch may be circumvented by using a switch with a slightly restricted number of possible permutations. In the next subsection, we discuss some multistage networks for multiprocessors. These networks are far less expensive than full crossbars or multiport memories for large multiprocessing systems. Moreover, the multistage networks are modular and easy to control. The modularity permits incremental expansion and repairability. A comparison of the three multiprocessor interconnection structures is given in Table 7.2.

7.2.3 Multistage Networks for Multiprocessors

In order to design multistage networks, we need to understand the basic principles involved in the construction and control of simple crossbar switches. Consider the 2×2 crossbar switch shown in Figure 7.28. This 2×2 switch has the capability

Table 7.2 Comparison of three multiprocessor hardware organizations

Multiprocessors with time shared bus:

1. Lowest overall system cost for hardware and least complex.
2. Very easy to physically modify the hardware system configuration by adding or removing functional units.
3. Overall system capacity limited by the bus transfer rate. Failure of the bus is a catastrophic system failure.
4. Expanding the system by the addition of functional units may degrade overall system performance (throughput).
5. The system efficiency attainable is the lowest of all three basic interconnection systems.
6. This organization is usually appropriate for smaller systems only.

Multiprocessors with crossbar switch:

1. This is the most complex interconnection system. There is a potential for the highest total transfer rate.
2. The functional units are the simplest and cheapest since the control and switching logic is in the switch.
3. Because a basic switching matrix is required to assemble any functional units into a working configuration, this organization is usually cost-effective for multiprocessors only.
4. Systems expansion (addition of functional units) usually improves overall performance. There is the highest potential for system efficiency such as for system expansion without reprogramming of the operating system.
5. Theoretically, expansion of the system is limited only by the size of the switch matrix, which can often be modularly expanded within initial design or other engineering limitations.
6. The reliability of the switch, and therefore the system, can be improved by segmentation and/or redundancy within the switch.

Multiprocessors with multiport memory:

1. Requires the most expensive memory units since most of the control and switching circuitry is included in the memory unit.
2. The characteristics of the functional units permit a relatively low cost uniprocessor to be assembled from them.
3. There is a potential for a very high total transfer rate in the overall system.
4. The size and configuration options possible are determined (limited) by the number and type of memory ports available; this design decision is made quite early in the overall design process and is difficult to modify.
5. A large number of cables and connectors are required.

of connecting the input A to either the output labeled 0 or the output labeled 1, depending on the value of some control bit c_A of the input A. If $c_A = 0$, the input is connected to the upper output, and if $c_A = 1$, the connection is made to the lower output. Terminal B of the switch behaves similarly with a control bit c_B. The 2×2 module also has the capability to arbitrate between conflicting requests. If both inputs A and B require the same output terminal, then only one of them will be connected and the other will be blocked or rejected.

The 2×2 switch shown in Figure 7.28 is not buffered. In such a switch, the performance may be limited by the switch setup time which is experienced each time a rejected request is resubmitted. To improve the performance, buffers can be inserted within the switch, as shown in Figure 7.29. Such a switch has also been shown to be effective for packet switching when used in a multistage network.

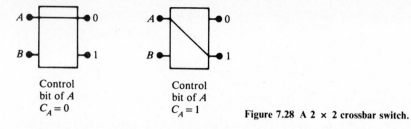

Figure 7.28 A 2 × 2 crossbar switch.

It is straightforward to construct a 1×2^n demultiplexer using the above described 2×2 module. This is accomplished by constructing a binary tree of these modules, as shown in Figure 7.30, for a 1×8 demultiplexer tree. The destinations are marked in binary. If the source A is required to connect to destination $(d_2 d_1 d_0)_2$, then the root node is controlled by bit d_2, the modules in the second stage are controlled by bit d_1, and the modules in the last stage are controlled by bit d_0. It is clear that A can be connected to any one of the eight output terminals. It is also obvious that input B can be switched to any one of the eight outputs. The method of constructing the 1×2^n demultiplexer tree can be extended to build a $2^n \times 2^n$ multistage network. Below we extend the tree network to devise a general multistage network called a banyan network.

A *banyan network* can be roughly described as a partially ordered graph divided into distinct levels. Nodes with no arcs fanning out of them are called *base* nodes and those with no arcs fanning into them are called *apex* nodes. The *fanout f* of a node is the number of arcs fanning out from the node. The *spread*

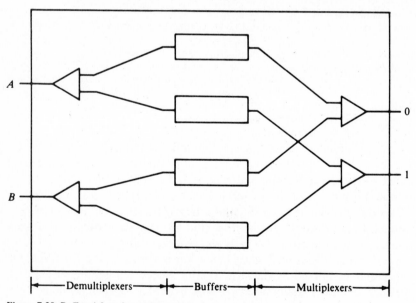

Figure 7.29 Buffered 2 × 2 crossbar switch.

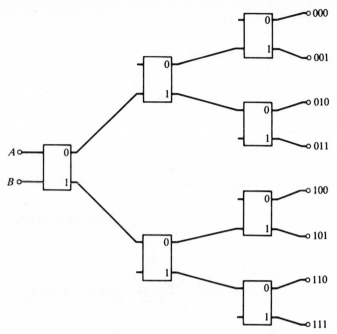

Figure 7.30 1-by-8 demultiplexer implemented with 2 × 2 switch boxes.

s of a node is the number of arcs fanning into it. An (f, s, l) banyan network can thus be described as a partially ordered graph with l levels in which there is exactly one path from every base to every apex node. The fanout of each nonbase node is f and the spread of each nonapex node is s. Each node of the graph is an $s \times f$ crossbar switch.

The banyan network can be derived from a uniform tree with fanout f. We illustrate the derivation of a $(2, 2, 2)$ banyan network from the two-level binary tree shown in Figure 7.31a. Since the spread is 2, it means that two arcs should be fanning into each nonroot node. Therefore, we replicate the rest to have s copies of the root and attach the root to the next level nodes, as shown in Figure 7.31b. To make the spread of the leaf nodes equal to two, replicate the top two levels (interleaving the second level nodes). Join the second level nodes to the leaf nodes to make the fanout of the second level nodes equal to 2 and the spread of the leaf nodes equal to 2. This completes the derivation of the $(2, 2, 2)$ banyan network and is shown in Figure 7.31c.

A banyan network has the advantage of providing a complete interconnection of one set of n devices to another set of n devices at a cost in switching circuitry that grows as $n \log n$. A crossbar switch, by contrast, grows as n^2. In general, an (f, s, l) banyan network can be defined as l recursions on an $s \times f$ crossbar switch. A cross point is thus a banyan of height 1. Hence different topologies of banyan networks can be implemented for multiprocessors. However, more studies need

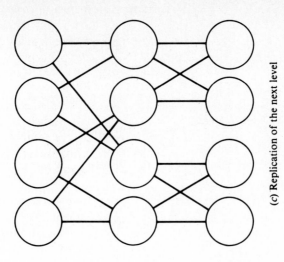

(a) A tree, fanout 2 (2 level)

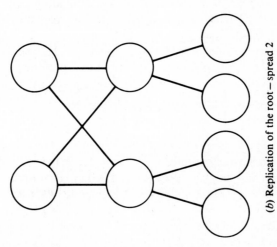

(b) Replication of the root – spread 2

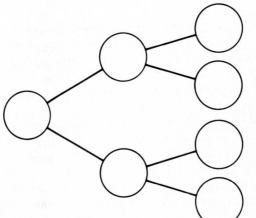

(c) Replication of the next level

Figure 7.31 Formation of a (2, 2, 2) Banyan graph.

to be performed to evaluate the cost effectiveness of these topologies under different multiprocessor work loads. Below, we discuss an implementation of a special type of banyan network called the delta network, which has been proposed for multiprocessors by Patel (1981).

Let an $a \times b$ crossbar module have the capability to connect any one of its a inputs to any one of the b outputs, where the outputs are labeled $0, 1, \ldots, b - 1$. An input terminal is connected to the output labeled d if the control digit supplied by the input is d, where d is a base-b digit. An $a \times b$ module also arbitrates between conflicting requests by accepting one of the requests and blocking or rejecting others.

A *delta network* is defined as an $a^n \times b^n$ switching network with n stages consisting of $a \times b$ crossbar modules. The interconnection or link patterns between stages is such that there exists a unique path of constant length from any source to any destination. Moreover, the path is digit controlled such that a crossbar module connects an input to one of its b outputs depending on a single base-b digit taken from the destination address. In a delta network, no input or output terminal of any crossbar module is left unconnected.

To systematize the link patterns between stages of the delta network, we define a q-shuffle of qc objects, denoted by S_{q*c} where q and c are some positive integers. S_{q*c} is a permutation of qc indices $\langle 0, 1, 2, \ldots, (qc - 1) \rangle$ and is defined as

$$S_{q*c}(i) = \left(qi + \left\lfloor \frac{i}{c} \right\rfloor \right) \bmod qc \tag{7.1}$$

for $0 \leq i \leq qc - 1$. An alternative $S_{q*c}(i)$ can be expressed as

$$S_{q*c}(i) = \begin{cases} qi \bmod(qc - 1) & \text{for } 0 \leq i < qc - 1 \\ i & \text{for } i = qc - 1 \end{cases} \tag{7.2}$$

A q-shuffle of qc playing cards can be viewed as follows. Divide the deck of qc cards into q piles of c cards each: top c cards $\langle 0, 1, \ldots, (c - 1) \rangle$ in the first pile, next c cards $\langle c, c + 1, \ldots, (2c - 1) \rangle$ in the second pile, and so on. Now pick the cards one at a time from the top of each pile, the first card from the top of pile one, the second card from the top of pile two, and so on in a circular fashion until all the piles of cards are exhausted. This new order of cards represents an S_{q*c} permutation of the previous order. Figure 7.32 illustrates an example of a 4 shuffle of 12 indices, namely S_{4*3}. From the above description, it is clear that a 2 shuffle is the well-known perfect shuffle discussed in Chapter 5.

In order to construct an $a^n \times b^n$ delta network, we use the a shuffle as the link pattern between every two consecutive stages of the network. If the destination D is expressed in a base-b system as $(d_{n-1}d_{n-2} \cdots d_1 d_0)_b$, where $D = \sum_{0 \leq j < n} d_j b^j$ and $0 \leq d_i < b$, then the base-b digit d_i controls the crossbar modules of stage $(n - i)$. The a-shuffle function is used to convert the outputs of a stage to the inputs of the next stage, where the inputs and outputs are numbered $0, 1, 2, \ldots$, starting at the

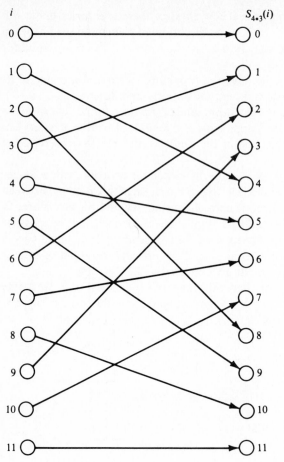

Figure 7.32 The 4 shuffle of 12 objects.

top. Figure 7.33 shows a general $a^n \times b^n$ delta network which has a^n sources and b^n destinations. Numbering the stages of the network as $1, 2, \ldots, n$, starting at the source side of the network requires that there be a^{n-1} crossbar modules in the first stage. The first stage then has $a^{n-1}b$ output terminals. This implies that stage two must have $a^{n-1}b$ input terminals, which requires $a^{n-2}b$ crossbar modules in the second stage. In general, the ith stage has $a^{n-i}b^{i-1}$ crossbar modules of size $a \times b$. Thus, the total number of $a \times b$ crossbar modules required in an $a^n \times b^n$ delta network can be found as $(a^n - n^n)/(a - b)$, for $a \neq b$ and nb^{n-1} for $a = b$. Two delta networks, one $4^2 \times 3^2$ and the other $2^3 \times 2^3$, derived from Figure 7.33 are shown in Figures 7.34 and 7.35, respectively; the interstage link patterns are 4 shuffle and 2 shuffle, respectively. Note that the destinations in Figures 7.34 and 7.35 are labeled in bases 3 and 2, respectively. It has been shown that the a-shuffle link pattern used between adjacent stages allows a source to connect to any destination by using the destination-digit control of each $a \times b$ crossbar module.

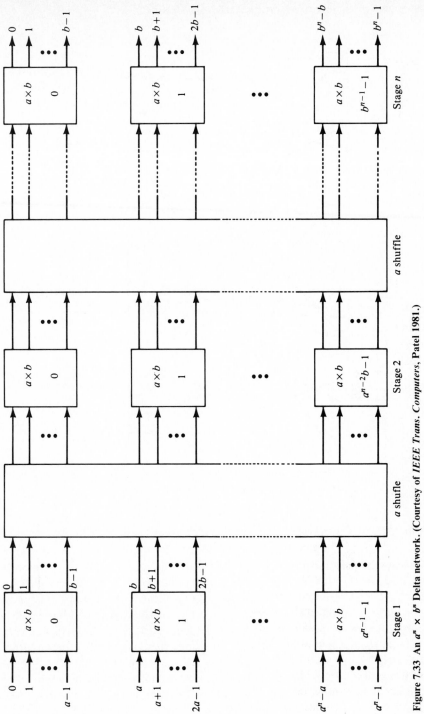

Figure 7.33 An $a^n \times b^n$ Delta network. (Courtesy of *IEEE Trans. Computers*, Patel 1981.)

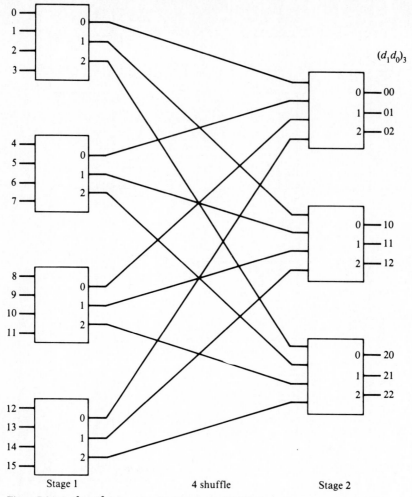

Figure 7.34 A $4^2 \times 3^2$ delta network. (Courtesy of *IEEE Trans. Computers*, Patel 1981.)

Note that the network of Figure 7.35 does not allow an identity permutation, which is useful if, say, memory module i is a "favorite" or home module of processor i. Therefore, identity permutation allows most of the memory references to be made without conflict. A simple renaming of the inputs of Figure 7.35 will permit an identity permutation. This is shown in Figure 7.36. In this case, if all 2×2 switches were in the straight position, then an identity permutation is generated.

In general, b is a power of 2 and a is very small, usually between 1 and 4. Figure 7.37 illustrates the functional block diagram of a 2×2 crossbar module. All single lines in the figure are 1-bit lines. The double lines on the INFO box represent address lines, incoming and outgoing data lines, and a read-write control line. The data lines may or may not be bidirectional. The function of the INFO box

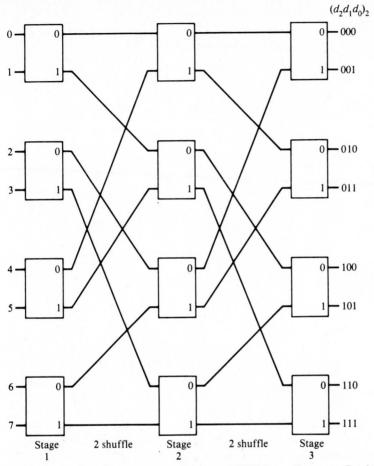

Figure 7.35 A $2^3 \times 2^3$ delta network. (Courtesy of *IEEE Trans. Computers*, Patel 1981.)

is that of a simple 2×2 crossbar; if the input X is 1, then a cross connection exists, and if X is 0, then a straight connection exists.

The function of the control box is to generate the signal X and provide arbitration. A request exists at an input port if the corresponding request line is 1. The destination digit provides the nature of the request; a 0 for the connection to the upper output port and a 1 for the lower port. In case of conflict, the request r_0 is given the priority and a busy signal $b_1 = 1$ is supplied to the lower input port. A busy signal is eventually transmitted to the source which originated the blocked request. The logic equations for all the labeled signals are given with the block diagram. For the INFO box, the equations are given for left to right direction. The parallel generation of X and $\overline{X}$ reduces one gate level.

The operation of a $2^n \times 2^n$ delta network using the above described 2×2 modules is as follows: Recall that there are n stages in this network. All processors requiring memory access must submit their requests at the same time by placing a

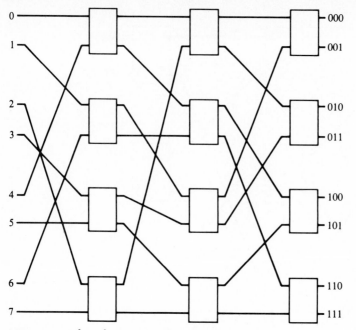

Figure 7.36 A $2^3 \times 2^3$ delta network to allow identity permutation.

1 on the respective request lines. If the busy line is 1, then the processor must re-submit its request. This can be accomplished simply by doing nothing; i.e., continue to hold the request line high. Thus the operation of the implementation described here is synchronous; that is, the requests are issued at fixed intervals at the same time. An asynchronous implementation is preferable if the network has many stages. However, such an implementation would require storage buffers for addresses, data and control in every module and also a complex control module. Thus, the cost of such an implementation might well be excessive.

7.2.4 Performance of Interconnection Networks

In this section, we analyze $p \times m$ crossbar networks and delta networks for processor-memory interconnections. Both networks are analyzed under identical assumptions for the purpose of comparison. We analyze the networks for finding the expected bandwidth given the rate of memory requests. Bandwidth is expressed in the average number of memory requests accepted per cycle. A cycle is defined as the time it takes for a request to propagate through the logic of the network plus the time needed to access a memory word plus the time used to return through the network to the source. We shall not distinguish the read or write cycles in this analysis. The analysis is based on the following assumptions:

1. Each processor generates random and independent requests for a word in memory. The requests are uniformly distributed over all memory modules.

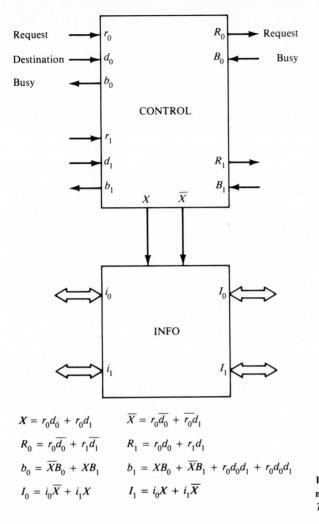

$$X = r_0 d_0 + r_0 d_1 \qquad \overline{X} = r_0 \overline{d_0} + \overline{r_0} d_1$$

$$R_0 = r_0 \overline{d_0} + r_1 \overline{d_1} \qquad R_1 = r_0 d_0 + r_1 d_1$$

$$b_0 = \overline{X} B_0 + X B_1 \qquad b_1 = X B_0 + \overline{X} B_1 + r_0 d_0 d_1 + r_0 d_0 d_1$$

$$I_0 = i_0 \overline{X} + i_1 X \qquad I_1 = i_0 X + i_1 \overline{X}$$

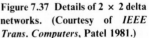

Figure 7.37 Details of 2 × 2 delta networks. (Courtesy of *IEEE Trans. Computers*, Patel 1981.)

2. At the beginning of every cycle, each processor generates a new request with a probability r. Thus, r is also the average number of requests generated per cycle by each processor.
3. The requests which are blocked (not accepted) are ignored; that is, the requests issued at the next cycle are independent of the requests blocked.

The last assumption is there to simplify the analysis. Although the model does not make proper account of rejections, it still serves a useful purpose. It can be solved exactly and it gives a lower bound on the expected bandwidth. In practice, of course, the rejected requests must be resubmitted during the next cycle or buffered in the module where the conflict occurs; thus the independent request assumption will not hold. Later, the last assumption will be relaxed to improve the model. Moreover, simulation studies performed by many authors for similar problems have shown that the probability of acceptance is only slightly lowered if the third assumption above is omitted. Thus the results of the analysis are fairly reliable and they provide a good measure for comparing different networks.

Analysis of crossbars Assume a crossbar of size $p \times m$ that is, p processors (sources) and m memory modules (destinations). In a full crossbar, two requests are in conflict if, and only if, the requests are to the same memory module. Therefore, in essence we are analyzing memory conflicts rather than network conflicts. Recall that r is the probability that a processor generates a request during a cycle. Let $q(i)$ be the probability that i requests arrive during one cycle. Then

$$q(i) = \binom{p}{i} r^i (1 - r)^{p-i} \tag{7.3}$$

where $\binom{p}{i}$ is the binomial coefficient.

Let $E(i)$ be the expected number of requests accepted by the $p \times m$ crossbar during a cycle, given that i requests arrived in the cycle. To evaluate $E(i)$, we know that from combinations the number of ways that i random requests can map to m distinct memory modules is m^i. Suppose now that a particular memory module is not requested. Then the number of ways to map i requests to the remaining $(m - 1)$ modules is $(m - 1)^i$. Thus, $m^i - (m - 1)^i$ is the number of maps in which a particular module is always requested. Thus the probability that a particular module is requested is $[m^i - (m - 1)^i]/m^i$. For every memory module, if it is requested, it means one request is accepted by the network for that module. Therefore, the expected number of acceptances, given i requests, is

$$E(i) = \frac{m^i - (m - 1)^i}{m^i} \cdot m = \left[1 - \left(\frac{m - 1}{m} \right)^i \right] m$$

Thus the expected bandwidth $B(p, m)$, that is, the average number of requests accepted per cycle, is

$$B(p, m) = \sum_{0 \leq i \leq p} E(i) \cdot q(i)$$

which simplifies to:

$$B(p, m) = m - m \left(1 - \frac{r}{m} \right)^p \tag{7.4}$$

Let us define the ratio of expected bandwidth to the expected number of requests generated per cycle as the probability of acceptance P_A. P_A is the probability that an arbitrary request will be accepted. Therefore

$$P_A = \frac{B(p, m)}{rp} = \frac{m}{rp} - \frac{m}{rp} \left(1 - \frac{r}{m} \right)^p \tag{7.5}$$

It is interesting to note the limiting values of $B(p, m)$ and P_A as p and m grow very large. Let $k = p/m$; then

$$\lim_{m \to \infty} \left(1 - \frac{r}{m}\right)^{km} = e^{-rk}$$

Thus for very large values of p and m

$$B(p, m) \simeq m(1 - e^{-rp/m}) \tag{7.6}$$

$$P_A \simeq \frac{m}{rp}(1 - e^{-rp/m}) \tag{7.7}$$

The above approximations are good within 1 percent of actual value when p and m are greater than 30 and within 5 percent when p and $m \geq 8$. Note that for a fixed ratio p/m, the bandwidth of Eq. 7.6 increases linearly with m.

Equation 7.5 was derived under the hypothesis of independent requests. In reality, however, a rejected request is not simply discarded but resubmitted during the next cycle, thereby increasing the request rate. We will not derive a detailed model that takes into account the exact behavior of a system with rejected requests. Instead, we will approximate the behavior by means of a simplifying assumption that makes the improved model more tractable and is still a bound on the exact model. We assume that the resubmitted request addresses the modules uniformly. A processor can be in one of two states, A or W. W is the state corresponding to a *wasted* cycle due to a rejected request. A is an *active* cycle during which a processor may issue a new request. The behavior of any one processor is described by the Markov graph of Figure 7.38.

Let q_A and q_W be the steady state probabilities that the processor is in state A and W, respectively. Solving for q_A and q_W, we obtain

$$q_A = \frac{P_A}{P_A + r(1 - P_A)} \tag{7.8}$$

and

$$q_W = 1 - q_A$$

The request rate r should be defined more precisely as the rate assuming conflict-free accesses. We refer to r as the static request rate. However, memory

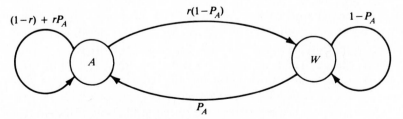

Figure 7.38 Markov graph for computing dynamic request rate r'.

requests are also made during each wasted cycle. Therefore, the memory modules encounter a dynamic request rate r' which is actually higher than the static request rate because of memory conflicts. r' can be obtained from the Markov graph as

$$r' = rq_A + q_W = \frac{r}{r + P_A(1 - r)} \tag{7.9}$$

Therefore Eq. 7.5 becomes

$$P_A = \frac{m}{r'p}\left[1 - \left(1 - \frac{r'}{m}\right)^p\right] \tag{7.10}$$

Equations 7.9 and 7.10 define an iterative process by which we can compute P_A for a given m, p, and r. r' can be initialized to r for the iterative process.

Thus, P_A is a measure of the wasted cycles of blocked requests. A higher P_A indicates a lower number of wasted cycles and a lower P_A indicates higher number of wasted cycles. The average number of wasted cycles $\bar{w}$ per request can be computed if we note that a request that is rejected i times consecutively before it is accepted waits for i cycles:

$$\bar{w} = \sum_{i=1}^{\infty} i(1 - P_A)^i P_A$$

$$= \frac{1 - P_A}{P_A} \tag{7.11}$$

Note that the reassignment of a rejected request (according to a uniform distribution among the memory modules) causes the model to overestimate the bandwidth. This is assumed to simplify the model. In practice, the requests are queued at the memory module and serviced by the module in a first-come-first-served fashion.

Analysis of delta networks Assume a delta network of size $a^n \times b^n$ constructed from $a \times b$ crossbar modules. Thus, there are a^n processors connected to b^n memory modules. We apply the result of Eq. 7.4 for a $p \times m$ crossbar to an $a \times b$ crossbar and then extend the analysis for the complete delta network. However, to apply Eq. 7.4 to any $a \times b$ crossbar module, we must first satisfy the assumptions of the analysis. We show below that the independent request assumption holds for every $a \times b$ module in a delta network.

Each stage of the delta network is controlled by a distinct destination digit (in base b) for the setting of individual $a \times b$ switches. Since the destinations are independent and uniformly distributed, so are the destination digits. Thus, for example, in some arbitrary stage i, an $a \times b$ crossbar uses digit d_{n-i} of each request; this digit is not used by any other stage in the network. Moreover, no digit other than d_{n-i} is used by stage i. Therefore, the requests at any $a \times b$ module are independent and uniformly distributed over b different destinations. Thus we can apply the result of Eq. 7.4 to any $a \times b$ module in the delta network.

Given the request rate r at each of the a inputs of an $a \times b$ crossbar module, the expected number of requests that it passes per time unit is obtained by setting $p = a$ and $m = b$ in Eq. 7.4, which is

$$b - b\left(1 - \frac{r}{b}\right)^a$$

Dividing the above expression by the number of output lines of the $a \times b$ module gives us the rate of requests on any one of b output lines:

$$1 - \left(1 - \frac{r}{b}\right)^a \tag{7.12}$$

Thus for any stage of a delta network, the output rate of requests, r_{out}, is a function of its input rate, r_{in}, and is given by

$$r_{\text{out}} = 1 - \left(1 - \frac{r_{\text{in}}}{b}\right)^a \tag{7.13}$$

Since the output rate of a stage is the input rate of the next stage, one can recursively evaluate the output rate of any stage starting at stage 1. In particular, the output rate of the final stage n determines the bandwidth of a delta network; that is, the number of requests accepted per cycle.

Let us define r_i to be the rate of requests on an output line of stage i. Then the following equations determine the bandwidth $B(a^n, b^n)$ of an $a^n \times b^n$ delta network, given r, the rate of requests generated by each processor:

$$B(a^n, b^n) = b^n r_n \tag{7.14}$$

where $\qquad r_i = 1 - \left(1 - \frac{r_{i-1}}{b}\right)^a \qquad$ and $\qquad r_0 = r$

The probability that a request will be accepted is

$$P_A = \frac{b^n r_n}{a^n r} \tag{7.15}$$

Since we do not have a closed-form solution for the bandwidth of delta networks (Eq. 7.14), we cannot directly compare the bandwidths of crossbar (Eq. 7.4) and delta networks. However, we present plots that compare the performance of crossbar and delta networks using Eqs. 7.5 and 7.15. Figure 7.39 shows the probability of acceptance, P_A, for $2^n \times 2^n$ and $4^n \times 4^n$ delta networks and $p \times p$ crossbar, when the request rate for each processor is $r = 1$. The curve marked delta -2 is for delta networks using 2×2 switches and delta -4 for delta networks using 4×4 switches. Notice that P_A for crossbar approaches a constant value as was predicted by Eq. 7.7. P_A for delta networks continues to fall as p grows. The model refinement developed for the crossbar switch can also be applied to delta networks iteratively and is left as an exercise for the reader.

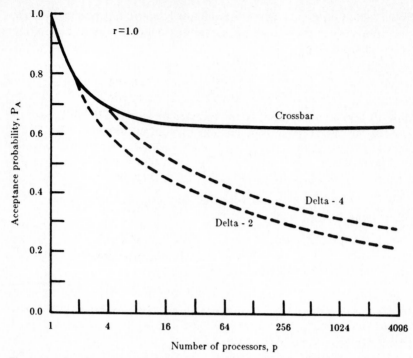

Figure 7.39 Probability of acceptance of $p \times p$ networks. (Courtesy of *IEEE Trans. Computers*, Patel 1981.)

7.3 PARALLEL MEMORY ORGANIZATIONS

This section addresses techniques for designing parallel memories for loosely and tightly coupled multiprocessors. The interleaving method presented is an extension of techniques applied to memory configurations for pipeline and vector processors. Many commercial multiprocessor systems are tightly coupled, where each processor has a private cache. The presence of multiple private caches introduces the problem of cache coherence or multicache consistency. Various solutions to cache-coherence problems are presented. Finally, we describe some simple models to evaluate the effectiveness of the various memory configurations.

7.3.1 Interleaved Memory Configurations

Low-order interleaving of memory modules is advantageous in multiprocessing systems when the address spaces of the active processes are shared intensively. If there is very little sharing, low-order interleaving may cause undesirable conflicts. Concentrating a number of pages of a single process in a given memory module of a high-order interleaved main memory is sometimes effective in reducing memory interference. In this case, a specific memory module M_i may be assigned to place most of the pages belonging to a process executing on processor i. Such a memory module M_i is called the *home memory* for processor i. If the entire set of active pages of a process being executed on processor i is contained in memory M_i, and if memory M_i contains no pages belonging to processes running on other processors, then processor i encounters no memory conflicts.

If every processor has the entire set of active pages of those processes that are running on it in its home memory, there will be no memory conflicts. The concept of home memory can be extended so that a set of modules $\{M_i\}$ are assigned as the home memories of processor i. This assumes that there are more memory modules than processors, so that at all times each memory module is associated with one processor. That is, $\{M_i\} \cap \{M_j\} = \phi$, for $i \neq j$. The home-memory organization for multiprocessors has an additional architectural advantage beyond the reduction in memory interference.

The processor-memory interconnection network (PMIN) of a multiprocessor system may be expensive, slow, and complicated. Figure 7.40 is an alternative organization in which each memory has two ports, one of which connects to the PMIN and one of which connects directly to the home processor. This topology

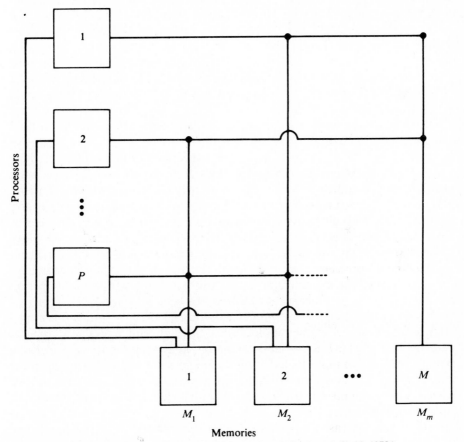

Figure 7.40 Home memory concept. (Courtesy of *IEEE Trans. Computers*, Smith 1978.)

permits enhanced access by each processor to its home memory by frequently avoiding switching time through the PMIN and permitting decreased cable lengths between processors and their home memories. Since PMIN participates in only a minority of all memory accesses with this organization, its speed becomes less critical and substantial cost savings may also be possible. This concept was applied in the design of Cm*. Home-memory organizations also permit significant gains in the reliability of system operation. A single memory failure when using a home-memory organization generally disables only a small subset of the processors currently running, that is, those with information in the failing memory.

The concurrent (C) access memory configuration described for pipeline processors can also be used for multiprocessors. For tightly coupled multiprocessors, a single C access configuration can be designed to match the bandwidth requirements of the processors. In this case, the main memory and the processors are on the opposite sides of the PMIN and references to memory by the processors must traverse the PMIN. Therefore, the processors encounter memory conflicts as well as transmission delays. To reduce these effects, a private cache is usually associated with each processor in a multiprocessor so that most of the referenced data and instructions can be found in the cache. However, the data bus width may affect the cost and transfer time of a block of data. For example, if each module has a data-transfer path of one 8-byte wide word and there are four memory modules on a bank of the C access configuration, then 32 bytes may be transferred in little more than the time required for one main memory cycle. Therefore, in a computer with a cache block size of 32 bytes only a little over one main memory cycle would be required to fetch all 32 bytes.

It should be noted that the cache is not usually interleaved, hence the arrival of the four words of information from main memory must be staggered slightly so as to allow the cache to accept each 8 bytes separately. A block of cache locations consists of contiguous memory locations. If the memory modules are interleaved on the low-order bits of the addresses, the block transfer will be inefficient. This occurs because consecutive memory locations of the block are in consecutive modules, and the delay incurred in setting up a path in the processor memory interconnection network for each access to a consecutive location of the block becomes very significant. Below we describe a more general parallel memory organization which can be used with a wide variety of multiple processor systems and in which memory module interleaving can be taken a step further to permit block transfer at even the cache bandwidth.

A two-dimensional memory organization called the L-M organization and arranged as l C-access configurations, each dimension with m modules, provides more flexibility. The L-M memory organization consists of $N(=2^n)$ identical memory modules arranged such that there are l lines or banks and m modules per line where $l = 2^\beta$ for integers β and n such that $0 \leq \beta \leq n$ $m = 2^{n-\beta}$ so that $lm = 2^n$. Again, a line refers to the address bus common to a set of m modules, as shown in Figure 7.41.

However, as a consequence of line and module sharing, the performance may be degraded. Furthermore, additional memory interference is introduced by this

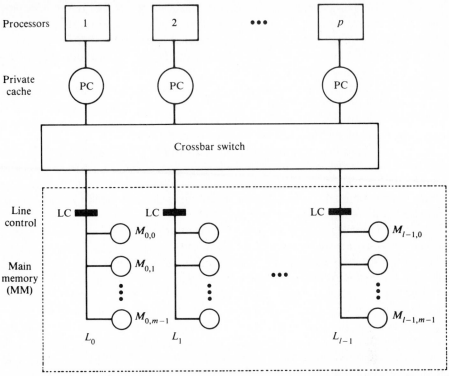

Figure 7.41 Multiprocessor system with private caches. (Courtesy of *IEEE Trans. Computers*, Briggs and Dubois 1983.)

organization. For a degenerate case in which there is one module per line, the memory conflict problem arises when two or more simultaneous memory requests reference the same module, hence the same line. For the two-dimensional memory, a conflict may also occur when a memory request references a busy line or a busy module on a line. A memory configuration characterized by (l, m) is a particular realization of the L-M memory organization.

Let us assume that a *write-back-write-allocate* cache replacement policy is adopted in the following discussion. Let w_b be the probability that the block frame to be replaced was modified. If a cache block frame which has not been modified is to be replaced, it is overwritten with the new block of data. However, a modified block frame that is to be replaced must be written to *main memory* (MM) before a block-read from MM is initiated. In this case, two consecutive transfers are made between the cache and MM. Hence, we assume that each time a cache miss occurs with probability w_b, a block-write to *MM* is required with probability w_b, followed by a block-read from MM.

One method of organizing the cache for block-reads and -writes is to assume that the two consecutive block transfers (one block-write followed by one block-read) are made between a processor and the same line. This assumption will be satisfied if a set-associative cache is used in which all the blocks that map to the same set are stored on the same line. This assumption implies that the number of sets is a multiple of the number of lines. Hence, in this method a cache miss requires the transfer of a $2b$-word block with a probability w_b and the transfer of a b-word with a probability $1 - w_b$.

The L-M memory organization is very cost-effective in matching the bandwidth of a cache memory which initiates block-transfer operations as a result of cache misses. The information is distributed in memory so that each block of a program resides on a line of memory. Consecutive words of a block are stored in consecutive modules on the same line. In this case, a line controller (LC) is associated with each line. The controller typically receives a cache request for a block transfer of size b and thereby issues b internal requests (IR) to consecutive modules on the line. The blocks in the memory are interleaved on the lines so that block i is assigned to modules on line $i \bmod \ell$.

When the main memory is used in the block-transfer mode, the address hold time or cycle of the memory module can be chosen to be equal to the cache cycle time in order to effectively utilize the line. In practice, the address cycle can be made as small as the cache cycle time by incorporating an address latch in each memory module. Let the cache cycle time be the unit time. Therefore, the memory cycle can be expressed as c time units. Also, the modules on a line are interleaved in a particular fashion so that the servicing of two memory requests could be overlapped on the same line. The modules on a line are interleaved so that a block of data of size $b(=2^x)$ is interleaved on consecutive modules on that line. Let line i and module j on that line be referred to as L_i and $M_{i,j}$, respectively, for $0 \le i \le l - 1$ and $0 \le j \le m - 1$. Then the kth word of the block of data which exists on line i is in module $k \bmod m$ on that line, for $0 \le k \le b - 1$. It is important to note that the first word of a block which exists on line i is in the first module $M_{i,0}$ of that line. If $b < m$, memory modules $M_{i,b}, M_{i,b+1}, \ldots, M_{i,m-1}$, will not be utilized since a block starts in module $M_{i,0}$. Hence, for effective utilization of memory modules, it is assumed that $b \ge m$.

When a block request is accepted by a line i, the line controller at that line issues b successive internal requests to consecutive modules on line i, starting from module $M_{i,0}$. It is assumed that these internal requests are issued at the beginning of every time unit. Therefore, the internal request for the kth word of the block will be issued to module $M_{i,j}$, where $j = k \bmod m$, for $0 \le k \le b - 1$. It is obvious that this set of b internal requests is not preemptible. Note that if $b > m$ or if the cache is set associative, the $(m + 1)$st internal request is for module $M_{i,0}$. Consequently, the first internal request must be completed by the time the $(m + 1)$st IR is issued. This constraint is satisfied if $c \le m$.

In order to visualize the concurrent servicing of two memory requests on the same line, we define a time unit, $\langle t, t + 1 \rangle$, as beginning at time t^+ and ending at time $(t + 1)^-$. Therefore, the successive IRs which are generated to modules on a line, in the servicing of a memory request, do not encounter any conflicts. If a memory request is accepted on line i at time t, then the IR for the kth word of a block of size b is initiated at time $t + k$ to module $M_{i,j}$ for $j = k \bmod m$ and

$0 \leq k \leq b - 1$. Since the memory module cycle is c, module $M_{i,j}$ will be busy in the intervals $\langle t + k, t + k + c \rangle$ for the values of j.

Since b and m are powers of 2 and $b \geq m$, then b/m is an integer ≥ 1. Therefore, each module on a line, i, which accepts a memory request for block transfer at time t receives b/m internal memory requests. In particular, the last IR to module $M_{i,0}$ is made at time $t + (b/m - 1)m = t + b - m$. Thus, the last interval in which module $M_{i,0}$ is busy (during the current block transfer) is

$$\langle t + b - m, t + b - m + c \rangle.$$

After this period, a new block-transfer request which addresses the line can be accepted. Because the current block transfer was initiated at time t, all block-transfer requests arriving at $t + 1, t + 2, \ldots, t + b - m + c - 1$ will find line i busy. Hence, to a memory request, the line is busy for $b - m + c$ time units. We refer to this as the *line service time*, S_i, of line i. However, the *actual service time*, A_i, of a memory request to line i is $b + c - 1$. We refer to the difference $A_i - S_i$ as the *drain time* $D_i = m - 1$. Since D_i is independent of i, we denote D_i by D for all i's. Hence, during S_i, any memory request made to line i will not be accepted but queued. At the end of S_i, the current request proceeds to the next stage where the data transfer is completed in time D. At the same time, a new request made to line i can be accepted. Therefore, the servicing of a memory request can be considered as proceeding in two stages of a pipeline.

7.3.2 Performance Trade-offs in Memory Organizations

In order to evaluate different multiprocessor memory configurations, we introduce a versatile but approximate model. This model is used to illustrate the performance trade-offs in a memory configuration. Each processor has a cache. We assume the interconnection network between the processor and memory to be a crossbar switch. The models developed for the crossbar in Section 7.2 are not applicable since they assume a unit time for the memory cycle. In practice, the main memory cycle c may vary for different memories and should be considered as an attribute of the memory configuration.

General model In each case, the multiprocessor system consists of p homogeneous processors and l banks or lines of interleaved memory. For generality, assume that the first stage of memory service time for modules of bank k is S_k. The drain (second stage service) time of each bank is D_k. Let q_k be the fraction of all references made to bank k. We denote by T the average "think time" spent within the processor nodes before a reference is made to a memory module. Figure 7.42 shows a representation of the model by a closed queueing network. We further represent the model by a state graph shown in Figure 7.43. In this graph, node A denotes an active state of the processor and node W, a waiting state. Node LT represents the state for the first part of the transfer during which the line is kept busy (line service time). The node DT represents the state in which a transfer is completed without holding the line. The state graph does not constitute a Markov chain since each

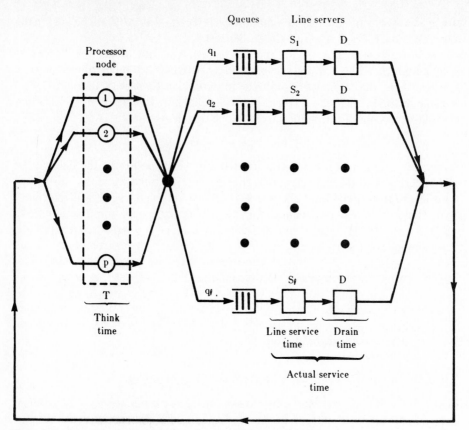

Figure 7.42 Closed queueing network model for a multiprocessor system.

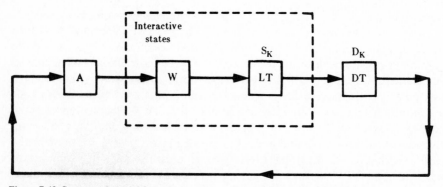

Figure 7.43 State graph model for memory requests in a tightly coupled multiprocessor.

state has a different average duration. Each processor goes through an independent state (state A) followed by interactive states (states W and LT) and another independent state (DT).

In an independent state, a processor executes on its own node without conflict. Interactive states are characterized by a potential for conflicts with other processors. Hence, during any LT state, the memory line is busy and no other processor can access the line. Let C be the average memory-request cycle time. The performance index is the average processor utilization U, defined as the average fraction of time spent by each processor in processing instructions. This performance index reflects the degree of matching between the processors and the memory organization.

We number the processors from 1 to p and the memory lines from 1 to l. Let

$$I_k(t) = [i_{k,1}(t), i_{k,2}(t), \ldots, i_{k,p}(t)] \tag{7.16}$$

for $k = 1, \ldots, l$, with $i_{k,j}(t) = 1$ if processor j is not waiting for or using line k, and $i_{k,j}(t) = 0$ if processor j is waiting for or using line k at time t.

$I_k(t)$ is called the *indicator vector* for line k at time t. Each component $i_{k,j}(t)$ indicates whether or not processor j is waiting for or holding line k. Note that a processor waits for or holds a line whenever it is in state W or LT (interactive states), respectively. Let X_k be the probability that a line k is busy and S_k is the average line service time of a request. Then

$X_k = \mathrm{Prob}[\text{at least one processor is waiting for or holding line } k]$

$\quad = 1 - \mathrm{Prob}[\text{no processor is waiting for or holding line } k]$

$\quad = 1 = \mathrm{Prob}[i_{k,1} \cdot i_{k,2} \cdots i_{k,p} = 1] = 1 - E[i_{k,1} \cdot i_{k,2} \cdots i_{k,p}]$

This last equality results from the fact that the expectation of a random variable taking only the values 0 and 1 is equal to the probability of the variable being 1. The rate of completed requests by line k is X_k/S_k.

In equilibrium, this rate can be equated to the rate of submitted requests to a line. To compute this second member of the equation, we note that a processor submits a request whenever it departs from state A. This occurs for each processor whenever a cycle in the network of Figure 7.43 is completed. Recall that C is the average time taken by such a cycle. The rate of submitted requests for the memory by any one processor is $1/C$. Since there are p requesting processors and each request is submitted with probability q_k to line k, the average rate of submitted requests to line k is pq_k/C.

Let Y be the average fraction of time a given processor is in an independent state. Hence, Y is also the probability of being in such a state. The symmetry of the system implies the same value of Y for all the processors. Since T is the average time in state A, $Y = (T + D)/C$. Substituting for $1/C$ in the equation for the average rate of submitted requests to a given line and equating this rate to the rate of completed request, we obtain $X_k = S_k p Y q_k/(T + D)$. Substituting for X_k, we have

$$E[i_{k,1} \cdot i_{k,2} \cdots i_{k,p}] + \rho_k Y = 1 \tag{7.17}$$

where $\rho_k = S_k p q_k/(T + D)$.

This equation is exact. However, the first term of the left hand side of the equation is very complex to estimate in general. The approximation consists in neglecting the interactions between processors. As a result of the approximation, the components of $I_k(t)$ are not correlated. This approximation performs best for a short and deterministic line-service time. Indeed, large instances of the line-service time are most likely to result in instantaneous longer queues and more interactions between the processors. Under the noncorrelation conditions

$$E[i_{k,1} \cdot i_{k,2} \cdots i_{k,p}] = E[i_{k,1}] \cdot E[i_{k,2}] \cdots E[i_{k,p}] \tag{7.18}$$

If we denote by Z_k the fraction of time spent by each processor waiting for or holding line k, Eq. 7.17 becomes $(1 - Z_k)^p + \rho_k Y = 1$ because of the symmetry of the system.

On the other hand, since a processor is either in an independent state or in an interactive state (waiting for or holding one of the lines), then, by the law of total probability, in a system with l lines we have

$$Y + \sum_{k=1}^{l} Z_k = 1 \tag{7.19}$$

We use Eq. 7.18 with the condition that $1 - \rho_k Y > 0$, $Z_k = 1 - (1 - \rho_k Y)^{1/p}$. Consequently, by the substitution for Z_k in Eq. 7.19 and rearranging, we obtain

$$Y = 1 - l + \sum_{k=1}^{l} (1 - \rho_k Y)^{1/p} \tag{7.20}$$

S_k is the mean line-service time and $T + D$ is the mean time between an exit from an interactive state and a visit to the next interactive state. Note that S_k can be found as the mean time that a processor spends holding a memory line k. Similarly, T is found as the mean time spent outside of an interactive state. Y can be solved by Newton's iterative method given that a unique solution exists for Y between 0 and $\min(1, 1/\rho_k)$. Let us illustrate the application of this model to the system mentioned earlier. For simplicity, assume that for these examples $q_k = 1/l$ and $S_k = S$ for all values of k. Then Eq. 7.20 becomes:

$$Y = \frac{1}{\rho} \left[1 - \left(\frac{Y + l - 1}{l} \right)^p \right] \tag{7.21}$$

where $\rho = pS/l(T + D)$.

Assume that in each of these processors, a machine cycle consists of an integer number, d, of cache cycles. Let θ be the probability that a memory request is issued by a processor to the cache controller in a machine cycle. Thus, the fraction of references made by the processor to the cache controller in each cache cycle is, $x = \theta/d$.

For the set-associative cache, if a block-write is not required (with a probability $1 - w_b$) on a cache miss, then the line which accepts the memory request is busy for $b - m + c$ time units. However, if a block-write is required (with probability w_b) in addition to the block-read, then two consecutive block transfers (each of size b)

are made uninterruptedly on the same memory line. In this case, the line that accepts the memory request is busy for $2b - m + c$ time units. Hence the mean line-service time is:

$$S = b(1 + w_b) - m + c \qquad (7.22)$$

Since $1 - h$ is the cache-miss ratio, the probability that a given cache cycle requires an access to memory is $x(1 - h)$. We account for the crossbar switch setup and traversal times by t_x. Hence the average time spent in state A is:

$$T = \frac{1}{x(1 - h)} + t_x \qquad (7.23)$$

Since the drain time, $D = m - 1$, we can determine Y from Eq. 7.21 for the multi-processor system with set-associative caches. The processor utilization, U, which is the fraction of time the processor is busy processing instructions is given by

$$U = \frac{1/[x(1 - h)]}{C} = \frac{1}{x(1 - h)C}$$

Since $C = (T + D)/Y$, the utilization can be rewritten as

$$U = \frac{Y}{x(1 - h)(T + D)} \qquad (7.24)$$

We illustrate the set-associative cache example with a multiprocessor system with $p = 16$ processors, $x = 0.4$, and $t_x = 0$ (infinitely fast crossbar). The cache hit ratio, $h = 0.95$, and the block size b is allowed to vary. The memory organization has a fixed number of modules per line ($m = 4$), but the number of lines vary. Also the memory module cycle time, c, varies. Figure 7.44 shows the application of Eqs. 7.21 through 7.24 for the given set of parameters.

This result assumes that the cache size is adjusted to give the same hit ratio when the block size is varied. An increase in the block size deteriorates the utilization. An operating region should be chosen where the utilization is acceptable. Note that for certain values of b and c, small values of l will give high utilization. This possible reduction in l gives the designer a choice. If for a small number of lines, $l < 16$, the utilization is acceptable, the designer can consider trade-offs with low-cost multiport memory.

7.3.3 Multicache Problems and Solutions

The presence of private caches in a multiprocessor necessarily introduces problems of *cache coherence*, which may result in data inconsistency. That is, several copies of the same data may exist in different caches at any given time. This is a potential problem especially in asynchronous parallel algorithms which do not possess explicit synchronization stages of the computation. For example, process A, which runs on processor i, produces data x, which is to be consumed by process B, which runs on processor $j \neq i$ asynchronously. Process A writes a new x into its cache while process B uses the old value of x in its cache because it is not aware of

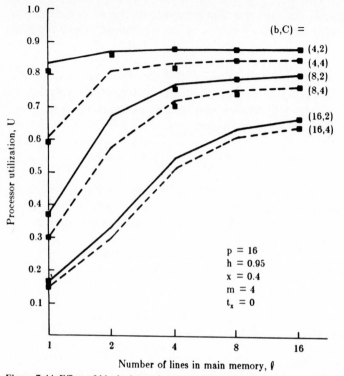

Figure 7.44 **Effect of block size and main memory speed on processor utilization for the set-associative cache. (Courtesy of *IEEE Trans. Computers*, Briggs and Dubois, Jan. 1983.)**

the new x. Process B may continue to use the old value of x in its cache unless it is informed of the presence of the new x in process A's cache so that a copy of it may be made in its cache. The possibility of having several processors using different copies of the same data must be avoided if the system is to perform correctly. Hence, data consistency must be enforced in the caches.

Another form of the data consistency problem occurs in a multiprogrammed multiprocessor system. In this case, a processor usually switches to other processes at the time of the arrival of external interrupt signals or page fault operations. If the suspended process migrates to another processor, the most recently updated data of this process might still be in the original processor's cache. Hence a process running on a new processor could use stale data in main memory. The new processor cannot recognize the data as stale, and thus would not be working with the process's proper context. Such an operation is incorrect and can result in subtle errors that are difficult to trace. In many multiprocessor systems such as the S-1, privileged instructions are provided to *sweep* the cache. The cache sweep operation is used to deliberately update main memory to reflect any changes in cache contents.

A system of caches is *coherent* if and only if a READ performed by any processor i of a main memory location x (which may be cached by other processors) always delivers the most recent value with the same address x. "Most recent" in this context has a special meaning in terms of a partial ordering of the READs and WRITEs of memory throughout the multiprocessor. However, for an intuitive understanding of the problem, it is sufficient to think of recency in terms of absolute time. In these terms, whenever a WRITE is done by one processor i to a memory location x, completion of the WRITE must guarantee that all subsequent READs of location x by any processor will deliver the new contents of x until another WRITE to x is completed.

The cache coherence problem exists only when the caches are associated with the processors. Designs have been proposed in which the caches are associated with the shared memory as shown in Figure 7.45. This avoids the cache coherence problem. This architecture is good for systems with a small number of processors. However, the potential gain in speed is then limited by the transmission delays through the interconnection network and by the conflicts at the caches. This technique has been shown to be adequate for multiprocessors where each processor is pipelined and executes multiple independent instruction streams.

Clearly, the cache coherence problem cannot be solved by a mere write-through policy. If a write-through policy is used, the main memory location is updated, but the possible copies of the variable in other caches are not automatically updated by the write-through mechanism. When a processor modifies a data in its cache, all the potential copies in other caches must be invalidated. "Write-through" is neither necessary nor sufficient for coherence.

Static coherence check Two different methods have been proposed to solve the cache coherence problem. The first method, called *static coherence check*, avoids

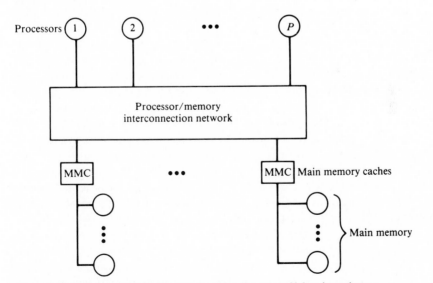

Figure 7.45 Caches associated with shared memory lines to avoid data inconsistency.

multiple copies by implementing different paths for shared writeable (*non-cacheable*) and private (*cacheable*) data. By data, we mean both code and operand. The shared data structures which are modifiable reside in main memory. They are never placed in the cache; that is, they are noncacheable. A reference to this shared data is made directly to main memory. Conversely, a read only segment of data which is shared by several processors need not be noncacheable. The cacheability of read only data reduces conflicts in main memory.

If t_m is the time to reference a datum in main memory, t_c the cache cycle time, and s the probability of referencing a shared modifiable datum, a lower bound on a datum reference is

$$(1 - s)t_c + st_m = t_c \left[(1 - s) + s \frac{t_m}{t_c} \right] \tag{7.25}$$

If the cycle ratio, t_m/t_c, is large (a typical value is 5), the performance of this scheme may be quite poor for algorithms with intense sharing, regardless of the cache size. Moreover, the requests for shared data increase contentions in the interconnection network and at the memory. The performance of this scheme can be improved by associating a high-speed memory or cache module with each memory line. This cache module is used to buffer the noncacheable data, thereby reducing the effective t_m and hence, the cycle ratio, t_m/t_c.

In a similar scheme which avoids these problems, the shared data is accessed through a shared cache while instruction fetches and private data references are made in private caches. Figure 7.46 illustrates this shared cache concept. Notice that the shared cache may consist of interleaved cache modules which may be connected to the processors and shared memory through an interconnection network. However, the complexity of this network is expected to be less than a full crossbar. All data references proceed at the cache speed except when conflicts occur at the shared cache or a miss occurs in either a private cache or the shared cache.

If the hit ratio is high enough in all caches, this scheme alleviates the contention problem at the main memory. The success of the shared cache concept relies on the relatively low rate of shared data references. Of course, the shared data may exhibit less locality than private data. However, the hit ratio in the shared cache improves as the degree of sharing of the shared variables increases. Indeed, a processor may find a shared variable in the shared cache even if it never referenced it before. Moreover, increasing the size of the shared cache is an effective method to improve the hit ratio.

The shared cache concept requires that data be tagged as private or shared. The tagging is basically static. *Static tags* are made during compile time and remain the same throughout the lifetime of the process. *Dynamic tags* are made during the execution of cooperating processes. A lookahead mechanism monitors the history of sharing of the data space in one phase and predicts the probability of sharing of the subspaces in the next phase. With this scheme, a data subspace could be in the shared cache for effective sharing in one phase and in the private caches in another phase, for efficient access, or vice-versa. The overhead may be unacceptable, as

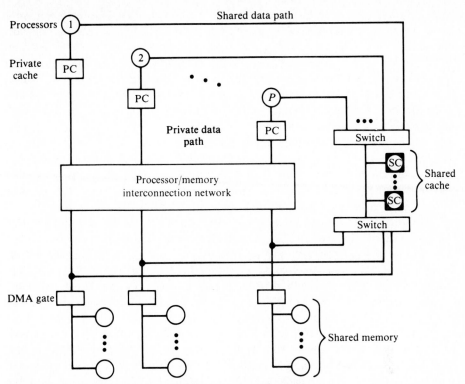

Figure 7.46 Multiprocessor system with private and shared data paths.

the caches must be flushed to main memory. Moreover, the migration of data sets can create constraints on the scheduler or loader. The tagging of data necessitates the compiler be designed to detect private and shared data. With the advent of such abstract and block-structured languages as concurrent Pascal, this can be accomplished by explicit indication of such data sets. It can be argued that the shared cache concept lacks flexibility.

Dynamic coherence check The second method for solving cache coherence is more flexible than the static coherence check, but also more complex and possibly more costly. In this scheme, called *dynamic coherence check*, multiple copies are allowed. However, whenever a processor modifies a location x in a cache block, it must check the other caches to invalidate possible copies. This operation is referred to as a *cross-interrogate* (XI). In the most rudimentary implementation of this method, the caches are tied on a high speed bus. When a local processor writes into a shared block in its cache, the processor sends a signal to all the remote caches to indicate that the "data at memory address x has been modified." At the same time, it writes through memory. Note that, to ensure correctness of execution, a processor which requests an XI must wait for an acknowledge signal from all other processors before it can complete the write operation. The XI invalidates the remote cache location corresponding to x if it exists in that cache.

When the remote processor references this invalid cache location, it results in a cache miss, which is serviced to retrieve the block containing the updated information.

For each write operation, $(n - 1)$ XIs result, where n is the number of processors. When n increases, the traffic on the high-speed bus becomes a bottleneck. Moreover, there is a potential for races if the XI requests are queued to accommodate the peak traffic on the bus. Some commercial multiprocessors with caches use this technique for a small number of processors. For example, the Honeywell 60/66 and Univac 1100/80 multiprocessors have cache-invalidate interfaces between every pair of caches. Note that the two sources of inefficiency for this technique are the necessity of a write-through policy, which increases the network traffic, and the redundant cache XIs which are performed. In the latter case, a cache is purged blindly whether or not it contains the data item x.

A more refined technique filters the XI requests before they are initiated. In a proposed design, the memory control element (MSC) maintains a central copy of the directories of all the caches. We will elaborate on a similar scheme called the *presence flag technique*, which assumes a write-back update policy. There are two central tables associated with the blocks of main memory (MM) (Figure 7.47). The first table is a two-dimensional table called the Present table. In this table, each entry $P[i, c]$ contains a *present* flag for the ith block in MM and the cth cache. If $P[i, c] = 1$, then the cth cache has a copy of the ith block of MM, otherwise it is zero. The second table is the *Modified* table and is one-dimensional. In this table, each entry $M[i]$ contains a *modified* flag for the ith block of MM. If $M[i] = 1$, it means that there exists a cache with a copy of the ith block more recent than the corresponding copy in MM. The Present and Modified tables can be implemented in a fast random-access memory.

The philosophy behind the cache coherence check is that an arbitrary number of caches can have a copy of a block, provided that all the copies are identical. They are identical if the processor associated with each of the caches has not attempted to modify its copy since the copy was loaded in its cache. We refer to such a copy as *read only* (RO) copy. In order to modify a block copy in its cache, a processor must own the block copy with *exclusive read only* (EX) or *exclusive read-write* (RW) access rights. A copy is held EX in a cache if the cache is the only one with the block copy and the copy has not been modified. Similarly, a copy is held RW in a cache if the cache is the only one with the block copy and the copy has been modified. Therefore, for consistency, only one processor can at any time own an EX or RW copy of a block.

To enforce the cache consistency rule, local flags are provided within each cache in addition to the global tables. A local flag $L[k, c]$ is provided for each block k in cache c. This flag indicates the state of each block in the cache. A block in a cache can be in one of three states: RO, EX, or RW. When a processor c fetches a block i on a read miss, the processor obtains an EX copy of the block, provided no other cache has a copy of block i and the fetch was for data. In other fetch misses, the block is assigned RO, as shown in Figure 7.48. The status information is recorded in the cache directory and global tables. The status is indicated

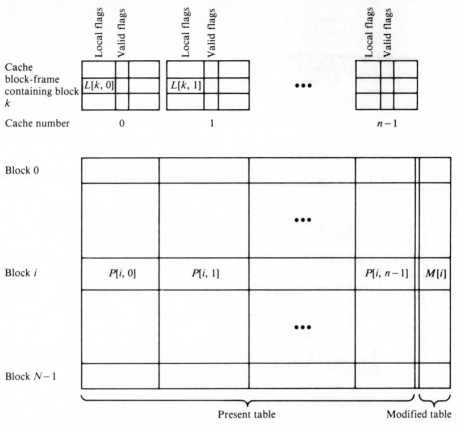

Figure 7.47 Organization of flags for dynamic solution to cache coherence.

in the global table by setting the appropriate present flag and clearing the corresponding modified bit.

As long as the copy of block i remains present in the cache, processor c can fetch it without any consistency check. If processor c attempts to store into its copy of block i, it must ensure that all other copies (if any) of block i are invalidated. To do this, the global table is consulted. It should indicate the processor caches that own a copy of block i. The modified bit for block i is updated in the global table to record the fact that processor c owns block i with RW access rights. Finally, the local $L[i, c]$ flag is set to RW to indicate that the block is modified. The flowchart for a store is given in Figure 7.49.

In this implementation, a block copy in a cache is invalidated whenever the cache receives a signal from some other processor attempting to store into it. Moreover, a cache which owns an RW copy may receive a signal from a remote cache requesting to own an RO copy. In this case, the RW copy's state is changed to RO.

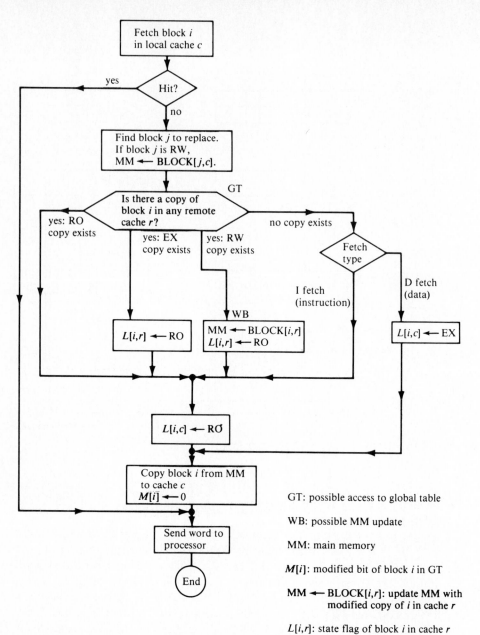

Figure 7.48 Coherence check for fetch operation.

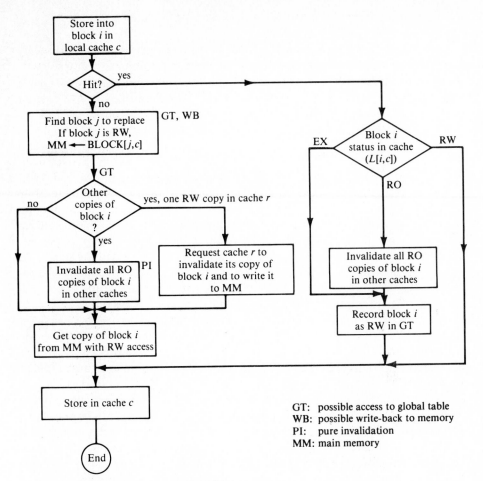

Figure 7.49 Coherence check for store operation.

There are four main sources of performance degradation in the dynamic coherence check algorithms shown in Figures 7.48 and 7.49. These sources are:

- Degradation of the average hit ratio due to block invalidation
- Traffic between caches to enforce consistency
- Concurrent access to the global tables resulting in conflicts
- Writeback due to invalidation of RW data

7.4 MULTIPROCESSOR OPERATING SYSTEMS

In this section, we discuss the operating system requirements for multiprocessors. First, a classification of multiprocessor operating systems is presented. We then discuss other system software supports needed for multiprocessing.

7.4.1 Classification of Multiprocessor Operating Systems

There is conceptually little difference between the operating system requirements of a multiprocessor and those of a large computer system utilizing multiprogramming. However, there is the additional complexity in the operating system when multiple processors must work simultaneously. This complexity is also a result of the operating system being able to support multiple asynchronous tasks which execute concurrently.

The functional capabilities which are often required in an operating system for a multiprogrammed computer include the resource allocation and management schemes, memory and dataset protection, prevention of system deadlocks and abnormal process termination or exception handling. In addition to these capabilities, multiprocessor systems also need techniques for efficient utilization of resources and, hence, must provide input-output and processor load-balancing schemes. One of the main reasons for using a multiprocessor system is to provide some effective reliability and graceful degradation in the event of failure. Hence, the operating system must also be capable of providing system reconfiguration schemes to support graceful degradation. These extra capabilities and the nature of the multiprocessor execution environment places a much heavier burden on the operating system to support automatically the exploitation of parallelism in the hardware and the programs being executed. An operating system which performs poorly will negate other advantages which are associated with multiprocessing. Hence, it is of utmost importance that the operating system for a multiprocessing computer be designed efficiently.

The presence of more than one processing unit in the system introduces a new dimension into the design of the operating system. The influence of a large number of processors on the design of an operating system is still a research problem. The modularity of processors and the interconnection structure among them affect the system development. Furthermore, communication schemes, synchronization mechanisms, and placement and assignment policies dominate the efficiency of the operating system. We introduce below only the basic configurations that have appeared in existing multiprocessor systems.

There are basically three organizations that have been utilized in the design of operating systems for multiprocessors, namely, *master-slave configuration*, *separate supervisor* for each processor, and *floating supervisor control*. For most multiprocessors, the first operating system available assumed the master-slave mode. This mode, in which the supervisor is always run on the same processor, is certainly the simplest to implement. Furthermore, it may often be designed by making relatively simple extensions to a uniprocessor operating system that includes full multiprogramming capabilities. Although the master-slave type of system is simple, it is normally quite inefficient in its control and utilization of the total system resources. The other two operating modes are superior to the master-slave in performance.

In a *master-slave* mode, one processor, called the master, maintains the status of all processors in the system and apportions the work to all the slave processors. An example of the master-slave mode is in the Cyber-170, where the operating system is executed by one peripheral processor P_0. All the other processors (central or peripheral) are treated as slaves to P_0. Another example is found in the DEC System 10, in which there are two identical processors. One of the processors is designated as master and the other as slave. The operating system runs only on the master, with the slave treated as a schedulable resource.

Since the supervisor routine is always executed in the same processor, a slave request via a trap or supervisor call instruction for an executive service must be sent to the master, which acknowledges the request and performs the appropriate service. The supervisor and its associated procedures need not be reentrant since there is only one processor that uses them. There are other characteristics of the master-slave operating system. Table conflicts and lock-out problems for system control tables are simplified by forcing a single processor to run the executive. However, this operating system mode causes the entire system to be very susceptible to catastrophic failures which require operation intervention to restart the master processor when an irrecoverable error occurs. In addition to the inflexibility of the overall system, the utilization of the slave processors may become appreciably low if the master cannot dispatch processes fast enough to keep the slaves busy. The master-slave mode is most effective for special applications where the work load is well defined or for asymmetrical systems in which the slaves have less capability than the master processor. It is the mode sometimes used if there are very few processors involved.

When there is a *separate supervisor system* (kernel) running in each processor, the operating system characteristics are very different from the master-slave systems. This is similar to the approach taken by computer networks, where each processor contains a copy of a basic kernel. Resource sharing occurs at a higher level, for example, via a shared file structure. Each processor services its own needs. However, since there is some interaction between the processors, it is necessary for some of the supervisory code to be reentrant or replicated to provide separate copies for each processor. Although each supervisor has its own set of private tables, some tables are common and shared by the whole system. This creates table access problems. The method used in accessing the shared resources depends on the degree of coupling among the processors. The separate supervisor operating system is not as sensitive to a catastrophic failure as a master-slave system. Also, each processor has its own set of input-output devices and files, and any reconfiguration of I/O usually requires manual intervention and possibly manual switching.

Unfortunately, the replication of the kernel in the processors would demand a lot of memory which may be underutilized, especially when compared with the utilization of the shared data structures. A static form of caching could be used to buffer frequently used portions of the operating system code, while the infrequently used code could be centralized in a shared memory. Unfortunately, the determination of which portions of operating system are frequently executed is relatively difficult to make and is likely to be dependent of the application workload.

The *floating supervisor control* scheme treats all the processors as well as other resources symmetrically or as an anonymous pool of resources. This is the most difficult mode of operation and the most flexible. In this mode, the supervisor routine floats from one processor to another, although several of the processors may be executing supervisory service routines simultaneously. This type of system can attain better load balancing over all types of resources. Conflicts in service requests are resolved by priorities that are either set statistically or under dynamic control. Since there is a considerable degree of sharing, most of the supervisory code must be reentrant. In this system, table-access conflicts and table lock-out delays cannot be avoided. It is important to control these accesses in such a way that system integrity is protected. This mode of operation has the advantages of providing graceful degradation and better availability of a reduced capacity system. Furthermore, it provides true redundancy and makes the most efficient use of available resources. Examples of operating systems that execute in this mode are the MVS and VM in the IBM 3081 and the Hydra on the C.mmp.

Most operating systems, however, are not pure examples of any of the three classes discussed above. The only generalization that is possible is that the first system produced is usually of the master-slave type and the ultimate being sought is the floating supervisor control. In Table 7.3, we summarize the major characteristics, advantages, and shortcomings of the above three types of operating systems for multiprocessor computers.

7.4.2 Software Requirements for Multiprocessors

One of the issues often raised in a discussion on multiprocessor software is the question of how it differs from uniprocessor software. In particular, how does software written to execute on multiple processors differ from that written to execute on the more familiar multiprogrammed uniprocessor environment? There are basically two sources of differences. These are the architectural attributes that are unique to the multiprocessor, and a new programming style peculiar to parallel applications. Such differences would warrant that the hardware and software of the system should provide facilities that are different from those found in conventional multiprogrammed uniprocessor environments. A multiprogrammed uniprocessor can simulate the multiple processor environment by creating multiple "virtual processors" for the users. For example, a Unix user routinely requests the concurrent execution of multiple programs with the output of one program "piped" as the input to the other. In this case, each program may be thought of as executing on a virtual processor. At this level of program execution there are few differences between a multiprogrammed uniprocessor system and a multiprocessor system. However, the presence of multiple processors and other replicated components usually increases the amount of management software that must be provided.

An architectural attribute that may affect programming in a multiprocessor system is nonhomogeneity. If the central processors are nonhomogeneous, that is, functionally different, they must be treated differently by software. For example, if one processor possesses emulation capability not possessed by another, some programs can only run to completion on the processor with the emulation capa-

Table 7.3 Operating system configurations for a multiprocessor computer

Master-slave operating system:

1. The executive routine is always executed in the same processor. If the slave needs service that must be provided by the supervisor, then it must request that service and wait until the current program on the master processor is interrupted and the supervisor is dispatched. The supervisor and the routines that it uses do not have to be reentrant since there is only the one processor using them.
2. Having a single processor executing the supervisor simplifies the table conflict and lock-out problem for control tables. The overall system is comparatively inflexible. This type of system requires comparatively simple software and hardware.
3. The entire system is subject to catastrophic failures that require operator intervention to restart when the processor designated as the master has a failure or irrecoverable error.
4. Idle time on the slave system can build up and become quite appreciable if the master cannot execute the dispatching routines fast enough to keep the slave(s) busy.
5. This type of operating system is most effective for special applications where the work load is well defined or for asymmetrical systems in which the slaves have less capability than the master processor.

Separate supervisor in each processor:

1. Each processor services it own needs. In effect, each processor (supervisor) has its own set of I/O equipment, files, etc.
2. It is necessary for some of the supervisory code to be reentrant or replicated to provide separate copies for each processor.
3. Each processor (actually each supervisor) has its own set of private tables, although some tables must be common to the entire system, and that creates table-access control problems.
4. The separate supervisor operating system is as sensitive as is the master-slave system; however, the restart of an individual processor that has failed will probably be quite difficult.
5. Because of the point immediately above, the reconfiguration of I/O usually requires manual intervention and possibly manual switching.

Floating-supervisor operating system:

1. The "master" floats from one processor to another, although several of the processors may be executing supervisor service routines at the same time.
2. This type of system can attain better load balancing over all types of resources.
3. Conflicts in service requests are resolved by priorities that can be set statically or under dynamic control.
4. Most of the supervisory code must be reentrant since several processors can execute the same service routine at the same time.
5. Table-access conflicts and table lock-out delays can occur, but there is no way to avoid this with multiple supervisors; the important point is that they must be controlled in such a way that system integrity is protected.

---

bility. Hence, software resource managers must provide appropriate dispatching mechanisms for such programs. Another example of software complexity occurs in a system with asymmetric main memory. In this case, not all processors can access all memory. This complicates the operating system software for resource management.

There is a second potential source of difference between multiprocessor and uniprocessor software. This is in the programming style peculiar to parallel applications. The basic unit of a program in execution is that of a process, an independent schedulable entity (a sequential program) that runs a processor and uses hardware and software resources. It may also execute concurrently with other processes, delayed (at least logically) only when it needs to wait to interact with one or more other processes. Hence, a parallel program can be said to consist of two or more interacting processes.

The potential of multiprocessing is achieved by enhancing its capability for parallel processing. Parallel processing can be indicated in a program explicitly or implicitly. For explicit parallelism, users must be provided with programming abstractions that permit them to indicate explicit parallelism when desired in a program. Implicit parallelism is detected by the compiler. In this case, the compiler scans the source program and recognizes the program flow. From this flow graph and other conditions, it detects nontrivial units of program statements which may be identified as a process. Some of these units may be independent and can be run concurrently with other processes.

In a multiprocessor system, synchronization takes on increased importance as it could create too high a penalty. This could significantly degrade system performance if the synchronization mechanisms are not efficient and the algorithms that use them are not properly designed. In some processors, the synchronization primitives are not implemented directly in hardware or microcode. Therefore, software alternatives must be provided. For example, the PDP-11 processors used for the C.mmp have been implemented with the semaphore-synchronization primitive in software, thereby taking a significant number of instructions. In an environment where processes need to synchronize often, this may be a major bottleneck.

Program-control structures are provided to aid the programmer in developing efficient parallel algorithms. Three basic nonsequential program-control structures have been identified. These control structures are characterized by the fact that the programmer need only focus on a small program and not on the overall control of the computation. The first example is the *message-based* organization which was used in the Cm* operating system. In this organization, computation is performed by multiple homogeneous processes that execute independently and interact via messages. The grain size of a typical process depends on the system.

The second example of a control structure is the *chore* structure. In this structure, all codes are broken into small units. The process that executes the unit of code (and the code itself) is called a *chore*. An important characteristic of a chore is that once it begins execution, it runs to completion. Hence, to avoid long waits, chores are basically small. They have relatively very little input and they reference only a few different objects. Moreover, they do not block and are noninterruptible. As part of its output, one chore might request the execution of a small set of additional chores. Examples of systems that use this structure are the Pluribus and the BCC-500.

Consider the memory-management portion of the operating system, which controls swapping between the main memory and a fixed-head disk. Sample chores may include (*a*) the disk command to request the transfer of a page of data between the disk and the memory, and (*b*) acknowledging completion of a disk-sector transmission and arranging for any subsequent action.

The third nonsequential control structure is that of *production systems*, now often used in artificial intelligence systems. Productions are expressions of the form ⟨antecedent, consequent⟩. Whenever the boolean antecedent evaluates to true, the consequent may be performed. In contrast to chores, production consequents may or may not include code which might block. In a production system, four scheduling strategies are often required (*a*) to control the selection of antecedents to be evaluated next, (*b*) to order (if necessary) the execution of selected antecedents, (*c*) to select the subset of runnable consequents to be executed, and (*d*) to order (if necessary) the execution of the selected consequents. Note that by the natures of all three control structures, they are all compatible with parallel execution.

The high degree of concurrency in a multiprocessor can increase the complexity of fault handling, especially in the recovery step. In a uniprocessor, it is always possible to eliminate parallelism by disabling interrupts and, if necessary, halting I/O activity. Software is needed to establish effective error recovery capability. This software, even with the aid of hardware mechanisms, may be quite complex. Understanding the behavior of running processes in a multiprocessor system is more complex than in uniprocessor environments. Although parallel programs may not be too complex to implement, there is a natural problem of nondeterminism in multiprocessors. Some efforts have been made to prove the correctness of parallel programs by researchers but extending these proofs to complex programs is still a formidable task.

7.4.3 Operating System Requirements

The basic goals for an operating system are to provide programmer interface (environment) to the machine, manage resources, provide mechanisms (system defined) to implement policies (user definable), and facilitate matching applications to the machine. It must also help achieve reliability. But this and other desirable attributes incur a cost that may be unacceptable. Guidelines should be established for trading performance for desirable attributes. The degree of transparency of the detailed machine that should be made available to the programmer should also be determined.

There are different levels of interaction in the specification of an operating system for multiprocessing systems. Asynchronous supervisor processes share the specification of the address-space management, process management, and synchronization levels. Efficient operating systems are designed to have a modular structure and hierarchical organization. This makes the detection and localization of errors easier. The classic functions of an operating system include the creation of objects such as processes and their domains, which include the memory segments. The management and sharing of segments, as was discussed in Chapter 2, are also important operating system functions. Other functions are the management of process communications through mailboxes or message buffers. Messages are used to define the interface between processes and help to reduce the number of ways an error can be propagated through the system.

In a multiprocessor system, processes can execute concurrently until they need to interact. Planned and controlled interaction is referred to as process communication or process synchronization. Process communication must take place through shared or global variables. Cooperating processes must communicate to synchronize or limit their concurrency. The relationship between two cooperating processes regarding a resource falls into one of two fundamental categories. They are either competitors or producers-consumers. Since process communication takes place through shared memory, competitors access this memory to seize and release permanent or *reusable* resources. Producers-consumers access this memory to pass temporary or *consumable* resources such as messages and signals.

In systems with multiple concurrent processes, the presence of resources such as unit record peripherals and tape drives which must not be used simultaneously by several processes (if program operation is to be correct) introduces the requirement for exclusive access to these devices. This requirement may also be imposed on shared objects such as a data segment during updating. Processes desiring exclusive access to a resource may compete for it. The same competition arises concerning access to what are called *virtual* resources, such as system tables and communication buffers between cooperating processes. Since it must be guaranteed that both processes do not access the buffer simultaneously, exclusive access to the buffer must be ensured. This exclusiveness of access is called *mutual exclusion* between processes. A request for mutual exclusion on the use of a resource implies the desire to reserve or release the resource. Process cooperation and competition may both be implemented if a mechanism is provided for process coordination or synchronization. This mechanism will be discussed in Section 8.1.

The above requirements for processor cooperation and competition have obvious implications on short- and medium-term scheduling of the multiple processors. If a desired resource or object is not available, the process requesting it must be suspended, blocked, or retry until it becomes available. There are often two levels of exclusiveness. One consists of the requirements for referral of access to a data structure (virtual resource) which may often be of short duration. The other is the requirement for, perhaps, a substantial delay until the physical resource, such as the processor or tape unit, becomes available. If the delay is short, it is not worthwhile to shift the attention of the processor from the process which is running on it to another process. If the delay exceeds the time required to switch the processor, the ability to shift attention may be vital for efficient utilization of the processor.

The sharing of the multiple processors may be achieved by placing the several processes together in shared memory and providing a mechanism for rapidly switching the attention of a processor from one process to another. This operation is often called *context switching*. Sharing of the processors introduces three subordinate problems:

1. The protection of the resources of one process from willful or accidental damage by other processes
2. The provision for communication among processes and between user processes and supervisor processes

3. The allocation of resources among processes so that resource demands can always be fulfilled

The goal of protection is to ensure that data and procedures are accessed correctly. When two or more processes wish to access a set of resources within the multiprocessor system, it is necessary to allocate the resources in such a way that the total resources of the system are not exceeded. Furthermore, if it is possible for a process to acquire a portion of the resources that it requires and then subsequently make a request for more, it is necessary to ensure that future demands can always be satisfied. As an example, suppose that the system has one card reader and one printer. Process one requests the card reader and process two requests the printer. If processes one and two subsequently request the printer and card reader, respectively, then the system is in a state where two processes are blocked indefinitely. This situation is called *deadlock* or *deadly embrace*. Methods for detecting and preventing deadlock, protection schemes and communication mechanisms for multiprocessor systems will be discussed in Chapter 8.

7.5 EXPLOITING CONCURRENCY FOR MULTIPROCESSING

A parallel program for a multiprocessor consists of two or more interacting processes. A process is a sequential program that executes concurrently with other processes. In order to understand a parallel program, it is first necessary to identify the processes and the objects that they share. In this section we study two approaches to designing parallel programs. One approach to be introduced below is to have explicit concurrency, by which the programmer specifies the concurrency using certain language constructs. The other approach is to have implicit concurrency. In this case, the compiler determines what can be executed in parallel. This approach is more appropriate for data-flow computations, to be discussed in Chapter 10.

7.5.1 Language Features to Exploit Parallelism

In order to solve problems in an MIMD multiprocessor system, we need an efficient notation for expressing concurrent operations. Processes are *concurrent* if their executions overlap in time. More precisely, two processes are concurrent if the first operation of one process starts before the last operation of the other process terminates. In this case, no prior knowledge is available about the speed at which concurrent processes are executed. In this section, we will discuss the concurrency explicitly indicated by the programmer.

One way to denote concurrency is to use FORK and JOIN statements. FORK spawns a new process and JOIN waits for a previously created process to terminate. Generally, the FORK operation may be specified in three ways: FORK A; FORK A, J; and FORK A J, N. The execution of the FORK A statement initiates another process at address A and continues the current process. The execution of the FORK A, J statement causes the same action as FORK A and also increments a counter at address J. FORK A, J, N causes the same action as FORK A and sets the counter at address J to N. In all usages of the FORK statements, the corresponding JOIN statement is expressed as JOIN J. The execution of this statement decrements the counter at J by one. If the result is 0, the process at address $J + 1$ is initiated, otherwise the processor executing the JOIN statement is released. Hence, all processes execute the JOIN terminals, except the very last one.

Application of these instructions for the control of three concurrent processes is shown in Figure 7.50. These instructions do not allow a path to terminate without encountering a junction point. The problem with FORK and JOIN is

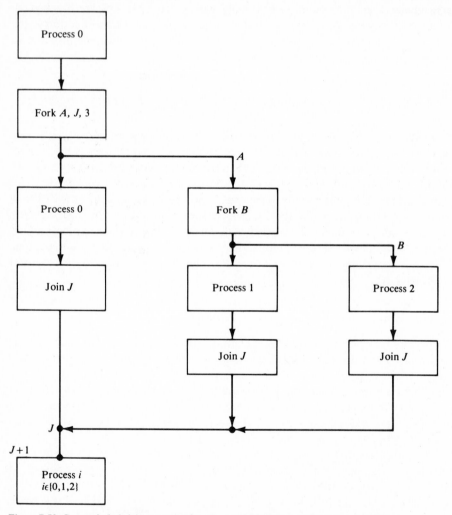

Figure 7.50 Conway's fork-join concept. (Courtesy of AFIPS Press *FJCC Proc.*, 1963.)

that, unless it is judiciously used, it blurs the distinction between statements that are executed sequentially and those that may be executed concurrently. FORK and JOIN statements are to parallel programming what the GO TO statement is to sequential programming. Also, because FORK and JOIN can appear in conditional statements and loops, a detailed understanding of program execution is necessary to enable the parallel activities. Nevertheless, when used in a disciplined manner, the statements are practical to enable parallelism explicitly. For example, FORK provides a direct mechanism for dynamic process creation, including multiple activation of the same program text.

An equivalent extension of the FORK-JOIN concept is the block-structured language originally proposed by Dijkstra. In this case, each process in a set of n processes $S_1, S_2, \cdots S_n$, can be executed concurrently by using the following **cobegin-coend** (or **parbegin-parend**) constructs:

$$
\begin{aligned}
&\textbf{begin} \\
&\quad S_0; \\
&\quad \textbf{cobegin } S_1; S_2; \ldots S_n; \textbf{ coend} \\
&\quad S_{n+1}; \\
&\textbf{end}
\end{aligned}
\qquad (7.25)
$$

The **cobegin** declares explicitly the parts of a program that may execute concurrently. This makes it possible to distinguish between shared and local variables, which in turn makes clear from the program text the potential source of interference. Figure 7.51 illustrates the precedence graph of the concurrent program given above. In this case, the block of statements between the **cobegin-coend** are executed concurrently only after the execution of statement S_0. Statement S_{n+1} is executed only after all executions of the statements $S_1, S_2, \ldots, S_n$ have been terminated. Since a concurrent statement has a single entry and a single exit, it is well suited

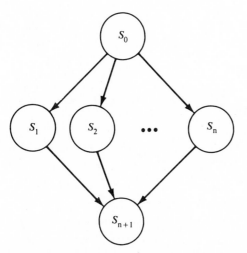

Figure 7.51 Precedence graph of the concurrent program.

to structured programming. The processes defined by the concurrent statement are completely independent of one another. The set of statements $S_1, S_2, \ldots, S_n$ are executed concurrently as disjoint processes. The disjointness implies that a variable v_i changed by statement S_i cannot be referenced by another statement S_j, where $j \neq i$. In other words, a variable subject to change by a process must be strictly private to that process, but disjoint processes can refer to common variables not changed by any of them.

Programs should be written so that it is simple for a compiler to check the degree of disjointness, possibly by scanning the program to recognize concurrent statements and variables accessed by them. The compiler must be able to distinguish between variables that can be changed by a statement and variables that can be referenced by a statement but not changed by it. These two kinds of variables are called the *variable* parameters and *constant* parameters of a statement.

To make the checking of disjointness manageable, it is often necessary to restrict the use of pointer variables and procedure parameters. For example, a pointer variable may be bound to a set of variables of a given type as

$$\textbf{var } \mathsf{i, j, k: integer: p: pointer to } \mathsf{i} \text{ or } \mathsf{j}; \tag{7.26}$$

This declaration indicates that variable p is a pointer to a particular set of integers. The notation enables a compiler and its run-time system to check that p always points to a variable of a well-defined type (in this case, an integer i or j).

The rule of disjointness enables the programmer to state explicitly that certain processes should be independent of one another. This depends on automatic detection of violations of this assumption. But as will be seen later, all multi-processing systems must occasionally permit concurrent processes to exchange data in a well-defined manner. The **cobegin-coend** notation hides this communication problem from the user, but it has to be solved at some other level.

Concurrent statements can be nested arbitrarily as in the following example, which is illustrated in Figure 7.52:

```
begin
    S₀;
    cobegin
    S₁
        begin S₂; cobegin S₃; S₄; S₅; coend S₆; end        (7.27)
        S₇;
    coend
    S₈;
end
```

Parallelism in the execution of statements may often be found in loops. Five primitives are listed below to allow the easy implementation of **parallel for** statements:

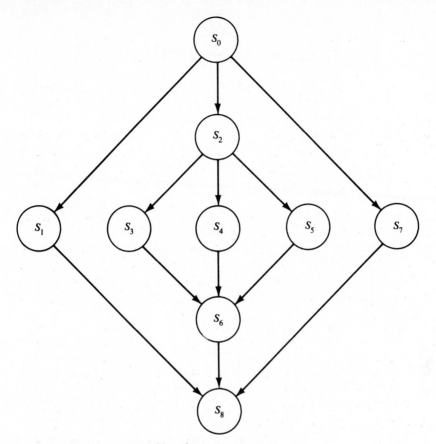

Figure 7.52 Precedence graph of nested concurrent processes.

- PREP: A parallel path counter, PPC, is initialized (PPC ← 1). (A stack of PPCs is kept in case of nested loops.)
- AND(L): Two-way fork. PPC ← PPC + 1. Process at address L is initiated and the current process is continued at the next instruction.
- ALSO(L): As above but without incrementing the PPC.
- JOIN: PPC ← PPC − 1. If PPC = 0, the PPC is "popped" and processing continues at the next instruction, else the processor executing the JOIN is released.
- IDLE: Terminates a path and releases the processor that was executing it.

Figure 7.53 shows the realization of a *parallel for* (**parfor**) statement using these instructions. Notice that statement S is executed for each value of i, and that this scheme is independent of the number of processors available in the system. Moreover, there is no need to state explicitly the relationship between the AND and JOIN primitives. Consider the matrix computation $C \leftarrow A \cdot B$, where A is

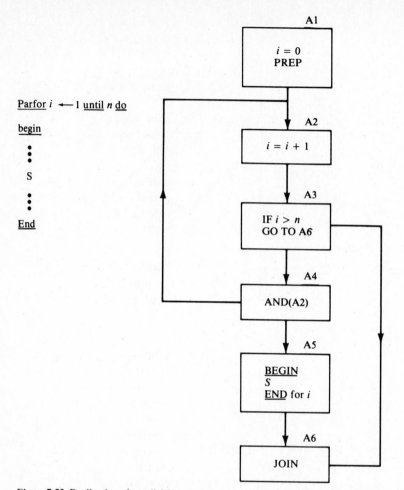

Figure 7.53 Realization of parallel for statement using defined primitives. (Courtesy of *ACM Computing Surveys*, **Baer 1973.)**

an $n \times n$ matrix and B and C are $n \times 1$ column vectors, for a very large n. The algorithm to compute the matrix C is given below using the **parfor** statement to spawn p independent processes. Assume that p divides n and $n/p = s$:

$$
\begin{aligned}
&\textbf{parfor } i \leftarrow 1 \textbf{ until } p \textbf{ do} \\
&\quad \textbf{begin} \\
&\qquad \textbf{for } j \leftarrow (i - 1)s + 1 \textbf{ until } s \cdot i \textbf{ do} \\
&\qquad \textbf{begin} \\
&\qquad\quad C(j) \leftarrow 0; \\
&\qquad\quad \textbf{for } k \leftarrow 1 \textbf{ until } n \textbf{ do} \\
&\qquad\qquad C(j) \leftarrow C(j) + A(j, k) \cdot B(k); \\
&\qquad \textbf{end} \\
&\quad \textbf{end}
\end{aligned}
\tag{7.28}
$$

Each process being spawned computes the statements between the outermost **begin-end** constructs for a different value of i. Hence, the computation of each group of $C(i)$ is done concurrently. Concurrent processes that access shared variables are called *communicating* processes. When processes compete for the use of shared resources, common variables are necessary to keep track of the requests for service.

A very common problem occurs when two or more concurrent processes share data which is modifiable. If a process is allowed to access a set of variables that is being updated by another process concurrently, erroneous results will occur in the computation. Therefore, controlled access of the shared variables should be required of the computations so as to guarantee that a process will have mutually exclusive access to the sections of programs and data which are nonreentrant or modifiable. Such segments of programs are called *critical* sections. The following assumptions are usually made regarding critical sections:

1. *Mutual Exclusion*: At most one process can be in a critical section at a time.
2. *Termination*: The critical section is executed in a finite time.
3. *Fair Scheduling*: A process attempting to enter the critical section will eventually do so in a finite time.

The mutually exclusive access to a set of shared variables can be accomplished by a number of constructs. An example is the MUTEXBEGIN and MUTEXEND constructs. Each construct alone does not enable a programmer to indicate whether a variable v should be private to a single process or shared by several processes. A compiler must recognize and guard any process interaction involving a shared variable v. The following is a notation used to declare a set of shared or common variables of type T: **var** v: **shared** T. Then a critical section may be defined by **csect** v **do** S. The definition associates a statement S with a common variable v and indicates that the statement S should have exclusive access to v. Critical sections referring to the same variable v exclude one another in time. By explicitly associating a critical section with the shared variable, the programmer informs the compiler of the sharing of this variable among concurrent processes, which is a deliberate exception to the rule of disjointness. At the same time, the compiler can check that a shared variable is used only inside critical sections and can generate code that implements mutual exclusion correctly. Critical sections referring to different variables can be executed in parallel, as shown in the following example:

```
var v: shared V;
var w: shared W;
cobegin                          (7.29)
    csect v do P;
    csect w do Q;
coend
```

The critical sections may also be nested as follows:

$$
\begin{aligned}
&\textbf{csect } v \textbf{ do} \\
&\textbf{begin} \\
&\qquad . . . \\
&\qquad \textbf{csect } w \textbf{ do } S; \\
&\qquad . . . \\
&\textbf{end}
\end{aligned}
\tag{7.30}
$$

However, there is a potential danger of deadlock, in which one or more processes are blocked waiting for events that will never occur. For example, two concurrent processes P_1 and P_2 may be deadlocked in the parallel program below if P_1 enters section v at the same time that P_2 enters w.

$$
\begin{aligned}
&\textbf{cobegin} \\
&P_1: \textbf{csect } v \textbf{ do csect } w \textbf{ do } S_1; \\
&P_2: \textbf{csect } w \textbf{ do csect } v \textbf{ do } S_2; \\
&\textbf{coend}
\end{aligned}
\tag{7.31}
$$

When process P_1 tries to enter its critical section w, it will be delayed because P_2 is already inside its critical section w. And process P_2 will be delayed trying to enter its section v because P_1 is already inside its section v.

The deadlock occurs because two processes enter their critical sections in opposite order and create a situation in which each process is waiting indefinitely for the completion of a region within the other process. This *circular wait* is a condition for deadlock. The deadlock is possible because it is assumed that a resource cannot be released (preempted) by a process waiting for an allocation of another resource. From this technique, an algorithm can be designed to find a subset of resources that would incur the minimum cost if preempted. This approach means that, after each preemption, the detection algorithm must be reinvoked to check whether deadlock still exists.

A process which has a resource preempted from it must make a subsequent request for the resource to be reallocated to it. As an example, we consider a system in which one process produces and sends a sequence of data items to another process that receives and consumes them. It is an obvious constraint that these data items cannot be received faster than they are sent. To satisfy this requirement, it is sometimes necessary to delay further execution of the receiving process until the sending process produces another data item. *Synchronization* is a general term for timing constraints of this type of communication imposed on interactions between concurrent processes.

The simplest form of interaction is an exchange of timing signals between two processes. A well-known example is the use of *interrupts* to signal the completion of asynchronous peripheral operations to the processor. Another type of timing signals, *events*, was used in early multiprocessing systems to synchronize concurrent processes. When a process decides to wait for an event, the execution of its next operation is delayed until another process signals the occurrence of the event.

The following program illustrates the transmission of timing signals from one process to another by means of a shared variable e of type *event*. Both processes are assumed to be cyclical. Notice that the concurrent operations *wait* and *signal* both access the same variable e.

```
var e: shared event;
cobegin
    cycle "sender"
    begin
        ... signal (e); ...
    end
    cycle "receiver"
    begin
        ... wait (e);
    end
coend
```

(7.32)

7.5.2 Detection of Parallelism in Programs

With reference to a sequential process, the term "parallelism" can be applied at several levels. Parallelism within a program can exist from the level of statements of procedural languages to the level of microoperations. In an MIMD multiprocessing environment, the general interest lies in parallelism of processes. The term "process" can be applied to a single statement or a group of statements which are self-contained portions of a computation.

Process parallelism can exist at a hierarchy of levels. For example, a group of statements is said to be processes at the first level. The statements within a procedure called by the main program would then be the second-level processes. If this procedure itself called another procedure, then the statements within the latter procedure would be the third level, and so on. Therefore, a sequentially organized program can be represented by a hierarchy of levels, as shown in Figure 7.54. Each block within a level represents a single process; as before, a process can represent a statement or a group of statements.

Once a sequentially organized program is resolved into its various levels, a fundamental consideration of parallel processing is recognizing processes within individual levels which can be executed in parallel. Assuming the existence of a system which can execute independent processes in parallel, this problem can be approached in two ways. We have already seen how process parallelism could be explicitly expressed by the programmer. If it is decided to make this indication independent of the programmer, then it is necessary to recognize the parallel executable processes implicitly by analysis of the source program.

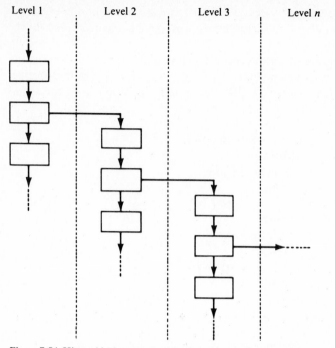

Level 1   Level 2   Level 3   Level n

Figure 7.54 Hierarchical representation of a sequentially organized program.

Data dependency is the main factor for the interprocess detection of parallelism. Consider several statements T_i of a sequentially organized program illustrated in Figure 7.55a. If the execution of statement T_3 is independent of the order in which statements T_1 and T_3 are executed (Figure 7.55a, b), then parallelism is said to exist between statements T_1 and T_2. They can, therefore, be executed in parallel, as shown in Figure 7.55c. This *commutativity* is a necessary but not a sufficient condition for parallel execution. There may exist, for instance, two statements which can be executed in either order but not in parallel. For example, an FFT computation produces its output in a scrambled order (bit reversed) as shown in Chapter 6. Therefore, there are two ways to perform FFT computations as shown below:

1. *Method one*
   a. Bit reverse the input.
   b. Perform the FFT.

2. *Method two*
   a. Perform the FFT.
   b. Bit reverse the output.

Thus performing the FFT and bit-reversal operations are two distinct processes which can be executed in alternate order with the same result. They cannot, however, be executed in parallel.

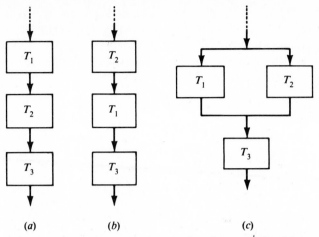

(a)   (b)   (c)

Figure 7.55 Sequential and parallel execution of a computational process.

The following *Bernstein condition* must be satisfied before sequentially organized processes can be executed in parallel. These are based on two separate sets of variables for each process T_i:

1. The *read* set I_i represents the set of all memory locations for which the first operation in T_i involving them is a fetch.
2. The *write* set O_i represents the set of all locations that are stored into in T_i.

The conditions under which two sequential processes T_1 and T_2 can be executed as two independent and concurrent processes is given below:

1. Locations in I_1 must not be destroyed by storing operations in O_2. The areas of memory from which task T_1 reads and onto which task T_2 writes should be mutually exclusive, that is,

$$I_1 \cap O_2 = \phi \tag{7.33}$$

2. By symmetry, exchanging the roles of T_1 and T_2,

$$I_2 \cap O_1 = \phi \tag{7.34}$$

Furthermore, to maintain the state of the machine (the contents of the total memory locations) when entering T_3 independently of the mode (parallel or sequential) of execution of T_1 and T_2, I_3 must be independent of the storing operations in T_1 and T_2, that is,

$$(O_1 \cap O_2) \cap I_3 = \phi \tag{7.35}$$

If one looks at T_i as a statement of a high-level language, then I_i and O_i represent, respectively, the input (those variables which appear only at the right of an assignment statement) and output data sets of T_i, respectively. Consider the following tasks, which represent Algol statements for evaluating three matrix arithmetic expressions. A, B, C, D, X, Y, and Z are each $n \times n$ matrices.

$$T_1; X \leftarrow (A + B) * (A - B)$$

$$T_2: Y \leftarrow (C - D) * (C + D)^{-1}$$

$$T_3: Z \leftarrow X + Y$$

For tasks T_1 and T_2, $I_1 = \{A, B\}$, $I_2 = \{C, D\}$, $O_1 = \{X\}$ and $O_2 = \{Y\}$. Since $I_1 \cap O_2 = \phi$, $I_2 \cap O_1 = \phi$, and $O_1 \cap O_2 = \phi$, tasks T_1 and T_2 can be executed in parallel. However task T_3 cannot be executed in parallel with either of T_1 or T_2 since $I_3 \cap O_2 \neq \phi$ or $I_3 \cap O_1 \neq \phi$. Hence, we can write a concurrent program to execute tasks T_1, T_2, and T_3 as follows:

```
begin
   cobegin
      X ← (A + B) * (A - B);
      Y ← (C - D) * (C + D)⁻¹;              (7.36)
   coend
   Z ← X + Y;
end
```

It is based on the above conditions that systems have been written for automatic detection of parallelism in source programs written in high-level languages. But the granularity of each of the processes created is usually small. At this point, it is desirable to clarify some possible misinterpretations of the implications of this method. The method does not try to determine whether any or all of the iterations within a loop can be executed simultaneously. Rather, the iterations executed sequentially are considered as a single task. Given a Pascal FOR statement, it is possible to detect if all executions of the loop must be performed sequentially or all of them can be executed simultaneously.

The total replication test can be approached at different levels of sophistication. Let $L = \{S_1, \ldots, S_i, \ldots, S_n\}$ be the statements composing the FOR loop. Then one can form the following input and output sets: $I_L = \bigcup_{j=1}^{n} I_j$, $O_L = \bigcup_{j=1}^{n} O_j$, where I_j and O_j are the input and output sets formed with variables referenced within L, with each subscripted array being an individual entry. If $I_L \cap O_L = \phi$, then all loop iterations can be replicated, for example:

```
for i ← 1 until n do
   begin
      A(i) ← B(i);
      C(i) ← D(i);                          (7.37)
   end
end
```

But if $I_L \cap O_L \neq \phi$, then one can look at the variables for which conflicts arise. If those are set before they are used, then the conflict is artificial and replication is permissible as, for example, in

$$
\begin{aligned}
&\textbf{for } i \leftarrow 1 \textbf{ until } n \textbf{ do} \\
&\textbf{begin} \\
&\quad A(i) \leftarrow f(A(i)); \\
&\quad T \leftarrow g(A(i)); \\
&\quad B(i) \leftarrow h(T); \\
&\textbf{end}
\end{aligned}
\tag{7.38}
$$

where a different T could be set aside for each replication. In practice, a compiler which incorporates an intelligent recognizer of parallelism with sufficient granularity is very difficult to implement. It is still a research problem. The recognizer often represents an overhead which may not be cost-effective for analyzing certain classes of programs in determining their parallel processability. The benefits of parallel processing obtained by using the recognizer will accrue only if the program is run many times in order that the initial overhead may be distributed over the many runs of the program.

7.5.3 Program and Algorithm Restructuring

The problem of decomposing a large program into many small concurrently executable (parallel processable) tasks has been studied for some time. Parallel processability permits faster execution times of programs and better utilization of resources in a multiprocessor computer. However, if a multiprocessor system is also capable of sequential processing of an instruction stream via a single processor, then some determination must be made as to whether or not multiprocessing will be beneficial. One of the necessary conditions of a program for parallel processing is that the program possesses many parallel paths.

A process consists of a number of computation steps. The time to execute the steps of the process is a random variable whose properties are often not well defined. When a number of processes cooperate concurrently to solve a given problem, there are a number of factors that contribute to the fluctuations in the execution time of a process. Some of these factors include memory contention, processor-scheduling policies, variations in processor speeds, and interrupts and variations in processing time due to input data distributions. This asynchronous behavior of processes leads to serious issues concerning the efficiency and correctness of the parallel algorithm. The unpredictably interleaved execution of the cooperating processes affects the correctness issue. The efficiency of the parallel algorithm may be reduced if synchronization is introduced to resolve the correctness issue. The effect of synchronization may also reduce the degree of concurrency in the algorithm.

There are a number of architectural factors that affect the decomposition of an algorithm for parallel processing. Some of these are the processor speed, memory access times, the memory bandwidth and its capacity. Depending on the architectural features, different aspects of the system may become the main bottlenecks in achieving a high level of concurrency.

The effective utilization of many multiprocessing computers is limited by the lack of a practical methodology for designing application programs to run on such computer systems. A major technique is to decompose algorithms for parallel execution. Two major issues in decomposition can be identified as partitioning and assignment. *Partitioning* is the division of an algorithm into procedures, modules and processes. *Assignment* refers to the allocation of these units to processors. These problems are among the most difficult and important in parallel processing. The emphasis below is to include communication factors as criteria for partitioning. Assignment techniques will be discussed in Section 8.4.

We will consider an example of an algorithm written for a uniprocessor and investigate the decomposition and restructuring of this algorithm for a multiprocessor system. The example is an image-processing algorithm called *histogramming*. A typical picture is represented by a rectangular array of picture elements (pixels). Each pixel has a small integer value (8 bits) between 0 and $b - 1$ (inclusive) that represents a gray scale value of a black-and-white picture or, for color images, the intensity of a primary color. Typically, $2 \leq b \leq 256$. Histogramming involves keeping track of the frequency of occurrence of each gray scale value; thus, for 8-bit pixels, b such frequencies (simple counters) must be maintained. Let *histog* $[0:b - 1]$ represent the array that keeps the count for the number of occurrences of the gray scale value $0, 1, \ldots, b - 1$. The rectangular picture is represented by the two-dimensional array of picture elements pixel $[0:m - 1, 0:n - 1]$, with m rows and n columns. If pixel $[i, j]$ represents the gray scale value of the pixel at coordinate i, j, then the following serially coded program will update the histogram to include the pixel at i, j:

```
    var pixel [0:m - 1, 0:n - 1];
    var histog[0:b - 1): integer;
  initial histog[0:b - 1] = 0; //initialize frequency counters//      (7.39)
    for i ← 0 until m - 1 do
       for j ← 0 until n - 1 do
          histog[pixel[i, j]] ← histog[pixel[i, j]] + 1;
```

The time complexity of this program is $0(mn)$.

This program can be restructured by realizing that the operation is iterative and scans a row of the image in the inner loop. Since there are m rows of the image, we can partition the image into p nonoverlapping and equal segments (assuming p divides m), where each segment has $m/p = s$ rows. We can then spawn a set of p processes to histogram the whole image, where each process is assigned to histogram a distinct segment of the image. However, the constraint is that all processes cooperate to form the histogram of the whole image; that is, they share the histog $[0:b - 1]$ array in updating the frequency counters. The degree of decomposition is thus p. In general, the value of p affects the performance of the algorithm. Using the **parfor** statement, the parallel algorithm to histogram the image may be written as follows:

```
var histog[0:b − 1]: integer: shared; //declare shared variables//
initial histog[0:b − 1] = 0; //initialize frequency counters//
   parfor i ← 1 until p do
      begin
         var pixel[(i − 1)s:  i − 1, 0:n − 1]: pixel;              (7.40)
            for k ← (i − 1)s until si − 1 do
               for j ← 0 until n − 1 do
                  csect histog[pixel[k, j]] do
                  histog[pixel[k, j]] ← histog[pixel[k, j]] + 1;
      end
```

Figure 7.56 illustrates the partitioning of the histogramming problem. Since the p processes share the histog $[0:b − 1]$ frequency counters, there may be a considerable degree of memory contention, assuming a tightly coupled system.

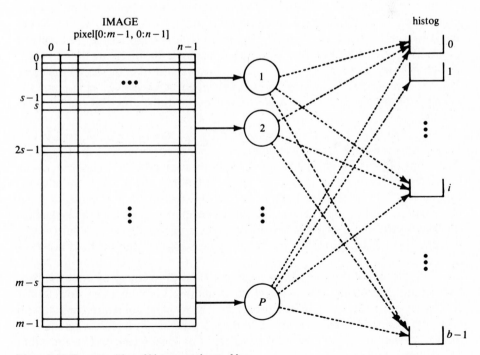

Figure 7.56 Decomposition of histogramming problem.

Also, the updating of each "*histog*" counter must be done in a mutually exclusive manner to avoid incorrect results. Hence, the counter update statement must be enclosed as a critical section. The degree of decomposition influences the degree of contention in this case. Without memory contention, the potential time complexity of each process is $0(sn)$. Since $s = m/p$, the decomposition of the problem into p processes has a potential speedup of p. This speedup is never achievable in practice, however.

We illustrate the effect of the placement of the process code, picture segments, and bins by considering the execution of this algorithm on three different multiprocessor architectures, each with p processors. In the first case, each of the p PEs consists of a processor and its local memory, which is attached to a time shared bus. In addition, a main memory, which is also attached to the bus, is shared by all the processors. Each PE contains the process code and its segment of the picture. The b bins are stored in the main memory. Since each PE contains a segment of the picture, the processors access the pixels without conflict. However, this architecture will cause excessive conflicts to the main memory because of concurrent accesses to the bins.

In the second case, the processors share the main memory through a crossbar switch. The process code and the entire picture elements are in memory. The bins are distributed across the memory modules. Therefore, in addition to conflicts of accesses to the process code and pixels, there are also conflicts of accesses to the bins.

In the third case, each processor of the second case has a private cache. Assume that the process code is small enough to reside in the cache; hence, we have faster access to code. Also assume that the cache is not large enough, so that the blocks of read only pixels are fetched into the cache on demand. The pixels are thus accessed at slightly faster than main memory speeds. However, the bins are shared writeable memory locations. Therefore, accesses to them cause excessive "ping-ponging" as copies of these bins are bounced from one cache to the other because of references for updates.

The effect of ping-ponging is considered by accesses to the bin histog[k] in a cache with write-back memory update policy. Suppose a remote cache C_j has the latest copy of bin k, which is now referenced by a local cache C_i. The reference in C_i results in a miss and causes C_j to update memory copy of bin k and also invalidate C_j's copy of bin k. Furthermore, C_i gets the copy of bin k from memory and increments it. In effect, processor i waits for two memory cycles each time a reference to a bin results in a miss when another processor has a copy of it. A subsequent reference by another processor to this bin ping-pongs the bin to the processor's cache.

If the degree of decomposition is greater than the number of available processors, the processing time of the histogramming problem is as slow as the completion time of the last of the p processes. The memory contention and mutual exclusion problems could be eliminated if each process has b bins to generate its local histogram for its segment of the picture in its local memory. The algorithm below illustrates the modification required to eliminate these problems.

```
var histog[0:b − 1]: integer; initial histog[0:b − 1] = 0;
var lhistog[1:,, 0:b − 1]: integer; //local bins//
initial lhistog[1:p, 0:b − 1] = 0;
parfor i ← 1 until p do
begin
    var pixel[(i − 1)s:si + 1, 0:n − 1]:pixel;
    var lhistog[i, 0:b − 1]:integer;                        (7.41)
    for k ← (i − 1)s until si + 1 do
        for j ← until n − 1 do
            lhistog[i, pixel[k, j]] ←  lhistog[i, pixel[k, j]] + 1;
end
for j ← 0 until b − 1 do //sum individual histograms//
    for i ← 1 until p do
        histog[j] ← histog[j] + lhistog[i, j];
```

However, extra overhead for synchronization is needed after the completion of all p processes to sum the individual histograms to obtain the overall histogram. The cost of the overhead is constant regardless of the size of the picture being processed. Slightly more local memory space is required to store the individual histograms, but this too is independent of the size of the picture being processed.

In general, the efficient implementation of an algorithm in a particular machine is largely shaped by the architecture of that machine. Relatively subtle changes in architecture can have extensive changes in the performance of the algorithm. The relationship between communication and computation is an important factor in designing effective parallel algorithms. One of the motivations for including communication in designing parallel programs is that the communication time can be greater than the computation time, based on data dependencies alone. The way in which data is distributed among processor memories can have a significant effect on the amount of required communication. By choosing the right data distribution, one may be able to design algorithms requiring less communication and thus reduce execution time.

The histogramming problem is unique in that a single copy of the data structure must be continually updated. If, for example, 2^{20} pixels (a 1024×1024 image) must be placed in b bins, the memory-contention problems in a parallel architecture can be formidable. As the processor speed increases relative to memory speed, it becomes necessary to reorganize the algorithms in which the number of data references made is minimized. For a machine like the C.mmp, where instruction execution and data references take about the same amount of time, an attempt to minimize the total number of executed instructions and data references should be equally made. As the processor speed increases, a larger proportion of the total time is spent in referencing data. This term soon dominates the total time and must be reduced in order to obtain significant speedup.

Also, as the capacity of the shared memory decreases, the algorithm should be decomposed to minimize the number of page faults between shared memory and disk. This means avoiding multiple passes through the data which increases the frequency of disk accesses. It is desirable to execute as many instructions as possible on the data in shared memory before bringing in a new page. In spite of this, if little computation is involved, an algorithm which makes efficient use of the data in shared memory will still run slowly, since the processor is forced to wait more often for data to be brought in from mass storage. A decrease in the bandwidth of the shared memory disk link or an increase in the disk access time will necessitate the same type of reorganization. Since more time is required to fill a buffer in shared memory, the algorithm must do all the computing that it can before initiating another transfer to or from file memory. Careful decomposition of the algorithms to be implemented on a machine may permit the use of slower disks and lower bandwidth channels between shared memory and disk.

In discussing the various approaches to partitioning, we emphasize the role of communication in program partitioning techniques. Unless the communication problem is effectively solved, delays due to communication bottlenecks may result. Partitioning methodologies for parallel programs evolved from two sources: (a) extensions to concepts that play a central role in sequential program design, especially data abstraction and information hiding concepts, and (b) techniques for synchronizing concurrent processes. The combination of the two sources has led to the concept of structuring systems as a set of concurrent processes that interact through monitors, which are discussed in Chapter 8. These approaches have been successful for real-time systems and operating systems designs which are based on a multiprogrammed uniprocessor system.

We formally define the partitioning problem as follows: Given an algorithm, specify the set of program units (modules or processes) that will implement the algorithm on a specified multiprocessor system in the most efficient manner. Efficiency can be measured by such criteria as the utilization of the processor or the speedup of the algorithm. One general partitioning guideline is based on the concept of *computation-communication* trade-offs. This concept is similar to the idea of space-time trade-offs in sequential programming. In partitioning, one can attempt to reduce the communication complexity by increasing the computation complexity. Another general guideline for partitioning algorithms is *clustering*. This method can be effectively applied to loosely coupled processing nodes. The basic idea is to form groups of modules in which the number of message transfers within groups is much greater than the number of transfers between groups.

A partitioning technique termed *recursive* or *iterative compute-combine* method can also be used in some cases. This approach is applicable to a broad class of problems. Examples are sorting and computing the maximum of a vector or unimodal function. The structure of the algorithm is a tree with the leaves representing the basic computations and the internal nodes representing the combination of results produced by the node descendants. Another technique is the *large army* technique. Taking advantage of parallel processing, one creates a large number of processes, each performing precisely the same function, such as in a search operation. When one of the processes achieves the collective goal, it notifies the others to cease the iteration and to reinitialize themselves for further iterations, if there are any.

Multiprocessors may not provide an effective means of increasing the execution speed of certain computationally expensive algorithms. The algorithm under examination may not lend itself to decomposition for a multiprocessing environment. The problems come from one or more critical sections of unevenly sized codes, which have to update a common data base (e.g., the same copy of a histogram). In these cases, synchronization can introduce significant overhead and the time lost by processes waiting for the same memory location may be large. Here, a uniprocessor which is N times as fast would be preferable to an N-processor system.

Conversely, algorithms which allow favorable scheduling of processes and/or the data to be partitioned into independent chunks often can run N times as fast given N processes. The extra synchronization overhead is small compared to the increase in the number of instructions executed per second. Maximum performance from an algorithm can only be obtained when it has been coded with the particular machine architecture in mind. Effective decomposition of algorithms is dependent on the programmer knowing the hardware capabilities and coding the algorithm to take advantage of the machine's capabilities.

7.6 BIBLIOGRAPHIC NOTES AND PROBLEMS

Multiprocessor hardware organizations and operating system configurations were surveyed in Enslow (1974, 1977). Commercial multiprocessors were comparatively studied in Satyanarayanan (1980), in which an annotated bibliography was given. Theoretical aspects of multiprocessor systems were discussed in Baer (1973, 1976). Experience using multiprocessor systems was summarized in Jones and Schwarz (1980). Reliability modeling of various multiprocessor architectures can be found in Hwang and Chang (1982). The Cm* material is based on the reports by Jones and Crehringer (1980).

An example of a crossbar design can be found in Wulf et al. (1981). Bain and Ahuja (1981) provided a comprehensive treatment of various arbitration algorithms for single bus structures. Patel (1981) introduced the delta network. Studies on packet switched networks can be found in Dias and Jump (1981) and in Chin and Hwang (1984). The Banyan networks were studied by Goke and Lipovski (1973). Parallel memory organizations for multiprocessing were treated by Briggs and Davidson (1977) and their uses in a system with caches by Briggs and Dubois (1983) and Yeh et al. (1983). The home memory concept was due to Smith (1978). Multicache coherence problems were studied by Dubois and Briggs (1982) and Censier and Feautrier (1978).

Concurrent programming techniques can be found in Andrews and Schneider (1983). Communication issues in developing parallel algorithms were studied in Lint and Agerwala (1981). An example of a multiprocessor operating system was given in Ousterhoust et al. (1980) for the Cm* system. Operating systems for multiprocessors were also treated in Ritchie (1973), Sites (1980), Habermann (1976), and Denning (1976). Load balancing among multiple processors was modeled in Ni and Hwang (1983). The FORK-JOIN concept is due to Conway

(1963). The primitives used to implement a PARALLEL FOR were studied in Gosden (1966). Synchronization primitives in concurrent systems are proposed by Dijkstra (1965, 1968). The extensions of semaphores can be found in Hoare (1974) and Hansen (1977). Automatic detection of parallelism can be found in Baer (1973). The conditions that determine whether two tasks can be executed in parallel were proved in Bernstein (1966). Techniques for recognition of parallel processable tasks were presented in Russel (1969) and Ramamoorthy and Gonzalez (1969). Program decomposition for multiprocessors is discussed in Hon and Reddy (1977).

Problems

7.1 Briefly describe the following terms associated with a multiprocessor system:

(a) Multiple computer system
(b) Multiprocessor system
(c) Loosely coupled multiprocessors
(d) Tightly coupled multiprocessors
(e) Homogeneous multiprocessors
(f) Heterogeneous multiprocessors
(g) A cluster of computer modules
(h) Private caches versus shared caches
(i) Context switching
(j) Semaphore for synchronization
(k) Time shared common buses
(l) Crossbar switches
(m) Multiport memory
(n) The delta network
(o) The L-M memory organization
(p) Multicache coherence problem
(q) Master-slave operating system
(r) Floating-supervisor system
(s) Mutual exclusion between processes
(t) Bus-arbitration algorithms
(u) Explicit parallelism
(v) Critical sections
(w) Computation-communication trade-offs

7.2 Assume a uniprocessor with cache. The main memory consists of 16 modules which can be interleaved in various ways. For each case below, indicate the number of memory cycles required per block transfer. Also indicate the reliability of each system by an integer k. A system is said to be k-reliable with respect to memory if it can keep functioning after k modules *taken at random* are disconnected. In the table, LSB means the least significant bit and MSB the most significant bit.

Interleaving	Block size	Bus width	Number of memory cycles	Reliability
4LSB	16 words	1 word		
2MSB-2LSB	16 words	8 words		
4	8 words	8 words		
1MS	4 words	8 words		
3MSB-1LSB	4 words	2 words		

7.3 The functions $S_{q*r}(i)$ and $f_{q*r}(i)$ from the Delta networks are defined as follows:

$$S_{q*r}(i) = \left(qi + \left[\frac{i}{r}\right]\right) \bmod qr \qquad \text{for } 0 \le i \le qr - 1$$

and

$$f_{q*r}(i) = \begin{cases} qi \bmod(qr - 1) & \text{for } 0 \le i \le qr - 2 \\ i & \text{for } i = qr - 1 \end{cases}$$

(a) Prove that $S_{q*r}(i) = f_{q*r}(i), \forall, 0 \le i \le qr - 1$.
(Hint: i can be written as $i = k_1 r + k_2$, where $0 \le k_2 < r$).
(b) Then show that f_{r*q} is the inverse of f_{q*r}. That is,

$$f_{r*q}(f_{q*r}(i)) = i$$

(c) Consider an $a^n \times b^n$ delta network which is implemented with $a \times b$ switch boxes.
(1) How many $a \times b$ switch boxes are required?
(2) What is the delay through the network if the delay through one box is D?

7.4 A three-processor system uses three multiport memory modules in a shared memory system in which each processor can access each memory module. Memory modules are assumed to be 100 percent reliable, but the processors fail with distressing frequency. 84 percent of the time, all three processors are working correctly, 15 percent of the time only two processors are usable, and 1 percent of the time only a single processor is functioning. The fraction of time during which no processor is working properly is negligible.

What is the average throughput in this system, as measured by the average number of memory modules active during a memory cycle? Use all of the assumptions of the multiprocessor model presented first in class. In particular, memory requests queued at a module at the start of a memory cycle but not serviced during that cycle remain queued at the module until they are eventually serviced. Do not worry about what happens immediately after a processor fails or is repaired; i.e., assume that the system is in steady state (with one, two, or three processors functioning) virtually all of the time.

7.5 In the common bus (time shared bus) organization shown in Figure 7.57, there are p parallel-pipeline processors and m memory modules. The arbiter randomly selects a request from the processors and puts it on the bus. After one time unit delay, the address (and data, if any) reaches all the memory parts. The appropriate module then gates-in the information. The module goes through a memory cycle of c time units long. The arbiter does not issue the selected request at time t if the addressed module is still going to be busy at time $t + 1$. Based on this description and the following assumptions, derive the memory bandwidth (average number of requests accepted per memory cycle) of this organization. Memory requests are random and uniformly distributed among all modules. The rejected requests are ignored. One request is issued by each processor at each time unit. No data dependency exists between any two requests.

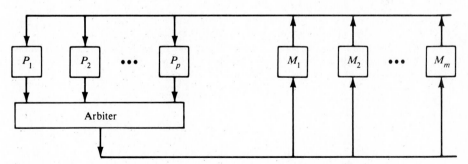

Figure 7.57 A bus-structured multiprocessor system with a centralized bus arbiter.

7.6 Consider a $p \times m$ crossbar switch connecting p processors to m memory modules. Assume only one input AND gate and OR gate (no wired-OR). Assume also that all variables are available in true and complemented form.

    (a) Estimate the number of gates in the switch, ignoring the decoders and the arbiter. Assume the data width to be w bits.

    (b) Design the decoder and arbiter for the above crossbar. Assume that the processor P_i has priority over P_j if $i < j$. Estimate the number of gates for this circuit.

7.7 We have considered an 8×8 delta network in Figure 7.35. Answer the following questions related to this interconnection network.

    (a) Does the network have a path between any processor and any memory module?

    (b) Let $(d_2 d_1 d_0)_2$ be the address of a memory module (MM) generated by a processor whose number is $(p_2 p_1 p_0)_2$. Let the control variables at stages 0, 1, and 2 be x_0, x_1, and x_2 respectively. The convention is

$$x_i = \begin{cases} 0 & \text{for straight connection} \\ 1 & \text{for crossed connection} \end{cases}$$

The requested MM address is passed through the successive stages to set up the path. Find the logic equations for x_0, x_1, x_2 as functions of d_0, d_1, d_2, and p_0, p_1, and p_2.

    (c) Assume that processor zero accesses MM2, processor four accesses MM4, and processor six accesses MM3. Show the paths for these three requests on Figure 7.35. Do these requests conflict?

7.8 Briefly characterize the *multicache coherence* problem and describe various methods that have been suggested to cope with the problem. Comment on the advantages and disadvantages of each method to preserve the coherence among multiple shared caches used in a multiprocessor system.

7.9 Distinguish among the following operating system configurations for multiprocessor computers. In each system configuration, name two example multiprocessor computers that have implemented an operating system similar to the configuration being discussed. Comment on the advantages, design problems, and shortcomings in each operating system configuration.

    (a) Master-slave operating system.

    (b) Separate supervisor system per processor.

    (c) Floating-point supervisor system.

7.10 Consider a computer with four processors P_1, P_2, P_3, P_4 and six memory modules M_1, $M_2, \ldots, M_6$. The four processors can be configured as an MIMD machine or as an SIMD machine. The illustrated memory access patterns are generated by the processors for the computation of six instructions with the data dependence graph shown in Figure 7.57. Each instruction needs to access the memory modules in, at most, three consecutive memory cycles. For SIMD mode, only the same instruction can access different modules simultaneously. For MIMD mode, no such restriction exists. When two or more processors access the same module in the same cycle, the request of the lower-numbered processor is granted, and the rest of the requests must wait for a later memory cycle.

    (a) For MIMD operation, different instructions can be executed by the four processors at the same time, subject only to data dependency. What is the average *memory bandwidth* (words/cycle) used in the execution of the above program in MIMD mode?

    (b) Repeat the same question for using the computer in SIMD mode. The four processors must execute the same instruction at the same time under SIMD mode.

7.11 Supposing each task is an *assignment statement*, restructure the following assignment statements using Bernstein's conditions so that we have maximum parallelism among tasks. Specify which of the three conditions you are using for the restructuring.

$$A = B + C$$

$$C = D + E$$

$$F = G + E$$

$$C = L + M$$

$$M = G + C$$

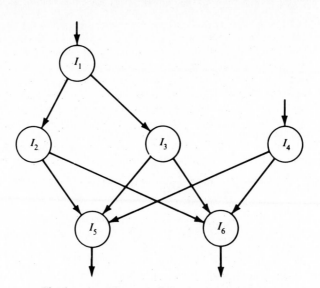

The data-dependency graph for the six instructions

Processors Instructions	P_1	P_2	P_3	P_4
I_1	M_2	M_4	M_3	M_2
I_2	M_1	M_3	M_2	M_6
I_3	M_4	M_6	M_5	M_6
I_4	M_3	M_4	M_4	M_2
I_5	M_2	M_2	M_2	M_1
I_6	M_1	M_5	M_5	M_1

(Entries are memory modules being requested to access by the processors)

Figure 7.58 Program graph and the memory access pattern for either an SIMD computer with 4 PEs or an MIMD multiprocessor with 4 processors in Problem 7.10.

Write your answer so that, when two assignment statements are put on the same line, it indicates that they can be processed in parallel. It is easier if you reset the order of precedence in a precedence graph. (Note: The statements executed after the restructuring should have the same result as the statements executed before restructuring.)

7.12 A *parallel computation* on an n-processor system can be characterized by a pair $\langle P(n), T(n) \rangle$, where $P(n)$ is the total number of unit operations to be performed and $T(n)$ is the total execution time in steps by the system. In a *serial computation* on a uniprocessor with $n = 1$, one can write $T(1) = P(1)$, because each unit operation requires one step to be executed. In general, we have $T(n) < P(n)$, if there is more than one operation to be performed per step by n processors, where $n \geq 2$. Five performance indices have been suggested below by Lee (1980) in comparing a parallel computation with a serial computation.

$$S(n) = \frac{T(1)}{T(n)} \quad \text{(The speedup)}$$

$$E(n) = \frac{T(1)}{n \cdot T(n)} \quad \text{(The efficiency)}$$

$$R(n) = \frac{P(n)}{P(1)} \quad \text{(The redundancy)}$$

$$U(n) = \frac{P(n)}{n \cdot T(n)} \quad \text{(The utilization)}$$

$$Q(n) = \frac{T^3(1)}{n \cdot T^2(n) \cdot P(n)} \quad \text{(The quality)}$$

(*a*) Prove that the following relationships hold in all possible comparisons of parallel to serial computations.

(1) $1 \leq S(n) \leq n$

(2) $E(n) = \dfrac{S(n)}{n}$

(3) $U(n) = R(n) \cdot E(n)$

(4) $Q(n) = \dfrac{S(n) \cdot E(n)}{R(n)}$

(5) $\dfrac{1}{n} \leq E(n) \leq U(n) \leq 1$

(6) $1 \leq R(n) \leq \dfrac{1}{E(n)} \leq n$

(7) $Q(n) \leq S(n) \leq n$

(*b*) Based on the above definitions and relationships, given physical meanings of these performance indices.

EIGHT

MULTIPROCESSING CONTROL AND ALGORITHMS

This chapter covers interprocess synchronization mechanisms, system deadlocks, protection schemes, multiprocessor scheduling, and parallel algorithms. These are important topics in developing a sophisticated operating system for a multiprocessor system. The parallel algorithms form the basis in using MIMD computers. For other related issues that have not been covered below, readers are advised to check the attached bibliographic notes.

8.1 INTERPROCESS COMMUNICATION MECHANISMS

Various interprocess communication schemes have been proposed by computer designers. This section enumerates some of the process-synchronization mechanisms implementable at the instruction level. High-level mechanisms such as the **P** and **V** primitives and conditional critical regions are then presented. Examples are given on the producer-consumer processes and the reader-writer problem using these mechanisms. The extension of conditional critical regions to monitors is also discussed.

8.1.1 Process Synchronization Mechanisms

Cooperating processes in a multiprocessor environment must often communicate and synchronize. Execution of one process can influence the other via communication. Interprocess communication employs one of two schemes: use of shared variables or message passing. Often the processes that communicate do so via a synchronization mechanism. A process executes with unpredictable speed and generates actions or events which must be recognized by another cooperating process. The set of constraints on the ordering of these events constitutes the set of synchronization required for the operating processes. The synchronization mechanism is used to delay execution of a process in order to satisfy such constraints.

Two types of synchronization are commonly employed when using shared variables. These are *mutual exclusion* and *condition synchronization*. We recall that mutual exclusion ensures that a physical or virtual resource is held indivisibly. Another situation occurs in a set of cooperating processes when a shared data object is in a state that is inappropriate for executing a given operation. Any process which attempts such an operation should be delayed until the state of the data object changes to the desired value as a result of other processes being executed. This type of synchronization is sometimes called condition synchronization. The mutual-exclusive execution of a critical section, S, whose access is controlled by a variable gate can be enforced by an entry protocol denoted by MUTEXBEGIN (gate) and an exit protocol denoted by MUTEXEND (gate). Alternatively, the effect of the entry and exit protocols can be expressed as **csect** gate **do** S.

There are certain problems associated with implementing the MUTEXBEGIN/ MUTEXEND construct. Execution of the MUTEXBEGIN statement should detect the status of the critical section. If it is busy, the process attempting to enter the critical section must wait. This can be done by setting an indicator to show that a process is currently in the critical section. Execution of the MUTEX-END statement should reset the status of the critical section to idle and provide a mechanism to schedule the waiting process to use the *critical section* (CS). One implementation is the use of the LOCK and UNLOCK operations to correspond to MUTEXBEGIN and MUTEXEND respectively. For these, consider that there is a single *gate* that each process must pass through to enter a CS and also leave it. If a process attempting to enter the CS finds the gate unlocked (open) it locks (closes) it as it enters the CS in one indivisible operation so that all other processes attempting to enter the CS will find the gate locked. On completion, the process unlocks the gate and exits from the CS. Assuming that the variable *gate* = 0(1) means that the gate is open (closed), the access to a CS controlled by the gate can be written as

```
LOCK (gate)
execute critical section
UNLOCK (gate)
```

The LOCK (x) operation may be implemented as follows:

```
var x: shared integer;
LOCK (x): begin
        var y: integer;
          y ← x;
        while y = 1 do y ← x; // wait until gate is open //
          x ← 1; // set gate to unavailable status //
        end
```

The UNLOCK(x) operation may be implemented as

$$\text{UNLOCK}(x): x \leftarrow 0;$$

The LOCK mechanism as shown is not satisfactory because two or more processes may find $x = 0$ before one reaches the $x \leftarrow 1$ statement. This can be remedied if the processor has an instruction that both tests and sets (modifies) a word. Such an instruction, called TEST_AND_SET(x) and available on the IBM S/370, tests and sets a shared variable x in a single *read-modify-write* memory cycle to produce a variable y. The read-modify-write operation must take place in one cycle so that the memory location, x, is not accessed and modified by another processor before the current processor completes the test-and-set operation. The indivisibility is usually accomplished by the requesting processor which holds the bus until the cycle is completed. Therefore the set of operations $\{y \leftarrow x; x \leftarrow 1\}$ is indivisible in the following definition of TEST_AND_SET(x):

```
      var x: shared integer;
TEST_AND_SET(x): begin
                   var y: integer;
                   y ← x;
                   If y = 0 then x ← 1;
                   end
```

The LOCK operation may be rewritten as

```
      var x: shared integer;
LOCK(x): begin
           var y: integer;
             Repeat {y ← TEST_AND_SET(x)} until y = 0;
           end
```

An important property of locks is that a process does not relinquish the processor on which it is executing while it is waiting for a lock held by another process. Thus, it is able to resume execution very quickly when the lock becomes available. However, this property may create problems for the error-recovery mechanism of the system when the processor which is executing the lock fails. The error-recovery procedure has to be sophisticated enough to ensure that deadlocks are not introduced as a result of the recovery process itself.

Another instruction used to enforce mutual exclusion of access to a shared variable in memory location m_addr is the *compare-and-swap* (CAS) instruction. This instruction is available on the IBM 370/168. A typical syntax of this instruction uses the two additional operands r_old and r_new, which are processor registers

(CAS r_old, r_new, m_addr). The action of the CAS instruction is defined as follows:

$$
\begin{aligned}
&\textbf{var } m\_addr: \textbf{ shared } address; \\
&\textbf{var } r\_old, r \; new: registers; \\
&\textbf{var } z: CAS \; flag; \\
&CAS: \text{if } r\_old = m\_addr \textbf{ then} \\
&\qquad \{m\_addr \leftarrow r\_new; z \leftarrow 1\} \\
&\qquad \textbf{else} \\
&\qquad\qquad \{r\_old \leftarrow m \; addr; z \leftarrow 0\}
\end{aligned}
$$

Notice that associated with the CAS instruction is a processor flag z. The flag is set if the comparison indicates equality. Again, the execution of the CAS instruction (that is, the IF statement) is an indivisible operation. We illustrate the use of the CAS instruction with a shared singly linked queue data structure (Figure 8.1), which is accessed concurrently by the two processes P_1 and P_2. The two operations which can be performed on the queue are ENQUEUE(X) and DEQUEUE. ENQUEUE(X) adds a node X to the "TAIL" of the queue and DEQUEUE returns a pointer to the deleted "HEAD" of the queue. HEAD and TAIL are shared global variables. Assuming that the queue is never empty (for simplicity), the ENQUEUE(X) primitive for a nonconcurrent system can be described as

```
Procedure ENQUEUE(X);
var P: pointer;    //P is local to each invocation //
begin
LINK(X) ← Λ;       //terminate last node's link//
P ← TAIL;
TAIL ← X;
LINK(P) ← X;       //attach new node to queue//
end
```

Suppose process P_1 requests to enqueue node X. While P_1 is executing the primitive, it gets interrupted by P_2, which requests to enqueue node Y to the same queue. Assume that the interruption occurs at the end of statement $P \leftarrow$ TAIL. Figure 8.1a illustrates the state of the queue at the time of interruption. If P_1 executes the procedure to completion after P_2 returns control to P_1, node X will be attached to the queue. However, node Y, which was added by P_2, would have been detached from the queue unintentionally. This error occurs because pointer P was not updated to point to the last node attached by process P_2. We can avoid this problem by using the CAS instruction to update P to point to the last attached node. This can be accomplished by replacing the TAIL $\leftarrow$ X statement with

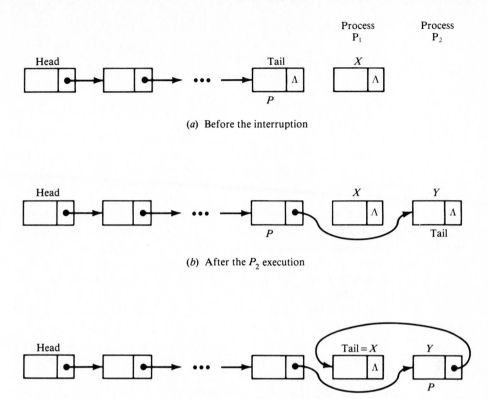

(a) Before the interruption

(b) After the P_2 execution

(c) Followed by the P_1 execution

Figure 8.1 Interleaved execution of ENQUEUE by process P_1 and process P_2.

"**repeat** CAS P, X, TAIL **until** TAIL = X". The modified ENQUEUE(X) primitive is shown below:

```
Procedure ENQUEUE(X);
var P: pointer;
begin
    LINK(X) ← Λ;
    P ← TAIL;
    repeat CAS P,X,TAIL until TAIL = X;
    LINK(P) ← X;
end
```

The CAS instruction ensures that the logical state (P) of the interrupted program is maintained on resumption of the interrupted program. Otherwise it updates the state P to the most recent value of TAIL.

Figure 8.1*b* shows the outcome of the execution of the primitive by P_2 followed by the completion of the execution of the primitive by P_1 (Figure 8.1*c*). The CAS instruction is more useful than the test-and-set instruction. An extension of the CAS instruction is the *compare double and swap*, also available on the IBM 370/168. There are other variations which enforce mutual exclusion. For example, the Honeywell 60/66 has the *load-accumulator-and-clear-memory-location* (LDAC) instruction.

The LOCK instruction using TAS has a drawback in that processes attempting to enter critical sections are busy accessing and testing common variables. This is called *busy-wait* or *spin-lock*, which results in performance degradation. The process cannot normally be context-swapped off its processor while it is waiting. Hence, the processor is said to be *locked out*. Such lock-out is only permitted in supervisor mode. In general, LOCK and UNLOCK primitives are not usually allowed to be executed in user mode because the user process may be swapped out while holding a critical section. On the other hand, if the user makes a supervisor call each time it attempts to access a critical section, the overhead will be greatly increased. Hence the CAS instruction was provided as an excellent mechanism of letting the user do some synchronization in user mode.

The performance degradation due to spin-locks is two-fold. When a processor is spinning, it actively consumes memory bandwidth that might otherwise have been used more constructively. If the spinning period is too long, a processor is not effectively utilized during that period. A number of methods have been proposed to reduce the degradation due to spin-locks. The first method is aimed at reducing the request rate to memory and, hence, the degree of memory conflicts. This is accomplished by delaying the reissuance of the lock request for an interval T. Thus, the LOCK(x) primitive, for example, can be modified as

```
LOCK(x): begin
            y ← TEST-AND-SET(x);
            while y ≠ 0 do
              begin
                PAUSE(T); //
                y ← TEST-AND-SET(x);
              end
         end
```

Note that the processor issuing the request may not be released unless T is large enough. The choice for T depends on the granularity of the resource being requested.

The second method is directed at relieving the processor of performing the lock access by incorporating a separate mechanism which processes lock requests. This can be accomplished in one of several ways. For example, the mechanism can continuously access the lock until it is available, as in the HEP machine.

Concurrently, the processor can execute another ready-to-run process in its local memory. When the processor is signaled by the mechanism that the lock has been allocated, it immediately resumes execution of the waiting process. Note resumption is immediate because the process was not swapped out. The busy-wait can be avoided if, in the first access to the lock, it is found busy. In this case, the process requesting it is blocked. When the lock becomes available, the mechanism is signaled so that the blocked process can be readied to resume execution. The latter scheme seems adequate for a mutually exclusive access to a resource with large granularity.

The distribution of locks in memory is an important factor in the performance of concurrent processes accessing lockable resources. For example, if all locks are stored in one memory module, the contention for these locks can become excessive. In a multiprocessor with private caches, the accesses to locks by the processors can cause excessive overhead because of consistency checks. However, contention for these locks can be partly relieved by distributing the locks into many blocks of memory.

Two primitive operations can be defined to *block* a process attempting to enter a busy critical section and *wake_up* the blocked process when the critical section becomes free. These primitives are

wake_up (p): if process p is logically blocked (that is, dormant), change its state to active; else set up a *wake-up waiting switch* (wws) to remember the wake-up call

block (p): if process p's wws is set, reset it and continue execution of the process; else change p's state to dormant

Using these operations requires a wake-up list which is updated dynamically. In order to prevent loss of information, wake-up signals that occur while a process is executing must be saved and a process should not be allowed to become dormant until all its wake-up signals have been serviced. The wake-up waiting switch (wws) is the mechanism used to save wake-up signals. A process identification tag is appended to the wake-up signal, which is used to route the signal to the appropriate receiving process. Hardware or software mechanisms may be used to implement the wws, which stores the wake-up signals on arrival until they are acknowledged. This may result in a potential race condition if the mechanism is improperly designed. Note that the blocking and unblocking operations constitute an overhead which may be significant if designed improperly.

Lock conflicts are resolved in the implementation of the busy-wait because a request that finds the lock busy waits until the lock is released. Serialization is thus enforced. Another synchronization primitive was proposed to permit some form of concurrency of access to a memory location while still enforcing some serialization. The format of this primitive is *fetch-and-add* (X, e), where X is a shared integer variable and e is an integer expression. Let the value of X be denoted by Y. We abbreviate the primitive as **F & A**(X, e), which is defined to return the old value of X and replace the contents of X by the sum $Y + e$ in one indivisible operation. If several fetch-and-add operations are initiated simultaneously by different processors on the shared variable X, the effect of these operations is exactly what it would be if they occurred in some unspecified serial order. That is, X is modified by the appropriate total increment and each operation yields the intermediate value of X corresponding to its position in the serial order. As an example, consider the two processors P_i and P_j which issue:

$$S_i \leftarrow \mathbf{F\&A}(X, e_i), \ S_j \leftarrow \mathbf{F\&A}(X, e_j)$$

respectively. Then S_i and S_j may contain Y and $Y + e_i$, respectively, or S_i and S_j may contain $Y + e_j$ and Y, respectively, depending on the priorities of P_i and P_j and the order of arrival of their requests. In either case, X becomes $Y + e_i + e_j$.

The fetch-and-add primitive can be implemented within the processor memory switch, as shown in Figure 8.2 for the example with two simultaneous fetch-and-adds directed at the same memory location X. In the example, it is assumed that P_i's request has a higher priority than P_j's. The switch forms $e_i + e_j$ and transmits $\mathbf{F\&A}(X, e_i + e_j)$ to the memory. At the same time, e_i is stored in the switch's register. On receipt of Y from memory as a result of $\mathbf{F\&A}(X, e_i + e_j)$, the switch transmits Y and $Y + e_i$ in response to requests $\mathbf{F\&A}(X, e_i)$ and $\mathbf{F\&A}(X, e_j)$, respectively.

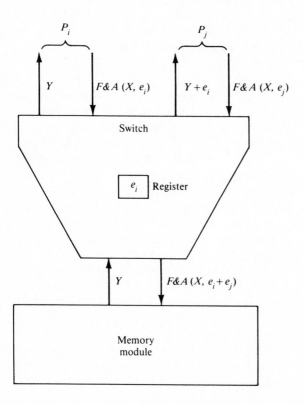

Figure 8.2 Implementation of the *Fetch-and-Add* primitive (F & A).

We illustrate a simple application of **F&A** in a multiprocessor environment. Suppose it is required that all processors which intend to access a given resource must first indicate their intentions by incrementing a common counter, X, in memory. An accurate count of these requests can be maintained if each processor indicates its intention by the statement **F&A**$(X, 1)$. Hence if two or more processors execute the statement simultaneously, X will contain the correct count of requests at the completion of all instructions. Note that the value returned to each processor as a result of execution of **F&A**$(X, 1)$ can be used as its position in the request queue.

Another synchronization primitive uses the semaphore, which consists of a counter, a process routine queue, and the two functions **P** and **V**. This is described in the next subsection. Although simple, semaphores are known to be sufficient solutions to synchronization problems for permanent-resource competitors and temporary-resource producers-consumers. However, semaphores are often very inconvenient in representing communication between processes. For this reason, most operating systems also provide other process-communication mechanisms. Two examples are events and messages.

Event primitives are typically provided by the two functions *wait* and *signal*. A process can wait on an event or a combination of events to be true. When another process signals an event, all processes waiting on that event are placed on the ready queue. Other variations are also possible. One potential problem with events is that a process has the possibility of waiting on an event that either never becomes true or was signaled earlier. A slight variation of waiting on an event, used especially in real-time systems, is waiting on a timing queue administered by the operating system for a specified time period to elapse.

Messages provide an even more flexible and direct method of interprocess communication, especially for producer-consumer relationships. Typical primitives are the functions *send* and *receive*, which allow a string of characters to be passed between processes. Implementation variations are numerous. For example, send may or may not wait for an acknowledgement. Receive usually waits if no message has been sent. The Intel iAPX 432 multiprocessor system uses the send and receive primitives.

8.1.2 Synchronization with Semaphores

Dijkstra invented the two operations **P** and **V**, which can be shared by many processes and which implement the mutual-exclusion mechanism efficiently. The **P** and **V** operations are called primitives and are assumed indivisible. They operate on a special common variable called a *semaphore*, which indicates the number of processes attempting to use the critical section:

var s: semaphore

Then the primitive **P**(s) acts as an open bracket or MUTEXBEGIN of a critical section; that is, it acts to acquire permission to enter. The $V(s)$ primitive is the MUTEXEND and records the termination of a critical section:

```
P(s): MUTEXBEGIN (s)
        s ← s - 1;
        If s < 0 then
        begin
        Block the process executing the P(s) and put it
        in a FIFO queue associated with the semaphore s;
        Resume the highest priority ready-to-run process;
        end
        MUTEXEND
V(s): MUTEXBEGIN (s)
        s ← s + 1;
        If s ≤ 0 then
        begin
        If an inactive process associated with semaphore s exists, then
        wake up the highest priority blocked process associated with s
        and put it in a ready list.
        end
        MUTEXEND
```

The semaphore s is usually initialized to 1. When s can take values of 0 or 1, it is called a *binary semaphore*, since it acts as a lock bit, allowing only one process at a time within an associated critical section. If s takes any integer value, it is called a *counting semaphore*. Notice that the $P(s)$ and $V(s)$ operations are modifying s and testing its status. $P(s)$ and $V(s)$ can be implemented in hardware or in software using locks.

One common use of synchronization mechanisms is to permit concurrent processes to exchange data during execution. The data or messages to be exchanged are usually stored in a circular buffer which is used to synchronize the speeds of the sending and receiving processes. Such a circular buffer is usually called a message buffer or *mailbox*.

For example, the Unix operating system provides an elegant form of message buffers called *pipes*. These are used as channels to stream data from one process to another. The typing of the "ls" command on the console in a Unix environment causes the files in the current directory to be "listed" on the console by running the "ls" process. If the user wishes to print the listing of the files on the printer, the two concurrent processes "ls" and "opr" may be used and are specified as "ls|opr." The "|" symbol specifies that a pipe should channel the output of "ls" to become the input to "opr." The "ls" process *produces* the list as an output into a pipe or buffer from which it is *consumed* and printed by the "opr" process, as illustrated in Figure 8.3.

Whenever a process produces sequences of output which are consumed by another process as input, there is said to be a producer-consumer relationship. A

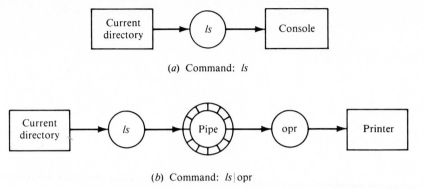

(a) Command: *ls*

(b) Command: *ls* | opr

Figure 8.3 Flow of data between two processes in UNIX.

message buffer may be considered to consist of a finite number of identical slots which are used for communication between the producer and consumer processes. If the number of slots is finite, the buffer is arranged as a circular buffer.

To demonstrate the communication between the producer and consumer processes, consider a finite buffer BUFFER of size n arranged as a circular queue in which the slot positions are named $0, 1, \ldots, n - 1$. There are the two pointers c and p, which correspond to the "head" and "tail" of a circular queue, respectively, as shown in Figure 8.4. The consumer consumes the message from the head c by updating c and then retrieving the message. Hence, c points to an empty slot before each consumption. The producer adds a message to the buffer by updating p before the add operation. Therefore, pointers p and c move counterclockwise and there can be a maximum of n message slots for consumption. Initially, $p = c = 0$, which indicates that the buffer is empty. Let the variables *empty* and *full* be used to indicate the number of empty slots and occupied slots, respectively. The *empty* variable is used to inform the producer of the number of available slots, while the

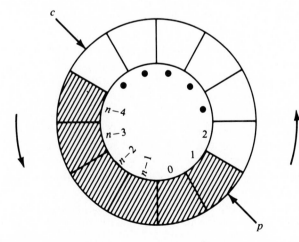

Figure 8.4 A circular message buffer with producer pointer p and consumer pointer c.

full variable informs the consumer of the number of messages needed to be consumed. The concurrent program below illustrates the actions of the producer and consumer processes. The producer or consumer will be suspended when *empty* = 0 or *full* = 0, respectively.

Example 8.1

```
shared record
        begin
        var p, c: integer;
        var empty, full: semaphore;
        var BUFFER [0:n − 1]: message;
        nd
  initial empty = n, full = 0, p = 0, c = 0;
cobegin
Producer: begin
        var m: message;
          Cycle
            begin
              Produce a message m;
              P(empty);
              p ← (p + 1) mod n;
              BUFFER [p] ← m; // place message in buffer//
              V(full)
            end
        end
Consumer: begin
        var m: message;
          Cycle
            begin
              P (full);
              c ← (c + 1) mod n;
              m ← BUFFER [c]; // remove message from buffer //
              V (empty);
              Consume message m;
            end
        end
  coend
```

The **P** and **V** operations may be extended for ease of problem formulation and clarity of solutions. The extended primitives **PE** and **VE** developed by Agerwala (1977) are indivisible and each operates on a set of semaphores which must be initialized to nonnegative values.

PE$(s_1, s_2, \ldots, s_n, \bar{s}_{n+1}, \ldots, \bar{s}_{n+m})$:

  MUTEXBEGIN

if for all i, $1 \leq i \leq n$, $s_i > 0$ **and for all** j, $1 \leq j \leq m$, $s_{n+j} = 0$

    then for all i, $1 \leq i \leq n$, $s_i \leftarrow s_i - 1$

      else the process is blocked and put in a set of queues associated

          with the set of semaphores $s_1, \ldots, s_n$;

  MUTEXEND

VE$(s_1, s_2, \ldots, s_n)$:

  MUTEXBEGIN

for all i, $1 \leq i \leq n$, $s_i \leftarrow s_i + 1$;

    wake-up highest priority process

    associated with set of semaphores $(s_1, \ldots, s_n)$;

  MUTEXEND

There is no association between s_i and $\bar{s}_j$. The $\bar{s}_j$ symbol is used for convenience to represent the semaphore s_j where $j > n$. The following examples are used to illustrate the application of the extended primitives.

Example 8.2: N processes, equal priority, m resources Each of N processes requires exclusive access to a subset of m distinct resources. The processes are granted access without any consideration of priorities. If two processes use disjoint subsets of resources, they may execute simultaneously. The solution is given below:

$$\textbf{var } r_1, r_2, \ldots, r_m: \textbf{semaphore}$$
$$\textbf{initial } r_1 = r_2 = \cdots = r_m = 1;$$

  Process i: **begin**

      PE $(r_a, r_b, \ldots, r_x)$;

      Use resource a, b, $\ldots$, x;

      VE $(r_a, r_b, \ldots, r_x)$

      end

Semaphore r_i is associated with resource i. If the PE primitive is completed successfully by a process, it indicates that resources a, b, $\ldots$, x are available and hence are allocated to the process.

Consider the application of this example in which processes X, Y, Z compete for card reader R, printer P, and tape unit T, as shown in Figure 8.5. Each process requires two of the resources simultaneously: X requires R and P, Y requires R and T, and Z requires P and T. The "Dining Philosophers' Problem" can be expressed as a special case of the above example (see Problems 8.6 and 8.7).

Example 8.3: N processes, N priorities, one resource Process i has higher priority than process $i + 1$, for $1 \leq i \leq N - 1$. The processes request access to a resource and are allocated the resource in a mutually exclusive manner

var r_R, r_p, r_T: **semaphore;**

initial $r_R = r_P = r_T = 1$;

cobegin

Process X: **begin** PE(r_R, r_P); use resource R and P; VE(r_R, r_P); **end**

Process Y: **begin** PE(r_R, r_T); use resource R and T; VE(r_R, r_T); **end**

Process Z: **begin** PE(r_P, r_T); use resource P and T; VE(r_P, r_T); **end**

coend

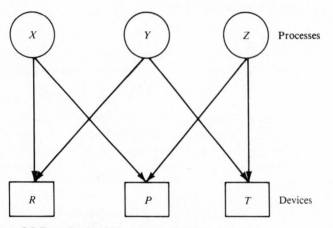

Figure 8.5 **Example of multiple resource allocation.**

based on the priorities. A request by a process is not honored until all higher priority requests have been granted. The resource is used nonpreemptively:

```
            var s₁,...,sₙ, R: semaphore
            initial s₁ = s₂ = ··· = sₙ = 0;
            initial R = 1;
Process i; begin
        VE (sᵢ); // register request of process i //
        PE (R,s̄₁,...,s̄ᵢ₋₁); // check to see if resource is available //
            // and if there are any outstanding requests //
            // made by higher priority processes //
        PE (sᵢ); // if not, grant resource to process i //
            // and withdraw outstanding request //
        Use resource;
        VE (R); // Return or deallocate resource //
        end
```

Note that the requesting process cannot be blocked on $PE(s_i)$ since a $VE(s_i)$ was executed earlier to register request. This example may be used in servicing prioritized interrupts. In this case the processes represent the interrupts and R represents the processor which services the interrupts.

The above example can be clarified further by considering a two-processor system that runs a supervisor process and a user process. If these two processes compete for a certain resource in the system *simultaneously*, the supervisor process should be given higher priority. The program segments of the supervisor and user processes that access the shared resource are shown below:

```
var     s, u, R: semaphore
initial s = u = 0;
initial R = 1;
Supervisor: begin          User: begin
            VE(s);               VE(u);
            PE(R);               PE(R, s);
            PE(s);               PE (u);
            Use Resource;        Use Resource;
            VE(R);               VE(R);
            end                  end
```

Notice that the constructs differ mainly in the second **PE** statements. Since the supervisor process is of a higher priority than the user process, it only checks to see if the resource is available [$PE(R)$], whereas the user process also checks to see if there is an outstanding request from the supervisor [$PE(R, s)$]. Since we are considering simultaneous execution of the user and supervisor codes, the execution of the $PE(R, s)$ statement will find $s = 1$, which was set by the $VE(s)$ operation in the supervisor process. Hence, the user process will be blocked until the resource is released by the supervisor.

Although, semaphores can be implemented using locks, they are more commonly accessed by system calls to the supervisor. The supervisor maintains two sets of lists or queues: *blocked* and *ready*. Descriptors for processes that are blocked on a semaphore are added to a block queue associated with that semaphore. For the generalized **P** and **V**, the set of blocked queues may be quite complex. However, execution of a **PE** or **VE** operation causes a trap to a supervisor routine which completes the operation. The ready list contains descriptors of processes that are ready to be assigned to a processor for execution. In a multiprocessor, with master-slave operating system, a single processor may be responsible for maintaining the ready list and assigning processes to the slave processors. The ready list may be shared in a multiprocessor with a distributed supervisor. In this case, the ready list may be accessed concurrently. Therefore, mutual exclusion must be ensured and can be accomplished by spin-locks, since enqueue and dequeue operations are fast on the ready list. Moreover, a processor that is attempting to access the ready list cannot execute any other process.

Semaphores are quite general and can be used to program almost any kind of synchronization. However, the use of the P and V primitives in a parallel algorithm makes the algorithm rather unstructured and prone to error. For example, omitting a **P** or **V**, or accidentally invoking a **P** on one semaphore and a **V** on another can have disastrous effects, since mutual exclusion would no longer be ensured. Also, when using semaphores, a programmer can forget to include in critical sections all statements that reference the shared modifiable objects. This, too, could cause errors in execution. Another problem with using semaphores is that both condition synchronization and mutual exclusion are implemented using the same pair of primitives. This makes it difficult to identify the purpose of a given **P** or **V** operation without a detailed trace of other effects on the semaphore.

8.1.3 Conditional Critical Sections and Monitors

Conditional critical section (CCS) was proposed by Hoare (1972) and Hansen (1972) to overcome most of the difficulties encountered with **P** and **V**s. This is a structured and highly user-oriented tool for specifying communication among concurrent processes. Their use allows direct expression of the fact that a process has to wait until an arbitrary condition on the shared variables holds. Interprocess communication in a system of concurrent processes is done by means of a shared variable v, which is composed of the component variables $v_1, v_2, \ldots, v_n$, as defined by:

$$\textbf{var v : shared record } v_1, \ldots, v_n: \langle type \rangle \textbf{ end}$$

The variable v is used to name a given resource. The global state of a system of processes is determined by the values of the shared variable v and the program counters of the single processes. The variables in v may only be accessed within CCS statements that name v. A CCS statement is of the form

$$\textbf{csect v do await } C:S$$

where C is a boolean expression and S is a statement list. Note that variables local to the executing process may also appear in the CCS statement:

A CCS statement delays the executing process until the condition, C, is true; S is then executed. The evaluation of C and execution of S are uninterruptible by other CCS statements that name the same resource. Thus, C is guaranteed to be true when execution of S begins. Mutual exclusion is provided by guaranteeing that execution of different CCS statements, each naming the same resource but not overlapped. Condition synchronization is provided by explicit boolean conditions in CCS statements.

We illustrate the use of the conditional critical sections by two applications. The first example is a solution to the producer-consumer problem. Assume that the two classes of processes (producers and consumers) communicate via a bounded circular buffer as in Figure 8.4. Access to this buffer must be mutually exclusive. Seven shared variables which are associated with the critical section v are used to indicate the global status of the system of processes.

Example 8.4 The variables *p* and *c* are as in Example 8.1. Variables *empty* and *full* are also integer variables denoting the number of slots empty or occupied respectively. Variables *np* and *nc* indicate the number of producers and consumers respectively, which are working on the buffer.

```
var v: shared record
              begin
              var p, c, empty, full, np, nc: integer;
              var BUFFER [0: n − 1]: message;
              end
initial empty = n, full = 0, p = 0, c = 0;
Procedure Enqueue (m: message)
   begin
      csect v do await empty > 0 and np = 0:
          begin
              np ← np + 1;
              empty ← empty − 1;
          end
       p ← (p + 1) mod n;
       BUFFER [p] ← m;
       csect v do full ← full + 1;
   end
Procedure Dequeue (m: message)
   begin
      csect v do await full > 0 and nc = 0:
          begin
              nc ← nc + 1;
              full ← full − 1;
          end
       c ← (c + 1) mod n;
       m ← BUFFER [c];
       csect v do empty ← empty + 1;
   end
```

The second example on the use of the conditional critical section is the solution of the reader-and-writer problem. Improper reading and writing of shared variables is the classic cause of difficulty in finding operating system bugs. The basic problem is that two sets of processes executing concurrently may interleave read and write operations in such a way that improper decisions are made and the shared variables are left in an improper state. This kind of bug is insidious, for it may only show up infrequently—and then the symptoms occur rarely or never repeat since they depend on a particular concurrency relationship.

In the reader-and-writer problem, there are reader and writer processes which share a common data segment. Any number of readers may access the segment simultaneously, but a writer must have exclusive access to it. To prevent a writer from waiting indefinitely long, it is necessary that no more readers be able to acquire the resource from the moment that a writer first wants to acquire it until the time it actually does acquire it. The variable *aw* indicates the number of writers that want to acquire the resource; *nw* and *nr* indicate the number of writers and readers, respectively, that have acquired the resource.

Example 8.5

```
          var v shared record aw, nw, nr    : integer end
          Initial aw = nw = nr = 0;
   Reader: begin
          csect v do await aw = 0: nr ← nr + 1;
          read segment;
          csect v do nr ← nr − 1;
          end
   Writer: begin
          csect v do
            begin
            aw ← aw + 1;
            await nr = 0 and nw = 0: nw ← nw + 1;
            end
          write to segment;
          csect v do begin
            nw ← nw − 1;
            aw ← aw − 1;
            end
          end
        end
```

All the process-synchronization methods we have discussed are logically equivalent in performing the synchronization or scheduling problem. However, some of them implement the solution to certain problems in a more complicated and inefficient manner than others. Therefore, they are not practically equivalent.

Monitors—*extension of conditional critical sections* A monitor is a shared data structure and a set of functions that access the data structure to control the synchronization of concurrent processes. This general definition includes semaphores, events, and messages as specific implementations. The notion of a monitor is not more powerful than these other techniques—just more general. While a process is a useful abstraction for multiprogramming, a monitor is a useful abstraction for process communication. Consequently, a programmer can ignore the implementation details of the resource when using it and can ignore how it is used when programming the monitor that implements it.

To assure the correctness of a program, it is useful to associate data structures with the operations performed on them. A monitor provides a body in which to

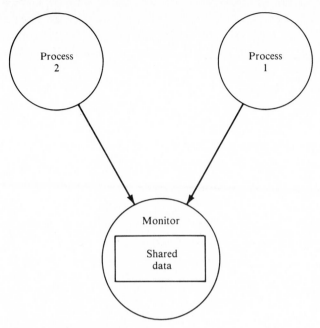

Figure 8.6 Monitor representation.

associate shared data structures with their critical sections. By so doing, the data structures are no longer shared or global, but local or hidden within the body of a monitor. In addition, process functions no longer contain critical sections. Instead, the critical sections are centralized and protected within the monitor functions. The restricted access to shared data structures provided by a monitor is even more attractive if it can be checked by a compiler. Many high-level languages today provide the means for controlling the scope of variable names.

Monitors provide support for processes to form a multiprogramming system. While a process is active in the sense that it performs a job, a monitor is passive in the sense that it only executes when called by a process. A monitor is necessary only when two or more processes communicate to ensure that they communicate properly. Figure 8.6 is a representation of two processes communicating through shared data encapsulated by a monitor.

A monitor consists of a set of *permanent variables* used to store the resource's state, and some procedures, which implement operations on the resource. A monitor also has initialization code for the permanent variables. This code is executed once before any procedure body is executed. The values of the permanent variables are retained between activations of monitor procedures and may be accessed only from within the monitor. Monitor procedures can have parameters and local variables, each of which takes on new values for each procedure activation. The structure of a monitor with name *mname* and procedures OP1, . . . , OPN is shown below.

```
mname monitor;
    var declarations of permanent variables
    procedure OP1 (parameters)
        var declarations of variables local to OP1
        begin
          code to implement OP1
        end
          :
        procedure OPN (parameters)
        var declarations of variables local to OPN
        begin
          code to implement OPN
        end
    begin
        code to initialize permanent variables
    end
```

The procedure OPJ within monitor *mname* can be invoked by executing

call *mname* · OPJ (arguments).

The execution of the procedures in a given monitor is guaranteed to be mutually exclusive. This ensures that the permanent variables are never accessed concurrently.

Pushing the monitor concept to its logical limit suggests that systems should be designed as collections of processes and monitors only. In this case, every data structure is local to either a process or monitor. This decomposition is valuable in large systems since it simplifies the problems of program validation and maintenance. If a data structure changes, it is clear which functions are affected, and the addition of a new process or monitor does not require the revalidation of unchanged components.

The current state of a monitor is defined by the monitor image, that is the memory associated with the monitor program. A monitor image represents either permanent or temporary resources that are the elements of process interaction. A process image is that portion of memory belonging to a process and defining its states. The process image changes with the execution of a program associated with the process. In the absence of process activity, process images and monitor images differ significantly. In this idle state, process images are of no importance and may vanish. However, monitor images—at least those representing permanent resources—must remain and resume a nonassigned state.

Monitor functions are reentrant but contain nonreentrant sections—i.e., critical sections. Indeed, monitor functions must be designed to protect against this. Monitor functions need not be considered as part of the monitor image. In fact, if two different monitor variables are accessed in the same way, a single copy of a program may be shared between the two monitors.

When a monitor function is called but is blocked from handling the request immediately, it may take several actions. It may immediately return a blocked indication, it may loop or busy-wait until the request can be handled, or it may place the process on a waiting queue for the resource requested. In the latter case, the waiting queue must be a part of the monitor data structure. In real-time systems, it is sometimes best to return a blocked indication and let the process decide whether to try again later or give up.

An operating system contains a kernel or nucleus which contains a few special processes to handle initialization and interrupts and a basic monitor to support the concept of a process. The basic monitor includes functions to switch environments between processes and to create, spawn, or fork a new process. The kernel is also one part of an operating system that executes in the privileged state.

Besides the kernel, an operating system consists of many monitors and a few processes. The processes include several kinds of I/O processes that are activated as needed and at least one active process to look for new jobs and create user processes for them. All monitors are part of the operating system and form the bulk of the system. They are used to manage the resources of the system. For example, monitors transmit messages between processes, control competing processes, enforce access rights, and communicate with I/O processes.

8.2 SYSTEM DEADLOCKS AND PROTECTION

With a high degree of concurrency in multiprocessors, deadlocks will arise when members of a group of processes which hold resources are blocked indefinitely from access to resources held by other processes within the group. We shall present some effective techniques for detecting, preventing, avoiding, and recovering from deadlocks. Also, we will discuss various protection mechanisms which can be used in a multiple process environment to ensure only authorized access to resources.

8.2.1 System Deadlock Problems

We use the following example to explain the cause of a system deadlock and the means to break a deadlock.

Example 8.6 Consider the three concurrent processes P_1, P_2, and P_3 sharing four distinct resources controlled by the four semaphores S_1, S_2, S_3, and S_4. All semaphores have an initial value 1. P-V primitives are used to specify the resource-request patterns shown in Figure 8.7a. Assume one unit of each resource type.

We use a directed graph in Figure 8.7b to show the possible resource-allocation ordering. The nodes correspond to resource semaphores, one per type. An edge (labeled P_k) from S_i to S_j means that resource S_i has been allocated to process P_k and P_k is requesting resource S_j. Following this rule, we

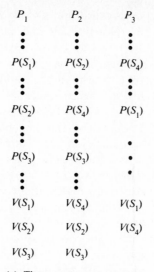

(a) Three concurrent processes

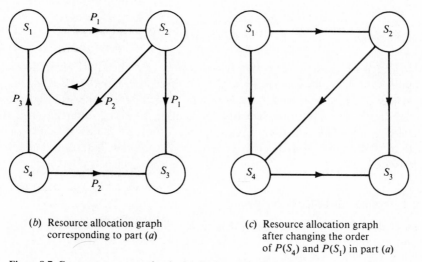

(b) Resource allocation graph
corresponding to part (a)

(c) Resource allocation graph
after changing the order
of $P(S_4)$ and $P(S_1)$ in part (a)

Figure 8.7 Concurrent processes for the deadlock study in Example 8.5.

obtain the *resource-allocation graph* in Figure 8.7b. The existence of a loop in the graph shows the possibility of a deadlock.

For example, the three nodes S_1, S_2, and S_4 form a loop in the clockwise direction. This means a deadlock situation in which resources S_1, S_2, and S_4 have been allocated to processes P_1, P_2, and P_3, respectively. P_1 is waiting for P_2 to release S_2, while P_2 is waiting for P_3 to release S_4, and P_3 is waiting for P_1 to release S_1. These three processes thus enter a *circular wait* situation, so that no process among the three can proceed. This situation is called *system deadlock* or "deadly embrace".

Suppose we modify the request pattern in process P_3 by exchanging the order of requests $P(S_4)$ and $P(S_1)$. A new resource-allocation graph results in Figure 8.7c, where the edge direction has been reversed from node S_1 to S_4. Since there are no loops in this modified graph, no circular wait will be possible. Thus deadlock can be avoided. Because of data dependencies or other reasons, the change of request order may not be permitted in general. Thus better techniques are needed to avoid deadlock. We shall show some of these techniques later.

In general, a deadlock situation may occur if one or more of the following conditions are in effect:

1. *Mutual exclusion*: Each task claims exclusive control of the resources allocated to it.
2. *Nonpreemption*: A task cannot release the resources it holds until they are used to completion.
3. *Wait for*: Tasks hold resources already allocated to them while waiting for additional resources.
4. *Circular wait*: A circular chain of tasks exists, such that each task holds one or more resources that are being requested by the next task in the chain.

The existence of these conditions effectively defines a state of deadlock in the previous example. In many ways, the first three conditions are quite desirable. For consistency, data records should be held until an update is complete. Similarly, preemption (the reclaiming of a resource by the system) cannot be done arbitrarily and must be supported by a *rollback* recovery mechanism, especially when data resources are involved. Rollback restores a process and its resources to a suitable previous state from which the process can eventually repeat its transactions.

Solutions to the deadlock problem have been classified as *prevention, avoidance, detection,* and *recovery* techniques. Prevention is the process of constraining system users so that requests leading to a deadlock never occur. For deadlock prevention, the system is designed so that one or more of the necessary conditions outlined above never hold. The scheduler then allocates resources so that the deadlocks will never occur. For deadlock avoidance, the scheduler controls resource allocation on the basis of advance information about resource usage so that deadlock is avoided. With deadlock detection and recovery, the scheduler gives resources to the process as soon as they become available and, when a deadlock is detected, the scheduler preempts some resources in order to recover the system from the deadlock situation.

Empirical observations have suggested that deadlock prevention mechanisms tend to undercommit resources while detection techniques give away resources so freely that prolonged blocking situations arise frequently. Avoidance schemes fall somewhere in between. Avoidance or prevention mechanisms must ensure that a deadlock will never occur for every request, resulting in undue process waits and run-time overhead. A prevention mechanism differs from an avoidance scheme in that the system need not perform run-time testing of potential allocations. In both prevention and avoidance cases, recovery from a system implementation error needs a rollback mechanism.

8.2.2 Deadlock Prevention and Avoidance

By restricting the behavior of the processes so that one of the necessary conditions for the occurrence of a deadlock is violated, deadlocks will never occur. This approach has been called *static prevention*, since the rule for allocating resources does not depend upon the current state of the system. One method is to relax the mutual-exclusion condition by permitting simultaneous access to resources by processes. This, for example, is possible in a read-only data object. However, in general the physical or logical properties of the resources may not always permit simultaneous access. Examples of these resources are card readers, printers, and critical sections of code. Hence, prevention of deadlock permitting simultaneous access to resources is impractical.

Similarly, the denial of the nonpreemption condition in a general case is unrealistic since physical resources such as line printers cannot be preempted. However, the nonpreemption condition can be waived for processors and memory pages which may be time-multiplexed among several processes. The forcible deallocation of a resource and the allocation of the resource to the preempting process may cause an intolerable overhead which, if not carefully controlled, may result in an inefficient utilization of resources. Another approach to preventing deadlock is to constrain each task to completely allocate all its required resources in advance of its execution. This limits the degree of concurrency and also under-utilizes the resources. This technique derives from the wait-for condition.

Finally, by constraining the resource types into a linear ordering, circular waiting can be prevented. In this method, the resource types are ordered into a resource hierarchy so that, for a system with m resource types, $R_1 < R_2 < \cdots < R_m$. If a task has been allocated a resource of type R_i, it can only request a resource R_j which is at a higher level so that $R_i < R_j$. The rule for releasing resources is that resource R_j must be released before R_i, if $R_i < R_j$. By this means, circular chains of blocked tasks cannot occur since each task requests resources in the same orderly way. A deadlock cannot occur in a system with linearly ordered resources. The feasibility of enforcing resource ordering by compile-time checks is a major advantage of this scheme. Restrictions on the allowable sequences of task requests force knowledgable use of the ordering rule. This technique is used in the IBM 370 series MVS operating system.

To avoid deadlocks in a multiprogrammed multiprocessing system in which the necessary conditions for deadlocks can exist, it is usually necessary to have some advance knowledge of the resource usage of processes. Sometimes deadlock avoidance techniques are called *dynamic prevention* methods since they attempt to allocate resources depending upon the current state of the system. These methods lead to better resource utilization.

One basic model that is assumed consists of a sequence of task steps during each of which the resource usage of the task remains constant. The execution of a task step first involves the acquisition of those resources needed by the given task step but not passed on by the previous task step. Next follows a period of execution during which the resource requirement remains invariant. Finally, at the completion of execution, all those resources not needed by the subsequent task step are released and returned to a pool of available resources.

Before discussing the avoidance techniques, it is convenient to describe another model for the resource-allocation system in a multiprocessor. A *resource-allocation system* (RAS) includes a set of n independent processes $P_1, P_2, \ldots, P_n$ $(n \geq 1)$, a set of m different types of resources $R_1, R_2, \ldots, R_m$ $(m \geq 1)$ so that each R_i has a fixed number of units c_i. The RAS also includes a scheduler that allocates the resources to the processes according to certain rules fulfilling some specified criteria.

The system state of a RAS is defined by $(\mathbf{W}, \mathbf{A}, \mathbf{f})$, where $\mathbf{W} = (\mathbf{w}_1, \mathbf{w}_2, \ldots, \mathbf{w}_n)$ is the *request matrix*, which has the dimensions n by m. The entry $\mathbf{w}_{ij} = \mathbf{w}_i(j)$ is the maximum number of additional units of resource R_j that the process P_i will need at one time to complete its task. $\mathbf{w}_i$ is the *want vector* for process $P_i \cdot \mathbf{A} = (\mathbf{a}_1, \mathbf{a}_2, \ldots, \mathbf{a}_n)$ is the *allocation matrix* $(n \times m)$. The entry $\mathbf{A}_{ij} = \mathbf{a}_i(j)$ is the number of units of resource R_j allocated to process P_i. $\mathbf{a}_i$ is the *allocation vector* for process P_i. The vector $\mathbf{f} = (f_1, f_2, \ldots, f_m)$ is the *free* (available) *resource vector* and $\mathbf{c} = (c_1, c_2, \ldots, c_m)$ is the *system capacity vector*. Since $f_j \leq c_j$ is the number of available units of resource type R_j, we can find f_j to be

$$f_j = c_j - \sum_{i=1}^{n} \mathbf{a}_i(j) \tag{8.1}$$

That is, the sum of the resources allocated and those available of type R_j must be equal to the total number of units of that type in the system.

When $\mathbf{A} = 0$, the system is in the initial state. In this state, $\mathbf{D} = (\mathbf{d}_1, \mathbf{d}_2, \ldots, \mathbf{d}_n) = W$ is called the *demand matrix* and $\mathbf{c} = \mathbf{f}$, where $\mathbf{d}_i$ is the demand vector for process P_i.

Certain basic assumptions are made regarding avoidance methods. Before a process enters the system, it is required to specify for each resource the maximum number of resource units it will ever need. There is no preemption and a process releases a resource after it has completed its task. Moreover, $\mathbf{d}_i \leq \mathbf{c}$ for all i.

A sequence of task steps $P_{e(1)}P_{e(2)} \cdots P_{e(k)}$ is called a *terminating sequence* for $(\mathbf{W}, \mathbf{A}, \mathbf{f})$, where $e(j)$ is the index of the process in the jth place, if

$$\mathbf{w}_{e(1)} \leq \mathbf{f} \tag{8.2}$$

and

$$\mathbf{w}_{e(i)} \leq \mathbf{f} + \sum_{j=1}^{i-1} \mathbf{a}_{e(j)} \qquad \text{for } 1 < i \leq k$$

Note that each occurrence of a process in the sequence goes through the following cycle: request resource, use resource, release resource. Hence the want vector for a process must not be greater than the free resource vector plus the "released" resource vector for the process to be run. A terminating sequence is *complete* if all processes are in the sequence.

The system state $(\mathbf{W}, \mathbf{A}, \mathbf{f})$ is *safe* if there is a complete terminating sequence for it; that is, if there is a way to allocate the resources claimed by the processes so that all of them can finish their task. The safeness of a state can be expressed as a *safe request matrix* $\mathbf{S}$, where S_{ij} is the maximum number of units of resource R_j that can be granted safely if process P_i requests them.

> **Example 8.7** If we restrict each process to making a single request for a finite number of units and the state of the system $(\mathbf{W}, \mathbf{A}, \mathbf{f})$ for three processes and two resource types is:
>
> $$\mathbf{W} = \begin{bmatrix} 1 & 0 \\ 2 & 2 \\ 0 & 1 \end{bmatrix} \qquad \mathbf{A} = \begin{bmatrix} 0 & 1 \\ 0 & 0 \\ 1 & 1 \end{bmatrix} \qquad \mathbf{f} = (1, 1)$$
>
> then the system is in a safe state. Notice that from Eq. 8.1, $\mathbf{c} = (2, 2)$ and $P_1 P_3 P_2$ is a complete terminating sequence. If P_2 requests only one unit of R_1, the system will be in a safe state, since in that case $P_3 P_1 P_2$ is a terminating sequence containing P_2. Therefore, $S_{2,1} = 1$. Similarly, if P_2 requests only one unit of R_2, $S_{2,2} = 1$. However, if P_2 requires at the same time one unit of R_1 and one unit of R_2, the request cannot be granted safely.

This example shows that the matrix $\mathbf{S}$ can be used only for single requests. If a process requires more than one resource, a rule stating the order in which the resources will be requested must be defined. In general, the computation of $\mathbf{S}$ may be time consuming. However, it is possible to compute $\mathbf{S}$ concurrently with process execution in a multiprocessor system. This reduces the overhead significantly.

8.2.3 Deadlock Detection and Recovery

The deadlock detection algorithm uses the information contained in a state of the system to decide whether or not a deadlock exists. For the case of a system with only one unit of each resource type, it is sufficient for the detection mechanism to find a circuit (circular wait) in the directed graph. Thus the deadlock detection mechanism maintains and examines a directed state graph to determine whether a circuit exists each time a resource is requested, acquired, or released by a task.

We can extend this technique to systems that have more than one unit of each resource type. Since a circuit in the state graph is only a necessary condition for a deadlock, a more elaborate state-detection mechanism is required. Using the notation developed previously, we recall that the free-resource vector $\mathbf{f}$ is such that its component f_j satisfies Eq. 8.1. Let $\mathbf{0}$ indicate a (row) zero vector, in which all components are zero. Also, $\mathbf{x} \leq \mathbf{y}$, where $\mathbf{x}$ and $\mathbf{y}$ are vectors, holds if and only if each pair of corresponding elements is related by $\leq$. The algorithm presented below is designed to reveal a deadlock by simply accounting for all possibilities of sequencing the tasks that remain to be completed. Suppose at time t the state of the system is given by $(\mathbf{W}, \mathbf{A}, \mathbf{f})$, where $\mathbf{W}$ is the want matrix, $\mathbf{A}$ the allocation matrix, and $\mathbf{f}$ the free-resource matrix. The following algorithm determines the existence of a deadlock at time t:

```
Procedure DETECT DEADLOCK
begin
Initialize Rows ← {1,2,...,n};
while i ∈ ROWS such that wᵢ ≤ v do
    begin
        ROWS ← ROWS − {i};
        v ← v − aᵢ;
    end
If ROWS ≠ φ then DEADLOCK;
end
```

The "while" statement searches for an index i in ROWS such that $\mathbf{a}_i \leq \mathbf{v}$. If none is found, a nonempty set in ROWS indicates the existence of a deadlock; otherwise, there is no deadlock. An important point to remember is that a program bug can cause a deadlock even in situations where deadlocks theoretically cannot occur. An ultimate time out can be a simple defensive check on the correctness of the system as well as a way to prevent indefinite deadlocks.

Given that a deadlock has occurred, perhaps the simplest approach to recovering from it would involve aborting each of the deadlocked tasks or, less drastically, aborting them in some sequence until sufficient resources are released to remove the deadlocks in the set of remaining tasks. Algorithms could also be designed that search for a minimum-sized set of tasks which, if aborted, would remove the deadlocks. A more general technique involves the assignment of a fixed cost b_i to the removal (forced preemption) of a resource of type R_i from a deadlocked task that is being aborted.

8.2.4 Protection Schemes

Protection is a mechanism which checks whether the concurrent processes are not trying, in case of error or malicious action, to exceed their rights in accessing the set of objects in the system. Protection should be distinguished from *security*, which is a policy used to denote mechanisms and techniques that control who may use or modify the computer system or the information stored in it. The protection mechanism protects one process from another. This includes the protection of the supervisor from the users and vice versa. The inclusion of an efficient protection scheme in a system also prevents the wide propagation of errors. The techniques of error confinement are based on hardware and firmware mechanisms of access control to entities or objects of the system. These mechanisms do not prevent occurrences of errors but are intended to limit their incidence on the protected objects. An addressing mechanism that decomposes the space of objects into *protected domains* is one scheme that makes the confinement and the non-propagation of errors easier. A *domain* is the set of objects that may be directly accessed by the process to which authorization is granted.

One common set of objects that is protected in a computer system is the set of memory locations. It is imperative to protect the address space of one task from the other by enforcing a separation of address space among different tasks. The protection of shared memory is classified into the protection of the physical and local address spaces.

The protection of physical address space could be accomplished by partitioning the physical memory into nonoverlapping blocks (page frames), each of which is assigned a lock. Each process has a key (often called an *access key*) as part of its process-identification word. Access to a block of memory by a process is granted if the process' access key fits the lock of the block. In fact, any process with a match-ing key can have access to the block. Hence, this scheme is not an effective protection mechanism if the blocks are shared by several processes.

Memory protection on the virtual address space is more effective. In systems that use base or relocation registers for mapping the virtual address to the physical address, protection is accomplished with *bounds registers*. Bounds registers specify the lower (base address) and upper bounds of the address space. An access by a process to memory outside the predefined bounds is trapped by the system as an access violation. This technique assumes that the address space for the process is in contiguous memory locations. The protection of the address space is further ensured since systems do not permit the modification of the bounds register by a user process. Sharing of address space by more than two concurrent processes is still difficult since the address space of each process is contiguous and the bounds registers perform linear mapping of addresses.

Another method for memory protection is for each task to have a segment table (ST), which consists of entries that include the set of access rights and the base address to pages or segments of the task. During the execution of a task, it uses the segment table base register (STBR) to obtain access by authenticat-ing the privileges of the processes, as shown in Figure 8.8. If the access-code field (AKR) of the virtual address matches the permitted access rights for the segment (acc) in STE(s), the segment is accessed. When a task switch occurs, the STBR is modified to point to the ST of the new task.

In process systems, there is a classic distinction between user privileges and supervisor privileges. The protection of supervisor processes from user processes is enforced partly by a hardware mechanism which defines two operating modes: supervisor mode and user mode. This can be accomplished by a single bit in the processor's control register. Generally, there are machine instructions, called *privileged instructions*, which are not executable by user processes. These instruc-tions can be considered the set of objects S which needs to be protected from the user that attempts execute access. The user domain in this case lacks all rights in the set $R = \{r \,|\, r = (s, \text{execute}), s \in S\}$. The protection is enforced by trapping the

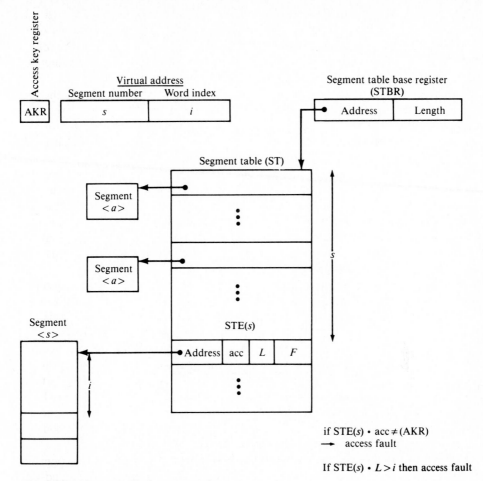

Figure 8.8 Address mapping in a segmented system.

user process that attempts to use $r \in R$. The user process can request to use a system procedure that contains privileged instructions by migrating from the user domain to the supervisor domain, where the supervisor can access $r \in R$ on behalf of the user process.

The multilevel protection scheme as implemented in Multics can be used effectively in multiprocessors. In this scheme, which is often called the *layered protection system*, the basic unit of protection is a segment. Segments are grouped into a set of n levels or classes. The layering scheme results in a nested ring structure consisting of n rings, as shown in Figure 8.9. Each level or class of segments is assigned to a distinct ring. Therefore, the implementation of the virtual address and the ST entry will have an extra field for representing the ring number of the segment.

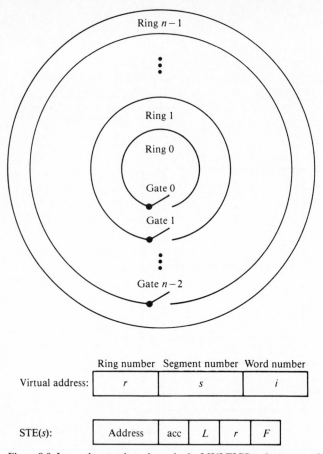

Ring number Segment number Word number

Virtual address:

r	s	i

STE(s):

Address	acc	L	r	F

Figure 8.9 Layered protection scheme in the MULTICS and segment table entries.

The access capabilities of ring r_i is a subset of ring r_j whenever ring $r_i > r_j$, for $r_i, r_j \in \{0, 1, \ldots, n - 1\}$. Access control is performed between classes and not within a class. Hence, one segment can reference another segment without a validation check if both segments are in the same class. However, the crossing of a ring boundary results in an access fault, which invokes the operating system to perform a validation check. If the crossing is from a ring r_i to ring $r_i + 1$, then the access is permitted. If the crossing is from ring r_i to ring $r_i - 1$, the operating system validates the permission. To call an inner ring, only certain entry points are permitted. These entry points are called *gates*. The segment which makes the call must present a valid key to match one of the locks at the gate. The validation process is performed by a *gatekeeper process*. The list of entry points corresponding to the set of locks is called a *gate list*.

In this system, segments that belong to a process can, for example, be assigned to a given ring. If the segments are shared by multiple processes, the disjointness of the classes of segments can be relaxed. A shared segment is assigned to a consecutive set of rings called an *access bracket*. In this case, the ring field in Figure 8.9 contains a set of two integers (low, high). A call from a segment in ring r_i to a segment with access bracket (n_1, n_2), will not fault if $n_1 \leq r_i \leq n_2$. However, if $r_i < n_1$, the access fault still occurs. A modified version of the layered protection scheme is used in the S-1 multiprocessor system. In most cases, however, the ring concept is not practical for more than three rings.

In order to provide useful conventions for sharing among processes, it is necessary to have a systematic way of describing what is to be shared and of controlling access to shared objects from various processes. This machinery can be described in terms of an idealized system called the object system, which consists of three major components: a set of objects X, a set of domains D, and an access matrix **A**. Objects are the protected entities. Typical objects are domains, files, processes and segments. Objects are assigned a unique name in the system, for example, by using a 64-bit counter. Recall that domains are entities which have access to objects. The property of a domain is that it has potentially different access than other domains. Note that objects do not necessarily belong to a domain but can be shared between domains.

The access of a domain to objects is determined by the access matrix **A**. Its rows are labeled by domain names and its columns by object names. Element $A[i, j]$ specifies the access which domain i has on object j. Each element consists of a set of strings called access attributes. Typical attributes are read (r), write (w), execute (x), wakeup (s). A domain has a y-access to an object if y is one of the attributes in that element of **A**. Associated with each attribute is a bit called the *copy flag* which controls the transfer of access.

The system itself attaches no significance to any access attribute except "owner" or to object names. Thus the relationship between, say, the file-handling module and the system is typical of the following: A user calls on the file-handler to create a file. The file-handler asks the system for a new object name n, which the system delivers from its stock of 2^{64} object names (e.g., by incrementing a 64-bit counter). The system gives the file-handler owner access to object n. The file-handler enters n in its own private tables, together with other information about the file which may be relevant (e.g., its disk address). It also gives its caller owner access to n and returns n to the caller as the name of the created file. Later, when some domain d tries to read from file n, the file-handler will examine $A[d, n]$ to see if "read" is one of the attributes of domain d, and refuse to do the read if it is not.

The sparsity of the access matrix A makes it impractical to represent as an ordinary matrix in memory. An alternative method, which is implementable, is to have a list T of pairs $\langle y: A[d, y] \rangle$ which is searched whenever the value of $A[d, x]$ is required. This pair is usually called *capability*. In general, a capability defines the rights (set of operations allowed) that a process has on an object. A capability is a system-maintained unforgettable ticket which, when presented, can be taken as incontestable proof that the presenter is authorized to have access to the object named in the ticket according to the access rights defined.

A finite sequence of capabilities is called a capability list or *C list*. A C list associated with a process defines the running environment (running domain) of the process at a given time; that is, the set of objects that it may use and the operations which it may perform on these objects, as shown in Figure 8.10. Process execution corresponds to running over a succession of domains: migrating from one domain to another expresses the variation of the flexibility of the process. Addressing by capabilities and system structuring by domains permit the solution of protection and error-confinement problems. These classic notions are the basis of numerous capability-based addressing systems such as the C.mmp Hydra and the Intel iAPX 432 system.

The resources in a domain of a process as shown in Figure 8.10 consist of the processor *register file* (RF), the *local memory* (LM), and the local capability list. Resources outside the domain are accessed only through capabilities stored in the local C list. Any domain can have access to any object if a capability for the object appears in its local C list. On a segment machine, capability lists can be supported by special segments (C list segments). A capability can be accessed by indexing into the C list, as shown in Figure 8.11. In this illustration, the capability is divided into four parts:

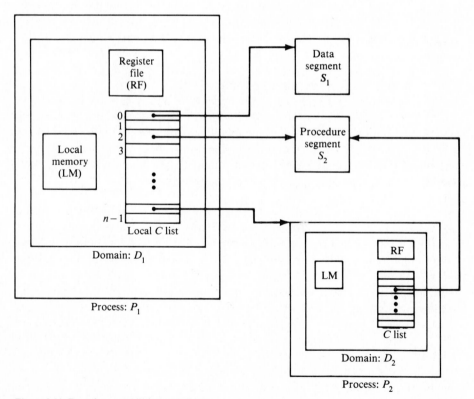

Figure 8.10 Domains, capabilities, and objects.

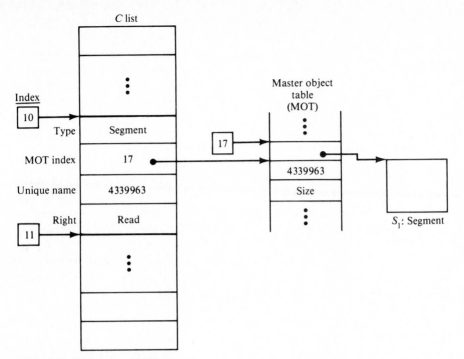

Figure 8.11 C-list and capabilities.

- A type definition of the designated object
- A pointer to a Master Object Table (MOT)
- An object identifier (unique name)
- A set of rights which defines the operations allowed on the object

The MOT entry pointed by the capability contains the absolute address of the object and its unique identifier. The MOT concept makes addressing of the object easy and a relocation of the object needs only the updating of an address in the MOT, even if this object is shared between several processes. It also makes the access slow.

In general, protection can be applied on an object or a path to the object. For example, the access-matrix concept applies the protection on the path, while the entry in the segment table applies it on the object. Protection placed on the access path to objects generally requires less overhead than protection placed on the objects. However, in some cases, both methods are required.

Capabilities have an advantage over privilege-checking in that the protection check is performed at the beginning of the object name interpretation without leaving the execution environment. Hence the error is confined to the execution environment. If a process refers to an object through C lists, it is impossible to name any object to which the process has no access rights. However, it can become wasteful in storage space and the overhead in loading and saving a C list upon activation and deactivation of the process can become substantial. If a parent process adds or deletes access rights to its C list regarding objects that are shared by its children processes, then the access rights must be modified for the several C lists of the children processes. This problem does not occur if the protection is on the object, since the change in access rights is made in one place—at the object.

8.3 MULTIPROCESSOR SCHEDULING STRATEGIES

In this section, we discuss the processor management techniques used in multiprocessor systems. The introduction of multiple processors complicates the scheduling problem. Deterministic and probabilistic models have been used to evaluate some scheduling schemes. Generally, finding an optimal algorithm for the processor scheduling problem in multiprocessors is computationally intractable. However, some dynamic-scheduling algorithms are close to optimal.

8.3.1 Dimensions of Multiple Processor Management

Multiprocessor management and scheduling have been a fertile source of interesting problems for researchers in the field of computer engineering. Replicated components, particularly those that are nonhomogeneous (heterogeneous) or asymmetric, increase the amount of management that must be provided by either the operating system or the application or both. In its most general form, the problem involves the scheduling of a set of processes on a set of processors with arbitrary characteristics in order to optimize some objective function. This involves the selection of a process for execution from a set of processes.

Basically, there are two resource-allocation decisions that are made in multiprocessing systems. One is where to locate code and data in physical memory—a *placement decision*; and the other is on which processor to execute each process—an *assignment decision*. These decisions are often trivial for a uniprocessor system in which assignments are dictated. Furthermore, the physical memory address space is accessible to the single processor in a uniprocessor system, hence the question of accessibility never occurs and memory-contention problems can be minimized by interleaving. Oftentimes, assignment decision is called processor management. It describes the managing of the processor as a shared resource among external users and internal processes. As a result, processor management consists of two basic kinds of scheduling: long-term external load scheduling and short-term internal process scheduling.

In general, active processes undergo different state transitions in the course of their lifetimes in the system. A process is in the *run* state if it is using a processor. A suspended process may enter the pool of *blocked processes*. A process is blocked if it cannot run because it is waiting for some external response, such as a wake-up signal, which may arrive to unblock it. The unblocking operation changes the status of the process to a *ready-to-run* or *ready* state, where it is eventually scheduled to a processor. Figure 8.12 illustrates the possible state transition experienced by a process. The scheduler at this level performs the *short-term process-scheduling* operation of selecting a process from the set of ready-to-run processes. The selected process is assigned to run on a processor. The *medium* and *long-term load-scheduling* operation is used to select and activate a new process to enter the processing environment. The activation of the new process causes it to be put on the ready list. Long-term load-scheduling also acts to control the degree of multiprocessing (that is, the number of active processes) in the system which, if excessive, may cause *thrashing* (see Chapter 2).

The process scheduler or dispatcher performs its function each time the running process is blocked or preempted. Its purpose is to select the next running process from the set of ready queues. The process scheduler resides in the kernel and can be considered a monitor for the ready queues. Since it is probably the most frequently executed program in the system, it should be fairly efficient to minimize operating system overhead.

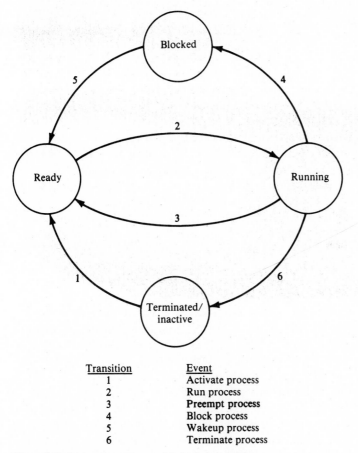

Transition	Event
1	Activate process
2	Run process
3	**Preempt process**
4	**Block process**
5	Wakeup process
6	Terminate process

Figure 8.12 States of a process and their state transitions.

The ready list can either be local or global. A local ready list may be associated with each multiprogrammed processor which has a local memory. Thus a process, once activated, may be bound to a processor. The local ready list reduces the access time of the list and, hence, the overhead encountered by the dispatcher. However, the local ready list concept discourages process migration. Moreover, under light system load, the processor utilization may not be equally distributed among all processors. To permit process migration, a global ready list which resides in the shared memory may be used. This has the disadvantage of requiring more overhead in saving and restoring process states by the process scheduler. However, the standard deviation of the processor utilization is small.

The general objectives of many theoretical scheduling algorithms are to develop processor assignments and scheduling techniques that use minimum numbers of processors to execute parallel programs in the least time. In addition, some develop algorithms for processor assignment to minimize the execution time of the parallel program when processors are available.

There are basically two types of models of processor scheduling, deterministic and nondeterministic. In *deterministic* models, all the information required to express the characteristics of the problem is known before a solution to the problem, that is, a *schedule*, is attempted. Such characteristics are the execution time of each task and the relationship between the tasks in the system. The objective of the resultant schedules is to optimize one or more of the evaluation criteria. For example, in deterministic models, the execution time of each process can either be interpreted as the maximum processing time or as the expected processing time. In the former case, the time to complete the schedule would be considered the maximum time to complete the system of processes, and in the latter case, the length of the schedule represents a rough estimate of the mean length of the computation. The motivation for this objective is that, in many cases, a poor schedule can lead to an unacceptable response time or utilization of system resources.

Deterministic models are not very realistic and do not take into consideration the irregular and unpredictable demands made on the multiprocessor system. Hence, stochastic models are often formulated to study the dynamic-scheduling techniques that take place in the system. In stochastic models, the execution time of a process is a random variable t with a given *cumulation distribution function* (**cdf**) F.

Processor scheduling implies that processes or tasks are to be assigned to a particular processor for execution at a particular time. Since many tasks can be candidates for execution, it is necessary to represent the collection of tasks in a manner which conveniently represents the relationships (if any) among the tasks. Generally, we will refer to a set of related processes as a *task system* or a *job*. A job, which consists of a set of processes, is represented as a precedence graph, as shown in Figure 8.13. The nodes in the graph are tasks which may represent independent operations or parts of a single program which are related to each other in time. The collection of nodes represents a set of processes $T = \{T_1, \ldots, T_n\}$, and the directed edge between nodes implies that a partial ordering or precedence

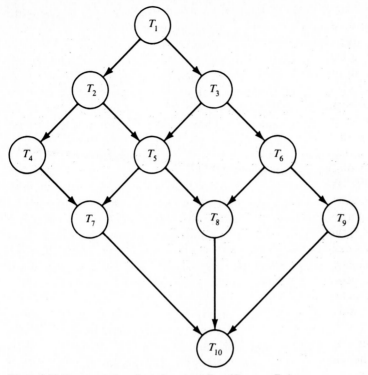

Figure 8.13 Representation of a task system, $T = (T_1, \ldots, T_{10})$.

relation $<$ exists between the processes. Therefore, if $T_i < T_j$, process T_i must be completed before T_j can be initiated. Processes with no predecessors are called *initial* processes (e.g., T_1), and those with no successors are called *final* processes (e.g., T_{10}). The individual nodes within a graph can be related to each other in a number of ways.

For example, it is possible for all processes in a graph to be independent of each other. In this case, there is no precedence relation or partial ordering between the processes and all the processes can be scheduled concurrently, provided there are enough processors available. The *width* of the task graph G, denoted by width(G), is the maximum size of any independent subset of processes. In Figure 8.13, $T_1 < T_2$, $T_1 < T_3$, $T_4 < T_7$, and $T_5 < T_7$. The width of the graph is 3. Associated with each node is a second attribute which refers to the time required by a hypothetical processor to execute the code represented by the node. Sometimes, this attribute is called the *weight* of the node. In a deterministic model, this attribute is a constant for each node, whereas, in a stochastic model, it is a random variable with a mean and standard deviation or a known distribution.

Given a computation graph and a multiprocessor system with p processors, a task assignment or a schedule must be developed such that it gives a description of the processes to be run and in what order as a function of time. The schedule must not violate any of the precedence relationships or the requirement that no more than one processor can be assigned to a task at any time.

In a multiprocessor system, one may associate a *process descriptor node* (PDN) with each executable and active process. This process may consist of a number of fields, as shown in Figure 8.14. The parent field is a pointer to the set of processes which initiated the process, the child field points to the set of processes to be initiated by the current process and the register state defines the register values of the given process. The kernel of the operating system uses the concept of PDNs to monitor the status of the processes.

In some systems, when processes are created, they exist as unrelated units, independent of each other. In other systems, the order of creation is remembered and a parent-child relationship is maintained between one process and the new process it creates. Both approaches have advantages and disadvantages. Typically, a child process is limited to using only those resources owned by its parent and is deallocated if its parent terminates. In most general-purpose systems, when a process is destroyed, its process image is returned to a pool of unallocated memory. However, in many dedicated or real-time systems, processes are never destroyed. Instead, they are created at compile time or initialization time and run forever, even at times when there is no work to do.

During the execution of a process on a processor, external stimuli such as interrupts may arrive and require urgent service because of input or output device constraints. If the interruption and subsequent resumption of the process in execution is permitted before its termination, *preemptive* scheduling is used. If

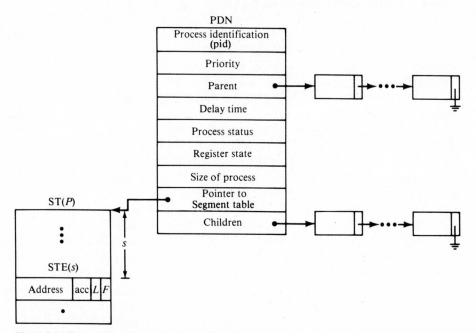

Figure 8.14 Process descriptor node of an active task.

interruption before process completion is not permitted, *nonpreemptive* or *basic* scheduling is applied. In general, preemptive disciplines generate schedules that are better than those generated by nonpreemptive disciplines. It is also true, however, that a certain penalty exists for preemptive schedules that do not exist in the nonpreemptive case. The penalty lies in the context-switching overhead, which consists of the system-interrupt processing and additional memory required to preserve the state of the interrupted process. This overhead may be acceptable if it occurs infrequently, however, in an environment in which preemption occurs frequently, unacceptable performance degradation may result.

Oftentimes, certain tasks may get preferential treatment over the others in a computer system. Systems in which this is true provide *priority scheduling.* In a priority-scheduling system, tasks are grouped into priority classes and numbered from 1 to *n*. It is usually assumed that the lower the priority-class number, the higher the priority; that is, tasks in priority class i are given preference over tasks in priority class j, if $i < j$. A good scheduling policy should be fair and maximize throughput; giving preference to high priority tasks, yet preventing "starvation" of low priority tasks.

Priority scheduling can be combined with preemptive or nonpreemptive scheduling to provide control policies. They are used to resolve a situation wherein a task of class i becomes a ready-to-run task when a task of class j is running in a processor, for $i < j$. In a *preemptive priority scheduling,* the running task is interrupted and the new task runs on that processor. A further refinement of this policy is the *preemptive-resume priority scheduling,* in which the task whose execution was interrupted continues execution at the point of interruption when the task is reassigned to run on the processor. In a *nonpreemptive priority* scheduling, the new ready-to-run process waits until the process currently running on the processor terminates its execution before it gains access to the processor.

Many parallel algorithms require the concurrent execution of multiple processes to achieve a significant performance speedup. The scheduling strategy plays a very important role in meeting the concurrency requirements. Usually the scheduler is designed as a mutually exclusive program which can only be executed by one process at any time. The problem which may be encountered is whether the scheduling of the set of concurrent processes cooperating in a job should be performed as a group or individually. Each process in the set could be assigned to a processor as it becomes available and runs the process immediately. Since this strategy depends on the dynamic availability of processors, the execution time of the job may be large and depends on the time the last process in the set is assigned.

If preemption of processes is permitted, the parallel processes of a job may be scheduled as a group. Processors executing low priority jobs may be preempted to release the processors for the parallel process system. The required number of processors for that job must be available before any process in the set is assigned for execution. It is, however, inefficient to allocate a processor to a process which has to delay its execution because its siblings (cooperating processes) have not yet been assigned to processors. This strategy limits the degree of decomposition to the total number of processors in the system.

A number of measures have been developed to evaluate the effectiveness of processor schedules. Some of these measures are (*a*) response or completion time, (*b*) speed-up ratio, and (*c*) processor utilization. The objectives for multiprocessor resource management and scheduling are the same performance objectives as for their uniprocessor counterparts, namely, maximizing throughput, minimizing response time, or completing processing of tasks in order of priority. Consequently, the multiprocessor schedulers have much in common with single processor schedulers.

8.3.2 Deterministic Scheduling Models

Deterministic schedules are usually displayed with timing diagrams called Gantt charts. We define some measures of performance based on Gantt charts. The flow time of a process is equal to the time its execution is completed. The flow time of a schedule is defined as the sum of the flow times of all processes in the schedule. For example, the flow times of processes T_1 and T_4 in Figure 8.15 are seven and two, respectively, while the flow time of the schedule is 25.5. The *mean flow time* is obtained by dividing the flow time of a schedule by the number of processes in the schedule. The *utilization* (or fractional busy time) of processors P_1, P_2, and P_3 is 0.93, 1.00, and 0.86, respectively. These utilization values are obtained by dividing the time during which the processor was busy by the total time during which it was available for execution. The *idle time* of P_1, P_2, and P_3 is 0.5, 0.0, and 1.0, respectively.

Figure 8.16 shows a process system schedule for a given program graph on two processors. The numbers associated with each node in the process graph represent the execution time of the process. Figure 8.16*b* gives the optimal schedule for the graph using two processors. Note that this schedule is achieved by keeping a processor idle even when there is a process to execute. Figure 8.16*c* shows that activating the schedulable process as soon as possible does not necessarily achieve an optimum schedule. The total execution time ET_1 of the process graph G on a uniprocessor is the sum of the numbers (weights) associated with each node. Hence, $ET_1 = 27$. From Figure 8.16*b*, the execution time on the two-processor system is $ET_2 = 15$. Therefore the speedup, $S_p = ET_1/ET_2 = \frac{27}{15} = 1.8$, for $p = 2$.

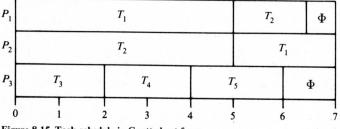

Figure 8.15 Task schedule in Gantt chart form.

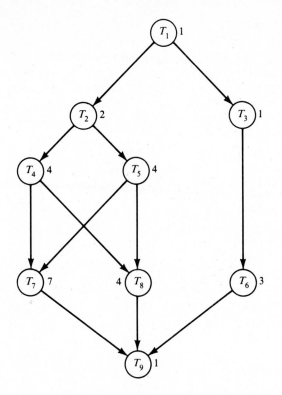

(a) Task graph G for a set of tasks

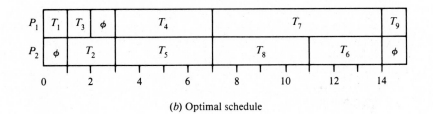

(b) Optimal schedule

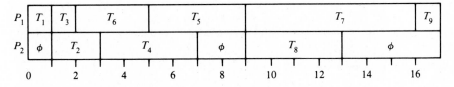

(c) Schedule when processors are activated as soon as possible

Figure 8.16 Task schedule in chart form, using p = 2 processors. (Courtesy of *ACM Computing Surveys*, Gonzalez, Sept. 1977.)

The mean utilization U_p of the p processor system in the case of Figure 8.16b is $U_p = (30 - 3)/30 = 0.9$, for $p = 2$. The reader can easily show that by increasing the number of processors to 3, the speedup does not increase. In fact, the utilization reduces to 0.6. Hence, the execution of the process graph in Figure 8.16a is most cost-effective on a two-processor system. The rationale behind the minimization of finishing or completion time is that system throughput can be maximized if the total computation time of each set of processes is minimized. *Throughput* is defined as the number of process sets processed per unit of time.

There are at least two reasons for minimizing the number of processors required to process a process system. The first and most obvious is cost. The second reason is the processor utilization. If the number of processors required to execute a set of processes in a given time is less than the total number of processors available, then the remaining processors can be used as backup processors for increased reliability and as background processors for noncritical computations.

A key issue in the study of processor scheduling is the amount of overhead or computation time needed to locate a suitable schedule. A scheduling algorithm is a procedure that produces a schedule for every given set of processes. An efficient scheduling algorithm is one that can locate a suitable schedule in an amount of time that is bounded in the length of the input by some polynomial. Construction of *optimal* schedules is NP-complete in many cases. NP-complete implies that an optimal solution may be very difficult to compute in the *worst* possible input case. However, construction of *suitable* schedules, that is, computing a reasonable answer for the typical input case, is not NP-complete. Therefore suitable schedules can be obtained for concurrent processes.

In this subsection, we examine deterministic schedules which can be used to optimize measures of performance. Unless stated explicitly, we assume a scheduling environment which consists of a number of identical processors, a set of processes with equal or unequal execution times and a (possibly empty) precedence order. First we consider preemptive schedules using two processors.

In order to understand the preemptive schedule (PS) on p processors, we define process graphs with mutually commensurable node weights. A set of nodes is said to be *mutually commensurable* if there exists a t such that each node weight is an integer multiple of t. In a preemptive schedule, a processor may be preempted from an executing process if such an action results in an improved measure of performance. The PS algorithms are due to Muntz and Coffman (1966).

Assume that the process graph consists of n independent processes with weights (process duration or execution times) of $t_1, t_2, \ldots, t_n$ and p processors. The optimal PS has a completion time of:

$$\omega = \max\left\{ \max_{1 \le i \le n} \{t_i\}, \frac{1}{p} \sum_{i=1}^{n} t_i \right\} \tag{8.3}$$

The optimal PS length cannot be less than the larger of the longest process or the sum of the execution times divided by the number of processors.

For their optimal algorithm, the set of nodes of unit weight in a graph are partitioned into a sequence of disjoint subsets such that all nodes in a subset are independent. All nodes in the same subset or at the same level are candidates for simultaneous execution or group scheduling. In a graph of N subsets or levels, the terminal node occupies the first level exclusively. Those nodes which may be executed during the unit time period preceding the execution of the terminal node occupy the second level, and so on. The initial or entrance node in the graph occupies the Nth level. Such an assignment of levels generate what is called *precedence partitions*.

In particular, the assignment procedure outlined above corresponds to the latest precedence partitions. That is, the assignment of nodes to levels is done in a manner which defers process initiation to the latest possible time without increasing the minimum completion time. Such a schedule is called the *latest-scheduling* strategy. This strategy assumes that the number of processors available is greater than or equal to the maximum number of processes at any level (width of G). This strategy may be contrasted with the *earliest-scheduling strategy*, which schedules a process as soon as a processor is available and the precedence constraints have been satisfied. Note that the earliest strategy produces earliest-precedence partitions.

For any arbitrary graph G, a precedence relation will exist between the subsets of the latest strategy due to the precedence which exists between the nodes in the original graph. A PS can be constructed for graph G by first scheduling the highest-numbered subset, then the subset at the next lower level, and so on. Note that when a subset consists of only one node, a node from the next lower subset is moved up if it does not violate the precedence constraints of the original graph. If each of the subsets is scheduled optimally, a *subset schedule* results. For two processors and equally weighted nodes, an optimal subset schedule for G is an optimal PS for G.

This result is extended to the case of graphs having mutually commensurable node weights. In order to generate the optimal result, it is necessary to convert graph G into another graph G_w in which all nodes have equal weights. This is done by taking a node of weight t_i and creating a sequence of n nodes such that $t_i = nt$, as illustrated in Figure 8.17. Note that the integrity of the original graph must be maintained. It can then be shown that an optimal subset schedule for G_w is an optimal PS for G, with $k = 2$.

In this approach, one must note whether the number of processes at any level is even or odd. If it is even, then all processes at that level can be executed in the minimum amount of time with no idle time for either of the two processors. If the number of processes is not a multiple of two, then the last three processes to be scheduled at that level can be executed in no less than $\frac{1}{2}$ unit, since all processes in G_w are of unit duration. By using the form shown in Figure 8.18, three processes in a given level can be executed in minimum time without processor idle time. Since scheduling in this manner ensures that no processor is idle, the subset sequence can be seen to generate a minimal-length PS. An example of the optimal PS algorithm is shown in Figure 8.19. For this example, the optimal subset sequence for G is $\{T_1\}, \{T_2, T_3\}, \{T_5, T_6, T_7\}, \{T_4, T_8\}, \{T_9, T_{10}\}, \{T_{11}\}$.

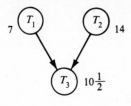

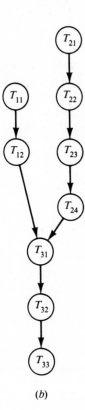

Figure 8.17 Comparison of a graph with mutually commensurable node weights with the corresponding graph having nodes of equal weight. (a) Graph G node weights $w_1 = 7$, $w_2 = 14$, $w_3 = 10 \ 1/2$; (b) graph G_w, $w = 3 \ 1/2$.

The optimal results derived above can be extended to the case in which any number of processors are allowed when the computation graph is a *rooted tree* and the node weights t_i are mutually commensurable. A *rooted tree* is one in which each node has at most one successor, with the exception of the root or terminal node, which has no successors. We discuss below some techniques for nonpreemptive schedules.

Recall that, in nonpreemptive or basic schedules, a processor assigned to a process is dedicated to that process until it is completed. The initial investigations discussed here develop optimal nonpreemptive two-processor schedules for arbitrary process orderings in which all processes are of unit duration. A particular

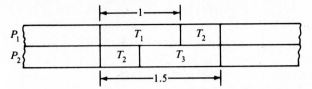

Figure 8.18 Minimum-time execution format for three unit tasks with two processors.

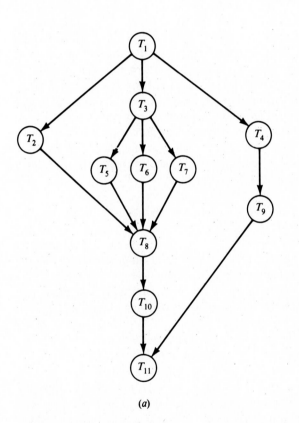

(a)

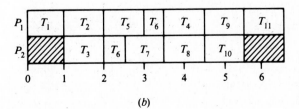

(b)

Figure 8.19 Illustration of subset sequence algorithm. (a) Graph G for a set of tasks, with all nodes having unit weight; (b) optimal preemptive schedule. (Courtesy of *ACM Computing Surveys*, Gonzales, Sept. 1977.)

simple class of scheduling algorithms for nonpreemptive schedules is the class of *list-scheduling algorithms*. A list-scheduling algorithm assigns distinct priorities to processes and allocates resources to the processes with highest priorities among those runnable at any time instant when the resource becomes free. A list schedule or list L for a graph G of n processes is denoted by $L = (T_1, T_2, \ldots, T_n)$ and represents some permutation of the n processes. A process is said to be ready if all of its predecessors have been completed. In using a list to generate a schedule, an idle processor is assigned to the first ready process found in the list. An algorithm for generating such an optimal list is described below.

The algorithm is a recursive procedure which begins by assigning subscripts in ascending order to the process (processes) which is (are) executed last owing to precedence constraints in the process graph. Notice that the set of successors of these processes is empty. Assignment proceeds "up the graph" in a manner that considers as candidates for the assignment of the next subscript all processes whose successors have already been assigned a subscript. Consideration of processes in this manner amounts to examining processes in a given latest-precedence partition, although the processes are not executed at a time that corresponds to this partition. In effect, the processes in a graph can be initially assigned subscripts in an arbitrary manner. This algorithm then reassigns subscripts in the method outlined above. The list is formed by listing the processes in decreasing subscript order, beginning with the last subscript assigned. The optimal schedule is formed by assigning ready processes in the list to idle processors. The algorithm is illustrated in Figure 8.20 by means of a process graph with reassigned subscripts, the resultant list L^*, and the optimal schedule.

The above algorithm does not always yield optimal results when the number of processors is increased beyond two, or when the number of processors is two and processes are allowed to have arbitrary durations. We describe a nonpreemptive scheduling method by Hu (1961). Two problems for process of unit duration were addressed. In the first case, given a fixed numbers of processors, it is required to determine the minimum time required to execute a process graph. The second case determines the number of processors required to process a graph in a given time.

We begin to arrive at a solution to these problems if we develop a labeling scheme for the nodes of the graph. A node T_i is given the label $\alpha_i = X_i + 1$, where X_i is the length of the longest path from T_i to the final node in the graph. Labeling begins with the final node, which is given the label $\alpha_1 = 1$. Nodes that are one unit removed from the final node are given the label 2, and so on. This labeling scheme makes it clear that the minimum time ω_{min} required to execute the graph is related to α_{max}, the node(s) with the highest numbered label, by

$$\omega_{min} \geq \alpha_{max}$$

The optimal solutions by Hu are limited to rooted trees. Using the labeling procedure described above, one can obtain an optimal schedule for p processors by processing a tree of unit-length processes in the following manner:

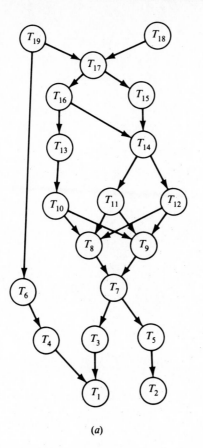

(a)

P_1	T_{19}	T_{17}	T_{16}	T_{14}	T_{12}	T_{10}	T_9	T_7	T_5	T_2
P_2	T_{18}	T_6	T_{15}	T_{13}	T_{11}	T_4	T_8	////	T_3	T_1

0   2   4   6   8   10

(b)

Figure 8.20 Illustration of Coffman and Graham algorithm. (a) **Task graph with reassigned subscripts** $L^* = (T_{19}, T_{18}, \ldots, T_1)$; (b) **optimal schedule. (Courtesy** *ACM Computing Surveys*, **Gonzales, Sept. 1977.)**

1. Schedule first the p (or fewer) nodes with the highest numbered label, i.e., the starting nodes. If the number of starting nodes is greater than p, choose p nodes whose α_i is greater than or equal to the α_i of those not chosen. In case of a tie, the choice is arbitrary.
2. Delete the p processed nodes from the graph. Let the term "starting node" now refer to a node with no predecessors.
3. Repeat steps 1 and 2 for the remainder of the graph.

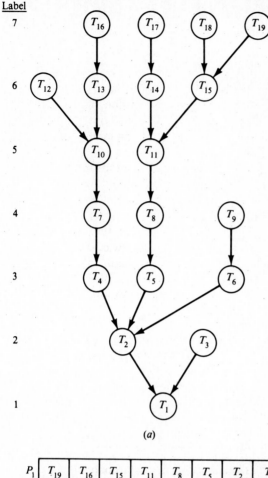

Label

(a)

P_1	T_{19}	T_{16}	T_{15}	T_{11}	T_8	T_5	T_2	T_1
P_2	T_{18}	T_{14}	T_{13}	T_{10}	T_7	T_4		
P_3	T_{17}	T_{12}	T_9	T_6	T_3			

(b)

Figure 8.21 Illustration of Hu's optimal algorithm. (*a*) Rooted tree labeled according to Hu's procedure; (*b*) optimal schedule for three processors. (Courtesy *ACM Computing Surveys*, Gonzalez, Sept. 1977.)

The schedules generated in this manner are optimal under the stated constraints. The labeling and scheduling procedures are quite simple to implement and are illustrated in Figure 8.21.

Recall that the minimum time required to execute a task graph by Hu's procedure is α_{max}. Suppose we wish to process a graph within a prescribed time t, where $t = \alpha_{max} + C$ and C is a nonnegative integer. The minimum number of processors p required to process the graph in time t is given by

$$p - 1 < \frac{1}{\gamma^* + C} \sum_{j=1}^{\gamma^*} \rho(\alpha_{max} + 1 - j) < p \tag{8.4}$$

where $\rho(i)$ denotes the number of nodes in the graph with label α_i and γ^* is the value of the constant γ, which maximizes the given expression. To illustrate this result, consider Figure 8.21. For $C = 0$, for example, value γ^* occurs when $\gamma = 1$ or $\gamma = 2$. This indicates that, in order to process the graph in minimum time, four processors are needed. For $C = 1$, $t = 8$ and γ^* occurs when $\gamma = 2$ or $\gamma = 5$, and three processors are required. Varying C further, we find that three processors are required when the processes must be processed within nine units, but only two processors are needed for a maximum processing time of 10 units.

Another study by Graham shows that, for a computing system with n identical processors in which processes are assigned arbitrarily to the processors, the completion time of the set of processes will not be more than twice the time required by an optimal schedule. This bound was derived in connection with the so-called *multiprocessor anomalies*. These anomalies are derived from the counterintuitive observation that the existence of one of the following conditions can lead to an increase in execution time:

1. Replace a given process list L by another list L', leaving the set of process times μ, the precedence order $<$, and the number of processors n unchanged.
2. Relax some of the restrictions of the partial ordering.
3. Decrease some of the execution times.
4. Increase the number of processors.

A general bound has been obtained by executing a set of processes twice. During the first execution, the processes are characterized by the parameters μ, $<$, L, n, and ω (the length of the schedule), and during the second execution by μ', $<'$, L', n', and ω' such that $\mu' \leq \mu$ and every constraint of $<'$ is also in $<$, i.e., $<'$ is contained in $<$. The result of this general bound is that

$$\frac{\omega'}{\omega} \leq 1 + \frac{n - 1}{n'} \tag{8.5}$$

This bound is the best possible, and, for $n = n'$, the ratio $2 - 1/n$ can be achieved by the variation of any one of L, μ, or $<$.

The above result was extended to a nonhomogeneous processor system by Liu and Liu. Suppose a multiprocessor system consists of n_i processors of speed μ_i, for $i = 1, 2, \ldots, k$, such that $\mu_1 > \mu_2 > \cdots > \mu_k \geq 1$, then

$$\frac{\omega'}{\omega} \leq \frac{\mu_1}{\mu_k} + 1 - \frac{\mu_1}{\sum\limits_{i=1}^{k} n_i \mu_i} \tag{8.6}$$

Example 8.8 Consider a system with one processor of speed five and five processors of speed one. By Eq. 8.6, we have

$$\frac{\omega'}{\omega} \leq \frac{5}{1} + 1 - \frac{5}{10} = \frac{11}{2}$$

Comparing this bound with that in Eq. 8.5 for a multiprocessor system with 10 identical processors of speed 1 (by substituting five identical processors of speed 1 for the processor of speed 5), the ratio $2 - \frac{1}{10}$ is achieved. The determination of a close to optimal schedule is more important for a heterogeneous system than for a homogeneous system.

Because of the limitations on optimal algorithms, bounds have been derived for the behavior of nonoptimal algorithms. The concept of precedence partitions can be used to generate bounds for processing time and the number of processors for graph structures whose nodes require unit-execution time. As indicated earlier, precedence partitions group processes into subsets to indicate the earliest and latest times during which processes can be initiated and still guarantee minimum execution time for the graph. This time is given by the number of partitions and is a measure of the longest path in the graph. For a graph of N levels, the minimum execution time is $\omega = N$ units. In order to execute a graph in this minimum time, the lower bound on the number of processors p required is given by

$$p \geq \max\left[\max_{1 \leq i \leq N} |L_i \cap E_i|, \max_{1 \leq i \leq N}\left[\frac{1}{i} \sum_{i=1}^{N} |L_i|\right] \right] \tag{8.7}$$

and the upper bound on the number of processors p required is given by

$$p \leq \min_{1 \leq i \leq N}\left[\max_{1 \leq i \leq N} |L_i|, \max_{1 \leq i \leq N} |E_i| \right] \tag{8.8}$$

In both cases, L_i and E_i refer to the ith latest and earliest precedence partitions, respectively, and $|x|$ represents the cardiality of the set x. The processes contained in $L_i \cap E_i$ are called *essential processes*. Those processes contained in the ith subset given by $L_i \cap E_i$ must be initiated $i - 1$ units after the start of the initial process in the graph to guarantee minimum execution time.

8.3.3 Stochastic Scheduling Models

Using nondeterministic techniques, the execution time of a process T_i is given by the random variable t_i, with cumulative distribution function F_i. Given a process graph G, let t_G be the random variable representing total execution time (the time from when all processes are started until the last process terminates). Assume t_G has a **cdf** F_G. There is a class of process graphs for which F_G can be expressed simply in terms of F_i. Below, we give a methodology, developed by Robinson (1979), for estimating F_G for this class.

Process graphs In order to determine the possible execution of job T, we define chains and simple process graphs. A subgraph of a process graph G is a *chain* if the set of processes in the subgraph are totally ordered. The length of a chain is the number of processes in the chain. If, in a chain, the initial process is T_i and the final process is T_j, we say it is a chain from T_i to T_j. A subgraph of a process graph G that is a chain is said to be a chain in G. In the following definition, a class of process graphs is defined for which F_G can be expressed simply in terms of the **cdfs** of process execution time F_i. Let $C_1, C_2, \ldots, C_m$ be all chains from initial to final processes in G. For each chain C_i containing processes $T_{i_1}, T_{i_2}, \ldots$, let X_i be the expression $x_{i_1} x_{i_2} \ldots$, formed by concatenating the polynomial variables $x_{i_1}, x_{i_2}, \ldots$, associated with processes $T_{i_1}, T_{i_2}, \ldots$, respectively. Then G is said to be *simple* if the polynomial $X(G) = X_1 + X_2 + \cdots + X_m$ can be factored so that each variable appears exactly once. Examples of simple and nonsimple process graphs are shown in Figure 8.22.

The class of parallel algorithms represented by simple process graphs are exactly those that can be written in block-structured languages with parallel blocks, provided no synchronization takes place between any of the components of a parallel block.

A set of processes is *independent* if, for any two processes T_i and T_j in the set, neither $T_i < T_j$ not $T_j < T_i$. In this example (Figure 8.22a), processes in set $\{T_1, T_2, T_4\}$ are independent. So also are processes in set $\{T_3, T_4\}$. Figure 8.22 shows some process graphs to explain the simplicity of graphs.

Let K be the number of processors in the system. If $K \geq \text{width}(G)$, each process in G begins execution immediately after the last predecessor completes. Let $C_1, C_2, \ldots, C_m$ be all the chains from initial to final processes in graph G. Also let the execution time of process T_i be t_i with **cdf** F_i. Then the total execution time of task system G is the maximum of the execution times of all the chains in G. That is,

$$t_G = \max_{1 \leq i \leq m} \sum_{T_j \in C_i} t_j \tag{8.9}$$

Note that $+$ and max are commutative and associative operations, respectively. Moreover, $+$ distributes over max. For example, $\max(a, b) + c = \max(a + c, b + c)$. Thus, if G is simple, the expression for t_G above can be factored in terms of max and $+$ so that each random variable appears only once. Then, if the t_i's are independent, the expression for F_G may be found by substituting F_i for t_i, $*$ (convolution) for $+$, and $\cdot$ (multiplication) for max in the expression for t_G. The convolution of **cdfs** F_1 and F_2 is written as follows:

$$F_1 * F_2(t) = \int_{-\infty}^{\infty} F_1(t - u) F_2 \, du \tag{8.10}$$

For the example in Figure 8.23, there are three chains, $C_1 = T_1 T_3 T_5$, $C_2 = T_2 T_3 T_5$, and $C_3 = T_3 T_5$. Therefore

$$t_G = \max\{(t_1 + t_3 + t_5), (t_t + t_3 + t_5), (t_4 + t_5)\}$$

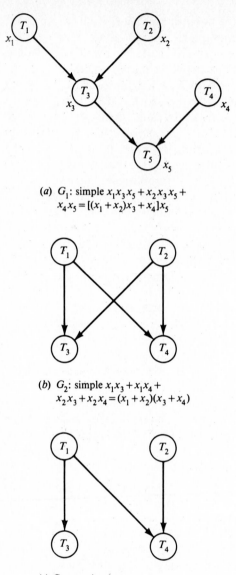

(a) G_1: simple $x_1 x_3 x_5 + x_2 x_3 x_5 + x_4 x_5 = [(x_1 + x_2) x_3 + x_4] x_5$

(b) G_2: simple $x_1 x_3 + x_1 x_4 + x_2 x_3 + x_2 x_4 = (x_1 + x_2)(x_3 + x_4)$

(c) G_3: nonsimple $x_1 x_3 + x_1 x_4 + x_2 x_4$

Figure 8.22 Examples of simple and nonsimple task graphs. (Courtesy *IEEE Trans. Software Engg.* Robinson, January 1979.)

Since $t_3 + t_5$ is common in the first two summations,

$$t_G = \max\{\max(t_1, t_2) + t_3 + t_5, t_4 + t_5\}$$

This expression can be factored further by noting that t_5 is common to both summations:

$$t_G = \max\{\max(t_1, t_2) + t_3, t_4\} + t_5 \qquad (8.11)$$

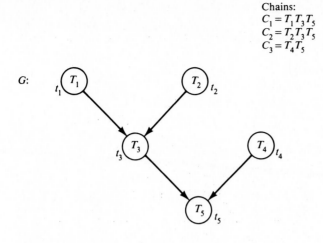

Chains:
$$C_1 = T_1 T_3 T_5$$
$$C_2 = T_2 T_3 T_5$$
$$C_3 = T_4 T_5$$

$$t_G = \max \{\Sigma\ t_j\} = \max \{(t_1 + t_3 + t_5), (t_2 + t_3 + t_5), (t_9 + t_5)\}$$

$$T_j \epsilon C_i = \max \{\max(t_1, t_2) + t_3, t_4\} + t_5 \quad \text{and} \quad 1 \le i \le m$$

$$F_G = \{(F_1 F_2) * (F_3 F_4)\} * F_5$$

Figure 8.23 Computation of t_G and F_G for task graph G. (Courtesy *IEEE Trans. Software Engg.*, Robinson, Jan. 1979.)

In Eq. 8.11, each random variable appears only once. Hence, F_G may be found by the substitution rule:

$$F_G = (((F_1 \cdot F_2) * F_3) \cdot F_4) * F_5 \tag{8.12}$$

As another example, consider the four-process merge-sort depicted by the process graph in Figure 8.24. Process S_i performs the sorting of one distinct subfile a_i, which is a fourth of file A. After the pair of either subfiles a_1 and a_2 or a_3 and a_4 are sorted, they are merged by the execution of process M_1 or M_2, respectively.

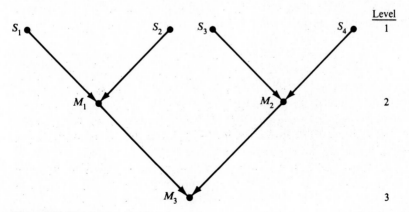

Figure 8.24 Four-process merge sort.

Merging is a method of combining two or more sorted files into a composite sorted file. In Figure 8.24, each M_i is a merge of the sorted subfiles produced by its immediate predecessors.

If all permutations of keys are equally likely, then the execution times of S_1, S_2, S_3, and S_4 have the same **cdf** and the execution times of M_1 and M_2 have the same **cdf**. Let the **cdf** of the execution times of the S_i's be F_1 and that of M_1 and M_2 be F_2. Furthermore, let the **cdf** of the execution time of M_3 be F_3. Then width$(G) = 4$. G is simple and the process-execution times are independent. Let the execution times of the S_i's and M_j be t_{S_i} and t_{M_j}, respectively. Hence, the execution time of the four-process merge-sort is

$$t_G = \max\{\max(t_{S_1}, t_{S_2}) + t_{M_1}, \max(t_{S_3}, t_{S_4}) + t_{M_2}\} + t_{M_3}$$

Since $t_{S_1}, t_{S_2}, t_{S_3}, t_{S_4}$ have the same **cdf** F_1 and t_{M_1}, t_{M_2} have the same **cdf** F_2, the **cdf** of t_{M_3} is F_3:

$$F_G = (F_1^2 * F_2) \cdot (F_1^2 * F_2) * F_3 = (F_1^2 * F_2)^2 * F_3 \qquad (8.13)$$

This should be compared with the **cdf** of the execution time for a one-process (sequential) merge-sort:

$$F_{\text{seq}} = F_1 * F_1 * F_1 * F_1 * F_2 * F_2 * F_3 \qquad (8.14)$$

since the execution time for the sequential merge-sort is

$$t_{\text{seq}} = t_{S_1} + t_{S_2} + t_{S_3} + t_{S_4} + t_{M_1} + t_{M_2} + t_{M_3} \qquad (8.15)$$

Notice that Eq. 8.15 assumes that the processing environment of the sequential merge-sort is the same as the concurrent merge-sort. In practice, this is not true, since the sequential merge-sort does not encounter interprocess-communication problems or memory conflicts which create overheads in the concurrent merge-sort. Hence, in practice, t_{seq} is usually less than that predicted by Eq. 8.15. In the next section, we consider the effect of these overheads on the performance of the algorithm.

Let μ_G and μ_{seq} be the mean execution times of the probability density functions $f_G = F'_G$ and $f_{\text{seq}} = F'_{\text{seq}}$, respectively. We can then estimate the theoretical speedup of the four-process merge-sort as

$$S_p = \frac{\mu_G}{\mu_{\text{seq}}} \qquad (8.16)$$

Equation 8.9 is not very useful when the **cdfs** of the process execution time are not known. Bounds can be derived for the mean execution time by using more limited knowledge about the execution times of processes. Let us denote the expected value of a random variable x by $E(x)$. The level of a process T in a process graph G is the maximum length of any chain in G from an initial process to T. The *depth* of G, denoted by depth(G), is the maximum level of any process. Given a process graph G with the number of available processors $K \geq$ width(G) and with the t_i independent, let $C_1, C_2, \ldots, C_m$ be all chains in G from initial to final processes. Also let H_i be the set of all processes of level i, for $1 \leq i \leq L$, where $L = \text{depth}(G)$. For any set of n random variables $\{x_i\}$,

$$E\left(\max_{1 \leq i \leq n} \{x_i\} \right) \geq \max_{1 \leq i \leq n} \{E(x_i)\} \tag{8.17}$$

from which the lower bound follows. For the upper bound, let $t_0 \equiv 0$ and define $f(i, j) = 0$ if $C_i \cap H_j$ is empty; otherwise $f(i, j)$ is the index of the single process in $C_i \cap H_j$. Then from Eq. 8.9,

$$t_G = \max_{1 \leq i \leq m} \left(\sum_{1 \leq j \leq L} t_{f(i, j)} \right) \leq \sum_{1 \leq j \leq L} \max_{1 \leq i \leq m} (t_{f(i, j)}) \tag{8.18}$$

Therefore

$$\max_{1 \leq i \leq m} \left(\sum_{T_j \in C_i} E(t_j) \right) \leq E(t_G) \leq \sum_{1 \leq i \leq L} E\left(\max_{T_j \in H_i} t_j \right) \tag{8.19}$$

The upper bound in Eq. 8.19 is useful only if something can be said about $E(\max\{t_j\})$. An applicable result from *order statistics* is that, if the random variables $x_1, x_2, \ldots, x_m$ are independent and identically distributed (i.i.d.) with the mean μ and standard deviation σ, then

$$E\left\{ \max_{1 \leq i \leq m} \{x_i\} \right\} \leq \mu + \frac{m - 1}{\sqrt{2m - 1}} \sigma \tag{8.20}$$

Hence, if the number of available processors $K \geq \text{width}(G)$, the t_i's are independent, $\text{depth}(G) = L$ and the m_j processes on level j have identically distributed execution times with the mean μ_j and standard deviation σ_j, then

$$\sum_{1 \leq j \leq L} \mu_j \leq E(t_G) \leq \sum_{1 \leq j \leq L} \left(\mu_j + \frac{m_j - 1}{\sqrt{2m_j - 1}} \sigma^j \right) \tag{8.21}$$

Queueing model Probabilistic models are often formulated to investigate the properties of dynamic scheduling methods that take the form of queueing systems. These require the specification of certain characteristics and attributes of the queueing system, such as the probability distribution functions of the interarrival times of processes, the service times of the processes, and the specification of the service discipline. The service or queueing discipline is the scheduling rule which determines both the sequence in which processes are executed and the processor-occupancy period each time a process is selected for service. A number of assumptions are usually made regarding queueing systems to make the analytical model tractable. These include the independence of processes and the statistical independence of the interarrival and service times.

A very simple model of scheduling in a multiprocessing system consists of p identical processing elements and a single infinite queue to which processes arrive. This model may be appropriate for a system with a global ready list and no preemptions. The mean processing time of processes on each processor is $1/\mu$ and the mean interarrival time of processes to the system is $1/\lambda$. Assuming that the service and interarrival times are exponentially distributed and the service discipline for processes is the common first-come-first-serve (FCFS), various performance factors can be obtained. Figure 8.25 illustrates the resulting queueing model in which processes arrive at a rate λ and are serviced at a rate μ. The utilization of the processors is

$$\rho = \frac{u}{p} \tag{8.22}$$

where u is the traffic intensity and is defined by $u = \lambda/\mu$. The mean response time of processes is [Kleinrock (1976)]

$$\overline{R}(\rho, u) = \frac{C(\rho, u)}{\mu p(1 - \rho)} + \frac{1}{\mu} \tag{8.23}$$

where $C(\rho, u)$ is Erlang's C formula and is given by

$$C(\rho, u) = \frac{u^p}{u^p + p!(1 - \rho) \sum_{n=0}^{p-1} \frac{u^n}{n!}}$$

There are a number of other scheduling algorithms, such as *round robin* (RR), preemptive, and nonpreemptive priority service disciplines, which can be modeled by the use of queueing systems. In an RR service discipline, each time a process is selected for execution, it is selected from the head of the ordered queue and allocated a fixed duration of run time called the *time slice* or *quantum*. If a process terminates execution before the end of the quantum, it departs from the processor. If at the

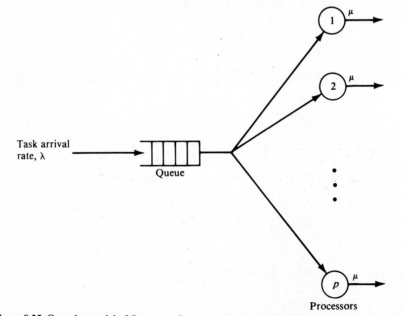

Figure 8.25 Queueing model of first-come-first-serve scheduling discipline in a multiprocessor system.

end of the quantum the process has not completed its execution (requires additional quantum), it is recycled to the end of the queue to await its next selection. New process arrivals simply join the end of the queue. The RR service discipline can be combined with the preemptive priority discipline to create a multilevel round-robin scheduling discipline. This discipline is used to give higher priority processes more frequent control than lower priority ones. Policies based on priority can be static (if the priority of a process remains fixed) or dynamic (if the priority of a process is allowed to change).

In the RR service discipline, a process in the run state is interrupted at the end of its quantum and may enter the ready state. An external event may cause the blocking of a running process. These transitions may necessitate a context switch. Furthermore, a running process can cause an explicit process switch by invoking a privileged instruction. For example, in the case of a fault, the process can cause a trap which switches context to the operating system, as in the IBM 370 supervisor call (SVC) instruction to be described in Chapter 9.

Long-term scheduling operations are used to control the load on the multiprocessor system by making decisions on activating new processes. One method to implement the schedule is to use priority queues for incoming processes. Prioritization of processes in a system may result in indefinite postponement of low priority processes if the arrival rate of the high priority processes is high. A set of processes which cooperate to solve a problem may be given higher priority than a single independent process.

Since there are many processors as well as memory modules to be scheduled, it may be useful to perform *group scheduling*, in which a set of related processes are assigned to processors to run simultaneously. Group scheduling can be extended to make placement decisions for groups of objects at a time, or to swap groups of related objects in and out. These different group schedulers have several possible advantages. First, if closely related processes run in parallel, blocking due to synchronization and frequency of context switching may be reduced. These will in effect aid in increasing performance. Second, if placement decisions are made for a group of objects with known reference patterns, the "distance" between the various processes and their referenced objects might be minimized. Hence, effective memory management for a set of related processes is easier since the time period for sharing is restricted to the short presence of the processes in the system. In general, a group assignment will not be very successful in lessening the number of context switches unless the processes within the group are "in step" so that few of them will be blocked from lack of input or other synchronization requirements.

8.4 PARALLEL ALGORITHMS FOR MULTIPROCESSORS

In this section, we describe and classify the various types of parallel algorithms. The characterization of parallel algorithms will help in the design and analysis of these algorithms. Some example algorithms are given. Techniques are shown to determine the performance of MIMD parallel algorithms.

8.4.1 Classification of Parallel Algorithms

Although extensive research has been performed on SIMD algorithms, there are few results available concerning the specification, design and analysis of MIMD multiprocessor algorithms. That is the basis for this section. A parallel algorithm for a multiprocessor is a set of k concurrent processes which may operate simultaneously and cooperatively to solve a given problem. If $k = 1$, it is called a *sequential algorithm.* To ensure that a parallel algorithm works correctly and effectively to solve a given problem, processes interact to synchronize and exchange data. Hence, in a task system, there may be some points where the processes communicate with other processes. These points are called *interaction points.* The interaction points divide a process into stages. Therefore, at the end of each stage, a process may communicate with some other processes before the next stage of the computation is initiated.

Because of the interactions between the processes, some processes may be blocked at certain times. The parallel algorithms in which some processes have to wait on other processes are called *synchronized algorithms.* Since the execution time of a process is variable, depending on the input data and system interruptions, all the processes that have to synchronize at a given point wait for the slowest among them. This worst case computation speed is a basic weakness of synchronized algorithms and may result in worse than expected speedup and processor utilization.

To remedy the problems encountered by synchronized parallel algorithms, *asynchronous parallel algorithms* exist for some set of problems. In an asynchronous algorithm, processes are not generally required to wait for each other and communication is achieved by reading dynamically updated global variables stored in shared memory. However, because of the concurrent memory accesses performed, conflicts may occur which will introduce some small delay in processes accessing common variables. For convenience, we shall often refer to synchronized and asynchronous parallel algorithms simply as synchronized and asynchronous algorithms, respectively.

Another alternative approach to constructing parallel algorithms is *macropipelining,* which is applicable if the computation can be divided into parts, called stages, so that the output of one or several collected parts is the input for another part. The program flow is illustrated in Figure 8.26. Because each computation part is realized as a separate process, communication costs may be high unless communication is achieved by address transmission. The question may arise as to whether to move the output data to the site of the next process in the pipeline or to move the next process, in particular its code, to the site of the data.

As an example, consider a simple pipeline compiler. Different processes are responsible for lexical analysis, syntax analysis, semantic analysis, optimization, and code generation. Source input is lexically analyzed and the recognized lexemes are input to the syntax-analysis process, thus building input for the semantic analyzer that, in turn, produces a tree for the code generator. Generated code is adapted by the final optimization process before being archived as the final

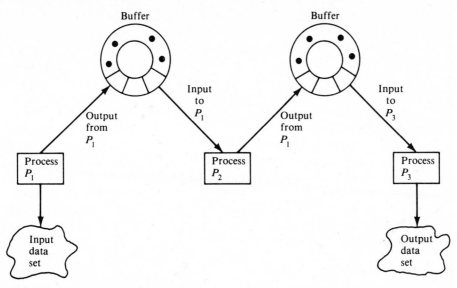

Figure 8.26 Program flow in macropipelines.

compiler output. Note that the processes that result from pipelining are hetero-geneous, while those resulting from partitioning are homogeneous.

The time taken to execute a fixed stage of a process is a random variable satisfying some cumulative distribution function. The fluctuations may be due to the variability of the processor's speeds and the input to the stage. A process may be blocked at the end of a stage because it is waiting for inputs in a synchronized algorithm or for the entering of a critical section in an asynchronous algorithm. The blocking time of a process is the total time that the process is blocked. If the multiprocessor system is heterogeneous, the execution time of a process will be smallest if the process is assigned to run on a faster processor. As an illustration of the variability due to input, we recall that the number of comparisons needed to sort n elements by the Quicksort algorithm ranges from $0(n \log_2 n)$ to $0(n^2)$, depending on the ordering of the input elements. The fluctuations in execution time may also result from delays due to memory conflicts, system interrupts, page faults, cache misses and the system work load. A typical source of nonnegligible overhead is that due to the execution of synchronization primitives. Synchroniza-tion primitives are needed for synchronizing processes and implementing critical sections.

An algorithm which requires execution on a multiprocessor system must be decomposed into a set of processes to exploit the parallelism. Two methods of decomposition naturally arise: static decomposition and dynamic decomposition. In *static decomposition*, the set of processes and their precedence relations are known before execution. In *dynamic decomposition*, the set of processes changes during execution. Static decomposition algorithms offer the possibility of very low process communication, provided the number of processes are small; however, their adaptability is limited. Dynamic decomposition algorithms can adapt effectively to variations in execution time of the process graph, but only at the expense of high process communication and other design overheads.

8.4.2 Synchronized Parallel Algorithms

A synchronized parallel algorithm is a parallel algorithm consisting of processes with the property that there exist a process such that some stage of the process is not activated until another process has completed a certain stage of its program. The synchronization can be performed by using the various synchronization primitives discussed in Section 8.1. For example, suppose it is required to compute the matrix $Z = A \cdot B + (C + D) \cdot (I + G)$ by maximum decomposition. A synchronized parallel algorithm may be constructed by creating three process P_1, P_2, and P_3, as shown in Figure 8.27. Processes P_1, P_2, and P_3 consist of two, one, and two stages, respectively, as shown below.

Example 8.9

```
var W, Y: shared real; var Sw, Sy: semaphore; initial Sw = Cy = 0;
cobegin
    Process P1: begin
                    V ← A × B; // stage 1 of P1 //
                    P(Sy);
                    Z ← V + Y; // stage 2 of P2 //
                end
    Process P2: begin
                    W ← C × D; // stage 1 of P2 //
                    V(Sw);
                end
    Process P3: begin
                    X ← I + G; // stage 1 of P3 //
                    P(Sw);
                    Y ← W + X; // stage 2 of P3 //
                    V(Sy);
                end
coend
```

Clearly, the activation of the second stage of process P_3 is subject to the condition that process P_2 is completed. Similarly, the second stage of P_1 cannot be initiated unless the second stage of P_3 is completed. Hence, the set of processes P_1, P_2, and P_3 is a synchronized parallel algorithm.

Since the time taken by a stage of a process is a random variable, synchronized algorithms have the drawback that some processes may be blocked at a given time, thereby degrading the performance of the algorithm. To illustrate the effect of the drawback, consider a synchronized algorithm with n processes. Assume

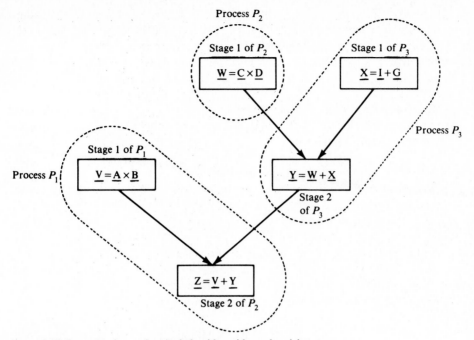

Figure 8.27 Example of a synchronized algorithm with synchronizing stages.

that this algorithm is run on a homogeneous multiprocessor system with n processors and the algorithm takes T_n. During the execution of the algorithm, let t_i denote the total time that i processes are running; that is, $n - i$ processes are blocked. Hence, $T_n = \sum_{i=0}^{n} t_i$. Assume that the algorithm can be run on a uniprocessor system in a time $T_1 \le \sum_{i=1}^{n} (i \cdot t_i)$. Therefore, the speedup S_n on an n-processor system is bounded by

$$S_n = \frac{T_1}{T_n} \le \frac{\sum\limits_{i=1}^{n} (i \cdot t_i)}{\sum\limits_{i=1}^{n} t_i} \qquad (8.24)$$

where $S_n \le n$ is obvious.

The degradation of performance can be clarified further by considering the class of synchronized parallel algorithms where only identical stages of processes are synchronized. Synchronized parallel algorithms which are adapted from SIMD algorithms are generally of this type. Consider the execution of a set of processes in which it is required to synchronize n identical stages and the time taken by the ith stage is a random variable t_i. Since the stages are all identical, the t_i's are identically distributed random variables with a mean, say, of t. Synchronization of the n stages means a new stage of any process can not be activated until all n stages are complete. Hence, the expected time taken by the synchronized stage of any process is the mean $\overline{T}$ of the random variable $T = \max_{1 \le i \le n}\{t_i\}$, rather than

t. In general, $\overline{T}$ is larger than t. The ratio $\overline{T}/t = \lambda_n$ is the *penalty factor* for synchronizing the n identical stages. If the penalty factor is large, the performance of the synchronized algorithm is largely degraded. The speedup bound S_n and the penalty factor λ_n give some indications of the performance of synchronized algorithms.

Synchronized iterative algorithms In practice, a large number of problems are solved by iterative methods. For example, zeros of function f may be computed by Newton's iteration method:

$$x_{i+1} = x_i - f'(x_i)^{-1}f(x_i) \tag{8.25}$$

where $f'(x)$ is the derivative of $f(x)$. The solution of a linear system of an equation by iteration is of the form

$$\mathbf{x}_{i+1} = \mathbf{A}\mathbf{x}_i + \mathbf{b} \tag{8.26}$$

where the $\mathbf{x}_i$, $\mathbf{b}$ are vectors each of size n and $\mathbf{A}$ is an $n \times n$ matrix.

A common application of iterative methods is in solving elliptic differential equations with boundary conditions (boundary-value problems). A simple but important equation of physics is Poisson's equation:

$$\frac{\partial^2 u}{\partial x^2} + \frac{\partial u^2}{\partial y^2} = f(x, y) \tag{8.27}$$

When $f(x, y) = 0$ for all x, y, this equation is known as the Laplace equation. The boundary-value problem consists of finding the function $u(x, y)$ that satisfies Eq. 8.27 within a closed region D and conditions prescribed on the boundary of D. Let D be a square domain in R^2. Also let the value of u be fixed on the boundary of D (denoted by $\overline{D}$). That is $u(x, y) = f(x, y)$ for all $x, y \in \overline{D}$. This is the Dirichlet problem. To solve this boundary-value problem on a digital computer, the domain D is sampled by superimposing a rectangular m by n grid or *mesh*. The distance between any two mesh points on any horizontal or vertical line is the *mesh width*, denoted by h. If h is small enough, we can approximate Eq. 8.27 by

$$\frac{\partial^2 u}{\partial x^2} \simeq \frac{u(x + h, y) + y(-h, y) - 2u(x, y)}{h^2}$$
$$\frac{\partial^2 u}{\partial y^2} \simeq \frac{u(x, y + h) + y(x, y - h) - 2u(x, y)}{h^2} \tag{8.28}$$

A discrete approximation to Eq. 8.27 is thus

$$4u(x, y) - y(x + h, y) - u(x - h, y) - u(x, h + h) - y(x, y - h) = -h^2 f(x, y) \tag{8.29}$$

Considering only the points in the mesh, we can rewrite Eq. 8.29 as

$$u_{i,j} = \tfrac{1}{4}(b_{i,j} + u_{i+1,j} + u_{i-1,j} + u_{i,j+1} + u_{i,j-1}) \tag{8.30}$$

for $i = 1, 2, \ldots, m$ and $j = 1, 2, \ldots, n$, where $u_{i,j} = u(ih, jh)$ and $b_{i,j} = -h^2 f(ih, jh)$. Equation 8.30 relates the update formula for any point (i, j) to only its nearest neighbors. A linear system of equations results in the $m \cdot n$ unknown values of the $\{u\}$ at all the points on the mesh inside D. Note that the dimension of the mesh is m by n.

The solution can be found iteratively by various methods. Two methods are discussed in this section. In the first method, we use a synchronized algorithm to solve the *partial differential equation* (PDE). In the next subsection, we will discuss an asynchronous algorithm to solve the PDE problem. However, in both cases, we assign a contiguous subset of the grid array $\{u_{i,j}\}$ to a process. One possible partitioning scheme is to make each subset consist of a number of consecutive rows of the grid. Thus, when the grid is stored in row-major format, a contiguous set of elements is allocated for each process. The synchronized algorithm consists of computing locally the values of the rth iterate $\{u_{i,j}^{(r)}\}$ from the values of the $(r - 1)$th iterate $\{u_{i,j}^{(r-1)}\}$ as follows:

$$u_{i,j}^{(r)} = \tfrac{1}{4}(b_{i,j} + u_{i+1,j}^{(r-1)} + u_{i-1,j}^{(r-1)} + u_{i,j+1}^{(r-1)} + u_{i,j-1}^{(r-1)})$$

When all processes have completed the computation of their iterates locally, the variables are updated in all other processes. It is after this synchronization step that the $(r + 1)$th iteration is initiated. This procedure is continued until the iterates converge to within an acceptable tolerance. The time in which a problem is solved depends both on the speedup and the convergence of the algorithm.

In general, an iterative algorithm can be described by an iterative function

$$\mathbf{x}_{i+1} = \phi(\mathbf{x}_i, \mathbf{x}_{i-1}, \ldots, \mathbf{x}_{i-d+1}) \tag{8.31}$$

where $\mathbf{x}_i \in R^n$.

The problems that can be formulated by an iteration function as described in Eq. 8.31 are numerous. They include relaxation methods for solving differential equations, solutions to linear and nonlinear systems of equations, and searches for extrema of functions. One approach to partitioning iterative algorithms for multiprocessors is to exploit the parallelism within the iteration function. Among all the possible partitions of ϕ, one tries to obtain a set of parallel tasks of the same size or, at least, of the same complexity so that the execution times of the tasks are *independent* and *identically distributed* (i.i.d.).

For example, in the case of Jacobi's iteration to solve a *linear system of equation* (LSE), Eq. 8.31 reduces to Eq. 8.26. If the system has a dimension n, we can allocate p processors, each updating n/p unknown iterates, assuming that n is divisible by p. This decomposition strategy of an iteration function is called *vertical* decomposition. In this case, if the matrix $\mathbf{A}$ has no sparsity structure, all the tasks have identical stochastic properties. Since some instances of the iterates x or some elements of the matrix $\mathbf{B}$ may be null, the processing time of each task is a random variable. However, the **cdf** of the processing time is the same for all tasks. This definition assumes also that the processors are identical and under control of the same integrated operation system. For example, one may observe that in the iteration of Eq. 8.25, the evaluations of f and f' at $\mathbf{x}_i$ can be done in parallel, and in the matrix iteration of Eq. 8.26, all the components of the vector x_{i+1} can be computed simultaneously. Another strategy to implement Eq. 8.31 on a multiprocessor is to exploit the fluctuations in the speed of a process. In this case, the idea is to use more than one process to compute the same function in parallel and expect that the process which obtains the result first takes less than the average time.

In the following discussion, we give an example of a synchronized algorithm that locates the zero of a monotonically increasing continuous function $f(x)$. It is assumed that $f(x)$ has opposite signs at the endpoints l and u such that the interval is $|u - l|$, as shown in Figure 8.28. The process terminates when $|u - l| < \varepsilon$, a permissible error. It should be noted that the algorithm presented can be easily modified to deal with discrete f, and thus can be used to search for a desired item in an ordered list.

The zero-searching algorithm is iterative and consists of n slave processes and a master process. The master process divides the given interval $u - l$ into $n + 1$ subintervals, each of size $\Delta = |(u - l)/(n + 1)|$. Each slave process i evaluates the function at $x_i + l + i\Delta$ as a stage of the process. When all of these evaluations complete, the master process compares the computed function values for the sign

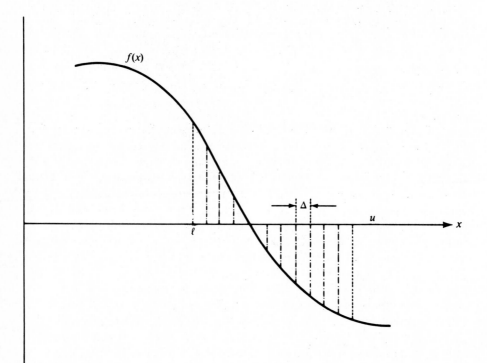

Figure 8.28 Finding the zero of a function $f(x)$ with 10 processors, where processor p_1 evaluates $f(x)$ at $x = l + i\Delta$. $\Delta = |u - l|/(n + 1)$.

change that indicates the presence of a root in a particular subinterval. This becomes the new interval of uncertainty to be subdivided for the next iteration. This cycle continues until the size of the interval containing the root is sufficiently reduced. The following example explains the zero-searching algorithm.

Example 10

```
real procedure rootf(f, l, u, n)
begin
function f;
var Δ, l, u, y[1:n]: shared real;
var i: shared integer;
while |u − l| > ε do
    begin
        Δ ← |u − l|/(n + 1); // compute subinterval //
        parfor i=1 until n do // create n slave process //
            begin
                y[i] ← f(l + iΔ); // evaluate function, f(x) //
            end
        l ← l + Δ; i ← 1; // obtain new interval of uncertainty //
        while sign (y[i] = sign (y[i + 1]) do
            begin
                l ← l + Δ; i ← i + 1;
            end
        u ← l + Δ;
    end
    z ← (l + u)/2; // zero of function, f(x), is z //
end procedure rootf
```

The key feature of this algorithm is the synchronization that occurs between the slave processes. Each slave process which completes its evaluation of the function is blocked. The two sequences of statements "$l \leftarrow l + \Delta; i \leftarrow i + 1;$" are not executed until all n slave processes have completed their evaluations of the function. Every slave process is awakened from the blocked state when the next iteration begins, and all the slave processes become eligible to resume execution simultaneously. The nature of the parallel solution demands this synchronization policy.

Let the time needed to evaluate f at a point in the interval be a random variable t with mean t, and time needed to determine the new uncertainty interval and to check the stopping criteria be another random variable c with mean c. For this example, we assume that $\bar{t} \gg \bar{c}$, so that c can be ignored in the analysis. It is also assumed that the execution time of the synchronization primitive can be ignored.

In evaluating the relative performance of the synchronized parallel zero-searching algorithm, we note that, on a uniprocessor, the binary search produces the best known search method and takes at most $[\log_2 |u − l|]$ function evaluations. Hence the expected running time is $[\log_2 |u − l|]t$.

For the synchronized parallel algorithm, it is clear that every iteration reduces the length of the interval of uncertainty by a factor of $n + 1$, when n slave processors are used. Therefore, the algorithm uses $[\log_{n+1}|u - l|]$ iterations and is optimal. However, the expected time for each iteration is $\lambda_n t$ rather than t, where λ_n is the penalty factor of synchronizing n function evaluations. Therefore, the expected running time of the algorithm is $[\log_{n+1}|u - l|] \cdot \lambda_n t$. Since the speedup is of the order of $\log n$, it performs poorly for large n. Hence when n is large a different search scheme that is efficient must be devised. The synchronized parallel algorithm can be inefficient when λ_n is large also, which usually happens when n is large.

Example 8.11 This example is a synchronized parallel algorithm which is iterative. In this case, the iteration function is decomposed so that each iteration step is performed by more than one process, and the processes are synchronized at the end of each iteration. Consider the solution of a linear system of equations with two concurrent processes, using Eq. 8.32. The most natural technique is to decompose each vector $\mathbf{x}_i$ into two segments $\mathbf{x}_i^{(1)}$ and $\mathbf{x}_i^{(2)}$, each of size $n/2$ (assuming n is divisible by 2) and update them by two parallel process as follows:

$$\begin{bmatrix} \mathbf{x}_{i+1}^{(1)} \\ \mathbf{x}_{i+1}^{(2)} \end{bmatrix} = \begin{bmatrix} \mathbf{A}_{11} & \mathbf{A}_{12} \\ \mathbf{A}_{21} & \mathbf{A}_{22} \end{bmatrix} \begin{bmatrix} \mathbf{x}_i^{(1)} \\ \mathbf{x}_i^{(2)} \end{bmatrix} + \begin{bmatrix} \mathbf{b}^{(1)} \\ \mathbf{b}^{(2)} \end{bmatrix} \qquad (8.32)$$

where $\mathbf{x}_{i+1}^{(1)} = \mathbf{A}_{11}\mathbf{x}_i^{(1)} + \mathbf{A}_{12}\mathbf{x}_i^{(2)} + \mathbf{b}^{(1)}$ and $\mathbf{x}_{i+1}^{(2)} = \mathbf{A}_{21}\mathbf{x}_i^{(1)} + \mathbf{A}_{22}\mathbf{x}_i^{(2)} + \mathbf{b}^{(2)}$.

That is, at an iteration step, each process updates half of the components and starts the next iteration only after both processes have completed updating their iterates.

8.4.3 Asynchronous Parallel Algorithms

In each asynchronous parallel algorithm, there is a set of global variables accessible to all processes. When a stage of a process is completed, the process reads some global variables. Based on the values of the variables read together with the results just obtained from the last stage, the process modifies a subset of the global variables and then activates the next stage or terminates itself. In many cases, in order to ensure logical correctness, the operations on global variables are programmed as critical sections.

Therefore, in an asynchronous algorithm, the communications between processes are achieved through the global variables or shared data and there is no explicit dependency between processes as in synchronized parallel algorithms. The main characteristic of an asynchronous parallel algorithm is that its processes never wait for inputs at any time but continue execution or terminate according to whatever information is currently contained in the global variables. However, it should be noted that processes may be blocked from entering critical sections which are needed in many algorithms.

For illustrative purposes, we show an asynchronous iterative algorithm corresponding to the familiar Newton's iteration for finding the zeros of a function $f(x)$. In this case, we conveniently create three global variables v_1, v_2, and v_3 to contain the current values of $f(x)$, $f'(x)$, and x, respectively. For example, after the $(i + 1)$th iteration of Eq. 8.25, $f(x_{i-1})$, $f'(x_{i-1})$, and x_i are updated as $f(x_i)$, $f'(x_i)$, and x_{i+1}, respectively. Suppose that the evaluation of $f'(x)$ is computationally more expensive than that of $f(x)$, then a reasonable asynchronous iterative algorithm consisting of two processes P_1 and P_2 can be defined as follows. Let process P_1 update variables v_1 and v_3, while process P_2 updates v_2. The program below shows a sketch of processes P_1 and P_2.

Example 8.12

```
function f, f';
var v₁, v₂, v₃: shared real;
    cobegin
Process P₁: begin
            while ⟨termination criteria S not satisfied⟩ do
              begin
                v₁ ← f(v₃);    // step 1 of P₁ //
                v₃ ← v₃ - v₂⁻¹ v₁;  // step 2 of P₁ //
                end
            end P₁
Process P₂: begin
            while ⟨termination criteria S not satisfied⟩ do
              v₂ ← f'(v₃); // step 1 of P₂ //
            end P₂
    coend
```

From the program it could be seen that, as soon as a process completes updating a global variable, it proceeds to the next updating by using the current values of the relevant variables without any delay. Suppose that the iterates are labeled in the order they are computed by step 2 of process P_1. Then, in general, the iterates generated do not satisfy the recurrence relation of Eq. 8.25. For example, if the initial values of the variables are $v_1 = f(x_0)$, $v_2 = f'(x_0)$ and $v_3 = x_1$, then the sequence and time period of step completions for each iteration within each process may be illustrated by a timing diagram, as shown in Figure 8.29. The number i on a demarcation on the timing diagram indicates the point where the ith iteration starts for that process. Then, for this illustration,

$$x_2 = x_1 - f'(x_0)^{-1} f(x_0)$$

$$x_3 = x_2 - f'(x_1)^{-1} f(x_2)$$

$$x_4 = x_3 - f'(x_2)^{-1} f(x_3)$$

From the concurrent program given above for P_1 and P_2, the recurrence relation that is generally followed by the execution of the processes is

$$x_{i+1} = x_i - f'(x_j)^{-1} f(x_i) \qquad (8.33)$$

where $j \leq i$. Therefore, the iterates generated by the asynchronous iterative algorithm are different from those generated by the sequential algorithm or synchronized iterative algorithms. It is difficult to derive any general theory for

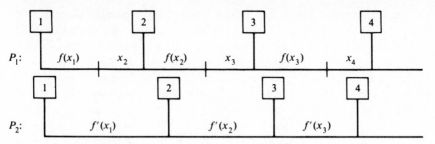

Figure 8.29 Time diagram for an asynchronous parallel algorithm.

the properties of the sequence $\{x_i\}$ because of the fluctuations of the speed of a process. Moreover, since the iterates generated by an asynchronous iterative algorithm in general do not satisfy any deterministic recurrence relation such as Eq. 8.25, it is difficult to obtain a general theory concerning conditions for convergence or the speed of convergence.

The design of an asynchronous iterative algorithm for a general iterative process (Eq. 8.31) involves the identification of some set of global variables $\{v[1], v[2], \ldots, v[n]\}$ such that each iterative step can be regarded as computing the new values of the v_i's from their old values. In general, it is desirable to choose the v_i's so that the updating of each v_i constitutes a significant portion of the work involved in one iteration. For example, consider the matrix iteration of Eq. 8.26. In this case, $v[i]$'s may be chosen as segments of equal size of the components in a vector iterate. After the $v[i]$'s have been chosen, concurrent processes which update the $v[i]$'s asynchronously can be defined as follows. Suppose there are n elements each in the vector $\mathbf{x}_i$ and $\mathbf{b}$. The set of global variables $\{v[1], v[2], \ldots, v[n]\}$ can be partitioned into p subsets, each of size $n/p = s$ (assuming that p divides n). The kth process updates the subset $\{v[(k-1)s+1], \ldots, v[ks]\}$, where $v[j]$ represents the current value of the jth component of the vector $\mathbf{x}_i$. Below is a p-process (Eq. 8.31) involves the identification of some set of global variables algorithms to solve the linear system of equations represented by Eq. 8.26.

Example 8.13

```
var v[1:n]: shared real;
parfor k = 1 until p do
   for i = (k - 1)s + 1 until ks do
      begin
      var acc: real;
      var A[(k - 1)s + 1: ks, 1: n] : real;
      var b[(k - 1)s + 1: ks] : real;
         acc ← 0.0;
         for j = 1 until n do
         acc ← acc + A[i,j] * v[j];
         v[i] ← acc + b[i];
      end
```

The above asynchronous iterative algorithms require parallelism inside the iteration function ϕ. It is possible to construct an asynchronous parallel algorithm to speed up the iterative process (Eq. 8.31) and not use any parallelism inside the iteration function ϕ. These algorithms, called *simple asynchronous* iterative algorithms, always generate the same sequence of iterates as the sequential algorithm. In general, these algorithms do not achieve speedup by sharing work; instead, the speedup is achieved by taking advantage of the fluctuations in the evaluation time. Below is an example of a simple asynchronous iterative algorithm which consists of k identical processes $P_1, \ldots, P_h$, each of which evaluates the iteration function ϕ by using the most recent iterates available at the time the evaluation is performed. In the concurrent program given below, i and x_i are global variables while j is local to the process. The value of variable i is the index of the iterate which was most recently computed; hence, the "if" statement is executed as a critical section.

```
var s: semaphore; initial s = 1;
var i, x[1:n] : shared : real;
parfor i ← 1 until k do
    begin
        while termination condition S not satisfied do
            begin
                j ← i + 1;
                x[j] ← φ (x[j − 1],x[j − 2], . . . ,x[j − d]);
                P(s);
                if i < j then i ← j;
                V(s);
            end
    end
```

The main advantage of simple asynchronous iterative algorithms is their general applicability. The algorithms are not restricted to numerical iterative processes only. In fact, they can be employed to speed up any sequence of processes. These algorithms are particularly attractive when decomposition of the processes is difficult. There are, however, some disadvantages. First, note that critical sections are needed in the algorithms. Second, it seems that unless fluctuations in computation time due to the system are large and coefficient of variation of the random variable t (time needed for one evaluation of the iteration ϕ by one process) is large, the speedup of the algorithm will be quite limited.

Concurrent quicksort algorithm In order to implement a parallel algorithm to sort an array of numbers, we discuss an example using the quicksort technique. The parallel algorithm consists of a variable number of processes which are created dynamically and assigned to processing elements (PE). The processes share the array of elements and a stack. The stack contains descriptors for continuous subsets of the array that have not yet been sorted. The stack must be accessed in a mutually exclusive manner. The stack is initialized to contain a single descriptor which describes the whole array.

In each pass, a process tries to pop a descriptor for a new subset from the shared stack. If successful, the process partitions the subset into two smaller ones consisting, respectively, of all elements less than and greater than some estimated median value. This median is computed as the mean of the first, last and middle elements of the subset. After this partitioning, a descriptor for the shorter of the new subsets is pushed onto the stack, and the longer subset is further partitioned in the same way. This procedure is continued until the number of elements in each subset is no more than a preselected threshold value. This subset may then be sorted in a single process using the simple insertion sort method.

The above parallel algorithm was implemented with a 20,480-element array and run on the Cm*. A brief description of the Cm* architecture was given in Section 7.1. Figure 8.30 shows the speedup of the parallel algorithm as a function of the number of processes for three operating environments. The speedup is relative to the speed of a uniprocess with the threshold value set to 10. The graphs are shown for a threshold value of 10. The three operating system environments consist of Smap, Medusa, and Staros. Smap is just a basic monitor with no operating

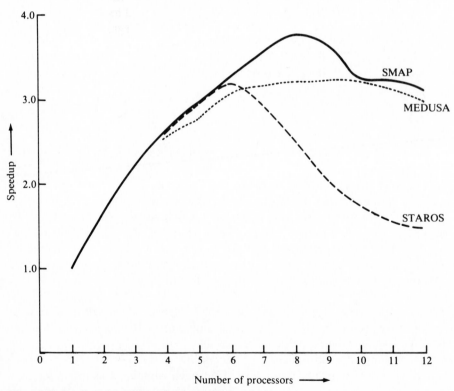

Figure 8.30 Speedup of parallel quicksort algorithm on Cm*.

system features. Medusa and Staros are two different operating systems designed for the Cm*. Notice the effect of the operating system on the performance of the algorithm. This is due to the overhead incurred by the invocation of the operating system functions for process scheduling and other chores. The performance peaks for a degree of decomposition between 6 and 8. This is due to the heavy contention of references to all the shared data located in one of the computer modules.

Asynchronous PDE A purely asynchronous method can be constructed to solve the PDE problem. In this method, each process updates the value of each point using the current values of immediate neighbors directly from the shared array so that it is available for other processes. This reduces the working space because no buffers are needed (as in the synchronized algorithm) and also assumes that the newest and probably the best approximation is used as soon as it is computed. The only variable that has to be locked against simultaneous use is the one that records the number of processes that have not finished their computations yet. This variable is accessed once per iteration. A counter is kept by each process to denote the number of performed iterations. Since each process has the same amount of work to do during each iteration, the value of its counter is a good measure of the relative speed of the process.

Experiments were performed on the Cm* to measure the performance of the asynchronous PDE algorithm using a 150 × 150 grid and fixed-point arithmetic. Figure 8.31 illustrates the speedup obtained with various degrees of decomposition

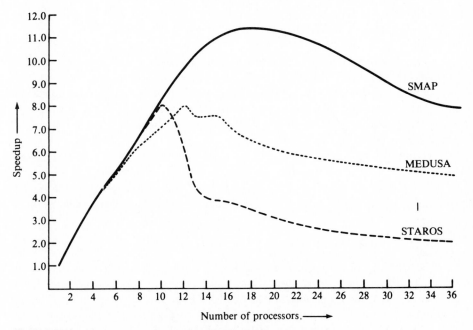

Figure 8.31 Speedup of purely asynchronous PDE algorithm on the Cm*.

and operating system environments. As long as most of the processes run in the cluster contain the global data, the speedup is almost linear. Otherwise, the speedup resembles that of the slowest process. In general, the distribution of the global data among the clusters will affect the performance. Also, the convergence depends on the relative speed of the various processes evaluating different parts of the grid. In general, asynchronous algorithms, if available, are preferred to synchronized algorithms provided the computations converge to the desired result.

8.4.4 Performance of Parallel Algorithms

Techniques developed in Section 8.3 do not account for the communication overhead caused by the interconnection topology. In this section, we study a methodology for evaluating the performance of a parallel algorithm which interacts with an architecture. Synchronized iterative algorithms are used as an example with loosely coupled multiprocessor systems. Finally, the effect of the degree of decomposition of a parallel algorithm on the performance is discussed.

Performance measures The effectiveness of a multiprocessor for a synchronized iterative algorithm depends on the performance features of the algorithm. In tightly coupled systems, performance is affected by memory interference. Conversely, the cost of interprocessor communication is the dominant factor for loosely coupled systems. In this section, we develop simple and approximate analytic models to estimate the relative effects of synchronization and interprocessor communication on the performance of a synchronized iterative algorithm. We recall from Section 8.4.2 that, in synchronized iterative algorithms, a cycle of operations is repeated until the result or a satisfying approximation to the result is obtained.

The model discussed here is for vectorial decomposition of iterative algorithms into i.i.d. tasks. The general case is very complex. Only the concurrent phase of the algorithm is modeled. Within each iteration, there may be a purely sequential phase which may include checking the convergence criterion after all processors are synchronized or when initiating a new iteration. Including such a sequential phase is a simple extension of the model.

An implementation of an algorithm on a given architecture is characterized by a set of performance features, $\{f_1, f_2, \ldots, f_N\}$, extracted from the analytical model. Let F be the *feature space* for the given architecture and algorithm. F can be seen as the product space of the one-dimensional spaces generated by each feature:

$$F = \{f_1\} \times \{f_2\} \times \cdots \times \{f_N\} \tag{8.33}$$

The topology of the space F is complex. The feature values may be real along some coordinate axes, and discrete along some others. A *performance index* for a given architecture is a real function defined on F by the analytical model. Local maxima of the index locate operating points in F where the architecture and the algorithm implementation are particularly well matched with respect to the index.

The power of analytical models resides in the estimation of the impact on the performance of a given feature or subset of features in isolation.

A symmetric multiprocessor system is made up of a set of identical processors. Generally the computation on each processor consists of a random number of instruction executions. The randomness in this number results, for example, from the evaluation of a function whose definition varies over its domain or of a function computed by a series expansion. In a minicomputer or a microprocessor, an instruction cycle consists of a variable number of machine cycles. Typical machine cycles are instruction fetch, operand fetch, and execution cycle. We will thus distinguish between memory access cycles and execution cycles. When a request for a memory word is rejected because of conflicts, the processor automatically retries by initiating a new memory access cycle. *Memory access time fluctuations* result. The execution part of an instruction cycle also has a random duration. Its duration may depend on the operand values. The number of machine cycles in the execution of an instruction is thus random, resulting in *execution time fluctuations*.

Since we are strictly concerned with the modeling of synchronized iterative processes, we concentrate on the efficient implementation of one iteration of any iterative algorithm with a given structure and size on an MIMD machine. In this framework, we consider the input data set for an algorithm described by Eq. 8.31 as including both the iterates x_k and the parameters defining Φ. In the case of an LSE, for example, these parameters are the system coefficients. Another cause of processing time fluctuations is the occurrence of external interrupts and page faults in the local or shared memories. To effectively isolate the performance of the algorithm on the architecture, we assume that each processor is uniprogrammed and that the memories are large enough to accommodate the address space of each process so that page faults do not occur. Moreover, external interrupts are disabled.

A loosely coupled multiprocessor system is one in which the processors access their instructions and data in their local memory. Thus, no memory access time fluctuation exists in this system. To communicate, the processors can initiate a data block transfer through their direct memory access (DMA) gate and high-speed bus (HSB) with broadcasting capability. The DMA gate has a fast communication memory (CM) which can be accessed also by the processor. To send a message to other processors, a processor stores the message in the CM, then initiates the transfer. The DMA controller of the sender monitors the bus. When it is free, a connection is established on the bus with the DMA controllers of the receivers, in time t_{Ab}. The message is transmitted on the bus and is simultaneously read by the receivers in time t_{Fb}. The total time the bus is busy for one message transfer is thus

$$t_{Cb} = t_{Ab} + t_{Fb} \tag{8.34}$$

The communication memory speeds up the transfers by reducing the overhead in each transfer. Moreover, the overlap between processing in the local memory and transfer between the communication memories is conflict free. If the CM is double buffered, the processor and the DMA controller can access it concurrently without conflicts. Under these conditions, t_{Cb} from Eq. 8.34 is deterministic for a given transfer.

To implement a synchronized algorithm on a loosely coupled system by vectorial decomposition, each of the P processors updates its subset of the iterates, then sends the values to the $(P - 1)$ other processors through the HSB. When a processor has received the updates from all the other processors, it can proceed to the next iteration.

Assume that the iterative algorithm is decomposed vectorially into P i.i.d. tasks. The P processors iterate through cycles in which they compute their subset of the iterates (processing phase), eventually communicate, and synchronize, as illustrated in Figure 8.32. The performance index is the efficiency factor E, defined as the fraction of time a processor is doing useful work. In a loosely coupled system, useful work is done during the entire processing phase only. This is not so in tightly coupled systems, where the cycles wasted in memory conflicts have to be deducted. This definition of the efficiency isolates the effect of the architecture on the performance. To compare the performance of the parallel algorithm with its corresponding sequential version, we would multiply the efficiency as defined here by a factor taking into account software restructuring or added software overhead in each iteration and by the ratio of the number of iterations required in both cases.

The techniques used to model the effect of synchronizations are drawn from order statistics. Let $T_{j:P}$ be the processing time of the jth processor to terminate (in the chronological order) when P processors are used. The estimation of the mean of $T_{j:P}$ is equivalent to the estimation of the mean of the jth order statistic among P independent samples drawn from the processing time distribution. For many distributions of interest, and for i.i.d. processes, the mean of $T_{j:P}$ is given by

$$m_{T_{j:P}} = m + 0_{j:P} \cdot \sigma \tag{8.35}$$

where m and σ are the mean and variance of the processing time, and $0_{j:P}$ is the mean of the jth order statistics among P samples drawn from the processing time distribution with mean 0 and variance 1. For example, for a *uniform* distribution,

$$0_{j:P} = \sqrt{2}\,\frac{2j - P - 1}{P + 1}$$

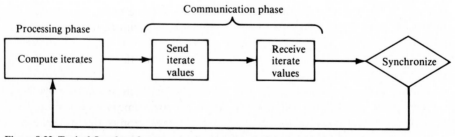

Figure 8.32 Typical flowchart for a process in a synchronized iterative algorithm.

For an *offset exponential* (an exponential plus a constant),

$$0_{j:P} = H_P - H_{P-i} - 1$$

where H_i is the ith harmonic number as defined by $\sum_{1 \leq k \leq i} 1/k$, for $i \geq 0$. For a *Gaussian*, no analytical formula has yet been found. The $0_{j:P}$ can, however, in this case be easily tabulated by using tables and recurrence relations.

The mean iteration time is then simply taken as the mean Pth order statistic among P independent samples:

$$m_I = m + 0_{P:P}\sigma \qquad (8.36)$$

where m_I is the mean iteration time, and $0_{P:P}$ depends uniquely on the distribution of the normalized processing time.

For these examples, a Gaussian processing-time distribution has been assumed. The choice is justified by the computation model defined earlier. A computation is seen as a random number of instruction cycles, each taking a random time. By an extension to the central limit theorem, the computation-time distribution tends to a Gaussian when the average number of instructions increases, provided the fluctuations of the number of instructions are small relative to the sum of the fluctuations of each individual instruction. The Gaussian was shown to predict quite accurately the speedup of iterative algorithms on C.mmp.

We present a model for evaluating the performance of iterative algorithms on a loosely coupled system. Let us denote the two buffers of the communication memory of a processor by CM[1] and CM[2]. In each cycle of a vectorially decomposed synchronized algorithm, each processor goes through the following phases:

1. Read the iterate updates received during the previous iteration in CM[1].
2. Update a subset of the iterates.
3. Write iterate updates in CM[1].
4. Initiate transfer of the iterate updates to the $(P - 1)$ other processors.
5. Wait for reception of all other iterate updates in CM[2].
6. Switch CM[1] and CM[2] and go to 1.

The first three phases comprise the processing time.

A high-speed bus has simultaneous read-write capability and takes advantage of the randomness of the processing times according to the scheme described. The time taken by a block transfer is given by Eq. 8.34. It is assumed to be the same for all processors. For the high-speed bus, we derive a lower bound on the mean iteration time m_I for any processing-time distribution with mean order statistics given by Eq. 8.35.

The first processor in chronological order to complete its processing phase (at time $T_{1:P}$) always finds the bus free. The total iteration time is at least $I \geq T_{1:P} + Pt_{Cb}$. We also have $I \geq T_{P:P} + t_{Cb}$, since at the termination of the last processor at $T_{P:P}$, one transfer at least has yet to take place. In general, when the jth processor is finished, there remain at least $(P - j + 1)$ transfers on the bus [it is effectively $(P - j + 1)$ when the processor finds the bus free], so that

$$I = \max_{j=1,\ldots,P} [T_{j:P} + (P - j + 1)t_{Cb}] \tag{8.37}$$

Assuming equal block transfer times, Eq. 8.37 is exact and can be used in a simulation when the processing time distribution is known.

In taking the average of Eq. 8.37, we note that, in general, if $x_1, \ldots, x_n$ are n random variables:

$$E\left(\max_{1 \leq i \leq n} \{x_i\}\right) \geq \max_{1 \leq i \leq n} \{E(x_i)\}$$

where $E(\max)$ is the average of the maxima and $E(x_i)$ is the average of x_i. According to this result, we write

$$m_I \geq \max_{j=1,\ldots,P} [m_0 + 0_{j:P} \cdot \sigma_0 + (P - j + 1)t_{Cb}] \tag{8.38}$$

Taking the lower bound for m_I, we can derive the efficiency as:

$$E = \frac{m_0}{m_I} \simeq \frac{m_0}{\max\limits_{j=1,\ldots,P} [m_0 + 0_{j:P}\sigma_0 + (P - j + 1)t_{Cb}]} = \frac{1}{1 + \Delta} \tag{8.39}$$

with

$$\Delta(P, C_0, t'_{Cb}) \simeq \max_{j=1,\ldots,P} [0_{j:P} \cdot C_0 + (P - j + 1) \cdot t'_{Cb}]$$

The set of performance features are P, C_0, $t'_{Cb} = t_{Cb}/m_0$ and $C_0 = \sigma_0/m_0$.

The efficiency factors for the loosely coupled system are displayed in Figure 8.33 as a function of the features. From these figures, it is clear that the high sensitivity of the performance index to the communication to computation times ratio t'_{Cb} limits the applicability of loosely coupled architectures for synchronized iterative algorithms. Such architectures are well matched for algorithms with a low communication to computation times ratio. However, when this ratio increases beyond a few percent, the efficiency decreases rapidly. This property reflects the power of a high-speed bus with broadcasting capability.

The above methodology can be used to study the degree of matching between an algorithm and a multiprocessor architecture. This methodology is based on extracting performance features for a class of algorithms and an architecture from an approximate analytical model. The features define a multidimensional space. A performance index is then a mapping from the feature space on the real line. Given the architecture, algorithms pertaining to the class defined by the hypothesis of the model can be partially ordered according to the value of the performance index. This ordering allows us to locate regions in the feature space where the architecture is well matched to algorithms in the class.

The difficulty of this approach is in striking a proper balance between the simplicity and tractability of the analytical model and its accuracy. As modeling

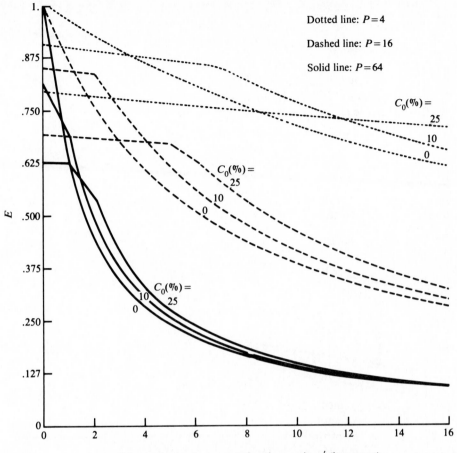

Dotted line: $P=4$

Dashed line: $P=16$

Solid line: $P=64$

$C_0(\%)=$

Communication to computation times ratio, t'_{cb}(in percent)

Figure 8.33 Efficiency versus feature t_{cb} for a loosely coupled system with a high speed. (Courtesy *IEEE Trans. Software Engg.*, Dubois and Briggs, July 1982.)

tools improve, the analytical model may be refined. Even if approximate, the feature space approach is much more realistic than complexity studies.

In Figure 8.34, cuts through the feature space are displayed. These cuts are two planes for each case. The index function E is represented by contours of equal index value. Loosely coupled systems are effective for processing-intensive computations (low values of feature t'_{Cb}). The regions with a high-efficiency factor shrink as the number of processes increases. Visualizing the feature space by cuts such as in Figure 8.34 is of great help in understanding the interaction between the architecture and the class of algorithms. Other architectures could be studied using the methodologies discussed.

The estimation of E is very important to the software designer for MIMD systems, since it is the proportionality factor between m_0 and m_1, the average iteration time (see Eq. 8.38 for example). As a result of the analysis, a given imple-

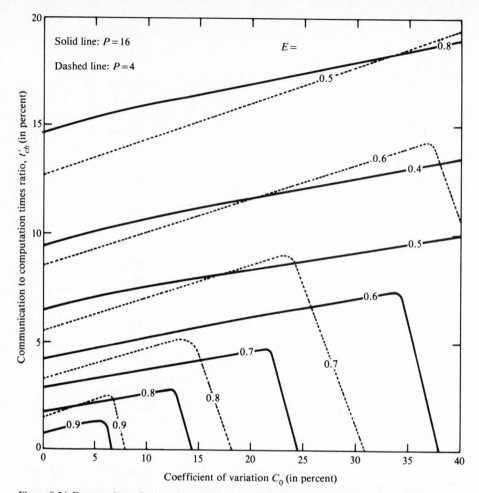

Figure 8.34 Feature planes for loosely coupled system with high-speed bus. (Courtesy of *IEEE Trans. Software Engg.*, Dubois and Briggs, July 1982.)

mentation may be revealed as inefficient for the architecture and may have to be restructured.

Effect of decomposition of performance Another interesting problem is to estimate the effect of the degree of decomposition of a given algorithm on the speedup in order to evaluate the optimum decomposition. For such a study, the assumptions on the computation to partition must be stronger. We use the equations derived in the previous section on the performance of synchronized algorithms.

We define a homogeneous computation as follows. Let SUM be a computation. SUM is seen as a random number of instruction cycles. If SUM can be partitioned into computation units with the same stochastic properties ("i.i.d units"), then it is said to be homogeneous with respect to the unit. Moreover, we assume a Gaussian distribution for the time taken by a computation unit for the same reasons as mentioned previously. This property is important so that the underlying processing-time distribution is preserved for all partitions of the computation. To obtain a decomposition of a homogeneous computation in i.i.d. tasks, we partition the computation into sets containing the same number of units. Each set defines a process. The number of such processes in the partition is the *degree of decomposition*, denoted by P since one processor is devoted to each process. The *maximum degree of decomposition* (PMAX) is obtained when each process contains only one computation unit.

A simple model for the mean and variance of the number of active cycles in a process of a homogeneous computation as a function of the decomposition is

$$m_0 = m_A + \frac{m_B}{P} \quad \text{and} \quad \sigma_0^2 = \sigma_A^2 + \frac{\sigma_B^2}{P} \tag{8.40}$$

m_A and σ_A^2 are the mean and variance of the fixed overhead independent of the decomposition, while m_B and σ_B^2 correspond to the mean and variance of the partitionable part of the computation.

As the degree of decomposition increases, the number of iterates to be computed by each process reduces proportionally (accounting for the second term in Eq. 8.40). The overhead term might include the initiation of a transfer through the high-speed bus. In most implementations, making a private copy of the iterate set will be required at the beginning of each iteration and should be accounted for in m_A and σ_A^2.

For the loosely coupled system, the block transfer time is modeled by

$$t_{Cb} = t_{Ab} + \frac{t_{Bb}}{P} \tag{8.41}$$

As in Eq. 8.35, the transfer time is deterministic and assumed identical for all the processes. The first term of Eq. 8.41 represents the transfer overhead (time between the reservation of the bus or memory module and the actual beginning of a transfer) plus the time taken possibly by the transfer of a fixed amount of information independent of the decomposition. Since the number of iterates computed by each process decreases proportionally to the decomposition, the transfer time decreases accordingly. Equation 8.41 means that the time to initiate a transfer t_{Ab} and the speed of the transfer are independent of the decomposition, an assumption not always verified for the bus system but nonetheless simple and realistic in most cases. The speedup, denoted by S_P, is defined as the ratio of the times taken by the algorithm on a uniprocessor and on a multiprocessor system when the degree of decomposition is P (with maximum PMAX). It is computed as follows for the case when $m_A \simeq \sigma_A^2 \simeq 0$.

For the loosely coupled architecture with a high-speed bus, we have

$$S_P \simeq \frac{P}{1 + \Delta_P} \tag{8.42}$$

with

$$\Delta_P = \underset{j=1,...,P}{\text{Max}} \left[0_{j:P} \cdot C_B \cdot \sqrt{P} + (P - j + 1) \cdot (P \cdot t'_{Ab} + t'_{Bb}) \right]$$

$$t'_{Ab} = \frac{t_{Ab}}{m_B}, \ t'_{Bb} = \frac{t_{Bb}}{m_B} \quad \text{and} \quad C_B = \frac{\sigma_B}{m_B}$$

Note that, contrary to the general study discussed earlier, the parameters are normalized in this section with respect to the total computation m_B.

The speedup curves are displayed in Figure 8.35. C_B (the coefficient of variation of the total computation) is shown to limit the optimum decomposition in most cases. Loosely coupled systems have a very good speedup when t'_{Bb} is small (0.1 percent) and $t'_A \simeq 0$. However, a nonnull constant term (Figure 8.36) in each

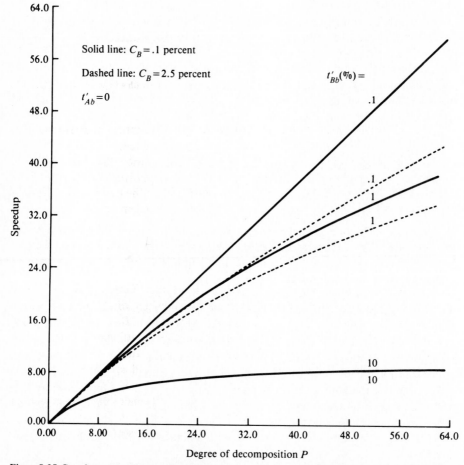

Figure 8.35 Speed-up versus decomposition for a loosely coupled system with a high-speed bus. (Courtesy of *IEEE Trans. Software Engg.*, Dubois and Briggs, July 1982.)

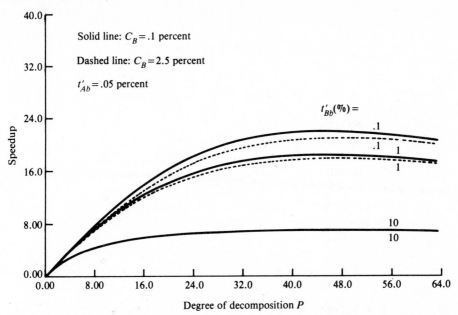

Solid line: $C_B = .1$ percent

Dashed line: $C_B = 2.5$ percent

$t'_{Ab} = .05$ percent

$t'_{Bb}(\%) =$

Figure 8.36 Speed-up versus decomposition for a loosely coupled system with a high-speed bus. (Courtesy of *IEEE Trans. Software Engg.*, Dubois and Briggs, July 1982.)

transfer causes the speedup to peak. In this latter case, the optimum decomposition is limited to a degree of 16 to 40 for the examples considered.

The speedup conceivably peaks out or saturates when the decomposition increases. This intuitive reasoning is confirmed quantitatively by the curves of Figure 8.34. These results can be used as a guideline by the compiler or the user for an effective decomposition of an MIMD iterative problem into tasks of similar statistical properties.

8.5 BIBLIOGRAPHIC NOTES AND PROBLEMS

Parallel algorithms for multiprocessors are analyzed in Kung (1976), including both synchronized and asynchronous algorithms. Other discussions including macropipelines can be found in Jones and Schwarz (1979). Baudet (1976) studied the performance of asynchronous parallel algorithms. Mathematical analysis of simple task graphs was developed in Robinson (1979). Iterative techniques for solving linear systems of equations are given in Conrad and Wallach (1977). Numerical methods are given in Dahlquist and Björch (1974). Performance of quicksort and PDE algorithms on Cm* is given in Deminet (1982). The performance of synchronized iterative algorithms was presented in Dubois and Briggs (1982a). Parallel tree search algorithms for multiprocessors can be found in Hwang and Yao (1977).

Some good sources of operating system design concepts are given in Coffman and Denning (1973), Habermann (1976), and Holt et al. (1978). A general overview of protection of information in computer systems was presented in Saltzer and Schroeder (1975). One of the earlier sources of information on protection mechanisms was given in Lampson (1974). A basic source of capability-based addressing schemes is in Fabry (1974). Application of capability-based addressing schemes to existing machines is presented in Lampson and Sturgis (1976) and Levy (1983). Another example of the implementation of protection schemes is in the Multics project Saltzer (1974). A complete overview of the deadlock problem is presented in Isloor and Marsland (1980). Some specific research in the solution to the deadlock problem are given in Coffman et al. (1971) and Holt (1972). Another comprehensive treatment of prevention, detection, and recovery of system deadlocks is given in Shoshani and Coffman (1970). An extension of such techniques to multiprocessor systems is given in Fontao (1971).

A general overview of process synchronization mechanisms is given in Madnick and Donovan (1974). The concepts of wakeup and block primitives are discussed in Habermann (1976). The wait and signal primitives are elaborated on in Stone (1980). The concept of pipes in the UNIX operating system can be found in Ritchie (1973). An application of synchronization primitives to the implementation of such pipes is given in Holt et al. (1978). An extension of the semaphore primitives developed by Dijkstra (1968) is presented in Agerwala (1977). The implementation of conditional critical regions and the construction of monitors are given in Schmid (1976). A general treatment of monitors is covered in Hoare (1974). Conditional critical regions were proposed by Hoare (1972) and Hansen (1972). Recently, concurrent programming was studied in Andrews and Schneider (1983).

A general overview of deterministic schedules is presented in Gonzalez (1977). Preemptive deterministic schedules have been researched in Muutz and Coffman (1969). Some nonpreemptive schedules are discussed in Coffman and Graham (1972) and Hu (1961). The multiprocessor anomalies are demonstrated in Graham (1972). The processor bounds are developed in Ramamoorthy et al. (1972) and Liu and Liu (1974). Probabilistic scheduling algorithms are presented in Coffman and Denning (1973). Load balancing in multiple processors is also studied in Ni and Hwang (1983). Traditional books on queueing theory such as Kleinrock (1975) are sources of information on probabilistic schedules. The group scheduling concept was discussed in Jones and Schwarz (1979).

Problems

8.1 Describe the following terminologies associated with multiprocessor operating systems and MIMD algorithms:

  (a) Mutual exclusion
  (b) The TEST-AND-SET instruction
  (c) The ENQUEUE and DEQUEUE operations
  (d) The **P** and **V** operators
  (e) Conditional critical sections
  (f) Deadlock prevention and avoidance
  (g) Deadlock detection and recovery

    (*h*) Protection versus security mechanisms
    (*i*) Deterministic versus stochastic scheduling
    (*j*) Multiprocessor anomalies
    (*k*) Synchronized versus asynchronous parallel algorithms
    (*l*) Degree of decomposition of a parallel algorithm

8.2 The following is a proposal to handle the "empty stack problem" of a stack that is used to structure a shared storage (or page) pool. GETSPACE is a procedure which returns a pointer to a free page. Before calling GETSPACE, a process should enter a critical section for stack inspection, for which purpose a global (shared variable) count STACKLENGTH records the current number of free pages. A process should not call GETSPACE until STACKLENGTH > 0. Similarly, there is a RELEASE (*i*) procedure, which releases page *i* to the page pool. Write two procedures: FREEPAGE—to get and return a pointer to a free page, and RETURN-PAGE (*i*)—to release page *i* using P and V primitives. (*Hint*: A binary semaphore mutex should be used to control access to the stack. Mutex is initialized to 1. Also use "STACKLENGTH" as a semaphore to control access to the variable STACKLENGTH for update).

8.3 Consider the following program:

$$\textbf{For } i = 1 \textbf{ to } n \textbf{ do}$$
$$\textbf{cobegin}$$
$$S_1[i]; S_2[i]; \ldots S[i];$$
$$\textbf{coend}$$

k processors are devoted to the above computation. Each computation $S_j[i]$, for $1 \le j \le k$ takes an unpredictable and random time to execute. Complete the program between the **begin** and **end** statements for process *j* using critical section (csect) on the shared variable, pcount, and P and V operations on the binary semaphores *s*. The primitives implement the synchronization of these *k* processors. *Hint*: The last processor to finish one iteration for one value of *i* updates pcount and "awakens" the other blocked processors through *s*.

    var pcount: **shared**; **initial** pcount = **k** − 1
    var s = {$s_1, \ldots, s$ } : **binary semaphore**; **initial** **s** = {1, 1, . . . , 1};
    {Process 1}:
        ⋮
    {Process j}:
      For ← 1 **to** *n* **do**
        begin
          . . .
          $\langle S_j(i) \rangle$
          . . .
        end
    {Process j + 1};
        ⋮

8.4 Assume that f_1 and f_2 are pointers to two sorted lists, each arranged as a circular doubly linked list with headnodes f_1 and f_2, respectively. f_1 and f_2 are sorted in ascending order and each node has three fields, namely, LLINK (left link), DATA, and RLINK (right link) (Figure 8.37). Write an asynchronous MIMD algorithm for two processes P_1 and P_2 to merge the files f_1 and f_2 into a sorted list f, also arranged as a circular list. Process P_1 retrieves from the fronts of f_1 and f_2 to produce a sorted sublist d_1, while P_2 retrieves from the rears of f_1 and f_2 to produce the sorted sublist d_2 until either f_1 or f_2 becomes empty. Attach the nonempty list to d_1 and d_2 to produce f. Return any unused node x to the storage pool with the operation POOL (*x*). Note that sublists d_1 and d_2 are initially empty.

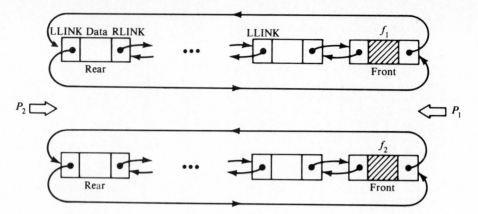

$P_2 \Rightarrow$ $\Leftarrow P_1$

For any node v,

If $v \neq f_1$ or f_2 and LLINK$(v) \neq f_1$ or f_2 then DATA(v) < DATA (LLINK(v))

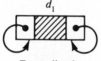

Empty list d_1

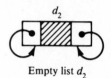

Empty list d_2

Figure 8.37 Parallel merging in Problem 8.4.

8.5 The following is a synchronized n-process MIMD algorithm to compute vector:

$$\mathbf{y} = \mathbf{A} \cdot \mathbf{x} + \mathbf{b}, \text{ where } \mathbf{y} \text{ is } n \times 1, \mathbf{A} \text{ is } n \times n, \mathbf{b} \text{ is } n \times 1$$

```
PROCESS:
{Parfor i ← until n − 1 do
    {y (i) ← 0;
      For j ← 0 until n − 1 do
         (i) ← y (i) + A (i, j) · x(j);
      y (i) ← y (i) + b (i);
    }
}
```

Assume that each assignment of the variable i in the **Parfor** statement takes c seconds. The time it takes to start or spawn a new process for a given i is a sum of independent random variables $\sum_{j=0}^{i} x_j - ic$ where x_j is exponentially distributed with mean time $1/(j + 1)\lambda$. What is the speedup S_n of the parallel process if multiplication and addition takes t_m and t_a seconds, respectively, on each processor and n concurrent processes are used? Also assume that $nc < 1/\lambda$. Then plot S_n versus n for values of $1/\lambda T =$ 0.1, 0.5, 0.8, 1, 2, 5, and 10.

8.6 Dijkstra's problem of dining philosophers (slightly generalized) is: There are n philosophers whose lives consist of alternately thinking and eating. The philosophers eat at a large circular table with a preassigned plate for each. Between two plates is a fork, which may be used by either adjacent philosopher. In order to eat, a philosopher must have two forks (one on his left and the other one on his right). Devise a control program of the general form: Note that the *n* philosophers may not necessarily follow the same control program to claim and release the forks.

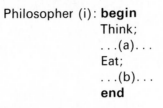

where (a) and (b) are code sections which claim and release the two forks, respectively. You should specify these two code sections such that the following properties are met:

(*a*) Use P-V for communication and synchronization.

(*b*) Allow a fork to be held by only one philosopher at a time.

(*c*) Use strictly local information, e.g., LEFT.FORK and RIGHT.FORK to indicate the two forks (resources) at both sides of each philosopher (process).

(*d*) Guarantee that no philosopher will starve, that is when the *n* processes enter a deadlock situation.

8.7 Solve the dining philosophers problem using (*a*) generalized *P* and *V*, (*b*) conditional critical regions.

8.8 Using *P-V* operations, write the synchronizing program for the task graph shown in Figure 8.38, where T_i' is the statement that controls the execution of task T_i. Solution should be of the following form:

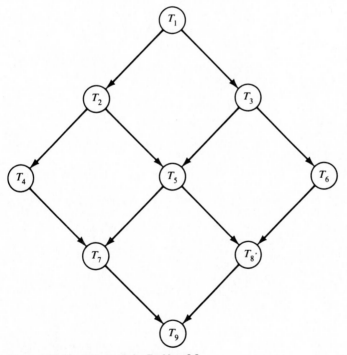

Figure 8.38 The task graph for Problem 8.8.

Define semaphore;
Initialization of semaphores;
cobegin
$T'_1:$
$T'_2:$
$\vdots$
$T'_7:$
$T'_8:$
$T'_9:$
coend

8.9 (a) Which combination of processes cause deadlock in the five process code segment programmed below? The processes are A, B, C, D, and E.

```
Begin
    shared record
        begin
            var S₁, S₂, S₃, S₄: semaphore;
            var blocked, unblocked: integer;
        end
    initial blocked = 0, unblocked = 1;
        initial S₁ = S₂ = S₃ = unblocked, S₄ = blocked;
    cobegin
        A: begin P(S₁); V(S₁); P(S₂); V(S₂) end;
        B: begin P(S₁), P(S₂); V(S₄); V(S₂); V(S₁) end;
        C: begin P(S₂); P(S₃); V(S₂); V(S₃) end
        D: begin P(S₄); P(S₂); P(S₁); V(S₁); V(S₂) end
        E: begin P(S₃); P(S₂); V(S₂); V(S₃) end
    coend
End
```

(b) Besides the combination of processes mentioned in your answer to part (a), which additional process(es) could be indefinitely blocked because of this deadlock?

(c) For the processes given, is deadlock inevitable, or does it depend on race conditions? Justify your answer.

(d) Assume that the skeletal code segment programmed above is an abbreviated version of a more complex program and that only the details of the semaphore-related code is shown here. Guarantee that all five processes in the real program complete by making a minor change to one of the skeletal processes.

8.10 Write a parallel algorithm to implement the concurrent Quicksort algorithm described on pages 625–626.

8.11 Show that the use of PE and VE could result in a deadlock or possibly starvation in a system of resources.

NINE

EXAMPLE MULTIPROCESSOR SYSTEMS

This chapter studies a number of existing multiprocessor systems. We begin with an introduction of the entire multiprocessor space. Two large multiprocessor projects are reviewed first. These are the early C.mmp system and the S-1 system currently under development. Then we study a number of commercially available multiprocessors, including some models in the IBM 370 series and the 3080 series, the Univac 1100 series, the Tandem Nonstop system, the HEP, and the Cray X-MP. A comprehensive literature guide on multiprocessors is given at the end of the chapter.

9.1 THE SPACE OF MULTIPROCESSOR SYSTEMS

Multiprocessor systems can be divided into two classes: the exploratory research computers and commercial multiprocessors. We consider a system to be exploratory if it is developed mainly for research purposes or for dedicated missions. Commercial multiprocessors are those systems that are available in the computer market. A summary of existing multiprocessors is given below. We leave the details of each system to subsequent sections. Some of the systems were studied in the previous two chapters.

9.1.1 Exploratory Systems

Three exploratory multiprocessors are covered in this book. The C.mmp and Cm* are both research multiprocessors developed at the Carnegie Mellon University. The C.mmp was developed in the early seventies. It consists of 16 PDP-11 mini-computers sharing a common memory via a 16 × 16 crossbar switch. We shall study the C.mmp architecture and its specially developed Hydra operating system in Section 9.2. The hierarchically structured Cm* has already been described in Chapter 7. The Cm* is still being used at CMU as a research vehicle. The C.mmp is no longer in operation now.

Another crossbar-structured multiprocessor is the S-1 system currently under development at the Lawrence Livermore National Laboratory. It is a 16-processor system. However, each uniprocessor in the S-1 is custom designed for a multiprocessing environment. The S-1, once completed, should be a gigaflops machine. We shall study its processor characteristics and software development in Section 9.3.

9.1.2 Commercial Multiprocessors

In Chapter 7, we have already studied several commercial multiprocessors, including the CDC Cyber-170, the Honeywell 60/66, and the DEC System 10. In Sections 9.4 and 9.5, we shall examine more large-scale multiprocessor systems, including the IBM System 370/168 and the IBM 3081 multiprocessors. In particular, we will focus on the details of the 370/168 MP and the 3081; both are dual-processor systems. In the Univac 1100 series, we shall study two multiprocessor systems: the model 1100/8x and the model 1100/9x systems, each of which has up to four processors.

Cray Research recently announced its multiprocessor model the Cray X-MP. This is a dual-processor system highly pipelined for both scalar and vector processing at high speed. Denelcor, Inc. developed the HEP computer, which can be configured to have up to 16 processors sharing multiple memories and peripherals via a packet switching network. We shall study HEP in Section 9.4. Most of the existing commercial multiprocessors operate essentially with multiple SISD operations at the highest program level; that is, single program multiprocessing and loosely coupled multiprogramming. The HEP is an *intrinsic* multiprocessor with real MIMD pipelined operations at the process level. To achieve fault-tolerant multiprocessing, we shall study the Tandem Nonstop multiple processor system. Multitasking techniques developed with the X-MP will be treated in Section 9.6.

In Table 9.1, we summarize the major architectural characteristics of those multiprocessor computers covered in this book. Speed improvement is only one of the concerns in using a multiprocessor computer. Enhanced reliability and availability and the promoting of resource sharing to achieve a high performance/cost ratio are also important factors in developing multiprocessors. The general trend for commercial machines is that high performance is achieved with multiple highly pipelined processors. The goal is to solve large user problems by multiple processors in a cooperative and effective manner. Most existing commercial systems have two to four processors. Only a few systems offer 16 processors like the Tandem and the HEP. Some research multiprocessors have more than 16 processors, like the Cm*, consisting of 50 LSI-11 processors in the system.

Table 9.1 Multiprocessor computer systems

Systems	Architectural features	Remarks
C.mmp	16 PDP-11s, Crossbar, Hydra OS	Section 9.2 (dismantled)
Cm*	50 LSI-11s, Hierarchical processor clusters, Medusa and Star OS	Section 7.1 (exploratory)
S-1	16 Mark IIA processors, Crossbar, Amber OS	Section 9.3 (under development)
IBM 370/168MP	Dual-processor systems, shared memory and separate I/O, Multiple Virtual Storage (MVS) OS	Sections 9.5.1 and 9.5.2
Univac 1100/8x, 1100/9x	Two- or four-processor systems, EXEC OS, shared memory and I/O	Section 9.5.3
Tandem /16	Up to 16 processors, dual-common buses, dual-ported controllers. Nonstop OS	Section 9.5.4
Cray X-MP	Dual processors with shared common memory and dedicated pipelines, COS	Section 9.6
Denelcor HEP	Up to 16 processors. Packet-switched network, MIMD pipelining	Section 9.4
IBM 3081, 3084	Two- or four-processor systems, shared memory and I/O devices, MVS and VM OS	Section 9.5.1
Cyber 170	Two processors with a central memory controller	Section 7.1.1
Honeywell 60/66	A three-processor system with triple redundancy	Section 7.1.1
PDP-10	Two-processor system with a master-slave or a symmetric configuration	Section 7.1.1

9.2 THE C.mmp MULTIPROCESSOR SYSTEM

This section reviews the architectural features of the C.mmp system and the kernel of its Hydra operating system. Reported performance of the C.mmp will be also examined in Section 9.2.3.

9.2.1 The C.mmp System Architecture

The C.mmp is composed of slightly modified Digital Equipment PDP-11/40E processors and built out of early 1970s technology. The average time to execute an instruction on a PDP-11/40 is approximately 2.5 μs. The architecture of the C.mmp is shown in Figure 9.1 for a given configuration that consists of 16 computer modules connected to 16 shared memory modules via a 16 × 16 crossbar switch (S.mp). The functional structure of a typical computer module in the C.mmp is shown in Figure 9.2. The shared memory provides a physical address space of 32 megabytes. The basic modifications made to the processors were to make user execution of certain privileged instructions illegal. Examples of these

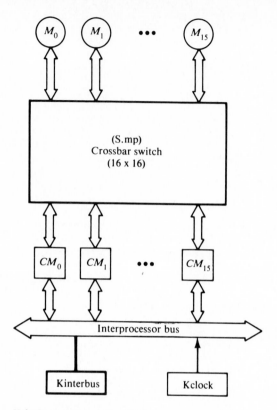

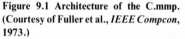

Kclock: common master clock

Kinterbus: interprocessor bus control

Figure 9.1 Architecture of the C.mmp. (Courtesy of Fuller et al., *IEEE Compcon*, 1973.)

instructions are HALT, RESET, WAIT, RTI (return from interrupt), and RTT (return from trap).

Further modifications were made to permit address-bounds checking on the stack pointer register R6. These modifications were required for software protection. The operating system is required to deposit some context information on the stack over protected procedure calls. RTI and RTT were modified since they modify the processor status, which must be protected because it is used to control the memory protection scheme. The PDP-11/40E processors were modified further to allow an extended writable control store.

Each processor has an 8K-byte local memory that is used primarily for operating system functions. The principal secondary memories of the C.mmp consist of four drives of 40M-byte disk controllers, three drives of 130M-byte disk controllers, and fixed head disks with zero latency controllers that are used for paging space. The peripheral devices are assigned to the Unibus of specific processors, as shown in Figure 9.2 for one processor. Hence there is no physical sharing of peripherals. A processor cannot initiate an I/O operation on a peripheral that

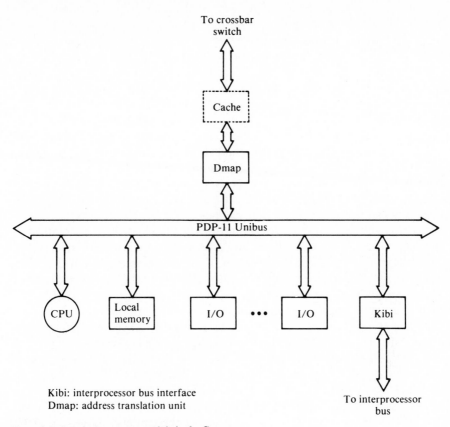

Figure 9.2 A typical computer module in the C.mmp.

is not on its Unibus. Fortunately, the operating system hides many of the asymmetries of the I/O subsystem from the user.

An interprocessor bus which connects the entire set of processors is used to perform the general function of interprocess communication. The bus provides a *common clock* (*Kclock*) as well as an *interprocessor control* (*Kinterbus*). These two logically and functionally separate features travel separate data paths, although they share a common control. Each processor has an *interbus interface* (*Kibi*) that defines the processor's bus address and makes available the bus functions to the software. The bus provides three basic functions, as described below.

The first function is to continuously broadcast a 60-bit 250-kHz nonrepeating clock (Kclock). This is done by multiplexing the clock value onto a 16-bit wide data path in four time periods, with low-order bits first. Any Kibi requesting a clock read waits for the initial time period and then buffers the four transmissions in four local holding registers available to the software. Clock values are often used for unique name generation in the operating system. The otherwise unused high-order four bits of the fourth local register are set to the processor number (bus address) to insure uniqueness when any number of Kibi's read the bus simultaneously. A countdown register is also maintained in each Kibi for interval timing. It may be initialized by a nonzero value in the program; a one is subtracted every 16 μs (timing supplied by the Kclock) and the process is interrupted when the register reaches zero.

The second and third bus functions are the interprocessor interrupts at three priority levels and the control mechanism. Each processor may interrupt, halt, continue or start any processor, including itself. These functions are used only when a drastic action such as systemwide reinitialization is necessary. The control operations are invoked by setting the bit(s) corresponding to the processor(s) to be controlled in a 16-bit register provided by the Kibi for the desired operation. A second 16-bit wide data path is eight-way time multiplexed. Each control operation is assigned a time period. As the appropriate period arrives, each Kibi ORs its control operation register onto the bus and clears the register.

Synchronization of bus accesses and operation specification are accomplished by the multiplexed time periods. The Kibi also inspects the bus to see if the specified operation is being invoked on its processor; if so, the action is performed. Setting the ith bit of the Kibi register to one associated with one of the functions will evoke that function on the ith processor. Thus, for example, moving a mask of all 1s into the halt register in each Kibi will stop the entire system. Although eight time periods are available, only six are used: three priority levels of interprocessor interrupt, halt, continue and start; the remaining two are ignored.

Probably the greatest limiting factor in building a large computing system from minicomputers is their small address space. In most cases, it is required to be able to address several million bytes of primary memory from the processors. The basic PDP-11 architecture is only capable of generating 16-bit addresses. Although the processor may generate only a 16-bit address, the Unibus supports an 18-bit address, and the shared memory uses a 25-bit address. An address relocation hardware *Dmap* associated with each processor performs the memory address translation. Its relationship with other bus components is shown in Figure 9.2. The processor-generated addresses are divided into eight pages, where each page is an 8K byte unit. Unibus addresses are divided into 32 pages, and the shared memory is divided into 4096 pages.

As shown in Figure 9.3, the two extra bits of the Unibus address are obtained from the program status register (PS) in the processor. These bits may not be altered by any user program. The user programs are actually bound to operate within the eight pages described by a subset of relocation registers. Such a subset is called a *space* and is named by the two bits $\langle 7:8 \rangle$ in the PS. With these two space bits, four address spaces can be specified as (0, 0), (0, 1), (1, 0) and (1, 1). Therefore, four sets of eight registers are provided in each relocation unit, although the stack page is common to all spaces to allow communication across spaces. One of these eight registers in a given address space can be selected by using the high-order three bits $\langle 13:15 \rangle$ of the 16-bit processor address word.

The four address spaces are the heart of the memory-protection mechanisms discussed later. The address-mapping registers and PS registers are both located

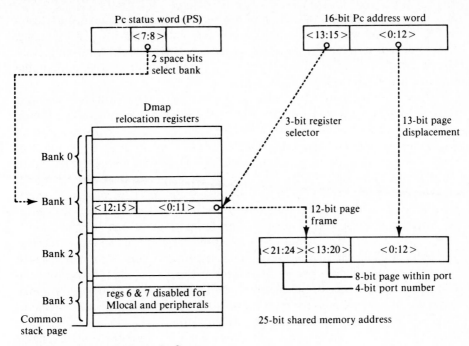

Figure 9.3 Address relocation in the C.mmp.

in the peripheral page, which is addressable via the (1, 1) space bits. The relocation registers in the space described by the (1, 1) space bits are the only ones that are directly addressable and are used exclusively by the kernel of the operating system. Hence, protecting the PS guarantees that no addressability changes may be made without the approval of the operating system. Direct addressability is accomplished by disabling two of the relocation registers in (1, 1) space, one each of Mlocal and the control register bank, for all peripheral devices (including Dmap). With these registers disabled, addresses pass along the unibus unchanged to be received by the addressed register or memory location.

Access to shared memory is performed in two stages: The *relocation* of the 18-bit processor-generated address into a 25-bit address space, and the *resolution* of contention in accessing that memory location. As illustrated in Figure 9.3, the Dmap intercepts the 18-bit unibus addresses (16-bit word plus the two space bits) and translates them as follows: the three high-order bits of the 16-bit word select a register from the bank specified by the space bits. The contents of the register provide a 12-bit page frame number; the remaining 13 bits from the address word are the displacement within that page. The two are concatenated to form the 25-bit mapping shared memory address. This transparency is performed for all memory accesses.

In addition to the 12 page frame bits, there are four bits in each relocation register used for control. They are designated as *no-page-loaded* (nonexistent memory), *write-protected* (read-only), *written-into* (dirty), and *cacheable* bits to control whether values from the page may be stored in a possible per-processor cache. The per-processor cache was planned but not implemented. The cacheable bit would have been used by the operating system to avoid cache consistency. This can be accomplished by indicating pages that are not both shared and writable. Shared and writable pages are never cached.

The shared memory address and (possibly) 16 bits of data, each parity checked, and two bits of access function data are sent to the cross-point switch. The address parity is checked at the switch interface. If the check fails, the request is aborted and the processor interrupted. Data parity is not checked until the data is read from memory. All parity is generated and data parity checked by the relocation unit (Dmap) interface to the bus from the switch.

The switch then routes the request to the memory port specified by the high-order four bits of the address. A port is requested by setting the processor's bit in an initial *request* register. Contention for the port is resolved by periodically gating the request register into a *queue* register, which is left-shifted as the port becomes available. The shifting creates a priority ordered queue: As a bit is shifted out, the corresponding processor is granted access to the port. Processor 15 is assigned the high-order bit; processor 0 the low-order bit, defining the priority. When the queue register is zero, all requests have been satisfied. The request register is again gated into the queue register, cleared, and a new cycle begins. A second request for the same port by a processor must enter via the request register, hence equality of service among the processors is maintained.

This two-level request mechanism also obscures the internal queue's priority ordering to the point that it is of virtually no importance outside the switch, preserving the symmetrical design of the cross-point. The switch's maximum concurrency (16 independent paths) is achieved if all processors request different ports. The cost of address translation, switch overhead (no contention), and round-trip cable overhead is about 1 μs. This is high by today's standards and is more than equal to the access time of the memory.

9.2.2 The Hydra Operating System

The operating system of the C.mmp was based on an experimental kernel called *Hydra*. The *kernel* is the "nucleus" of an operating system. However, we will use the term "kernel" synonymously with an operating system. Hydra was designed as a logically distributed system so that any processor can execute the kernel. Also, more than one processor can execute the kernel concurrently. This parallelism is enhanced by using locks on various data structures and not on the code that references them. There were two basic goals in the design of Hydra. One was to supply primitives that allow most of the facilities generally provided by an operating system to be written as user programs. This will permit the operating system to be effectively tailored to each user's needs. The other goal was to permit any number of user level definitions of a facility to coexist at the same time. These goals suggest that the kernel be designed as a collection of basic or *kernel mechanisms* of universal user applicability on the C.mmp.

In order to facilitate the design of the kernel mechanisms, the separation of mechanism and policy is required. This principle is called policy-mechanism separation. Such separation contributes to the flexibility of the system because it leaves the complex decisions to the user. Policies are generally encoded in user-level software which is external to, but communicates with, the kernel. Mechanisms are provided in the kernel to implement these policies. The kernel mechanisms are used to provide a protected image of the hardware operation. For example, a user is not permitted to manipulate I/O device control registers, as doing so may allow the user to inadvertently overwrite a protected portion of memory. Although the policy-mechanism separation philosophy is desirable, there are instances in which a kernel mechanism may actually be a parameterized policy. *Parameterized policy* provides the means by which overall long-term policies can be enforced by user-level software and simultaneously can avoid excessive domain-switching mechanisms for decisions which require a fast response. An example of such a policy will be given later.

The testing of Hydra is facilitated by providing language constructs which permit *abstractions* of data. Such abstractions define data types by specifying the storage structures used and a set of functions which operate on it. A property of data abstraction is that the details of representation and manipulation are hidden from the user. This technique is used in the design of the Hydra to enhance the protection mechanism by extending the type definition to specify the representation of virtual resources and the nature of the implementation of various operations on a particular type of resource. Examples of virtual resources are file, directory, semaphore, and page. One of the elegant features of Hydra is that it is an *object-oriented* system. All information is encapsulated in structures called objects which are accessed only through capabilities. Hence, Hydra has capability-based protection mechanisms to support the philosophy discussed.

The set of objects a process can access is its address space. Objects are of variable size and consist of a data part and a capability list (C list). The data part can be expressed as a tuple: representation and type. The *representation* component contains the information and the *type* of an object indicates the nature of the resource. The C list consists of a set of capabilities. The capability is represented by a tuple: unique-name and access rights. The *unique-name* of an object is generated using the 60-bit clock described previously. A process may only perform those operations on an object that are permitted by the *access rights* in the capability through which the process named the object.

The basic unit of a schedulable entity in Hydra is a process. An active process is not bound to a processor. Therefore, a process may migrate from one processor to another during its lifetime. The set of objects defined by the capabilities of a process at a given time defines the execution environment and, hence, the protection environment. This record of the execution environment of a process is called the *local name space* (LNS), an object type.

Another object type often used is the procedure. A *procedure* object contains a list of references to other objects which must be accessed during the execution of the procedure's code. A procedure is thus considered a static entity, There is a unique LNS for each invocation of the procedure. This LNS disappears after the procedure terminates.

Moreover, a procedure object may contain *templates* which characterize the actual parameters expected by the procedure. When the procedure is called, the slots in the LNS which correspond to parameter templates in the procedure object are filled with "normal" capabilities derived from the actual parameters supplied by the caller. This derivation is the heart of the protection-checking mechanism, and the template defines the checking to be performed. If the caller's rights are adequate, a capability is constructed in the new LNS. This LNS references the object passed by the caller and contains rights specified in the template.

System interrupts were provided in the C.mmp architecture to facilitate inter-processor communication. An analogous software mechanism is provided at the user level by the kernel. This mechanism, called *control interrupts*, is used for interprocess communication. When it occurs and is directed to a process, the receiver process transfers control asynchronously to a special address specified by the user. This address is within the addressing domain in which the process is executing at the time. A 16-bit mask is specified by the process that sends a control interrupt. These bits are compared with a mask in the receiver process, and the receiver process is interrupted only if there is a match between one or more bits. Hence adequate protection is maintained. Control interrupts are generally slow; however, they have some properties that make them desirable for error recovery.

The operating system provides an elegant message system for handling com-munications between processes and thus encourages the use of cooperating processes. The message system uses objects called ports as gateways for processes to send and receive messages between processes. Each port has a set of logical terminals called *channels* which are used to connect between sender and receiver processes. There are basically two types of channels: input and output. Messages are sent from output channels and received in input channels. Two processes can communicate if they each have a capability for the other's port and if a com-munication path is established between the ports.

To establish a path between the two ports, the output channel of one is connected to the input channel of the other and vice versa. Each port provides a message slot which is a buffer that is used to queue messages. This slot also provides a local mechanism to name messages. The message system can operate in two modes: nonacknowledgement and acknowledgement. In the first mode, the sender sends a message and continues processing without waiting for a reply. Operations in the second require a reply to a send message. A process that attempts to receive a message before its arrival is suspended until the arrival of the message, whereupon the process is unblocked. The message system is also used in I/O communication to provide transparency of the asymmetries of the I/O structure at the user level.

The message system is not very efficient, thus two other synchronization mechanisms, locks and semaphores, are provided. Two types of locks exist in the Hydra. The *kernel lock* makes use of hardware facilities such as interprocessor interrupts which are not available at the user level and therefore can be used only in the implementation of the Hydra. The *spin lock* is available to users as it does not use privileged instructions to implement it. The kernel locks, which are used primarily to provide mutual exclusion for operations on various system queues and tables, pervade the implementation of the kernel.

The kernel lock consists of three components: the lock byte, the sublock byte, and the processor mask word. The lock byte maintains a counter of the number of processes waiting for the lock. A process which wishes to obtain the lock indivisibly increments and tests the lock byte with a single PDP-11 instruction; if the result indicates that the lock is free, it is then locked and the locking process can execute its critical code. Otherwise, the process sets the bit corresponding to its processor in the processor mask word and executes a WAIT instruction with all interrupts except the highest priority IPI (interprocessor interrupt) disabled.

When a process is ready to unlock the lock, it indivisibly decrements and tests the count in the lock byte; if the result indicates that no other processes are waiting, the lock is unlocked and normal execution can continue. If other processes are waiting, the unlocking process sets the sublock byte to one and sends an IPI to every processor with a bit set in the processor mask. These processors resume after their WAIT instructions and indivisibly decrement and test the sublock byte. One random processor will discover the count to be zero, remove itself from the mask of waiting processors, and execute its process's critical code. The other processors go back to waiting.

One disadvantage of locks is that a process which waits during the execution of a kernel or spin lock does not relinquish the processor on which the process is executing. Kernel locks have another disadvantage which involves the overhead of invoking lock and unlock primitives. This overhead is minimized by storing the code for the kernel lock primitives in the processor's local memory. In this case, there is no memory contention and no contention for the lock. However, spin locks have one major disadvantage over kernel locks: When a processor is spinning, it accesses shared memory and thus consumes memory bandwidth which might have been used more constructively.

Generally, when the probability of waiting is low, the lock primitives are very efficient. A study performed on the C.mmp indicates that, although a process may spend over 60 percent of its time executing kernel code, only about 10 percent of accesses to locks cause locking. Moreover, the total fraction of time spent by processors waiting for locks is less than 1 percent. The study also shows that operations performed on data structures while they are locked are small. The overall average time spent in a critical section is about 300 μs.

Situations often arise in which lengthy blocking cannot be avoided in a system. In such cases, using the lock primitive will result in excessive waste of resources. For example, after a process issues an I/O request, a significant amount of time may elapse before its completion. In other cases, relatively large sections of code may require exclusive use of a data structure. In each case, when lengthy blocking is possible, Hydra provides two types of semaphore mechanisms, *kernel semaphore* (**K-Sem**) and *policy semaphore* (**P-Sem**). Both are implementations of the generalized or counting semaphores. The main difference between the semaphore and lock mechanisms is that, if a process blocks as a result of executing a **P** operation on a semaphore, some of the resources belonging to the blocked process will be relinquished until the process is able to resume execution. **K-Sems** are designed to be most efficient when no blocking occurs. Under these conditions, they are about as efficient as lock primitives. When blocking occurs, **K-Sems** are considerably more time consuming. Blocking requires the manipulation of the process queue and, in the case of a **P** operation, saving the state of the blocking process. If the average blocking period is large, the context-swap overhead of about 8 ms needed to block and wake up a process is significant. If the blocking period is less than the context-swap time, then the use of a **K-Sem** actually decreases overall system throughput as a result of processor thrashing.

When a suspended process is unblocked, it may have to wait until the resources it requires are released by higher priority processes which are competing for them. A policy of fairness among competing users is enforced by providing a more conservative form of semaphore mechanism. This **P-Sem** has an additional feature. After a predetermined wait time elapses, the primary memory belonging to the blocked process is made eligible for swap-out to a drum and the process is returned to its policy module for reconsideration of long- or medium-term scheduling. The short-term scheduler is called *kernel multiprogramming system* (KMPS). This is a mechanism which one or several policy modules may control via parameterization. Hence, KMPS is an example of a parameterized policy.

For fair multiplexing of all processors, the KMPS ensures the execution of the highest priority feasible process by using a preemptive priority resume policy. Processes within the same priority are scheduled in a round-robin fashion. The scheduling parameters of a process are its priority, a processor mask, and a maximum working set size. The priority is an integer value between 0 and 255, inclusive. The processor mask indicates the subset of processors on which the process can execute. The mask is required because of the earlier heterogeneity of the processors and the asymmetry of the I/O subsystem. The three parameters are set by the policy module. Under certain circumstances, the KMPS will return a process to its policy module. An example of this occurs if the KMPS blocks on a policy module's semaphore.

9.2.3 Performance of the C.mmp

Experience with the C.mmp shows that unavailability of the crossbar switch used did not pose a problem. Hard failures of the switch were rare, perhaps because of the regularity of its structure. The processors, memory modules, and the inter-processor bus were far less reliable by comparison. This demonstrates that the term "reliability" is relative. Although hard switch failures have been very rare, one observed type of transient error demonstrates some of the difficulties in successfully achieving logically distributed responsibility. When a process or device is accessing memory through the switch, the accessed module is unavailable to other processors or devices for the duration of the transaction.

A device controller experiencing an error may sometimes abort a transfer without correctly terminating the protocol between its unibus and the switch, with the result that the accessed memory module is "hung" with all its access paths blocked indefinitely. While the distributed nature of the switch allows access paths to other memories to function normally, any other processor trying to access the hung memory will also wait indefinitely. It is impossible to detect or to recover from this condition with software; only a manual reset can clear the memory and free the waiting processors. This problem uncovers a basic design flaw in the switch: its correct functioning depends on the correct functioning of its attached devices. The problem was minimized by modifications to the controllers. A better solution is for all switch transactions to "time-out" automatically after a predetermined period.

In any system, three basic steps are required to handle faults successfully: detection, diagnosis, and recovery. Fault detection is enhanced by system modularity and consistency checking. All techniques for consistency checking utilize some degree of redundancy in order to recognize inconsistencies. The self-identifying data structure employed for type checking within the Hydra kernel illustrates one set of types of redundancy. Many errors can be detected by associating watchdog timers with important system resources. This is a natural approach in a multiprocessor, where components can monitor each other relatively easily. Implementations of this technique differ, but the basic idea is that the timer will in some way raise an error-condition indicator if it is not reset within some specified time limit.

In the Hydra, a watchdog mechanism of this type has been implemented to detect processors that halt or become trapped in endless loops. The watchdog depends on a word in main memory that is shared by all processors. One bit in this word is assigned to each of the processors; if a processor is correctly executing Hydra, it should frequently execute code, causing it to set its designated bit. Every 4 s each processor also checks whether other processors have set their bits. Thus each processor must set its bit at least once every 4 s or it will be detected as malfunctioning and error recovery will be initiated. Diagnosis in the C.mmp/Hydra is carried out by a mechanism called the *suspect-monitor*, which is invoked whenever a serious error is detected. The processor that detects the error is designated the *suspect*, and the rest of the system is quiesced.

One processor is then chosen at random to act as the *monitor*. The monitor processor tests the suspect by stepping it through a simple diagnostic, following the suspect through each step in the diagnostic by watching a shared word of memory. Any failure in this sequence is grounds for removing the suspect processor from the configuration immediately. If the diagnostic completes successfully, the error is logged on disk and more extensive steps are taken to try to determine its cause. The exact tests depend on the nature of the error but include an extended processor diagnostic and attempts to retry memory fetches that caused parity failures.

Early versions of the suspect-monitor proved ineffective despite the extensive testing performed. This was due to transient errors which occur infrequently except under heavy loads. Thus, the suspect diagnostic rarely caught a processor in the act of failure, and yet another failure often occurred soon after the system was restarted. Such restarts are fast, typically taking less than 2 min; hence relatively high availability was maintained. However, the loss of user jobs represents an extreme inconvenience. The suspect-monitor system's capabilities was improved by providing a system of processor-error counters. These counters record the occurrence of particular errors on each processor, and if they exceed a threshold for total errors or for a particular error class, the offending processor is amputated or removed from the configuration or quiesced. The counters are also periodically right-shifted, causing them to decay over time so that they measure error frequency rather than simply providing an error count. A flaw in this scheme is that error counters are maintained for processors only. The processor that detects an error is charged with causing it, even if no concrete evidence to that effect exists; the error may actually have been caused by another processor, bad memory, or even by software. In practice, the high degree of symmetry among the processors makes it improbable that one processor will detect an error for which it is not responsible with a high enough frequency to exceed its error threshold.

It was found that parity errors are the single most common failure mode. While hard failures occur regularly, most parity failures are transient, suggesting that perhaps error counters should be implemented for memory pages as well as for processors. Although considerable emphasis was placed on error detection and diagnosis in the C.mmp/Hydra, the recovery mechanisms are insufficient to preserve integrity of smaller granules of computation.

To demonstrate the effect of memory contention in an execution environment of the C.mmp, an experiment is described below. This experiment consists of finding the root or zero of a function. The parallel algorithm used to solve this problem was described in Section 8.4.2. There are two implementations of the algorithm. In the first case, the code of the algorithm was stored in a single memory page which was shared by all processes. The second implementation of the algorithm provided separate pages of code for each process. Therefore, the first implementation will encounter more memory conflicts. The experiments were conducted on a C.mmp configuration consisting of Model 20 and 40 PDP-11s. The Model 20 is typically 50 to 60 percent slower than the Model 40. Figure 9.4 illustrates the effect of memory contention on the performance of the two implementations of the root-finder algorithm. Notice that, beyond a certain threshold, an increase in the number of processors will produce a negative effect on the performance for the implementation with shared code page.

This algorithm was also used to study the performance of the various synchronization primitives discussed above. Recall that the key feature of the parallel algorithm is that it is synchronous. The nature of the parallel solution demands the synchronization policy. Figure 9.5 shows the elapsed time required by the root-finder algorithm for varying numbers of slave processes and four different synchronization mechanisms. For these measurements, the function-evaluation time was distributed normally with a mean of 72 ms and a standard deviation of 18 ms. The parameter e refers to the wait-time constant for policy semaphores. The curve labeled PMO corresponds roughly to the case where $e = 0$. While

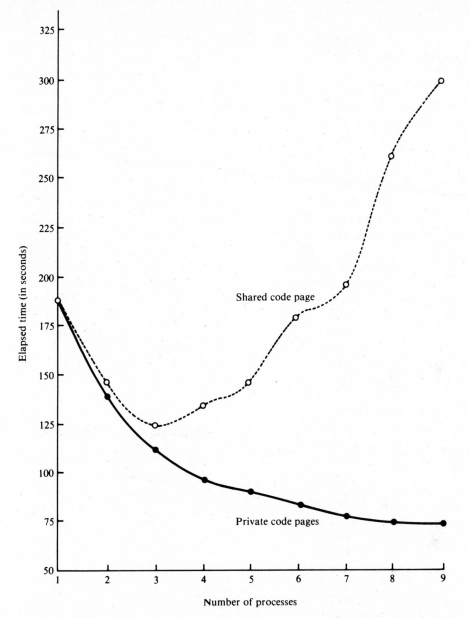

Figure 9.4 Performance degradation due to memory contentions. (Courtesy of Oleinick, Carnegie-Mellon University, 1978.)

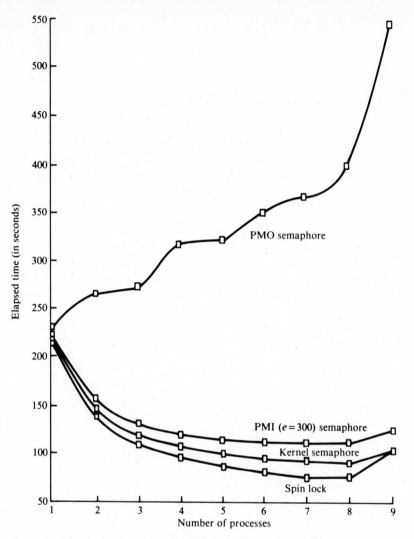

Figure 9.5 Effect on performance of different synchronization mechanisms. (Courtesy of Oleinick, Carnegie-Mellon University, 1978.)

many factors affect the performance of this algorithm, the damaging effect of an inappropriate synchronization mechanism is clearly demonstrated.

9.3 THE S-1 MULTIPROCESSOR SYSTEM

The system architecture of the S-1 multiprocessor system is presented below. The system is being developed under the auspices of the United States Navy. Described below are the basic organization and characteristics of the uniprocessor Mark IIA used in the S-1 construction. This processor is expected to have a performance level comparable to the Cray-1. The S-1 consists of 16 uniprocessors which share 16 memory banks via a crossbar switch. Each processor has a private cache. The software development to be presented includes the operating system for the S-1.

9.3.1 The S-1 System Architecture

The S-1 multiprocessor system is developed to perform computations at an unprecedented aggregate rate on a wide variety of scientific problems. It can be described as a high-speed general-purpose multiprocessor. The S-1 is implemented with the S-1 uniprocessors called Mark IIAs. For a large class of numerical problems, the Mark IIA is expected to achieve a computation rate roughly an order magnitude greater than that of the Cray-1 computer. Figure 9.6 shows the logical structure of a typical S-1 multiprocessor. This structure includes 16 independent Mark IIA uniprocessors which share 16 memory banks through a crossbar switch. Each memory bank can contain up to 2^{30} bytes of semiconductor memory and hence a total physical address space of 16 gigabytes (2^{34}).

Large memories are crucial for the efficient solution of many large problems such as those found in the three-dimensional physical simulations of the Monte Carlo intensive studies. These studies are of great current interest in applications ranging from incompressible fluid flow studies to acoustic ray tracing in highly stratified media. The large memory addressability of the S-1 essentially eliminates the programming cost associated with managing multiple types of computer system storage. Each processor-to-memory bank connection can transfer one word per 50 ns, resulting in a peak data-transfer rate of 320 M words/s.

The crossbar switch is designed to provide access for multiple memory requests. The service discipline for memory requests is such that no processor gets two accesses to a memory bank while another is attempting to access the same bank. The crossbar switch also handles interprocessor communications. The S-1 multiprocessor system has the capability of using dual crossbar switches for reliability and a front-end (diagnostic-maintenance) processor to remove a failing switch and substitute an alternate switch. Although the growth rate of such a "square" crossbar is asymptotically $O(N^2)$, where N is the number of processors or memory banks, the S-1 crossbar is estimated to cost somewhat less than a single S-1 uniprocessor. Less than 25 percent of the switch, or 0.8 percent of the total system cost, exhibits an $O(N^2)$ growth rate. The remainder of the system cost exhibits an $O(N)$ growth rate. This is valid if we assume that half of the total system cost is invested in the memory. This suggests that it is economically feasible to implement crossbar switches for multiprocessor systems with more than 16 processors. However, this suggestion cannot be drawn for a multiprocessor with low-cost processors, where the cost of the crossbar switch may dominate.

Each processor in the S-1 has a private cache which is transparent to the user. As discussed in Section 7.3, the association of a private cache with each processor introduces the problem of cache consistency. To solve the cache coherence problem, the S-1 multiprocessor includes a design closely related to the dynamic model discussed in Section 7.3. In the S-1, a small tag is associated with each line or block

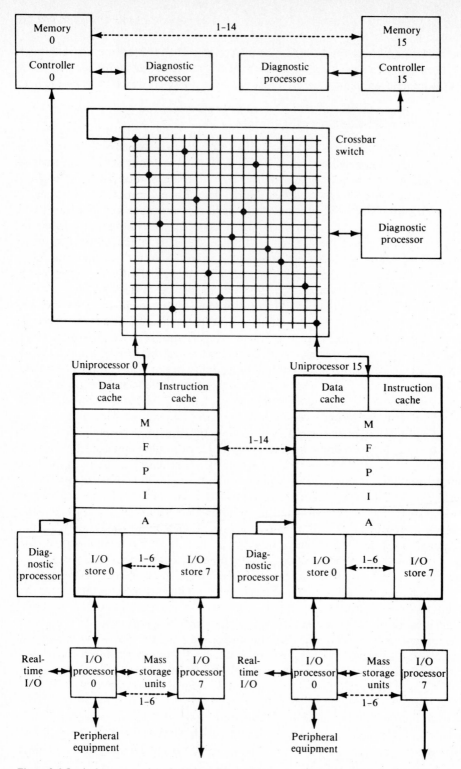

Figure 9.6 Logical structure of the S-1 Mark IIA multiprocessor. (Courtesy of S-1 project at Lawrence Livermore National Laboratory, 1979.)

(a set of 16 words) in the physical memory. This tag identifies the unique member uniprocessor (if any) which has been granted permission to retain (that is, own) the block with write access. It also identifies all processors which own the line with read access.

The memory controller allows multiple processors to own a line with read access. However, it responds with a special error flag when a request is received to grant read or write access for any block which is already owned with write access. The special flag is also set when a request is received to grant write access for any block which is already owned with read access. Any uniprocessor receiving such an access denial is responsible for requesting other uniprocessors to flush or purge the contested block from their private caches. It does this by using send and receive messages via the interprocessor-interrupt mechanism within the crossbar switch. The procedure outlined above thus dynamically maintains cache consistency.

The S-1 design provides a somewhat unconventional I/O subsystem which consists of many microcoded I/O channels. Each channel is managed by an I/O processor. The I/O subsystem also contains I/O buffers or memories which are accessible as part of the S-1 processor's address space. There is a 2K single-word buffer for each channel. These I/O memories are shared between an S-1 processor and an I/O processor. On output, data is placed into the I/O memory and then the I/O processor is signalled to transmit the data to the device. Input is handled similarly. These I/O memories are managed and assigned through the address-space management mechanism of the S-1 processor. Thus processes may perform I/O to devices if they have access to the I/O memory shared with that I/O processor. The S-1 architecture places little constraints on the I/O processor, which may be a commercially available minicomputer or specially designed hardware.

The I/O interconnection structure is designed to be simple and possess some degree of fault tolerance. Each I/O peripheral processor may be connected to input-output ports on at least two uniprocessors, so that the failure of a single uniprocessor does not isolate any input-output device from the multiprocessor system. This fault-tolerance approach is used extensively in the design of the S-1 to achieve high reliability and availability. For reliability, all single-bit errors that occur in memory transactions are automatically corrected, and all double-bit errors are detected regardless of whether the errors occur in the crossbar switch or in the memory system. The crossbar can be configured to keep a backup copy of every datum in memory so that the failure of any memory bank will not entail the loss of crucial data. System maintenance is facilitated by connecting a diagnostic computer to each uniprocessor, each crossbar switch, and each memory bank. This diagnostic computer can probe, report, and change the internal state of all modules that it monitors.

9.3.2 Multiprocessing Uniprocessors

The performance of each Mark IIA is achieved by extensive pipelining due to advances in microcode, hardware structure, and implementation technology.

Each uniprocessor has a virtual address space of 2^{29} thirty-six-bit words, uniformly addressable in quarterwords, halfwords, singlewords, and doublewords. The processor has 16 register sets for fast context switching and each register set has 32 general-purpose 36-bit registers. Two registers are used to maintain the processor and user status. The virtual address space is segmented to promote modular sharing and separate access for each user or task. Variable size segments are implemented and bounds checking is performed for reliability. The protection mechanism used in each processor is similar to the ring protection system in the Multics. Separate address spaces are allowed for each of the four rings which provide concentric levels of privilege. Gates at each level provide the necessary protection interface for procedure calls to the kernel.

Facilities are included to perform arithmetic and logical operations on various data types. The data types include boolean, integer, floating-point with a set of rounding modes, complex, vectors and matrices. The instruction set is optimized to contain features for compilers and for operating system efficiency as well as for arithmetic-intensive and real-time applications. In addition, special I/O instructions are provided to manipulate the contents of the I/O buffer. The interrupt architecture consists of vectored interrupts with vector locations which can be changed dynamically. Interrupts can be individually enabled or disabled and can be programmed in eight priority levels. The processor priority is also able to be reset. The uniprocessor has been designed to permit high-speed emulation of general instruction set architectures.

The uniprocessor is designed especially to facilitate pipelined parallelism in the fetching and decoding of instructions, the associated fetching of instruction operands, and the eventual execution of instructions. The preparation and execution of instructions that specify both scalar and vector operations are pipelined. Every instruction proceeds through multiple pipeline stages, including instruction preparation, operand preparation, and execution. Figure 9.7 depicts the internal logical structure of the S-1 Mark IIA uniprocessors. The processor consists of five major sections which are extremely fast, relatively special-purpose programmable controllers that operate in parallel to provide high performance.

Four sections that form the instruction pipeline are for instruction fetch (F sequencer), instruction decode (P sequencer), operand preparation (I sequencer), and arithmetic execution (A module). These sections are internally pipelined to achieve a maximum instruction-issue rate of one instruction per 50 ns, which is equivalent to a maximum data throughput rate of 720 million bytes/s. The maximum computation rate of the pipeline is 400 megaflops. The sequencers and the A module are heavily microcode controlled with a total of 2.5 million control store bits with a total microword width of 996 bits. A microcode is an architecture which defines very low-level program that precisely specifies the operation of every pipeline stage.

Figure 9.8 shows the instruction unit pipeline diagram to consist of 11 major segments. Some stages of the pipeline, particularly those dealing with operand-address arithmetic and instruction execution, necessarily have a wide variety of functions, since the pipeline must process a wide variety of instructions. This

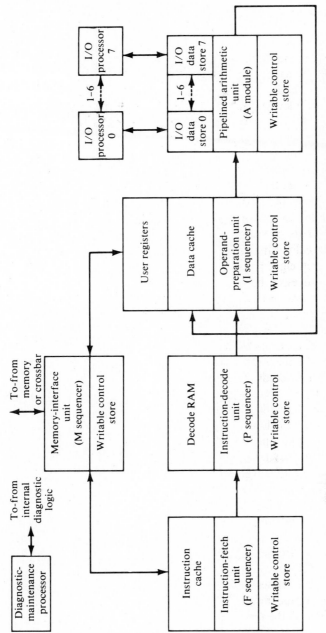

Figure 9.7 The internal logical structure of the S-1 Mark IIA uniprocessor. (Courtesy of S-1 project at Lawrence Livermore National Laboratory, 1979.)

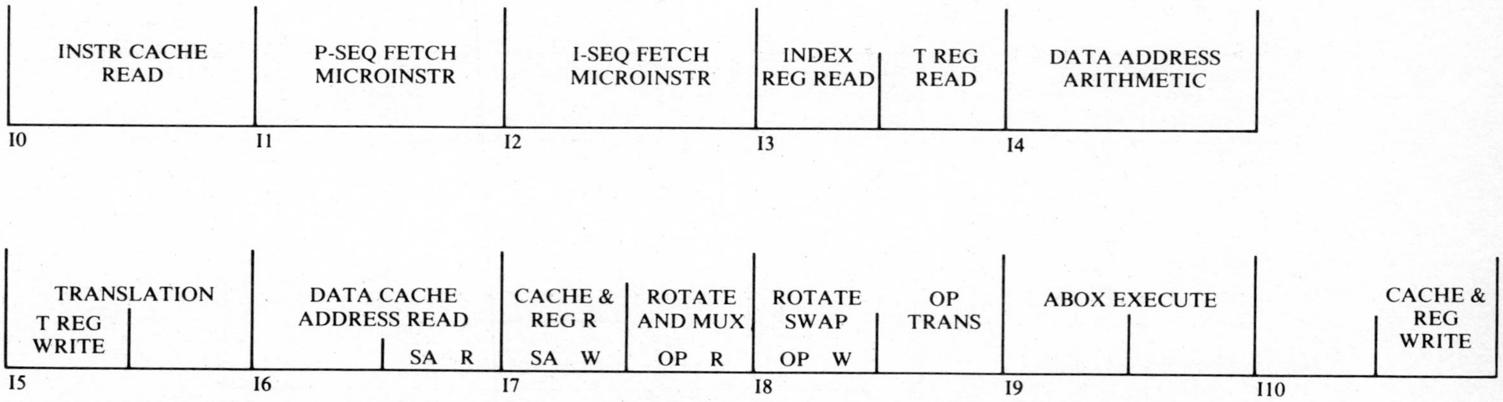

INSTR CACHE READ	P-SEQ FETCH MICROINSTR	I-SEQ FETCH MICROINSTR	INDEX REG READ	T REG READ	DATA ADDRESS ARITHMETIC
I0	I1	I2	I3	I4	

TRANSLATION T REG WRITE	DATA CACHE ADDRESS READ SA R	CACHE & REG R SA W	ROTATE AND MUX OP R	ROTATE SWAP OP W	OP TRANS	ABOX EXECUTE	CACHE & REG WRITE
I5	I6	I7	I8	I9			I10

Figure 9.8 Instruction unit pipeline diagram in S-1. (Courtesy of S-1 Project at Lawrence Livermore National Laboratory, 1979.)

variability in operation is effected through the extensive use of microcode. The variability built into the microcode-controlled pipeline also facilitates high performance emulation of other computers. The instruction sequence starts with an instruction cache read. The private cache associated with each processor is partitioned into instruction cache and data cache to achieve a high bandwidth. Each cache is organized as a four-way set-associative memory with 16 words per block. Both caches are vector-structured; that is, in the instruction cache, a cache read can retrieve three consecutive instruction words starting at any word boundary. In the data cache, reads can retrieve eight consecutive halfwords starting at any halfword boundary. The instruction and data caches have capacities of 16K bytes and 64K bytes, respectively. The cache replacement policy is the least recently used algorithm.

The M sequencer predecodes instructions when loading the instruction cache from memory on a cache miss. Predecoded information includes instructions of a length of one, two or three words, branch offset and branch prediction. The predecoding of instructions allows branches which are relative to the program counter (PC) to be computed in one cycle within 8K bytes of the PC. Branch instructions are predicted to allow the pipeline processing to continue. The success or failure of previous predictions are used to make better predictions. This is facilitated by recording the prediction for each location in the instruction cache with a single bit. For the first execution, an initial prediction is used based on the instruction type. A prediction failure causes an opposite prediction to be tried on the next execution. This technique has been found to correctly predict about 98 percent of all instructions for a typical compilation.

The P sequencer is used to calculate constants and register operands. Each P sequencer instruction calls an I sequencer subroutine. The I sequencer subsequently calculates all operand types and complex branch addresses. An operand queue (not shown) exists between the I sequencer and the pipelined arithmetic A module to buffer up to 16 operands of 1 to 16 bytes each. This buffering smooths out the flow of operands between the I sequencer and the A module. Also, the write queue (not shown) is placed between the A module and the data cache or register to keep track of pending writes from the A module. This queue also detects attempts by the A module to use data-cache locations which have been scheduled to be written by other units (such as other processors). The A module, which runs at twice the rate of other segments, performs the execution part of instruction processing.

The address-translation mechanism ingeniously maps a 31-bit virtual address into a 34-bit physical address, providing both segmentation and paging. It provides four different virtual address spaces, one per ring, which may overlap. A page is 4096 quarterwords long. Because a single address space may contain as many as 2^{19} pages, it is evident that the page mapping tables may themselves be paged. The address translation mechanism has four different steps. Instead of a giant page table of 2^{19} entries, it uses many little page tables each of 16 entries long. Hence, not every page table needs to be in memory at once. The 16 pages pointed to by one page table make up a *segmentito*.

A giant table called a *descriptor segment* contains a pointer to each of the (at most) 2^{15} page tables for each of the four virtual address spaces. Hence, there are at most 2^{17} page tables. If the descriptor segment were placed in memory permanently, an address reference would require two translations: one to find the proper page table and another to find the proper page. However, the descriptor segment itself is composed of pages which are grouped into segmentitos, so that an address reference would first require two translations. The first finds the appropriate point in the descriptor segment, and then two more translations find the target address. Figure 9.9 traces the entire address translation process.

A register called the *descriptor segment pointer* holds the 34-bit physical address of the first word of the *descriptor segmentito table* (DST). Because the descriptor segment points to (at most) four sets of 2^{15} segmentitos and each pointer requires eight quarterwords, the descriptor segment never exceeds 2^{20} quarterwords. That translates into a maximum of 16 segmentitos, which implies that there are at most 16 entries (called *segmentito table entries*) in the DST. The two-bit number of the ring being accessed together with the least two bits of the virtual address select an entry from the 16 in the DST. In turn, that entry points to the physical address of the first word of a *descriptor page table* (DPT), which has an entry (called a *page table entry*) for each of the 16 pages comprising that segmentito. Bits $\langle 28:25 \rangle$ of the virtual address select one entry from the 16 in that particular DPT, which points to one page of the descriptor segment itself. The descriptor segment contains pointers to segmentitos that make up the four virtual address spaces. The address translation process can be followed through to obtain the physical address.

It should be noted that the entire mapping structure provided need not be used. A segmentito or page table entry may be full either because the corresponding segmentito or page is absent from memory or because the virtual address space in question is smaller than the maximum allowable size. The address translation process outlined above will be inefficient if every address translation goes through many indirect references. This is alleviated by providing *map cache units* (lookaside buffers) which hold the most recent translations.

In addition, each map contains an 11-bit address-space identification field which allows translations for multiple users to coexist in the map caches. The instruction address translation unit is one-way set-associative with 1024 entries. Two copies are provided to translate addresses of the beginning and end of multiple-word instructions to avoid faulting within an instruction. The operand address translation unit is four-way set-associative with 1024 entries. Two copies are also provided to translate addresses of the beginning and end of multiple-word operands in an instruction. This scheme also avoids faulting within an instruction cycle.

The expected performance of Mark IIA uniprocessors is compared with the CDC 7600 and the Cray-1 on several important benchmark miniprograms in Table 9.2. Notice that the Mark IIA computes these benchmarks at roughly the same speed as the Cray-1 and almost twice the speed of the CDC 7600. The Cray-1 has a performance of two to four times greater than the CDC 7600. The S-1 results assume the use of 36-bit floating-point numbers. However, neither the CDC 7600

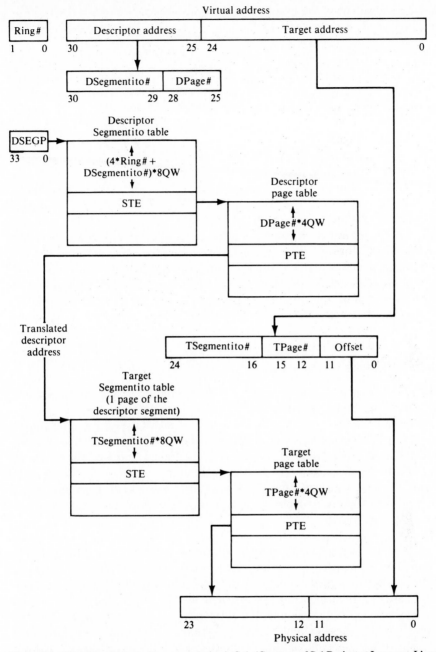

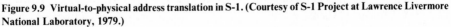

Figure 9.9 Virtual-to-physical address translation in S-1. (Courtesy of S-1 Project at Lawrence Livermore National Laboratory, 1979.)

Table 9.2 Comparison of the expected performances of the S-1 Mark IIA Uniprocessor, the Cray-1, and the CDC 7600.

		Computation rate, megaflops				
		S-1 Mark IIA		Cray-1		
Miniprogram	Miniprogram function	Scalar	Vector	Scalar	Vector	CDC 7600
1	Hydro excerpt	9.1	59	9.3	71	5.3
2	Unrolled inner product	11	74	8.8	47	6.6
3	Inner product	8.0	65	4.4	62	4.6
5	Tridiagonal elimination	7.5	7.5	7.6	7.6	4.0
7	Equation-of-state excerpt	13	46	12.6	80	7.3

nor the Cray-1 provides a low-precision floating-point format. The Cray-1 has only a 64-bit word format. For signal or real-time processing applications, the Mark IIA is expected to perform about four times better than the Cray-1. The S-1 Mark IIA uniprocessor is built out of ECL 100K medium-scale integrated circuits in performance-critical areas and ECL 10K circuits elsewhere. However, the S-1 is still not realized and the expected performance being reported may be rather optimistic.

9.3.3 S-1 Software Development

The major software areas addressed for the S-1 multiprocessor system are the programming language support, single-user and multiuser operating systems. the advanced operating system, and the system design facility. Basic languages supported by S-1 include Pascal, Fortran, C, Ada, New Implementation of LISP (NIL), and FASM—the Mark IIA assembler. The Pascal compiler was enhanced with improved type definition, module definition, exception handling, and additional control constructs. The C language will be based on the Unix implementation and can be easily transported to the single-user, multiuser and advanced operating system.

The *single-user operating system* (OS-0) is a simple stand-alone system which runs a single task at a time and provides only basic I/O functions. The OS-0 was operational on the Mark I processor and used in the hardware system design tool. The OS-0 is also designed to support the testing of processors and provide a minimal base for other operating systems. The *multiuser operating system* (OS-1) to be developed will be based on the Unix operating system because it is a small, relatively powerful system and has demonstrated a suitability for transport. Moreover, it is well known to a large community and has a large body of software available from the user community.

The advanced operating system for the S-1 is the full-functionality *Amber*. The Amber supports a mix of applications which include real-time systems (e.g., signal processing), interactive use (e.g., program development), computation-intensive problems (e.g., physical simulation), and secure environments for data. It also supports full use of the S-1 architectural features by providing multiprocessor support, the management of large, segmented address space, and exploitation of reliability features. The Amber O/S combines functions of the file system and virtual memory. The file directory structure is hierarchical and tree structured. Files are represented as segments. Segmentation facilitates dynamic linking. A demand-paging policy is used to copy pages directly between disk records and main memory. Page replacement works globally on all of main memory and uses the approximate least-recently-used algorithm for eviction of pages. The LRU is not always optimal for some applications such as real-time applications. In such cases, other placement and replacement algorithms are used.

The Amber O/S supports multitasking by the division of problems into co-operating tasks. It also provides low- and high-level scheduling features. The low-level features provide simple mechanisms for real-time applications. Examples are priority scheduling with round-robin queues, dedicated processor assignments, and interrupt processing. The high-level scheduler may implement complex features such as resource allocation and load balancing on multiprocessor configurations. Interprocess communication techniques such as message channels are provided. Other synchronization techniques supported are software interrupts and event notifications. Time-outs on event waits are also implemented. The Amber also possesses features to enhance availability and maintainability. Time-outs on all waits and suspension of processes are performed to prevent deadlock situations. Monitor tasks run concurrently with user and system tasks to detect hardware malfunctions.

9.4 THE HEP MULTIPROCESSOR SYSTEM

The Heterogenous Element Processor (HEP) is a large-scale scientific multi-processor system which can execute a number of sequential (SISD) or parallel (MIMD) programs simultaneously. The system contains up to 16 process execution modules (PEM) and up to 128 data memory modules (DMM). The PEMs or DMMs are connected with the I/O and control subsystem via a high-speed switching network. The PEM is the computational element of the HEP. In this section, we describe the architecture of the HEP, the organization of the PEM, and extensions made to the programming language to facilitate parallel processing on the HEP.

9.4.1 The HEP System Architecture

The HEP is the first commercially available MIMD multiprocessor system. An example configuration of the HEP with 28 switching nodes is shown in Figure 9.10. This configuration consists of four PEMs, four DMMs, a mass-storage subsystem, an I/O control processor, and node connections to four other devices. We shall describe the mass-storage subsystem and the switch network in this

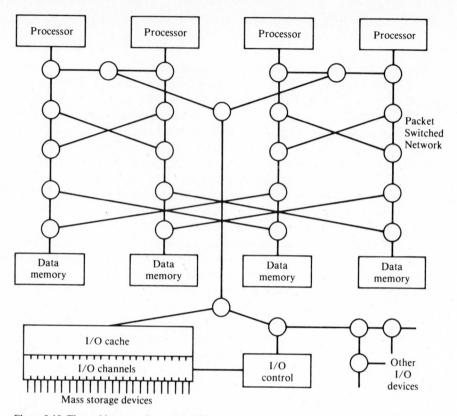

Figure 9.10 The architecture of a typical HEP system with four processors. (Courtesy of Denelcor, Inc., 1982.)

section. All instructions and data words in the HEP are 64 bits wide, although data references within the PEM can access halfword, quarterword, and bytes.

The mass-storage subsystem The mass-storage subsystem consists of three major components. A large MOS buffer memory provides an I/O cache function to mask the seek and rotational delays of disks. Disk storage modules provide storage increments of 600 megabytes. I/O channels couple the disk storage modules to the I/O cache and are controlled by the I/O control processor. Figure 9.11 illustrates the components of the mass-storage subsystem. The cache memory, which is eight-way interleaved with a 400-ns cycle time, may be expanded from the initial 8 megabytes to 128 megabytes in increments of 8 megabytes. Cache accesses are only in full words; at peak rate, a word can be accessed every 50 ns. The system can handle up to 32 I/O channels, with each channel supporting a transfer rate of up to 2.5 megabytes/s. Therefore, the cache memory can accommodate all channels simultaneously, thus yielding a potential transfer rate of 80 megabytes/s.

Figure 9.12 identifies the relationship of the various elements in the mass-storage subsystem (MSS). In this figure, a PDP 11/44 is used as an I/O and control

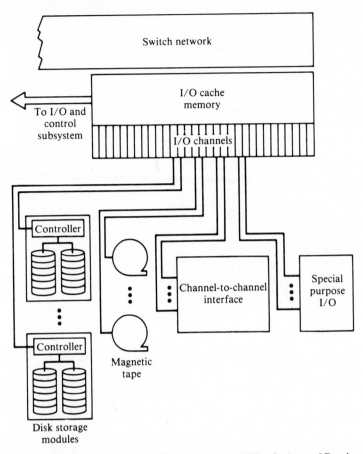

Figure 9.11 The mass storage system (MSS) in the HEP. (Courtesy of Denelcor, Inc., 1982.)

processor (IOCP) to control the communication between the disk controllers and their interfaces to cache memory. This control is accomplished via an IOP command bus. In particular, the IOCP is used by the HEP system software as the scheduler for all I/O activities on the MSS. The IOCP also has direct access to cache memory control for data transmission via an allocated channel. This permits the IOCP to have direct access to data in the cache memory. Each disk storage module consists of two disk drives. One of the first two drives is dual ported in order to permit a direct connection from the drive to a disk controller in the PDP 11/44. This allows initial program load drive-0.

Each of the IOPs (1 through 31) consists of an IOCP bus interface, an I/O controller and a cache interface. The IOP bus interface has access to the PDP 11/44 unibus via the IOP command bus and an IOP controller interface. This extends the PDP 11/44 addressing capability to the IOP bus interface. All the I/O channels are converted to an IOP *snapshot* device in the cache memory control. This device scans the status of all 32 channels and can service a request to transfer

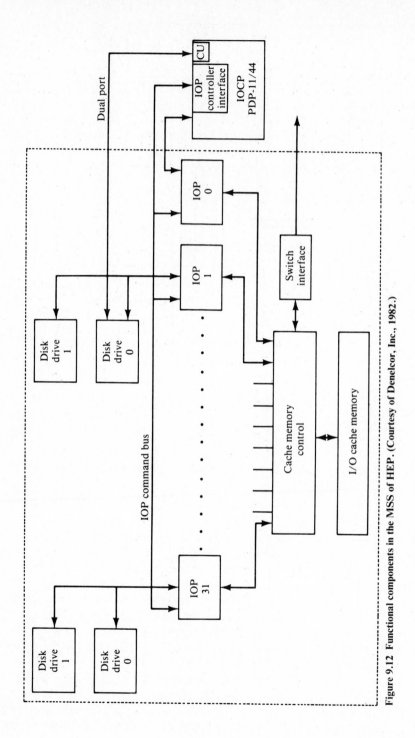

Figure 9.12 Functional components in the MSS of HEP. (Courtesy of Denelcor, Inc., 1982.)

a word for a channel every 100 ns. Cache memory request messages are received from the switch network through the switch interface. This interface is coupled to a switch node and can service a memory request from the switch every 100 ns.

The packet switching network The HEP switch is a synchronous, pipelined, packet-switched network consisting of an arbitrary number of nodes. Each node, which consists of three full duplex ports, is connected to its neighbors. These neighbors may be PEMs, DMMs, subsystems, or other nodes. Figure 9.13 depicts the HEP switching node. Each node receives three message packets on each of its three ports every 100 ns and attempts to route the messages in such a way that

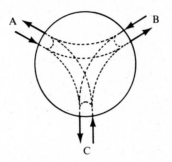

(*a*) Bidirectional three-ported switch node

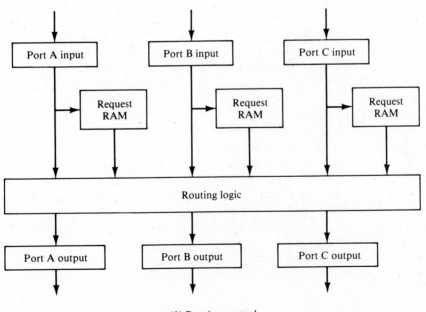

(*b*) Routing control

Figure 9.13 Switching node in the HEP's interconnection network. (Courtesy of Denelcor, Inc., 1982.)

the distance from each message to its addressed destination is reduced. This is accomplished by incorporating within each node three routing tables (one per port), which are loaded when the system is configured. Thus, each switch node is programmed to know the best output port routing to the final destination. Such programmed routing techniques allow for alternate routing to bypass a faulty component. In practice, the actual routing is determined by the best routing path and by priority in the case of conflicts. The priority is implemented by the use of age counters which increment with each nonoptimal routing.

A unique feature of the switching network is that the switch nodes do not enqueue packets. These packets are routed by the switch nodes every 50 ns regardless of port contention. The modularity of the switching network permits field expandability. The increased memory access times that result from the greater physical distances between the PEMs and the DMMs can be compensated for in two ways. Each PEM contains a local memory large enough to buffer most of the program codes. Since each switch node is pipelined, each processor can execute a large number of instruction streams concurrently.

9.4.2 Process Execution Modules

The PEM is designed to execute multiple independent instruction streams on multiple data streams simultaneously. This is accomplished by pipelining each PEM with multiple functional units. Before presenting the organization of the PEM, we illustrate how the concurrency in execution of the MIMD streams is implemented. In the first case, consider a single instruction (SISD) stream which is being executed by a conventional (SISD) processor, as shown in Figure 9.14a. Very little overlap in execution can be achieved. Even with instruction-lookahead capability, the dependency constraints resulting from conditional branch instructions limited the concurrency significantly. So also are the SIMD processors in Figure 9.14b. These are vector-oriented computations. Because of the occurrence of conditional branch instructions, the performance may be degraded. The machine may have to wait for the total completion of the instruction before proceeding. That is, the conditional branches could not make use of the replicated hardware.

However, by providing multiple independent instruction streams executing multiple data streams in a pipelined execution environment, maximum parallelism can be achieved. For the example shown in Figure 9.14c, while an ADD is in progress for one process, a multiply may be executing for another, a divide for a third and a branch for a fourth. Because the multiple instructions executed concurrently by an MIMD machine are independent of each other, the execution of one instruction does not influence the execution of other instructions and full parallelism in processing may be achieved. Note, however, that a single process does not achieve any speedup in such a scheme as was accomplished in the IBM 360/91 system.

Each PEM consists of its own program memory and an instruction processing unit (IPU), as shown in Figure 9.15. The program memory in each PEM has a capacity ranging from 1 to 8 megabytes. Instructions of active processes which are

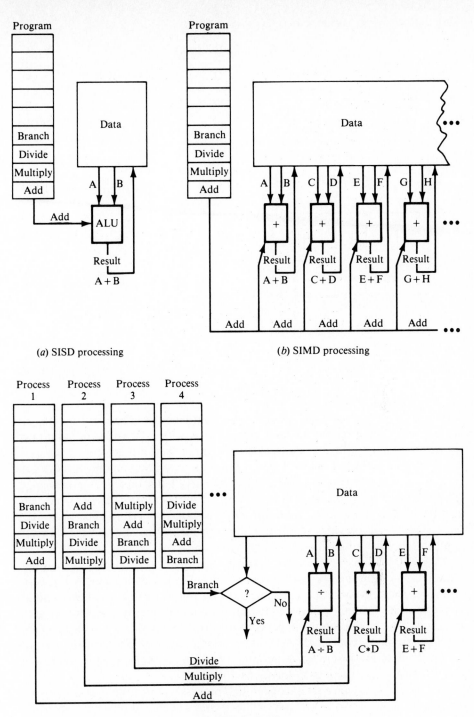

(a) SISD processing

(b) SIMD processing

(c) MIMD processing

Figure 9.14 Achieving maximal parallelism with replicated hardware in the HEP. (Courtesy of Denelcor, Inc., 1982.)

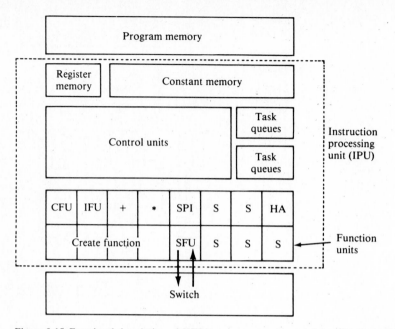

Figure 9.15 Functional description of HEP's process execution module. (Courtesy of Denelcor, Inc., 1982.)

allocated to a PEM are buffered in the program memory. These instructions are fetched from the program memory every 100 ns with concurrent decoding and execution of previously fetched instructions, as depicted in Figure 9.16. Up to 50 instructions may be in various stages of execution operating on one or more data streams simultaneously. However, the instruction fetch unit does not seem to permit simultaneity in instruction fetches and decodes. Also, there is only one instruction fetch unit in the PEM. For these reasons, the performance of the HEP processor may be limited to one instruction cycle per 100 ns. This may subsequently limit the effective utilization of the functional units.

The IPU in each PEM includes 2048 interchangeable general-purpose registers, as well as constant memory and function units. The constant memory is used to store user program constants and is read-only by user programs. The 4096 locations in the constant memory eliminate the need for data memory accesses for program constants. The function units implement the HEP instruction set, which includes extensions used to coordinate MIMD processing. In addition, the IPU has provisions for four expansion function units. These units may be used for custom or special-purpose instructions at the user's option.

In the HEP system, a set of cooperating processes constitute a *task*. Tasks and processes can be of two types: user or supervisor. The execution environment of a task is its *task domain*, which is defined by a 64-bit *task status word* (TSW). The TSW provides protection and relocation information for each task by a specification partition of the program, constant, register and data memories into areas.

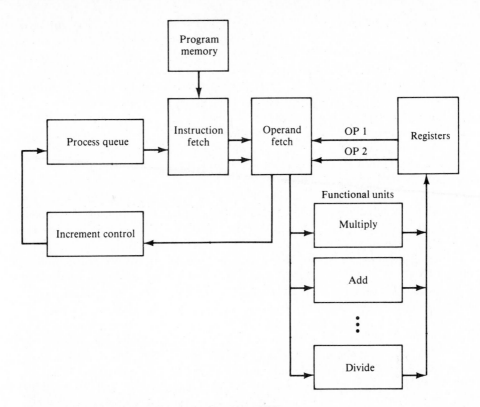

Figure 9.16 Instruction execution and data flow in the HEP.

This information is encoded as the program base, program limit, data base, data limit, constant base, register base, and register limit. All virtual addressing to operands is relative to the base addresses in the memory area in which they are stored. A *task status register* is used to hold the TSW for each task domain. A 16-entry task queue, where each entry contains a unique TSW, is used to implement a simple first-in first-out discipline in deciding which ready-to-run task to schedule. The task queue is equally divided for user and supervisor tasks.

In addition to the TSW, there is a *process status word* (PSW), which contains a 20-bit program counter and other state information for a HEP process. Each PSW points to an instruction that is ready for execution. There is a *process tag* (PT) in the task queue for each PSW that points to an instruction that is ready for execution. When a task is first initiated, it has only one PSW; that is, one process. The software creates additional PSWs as new processes are created to initiate parallel processing within a task. There is a PSW queue which can hold a total of 128 PSWs: 64 for user processes and 64 for supervisor processes.

These PSWs in the process queue circulate in a control loop which includes an incrementer and a pipeline delay. The delay is such that a particular PSW cannot circulate around the control loop any faster than data can circulate around the data loop consisting of general-purpose registers and the function units. As the program counter in a circulating PSW increments to point to successive instructions in program memory, the function units are able to complete each instruction in time to allow the next instruction for that PSW to be influenced by its effects. The control and data loops are pipelined in eight 100-ns segments, so that as long as at least eight PSWs are in the control loop, the processor executes 10 MIPS. However, a particular process cannot execute faster than 1.25 MIPS, and will execute at a lesser rate if more than eight PSWs are in the control loop.

The instruction issuing operation maintains a fair allocation of resources between tasks first and between processes within a task second. The main schedule contains 16 task queues, each containing up to 64 PTs. A secondary queue called the snapshot queue records the head PT in each task queue each time the snapshot queue becomes empty. PTs arriving one at a time from the snapshot queue cause the issuing of an instruction from the corresponding process into the execution pipeline.

A control unit cooperates with the function units to execute instructions in the IPU. The control unit selects an instruction for execution from one of the task queues, fetches the instruction, addresses the operands, and passes the instruction operation code and the operands to one of the function units to perform the specified operation. There are two types of function units: *synchronous* and *asynchronous*. The synchronous function units are pipelined with eight linear segments and a segment time of 100 ns. Thus, instructions are completed in 800 ns. Examples of synchronous function units are the floating-point adder (+), the multiplier function (*), the integer function unit (IFU), the create function unit (CFU), the hardware access (HA) unit, and the system performance instrument (SPI).

The CFU performs all operations affecting the PSWs. This includes activating and terminating processes, incrementing the program counter in a PSW that has had an instruction executed, and executing branch and supervisor call instructions. The HA executes all instructions to read or write program memory and performs bit encode and decode operations. The SPI collects data for performance measurement and monitoring counters and tracks the number of instructions executed by tasks. This allows billing the user for the amount of work done regardless of the time required because of overheads.

Asynchronous function units do not necessarily complete their operations within 800 ns. Examples of such function units are the divider (÷) and the scheduler (SFU). The divide function unit consists of up to eight individual divider modules which asynchronously execute 64-bit floating-point divide instructions. Divide instructions are initiated at a rate of one every 100 ns until all divider modules are busy. Each module can execute a divide instruction every 1700 ns. This is the only function unit in the IPU that is not pipelined. The SFU is both synchronous and asynchronous, and executes all instructions involving data transfers between register memory and data memory. Transfers that pass through the switch are executed asynchronously; all others are executed synchronously. The SFU can accept a new instruction every 100 ns.

When a data-transfer instruction is executed, the SFU sends a switch message packet containing a 32-bit data memory address, a return address identifying both processor and process, and 64 bits of data if a store instruction was executed. The SFU also removes the process that executed the instruction from the control loop and does not reinsert it until a response packet is received from the switch. When that response packet arrives, the SFU writes the data portion of the response in the appropriate register if a load instruction was executed. In order to perform these functions, the SFU is equipped with a queue similar to the queue in the control loop of the processor proper, and a process migrates freely between these two queues as it initiates and completes data-memory reference instructions. An important consequence is that while processes are in the SFU queue they are not present in the control loop queue and thus do not consume the valuable computational cycles while memory operation references are in progress.

The waiting period experienced by a process which encountered a conflicting access to memory or a busy resource does not cause the IPU to remain idle. In fact, the IPU switches context every 100-ns cycle. The rapid context switching is facilitated by its hardware implementation. Recall that the IPU has a program status register and 40 general-purpose registers for each user process. These register sets eliminate the need to save and restore program context when switching between users. Thus, the IPU multiplexes the execution of instructions from up to 128 instruction streams. This is done because the initiation of an instruction execution must often wait for the results from the instruction immediately preceding it. The IPU uses this waiting time to initiate instructions from other active instruction streams. From 8 to 12 processes are usually sufficient for the IPU to use all instruction cycles and thus achieve the 10 MIPS execution rate.

Protection mechanism Protection of one user process from another is accomplished in HEP by various techniques. Nonprivileged processes in separate task domains are prohibited from reading and writing the other's general-purpose registers and data memory by hardware address checking. All addresses are bounds-checked against values in the TSW and access denied or permitted accordingly. Nonprivileged processes are also prohibited from directly initiating I/O and from modifying program memory, constant memory, the task and process queues. A user process cannot change the environments of other user processes unless there is controlled cooperation and their task domains overlap.

Synchronization mechanism Cooperating processes synchronize by means of accesses to shared data. In HEP, this facility is provided by associating an access state with each register memory and data memory location. In data memory, the access states are **full** and **empty**; a load instruction can be made to wait until the addressed location is **full** and indivisibly (i.e., without allowing an intervening reference to the location) set the location **empty**. Similarly, a store instruction can wait for **empty** and then set **full** at any location in data memory. In register memory, an instruction can require that both sources be **full** and the destination **empty**, and then set both sources **empty** and the destination **full**. To ensure the indivisibility of this kind of operation, the third access state **reserved** is implemented in the registers. The destination register is set **reserved** when the source data is sent to the function units, and only when the function unit stores the result is the destination set **full**. No instruction can successfully execute if any of the registers it uses is **reserved**.

A process failing to execute an instruction because of an improper register access state is merely reinserted in the queue with an unincremented program counter so that it will reattempt the instruction on its next turn for execution. A program executing a load or store instruction that fails because of an improper data-memory access state is reinserted in the SFU queue and generates a new switch message on its next attempt.

9.4.3 Parallel Processing on the HEP

Extensions were made to Fortran 77 in HEP to provide language support for parallel processing. A special data type called the *asynchronous variable* was introduced to enable synchronization between cooperating and competing processes. The asynchronous variable type uses the access-state capability of the HEP hardware to support the correct interaction between processes. An asynchronous variable is identified with a $ before the variable name. Such a variable may be written into only when its location is **empty** and may only be fetched when it is **full**. Either operation on an asynchronous variable that does not meet these requirements waits under hardware control until the proper access state is set by a parallel process.

The access state of each asynchronous variable is initially set **empty** or **full** by the program. The HEP Fortran 77 provides two statements and five specially designed intrinsic functions for manipulating and testing access states.

Single statements

> A = $Q   //Wait for full, read and set empty//
> $Q = A   //Wait for empty, write and set full//

Intrinsic functions

> A = VALUE($Q)   //Access the value, regardless of state//
> A = SETE($Q)   //Read regardless of state and set empty//

A = WAITF($Q)   //Wait for full, but do not set empty//
L = FULL($Q)   //Test for full access state and return logical result//
L = EMPTY($Q)   //Test for empty access state and return logical result//

A PURGE statement is used to unconditionally set the access state to **empty**.

Another class of extensions were made to Fortran 77 to allow parallel process creation (similar to FORK) and termination (JOIN). The first statement, called CREATE, is syntactically similar to a Fortran CALL, but it causes the created subroutine to run in parallel with its creator. Another statement, called RESUME, is syntactically like a RETURN from a subroutine. However, it causes the caller of a subroutine to resume execution in parallel with the subroutine. If a subroutine was CREATEd, a RESUME has no effect. On the other hand, a RETURN causes the termination of the process if it was CREATEd or if it previously executed a RESUME.

HEP Fortran generates fully reentrant code and dynamically allocates registers and local variables in data memory as required by the program. Hence, it is easy to create several processes which simultaneously execute identical programs on different data. This can be accomplished by placing a CREATE statement in a loop so that several parallel processes will execute identical programs on different local data. An example of the implementation of parallel operations in the HEP is given below.

Example 9.1

```
        PURGE $IP, $NP
        $NP = NPROCS
        DO 10 I = 2, NPROCS
        $IP = I - 1
        CREATE S($IP,$NP)
           10 CONTINUE
            $IP = NPROCS
            CALL S($IP,$NP)
C       WAIT FOR ALL PROCESSES TO FINISH
        20 N = $NP
           $NP = N
           :
           :
           IF (N .NE. 0) GO TO 20
           SUBROUTINE S($ IP, $NP)
           MYNUM = $IP
           :
           :
           $NP = $NP - 1
           RETURN
           END
           :
```

In this example, the program creates NPROCS-1 processes all executing subroutine S, and then itself executes the subroutine S by calling it, with the result that NPROCS processes are ultimately executing S. The parameter $IP is used here to identify each process uniquely. Since parameter addresses rather than values are passed, $IP is asynchronous and is filled by the creating program and emptied within S. This prevents the creating program from changing the value of $IP until S has made a copy of it. The asynchronous variable $NP is used to record the number of processes executing S. When S is finished, $NP is decremented, and when the creating program discovers that $NP has reached zero, all NPROCS processes have completed execution of S (excepting possibly the RETURN statement).

The following example considers converting a serial code into a parallel program in order to speed up the execution on the HEP.

```
           DIMENSION A(270), B(270), C(270), D(270)
           ⋮
           N = 270
           E = 0.0
           DO 100 I = 1, N
           A(I) = A(I)**SIN(B(I))
           IF (SIN(A(I)).GT.COS(C(I))) GO TO 10
           A(I) = A(I) + C(I)
           GO TO 20
    10     A(I) = A(I) - D(I)
    20     E = E + A(I)**2
    100    CONTINUE
           ⋮
```

(*a*) Serial code.

```
           COMMON A(270), B(270), C(270), D(270), $E
           ⋮
           L = 270
           N = 20
           PURGE $E, $IN, $IW
           $E = 0.0
           $IN = 1
           $IW = 0
           DO 100 I = 1, N
           CREATE DOALL ($IN, $IW, L)
    100    CONTINUE
    200    IF (VALUE ($IW).L.T.L) GO TO 200
           ⋮
           SUBROUTINE DOALL ($IN, $IW, L)
           COMMON A(270), B(270), C(270), D(270), $E
    1      I = $IN
           $IN = I + 1
           IF (I.GT.L) GO TO 30
           A(I) = A(I)**SIN(B(I))
           IF (SIN(A(I)).GT.COS(C(I))) GO TO 10
           A(I) = A(I) + C(I)
           GO TO 20
    10     A(I) = A(I) - D(I)
    20     $E = $E + A(I)**2
           $IW = $IW + 1
           GO TO 1
    30     RETURN
```

(*b*) Parallel version.

Figure 9.17 Algorithm restructuring example in using HEP for parallel processing.

Example 9.2 The serial code shown in Figure 9.17*a* manipulates the linear array *A* with 270 elements and accumulates the square of the components of A in a variable E. The asynchronous variables $E, $IN and $IW are introduced in the parallel version of the program shown in Figure 9.17*b* $E is used to mutually exclusively accumulate the square of A(*i*)'s when they are updated. The parallel version creates 20 processes so that the granularity is significant enough to have nontrivial processes. $IN is used to control accesses to unique components of A and $IN is used to terminate the parallelism when all components of A have been updated and $E computed.

Another common technique allows processes to schedule themselves. In the simplest case, a number of totally independent computational steps are to be performed that significantly exceeds the number of processes available; moreover, the execution time of the steps may be widely varying. Self-scheduling allows each process to acquire the next computational step dynamically when it finishes the previous one.

Example 9.3 The following example has a subroutine T which is to be executed 400 times. All iterations are assumed to be independent; i.e., none of the iterations uses the output of any of the others. Four processes are initiated to do the processing. The variable $START is used to keep track of the iteration count and to assure that only 400 iterations are started. $DONE is used to assure that all 400 iterations have completed before the main program continues. Statement 5 in the main program will cause the main program to nonbusy wait (i.e., consume no "CPU" cycles) for the 400th iteration to complete and $ALLDONE to be set full by statement 99:

```
        PURGE $START, $DONE, $ALLDONE
        $START = 0
        $DONE = 0
        CREATE T ($START, $DONE, $ALLDONE)
        CREATE T ($START, $DONE, $ALLDONE)
        CREATE T ($START, $DONE, $ALLDONE)
        CALL T ($START, $DONE, $ALLDONE)
    5   DUMMY = $ALLDONE
        :
        END
        SUBROUTINE T ($START, $DONE, $ALLDONE)
   10   1 = 1 + 1
        IF (I.G.E.400) GO TO 99
        :
        $DONE = $DONE + 1
        GO TO 10
   99   IF (VALUE ($DONE).EQ.400) $ALLDONE = 1
        RETURN
        END
```

Self-scheduling is an excellent technique for programs which have steps with widely varying execution times because it balances the work load among available processes. There are many other techniques which have been used to exploit the HEP's parallel architecture.

There are many applications of the HEP machine. It has been suggested to handle the traditional multiprogramming of SISD programs. The application for which HEP was originally designed was the solution of large-scale systems of differential equations, such as those describing flight dynamics problems. Another problem for which the HEP is suitable is the partial differential equations describing continuous meshes. An application area for which the HEP would have a tremendous potential is in the simulation of a discrete event system or process-driven simulation. However, the application areas for HEP are not limited to the above. The architecture is quite flexible for a wide variety of applications.

9.5 MAINFRAME MULTIPROCESSOR SYSTEMS

This section describes some commerical multiprocessor mainframe systems. The systems to be described do not achieve their performance by decomposing a user SISD algorithm into MIMD processes. Instead, the multiprocessor operating systems achieve concurrency through explicit parallelism. The system performance is achieved by mostly concurrent execution of independent and noninteracting user processes. Most commercial multiprocessors offer fairly loose coupling. Of course, the degree of coupling varies from system to system.

9.5.1 IBM 370/168MP, 3033, and 3081

The architecture of the IBM System/370 is extended from the IBM System/360. A series of models were developed in the System/370. Different models in the System/370 represent different performance levels. Most models of the System/370 are SISD machines with a uniprocessor. Multiprocessing is only an added-on feature of the series for the top of line in performance. In 1966, the IBM S/360 Model 67 was introduced as a dual-processor time-sharing system. The S/360 Model 65 MP is a dual-processor version of the standard Model 65. In 1974, the IBM S/370 Models 158 MP and 168 MP were introduced as dual-processor systems with shared real and virtual shortage. In 1976, IBM introduced the S/370 Models 158 AP and 168 AP as asymmetric multiprocessors. The code MP stands for *multiprocessing* and AP for *attached processing*. In this section, we describe the architectural evolution of the IBM 370/168 for both MP and AP. Processor and operating system features for various 370/168 multiprocessor configurations are then reviewed with emphasis on their capabilities. We will also compare the 370/168 MP with the enhanced IBM 3033 and 3081 multiprocessor systems.

A uniprocessor IBM 370/168 configuration is shown in Figure 9.18. The main memory is divided into four logical storage units (LSU), which form a four-way interleaved memory system. The memory access and conflict resolution is con-

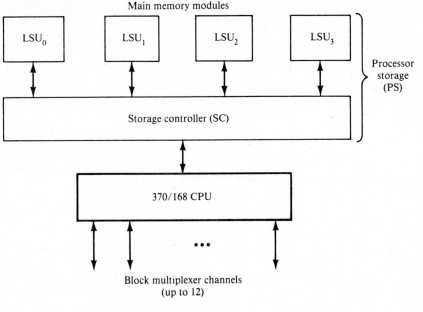

Main memory modules

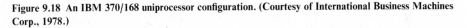

LSU: logical storage unit

Figure 9.18 An IBM 370/168 uniprocessor configuration. (Courtesy of International Business Machines Corp., 1978.)

trolled by the storage controller. There is only one central processing unit (CPU) which contains the pipelined instruction decode and execution units together with a fast cache. Multiple I/O channels can be connected to the CPU. Each channel is a specialized I/O processor with a simple I/O instruction set and operates asynchronously with the CPU. An AP configuration for the IBM 370/168 is illustrated in Figure 9.19. It is extended from the uniprocessor configuration by attaching an attached processing unit (APU).

The APU is almost identical to the standard 370/168 CPU except no I/O channels can be attached to it. Both the CPU and APU have their own caches. The cache coherence problem is resolved by using the cache invalidate (CI) lines between the CPU and APU. The interprocessor communication (IPC) lines are used for exchanging information or interrupt signals directed between the two processors. The structure is considered asymmetric because the APU is devoted exclusively to computation and the CPU handles both internal computation and I/O communications. The multisystem control unit (MCU) performs the interconnection switching functions between the processors and the shared memory modules.

An MP configuration of the IBM 370/168 is shown in Figure 9.20. Instead of attaching an APU, another CPU is used to form a symmetric dual-processor system. This MP configuration is composed of two 370/168 uniprocessor systems with shared memories. The two CPUs have equal capabilities. Two sets of I/O

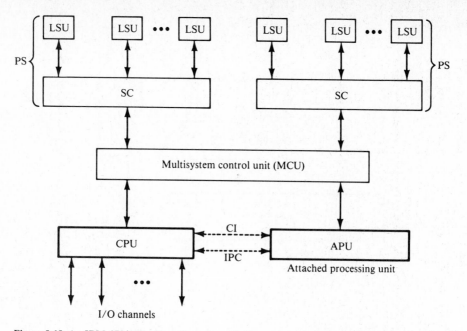

Figure 9.19 An IBM 370/168 AP configuration. (Courtesy of International Business Machines Corp., 1978.)

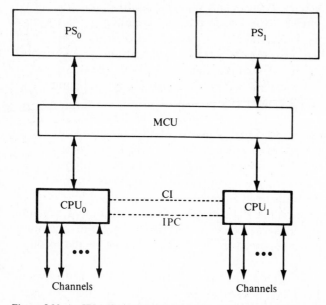

Figure 9.20 An IBM 370/168 MP configuration. (Courtesy of International Business Machines Corp., 1978.)

channels attached to each CPU are mutually exclusive and cannot communicate with each other directly. The MCU provides the necessary interconnection hardware between the two CPUs and shared memories. It also contains a configuration control panel for the purpose of manual systems reconfiguration.

In the IBM 370/158 MP configuration, two processors share from 1 to 8 million bytes of main storage. Each processor has a separate 8K-byte cache with 230-ns access time of 8 bytes. The two processors in the 370/168 MP share from 2 to 16 million bytes of main storage. Each CPU has either an 8K-byte or 16K-byte cache with a reduced 80-ns access time of 8 bytes. The model 158 has 10 block multiplexor channels, while the model 168 can have up to 22 block multiplexor channels. The block multiplexor channels permit concurrent processing of multiple channel programs for various speed peripheral devices, as was illustrated in Section 2.5. The Model 168 is enhanced from the Model 158 mainly in the area of memory and I/O subsystems. Their CPUs essentially have the same capabilities.

The 370/168 MP configuration is considered loosely coupled because two separate copies of operating systems are running in the two CPUs. An IBM 370/168 uniprocessor system can also be reconfigured to a tightly coupled multiprocessing system of dual CPUs with shared memories and shared I/O devices, as shown in Figure 9.21. The two CPUs are tightly coupled by a single copy of the operating system in the shared memory. A tightly coupled CPU pair can also be loosely coupled with another uniprocessor CPU to form a mixture multiprocessor system, as demonstrated in Figure 9.22. This is really a tightly coupled multiprocessor in a loosely coupled configuration. The tightly coupled dual CPU and the uniprocessor share some direct-access devices, such as disk, and some tape units. A channel-to-channel adaptor can be used to link the two CPU modules. Each CPU module still has some private channels connecting to some private I/O and secondary devices, like the 3330 disk storage subsystems.

The IBM 3033 system The 3033 multiprocessor complex consists of two 3033 Model M processors, two 3036 consoles, and the 3038 multiprocessor communications unit (MCU). Figure 9.23 shows a conceptual relationship between the MCU and processor functions. The 3033 attached processor complex consists of a 3033 Model A processor, the 3042 attached processor, two 3036 consoles, and the 3038 MCU.

The MCU for the multiprocessor-attached processor models provides prefixing, interprocessor communication, cache (high-speed buffer) and storage update communication, sharing of processor storage, configuration-partitioning control, synchronization facilities, and communication of changes to the storage protection keys.

The MCU also enables both processors in an MP configuration to access all of processor storage while retaining the overlap capability in storage operations permitted by eight-way interleaving. This means that both processors can have concurrent storage operations in progress with a varying degree of overlap depending upon the particular sequence of LSU accesses. The configuration and partitioning control in an MP system provides a variety of storage configuration options

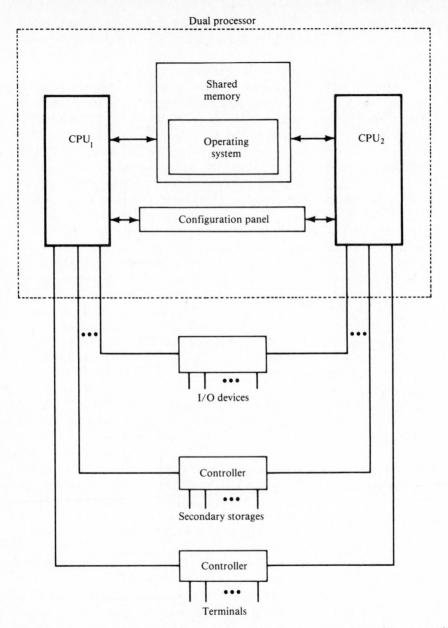

Figure 9.21 A tightly coupled IBM dual processor system with a single copy of operating system residing in the shared memory.

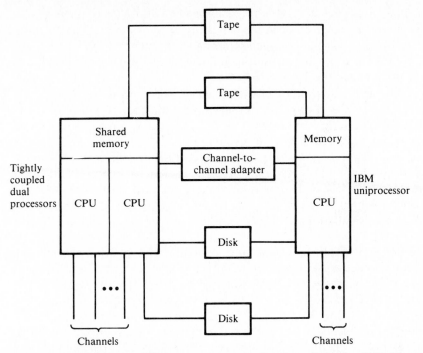

Figure 9.22 A tightly coupled IBM dual-processor system loosely coupled with an IBM uniprocessor.

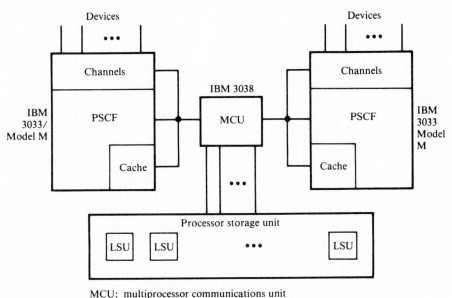

MCU: multiprocessor communications unit
PSCF: processor storage control function

Figure 9.23 The IBM 3033 multiprocessor complex. (Courtesy of International Business Machines Corp., 1978.)

which can apportion the storage either independently to each processor for uni-processor mode or shared between the two processors for multiprocessor mode. The 3033 MP complex achieves its high performance through higher interprocessor communication, better cache and storage protection and faster access to shared processor storage than the 370/168 MP.

The 3033 MP contains another improvement over the 168 MP and AP, in that the priority bit mechanism has two levels. Low-level bits compete with low-level bits and high-level bits compete with high-level bits but, as might be suspected from the names, a high-level bit can preempt a low-level bit. The 3033 with its enhanced buffering can, at times, sustain an exceptionally long string of storage requests, so this facility prevents a high-priority request on one processor from being unnecessarily delayed by low-priority activity on the other. The 3033 MP performance has been stated to be 1.6 to 1.8 times that of the 3033 uniprocessor system, based on simulation results and running experience.

The IBM 3081 system The IBM 3081 processor unit has a symmetric organization of two central processors, each with a 26-ns machine cycle time, and executes IBM System/370 instructions at approximately twice the rate of the IBM 3033. One of the goals set in the design of the 3081 was better price/performance index over the System/370 and 303x series. The other goal was upward compatibility with those product lines. Furthermore, it was designed to have improved reliability, availability, and serviceability through new technology and partitioning and packaging schemes. One of the major achievements in packaging is the development of a field replaceable unit called a thermal conduction module (TCM), which contains up to 130 IC chips on one substrate. With these TCMs, a large board called a clark board was developed. Each board contains up to either six or nine TCMs, which made it possible to package the entire processor unit on four boards in one frame.

The 3081 processor unit organization shown in Figure 9.24 consists of five subsystems: two central processors, the system controller, the main storage, and the external data controller (EXDC). The 3081 is called a *dyadic processor* since it is configured as two identical processors that share a system controller and EXDC within one frame. Furthermore, they act as a tightly coupled multiprocessor which cannot be decoupled to act as two independent uniprocessors as in the IBM 3033. The configuration is symmetrical because each processor has the same priority and operational characteristics with respect to the central storage and channels. Each processor has access to channels and to central storage via the controller.

The processors share main storage, which could be 16, 24, or 32 megabytes. A segment of main memory called the system area is reserved for microcode. This area also contains unit control words (UCWs) for I/O devices and system tables and directories. Hence, the system area is not accessible to user programs. The main storage is organized as a card-on-board package and is two-way interleaved. Each board, which contains 4M bytes of main memory, is called the basic storage module. This module is configured so that a block (128 bytes) of data can be

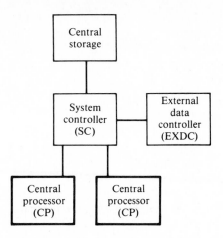

Figure 9.24 The IBM 3081 system components. (Courtesy of International Business Machines Corp., 1980.)

accessed with a single operation to efficiently transfer a block between the processor and memory. The interleaving scheme uses doubleword, which is the basic unit of memory operation, and a 2K-byte address across the 4M-byte modules. The 2K byte segment, which was chosen to minimize the complexity of memory reconfiguration, can thus be independently accessed.

The system controller provides the paths and controls the communications between the main memory and other subsystems. The basic data-bus width of all units connecting to the controller is 8 bytes with a data transfer rate of 8 bytes per machine cycle. The bus is bidirectional. The controller also contains the storage protect keys and time-of-day clock and manages an eight-position queue containing storage requests. The 3081 can support up to 24 channels, which can be of either the byte-multiplexer or block-multiplexer type. Channels are controlled by the EXDC. The EXDC consists of two types of microcode-controlled elements. One of the elements handles the control of I/O instructions and interrupts. The other handles the data control sequencing and provides buffering for each group of eight channels.

Each processor consists of five functional elements, as shown in Figure 9.25, and packaged within a nine-TCM board. The processor is not a pipelined processor as in the IBM System 370/168. However, it has an effective instruction prefetching capability. Each processor has three separate execution elements, a buffer control element, and a control store element. The execution elements are the instruction elements, variable-field element, and execution element. The instruction element controls the instruction sequencing of a processor by initiating requests for instructions and attempting to maintain an instruction buffer of four doublewords locally. It performs the instruction-decode and operand-address generation functions and initiates all requests for operands. It also executes all arithmetic and logical operations.

The variable-field element operates under horizontal microcode control, executes all variable length, storage-to-storage instructions. Within it is a decimal adder and its associated input and output regions. In executing the specified set

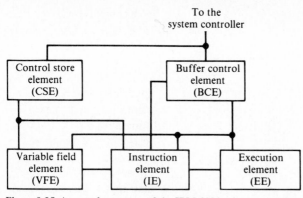

Figure 9.25 A central processor of the IBM 3081. (Courtesy of International Business Machine Corp., 1980.)

of instructions, it operates together with the instruction element, which performs operand fetches and stores in parallel. The execution element executes fixed-point multiply and divide instructions. It also executes conversion-type instructions (e.g. binary to decimal) and floating-point instructions. The control store element controls the sequencing of the horizontal microcode of the processor.

The buffer control element contains the 32K- or 64K-byte cache, which uses a write-back main memory update policy. The block size is 128 bytes and the cache is four-way set-associative with a least-recently-used replacement algorithm. The cache has a two-cycle access with the virtual-to-real address translation performed in parallel. The write-back policy used in the 3081 is different from the write-through policy used in the 3033. Simulation studies showed that the write-back policy was better on the 3081 as soon as the memory-access time exceeded about ten machine cycles. Also, the write-back policy facilitated a checkpoint-retry algorithm for the processor. The checkpoint-retry mechanism is a hardware device which can be used to establish a checkpoint at some instruction N. At this instruction, the contents of the processor registers are saved in a backup register set. As program execution continues, any store into the cache will cause the old value of a changed doubleword to be saved in a push-down stack. If an error condition occurs, the processor registers can be restored to their original state at the last checkpoint and the process can be restarted.

Since each processor has a cache, the write-back policy adopted creates a data consistency problem which is managed by the system controller. The controller implements the global table similar to Section 7.3. This table is used to enforce consistency. The dynamic coherence scheme is used in the 3081. The difference is that when a processor requests a fetch of block which is held exclusive and modified in remote cache, the copy of the block is updated in memory. Furthermore, the copy in the remote cache is invalidated instead of changing state to read-only. Thereafter, the local processor fetches the block from memory. An algorithm which predicts the usage of a block of data was developed to minimize the performance overhead of status changes and invalidation. A four-processor system (the IBM 3084) can be configured by a set of two 3081s in either MP or AP mode.

9.5.2 Operating System for IBM Multiprocessors

All IBM 360 and 370 models have a 32-bit word divided into 4 bytes that are byte addressable for business-oriented (character strings) applications. The System/370 instruction set includes fixed-point and floating-point arithmetic operations, character manipulation, binary as well as decimal arithmetic computations plus a number of system control instructions. There are sixteen general-purpose registers, four floating-point registers, and sixteen control registers in the CPU. The control registers are mainly used for executing the system control sequence in the operating system. There is also a 64-bit program status word (PSW) register. This PSW is primarily used by user programs in indicating the status of interrupts, overflow or underflow, and even functions as an extra program counter.

In order to facilitate multiprocessing, the IBM 370/168 has the following special features in addition to those uniprocessor models in the System/370 series. Each CPU use a block of 4K words to hold key status and control sequences. Prefixing capability is provided to logically assign this block to each CPU in a separate physical block in the shared memory. A time-of-day feature is built into the system to synchronize the clocks of two CPUs in MP mode. Interprocessor communication mechanisms are provided to signal a CPU or to respond to the signal sent by another CPU. There are five different interrupt classes in S/370 including program interrupts, I/O interrupts, external interrupts, machine-check interrupts, and service-call interrupts to allow communications among user and system programs. The PSW register is used to facilitate the interrupt services.

Instructions related to I/O operations are treated as privileged instructions. The execution of these privileged instructions is controlled by the bit pattern in the PSW register. Memory protection has been mechanized with the aid of the PSW register. Other interesting functions of the 370/168 processors include dynamic address translation to support the virtual storage operating system. The virtual address space can cover up to 16 million bytes for any physical main memory space from 2 million bytes to 16 million bytes in 1 million-byte increments. Error checking and error correction capabilities are also built into the main memory. Instruction retry and I/O command retry capabilities are also provided to reduce the number of system failures.

The degree of coupling between two processors in a multiprocessor system is determined by the capabilities of the operating system. The IBM 370/168 runs with an Operating System/Virtual Storage 2 (OS/VS2), which is revised from the standard S/370 operating system. This OS/VS2 is a time-sharing multiprocessing system in a virtual storage environment supporting either a tightly coupled system or a loosely coupled configuration. Two important features of multiprocessing in various 370/168 configurations are the separation of architectural configurations

(AP, MP or others) from the implementation of system control mechanisms and the sophistication of the interprocessor communication mechanisms.

For a tightly coupled dual-processor 370/168 MP system (Figure 9.21), five important features have been developed in the OS/VS2 to support the multi-processing (MP) hardware. These features are listed below:

1. A serialization technique called locking is provided to disable across CPUs. It allows mutually exclusive functions to run in parallel on an MP system.
2. The service management provides a new unit of dispatchability in the system which has less overhead and better performance in encouraging parallelism in system functions.
3. The CPU affinity provides a way for forcing an emulatory job step to a particular CPU having the desired hardware feature.
4. The dispatching supports the changes in MP functions and in multiple address spaces.
5. The alternate CPU recovery (ACR) invokes a special purpose when a CPU is detected malfunctioning.

Various 370/168 MP configurations have been installed with special hardware-software error-recovery mechanisms. When an error is detected on a processor, an interrupt service is generated to recover that processor, if possible. If the interrupt handler realizes that recovery is impossible, an SIGP instruction is issued to specify an emergency alert as the order code. The OS/VS2 uses a linear ordering scheme to avoid system deadlock. The error-recovery software will incrementally execute all tasks holding locks until the deadlock crisis is avoided. Reconfiguration of the 370/168 system is done through operator intervention. An MP system can be divided into two independent uniprocessor systems. The APU in an AP configuration can be disabled without paralyzing the whole system. However, a failure of the CPU in an AP configuration will result in the failure of the entire system.

9.5.3 Univac 1100/80 and 1100/90 Series

Large-scale mainframe computer systems in the Univac 1100 series are described in this section. Beginning with the 1107 in 1962, the 1100 series has progressed through a succession of compatible computer models to the latest 1100/80 and 1100/90. We first review the architectural evolution in the series and then discuss the details of the models 1100/80 and 1100/90 and their operating system and language requirements.

Architectural evolution of Univac 1100 series The 1100 series hardware architecture is based on a 36-bit word, one's complement structure which obtains one operand from storage and one from a high-speed register, or two operands from high-speed registers. The 1100 Operating System is designed to support a symmetrical multiprocessor configuration simultaneously providing multiprogrammed batch,

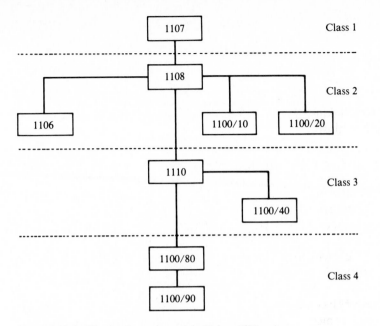

Figure 9.26 Architectural genealogy of the Univac 1100 series.

time-sharing, and transaction environments. The evolution of the Univac 1100 series is depicted in Figure 9.26. Although the basic architecture has remained the same since the 1107, the series has progressed through four architectural classes and 24 different processor-system configurations.

The 1107 was originally designed for batch-oriented scientific and engineering applications. The architectural and the operating system evolutions reflect a continuing push towards more efficient interactive and business-oriented capabilities. One of the strongest features of the 1100 series is its multiprocessor capability. Multiprocessor configurations have been in general use since the introduction of the first 1108 multiprocessor system in 1968. The System 1108 was the first commercially available general-purpose computer to support a completely symmetrical multiprocessor system; i.e., all processors share the same memory, I/O channels, and a single copy of the executive system. The major improvement of the 1108 system over the 1107 was increased throughput and enhanced protection in multiprogramming environments. The primary new feature which provided these improvements was a relative-addressing structure which created a dynamic relocation capability. In addition to faster unit processor operation, multiprocessor configurations were introduced which offered higher performance and greater system availability.

Newer versions of the 1108 system are designed to be tightly coupled symmetric multiprocessors, as shown in Figure 9.27. Each of the main storage units is multiported. The **TEST-AND-SET** instruction was added to facilitate interprocess synchronization. This instruction causes the storage unit to read a semaphore bit

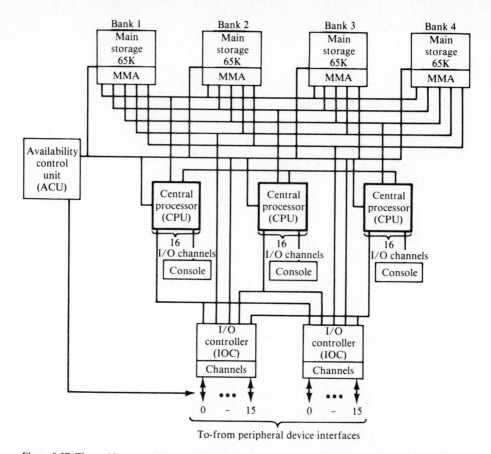

Figure 9.27 The architecture of Univac 1108 multiprocessor. (Courtesy of Sperry Rand Corp., 1965.)

and then, without allowing any other processor to access the same memory word, to set the semaphore bit. If the semaphore was initially set, an interrupt occurs (indicating that the item protected by this semaphore is already used). At this point, the interrupted process is queued until the semaphore is cleared. If the semaphore was initially clear, the next instruction is executed. Execution of the **TEST-AND-SET** instruction must precede the use of any data where erroneous results could be produced by two or more instruction streams operating on these data concurrently.

The introduction of the multiprocessor version of the 1108 led to the development of a new kind of system component called the availability control unit (ACU). This unit allows partitioning of the system into three smaller independent systems for debugging of either hardware or software on one system, while normal operation (at reduced throughput) continues on the remainder of the system. Each processor periodically sends a signal to the ACU indicating that the processor is still functioning and the executive is still in control. If the ACU does not receive all

Table 9.3 The Univac 1100 series models

	Model			
Features	1108	1110	1100/80	1100/90
First delivery	1962	1972	1977	1982
Maximum number processors	2	4	4	4
Maximum number I/O processors	2	4	4	4
Integer add time (ns)	750	300	200	60
Storage structure	One level	Primary/extended	Cache/main	Cache/main Cache/disk
Instruction set	151	206	201	238

the expected signals within a predetermined time, an automatic recovery sequence is initiated.

The functional characteristic of various 1100 systems are summarized in Table 9.3. Readers can see the evolutional changes in processor features, memory structures, hardware technologies, and instruction sets from 1108 to 1100/90 in 20 years. The 1110 was the first processor in the 1100 series constructed entirely of integrated circuits (mainly with high-speed TTL). Through a chronological development of the 1100/20, 40, and 10 systems, the 1100/80 and 1100/90 systems merged as the latest product in the series.

The Univac 1100/80 systems The 1100/80 performs an add instruction in only 200 ns. Important features of the 1100/80 architecture and design approaches are listed below:

1. Addressable memory is returned to a single level structure.
2. The effective memory speed is increased by using a user-transparent cache.
3. Single-bit-error correction and double-bit error detection are on main memory.
4. The arithmetic-logic unit is microprogrammed.
5. Instructions have been added to accelerate user and executive common functions.
6. This is automatic recovery from system failures.

A uniprocessor 1100/80 system is shown in Figure 9.28. The system is organized with a central processor and an I/O unit attached to main storage units through a storage interface unit. The storage interface unit contains a cache to speed up memory reference. Peripherals are connected to the storage interface unit through channels in the I/O units. This configuration is called a 1×1 system, for it consists of one processor and one I/O unit. In general, 1100/80 systems are designated as $M \times N$ configurations, where M is the number of processors and N the number of I/O units. Configurations 1×1, 2×2, and 4×4 are possible. In a 2×2 system (Figure 9.29), two processors and two I/O units are connected to a storage

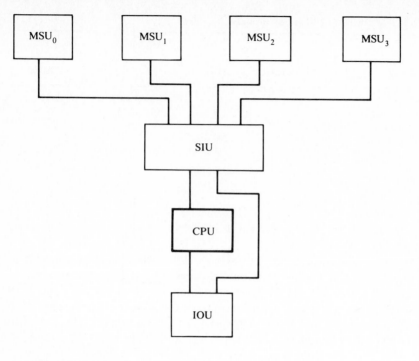

MSU: main storage unit
SIU: storage interface unit
IOU: I/O unit

Figure 9.28 A single-processor Univac 1100/80 configuration. (Courtesy of *Comm. of ACM*, Borgerson et al., 1978.)

interface unit. There is still only one cache, which is common to both processors and located in the storage interface unit.

Figure 9.30 depicts a 4 × 4 system. A second storage interface unit with its own independent cache is now present and connected to the two additional processors and I/O units. The two storage interface units have a cache invalidate interface which ensures that if both caches contain copies of the same data, altering the copy in one cache will cause the corresponding copy in the other to be marked as invalid.

Main memory is a common resource for all processors and I/O units and is accessed by them via the corresponding storage interface units. There can be up to four main storage units, each containing from 512K to 1M words of memory. Each main storage unit is connected to both storage interface units and can be two-way interleaved. Processors are connected to each other by interprocessor interrupt interfaces, which permit a processor to cause an interrupt in any other processor. An I/O unit is electrically connected to only one storage interface unit and to the processors on that storage interface unit. As a result, a processor can handle I/O only on I/O connected to the same storage interface unit as itself.

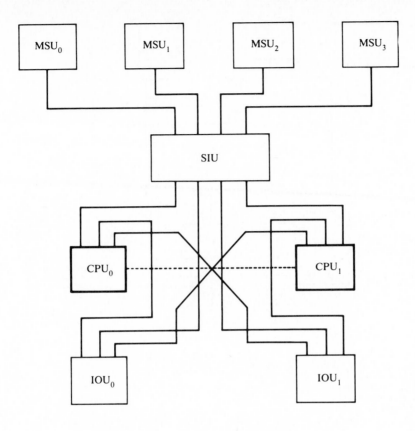

-------------------- : interprocessor interrupt lines

MSU: main storage unit
SIU: storage interface unit
IOU: I/O unit

Figure 9.29 A dual-processor Univac 1100/80 configuration. (Courtesy of *Comm. of ACM*, Borgerson et al., 1978.)

The central processor of an 1100/80 has a 36-bit word length and a reasonably rich repertoire of fixed-point, floating-point, data-movement, and character-manipulation instructions. The architecture is essentially register-oriented, with separate index registers and accumulators. Most double-operand instructions have one operand in a register and one in memory. Central to the architecture of this system is a set of 128 words called the general register set (GRS). Programs can address 16 index registers and 16 accumulators.

The 1100/80 is installed with a new group of instructions to accelerate common functions for both users and the executive. These include several context-switching instructions such as save and restore system status and load and store GRS, and user-oriented instructions, including new constant storage and memory increment

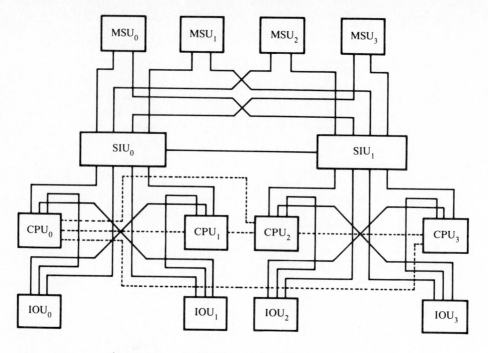

------------------ : interprocessor interrupt lines

MSU: main storage unit
SIU: storage interface unit
IOU: I/O unit

Figure 9.30 A four-processor Univac 1100/80 configuration. (Courtesy of *Comm. of ACM*, Borgerson et al., 1978.)

and decrement instructions. Two new instructions were also added to support the autorecovery feature of the 1100/80. These instructions reset the autorecovery timer and toggle the autorecovery path. When autorecovery is enabled and the system software does not reset the automatic recovery timer within the preset time interval, the system transition unit (similar to the ACU of the 1108) clears, reloads, and reinitiates the system. Two recovery paths are provided. The alternative recovery path is system initiated when an attempted automatic recovery fails. The instructions mentioned above provide for software resetting of the automatic recovery time and for selection of the first automatic recovery path to be used by the next recovery attempt.

The 1100/80 introduced instructions to aid the address-space manipulator. The most significant new instruction transfers a two-word segment descriptor directly from the segment descriptor table to the segment descriptor register, saves the previous contents of the segment descriptor register, and branches. The granularity of segment sizes has been improved on the 1100/80. Segments can be as large as 262K words and can be specified in 64-word granules beginning on any 512-word boundary and ending on any 64-word boundary.

Input-output channels on the 1100/80 are available in two forms. Word channels are available that are compatible with the 1110 system. Additionally, intelligent byte channels are available that allow the direct usage of byte-oriented peripheral equipment. The 1100/80 uses a high-speed cache memory between the processor and main storage. The cache memory is transparent to the user. It is constructed of emitter-coupled logic storage elements and contains up to 16K words; these words are the most recently used contents of main storage. The physical main storage capacity was increased to a maximum of 4M words of MOS memory. Single-bit error correction and double-bit error detection are provided.

The Univac 1100/90 systems The Univac 1100/90 multiprocessors are the most recent systems by Sperry Univac. The systems permit one, two, three, or four central processing units (CPU) as 1100/91, 1100/92, 1100/93, and 1100/94 systems, respectively. The 1100/9x is an x-by-x system containing x CPUs and x I/O processors, which can be tightly coupled. Figure 9.31 shows an example of a four-by-four system. However, loosely coupled configurations are also possible in which there are two independent systems sharing one mass storage subsystem.

The 1100/94 system configuration, in addition to having four CPUs and four I/O processors, contains four main storage units (MSU) and two system support processors. Each CPU is pipelined with an 8K word instruction cache and an 8K word data cache. A word is 36 bits wide. Each cache is organized into 256 sets with four blocks per set. Each block contains eight words. The CPU uses a virtual addressing scheme with 2^{36} words of address space. The initial address is divided into four portions. A segmentation scheme is used with a maximum of 262,144 segments. A write-through policy is used to update the MSU. On a write to shared data in a local cache, all caches in other CPUs containing a copy of the block are invalidated.

Each MSU contains four independent banks. A block read is a single reference resulting in four doubleword transfers with a 600-ns cycle time. A doubleword read is accomplished in 360 ns. The 1100/90 systems use the same system software as the 1100/80 systems for upward compatibility.

Operating system features in Univac 1100 series The operating system structure for the 1100 series consists of multiple layers of software, as shown in Figure 9.32. The structure of the kernel of the operating system is discussed here. The 1100 series executive system is called EXEC. A user's request to EXEC is made by executing a software interrupt instruction called *executive request interrupt* (ERI). Execution of this instruction in a processor causes a transfer of control to the executive. The EXEC has an input-output control routine concept called a symbiont (spooling routine). These routines overlap read, print, and punch operations with program execution. The EXEC also possesses multiprogramming capabilities designed to operate in both a multiprogram and multiprocessor

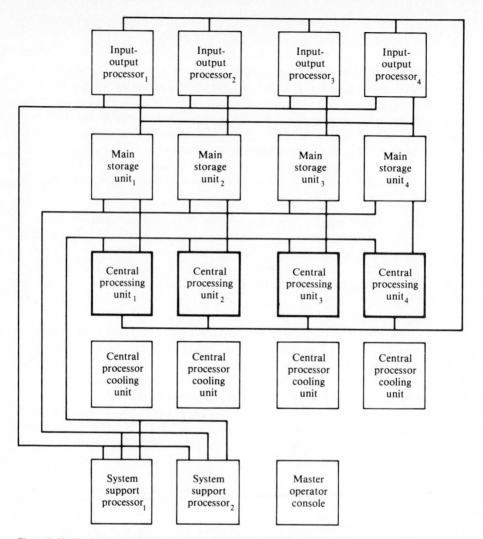

Figure 9.31 The Univac 1100/94 system with four processors. (Courtesy of Sperry Rand Corp., 1983.)

environment. Moreover, it supports a concurrent mix of batch, remote batch, remote batch, demand and transaction programs.

Particular emphasis is placed on demand mode also known as time sharing. All system facilities available in batch mode are also available in demand mode; the same *run stream* can be used in either batch mode or demand mode without change. A run stream is a collection of user service requests used for batch, remote batch, and demand. Included in the run stream are any data images supporting each service request. The run stream is formulated using a control language consisting of service requests. A task is an individual service request, to assign a tape, for example, or to perform a compilation within a run stream.

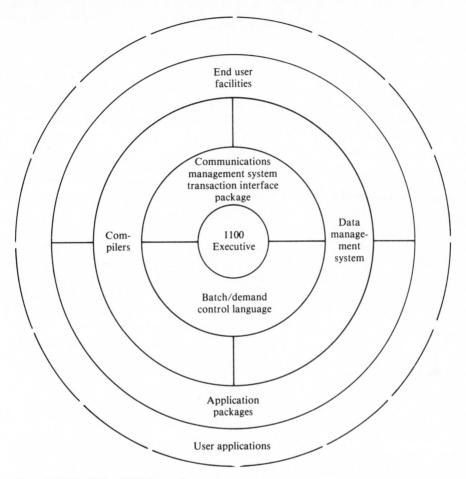

Figure 9.32 The Univac/EXEC operating system.

The origin of a program is in symbolic elements within the run stream. These elements are then compiled to form relocatable elements which are collected (bound) with other relocatable elements to form an absolute element (the program). The term "absolute" refers to the program relative-address solution only; the relative-addressing capability of the hardware allows the program to be loaded (or swapped and reloaded) and executed anywhere within main storage. References to shared segments of both user code and system libraries are resolved during execution.

A batch stream which enters the system is first processed by the symbiont complex. This complex disassociates the run stream from the relatively slow unit-record device speeds and allows tasks to proceed at higher mass-storage speeds. The run stream is scanned for facility allocation and prescheduling. Multiple asynchronous input-output services are allowed. This is particularly important in a multiprogramming-multiprocessing environment.

After staging in a mass-storage schedule queue, the run stream is processed by the coarse scheduler, which is responsible for the scheduling, selecting, and activating of the run stream. The run is assigned a temporary program file in which intermediate results, such as compiler output or text editor output, are held until termination, when the file is released. The results may be retained by directing them instead to a permanent file or copying the contents of the temporary file prior to termination. Demand runs are scheduled for immediate activation; batch runs are scheduled on a user-selected priority basis. A major batch-scheduling consideration at this point is the availability of facilities such as tape devices. When necessary facilities are available, the program is then queued for main storage allocation.

The dynamic allocator, which has the responsibility for the distribution of main storage space among users, removes the program on a priority basis. The main functions of the dynamic allocator include the allocation and release of main storage and the initial load, swap-out, and reload of programs. The decisions of the dynamic allocator are facilitated by relative addressing, which allows the program to be loaded anywhere in memory. The program may be partitioned into multiple segments which need not be loaded contiguously. Segments (usually shared) that were not a part of the initial program may be referenced (and loaded) dynamically. This facility allows for greater program protection and re-entrancy efficiency. It also allows each segment to be loaded into a separate memory module, thus reducing the effective instruction execution time through storage unit overlap.

A switch list is used by the 1100 EXEC to control an executing program. The program may fork into any number of asynchronous execution paths called activities, each of which is independently scheduled (except for synchronization requests). It is given main memory space and a time slice under the control of a unique switch list entry. The executing activity requests 1100 executive services through a set of executive requests. These perform services such as input-output, control statement processing, and activity activation. An I/O operation can be requested by a user program. If the request is not to an I/O unit on the same storage interface unit as the processor that is running the program, the processor will signal another processor on the other storage interface unit. The I/O operation is then initiated by this processor. The signalling is performed via the interprocessor interrupt mechanism. On completion of the I/O transaction for this request, the I/O unit sends a completion interrupt signal. One of the processors on the same interface handles this interrupt for eventual notification of the user program which requested the I/O transaction.

The dispatcher allocates real processor time slices to outstanding activities according to the priority and needs of the respective activities. In a multiprocessor system, any available processor may be assigned to execute the next time slice. Thus, an activity may execute successive time slices on different processors, or two parallel activities within the same program may be executing concurrently on different processors. Upon completion of processing within an activity, a request for normal or abnormal termination is made. After all activities within a task have terminated, the task is terminated and control is returned to the coarse scheduler. We have only sketched the EXEC operations here. Interested readers should check with the Univac EXEC manuals for details.

9.5.4 The Tandem Nonstop System

On-line computing with continuous availability is in high demand in many business applications. Certain applications, such as automatic toll billing for telephone systems, lose money each minute the system is down and the losses are irrecoverable. The Tandem-16 Nonstop system was designed to offer better availability than most existing multiple processor computers. The system is organized around three types of components: the processors, device controllers, and system buses (Figure 9.33). The processors are interconnected by the *dynabus*, which consists of two buses. The device controllers are each connected to two independent I/O channels, one from each processor on its side. The system is designed to continue operation through any single failure and to allow on-line repairing without affecting the rest of the system. The on-line maintenance was a key factor in using dual power supplies in the system.

Each processor includes a 16-bit CPU, a main memory, a bus control, and an I/O channel (Figure 9.34). Up to 2M bytes of main memory are available. The processor module is viewed by the user as a stack-oriented computer with a virtual memory system capable of supporting multiprogramming. The CPU is a microprogrammed processor consisting of eight registers which can be used as general-purpose registers, an ALU, and several miscellaneous flags and counters. The instruction set includes arithmetic operations, logical operations, procedure calls and exits, interprocessor SENDs, and I/O operations. The system has 16 interrupt levels which include bus data received, I/O transfer completion, memory error, interval time, page fault, privileged instruction violation, etc. Packets are the primitive data transferred over the dynabus.

Main memory is organized in physical pages of 1K words. Up to one megaword of memory may be attached to a processor. In a semiconductor memory system, there are six check bits per word to provide single error correction and double error detection. The semiconductor memory with error correction is more reliable than core. Battery backup provides short-term nonvolatility of the semiconductor memory system.

Memory is logically divided into four address spaces. These are the virtual address spaces of the machine; both the system and the user have separate code spaces and data spaces. The code space is unmodifiable and the data space can be viewed either as a stack or a random-access memory, depending on the adressing mode used. Each virtual address space has 46K words. Four maps are provided, one for each logical address space. The map access time and the delay by error correction are included in the 500-ns cycle time of the semiconductor memory system. The high-level language provided on the Tandem 16 system is the TAL, a block-structured, ALGOL-like language.

Multiple processors in Tandem-16 communicate with each other over the X bus and Y bus shown in Figure 9.35. Bus access is determined by two independent

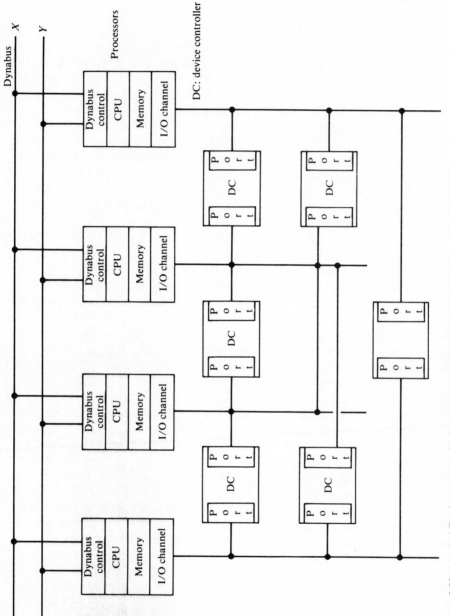

Figure 9.33 A typical Tandem system with four processors. (Courtesy of Tandem Computer, Inc., 1978.)

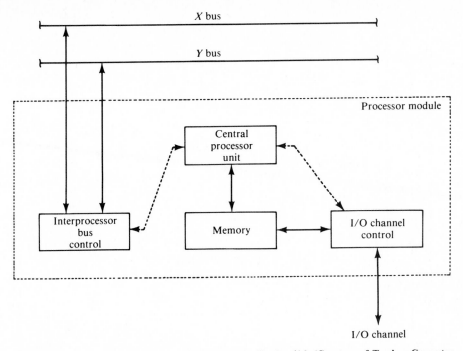

Figure 9.34 System components in one processor of the Tandem/16. (Courtesy of Tandem Computer, Inc., 1978.)

interprocessor bus controllers. There are two sets of radial connections from each bus controller to each processor module. They distribute clocks for synchronous transmission over the bus. No failed processor can dominate the dynabus utilization. Each bus has a clock associated with it, running independently of the processor clocks.

The dynabus interface controller consists of three high-speed caches, two of which are associated with the two buses and one is an output queue that can be switched between the two buses. Each caches has 16 words and all bus transfers are made from cache to cache. All components attaching to the buses are kept physically distinct, so that no single component failure can contaminate both buses simultaneously. Also, the controller has clock synchronization and interlock circuitry. All processors communicate in a point-to-point manner using this shared bus configuration.

For any interprocessor data transfer, one processor is the sender and the other is the receiver. Before a processor can receive data over a bus, the operating system must configure an entry in a table known as the *bus receive table* (BRT). Each BRT entry contains the address where the incoming data is to be stored, the sequence number of the next packet, the send processor number, the receiver processor number, and the number of words to be transfered. A SEND instruction is executed in the sending processor, which specifies the bus to be used, the intended

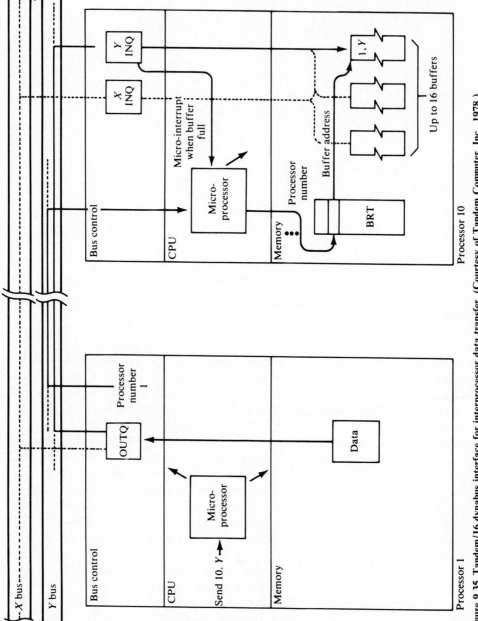

Figure 9.35 Tandem/16 dynabus interface for interprocessor data transfer. (Courtesy of Tandem Computer, Inc., 1978.)

receiver, and the number of words to be sent. The sending processor's CPU stays in the SEND instruction until the data transfer is completed. Up to 65,535 words can be sent in a single SEND instruction. While the sending processor is executing the SEND instruction, the dynabus control logic in the receiving processor is storing the data away according to the appropriate BRT entry. In the receiving processor, this occurs simultaneously with its program execution.

A message is divided into packets of 16 words. The sending processor fills its outgoing queue with these packets, requests a bus transfer, and transmits upon grant of the bus by the bus controller. The receiving processor fills the incoming queue associated with the bus and issues a microinterrupt to its own CPU. The CPU checks the BRT entry accordingly. The BRT entries are four words that include a transfer buffer address, a sequence number, and the sender and receiver processor numbers. Error recovery action is to be taken in case the transfer is not completed within a time-out interval. These parameters are placed on a register stack and are dynamically updated so that the SEND instruction is interruptible on packet boundaries.

All I/O is done on a direct memory access basis through a microprogrammed, multiplexed channel with a block size determined by the individual controller. All the controllers are buffered so that all transfers over the I/O channel are at memory speed (4M bytes/s) and never wait for mechanical motion since the transfers always come from a buffer in the controller rather than from the actual I/O device. There exists the I/O Control Table (IOC) in the system data space of each processor that contains a two-word entry for each of the 256 possible I/O devices attached to the I/O channel. These entries contain a byte count and virtual address in the system data space for I/O data transfers. The I/O channel moves the IOC entry to active registers during the connection of an I/O controller and restores the updated values to the IOC upon disconnection. The channel transfers data in parallel with program execution. The memory system priority always permits I/O accesses to be handled before CPU or dynabus accesses.

The dual-ported I/O device controllers provide the interface between the I/O channel and a variety of peripheral devices. Each controller contains two independent I/O channel ports so that it can never simultaneously cause failure of both ports. Each port attached to an I/O channel must be assigned a controller number and a priority distinct from other ports attached to the same I/O channel. Logically only one of the two ports of an I/O controller is active; the other port is utilized only in the event of a path failure to the primary port. If a processor determines that a given controller is malfunctioning on its I/O channel, it can issue a command that logically disconnects the port from the controller. This does not affect the ownership status. If the problem is within the port, an alternate path can be used.

Each disk drive in the system may be dual-ported. Each port of a disk drive is connected to an independent disk controller. Each of the disk controllers are also dual-ported and connected between two processors. A string of up to each drives (four mirrored pairs) can be supported by a pair of controllers in this manner. The disk controller is buffered and absolutely immune to overruns. All data transferred over the bus is parity checked in both directions, and errors are reported via the interrupt system. A watchdog timer in the I/O channel detects if a nonexistent I/O controller has been addressed, or if a controller stops responding during an I/O sequence. In case of channel failure, the path switching between devices and controller is demonstrated in Figure 9.36, where an alternate path is chosen to provide the access of the disk.

The operating system of Tandem is called the Guardian. It is a "nonstop" operating system designed to achieve the following capabilities:

1. It should be able to remain operational after any single detected module or bus failure.
2. It should allow any module or bus to be repaired on-line and then reintegrated into the system.
3. It is to be implemented with high reliability provided by the hardware but not negated by software problems.
4. It should support all possible hardware configurations, ranging from a two-processor, diskless system through a sixteen-processor system with billions of bytes of disk storage.
5. It should hide the physical configuration as much as possible so that applications could be written to run on a great variety of system configurations.

The Guardian resides in each processor but is aware of all other processors. In fact, the operating systems in different processors constantly monitor each other's performance. The instant one processor's operating system fails to respond correctly, other processors assume that it is failing and take over its work load. Obviously, this requires a great deal of communication among the processors. This requires a process to be able to address the system resources by a logical name rather than by a physical address. The Guardian operating system is designed in a top down manner with three levels of well-defined interfaces, as shown in Figure 9.37. It is based on the concept of processes sending messages to other processes.

All resources in the system are considered to be files, and each resource has a logical file name. Communication between an application process and any resource (disk, tape, another process, etc.) is via the file system. The file system knows only the logical name of the intended recipient of a message. It passes the message to the message system, which then determines the physical location of the recipient. The message system is a software analog of the dynabus. It handles automatic path retries in case of path errors. Because application programs deal only with logical file names, the system offers total geographic independence of resources. The programmer views this multiprocessor system as a single processor with resources available through file system calls.

The processes and messages are further elaborated with abstraction. Each processor module has one or more processes residing in it. A process is initially created in a specific processor and may not execute in another processor. Each process has an execution priority assigned to it. Processor time is allocated to the

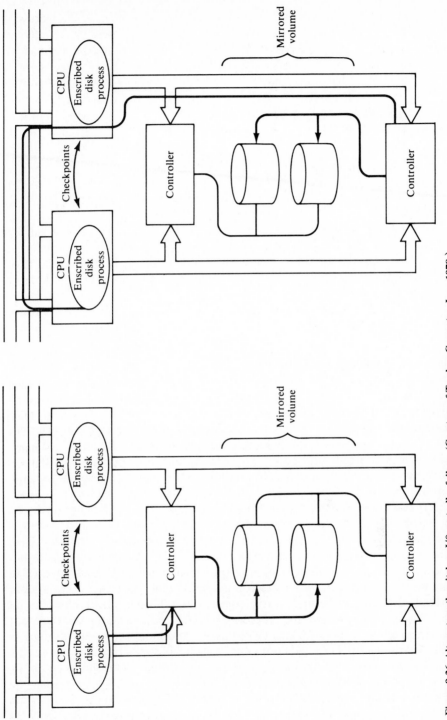

Figure 9.36 Alternate path switch on I/0 controller failure. (Courtesy of Tandem Computer, Inc., 1978.)

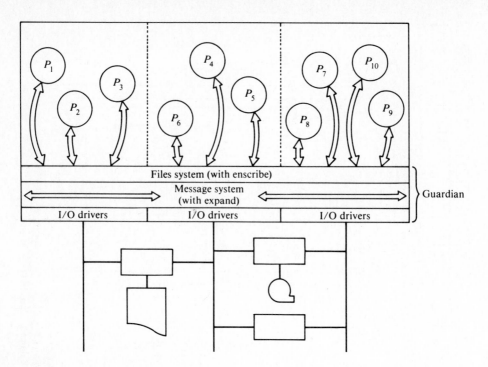

Figure 9.37 The Guardian operating system.

highest priority process. Process-synchronization primitives include counting semaphores and process local event flags. Semaphore operations are performed via the functions **PSEM** and **VSEM**, similar to Dijkstra's **P** and **V** operators. Semaphores may only be used for synchronization between processes within the same processor. They are typically used to control access to resources such as resident memory buffers, message control blocks, and I/O controllers.

The message system provides five primitive operations, which are illustrated in Figure 9.38 in the context of a process making an inquire to the process. A process sends a message to the appropriate server process via a procedure LINK. The message will consist of parameters denoting the type of inquires and data needed. The message will be queued in the server process, setting an event flag, and then the requester process may continue executing. The server process calls a procedure to return the first message queued. It will then obtain a copy of the requestor's data by calling the procedure READLINK. Next, the server process will process the request. The status of the operation and the result will then be returned by the WRITELINK procedure, which will signal the requester process via another event flag. Finally, the requester process will complete its end of the transaction by calling the BREAKLINK procedure.

The message system is designed to obtain resources needed for message transmission (control blocks) at the start of a message-transfer request. Once the

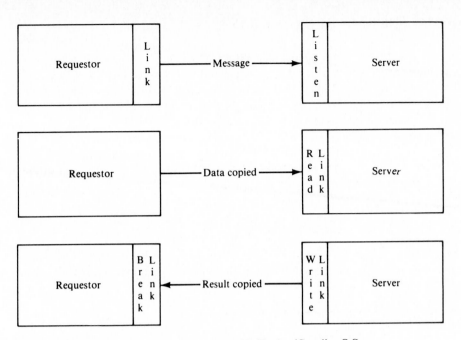

Figure 9.38 The message system primitive developed in Tandem/Guardian O.S.

LINK has been successfully completed, both processes are assured that sufficient resources are in hand to complete the message transfer. Furthermore, a process may reserve some control blocks to guarantee that it will always be able to send messages to respond to a request from its message queue. Such a resource control assures that deadlocks are prevented by complex producer-consumer interactions.

The Guardian is constructed of processes which communicate with messages. Fault tolerance is provided by duplication of both hardware and software components. Access to I/O devices is provided by process pairs consisting of a primary process and a backup process. The primary process must check out state information to the backup process so that the backup may take over on a failure. Requests to these devices are routed using the logical device name or number so that the request is always routed to the primary process. The result is a set of primitives and protocols which allow recovery and continued processing in spite of single failures in bus, processor, or I/O device.

A "network" system can link up to 255 Tandem-16 systems. The Guardian-Expand Network system can extend the dynabus into a long-range network. To a user at a terminal, the entire network appears to be a single Tandem-16 system. The network maintains the geographic independence of resources. Any resource in the network can be addressed by its logical file name without regard for its physical location. However, a configuration option allows users to reserve processors for local processing requirements, thereby excluding those processors from the network.

9.6 THE CRAY X-MP AND CRAY-2

The Cray X-MP is a multiprocessor extension of the Cray-1. It contains two Cray-1-like processors with shared memory and I/O subsystems. The first X-MP was installed in later 1983. Cray Research is currently also developing a four-processor Cray-2. In this section, we describe the system architecture of X-MP and examine its vector processing and multitasking capabilities. We will examine the multiprocessing performance of X-MP for both compute-bound and I/O-bound applications. The details of Cray-2 were not available at the time this book was published. However, some target specifications of Cray-2 will be indicated simply to show the trend of development.

9.6.1 Cray X-MP System Architecture

The system organization of the Cray X-MP is shown in Figure 9.39. The mainframe features two identical CPUs and a multiport memory shared by both

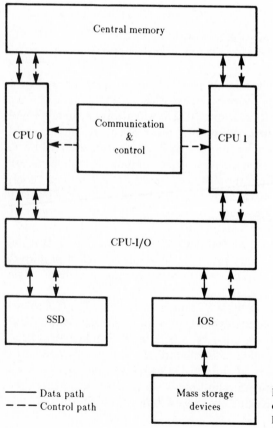

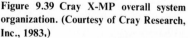

Figure 9.39 Cray X-MP overall system organization. (Courtesy of Cray Research, Inc., 1983.)

processors. Each CPU has an internal structure very similar to Cray-1. However, there are three ports per CPU (instead of two ports in Cray-1). The extra port is added to allow communication between the two CPUs via a communication and control unit.

Shared central memory The two processors share a central bipolar memory with 4M 64-bit words. This shared memory is organized in 32-way interleaved memory banks (twice that of Cray-1). All banks can be accessed independently and in parallel during each machine clock period. Each processor has four parallel memory ports (four times that of Cray-1) connected to this central memory, two for *vector fetches*, one for *vector store*, and one for independent I/O operations. The multiport memory has built-in conflict resolution hardware to minimize the delay and maintain the integrity of all memory references to the same bank at the same time, from all processor's ports. The interleaved multiport memory design coupled with shorter memory cycle time provides a high-performance and balanced memory organization with sufficient bandwidth (eight times that of Cray-1) to support simultaneous high-speed CPU and I/O operations.

The CPU of X-MP Throughout the two CPUs, 16-gate array integrated circuits are used. These circuits, which are faster and denser than the circuitry used in the Cray-1, contributed to a clock cycle time of 9.5 ns and a memory bank cycle time of 38 ns. Proven cooling and packaging techniques have also been used on the Cray X-MP to ensure high system reliability.

Each CPU is basically a Cray-1 processor with additional features to permit multiprocessing. Within each CPU are four instruction buffers, each with 128 16-bit instruction parcels, twice the capacity of the Cray-1 instruction buffers. The instruction buffers of each CPU are loaded from memory at the burst rate of 8 words per clock period. The contents of the exchange package have been augmented to include cluster number and processor number. Increased protection of data is also made possible through a separate memory field for user programs and data. Exchange sequences occur at the rate of 2 words per clock period on the X-MP.

Operational registers and functional pipelines are among the features providing compatibility with the Cray-1. There are 13 functional pipes and A, B, S, T, and V registers as in Cray-1. With a basic machine cycle of 9.5 ns, the X-MP is capable of an overall instruction issue rate of over 200 MIPS. Computation rates of over 400 megaflops are possible, and combined arithmetic/logical operations can exceed 1000 million operations per second.

CPU intercommunication The CPU intercommunication section comprises three clusters of shared registers for interprocessor communication and synchronization. Each cluster of shared registers consists of eight 24-bit shared address (SB) registers, eight 64-bit shared scalar (ST) registers, and thirty-two 1-bit synchronization (SM) registers. Under operating system control, a cluster may be allocated to both, either, or none of the processors. The cluster may be accessed by any processor to which it is allocated in either user or system mode. A 64-bit real-time clock is shared by the processors.

Solid-state storage device (SSD) A new and large CPU-driven *solid-state storage device* (SSD) is designed as an integral part of the mainframe with very high block transfer rate. This can be used as a fast-access device for large prestaged or intermediate files generated and manipulated repetitively by user programs, or used by the system for job "swapping" space and temporary storage of system programs. The SSD design with its large size (32 megawords), typical rate of 1000 megabytes/s (250 times faster than disk), and much shorter access time (less than 0.5 ms, 100 times faster than disk), coupled with the high-performance multiprocessor design, will enable the user to explore new application algorithms for solving bigger and more sophisticated problems in science and engineering. The concept of SSD is illustrated in Figure 9.40. It performs much better than that of the disk due to its shorter access time and faster transfer rate.

I/O subsystem (IOS) The I/O subsystem, which is an integral part of the X-MP system, also contributes to the system's overall performance. The I/O subsystem (compatible with Cray-1/2) offers parallel streaming of disk drives, I/O buffering (8 megawords maximum size) for disk-resident and buffer memory-resident datasets, high-performance on-line tape handling, and common device for front-end system communication, networking, or specialized data acquisition. The IOP design enables faster and more efficient asynchronous I/O operations for data access and deposition of initial and final outputs through high-speed channels (each channel has a maximum rate of 850 megabytes/s, and a typical rate of 40 megabytes/s, 10 times faster than disk), while relieving the CPUs to perform computation-intensive operations.

Interfaces to front-end computers The Cray X-MP is interfaced to front-end computer systems through the I/O subsystem. Up to three front-end interfaces per I/O subsystem, identical to those used in the Cray-1, can be accommodated. Front-end

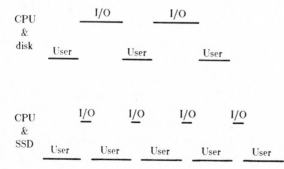

Figure 9.40 The concept of SSD in Cray X-MP as compared with the use of disks.

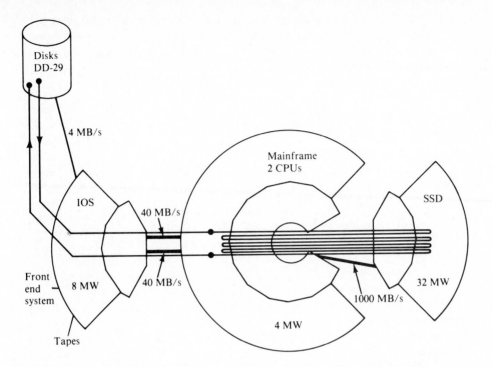

Figure 9.41 The data flow and transfer rates in Cray X-MP. (Courtesy of Cray Research, Inc., 1983.)

interfaces compensate for differences in channel widths, word size, logic levels, and control protocols, and are available for a variety of front-end systems. The X-MP can be connected to front-end machines like IBM/MVS, CDC NOS, and NOS/BE, systems.

The data flow patterns and data transfer rates among the mainframe (two CPUs and main memory of 4 megawords), the SSD, the IOS, the external disks and tapes, and the front-end system are illustrated in Figure 9.41. The high-speed transfer rates between the mainframe and SSD (1000 megabytes/s) and between the mainframe and IOS (80 megawords/s) make the system suitable for solving large-scale scientific problems, which are both computation-intensive and I/O demanding.

9.6.2 Multitasking on Cray X-MP

The X-MP is designed to be a general purpose multiprocessor system for multi-tasking applications. It can run independent tasks of different jobs on two pro-cessors. Program compatibility with Cray-1 is maintained for all tasks. It can also run related tasks of a single job on two processors. The two processors are tightly coupled through shared memory and shared registers. The system has low overhead of task initiation for multitasking. Typically O(1 μs) to O(1 ms) times is needed, depending on granularity of the tasks and software implementation techniques.

The two processors can assume various flexible architectural clustering patterns. Faster exchange for switching machine state between tasks is provided. Hardware supports the separation of memory segments for each user's data and program to facilitate concurrent programming.

Let $p = 2$ be the number of physical processors in the system. Listed below are various processor clustering patterns that are challenged in the design of X-MP. The Cray Operating System (COS) has been designed to control the allocation of the clusters of shared registers to the CPU in either user or supervisor mode.

1. All processors are identical and symmetric in their programming functions, i.e., there is no permanent master-slave relation existing between all processors.
2. A cluster of k processors ($0 \leq k \leq p$) can be assigned to perform a single task.
3. Up to $p + 1$ processor clusters can be assigned by the operating system.
4. Each cluster contains a unique set of shared data and synchronization registers for the intercommunication of all processors in a cluster.
5. Each processor in a cluster can run in either monitor or user mode controlled by the operating system.
6. Each processor in a cluster can asynchronously perform either scalar or vector operations dictated by user programs.
7. Any processor running in monitor mode can interrupt any other processor and cause it to switch from user mode to monitor mode.
8. Detection of system deadlock is provided within the cluster.

The vector performance of each processor is improved through faster machine clock, parallel memory ports, and hardware automatic "flexible chaining" features. These new features allow simultaneous memory fetches, arithmetic, and memory store operations in a series of related vector operations (this contrasts to the "fixed chaining" and unit-directional vector fetch/store in Cray-1). As a result, the processor design provides higher speed and more balanced vector processing capabilities for both long and short vectors, characterized by heavy register-to-register or heavy memory-to-memory vector operations.

Example 9.4 Vector computations on X-MP are illustrated in Figure 9.42 for the following computation:

$$A = B + S * D$$

where boldface letters denote vector quantities. Using three memory ports per processor, the hardware automatically "chains" through all five vector operations such that one result per clock period can be delivered.

$$A = B + s * D$$

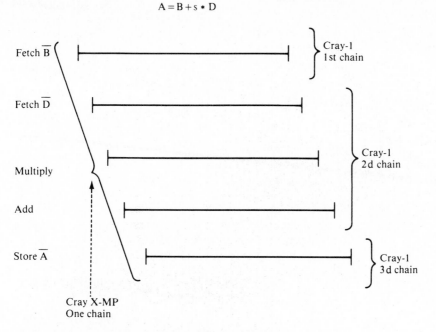

Figure 9.42 Pipeline chaining in Example 9.4 for Cray X-MP.

Multitasking exploits another dimension of parallelism beyond that provided by vectorization. So far, *vectorization* has been focused on the low-level parallelism, primarily among independent and statement-oriented operations from single-job programs. The *multitasking* offers a high-level parallelism among independent algorithms, which are job/program/loop-oriented to achieve both single and multijob performance. Combining both vectorization and multitasking, one can explore new and faster parallel algorithms at several levels, as listed below:

1. Multitasking at the job level (Figure 9.43a)
2. Multitasking at the job-step level (Figure 9.43b)
3. Multitasking at the program level (Figure 9.44)
4. Multitasking at the loop level (Figure 9.45)

When this book was published, software support for multitasking at the job level (Figure 9.43a), the program level (Figure 9.44), and the loop level (Figure 9.45) were available from Cray Research. However, the feasibility of implementing multitasking at the job-step level (Figure 9.43b) is still under further study. In what follows, we show three examples to illustrate the concept of multitasking, in particular, for the X-MP multiprocessor system.

(a) Multitasking at the job level

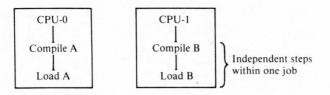

(b) Multitasking at the job-step level

Figure 9.43 Multitasking at job levels for Cray X-MP.

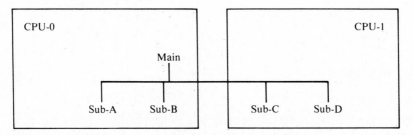

Figure 9.44 Multitasking at the program level for Cray X-MP.

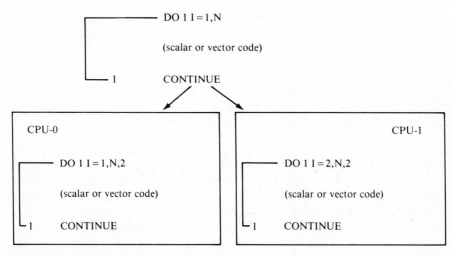

Figure 9.45 Multitasking at the loop level for Cray X-MP.

Example 9.5 Multitasking of vector code and scalar code is illustrated in Figure 9.46 for the following two loop computations, respectively.

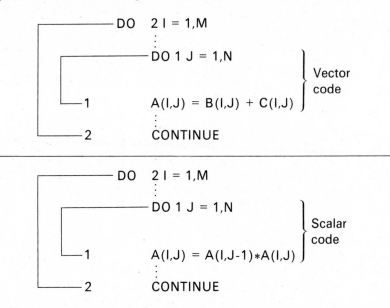

Example 9.6 Multitasking by processor pipelining (macropipelining introduced in Chapter 1) is illustrated in Figure 9.47 for the following loop computations, where S1 and S2 stand for the two vector computations involved.

```
      DO 1 I = 2,N
      A(I) = A(I − 1) + B(I)   S1
      D(I) = A(I) + C(I)       S2
    1 CONTINUE
```

9.6.3 Performance of Cray X-MP

In this section, the performance of X-MP is evaluated with theoretical predictions and benchmark timings as reported by the designers. The X-MP processor design is well-balanced for processing both scalar and vector codes. At the end, we sketch the Cray-2, which is still under development.

The overall effective performance of each processor in execution of typical user programs with interspersing scalar and vector codes (usually short vectors) is ensured through fast data flow between scalar and vector functional units, short memory access time for vector and scalar references, as well as small start-up time for scalar and vector operations. As a result of this design characteristic, the machine can perform very well in real programming environments using standard compiler, without resorting to an enormous amount of hand-coding or even restructuring of the original application algorithms. Certainly, as the code is more

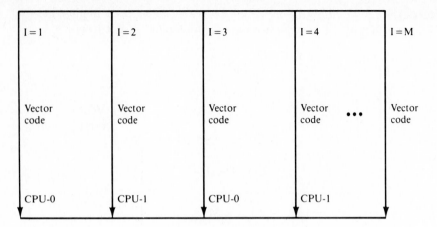

Figure 9.46 Multitasking in Example 9.5 among two CPUs in Cray X-MP.

vectorized, and the vector length is becoming longer, an even better performance can be achieved.

With a 9.5-ns clock rate, the peak speed of one CPU in X-MP is 210 megaflops and that of using two CPUs (dedicated to multitasking of a single large job) is 420 megaflops. We assume one *unit* to be based on compiler-generated code running on Cray 1/S. This means that the "minimum" 1-CPU rate is 1 and that of 2-CPU is 2. Let "typical" be the cases of small-to-medium size vectors encountered in typical programs. Let "maximum" refer to the cases of very long vectors. The performance of various types of programs relative to that of Cray 1/S is summarized in Table 9.4. The unit for I/O rate is based on measured time per sector.

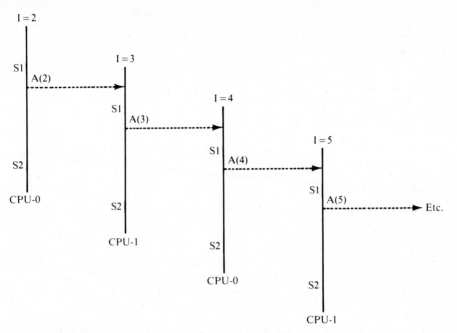

Figure 9.47 Multitasking by processor pipelining in Example 9.6.

Some benchmark timings on X-MP are reported by the Cray Research designers. Table 9.5 shows the timing on various vector loop families with respect to three representative vector lengths. The improvement of X-MP over Cray 1/S on typical vector loops ranges from 1.5 to 3.0 with respect to increasing vector lengths. It has been also reported that for general linear algebra (Fortran) benchmark programs, the speedup factor of X-MP over Cray 1/S ranges from 2.77 to 3.27.

Table 9.4 Overall performance of the Cray X-MP relative to Cray 1/S and disk

1-CPU rate	(Peak 210 megaflops)	
Minimum:	1 (Cray 1/S)	
Typical:	Scalar-dominated 1.5	
	Vector-dominated 2.0	
Maximum:	4	

2-CPU rate	(Peak 420 megaflops)	
Minimum:	2	
Typical:	Scalar-dominated 3.0	
	Vector-dominated 4.9	
Maximum:	4	

I/O rate	Access time	Transfer rate
Disk	1	1
SSD	0.01	250

Table 9.5 Vector loop families benchmark timing on X-MP over Cray 1/S

Vector loop families	Short vector (VL = 8)	Medium vector (VL = 128)	Long vector (VL = 1024)
$A = B$	1.1	1.8	2.1
$A = B + C$	1.2	2.2	2.7
$A = B * C$	1.5	2.6	3.3
$A = B/C$	1.5	1.9	2.0
$A = B + C + D$	1.5	2.7	3.2
$A = B + C * D$	1.4	2.9	3.6
$A = B + s * D$	1.3	3.0	4.0
$A = B + C + D + E$	1.3	2.3	2.7
$A = B + C + D * E$	1.6	2.5	2.9
$A = B * C + D * E$	1.3	2.5	3.1
$A = B + C * D + E * F$	1.5	2.1	2.2
Typical	1.5	2.5	3.0

Theoretically, we can roughly analyze the total speedup of X-MP over a scalar processor as follows: Vectorization offers a speedup of 10 to 20 over scalar processing, depending on actual code and vector length. Multitasking offers an additional speedup of $S_m \leq 2$, depending on task size and relative multitasking overhead. The total speedup over scalar processing is thus equal to $S = S_m \times (10$ to 20). In the benchmark, SPECTRAL, for short-term weather forecasting, the actual 2-CPU speedup has been measured as $S_m = 1.89$ over 1-CPU. Therefore, we obtain $S = 18$ to 38 under the assumption that $S_m = 1.8$ to 1.9.

We describe below a model developed by Ingrid Bucher (1983) to evaluate the performance of Cray X-MP in environments with different work loads. Work loads on the X-MP can be characterized by three types of execution requirements: *scalar* mode, *vector* mode, and *concurrent* mode. The scalar mode is characterized by a process code being executed sequentially either for reasons of logic or because it is too costly to vectorize. In the vector mode, a process code is vectorizable and executed in the vector section of the processor. In this mode the process granularity is small. In the concurrent mode, the process code is decomposed into cooperating processes and can be executed on more than one processor. The process granularity is large enough to overcome the communication and process creation overheads.

Let S_s, S_v, and S_c represent the rates at which a machine can execute scalar, vector, and concurrent codes, respectively. Also, let F_s, F_v, and F_c be the fractions of the work load that can be executed only in scalar, vector, and concurrent modes, respectively. Therefore the time required to execute this work load is proportional to

$$T = \frac{F_s}{S_s} + \frac{F_v}{S_v} + \frac{F_c}{S_c} \equiv \frac{1}{S_{eff}} \tag{9.1}$$

where S_{eff} is the work load–dependent effective speed of the machine. Equation 9.1 implies that the slowest of the execution speeds will critically influence the effective speed unless the fractional work load F associated with it is negligibly small.

The weight factors F_s, F_v, and F_c have to be determined empirically from the work load and adjusted by projections of how the work load will evolve in the future. In general, the choice of machine configurations may influence the characteristics of the work load. For example, a machine with high concurrent speed may encourage more Monte Carlo simulations. A satisfactory measure that is independent of machine architecture and compiler optimization and characterizes the amount of computational work done is desirable. A generally accepted metric for the execution speed of supercomputers is the megaflops. However, this metric does not include much of the work done. Examples of such work are the logical operations, integer arithmetic, and table hookups. Because of the highly parallel architecture of each processing unit, these operations may often be performed in parallel with the floating-point work. Nevertheless, we adopt the megaflops measure.

In the vector mode, the time required to perform operations on vectors of length N is a linear function of N given by

$$T = T_{\text{start}} + N\Delta \tag{9.2}$$

where T_{start} is the startup time for the vector operation and Δ is the time per result elements. For example, the Cray X-MP has shorter startup and element times for its vector operations than the Cray-1S and therefore clearly has the superior vector processor. The vector execution speed can be estimated by

$$S_v = \frac{N}{T} = \frac{1}{\Delta + T_{\text{start}}/N} \tag{9.3}$$

Note, however, that the average time to process a vector length N has a more complicated relationship than Eq. 9.2, because vectors of length $N > 64$ are stripmined in sections of length 64.

Not all vector operations follow the simple relationship shown in Eq. 9.2. For the Cray-1S, vectors must have a constant stride (distance between memory locations), but the stride need not be 1. However, for many repetitive operations, data are not stored in memory in a regular pattern. Hence we can identify these types of vector operations:

1. Vector operations for vectors stored in continuous locations
2. Operations for vectors stored with constant stride
3. Operations for vector operands stored in irregular locations in memory

Operands stored in irregular locations must be gathered, and the results may have to be scattered back into memory. The Cray-1S performs, gathers, and scatters in scalar mode only. Therefore, we can modify the execution rate in the vector mode by

$$\frac{1}{S_v} = \frac{F_1}{S_{v1}} + \frac{F_2}{S_{v2}} + \frac{F_3}{S_{v3}} \tag{9.4}$$

where S_{v1}, S_{v2}, and S_{v3} are the vector speeds for operands stored in continuous memory location, locations with constant stride > 1, and random locations, respectively. F_1, F_2, and F_3 are the corresponding fractions of the vectorizable work load.

The number of *loads* and *store* per floating-point operation greatly influences the vector speed. For some typical vector codes, measurements indicate that 0.6 to 1.0 *loads* and 0.2 to 0.5 *stores* were observed per floating-point operation. Therefore, the floating Fortran statement

$$V1(I) = S1 * V2(I) + S2 * V3(I) \tag{9.5}$$

produces the typical code. Further, two such statements are contained in a typical DO loop, reducing the startup time for the other loop per floating-point operation by a factor of 2 for the X-MP.

Table 9.6 contains values for vector speeds for a work load similar to that at the Los Alamos Laboratory. Table 9.7 indicates the values for a more ideal work load. Note the effective speeds are degraded by only small amounts due to the slow components. Measurements of the scalar speed S_s is performed by running a bench program. For example, the scalar speeds for Cray-1S and one of two processors of the Cray X-MP are 4.2 and 5.4, respectively.

For the asynchronous concurrent mode, there are communication overheads and portions of the parallel algorithm that must be executed sequentially. Let F_c be the fraction of code that can be executed in parallel mode on an arbitrary number of P processors, with the remainder F_{seq} of it to be executed sequentially. Then the execution time of the concurrent algorithm is proportional to

$$\frac{1}{S_c} = \frac{F_c}{P * S_s} + \frac{F_{seq}}{S_s} + P * T_{comm} \tag{9.6}$$

Table 9.6 Characteristic vector speeds (megaflops) for vector length = 100 and work load $F_s = 0.78$, $F_v = 0.20$, $F_c = 0.02$. (Courtesy of *ACM Sigmetrics*, Bucher 1983)

Machine	S_{v1} Vector speed for continuous vectors	S_{v2} Vector speed for constant stride	S_{v3} Vector speed for random access	S_v Effective vector speed
Cray-1S	58	56	5	46
Cray X-MP*	107	101	6	79

* One of two processors.

Table 9.7 Characteristic vector speeds (megaflops) for vector length = 500 and ideal work load $F_s = 0.85, F_v = 0.15, F_c = 0.00$. (Courtesy of *ACM Sigmetrics*, Bucher 1983)

Machine model	S_1 Vector speed for continuous vectors	S_2 Vector speed for constant stride	S_3 Vector speed for random access	S_v Effective vector speed
Cray-1S	66	65	5	66
Cray X-MP*	133	132	6	133

* One of two processors.

where S_s is the speed for executing the sequential portion of code and T_{comm} is the communication overhead. Using Eq. 9.1 and results described earlier, we can compile characteristic speeds of Cray-1S, Cray X-MP, and some hypothetical machines for two work loads with differing characteristics. In Tables 9.8 and 9.9, the machines in quotes are hypothetical machines and the numbers in parentheses are postulated numbers for hypothetical machines.

From these tables, it is obvious that the effective speed of a supercomputer is strongly work load–dependent. The slowest characteristic speed will affect the effective speed critically unless the fraction of the work load associated with that speed is negligibly small. It acts like a bottleneck. The most effective way to speed up a machine is to increase this speed or to decrease the fraction of work associated with it. The results also show that speeding up the fastest characteristic speed of a supercomputer will markedly improve its effective speed, only if the fraction of the work load running at that speed is close to 1. If this is not the case, the installation of additional vector pipelines on a vector computer will not be effective.

In summary, the Cray X-MP has 8 times Cray-1 memory bandwidth with guaranteed chaining of linked vector operations. Compared to Cray-1, the X-MP offers 1.25 to 3.75 speedup for single job and 2.5 to 5 times throughput on CPU

Table 9.8 Characteristic speeds (megaflops) for Cray-1S, Cray X-MP, and a hypothetical machine for vector length = 100, with work load $F_s = 0.20$, $F_v = 0.60$, and $F_c = 0.20$. (Courtesy of *ACM Sigmetrics*, Bucher 1983)

Machine	S_s	S_v	S_c	S_{eff}
Cray-1S	4.2	46	4.2	9.2
Cray X-MP (1 processor)	5.4	79	5.4	12.2
Cray X-MP (2 processors)	5.4	(158)	(10.8)	(16.8)
"Cray X-MP" (4 processors)	5.4	(316)	(21.6)	(20.7)

Table 9.9 Characteristic speeds (megaflops) for Cray-1S, Cray X-MP, and a hypothetical machine for vector length = 500, with work load $F_s = 0.10$, $F_v = 0.80$ and $F_c = 0.10$. (Courtesy of *ACM Sigmetrics*, Bucher 1983)

Machine	S_s	S_v	S_c	S_{eff}
Cray-1S	4.2	46	4.2	16.7
Cray X-MP (1 processor)	5.4	133	5.4	23.2
Cray X-MP (2 processors)	5.4	(266)	(10.8)	(32.5)
"Cray X-MP" (4 processors)	5.4	(532)	(21.6)	(40.6)

dominated job mix. The improvement in speed is due to two processors scheduled by the COS, shorter clock period, higher memory bandwidth, and guaranteed chaining. Like the Cray-1, the X-MP is good for both short and long vector processing. A general guideline to explore the computing power in X-MP is to partition tasks at the highest level to apply multitasking and then to vectorize tasks at the lower levels as much as possible.

The Cray-2 Cray Research, Inc. is currently developing the Cray-2, which is expected to have 6 times speedup in scalar and 12 times speedup in vector operations over the Cray-1. Cray-2 is planned to have four processors using 32 M words of main memory. The CPU cycle time is targeted to be 4 ns. The I/O will be improved 20 times from current Cray-1 capability. It has been suggested that 16-gate ECL chips will be used in Cray-2. Highly densed logic and memory modules will be cooled by immersion in inert fluorocarbon liquid. The longest wire length is confined to 16 in. The system is planned to be housed in a circular frame 38 inches in diameter and 26 inches in height, a rather condensed size for a supercomputer. The Cray-2 is expected to become available in the late 1980s.

9.7 BIBLIOGRAPHIC NOTES AND PROBLEMS

The original design of C.mmp architecture is described in Wulf et al. (1972). The final C.mmp architecture is described in Fuller and Harbison (1978). The experience of the C.mmp among other multiprocessors is presented in Jones and Schwartz (1980). Reliability of C.mmp has been studied in Siewiorek et al. (1978). The Hydra operating system is described in Wulf et al. (1981). Oleinick (1978) studied parallel algorithms for the C.mmp. Marathe and Fuller (1977) evaluated the C.mmp architecture and the Hydra kernel.

The S-1 multiprocessor has been reported in Widdoes (1980). Lawrence Livermore National Laboratory has published a series of reports on the S-1 project at the Lawrence Livermore National Laboratory (1981). IBM System/370 architecture was assessed in Case and Pedegs (1978). IBM 3033 and 3081 are described in IBM (1978, 1983). Programming and operating system design considerations of tightly coupled IBM multiprocessor system are given in Arnold et al. (1974) which includes an overview of the OS/VS2 MVS. Functional characteristics of 370/168 can be found in the IBM manual IBM (1979). System description of the Denelcor HEP computer is extracted from technical notes by Denelcor, Inc. (1983) and a report by Smith and Fink (1980). Jordan (1983) has studied the performance of the HEP. The material on the Cray X-MP and Cray-2 is based on Chen (1983) and some technical presentations by Cray Research, Inc. Bucher (1983) developed the performance models for Cray X-MP.

The evolution of the Sperry Univac 1100 series is reported in Borgerson et al. (1978). The detailed description of Univac 1100/80 systems can be found in several Sperry Univac manuals on the processor and storage, hardware system, programming, and executive systems. An introductory treatment of commercial multiprocessor systems, including the IBM 370/168, CDC Cyber-170, Honeywell Series 60 Level 66, Univac 1100/80, Burroughs B7700, and DEC System 10 Model KL-10, C.mmp, and C.m*, is given in Satyanarayanan (1980) plus an annotated bibliography up to 1979. Surveys of earlier multiprocessors can be found in Enslow (1974, 1977). A recent tutorial text on supercomputers by Hwang and Kuhn (1984) covers recent vector processors and multiprocessor systems. The Tandem Nonstop system is described in Katzman (1978). Recently, there are a number of research multiprocessors reported by Gajski et al. (1983), Gottlieb et al. (1983), and Fritsch et al. (1983).

Problems

9.1 Determine the evaluation time of the arithmetic expression

$$S = A[1]B[1] + A[2]B[2] + A[3]B[3] + A[4]B[4]$$

in each of the following computer systems:
    (*a*) An SISD system with a general-purpose PE
    (*b*) A multifunction SISD system with one adder and one multiplier
    (*c*) An SIMD system with four PEs
    (*d*) An MIMD system with four processors
The addition and multiplication require two and four time units, respectively. Memory-access time due to instruction and data fetch are ignored. The data-transfer time from one PE to another PE is assumed to be one time unit in SIMD and MIMD systems, whereas it is ignored in SISD and multifunction systems. In an SIMD system, the interconnection of PEs is in a linear circular fashion; i.e., each PE is connected to two neighboring PEs. In an MIMD, each PE can directly communicate with other PEs.

9.2 Three types of switch boxes are used to design a multistage interconnection network for an MIMD system. A square switch has two inputs and two outputs. An arbitration switch has two inputs and one output. A distribution switch has one input and two outputs. You are asked to design an 8 × 4 interconnection network using these switch modules.
    (*a*) Use the minimum number of switch modules to construct the 8 × 4 network with a unique path between any source and any destination.
    (*b*) Repeat (*a*) for a 4 × 8 network.
    (*c*) There are many ways to construct a $2^m \times 2^n$ network, if $m > n$. Comment on the better choices

among all the possible configurations in terms of hardware requirements and expected network performance.

9.3 Consider the storage of a symmetric n-by-n matrix $\mathbf{A} = (a_{ij})$ in a memory system with n parallel modules, where n is a perfect square. Devise storage schemes to satisfy each of the following requirements. It is assumed that only $[n/2]$ rows of the matrix are to be stored if n is odd, and $[n/2] + 1$ rows are needed if n is even. Each memory module has a separate index register to keep track of the allocation.

(a) It is required to access any row or any column in one memory cycle. For example, we want to access the elements a_{13}, a_{23}, and a_{33} in one cycle, or the elements a_{43}, a_{53}, a_{63}, a_{73}, a_{83}, and a_{93} in another cycle.

(b) It is required to access any row or any nonoverlapping square of blocks as in the example below:

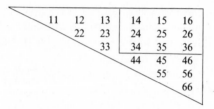

(c) Illustrate your memory allocation schemes for (a) and (b) with $N = 9$ and $N = 16$, respectively. Is it possible to achieve (a) and (b) with the same scheme?

9.4 Answer the following questions associated with the C.mmp system:

(a) Explain the special system instructions HALT, RESET, WAIT, RTI, and RTT developed for the PDP-11 processors in the C.mmp.

(b) Explain the function of the *Dmap* and of the *interprocessor bus* installed in the C.mmp.

(c) What are the special features built into the *Hydra* operating system?

9.5 Answer the following questions on the S-1 multiprocessor project:

(a) Explain the use of separate data cache and instruction cache in the pipelined design of the S-1 Mark IIA uniprocessors.

(b) Explain the virtual-to-physical address translation scheme used in the S-1 system.

(c) What are the special features in the *Amber* operating system that facilitates multiprocessing?

9.6 Answer the following questions for the HEP multiprocessor:

(a) Distinguish between the conventional SISD pipelining and the MIMD pipelining introduced in the HEP.

(b) Explain the design and priority operations of the packet-switching interconnection network developed in the HEP.

(c) Explain the synchronization and protection mechanisms developed in the HEP.

9.7 Answer the following questions for the IBM multiprocessors:

(a) Distinguish the Attached Processing (AP) mode from the Multiprocessing (MP) mode in various IBM multiprocessors.

(b) What are the improvements of the IBM 3081 over the IBM 370/168MP and IBM 3033 in both technologies and designs?

(c) What are the multiprocessing features in the IBM OS/VS2 operating system?

9.8 Answer the following questions for the Univac 1100 series:

(a) Describe the increase of multiprocessing capability in various $M \times N$ configurations of the Univac 1100/80.

(b) What are the improvements made in Univac 1100/90 multiprocessors over the Univac 1100/80 models?

(c) Explain the functional structure of the kernel of the EXEC operating system.

9.9 Answer the following questions for the Tandem nonstop system:

(a) Why can the Tandem multiprocessor tolerate all single failures in the system?

(b) Explain the alternate path switching between devices and controllers in the Tandem/16.

(c) Describe the message system developed in the Guardian operating system.

9.10 Answer the following questions for the Cray X-MP system:

(a) Explain the inter-CPU communication structure in the Cray X-MP.

(b) Explain the functions of the Solid-State Storage Device (SSD) and of the I/O Subsystem (IOS) in the Cray X-MP.

(c) Explain the improvements made in the Cray X-MP over its predecessor, the Cray-1.

9.11 A computing system has 10 tape drives available. All jobs that run on the system require a maximum of four tape drives to complete, but we know that they start by running for a long period with only three; they request the one remaining drive for a short period when needed near the end of their operation. (There is an endless supply of these jobs.)

(a) If the job scheduler operates with the policy that it will not start a job unless there are four unassigned drives, and it assigns those four drives to a job for its entire duration, what is the maximum number of jobs that can be in progress at once? What are the minimum and maximum number of drives that may actually be idle as a result of this policy?

(b) Figure out a better scheduling policy to improve the drive utilization rate and at the same time to avoid a system deadlock. What is the maximum number of jobs that can be in progress in your new policy? What are the minimum and maximum numbers of drives that may be idle as a result of this policy?

9.12 *Chained vector time (chime)* is a useful term for discussing vector operation timing. Cray X-MP can combine several chimes implementable on a Cray-1 into a single long chime. Give an example vector computation sequence (more involved than that shown in Example 9.4) to show the advantages of using X-MP over the use of Cray-1.

CHAPTER TEN

DATA FLOW COMPUTERS AND VLSI COMPUTATIONS

Computer architects have been constantly searching for new approaches to designing high-performance machines. Data flow and VLSI offer two mutually supportive approaches towards the design of future supercomputers. In this chapter, we study the requirements of data-driven computations, functional programming languages, and various data flow system architectures that have been challenged in recent years. In the VLSI computing area, we introduce topological structures of multiprocessor arrays for large-scale numeric computations and for symbolic manipulations. Techniques for directly mapping parallel algorithms into hardware structures will be studied. VLSI architectures for designing large-scale matrix arithmetic solvers are presented based on matrix partitioning and algorithmic decomposition. Potential applications of some of these VLSI computing structures are demonstrated for real-time image processing.

10.1 DATA-DRIVEN COMPUTING AND LANGUAGES

Data flow computers are based on the concept of *data-driven* computation, which is drastically different from the operation of a conventional von Neumann machine. The fundamental difference is that instruction execution in a conventional computer is under program-flow control, whereas that in a data flow computer is driven by the data (operand) availability. We characterize below these two types of computers. The basic structures of data flow computers and their advantages and shortcomings will be discussed in subsequent sections.

Jack Dennis (1979) of MIT has identified three basic issues towards the development of an ideal architecture for future computers. The first is to achieve a high performance/cost ratio; the second is to match the ratio with technological progress; and the third is to offer better programmability in application areas.

The data flow model offers an approach to meet these demands. The recent progress in the VLSI microelectronic area has provided the technological basis for developing data flow computers.

10.1.1 Control Flow vs. Data Flow Computers

The concepts of *control flow* and *data flow* computing are distinguished by the control of computation sequences in two distinct program representations. In the control flow program representations shown in Figure 10.1, the statement

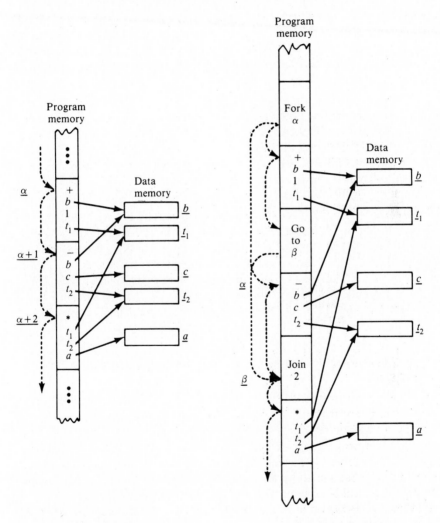

(a) Sequential control flow   (b) Parallel control flow

Figure 10.1 Instruction execution in a control flow computer for the computation of $a = (b + 1) * (b - c)$ using shared data memory.

$a = (b + 1) * (b - c)$ is specified by a series of instructions with an explicit flow of control. Shared memory cells are the means by which data is passed between instructions. Data (operands) are referenced by their memory addresses (variables). In Figure 10.1, solid arcs show the access to stored data, while dotted arcs indicate the flow of control.

In the traditional *sequential control flow* model (von Neumann), there is a single thread of control, as shown in Figure 10.1a, which is passed from instruction to instruction. Explicit control transfers are caused by using operators like GO TO. In the *parallel control flow* model (Figure 10.1b), special parallel control operators such as FORK and JOIN are used to explicitly specify parallelism. These operators allow more than one thread of control to be active at an instant and provide means for synchronizing these threads, as demonstrated in Figure 10.1b. All underlined variables refer to addresses of operands and instructions. Special features are identified below for either the sequential or parallel control flow model:

- Data is passed between instructions via references to shared memory cells.
- Flow of control is implicitly sequential, but special control operators can be used explicitly for parallelism.
- Program counters are used to sequence the execution of instruction in a centralized control environment.

In a data flow computing environment, instructions are activated by the availability of data tokens as indicated by the ( ) in Figure 10.2. Data flow programs are represented by directed graphs, which show the flow of data between instructions. Each instruction consists of an operator, one or two operands, and one or more destinations to which the result (data token) will be sent. Three snapshots of the data flow graph for $a = (b + 1) * (b - c)$ are shown in Figure 10.3. The dots correspond to data tokens being passed between instructions. Listed below are interesting features in the data flow model:

- Intermediate or final results are passed directly as data token between instructions.
- There is no concept of shared data storage as embodied in the traditional notion of a variable.
- Program sequencing is constrained only by data dependency among instructions.

Control flow computers have a *control-driven* organization. This means that the program has complete control over instruction sequencing. Synchronous computations are performed in control flow computers using centralized control. Data flow computers have a *data-driven* organization that is characterized by a passive examine stage. Instructions are examined to reveal the operand availability, upon which they are executed immediately if the functional units are available.

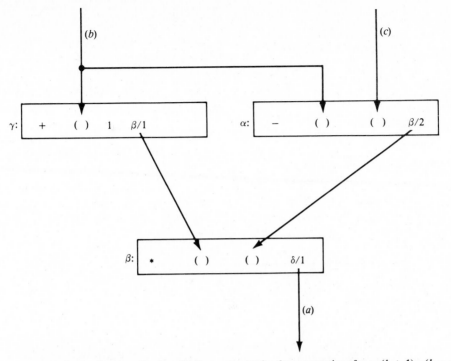

Figure 10.2 Instruction execution in a dataflow computer for the computation of $a = (b + 1) * (b - c)$ **by direct data forwarding.**

This data-driven concept means *asynchrony*, which means that many instructions can be executed simultaneously and asynchronously. A high degree of implicit parallelism is expected in a data flow computer. Because there is no use of shared memory cells, data flow programs are free from side effects. In other words, a data flow operation is purely functional and produces no side effects such as the changes of a memory word. Operands are directly passed as "tokens" of values instead of as "address" variables. Data flow computations have no far-reaching effects. This locality of effect plus asynchrony and functionality make them suitable for distributed implementation.

Information items in a data flow computer appear as *operation packets* and *data tokens*. An operation packet is composed of the opcode, operands, and destinations of its successor instructions, as shown in Figure 10.2. A data token is formed with a result value and its destinations. Many of these packets or tokens are passed among various resource sections in a data flow machine. Therefore, the machine can assume a packet communication architecture, which is a type of distributed multiprocessor organization.

Data flow machine architectures Depending on the way of handling data tokens, data flow computers are divided into the *static model* and the *dynamic model*, as introduced in Figure 10.4 and Figure 10.5, respectively. In a static data flow

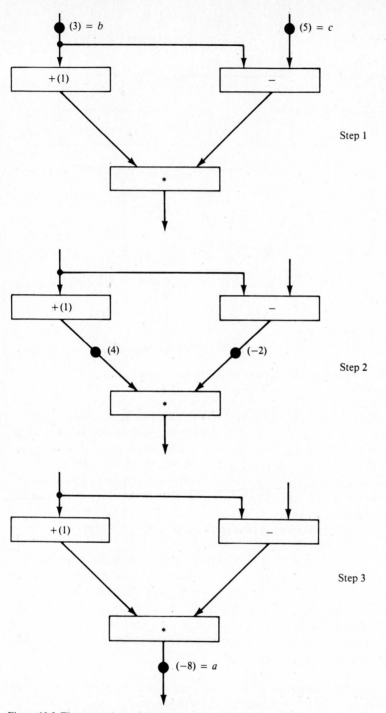

Figure 10.3 Three snapshots of the dataflow computation for $a = (b + 1) * (b - c)$.

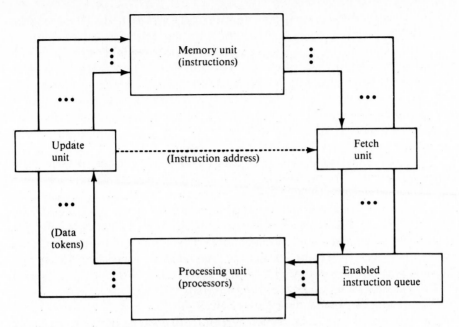

Figure 10.4 A static dataflow computer organization.

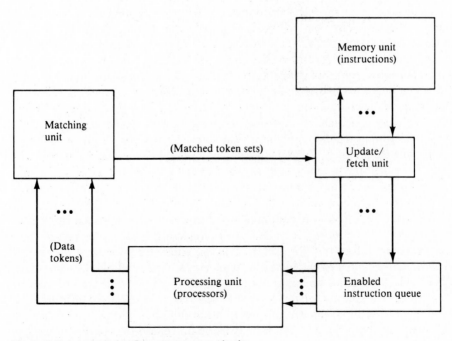

Figure 10.5 A dynamic dataflow computer organization.

machine, data tokens are assumed to move along the arcs of the data flow program graph to the operator nodes. The nodal operation gets executed when all its operand data are present at the input arcs. Only one token is allowed to exist on any arc at any given time, otherwise the successive sets of tokens cannot be distinguished. This architecture is considered static because tokens are not labeled and *control tokens* must be used to acknowledge the proper timing in transferring data tokens from node to node. Jack Dennis and his research group at the MIT Laboratory for Computer Science is currently developing a static data flow computer.

A dynamic data flow machine uses *tagged tokens*, so that more than one token can exist in an arc. The tagging is achieved by attaching a label with each token which uniquely identifies the context of that particular token. This dynamically tagged data flow model suggests that maximum parallelism can be exploited from a program graph. If the graph is cyclic, the tagging allows dynamically unfolding of the iterative computations. Dynamic data flow computers include the Manchester machine developed by Watson and Gurd at the University of Manchester, England, and the Arvinds machine under development at MIT, which is evolved from an earlier data flow project at the University of California at Irvine.

The two packet-communication organizations are based on two different schemes for synchronizing instruction execution. A point of commonality in the two organizations is that multiple processing elements can independently and asynchronously evaluate the executable instruction packets. In Figure 10.4, the data tokens are in the input pool of the update unit. This update unit passes data tokens to their destination instructions in the memory unit. When an instruction receives all its required operand tokens, it is enabled and forwarded to the enabled queue. The fetch unit fetches these instructions when they become enabled.

In Figure 10.5, the system synchronization is based on a matching mechanism. Data tokens form the input pool of the matching unit. This matching unit arranges data token into pairs or sets and temporarily stores each token until all operands are compared, whereupon the matched token sets are released to the fetch-update unit. Each set of matched data tokens (usually two for binary operations) is needed for one instruction execution. The fetch-update unit forms the enabled instructions by merging the token sets with copies sent to their consumer instructions. The matching of the special tags attached to the data tokens can unfold iterative loops for parallel computations. We shall further discuss this tagged-token concept in later sections.

Both static and dynamic data flow architectures have a pipelined ring structure. If we include the I/O, a generalized architecture is shown in Figure 10.6. The ring contains four resource sections: the *memories*, the *processors*, the *routing network*, and the *input-output unit*. The memories are used to hold the instruction packets. The processing units form the task force for parallel execution of enabled instructions. The routing network is used to pass the result tokens to their destined instructions. The input-output unit serves as an interface between the data flow computer and the outside world. For dynamic machines, the token matching is performed by the I/O section.

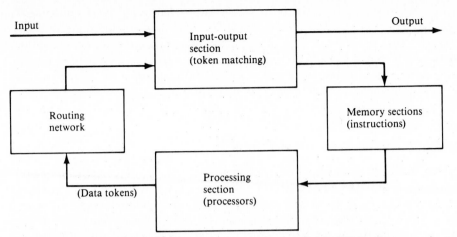

Figure 10.6 A ring-structured dataflow computer organization including the I/O functions.

Most existing data flow machine prototypes are built as an attached processor to a host computer, which handles the code translation and I/O functions. Eventually, computer architects wish to build stand-alone data flow computers. The basic ring structure can be extended to many improved architectural configurations for data flow systems. For example, one can build a data flow system with multiple rings of resources. The routing network can be divided into several functionally specialized packet-switched networks. The memory section can be subdivided into cell blocks. We shall describe variants of data flow computer architecture in Section 10.2.

Major design issues Toward the practical realization of a data flow computer, we identify below a number of important technical problems that remain to be solved:

1. The development of efficient data flow languages which are easy to use and to be interpreted by machine hardware
2. The decomposition of programs and the assignment of program modules to data flow processors
3. Controlling and supporting large amounts of interprocessor communication with cost-effective packet-switched networks
4. Developing intelligent data-driven mechanisms for either static or dynamic data flow machines
5. Efficient handling of complex data structures, such as arrays, in a data flow environment
6. Developing a memory hierarchy and memory allocation schemes for supporting data flow computations
7. A large need for user acquaintance of functional data flow languages, software supports, data flow compiling, and new programming methodologies
8. Performance evaluation of data flow hardware in a large variety of application domains, especially in the scientific areas

Approaches to attack the above issues and partial solutions to some of them will be presented in subsequent sections. We need first to understand the basic properties of data flow languages. After all, the data flow computers are language-oriented machines. In fact, research on data flow machines started with data flow languages. It is the rapid progress in VLSI that has pushed the construction of several hardware data flow prototypes in recent years.

10.1.2 Data Flow Graphs and Languages

There is a need to provide a high-level language for data flow computers. The primary goal is to take advantage of implicit parallelism. Data flow computing is compatible with the use of dependence graphs in program analysis for compiling in a conventional computer. An efficient data flow language should be able to express parallelism in a program more naturally, to promote programming productivity, and to facilitate close interactions between algorithm constructs and hardware structures. Examples of data flow languages include the Irvine Dataflow (ID) language and the Value Algorithmic Language (VAL) among several *single assignment* and *functional programming* languages that have been proposed by computer researchers

In a maximum parallel program, the sequencing of instructions should be constrained only by data dependencies and nothing else. Listed below are useful properties in a data flow language. We shall describe their implications and usages separately.

- Freedom from side effects based on functional programming
- Locality of effect without far-reaching data dependencies
- Equivalence of instruction-sequencing constraints with data dependencies
- Satisfying single-assignment rule with aliasing
- Unfolding of iterative computations into parallelism
- Lack of "history sensitivity" in procedures calls

Data flow graphs In a conventional computer, program analysis is often performed at compile time to yield better resource utilization and code optimization and at run time to reveal concurrent arithmetic logic activities for higher system throughput. For an example, we analyze the following Fortran program:

Example 10.1

1. $P = X + Y$ must wait for inputs X and Y
2. $Q = P \div Y$ must wait for instruction 1 to complete
3. $R = X \times P$ must wait for instruction 1 to complete
4. $S = R - Q$ must wait for instructions 2 and 3 to complete
5. $T = R \times P$ must wait for instruction 3 to complete
6. $U = S \div T$ must wait for instruction 4 and 5 to complete

Permissible computation sequences of the above program on a serial computer include the following five:

$$(1, 2, 3, 4, 5, 6)$$
$$(1, 3, 2, 5, 4, 6)$$
$$(1, 3, 5, 2, 4, 6)$$
$$(1, 2, 3, 5, 4, 6)$$
$$(1, 3, 2, 4, 5, 6)$$

On a parallel computer, it is possible to perform these six operations (1, [2 and 3 simultaneously], [4 and 5 simultaneously], 6) in three steps instead of six steps.

The above program analysis can be represented by the data flow graph shown in Figure 10.7. A *data flow graph* is a directed graph whose nodes correspond to operators and arcs are pointers for forwarding data tokens. The graph demonstrates sequencing constraints (consistent with data dependencies) among instructions. In a data flow computer, the machine level program is represented by data flow graphs. The firing rule of instructions is based on the data availability.

Two types of links on data flow graphs are depicted in Figure 10.8. The purpose is to distinguish those for numerical data from those for boolean variables.

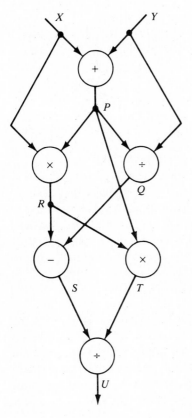

Figure 10.7 A dataflow graph for the computation of $U = f(X, Y) = (X \times (X + Y) - (X + Y) \div Y) \div (X \times (X + Y) \times (X + Y))$.

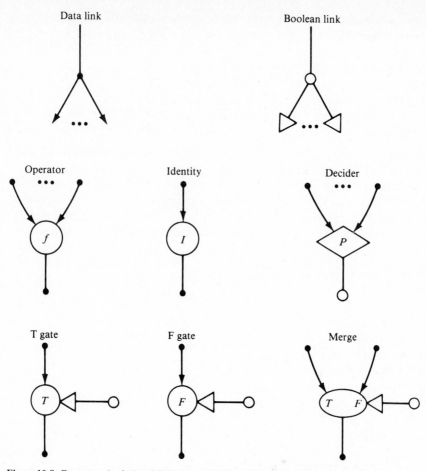

Figure 10.8 Operators (nodes) and links (arcs) for the construction of dataflow graphs.

Numerical data links transmit integer, real, or complex numbers and boolean links carry only boolean values for control purposes. Figure 10.8 presents various operator types for constructing data flow graphs. An *identity* operator is a special operator that has one input arc and transmits its input value unchanged. *Deciders, gates,* and *merge* operators are used to represent conditional or iterative computation in data flow graphs. A decider requires a value from each input arc and produces the truth value resulting from applying the predicate P to the values received.

Control tokens bearing boolean values control the flow of data tokens by means of the T gates, the F gates, and the merge operators. A T gate passes a data token from its data input arc to its output arc when it receives the true value on its control input arc. It will absorb a data token from its data input arc and place nothing on its output arc if it receives a false value. An F gate has similar behavior, except the sense of the control value is reversed. A merge operator has T and F data input arcs and a truth-value control arc. When a truth value is received, the merge actor places the token from the true input arc on its output arc. The token on the other unused input arc is discarded. Similarly, the false input is passed to the output, when the control arc is false.

Example 10.2 The following iterative computation is represented by the data flow graph in Figure 10.9, using some of the operators and graph links specified in Figure 10.8. The integer power $z = x^n$ of an input number x is desired:

$$\begin{aligned}
&\textbf{input x,n} \\
&\quad y=1\,;i=n \\
&\quad \textbf{while } i>0 \textbf{ do} \\
&\quad\quad \textbf{begin } y=y*x;i=i-1 \textbf{ end} \\
&\quad z=y \\
&\textbf{output } z
\end{aligned} \qquad (10.1)$$

The successive values assumed by the loop variables y and i pass through the links labeled in the program graph. The decider emits a token carrying the true value each time execution of the loop body is required. When the firing of the decider yields a false, the value of y is routed to the output link z. Note the presence of tokens carrying false values on the input arcs of the merge operators. These tokens allow the merge operator to initiate execution of the loop by passing initial values for the loop variables. The initial values of the control token are marked as *false* in Figure 10.9.

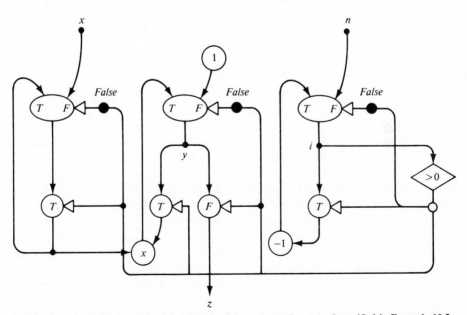

Figure 10.9 The dataflow graph representation of the computation $z = x^n$ specified in Example 10.2.

Data flow graphs form the basis of data flow languages. We briefly describe below some attractive properties of data flow languages.

Locality of effect This property can be achieved if instructions have no unnecessary far-reaching data dependencies. In Algol or Pascal, blocks and procedures provide some locality by making assignment only to local variables. This means that global assignments and common variables should be avoided. Data flow languages generally exhibit considerable locality. Assignment to a formal parameter should be within a definite range. Therefore, block structures are highly welcome in a data flow language.

Freedom from side effects This property is necessary to ensure that data dependencies are consistent with sequencing constraints. Side effects come in many forms, such as in procedures that modify variables in the calling program. The absence of global or common variables and careful control of the scopes of variables make it possible to avoid side effects. Another problem comes from the aliasing of parameters. Data flow languages provide "call by value" instead of the "call by reference." This essentially solves the aliasing problem. Instead of having a procedure modify its arguments, a "call by value" procedure copies its arguments. Thus, it can never modify the arguments passed from the calling program. In other words, inputs and outputs are totally isolated to avoid unnecessary side effects.

Single assignment rule This offers a method to promote parallelism in a program. The rule is to forbid the use of the same variable name more than once on the left-hand side of any statement. In other words, a new name is chosen for any redefined variable, and all subsequent references are changed to the new name. This concept is shown below:

$$
\begin{array}{ll}
X := P - Q & X := P - Q \\
X := X \times Y \quad \rightarrow & X1 := X \times Y \\
W := X - Y & W := X1 - Y
\end{array}
\tag{10.2}
$$

The statements on the right are made to satisfy the single assignment rule. It greatly facilitates the detection of parallelism in a program. Single assignment rule offers clarity and ease of verification, which generally outweighs the convenience of reusing the same name. Single assignment rule was first proposed by Tesler and Enea in 1968. It has been applied in developing the French data flow computer LAU and the Manchester data flow machine in England.

Unfolding iterations A programming language cannot be considered as effective if it cannot be used to implement iterative computations efficiently. Iterative computations are represented by "cyclic" data flow graphs, which are inherently sequential. In order to achieve parallel processing, iterative computations must be unfolded. Techniques have been suggested to use tagged tokens to unfold activities embedded in a cyclic data flow graph. In a conventional machine, the same operation must be sequentially performed in successive iterations.

We define each distinct evaluation of an operator as an *activity*. Unique names can be created by tagging repeated evaluations of the same operator in different iterations. A tagged token is formed with two parts: ⟨data, destination activity name⟩. The destination activity is a unique name which identifies the context in which a code block is invoked, the code block name, the instruction number within the code block, and the iteration number associated with the looping index value. This tagged information will unfold iterative computations in a recursive manner because the context tag may be itself an activity name.

Arvind and Gostelow (1978) have proposed a *U-interpreter*, which is part of the data flow language ID. The U-interpreter is used to unfold iterations. This notion of labeling computational activities, coupled with some rules for manipulating the activity names, should help to enhance the parallelism in programs written in any functional or data flow language. Special hardware structures are needed to exploit the practical benefits in designing a data flow architecture with tagged tokens. Such a dynamic architecture (Figure 10.5) needs to match the tags of many data tokens before they can be paired to enable parallel computations asynchronously.

10.1.3 Advantages and Potential Problems

Pros and cons of data flow computers are discussed in this section. Due to their strong appeal to parallelism, data flow techniques have attracted a great deal of attention in recent years. We assess first the advantages and then examine the opposition opinions. The development of data flow computers and languages is still in its infancy stage. The research community is currently divided in opinions. It is too early to draw a final conclusion because the success of data flow computing depends heavily on high technology and its matching with applications. However, it is commonly recognized that more research and development challenges should continue in this area. The idea of data-driven computation is rather old, but only in recent years have architectural models with anticipated performance been developed.

Most advantages are claimed by researchers in this area. The claimed advantages were only partially supported by performance analysis and simulation experiments. Operational statistics are not available from existing prototype data flow machines. Therefore, some of the claimed advantages are still subject to further verification. Data flow computers are advantageous in many respects over the traditional von Neumann machines. These aspects are elaborated below in terms of projected performance, matching technology, and programming productivity.

Highly concurrent operations Parallelism can be easily exposed in a data flow program graph. The data flow approach offers a possible solution to the problem of efficiently exploiting concurrency of computation on a large scale. It benefits not only regularly structured but also arbitrary parallelism in programs. The direct use of values instead of names of value containers (addresses) enables purely functional programming without side effects. Asynchronous parallelism can be exploited at the instruction level or at the procedure level. Inherently sequential computations can be unfolded to enable parallelism. The data flow approach has applied pipelining, array processing, and multiprocessing techniques discussed in previous chapters for control flow computers.

The data flow language does not introduce instruction-sequencing constraints other than the ones imposed by data dependencies in the algorithm. In theory, maximum parallelism can be achieved if sufficient resources are provided. This approach extends naturally to an arbitrary number of processors in the system. The speedup should be linearly proportional to the increase of processor number. The high concurrency in a data flow computer is supported by easier program verification, better modularity and extendability of hardware, reduced protection problems, and superior confinement of software errors.

Matching with VLSI technology Recall the basic architecture of a data flow computer (Figure 10.6). The memory section contains instruction cells which can be uniformly structured in large-scale memory arrays. The pool of processing units and the network of packet switches can be each also regularly structured with modular cells. All this homogeneity and modularity in cellular structures contributes to the suitability of VLSI implementation of major components in a data flow computer. As introduced in Chapter 1, the impressive progress in microelectronics technology has made it possible to challenge the fabrication of large arrays of processors, memories, and switches on VLSI chips.

The interconnection between chips can be built into highly densed packaging systems. It is fair to say that data flow machine architecture matches nicely with the technological supports that we anticipate to have. The potential of VLSI and VHSIC technologies can be fully exploited in the development of data flow machines. The operations in a data flow computer may be asynchronous. However, the hardware components can be designed with synchronous functional pipes and clocked memory and switch arrays. With more lessons to be learned and the data flow hardware properly evaluated, it would be appropriate to consider VLSI implementation of some large-scale data flow systems.

Programming productivity In a control flow vector processor or a multiprocessor system, the percentage of code that can be vectorized ranges from 10 to 90 percent across a broad range of scientific applications. The nonvectorizable code (scalar operations) tends to become a bottleneck. Automatic vectorization requires sophisticated data flow analysis, which is difficult in Fortran because of the side effects caused by the global scope and aliasing of variables. A well-designed data flow computer should be able to overcome these difficulties and to remove the bottleneck caused by assorted scalar operations.

It has been claimed by many computer researchers that functional programming languages will increase the software productivity as compared to the imperative languages like Fortran and Pascal. This is especially true when the computing environment demands a high degree of parallel processing to achieve a prespecified level of performance. Intuitively, this assertion is valid for certain algorithm constructs and work-load distributions. However, more empirical results are needed to prove its validity for general scientific computations.

Shortcomings of data flow computing Critics of the data flow approach have pointed out quite a number of potential problems in the development and application of data flow computers at the instruction level. It is instructional to learn from these reserved positions and to explore other alternatives to achieve high performance. In the conventional computer with centralized control hardware, an imperative language such as Fortran is used and an intelligent compiler is needed to normalize the program and to generate the dependence graph, which guides the vectorization and optimization processes we have studied in previous chapters. High-level use of the dependence graph is practiced here primarily at compile time. The major advantages of this high-level approach are summarized below:

- There is no need to use a new functional programming language, which ordinary programmers may be reluctant to learn.
- Existing software assets for vectorizing, compiling, and dedicated application software can continue to be utilized.
- Data flow analysis at the higher level of procedures and loops will result in less overhead when averaged over all instructions to be executed.

In the data flow approach, special functional programming languages must be used which can be easily compiled into a dependence graph. The object code is generated to efficiently map the dependence graph onto the data flow machine with distributed control hardware. Some advantages of high-level data flow machines become potential shortcomings in the data flow computer, which exploits parallelism at the lowest level of instruction execution. Apparent disadvantages of instructional-level data flow computers are summarized below:

1. The data driven at instruction level causes excessive pipeline overhead per instruction, which may destroy the benefits of parallelism. The long pipeline filling problem is attributed to queueing all enabled instructions at the input ports of every subsystem in the data flow ring. The queue lengths absorb some of the parallelism in a program, thus, performance becomes weak for improper buffering and traffic congestion.
2. Data flow programs tend to waste memory space for the increased code length due to the single assignment rule and the excessive copying of data arrays. The damaging effects of the memory access conflict problem are so far not well addressed by data flow researchers.
3. When a data flow computer becomes large with high numbers of instruction cells and processing elements, the packet-switched network used becomes cost-prohibitive and a bottleneck to the entire system.

4. Some critics feel that data flow has a good deal of potential in small-scale or very large-scale parallel computer systems, with a raised level of control. For medium-scale parallel systems, data flow competes less favorably with the existing pipeline, array, and multiprocessor computers. We shall further discuss this assessment in Section 10.2.3.

10.2 DATA FLOW COMPUTER ARCHITECTURES

Several interesting data flow computer architectures are studied in this section. The intent is to identify related architectural concepts rather than to describe the implementation details. We shall start with static data flow computers represented by the Dennis machine at MIT. Then we describe several ring-structured, dynamic data flow computers, including the original Irvine machine and its successor machine at MIT, the EDDY system in Japan, and the Manchester machine in England. Several specially designed data flow systems will be briefly examined, including the Utah machine, the French LAU system, and the Newcastle data-control flow computer. Design alternatives of data flow computers will also be discussed to inspire future development.

10.2.1 Static Data Flow Computers

Jack Dennis and his associates at MIT have pioneered the area of data flow research. They have developed a static data flow computing model and the associated language supports. There are two interesting data flow projects at MIT. For identification purpose, we distinguish them by calling them the Dennis machine and the Arvind machine. The Dennis machine has a static architecture, whereas the Arvind machine is dynamic, using tagged tokens and colored activities.

Data flow graphs used in the Dennis machine must follow a static execution rule that only one data token can occupy an arc at an instant. This leads to a static firing rule that an instruction is enabled if a data token is present on each of its input arcs and no token is present on any of its output arcs. Thus, the program graph contains control tokens as well as data tokens, both contributing to the enabling of an instruction. These control tokens act as acknowledge signals when data tokens are removed from output arcs.

The Dennis machine is designed to exploit the concurrency in programs represented by static data flow graphs. The structure of this data flow computer is shown in Figure 10.10; it consists of five major sections connected by channels through which information is sent in the form of discrete tokens (packets):

- *Memory* section consists of instruction cells which hold instructions and their operands.
- *Processing* section consists of processing units that perform functional operations on data tokens.

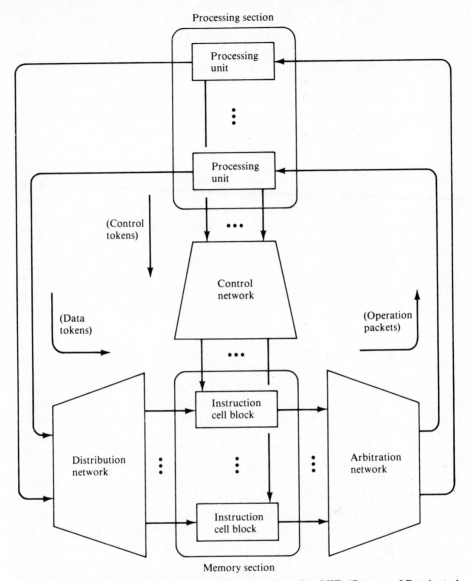

Figure 10.10 The static dataflow computer architecture proposed at MIT. (Courtesy of Dennis et al., 1979.)

- *Arbitration* network delivers operation packets from the memory section to the processing section.
- *Control* network delivers a control token from the processing section to the memory section.
- *Distribution* network delivers data tokens from the processing section to the memory section.

Instructions held in the memory section are enabled for execution by the arrival of their operands in data tokens from the distribution network and control tokens from the control network. Enabled instructions, together with their operands, are sent as operation packets to the processing section through the arbitration network. The results of instruction execution are sent through the distribution network and the control network to the memory section, where they become operands of other instructions. Each instruction cell has a unique address, the cell identifier. An occupied cell holds an instruction consisting of an operation code and several destinations. Each destination contains a destination address, which is a cell identifier, and additional control information used by processing units to generate result tokens. An instruction represents one or more operators of the program graph, together with its output links. Instructions are linked together through destination addresses stored in their destination fields.

Each instruction cell contains receivers which await the arrival of token values for use as operands by the instruction. Once an instruction cell has received the necessary operand tokens and acknowledge signals, the cell becomes enabled and sends an operation packet consisting of the instruction and the operand values to the appropriate processing unit through the arbitration network. Note that the acknowledge signals are used to correctly implement the firing rule for program graphs.

The arbitration network provides a path from each instruction cell to each processing unit and sorts the operation packets among its output ports according to the operation codes of the instructions they contain. For each operation packet received, a processing unit performs the operation specified by the instruction using the operand values in the packet and produces one or more result tokens, which are sent to instruction cells through the control network and distribution network. Each result token consists of a result value and a destination address derived from the instruction being processed by the processing unit. There are control tokens containing boolean values or acknowledge signals, which are sent through the control network, and data packets containing integer or complex values, which are sent through the distribution network.

The two networks deliver result tokens to receivers of instruction cells as specified by their destination address fields; that is, data packets are routed according to their destination address. The arrival of a result token at an instruction cell either provides one of the receivers of the cell with an operand value or delivers an acknowledge signal; if all result tokens required by the instruction in the cell have been received, the instruction cell becomes enabled and dispatches its contents to the arbitration network as a new operation packet.

The functions performed by the processing unit are distributed among several sections of the data flow processor. The operations specified by instructions are carried out in the processing section, but control of instruction sequencing is a function of the control network, and the decoding of operation codes is partially done within the arbitration network. The address fields (destination addresses) of instructions specify where the results should be sent instead of addressing a shared memory cell. Instead of instructions fetching their operands, the operand values are sent to the instructions.

All communication between subsystems in the Dennis machine is by packet transmission over the channels. The transmission of packets over each channel uses an asynchronous protocol so that the five sections of the computer can operate independently without using central timing signals. Systems organized to operate in this manner are said to have the packet communication architecture.

The instruction cells are assumed to be physically independent, so at any time many of them may be enabled. The arbitration network should be designed to allow many instruction packets to flow through it concurrently. Similarly, the control network and the distribution network should be designed to distribute dense streams of control and data packets back to the instruction cells. In this way, both the appetites of pipelining and parallelism are satisfied. The arbitration, distribution, and control networks of the data flow processor are examples of packet-switched routing networks that perform the function of directing packets to many functional units of the processor. If the parallelism represented in the data flow graph is to be fully exploited, routing networks must have a high bandwidth.

When the number of instruction cells becomes large, the three networks shown in Figure 10.10 may become exceedingly large and thus cost prohibitive. One approach that has been suggested to overcome this difficulty is to use the concept of *cell blocks*. A cell block is a collection of instruction cells which share the same set of input and output ports from the distribution, control, and arbitration networks. The cell-block implementation and its use in the machine architecture are demonstrated in Figure 10.11. By using shared I/O ports, the arbitration networks can be partitioned into subnetworks of significantly smaller sizes; so can the other networks in the system.

In Figure 10.12, we show an example design of the cell block-structured data flow multiprocessor system. The system consists of four processors and 32 cell blocks. Three building blocks can be used to construct the 32×4 arbitration network and the 4×32 distribution network. Illustrated in Figure 10.13 are the 2×1 arbiter, the 1×2 distributor, the 2×2 switch, and the 3×2 switch used in the network constructions in Figure 10.12 and Figure 10.14, respectively. The distributors are blocking free. The arbiter can pass only one input to its output. The 2×2 switch has nine possible states, two of which may cause blocking. The 3×2 switch has 27 states, 14 of which will cause blocking. Whenever a blocking takes place, only one of the conflicting requests can get through the switch.

The blocked requests will be discarded in an unbuffered network and the requests will be resubmitted. For a packet-switched network with buffers at the inputs of the switches or arbiters, the blocked requests will be held waiting to be passed to the output ports in a later time. The buffered Delta networks discussed in Chapter 7 can be modified to be used in a data flow environment. An example buffered arbitration network of size 27×8 is shown in Figure 10.14. Each input

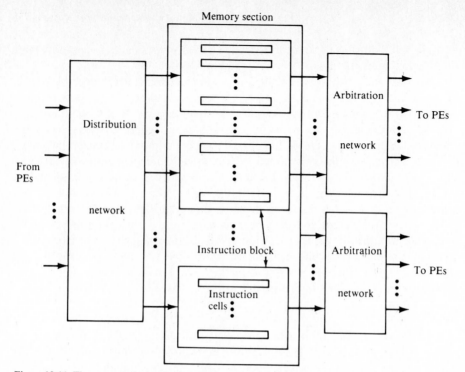

Figure 10.11 The concept of grouping instruction cells into cell blocks.

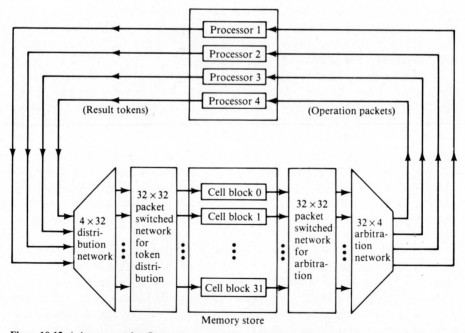

Figure 10.12 A 4-processor dataflow computer with 32 cell blocks interconnected by a 32 × 4 arbitration network and a 4 × 32 distribution network.

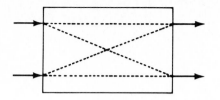

(*a*) A 2-by-2 switch

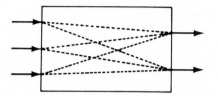

(*b*) A 3-by-2 switch

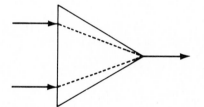

(*c*) A 2-by-1 arbiter

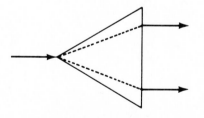

(*d*) A 1-by-2 distributor

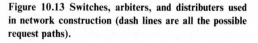

Figure 10.13 Switches, arbiters, and distributers used in network construction (dash lines are all the possible request paths).

port of the 3 × 2 switch has a buffer. A round-robin scheme can be used to resolve conflicts among multiple requests destined to the same output ports.

Since the arbitration network has many inputs, a serial format is appropriate for packet transfer between instruction cells (or cell blocks) and the arbitration network to reduce the number of connections needed. However, to achieve a high rate of packet flow at the output ports, a parallel format is required. For this

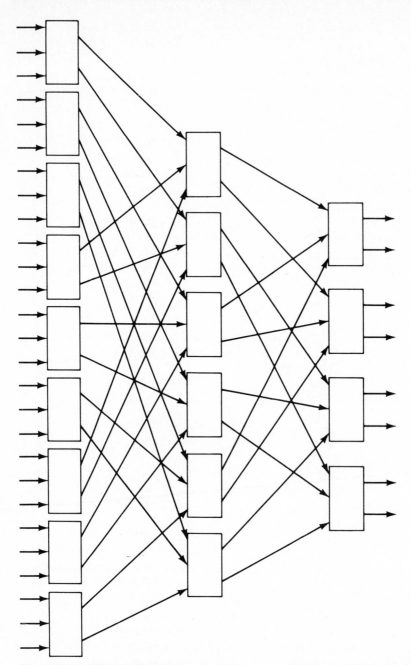

Figure 10.14 A 27-by-8 buffered Delta network for resource arbitration in a Delta network.

reason, serial-to-parallel conversion is done within the buffers as a packet travels through the arbitration network. Parallel-to-serial conversion is performed in the distribution network for similar reasons. The control network is usually unbuffered with direct circuit-switching paths.

The data flow project led by Dennis at MIT is undergoing four stages of development:

1. The construction of a four PE prototype machine to support language concepts of scalar variables, conditionals, and iterations used in signal processing
2. The extension of the scalar data flow machine to a vector/scalar processor to support data structures for scientific computations and to develop a user programming language
3. The overcoming of the program size limitation of stages one and two by adding cache memories and backup storage areas for inactive programs
4. The building of a general-purpose data flow computer which stands alone, compiles its own program, and runs a time-sharing service to multiple users

Currently, the prototype hardware is under construction and a compiler is being written for the VAL programming language. A number of supportive projects on fault tolerance, data flow hardware description languages, etc., are also in progress at MIT's Laboratory for Computer Science.

10.2.2 Dynamic Data Flow Computers

Three dynamic data flow projects are introduced below. In dynamic machines, data tokens are *tagged* (labelled or colored) to allow multiple tokens to appear simultaneously on any input arc of an operator node. No control tokens are needed to acknowledge the transfer of data tokens among instructions. Instead, the matching of token tags (labels or colors) is performed to merge them for instructions requiring more than one operand token. Therefore, additional hardware is needed to attach tags onto data tokens and to perform tag matching. We shall first present the Arvind machine, followed by the EDDY system and the Manchester data flow machine.

The development of the Irvine data flow machine was motivated by the desire to exploit the potential of VLSI and to provide a high-level, highly concurrent program organization. This project originated at the University of California at Irvine and now continues at the Massachusetts Institute of Technology by Arvind and his associates. The architecture of the original Irvine machine is conceptually shown in Figure 10.15. The ID programming language was developed for this machine. This machine has not been built; but extensive simulation studies have been performed on its projected performance.

The Irvine machine was proposed to consist of multiple PE clusters. All PE clusters (physical domains) can operate concurrently. The physical domains are interconnected by two system buses. The token bus is a pair of bidirectional

A physical domain

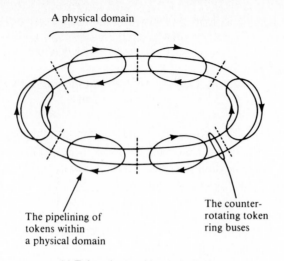

The pipelining of
tokens within
a physical domain

The counter-
rotating token
ring buses

(a) Token rings and local pipelining

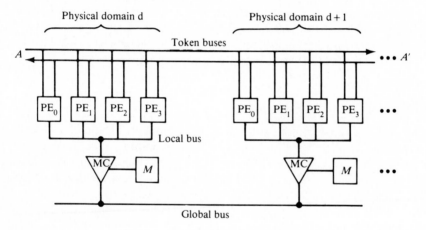

(b) Processor clusters and interconnection buses

Figure 10.15 The Irvine dataflow computer. (Courtesy of *IEEE Trans. Computers*, Gostelow and Thomas, October 1980.)

shift-register rings. Each ring is partitioned into as many slots as there are PEs and each slot is either empty or holds one data token. Obviously, the token rings are used to transfer tagged tokens among the PEs.

Each cluster of PEs (four PEs per cluster, as shown in Figure 10.15) shares a local memory through a local bus and a memory controller. A global bus is used to transfer data structures among the local memories. Each PE must accept all tokens that are sent to it and sort those tokens into groups by activity name. When all input tokens for an activity have arrived (through tag matching), the PE must execute that activity. The U-interpreter can help implement iterative or procedure computations by mapping the loop or procedure instances into the PE clusters for parallel executions.

The Arvind machine at MIT is modified from the Irvine machine, but still based on the ID language. Instead of using token rings, the Arvind machine has chosen to use an $N \times N$ packet switch network for inter-PE communications as demonstrated in Figure 10.16a. The machine consists of N PEs, where

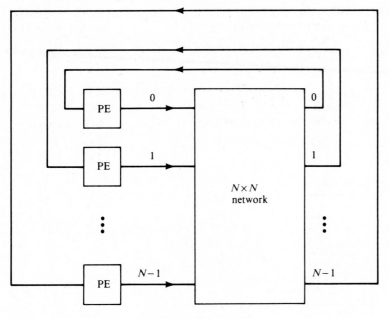

(*a*) The machine architecture

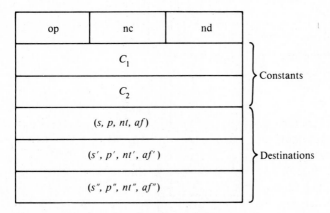

(*b*) A typical instruction

Figure 10.16 Arvind's dataflow machine organization and instruction format. (Courtesy of Arvind et al., Sept. 1980.)

each PE is a complete computer with an instruction set, a memory, tag-matching hardware, etc. Activities are divided among the PEs according to a mapping from tags to PE numbers. Each PE uses a statistically chosen assignment function to determine the destination PE number.

A general format for instructions is shown in Figure 10.16*b*, where *op* is the opcode, *nc* is the number of constants (maximum of two) stored in the instruction, and *nd* is the number of destinations for the result token. Each destination is identified by four fields (*s*, *p*, *nt*, *af*); where *s* is the destination address, *p* indicates the input port at the destination instruction, *nt* indicates the number of tokens needed to enable the destination instruction, and *af* indicates the assignment function to be used in selecting the PE for the execution of the destination instruction.

The functional structure of each PE is shown in Figure 10.17. The input section has a register which if empty can accept a token either from the communication system or from the output section of the same PE. Each activity requires

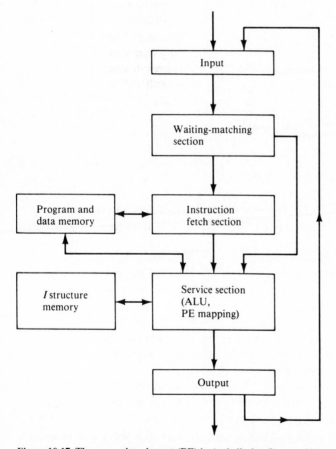

Figure 10.17 The processing element (PE) in Arvind's dataflow machine at MIT.

either one or two tokens, as indicated by the *nt* field of a token. If the activity corresponding to the input token requires another token, the waiting-matching section is informed. The latter has a buffer to hold those tokens for which another token with a matching tag has not yet arrived. Whenever the tags of two tokens match, both tokens are moved to the instruction-fetch buffer. Based on the statement number part of the tag, an instruction from the local program memory is fetched.

If a match for the tag of the input token is not found and the waiting-matching buffer is full, a refusal to accept the token will cause a deadlock. Therefore, if the buffer-full condition exists, the token has to be stored somewhere else and retrieved at a later time. After the instruction has been fetched, an operation packet containing the operation code, the operands, and the destinations is formed and sent to the service section. The service section contains a floating-point ALU and the hardware to calculate new activity names and destination PE numbers.

The *I structure* is a special tagged memory for storing arraylike data structures with constraints on their creation and access. Essentially, an element of an I structure can be defined only once. A presence bit is associated with every element of an I structure. An attempt to read an element whose presence bit is not set causes the read to be deferred. The use of I structures can avoid excessive array copying. The service section also processes the memory operations except I structure reads. After the ALU or the memory produces the result and the new tags and destination PE numbers have been computed, the result tokens are sent to the output section. Since it is possible to encounter delays in transmitting a token through the communication network, some buffer space is provided in the output section.

A separate section to hold deferred reads (i.e., requests to read an element of an I structure before it has been produced) is needed to avoid the blocking of the service section. Every unsuccessful read request will be marked and set aside. An unusual feature of the PE is that it has no program counter. Instead, it maintains a list of enabled activities in the service section and can execute them in any order. A PE will have 100 percent ALU utilization as long as there is at least one enabled activity in the service queue at any given time instant.

A group of PEs known as a *physical domain* is allocated whenever a procedure or a loop is invoked. All activities of the invoked procedure (or loop) take place within the physical domain except those activities which are caused by an operator that changes the context part. The activities of a procedure (loop) can be distributed within a physical domain on the basis of the instruction number of the iteration number of an activity name. Tag matching may contribute to additional overhead, which is potentially a performance bottleneck for dynamic data flow computers.

In order to include the possibility of activating several code blocks (not necessarily distinct from each other) within a physical domain, one can assign a different *color* to each activation. However, only a finite number of colors are allowed within a physical domain and, if all colors of a physical domain are in use, no new loop or procedure activation can be scheduled on it. Colors are released when a loop or procedure terminates. Sharing of code blocks within a physical domain is feasible because all invocations carry different colors. Several color registers are used in each PE. This will help distribute logical activities to PEs on a resource-sharing basis. Coloring will increase resource utilization and thus total system throughput.

In Japan, the development of a scientific data flow machine called EDDY (Experimental system for Data Driven processor arraY) is in progress. The hardware consists of 4×4 PEs and two broadcast control units (BCUs), as shown in Figure 10.18. Each PE is composed of two microprocessors (Z8001) and is connected directly with eight neighboring PEs. The broadcast control can load or unload programs and data to or from all PEs, in column or row, at the same time.

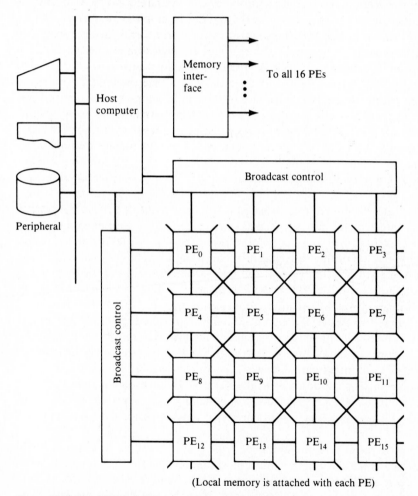

(Local memory is attached with each PE)

Figure 10.18 The EDDY dataflow machine in Japan. (Courtesy of *Conf. Proc. 10th Annual Symp. Computer Architecture*, Takakashi and Amamiya, June 1983.)

The software system implemented on each Z8001 "simulates" the circular pipeline data flow control of the PE in detail, using logical simulation clocks. It generates statistical data, such as operation rates of the function units and average queue length. The simulation results will be used to help develop the custom-designed PE hardware. The functional language to be used in EDDY is called VALID.

The custom-designed PE is a circular pipeline consisting of an instruction memory section, operand memory section, operation section and communication section, as shown in Figure 10.19. On the arrival of each operand token, the instruction memory fetches its operation node and sends both the fetched instruction and operand data to the operand memory section. If the arrived data is an operand for a two-operand operation, the operand memory searches for its paired partner associatively. When the paired operand is found, an operation packet is constructed and sent to the operation section. When no paired operand is found, the arrived data token is stored in the operand memory with a key attached.

All data tokens are tagged, which represents their execution environment so as to allow more than one token to be travelling on an arc. In order to realize highly distributed control, it is important to decentralize the tagging control. It is also necessary to mechanize the tagging control so as to extract maximal parallelism. The EDDY system uses a mixed strategy with both *static* tagging and *dynamic* tagging. In static tagging, execution environments are predefined and a

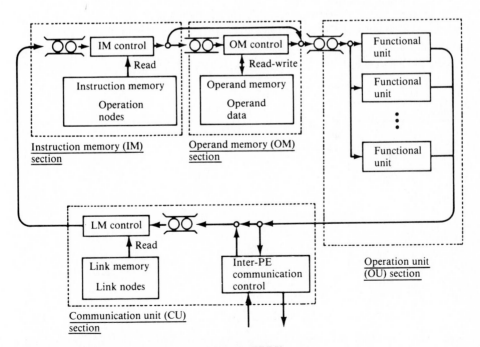

Figure 10.19 The functional design of each PE in the EDDY system.

unique tag is assigned to each of them. In dynamic tagging, tags are assigned to each environment dynamically. An execution environment is represented by a (tag) name.

The environment name and opcode are used as a key for the associative search. The operation section consists of several functional units including some number crunchers. The communication section consists of final link memory and an inter-PE communication controller. This controller sends result packets to link memory or to other PEs and also receives result packets from other PEs and transmits them to its own link memory.

The data flow project at Manchester University has included the design of the high-level, single-assignment programming language Lapse; the implementation of translators for Lapse and a subset of Pascal; and the production of a detailed stimulator for the Manchester compute architecture. Currently the group is completing a 20-processor data flow computer prototype.

The Manchester machine also assumes a ring structure, as demonstrated in Figure 10.20. Five functional blocks communicate in clockwise direction around a ring. A token package is the main unit of information and comprises a data-value, label, and destination node pointer. The *matching unit* groups tokens. When sufficient tokens arrive to fire a node, an appropriate group package finds a destination node description in the *node store*. An executable package [containing operator, operands, label, and pointer(s) to further destination node(s)] is sent to the processing unit for execution. The *switch* handles external input/output. The *token queue* saves excess tokens generated at about the same time.

Parallel data-driven rings have been suggested to extend the Manchester machine (Figure 10.21). Very high processing rates may be achieved by connecting multiple numbers of pipelined rings in this approach. A unidirectional pipelined exchange switch is modularly extensible and of relatively simple form as compared

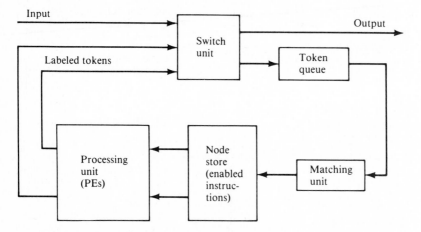

Figure 10.20 The Manchester dataflow computer organization. (Courtesy of AFIPS *Proc. of NCC*, Watson and Gurd, June 1979.)

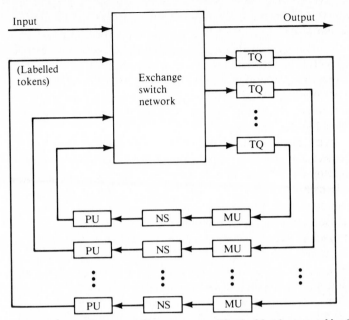

Figure 10.21 Multiple ring architecture proposed for the Manchester machine (TQ: Token Queue; MU: Matching Unit; NS: Node Store; PU: Processing Unit). (Courtesy of *Computer Design*, Gurd and Watson, July 1980.)

to a crossbar switch, for example. In such a very large system, the major problem is to distribute the work load evenly among multiple data flow rings demonstrated in the figure.

10.2.3 Data Flow Design Alternatives

There are several data flow projects that have special architectural approaches different from the static or dynamic machines described in previous sections. In fact, the first operational data flow machine in the USA is the Data-Driven Machine (DDM-1) designed by A. Davis and his colleagues in 1976. The program and machine organization are based on the concept of recursion, markedly different from the previous data flow systems we have examined. The computer is composed of a hierarchy of computing elements (processor-memory pairs), where each element is logically recursive and consists of further offspring elements.

Logically the DDM architecture is tree structured, with each computing element being connected to a parent element (above) and up to eight offspring elements (below), which it supervises. The DDM project is currently located at the University of Utah. It is operational and communicates with a DEC-20/40, which is used for software support of compilers, simulators, and performance measurement programs.

In Toulouse, France, a data flow system called LAU has been constructed with 32 bit-slice microprocessors interconnected by multiple buses. The LAU programming language is based on single assignment rule, but the computer's program organization is based on control flow concepts. In the computer, data are passed via sharable memory cells that are accessed through addresses embedded in instructions. Seperate control signals are used to enable instructions.

In Newcastle, England, another data flow system is under development. This system uses both data tokens and control tokens to enable instruction execution. The Newcastle system is a combination of the data flow and control flow mechanisms in one integrated system approach.

Up to 1983, only the DDM at Utah, the EDDY in Japan, the Manchester machine, and the French LAU system are operational data flow computers. There are many other research projects that are devoted to various aspects of data flow computing. Most data flow projects emphasize run-time simultaneity at the instruction level. Unless the program being executed is embedded with a high degree of parallelism, the performance of such instruction-level data-driven computers could be very poor because of high system overhead in detecting the parallelism and in scheduling the available resources. Two design alternatives to the data flow approach are discussed below. These modified approaches offer higher machine compatibility and better utilization of the existing software assets.

Dependence-driven approach This approach was independently proposed by Gajski et al. (1982), and by Motooka et al. (1981). The idea is to raise the level of parallelism to *compound-function* (procedure) level at run time. A compound function is a collection of computational tasks that are suitable for parallel processing by multiprocessors. Listed below are six compound functions investigated by the research group at the University of Illinois:

- Array (vector matrix) operations
- Linear recurrence
- For-all loops
- Pipeline loops
- Blocks of assignment statements
- Compound conditional statements

A program is a dependence graph connecting the compound-function nodes. *Dependence-driven* refers to the application of data flow principles over multiple compound-function nodes. In a sense, it is procedure driven. Instead of using data flow languages, traditional high-level language programs can be used in this dependence-driven approach (Figure 10.22). Additional program transformation packages should be developed to convert ordinary language programs to dependence graphs and to generate codes from dependence graphs. A hardware organization needed for dependence-driven computations is illustrated in Figure 10.23. Such a dependence-driven machine has a global controller for multiple processor clusters and shared memory and other resources, instead of decentralized control as emphasized in a data-driven machine.

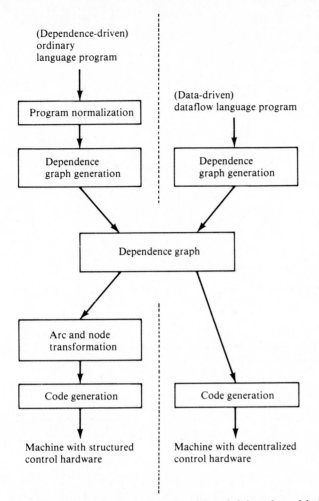

Figure 10.22 Comparison between data-driven and dependence-driven computing models. (Courtesy of IEEE *Computer*, **Gajski et al., February 1982.)**

A second opinion has been expressed on data flow machines and languages by the dependence-driven researchers. Two questions were raised: First, are data flow languages marketable? To date, the high-speed computer market has been dominated by conservatism and software compatibility. Can data flow languages, as currently proposed, overcome this conservatism? Second, will data flow languages enhance programmer productivity? Although data flow researchers have made some claims to this effect, they remain unsubstantiated.

Dependence-driven researchers felt that, in small-scale parallel systems, data flow principles have been successfully demonstrated. When simultaneity is low, irregular, and run time–dependent, data flow might be the architecture of choice. In very large-scale parallel systems, data flow principles still show some potential

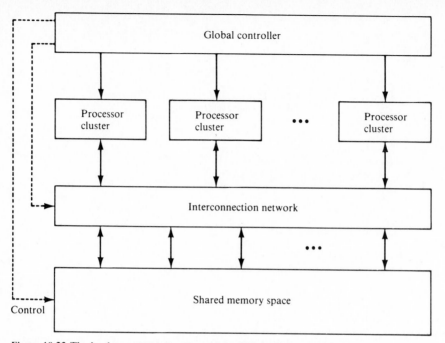

Figure 10.23 The hardware structure suggested for high-level data flow computing, for either the dependence-driven model or the event-driven model.

for high-level control. It is in medium-scale parallel systems that data flow has little chance of success. Pipelined, parallel, and multiprocessor systems are all effective in this range. For data flow processing to become established here, its inherent inefficiencies must be overcome.

Multilevel event-driven approach The dependence-driven was generalized to an event-driven approach by Hwang and Su (1983c). An *event* is a logical activity which can be defined at the job (program) level, the procedure level, the task level, or at the instruction level after proper *abstraction* or *engrossment*, as illustrated in Figure 10.24. Hierarchical scheduling is needed in this event-driven approach. A mechanism for program abstraction needs to be developed. Such a mechanism must not require high system overhead. It could be implemented partially at compile time and partially at run time. The choice depends on the performance criteria to be used in promoting parallel processing at various levels. Hierarchical scheduling of resources is the most challenging part of research in this approach.

Heuristic algorithms are needed for scheduling multiple events to the available resources in an event-driven computer. Instead of using the first-in, first-out (FIFO) scheduling policy on all enabled activities, as in a data-driven computer, this approach considers the use of *priority queues* in the event scheduling. The priority is determined by pre-run-time estimating of the time-space complexities of all enabled events. The optimal mapping of logical events to physical resources has

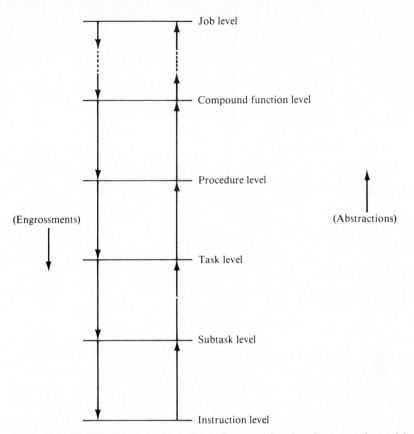

Figure 10.24 Multilevel program abstraction in the event-driven data flow computing model.

proven to be NP-complete. The heuristics using priority queues will result in nearly optimal performance, if the complexity estimations are sufficiently accurate. Intuitively, a multilevel event-driven approach should be more appealing to general-purpose computer design which uses both data flow and control flow mechanisms. Due to the complexity in hierarchical control, many research and development efforts are still needed to make this approach workable and cost effective.

For research-oriented readers, we identify below a number of important issues that demand further efforts towards the development of workable data flow multiprocessor systems.

1. The design of a machine instruction set and high-level data flow languages
2. The design of the packet communication networks for resource arbitration and for token distribution
3. The development of data flow processing elements and the structured memory
4. The development of activity control mechanisms and data flow operating system functions

5. Overhead estimations of data flow computers, including development overhead, execution overhead, and application overhead
6. Performance analysis of data flow machines for irregular parallelism with intermix of scalar and vector computations
7. Relative performance of asynchronous data flow machines as compared with synchronous SIMD, MIMD, or pipeline computers
8. The development of program debugging tools and tuning mechanisms

Data flow offers a viable approach to improve today's computer performance. The development of data flow computers is in its infancy stage. With the push of VLSI computing structures, we can anticipate an important role of data flow mechanisms and their variations in future computers.

10.3 VLSI COMPUTING STRUCTURES

Highly parallel computing structures promise to be a major application area for the million-transistor chips that will be possible in just a few years. Such computing systems have structural properties that are suitable for VLSI implementation. Almost by definition, parallel structures imply a basic computational element repeated perhaps hundreds or thousands of times. This architectural style immediately reduces the design problem by similar orders of magnitude. In this section, we examine some VLSI computing structures that have been suggested by computer researchers. We begin with a characterization of the systolic architecture. Then we describe methodologies for mapping parallel algorithms into processor arrays. Finally, we present the reconfigurable processor arrays for designing algorithmically specialized machines. Only globally structured, cellular array structures are presented below. Modularly structured VLSI computing structures will be presented in Section 10.4. Described below are key attributes of VLSI computing structures.

Simplicity and regularity Cost effectiveness has always been a major concern in designing special-purpose VLSI systems; their cost must be low enough to justify their limited applicability. Special-purpose design costs can be reduced by the use of appropriate architectures. If a structure can truly be decomposed into a few types of building blocks which are used repetitively with simple interfaces, great savings can be achieved. This is especially true for VLSI designs where a single chip comprises hundreds of thousands of identical components. To cope with that complexity, simple and regular designs are essential. VLSI systems based on simple, regular layout are likely to be modular and adjustable to various performance levels.

Concurrency and communication Since the technological trend clearly indicates a diminishing growth rate for component speed, any major improvement in computation speed must come from the concurrent use of many processing elements.

The degree of concurrency in a VLSI computing structure is largely determined by the underlying algorithm. Massive parallelism can be achieved if the algorithm is designed to introduce high degrees of pipelining and multiprocessing. When a large number of processing elements work simultaneously, coordination and communication become significant—especially with VLSI technology where routing costs dominate the power, time, and area required to implement a computation. The issue here is to design algorithms that support high degrees of concurrency, and in the meantime to employ only simple, regular communication and control to allow efficient implementation. The locality of interprocessor communications is a desired feature to have in any processor arrays.

Computation intensive VLSI processing structures are suitable for implementing *compute-bound* algorithms rather than *I/O-bound* computations. In a compute-bound algorithm, the number of computing operations is larger than the total number of input and output elements. Otherwise, the problem is I/O bound. For example, the matrix-matrix multiplication algorithm represents a compute-bound task, which has $O(n^3)$ multiply-add steps, but only $O(n^2)$ I/O elements. On the other hand, adding two matrices is I/O bound, since there are n^2 adds and $3n^2$ I/O operations for the two input matrices and one output matrix. The I/O-bound problems are not suitable for VLSI because VLSI packaging must be constrained with limited I/O pins. A VLSI device must balance its computation with the I/O bandwidth. Knowing the I/O-imposed performance limit helps prevent overkill in the design of a special-purpose VLSI device.

10.3.1 The Systolic Array Architecture

The choice of an appropriate architecture for any electronic system is very closely related to the implementation technology. This is especially true in VLSI. The constraints of power dissipation, I/O pin count, relatively long communication delays, difficulty in design and layout, etc., all important problems in VLSI, are much less critical in other technologies. As a compensation, however, VLSI offers very fast and inexpensive computational elements with some unique and exciting properties. For example, bidirectional transmission gates (pass transistors) enable a full barrel shifter to be configured in a very compact NMOS array.

Properly designed parallel structures that need to communicate only with their nearest neighbors will gain the most from very-large-scale integration. Precious time is lost when modules that are far apart must communicate. For example, the delay in crossing a chip on polysilicon, one of the three primary interconnect layers on an NMOS chip, can be 10 to 50 times the delay of an individual gate. The architect must keep this communication bottleneck uppermost in his mind when evaluating possible structures and architectures for implementation in VLSI.

The *systolic* architectural concept was developed by Kung and associates at Carnegie-Mellon University, and many versions of systolic processors are being designed by universities and industrial organizations. This subsection reviews the basic principle of systolic architectures and explains why they should result in cost-effective, high-performance, special-purpose systems for a wide range of potential applications.

A systolic system consists of a set of interconnected cells, each capable of performing some simple operation. Because simple, regular communication and control structures have substantial advantages over complicated ones in design and implementation, cells in a systolic system are typically interconnected to form a systolic array or a systolic tree. Information in a systolic system flows between cells in a pipelined fashion, and communication with the outside world occurs only at the "boundary" cells. For example, in a systolic array, only those cells on the array boundaries may be I/O ports for the system.

The basic principle of a systolic array is illustrated in Figure 10.25. By replacing a single processing element with an array of PEs, a higher computation throughput can be achieved without increasing memory bandwidth. The function of the memory in the diagram is analogous to that of the heart; it "pulses" data through the array of PEs. The crux of this approach is to ensure that once a data item is brought out from the memory it can be used effectively at each cell it passes. This is possible for a wide class of compute-bound computations where multiple operations are performed on each data item in a repetitive manner.

Suppose each PE in Figure 10.25 operates with a clock period of 100 ns. The conventional memory-processor organization in Figure 10.25a has at most a performance of 5 million operations per second. With the same clock rate, the systolic array will result in 30 MOPS performance. This gain in processing speed can also be justified with the fact that the number of pipeline stages has been increased six times in Figure 10.25b. Being able to use each input data item a number of times is just one of the many advantages of the systolic approach. Other advantages include modular expansionability, simple and regular data and

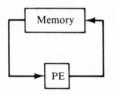

(a) The conventional processor

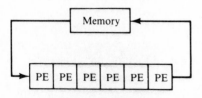

(b) A systolic processor arrray

Figure 10.25 The concept of systolic processor array. (Courtesy of IEEE *Computer*, Kung, January 1981.)

control flows, use of simple and uniform cells, elimination of global broadcasting, limited fan-in and fast response time.

Basic processing cells used in the construction of systolic arithmetic arrays are the *additive multiply* cells specified in Figure 3.29. This cell has the three inputs a,b,c, and the three outputs $a = a$, $b = b$, and $d = c + a * b$. One can assume six interface registers are attached at the I/O ports of a processing cell. All registers are clocked for synchronous transfer of data among adjacent cells. The additive-multiply operation is needed in performing the inner product of two vectors, matrix-matrix multiplication, matrix inversion, and L-U decomposition of a dense matrix.

Illustrated below is the construction of a systolic array for the multiplication of two banded matrices. An example of band matrix multiplication is shown in Figure 10.26a. Matrix **A** has a bandwidth $(3 + 2) - 1 = 4$ and matrix **B** has a bandwidth $(2 + 3) - 1 = 4$ along their principal diagonals. The product matrix $C = A \cdot B$ then has a bandwidth $(4 + 4) - 1 = 7$ along its principal diagonal. Note that all three matrices have dimension $n \times n$, as shown by the dotted entries. The matrix of bandwidth w may have ω diagonals that are not all zeros. The entries outside the diagonal band are all zeros.

It requires $w_1 \times w_2$ processing cells to form a systolic array for the multiplication of two sparse matrices of bandwidths w_1 and w_2, respectively. The resulting product matrix has a bandwidth of $w_1 + w_2 - 1$. For this example, $w_1 \times w_2 = 4 \times 4 = 16$ multiply cells are needed to construct the systolic array shown in Figure 10.26b. It should be noted that the size of the array is determined by the bandwidths w_1 and w_2, independent of the dimension $n \times n$ of the matrices. Data flows in this diamond-shaped systolic array are indicated by the arrows among the processing cells.

The elements of $\mathbf{A} = (a_{ij})$ and $\mathbf{B} = (b_{ij})$ matrices enter the array along the two diagonal data streams. The initial values of $\mathbf{C} = (c_{ij})$ entries are zeros. The outputs at the top of the vertical data stream give the product matrix. Three data streams flow through the array in a pipelined fashion. Let the time delay of each processing cell be one unit time. This systolic array can finish the band matrix multiplication in T time units, where

$$T = 3n + \min(w_1, w_2) \tag{10.3}$$

Therefore, the computation time is linearly proportional to the dimension n of the matrix. When the matrix bandwidths increase to $w_1 = w_2 = n$ (for dense matrices **A** and **B**), the time becomes $O(4n)$, neglecting the I/O time delays. If one used a single additive-multiply processor to perform the same matrix multiplication, $O(n^3)$ computation time would be needed. The systolic multiplier thus has a speed gain of $O(n^2)$. For large n, this improvement in speed is rather impressive.

VLSI systolic arrays can assume many different structures for different compute-bound algorithms. Figure 10.27 shows various systolic array configurations and their potential usage in performing those computations is listed in Table 10.1. These computations form the basis of signal and image processing, matrix arithmetic, combinatorial, database algorithms. Due to their simplicity and

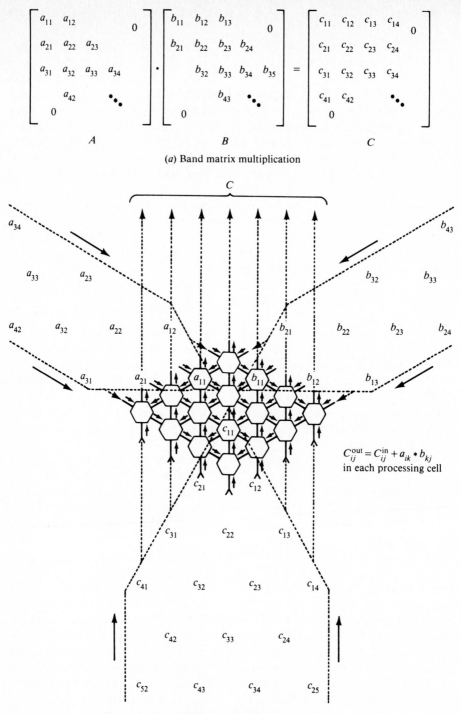

(a) Band matrix multiplication

$$C_{ij}^{out} = C_{ij}^{in} + a_{ik} * b_{kj}$$
in each processing cell

(b) The systolic array

Figure 10.26 A systolic array for band matrix multiplication. (Courtesy of *Proc. of the Symposium on Sparse Matrix Computing and Their Applications*, Kung and Leiserson, November 1978.)

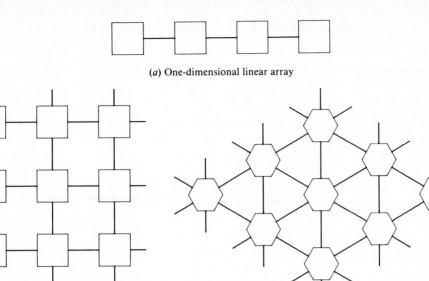

(a) One-dimensional linear array

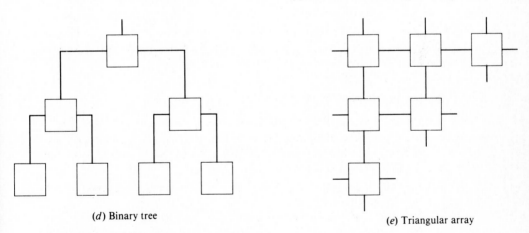

(b) Two-dimensional square array

(c) Two-dimensional hexagonal array

(d) Binary tree

(e) Triangular array

Figure 10.27 Various systolic array configurations.

strong appeal to intuition, systolic techniques attracted a great deal of attention recently. However, the implementation of systolic arrays on a VLSI chip has many practical constraints.

The major problem with a systolic array is still in its I/O barrier. The globally structured systolic array can speed-up computations only if the I/O bandwidth is high. With current IC packaging technology, only a small number of I/O pins can be used for a VLSI chip. For example, a systolic array of n^2 step processors can perform the L-U decomposition in $4n$ time units. However, such a systolic array in a single chip may require $4n \times w$ I/O terminals, where w is the word length.

Table 10.1 Computation functions and desired VLSI structures

Processor array structure	Computation functions
1-D linear arrays	Fir-filter, convolution, discrete Fourier transform (DFT), solution of triangular linear systems, carry pipelining, cartesian product, odd-even transportation sort, real-time priority queue, pipeline arithmetic units.
2-D square arrays	Dynamic programming for optimal parenthesization, graph algorithms involving adjacency matrices.
2-D hexagonal arrays	Matrix arithmetic (matrix multiplication, L-U decomposition by Gaussian elimination without pivoting, QR-factorization), transitive closure, pattern match, DFT, relational database operations.
Trees	Searching algorithms (queries on nearest neighbor, rank, etc., systolic search tree), parallel function evaluation, recurrence evaluation.
Triangular arrays	Inversion of triangular matrix, formal language recognition.

For large n (say $n \geq 1000$) with typical operand width $w = 32$ bits, it is rather impractical to fabricate an $n \times n$ systolic array on a monolithic chip with over $4n \times w = 12,000$ I/O terminals. Of course, I/O port sharing and time-division multiplexing can be used to alleviate the problem. But still, I/O is the bottleneck. Until the I/O problem can be satisfactorily solved, the systolic arrays can be only constructed in small sizes. The modular VLSI approach to be described in Section 10.4 offers an alternative to overcome this difficulty.

10.3.2 Mapping Algorithms into VLSI Arrays

Procedures to map cyclic loop algorithms into special-purpose VLSI arrays are described below. The method is based on mathematical transformation of the index sets and the data-dependence vectors associated with a given algorithm. After the algorithmic transformation, one can devise a more efficient array structure that can better exploit parallelism and pipelining by removing unnecessary data dependencies.

The exploitation of parallelism is often necessary because computational problems are larger than a single VLSI device can process at a time. If a parallel algorithm is structured as a network of smaller computational modules, then these modules can be assigned to different VLSI devices. The communications between these modules and their operation control dictates the structure of the VLSI system and its performances. In Figure 10.28, a simplistic organization of a computer system is shown consisting of several VLSI devices shared by two processors through a resource arbitration network.

The I/O bottleneck problem in a VLSI system presents a serious restriction imposed on the algorithm design. The challenge is to design parallel algorithms which can be partitioned such that the amount of communication between modules is as small as possible. Moreover, data entering the VLSI device should be utilized exhaustively before passing again through the I/O ports. A global model of the VLSI processor array can be formally described by a 3-tuple (G, F, T); where G is

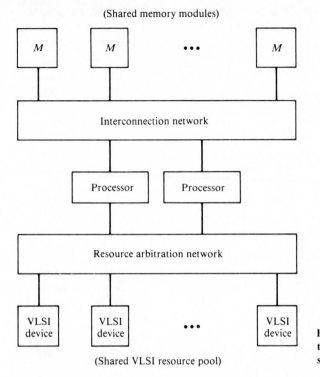

(Shared memory modules)

(Shared VLSI resource pool)

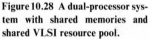

Figure 10.28 A dual-processor system with shared memories and shared VLSI resource pool.

the network geometry, F is the cell function, and T is the network timing. These features are described below separately.

The *network geometry G* refers to the geometrical layout of the network. The position of each processing cell in the plane is described by its Cartesian coordinates. Then, the interconnection between cells can easily be described by the position of the terminal cells. These interconnections support the flow of data through the network; a link can be dedicated only to one data stream of variables or it can be used for the transport of several data streams at different time instances. A simple and regular geometry is desired to uphold local communications.

The *functions F* associated to each processing cell represent the totality of arithmetic and logic expressions that a cell is capable of performing. We assume that each cell consists of a small number of registers, an ALU, and control logic. Several different types of processing cells may coexist in the same network; however, one design goal should be the reduction of the number of cell types used.

The *network timing T* specifies for each cell the time when the processing of functions F occurs and when the data communications take place. A correct timing assures that the right data reaches the right place at the right time. The speed of the data streams through the network is given by the ratio between the distance of the communication link over the communication time. Networks with constant data speeds are preferable because they require a simpler control logic.

The basic structural features of an algorithm are dictated by the data and control dependencies. These dependencies refer to precedence relations of computations which need to be satisfied in order to compute correctly. The absence of dependencies indicates the possibility of simultaneous computations. These dependencies can be studied at several distinct levels: blocks of computations level, statement (or expression) level, variable level, and even bit level. Since we concentrate on algorithms for VLSI systolic arrays, we will focus only on data dependencies at the variable level.

Consider a Fortran loop structure of the form:

$$
\begin{aligned}
&\text{DO} \quad 10 \qquad I^1 = l^1, u^1 \\
&\text{DO} \quad 10 \qquad I^2 = l^2, u^2 \\
&\quad \vdots \\
&\text{DO} \quad 10 \qquad I^n = l^n, u^n \\
&\qquad S_1(I) \\
&\qquad S_2(I) \\
&\quad \vdots \\
&\qquad S_N(I) \\
&\text{10 CONTINUE}
\end{aligned}
\tag{10.4}
$$

where l^j and u^j are integer-valued linear expressions involving $I^1, \ldots, I^{j-1}$ and $\mathbf{I} = (I^1, I^2, \ldots, I^n)$ is an index vector. $S_1, S_2, \ldots, S_N$ are assignment statements of the form $x = \mathrm{E}$ where x is a variable and E is an expression of some input variables.

The index set of the loop in Eq. 10.4 is defined by:

$$
S^n(\mathbf{I}) = \{(I^1, \ldots, I^n): l^1 \le I^1 \le u^1, \ldots, l^n \le I^n \le u^n\}
\tag{10.5}
$$

Consider two statements $S(\mathbf{I}_1)$ and $S(\mathbf{I}_2)$ which perform the functions $f(\mathbf{I}_1)$ and $g(\mathbf{I}_2)$, respectively. Let $V_1(f(\mathbf{I}_1))$ and $V_2(g(\mathbf{I}_2))$ be the output variables of the two statements respectively.

Variable $V_2(g(\mathbf{I}_2))$ is said to be *dependent* on variable $V_1(f(\mathbf{I}_1))$ and denote $V_1(f(\mathbf{I}_1)) \rightarrow V_2(g(\mathbf{I}_2))$, if (i) $\mathbf{I}_1 > \mathbf{I}_2$ (less than in the lexicographical sense); (ii) $f(\mathbf{I}_1) = g(\mathbf{I}_2)$; and (iii) $V_1(f(\mathbf{I}_1))$ is an input variable in statement $S(\mathbf{I}_2)$. The difference of their index vectors $\mathbf{d} = \mathbf{I}_1 - \mathbf{I}_2$ is called the *data-dependence vector*. In general, an algorithm is characterized by a number of data-dependence vectors, which are functions of elements of the index set defined in Eq. 10.5. There is a large class of algorithms which have fixed or constant data dependence vectors.

The transformation of the index sets described above is the key towards an efficient mapping of the algorithm into special-purpose VLSI arrays. The following procedure is suggested to map loop algorithms into VLSI computing structures.

Mapping procedure
1. Pipeline all variables in the algorithm.
2. Find the set of data-dependence vectors.
3. Identify a valid transformation for the data-dependence vectors and the index set.
4. Map the algorithm into hardware structure.
5. Prove correctness and analyze performance.

We consider an example algorithm to illustrate the above procedure: the L-U decomposition of a matrix **A** into lower- and upper-triangular matrices by

Gaussian elimination without pivoting. It is shown that better interconnection architectures can be formally derived by using appropriate algorithm transformations.

Example 10.3 The L-U decomposition algorithm is expressed by the following program:

$$
\begin{aligned}
&\textbf{for } k \leftarrow 0 \textbf{ until } n-1 \textbf{ do} \\
&\quad \textbf{begin} \\
&\qquad u_{kk} \leftarrow 1/a_{kk} \\
&\qquad \textbf{for } j \leftarrow k+1 \textbf{ until } n-1 \textbf{ do} \\
&\qquad\quad u_{kj} \leftarrow a_{kj} \\
&\qquad \textbf{for } i \leftarrow k+1 \textbf{ until } n-1 \textbf{ do} \\
&\qquad\quad l_{ik} \leftarrow a_{ik} u_{kk} \\
&\qquad \textbf{for } i \leftarrow k+1 \textbf{ until } n-1 \textbf{ do} \\
&\qquad\quad \textbf{for } j \quad k+1 \textbf{ until } n-1 \textbf{ do} \\
&\qquad\qquad a_{ij} \leftarrow a_{ij} + l_{ik} u_{kj} \\
&\quad \textbf{end.}
\end{aligned}
$$

(10.6)

This program can be rewritten into the following equivalent form in which all the variables have been pipelined and all the data broadcasts have been eliminated:

$$
\begin{aligned}
&\textbf{for } k \leftarrow 0 \textbf{ until } n-1 \textbf{ do} \\
&\quad \textbf{begin} \\
1:&\qquad i \leftarrow k; \\
&\qquad j \leftarrow k; \\
&\qquad u^i_{kj} \leftarrow 1/a^k_{tj} \\
&\qquad \textbf{for } j \leftarrow k+1 \textbf{ until } n-1 \textbf{ do} \\
2:&\qquad \textbf{begin} \\
&\qquad\quad i \leftarrow k; \\
&\qquad\quad u^i_{kj} \leftarrow a^k_{ij} \\
&\qquad \textbf{end} \\
&\qquad \textbf{for } i \leftarrow k+1 \textbf{ until } n-1 \textbf{ do} \\
3:&\qquad \textbf{begin} \\
&\qquad\quad j \leftarrow k; \\
&\qquad\quad u^i_{kj} \leftarrow u^{i-1}_{kj}; \\
&\qquad\quad l^j_{ik} \leftarrow a^k_{ij} \cdot u^i_{kj} \\
&\qquad \textbf{end} \\
&\qquad \textbf{for } i \leftarrow k+1 \textbf{ until } n-1 \textbf{ do} \\
&\qquad\quad \textbf{for } j \leftarrow k+1 \textbf{ until } n-1 \textbf{ do} \\
4:&\qquad\quad \textbf{begin} \\
&\qquad\qquad l^j_{ik} \leftarrow l^{j-1}_{ik}; \\
&\qquad\qquad u^i_{kj} \leftarrow u^{i-1}_{kj}; \\
&\qquad\qquad a^k_{ij} \leftarrow a^{k-1}_{ij} - l^{j-1}_{ik} u^{i-1}_{kj} \\
&\qquad\quad \textbf{end} \\
&\quad \textbf{end}
\end{aligned}
$$

(10.7)

The data dependencies for this three-loop algorithm have the nice property that

$$\mathbf{d}_1 = (1, 0, 0)^T$$

$$\mathbf{d}_2 = (0, 1, 0)^T \qquad (10.8)$$

$$\mathbf{d}_3 = (0, 0, 1)^T$$

We write the above in matrix form $\mathbf{D} = [\mathbf{d}_1, \mathbf{d}_2, \mathbf{d}_3] = \mathbf{I}$. There are several other algorithms which lead to these simple data dependencies, and they were among the first to be considered for the VLSI implementation.

The next step is to identify a linear transformation $\mathbf{T}$ to modify the data dependencies to be $\mathbf{T} \cdot \mathbf{D} = \Delta$, where $\Delta = [\delta_1, \delta_2, \delta_3]$ represents the modified data dependencies in the new index space, which is selected a priori. This transformation $\mathbf{T}$ must offer the maximum concurrency by minimizing data dependencies and $\mathbf{T}$ is a bijection. A large number of choices exist, each leading to a different array geometry. We choose the following one:

$$\mathbf{T} = \begin{bmatrix} 1 & 1 & 1 \\ 0 & 1 & 0 \\ 0 & 0 & 1 \end{bmatrix} \quad \text{such that} \quad \begin{bmatrix} \hat{k} \\ \hat{i} \\ \hat{j} \end{bmatrix} = \mathbf{T} \cdot \begin{bmatrix} k \\ i \\ j \end{bmatrix} \qquad (10.9)$$

The original indices k, i, j are being transformed by $\mathbf{T}$ into $\hat{k}, \hat{i}, \hat{j}$. The organization of the VLSI array for $n = 5$ generated by this $\mathbf{T}$ transformation is shown in Figure 10.29.

In this architecture, variables a_{ij}^k do not travel in space, but are updated in time. Variables l_{ij}^k move along the direction $\hat{j}$ (east with a speed of one grid per

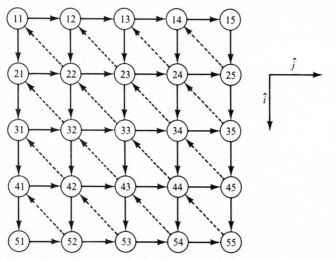

Figure 10.29 A square systolic array for L-U decomposition ($n = 5$) in Example 10.3. (Courtesy of *IEEE Proceedings*, Moldovan, January 1983.)

time unit), and variables u_{ij}^k move along the direction $\hat{i}$ (south) with the same speed. The network is loaded initially with the coefficients of **A**, and at the end the cells below the diagonal contain **L** and the cells above the diagonal contain **U**.

The processing time of this square array is $3n - 5$. All the cells have the same architecture. However, their functions at one given moment may differ. It can be seen from the program in statement (10.7) that some cells may execute loop four, while others execute loops two or three. If we wish to assign the same loops only to specific cells, then the mapping must be changed accordingly.

For example, the following transformation:

$$\mathbf{T'} = \begin{bmatrix} 1 & 1 & 1 \\ -1 & 1 & 0 \\ -1 & 0 & 1 \end{bmatrix}$$

introduces a new data communication link between cells toward north-west. These new links will support the movement of variables a_{ij}^k. According to this new transformation, the cells of the first row always compute loop two, the cells of the first column compute loop three, and the rest compute loop four. The reader can now easily identify some other valid transformations which will lead to different array organizations.

The design of algorithmically specialized VLSI devices is at its beginning. The development of specialized devices to replace mathematical software is feasible but still very costly. Several important technical issues remain unresolved and deserve further investigation. Some of these are: I/O communication in VLSI technology, partitioning of algorithms to maintain their numerical stability, and minimization of the communication among computational blocks.

10.3.3 Reconfigurable Processor Array

Algorithmically specialized processors often use different interconnection structures. As demonstrated in Figure 10.30, five array structures have been suggested for implementing different algorithms. The *mesh* is used for dynamic programming. The *hexagonally connected mesh* was shown in the previous section for L-U decomposition. The *torus* is used for transitive closure. The *binary tree* is used for sorting. The *double-rooted tree* is used for searching. The matching of the structure to the right algorithm has a fundamental influence on performance and cost effectiveness.

For example, if we have an $n \times n$ mesh-connected microprocessor structure and want to find the maximum of n^2 elements stored one per processor, $2n - 1$ steps are necessary and sufficient to solve the problem. But a faster algorithmically specialized processor for this problem uses a tree machine to find the solution in $2 \log n$ steps. For large n, this is a benefit worth pursuing. Again, a bus can be introduced to link several differently structured multiprocessors, including mesh- and tree-connected multiprocessors. But the bus bottleneck is quite serious. What we need is a more polymorphic multiprocessor that does not compromise the benefits of VLSI technology.

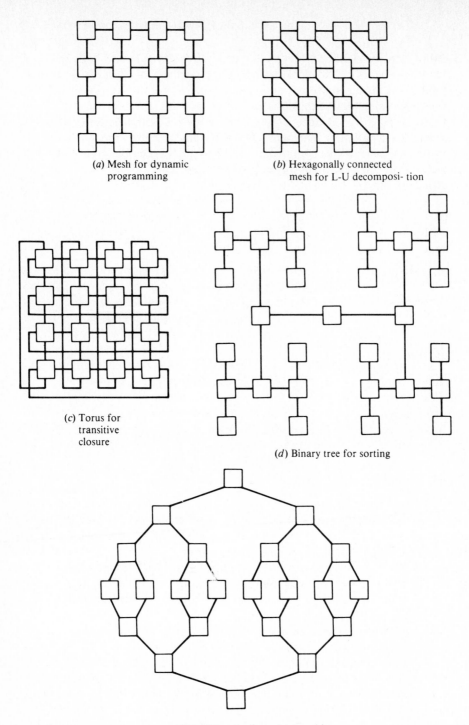

(a) Mesh for dynamic
programming

(b) Hexagonally connected
mesh for L-U decomposi- tion

(c) Torus for
transitive
closure

(d) Binary tree for sorting

(e) Doubly rooted tree for searching

Figure 10.30 Algorithmically specialized processor array configurations. (Courtesy of IEEE *Computer***,**
Snyder, January 1982.)

A family of reconfigurable processor arrays is introduced in this section. This configurable array concept was first proposed in 1982 by Lawrence Snyder at Purdue University. Each configurable VLSI array is constructed with three types of components: a collection of processing elements, a switch lattice, and an array controller. The *switch lattice* is the most important component and the main source of differences among family members. It is a regular structure formed from programmable switches connected by data paths. The PEs are not directly connected to each other, but rather are connected at regular intervals to the switch lattice. Figure 10.31 shows three examples of switch lattices. Generally, the layout will be square, although other geometries are possible. The perimeter switches are connected to external storage devices. With current technology, only a few PEs and switches can be placed on a single chip. As improvements in fabrication technology permit higher device densities, a single chip will be able to hold a larger region of the switch lattice.

Each switch in the lattice contains local memory capable of storing several configuration settings. A configuration setting enables the switch to establish a direct static connection between two or more of its incident data paths. For example, we achieve a mesh interconnection pattern of the PEs for the lattice in Figure 10.31a by assigning north-south configuration settings to alternate switches in odd-numbered rows and east-west settings to switches in the odd-numbered columns. Figure 10.32a illustrates the configuration; Figure 10.32b gives the configuration settings of a binary tree.

The controller is responsible for loading the switch memory. The switch memory is loaded preparatory to processing and is performed in parallel with the PE program memory loading. Typically, program and switch settings for several phases can be loaded together. The major requirement is that the local configuration settings for each phase's interconnection pattern be assigned to the same memory location in all switches.

Switch lattices It is convenient to think of the switches as being defined by several characteristic parameters:

- m—the number of wires entering a switch on one data path (path width)
- d—the degree of incident data paths to a switch
- c—the number of configuration settings that can be stored in a switch
- g—the number of distinct data-path groups that a switch can connect simultaneously.

The value of m reflects the balance struck between parallel and serial data transmission. This balance will be influenced by several considerations, one of which is the limited number of pins on the package. Specifically, if a chip hosts a square region of the lattice containing n PEs, then the number of pins required is proportional to $m\sqrt{n}$.

The value of d will usually be four, as in Figure 10.31a, or eight, as in Figure 10.31c. Figure 10.31b shows a mixed strategy that exploits the tendency of switches

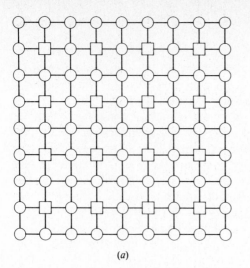

(a)

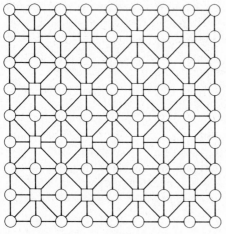

(b)

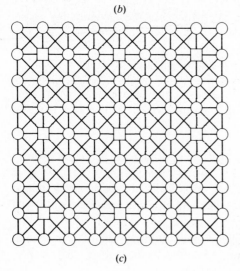

(c)

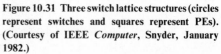

Figure 10.31 Three switch lattice structures (circles represent switches and squares represent PEs). (Courtesy of IEEE *Computer*, Snyder, January 1982.)

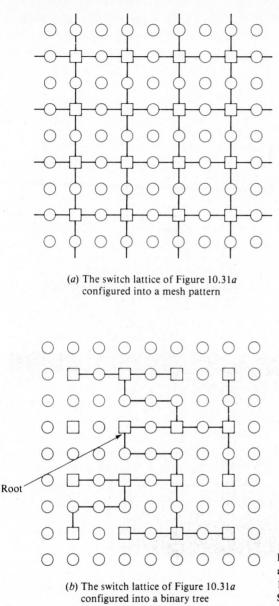

(a) The switch lattice of Figure 10.31a
configured into a mesh pattern

Root

(b) The switch lattice of Figure 10.31a
configured into a binary tree

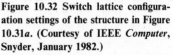

**Figure 10.32 Switch lattice configura-
ation settings of the structure in Figure
10.31a. (Courtesy of IEEE *Computer*,
Snyder, January 1982.)**

to be used in two different roles. Switches at the intersection of the vertical and
horizontal switch corridors tend to perform most of the routing, while those
interposed between two adjacent PEs act more like extended PE ports for selecting
data paths from the "corridor buses." The value of c is influenced by the number
of configurations that may be needed for a multiphase computation and the
number of bits required per setting.

The *crossover capability* is a property of switches and refers to the number of distinct data-path groups that a switch can simultaneously connect. Crossover capability is specified by an integer g in the range 1 to $d/2$. Thus, 1 indicates no crossover and $d/2$ is the maximum number of distinct paths intersecting at a degree d switch.

It is clear that lattices can differ in several ways. The PE *degree*, like the switch degree, is the number of incident data paths. Most algorithms of interest use PEs of degree eight or less. Larger degrees are probably not necessary since they can be achieved either by multiplexing data paths or by logically coupling processing elements, e. g., two degree-four PEs could be coupled to form a degree-six PE where one PE serves only as a buffer.

The number of switches that separate two adjacent PEs is called the *corridor width*, w. (See Figure 10.31c for a $w = 2$ lattice.) This is perhaps the most significant parameter of a lattice since it influences the efficiency of PE utilization, the convenience of interconnection pattern embeddings, and the overhead required for the polymorphism.

Pattern embedding A given interconnection pattern can be embedded in a programmable switch lattice. We say that the switch lattice "hosts" the given pattern. Figure 10.33 shows the embedding of the complete bipartite graph in the lattice of Figure 10.31c where the center column of PEs is unused. Increasing the corridor width improves processor utilization when the complex interconnection patterns must be embedded because it provides more data paths per unit area.

For most of the algorithmically specialized processors arrays, a corridor width of two suffices to achieve optimal or near optimal PE utilization. However, to be sure of hosting all planar interconnection patterns of n nodes with reasonably complete processor utilization, a width proportional to log n may be necessary. It is possible, using basis elements of 15-node trees embedded in 4×4 square regions of the lattice, to achieve a completely planar embedding of a 255-node complete binary tree (Figure 10.34) into the lattice of Figure 10.31a. There is only one unused PE in this planar embedding, as marked by the darkened square at the lower right corner.

By integrating programmable switches with the processing elements, the computer achieves a polymorphism of interconnection structure that also preserves locality. This enables us to compose algorithms that exploit different interconnection patterns. In addition to responding to problems of different sizes and characteristics, the flexibility of integrated switches provides substantial fault tolerance. The above reconfigurable processor array embedded in the switch lattice is a good candidate for *waver-scale integration* (WSI). WSI has been previously attempted by discretionary wiring. Due to the additional masking steps required, this has not proved to be practical. Other researchers are currently investigating laser restructuring and fuse-blowing approaches to implementing WSI.

The concept of WSI implementation of the reconfigurable switch lattice is illustrated in Figure 10.35. A 9×9 grid of building blocks is patterned on a 4-inch wafer. Multiple 2×2 virtual lattices are mapped into a 4×3 building block,

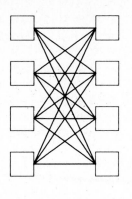

(*a*) Bipartite
graph

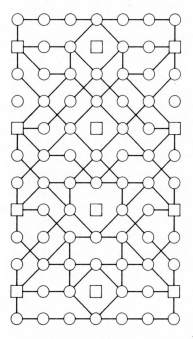

(*b*) Embedding of the
bipartite graph

**Figure 10.33 A bipartite graph embedded into the lattice of
Figure 10.31*c* using a switch with a crossover value $g = 2$.
(Courtesy of IEEE *Computer*, Snyder, January 1982.)**

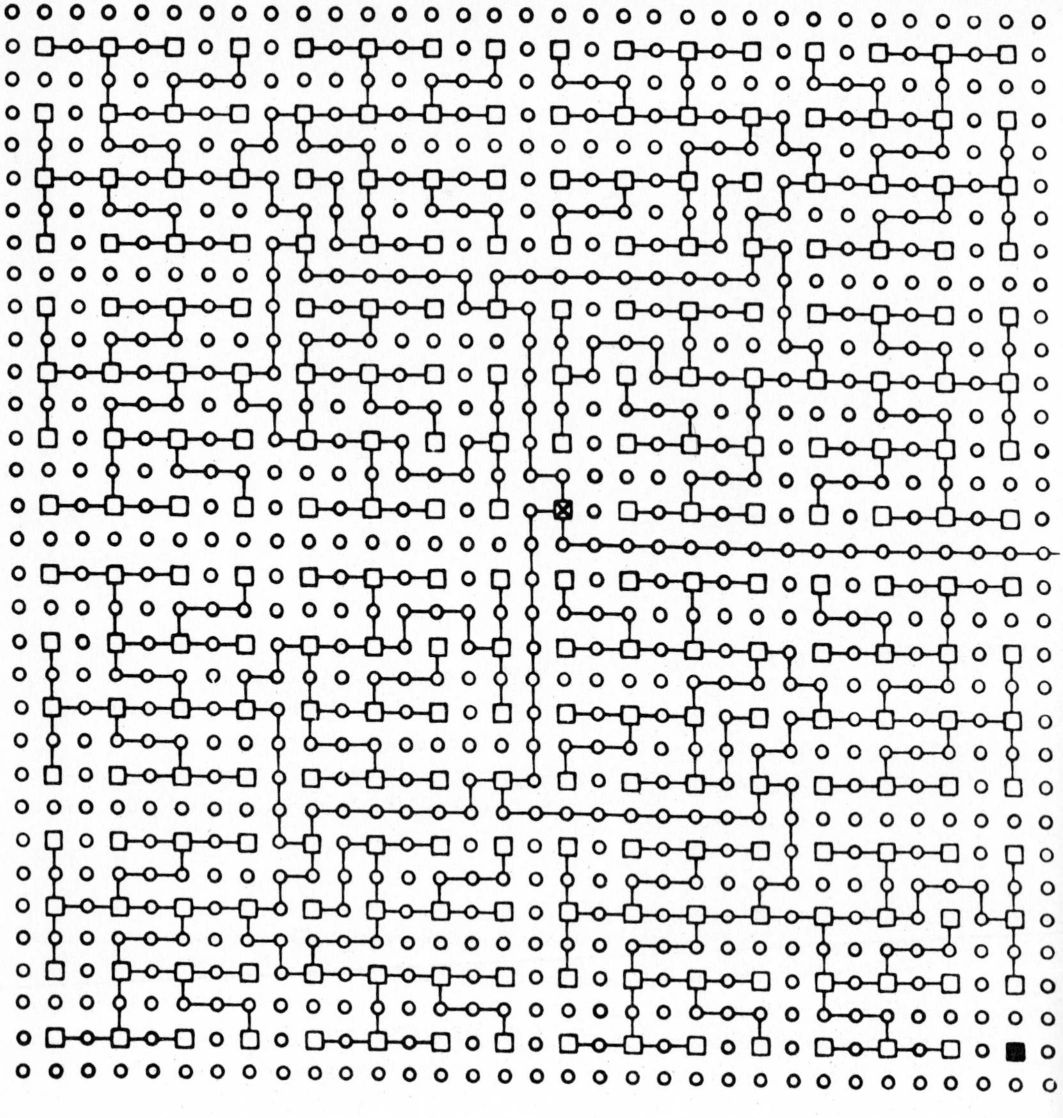

Spare

Figure 10.34 Planar embedding of a 255-node binary tree into the switch lattice of Figure 10.31a (the root of the tree is at the center of the lattice). (Courtesy of IEEE *Computer*, Snyder, January 1982.)

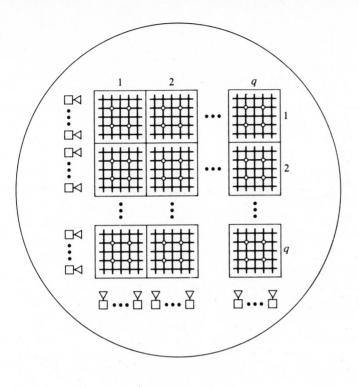

$\triangleleft$ Bonding pad

$\square$ Driver

Figure 10.35 Layout of a Wafer Scale Integrated (WSI) processor array. (Courtesy of K. S. Hedlun, Ph.D. Thesis, Purdue University, June 1982).

as illustrated in Figure 10.36. WSI implementation of highly parallel computing structures, either static function or programmable, demands high yield on the wafer. To implement a wafer scale system, all PEs on a wafer are tested, and then the good PEs are connected together. The wafer is structured so that the presence of faulty PEs is masked off and only functional PEs are used.

With current technology, machines with over 300 processors per wafer can be fabricated. These wafer-scale machines will be cheaper, faster, and more reliable than their counterparts implemented with single chip components. However, many practical problems of testing, routing around a faulty PE, power consumption, synchronization, and packaging remain to be solved. Both VLSI and WSI computing structures are being vigorously sought by parallel computing specialists. Three dimensional VLSI computing structures were also recently proposed, in which multi-layer devices are demanded.

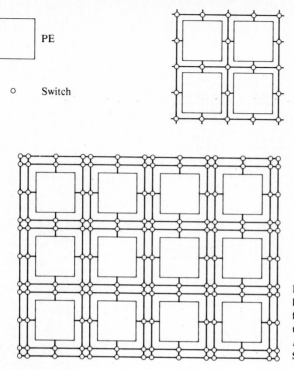

□   PE

○   Switch

Figure 10.36 A 2 × 2 virtual lattice and a 4 × 3 building block for WSI implementation. (Courtesy of *Proc. of Int'l Conf. on Parallel Processing*, Hedlund and Snyder, August 1982.)

10.4 VLSI MATRIX ARITHMETIC PROCESSORS

In this section, we describe modular VLSI architectures for implementing large-scale matrix arithmetic processors. We begin with the cellular design of several primitive matrix arithmetic modules. A class of partitioned matrix algorithms and their pipelined network implementations are then presented. Performance analysis is given for these VLSI matrix arithmetic solvers. Finally, we show how these matrix solvers can be used for real-time image processing.

10.4.1 VLSI Arithmetic Modules

Four primitive VLSI arithmetic modules are functionally introduced in Figure 10.37. These VLSI devices are building blocks for implementing the partitioned matrix algorithms to be studied shortly. These modules are used to perform $m \times m$ submatrix or m-element subvector computations. Each module is constructed with a cellular array of multipliers, dividers, and interface latches for pipelined operations. The schematic logic designs of these primitive VLSI chips are described below.

The D module is for *L-U decomposition* of an intermediate $m \times m$ submatrix $\hat{A}_{rr} = L_{rr} \cdot U_{rr}$ along the principal diagonal of a given matrix $\mathbf{A}$ ($\hat{A}_{rr}$ will be defined

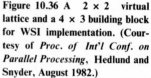

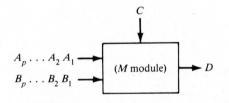

A → **(D module)** → L, U

$$\begin{bmatrix} a_{11} & a_{12} & a_{13} \\ a_{21} & a_{22} & a_{23} \\ a_{31} & a_{32} & a_{33} \end{bmatrix} = \begin{bmatrix} 1 & 0 & 0 \\ l_{21} & 1 & 0 \\ l_{31} & l_{32} & 1 \end{bmatrix} \cdot \begin{bmatrix} u_{11} & u_{12} & u_{13} \\ 0 & u_{22} & u_{23} \\ 0 & 0 & u_{33} \end{bmatrix}$$

(*a*) Submatrix decomposition module

U → **(I module)** → $U^{-1} = V$

$$\begin{bmatrix} u_{11} & u_{12} & u_{13} \\ 0 & u_{22} & u_{23} \\ 0 & 0 & u_{33} \end{bmatrix}^{-1} = \begin{bmatrix} v_{11} & v_{12} & v_{13} \\ 0 & v_{22} & v_{23} \\ 0 & 0 & v_{33} \end{bmatrix}$$

(*b*) Submatrix inverter

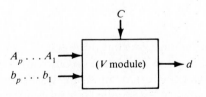

C →
$A_p \ldots A_2 A_1$ →, $B_p \ldots B_2 B_1$ → **(M module)** → D

$D = C + \sum_{i=1}^{p} A_i \cdot B_i$ where C, D, and $\{A_i$ and B_i for $i = 1, \ldots, p\}$ are $m \times m$ matrices.

(*c*) Matrix multiplier

C →
$A_p \ldots A_1$ →, $b_p \ldots b_1$ → **(V module)** → d

$d = c + \sum_{i=1}^{p} A_i \cdot b_i$ where c, d, $\{b_i$ for $i = 1, \ldots, p\}$ are $m \times 1$ column vectors, and $\{A_i$ for $i = 1, \ldots, p\}$ are $m \times m$ matrices.

(*d*) Matrix-vector multiplier

Figure 10.37 VLSI arithmetic modules for matrix computations. (Courtesy of *IEEE Trans. Computers*, Hwang and Cheng, December 1982.)

shortly). The I module is for the *inversion* of a triangular $m \times m$ submatrix. The input-output arithmetic specifications of these VLSI modules are given in the drawing. Both D and I modules have a fixed delay of 2m time units. One time unit equals the time required to perform one multiply-add operation $a \times b + c = d$, or one divide operation $a/b = c$, by one step processor in the cellular arrays shown in Figure 10.38 and Figure 10.39.

The M module is the predominant device to be used in the construction of various matrix solvers. *Accumulative chain matrix multiplications* are performed by an M module as specified in Figure 10.40. The number p of pairs of $m \times m$ matrices to be multiplied and added is determined by the external input sequence. Therefore, the time delay of an M module is equal to $p \cdot m + 1$. The V module is modified from the M module for *accumulative submatrix-vector multiplications*. The delay of a V module is also measured as $p \cdot m + 1$. Because each D, I, or M module contains an array of about m^2 step processors, their interior chip complexity is $O(m^2)$. Each V module contains a pipeline of m step processors and thus has an interior chip complexity of $O(m)$. The time delays of each D or I module has an order $O(m)$ and those for M and V modules are $O(m \cdot p)$, depending on the number of input pairs to be processed.

10.4.2 Partitioned Matrix Algorithms

Based on the state-of-the-art electronic and packaging technologies, we can only expect VLSI arithmetic devices designed to implement regularly structured functions with limited I/O terminals. A modular approach to achieve VLSI matrix arithmetic is amenable from the viewpoints of feasibility and applicability. A matrix partitioning approach is presented below to overcome those technological constraints in constructing large-scale matrix processors. Four partitioned algorithms are described below for modular VLSI implementation:

- L-U decomposition by a variant of Gaussian elimination
- Normal inversion of a nonsingular triangular matrix
- Multiplication of two compatible matrices
- Solving a triangular system of equations by back substitution

L-U decomposition by partitioning A partitioned approach is proposed to circumvent the I/O problem of systolic arrays by using $m \times m$ VLSI modules, where m is smaller than n in at least two orders of magnitude. Of course, I/O port sharing and time-division multiplexing are often used to satisfy the IC packaging constraints, even for small m. The partitioned triangular decomposition is illustrated in Figure 10.41. The given matrix $\mathbf{A} = (a_{ij})$ is partitioned into k^2 submatrices of the order $m \times m$ each. The submatrix computation sequence is identified in steps. This method is equivalent to Crout's method when $m = 1$. However, we consider nontrivial cases where $m = 2$.

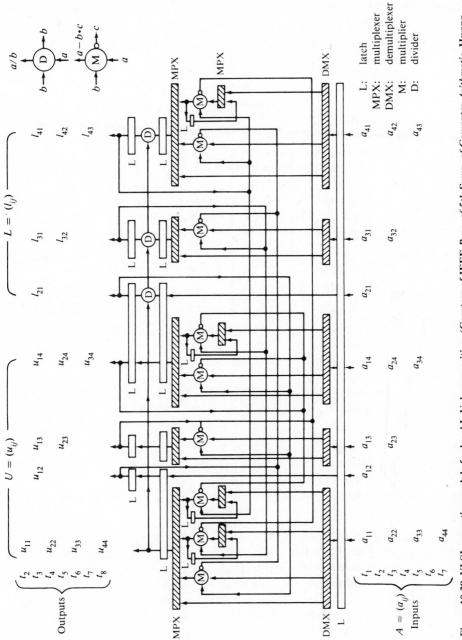

Figure 10.38 VLSI computing module for local L–U decomposition. (Courtesy of IEEE *Proc. of 5th Symp. of Computer Arithmetic*, Hwang and Cheng, May 1981.)

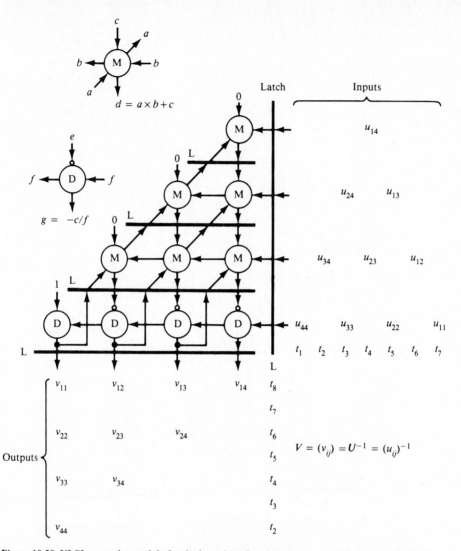

Figure 10.39 VLSI computing module for the inversion of a triangular matrix. (Courtesy of IEEE Proc. of 5th Symp. on Computer Arithmetic, Hwang and Cheng, May 1981.)

At step one, L-U decomposition of submatrix A_{11} is performed using a D module to generate the two triangular submatrices L_{11} and U_{11} such that $A_{11} = L_{11} \cdot U_{11}$. Two I modules are used to compute the inverse submatrices L_{11}^{-1} and U_{11}^{-1} at step two. The following matrix multiplications are then performed by $2(k-1)$ M modules in parallel at step 2.

$$L_p = A_{p1} \cdot U_{11}^{-1} \qquad \text{for } p = 2, 3, \ldots, k$$

$$U_{1q} = L_{11}^{-1} \cdot A_{1q} \qquad \text{for } q = 2, 3, \ldots, k \tag{10.11}$$

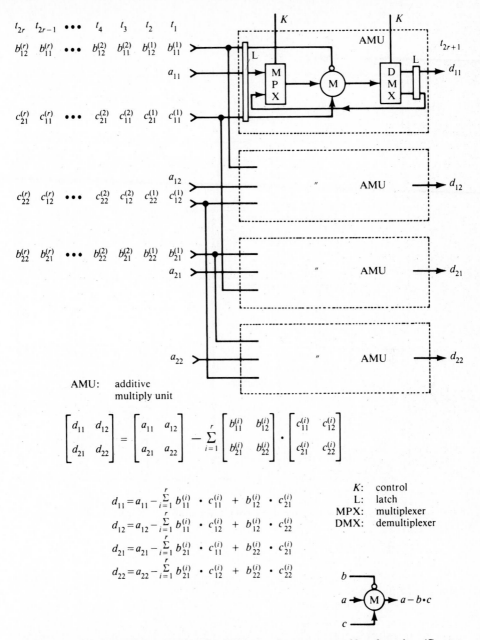

Figure 10.40 VLSI arithmetic module for the multiplication of two sequences of 2 × 2 matrices. (Courtesy of IEEE *Proc. of 5th Symposium of Computer Arithmetic*, Hwang and Cheng, May 1981.)

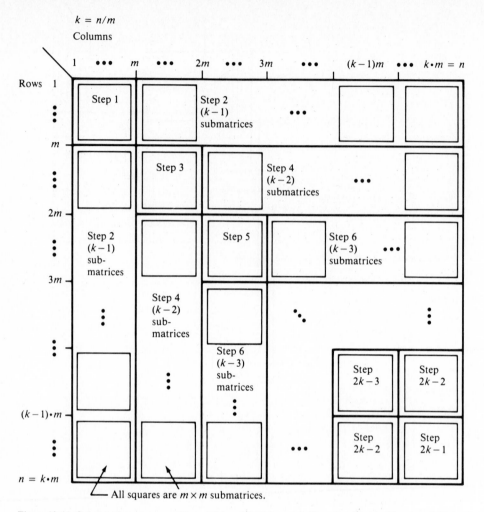

Figure 10.41 Computation sequence of the partitioned L-U decomposition algorithm by Hwang and Cheng (1982).

In subsequent steps, we generate the following intermediate submatrices using the M modules:

$$\hat{A}_{pq} = A_{pq} - \sum_{s=1}^{r-1} L_{ps} \cdot U_{sq} \qquad \text{for } p, q = 2, 3, \ldots, k \qquad (10.12)$$

Local L-U decompositions are then performed on $\hat{A}_{rr}$ at successively odd-numbered steps along the principal diagonal as shown in Figure 10.41:

$$L_{rr} \cdot U_{rr} = \hat{A}_{rr} \qquad \text{for } r = 2, 3, \ldots, k \qquad (10.13)$$

The remaining off-diagonal submatrices L_{pr} and U_{rq} are computed by inverting the diagonal submatrices U_{rr} and L_{rr} and then multiplying them by intermediate submatrices $\hat{A}_{pr}$ and $\hat{A}_{rq}$ at successively even-numbered steps. For $r = 2, 3, \ldots, k$, we compute

$$\begin{cases} L_{pr} = \hat{A}_{pr} \cdot U_{rr}^{-1} & \text{for } p = r + 1, \ldots, k \\ U_{rq} = L_{rr}^{-1} \cdot \hat{A}_{rq} & \text{for } q = r + 1, \ldots, k \end{cases} \tag{10.14}$$

The partitioned L-U decomposition is exemplified below. Each capital entry in the matrix **A** represents an $m \times m$ submatrix. The given matrix has an order n. We assume $n = m \cdot k$ for some integer k. The given matrix **A** is thus partitioned into $k^2 = n^2/m^2$ submatrices. The L-U decomposition of matrix **A** can be done in $2k - 1$ submatrix steps. All the diagonal elements of **L** are equal to 1. All diagonal submatrices of **U** are upper triangular matrices. The following example corresponds to the case of $k = n/m = 3$:

Example 10.4

$$\mathbf{A} = \begin{pmatrix} A_{11} & A_{12} & A_{13} \\ A_{21} & A_{22} & A_{23} \\ A_{31} & A_{32} & A_{33} \end{pmatrix}$$

$$= \begin{pmatrix} L_{11} & 0 & 0 \\ L_{21} & L_{22} & 0 \\ L_{31} & L_{32} & L_{33} \end{pmatrix} \cdot \begin{pmatrix} U_{11} & U_{12} & U_{13} \\ 0 & U_{22} & U_{23} \\ 0 & 0 & U_{33} \end{pmatrix} = \mathbf{L} \cdot \mathbf{U}$$

1. $A_{11} = L_{11} \cdot U_{11}$ (D module)

2. $L_{21} = A_{21} \cdot U_{11}^{-1}; L_{31} = A_{31} \cdot U_{11}^{-1}$

    $U_{12} = L_{11}^{-1} \cdot A_{12}; U_{13} = L_{11}^{-1} \cdot A_{13}$ (I modules and M modules)

3. $\hat{A}_{22} = A_{22} - L_{21} \cdot U_{12} = L_{22} \cdot U_{22}$

    $\hat{A}_{23} = A_{23} - L_{21} \cdot U_{13}; \hat{A}_{32} = A_{32} - L_{31} \cdot U_{12}$ (M modules and D modules)

4. $U_{23} = L_{22}^{-1} \cdot \hat{A}_{23}; L_{32} = \hat{A}_{32} \cdot U_{22}^{-1}$ (I modules and M modules)

5. $\hat{A}_{33} = A_{33} - (L_{31} \cdot U_{13} + L_{32} \cdot U_{23}) = L_{33} \cdot U_{33}$ (M modules and D modules)

The above interactive procedures are summarized in Figure 10.42 for partitioned L-U decomposition of any groups of any nonsingular dense matrix **A** of

ALGORITHM (Partitioned L-U Decomposition)

Inputs:

An $n \times n$ dense matrix $\mathbf{A} = (a_{ij})$ partitioned into $k^2 m \times m$ submatrices A_{ij} for $i, j = 1, 2, \ldots, k$, where $n \equiv k \cdot m$.

Outputs:

$k \cdot (k + 1)$ submatrices L_{pq} for $q \le p \equiv 1, 2, \ldots, k$ and U_{rs} for $s \ge r \equiv 1, 2, \ldots, k$, each of order $m \times m$.

Procedures:

(1) Decompose A_{11} into L_{11} and U_{11} such that $L_{11} \cdot U_{11} = A_{11}$.

(2) Compute inverse matrices L_{11}^{-1} and U_{11}^{-1};

Compute $L_{p1} = A_{p1} \cdot U_{11}^{-1}$; $U_{1p} = L_{11}^{-1} \cdot A_{1p}$, for $p = 2, 3, \ldots, k$.

(3) **For** $q \leftarrow 2$ **to** $(k - 1)$ **step 1 do**

$$\text{Compute } \hat{A}_{qq} = A_{qq} - \sum_{s=1}^{q-1} L_{qs} \cdot U_{sq};$$

$$\text{Decompose } \hat{A}_{qq} = L_{qq} \cdot U_{qq};$$

Compute the matrices L_{qq}^{-1} and U_{qq}^{-1}.

For $p \leftarrow (q + 1)$ **to** k **step 1 do**

$$\text{Compute } \hat{A}_{pq} = A_{pq} - \sum_{s=1}^{r-1} L_{ps} \cdot U_{sq};$$

$$\text{and } \hat{A}_{pq} = A_{qp} - \sum_{s=1}^{r-1} L_{qs} \cdot U_{sp} \text{ for } r = \min(p, q);$$

$$\text{Compute } L_{pq} = \hat{A}_{pq} \cdot U_{qq}^{-1}; U_{qp} = L_{qq}^{-1} \cdot \hat{A}_{qp}.$$

Repeat

Repeat

(4) Compute $\hat{A}_{kk} = A_{kk} - \sum_{s=1}^{k-i} L_{ks} \cdot U_{sk}$

Decompose $\hat{A}_{kk} = L_{kk} \cdot U_{kk}$

Figure 10.42 Partitioned algorithm for L-U decomposition. (Courtesy of *IEEE Trans. Computers*, Hwang and Cheng, 1982.)

order n. Submatrix computations are specified in groups. Each group can be computed in parallel by multiple VLSI modules. Submatrix computations can also be computed in sequential order, if only a limited number of VLSI chips are available.

Matrix inversion and multiplication A partitioned algorithm is described for iterative inversion of an $n \times n$ nonsingular triangular matrix using I and M modules. For clarity, we demonstrate the partitioning method by finding the inverse of an example $4m \times 4m$ upper triangular matrix $U = (u_{ij})$ with $m \times m$ modules. The inverse matrix $V = (v_{ij}) = U^{-1}$ is partitioned into $k^2 = (n/m)^2 = (4m/n)^2 = 4^2 = 16$ submatrices, as exemplified below:

Example 10.5

$$\mathbf{U}^{-1} = \begin{pmatrix} U_{11} & U_{12} & U_{13} & U_{14} \\ 0 & U_{22} & U_{23} & U_{23} \\ 0 & 0 & U_{33} & U_{34} \\ 0 & 0 & 0 & U_{44} \end{pmatrix}^{-1}$$

$$= \begin{pmatrix} V_{11} & V_{12} & V_{13} & V_{14} \\ 0 & V_{22} & V_{23} & V_{24} \\ 0 & 0 & V_{33} & V_{34} \\ 0 & 0 & 0 & V_{44} \end{pmatrix} = \mathbf{V}$$

1. $V_{11} = U_{11}^{-1}$; $V_{22} = U_{22}^{-1}$; $V_{33} = U_{33}^{-1}$; $V_{44} = U_{44}^{-1}$ (I modules)

2. $V_{12} = -V_{11} \cdot (U_{12} \cdot V_{22})$; $V_{23} = -V_{22} \cdot (U_{23} \cdot V_{33})$;

   $V_{34} = -V_{33} \cdot (U_{34} \cdot V_{44})$ (M modules)

3. $V_{13} = -V_{11} \cdot (U_{12} \cdot V_{23} + U_{13} \cdot V_{33})$

   $V_{24} = -V_{22} \cdot (U_{23} \cdot V_{34} + U_{24} \cdot V_{44})$ (M modules)

4. $V_{14} = -V_{11} \cdot (U_{12} \cdot V_{24} + U_{13} \cdot V_{34} + U_{14} \cdot V_{44})$ (M modules)

Partitioned multiplication of two large $n \times n$ matrices, say $\mathbf{A} \cdot \mathbf{B} = \mathbf{C}$, is rather straightforward. We include it here for completeness. Basically, each $m \times m$ submatrix C_{pq} of matrix $\mathbf{C}$ is obtained by performing $C_{pq} = \sum_{r=1}^{k} A_{pr} \cdot B_{rq}$, by one M module for each $p, q = 1, 2, \ldots, k$, where $km = n$ and A_{pr} and B_{rq} are $m \times m$ submatrices of the input matrices $\mathbf{A}$ and $\mathbf{B}$ respectively.

Triangular linear system solver The VLSI solution of a triangular linear system of equations can be done in k back-substitution steps. In the following example, $\mathbf{x}_i$ and $\mathbf{b}_i$ for $i = 1, 2, \ldots, k$ are $m \times 1$ subvectors and U_{ij} are $m \times m$ submatrices:

Example 10.6

$$\begin{bmatrix} U_{11} & U_{12} & U_{13} & U_{14} \\ 0 & U_{22} & U_{23} & U_{24} \\ 0 & 0 & U_{33} & U_{34} \\ 0 & 0 & 0 & U_{44} \end{bmatrix} \cdot \begin{bmatrix} \mathbf{x}_1 \\ \mathbf{x}_2 \\ \mathbf{x}_3 \\ \mathbf{x}_4 \end{bmatrix} = \begin{bmatrix} \mathbf{b}_1 \\ \mathbf{b}_2 \\ \mathbf{b}_3 \\ \mathbf{b}_4 \end{bmatrix}$$

1. $\mathbf{x}_4 = U_{44}^{-1} \cdot \mathbf{b}_4$ (I modules and V modules)

2. $\mathbf{x}_3 = U_{33}^{-1} \cdot (\mathbf{b}_3 - U_{34} \cdot \mathbf{x}_4)$ (I modules and V modules)

3. $\mathbf{x}_2 = U_{22}^{-1} [\mathbf{b}_2 - (U_{23} \cdot \mathbf{x}_3 + U_{24} \cdot \mathbf{x}_4)]$ (I modules and V modules)

4. $\mathbf{x}_1 = U_{11}^{-1} \cdot [\mathbf{b}_1 - (U_{12} \cdot \mathbf{x}_2 + U_{13} \cdot \mathbf{x}_3 + U_{14} \cdot \mathbf{x}_4)]$ (I modules and V modules)

In general, $k = n/m$ steps are needed in the back substitution. Matrix $\mathbf{U}$ is partitioned into $k \times (k + 1)/2$ submatrices of order $m \times m$ each. The solution vector $\mathbf{x}$ is divided into k subvectors.

10.4.3 Matrix Arithmetic Pipelines

Several matrix arithmetic processors are described below using those VLSI arithmetic modules as building blocks. These matrix networks will be used in Section 10.4.4 for the implementation of a feature extractor and a pattern classifier. The first network is for L-U decomposition of an $n \times n$ matrix $\mathbf{A}$. The second one is for the inversion of a triangular matrix of order n. The third one is for partitioned matrix multiplication, and the fourth one is for solving a triangular system of equations. With a pipelined architecture, only linear number $O(n/m)$ of VLSI chips is needed. The projected speedup of $O(n^3)/O(n^2/m)$ or $O(n^2)/O(n)$ is rather impressive for $n \gg m$ in real-time computations.

Matrix arithmetic solvers An L-U decomposition network is designed in Figure 10.43 for the computations in Example 10.4. In general, such a VLSI network needs to use one D module, two I modules, and $2k - 1$ M modules. These VLSI arithmetic modules are interfaced with high-speed latch memories to yield pipelining operations with feedback connections. Multiplexers are used to select the appropriate input to the functional modules at different steps. Note that the steps are divided according to submatrix operations. Each step may require a different number of pipeline cycles to complete the operation. To decompose an $n \times n$ matrix $\mathbf{A}$ into the two triangular matrices $\mathbf{L}$ and $\mathbf{U}$ such that $\mathbf{A} = \mathbf{L} \cdot \mathbf{U}$, the network requires $O(n^2/m)$ time with a total module count of $O(n/m)$. It requires $O(n^3)$ time delay for implementing the same algorithm on a uniprocessor computer.

Parallel M modules can be used to perform the partitioned matrix multiplications, as demonstrated in Figure 10.44 for the case of $k = n/m = 3$. $O(n^2/m)$ time is required with the use of $O(n/m)$ M modules. Moreover, one can achieve $O(n)$ time at the expense of using $O(n^2/m^2)$ M modules for partitioned matrix multiplication.

The matrix inversion algorithm in Example 10.5 is realized by the pipelined matrix network in Figure 10.45. In general, inverting a triangular matrix of order n requires the use of k I modules and $2(k - 1)$ M modules. Thus, the total module count equals $k + 2(k - 1) = 3k - 2 = O(k) = O(n/m)$ for $n \gg m$. The input assignments and data flows at intermediate and output terminals are also specified in the drawing. The total time delay in using this network to generate the inverse matrix $\mathbf{V} = \mathbf{U}^{-1}$ is equal to $O(n^2/m)$ for $n \gg m$.

Figure 10.46 shows the pipelined network for solving a triangular system of equations, as demonstrated in Example 10.6. In general, the network requires one I module and $[(n + m + 2)/(2m + 2)]$ V modules. The time delay of this network is $O(n)$ with the use of $O(n/m)$ V modules.

Performance analysis VLSI module requirements and the speed complexity of the above matrix algorithms are analyzed below. We consider two architectural

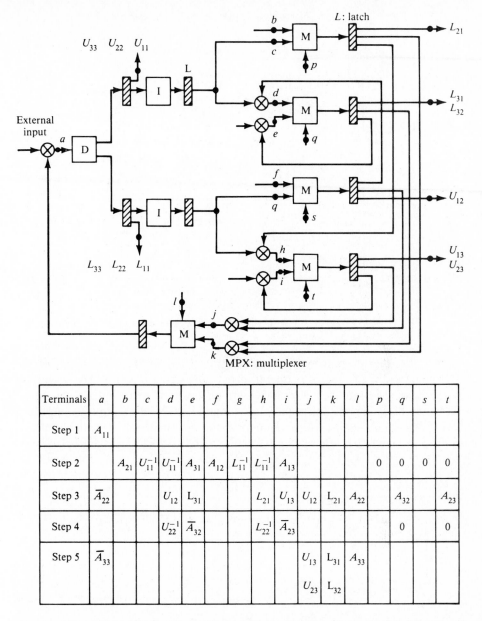

Terminals	a	b	c	d	e	f	g	h	i	j	k	l	p	q	s	t
Step 1	A_{11}															
Step 2		A_{21}	U_{11}^{-1}	U_{11}^{-1}	A_{31}	A_{12}	L_{11}^{-1}	L_{11}^{-1}	A_{13}				0	0	0	0
Step 3	$\overline{A}_{22}$			U_{12}	L_{31}			L_{21}	U_{13}	U_{12}	L_{21}	A_{22}		A_{32}		A_{23}
Step 4				U_{22}^{-1}	$\overline{A}_{32}$			L_{22}^{-1}	$\overline{A}_{23}$					0		0
Step 5	$\overline{A}_{33}$									U_{13}	L_{31}	A_{33}				
										U_{23}	L_{32}					

Figure 10.43 Arithmetic pipeline for partitioned L-U decomposition (Example 10.4). (Courtesy of *Computer Vision, Graphics, and Image Processing***, Hwang and Su, 1983a.)**

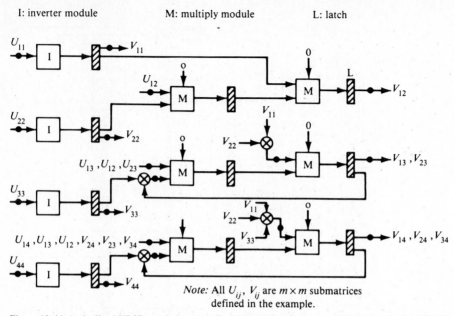

I: inverter module   M: multiply module   L: latch

Note: All U_{ij}, V_{ij} are $m \times m$ submatrices
defined in the example.

Figure 10.44 A pipelined VLSI matrix inverter (Example 10.5). (Courtesy of *Computer Vision, Graphics and Image Processing*, Hwang and Su, 1983a.)

configurations for the partitioned matrix arithmetic algorithms. In a *strictly parallel* configuration, all submatrix operations at each step are performed in parallel by multiple VLSI modules. This implies minimum time delay in each step. The total time delay among all steps is also minimized by overlapping some step operations. In a *serial-parallel* configuration, the number of available VLSI modules in each step is upper bounded. Thus, some parallel-executable operations

One modular
step

$A_{13}\ A_{12}\ A_{11}$ $A_{13}\ A_{12}\ A_{11}$ $A_{13}\ A_{12}\ A_{11}$ → M → C_{13} C_{12} C_{11}

$A_{23}\ A_{22}\ A_{21}$ $A_{23}\ A_{22}\ A_{21}$ $A_{23}\ A_{22}\ A_{21}$ → M → C_{23} C_{22} C_{21}

$A_{33}\ A_{32}\ A_{31}$ $A_{33}\ A_{32}\ A_{31}$ $A_{33}\ A_{32}\ A_{31}$ → M → C_{33} C_{32} C_{31}

$B_{33}\ B_{23}\ B_{13}$ $B_{32}\ B_{22}\ B_{12}$ $B_{31}\ B_{21}\ B_{11}$

Figure 10.45 Partitioned matrix multiplication using the M module specified in Figure 10.40.

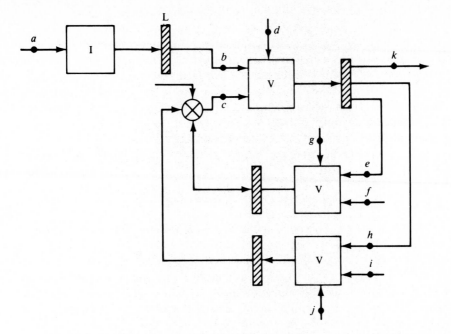

| Steps | Input terminals | | | | | | | | | | Outputs |
	a	b	c	d	e	f	g	h	i	j	k
Step 1	U_{44}	U_{44}^{-1}	b_4	0							x_4
Step 2	U_{33}	U_{33}^{-1}	b_3	0	x_4	U_{34}	b_3				x_3
Step 3	U_{22}	U_{22}^{-1}	b_2	0				x_3 x_4	U_{23} U_{24}	b_2	x_2
Step 4	U_{11}	U_{11}^{-1}	b_1	0	x_2 x_3 x_4	U_{12} U_{13} U_{14}	b_1				x_1

Figure 10.46 A VLSI triangular system solver (Example 10.6). (Courtesy of *Computer Vision, Graphics, and Image Processing*, Hwang and Su, 1983a.)

may have to be executed sequentially. Of course, serial-parallel operations will result in longer time delays because of limited hardware modules.

To implement the partitioned L-U decomposition algorithm, we need to use one D module, two I modules, and large number of M modules. The number of needed M modules depends on the chosen architectural configuration. The partitioned L-U decomposition can be realized in $O(n)$ time with $O(n^2/m^2)$ VLSI modules each with interior chip complexity $O(m^2)$. Using a uniprocessor, $O(n^3)$ time steps are needed to perform the L-U decomposition. It is interesting to note that, with the partitioned approach, the triple product of the *chip count* $O(n^2/m^2)$, the *compute time* $O(n)$, and the *chip size* $O(m^2)$ yields the uniprocessor compute time $O(n^3)$; that is:

$$O(n^2/m^2) \cdot O(n) \cdot O(m^2) = O(n^3) \tag{10.15}$$

This property is called *conservation law* between available hardware chips and achievable speed.

The chip count $O(n^2/m^2)$ is too high to be of practical value because of the fact that $n \gg m$. Therefore, we have to bound the chip count with a linear order $O(n/m)$ in a serial-parallel implementation of the partitioned matrix algorithm. One can use $2n/m - 1$ M modules to implement a serial-parallel architecture for L-U decomposition as shown in Figure 10.42. Using $O(n/m)$ modules yields a prolonged time delay $O(n^2/m)$ for $n \gg m \gg 1$.

The conservation law is again preserved in serial-parallel architecture; that is:

$$O(n/m) \cdot O(n^2/m) \cdot O(m^2) = O(n^3) \tag{10.16}$$

Similar analysis can be made to estimate the chip counts and time delays for partitioned matrix inversion and multiplication. In Table 10.2, we show that the first three matrix algorithms can each be implemented by $O(n^2/m^2)$ VLSI modules with $O(n)$ time delays for the strictly parallel architecture, and by $O(n/m)$ modules with $O(n^2/m)$ time for the serial-parallel configuration. Multiplication needs to use M modules exclusively. To solve a triangular LSE, the total time delay is $O(n)$ and $O(n/m)$ VLSI modules are used. The strictly parallel architecture is suggested for constructing a VLSI triangular system solver. Again the conservation law holds as:

$$O(n/m) \cdot O(n) \cdot O(m) = O(n^2) \tag{10.17}$$

where $O(n^2)$ is the compute time of using a uniprocessor to solve triangular system of algebraic equations.

It is obvious that trade-offs exist between the module counts and time delays of all partitioned matrix algorithms. By presetting a speed requirement, one can decide the minimum number of VLSI modules needed to achieve the desired speed performance. On the other hand, one can predict the speed performance under prespecified hardware allowance. This trade-off study is necessary for cost-effective design of large-scale matrix system solvers.

Table 10.2 Hardware requirements and speed performances of partitioned VLSI matrix algorithms

| | VLSI architecture and complexity | | | |
| | Strictly parallel architectures with minimum time delays | | Serial-parallel architecture with bounded number of VLSI modules | |
Matrix algorithm	VLSI module count and module types	Total compute time	VLSI module count and module types	Total compute time
L-U decomposition	$O(n^2/m^2)$ D, I, M*	$O(n)$	$O(n/m)$ D, I, M*	$O(n^2/m)$
Inversion of triangular matrix	$O(n^2/m)$ I, M*	$O(n)$	$O(n/m)$ I, M*	$O(n^2/m)$
Matrix multiplication	$O(n^2/m^2)$ M*	$O(n)$	$O(n/m)$ M*	$O(n^2/m)$
Solving triangular linear system of equations	$O(n/m)$ I, V*	$O(n)$		

Note: All measures are based on the assumption $n \gg m \gg 1$, where n is the matrix order and m is the VLSI module size.

* Predominating VLSI modules to be used.

10.4.4 Real-Time Image Processing

A computational model for a statistical image analysis system is illustrated in Figure 10.47. All pattern vectors $\mathbf{x}$ (the raw patterns to be recognized) form the input space $\mathbf{V}_n$. To design a feature extractor, one has to produce a set of m transformation vectors $\{\mathbf{d}_i | i = 1, 2, \ldots, m\}$ from a set S of training samples with known classes. Each $\mathbf{d}_i$ is an n-dimensional column vector. We denote the jth sample of class s as $\mathbf{x}_j^{(s)}$. The output of the extractor is the feature vector $\mathbf{y}$, which is related to the input $\mathbf{x}$ by a linear transformation $\mathbf{y} = \mathbf{D} \cdot \mathbf{x}$, where $\mathbf{D} = [\mathbf{d}_1, \mathbf{d}_2, \ldots, \mathbf{d}_m]^T$ is an $m \times n$ transformation matrix.

VLSI feature extraction Foley and Sammon (1975) have introduced a discriminating method to generate an optimal set of transformation vectors based on maximum separability instead of best picture fitting. The Foley-Sammon algorithm is modified below to allow modular implementation of a feature extractor by the proposed VLSI hardware.

Let n_s be the number of training samples and $\mathbf{m}_s$ be the sample mean for class s. The sample offset $\mathbf{z}_j^{(s)}$ is a column vector formed by the following vector subtraction:

$$\mathbf{z}_j^{(s)} = \mathbf{x}_j^{(s)} - \mathbf{m}_s \qquad \text{for } j = 1, 2, \ldots, n_s$$

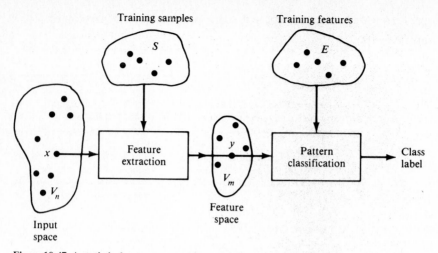

Figure 10.47 A statistical pattern recognition system.

The sample offset matrix $\mathbf{Z}_s$ is an $n \times n_s$ matrix formed by $\mathbf{Z}_s = [\mathbf{z}_1^{(s)}, \mathbf{z}_2^{(s)}, \ldots, \mathbf{z}_n^{(s)}]$. A within-class scatter matrix $\mathbf{S}_s$ is obtained by performing an orthogonal matrix multiplication, where $\mathbf{S}_s$ is an $n \times n$ matrix:

$$\mathbf{S}_s = \mathbf{Z}_s \cdot \mathbf{Z}_s^T \tag{10.18}$$

A weighted scatter matrix $\mathbf{A}$ is defined below for classes s and t. The fraction C, where $0 \le C \le 1$, is determined by a generalized Fisher criterion:

$$\mathbf{A} = C \cdot \mathbf{S}_s + (1 - C) \cdot \mathbf{S}_t \tag{10.19}$$

Let $\mathbf{m} = \mathbf{m}_s - \mathbf{m}_t$ be the mean difference. We define an $h \times h$ matrix $\mathbf{B}_h = (b_{ij})$ for $h = 1, 2, \ldots, m - 1$, where $b_{ij} = \mathbf{d}_i^T \cdot \mathbf{A}^{-1} \cdot \mathbf{d}_j$ for $1 \le i, j \le h$. Foley-Sammon algorithm is summarized below:

Foley-Sammon feature extraction algorithm

1. Initialize $i = 1$ and $\mathbf{B}_1^{-1} = b_{11}^{-1}$. Compute $\mathbf{d}_1$ by

$$\mathbf{d}_1 = \alpha_1 \cdot \mathbf{A}^{-1} \cdot \mathbf{m} \tag{10.20}$$

   where α_1 is a scalar constant satisfying $\mathbf{d}_1 \cdot \mathbf{d}_1^T = 1$ and

$$\alpha_1^2 = (\mathbf{m}^T \cdot [\mathbf{A}^{-1}]^2 \cdot \mathbf{m})^{-1}$$

2. Increment $i \leftarrow i + 1$. Halt, if $i > m$.
3. Compute the ith transformation vector $\mathbf{d}_i$ by

$$\mathbf{d}_i = \alpha_i \cdot \mathbf{A}^{-1} \cdot (\mathbf{m} - [\mathbf{d}_1, \mathbf{d}_2, \ldots, \mathbf{d}_{i-1}] \cdot \mathbf{B}_{i-1}^{-1} \cdot \mathbf{w}) \tag{10.21}$$

   where $\mathbf{w} = [1/\alpha_1, 0, 0, \ldots, 0]^T$ is a column vector with $(i - 1)$ elements, and α_i satisfies $\mathbf{d}_i^T \cdot \mathbf{d}_i = 1$. Go to step 2.

The above computations involve the inversions of **A** and $\mathbf{B}_i = 1, 2, \ldots, m$, which are very lengthy. Instead of performing recursive matrix inversion, a block-partitioning method is used to generate the inverse matrices $\mathbf{A}^{-1}$ and $\mathbf{B}_i^{-1}$. In a feature extraction process, matrix computations include $\mathbf{Z}_s \cdot \mathbf{Z}_s^T$, $\mathbf{Z}_t \cdot \mathbf{Z}_t^T$, and $[\mathbf{d}_1, \mathbf{d}_2, \ldots, \mathbf{d}_{i-1}] \cdot \mathbf{B}_{i-1}^{-1}$, $\mathbf{A}^{-1}$ and $\mathbf{B}_i^{-1}$ for all $i = 1, 2, \ldots, m-1$. Figure 10.48 shows the functional design of a VLSI feature extractor. This extractor is constructed with three subsystems: scatter matrix generator, matrix inverter, and feature generator, as shown by dash-line boxes. The vector subtractor is implemented with modified V modules for generating $\mathbf{Z}_s$, $\mathbf{Z}_s^T$, $\mathbf{Z}_t$, $\mathbf{Z}_t^T$, and the mean difference **m** used in the above algorithm. Two matrix multiply networks (Figure 10.44) are used to perform the orthogonal matrix multiplications. Each network contains n/m M modules. The weighted matrix adder can be implemented by n/m M modules with some special constant inputs.

The inversion of the scatter matrix **A** is done by employing an L-U decomposition network (Figure 10.43), two triangular matrix inverters (Figure 10.45), and one multiply network to yield the computation $\mathbf{A}^{-1} = (\mathbf{L} \cdot \mathbf{U})^{-1} = \mathbf{U}^{-1} \cdot \mathbf{L}^{-1}$. The inverse matrices $\mathbf{B}_i^{-1}$ for $i = 2, 3, \ldots, m-1$ can be similarly generated by this matrix inverter. Let $\mathbf{D}_i = [\mathbf{d}_1, \mathbf{d}_2, \ldots, \mathbf{d}_i]$. The matrix multiplications $\mathbf{D}_i \cdot \mathbf{B}_i^{-1}$ are performed by the same matrix multiply network generating the scatter matrix $\mathbf{S}^t$. If i/r is not an integer, the matrices $\mathbf{D}_i$ and $\mathbf{B}_i^{-1}$ can also be augmented with zeros and the identity matrix in order to use standard VLSI modules. The above computations are recursively performed by the transformation vector generator. This generator can be implemented by V modules with modified constant inputs. The matrix-vector multiplier is implemented with V modules.

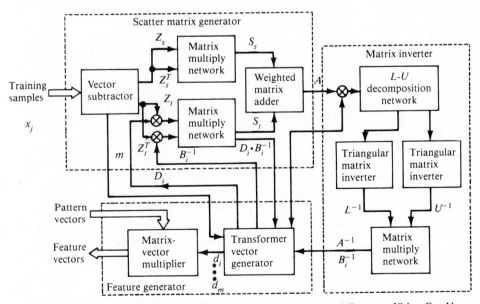

Figure 10.48 The schematic design of a VLSI pattern classifier. (Courtesy of *Computer Vision, Graphics, and Image Processing,* **Hwang and Su, November 1983.)**

VLSI pattern classification Linear discriminant functions can be used for pattern classification. To distinguish among p pattern classes, $p(p-1)/2$ pairwise discriminant functions are needed. A linear discriminant function between two distinct classes is defined by:

$$F(\mathbf{y}) = \mathbf{v}^T \cdot \mathbf{y} + \alpha \qquad (10.22)$$

where $\mathbf{y} = (y_1, y_2, \ldots, y_m)^T$ is the feature vector, $\mathbf{v} = (v_1, v_2, \ldots, v_m)^T$ is called the discriminant vector and α is a scalar threshold constant. The discriminant vector $\mathbf{v}$ and threshold constant α are determined with the aid of a set E of training features with known class labels. The feature pattern $\mathbf{y}$ is classified into class s if $F(\mathbf{y}) \geq 0$, and into class t, if otherwise.

Fisher's method is used to generate the discriminant vector $\mathbf{v}$ from training features. The threshold constant α can be set to "zero" with an appropriate choice of the coordinate system. Let $\mathbf{y}_j^{(s)}$ be the jth training feature vector of class s, for $j = 1, 2, \ldots, m_s$. The feature mean difference is $\mathbf{f} = \mathbf{f}_s - \mathbf{f}_t$ and feature offset vector is $\mathbf{w}_j^{(s)} = \mathbf{y}_j^{(s)} - \mathbf{f}_s$. An $m \times m_s$ feature offset matrix $\mathbf{W}_s = [\mathbf{w}_1^{(s)}, \mathbf{w}_2^{(s)}, \ldots, \mathbf{w}_{m_s}^{(s)}]$ is defined for each class. The covariance matrix for class s is computed by:

$$\sum_s = \frac{1}{m_s - 1} \cdot \mathbf{W}_s \cdot \mathbf{W}_s^T \qquad (10.23)$$

where $\sum_s$ has dimension $m \times m$. The following computation steps are needed to generate the discriminant vectors needed for pattern classification.

A linear pattern classification algorithm
1. Compute $\mathbf{f} = \mathbf{f}_s - \mathbf{f}_t$ and the feature offset matrices $\mathbf{W}_s$ by subtracting the mean $\mathbf{f}_s$ from each training feature $\mathbf{y}_j^{(s)}$ for $j = 1, 2, \ldots, m_s$.
2. Generate matrices $\sum_s$ and $\sum_t$ using Eq. 10.23.
3. Solve the following linear system of equations to determine the discriminant vector $\mathbf{v}$:

$$\left(\sum_s + \sum_t \right) \cdot \mathbf{c} = \mathbf{f} \qquad (10.24)$$

Functional design of a VLSI pattern classifier based on the above algorithm is sketched in Figure 10.49. The schematic design of the covariance matrix generator is similar to the scatter matrix generator in Figure 10.48. The linear system solver is composed of an L-U decomposition network (Figure 10.43) and a triangular system solver (Figure 10.46). This matrix solver is needed to solve the dense system specified in Eq. 10.24. The Fisher classifier is essentially a threshold decision unit (Eq. 10.22) which can be easily implemented by some combinational logic circuits and the modified V modules. The VLSI approaches to both feature extraction and pattern classification can result in significant speedups of

$$\frac{O(n^3)}{O(n^2/m)} \quad \text{or} \quad \frac{O(n^3)}{O(n)} \qquad (10.18)$$

This will make it possible to achieve real-time image processing.

Feature extraction and pattern classification are initial candidates for possible VLSI implementation. VLSI computing structures have been proposed for

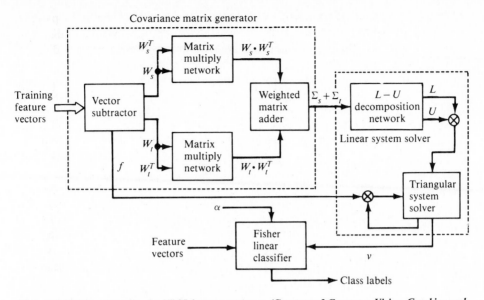

Figure 10.49 The schematic of a VLSI feature extractor. (Courtesy of *Computer Vision, Graphics, and Image Processing*, Hwang and Su, November 1983.)

general signal/image processing applications. Other methods, such as the eigen-vector approaches to feature selection and Bayes quadratic discriminant functions, should also be realizable with VLSI hardware. It is highly desirable to develop VLSI computing structures also for smoothing, image registration, edge detection, image segmentation, texture analysis, multistage feature selection, syntactic pattern recognition, pictorial query processing, and image database management. The potential merit lies not only in speed gains, but also in reliability and cost effectiveness.

10.5 BIBLIOGRAPHIC NOTES AND PROBLEMS

The data flow approach to designing high-performance computers was pioneered by Dennis (1974), among many other researchers. A good distinction between control flow computers and data flow computers can be found in Treleaven et al. (1982). A special issue on data flow system appeared in the IEEE *Computer Magazine* in February 1982. This issue contains several introductory articles on data flow languages, machine architectures, and some critics' opinions. Static data flow machines are described in Dennis et al. (1979) and Dennis (1980). Data flow languages have been studied in Tesler and Enea (1968), Backus (1978), Ackerman and Dennis (1979), Arvind et al. (1978), and Arvind and Gostelow (1982). Potential problems of the data flow approach are assessed by Gajski et al. (1982).

The Irvine data flow machine with tagged tokens is reported in Arvind and Gostelow (1977), Gostelow and Thomas (1980), and Thomas (1981). The

Manchester machine is reported in Gurd and Watson (1980). The MIT dynamic data flow project has been described in Arvind et al. (1980) and Arvind (1983). The EDDY system is described in Takahashi and Amamiya (1983). The French LAU system is described in Syre et al. (1977, 1980). The Utah machine is described in Davis (1978). The Newcastle control data flow machine is described in Treleaven (1978). The dependence-driven approach was proposed by Gajski et al. (1981). The event-driven approach using priority queues was suggested by Hwang and Su (1983c). Packet switching networks for dataflow multiprocessors were treated in Dias and Jump (1981) and in Chin and Hwang (1983).

Systolic array for VLSI computation was suggested by Kung and Leiserson (1978). A review of the systolic architecture can be found in Kung (1982). An assessment of VLSI for highly parallel computing is given by Fairburn (1982). The material on mapping algorithms into VLSI arrays is based on the work by Moldovan (1983). Reconfigurable processor-switch lattices are based on the work of Snyder (1982). Water scale integration of the switch lattice is studied in Hedlund's Thesis (1982). Partitioned matrix algorithms and VLSI image processing structures are based on the work by Hwang and Cheng (1982) and by Hwang and Su (1983a). A wavefront approach to designing cellular processor arrays can be found in S. Y. Kung et al. (1982). The 3-dimensional VLSI architecture was treated in Grinberg et al (1984).

Problems

10.1 Describe the following terms associated with data flow computers and languages:

(a) Control flow computers

(b) Data-driven computations

(c) Static data flow computers

(d) Dynamic data flow computers

(e) Data flow graphs and languages

(f) Single-assignment rule

(g) Unfolding of iterative computations

(h) Freedom from side effects

(i) Dependence-driven computation

(j) Coloring technique

(k) Event-driven computation

10.2 Draw data flow graphs to represent the following computations:

(a) **If** $(a=b)$ **and** $(c<d)$ **then** $c \leftarrow c - a$
                                        else $c \leftarrow c + a$

(b) **For** $i \leftarrow 1$ **until** m **do**
    begin
       $C(i) \leftarrow 0$
       For $j \leftarrow 1$ **until** n **do**
          $C[i] \leftarrow C[i] + a[i,h] * b[j]$
    end

(c) $Z = N! = N \times (N - 1) \times (N - 2) \times \ldots \times 2 \times 1$

You are allowed to use the *merge operator*, the *true gate*, the *false gate*, the *multiply operator*, the *add* or *subtract operator*, the *logical and* the *compare operator* in your graph construction.

10.3 It is desired to construct a packet-switched arbitration network for a static data flow computer similar to the Dennis machine at MIT. Use 5×2 switch boxes as building blocks to construct the network. A unique addressing path is demanded in the network.

(a) Design the 5×2 switch box with multiplexers, demultiplexers, and buffers. Switch control mechanism should be explained.

(b) Construct a $5^3 \times 2^3$ buffered Delta network with the 5×2 switch boxes to be used for arbitration purpose. Show all the interconnections between stages.

(c) There are 243 possible states of a typical 5×2 switch box. Each input port sends one request to be connected to one of the two output ports or none. Assuming that all states are equally probable, derive the blocking probability of a typical 5×2 switch box. When the switch is in a nonblocking state, all requests from input ports are connected to distinct output ports without conflicts. Whenever two or more input requests are destined to the same output port, the switch is entering a blocking state. The blocking probability indicates the chance that a switch may be blocked.

(d) Repeat the same question in part (b) for a 2×2 switch box. Compare the blocking probabilities between 5×2 and 2×2 switch boxes. Which one has higher blocking probability?

(e) Based on the blocking probability found in part (c), derive an expression to represent the network blocking probability, if requests from all 125 input ports are equally probable and their destination distribution is uniform among the eight output ports.

10.4 (a) Use 8×8 switch boxes to construct a 64×64 routing network for the Arvind machine with 64 PEs. Label all the input-output ports and show all the interconnections among the 8×8 boxes.

(b) Show how to join two 64×64 networks to form a network of size 112×112. Some outputs of one network can be connected to some inputs of the network in the joining process.

(c) Suppose that each 8×8 switch box has a delay of D. Analyze the delays of the 64×64 network and of the 112×128 network separately, under no blocking conditions.

10.5 Given a sequence of weights $\{\omega_1, \omega_2, \ldots, \omega_k\}$ and an input sequence of signals $\{x_1, x_2, \ldots, \omega_k\}$, design two linear systolic arrays with k processing cells to solve the convolution problem

$$y_i = \omega_1 x_1 + \omega_2 x_2 + \cdots + \omega_k x_k \tag{10.27}$$

(a) In the first design, you are given the unidirectional cells which compute $y_{out} \leftarrow y_{in} + \omega \cdot x_{in}$ as shown in Figure 10.50a. Explain your design, the distribution of the inputs, and the systolic flow of the partial results y_i's from left to right.

(b) In the second design, you are given the bidirectional cells which compute $y_{out} \leftarrow y_{in} + \omega \cdot x_{in}$ and $x_{out} \leftarrow x_{in}$, as shown in Figure 10.50b. Explain the design and operation of this systolic convolution array.

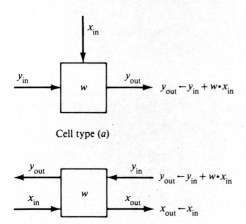

Cell type (a)

Cell type (b)

Figure 10.50 Processing cell types for the construction of a linear systolic array for one-dimensional convolution (Problem 10.5).

(c) Comment on the advantages and drawbacks in each design:

Note that in both designs (a) and (b), weights are preloaded to the cells, one at each cell, and stay at cells throughout the computation. In design (b), the x_i's and the y_i's move systolically in opposite directions.

10.6 Consider the implementation of the partitioned L-U decomposition algorithm (Figure 10.42) with the VLSI matrix arithmetic modules shown in Figure 10.37. We will analyze the hardware and time complexities: the module count M and the compute time T for chip complexity $C = O(m^2)$ in each of the following architectural configurations:

(a) In serial-parallel implementation, prove that $M = O(n/m)$ and $T = O(n^2/m)$.

(b) For strictly parallel implementation, prove that $M = O(n^2/m^2)$ and $T = O(n)$.

In the above proofs, n is the given matrix size and m is the VLSI module size. It is assumed that n is much greater than m.

10.7 Consider the VLSI implementation of an optimal parenthesization algorithm based on integer programming. A string of n matrices is multiplied:

$$M = M_1 \times M_2 \times \cdots \times M_n \tag{10.28}$$

Let $r_0, r_1, \ldots, r_n$ be the dimensions of the n matrices with r_{i-1} and r_i dimensions of M_i. Denote by m_{ij} the minimum cost of computing the product $M_i \cdot M_{i+1} \cdots M_j$. The algorithm which produces m_{in} is given below:

```
for i←1 to n do mᵢᵢ←0
  for 1←1 to n−1 do
    for i←1 to n−1 do
      begin
      j←i+1
      mᵢⱼ←MIN (mᵢₖ+mₖ₊₁,ⱼ+rᵢ₋₁rₖrⱼ)
            i<k<j
      end
```

Following the mapping procedure in Section 10.3.2, transform the above algorithm into a suitable form which can be implemented by the triangular array shown in Figure 10.50. All the processing cells perform the same functions to be defined in your transformed algorithm.

[*Hint*: One possible transformation of the indices $\mathbf{T}: (l, i, k) \to (\hat{l}, \hat{i}, \hat{k})$ is given by $\hat{l} = \max(2l + i - k, l - i + k + 1): \hat{i} = l + k;$ and $\hat{k} = -k$.].

10.8 Develop a cellular array processor for implementing a tridiagonal linear system solver. Specify the cell functions. the VLSI array structure, and the data flow patterns in the cellular array. You have freedom in choosing either a global systolic approach or a modular pipelined approach based on "block" partitioning and back substitution. Comment on the speed and hardware complexities in your design.

10.9 Consider the program graph shown in Figure 10.51. The critical path is $a, b, c_1, c_2, \ldots, c_8$, which results in a lower bound on execution of 13 time units, assuming that division takes 3 time units, multiplication 2, and addition 1. A hypothetical data flow computer has four processing units, each capable of executing any function. We idealize the machine by assuming that memory and interconnection delays are zero. In each of the following machine utilizations, show the schedule (a time-space diagram similar to that in Figure 3.46) of the 24 computing events (8 *divisions*, 8 *multiplications*, and 8 *additions*) and indicate the total execution time and utilization rate of processors.

(a) Use only one processor to perform sequential execution, one operation at a time.

(b) Use three processors to perform static data flow computations with a one-token-per-arch policy. Note that the three processors can be pipelined to execute a block of statements inside the loop.

(c) Use four processors to perform dynamic data flow computations such that tokens are labeled and logical events are colored to share the available resources.

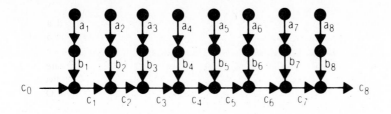

$$\textbf{input } d,e,f$$
$$c_0 = 0$$
$$\textbf{for } i \textbf{ from } 1 \textbf{ to } 8 \textbf{ do}$$
$$\textbf{begin}$$
$$a_i := d_i \div e_i$$
$$b_i := a_i * f_i$$
$$c_i := b_i + c_{i-1}$$
$$\textbf{end}$$
$$\textbf{output } a,b,c$$

Figure 10.51 A program graph for Prob. 10.9. (Courtesy of IEEE *Computer*, Gajski, et al., Feb. 1982.)

(*d*) Apply a random scheduling policy on four processors.

(*e*) Using a control flow vector machine with a "perfect" vectorizing compiler, which could detect the recurrence and achieve full vectorization. Note that intermediate variables can be introduced to completely balance the computing load among the four processors.

Hint: Parts (*c*) and (*e*) should result in the same minimum execution time. However, processor utilization rates would be different.

10.10 Consider a square matrix $B = A + C$, where A, B, and C are all $n \times n$ matrices, the inverse A^{-1} of matrix A is known and the rank of matrix C equals k for some $k \leq n$. You are asked to design a cellular array of processors to find the inverse, B^{-1} of matrix B, given the above conditions.

(*a*) Construct the VLSI processor array to find B^{-1} given A^{-1} and rank $(C) = k = 1$.

(*b*) Modify the design in part (*a*) to find B^{-1} given A^{-1} and rank $(C) = k > 1$.

BIBLIOGRAPHY

Ackerman, W. B., and Dennis, J. B., "VAL—A Value-Oriented Algorithmic Language," *TR-218*, Lab. for Computer Science, MIT, June 1979.

Agerwala, T., "Some Extended Semaphore Primitives," *Acta Informatica 8*, Springer Verlag, 1977.

Agrawal, D. P., "Graph Theoretical Analysis and Design of Multistage Interconnection Networks," *IEEE Trans. on Comp.*, C-32, July 1983, pp. 637–648.

Algiere, J. L., and Hwang, K., "Sparse Matrix Techniques for Circuit Analysis on the Cyber 205," *TR-EE 83-40*, Purdue University, W. Lafayette, Indiana, October 1983.

Amdahl Corp., *Amdahl 470 V/6 Machine Reference Manual*, Sunnyvale, California, 1975.

Amdahl, G. M., Blaauw, G. A., and Boorks, F. J., Jr., "Architecture of the IBM System/360," *IBM Journ. of Res. and Dev.*, vol. 8, no. 2, 1964, pp. 87–101.

Anderson, D. W., Earle, J. G., Goldschmidt, R. E., and Powers, D. M., "The IBM System/360 Model 91: Floating-Point Execution Unit," *IBM Journ. of Res. and Dev.*, January 1967a, pp. 34–53.

Anderson, D. W., Sparacio, F. A., and Tomasulo, R. M., "The IBM System/360 Model 91: Machine Philosophy and Instruction Handling," *IBM Journ. of Res. and Dev.*, vol. 11, no. 1, 1967b, pp. 8–24.

Anderson, J. P., Hoffman, S. A., Shifman, J., and Williams, R. J., "D825-A Multiple Computer System for Command and Control," *Proc. AFIPS Fall Joint Computer Conference*, vol. 22, 1962, pp. 86–96.

Andrews, G. J., and McGraw, J. R., "Language Features for Parallel Processing and Resource Control," *Proceedings of the Conference on Design and Implementation of Programming Languages*, Ithaca, N.Y., October 1976.

Andrews, G. R., and Schneider, F. B., "Concepts and Notations for Concurrent Programming," *ACM Computing Surveys*, vol. 15, March 1983, pp. 3–43.

Arnold, C. N., "Performance Evalution of Three Automatic Vectorizer Packages," *Proc. of Int'l. Conf. Parallel Proc.*, 1982, pp. 235–242.

Arnold, J. S., Casey, D. P., and McKinstry, R. H., "Design of Tightly-Coupled Multiprocessing Programming," *IBM Systems Journal*, no. 1, 1974.

Arvind and Gostelow, K. P., "A Computer Capable of Exchanging Processors for Time," *Proc. 1977 IFIP Congress*, North-Holland, Amsterdam, 1977.

Arvind and Gostelow, K. P., "The U Interpreter," *IEEE Comp.*, vol. 15, no. 2, Feb. 1982, pp. 42–50.

Arvind and Iannucci, R. A., "A Critique of Multiprocessing von Neumann Style," *Proc. 10th Ann. Symp. Computer Architecture*, June 1983, pp. 426–436.

Arvind, Kathail, V., and Pingali, K., "A Data Flow Architecture with Tagged Tokens," *Technical Memo 174*, Lab. for Computer Science, MIT, Sept. 1980.

Association of Computing Machinery, "Special Issue on Computer Architecture," *Comm. of ACM*, vol. 21, no. 1, Jan. 1980.

Backus, J., "Can Programming Be Liberated from the von Neumann Style? A Functional Style and Its Algebra of Programs," *Comm. of ACM*, vol. 21, no. 8, Aug. 1978, pp. 613–641.

Baer, J. L., "A Survey of Some Theoretical Aspects of Multiprocessing," *ACM Computing Surveys*, vol. 5, no. 1, March 1973, pp. 31–80.

Baer, J. L., "Multiprocessing Systems," *IEEE Trans. on Comp.*, C-25, Dec. 1976, pp. 1271–1277.

Baer, J. L., *Computer Systems Architectures*, Computer Science Press, Potomac, Maryland, 1980.

Baer, J. L., and Bovet, D. P., "Compilation of Arithmetic Expressions for Parallel Computations," *Proc. IFIP Congress 1968*, North-Holland, Amsterdam, 1968; pp. 340–346.

Baer, J. L., and Ellis, C., "Model, Design, and Evaluation of a Compiler for a Parallel Processing Environment," *IEEE Trans. on Soft. Eng.*, SE-3, Nov. 1977, pp. 394–405.

Bain, W. L., Jr., and Ahuja, S. R., "Performance Analysis of High-Speed Digital Buses for Multiprocessing Systems," *Proc. 8th Ann. Symp. Computer Architecture*, May 1981, pp. 107–131.

Banerjee, U., Gajski, D., and Kuck, D., "Accessing Sparse Arrays in Parallel Memories," *Journ. of VLSI and Computer Systems*, vol. 1, no. 1, 1983, pp. 69–99.

Barke, D. F., ed., *Very Large Scale Integration (VLSI): Fundamentals and Applications*, Springer-Verlag, New York, 1980.

Barnes, G. H., Brown, R. M., Kato, M., Kuck, D. J., Slotnick, D. L., and Stokes, R. A., "The ILLIAC IV Computer," *IEEE Trans. on Computers*, Aug. 1968, pp. 746–757.

Baskett, F., and Keller, T. W., "An Evaluation of the CRAY-1 Computer," *High Speed Computer and Algorithm Organization*, Kuck, et al., eds., Academic Press, New York, 1977, pp. 71–84.

Baskett, F., and Smith, A. J., "Interference in Multiprocessor Computer Systems with Interleaved Memory," *Comm. of ACM*, vol. 19, no. 6, June 1976, pp. 327–334.

Batcher, K. E., "STARAN Parallel Processor System Hardware," *Proc. AFIPS-NCC*, vol. 43, pp. 405–410.

Batcher, K. E., "The Flip Network in STARAN," *Int'l. Conf. Parallel Proc.*, Aug. 1976, pp. 65–71.

Batcher, K. E., "The Multi-dimensional Access Memory in STARAN," *IEEE Trans. on Comps.*, 1977, pp. 174–177.

Batcher, K. E., "Design of a Massively Parallel Processor," *IEEE Trans. on Comp.*, C-29, Sept. 1980, pp. 836–840.

Baudet, G. M., "Asynchronous Iterative Methods for Multiprocessors," *Journ. of ACM*, vol. 25, no. 2, Apr. 1978, pp. 226–244.

Bauer, L. H., "Implementation of Data Manipulating Functions on the STARAN Associative Array Processor," *Proc. Sagamore Comp. Conf. Parallel Proc.*, Aug. 1974, pp. 209–227.

Bell, C. G., Mudge, J. C., and McNamara, J., *Computer Engineering: A DEC View of Hardware Systems Design*, Digital Press, Bedford, Mass., 1978.

Bell, J., Casasent, D., and Bell, C. G., "An Investigation of Alternative Cache Organizations," *IEEE Trans. on Comp.*, C-23, Apr. 1974, pp. 346–351.

Benes, V. E., *Mathematical Theory of Connecting Networks and Telephone Traffic*, Academic Press, New York, 1965.

Bensoussan, A., Clingen, C. T., and Daley, R. C., "The MULTICS Virtual Memory: Concepts and Design," *Comm. of ACM*, vol. 15, May 1972, pp. 308–315.

Bernstein, A. J., "Analysis of Programs for Parallel Processing," *IEEE Trans. Elec. Comp.*, E-15, Oct. 1966, pp. 746–757.

Berra, P. B., and Oliver, E., "The Role of Associative Array Processors in Database Machine Architecture," *IEEE Comp.*, Mar. 1979, pp. 53–61.

Bhandarkar, D. P., "Analysis of Memory Interference in Multiprocessors," *IEEE Trans. on Comp.*, C-24, Sept. 1975, pp. 897–908.

Bhandarkar, D. P., "Some Performance Issues in Multiprocessor System Design," *IEEE Trans. on Comp.*, C-26, no. 5, May 1977, pp. 506–511.

Blaauw, G., "Computer Architecture," *Electronische Rechenanlagen*, vol. 14, no. 4, 1972, pp. 154–160.

Blaauw, G., *Digital Systems Implementation*, Prentice-Hall, Englewood Cliffs, N.J., 1976.

Bode, A., and Händler, W., *Rechnerarchitektur: Grundlagen und Verfahren*, Springer-Verlag,, Berlin (volumes 1 and 2), 1980, 1982.

Borgeson, B. R., Hanson, M. L., and Hartley, P. A., "The Evolution of the Sperry Univac 1100 Series: A History, Analysis, and Projection," *Comm. of ACM*, vol. 21, no. 1, Jan. 1978, pp. 25–43.

Bouknight, W. J., Denenberg, S. A., McIntyre, D. E., Randall, J. M., Sameh, A. H., and Slotnick, D. L., "The Illiac IV System," *Proc. IEEE*, vol. 60, no. 4, Apr. 1972, pp. 369–388.

Bovet, D. P., and Vanneschi, M., "Models and Evaluation of Pipeline Systems," *Computer Architectures and Networks* (Gelenbe and Mahl, eds.), North Holland, Amsterdam, 1976, pp. 99–111.

Brent, R., "The Parallel Evaluation of General Arithmetic Expressions," *Journ. of ACM*, vol. 21, no. 2, Apr. 1974, pp. 201–206.

Briggs, F. A., "Performance of Memory Configurations for Parallel-Pipelined Computers," *Proc. 5th Ann. Symp. Computer Architecture*, Apr. 1978, pp. 202–209.

Briggs, F. A., "Effects of Buffered Memory Requests in Multiprocessor Systems," *Proc. ACM/SIGMETRICS Conf. on Simulation, Measurement and Modeling of Comput. Systems*, 1979, pp. 73–81.

Briggs, F. A., and Davidson, E. S., "Organization of Semiconductor Memories for Parallel-Pipelined Processors," *IEEE Trans. on Comp.*, Feb. 1977, pp. 162–169.

Briggs, F. A., and Dubois, M., "Modeling of Synchronized Iterative Algorithms for Multiprocessors," *Proc. 18th Ann. Allerton Conf. on Communication, Control and Computing*, Oct. 1980, pp. 554–563.

Briggs, F. A., and Dubois, M., "Performance of Cache-Based Multiprocessors," *Proc. ACM/SIGMETRICS Conf. on Measurement and Modeling of Computer Systems*, Sept. 1981.

Briggs, F. A., and Dubois, M., "Effectiveness of Private Caches in Multiprocessor Systems with Parallel-Pipelined Memories," *IEEE Trans. on Comp.*, C-32, no. 1, Jan. 1983, pp. 48–59.

Briggs, F. A., Dubois, M., and Hwang, K., "Throughput Analysis and Configuration Design of a Shared-Resource Multiprocessors Systems: PUMPS," *Proc. 8th Ann. Symp. Computer Architecture*, May 1981, pp. 67–80.

Briggs, F. A., Fu, K. S., Hwang, K., and Patel, J. H., "PM^4: A Reconfigurable Multiprocessor System for Pattern Recognition and Image Processing," *Proc. of NCC, AFIPS*, June 1979, pp. 255–265.

Briggs, F. A., Fu, K. S., Hwang, K., and Wah, B. W., "PUMPS Architecture for Pattern Analysis and Image Database Management," *IEEE Trans. on Comp.*, C-31, no. 10, Oct. 1982, pp. 969–982.

Browning, S. A., "The Tree Machine: A Highly Concurrent Computing Environment," Ph.D. Thesis, Dept. of Computer Science, Cal. Tech., Pasadena, 1980.

Bucher, I. Y., "The Computational Speed of Supercomputers," *Proc. ACM/SIGMETRICS Conf. on Measurement and Modeling of Computer Systems*, Aug. 1983, pp. 151–165.

Bucholz, W., *Planning a Computer System: Project Stretch*, McGraw-Hill, New York, 1962.

Budnik, P. P., and Kuck, D. J., "The Organization and Use of Parallel Memories," *IEEE Trans. on Comp.*, vol. 20, Dec. 1971, pp. 1566–1569.

Burnett, G. J., and Coffman, E. G., "A Study of Interleaved Memory Systems," *Proc. Spring Joint Computer Conf., AFIPS*, SJCC, vol. 36, 1970, pp. 467–474.

Burroughs Co., "BSP: Overview Perspective, and Architecture," document no. 61391, Feb. 1978*a* (30 pages).

Burroughs Co., "BSP: Floating Point Arithmetic," document no. 61416, 1978*b* (27 pages).

Burroughs Co., "BSP: Implementation of FORTRAN," document no. 16391, Nov. 1977 (18 pages).

Buzen, J. P., "I/O Subsystem Architecture," *Proc. IEEE*, *63*, June 1975, pp. 871–879.

Cappa, M., and Hamacher, V. C., "An Augmented Iterative Array for High-Speed Array Division," *IEEE Trans. on Comp.*, C-22, Feb. 1973, pp. 172–175.

Carlson, W. W., and Hwang, K., "On Structural Data Accessing in Dataflow Computers," *Proc. 1st Int'l. Conf. Computers and Applications*, Beijing, China, June 1984.

Case, R. P., and Padegs, A., "Architecture of the IBM System 370," *Comm. of ACM*, vol. 21, no. 1, 1978, pp. 73–96.

Censier, L. M., and Feautrier, P., "A New Solution to Coherence Problems in Multicache Systems," *IEEE Trans. on Comp.*, C-27, Dec. 1978, pp. 1112–1118.

Chamberlin, D. D., "Parallel Implementation of a Single Assignment Language," *Ph.D. Thesis*, Stanford Univ., Calif., 1971.

Chamberlin, D. D., Fuller, S. H., and Liu, L. Y., "An Analysis of Page Allocation Strategies for Multiprogramming Systems with Virtual Memory," *IBM Journ. of Res. and Dev.*, 1973.

Chandy, K. M., "Models for the Recognition and Scheduling of Parallel Tasks on Multiprocessor Systems," *Bulletin of the Operations Research Society of America*, vol. 23, suppl. 1, Spring 1975, p. B-117.

Chang, D., Kuck, D. J., and Lawrie, D. H., "On the Effective Bandwidth of Parallel Memories," *IEEE Trans. on Comp.*, C-26, no. 5, May 1977, pp. 480–490.

Charlesworth, A. E., "An Approach to Scientific Array Processing: The Architecture Design of the AP-120B/FPS-164 Family," *IEEE Comp.*, Dec. 1981, pp. 12–30.

Chen, N. F., and Liu, C. L., "On a Class of Scheduling Algorithms for Multiprocessor Computing Systems," *Proc. Conf. on Parallel Proc.*, Raquette Lake, N.Y., August 1974.

Chen, S. C., "Speedup of Iterative Programs in Multiprocessor Systems," *Ph.D. Thesis*, Univ. of Ill. at Urb.-Champ., Dept. of Computer Science, no. 75-694, Jan. 1975.

Chen, S. C., "Large-Scale and High-Speed Multiprocessor System for Scientific Applications: Cray X-MP Series," *Proc. NATO Advanced Research Workshop on High-Speed Computing*, J. Kawalik, editor, Springer Verlag, Jülich, W. Germany, June 20–22, 1983.

Chen, T. C., "Parallelism, Pipelining, and Computer Efficiency," *Computer Design*, Jan. 1971, pp. 69–74.

Chen, T. C., "Overlap and Pipeline Processing," in *Introduction to Computer Architecture*, Chap. 9 (Stone, ed.), Science Research Associates, Inc., Chicago, 1980, pp. 427–486.

Chin, C. Y., and Hwang, K., "Connection Principles of Multipath Packet Switching Networks," *Proc. 11th Ann. Symp. Computer Architecture*, Ann Arbor, Mich., June 1984.

Chow, C. K., "On Optimization of Storage Hierarchies," *IBM Journ. of Res. and Dev.*, May 1974, pp. 194–203.

Chu, Y., *High Level Language Computer Architecture*, Academic Press, New York, 1975.

Chu, Y., and Abrams, M., "Programming Languages and Direct-Execution Computer Architecture," *IEEE Comp.*, vol. 14, July 1981, pp. 22–40.

Coffman, E. G., "Bounds on Parallel Processing of Queues with Multiple Jobs," *Naval Research Logical Quarterly*, 14, Sept. 1967, pp. 345–366.

Coffman, E. G., Elphick, M. J., and Shoshani, A., "System Deadlocks." *ACM Computer Surveys*, 3, 1971, pp. 67–78.

Coffman, E. G., and Denning, P. J., *Operating Systems Theory*, Prentice-Hall, Englewood Cliffs, N.J., 1973.

Coffman, E. G., and Graham, R. L., "Optimal Scheduling for Two Processor Systems," *Acta Informatica*, vol. 1, 1972, pp. 200–213.

Coffman, E. G., and Ryan, T. J., Jr., "A Study of Storage Partitioning Using a Mathematical Model of Locality," *Comm. of ACM*, vol. 15, Mar. 1972, pp. 185–190.

Coffman, E. G., ed., *Computer and Job-Shop Scheduling Theory*, John Wiley, New York, 1976.

Cohen, E., and Jefferson, D., "Protection in the Hydra Operating System," *Proc. 5th Symp. on Operating System Principles*, Nov. 1975, pp. 141–160.

Cohen, T., "Structured Flowcharts for Multiprocessing," *Computer Languages*, vol. 13, no. 4, 1978, pp. 209–226.

Connors, W. D., Florkowski, J. H., and Patton, S. K., "The IBM 3033: An Inside Look," *Datamation*, May 1979, pp. 198–218.

Conrad, V., and Wallach, "Iterative Solution of Linear Equations on a Parallel Processor System," *IEEE Trans. on Comp.*, Sept. 1977, pp. 838–847.

Conti, C. J., "Concepts for Buffer Storage," *Computer Group News*, 2, Mar. 1969, pp. 9–13.

Conti, C. J., Gibson, D. H., and Pikowsky, S. H., "Structural Aspects of the System 360/85; General Organization," *IBM Systems Journ.*, 1968, pp. 2–14.

Control Data Corp., *Control Data STAR-100 Features Manual*, St. Paul, Minn., pub. no. 60425500, Oct. 1973.

Control Data Corp., *Control Data STAR-100 FORTRAN Language Version 2 Reference Manual*, St. Paul, Minn., pub. no. 60386200, 1976.

Control Data Corp., *CDC Cyber 200 Operating System 1.4 Reference Manual*, St. Paul, Minn., pub. no. 60457000, vol. 1, 1979a.

Control Data Corp., *CDC Cyber 200 Fortran Language 1.4 Reference Manual*, St. Paul, Minn., pub. no. 60456040, 1979*b*.

Control Data Corp., *CDC Cyber 200/Model 205 Technical Description*, St. Paul, Minn., Nov. 1980.

Conway, M., "A Multiprocessor System Design," *Proc. AFIPS Fall Joint Comput. Conf.*, Spartan Books, N.Y., 1963, pp. 139–146.

Cooper, R. G., "The Distributed Pipeline," *IEEE Trans. Comp.*, Nov. 1977, pp. 1123–1132.

Cordennier, V., "A Two Dimension Pipelined Processor for Communication in a Parallel System," *Proc. 1975 Sagamore Comp. Conf. Parallel Proc.*, 1975, pp. 115–121.

Crane, B. A., Gilmartin, M. J., Huttenhoff, J. H., Rus, P. T., and Shively, R. R., "PEPE Computer Architecture," *IEEE Compcon*, 1972, pp. 57–60.

Cray Research, Inc., *CRAY-1 Computer System Hardware Reference Manual*, Bloomington, Minn., pub. no. 2240004, 1977.

Cray Research, Inc., *CRAY-1 Computer System Preliminary CRAY FORTRAN (CFT) Reference Manual*, Bloomington, Minn., pub. no. 2240009, 1978.

Cray Research Inc., *CRAY-1 Fortran (CFT) Reference Manual*, Bloomington, Minn., pub. no. 2240009, Dec. 1979*b*.

Gustafson, R. N., and Sparacio, F. J., "IBM 3081 Processor Unit: Design Considerations and Design Process," *IBM Journ. of Res. and Dev.*, vol. 26, no. 1, Jan. 1982, pp. 12–21.

Daley, R. C., and Dennis, J. B., "Virtual Memory Process and Sharing in Multics," *Comm. of ACM*, vol. 11, May 1968, pp. 306–311.

Datawest Corp., "Real Time Series of Microprogrammable Array Transform Processors," Prod. Bulletin Series B, 1979.

Davidson, E. S., "The Design and Control of Pipelined Function Generators," *Proc. 1971 Int'l. IEEE Conf. on Systems, Networks, and Computers*, Oaxtepec, Mexico, Jan. 1971, pp. 19–21.

Davidson, E. S., "Scheduling for Pipelined Processors," *Proc. 7th Hawaii Conf. on System Sciences*, 1974, pp. 58–60.

Davidson, E. S., Thomas, D. P., Shar, L. E., and Patel, J. H., "Effective Control for Pipelined Computers," *COMPCON Proc.*, IEEE 75CH0920-9C, 1975, pp. 181–184.

Davis, A. L., "The Architecture and System Methodology of DDM1: A Recursively Structured Data Driven Machine," *Proc. 5th Ann. Symp. on Computer Architecture*, 1978, pp. 210–215.

Davis, C. G., and Vouch, R. L., "Ballistic Missile Defense: A Supercomputer Challenge," *IEEE Comp.*, Nov. 1980, pp. 37–46.

Deitel, H. M., *An Introduction to Operating Systems*, Addison-Wesley, Reading, Mass. 1984.

Deminet, J., "Experience with Multiprocessor Algorithms," *IEEE Trans. on Comp.*, C-31, Apr. 1982, pp. 278–288.

Denelcor, Inc., *Heterogeneous Element Processor: Principles of Operation*, April 1981.

Denning, P. J., "The Working Set Model for Program Behavior," *Comm. of ACM*, vol. 11, no. 5, 1968, pp. 323–333.

Denning, P. J., "Operating Systems Principles for Data Flow Networks," *IEEE Comp.*, July 1978, pp. 86–96.

Denning, P. J., "Working Sets Past and Present," *IEEE Trans. on Soft. Eng.*, SE-6, no. 1, Jan. 1980.

Denning, P. J., "Virtual Memory," *ACM Computing Surveys*, 2, Sept. 1970, pp. 153–189.

Denning, P. J., and Graham, G. S., "Multiprogrammed Memory Management," *Proc. IEEE*, vol. 63, June 1975, pp. 924–939.

Denning, P. J., and Schwartz, S. C., "Properties of the Working Set Model," *Comm. of ACM*, vol. 15, 1972.

Dennis, J. B., "Data Flow Supercomputers," *IEEE Comp.*, Nov. 1980, pp. 48–56.

Dennis, J. B., "First Version of a Data Flow Procedure Language," in *Lecture Notes in Computer Science*, 19, Springer-Verlag, Berlin, 1974, pp. 362–376.

Dennis, J. B., Leung, C. K., and Misunas, D. P., "A Highly Parallel Processor Using a Data Flow Machine Language," *CSG Memo 134-1*, Lab. for Computer Science, MIT, June 1979.

Dennis, J. B., and Misunas, D. P., "A Preliminary Architecture for a Basic Data Flow Processor," *Proc. Second Ann. Symp. on Computer Architecture*, IEEE, Jan. 1975, pp. 126–132.

Dennis, J., and Rong, G., "Maximum Pipelining of Array Operations on Static Dataflow Machine," *Proc. 1983 Int'l. Conf. Parallel Proc.*, August 23–26, 1983.

Dennis, J. B., and Weng, K., "Application of Dataflow Computation to the Weather Problem," *High Speed Computer and Algorithm Organization*, Kuck, et al., eds., New York: Academic Press, New York, 1977, pp. 143–157.

Despain, A. M., and Patterson, D. A., "X-tree—A Tree Structured Multiprocessor Computer Architecture," *Proc. 5th Ann. Symp. on Computer Architecture*, 1978, pp. 144–151.

Dias, D. M., and Jump, J. R., "Analysis and Simulation of Buffered Delta Networks," *IEEE Trans. on Comp.*, C-30, Apr. 1981*a*, pp. 273–282.

Dias, D. M., and Jump, J. R., "Packet Switching Interconnection Networks for Modular Systems," *IEEE Comp.*, Dec. 1981*b*, pp. 43–53.

Dijkstra, E. W., "Solution of a Problem in Concurrent Programming," *Comm. of ACM*, vol. 8, Sept. 1965, pp. 569–570.

Dijkstra, E. W., "Cooperating Sequential Processes," *Programming Languages*, F. Genuys, ed., Academic Press, New York, 1968, pp. 43–112.

Dorr, F. W., "The Cray-1 at Los Alamos," *Datamation*, Oct. 1978, pp. 113–120.

Dowsing, R. D., "Processor Management in a Multiprocessor System," *Electronic Letters*, vol. 12, no. 24, Nov. 1976.

Dubois, M., "Analytical Methodologies for the Evaluation of Multiprocessing Structures," *Ph.D. Thesis*, Purdue Univ., Ind., 1982.

Dubois, M., and Briggs, F. A., "Effects of Cache Coherency in Multiprocessors," *IEEE Trans. on Comp.*, C-31, no. 11, Nov. 1982*a*.

Dubois, M., and Briggs, F. A., "Performance of Synchronized Iterative Processes in Multiprocessor Systems," *IEEE Trans. on Soft. Eng.*, July 1982*b*, pp. 419–431.

Duff, M. J. B., ed., *Computing Structures for Image Processing*, Academic Press, London, 1983.

El-Ayat, K. A., "The Intel 8089: An Integrated I/0 Processor," *IEEE Comp.*, vol. 12, no. 6, June 1979, pp. 67–78.

Emer, J. S., and Davidson, E. S., "Control Store Organization for Multiple Stream Pipelined Processors," *Proc. 1978 Int'l. Conf. Parallel Proc.*, 1978, pp. 43–48.

Enslow, P. H., "Multiprocessor Organization," *Computing Surveys*, vol. 9, Mar. 1977, pp. 103–129.

Enslow, P. H., ed., *Multiprocessors and Parallel Processing*, Wiley-Interscience, New York, 1974.

Evans, D. J., ed., *Parallel Processing Systems*, Cambridge Univ. Press, England, 1982.

Evensen, A. J., and Troy, J. L., "Introduction to the Architecture of a 288-Element PEPE," *Proc. Sagamore Conf. Parallel Proc.*, 1973, pp. 162–169.

Fabry, R. S., "Capability-based Addressing," *Comm. of ACM*, vol. 17, July 1974, pp. 403–412.

Faggin, F., "How VLSI Impacts Computer Architecture," *IEEE Spectrum*, 15, May 1978, pp. 28–31.

Fairbairn, D. G., "VLSI: A New Frontier for System Designers," *IEEE Comp.*, Jan. 1982, pp. 87–96.

Feierbach, G., and Stevenson, D. K., "The Phoenix Array Processing System," *Phoenix Project Memo. 7*, NASA Ames Research Center, Mountain View, Calif., Nov. 1978.

Feldman, J. D., and Fulmer, L. C., "RADCAP:- Operational Parallel Processing Facility," *Proc. Nat'l Comp. Conf.*, AFIPS, 1974, pp. 7–15.

Feller, W., *An Introduction to Probability Theory and its Applications*, vol. 1, Wiley, New York, 1970.

Femt, T. Y., "Some Characteristics of Associative/Parallel Processing," *Proc. 1972 Sagamore Comp. Conf.*, Syracuse Univ., 1972, pp. 5–16.

Feng, T. Y., "Data Manipulation Functions in Parallel Processors and Their Implementations," *IEEE Trans. on Comp.*, C-23, no. 3, Mar. 1974, pp. 309–318.

Feng, T. Y., ed., "Parallel Processors and Processing," special issue, *ACM Computing Surveys*, vol. 9, no. 1, Mar. 1977*a*.

Feng, T. Y., "Parallel Processors and Processing," *Class Notes*, Wayne State Univ., Detroit, Michigan (unpublished), 1977*b*.

Feng, T. Y., "A Survey of Interconnection Networks," *IEEE Comp.*, Dec. 1981, pp. 12–27.

Fennell, K. D., and Lesser, V. R., "Parallelism in Artificial Intelligence Problem Solving: A Case Study of Hearsay II," *IEEE Trans. on Comp.*, Mar. 1977, pp. 98–111.

Ferrari, D., "An Analytic Study of Memory Allocation in Multiprocessing System," *Computer Architecture and Networks*, Gelenbe and Mahl, eds., North-Holland, Amsterdam, 1974.

Ferrari, D., Gelenbe, E., and Mahl, R., "An Analytic Study of Memory Allocation in Multiprocessor Systems," *Proc. Conf. on Computer Architecture and Networks*, France, August 1974.

Floating Point System, Inc., *AP-120B Processor Handbook*, Portland, Oregon, pub. no. 7259-02, May 1976.

Flynn, M. J., "Very High-Speed Computing Systems" *Proc. IEEE*, vol. 54, 1966, pp. 1901–1909.

Flynn, M. J., "Some Computer Organization and Their Effectiveness," *IEEE Trans. on Comp.*, C-21, no. 9, Sept. 1972, pp. 948–960.

Flynn, M. J., "The Interpretive Interface: Resources and Program Representation in Computer Organization," *High Speed Computer and Algorithm Organization*, Kuck et al., Academic Press, New York, 1977, pp. 41–69.

Flynn, M. J., and Amdahl, G. M., "Engineering Aspects of Large High Speed Computer Design," *Proc. Symp. Microelectronics and Large Systems*, Spartan Press, Washington, D.C., 1965, pp. 77–95.

Flynn, M. J., Podvin, A., and Shmizu, K., "A Multiple Instruction Stream with Shared Resources," *Parallel Processor Systems, Technologies, and Applications*, Hobbs, ed., Spartan Books, Washington, D.C., 1970, pp. 251–286.

Fontao, R. O., "A Concurrent Algorithm for Avoiding Deadlocks in Multiprocess Multiple Resonance Systems," *Proc. 3d Symp. Operating System Principles*, Oct. 1971.

Foster, C. C. (1976). *Content-Addressable Parallel Processors*, Van Nostrand Reinhold Co., New York, 1976.

Franta, W. R., and Houle, P. A., "Comments on Models of Multiprocessor Multi-Memory Bank Computer Systems," *Proc. 1974 Winter Simulation Conf.*, vol. I, Washington, D.C., Jan. 1974.

Fritsch, G., Kleinoeder, W., Linster, C. U., and Volkert, J., "EMSY 85: The Erlangen Multiprocessor System for a Broad Spectrum of Applications," *Proc. 1983 Int'l. Conf. on Parallel Proc.*, August 1983, pp. 325–330.

Fuller, S. H., and Harbison, S. P., *The C.mmp Multiprocessor*, Technical Report, Carnegie-Mellon Univ., Computer Science Dept., 1978.

Fuller, S. H., Swan, R., and Wulf, W. A., "The Instrumentation of C.mmp: A Multi-miniprocessor," *IEEE Compcon*, 1973.

Gajski, D. D., "An Algorithm for Solving Linear Recurrence Systems on Parallel and Pipelined Machines," *IEEE Trans. on Comp.*, Mar. 1981, pp. 190–205.

Gakski, D. D., Kuck, D. J., and Padua, D. A., "Dependence Driven Computation," *Proc. COMCON Spring*, Feb. 1981, pp. 168–172.

Gajski, D., Kuck, D., Lawrie, D., and Sameh, A., "Cedar—A Large Scale Multiprocessor," *Proc. 1983 Int'l. Conf. on Parallel Proc.*, Aug. 1983, pp. 524–529.

Gajski, D. D., Panda, D. A., Kuck, D. J., and Kuhn, R. H., "A Second Opinion on Dataflow Machines and Languages," *IEEE Comp.*, Feb. 1982, pp. 58–70.

Gajski, D. D., and Rubinfield, L. P., "Design of Arithmetic Elements for Burroughs Scientific Processor," *Proc. 4th Symp. Computer Arithmetic*, Oct. 1978, pp. 245–256.

Gao, Q. S., and Zhang, X., "Cellular Vector Computer of Vertical and Horizontal Processing with Vertical Common Memory," *Journ. of Computers*, no. 1, Jan. 1979, pp. 1–12 (in Chinese).

Gao, Q. S., and Zhang, X., "Another Approach to Making Supercomputer by Microprocessors— Cellular Vector Computer of Vertical and Horizontal Processing with Virtual Common Memory," *Int. Conf. Parallel Proc.*, Aug. 1980, pp. 163–164.

Gaudet, G., and Stevenson, D., "Optimal Sorting Algorithms for Parallel Computers," *IEEE Trans. on Comp.*, C-27, Jan. 1978, pp. 84–87.

Gecsei, J., and Lukes, J. A., "A Model for the Evaluation of Storage Hierarchies," *IBM Systems Journ.*, no. 2, 1974, pp. 163–178.

Ginsberg, M., "Some Numerical Effects of A FORTRAN Vectorizing Compiler on A Texas Instruments Advanced Scientific Computer," *High Speed Computer and Algorithm Organization*, Kuck, et al., eds., Academic Press, New York, 1977, pp. 461–62.

Goke, R., and Lipovski, G. J., "Banyan Networks, for Partitioning on Multiprocessor Systems," *Proc. 1st Ann. Symp. Computer Architecture*, 1973, pp. 21–30.

Gonzalez, M. J., "Deterministic Processor Scheduling," *Computing Surveys*, vol. 9, no. 3, Sept. 1977, pp. 173–204.

Gonzalez, M. J., and Ramamoorthy, C. V., "Recognition and Representation of Parallel Processable Streams in Computer Programs," in *Parallel Processor Systems*, Technologies and Applications, Macmillan Ltd., London, England, 1970.

Gonzalez, M. J., and Ramamoorthy, C. V., "Parallel Task Execution in a Decentralized System," *IEEE Trans. on Comp.*, C-21, Dec. 1972, 1310–1322.

Gonzalez, T., and Sahni, S., "Preemptive Scheduling of Uniform Processor Systems," *Journ. of ACM*, vol. 25, no. 1, Jan. 1978, pp. 92–101.

Goodman, J. R. "An Investigation of Multiprocessor Structures and Algorithms for Database Management," *UCB/ERL M81/83*, Dept. of EECS, Univ. of Calif., Berkeley, 1981.

Goodyear Aerospace Co., "Massively Parallel Processor (MPP)," Tech. Report GER-16684, July 1979.

Gosden, J. A., "Explicit Parallel Processing Description and Control in Programs for Multi and Uni-processor Computers," *AFIPS Fall Joint Comput. Conf.*, Spartan Books, N.Y., 1966, pp. 651–660.

Gostelow, K. P., and Thomas, R. E., "Performance of a Simulatec Dataflow Computer," *IEEE Trans. on Comp.*, Oct. 1980, pp. 905–919.

Gottlieb, A., Grishman, R., Kruskal, C. P., McAaliffe, K. P., Randolph, L., and Snir, M., "The NYU Ultracomputer-Designing an MIMD Shared Memory Parallel Computer," *IEEE Trans. on Comp.*, Feb. 1983, pp. 175–189.

Graham, G. S., A Study of Program and Memory Policy Behavior, *Ph.D. Thesis*, Purdue Univ., Ind., 1976.

Graham, R. L., "Bounds on Multiprocessing Anomalies and Packing Algorithms," *Proc. AFIPS 1972 Spring Joint Comp. Conf.*, 40, AFIPS Press, Montvale, N.J., 1972, pp. 205–217.

Graham, W. R., "The Parallel and the Pipeline Computers," *Datamation*, Apr. 1970, pp. 68–71.

Grimsdale, R. L., and Johnson, D. M., "A Modular Executive for Multiprocessor Systems," *Proc. Conf. on Trends in One-Line Computer Control Systems*, Sheffield, England, Apr. 1972.

Grinbert, J., Nudd, G. R., and Etchella, R. D., "A Cellular VLSI Architecture," *IEEE Comp.*, Jan. 1984.

Grohoski, G. R., and Patel, J. H., "A Performance Model for Instruction Prefetch in Pipelined Instruction Units," *Proc. 1982 Int'l. Conf. Parallel Proc.*, August 24–27, 1982, pp. 248–252.

Gula, J. L., "Operating System Considerations for Multiprocessor Architecture," *Proc. 7th Texas Conf. on Computing Systems*, Houston, Nov. 1978.

Gurd, J., and Watson, I., "Data Driven System for High Speed Parallel Computing," *Computer Design*, Parts I & II, June & July 1980.

Habermann, A. N., *Introduction to Operating System Design*, Science Res. Assoc., 1976.

Hallin, T. G., and Flynn, M. J., "Pipelining of Arithmetic Functions," *IEEE Trans. on Comp.*, Aug. 1972, pp. 880–886.

Händler, W., "The Impact of Classification Schemes on Computer Architecture," *Proc. 1977 Int. Conf. on Parallel Proc.*, pp. 7–15.

Hansen, P. B., "The Programming Language Concurrent Pascal," *IEEE Trans. on Soft. Eng.*, 1, 2, June 1975, pp. 199–207.

Hansen, P. B., *Concurrent Pascal*, Prentice-Hall, New York, 1978.

Hansen, P. B., *The Architecture of Concurrent Programs*, Prentice-Hall, Englewood Cliffs, N.J., 1977.

Harris, J. A., and Smith, D. R., "Hierarchical Multiprocessor Organizations," *Proc. 4th Symp. on Computer Architecture*, 1977.

Hayes, J. P., *Computer Architecture and Organization*, McGraw-Hill, New York, 1978.

Hedlund, K. S., "Wafer Scale Integration of Parallel Processors," Ph.D. Thesis, Comp. Science Dept., Purdue Univ., Ind., 1982.

Hellerman, H., *Digital Computer System Principles*, McGraw-Hill, New York, 1967, pp. 228–229.

Hellerman, H., and Smith, H. J., Jr., "Throughput Analysis of Some Idealized Input, Output, and Compute Overlap Configurations," *Computing Surveys*, 2, June 1970, pp. 111–118.

Higbie, L. C., "Applications of Vector Processing," *Computer Design*, Apr. 1978, pp. 139–145.

Higbie, L. C., "Supercomputer Architecture," *IEEE Comp.*, 6, Dec. 1973, pp. 48–58.

Hintz, R. G., and Tate, D. P., "Control Data STAR-100 Processor Design," *COMPCON Proc.*, Sept. 1972, pp. 1–4.

Hoare, C. A. R., "Towards a Theory of Parallel Programming," *Operating Systems Techniques*, C. A. R. Hoare, ed., Academic Press, New York, 1972.

Hoare, C. A. R., "Monitors: An Operating System Structuring Concept," *Comm. of ACM*, vol. 17, no. 10, Oct. 1974, pp. 549–557.

Hockney, R. W., and Jesshope, C. R., *Parallel Computers: Architecture, Programming and Algorithms*, Adam Hilger Ltd., Bristol, England, 1981.

Holley, L. H., Parmlee, R. P., et al., "VM/370 Asymmetric Multiprocessing," *IBM Systems Journ.*, vol. 18, no. 1, 1979.

Holt, R. C., "Some Deadlock Properties of Computer Systems," *ACM Computing Surveys*, 4, Sept. 1972, 179–195.

Holt, R. C., Graham, G. S., Lazowska, E. D., and Scott, M. A., *Structured Concurrent Programming with Operating Systems Applications*, Addison-Wesley, Mass., 1978.

Hon, R., and Reddy, D. R., "The Effect of Computer Architecture on Algorithm Decomposition and Performance," *High-Speed Computers and Algorithm Organization*, Kuck, et al., ed., Academic Press, New York, 1977, pp. 411–421.

Hoogendoorn, C. H., "A General Model for Memory Interference in Multiprocessors," *IEEE Trans. on Comp.*, C-26, no. 10, Oct. 1977*a*, pp. 998–1005.

Hoogendoorn, C. H., "Reduction of Memory Interference in Multiprocessor Systems," *Proc. 4th Ann. Symp. on Computer Architecture*, Silver Springs, MD, Mar. 1977*b*, pp. 179–183.

Hsiao, D. K., "Data Base Computers," in *Advances in Computers*, vol. 19, Yovits, ed., Academic Press, New York, 1980, pp. 1–64.

Hsiao, D. K., ed., *Advanced Database Machine Architecture*, Prentice-Hall, Englewood Cliffs, N.J., 1983.

Hu, T. C., "Parallel Sequencing and Assembly Line Problems," *Oper. Res.*, vol. 9, no. 6, Nov.-Dec., 1961, pp. 841–848.

Hufnagel, S., "Comparison of Selected Array Processor Architecture," *Computer Design*, Mar. 1979, pp. 151–158.

Hwang, K., "Fault-Tolerant Microprogrammed Digital Controller Design," *IEEE Trans. on Industrial Electronics and Control Instrumentation*, Aug. 1976, pp. 200–207.

Hwang, K., "Global and Modular Two's Complement Array Multipliers," *IEEE Trans. on Comp.*, Apr. 1979*a*, pp. 300–306.

Hwang, K., *Computer Arithmetic: Principles, Architecture and Design*, Wiley, New York, 1979*b*.

Hwang, K., "VLSI Computer Arithmetic for Real-Time Image Processing," Chap. 7, *VLSI Electronics: Microstructure Science*, vol. 7, Einpruch, ed., Academic Press, New York, 1984.

Hwang, K., and Chang, T. P., "Combinatorial Reliability Analysis of Multiprocessor Computers," *IEEE Trans. Reliability*, vol. R-31, no. 5, Dec. 1982, pp. 469–473.

Hwang, K., and Cheng, Y. H., "Partitioned Matrix Algorithms for VLSI Arithmetic Systems," *IEEE Trans. on Comp.*, C-31, no. 12, Dec. 1982, pp. 1215–1224.

Hwang, K., Chin, C. Y., and Ni., L. M., "Adaptive Path-Directed Routing for Packet Switched Computer Networks," *TR-EE 83-37*, Purdue Univ., Ind., 1983.

Hwang, K., and Fu, S. K., "Integrated Computer Architectures for Image Processing and Database Management," *IEEE Comp.*, vol. 16, no. 1, Jan. 1983, pp. 51–61.

Hwang, K., and Kuhn, R. H., eds. *Tutorial on Supercomputers Design and Applications*, IEEE Computer Society Press (in press).

Hwang, K., and Ni, L. M., "Resource Optimization of a Parallel Computer for Multiple Vector Processing," *IEEE Trans. on Comp.*, C-29, Sept. 1980, pp. 831–836.

Hwang, K., and Su., S. P., "VLSI Architectures of Feature Extraction and Pattern Classification," *Computer Vision, Graphics, and Image Processing*, vol. 24, Academic Press, New York, Nov. 1983*a*, pp. 215–228.

Hwang, K., and Su, S. P., "Priority Scheduling in Event-Driven Dataflow Computers," *TR-EE 83-86*, Purdue Univ., Ind. Dec. 1983*b*.

Hwang, K., and Su, S. P., "Multitask Scheduling in Vector Supercomputers," *TR-EE 83-52*, Purdue Univ., Ind., Dec. 1983*c*.

Hwang, K., Su, S. P., and Ni, L. M., "Vector Computer Architecture and Processing Techniques," *Advanced in Computers*, vol. 20, Yovits, ed., Academic Press, New York, 1981, pp. 115–197.

Hwang, K., and Yao, S. B., "Optimal Batched Searching of Tree-Structural Files in Multiprocess Computer System," *Journ. of Assoc. of Comp. Mach.*, vol. 24, no. 3, July 1977, pp. 441–454.

IBM Corp., *IBM System/360 and System/370 I/O Interface Channel to Control Unit*, form GA22-6974-3, 1976.

IBM Corp., *IBM 3838 Array Processor Functional Characteristics*, no. 6A24-3639-0, file no. S370-08, Endicott, N.Y., Oct. 1976.

IBM Corp., *IBM System/370 Model 168 Functional Characteristics*, form no. GA22-7010-4, 1976.

IBM Corp., *3033 Processor Complex Theory of Operation/Diagrams Manual*. vols. 1–5, SY22-7001 through SY22-7005, Jan. 1978.

IBM Corp., "Special Issue on IBM 3081," *IBM Journ. of Res. and Dev.*, vol. 26, no. 1, Jan. 1982, pp. 2–29.

IBM Corp., *System/370 Principles of Operation*, GA22-7000-4, 1974.

Isloor, S. S., and Marsland, T. A., "The Deadlock Problem: An Overview," *IEEE Computer*, vol. 13, no. 9, Sept. 1980.

Jain, N., *Performance Study of Synchronization Mechanisms in a Multiprocessor. Ph.D. Thesis*, Carnegie-Mellon Univ., 1979.

Jensen, J. E., and Baer, J. L., "A Model of Interference in a Shared Resource Multiprocessor," *Proc. 3d Ann. Symp. on Computer Architecture*, Clearwater, Fla., Jan. 1976, pp. 52–57.

Jin, L., "A New General-Purpose Distributed Multiprocessor Structure," *Proc. Int'l. Conf. on Parallel Proc.*, Aug. 1980, pp. 153–154.

Johnson, L., "Gaussian Elimination on Sparse Matrices and Concurrency," *Tech. Report 4087:TR:80*, Dept. of Computer Science, Cal. Tech., Pasadena, 1980.

Jones, A. K., and Gehringer, E. F. (Editor), "Cm* Multiprocessor Project: A Research Review," *Tech. Rept. CMU-CS-80-131*, Carnegie-Mellon Univ., July 1980.

Jones, A. K., and Schwarz, P., "Experience Using Multiprocessor Systems: A Status Report," Dept. of Computer Science, Carnegie-Mellon Univ., Tech. Report CMU-CS-79-146, Oct. 1979.

Jordan, H. F., "Performance Measurement of HEP-A Pipelined MIMD Computer," *Proc. 10th Ann. Symp. Computer Architecture*, June 1983, pp. 207–212.

Jordan, H. F., Scalabrin, M., and Calvert, W., "A Comparison of Three Types of Multiprocessor Algorithms," *Proc. 1979 Int'l. Conf. on Parallel Proc.*, Bellaire, MI, Aug. 1979, pp. 231–238.

Jump, J. R., and Ahuja, S. R., "Effective Pipelining of Digital Systems," *IEEE Trans. on Comp.*, Sept. 1978, pp. 855–865.

Kaplan, K. R., and Winder, R. V., "Cache-Based Computer Systems," *Computer*, 6, Mar. 1973, 30–36.

Karp, K. M., and Miller, R. E., "Properties of a Model for Parallel Computations: Determinancy, Terminating, Queueing," *SIAM Journal of Applied Mathematics*, vol. 24, Nov. 1966, pp. 1390–1411

Karplus, W. J., and Cohen, D., "Architectural and Software Issues in the Design and Application of Peripheral Array Processors," *IEEE Comp.*, Sep. 1981, pp. 11–17.

Kartashev, S. I., and Kartashev, S. P., "Problems of Designing Supersystems with Dynamic Architectures," *IEEE Trans. on Comp.*, Dec. 1980, pp. 1114–1132.

Kascic, M. J., *Vector Processing on the Cyber 200*, Control Data Corp, 1979 (38 pages).

Katzan, H., *Computer Organization and the System/360*, Van Nostrand Reinhold, New York, 1971.

Kaufman, M., "An Almost-optimal Algorithm for the Assembly-line Scheduling Problem," *IEEE Trans. on Comp.*, C-23, Nov. 1974, pp. 1169–1174.

Keller, R. M., "Look-Ahead Processors," *ACM Computing Surveys*, vol. 7, no. 4, Dec. 1975, pp. 177–195.

Keller, R. M., Patil, S. S., and Lindstrom, G., "A Loosely Coupled Applicative Multiprocessing System," *Proc. Nat'l. Computer Conf.*, AFIHS Press, 1979.

Kennedy, K., "Optimization of Vector Operations in an Extended Fortran Compiler," *IBM Research Report*, RC-7784, 1979.

Kinney, L. L., and Arnold, R. G., "Analysis of a Multiprocessor System with a Shared Bus," *Proc. 5th Ann. Symp. on Computer Architecture*, Palo Alto, CA, Apr. 1978, pp. 89–95.

Kleinrock, L. *Queueing Systems: Theory and Applications*, Wiley, New York, 1975.

Knuth, D. E., and Rao, G. S., "Activity in Interleaved Memory," *IEEE Trans. on Comp.*, C-24, no. 9, Sept. 1975, pp. 943–944.

Kober, R., and Kuznia, C., "SMS—A Multiprocessor Architecture for High-Speed Numerical Calculations," *Proc. Int'l. Conf. Parallel Proc.*, 1978, pp. 18–23.

Kogge, P. M., "The Microprogramming of Pipelined Processors," *Proc. 4th Ann. Conf. Computer Architecture*, IEEE no. 77CH 1182-5C, Mar. 1977a, pp. 63–69.

Kogge, P. M., "Algorithm Development for Pipelined Processors," *Proc. 1977 Int'l. Conf. Parallel Proc.*, IEEE no. 77 CH1253-4C, Aug. 1977b, p. 217.

Kogge, P. M., *The Architecture of Pipelined Computers*, McGraw-Hill, New York, 1981.

Kogge, P. M., and Stone, H. S., "A Parallel Algorithm for the Efficient Solution of a General Class of Recurrence Equations," *IEEE Trans. on Comp.*, C-22, 1973, pp. 786–793.

Kosinski, P. R., "A Data Flow Programming Language," *Report RC4264*, IBM, T. J. Watson Research Center, Yorktown Heights, N.Y., Mar. 1973.

Kozdrowicki, E. W., and Theis, D. J., "Second Generation of Vector Supercomputers," *IEEE Computer*, Nov. 1980, pp. 71–83.

Kraley, M. F., "The Pluribus Multiprocessor," *Digest of Papers, 1975 Int'l. Symp. on Fault-Tolerant Computing*, Paris, France, June 1975, p. 251.

Kuck, D. J., "Parallel Processing of Ordinary Programs," in *Advances in Computers*, vol. 15, Rubinoff and Yovits, eds., Academic Press, New York, 1976, pp. 119–179.

Kuck, D. J., "Illiac IV Software and Application Programming," *IEEE Trans. on Comp.* Aug. 1968, pp. 746–757.

Kuck, D. J., "A Survey of Parallel Machine Organization and Programming," *ACM Computing Surveys*, vol. 9, no. 1, Mar. 1977, pp. 29–59.

Kuck, D. J., *The Structure of Computers and Computations*, vol. 1, Wiley, New York, 1978.

Kuck, D. J., Kuhn, R. H., Padua, D. A., Leasure, B., and Wolfe, M., "Dependence Graphs and Compiler Optimizations," *Proc. 8th ACM Symp. Principles Programming Languages*, Jan. 1981, pp. 207–218.

Kuck, D. J., Lawrie, D. H., and Sameh, A. H., eds. *High Speed Computer and Algorithm Organization*, Academic Press, New York, 1977.

Kuck, D. J., and Stokes, R. A., "The Burroughs Scientific Processor (BSP)" *IEEE Trans. on Comp.*, C-31, no. 5, May 1982, pp. 363–376.

Kuhn, R. H., "Optimization and Interconnection Complexity for: Parallel Processors, Single-Stage Networks, and Decision Trees," *Ph.D. Thesis*, Univ. of Ill. at Urb-Champ., Dep. of Computer Science, no. 80-1009, Feb. 1980.

Kuhn, R. H., and Padau, D. A., eds., *Tutorial on Parallel Processing*, IEEE Computer Society Press, order no. 367, Los Angeles, 1981.

Kulisch, U. W., and Miranker, W. L., eds., *A New Approach to Scientific Computation*, Academic Press, New York, 1983.

Kung, H. T., "Synchronized and Asynchronous Parallel Algorithms for Multiprocessors," *Algorithms and Complexity: Recent Results and New Directions*, Traub, ed., Addison-Wesley, 1976.

Kung, H. T., "The Structure of Parallel Algorithms," *Advances in Computers*, vol. 19, Yovits, ed., Academic Press, New York, 1980, pp. 65–112.

Kung, H. T., "Why Systolic Architectures," *IEEE Comp.*, Jan. 1982, pp. 37–46.

Kung, H. T., and Leiserson, C. E., "Systolic Arrays (for VLSI)," *Spare Matrix Proc.*, Duff, et al., eds., Society of Indust. and Appl. Math., Philadelphia, Pa., 1978, pp. 245–282.

Kung, S. Y., Arun, K. S., Galezer, R. J., Rao, D. V. B., "Wavefront Array Processor: Language, Architecture, and Applications," *IEEE Trans. on Comp.* C-31, no. 11, Nov. 1982, pp. 1054–1066.

Kurinckx, A., and Pujolle, G., "Analytic Methods for Multiprocessor Modeling," *4th Int'l. Symp. on Modeling and Performance Evaluation of Computer Systems*, Part II, Vienna, Austria, Feb. 1979.

Kurtzberg, J. M., "On the Memory Conflict Problem in Multiprocessor Systems," *IEEE Trans. on Comp.*, C-23, no. 3, Mar. 1974, pp. 286–293.

Lamport, L., "A New Solution of Dijkstra's Concurrent Programming Problem," *Comm. of ACM*, vol. 17, Aug. 1974, pp. 453–454.

Lamport, L., "The Synchronization of Independent Processes," *Acta Informatica*, vol. 7, no. 1, 1976, pp. 15–34.

Lamport, L., "Proving the Correctness of Multiprocess Programs," *IEEE Trans. on Soft. Eng.*, SE-3, no. 2, Mar. 1977, pp. 125–143.

Lampson, B. W., "Dynamic Protection Structures," *1969 Fall Joint Computer Conference*, AFIPS Press, 1969, pp. 27–38.

Lampson, B. W., "Protection," *Operating Systems Review* 8(1), Jan. 1974.

Lampson, B. W., and Sturgis, H. E., "Reflections on an Operating System Design," *Comm. of ACM*, vol. 19, May 1976, pp. 251–265.

Lane, W. G., "Input/Output Processing," *Introduction to Computer Architecture*, Stone, ed., SRA Inc., 1978, pp. 275–316.

Lang, D. E., Agerwala, T. K., and Chandy, K. M., "A Modeling Approach and Design Tool for Pipelined Central Processors," *Proc. 6th Ann. Symp. on Computer Architecture*, Apr. 1979, pp. 122–129.

Lang, T., and Stone, H. S., "A Shuffle-Exchange Network with Simplified Control," *IEEE Trans. on Comp.*, C-25, Jan. 1976, pp. 55–56.

Larson, A. G., "Cost-Effective Processor Design with an Application to Fast Fourier Transform Computers," Ph.D. Thesis, Stanford Univ., 1973.

Larson, A. G., and Davidson, E. S., "Cost-Effective Design of Special-Purpose Processors: A Fast Fourier Transform Case Study," *Proc. 11th Allerton Conf.*, 1973, pp. 547–557.

Lawrence Livermore Laboratory. "The S-1 Project: *Annual Reports*," vol. 1 Architecture, vol. 2 Hardware, and vol. 3 Software, UCID-18619, Univ. of Calif., Livermore, 1979.

Lawrie, D. H., "Access and Alignment of Data in an Array Processor," *IEEE Trans. on Comp.*, C-24, no. 12, Dec. 1975, pp. 1145–1155.

Lawrie, D. H., Layman, T., Baer, D., and Randal, J. M., "Glypnir—A Programming Language for ILLIAC IV," *Comm. of ACM*, vol. 18, Mar. 1975, pp. 157–164.

Lawrie, D. H., and Vora, C. R., "The Prime Memory System for Array Access," *IEEE Trans. on Comp.*, C-31, no. 5, Oct. 1982, pp. 435–442.

Lee, R. B-L., "Empirical Results on the Speed, Efficiency, Redundancy and Quality of Parallel Computations," *Int'l. Conf. Parallel Proc.*, Aug. 1980, pp. 91–96.

Levy, H. M., *Capability-Based Computer Systems*, Digital Press, 1983.

Levy, H. M., and Eckhouse, R. H., Jr., *Computer Programming and Architecture—The Vax-11*, Digital Press, 1980.

Li, H. F., "Scheduling Trees in Parallel Pipelined Processing Environments," *IEEE Trans. on Comp.*, Nov. 1977, pp. 1101–1112.

Lincoln, N. R., "Technology and Design Trade Offs in the Creation of a Modern Supercomputer," *IEEE Trans. on Comp.*, C-31, no. 5, May 1982, pp. 363–376.

Lint, B., and Agerwala, T., "Communication Issues in the Design and Analysis of Parallel Algorithms," *IEEE Trans. on Soft. Eng.*, SE-7, no. 2, Mar. 1981, pp. 174–188.

Lipovski, G. J., and Malek, M., "A Theory for Multicomputer Interconnection Networks," *Tech. Report TRAC-40*, Univ. of Texas, Austin, Mar. 1981.

Lipovski, G. J., and Tripathi, A., "A Reconfigurable Varistructured Array Processor," *Proc. 1977 Int'l. Conf. on Parallel Proc.*, 1977, pp. 165–174.

Liptay, J. S., "Structural Aspects of System 360/85; The Cache," *IBM Systems Journ.*, 7, 1969, pp. 15–21.

Liu, J. W. S., and Liu, C. L., "Bounds on Scheduling Algorithms for Heterogeneous Computing Systems," *Proc. IFIP Congress* 74, 1974, pp. 349–353.

Liu, J. W. S., and Liu, C. L., "Performance Analysis of Multiprocessor Systems Containing Functionally Dedicated Processors," *Acta Informatica*, vol. 10, no. 1, 1978, pp. 95–104.

Loomis, H. H., "The Maximum Rate Accumulator," *IEEE Trans. on Comp.*, vol. EC-15, no. 4, Aug. 1966, pp. 628–639.

Lorin, H. (1972). *Parallelism in Hardware and Software*, Prentice-Hall, Englewood Cliffs, N.J., 1972.

Madnick, S. E., and Donovan, J. J., *Operating Systems*, McGraw-Hill, New York, 1974.

Majithia, J. C., "Cellular Array for Extraction of Squares and Square Roots of Binary Numbers," *IEEE Trans. on Comp.*, C-20, no. 12, Dec. 1970, pp. 1617–1618.

Marathe, M., and Fuller, S. H., "A Study of Multiprocessor Contention for Shared Data in C.mmp.," *ACM/SIGMETRICS Conf.*, Washington, D.C., Dec. 1977.

Matick, R. E., *Computer Storage Systems and Technology*, Wiley, New York, 1977.

Matick, R. E., "Memory and Storage," *Introduction to Computer Architecture*, Stone, ed., SRA Inc., 1980, pp. 205–274.

Mattson, R. L., Gecsei, J., Slutz, D. R., and Traiger, I. L., "Evaluation Techniques for Storage Hierarchies," *IBM Systems Journ.*, 9, 1970, 78–117.

Mazare, G., "Multiprocessor Systems," *Proc. 1974 CERN School of Computing*, Godysund, Norway, Aug. 1974.

McGraw, J. R., "Data Flow Computing—Software Development," *IEEE Trans. on Computers*, Dec. 1980, pp. 1095–1103.

Mead, C., and Conway, L., *Introduction to VLSI Systems*, Addison-Wesley, Mass., 1980.

Miranker, G. S., "Implementation of Procedures on a Class of Data Flow Processors," *Proc. Int'l. Conf. Parallel Proc.*, IEEE no. 77CH 1253-4C, 1977, pp. 77–86.

Miura, K., and Uchida, K., "FACOM Vector Processor VP-100/VP-200," *Proc. NATO Advanced Research Workshop on High-Speed Computing*, Jülich, W. Germany, Springer-Verlag, June 20–22, 1983.

Moldovan, D. I., "On the Design of Algorithms for VLSI Systolic Array," *Proc. IEEE*, Jan. 1983, pp. 113–120.

Moto-oka, T., "Overview to the Fifth Generation Computer System Project," *Proc. 10th Ann. Symp. Computer Architecture*, June 1983, pp. 417–422.

Moto-oka, T., and Fuchi, K., "The Architectures in the Fifth Generation Computers," *Proc. 1983 IFIP Congress*, North-Holland, Amsterdam, 1983, pp. 589–602.

Mrosousky, I., Wong, J. Y., and Lampe, H. W., "Construction of a Large Field Simulator on a Vector Computer," *Journal of Petroleum Tech.*, Dec. 1980, pp. 2253–2264.

Mueller, P. T., Siegel, L. J., and Siegel, H. T., "Parallel Algorithms for the Two-dimensional FFT," *Proc. 5th Int'l. Conf. on Pattern Recog. and Image Proc.*, Dec. 1980, pp. 497–502.

Muntz, R. R., and Coffman, E. G., "Optimal Preemptive Scheduling on Two Processor Systems," *IEEE Trans. on Comp.*, C-18, Nov. 1969, pp. 1014–1020.

Muraoka, Y., "Parallelism Exposure and Exploitation in Programs," Ph.D. Thesis, Univ. of Ill. at Urb.-Champ., Dept. of Computer Science 71-424, Feb. 1971.

Myers, G. J., *Advances in Computer Architecture*, Wiley, New York, 1978.

Nassimi, D., and Sahni, S. H., "Data Broadcasting in SIMD Computers," *Proc. Int'l. Conf. Parallel Proc.*, Aug. 1980, pp. 325–326.

Nessett, D. M., "The Effectiveness of Cache Memories in a Multiprocessor Environment," *Australian Computer Journ.*, vol. 7, no. 1, Mar. 1975, pp. 33–38.

Newton, G., "Deadlock Prevention, Detection and Resolution: An Annotated Bibliography," *ACM Operating Sys. Review*, vol. 13, no. 2, Apr. 1979, pp. 33–44.

Newton, R. S., "An Exercise in Multiprocessor Operating System Design," *Agard Conf. Proc. No. 149 on Real-Time Computer-based Systems*, NATO Advisory Group on Aerospace R & D, Athens, Greece, May 1974.

Ni, L. M., "Performance Optimization of Parallel Processing Computer Systems," *Ph.D. Thesis*, School of Electrical Engineering, Purdue Univ., Ind., Dec. 1980.

Ni, L. M., and Hwang, K., "Performance Modeling of Shared Resource Array Processors," *IEEE Trans. on Soft. Eng.*, SE-7, no. 4, July 1981, pp. 386–394.

Ni, L. M., and Hwang, K., "Vector Reduction Methods for Arithmetic Pipeline," *Proc. 6th Symp. on Computer Arithmetic*, June 20–22, 1983, pp. 144–150.

Nolen, J. S., Kuba, D. W., and Kascic, M. J., Jr., "Application of Vector Processors to the Solution of Finite Difference Equations," *AIME 5th Symp. Reservoir Simulation*, Feb. 1979, pp. 37–44.

Nutt, G. J., "A Parallel Processor Operating System," *IEEE Trans. on Soft. Eng.*, SE-3, no. 6, Nov. 1977a, pp. 467–475.

Nutt, G. J., "Memory and Bus Conflict in an Array Processor," *IEEE Trans. on Comp.*, June 1977*b*, pp. 514–521.

Oleinick, P. N., The Implementation and Evaluation of Parallel Algorithms on C.mmp, Ph.D. Dissertation, Carnegie-Mellon Univ., 1978.

Oleinick, P. H., and Fuller, S. H., "The Implementation and Evaluation of a Parallel Algorithm on C.mmp," *Technical Report*, Carnegie-Mellon Univ. Computer Science Dept., Dec. 1977.

Orcutt, S. E., "Computer Organization and Algorithms for Very High-Speed Computations," *Ph.D. Thesis*, Stanford University, Calif., 1974.

Ousterhout, J. K., "Partitioning and Cooperation in a Distributed Multiprocessor Operating System: Medusa," *Ph.D. Thesis*, Carnegie-Mellon Univ., April 1980.

Owen, G. J., "Rollback—A Method of Process and System Recovery," *Proc. Conf. on Soft. Eng. for Telecommunication Switching Systems*, Colchester, England, Apr. 1973.

Owicki, S., and Gries, D., "Verifying Properties of Parallel Programs: An Axiomatic Approach," *Comm. of ACM*, vol. 19, 5, May 1976, pp. 279–85.

Padua, D. A., Kuck, D. J., and Lawrie, D. H., "High-Speed Multiprocessors and Compilation Techniques," *IEEE Trans. on Comp.*, C-29, Sept. 1980, pp. 763–776.

Panda, D. A., Kuck, D. J., and Lawrie, D. H., "High-Speed Multiprocessors and Compiling Techniques," *IEEE Trans. on Comp.*, Sept. 1980, pp. 763–776.

Parasuraman, B., "Pipelined Architectures for Microprocessor," *COMPCON Proc.*, 1976, pp. 225–228.

Parnas, D. L., "On the Criteria to Be Used in Decompositng Systems into Modules," *Comm. of ACM*, vol. 15, Dec. 1972.

Patel, J. H., "Improving the Throughput of Pipelines with Delays and Buffers," *Ph.D. Thesis*, University of Illinois at Urb.-Champ., 1976.

Patel, J. H., "Pipelines with Internal Buffers," *Proc. 5th Ann. Symp. on Computer Architecture*, Apr. 1978, pp. 249–254.

Patel, J. H., "Performance of Processor-Memory Interconnections for Multiprocessors," *IEEE Trans. on Comp.*, Oct. 1981, pp. 771–780.

Paul, G., "Large-Scale Vector/Array Processors," *IBM Research Report*, RC 7306, Sept. 1978 (24 pages).

Paul, G., and Wilson, M. W., *The VECTRAN Language: An Experimental Language for Vector/Matrix Array Processing*, IBM Palo Alto Scientific Center Report 6320–3334, Aug. 1975.

Pearce, R. C., and Majithia, J. C., "Analysis of a Shared Resource MIMD Computer Organization," *IEEE Trans. on Comp.*, C-27, no. 1, Jan. 1978, pp. 64–67.

Pease, M. C., "An Adaptation of the Fast Fourier Transform for Parallel Processing," *Journ. of ACM*, vol. 15, Apr. 1968, pp. 252–264.

Pease, M. C., "The Indirect Binary n-cube Microprocessor Array," *IEEE Trans. on Comp.*, C-25, May 1977, pp. 458–473.

Perrott, R. H., "A Language for Array and Vector Processors," *ACM Trans. on Programming Languages and Systems*, vol. 1, no. 2, Oct. 1979, pp. 177–195.

Peterson, J. L., "Petri Nets," *ACM Computing Surveys*, 3028: Sept. 1977, pp. 223–252.

Pradhan, D. K., and Kodandapani, K. L., "A Uniform Representation of Single- and Multistage Interconnection Networks Used in SIMD Machines," *IEEE Trans. on Comp.*, Sept. 1980, pp. 777–790.

Prasad, N. S., *Architecture and Implementation of Large Scale IBM Computer Systems*, Q.E.D. Information Sciences, Inc., Wellesley, Mass., 1981.

Preparata, F. P., "Parallelism in Sorting," *Proc. 1977 Int'l. Conf. on Parallel Proc.*, Detroit, Mich., Aug. 1977, pp. 202–206.

Preparata, F. P., and Vuillemin, J. E., "The Cube-Connected Cycles: A Versatile Network for Parallel Computation," *Proc. 20th Symp. Foundations of Computer Science*, 1979, pp. 140–147.

Preston, K., Duff, M. J. B., Levialdi, D. S., Norgren, P. E., and Toriwaki, J. I., "Basics of Cellular Logic With Some Applications in Medical Image Processing," *Proc. IEEE*, May 1979, pp. 826–856.

Prieve, B.'B., and Fabry, R. S., "VMIN—An Optimal Variable-Space Page Replacement Algorithm," *Comm. of ACM*, vol. 19, May 1976, 295–297.

Purcell, C. J., "The Control Data STAR-100—Performance Measurements," *AFIPS NCC Proc.*, 1974, pp. 385–387.

Radoy, C. H., and Lipovski, G. J., "Switched Multiple Instruction Multiple Data Stream Processing," *Proc. 2d Ann. Symp. Computer Architecture*, 1974, pp. 183–187.

Ramamoorthy, C. V., Chandy, K. M., and Gonzalez, M. J., "Optimal Scheduling Strategies in a Multiprocessor System," *IEEE Trans. on Comp.*, C-21, 2, Feb. 1972, pp. 137–146.

Ramamoorthy, C. V., and Gonzalez, M. J., "Recognition and Representation of Parallel Processable Streams in Computer Programs, II (Task/Process Parallelism)," *Proc. ACM 24th Nat. Conf.*, ACM, New York, 1969, 387–397.

Ramamoorthy, C. V., and Kim, K. H., "Pipelining—The Generalized Concept and Sequencing Strategies," *NCC Proc.*, AFIPS Press, 1974, pp. 289–97.

Ramamoorthy, C. V., and Li, H. F., "Sequencing Control in Multifunctional Pipeline Systems," *Proc. 1975 Sagamore Comp. Conf. on Parallel Proc.*, 1975, pp. 79–89.

Ramamoorthy, C. V., and Li, H. F., "Pipeline Architecture," *ACM Computing Surveys*, vol. 9, no. 1, Mar. 1977, pp. 61–102.

Rao, G. S., "Performance Analysis of Cache Memories," *Journ. of Assoc. of Comp. Mach.*, vol. 25, no. 3, 1978, pp. 378–395.

Rau, B. R., and Rossman, G. E., "The Effect of Instruction Fetch Strategies upon the Performance of Pipelined Instruction Units," *Proc. 4th Ann. Symp. Computer Architecture*, IEEE 77CH 1182-5C, 1977, pp. 80–89.

Raw, B. R., "Program Behavior and the Performance of Interleaved Memories," *IEEE Trans. on Comp.*, C-28, no. 3, Mar. 1979, pp. 191–199.

Reilly, J., Sutton, A., Nasser, R., and Griscom, R., "Processor Controller for the IBM 3081," *IBM Journ. of Res. and Dev.*, vol. 26, no. 1, Jan., pp. 22–29.

Rice, J., *Matrix Computations and Mathematical Software*, McGraw-Hill, New York, 1981.

Ritchie, D. M., and Thompson, K., "The UNIX Time Sharing System," *Comm. of ACM*, vol. 17, July 1974, pp. 365–375.

Robinson, J. T., "Some Analysis Techniques for Asynchronous Multiprocessor Algorithms," *IEEE Trans. on Soft. Eng.*, Jan. 1979, pp. 24–30.

Rodrique, G., ed., *Parallel Computations*, Academic Press, New York, 1982.

Rodrique, G., Giroux, E. D., and Pratt, M., "Perspective on Large-Scale Scientific Computations," *IEEE Comp.*, Oct. 1980, pp. 65–80.

Roesser, R. P., "Two-Dimensional Microprocessor Pipelines for Image Processing," *IEEE Trans. on Comp.*, Feb. 1978, pp. 144–56.

Rohrbacher, D., and Potter, J. L., "Image Processing with STARAN Parallel Computer," *IEEE Comp.*, Aug., pp. 54–59.

Rosene, A. F., "Memory Allocation for Multiprocessors," *IEEE Trans. on Electronic Computers*, vol. 16, no. 5, Oct. 1967, pp. 659–665.

Rumbaugh, J., "A Data Flow Multiprocessor," *IEEE Trans. on Comp.*, C-26, no. 2, Feb. 1977, pp. 138–146.

Russell, E. C., "Automatic Program Analysis," *Ph.D. Thesis*, Dep. of Electrical Engineering, Univ. of Calif., Los Angeles, 1969.

Russell, R. M., "The Cray-1 Computer System," *Comm. of ACM*, Jan. 1978, pp. 63–72.

Saltzer, J. H., "A Simple Linear Model of Demand Paging Performance," *Comm. of ACM*, vol. 17, April 1974.

Saltzer, J. H., and Schroeder, M. D., "The Protection of Information in Computer Systems," *Proc. IEEE*, Sept. 1975, pp. 1238–1308.

Sameh, A. H., "Numerical Parallel Algorithms—A Survey," *High-Speed Computers and Algorithm Organization*, Kuck, et al., eds., Academic Press, 1977, pp. 207–228.

Sastry, K. V., and Kain, R. Y., "On the Performance of Certain Multiprocessor Computer Organizations," *IEEE Trans. on Comp.*, vol. C-24, no. 11, Nov. 1975, pp. 1066–1074.

Satyanarayanan, M., *Multiprocessors: A Comparative Study*, Prentice-Hall, Englewood Cliffs, N.J., 1980.

Schaefer, D. H., "Spatially Parallel Architectures: An Overview," *Computer Design*, Aug. 1982, pp. 117–124.

Schmid, H. A., "On the Efficient Implementation of Conditional Critical Regions and the Construction of Monitors," *Acta Informatica* 6, Springer-Verlag, 1976, pp. 227–249.

Schwartz, J. T., "Ultra-Computers," *ACM Trans. Programming Languages and Systems*, vol. 2, no. 4, 1980, pp. 484–521.

Senzig, D. N., and Smith, R. V., "Computer Organization for Array Processing," *AFIPS FJCC Proc.* (part I), 1965, pp. 117–128.

Sethi, A. S., and Deo, N., "Interference in Multiprocessor Systems with Localized Memory Access Probabilities," *IEEE Trans. on Comp.*, vol. C-28, no. 2, Feb. 1979.

Shapiro, H. D., "A Comparison of Various Methods for Detecting and Utilizing Parallelism in a Single Instruction Stream," *Proc. 1977 Int'l. Conf. Parallel Proc.*, IEEE No. 77CH 1253-4C, 1977, pp. 67–76.

Shar, L. E., "Design and Scheduling of Statistically Configured Pipelines," *Digital Systems*, Lab Report SU-SEL-72-042, Stanford University, Stanford, Calif., Sept. 1972.

Shar, L. E., and Davidson, E. S., "A Multiminiprocessor System Implemented Through Pipelining," *IEEE Comp.*, Feb. 1975, pp. 42–51.

Shen, J. P., and Hayes, J. P., "Fault Tolerance of a Class of Connecting Networks," *Proc. 7th Symp. Computer Architecture*, 1980, pp. 61–71.

Shoshani, A., and Coffman, E. G., Jr., "Sequencing Tasks in Multiprocess, Multiple Resource Systems to Avoid Deadlocks," *Proc. 11th Ann. Symp. Switching and Automata Theory*, Oct. 1970, pp. 225–233.

Siegel, H. J., "A Model of SIMD Machines and a Comparison of Various Interconnection Networks," *IEEE Trans. on Comp.*, vol. C-28, no. 12, Dec. 1979a, pp. 907–917.

Siege, H. J., "Interconnection Networks for SIMD Machines," *IEEE Comp.*, June 1979b, pp. 57–65.

Siegel, H. J., "The Theory Underlying the Partitioning of Permutation Networks," *IEEE Trans. on Comp.*, vol. C-29, no. 9, Sept. 1980, pp. 791–800.

Siegel, H. J., *Interconnection Networks for Large-Scale Parallel Processing: Theory and Case Studies*, Lexington Books, Lexington, Mass. 1984.

Siewiorek, D. P., et al., "A Case Study of C.mmp, Cm* and C.vmp, Part I: Experience with Fault-Tolerance in Multiprocessor Systems," *Proc. IEEE*, vol. 66, no. 10, Oct. 1978, pp. 1178–1199.

Siewiorek, D., Bell, C. G., and Newell, A., *Principles of Computer Structures*, McGraw-Hill, New York, 1980.

Sites, R. L., "Operating Systems and Computer Architecture," in *Introduction to Computer Architecture* (Stone, ed.), SRA Inc., 1980, pp. 591–643.

Slotnick, D. L., "Unconventional Systems," *Computer Design*, Dec. 1982, pp. 49–52.

Slotnick, D. L., Borck, W. C., and McReynolds, R. C., "The SOLOMON Computer," *Proc. of AFIPS Fall Joint Comp. Conf.*, Wash. D.C., 1962, pp. 97–107.

Smith, A. J., "A Modified Working-Set Paging Algorithm," *IEEE Trans. on Comp.*, C-29, Sept. 1976, 907–914.

Smith, A. J., "Multiprocessor Memory Organization and Memory Interference," *Comm. of ACM*, vol. 20, no. 10, Oct. 1977, pp. 754–761.

Smith, A. J., "A Comparative Study of Set-Associative Memory Mapping Algorithms and Their use for Cache and Main Memory," *IEEE Trans. Soft. Eng.*, vol. SE-4, March 1978, pp. 121–130.

Smith, A. J., "Cache Memories," *ACM Computing Surveys*, vol. 14, no. 3, Sept. 1982, pp. 473–530.

Smith, B. J., "A Pipelined Shared Resources MIMD Computer," *Proc. 1978 Int'l. Conf. on Parallel Proc.*, 1978, pp. 6–8.

Smith, B. J., "Architecture and Applications of the HEP Multiprocessor Computer System," *Real Time Signal Processing IV*, vol. 298, Aug. 1981.

Smith, J. W., "Cooperation and Competition: An Approach to Parallel Computation," *Proceedings of Southeaston 1979*, Roanoake, Virg., Apr. 1979.

Snyder, L., "Introduction to the Configurable Highly Parallel Computer," *IEEE Comp.*, Jan. 1982, pp. 47–64.

Sperry Univac., *The Univac Series 1100 Announcement*, May 1982.

Steele, G. L., "Multiprocessing Compactifying Garbage Collection," *Comm. of ACM*, vol. 18, no. 9, Sept. 1975, pp. 495–508.

Stephenson, C. M., "Control of a Variable Configuration Pipelined Arithmetic Unit," *Proc. 11th Allerton Conf.*, Oct. 1973, pp. 558–567.

Stevens, K., "CFD—A FORTRAN-like Language for the Illiac IV," *SIGPLAN Notices*, March 1975, pp. 72–80.

Stevenson, D. K., "Numerical Algorithms for Parallel Computers," *Proc. Nat'l. Computer Conf.*, AFIPS Press, vol. 49, 1980, pp. 357–361.

Stokes, R. A., "Burroughs Scientific Processor," in *High Speed Computer and Algorithm Organization* (Kuck, et al., eds.) Academic Press, New York, 1977, pp. 85–89.

Stone, H. S., "Parallel Processing with a Perfect Shuffle," *IEEE Trans. on Comp.*, vol. C-20, Feb. 1971, pp. 153–161.

Stone, H. S., "An Efficient Parallel Algorithm for the Solution of a Tridiagonal Linear System of Equations," *Journ. of ACM*, vol. 20, 1973, pp. 27–38.

Stone, H. S., "Multiprocessor Scheduling with the Aid of Network Flow Algorithms," *IEEE Trans. on Soft. Eng.*, vol. SE-5, no. 1, Jan. 1977, pp. 85–93.

Stone, H. S., "Sorting on STAR," *IEEE Trans. on Comp.*, March 1978, pp. 138–46.

Stone, H. S., "Parallel Computers," Chap. 8 in *Introduction to Computer Architecture* (Stone, ed.), SRA, 1980, pp. 363–426.

Stout, Q. F., "Sorting, Merging, Selecting, and Filtering on Tree and Pyramid Machines," *Proc. 1983 Int'l. Conf. Parallel Processing*, 1983, pp. 214–221.

Strecker, W., "Cache Memories for PDP-11 Family Computers," *Proc. 3rd Symp. on Comp. Arch.*, 1976, 155–157.

Su, S. P., "Pipelining and Dataflow Techniques for Designing Supercomputers," *Ph.D. Thesis*, School of E.E., Purdue University, Dec. 1982.

Sugarman, R., "Superpower Computers," *IEEE Spectrum*, Apr. 1980, pp. 28–34.

Sutherland, I. E., and Mead, C. A., "Microelectronics and Computer Science," *Scientific American*, vol. 237, 1977, pp. 210–229.

Swan, R. J., Bechtholsheim, A., Lai, K. W., and Ousterhout, J. K., "The Implementation of the Cm* Multimicroprocessor," *Proc. AFIPS 1977 Nat. Comp. Conf.*, 46, AFIPS Press, Montvale, N.J., 1977, pp. 645–655.

Syre, J. C., Comte, D., and Hifdi, N., "Pipelining, Parallelism and Asynchronism in the LAU System," *Proc. 1977 Int. Conf. on Parallel Processing*, 1977, pp. 87–92.

Syre, J. C., et al., "The Data Driven LAU Multiprocessor System: Results and Perspectives," in *Information Processing 80* (Lavington, S. H., ed.), North Holland, New York, 1980.

Takahashi, N., and Amamiya, M., "A Dataflow Processor Array System: Design and Analysis," *Proc. of the 10th Int'l. Symp. on Computer Architecture*, June 13–17, 1983, pp. 243–251.

Tanenbaum, A., "Implication of Structured Programming for Computer Architecture," *Comm. of ACM*, 21, Mar. 1978, pp. 237–246.

Tang, C. K., "Cache System Design in the Tightly Coupled Multiprocessor System," *Proc. AFIPS 1976 Nat. Comp. Conf.*, 45, AFIPS Press, Montvale, N.J., 1976, pp. 749–753.

Tanimoto, S. L., "A Pyramidal Approach to Parallel Processing," *Proc. 10th Annual Symp. Computer Architecture*, Sweden, 1983, pp. 372–378.

Tannenbaum, A. S., *Structured Computer Organization*, Prentice-Hall, Englewood Cliffs, N.J., 1976.

Tesler, L. G., and Enea, H., "A Language for Concurrent Processes," *Proc. SJCC*, AFIPS Press, 1968.

Texas Instruments, Inc., "Description of the ASC System: Parts 1 to 5, Manual Nos. 934662 to 934666, 1971.

Texas Instruments, Inc., *ASC FORTRAN Reference Manual*, Pub. No. 930044, 1972.

Theis, D. J., "Special Tutorial: Vector Supercomputers," *IEEE Comp.*, Apr. 1974, pp. 52–61.

Thomas, A. T., and Davidson, E. S., "Scheduling of Multiconfigurable Pipelines," *Proc. 12th Allerton Conf.*, Univ. of Illinois, Urbana, 1974, pp. 658–69.

Thomas, R. E., "A Dataflow Architecture with Improved Asymptotic Performance," *Ph.D. Thesis*, Dept. of Computer Science, Univ. of Calif., Irvine, Apr. 1981.

Thompson, C. D., "Generalized Connection Networks for Parallel Processor Intercommunication," *IEEE Trans. Comp.*, vol. C-27, no. 12, Dec. 1978, pp. 1119–1126.

Thompson, C. D., and Kung, H. T., "Sorting on a Mesh-Connected Parallel Computer," *Comm. of ACM*, vol. 20, no. 4, Apr. 1977, pp. 263–271.

Thompson, S. D., "A Complexity Theory for VLSI," *Ph.D. Thesis*, Dept. of Computer Science, Carnegie-Mellon University, Pittsburgh, Penn. Sept. 1980.

Thornton, J. E., *Design of a Computer, the Control Data 6600*, Scott, Foresman and Co., Glenview, Ill., 1970.

Thurber, K. J., *Large Scale Computer Architecture—Parallel and Associative Processors*, Hayden Book Co., N.J., 1976.

Thurber, K. J., "Parallel Processor Architectures—Part I: General Purpose System," *Computer Design*, Jan. 1979a, pp. 89–97.

Thurber, K. J., "Parallel Processor Architectures—Part II: Special Purpose Systems," *Computer Design*, Feb., 1979b, pp. 103–114.

Thurber, K. J., and Masson, G. M., *Distributed Processor Communication Architecture*. Lexington Books, Lexington, Mass., 1979.

Thurber, K. J., and Wald, L. D., "Associative and Parallel Processors," *ACM Computing Surveys*, vol. 7, Dec. 1975, pp. 215–255.

Tjaden, G. S., and Flynn, M. J., "Representation of Concurrency with Ordering Matrices," *IEEE Trans. on Comp.*, vol. C-22, no. 8, Aug. 1973, pp. 752–761.

Tokoro, M., "On the Working Set Concept for Dataflow Machine," *Proc. of 10th Ann. Symp. Computer Architecture*, June 1983, pp. 90–97.

Tomasulo, R. M., "An Efficient Algorithm for Exploiting Multiple Arithmetic Units," *IBM Journ. of Res. and Dev.*, vol. 11, no. 1, Jan. 1967, pp. 25–33.

Treleaven, P. C., "Exploiting Program Concurrency in Computing Systems," *IEEE Comp.*, 12, Jan. 1979, pp. 42–50.

Treleaven, P. C., Brownbridge, D. R., and Hopkins, R. P., "Data Driven and Demand-Driven Computer Architecture," *ACM Computing Surveys*, March 1982, pp. 93–144.

Ullman, J. D., *Computational Aspects of VLSI*, Computer Science Press, Rockville, Md., 1984.

Uhr, L., *Algorithm-Structured Computer Arrays and Networks*, Academic Press, New York, 1984.

Vick, C. R., and Merwin, R. E., "An Architecture Description of a Parallel Processing Element," *Proc. Int'l Workshop on Computer Architecture*, 1973.

Walker, L. L., "Multiprocessor Operating System Design," in *Operating Systems, International Computer State of the Art Report*, Infotech Ltd., Maidenhead, England, 1972.

Waser, S., and Flynn, M. T., *Introduction to Arithmetic for Digital Systems Designers*, Holt, Rinehart and Winston, New York, 1982.

Watson, R. W., *Timesharing System Design Concepts*, McGraw-Hill, New York, 1970.

Watson, W. J., "The TI ASC—A Highly Modular and Flexible Super Computer Architecture," *Proc. AFIPS Fall Joint Computer Conf.*, AFIPS Press, Montvale, N.J., 1972, pp. 221–228.

Watson, W. J., and Carr, H. M., "Operational Experiences with the TI Advanced Scientific Computer," *AFIPS NCC Proc.*, 1974, pp. 389–97.

Weckes, S., "A Design for a Multiple Processor Operating Environment," *Digest of Papers, COMPCON 73*, San Francisco, Calif., March 1973, pp. 143–146.

White, C. H. (ed.), *Multiprocessor Systems, International Computer State of the Art Report*, Infotech Ltd., Maidenhead, England, 1976.

Widdoes, L. C., Jr., "The S-1 Project: Developing High-Performance Digital Computers," *Digest of Papers: IEEE Compcon 80*, Spring 1980, pp. 282–291.

Wilkes, M. V., *Time-Sharing Computer System*, 2d ed., Elsevier, New York, 1972.

Wittmayer, W. R., "Array Processor Provides High Throughput Rates," *Computer Design*, March 1978, pp. 93–100.

Wu, C. L., and Feng, T. Y., "Fault Diagnosis for a Class of Multistage Interconnection Networks," *Proc. 1979 Int'l. Conf. Parallel Processing*, 1979, pp. 269–278.

Wu, C. L., and Feng, T. Y., "On a Class of Multistage Interconnection Networks," *IEEE Trans. on Comp.*, vol. C-29, no. 8, Aug. 1980, pp. 694–702.

Wu, C. L., and Feng, T. Y., "Universitility of the Shuffle Exchange Network," *IEEE Trans. on Computers*, vol. C-30, no. 5, May 1981, pp. 324–331.

Wulf, W. A., and Bell, C. G., "C.mmp—A Multi-miniprocessor," *Proc. AFIPS Fall Joint Computer Conference*, vol. 41, AFIPS Press, Montvale, N.J., 1972, pp. 765–777.

Wulf, W. A., et al., "Overview of the Hydra Operating System," in *Proc. of the 5th Symp. on Operating System Principles*, ACM, Nov. 1975, Austin, pp. 122–131.

Wulf, W. A., Levin, R., and Harbison, S. P., *HYDRA/C.mmp: An Experimental Computer System*, McGraw-Hill, N.Y., 1981.

Yau, S. S., and Fung, H. S., "Associative Processor Architecture—A Survey," *ACM Computing Surveys*, March 1977, vol. 9, no. 1, pp. 3–28.

Yeh, P. C., "Shared Cache Organization for Multiple-Stream Computer Systems," Coordinated Science Lab., Univ. of Ill., Tech. Rep. R-904, Jan. 1981.

Yeh, P. C., Patel, J. H., and Davidson, E. S., "Shared Cache for Multiple Stream Computer Systems," *IEEE Trans. on Comp.*, vol. C-32, no. 1, Jan, 1983, pp. 38–47.